Upgrading and Repairing PCs

Eighth Edition

que®

Upgrading and Repairing PCs

Eighth Edition

Scott Mueller

Upgrading and Repairing PCs, Eighth Edition

Copyright© 1998 by Que® Corporation

All rights reserved. Printed in the United States of America. No part of this book may be used or reproduced in any form or by any means, or stored in a database or retrieval system, without prior written permission of the publisher except in the case of brief quotations embodied in critical articles and reviews. Making copies of any part of this book for any purpose other than your own personal use is a violation of United States copyright laws. For information, address Que Corporation, 201 W. 103rd Street, Indianapolis, IN, 46290. You may reach Que's direct sales line by calling 1-800-428-5331.

Library of Congress Catalog No.: 97-68686

ISBN: 0-7897-1295-4

This book is sold *as is*, without warranty of any kind, either express or implied, respecting the contents of this book, including but not limited to implied warranties for the book's quality, performance, merchantability, or fitness for any particular purpose. Neither Que Corporation nor its dealers or distributors shall be liable to the purchaser or any other person or entity with respect to any liability, loss, or damage caused or alleged to have been caused directly or indirectly by this book.

99 98   9 8 7 6 5 4

Interpretation of the printing code: The rightmost double-digit number is the year of the book's printing; the rightmost single-digit number, the number of the book's printing. For example, a printing code of 98-8 shows that the eighth printing of the book occurred in 1998.

All terms mentioned in this book that are known to be trademarks or service marks have been appropriately capitalized. Que cannot attest to the accuracy of this information. Use of a term in this book should not be regarded as affecting the validity of any trademark or service mark.

Screen reproductions in this book were created using Collage Plus from Inner Media, Inc., Hollis, NH.

Back cover photograph Copyright© 1997 Black/Toby Photography

Composed in *Stone Serif* and *MCPdigital* by Que Corporation

Contents at a Glance

Introduction	1	
Introduction	**7**	
1 Personal Computer Background	9	
2 Overview of System Features and Components	15	
3 System Teardown and Inspection	27	

Input/Output Hardware	**333**
9 Input Devices	335
10 Video Display Hardware	385
11 Communications and Networking	429
12 Audio Hardware	489

Primary System Components	**77**
4 Motherboards	79
5 Bus Slots and I/O Cards	105
6 Microprossor Types and Specifications	159
7 Memory	223
8 The Power Supply	291

Mass Storage	**517**
13 Floppy Disk Drives	519
14 Hard Disk Drives	567
15 Hard Disk Interfaces	627
16 Hard Disk Drive Installation	687
17 CD-ROM Drives	723
18 Tape and Other Mass-Storage Drives	759

System Assembly Maintenance 791
19 Building a System 793
20 Portable Systems 809

Troubleshooting and Diagnostics 835
21 Software and Hardware Diagnostic Tools 837
22 Operating Systems Software and Troubleshooting 873
23 IBM Personal Computer Family Hardware 925
24 A Final Word 979

Appendixes 987
A Vendor List 989
B Glossary 1039

Index 1101

Contents

Introduction   **1**

    What Are the Main Objectives
        of This Book? 3
    Who Should Use This Book? 3
    What Is in This Book? 4

I Introduction   7

1 Personal Computer Background   9

    Personal Computing History 9
    The IBM Personal Computer 11
    The IBM-Compatible Marketplace
        16 Years Later 13

2 Overview of System Features and Components   15

    Types of Systems 15
    Documentation 17
        Basic System Documentation 18
        Component and Peripheral Documentation 19
        Chip and Chipset Documentation 21
    Manufacturer-Specific Documentation 23
    Warranties and Service Contracts 23

3 System Teardown and Inspection   27

    Using the Proper Tools 27
        Hand Tools 28
        Soldering and Desoldering Tools 30
    Using Proper Test Equipment 33
        Wrap Plugs (Loopback Connectors) 33
        Meters 34
        Logic Probes and Logic Pulsers 35
        Outlet Testers 35
        SIMM Testers 36
    Chemicals 37
    A Word About Hardware 39
        Types of Hardware 39
        English versus Metric 40

Disassembly and Reassembly Procedures 40
    Disassembly Preparation 41
    System Disassembly 45
    Motherboard Installation 52
Preventive Maintenance and Backups 57
Developing a Preventive Maintenance Program 58
    Active Preventive Maintenance Procedures 58
    Hard Disk Maintenance 67
    Passive Preventive Maintenance Procedures 69

II Primary System Components   77

4 Motherboards   79

Replacement Motherboards 79
Knowing What to Look For (Selection Criteria) 79
    Documentation 83
    ROM BIOS Compatibility 84
    Using Correct Speed-Rated Parts 89
Motherboard Form Factors 90
    Backplane Systems 91
    Full-Size AT 92
    Baby-AT 92
    LPX 93
    ATX 94
    NLX 97
Motherboard Interface Connectors 98
Motherboard CMOS RAM Addresses 101

5 Bus Slots and I/O Cards   105

What Is a Bus? 105
    The Processor Bus 105
    The Memory Bus 107
    The Address Bus 108
The Need for Expansion Slots 108
Bus Mastering 109
Types of I/O Buses 109
    The ISA Bus 110
    The Micro Channel Bus 115
    The EISA Bus 117
    Automated Setup 120
    Local Buses 120
    FireWire (IEEE-1394) 138
    Universal Serial Bus (USB) 139
System Resources 140
    Interrupts (IRQs) 140
    DMA Channels 145
    I/O Port Addresses 147

Resolving Resource Conflicts 148
    Resolving Conflicts Manually 149
    Using a System-Configuration Template 150
    Heading Off Problems: Special Boards 154
    Plug and Play Systems 156

6 Microprocessor Types and Specifications   159

Processor Specifications 159
    Data Bus 159
    Internal Registers 162
    Address Bus 162
    Processor Speed Ratings 163
Intel Processors 166
    8088 and 8086 Processors 166
    80186 and 80188 Processors 167
    286 Processors 167
    386 Processors 168
    386DX Processors 169
    386SX Processors 170
    386SL Processors 170
    486 Processors 171
    OverDrive Processors and Sockets 182
    Pentium 193
    Pentium Pro Processor 201
    Pentium II 203
Intel-Compatible Processors 204
    AMD Processors 205
    Cyrix 205
Math Coprocessors 206
    8087 Coprocessor 208
    80287 Coprocessor 209
    80387 Coprocessor 209
    Weitek Coprocessors 210
    80487 Upgrade 210
Processor Tests 210
    Known Defective Chips 211
    Pentium Processor Models and Steppings 215
    Other Processor Problems 222
    Heating and Cooling Problems 222

7 Memory   223

The System Logical Memory Layout 223
    Conventional (Base) Memory 224
    Upper Memory Area (UMA) 224
    Extended Memory 242
    Expanded Memory 244
    Preventing ROM BIOS Memory Conflicts and Overlap ... 246

ROM Shadowing 246
Total Installed Memory versus Total Usable Memory 248
Adapter Memory Configuration and Optimization 250
Taking Advantage of Unused Upper Memory 252
Physical Memory 256
RAM Chips 257
Physical Storage and Organization 257
Memory Banks 259
Parity Checking 261
SIMMs and DIMMs 264
SIMM Pinouts 269
RAM Chip Speed 271
EDO RAM 272
SDRAM 272
Upgrading by Increasing System Memory 273
Upgrade Strategies 273
Adding Motherboard Memory 274
Selecting and Installing Memory Chips, SIMMs,
  or DIMMs 274
Adding Adapter Boards 280
Installing Memory 281
Upgrading the ROM BIOS 283
Keyboard-Controller Chips 286
BIOS Manufacturers and Vendors 286
Special ROM BIOS-Related Problems 287
Changes to an Existing BIOS 288

8 The Power Supply   291

Power Supply Function and Operation 291
Power Supply Form Factors 293
Power Supply Connectors 299
The Power_Good Signal 303
Power Supply Loading 304
Power-Supply Ratings 305
Power Supply Specifications 307
Power-Use Calculations 308
Leave It On or Turn It Off? 310
Energy Star Systems 312
Power Supply Problems 313
Power Supply Troubleshooting 314
Digital Multi-Meters 316
Specialized Test Equipment 318
Repairing the Power Supply 319
Obtaining Replacement Units 321
Deciding on a Power Supply 321
Sources for Replacement Power Supplies 322

Using Power-Protection Systems 323
    Surge Suppressers (Protectors) 325
    Phone Line Surge Protectors 325
    Line Conditioners 326
    Backup Power 326
RTC/NVRAM Batteries 329

III Input/Ouput Hardware   333

9 Input Devices   335

Keyboards 335
    Types of Keyboards 335
    Keyboard Technology 342
    Keyboard Troubleshooting and Repair 361
    Reference Material 367
Mice 368
    Microsoft IntelliMouse 370
    Mouse Interface Types 371
    Mouse Troubleshooting 373
    Trackpoint II/III 377
    Glidepoint 381
Game Adapter (Joystick) Interface 381

10 Video Display Hardware   385

Monitors 385
    Display Technologies 386
    Monochrome versus Color 388
    The Right Size 389
    Monitor Resolution 390
    Interlaced versus Noninterlaced 391
    Energy and Safety 391
    Monitor Buying Criteria 392
Video Cards 396
    Obsolete Display Adapters 396
    VGA Adapters and Displays 404
    VESA SVGA Standards 410
    Video Memory 412
    Improving Video Speed 414
    Video Card Buying Criteria 417
    Chipsets 417
    Video Cards for Multimedia 418
System Video Information 424
    Monitor ID Pins 424
    Advanced Power Management (APM) 424
Adapter and Display Troubleshooting 425

11 Communications and Networking — 429

Using Communications Ports and Devices 429
    Serial Ports 429
    High-Speed Serial Ports 434
    Serial Port Configuration 435
    Modem Standards 436
    Integrated Services Digital Network (ISDN) 444
    56K Modems 445
    Parallel Ports 446
    Parallel-Port Configuration 451
    Testing Serial Ports 453
    Testing Parallel Ports 455
Future Serial and Parallel Port Replacements 455
    USB (Universal Serial Bus) 456
    IEEE 1394 457
Understanding the Components of a LAN 457
    Workstations 459
    File Servers 460
    Evaluating File Server Hardware 461
    Network Interface Cards (NICs) 464
    LAN Cables 471
    Using Twisted Pair Cable 471
    Using Coaxial Cable 471
    Using Fiber-Optic Cable 473
    Network Topologies 474
Selecting the Proper Cable 476
Examining Protocols, Frames, and Communications 478
    Using Frames that Contain Other Frames 479
    Using the OSI Reference Model 480
    Using Low-Level Protocols 482
Evaluating High-Speed Networking Technologies 483
    Using the Fiber Distributed Data Interface 484
    Using 100Mbps Ethernet 484
    Using ATM 486
TCP/IP and the Internet 486
    Connecting to the Internet 487

12 Audio Hardware — 489

Sound Card Applications 489
    Games 490
    Multimedia 491
    MIDI 492
    Presentations 493
    Recording 493
    Voice Annotation 494
    Voice Recognition 494
    Proofreading 495

Audio CDs	495
Sound Mixer	495
Sound Card Concepts and Terms	495
The Nature of Sound	495
Game Standards	496
Frequency Response	496
Sampling	497
8-Bit versus 16-Bit	497
The CD-ROM Connection	498
Sound File Formats	499
Sound Reproduction	499
Compression/Decompression	499
Sound Card Characteristics	499
Compatibility	499
Sampling	500
Stereo versus Mono	500
CD-ROM Connector	501
Data Compression	501
MIDI Interface	501
Bundled Software	502
Multi-Purpose Digital Signal Processors	502
Sound Drivers	502
Connectors	502
Volume Control	504
Sound Card Options	504
Speakers	504
Microphone	506
Joysticks	506
MIDI Connector	507
Synthesizer	507
Sound Card Installation	507
Installing the Sound Card	508
Using Your Stereo Instead of Speakers	509
Troubleshooting Sound Card Problems	510
Hardware (Resource) Conflicts	510
Other Sound Card Problems	512

IV Mass Storage   517

13 Floppy Disk Drives   519

Development of the Floppy Disk Drive	519
Drive Components	520
Read/Write Heads	520
The Head Actuator	523
The Spindle Motor	524
Circuit Boards	525
The Faceplate	525
Connectors	525

Drive-Configuration Devices 527
    Drive Select 527
    Terminating Resistors 529
    Diskette Changeline 530
    Media Sensor 533
The Floppy Disk Controller 534
Disk Physical Specifications and Operation 536
    Disk Magnetic Properties 538
    Logical Operation 540
Types of Floppy Drives 544
    The 360K 5 1/4-Inch Drive 545
    The 1.2M 5 1/4-Inch Drive 545
    The 720K 3 1/2-Inch Drive 546
    The 1.44M 3 1/2-Inch Drive 547
    The 2.88M 3 1/2-Inch Drive 548
    Handling Recording Problems with 1.44M
        3 1/2-Inch Drives 549
Analyzing Floppy Disk Construction 551
    Floppy Disk Media Types and Specifications 554
    Caring for and Handling Floppy Disks and Drives 556
    Airport X-Ray Machines and Metal Detectors 557
Drive-Installation Procedures 559
Troubleshooting and Correcting Problems 560
    "Phantom Directory" (Disk Change) Problems 560
    Off-Center Disk Clamping 561
Repairing Floppy Drives 562
    Cleaning Floppy Drives 562
    Aligning Floppy Disk Drives 563
Floptical Drives 564
    21M Floptical Drives 564
    Iomega Zip Drives 565
    LS-120 (120M) Floptical Drives 565

14 Hard Disk Drives   567

Definition of a Hard Disk 567
    Capacity Measurements 568
    Hard Drive Advancements 568
    Areal Density 568
Hard Disk Drive Operation 569
    The Ultimate Hard Disk Drive Analogy 570
    Magnetic Data Storage 572
    Data Encoding Schemes 575
    Encoding Scheme Comparisons 579
    Sectors 580
Basic Hard Disk Drive Components 588
    Hard Disk Platters (Disks) 588
    Recording Media 589
    Read/Write Heads 591
    Read/Write Head Designs 592

Head Sliders	595
Head Actuator Mechanisms	596
Air Filters	607
Hard Disk Temperature Acclimation	608
Spindle Motors	609
Spindle Ground Strap	610
Logic Boards	611
Cables and Connectors	612
Configuration Items	613
The Faceplate or Bezel	613
Hard Disk Features	615
Reliability	615
Performance	615
Shock Mounting	622
Cost	623
Capacity	623
Specific Recommendations	624

15 Hard Disk Interfaces   627

Interfaces Choices	627
The ST-506/412 Interface	629
Encoding Schemes and Problems	629
The ESDI Interface	632
The IDE Interface	633
IDE Origins	635
IDE Bus Versions	635
XT-Bus (8-Bit) IDE	650
MCA IDE	651
Introduction to SCSI	653
IDE versus SCSI	681
Performance	681
SCSI versus IDE: Advantages and Limitations	682
Recommended Aftermarket Controllers and Host Adapters	683
Recommended SCSI Host Adapters	683
Disk Hardware and Software Limitations	684
Disk Interface Capacity Limitations	684
ROM BIOS Capacity Limitations	686
Operating System Capacity Limitations	686

16 Hard Disk Drive Installation   687

Hard Disk Installation Procedures	687
Controller Configuration	688
Physical Installation	694
System Configuration	695
Formatting and Software Installation	698
Hard Disk Drive Troubleshooting and Repair	718
17xx, 104xx, and 210xxxx Hardware Error Codes	719

17 CD-ROM Drives   723

- What Is a CD-ROM? 723
  - CD-ROM, a Brief History 724
  - CD Technology 724
  - Inside Data CDs 726
- What Types of Drives Are Available? 728
  - CD-ROM Drive Specifications 728
  - Interface 731
  - Loading Mechanism 733
  - Other Drive Features 735
- CD-ROM Disc and Drive Formats 736
  - Data Standard: ISO 9660 737
  - High Sierra Format 737
  - CD-DA (Digital Audio) 738
  - CD+ 738
  - PhotoCD 738
  - CD-ROM-XA or Extended Architecture 740
  - CD-R 741
  - CD-E 742
  - DVD (Digital Versatile Disc) 742
- Multimedia CD-ROM 743
- Installing Your Drive 744
  - Avoiding Conflict: Get Your Cards in Order 745
  - Drive Configuration 745
  - External (SCSI) CD-ROM Hook-Up 746
  - Internal Drive Installation 747
  - Ribbon Cable and Card Edge Connector 748
  - SCSI Chains: Internal, External, a Little of Both 750
  - CD-ROM Software on Your PC 752
- Software Loading 754
  - CD-ROM in Microsoft Windows 3.x 755
  - CD-ROM in Windows 95 and Windows NT 4.0 755
- Troubleshooting CD-ROMs 756

18 Tape and Other Mass-Storage Drives   759

- Tape Backup Drives 759
  - The Origins of Tape Backup Standards 761
  - The QIC Standards 761
  - Common QIC Tape Backup Types 764
  - Newer High-Capacity QIC-Standard Drives 767
  - QIC-Tape Compatibility 768
  - Other High-Capacity Tape Drive Standards 769
  - Choosing a Tape Backup Drive 773
  - Tape Drive Installation Issues 775
  - Tape Drive Backup Software 778

Removable Storage Drives 780
    Types of Removable Media Drives 780
    Magnetic Media Drives 781
    Magneto-Optical Drives 783
    Comparing Removable Drives 785
    Write-Once, Read Many (WORM) Drives 786
    Compact Disc Recordable (CD-R) Drives 787

V System Assembly Maintenance   791

19 Building a System   793

System Components 794
    Case and Power Supply 794
    Motherboard 795
    I/O Ports 803
    Floppy Disk Drive 804
    Hard Disk Drive 804
    CD-ROM Drive 804
    Keyboard and Pointing Device (Mouse) 805
    Video Card and Display 805
    Sound Card and Speakers 806
    Accessories 806
System Assembly 807
Sources and Suppliers 807

20 Portable Systems   809

Form Factors 809
    Laptops 810
    Notebooks 810
    Subnotebooks 811
Portable System Designs 811
Upgrading and Repairing Portables 812
Portable System Hardware 813
    Displays 813
    Processors 817
    Memory 819
    Hard Disk Drives 819
    Removable Media 820
    PC Cards 821
    Keyboards 826
    Pointing Devices 827
    Batteries 828
Peripherals 830
    External Displays 830
    Docking Stations 832
    Connectivity 833

VI Troubleshooting and Diagnostics — 835

21 Software and Hardware Diagnostic Tools — 837

Diagnostics Software 837
The Power-On Self Test (POST) 838
    What Is Tested? 838
    POST Audio Error Codes 839
    POST Visual Error Codes 842
    I/O Port POST Codes 842
IBM Diagnostics 843
    IBM Advanced Diagnostics 843
General-Purpose Diagnostics Programs 864
    AMIDiag 864
    Checkit Pro 865
    Microscope 865
    Norton Utilities Diagnostics 866
    PC Technician 867
    QAPlus/FE 867
Disk Diagnostics 868
    Drive Probe 869
    Disk Manager 869
Data Recovery Utilities 870
Shareware and Public-Domain Diagnostics 871

22 Operating Systems Software and Troubleshooting — 873

Disk Operating System (DOS) 873
    Operating System Basics 874
    The System ROM BIOS 875
    DOS Components 877
    IO.SYS (or IBMBIO.COM) 878
    MSDOS.SYS (or IBMDOS.COM) 878
    The Shell or Command Processor (COMMAND.COM) ... 878
    DOS Command File Search Procedure 879
    DOS Versions 881
    The Boot Process 882
    How DOS Loads and Starts 882
    File Management 888
    DOS File Space Allocation 888
    Interfacing to Disk Drives 889
    DOS Structures 895
    Potential DOS Upgrade Problems 905
    Known Bugs in DOS 906
    DOS Disk and Data Recovery 907
    The *RECOVER* Command 916
    ScanDisk 918
    Third-Party Programs 918

　　　　　Memory-Resident Software Conflicts 918
　　　　　Hardware Problems versus Software Problems 919
　　Windows 95 919
　　　　　Windows 95 and DOS Compared 920
　　　　　FAT32 921
　　Windows NT 922

23 IBM Personal Computer Family Hardware　　　925

　　System-Unit Features by Model 926
　　An Introduction to the PC (5150) 927
　　　　　PC Models and Features 928
　　　　　PC BIOS Versions 930
　　　　　PC Technical Specifications 932
　　An Introduction to the PC Convertible (5140) 936
　　　　　PC Convertible Specifications and Highlights 938
　　　　　PC Convertible Models and Features 939
　　An Introduction to the XT (5160) 941
　　　　　XT Models and Features 943
　　　　　XT BIOS Versions 945
　　　　　XT Technical Specifications 946
　　An Introduction to the Portable PC 951
　　An Introduction to the AT 955
　　　　　AT Models and Features 958
　　　　　AT BIOS Versions 962
　　　　　AT Technical Specifications 966
　　An Introduction to the XT Model 286 971
　　　　　XT Model 286 Models and Features 973
　　　　　XT Model 286 Technical Specifications 974

24 A Final Word　　　979

　　Manuals 980
　　Machines 982
　　Modems 984
　　Magazines 985
　　The Appendixes 985
　　In Conclusion 986

VII Appendixes　　　987

A Vendor List　　　989

B Glossary　　　1039

Index　　　1101

Credits

President
Roland Elgey

Senior Vice President/Publishing
Don Fowley

Publisher
Joseph B. Wikert

Publishing Director
Brad R. Koch

Manager of Publishing Operations
Linda H. Buehler

General Manager
Joe Muldoon

Director of Editorial Services
Carla Hall

Managing Editor
Thomas F. Hayes

Acquisitions Editor
Angela Wethington

Product Director
Robert Bogue

Production Editor
Lisa M. Gebken

Product Marketing Manager
Kourtnaye Sturgeon

Assistant Product Marketing Manager
Gretchen Schlesinger

Technical Editor
Jerry Cox

Media Development Specialist
David Garratt

Technical Support Specialist
Nadeem Muhammed

Acquisitions Coordinators
Michelle R. Newcomb
Tracy M. Williams

Software Relations Coordinator
Susan D. Gallagher

Editorial Assistant
Jeff Chandler

Book Designer
Ruth Harvey

Cover Designer
Dan Armstrong

Production Team
Bryan Flores
Trey Frank
Tony McDonald
Tim Neville
Sossity Smith
Lisa Stumpf

Indexer
Ginny Bess

Que would also like to acknowledge the following contributors:
Robert Bogue, **Kevin Kloss**, **Steve Schafer**, **Keith Underdahl**, and **Craig Zacker**.

Composed in ***Stone Sans*** and ***Stone Serif*** by Que Corporation.

Dedication

To my family:

Lynn, Amanda and Emerson

Yet another edition completed, just in time to begin writing the next one. This book has become a full-time job!

Biography

Scott Mueller is president of Mueller Technical Research, an international personal computer research and corporate training firm. Since 1982, MTR has specialized in the industry's longest running, most in-depth, accurate, and effective corporate technical training seminars, maintaining a client list that includes Fortune 500 companies, the U.S. and foreign governments, major software and hardware corporations, as well as PC enthusiasts and entrepreneurs. His seminars have been presented to thousands of PC professionals throughout the world.

Scott Mueller has developed and presented personal computer training courses in all areas of PC hardware and software. He is an expert in PC hardware, operating systems, data-recovery techniques, and local area networks. MTR seminars are available on an on-site contract basis or publicly through the American Research Group (ARG). For more information about a custom computer training seminar for your organization, contact:

> Mueller Technical Research
> 21718 Mayfield Lane
> Barrington, IL 60010-9733
> (847) 726-0709
> (847) 726-0710 Fax
> Internet: 73145.1566@compuserve.com

For more information about attending a public seminar, contact:

> American Research Group
> 114 Edinburgh South, Suite 200
> Cary, NC 27512
> (919) 461-8600
> (919) 461-8846 Fax
> http://www.arg.com
> email: questions@arg.com

Scott has many popular books, articles, and course materials to his credit, including *Upgrading and Repairing PCs*, which has sold more than 1 million copies, making it by far the most popular PC hardware book on the market today. His 2-hour video, titled *"Your PC-The Inside Story,"* is available through LearnKey, Inc. For ordering information, contact:

LearnKey, Inc.
1845 West Sunset Boulevard
St. George, UT 84770
(800) 937-3279
(801) 674-9733
(801) 674-9734 Fax

If you have questions about PC hardware, suggestions for the next version of the book, or any comments in general, send them to Scott via email. Correspondence through standard mail takes him much longer to answer!

When he is not working on PC related books or teaching seminars, Scott can usually be found in the garage working on his LT4 powered '94 Impala SS, LT4 powered '95 Caprice 9C1 (police package), or Buick Turbo V6 powered '89 Trans Am, as well as various other performance car related projects. He can also be found testing the vehicles at the local drag strip, or showing them off at car shows or the local cruise/drive-in scene.

Acknowledgments

This 8th edition is the product of a great deal of additional research and development over the previous editions. Several people have helped me with both the research and production of this book. I would like to thank the following people:

First, a very special thanks to my Wife and partner, Lynn. This book continues to be an incredible burden on both our business and family life, and she has put up with a lot! Lynn is excellent at dealing with the many companies we have to contact for product information and research. She is the backbone of MTR.

Thanks to Lisa Carlson of Mueller Technical Research for helping with product research and office management. She has fantastic organizational skills that have been a tremendous help in managing all of the information that comes into and goes out of this office. Thanks to John Rourke, who not only teaches many of the MTR seminars, and who also is the designer and creator of the Discovery card, which is the first card on the market for troubleshooting IRQ and DMA conflicts.

Thanks to all of the companies who have provided hardware, software, and research information that has been helpful in developing this book. Thanks to David Means for feedback from the trenches about various products and especially data recovery information.

I would like to offer a special thanks to the people at Que that have made this book possible. Thanks also to all of the editors and staff who work so hard to get these books out!

Thanks to all of the readers who have emailed me with suggestions concerning this book; I welcome all of your comments. A special thanks to Paul Reid, who always has many suggestions to offer for improving the book and making it more accurate.

Finally, I would like to thank the more than ten thousand people who have attended my Seminars; you may not realize how much I learn from each of you and your questions! Thanks also to those of you on the Internet and CompuServe forums with both questions and answers, from which I have also learned a great deal.

We'd Like to Hear from You!

Que Corporation has a long-standing reputation for high-quality books and products. To ensure your continued satisfaction, we also understand the importance of customer service and support.

Tech Support

If you need assistance with the information in this book or with a CD/disk accompanying the book, please contact Macmillan Technical Support by phone at 317/581-3833 or via email at **support@mcp.com**.

Orders, Catalogs, and Customer Service

To order other Que or Macmillan Computer Publishing books, catalogs, or products, please contact our Customer Service Department:

    Phone: 800/858-7674

    Fax: 800/882-8583

    International Fax: 317/228-4400

Or visit our online bookstore:

    http://www.mcp.com/

Introduction

Welcome to *Upgrading and Repairing PCs*, 8th Edition. This book is for people who want to upgrade, repair, maintain, and troubleshoot computers. It covers the full range of PC-compatible systems from the oldest 8-bit machines to the latest in high-end 64-bit workstations.

In addition, this book covers state-of-the-art hardware and accessories that make the most modern personal computers easier, faster, and more productive to use. Hardware coverage includes all of the Intel and Intel-compatible processors through the Pentium, Pentium Pro, and new Pentium II CPU chips; new cache and main memory technology; PCI local bus technology; CD-ROM drives; tape backups; sound boards; PC-Card and Cardbus devices for laptops; IDE and SCSI-interface devices; larger and faster hard drives; and new video adapter and display capabilities.

The comprehensive coverage of the PC-compatible personal computer in this book has consistently won acclaim since debuting as the first book of its kind on the market in 1988. Now with the release of this eighth edition, *Upgrading and Repairing PCs* continues its place as not only the best selling book of its type, but also the most comprehensive and easily used reference on even the most modern systems—those based on cutting-edge hardware and software. The book examines PCs in-depth, outlines the differences among them, and presents options for configuring each system at the time you purchase it.

Sections of this book provide detailed information about each internal component of a personal computer system, from the processor to the keyboard and video display. The book examines the options available in modern, high-performance PC configurations, and how to use them to your advantage; it focuses on much of the hardware and software available today and specifies the optimum configurations for achieving maximum benefit for the time and money you spend. At a glance, here are the major system components and peripherals covered in this edition of *Upgrading and Repairing PCs*:

Introduction

- Pentium II, Pentium Pro, Pentium, 486, and earlier central processing unit (CPU) chips.
- The latest processor upgrade socket and slot specifications.
- New motherboard chipsets and designs, including the ATX form factor.
- Special bus architectures and devices, including high-speed PCI (Peripheral Component Interconnect) and VL-Bus (VESA Local), EISA (Extended Industry Standard Architecture), and MCA (Micro Channel Architecture).
- Bus resources which often conflict such as Interrupt ReQuest (IRQ) lines, Direct Memory Access (DMA) channels, and Input Output (I/O) port addresses.
- Plug and Play architecture.
- Larger, faster hard drives and hard drive interfaces, including EIDE and SCSI.
- Floppy drives, including 360K, 1.2M, 1.44M, and 2.88M drives.
- New storage devices such as DVD, CD-ROM, and Magneto-Optical drives.
- Increasing system memory capacity with SIMM and DIMM modules.
- New types of memory including Synchronous Pipeline Burst cache, EDO RAM, Burst EDO, and Synchronous DRAM.
- Large-screen Super VGA monitors and high-speed graphics adapter cards.
- Peripheral devices such as CD-ROM drives, sound boards, and tape backups.
- PC-Card and Cardbus devices for laptops.

This book also shows you how to troubleshoot the kind of hardware problems that can make PC upgrading and repairing difficult. Troubleshooting coverage includes IRQ, DMA channel, and I/O Port addressees, as well as memory address conflicts. This book tells you how to avoid problems with these system resources, and how to make installing a new adapter board in your computer a simple plug-and-play operation. This book also focuses on software problems, starting with the basics of how DOS or another operating system works with your hardware to start up your system. You also learn how to troubleshoot and avoid problems involving system hardware, the operating system, and applications software such as word processors or spreadsheets.

This book is the result of years of research and development in the production of my PC hardware, operating system, and data recovery seminars. Since 1982, I have personally taught (and still teach) thousands of people about PC troubleshooting, upgrading, maintenance, repair, and data recovery. This book represents the culmination of many years of field experience as well as knowledge culled from the experiences of thousands of others. What originally started out as a simple course workbook has grown over the years into a complete reference on the subject. Now you can benefit from this experience and research.

What Are the Main Objectives of This Book?

Upgrading and Repairing PCs focuses on several objectives. The primary objective is to help you learn how to maintain, upgrade, and repair your PC system. To that end, *Upgrading and Repairing PCs* helps you fully understand the family of computers that has grown from the original IBM PC, including all PC-compatible systems. This book discusses all areas of system improvement such as floppy disks, hard disks, central processing units, math coprocessors, and power-supply improvements. The book discusses proper system and component care; it specifies the most failure-prone items in different PC systems, and tells you how to locate and identify a failing component. You'll learn about powerful diagnostics hardware and software that enable a system to help you determine the cause of a problem and how to repair it.

The PC-compatible microcomputer family is rapidly moving forward in power and capabilities. Processor performance increases with every new chip design. *Upgrading and Repairing PCs* helps you gain an understanding of each of the CPU chips used in PC-compatible computer systems.

This book covers the important differences between major system architectures—the original Industry Standard Architecture (ISA), Extended Industry Standard Architecture (EISA), and Micro Channel Architecture (MCA). The most modern systems use special local bus architectures and adapter cards to get top speed from system peripherals such as video adapter cards and hard drives. Besides ISA, EISA, and MCA, these local bus architectures include PCI (Peripheral Component Interconnect) and VL-Bus devices. *Upgrading and Repairing PCs* covers each of these system architectures and their adapter boards to help you make decisions about which kind of system you may want to buy in the future, and how to upgrade and troubleshoot such systems.

The amount of storage space available to modern PCs is increasing geometrically. *Upgrading and Repairing PCs* covers storage options ranging from larger, faster hard drives to state-of-the-art storage devices. In addition, this book provides detailed information on upgrading and troubleshooting the system's RAM.

When you finish reading this book, you should have the knowledge to upgrade as well as troubleshoot and repair almost all systems and components.

Who Should Use This Book?

Upgrading and Repairing PCs is designed for people who want a thorough understanding of how their PC systems work. Each section fully explains common and not-so common problems, what causes problems, and how to handle problems when they arise. You will gain an understanding of disk configuration and interfacing, for example, that can improve your diagnostic and troubleshooting skills. You'll develop a feel for what goes on in a system so that you can rely on your own judgment and observations and not some table of canned troubleshooting steps. This book is for people who are truly interested in their systems and how they operate.

Upgrading and Repairing PCs is written for people who select, install, configure, maintain, and repair systems they or their companies use. To accomplish these tasks, you need a level of knowledge much higher than that of an average system user. You must know exactly which tool to use for a task and how to use the tool correctly. This book can help you achieve this level of knowledge.

What Is in This Book?

Part I of this book serves primarily as an introduction. Chapter 1 begins with an introduction to the development of the original IBM PC and PC-compatibles. Chapter 2 provides information about the different types of systems you encounter and what separates one type of system from another, including the types of system buses that differentiate systems. Chapter 2 also provides an overview of the types of PC systems that help build a foundation of knowledge essential for the remainder of the book. Chapter 3 discusses the physical disassembly and reassembly of a system.

Part II covers the primary system components of a PC. Chapter 4 begins this part with a discussion of the components in a PC system by covering the motherboard. Chapter 5 continues this discussion by focusing on the different types of expansion slots and bus types found in PC systems. Chapter 6 goes into detail about the central processing unit (CPU), or main processor, including those from Intel as well as other companies. Chapter 7 gives a detailed discussion of PC memory, from basic architecture to the physical chips and SIMMs themselves. Chapter 8 is a detailed investigation of the power supply, which remains as the primary cause for PC system problems and failures.

Part III is about input/output hardware and begins with Chapter 9 on input devices. This chapter includes coverage of keyboards, pointing devices, and the game port. Chapter 10 discusses video display hardware, including video adapters and monitors. Chapter 11 is a detailed discussion of communications and networking hardware, while Chapter 12 focuses on audio hardware, including sound boards and speaker systems.

Part IV is about mass storage systems and leads off with Chapter 13 on floppy disk drives and controllers. Chapter 14 is a detailed discussion of hard disk drives and drive technology. Chapter 15 covers hard disk interfaces, including IDE and SCSI, in-depth. Chapter 16 details the installation requirements and procedures for a hard disk. This information is invaluable when you install drives as either replacements or upgrades in a system, and if you troubleshoot and repair malfunctioning drives. Chapter 17 is about CD-ROM drives, and Chapter 18 covers tape and other mass storage drives.

Part V covers system assembly and maintenance and starts off with Chapter 19 on buying or building a PC-compatible system as well as system upgrades and improvements. This information is especially useful if you make purchasing decisions and also serves as a general guideline for features that make a certain compatible computer a good or bad choice. The more adventurous can use this information to assemble their own custom system from scratch. Chapter 20 covers portable systems including laptop and notebook systems. It also focuses on all of the technology unique and peculiar to portable systems such as display, battery, and other technologies.

Part VI covers troubleshooting and diagnostics and starts off with Chapter 21 on diagnostic tools. Chapter 22 covers operating system software and troubleshooting, as well as data recovery. Chapter 23 covers in considerable depth the original classic IBM PC, XT, and AT computers. All modern compatibles are based on these systems, so this information can serve as a useful reference. This information is useful not only for supporting actual IBM equipment, but also for PC-compatible systems not supplied with extensive documentation. You learn how to compare systems with the original IBM standard, and see how far we have come since these original cornerstone systems were introduced.

Chapter 24 gives your experience closure by tying all the technologies together and providing suggestions on additional places to find information.

Appendix A provides an extremely well-detailed vendor list useful for finding suppliers and vendors for necessary hardware and software. Appendix B provides an informative glossary.

I believe that *Upgrading and Repairing PCs* will prove to be the best book of its kind on the market. It offers not only the breadth of PC-compatible equipment, but also much in-depth coverage of each topic. This book is valuable as a reference tool for understanding how various components in a system interact and operate, and as a guide to repairing and servicing problems you encounter. *Upgrading and Repairing PCs* is far more than just a repair manual; I sincerely hope that you also enjoy it.

Part I

Introduction

1 Personal Computer Background

2 Overview of System Features and Components

3 System Teardown and Inspection

Chapter 1

Personal Computer Background

Many discoveries and inventions have directly and indirectly contributed to the development of the personal computer. Examining a few important developmental landmarks can help bring the entire picture into focus.

Personal Computing History

A modern digital computer is largely a collection of electronic switches. These switches are used to represent, as well as to control, the routing of data elements called *binary digits* (or *bits*). Because of the on or off nature of the binary information and signal routing used by the computer, an efficient electronic switch was required. The first electronic computers used vacuum tubes as switches, and although the tubes worked, they had many problems.

The tube was inefficient as a switch. It consumed a great deal of electrical power and gave off enormous heat—a significant problem in the earlier systems. Primarily because of the heat they generated, tubes were notoriously unreliable—one failed every couple hours or so in the larger systems.

The invention of the transistor, or semiconductor, was one of the most important developments leading to the personal computer revolution. The transistor was invented in 1948 by Bell Laboratories engineers John Bardeen, Walter Brattain, and William Shockley. The transistor, which essentially functions as a solid-state electronic switch, replaced the much less suitable vacuum tube. Because the transistor was so much smaller and consumed significantly less power, a computer system built with transistors was much smaller, faster, and more efficient than a computer system built with vacuum tubes.

The conversion to transistors began the trend toward miniaturization that continues to this day. Today's small laptop (or palmtop) PC systems, which run on batteries, have more computing power than many earlier systems that filled rooms and consumed huge amounts of electrical power.

In 1959, engineers at Texas Instruments invented the *integrated circuit (IC)*, a semiconductor circuit that contains more than one transistor on the same base (or substrate material) and connects the transistors without wires. The first IC contained only six transistors. By comparison, the Intel Pentium Pro microprocessor used in many of today's high-end systems has more than 5.5 million transistors, and the integral cache built into some of these chips contains as many as an additional 32 million transistors! Today, many ICs have transistor counts in the multimillion range.

In 1969, Intel introduced a 1K-bit memory chip, which was much larger than anything else available at the time. (1K bits equals 1,024 bits, and a byte equals 8 bits. This chip, therefore, stored only 128 bytes—not much by today's standards.) Because of Intel's success in chip manufacturing and design, Busicomp, a Japanese calculator manufacturing company, asked Intel to produce 12 different logic chips for one of its calculator designs. Rather than produce 12 separate chips, Intel engineers included all the functions of the chips in a single chip.

In addition to incorporating all the functions and capabilities of the 12-chip design into one multipurpose chip, the engineers designed the chip to be controlled by a program that could alter the function of the chip. The chip then was generic in nature, meaning that it could function in designs other than calculators. Previous designs were hard-wired for one purpose, with built-in instructions; this chip would read from memory a variable set of instructions that would control the function of the chip. The idea was to design almost an entire computing device on a single chip that could perform different functions, depending on what instructions it was given.

The first microprocessor—the Intel 4004, a 4-bit processor—was introduced in 1971. The chip operated on 4 bits of data at a time. The successor to the 4004 chip was the 8008 8-bit microprocessor, introduced in 1972.

In 1973, some of the first microcomputer kits based on the 8008 chip were developed. These kits were little more than demonstration tools and did little except blink lights. In late 1973, Intel introduced the 8080 microprocessor, which was 10 times faster than the earlier 8008 chip and addressed 64K of memory. This breakthrough was the one that the personal computer industry had been waiting for.

MITS introduced the Altair kit in a cover story in the January 1975 issue of *Popular Electronics* magazine. The Altair kit, considered to be the first personal computer, included an 8080 processor, a power supply, a front panel with a large number of lights, and 256 bytes (not kilobytes) of memory. The kit sold for $395 and had to be assembled. The computer included an open architecture bus (slots) that prompted various add-ons and peripherals from aftermarket companies. The new processor inspired other companies to write programs, including the CP/M (Control Program for Microprocessors) operating system and the first version of the Microsoft BASIC (Beginners All-purpose Symbolic Instruction Code) programming language.

IBM introduced what can be called its first *personal computer* in 1975. The Model 5100 had 16K of memory, a built-in 16-line-by-64-character display, a built-in BASIC language interpreter, and a built-in DC-300 cartridge tape drive for storage. The system's $9,000 price placed it out of the mainstream personal computer marketplace, which was dominated by experimenters (affectionately referred to as *hackers*) who built low-cost kits ($500 or so) as a hobby. The IBM system obviously was not in competition for this low-cost market and did not sell well.

The Model 5100 was succeeded by the 5110 and 5120 before IBM introduced what we know as the IBM Personal Computer (Model 5150). Although the 5100 series preceded the IBM PC, the older systems and the 5150 IBM PC had nothing in common. The PC IBM turned out was more closely related to the IBM System/23 DataMaster, an office computer system introduced in 1980. In fact, many of the engineers who developed the PC at IBM had originally worked on the DataMaster.

In 1976, a new company called Apple Computer introduced the Apple I, which sold for $695. This system consisted of a main circuit board screwed to a piece of plywood; a case and power supply were not included. Only a few of these computers were made, and they reportedly have sold to collectors for more than $20,000. The Apple II, introduced in 1977, helped set the standard for nearly all the important microcomputers to follow, including the IBM PC.

The microcomputer world was dominated in 1980 by two types of computer systems. One type, the Apple II, claimed a large following of loyal users and a gigantic software base that was growing at a fantastic rate. The other type, CP/M systems, consisted not of a single system but of all the many systems that evolved from the original MITS Altair. These systems were compatible with one another and were distinguished by their use of the CP/M operating system and expansion slots, which followed the S-100 (for slots with 100 pins) standard. All these systems were built by a variety of companies and sold under various names. For the most part, however, these companies used the same software and plug-in hardware. It is interesting to note that none of these systems were PC-compatible, or Mac-compatible, the two primary standards in place today!

The IBM Personal Computer

At the end of 1980, IBM decided to truly compete in the rapidly growing low-cost personal computer market. The company established what then was called the Entry Systems Division, located in Boca Raton, Florida, to develop the new system. This small group consisted of 12 engineers and designers under the direction of Don Estridge; the team's chief designer was Lewis Eggebrecht. The division developed IBM's first real PC. (IBM considered the 5100 system, developed in 1975, to be an intelligent programmable terminal rather than a genuine computer, even though it truly was a computer.) Nearly all these engineers had been moved to the new division from the System/23 DataMaster project, which in 1980 introduced a small office computer system that was the closest predecessor to the IBM PC.

Much of the PC's design was influenced by the DataMaster's design. In the DataMaster's single-piece design, the display and keyboard were integrated into the unit. Because these features were limiting, they became external units on the PC, although the PC keyboard layout and electrical designs were copied from the DataMaster.

Several other parts of the IBM PC system also were copied from the DataMaster, including the expansion bus (or input/output slots), which included not only the same physical 62-pin connector but also almost identical pin specifications. This copying was possible because the PC used the same interrupt controller as the DataMaster and a similar direct memory access (DMA) controller. Expansion cards already designed for the DataMaster could then be easily re-designed to function in the PC.

The DataMaster used an Intel 8085 CPU, which had a 64K address limit, as well as an 8-bit internal and external data bus. This arrangement prompted the PC design team to use the Intel 8088 CPU, which offered a much larger (1M) memory address limit, and an internal 16-bit data bus, but only an 8-bit external data bus. The 8-bit external data bus and similar instruction set allowed the 8088 to be easily interfaced into the earlier DataMaster designs.

Estridge and the design team rapidly developed the design and specifications for the new system. In addition to borrowing from the System/23 DataMaster, the team studied the marketplace, which also had enormous influence on the IBM PC's design. The designers looked at the prevailing standards, learned from the success of those systems, and incorporated into the new PC all the features of the popular systems—and more. With the parameters for design made obvious by the market, IBM produced a system that filled its niche in the market perfectly.

IBM brought its system from idea to delivery in one year by using existing designs and purchasing as many components as possible from outside vendors. The Entry Systems Division was granted autonomy from IBM's other divisions and could tap resources outside the company, rather than go through the bureaucratic procedures that required exclusive use of IBM resources. IBM contracted out the PC's languages and operating system to a small company named Microsoft. That decision would be the major factor in establishing Microsoft as the dominant force in PC software today.

> **Note**
> It is interesting to note that IBM had originally contacted Digital Research (the company that created CP/M, then the most popular Personal Computer operating system) to have them develop an operating system for the new IBM PC, but they were leery of working with IBM, and especially balked at the non-disclosure agreement IBM wanted them to sign. Microsoft jumped on the opportunity left open by Digital Research, and as a result has become one of the largest software companies in the world. IBM's use of outside vendors in developing the PC was an open invitation for the aftermarket to jump in and support the system—and it did.

On Wednesday, August 12, 1981, a new standard was established in the microcomputer industry with the debut of the IBM PC. Since then, hundreds of millions of PC-compatible systems have been sold as the original PC has grown into an enormous family of computers and peripherals. More software has been written for this computer family than for any other system on the market.

The IBM-Compatible Marketplace 16 Years Later

In the more than 16 years since the original IBM PC was introduced, many changes have occurred. The IBM-compatible computer, for example, advanced from a 4.77MHz 8088-based system to 300MHz or faster Pentium II-based systems—nearly *2,000 times faster* than the original IBM PC (in actual processing speed, not just clock speed). The original PC had only one or two single-sided floppy drives that stored 160K each using DOS 1.0, whereas modern systems easily can have 10G (10 billion bytes) or more of hard disk storage. A rule of thumb in the computer industry is that available processor performance and disk-storage capacity at least double every two to three years. Since the beginning of the PC industry, this pattern has shown no sign of changing.

In addition to performance and storage capacity, another major change since the original IBM PC was introduced is that IBM is not the only manufacturer of "PC-compatible" systems. IBM originated the PC-compatible standard, of course, and it continues to set standards that compatible systems follow, but the company does not dominate the PC market as it did originally. More often than not, new standards in the PC industry are developed by companies and organizations other than IBM. Today it is Intel and Microsoft who are primarily responsible for developing and extending the PC hardware and software standards, respectively. Some have even taken to calling PCs "Wintel" systems, owing to the dominance of those two companies.

Even so, there are literally hundreds of system manufacturers producing computers that are fully PC compatible, not to mention the thousands of peripheral manufacturers whose components expand and enhance PC-compatible systems.

PC-compatible systems have thrived, not only because compatible hardware can be assembled easily, but also because the primary operating system was available not from IBM but from a third party (Microsoft). The core of the system software is the BIOS (Basic Input Output System), and this was also available from third-party companies like AMI, Award, Phoenix, and others. This situation allowed other manufacturers to license the operating system and BIOS software and to sell their own compatible systems. The fact that DOS borrowed the functionality and user interface from both CP/M and UNIX probably had a lot to do with the amount of software that became available. Later, with the success of Windows, there would be even more reasons for software developers to write programs for PC-compatible systems.

One of the reasons why Apple Macintosh systems will likely never enjoy the success of PC-compatibles is that Apple controls all the software (BIOS and OS), and until recently had not licensed any of it to other companies for use in compatible systems. Apple now seems to recognize this flawed stance because they have begun to license this software; however, it seems too late for them to effectively compete with the PC-compatible juggernaut. It is fortunate for the computing public as a whole that IBM created a more open and extendible standard. The competition among manufacturers and vendors of PC-compatible systems is the reason why such systems offer so much performance and so many capabilities for the money.

The IBM-compatible market continues to thrive and prosper. New technology continues to be integrated into these systems, enabling them to grow with the times. Because of the high value that these types of systems can offer for the money and the large amount of software that is available to run on them, PC-compatible systems likely will dominate the personal computer marketplace for perhaps the next 15 to 20 years as well.

Chapter 2

Overview of System Features and Components

This chapter discusses the differences in system architecture among PC-compatible systems and also explains memory structure and use. In addition, the chapter discusses how to obtain the documentation necessary for maintaining and upgrading your computer.

Types of Systems

Many types of PC-compatible systems are on the market today. Most systems are similar, but a few important differences in system architecture have become more apparent as operating environments (such as Windows and OS/2) have increased in popularity. Operating systems such as OS/2 1.x and Windows 3.1 require at least a 286 CPU platform on which to run. OS/2 2.x, 3.x (Warp), and Windows 95 will run on a 386 system, and Windows NT 4.x requires at least a 486 CPU to run. Knowing and understanding the differences among these hardware platforms will enable you to plan, install, and use modern operating systems and applications in order for you to use the hardware optimally.

All PC-compatible systems can be broken down into two basic system types, or *classes*, of hardware:

- 8-bit (PC/XT-class) systems
- 16/32/64-bit (AT-class) systems

The term *PC* stands for *personal computer*, *XT* stands for an *eXTended PC*, and *AT* stands for an *Advanced Technology PC*. The terms *PC*, *XT*, and *AT* as used here are taken from the original IBM systems of those names. The XT basically was a PC system that included a hard disk for storage in addition to the floppy drive(s) found in the basic PC system. These systems had an 8-bit 8088 processor and an 8-bit Industry Standard Architecture (ISA) Bus for system expansion. The *bus* is the name given to expansion slots in which additional plug-in circuit boards can be installed. The 8-bit designation comes from the fact that the ISA Bus found in the PC/XT class systems can send or receive only 8 bits of data in a single cycle. The data in an 8-bit bus is sent along eight wires simultaneously, in parallel.

More advanced systems are said to be *AT-class,* which indicates that they follow certain standards and follow the basic design first set forth in the original IBM AT system. *AT* is the designation IBM applied to systems that first included more advanced 16-bit (and later, 32- and 64-bit) processors and expansion slots. AT-class systems must have any processor that is compatible with Intel 286 or higher processors (including the 386, 486, Pentium, Pentium Pro, and Pentium II processors) and must have a 16-bit or greater system bus. The system bus architecture is central to the AT system design.

The first AT-class systems had a 16-bit version of the ISA Bus, which is an extension of the original 8-bit ISA Bus found in the PC/XT-class systems. Eventually, several expansion slot or bus designs were developed for AT-class systems, including those in the following list:

- 16-bit ISA Bus
- 16/32-bit Extended ISA (EISA) Bus
- 16/32-bit PS/2 Micro Channel Architecture (MCA) Bus
- 16-bit PC-Card (PCMCIA) Bus
- 32-bit Cardbus (PCMCIA) Bus
- 32-bit VESA Local (VL) Bus
- 32/64-bit Peripheral Component Interconnect (PCI) Bus
- Accelerated Graphics Port (AGP)

A system with any of these types of expansion slots is by definition an AT-class system, regardless of the actual Intel or Intel-compatible processor used. AT-type systems with 386 or higher processors have special capabilities not found in the first generation of 286-based ATs. The 386 and higher systems have distinct capabilities regarding memory addressing, memory management, and possible 32- or 64-bit wide access to data. Most systems with 386DX or higher chips also have 32-bit bus architectures to take full advantage of the 32-bit data transfer capabilities of the processor.

Most PC systems today incorporate 16-bit ISA slots for backward compatibility and lower function adapters, and PCI slots for truly high performance adapters. Most portable systems use PC-Card and Cardbus slots in the portable unit, as well as ISA and PCI slots in optional docking stations.

Chapter 5, "Bus Slots and I/O Cards," contains a great deal of in-depth information on these and other PC system buses, including technical information such as pinouts, performance specifications, and bus operation and theory.

Table 2.1 summarizes the primary differences between the older 8-bit (PC/XT) systems and a modern AT system. This information distinguishes between these systems and includes all IBM and compatible models.

Table 2.1 Differences Between PC/XT and AT Systems

System Attributes	(8-bit) PC/XT Type	(16/32/64-bit) AT Type
Supported processors	All x86 or x88	286 or higher
Processor modes	Real	Real/Protected/Virtual Real
Software supported	16-bit only	16 or 32-bit
Expansion slot width	8-bit	16/32/64-bit
Slot type	ISA only	ISA, EISA, MCA, PC-Card, Cardbus, VL-Bus, PCI
Hardware interrupts	8 (6 usable)	16 (11 usable)
DMA channels	4 (3 usable*!8 (7 usable)	
Maximum RAM	1M	16M/4G or more
Floppy controller speed	250 Kbit/sec	250/300/500/1,000 Kbit/sec
Standard boot drive	360K or 720K	1.2M/1.44M/2.88M
Keyboard interface	Unidirectional	Bi-directional
CMOS memory/clock	None standard	MC146818 compatible
Serial-port UART	8250B	16450/16550A

The easiest way to identify a PC/XT (8-bit) system would be by the 8-bit ISA expansion slots. No matter what processor or other features the system had, if all of the slots are 8-bit ISA, then the system would be a PC/XT. AT (16-bit plus) systems can be similarly identified by having 16-bit or greater slots of any type. These could be ISA, EISA, MCA, PCCard (formerly PCMCIA), Cardbus, VL-Bus, or PCI. Using this information, you can properly categorize virtually any system as a PC/XT type or an AT type. There really have been no PC/XT type (8-bit) systems manufactured for many years. Unless you are in a computer museum, virtually every system you would encounter today is based on the AT type design!

For more information on the other architectural differences between these types of systems, consult the various sections of the book that deal with each system component.

Documentation

One of the biggest problems in troubleshooting, servicing, or upgrading a system is having proper documentation. I believe that good documentation is critical for system support and future upgrade capability. Because it can be a problem getting documentation on systems or components that are older, the time to acquire documentation is when the system or components are new.

There are several types of documentation available to cover a given system:

- *System-level documentation.* The system-specific manual(s) put together by the system manufacturer or assembler. Some companies break this down further into Operations, Technical Reference, and Service manuals.

- *Component-level documentation.* The specific OEM (Original Equipment Manufacturer) manuals for each major component such as the motherboard, video card, hard disk, floppy drive, CD-ROM drive, modem, network card, SCSI adapter, and so on.

- *Chip- and chipset-level documentation.* The most specific and technical manuals which cover items such as the processor, motherboard chipset, super I/O chip, BIOS, memory modules, video chipset, and various disk controller, SCSI bus interface, network interface, and other chips used throughout the system.

The system- and component-level documentation is essential for even the most basic troubleshooting and upgrading tasks. More technical literature such as the chip- and chipset-level documentation is probably necessary only for software and hardware developers who have more special requirements. However, if you are like me and really want to know as much about a system as possible, then you will find as I do that having the chip- and chipset-level documentation can give you insights and information about a system you simply can't get otherwise. This section will examine all of this documentation and, most importantly, explain how to get it!

Basic System Documentation

When you purchase a complete system, it should include a basic set of documentation. What you actually get will vary widely depending on what type of system you get and who put it together.

Name-brand manufacturers such as IBM, Compaq, Hewlett-Packard, Toshiba, Packard Bell, and others will almost certainly include custom manuals they have developed specifically for each system they sell. For those types of systems which use proprietary components, you should contact the manufacturer for their specific documentation.

Companies who assemble or build systems out of industry standard components may either produce their own documentation, or simply include the documentation that is included with the components they install in their systems. Most of the larger system assemblers such as Gateway, Dell, Micron, Midwest Micro, and others will also have their own custom-produced documentation for the main system unit, and may even have custom manuals for many of the individual system components.

This type of documentation is useful for people setting up a system for the first time or for performing simple upgrades, but often lacks the detailed technical reference information needed by somebody who might be troubleshooting the system or upgrading it beyond what the manufacturer or assembler had originally intended. In that case, you are better off with any of the OEM component manuals which are available directly from the component or peripheral manufacturers themselves.

Most of the smaller system assemblers will forego any custom-produced system documentation and simply include the component level manuals for the components they are including in the assembled system. For example, if an Asus motherboard and STB video card were included in a particular system, then the manuals from Asus and STB which originally came with those products would be included with the assembled system.

> **Getting Documentation from an Assembler**
>
> Some system assemblers like to keep the component documentation and not include it with the systems they build. This forces the purchaser of the systems to go back to the assembler for any support or technical information, and also tends to make the purchaser believe that the assembler actually manufactured the system rather than simply assembled it using off-the-shelf components. I would not recommend purchasing from any system assembler who did not include all of the documentation for the individual system components they are installing.

The standard manuals included with most system components and peripherals contain basic instructions for system setup, operation, testing, relocation, and option installation. Some sort of basic diagnostics disk (sometimes called a *Diagnostics and Setup* or *Reference Disk*) normally is included with a system as well. Often the diagnostics are simply a custom labeled version of a commonly available commercial diagnostic program.

> **Tip**
>
> Most system vendors and equipment manufacturers have jumper settings and manuals available on their Web sites in downloadable form. Appendix A contains a list of vendors and their Web sites.

Component and Peripheral Documentation

It is a well-known fact that many systems sold today are not really manufactured as a custom unit by a single company but instead are assembled out of standard off-the-shelf components that are available on the open market. In fact, I normally recommend that people purchase exactly that type of system, because all of the components conform to known standards and can easily be replaced or upgraded later.

Even proprietary manufactured systems such as IBM, Compaq, Hewlett-Packard, Packard Bell, and others use at least some off-the-shelf standard components (disk drives, for example). To fully document a system, I recommend you take an inventory of the standard components used, and collect all of the OEM documentation or product manuals for them.

This process is simple; when I am supporting a given system, I first disassemble it and write down all of the information on each of the components inside. Sometimes you will need to do a little more investigating or even ask the company who assembled the system exactly what components they included. Most components such as hard disks, CD-ROM drives, video cards, sound cards, network cards, and more are pretty easy to identify. Somewhere on the device or card there should be a label indicating at least the manufacturer and usually also the model number. From this, you can look up the manufacturer in the vendor listing in Appendix A of this book. Using that information, you can contact the company via telephone, fax, or Internet Web site to obtain the complete documentation on their products.

Motherboards can be tricky to identify because not all manufacturers mark them clearly. In that case, you are best off contacting the company who sold you the computer to ask them exactly what motherboard you have. Don't be afraid to ask the company exactly what motherboard or other components they are installing in the systems they sell. If they can't or won't answer, you may be better off purchasing from a different company in the future. If the company who sold the system is no longer available or cannot help, check the paperwork that came with the system. Sometimes there are clues in the original paperwork that might indicate what motherboard your system includes. Most of the popular motherboard manufacturers are listed in the vendor list in Appendix A.

You will also find a listing in the vendor list for MicroHouse. They sell a reference manual called the *Encyclopedia of Main Boards*, which has information on hundreds of different PC-compatible motherboards. As a last resort, you might be able to identify your board by comparing it to those shown in their book. In their motherboard encyclopedia, you will find information about the jumper and switch settings of most PC boards on the market.

As an example, one system I worked on is a Gateway P6 (Pentium Pro) 200MHz system which included the following industry standard components:

Motherboard:	Intel VS440FX "Venus"
Video Card:	STB Velocity 3D
Hard Disk:	Quantum Fireball TM3840A
Floppy Drive:	Panasonic JU-256
CD-ROM Drive:	Mitsumi FX120

Many of the larger system assemblers like Gateway and Dell have been using Intel motherboards. Most motherboards today use Intel processors and chipsets, but some people may not be aware that Intel makes complete PC motherboards as well. Even so, Gateway did not include the actual Intel motherboard or other component manuals but instead included their own custom manuals for the motherboard, video card, hard disk, and CD-ROM drive. By contacting the individual companies directly over the Internet and via the telephone, I was able to obtain more detailed documentation on all of these products. Many times the OEM documentation or product manuals can be downloaded directly from the respective companies' Web sites, often in the form of Adobe Acrobat .PDF files, which you can read with the Acrobat reader available for free for downloading from Adobe.

> **Note**
>
> Not all of these manuals are available online, and even if they are, it is still nice to have the printed manuals or datasheets in your documentation library for future reference.

Chip and Chipset Documentation

If you really want the ultimate in documentation for your system, I highly recommend getting the documentation for the various chips and chipsets in your system. This would include specific manuals for each of the major chip-level components in the system—such as the processor, motherboard chipset, BIOS, super I/O chipset, and so on. Before you can get this documentation, you must first identify all of the relevant chips and chipsets in your system.

The process is relatively simple. Look at the documentation for each major component, especially the motherboard. The OEM motherboard documentation should tell you which chipset is used on the board, which processors are supported, and which super I/O chip is used. From the OEM documentation you have on your system components, you should be able to find out what the following major chip and chipsets are:

Processor   Super I/O Chip

Motherboard Chipset   Video Chipset

ROM BIOS

If your motherboard has an integrated video card, then the video chipset type will be listed there also. If you have a separate video card, then look in the video card manual and it should clearly identify the video chipset used.

The most important chips you will want to identify are on the motherboard. The first thing you would want to identify is the processor. This should be relatively easy; most PC systems use Intel processors. A small percentage of systems use AMD or Cyrix processors, or versions of these processors sold under other names. The documentation that comes with the system will normally identify which brand of processor you have, and which model and speed it is.

If you aren't sure what processor is in the system, software programs such as the MSD (Microsoft Diagnostics) program are included with Windows, or a system diagnostic you purchase such as the Norton Utilities.

Normally the processor is the largest chip on the motherboard, and can often be identified by simply reading the information stamped on it. In some cases, the processor will have a heat sink or fan attached to the top, in which case you may have to either remove the heat sink or fan to read the information stamped on top of the chip, or simply remove the entire processor and heat sink or fan assembly to read the information stamped on the bottom of the chip.

The chipset is difficult for software to determine, so you will either have to find out which chipset you have from the motherboard documentation or by first-hand inspection. The motherboard chipset normally consists of several large chips on the board; there are chipsets that use anywhere from one to six chips. Generally each chip in the set will have a part number stamped on it, but the chipset itself will be named after the main chip. The Pentium Pro board I mentioned had two chips labeled 82441FX and 82442FX; these are both a part of what Intel calls the *440FX chipset*.

Finding out the manufacturer of the motherboard BIOS is easy; that is normally found in the motherboard manual. It is also displayed, along with the exact version number you have, every time you power the system on. Most systems today use an AMI, Award, or Phoenix BIOS, but there are several other manufacturers as well.

Virtually all motherboards built in the '90s and later include a special interface chip called a super I/O chip. This is a single chip device that normally includes the following components:

- Primary and secondary IDE host adapters
- Floppy controller
- Two serial ports
- One parallel port

Some do not include the IDE host adapters, such as the National Semiconductor 87308 used in the Pentium Pro motherboard I have been referring to. That particular chip also includes an 8042-style keyboard controller and a MC146818-style real-time clock with nonvolatile CMOS RAM. Other super I/O chips may include a game (joystick) interface as well. Obtaining the documentation for your particular super I/O chip will of course tell you exactly what it's capabilities are.

Another important chipset in a system is the *video chipset*. This is normally found on the video card, or on the motherboard if the motherboard has built-in video. The OEM video card or motherboard documentation should tell you exactly which video chipset you have. If not, then you can use free software such as MSD or commercial programs such as Norton Utilities to identify which chipset you have without even opening up the case. A last resort would be to open the system and read the part number right off of the video chipset, which is usually the largest chip on the video card.

Using as an example a Pentium Pro 200MHz system as an example, I found it contained the following main chip and chipset components:

Processor:	Intel Pentium Pro
Motherboard Chipset:	Intel 440FX "Natoma"
ROM BIOS:	AMI
Super I/O Chip:	National Semiconductor PC87308
Video Chipset:	S3 Inc. ViRGE/VX

Note that this particular motherboard did not have the video integrated, so the video chipset was on the video card.

From this documentation, I learned about the capability to increase the clock multiplier setting on the motherboard to an otherwise undocumented 3.5x, which resulted in running the Pentium Pro 200 chip at 233MHz! I was also able to get more information on the various serial, parallel, and disk controllers contained in the super I/O chip, and learned more about the advanced CMOS settings in the BIOS Setup routines.

For example, I often get questions about the Advanced CMOS settings. Most people assume that these settings would be described in their ROM BIOS documentation because the ROM-based CMOS Setup program in their system controls these settings. If you contact the BIOS manufacturer or read the BIOS documentation, you will quickly find out that the ROM BIOS manufacturer knows little or nothing about these settings. In fact, these settings actually have little or nothing to do with the particular ROM BIOS used, and everything to do with the particular motherboard *chipset* used. You can find descriptions of all these settings in the documentation for your motherboard chipset, which can be obtained from the chipset manufacturer.

Manufacturer-Specific Documentation

If your system is from a name-brand manufacturer—such as IBM, Compaq, Hewlett-Packard, Toshiba, and others—then there may be a wealth of information available in manufacturer-specific manuals and documentation. Because of the specific nature of the information in these types of manuals, you most likely will have to obtain it from the manufacturer of the system.

The process of obtaining other manufacturers' manuals may (or may not) be easy. Most large companies run responsible service and support operations that provide technical documentation. Other companies either do not have or are unwilling to part with such documentation, in an effort to protect their service departments (and their dealers' service departments) from competition. Contact the manufacturer directly; the manufacturer can direct you to the correct department so that you can inquire about this information. Information on how to contact most PC manufacturers can be found in the vendor listing in Appendix A of this book.

Warranties and Service Contracts

Extended warranties are a more recent trend in the computer industry. With the current fierce competition among hardware vendors, a good warranty is one way for a specific manufacturer to stand out from the crowd. Although most companies offer a one-year warranty on their systems, others offer longer warranty periods, such as three years or more.

In addition to extended-length warranties, some manufacturers offer free or nearly free on-site service during the warranty period. Many highly competitive mail-order outfits offer service such as this for little or no extra cost.

Chapter 2—Overview of System Features and Components

> **Tip**
>
> Most companies offer extended-length warranties and free or low-cost on-site service. If your system is "mission-critical," meaning it absolutely must be functioning all the time (such as with a network file, database, or application server), you might want to consider an on-site service contract. Such contracts are usually overkill for a standard PC.

In most normal cases, service contracts are not worth the price. In the retail computer environment, a service contract is often a way for a dealer or vendor to add income to a sale. Most annual service contracts add 5 to 10 percent of the cost of the system. A service contract for a $5,000 system, for example, costs $250 to $500 per year. Just as in the auto industry, salespeople in the computer industry are trained to vigorously sell service contracts. Extra cost warranties or service contracts are largely unnecessary except in special situations.

> **Note**
>
> Retail computer stores, electronics stores, and PC distributors make almost no money on the home PC you buy. Stiff price competition has taken away any profit they might make. However, add-ons—such as service contracts, surge suppressors, mouse pads, and so on—are very high-margin items. Stores make their money by selling the extras, not the computer itself.

The high prices of service contracts also might affect the quality of service you receive. Technicians could try to make their work seem more complex than it actually is to make you believe that the contract's price is justified. For example, a service technician might replace your hard disk or entire motherboard with a spare when all you need is low-level formatting for the hard disk or a simple fix for the motherboard such as a single memory chip. A "defective" drive, for example, probably is just returned to the shop for low-level formatting. Eventually, it ends up in somebody else's system. Replacing a part is faster and leaves the impression that your expensive service contract is worth the price because you get a "new" part. You might be much less impressed with your expensive service contract if the service people visit, do a simple troubleshooting procedure, and then replace a single $2 cable or spend 15 minutes reformatting the hard disk.

With some basic troubleshooting skills, simple tools, and a few spare parts, you can eliminate the need for most of these expensive service contracts. Unfortunately, some companies practice deceptive servicing procedures to justify the expensive service contracts they offer. Users are made to believe that these types of component failures are the norm, and they have a mistaken impression about the overall reliability of today's systems.

> **Tip**
>
> If you have many systems, you can justify carrying a spare-parts inventory, which can also eliminate the need for a service contract. For less than what a service contract costs for five to 10 systems, you often can buy a complete spare system each year. Protecting yourself with extra

> equipment rather than service contracts is practical if you have more than 10 computers of the same make or model. For extremely time-sensitive applications, you might be wise to buy a second system along with the primary unit—such as in a network file-server application. Only you can make the appropriate cost-justification analysis to decide whether you need a service contract or a spare system.

In some instances, buying a service contract can be justified and beneficial. If you have a system that must function at all times and is so expensive that you cannot buy a complete spare system, or for a system in a remote location far away from a centralized service operation, you might be wise to invest in a good service contract that provides timely repairs. Before contracting for service, you should consider your options carefully. These sources either supply or authorize service contracts:

- Manufacturers
- Dealers or vendors
- Third parties

Although most users take the manufacturer or dealer service, sometimes a third party tries harder to close the deal; for example, it sometimes includes all the equipment installed, even aftermarket items the dealers or manufacturers don't offer. In other cases, a manufacturer might not have its own service organization; instead, it makes a deal with a major third-party nationwide service company to provide authorized service.

After you select an organization, several levels of service often are available. Starting with the most expensive, these levels of service typically include:

- Four-hour on-site response
- Next-day on-site response
- Carry-in/ship-in, or "depot," service

The actual menu varies from manufacturer to manufacturer. For example, IBM offers only a full 24-hours-a-day, 7-days-a-week, on-site service contract. IBM claims that a technician is dispatched usually within four hours of your call. For older systems, but not the PS/2, IBM also offers a courier or carry-in service contract. Warranty work, normally a customer carry-in depot arrangement, can be upgraded to a full on-site contract for only $40. After the first-year $40 contract upgrade expires, you can continue the full on-site service contract for standard rates.

If you have ever bought a service contract, you may be surprised by the pricing. In most cases, the price will be so high that you will only be able to justify it for mission-critical systems such as file servers.

Chapter 3

System Teardown and Inspection

This chapter examines procedures for tearing down and inspecting a system. The chapter describes the types of tools required, the procedure for disassembling the system, and the various components that make up the system. A special section discusses some of the test equipment you can use when troubleshooting a system; another section covers some problems you may encounter with the hardware (screws, nuts, bolts, and so on).

Using the Proper Tools

To troubleshoot and repair PC systems properly, you need a few basic tools. If you intend to troubleshoot and repair PCs professionally, there are many more specialized tools you will want to purchase. These advanced tools allow you to more accurately diagnose problems and make the jobs easier and faster. The basic tools that should be in every troubleshooter's toolbox are:

- Simple hand tools for basic disassembly and reassembly procedures, including a flat blade and Phillips screwdrivers (both medium and small sizes), tweezers, an IC extraction tool, and a parts grabber or *hemostats*

- Diagnostics software and hardware for testing components in a system

- A multimeter that allows accurate measurement of voltage and resistance

- Chemicals, such as contact cleaners, component freeze sprays, and compressed air for cleaning the system

- Foam swabs, or cotton swabs if foam isn't available

- Small wire ties for "dressing" or organizing wires

Some environments may also have the resources to purchase the following, although it's not required for most work:

- Memory testing machines, which are used to evaluate the operation of SIMMs (Single Inline Memory Modules), DIP (Dual Inline Pin) chips, and other memory modules

Chapter 3—System Teardown and Inspection

- Serial and parallel wrap plugs to test serial and parallel ports
- A network cable scanner, if a network is used
- A serial breakout box if a lot of the systems operate over serial cables, such as UNIX dumb terminals

In addition, an experienced troubleshooter will probably want to have soldering and desoldering tools to fix bad serial cables. These tools are discussed in more detail in the following section. Diagnostics software and hardware are discussed in Chapter 21, "Software and Hardware Diagnostic Tools."

Hand Tools

When you work with PC systems, it immediately becomes apparent that the tools required for nearly all service operations are very simple and inexpensive. You can carry most of the required tools in a small pouch. Even a top-of-the-line "master mechanics" set fits inside a briefcase-size container. The cost of these tool kits ranges from about $20 for a small service kit to $500 for one of the briefcase-size deluxe kits. Compare these costs with what might be necessary for an automotive technician. Most automotive service techs spend $5,000 to $10,000 or more for the tools they need. Not only are PC tools much less expensive, but I can tell you from experience that you don't get nearly as dirty working on computers as you do working on cars.

In this section, you learn about the tools required to make a kit that is capable of performing basic, board-level service on PC systems. One of the best ways to start such a set of tools is a small kit sold especially for servicing PCs.

The following list shows the basic tools that you can find in one of the small PC tool kits that sell for about $20:

- 3/16-inch nut driver
- 1/4-inch nut driver
- Small Phillips screwdriver
- Small flat-blade screwdriver
- Medium Phillips screwdriver
- Medium flat-blade screwdriver
- Chip extractor
- Chip inserter
- Tweezers
- Claw-type parts grabber
- T10 and T15 Torx drivers

> **Note**
> Some tools aren't recommended because they are of limited use. However, they normally come with these types of kits.

You use nut drivers to remove the hexagonal-headed screws that secure the system-unit covers, adapter boards, disk drives, power supplies, and speakers in most systems. The nut drivers work much better than conventional screwdrivers.

Because some manufacturers have substituted slotted or Phillips-head screws for the more standard hexagonal-head screws, standard screwdrivers can be used for those systems.

You use the chip-extraction and insertion tools to install or remove memory chips (or other smaller chips) without bending any pins on the chip. Usually, you pry out larger chips, such as some microprocessors or ROMs, with the small screwdriver. Larger processors such as the 486, Pentium, or Pentium Pro chips require a chip extractor if they are in a standard *LIF (Low Insertion Force)* socket. These chips have so many pins on them that a large amount of force is required to remove them, despite the fact that they call the socket "low insertion force." If you use a screwdriver on a large physical-size chip like a 486 or Pentium, you risk cracking the case of the chip and permanently damaging it. The chip extractor tool for removing these chips has a very wide end with tines that fit between the pins on the chip to distribute the force evenly along the chip's underside. This will minimize the likelihood of breakage. Most of these types of extraction tools must be purchased specially for the chip you're trying to remove.

Fortunately, motherboard designers have seen fit to use mostly *ZIF (Zero Insertion Force)* sockets on systems with 486 and larger processors. The ZIF socket has a lever which when raised releases the grip on the pins of the chip, allowing it to be easily lifted out with your fingers.

The tweezers and parts grabber can be used to hold any small screws or jumper blocks that are difficult to hold in your hand. The parts grabber is especially useful when you drop a small part into the interior of a system; usually, you can remove the part without completely disassembling the system.

Finally, the Torx driver is a special, star-shaped driver that matches the special screws found in most Compaq systems and in many other systems as well.

Although this basic set is useful, you should supplement it with some other small hand tools, such as:

- Needlenose pliers
- Hemostats
- Wire cutter or wire stripper
- Vise or clamp
- File
- Small flashlight

Pliers are useful for straightening pins on chips, applying or removing jumpers, crimping cables, or grabbing small parts.

Hemostats are especially useful for grabbing small components, such as jumpers.

The wire cutter or stripper, obviously, is useful for making or repairing cables or wiring.

The metric nut drivers can be used in many clone or compatible systems as well as in the IBM PS/2 systems, all of which use metric hardware.

The tamperproof Torx drivers can be used to remove Torx screws with the tamper-resistant pin in the center of the screw. A tamperproof Torx driver has a hole drilled in it to allow clearance for the pin.

You can use a vise to install connectors on cables and to crimp cables to the shape you want, as well as to hold parts during delicate operations. In addition to the vise, Radio Shack sells a nifty "extra hands" device which has two movable arms with alligator clips on the end. This type of device is very useful for making cables or for other delicate operations where an extra set of hands to hold something might be useful.

You can use the file to smooth rough metal edges on cases and chassis, as well as to trim the faceplates on disk drives for a perfect fit.

The flashlight can be used to illuminate system interiors, especially when the system is cramped and the room lighting is not good. I consider this tool to be essential.

Another consideration for your tool kit is an *ESD (electrostatic discharge) protection kit*. This kit consists of a wrist strap with a ground wire and a specially conductive mat, also with its own ground wire. Using a kit like this when working on a system will help to ensure that you never accidentally zap any of the components with a static discharge.

> **Note**
>
> You can work without an ESD protection kit, if you're disciplined and careful about working on systems. If you don't have an ESD kit available, you should leave the computer plugged in, so that the power cord connects the chassis of the PC to ground. Then make sure that you remain in constant or nearly constant contact with the case. It's easy to rest an arm or elbow on some part of the case while working inside the computer.

The ESD kits, as well as all the other tools and much more, are available from a variety of tool vendors. Specialized Products Company and Jensen Tools are two of the most popular vendors of computer and electronic tools and of service equipment. Their catalogs show an extensive selection of very high-quality tools. (These companies and several others are listed in Appendix A, "Vendor List.") With a simple set of hand tools, you will be equipped for nearly every PC repair or installation situation. The total cost of these tools should be less than $150, which is not much considering the capabilities they give you.

Soldering and Desoldering Tools

In certain situations—such as repairing a broken wire, making cables, reattaching a component to a circuit board, removing and installing chips that are not in a socket, or adding jumper wires or pins to a board—you must use a soldering iron to make the repair.

Although virtually all repairs these days are done by simply replacing the entire failed board, you may need a soldering iron in some situations. The most common case would be where there was physical damage to a system, such as where somebody had ripped the keyboard connector off of a motherboard by pulling on the cable improperly. Simple soldering skills could save the motherboard in this case.

Most motherboards these days include I/O components such as serial and parallel ports. Many of these ports are fuse-protected on the board; however, the fuse is usually a small soldered-in component. These fuses are designed to protect the motherboard circuits from damage from an external source. If a short circuit or static charge from an external device blows these fuses, the board can be saved if you can replace them.

To perform minor repairs such as these, you need a low-wattage soldering iron—usually about 25 watts. More than 30 watts generates too much heat and can damage the components on the board. Even with a low-wattage unit, you must limit the amount of heat to which you subject the board and its components. You can do this with quick and efficient use of the soldering iron, as well as with the use of heat-sinking devices clipped to the leads of the device being soldered. A *heat sink* is a small metal clip-on device designed to absorb excessive heat before it reaches the component that the heat sink is protecting. In some cases, you can use a pair of hemostats as an effective heat sink when you solder a component.

To remove components that originally were soldered into place from a printed circuit board, you can use a soldering iron with a *solder sucker*. This device normally is constructed as a small tube with an air chamber and a plunger-and-spring arrangement. (I do not recommend the squeeze-bulb type of solder sucker.) The unit is "cocked" when you press the spring-loaded plunger into the air chamber. When you want to remove a device from a board, you use the soldering iron from the underside of the board, and heat the point at which one of the component leads joins the circuit board until the solder melts. As soon as melting occurs, move the solder-sucker nozzle into position, and press the actuator. This procedure allows the plunger to retract and creates a momentary suction that inhales the liquid solder from the connection and leaves the component lead dry in the hole.

Always do the heating and suctioning from the underside of a board, not from the component side. Repeat this action for every component lead joined to the circuit board. When you master this technique, you can remove a small component in a minute or two with only a small likelihood of damage to the board or other components. Larger chips that have many pins can be more difficult to remove and resolder without damaging other components or the circuit board.

> **Tip**
>
> These procedures are intended for Through-Hole devices only. These are components whose pins extend all the way through holes in the board to the underside. Surface mount devices are removed with a completely different procedure, using much more expensive tools. Working on surface-mounted components is beyond the capabilities of all but the most well-equipped shops.

If you intend to add soldering and desoldering skills to your arsenal of capabilities, you should practice. Take a useless circuit board and practice removing various components from the board, then reinstall the components. Try to remove the components from the board by using the least amount of heat possible. Also, perform the solder-melting operations as quickly as possible, limiting the time that the iron is applied to the joint. Before you install any components, clean out the holes through which the leads must project and mount the component in place. Then apply the solder from the underside of the board, using as little heat and solder as possible.

Attempt to produce joints as clean as the joints that the board manufacturer performed by machine. Soldered joints that do not look clean may keep the component from making a good connection with the rest of the circuit. This "cold-solder joint" normally is created because you have not used enough heat. *Remember that you should not practice your new soldering skills on the motherboard of a system that you are attempting to repair!* Don't attempt to work on real boards until you are sure of your skills. I always keep a few junk boards around for soldering practice and experimentation.

> **Tip**
>
> When first learning to solder, you may be tempted to set the iron on the solder and leave it there until the solder melts. If the solder doesn't melt immediately when applying the iron to it, you're not transferring the heat from the iron to the solder efficiently. This means that either the iron is dirty, or there is debris between it and the solder. To clean the iron, take a wet sponge and drag it across the tip of the iron.
>
> If after cleaning the iron there's still some resistance, try to scratch the solder with the iron when it's hot. Generally, this removes any barriers to heat flow and will instantly melt the solder.

No matter how good you get at soldering and desoldering, some jobs are best left to professionals. Components that are surface-mounted to a circuit board, for example, require special tools for soldering and desoldering, as do other components that have high pin densities.

I upgraded an IBM P75 portable system by replacing the 486DX-33 processor with a 486DX2-66 processor. This procedure normally would be simple (especially if the system uses a ZIF socket), but in this particular system, the 168-pin 486DX chip was soldered into a special processor card. To add to the difficulty, there were surface-mounted components on both sides of the card—even the solder side.

Needless to say, this was a very difficult job that required a special piece of equipment called a *hot air rework station*. The hot air rework station uses blasts of hot air to solder or desolder all of the pins on a chip simultaneously. To perform this replacement job, the components on the solder side of the board were protected with special heat-resistant masking tape, while the hot air was directed at the 168 pins of the 486 chip, allowing it to be removed. Then the replacement chip was inserted into the holes in the board, a special solder paste was applied to the pins, and the hot air was used again to solder all 168 pins simultaneously.

The use of professional equipment such as this resulted in a perfect job that cannot be told from the factory original. Attempting a job like this with a conventional soldering iron probably would have damaged the expensive processor chips, as well as the even more expensive multilayer processor card.

Using Proper Test Equipment

In some cases, you must use specialized devices to test a system board or component. This test equipment is not expensive or difficult to use, but it can add much to your troubleshooting abilities. I consider a voltmeter to be required gear for proper system testing. A *multimeter* can serve many purposes, including checking for voltage signals at different points in a system, testing the output of the power supply, and checking for continuity in a circuit or cable. An outlet tester is an invaluable accessory that can check the electrical outlet for proper wiring. This capability is useful if you believe that the problem lies outside the computer system itself.

Wrap Plugs (Loopback Connectors)
For diagnosing serial- and parallel-port problems, you need *wrap plugs* (also called *loopback connectors*), which are used to circulate, or wrap, signals. The plugs enable the serial or parallel port to send data to itself for diagnostic purposes.

Several types of wrap plugs are available. You need one for the 25-pin serial port, one for the 9-pin serial port, and one for the 25-pin parallel port (see Table 3.1). Many companies, including IBM, sell the plugs separately. IBM also sells a special version that includes all three types in one plug.

Table 3.1 Wrap Plug Types	
Description	**IBM Part Number**
Parallel-port wrap plug	8529228
Serial-port wrap plug, 25-pin	8529280
Serial-port wrap plug, 9-pin (AT)	8286126
Tri-connector wrap plug	72X8546

The handy tri-connector unit contains all commonly needed plugs in one compact unit. The unit costs approximately $30 from IBM. Be aware that most professional diagnostics packages (especially the ones that I recommend) include the three types of wrap plugs in the package; you may not need to purchase them separately. If you're handy, you can even make your own wrap plugs for testing. I include wiring diagrams for the three types of wrap plugs in Chapter 11, "Communications and Networking." In that chapter, you also will find a detailed discussion of serial and parallel ports.

Beyond a simple wrap plug, you can use a *breakout box*. These are usually DB25 connector devices which allow you to make custom temporary cables or even to monitor signals on a cable. For most PC troubleshooting use, one of the "mini" breakout boxes works well and is inexpensive.

Meters

Many troubleshooting procedures require that you measure voltage and resistance. You take these measurements by using a handheld Digital Multi-Meter (DMM). The meter can be an analog device (using an actual meter) or a digital-readout device. The DMM has a pair of wires called *test leads* or *probes*. The test leads make the connections so that you can take readings. Depending on the meter's setting, the probes measure electrical resistance, direct-current (DC) voltage, or alternating-current (AC) voltage.

Usually, each system-unit measurement setting has several ranges of operation. DC voltage, for example, usually can be read in several scales, to a maximum of 200 millivolts (mv), 2v, 20v, 200v, and 1,000v. Because computers use both +5 and +12v for various operations, you should use the 20v maximum scale for making your measurements. Making these measurements on the 200mv or 2v scale could "peg the meter" and possibly damage it because the voltage would be much higher than expected. Using the 200v or 1,000v scale works, but the readings at 5v and 12v are so small in proportion to the maximum that accuracy is low.

If you are taking a measurement and are unsure of the actual voltage, start at the highest scale and work your way down. Most of the better meters have autoranging capability: The meter automatically selects the best range for any measurement. This type of meter is much easier to operate. You just set the meter to the type of reading you want, such as DC volts, and attach the probes to the signal source. The meter selects the correct voltage range and displays the value. Because of their design, these types of meters always have a digital display rather than a meter needle.

> **Caution**
>
> Whenever using a multimeter to test any voltage that could potentially be 110v or above, always use one hand to do the testing, not two. Either clip one lead to one of the sources and probe with the other, or hold both leads in one hand.
>
> If you are holding a lead in each hand and accidentally slip, you can very easily become a circuit, allowing power to conduct or flow through you. When the power is flowing from arm to arm, the path of the current is directly across the heart. Hearts have a tendency to quit working when subjected to high voltages. They're funny that way.

I prefer the small digital meters; you can buy them for only slightly more than the analog style, and they're extremely accurate, as well as much safer for digital circuits. Some of these meters are not much bigger than a cassette tape; they fit in a shirt pocket. Radio Shack sells a good unit (made for Radio Shack by Beckman) in the $25 price range; the meter is a half-inch thick, weighs 3 1/2 ounces, and is digital and autoranging as well. This type of meter works well for most, if not all, PC troubleshooting and test uses.

> **Caution**
>
> You should be aware that many analog meters can be dangerous to digital circuits. These meters use a 9v battery to power the meter for resistance measurements. If you use this type of meter to

measure resistance on some digital circuits, you can damage the electronics, because you essentially are injecting 9v into the circuit. The digital meters universally run on 3 to 5v or less.

Logic Probes and Logic Pulsers

A *logic probe* can be useful for diagnosing problems in digital circuits. In a *digital circuit*, a signal is represented as either high (+5v) or low (0v). Because these signals are present for only a short time (measured in millionths of a second) or oscillate (switch on and off) rapidly, a simple voltmeter is useless. A logic probe is designed to display these signal conditions easily.

Logic probes are especially useful for troubleshooting a dead system. By using the probe, you can determine whether the basic clock circuitry is operating and whether other signals necessary for system operation are present. In some cases, a probe can help you cross-check the signals at each pin on an Integrated Circuit chip. You can compare the signals present at each pin with the signals that a known-good chip of the same type would show—a comparison that is helpful in isolating a failed component. Logic probes can be useful for troubleshooting some disk drive problems by enabling you to test the signals present on the interface cable or drive-logic board.

A companion tool to the probe is the logic pulser. A *pulser* is designed to test circuit reaction by delivering into a circuit a logical high (+5v) pulse, usually lasting 1 1/2 to 10 millionths of a second. Compare the reaction with that of a *known-functional circuit*. This type of device normally is used much less frequently than a logic probe, but in some cases, it can be helpful for testing a circuit.

Outlet Testers

Outlet testers are very useful test tools. These simple, inexpensive devices, which are sold at hardware stores, are used to test electrical outlets. You simply plug the device in, and three LEDs light in various combinations, indicating whether the outlet is wired correctly.

Although you may think that badly wired outlets would be a rare problem, I have seen a large number of installations in which the outlets were wired incorrectly. Most of the time, the problem seems to be in the ground wire. An improperly wired outlet can result in flaky system operation, such as random parity checks and lockups. With an improper ground circuit, currents can begin flowing on the electrical ground circuits in the system. Because the system uses the voltage on the ground circuits as a comparative signal to determine whether bits are 0 or 1, a floating ground can cause data errors in the system.

Once, while running one of my PC troubleshooting seminars, I was using a system that I literally could not approach without locking it up. Whenever I walked past the system, the electrostatic field generated by my body interfered with the system, and the PC locked up, displaying a parity-check error message. The problem was that the hotel I was using was very old and had no grounded outlets in the room. The only way I could prevent the system from locking up was to run the class in my stocking feet, because my leather-soled shoes were generating the static charge.

Other symptoms of bad ground wiring in electrical outlets are continuous electrical shocks when you touch the case or chassis of the system. These shocks indicate that voltages are flowing where they should not be. This problem also can be caused by bad or improper grounds within the system itself. By using the simple outlet tester, you can quickly determine whether the outlet is at fault.

If you just walk up to a system and receive an initial shock, it's probably just static electricity. Touch the chassis again without moving your feet. If you receive another shock, there is something *very* wrong. In this case, the ground wire actually has voltage applied to it. You should have a professional electrician come out immediately.

If you don't like being a human rat in an electrical experiment, you can test the outlets with your multimeter. First, remember to hold both leads in one hand. Test from one blade hole to another. This should read between 110–125v depending upon the electrical service in the area. Then check from each blade to the ground (the round hole). One blade hole, the smaller one, should show a voltage almost identical to the one that you got from the blade hole-to-blade hole test. The larger blade hole when measured to ground should show less than 0.5v.

Because ground and neutral are supposed to be tied together at the electrical panel, much difference indicates that they are not tied together. However, small differences can be accounted for by the fact that there may be current from other outlets down the line flowing on the neutral, and there isn't any on the ground.

If you don't get the results you expect, call an electrician to test the outlets for you. More weird computer problems are caused by improper grounding, and other power problems, than people like to believe.

SIMM Testers

I now consider a SIMM test machine a virtually mandatory piece of gear for anybody serious about performing PC troubleshooting and repair as a profession. These are basically small test machines designed to evaluate SIMM and other types of memory modules including individual chips such as cache memory. They can be somewhat expensive, costing upwards of $1,000 to $2,500 or more, but these types of machines are the only truly accurate way to test memory.

Without one of these testers, you are relegated to testing memory by running a diagnostic program on the PC and testing the memory as it is installed. This can be very problematic, as the memory diagnostic program can do only two things to the memory: write and read. A SIMM tester can do many things that a memory diagnostic running in a PC cannot do, such as:

- Identify the type of memory
- Identify the memory speed
- Identify whether the memory has parity or is using bogus parity emulation
- Vary the refresh timing and access speed timing

- Locate single-bit failures
- Detect power and noise-related failures
- Detect solder opens and shorts
- Isolate timing-related failures
- Detect data-retention errors

No conventional memory diagnostic software can do these things because it has to rely on the fixed-access parameters set up by the memory controller hardware in the motherboard chipset. This prevents the software from being able to alter the timing and methods used to access the memory. You end up with memory that will fail in one system and work in another, when it is in fact actually bad. This can allow intermittent problems to occur, and be almost impossible to detect.

The bottom line is that there is no way that truly accurate memory testing can be done in a PC; a SIMM tester is required for comprehensive and accurate testing of memory. With the price of a typical 32M memory module at more than $200, the price of a SIMM tester can be justified very easily in a shop environment where a lot of PCs will be tested. One of the SIMM testers I recommend the most is the SIGMA LC by Darkhorse Systems. See the vendor list in Appendix A for more information. Also see Chapter 7, "Memory," for more information on memory in general.

Chemicals

Chemicals can be used to help clean, troubleshoot, and even repair a system. For the most basic function—cleaning components, electrical connectors, and contacts—one of the most useful chemicals was 1,1,1 trichloroethane. This substance was a very effective cleaner. This chemical was used to clean electrical contacts and components, and did not damage most plastics and board materials. In fact, trichloroethane could be very useful for cleaning stains on the system case and keyboard. Electronic chemical-supply companies are now offering several replacements for trichloroethane because it is being regulated as a chlorinated solvent, along with CFCs (chlorofluorocarbons) such as freon.

A unique type of contact enhancer and lubricant called *Stabilant 22* is currently on the market. This chemical, which is applied to electrical contacts, greatly enhances the connection and lubricates the contact point; it is much more effective than conventional contact cleaners or lubricants.

Stabilant 22 is a liquid-polymer semiconductor; it behaves like liquid metal and conducts electricity in the presence of an electric current. The substance also fills the air gaps between the mating surfaces of two items that are in contact, making the surface area of the contact larger and also keeping out oxygen and other contaminants that can oxidize and corrode the contact point.

This chemical is available in several forms. Stabilant 22 itself is the concentrated version, whereas Stabilant 22a is a version diluted with isopropanol in a 4:1 ratio. An even more diluted 8:1-ratio version is sold in many high-end stereo and audio shops under the name Tweek. Just 15ml of Stabilant 22a sells for about $40, whereas a liter of the concentrate costs about $4,000!

As you can plainly see, Stabilant 22 is fairly expensive, but very little is required in an application, and nothing else has been found to be as effective in preserving electrical contacts. (NASA uses the chemical on spacecraft electronics.) An application of Stabilant can provide protection for up to 16 years, according to its manufacturer, D.W. Electrochemicals. You will find the company's address and phone number in the vendor list in Appendix A.

Stabilant is especially effective on I/O slot connectors, adapter-card edge and pin connectors, disk drive connectors, power-supply connectors, and virtually any connector in the PC. In addition to enhancing the contact and preventing corrosion, an application of Stabilant lubricates the contacts, making insertion and removal of the connector easier.

Compressed air often is used as an aid in system cleaning. Normally composed of freon or carbon dioxide (CO_2), compressed gas is used as a blower to remove dust and debris from a system or component. Be careful when you use these devices: Some of them can generate a tremendous static charge as the compressed gas leaves the nozzle of the can. Be sure that you are using the kind approved for cleaning or dusting computer equipment, and consider wearing a static grounding strap as a precaution. Freon TF is known to generate these large static charges; Freon R12 is less severe.

Of course, because both chemicals damage the ozone layer, most suppliers are phasing them out. Expect to see new versions of these compressed-air devices with CO_2 or some other less-harmful propellant.

When using these compressed air products, make sure you hold the can upright so that only gas is ejected from the nozzle. If you tip the can, the raw propellant will come out, which is wasteful. This operation should be performed on equipment which is powered off to minimize any chance of damage through short circuiting or bumping anything.

Caution

If you use any chemical that contains the propellant Freon R12 (dichlorodifluoromethane), *do not expose the gas to an open flame or other heat source*. If you burn this substance, a highly toxic gas called *phosgene* is generated. Phosgene, used as a choking gas in World War I, can be deadly.

Freon R12 is the substance that was used in most automobile air-conditioning systems before 1995. Automobile service technicians are instructed *never* to smoke near air-conditioning systems. By 1996, the manufacture and use of these types of chemicals have been either banned or closely regulated by the government, and replacements have been found. For example, virtually all new car automobile air-conditioning systems have been switched to a chemical called R-134a. The unfortunate side effect of this situation is that all the replacement chemicals are much more expensive than freon.

Related to compressed-air products are *chemical-freeze sprays*. These sprays are used to cool a suspected failing component quickly so as to restore it to operation. These substances are not used to repair a device, but to confirm that you have found the failed device. Often, a component's failure is heat-related; cooling it temporarily restores it to normal operation. If the circuit begins operating normally, the device that you are cooling is the suspect device.

A Word About Hardware

This section discusses some problems that you may encounter with the hardware (screws, nuts, bolts, and so on) used in assembling a system.

Types of Hardware

One of the biggest aggravations that you encounter in dealing with various systems is the different hardware types and designs that hold the units together.

For example, most system hardware types use screws that can be driven with 1/4-inch or 3/16-inch hexagonal drivers. IBM used these screws in all its original PC, XT, and AT systems, and most compatible systems use this standard hardware as well. Some manufacturers use different hardware. Compaq, for example, uses Torx screws extensively in most of its systems. A Torx screw has a star-shape hole driven by the correct-size Torx driver. These drivers carry size designations: T-8, T-9, T-10, T-15, T-20, T-25, T-30, T-40, and so on.

A variation on the Torx screw is the tamperproof Torx screw found in power supplies and other assemblies. These screws are identical to the regular Torx screws, except that a pin sticks up from the middle of the star-shape hole in the screw. This pin prevents the standard Torx driver from entering the hole to grip the screw; a special tamperproof driver with a corresponding hole for the pin is required. An alternative is to use a small chisel to knock out the pin in the screw. Usually, a device that is sealed with these types of screws is considered to be a complete replaceable unit that rarely, if ever, needs to be opened.

Many manufacturers also use the more standard slotted-head and Phillips-head screws. Using tools on these screws is relatively easy, but tools do not grip these fasteners as well as hexagonal head or Torx screws do, and the heads can be rounded off more easily than other types can. Extremely cheap versions tend to lose bits of metal as they're turned with a driver, and the metal bits can fall onto the motherboard. Stay away from cheap fasteners whenever possible; the headaches of dealing with stripped screws aren't worth it.

Some case manufacturers are making cases which snap together or use thumb screws. These are usually advertised as "no-tool" cases because you literally do not need any tools to take out the cover and many of the major assemblies.

Curtis sells special nylon plastic thumb screws that fit most normal cases and can be used to replace the existing screws to make opening the case a no-tool proposition. You should still always use metal screws to install internal components such as adapter cards, disk drives, power supplies, and the motherboard because the metal screws provide a ground point for these devices.

English versus Metric

Another area of aggravation with hardware is the fact that two types of thread systems are available: English and metric. IBM used mostly English-threaded fasteners in its original line of systems, but many other manufacturers used metric-threaded fasteners in their systems.

The difference becomes apparent especially with disk drives. American-manufactured drives sometimes use English fasteners; drives made in Japan or Taiwan usually use metric fasteners. Whenever you replace a floppy drive in an older PC-compatible unit, you encounter this problem. Try to buy the correct screws and any other hardware, such as brackets, with the drive, because they may be difficult to find at a local hardware store. Many of the drive manufacturers offer retail drive kits that include these components. The OEM's drive manual lists the correct data about a specific drive's hole locations and thread size.

Hard disks can use either English or metric fasteners; check your particular drive to see which type it uses. Most drives today seem to use metric hardware.

> **Caution**
>
> Some screws in a system may be length-critical, especially screws that are used to retain hard disk drives. You can destroy some hard disks by using a mounting screw that's too long; such a screw can puncture or dent the sealed disk chamber when you install the drive and fully tighten the screw. When you install a new drive in a system, always make a trial fit of the hardware to see how far the screws can be inserted into the drive before they interfere with components of the drive. When you're in doubt, the drive manufacturer's OEM documentation will tell you precisely what screws are required and how long they should be.

Disassembly and Reassembly Procedures

The process of physically disassembling and reassembling systems isn't difficult. Because of marketplace standardization, only a couple of different types and sizes of screws (with a few exceptions) are used to hold the systems together. Also, the physical arrangement of the major components is similar even among systems from different manufacturers. In addition, a typical system does not contain many components today.

This section covers the disassembly and reassembly procedure in the following sections:

- Case or cover assembly
- Adapter boards
- Disk drives
- Power supply
- Motherboard

This section discusses how to remove and install these components for several different types of systems. With regard to assembly and disassembly, it is best to consider each system by the type of case that the system uses. All systems that have AT-type cases, for example, are assembled and disassembled in much the same manner. Tower cases basically are AT-type cases turned sideways, so the same basic instructions apply to those cases as well. Most Slimline and XT style cases are similar; these systems are assembled and disassembled in much the same way.

The following section lists disassembly and reassembly instructions for several case types, including those for all standard IBM-compatible systems.

Disassembly Preparation

Before you begin disassembling any system, you must be aware of several issues. One issue is *ESD (electrostatic discharge) protection*. The other is recording the configuration of the system, with regard to the physical aspects of the system (such as jumper or switch settings and cable orientations) and to the logical configuration of the system (especially in terms of elements such as CMOS settings).

ESD Protection. When you are working on the internal components of a system, you need to take the necessary precautions to prevent accidental static discharges to the components. At any time, your body can hold a large static voltage charge that can easily damage components of your system. Before I ever put my hands into an open system, I first touch a grounded portion of the chassis, such as the power supply case. This action serves to equalize the charges that the device and I would be carrying. The key here is to leave the device computer in. By leaving the computer plugged in, you're allowing the static electricity to drain off safely to ground, rather than forcing the components of the system to accept the jolt.

In past editions of this book, it's been recommended that you unplug your systems. This is still true where you're concerned that you may accidentally power on the system while working on it. However, if this is not a concern, you should leave the computer plugged in.

High-end workbenches at repair facilities have the entire bench grounded, so it's not as big a problem; however, you need something to be a good ground source to prevent current from building up in you, and the best source is in the power cord that connects the computer to the wall.

A more sophisticated way to equalize the charges between you and any of the system components is to use an ESD protection kit. These kits consist of a wrist strap and mat, with ground wires for attachment to the system chassis. When you are going to work on a system, you place the mat next to or partially below the system unit. Next, you clip the ground wire to both the mat and the system's chassis, tying the grounds together. Then you put on the wrist strap and attach that wire to a ground as well. Because the mat and system chassis are already wired together, you can attach the wrist-strap wire to the system chassis or to the mat itself. If you are using a wrist strap without a mat, clip the wrist-strap wire to the system chassis. When clipping these wires to the chassis, be sure to use an area that is free of paint so that a good ground contact can be achieved. This setup ensures that any electrical charges are carried equally by you and any of the components in the system, preventing the sudden flow of static electricity that can damage the circuits.

As you remove disk drives, adapter cards, and especially delicate items such as the entire motherboard, as well as SIMMs or processor chips, you should place these components on the static mat. I see some people putting the system unit on top of the mat, but the unit should be alongside the mat so that you have room to lay out all the components as you remove them. If you are going to remove the motherboard from a system, be sure that you leave enough room for it on the mat.

If you do not have such a mat, simply place the removed circuits and devices on a clean desk or table. Always pick up a loose adapter card by the metal bracket used to secure the card to the system. This bracket is tied into the ground circuitry of the card, so by touching the bracket first, you prevent a discharge from damaging the components of the card. If the circuit board has no metal bracket (a motherboard, for example), handle the board carefully by the edges, and try not to touch any of the components.

> **Caution**
>
> Some people have recommended placing loose circuit boards and chips on sheets of aluminum foil. *This procedure is absolutely not recommended and can actually result in an explosion!* Many motherboards, adapter cards, and other circuit boards today have built-in lithium or ni-cad batteries. These batteries react violently when they are shorted out, which is exactly what you would be doing by placing such a board on a piece of aluminum foil. The batteries will quickly overheat and possibly explode like a large firecracker (with dangerous shrapnel). Because you will not always be able to tell whether a board has a battery built into it somewhere, the safest practice is to never place any board on any conductive metal surface, such as foil.

Recording Setup and Configuration. Before you power off the system for the last time to remove the case, you should learn, and record, several things about the system. Often when working on a system, you intentionally or accidentally wipe out the CMOS Setup information. Most systems use a special battery-powered CMOS clock and data chip that is used to store the system's configuration information. If the battery is disconnected, or if certain pins are accidentally shorted, you can discharge the CMOS memory and lose the setup. The CMOS memory in most systems is used to store simple things such as how many and what type of floppy drives are connected, how much memory is in the system, and the date and time.

A critical piece of information is the hard disk type settings. Although you or the system can easily determine the other settings the next time you power on the system, the hard disk type information is another story. Most modern BIOS software can read the type information directly from most IDE and all SCSI drives. With older BIOS software, however, you have to explicitly tell the system the parameters of the attached hard disk. This means that you need to know the current settings for cylinders, heads, and sectors per track.

Some BIOS software indicates the hard disk only by a type number, usually ranging from 1–50. Be aware that most BIOS programs use type 47 or higher for what is called a *user-definable type*, which means that the cylinder, head, and sector counts for this type were entered manually and are not constant. These user-definable types are especially important to write down, because this information may be very difficult to figure out later when you need to start the system.

Modern Enhanced IDE drives will also have additional configuration items that should be recorded. These include the translation mode and transfer mode. With drives larger than 528M, it is important to record the translation mode, which will be expressed differently in different BIOS versions. Look for settings like CHS (Cylinder Head Sector), ECHS (Extended CHS), Large (which equals ECHS), or LBA (Logical Block Addressing). If you reconfigure a system and do not set the same drive translation as was used originally with that drive, then all the data may be inaccessible. Most modern BIOS have an autodetect feature that automatically reads the drive's capabilities and sets the CMOS settings appropriately. Even so, there have been some problems with the BIOS not reading the drive settings properly, or where someone had overridden the settings in the previous installation. With translation, you have to match the setting to what the drive was formatted under previously if you want to read the data properly.

The speed setting is a little more straightforward. Older IDE drives can run up a speed of 8.3M/sec, which is called *PIO (Programmed I/O) mode 2*. Newer EIDE drives can run PIO Mode 3 (11.1M/sec) or PIO Mode 4 (16.6M/sec). Most BIOSes today allow you to set the mode specifically, or you can use the autodetect feature to automatically set the speed. For more information on the settings for hard disk drives, refer to Chapter 15, "Hard Disk Interfaces."

If you do not enter the correct hard disk type information in the CMOS setup program, you will not be able to access the data on the hard disk. I know of several people who lost some or all of their data because they did not enter the correct type information when they reconfigured their systems. If this information is incorrect, the usual results are a `Missing operating system` error message when the system starts and the inability to access the C drive.

Some of you may be thinking that you can just figure out the parameters by looking up the particular hard disk in a table. Unfortunately, this method works only if the person who set up the system originally entered the correct parameters. I have encountered a large number of systems in which the hard disk parameters were not entered correctly; the only way to regain access to the data is to determine, and then use, the same incorrect parameters that were used originally. As you can see, no matter what, you should record the hard disk information from your setup program.

Most systems have the setup program built right into the ROM BIOS software itself. These built-in setup programs are activated by a hot-key sequence such as Ctrl+Alt+Esc or Ctrl+Alt+S if you have a Phoenix ROM. Other ROMs prompt you for the setup program every time the system boots, such as with the popular AMI BIOS. With the AMI, you simply press the Delete key when the prompt appears on-screen during a reboot.

When you get the setup program running, record all the settings. The easiest way to do this is to print it out. If a printer is connected, press Shift+Print Screen; a copy of the screen display will be sent to the printer. Some setup programs have several pages of information, so you should record the information on each page as well.

Many setup programs, such as those in the AMI BIOS, allow for specialized control of the particular chipset used in the motherboard. These complicated settings can take up several screens of information, all of which should be recorded. Most systems will return all these settings to a default state when the battery is removed, and you lose any custom settings that were made.

MCA and EISA bus systems have a very sophisticated setup program that stores not only the motherboard configuration but also configurations for all the adapter cards. Fortunately, the setup programs for these systems have the capability to save the settings to a file on a floppy disk so that they can be restored later.

To access the setup program for most of these systems, you need the Setup or Reference Disk for the particular system. Some systems, such as various IBM PS/2 and Compaq systems, store a complete copy of the Reference or Setup Disk in a hidden partition of the hard disk. When these systems boot up, the cursor jumps to the right side of the screen for a few seconds. During this time, if you press Ctrl+Alt+Insert for IBM systems or F10 for Compaq systems, the hidden setup programs should load. Other manufacturers will use different keystrokes to activate the setup program or hidden partition, so consult your documentation to find the correct keystrokes for your particular system.

There are programs which advertise the ability to save all of your CMOS settings to disk, allowing you to reload them later. This works as long as the program is designed to work with your specific BIOS, but unfortunately there is no such program that works properly with all of the different BIOS versions on the market today. If you use such a program, be sure it is compatible with your system before proceeding.

Recording Physical Configuration. While you are disassembling a system, it is a good idea to record all the physical settings and configurations within the system, including jumper and switch settings, cable orientations and placement, ground-wire locations, and even adapter-board placement. Keep a notebook handy for recording these items, and write down all the settings in the book.

It is especially important to record all the jumper and switch settings on every card that you remove from the system, as well as those on the motherboard itself. If you accidentally disturb these jumpers or switches, you will know how they were originally set. This knowledge is very important if you do not have all the documentation for the system handy. Even if you do, undocumented jumpers and switches often do not appear in the manuals but must be set a certain way for the item to function. It is very embarrassing, to say the least, if you take apart somebody's system and then cannot make it work again because you disturbed something. If you record these settings, you will save yourself the embarrassment.

Also record all cable orientations. Most name-brand systems use cables and connectors that are keyed so that they cannot be plugged in backward, but most generic compatibles do not have this added feature. In addition, it is possible to mix up hard disk and floppy cables. You should mark or record what each cable was plugged into and its proper orientation. Ribbon cables usually have an odd-colored (red, green, blue, or black) wire at one end that indicates pin 1. There may also be a mark on the connector such as a triangle or even the number 1. The devices into which the cables are plugged also are marked in some way to indicate the orientation of pin 1. Often there will be a dot next to the pin 1 side of the connector, or there may be a 1 or other mark. In some cases, the cables and connectors will be keyed such that they can only go in one way.

Although cable orientation and placement seem to be very simple, we rarely get through the entire course of my PC troubleshooting seminars without at least one group of people having cable-connection problems. Fortunately, in most cases (excepting power cables), plugging in any of the ribbon cables inside the system backward rarely causes any permanent damage.

Power and battery connections are exceptions; plugging them in backward in most cases will cause damage. In fact, plugging the motherboard power connectors in backward or in the wrong plug location will put 12v where only 5v should be—a situation that can cause components of the board to violently explode. I know of several people who have facial scars caused by shrapnel from exploding components caused by improper power supply connections! As a precaution, I always like to turn my face away from the system when I power it on for the first time.

Plugging the CMOS battery in backward can damage the CMOS chip itself, which usually is soldered into the motherboard; in such a case, the motherboard itself must be replaced.

Finally, it is a good idea to record miscellaneous items such as the placement of any ground wires, adapter cards, and anything else that you may have difficulty remembering later. Some configurations and setups are particular about which slots the adapter cards are located in; it usually is a good idea to put everything back exactly the way it was originally, especially in MCA and EISA bus systems.

Now that you have made the necessary preparations and taken the necessary precautions, you can actually begin working on the systems.

System Disassembly

Disassembling most systems normally requires only a few basic tools: a 1/4-inch nut driver or Phillips-head screwdriver for the external screws that hold the cover in place, and a 3/16-inch nut driver or Phillips-head screwdriver for all the other screws. A needle-nose pliers can also help in removing motherboard standoffs, jumpers, and stubborn cable connectors.

An antistatic mat is useful for placing components on while they are out of the system chassis to protect them from static. If you don't have a mat, then any nonmetallic static-free surface can suffice as a work area.

Removing the Cover. To remove the case cover, follow these steps:

1. Power off the system. Disconnect all of the cables at the back of the case, including the power cable.

2. Examine your case to determine how to remove the cover. Remove the screws holding the case cover on the chassis. These are normally around the rim of the

cover and are normally in the rear; however, in some cases, the screws are behind the front plastic faceplate or bevel (see Figure 3.1).

FIG. 3.1 Remove the screws that hold the cover in place.

3. Once the screws are removed, grasp the cover and slide or lift it off. Some covers slide toward the back and some to the front; some lift straight up.

4. Now is a good time to connect the wrist strap or antistatic mat if you have one. Wear the wrist strap on one wrist and clip the wire end to a metal part of the case. Clip the wire from the mat to the case as well. This will keep you and the equipment at the same electrical potential and prevent any damage due to static electricity.

Removing Adapter Boards. To remove all the adapter boards from the system unit, first remove the system-unit cover, as described in the previous section. Then proceed as follows for each adapter:

1. Note which slots each adapter is in; if possible, make a diagram or drawing.

2. Remove the screw that holds the adapter in place (see Figure 3.2).

3. Note the positions of any cables that are plugged into the adapter before you remove them. In a correctly wired system, the colored stripe on one side of the ribbon cable always denotes pin 1. Some connectors have keys that enable them to be inserted only the correct way.

Disassembly and Reassembly Procedures 47

Used with permission from IBM Corporation.

FIG. 3.2 Remove the screw that holds the adapter in place.

4. Remove the adapter by lifting with even force at both ends.

5. Note the positions of any jumpers or switches on the adapter, especially when documentation for the adapter is not available. Even when documentation is available, manufacturers often use undocumented jumpers and switches for special purposes, such as testing or unique configurations. It's a good idea to know the existing settings, in case they are disturbed later.

Removing Disk Drives. Removing drives is very easy. The procedure is similar for all types of drives, such as floppy, hard disk, CD-ROM, and even tape drives.

Special rails or brackets are attached to the sides of the drives, and the drives slide into the system-unit chassis on these rails or brackets. The chassis has guide tracks for the rails, which enable you to remove the drive from the front of the unit without having to access the side to remove any mounting screws. The rails normally are made of plastic or fiberglass, but they can be made of metal in some systems. It should be noted that any brackets or rails should remain attached to the drive while you are removing or installing it.

Always back up hard disks completely before removing disks from the system. A backup is important because the possibility always exists that data will be lost or the drive damaged by rough handling.

48   Chapter 3—System Teardown and Inspection

To remove the drives, first remove the cover as described earlier. Then proceed as follows:

1. Depending on the specific case design, drives may be mounted using special brackets or rails. Locate the screws holding each drive bracket or drive assembly in the case and remove them. Some drives will slide out on rails, or be removed with the bracketry still attached to the drive itself.

2. Disconnect from the drives the power cables, data cables, and any ground wires if present (see Figures 3.3 and 3.4). In a correctly wired system, the colored stripe on one side of the ribbon cable always denotes pin 1. The power connector is shaped so that it can be inserted only the correct way.

3. Slide the drive completely out of the unit.

FIG. 3.3   Disconnect the hard drive power cable, signal and data cables, and ground wire.

Removing the Power Supply. The power supply is mounted in the system unit with several (normally four) screws in the rear and sometimes interlocking tabs on the bottom. Removing the power supply may require that you slide the disk drives forward for clearance when you remove the supply.

To remove the power supply, first remove the cover, then proceed as follows:

1. Remove the power-supply retaining screws from the rear of the system-unit chassis (see Figure 3.5).

Disassembly and Reassembly Procedures **49**

FIG. 3.4 Disconnect the floppy drive power cable, signal cable, and ground wire.

FIG. 3.5 Remove the power-supply retaining screws from the rear of the chassis.

2. Disconnect the cables from the power supply to the motherboard (see Figure 3.6), and then disconnect the power cables from the power supply to the disk drive. Always grasp the connectors themselves; never pull on the wires.

3. Lift the power supply out of the chassis.

Used with permission from IBM Corporation.

FIG. 3.6 Disconnect the cables from the power supply to the motherboard.

Removing the Motherboard. After all adapter cards are removed from the unit, you can remove the motherboard. The motherboard is normally held in place by several screws, and may also use plastic standoffs that elevate the board from the metal chassis so that the bottom of the board does not touch the chassis and cause a short.

You should not separate the standoffs from the motherboard before removing it from the chassis; instead, remove the board and the standoffs as a unit. The standoffs normally slide into slots in the chassis. When you reinstall the motherboard, make sure that the standoffs are located in their slots properly. If one or more standoffs do not engage the chassis properly, you may crack the motherboard when you tighten the screws or install adapter cards.

To remove the motherboard, first remove all adapter boards from the system unit, as described earlier. Then proceed as follows:

1. If the motherboard has onboard floppy, hard disk, serial, or parallel ports, document those cable connections and mark them before disconnecting them.

2. There are numerous small wires that go from the front panel on the case to the motherboard. Before disconnecting them, document the wire connections to the motherboard, and use some masking tape or some kind of label to mark the small wire connectors as you take them off the motherboard. Marking these wires will save you a lot of time later during the installation.

3. If there is an active heat sink in the CPU which incorporates a fan, unplug the power lead to the CPU fan.

4. If you have not already removed the power supply, document how the power supply cables are plugged into the motherboard, and disconnect the power supply connections to the board.

5. Locate and remove the motherboard retaining screws, making sure you save any plastic washers that might be used.

6. Slide the motherboard away from the power supply about a half-inch, until the standoffs have disengaged from their mounting slots (see Figure 3.7).

7. Lift the motherboard up and out of the chassis. Place it on a static-free surface, such as an antistatic mat.

8. Remove the CPU and any memory modules you want to reuse later.

FIG. 3.7 Disengage standoffs from their mounting slots.

Removing SIMMs or DIMMs. One benefit of using single or dual inline memory modules (SIMMs or DIMMs) is that they're easy to remove or install. When you remove memory modules, remember that because of physical interference, you must remove the memory-module package that is closest to the disk drive bus-adapter slot before you remove the package that is closest to the edge of the motherboard. This procedure describes removing a SIMM device; note that a DIMM is also removed in exactly the same way. The only difference is that a DIMM is slightly longer and has more contacts than a SIMM device.

To remove a SIMM (or DIMM) properly, follow this procedure:

1. Gently pull the tabs on each side of the SIMM or DIMM socket outward.
2. Rotate or pull the SIMM or DIMM up and out of the socket (see Figure 3.8).

FIG. 3.8 Removing a SIMM or DIMM.

> **Caution**
>
> Be careful not to damage the connector. If you damage the motherboard memory connector, you could be looking at an expensive repair. Never force the module; it should come out easily. If it doesn't, you are doing something wrong.

Motherboard Installation

If you are installing a new motherboard, unpack the motherboard and check to make sure you have everything that should be included. If you purchase a new board, normally you should get at least the motherboard itself, some I/O cables, and a manual. If you ordered the motherboard with a processor or memory, it will normally be installed on the board for you, but may also be included separately. Some board kits will include an antistatic wrist strap to help prevent damage due to static electricity when installing the board.

Prepare the New Motherboard. Before a new motherboard can be installed, it must be set up properly to accept the processor. Most newer motherboards have jumpers which control both the CPU speed as well as the voltage supplied to it. If these are set incorrectly, the system may not operate at all, operate erratically, or possibly even damage the CPU. If you have any questions about the proper settings, contact the vendor who sold you the board before making any jumper changes.

Most processors today run hot enough to require some form of heat sink to dissipate heat from the processor. To install the processor and heat sink, use the following procedures:

1. Take the new motherboard out of the antistatic bag it was supplied in, and set it on the bag or the antistatic mat if you have one.

2. Refer to the motherboard manufacturer's manual to set the jumpers to match the CPU you are going to install. Look for the diagram of the motherboard to find the jumper location, and look for the tables for the right settings for your CPU. If the CPU was supplied already installed on the motherboard, then the jumpers should already be correctly set for you, but it is still a good idea to check them.

3. Find pin 1 on the processor; it is usually denoted by a corner of the chip that is marked by a dot or a bevel in that corner. Next, find the corresponding pin 1 of the ZIF socket for the CPU on the motherboard. Pin 1 is usually marked on the board, or there is a bevel in one corner of the socket. Insert the CPU into the ZIF socket by lifting the release lever, aligning the pins on the processor with the holes in the socket, and pushing it down into place. If the processor does not go all the way into the socket, then check for possible interference or pin alignment problems. When the processor is fully seated in the socket, push the locking lever on the socket down to secure the processor.

4. If the CPU does not already have a heat sink attached to it, then attach it now. Most heat sinks will either clip directly to the CPU or to the socket with one or more retainer clips. Be careful when attaching the clip to the socket; you don't want it to scrape against the motherboard, which might damage circuit traces or components. In most cases, it is a good idea to put a dab of heat sink thermal transfer compound (normally a white-colored grease) on the CPU before installing the heat sink. This prevents any air gaps and allows the heat sink to work more efficiently.

Install Memory Modules. In order to function, the motherboard must have memory installed on it. Modern motherboards use either SIMMs or DIMMs. Depending on the module type, it will have a specific method of sliding into and clipping to the sockets. Normally, you install modules in the lowest numbered sockets or banks first. Note that some boards will require modules to be installed in pairs or even four at a time. Consult the motherboard documentation for more information on which sockets to use first and in what order, and how to install the specific modules the board uses.

Memory modules are normally keyed to the sockets by a notch on the side or on the bottom, so they can only go in one way. Reverse the procedure discussed in the section "Removing SIMMs or DIMMs" for removing the modules to install them instead.

Mount the New Motherboard in the Case. The motherboard will attach to the case with one or more screws and often several plastic standoffs. If you are using a new case, you may have to attach one or more metal spacers or plastic standoffs in the proper holes before you can install the motherboard. Use the following procedure to install the new motherboard in the case:

1. If plastic standoffs were used, you may need to take them out of the old motherboard. Using a needlenose pliers, carefully squeeze the top of each standoff and push it carefully through the board.

2. Find the corresponding holes in the new motherboard for the metal spacers and plastic standoffs. You should use metal spacers wherever there is a ring of solder around the hole. Use plastic standoffs where there is not the ring of solder. Screw any metal spacers into the new case in the proper positions to align with the screw holes in the motherboard.

3. Insert any plastic standoffs directly into the new motherboard from underneath until they snap into place.

4. Install the new motherboard into the case by setting it down so any standoffs engage the case. Often you will have to set the board into the case and slide it sideways to engage the standoffs into the slots in the case. When the board is in the proper position, the screw holes in the board should be aligned with any of the metal spacers or screw holes in the case.

5. Take the screws and any plastic washers that were previously used, and screw the motherboard to the case.

Connect the Power Supply. Newer ATX-style motherboards have a single power connector which can only go on one way. Baby-AT and other style board designs usually have two separate six-wire power connectors from the power supply to the board, which may not be keyed and therefore may be interchangeable. Even though it may be possible to insert them several ways, only one way is correct! These power leads are usually labeled P8 and P9 in most systems. The order in which they are put on the board is crucial; if you install them backwards, you might cause damage to the motherboard when you power it up. Many systems also use a CPU cooling fan which should be connected as well. To attach the power connectors from the power supply to the motherboard:

1. If the system uses a single ATX-style power connector, then plug it in; it can only go on one way.

    If two separate six-wire connectors are used, the two black ground wires on the ends of the connectors must meet in the middle. Align the power connectors such that the black ground wires are adjacent to one another and plug the connectors in. Consult the documentation with your board to make sure the power supply connection is correct.

2. Plug in the power lead for the CPU fan if one is used. The fan will either connect to the power supply via a disk drive power connector, or it may connect directly to a fan power connector directly on the motherboard.

Connect I/O and Other Cables to the Motherboard. There are several connections that must be made between a motherboard and the case. These include LEDs for the hard disk and power, an internal speaker connection, a reset button, and a de-turbo button on some systems. Most modern motherboards also have several built-in I/O ports which have to be connected. This would include dual IDE host adapters, a floppy controller, dual serial ports, and a parallel port. Some boards will also include additional items such as built-in video, sound, or SCSI adapters.

If the board is an ATX type, the connectors for all of the external I/O ports are already built into the rear of the board. If you are using a Baby-AT type board, then you may have to install cables and brackets to run the serial, parallel, and other external I/O ports to the rear of the case. If your motherboard has on-board I/O, use the following procedures to connect the cables:

1. Connect the floppy cable between the floppy drives and the 34-pin floppy controller connector on the motherboard.

2. Connect the IDE cables between the hard disk, IDE CD-ROM, and IDE tape drives and the 40-pin primary and secondary IDE connectors on the motherboard. Normally, you will use the primary IDE channel connector for hard disks only and the secondary IDE channel connector to attach an IDE CD-ROM or tape drive.

3. On non-ATX boards, a 25-pin female cable port bracket is normally used for the parallel port. There are usually two serial ports: a 9-pin, and either another 9-pin or a 25-pin male connector port. Align pin 1 on the serial and parallel port cables with pin 1 on the motherboard connector and plug them in.

4. If the ports don't have card slot type brackets or if you need all of your expansion slots, there may be port knockouts on the back of the case you can use instead. Find ones that fit the ports, and push them out, removing the metal piece covering the hole. Unscrew the hex nuts on either side of the port connector and position it in the hole. Install the hex nuts back in through the case to hold the port connector in place.

5. Most newer motherboards also include a built-in mouse port. If the connector for this port is not built into the back of the motherboard (usually next to the keyboard connector), then you will probably have a card bracket type connector to install. In that case, plug the cable into the motherboard mouse connector and then attach the external mouse connector bracket to the case.

6. Attach the front panel switch, LED, and internal speaker wires from the case front panel to the motherboard. If they are not marked on the board, check where each one is on the diagram in the motherboard manual.

Install Bus Expansion Cards. Most systems use expansion cards for video, network interface, sound, and SCSI adapters. These cards will be plugged into the bus slots present on the motherboard. To install these cards:

1. Insert each card by holding it carefully by the edges, making sure not to touch the chips and circuitry. Put the bottom edge finger connector into a slot that fits. Firmly press down on the top of the card, exerting even pressure, until it snaps into place.

2. Secure each card bracket with a screw.

3. Attach any internal cables you may have removed earlier from the cards.

Replace the Cover and Connect External Cables. Now the system should be nearly assembled. All that remains is installing the cover assembly and connecting any external devices which are cabled to the system. I usually don't like to install the case cover screws until I have tested the system and I am sure everything is working properly! Often I will find that a cable has been connected improperly, or some jumper setting is not correct, requiring that I remove the cover to repair the problem. Use the following procedure to complete the assembly:

1. Slide the cover back on the case.

2. Before powering up the system, connect any external cables. Most of the connectors are D-shaped and only go in one way.

3. Plug the 15-pin monitor cable into the video card female connector.

4. Attach the phone cord to the modem, if any.

5. Plug the round keyboard cable into the keyboard connector, and the mouse into the mouse port or serial port if a serial mouse is being used.

6. If you have any other external cabling such as joystick or audio jacks to a sound card, attach them now as well.

Run the Motherboard BIOS Setup Program (CMOS Setup). Now that everything is connected, you can power up the system and run the system configuration or setup program. This will allow you to configure the motherboard to the installed devices, as well as to set the system date and time. The system will also test itself to determine if there are any problems:

1. Power on the monitor first, and then the system unit. Observe the operation via the screen and listen for any beeps from the system speaker.

2. The system should automatically go through a Power On Self Test (POST) consisting of video BIOS checking, RAM test, and usually an installed component report. If there is a fatal error during the POST, you may not see anything on the screen and the system may beep several times indicating a specific problem. Check the motherboard or BIOS documentation to determine what the beep codes mean.

3. If there are no fatal errors, you should see the POST display on the screen. Depending on the type of motherboard BIOS, such as Phoenix, AMI, Award, or others, you need to press a key or series of keys to interrupt the normal boot sequence and get to the setup program screens which allow you to enter important system information. Normally the system will indicate via the on-screen display which key to press to activate the BIOS setup program during the POST, but if not, then check the motherboard manual for the key(s) to press to enter the BIOS Setup.

4. Once the setup program is running, use the setup program menus to enter the current date and time, your hard drive settings, floppy drive types, video cards,

keyboard settings, and so on. Most newer motherboard BIOS can autodetect the hard drive, so you should not have to manually enter any parameters for it.

5. Follow the instructions on the screen or in the motherboard manual to save the settings and exit the setup menu.

At this point, the system should boot normally from either a floppy disk or hard disk. If there are any problems, turn to the troubleshooting section of the motherboard manual. When you are sure the system is up and running successfully, power it off and screw the chassis cover securely to the case.

Now your new motherboard should be installed and your system successfully upgraded or repaired.

Preventive Maintenance and Backups

Preventive maintenance is the key to obtaining years of trouble-free service from your computer system. A properly administered preventive maintenance program pays for itself by reducing problem behavior, data loss, component failure, and by ensuring a long life for your system. In several cases, I have "repaired" an ailing system with nothing more than a preventive maintenance session. Preventive maintenance also increases your system's resale value because it will look and run better.

You will also learn the importance of creating backup files of data and the various backup procedures available. A sad reality in the computer repair and servicing world is that hardware can always be repaired or replaced, but data cannot. Most hard disk troubleshooting and service procedures, for example, require that a low-level format be performed. This low-level format overwrites any data on the disk.

Most of the discussion of backing up systems in this chapter is limited to professional solutions that require special hardware and software. Backup solutions that employ floppy disk drives, such as the DOS backup software, are insufficient and too costly in most cases for hard disk backups. It would take 2,867 1.44M floppy disks, for example, to back up the 4G hard disk in my portable system! That would cost more than $1,000 in disks, not to mention the time involved. A DAT (Digital Audio Tape) or Travan tape system, on the other hand, can put 4G to 8G or more on a single $5 to $30 tape.

Although the tape drive itself will cost up to $500 or more, the media costs are really far more significant than the cost of the drive. If you are doing responsible backups, you will have at least three sets of media for each system you are backing up. The media sets would be used on a rotating basis, and one of them should be moved offsite. The media sets should be changed out at an interval of a year or less to prevent excessive wear. If you are backing up more than one system, these media costs will add up quickly.

You should also factor in the cost of time. If a backup requires manual intervention to change the media during the backup, I don't recommend it. A backup system should be able to fit a complete backup on a single tape so that the backup can be performed unattended. If someone has to hang around to switch tapes every so often, the backup becomes a real chore and is less likely to be performed. Also, every time a media change occurs, there is a substantial increase in the likelihood of errors and problems that may not be realized until a restore is performed. A backup is far more important than most people realize, and spending a little more on a quality piece of hardware like a Travan or DAT drive will pay off in the long run with greater reliability, lower media costs, higher performance, and unattended backups that contain the entire system file structure.

Developing a Preventive Maintenance Program

Developing a preventive maintenance program is important to everyone who uses or manages personal computer systems. Two types of preventive maintenance procedures exist—active and passive.

Active preventive maintenance includes steps you apply to a system that promote a longer, trouble-free life. This type of preventive maintenance primarily involves periodic cleaning of the system and its components. This section describes several active preventive maintenance procedures, including cleaning and lubricating all major components, reseating chips and connectors, and reformatting hard disks.

Passive preventive maintenance includes steps you can take to protect a system from the environment, such as using power-protection devices; ensuring a clean, temperature-controlled environment; and preventing excessive vibration. In other words, passive preventive maintenance means treating your system well. This section also describes passive preventive maintenance procedures.

Active Preventive Maintenance Procedures

How often you should implement active preventive maintenance procedures depends on the system's environment and the quality of the system's components. If your system is in a dirty environment, such as a machine shop floor or a gas station service area, you might need to clean your system every three months or less. For normal office environments, cleaning a system every one to two years is usually fine. However, if you open your system after one year and find dust bunnies inside, you should probably shorten the cleaning interval.

Other hard disk preventive maintenance procedures include making periodic backups of critical areas, such as boot sectors, file allocation tables (FATs), and directory structures on the disk. Also defragmenting a hard disk should be performed periodically, normally right after any backups.

Cleaning a System. One of the most important operations in a good preventive maintenance program is regular and thorough cleaning of the system. Dust buildup on the internal components can lead to several problems. One is that the dust acts as a thermal insulator, which prevents proper system cooling. Excessive heat shortens the life of system components and adds to the thermal stress problem caused by wider temperature changes between power-on and power-off states. Additionally, the dust may contain conductive elements that can cause partial short circuits in a system. Other elements in dust and dirt can accelerate corrosion of electrical contacts and cause improper connections. In all, the removal of any layer of dust and debris from within a computer system benefits that system in the long run.

Most non-ATX PC-compatible systems use a forced-air cooling system that allows for even cooling inside the system. A fan is mounted in, on, or near the power supply and pushes air outside. This setup depressurizes the interior of the system relative to the outside air. The lower pressure inside the system causes outside air to be drawn into openings in the system chassis and cover. This draw-through, or depressurization, is the most efficient cooling system that can be designed without an air filter. Air filters typically are not used with depressurization systems because there is no easy way to limit air intake to a single port that can be covered by a filter.

Some industrial computers and ATX systems use a forced-air system that uses the fan to pressurize, rather than to depressurize, the case. This system forces air to exhaust from any holes in the chassis and case or cover. The key to the pressurization system is that all air intake for the system is at a single location—the fan. The air flowing into the system therefore can be filtered by simply integrating a filter assembly into the fan housing. The filter must be cleaned or changed periodically. Because the interior of the case is pressurized relative to the outside air, airborne contaminants are not drawn into the system even though it may not be sealed. Any air entering the system must pass through the fan and filter housing, which removes the contaminants. Pressurization cooling systems are used primarily in industrial computer models designed for extremely harsh environments.

Most systems you have contact with are depressurization systems. Mounting any sort of air filter on these types of systems is impossible because air enters the system from too many sources. With any cooling system in which incoming air is not filtered, dust and other chemical matter in the environment is drawn in and builds up inside the computer. This buildup can cause severe problems if left unchecked.

One problem that can develop is overheating. The buildup of dust acts as a heat insulator, which prevents the system from cooling properly. Some of the components in a modern PC can generate an enormous amount of heat that must be dissipated for the component to function. The dust also might contain chemicals that conduct electricity. These chemicals can cause minor current shorts and create electrical signal paths where none should exist. The chemicals also cause rapid corrosion of cable connectors, socket-installed components, and areas where boards plug into slots. All can cause intermittent system problems and erratic operation.

> **Tip**
>
> Cigarette smoke contains chemicals that can conduct electricity and cause corrosion of computer parts. The smoke residue can infiltrate the entire system, causing corrosion and contamination of electrical contacts and sensitive components such as floppy drive read/write heads and optical drive lens assemblies. You should avoid smoking near computer equipment and encourage your company to develop and enforce a similar policy.

Floppy disk drives are particularly vulnerable to the effects of dirt and dust. Floppy drives are a large "hole" within the system through which air continuously flows. Therefore, they accumulate a large amount of dust and chemical buildup within a short time. Hard disk drives do not present quite the same problem. Because the head disk assembly (HDA) in a hard disk is a sealed unit with a single barometric vent, no dust or dirt can enter without passing through the barometric vent filter. This filter ensures that contaminating dust or particles cannot enter the interior of the HDA. Thus, cleaning a hard disk requires simply blowing the dust and dirt off from outside the drive. No internal cleaning is required.

Disassembly and Cleaning Tools. To properly clean the system and all the boards inside requires certain supplies and tools. In addition to the tools required to disassemble the unit, you should have these items:

- Contact cleaning solution
- Canned air
- A small brush
- Lint-free foam cleaning swabs
- Antistatic grounding wrist strap

You also might want to acquire these optional items:

- Foam tape
- Low-volatile room-temperature vulcanizing (RTV) sealer
- Silicone type lubricant
- Computer vacuum cleaner

These simple cleaning tools and chemical solutions will allow you to perform most common preventive maintenance tasks.

Chemicals. You can use several different types of cleaning solutions with computers and electronic assemblies. Most fall into the following categories:

- Standard cleaners
- Contact cleaner/lubricants
- Dusters

> **Tip**
>
> The makeup of many of the chemicals used for cleaning electronic components has been changing because many of the chemicals originally used are now considered environmentally unsafe. They have been attributed to damaging the earth's ozone layer. Chlorine atoms from chlorofluorocarbons (CFCs) and chlorinated solvents attach themselves to ozone molecules and destroy them. Many of these chemicals are now strictly regulated by federal and international agencies in an effort to preserve the ozone layer. Most of the companies that produce chemicals used for system cleaning and maintenance have had to introduce environmentally safe replacements. The only drawback is that many of these safer chemicals cost more and usually do not work as well as those they replace.

Many specific chemicals are used in cleaning and dusting solutions, but five types are of particular interest. The EPA has classified ozone-damaging chemicals into two classes, Class I and Class II. Chemicals that fall into these two classes have their usage regulated. Other chemicals are nonregulated. Class I chemicals include:

- Chlorofluorocarbons (CFCs)
- Chlorinated solvents

Class I chemicals can only be sold for use in professional service and not to consumers. A law that went into effect on May 15, 1993, requires that the containers for Class I chemicals be labeled with a warning that the product "contains substances that harm public health and the environment by destroying ozone in the atmosphere." Additionally, electronics manufacturers and other industries must also apply a similar warning label to any products that use Class I chemicals in the production process. This means that any circuit board or computer that is manufactured with CFCs will have this label.

The most popular Class I chemicals are the various forms of freon, which are CFCs. A very popular cleaning solution called 1,1,1 Trichloroethane is a chlorinated solvent and also is strictly regulated. Up until 1995, virtually all computer or electronic cleaning solutions contained one or both of these chemicals. While you can still purchase them, regulations and limited production have made them more expensive and more difficult to find.

Class II chemicals include *hydrochlorofluorocarbons (HCFCs)*. These are not as strictly regulated as Class I chemicals because they have a lower ozone depletion potential. Many cleaning solutions have switched to HCFCs because they do not require the restrictive labeling required by Class I chemicals and are not as harmful. Most HCFCs have only one-tenth the ozone damaging potential of CFCs.

Other nonregulated chemicals include *volatile organic compounds (VOCs)* and *hydrofluorocarbons (HFCs)*. These chemicals do not damage the ozone layer but actually contribute to ozone production which, unfortunately, appears in the form of smog or ground level pollution. Pure isopropyl alcohol is an example of a VOC that is commonly used in electronic part and contact cleaning. HFCs are used as a replacement for CFCs because the HFCs do not damage the ozone layer.

The Environmental Protection Agency has developed a method to measure the ozone damaging capability of a chemical. The *Ozone Depletion Potential (ODP)* of a chemical solution is the sum of the depletion potentials of each of the chemicals used in the solution by weight. The ODP of Freon R12 (Automotive Air Conditioning Freon) is 1.0 on this scale. Most modern CFC replacement chemicals have an ODP rating of 0.0 to 0.1, as opposed to those using CFCs and chlorinated solvents that usually have ODP ratings of 0.75 or higher.

Standard Cleaners. Standard cleaning solutions are available in a variety of types and configurations. You can use pure isopropyl alcohol, acetone, freon, trichloroethane, or a variety of other chemicals. Most board manufacturers and service shops are now leaning toward the alcohol, acetone, or other chemicals that do not cause ozone depletion and comply with government regulations and environmental safety.

You should be sure that your cleaning solution is designed to clean computers or electronic assemblies. In most cases, this means that the solution should be chemically pure and free from contaminants or other unwanted substances. You should not, for example, use drugstore rubbing alcohol for cleaning electronic parts or contacts because it is not pure and could contain water or perfumes. The material must be moisture-free and residue-free. The solutions should be in liquid form, not a spray. Sprays can be wasteful, and you almost never spray the solution directly on components. Instead, wet a foam or chamois swab used for wiping the component. These electronic-component cleaning solutions are available at any good electronics parts stores.

Contact Cleaner/Lubricants. These are very similar to the standard cleaners but include a lubricating component. The lubricant eases the force required when plugging and unplugging cables and connectors, which reduces strain on the devices. The lubricant coating also acts as a conductive protectant that insulates the contacts from corrosion. These chemicals can greatly prolong the life of a system by preventing intermittent contacts in the future.

Contact cleaner/lubricants are especially effective on I/O slot connectors, adapter card edge and pin connectors, disk drive connectors, power supply connectors, and virtually any connectors in the PC. Refer to the earlier section "Chemicals" for more information on contact enhancers and lubricants.

Dusters. Compressed gas often is used as an aid in system cleaning. The compressed gas is used as a blower to remove dust and debris from a system or component. Originally, these dusters used CFCs such as freon, while modern dusters now use HFCs or carbon dioxide, neither of which is damaging to the ozone layer. Be careful when you use these devices because some of them can generate a static charge when the compressed gas leaves the nozzle of the can. Be sure that you are using the kind approved for cleaning or dusting off computer equipment, and consider wearing a static grounding strap as a precaution. The type of compressed-air cans used for cleaning camera equipment can sometimes differ from the type used for cleaning static-sensitive computer components.

Related to compressed-air products are chemical-freeze sprays. These sprays are used to quickly cool down a suspected failing component, which often temporarily restores it to operation. These substances are not used to repair a device, but to confirm that you have found a failed device. Often, a component's failure is heat-related and cooling it temporarily restores it to function. If the circuit begins operating normally, the device you are cooling is the suspect device.

Vacuum Cleaners. Some people prefer to use a vacuum cleaner instead of canned gas dusters for cleaning a system. Canned gas is usually better for cleaning in small areas. A vacuum cleaner is more useful when you are cleaning a system loaded with dust and dirt. You can use the vacuum cleaner to suck out dust and debris instead of blowing them on other components, which sometimes happens with canned air. For outbound servicing (when you are going to the location of the equipment instead of the equipment coming to you), canned air is easier to carry in a tool kit than a small vacuum cleaner. There are also tiny vacuum cleaners available for system cleaning. These small units are easy to carry and may serve as an alternative to compressed air cans.

There are special vacuum cleaners specifically designed for using on and around electronic components. They are designed to minimize ESD while in use. If you are using a regular vacuum cleaner and not one specifically designed with ESD protection, then you should take precautions such as wearing a grounding wrist strap. Also be careful if the cleaner has a metal nozzle not to touch it to the circuit boards or components you are cleaning.

Brushes and Swabs. A small brush (makeup, photographic, or paint) can be used to carefully loosen accumulated dirt and dust before spraying with canned air or using the vacuum cleaner. Be careful about generating static electricity. In most cases, the brushes should not be used directly on circuit boards but should be used instead on the case interior and other parts such as fan blades, air vents, and keyboards. Wear a grounded wrist strap if you are brushing on or near any circuit boards, and brush slowly and lightly to prevent static discharges from occurring.

Use cleaning swabs to wipe off electrical contacts and connectors, disk drive heads, and other sensitive areas. The swabs should be made of foam or synthetic chamois material that does not leave lint or dust residue. Unfortunately, proper foam or chamois cleaning swabs are more expensive than the typical cotton swabs. Do not use cotton swabs because they leave cotton fibers on everything they touch. Cotton fibers are conductive in some situations and can remain on drive heads, which can scratch disks. Foam or chamois swabs can be purchased at most electronics supply stores.

One item to avoid is an eraser for cleaning contacts. Many people (including myself) have recommended using a soft pencil-type eraser for cleaning circuit board contacts. Testing has proven this to be bad advice for several reasons. One is that any such abrasive wiping on electrical contacts generates friction and an ESD. This ESD can be damaging to boards and components, especially with newer low-voltage devices made using new technology. These devices are especially static-sensitive, and cleaning the contacts without a proper liquid solution is not recommended. Also, the eraser will wear off the gold coating on many contacts, exposing the tin contact underneath, which will rapidly corrode when exposed to air. Some companies sell premoistened contact cleaning pads that are soaked in a proper contact cleaner and lubricant. These pads are safe to wipe on conductor and contacts with no likelihood of ESD damage or abrasion of the gold plating.

Silicone Lubricants. Silicone lubricants are used to lubricate the door mechanisms on floppy disk drives and any other part of the system that may require clean, non-oily lubrication. Other items you can lubricate are the disk drive head slider rails or even printer-head slider rails, which allow for smooth operation.

Using silicone instead of conventional oils is important because silicone does not gum up and collect dust and other debris. Always use the silicone sparingly. Do not spray it anywhere near the equipment as it tends to migrate and will end up where it doesn't belong (such as on drive heads). Instead, apply a small amount to a toothpick or foam swab and dab the silicone on the components where needed. You can use a lint-free cleaning stick soaked in silicone lubricant to lubricate the metal print-head rails in a printer.

Remember that some of the cleaning operations described in this section might generate a static charge. You may want to use antistatic grounding strap in cases in which static levels are high to ensure that you do not damage any boards as you work with them.

Obtaining Required Tools and Accessories. Most cleaning chemicals and tools can be obtained from a number of electronics supply houses, or even your local Radio Shack. A company called Chemtronics specializes in chemicals for the computer and electronics industry. These and other companies that supply tools, chemicals, and other computer and electronic cleaning supplies are listed in the vendor list in Appendix A. With all these items on hand, you should be equipped for most preventive maintenance operations.

Disassembling and Cleaning Procedures. To properly clean your system, it must be at least partially disassembled. Some people go as far as to remove the motherboard. Removing the motherboard results in the best possible access to other areas of the system; but in the interest of saving time, you probably need to disassemble the system only to where the motherboard is completely visible.

All plug-in adapter cards must be removed, along with the disk drives. Although you can clean the heads of a floppy drive with a cleaning disk without opening the system unit's cover, you probably will want to do more thorough cleaning. In addition to the heads, you also should clean and lubricate the door mechanism and clean any logic boards and connectors on the drive. This procedure usually requires removing the drive.

Next, do the same procedure with a hard disk: Clean the logic boards and connectors, as well as lubricate the grounding strap. To do so, you must remove the hard disk assembly. As a precaution, be sure it is backed up before removal.

Reseating Socketed Chips. A primary preventive maintenance function is to undo the effects of chip creep. As your system heats and cools, it expands and contracts, and the physical expansion and contraction causes components that are plugged into sockets to gradually work their way out of those sockets. This process is called *chip creep*. To correct its effects, you must find all socketed components in the system and make sure that they are properly reseated.

In most systems, all the memory chips are socketed or are installed in socketed SIMMs or DIMMs. SIMM/DIMM devices are retained securely in their sockets by a positive latching mechanism and cannot creep out. *Memory SIPP (Single Inline Pin Package) devices* (SIMMs with pins rather than contacts) are not retained by a latching mechanism and therefore can creep out of their sockets. Standard socketed memory chips are prime candidates for chip creep. Most other logic components are soldered in. You can also expect to find the ROM chips, the main processor or CPU, and the math coprocessor in sockets. In most systems, these items are the only components that are socketed; all others are soldered in.

Exceptions, however, might exist. A socketed component in one system might not be socketed in another—even if both are from the same manufacturer. Sometimes this difference results from a parts-availability problem when the boards are manufactured. Rather than halt the assembly line when a part is not available, the manufacturer adds a socket instead of the component. When the component becomes available, it is plugged in and the board is finished. Many newer systems place the CPU in a ZIF socket, which has a lever that can release the grip of the socket on the chip. In most cases, there is very little creep with a ZIF socket.

To make sure that all components are fully seated in their sockets, place your hand on the underside of the board and then apply downward pressure with your thumb (from the top) on the chip to be seated. For larger chips, seat the chip carefully in two movements, and press separately on each end of the chip with your thumb to be sure that the chip is fully seated. (The processor and math coprocessor chips can usually be seated in this manner.) In most cases, you hear a crunching sound as the chip makes its way back into the socket. Because of the great force sometimes required to reseat the chips, this operation is difficult if you do not remove the board.

For motherboards, forcibly seating chips can be dangerous if you do not directly support the board from the underside with your hand. Too much pressure on the board can cause it to bow or bend in the chassis, and the pressure can crack it before seating takes place. The plastic standoffs that separate and hold the board up from the metal chassis are spaced too far apart to properly support the board under this kind of stress. Try this operation only if you can remove and support the board adequately from underneath.

You may be surprised to know that, even if you fully seat each chip, they might need reseating again within a year. The creep usually is noticeable within a year or less.

Cleaning Boards. After reseating any socketed devices that may have crept out of their sockets, the next step is to clean the boards and all connectors in the system. For this step, use the cleaning solutions and the lint-free swabs.

First, clean the dust and debris off the board and then clean any connectors on the board. To clean the boards, it is usually best to use a vacuum cleaner designed for electronic assemblies and circuit boards or a duster can of compressed gas. The dusters are especially effective at blasting any dust and dirt off the boards.

Also, blow any dust out of the power supply, especially around the fan intake and exhaust areas. You do not need to disassemble the power supply to do this; just use a duster can and blast the compressed air into the supply through the fan exhaust port. This will blow the dust out of the supply and clean off the fan blades and grill, which will help with system airflow.

> **Caution**
>
> Be careful with ESD, which can damage components when cleaning electronic components. Take extra precautions in the dead of winter in an extremely dry, high-static environment. You can apply antistatic sprays and treatments to the work area to reduce the likelihood of ESD damage.
>
> An antistatic grounding wrist strap is recommended. This should be connected to a ground on the card or board you are wiping. This strap ensures that no electrical discharge occurs between you and the board. An alternative method is to keep a finger or thumb on the ground of the motherboard or card as you wipe it off. It is easier to ensure proper grounding while the motherboard is still installed in the chassis, so it is a good idea not to remove it.

Cleaning Connectors and Contacts. Cleaning the connectors and contacts in a system promotes reliable connections between devices. On a motherboard, you will want to clean the slot connectors, power supply connectors, keyboard connector, and speaker connector. For most plug-in cards, you will want to clean the edge connectors that plug into slots on the motherboard as well as any other connectors, such as external ones mounted on the card bracket.

Submerge the lint-free swabs in the liquid cleaning solution. If you are using the spray, hold the swab away from the system and spray a small amount on the foam end until the solution starts to drip. Then, use the soaked foam swab to wipe the connectors on the boards. Presoaked wipes are the easiest to use. Simply wipe them along the contacts to remove any accumulated dirt and leave a protective coating behind.

On the motherboard, pay special attention to the slot connectors. Be liberal with the liquid; resoak the foam swab repeatedly, and vigorously clean the connectors. Don't worry if some of the liquid drips on the surface of the motherboard. These solutions are entirely safe for the whole board and will not damage the components.

Use the solution to wash the dirt off the gold contacts in the slot connectors, and then douse any other connectors on the board. Clean the keyboard connector, the grounding positions where screws ground the board to the system chassis, power-supply connectors, speaker connectors, battery connectors, and so on.

If you are cleaning a plug-in board, pay special attention to the edge connector that mates with the slot connector on the motherboard. When people handle plug-in cards, they often touch the gold contacts on these connectors. Touching the gold contacts coats them with oils and debris, which prevents proper contact with the slot connector when the board is installed. Make sure that these gold contacts are free of all finger oils and residue. It is a good idea to use one of the contact cleaners that has a conductive lubricant, which both allows connections to be made with less force and also protects the contacts from corrosion.

You will also want to use the swab and solution to clean the ends of ribbon cables or other types of cables or connectors in a system. Clean the floppy drive cables and connectors, the hard disk cables and connectors, and any others you find. Don't forget to clean the edge connectors that are on the disk drive logic boards, as well as the power connectors to the drives.

Cleaning the Keyboard and Mouse. Keyboards and mice are notorious for picking up dirt and garbage. If you have ever opened up an older keyboard, you often will be amazed at the junk you will find in there.

To prevent problems, it is a good idea to periodically clean the keyboard with a vacuum cleaner. An alternative method is to turn the keyboard upside down and shoot it with a can of compressed gas. This will blow out the dirt and debris that has accumulated inside the keyboard and possibly prevent future problems with sticking keys or dirty keyswitches.

If a particular key is stuck or making intermittent contact, you can soak or spray that switch with contact cleaner. The best way to do this is to first remove the keycap and then spray the cleaner into the switch. This usually does not require complete disassembly of the keyboard. Periodic vacuuming or compressed gas cleaning will prevent more serious problems with sticking keys and keyswitches.

Most mice are easily cleaned. In most cases, there is a twist-off locking retainer that keeps the mouse ball retained in the body of the mouse. By removing the retainer, the ball will drop out. After removing the ball, you should clean it with one of the electronic cleaners. I would recommend a pure cleaner instead of a contact cleaner with lubricant because you do not want any lubricant on the mouse ball. Then you should wipe off the rollers in the body of the mouse with the cleaner and some swabs.

Periodic cleaning of a mouse in this manner will eliminate or prevent skipping or erratic movement that can be frustrating. I also recommend a mouse pad for most ball-type mice because the pad will prevent the mouse ball from picking up debris from your desk.

Mice often need frequent cleaning before they start sticking and jumping, which can be frustrating. If you never want to clean a mouse again, I suggest you look into the Honeywell mouse. These mice have a revolutionary new design that uses two external wheels rather than the conventional ball and roller system. The wheels work directly on the desk surface and are unaffected by dirt and dust. Because the body of the mouse is sealed, dirt and dust cannot enter it and gum up the positional sensors. I find this mouse excellent to use with my portable system because it works well on any surface. This mouse is virtually immune to the sticking and jumping that plagues ball and roller designs and never needs to be cleaned, so it is less frustrating than conventional mice.

Other pointing devices requiring little or no maintenance are the IBM designed Trackpoint and similar systems introduced by other manufacturers, such as the Glidepoint by Alps. These devices are totally sealed, and use pressure transducers to control pointer movement. Because they are sealed, cleaning need only be performed externally, and is as simple as wiping the device off with a mild cleaning solution to remove oils and other deposits that have accumulated from handling them.

Hard Disk Maintenance

Certain preventive maintenance procedures protect your data and ensure that your hard disk works efficiently. Some of these procedures actually minimize wear and tear on your drive, which will prolong its life. Additionally, a high level of data protection can be implemented by performing some simple commands periodically. These commands provide methods for backing up (and possibly later restoring) critical areas of the hard disk that, if damaged, would disable access to all your files.

Defragmenting Files. Over time, as you delete and save files to a hard disk, the files become *fragmented*. This means that they are split into many noncontiguous areas on the disk. One of the best ways to protect both your hard disk and the data on it is to periodically defragment the files on the disk. This serves two purposes. One is that by ensuring that all of the files are stored in contiguous sectors on the disk, head movement and drive wear and tear will be minimized. This has the added benefit of improving the speed at which files will be retrieved from the drive by reducing the head thrashing that occurs every time a fragmented file is accessed.

The second major benefit, and in my estimation the more important of the two, is that in the case of a disaster where the FATs and root directory are severely damaged, the data on the drive can usually be recovered very easily if the files are contiguous. On the other hand, if the files are split up in many pieces across the drive, it is virtually impossible to figure out which pieces belong to which files without an intact FAT and directory system. For the purposes of data integrity and protection, I recommend defragmenting your hard disk drives on a weekly basis, or immediately after you perform any major backup.

Three main functions are found in most defragmenting programs:

- File defragmentation
- File packing (Free Space Consolidation)
- File sorting

Defragmentation is the basic function, but most other programs also add file packing. Packing the files is optional on some programs because it usually takes additional time to perform. This function packs the files at the beginning of the disk so that all free space is consolidated at the end of the disk. This feature minimizes future file fragmentation by eliminating any empty holes on the disk. Because all free space is consolidated into one large area, any new files written to the disk will be able to be written in a contiguous manner with no fragmentation necessary.

The last function, file sorting, is not usually necessary and is performed as an option by many defragmenting programs. This function adds a tremendous amount of time to the operation, and has little or no effect on the speed at which information is accessed. It can be somewhat beneficial for disaster recovery purposes because you will have an idea of which files came before or after other files if a disaster occurs. These benefits would be minimal compared to having the files be contiguous no matter what their order. Not all defragmenting programs offer file sorting, and the extra time it takes is probably not worth any benefits you will receive. Other programs can sort the order that files are listed in directories, which is a quick and easy operation compared to sorting the file ordering the disk.

Checking for Virus Programs. Both Microsoft and IBM now provide standard antivirus software in DOS. The Microsoft Anti-Virus program is actually a reduced function version of the Central Point Anti-Virus software. IBM has written a package called the IBM Anti-Virus program. Many aftermarket utility packages are available that will scan for and remove virus programs. One of the best known is the McAfee Associates' SCAN program, which is also one of the easiest to run because it is a command-line utility. The McAfee program is also distributed through BBS systems and is often site-licensed to large companies.

Because Windows 95 does not include an antivirus program, you may want to invest in one of the aftermarket utilities such as the McAfee program.

No matter which of these programs you use, it is a good idea to perform a scan for virus programs periodically, especially before making hard disk backups. This will help to ensure that you catch any potential virus problem before it spreads and becomes a major hassle.

Passive Preventive Maintenance Procedures

Passive preventive maintenance involves taking care of the system in an external manner: basically, providing the best possible environment—both physical as well as electrical—for the system to operate in. Physical concerns are conditions such as ambient temperature, thermal stress from power cycling, dust and smoke contamination, and disturbances such as shock and vibration. Electrical concerns are items such as ESD, power-line noise, and radio-frequency interference. Each of these environmental concerns is discussed in this section.

Examining the Operating Environment. Oddly enough, one of the most overlooked aspects of microcomputer preventive maintenance is protecting the hardware—and the sizable financial investment it represents—from environmental abuse. Computers are relatively forgiving, and they are generally safe in an environment that is comfortable for people. Computers, however, are often treated with no more respect than desktop calculators. The result of this type of abuse is many system failures.

Before you acquire a system, prepare a proper location for your new system, free of airborne contaminants such as smoke or other pollution. Do not place your system in front of a window: The system should not be exposed to direct sunlight or temperature variations. The environmental temperature should be as constant as possible. Power should be provided through properly grounded outlets, and should be stable and free from electrical noise and interference. Keep your system away from radio transmitters or other sources of radio frequency energy. This section examines these issues in more detail.

Heating and Cooling. Thermal expansion and contraction from temperature changes place stress on a computer system. Therefore, keeping the temperature in your office or room relatively constant is important to the successful operation of your computer system.

Temperature variations can lead to serious problems. You might encounter excessive chip creep, for example. If extreme variations occur over a short period, signal traces on circuit boards can crack and separate, solder joints can break, and contacts in the system undergo accelerated corrosion. Solid-state components such as chips can be damaged also, and a host of other problems can develop.

Temperature variations can play havoc with hard disk drives. Writing to a disk at different ambient temperatures can, on some drives, cause data to be written at different locations relative to the track centers. Read and write problems then might accelerate later.

To ensure that your system operates in the correct ambient temperature, you first must determine your system's specified functional range. Most manufacturers provide data about the correct operating temperature range for their systems. Two temperature specifications might be available, one indicating allowable temperatures during operation and another indicating allowable temperatures under nonoperating conditions. IBM, for example, indicates the following temperature ranges as acceptable for most of its systems:

System on: 60 to 90° Fahrenheit

System off: 50 to 110° Fahrenheit

For the safety of the disk and the data it contains, avoid rapid changes in ambient temperatures. If rapid temperature changes occur—for example, when a new drive is shipped to a location during the winter and then brought indoors—let the drive acclimate to room temperature before turning it on. In extreme cases, condensation forms on the platters inside the drive HDA—disastrous for the drive if you turn it on before the condensation can evaporate. Most drive manufacturers specify a timetable to use as a guide in acclimating a drive to room temperature before operating it. You usually must wait several hours to a day before a drive is ready to use after it has been shipped or stored in a cold environment. They normally advise that you leave the drive in the packing until it is acclimatized. Removing the drive from a shipping carton when extremely cold will increase the likelihood of condensation forming as the drive warms up.

Most office environments provide a stable temperature in which to operate a computer system, but some do not. Be sure to give some consideration to the placement of your equipment.

Power Cycling (On/Off). As you have just learned, the temperature variations a system encounters greatly stress the system's physical components. The largest temperature variations a system encounters, however, are those that occur during system warm-up when you initially turn it on. Turning on (also called *powering on*) a cold system subjects it to the greatest possible internal temperature variations. For these reasons, limiting the number of power-on cycles a system is exposed to greatly improves its life and reliability.

If you want a system to have the longest and most trouble-free life possible, you should limit the temperature variations in its environment. You can limit the extreme temperature cycling in two simple ways during a cold startup: Leave the system off all the time or leave it on all the time. Of these two possibilities, of course, you want to choose the latter option. Leaving the power on is the best way I know to promote system reliability. If your only concern is system longevity, the simple recommendation would be to keep the system unit powered on (or off!) continuously. In the real world, however, there are more variables to consider, such as the cost of electricity, the potential fire hazard of unattended running equipment, and other concerns as well.

If you think about the way light bulbs typically fail, you can begin to understand that thermal cycling can be dangerous. Light bulbs burn out most often when you first turn them on, because the filament must endure incredible thermal stresses as it changes temperature—in less than one second—from ambient to several thousands of degrees. A bulb that remains on continuously lasts longer than one that is turned on and off repeatedly.

Where problems can occur immediately at power-on is in the power supply. The startup current draw for the system and for any motor during the first few seconds of operation is very high compared to the normal operating-current draw. Because the current must come from the power supply, the supply has an extremely demanding load to carry for the first few seconds of operation, especially if several disk drives will be started. Motors have an extremely high power-on current draw. This demand often overloads a marginal circuit or component in the supply and causes it to burn or break with a "snap." I have seen several power supplies die the instant a system was powered up. To enable your equipment to have the longest possible life, try to keep the temperature of solid-state components relatively constant, and limit the number of startups on the power supply. The only way I know to do so is to leave the system on.

Although it sounds as though I am recommending that you leave all of your computer equipment on 24 hours a day, seven days a week, I no longer recommend this type of operation. A couple of concerns have tempered my urge to leave everything running continuously. One is that an unattended system that is powered on represents a fire hazard. I have seen monitors start themselves on fire after internally shorting, and systems whose cooling fans have frozen, enabling the power supply and entire system to overheat. I do not leave any system running in an unattended building. Another problem is wasted electrical power. Many companies have adopted austerity programs that involve turning lights and other items off when not in use. The power consumption of some of today's high-powered systems and accessories is not trivial. Also, an unattended operating system is more of a security risk than one that is powered off and locked.

Realities—such as the fire hazard of unattended systems running during night or weekend hours, security problems, and power-consumption issues—might prevent you from leaving your system on all the time. Therefore, you must compromise. Power on the system only one time daily. Don't power the system on and off several times every day. This good advice is often ignored, especially when several users share systems. Each user powers on the system to perform work on the PC and then powers off the system. These systems tend to have many more problems with component failures.

If you are in a building with a programmable thermostat, you have another reason to be concerned about temperatures and disk drives. Some buildings have thermostats programmed to turn off the heat overnight or over the weekend. These thermostats are programmed also to quickly raise the temperature just before business hours every day. In Chicago, for example, outside temperatures in the winter can dip to –20° (not including a wind-chill factor). An office building's interior temperature can drop as low as 50° during the weekend. When you arrive Monday morning, the heat has been on for only an hour or so, but the hard disk platters might have not yet reached even 60° when you turn on the system unit. During the first 20 minutes of operation, the disk platters rapidly rise in temperature to 120° or more. If you have an inexpensive stepper motor hard disk and begin writing to the disk at these low temperatures, you are setting yourself up for trouble. Again, many systems with these "cheap" drives don't even boot properly under these circumstances and must be warmed up before they even boot DOS.

> **Tip**
>
> If you do not leave a system on continuously; at least give it 15 minutes or more to warm up after a cold start before writing to the hard disk. Power up the system and go get a cup of coffee, read the paper, or do some other task. This practice does wonders for the reliability of the data on your disk, especially cheaper units.

If you do leave your system on for long periods of time, make sure that the screen is blank or displays a random image if the system is not in use. The phosphor on the picture tube can burn if a stationary image is left on-screen continuously. Higher-persistence phosphor monochrome screens are most susceptible, and the color displays with low-persistence phosphors are the least susceptible. If you ever have seen a monochrome display with the image of some program permanently burned in—even with the display off—you know what I mean. Look at the monitors that display flight information at the airport—they usually show some of the effects of phosphor burn.

Most modern displays that have power-saving features can automatically enter a standby mode on command by the system. If your system has these power-saving functions, enable them as they will help to reduce energy costs as well as preserve the monitor.

Screen savers or blankers will either blank the screen completely or display some sort of moving random image to prevent burn-in. This can be accomplished by either a manual or automatic procedure as follows:

- *Manual.* Turn the brightness and contrast levels all the way down, or even turn off the display completely. This technique is effective but it is a manual method; you must remember to do it.

- *Automatic.* Many types of programs can cause the screen to blank or display random images automatically at a predetermined interval. Screen savers are built in to most graphical user interfaces (GUIs) such as Windows and OS/2. These can easily be enabled, and you can also specify the time delay before they activate. If you run under plain DOS, you can use a number of public domain as well as commercial screen saver programs. These programs usually run as *terminate-and-stay-resident (TSR) programs*. The program watches the clock as well as the keyboard and mouse ports. If several minutes pass with nothing typed at the keyboard or no mouse movement, the program activates and either shuts off all signals to the display or creates an image that moves around on the screen to prevent burn-in.

Screen savers are obsolete in a modern green PC that features power management capabilities. In fact, in these systems, using a screen saver can defeat the power management functions by keeping the hard disk drive and the screen fully powered up at all times. With the built-in power management found in most system BIOS as well as Windows 95, screen savers are more for entertainment than to serve a practical purpose.

Static Electricity. Static electricity can cause numerous problems within a system. The problems usually appear during the winter months when humidity is low or in extremely dry climates where the humidity is low year-round. In these cases, you might need to take special precautions to ensure that the system functions properly.

Static discharges outside a system-unit chassis are rarely a source of permanent problems within the system. The usual effect of a static discharge to the case, keyboard, or even in close proximity to a system is a parity check (memory) error or a locked-up system. In some cases, I have been able to cause parity checks or system lockups by simply walking past a system. Most static-sensitivity problems such as this are caused by improper grounding of the system power. Be sure that you always use a three-prong, grounded power cord plugged into a properly grounded outlet. If you are unsure about the outlet, you can buy an outlet tester at most electronics supply or hardware stores for only a few dollars.

Whenever you open a system unit or handle circuits removed from the system, you must be much more careful with static. You can permanently damage a component with a static discharge if the charge is not routed to a ground. I usually recommend handling boards and adapters first by a grounding point such as the bracket to minimize the potential for static damage.

An easy way to prevent static problems is with good power-line grounding, which is extremely important for computer equipment. A poorly designed power-line grounding system is one of the primary causes of poor computer design. The best way to prevent static damage is to prevent the static charge from getting into the computer in the first place. The chassis ground in a properly designed system serves as a static guard for the computer, which redirects the static charge safely to ground. For this ground to be complete, therefore, the system must be plugged into a properly grounded three-wire outlet.

If the static problem is extreme, you can resort to other measures. One is to use a grounded static mat underneath the computer. Touch the mat first before you touch the computer to ensure that any static charges are routed to ground and away from the system unit's internal parts. If problems still persist, you might want to check out the electrical building ground. I have seen installations in which three-wire outlets exist but are not grounded properly. You can use an outlet tester to be sure that the outlet is wired properly.

Power-Line Noise. To run properly, a computer system requires a steady supply of clean noise-free power. In some installations, however, the power line serving the computer serves heavy equipment also, and the voltage variations resulting from the on-off cycling of this equipment can cause problems for the computer. Certain types of equipment on the same power line also can cause *voltage spikes*—short transient signals of sometimes 1,000v or more—that can physically damage a computer. Although these spikes are rare, they can be crippling. Even a dedicated electrical circuit used only by a single computer can experience spikes and transients, depending on the quality of the power supplied to the building or circuit.

During the site-preparation phase of a system installation, you should be aware of these factors to ensure a steady supply of clean power:

- If possible, the computer system should be on its own circuit with its own circuit breaker. This setup does not guarantee freedom from interference, but it helps.

- The circuit should be checked for a good, low-resistance ground, proper line voltage, freedom from interference, and freedom from *brownouts* (voltage dips).

- A three-wire circuit is a must, but some people substitute grounding-plug adapters to adapt a grounded plug to a two-wire socket. This setup is not recommended; the ground is there for a reason.

- Power-line noise problems increase with the resistance of the circuit, which is a function of wire size and length. To decrease resistance, therefore, avoid extension cords unless absolutely necessary, and then use only heavy-duty extension cords.

- Inevitably, you will want to plug in other equipment later. Plan ahead to avoid temptations to use too many items on a single outlet. If possible, provide a separate power circuit for noncomputer-related accessories.

Air conditioners, coffee makers, copy machines, laser printers, space heaters, vacuum cleaners, and power tools are some of the worst corrupters of a PC system's power. Any of these items can draw an excessive amount of current and play havoc with a PC system on the same electrical circuit. I've seen offices in which all the computers begin to crash at about 9:05 A.M. daily, which is when all the coffee makers are turned on!

Also, try to ensure that copy machines and laser printers do not share a circuit with other computer equipment. These devices draw a large amount of power.

Another major problem in some companies is partitioned offices. Many of these partitions are prewired with their own electrical outlets and are plugged into one another in a sort of power-line daisy chain, similar to chaining power strips together. I pity the person in the cubicle at the end of the electrical daisy chain, who will have very flaky power!

As a real-world example of too many devices sharing a single circuit, I can describe several instances in which a personal computer had a repeating parity-check problem. All efforts to repair the system had been unsuccessful. The reported error locations from the parity-check message also were inconsistent, which normally indicates a problem with power. The problem could have been the power supply in the system unit or the external power supplied from the wall outlet. This problem was solved one day as I stood watching the system. The parity-check message was displayed at the same instant someone two cubicles away turned on a copy machine. Placing the computers on a separate line solved the problem.

By following the guidelines in this section, you can create the proper power environment for your systems and help to ensure trouble-free operation.

Radio-Frequency Interference. *Radio-frequency interference (RFI)* is easily overlooked as a problem factor. The interference is caused by any source of radio transmissions near a computer system. Living next door to a 50,000-watt commercial radio station is one sure way to get RFI problems, but less powerful transmitters cause problems, too. I know of many instances in which portable radio-telephones have caused sporadic random keystrokes to appear, as though an invisible entity were typing on the keyboard. I also have seen RFI cause a system to lock up. Solutions to RFI problems are more difficult to state because every case must be handled differently. Sometimes, reorienting a system unit eliminates the problem because radio signals can be directional in nature. At other times, you must invest in specially shielded cables for cables outside the system unit, such as the keyboard cable.

One type of solution to an RFI noise problem with cables is to pass the cable through a *toroidal iron core*, a doughnut-shaped piece of iron placed around a cable to suppress both the reception and transmission of electromagnetic interference (EMI). If you can isolate an RFI noise problem in a particular cable, you often can solve the problem by passing the cable through a toroidal core. Because the cable must pass through the center hole of the core, it often is difficult, if not impossible, to add a toroid to a cable that already has end connectors installed.

Radio Shack sells a special snap-together toroid designed specifically to be added to cables already in use. This toroid looks like a thick-walled tube that has been sliced in half. You just lay the cable in the center of one of the halves, and snap the other half over the first. This type of construction makes it easy to add the noise-suppression features of a toroid to virtually any existing cable.

IBM also makes a special 6-foot long PS/2 keyboard cable with a built-in toroid core (part number 27F4984) that can greatly reduce interference problems. This cable has the smaller six-pin DIN (PS/2 style) connector at the system end and the standard SDL (Shielded Data Link) connector at the keyboard end; it costs about $40.

The best, if not the easiest, way to eliminate the problem probably is to correct it at the source. You likely won't convince the commercial radio station near your office to shut down, but if you are dealing with a small radio transmitter that is generating RFI, sometimes you can add to the transmitter a filter that suppresses spurious emissions. Unfortunately, problems sometimes persist until the transmitter is either switched off or moved some distance away from the affected computer.

Dust and Pollutants. Dirt, smoke, dust, and other pollutants are bad for your system. The power-supply fan carries airborne particles through your system, and they collect inside. If your system is used in an extremely harsh environment, you might want to investigate some of the industrial systems on the market designed for harsh conditions. IBM used to sell industrial-model XT and AT systems but discontinued them after introducing the PS/2. IBM has licensed several third-party companies to produce industrial versions of PS/2 systems.

Compatible vendors also have industrial systems; many companies make special hardened versions of their systems for harsh environments. Industrial systems usually use a different cooling system from the one used in a regular PC. A large cooling fan is used to pressurize the case rather than depressurize it, as most systems do. The air pumped into the case passes through a filter unit that must be cleaned and changed periodically. The system is pressurized so that no contaminated air can flow into it; air flows only outward. The only way air can enter is through the fan and filter system.

These systems also might have special keyboards impervious to liquids and dirt. Some flat-membrane keyboards are difficult to type on, but are extremely rugged; others resemble the standard types of keyboards but have a thin, plastic membrane that covers all the keys. You can add this membrane to normal types of keyboards to seal them from the environment.

A new breed of humidifier can cause problems with computer equipment. This type of humidifier uses ultrasonics to generate a mist of water sprayed into the air. The extra humidity helps cure problems with static electricity resulting from a dry climate, but the airborne water contaminants can cause many problems. If you use one of these systems, you might notice a white ash-like deposit forming on components. The deposit is the result of abrasive and corrosive minerals suspended in the vaporized water. If these deposits collect on the system components, they can cause all kinds of problems. The only safe way to run one of these ultrasonic humidifiers is with pure distilled water. If you use a humidifier, be sure it does not generate these deposits.

If you do your best to keep the environment for your computer equipment clean, your system will run better and last longer. Also, you will not have to open your unit as often for complete preventive maintenance cleaning.

Part II

Primary System Components

4   Motherboards

5   Bus Slots and I/O Cards

6   Microprocessor Types and Specifications

7   Memory

8   The Power Supply

Chapter 4
Motherboards

Easily the most important component in a PC system is the main board or motherboard. Some companies, such as IBM, refer to the motherboard as a system board or planar. The terms *motherboard*, *main board*, *system board*, and *planar* are interchangeable. In this chapter, we will examine the different types of motherboards available, as well as those components usually contained on the motherboard and motherboard interface connectors.

Replacement Motherboards

Some manufacturers go out of their way to make their systems as physically incompatible as possible with any other system. Then replacement parts, repairs, and upgrades are virtually impossible to find—except, of course, from the original system manufacturer, at a significantly higher price than the equivalent part would cost to fit a standard PC-compatible system.

For example, if the motherboard in my current AT-chassis system (or any system using a Baby-AT motherboard and case) dies, I can find any number of replacement boards that will bolt directly in, with my choice of processors and clock speeds, at very good prices. If the motherboard dies in a newer IBM, Compaq, Hewlett-Packard, Packard Bell, Gateway, AST, or other proprietary shaped system, you'll pay for a replacement available only from the original manufacturer, and you have little or no opportunity to select a board with a faster or better processor than the one that failed. In other words, upgrading or repairing one of these systems via a motherboard replacement is difficult and usually not cost-effective.

Knowing What to Look For (Selection Criteria)

As a consultant, I am often asked to make a recommendation for purchases. Making these types of recommendations is one of the most frequent tasks a consultant performs. Many consultants charge a large fee for this advice.

Without guidance, many individuals don't have any rhyme or reason to their selections and instead base their choices solely on magazine reviews or, even worse, on some personal bias. To help eliminate this haphazard selection process, I have developed a simple checklist that will help you select a system. This list takes into consideration several important system aspects overlooked by most checklists. The goal is to ensure that the selected system truly is compatible and has a long life of service and upgrades ahead.

It helps to think like an engineer when you make your selection. Consider every aspect and detail of the motherboards in question. For instance, you should consider any future uses and upgrades. Technical support at a professional (as opposed to a user) level is extremely important. What support will be provided? Is there documentation, and does it cover everything else?

In short, a checklist is a good idea. You can use the following check list to evaluate any PC-compatible system. You might not have to meet every one of these criteria to consider a particular system, but if you miss more than a few of these checks, consider staying away from that system. The items at the top of the list are the most important, and the items at the bottom are perhaps of lesser importance (although I think each item is important). The rest of this chapter discusses in detail the criteria in this checklist:

- *Processor*. A Pentium motherboard should use as a minimum the second-generation 3.3v Pentium processor, which has a 296-pin Socket 5 or Socket 7 configuration that differs physically from the 273-pin Socket 4 first-generation design. Pentium motherboards with the Socket 7 configuration also support newer processors with MMX technology, including AMD's K6. All second-generation Pentiums (75MHz and up) are fully SL Enhanced. Newer Pentium Pro and Pentium II processors have their own unique motherboard configurations, and are not compatible with other Pentium-based motherboards.

- *Processor Sockets*. A Pentium motherboard should have at least one ZIF socket that follows the Intel Socket 7 (321-pin) specification. The Socket 7 with an adjacent VRM (Voltage Regulator Module) socket will allow the best selection of future Pentium processors that will be available at higher speeds. Although Socket 5 is similar to Socket 7, many of the newer and faster Pentiums—including the MMX equipped processors—require Socket 7. Pentium Pro (P6) motherboards use Socket 8, and many are set up for multiple processors. Before going to the expense of buying a multi-processor board, ensure that your operating system is able to handle it. For instance, while Windows 95 cannot really benefit from more than one CPU, Windows NT, OS/2, and some others may run considerably faster.

- *Motherboard Speed*. A Pentium or Pentium Pro motherboard should run at 60 or 66MHz and be speed-switchable between these speeds. Notice that all the Pentium and Pentium Pro processors sold today run at a multiple of the motherboard speed. For example, Pentium 75 runs at a motherboard speed of 50MHz; Pentium 60, 90, 120, 150, and 180MHz chips run at a 60MHz base motherboard speed; and the Pentium 66, 100, 133, 166, and 200 run at a 66MHz motherboard speed setting.

The Pentium Pro 150, 180, and 200 run at 50, 60, and 66MHz speeds, respectively. All components on the motherboard (especially cache memory) should be rated to run at the maximum allowable motherboard speed.

- *Cache Memory.* All Pentium motherboards should have 256K to 512K of Level 2 cache on-board. Most Pentium Pro processors have a built-in 256K or 512K Level 2 cache, but may also have more Level 2 cache on the motherboard for even better performance. The Level 2 cache should be of a Write-Back design, and must be populated with chips that are fast enough to support the maximum motherboard speed, which should be 15ns or faster for 66MHz maximum motherboard speeds. For Pentium boards, the cache should be a Synchronous SRAM (Static RAM) type, which is also called *Pipelined Burst SRAM*.

- *SIMM Memory.* All Pentium and Pentium Pro motherboards should use either 72-pin SIMMs or 168-pin DIMMs (Dual In-line Memory Modules). Due to the 64-bit design of these boards, the 72-pin SIMMs must be installed in matched pairs, while DIMMs are installed one at a time (one per 64-bit bank). Carefully consider the total amount of memory that the board supports. While 16M is regarded as a bare minimum for today's memory-hungry applications, you may actually require much more. Pentium motherboards should support at least 128M, and many current Pentium II boards support more than 1G! A motherboard should contain at least four memory sockets (72-pin, 168-pin, or a combination) and the more the better. For maximum performance, look for systems that support SDRAM (Synchronous DRAM) or EDO (Extended Data Out) type SIMMs/DIMMs. The SIMMs should be rated at 70ns or faster.

  Mission-critical systems ideally should use Parity SIMMs and ensure that the motherboard fully supports parity checking or even ECC (Error Correcting Code) as well. Note that the popular Intel Triton Pentium chipset (82430FX) does not support parity checked memory at all, but their other Pentium chipsets such as the older Neptune (82430NX) and newer Triton II (82430HX) do indeed offer parity support. Triton II even offers ECC capability using standard parity SIMMs. All the current Pentium Pro chipsets also support Parity memory and are ideal for file servers and other mission critical use when equipped with parity SIMMs or DIMMs.

- *Bus Type.* Pentium, Pentium Pro, and Pentium II motherboards should have three or four ISA bus slots and three or four PCI local bus slots. Take a look at the layout of the slots to ensure that cards inserted in them will not block access to memory sockets, or be blocked by other components in the case.

- *BIOS.* The motherboard should use an industry-standard BIOS such as those from AMI, Phoenix, Microid Research, or Award. The BIOS should be of a Flash ROM or EEPROM (Electrically Erasable Programmable Read Only Memory) design for easy updating. The BIOS should support the Plug and Play (PnP) specification, Enhanced IDE or Fast ATA, as well as 2.88M floppy drives. APM (Advanced Power Management) support should be built into the BIOS as well.

- *Form Factor.* For maximum flexibility, the Baby-AT form factor is still a safe bet. It can be installed in the widest variety of case designs, and is retrofittable in most systems. For the greatest performance and future flexibility, many newer motherboards and systems incorporate the new ATX form factor, which has distinct performance and functional advantages over Baby-AT. Additionally, the new NLX form factor has been developed by Intel as an improvement on the ATX. Although it is new, the NLX specification is supported by a number of manufacturers, so it could prove to be a popular board in the coming years.

- *Built-in interfaces.* Ideally, a motherboard should contain as many built-in standard controllers and interfaces as possible (except video). A motherboard should have a built-in floppy controller that supports 2.88M drives, built-in primary and secondary local bus (PCI or VL-Bus) Enhanced IDE (also called Fast ATA) connectors, two built-in high-speed serial ports (must use 16550A type buffered UARTs), and a built-in high-speed parallel port (must be EPP/ECP-compliant). A built-in PS/2 type mouse port should be included, although one of the serial ports can be used for a mouse as well.

  Some newer systems, particularly those with ATX and NLX form factors, should include a built-in USB (Universal Serial Bus) port. USB ports will become a "must-have" item on multimedia systems in the near future. A built-in SCSI port is a bonus as long as it conforms to ASPI (Advanced SCSI Programming Interface) standards. Built-in network adapters are acceptable, but usually an ISA slot card network adapter is more easily supported via standard drivers and is more easily upgraded as well. Built-in video adapters are also a bonus in some situations, but because there are many different video chipset and adapter designs to choose from, generally there are better choices in external local bus video adapters. The same goes for built-in sound cards; they usually offer basic Sound Blaster compatibility and function, but often do not include other desirable features found on most plug-in sound cards, such as wavetable support.

- *Plug and Play (PnP).* The motherboard should fully support the Intel PnP specification. This will allow automatic configuration of PCI adapters as well as PnP ISA adapters.

Tip

Even if a motherboard doesn't list that it's PnP-compatible, it may be. PCI motherboards are required to be PnP-compatible, as it is a part of the PCI standard.

- *Power Management.* The motherboard should fully support SL Enhanced processors with APM (Advanced Power Management) and SMM (System Management Mode) protocols that allow for powering down various system components to different levels of readiness and power consumption.

- *Motherboard Chipset.* Pentium and Pentium MMX motherboards should use a high-performance chipset—preferably one that allows parity checking, such as the Intel

Triton II (430HX). The popular original Intel Triton (430FX) chipset, along with the newer 430TX and 430VX chipsets, does not support parity-checked memory. For critical applications using Pentium motherboards where accuracy and data integrity is important, I recommend you use a board based on the Triton II (430HX) chipset or any others like it that support ECC memory using true parity memory modules. As a bonus, the 430HX chipset supports USB and dual CPUs, making it truly versatile.

Pentium Pro and Pentium II motherboards currently have the high-end Orion (450KX and 450GX) chipsets, as well as the less expensive Natoma (440FX) chipset. All three chipsets support parity memory, USB, and multiple CPUs, and are suitable for critical application use.

- *Documentation.* Good technical documentation is a requirement. Documents should include information on any and all jumpers and switches found on the board, connector pinouts for all connectors, specifications for cache RAM chips, SIMMs, and other plug-in components, and any other applicable technical information. I would also acquire separate documentation from the BIOS manufacturer covering the specific BIOS used in the system, as well as the data books covering the specific chipset used in the motherboard. Additional data books for any other controller or I/O chips on-board are a bonus, and may be acquired from the respective chip manufacturers.

  Another nice thing to have is available online support and documentation updates, although this should not be accepted in place of good hardcopy manuals.

You may notice that these selection criteria seem fairly strict and may disqualify many motherboards on the market, including what you already have in your system! These criteria will, however, guarantee you the highest quality motherboard offering the latest in PC technology that will be upgradable, expandable, and provide good service for many years. Most of the time I recommend purchasing boards from better-known motherboard manufacturers such as Intel, SuperMicro, Micronics, AMI, Biostar, Tyan, Asus, and so on. These boards might cost a little more than others that you have never heard of, but there is some safety in the more well-known brands; that is, the more boards that they sell, the more likely that any problems will have been discovered by others and solved long before you get yours. Also, if service or support are needed, the larger vendors are more likely to be around in the long run.

Documentation

As mentioned, extensive documentation is an important factor to consider when you're planning to purchase a motherboard. Most motherboard manufacturers design their boards around a particular chipset, which actually counts as the bulk of the motherboard circuitry. There are a number of manufacturers offering chipsets, such as Intel, Opti, VIA, SiS, and others. I recommend obtaining the data book or other technical documentation on the chipset directly from the chipset manufacturer.

One of the more common questions I hear about a system relates to the BIOS Setup program. People want to know what the "Advanced Chipset Setup" features mean and what the effects of changing them will be. Often they go to the BIOS manufacturer thinking that the BIOS documentation will offer help. Usually, however, people find that there is no real coverage of what the chipset setup features are in the BIOS documentation. You will find this information in the data book provided by the chipset manufacturer. Although these books are meant to be read by the engineers who design the boards, they contain all the detailed information about the chipset's features, especially those that might be adjustable. With the chipset data book, you will have an explanation of all the controls in the Advanced Chipset Setup section of the BIOS Setup program.

Besides the main chipset data books, I also recommend collecting any data books on the other major chips in the system. This would include any floppy or IDE controller chips, Super I/O chips, and of course the main processor. You will find an incredible amount of information on these components in the data books.

> **Caution**
>
> Most chipset manufacturers only make a particular chip for a short time, rapidly superseding it with an improved or changed version. The data books are only available during the time the chip is being manufactured, so if you wait too long, you will find that such documents may no longer be available. The time to collect documentation on your motherboard is *now*!

ROM BIOS Compatibility

The issue of ROM BIOS compatibility is important. If the BIOS is not compatible, any number of problems can result. Several reputable companies that produce compatibles have developed their own proprietary ROM BIOS that works just like IBM's. Also, many of the compatibles' OEMs have designed ROMs that work specifically with additional features in their systems while effectively masking the effects of these improvements from any software that would "balk" at the differences.

OEMs. Many OEMs (Original Equipment Manufacturers) have developed their own compatible ROMs independently. Companies such as Compaq and AT&T have developed their own BIOS products which are comparable to those offered by AMI, Phoenix, and others. These companies also offer upgrades to newer versions that often can offer more features and improvements or fix problems with the older versions. If you use a system with a proprietary ROM, make sure that it is from a larger company with a track record and one that will provide updates and fixes as necessary. Ideally, upgrades should be available for download from the Internet.

Several companies have specialized in the development of a compatible ROM BIOS product. The three major companies that come to mind in discussing ROM BIOS software are American Megatrends, Inc. (AMI), Award Software, and Phoenix Software. Each company licenses its ROM BIOS to a motherboard manufacturer so that the manufacturer can worry about the hardware rather than the software. To obtain one of these ROMs for a motherboard, the OEM must answer many questions about the design of the system so that the proper BIOS can be either developed or selected from those already designed. Combining a ROM BIOS and a motherboard is not a haphazard task. No single, generic, compatible ROM exists, either. AMI, Award, Microid Research, and Phoenix ship to different manufacturers many variations of their BIOS code, each one custom-tailored to that specific system, much like DOS can be.

A good source of information on currently available BIOS products is available from the System Optimization Web site at:

http://www.sysopt.com/bios.html

On the Web

AMI. Although AMI customizes the ROM code for a particular system, it does not sell the ROM source code to the OEM. An OEM must obtain each new release as it becomes available. Because many OEMs don't need or want every new version developed, they might skip several version changes before licensing a new one. The AMI BIOS is currently the most popular BIOS in PC systems today. Newer versions of the AMI BIOS are called *Hi-Flex* due to the high flexibility found in the BIOS configuration program. The AMI Hi-Flex BIOS is used in Intel, AMI, and many other manufacturers' motherboards. One special AMI feature is that it is the only third-party BIOS manufacturer to make its own motherboard.

During powerup, the BIOS ID string is displayed on the lower-left of the screen. This string tells you valuable information about which BIOS version you have, as well as certain settings which are determined by the built-in setup program.

> **Tip**
>
> A good trick to help you view the BIOS ID string is to shut down and either unplug your keyboard, or hold down a key as you power back on. This will cause a keyboard error, and the string will remained displayed.

The primary BIOS Identification string (ID String 1) is displayed by any AMI BIOS during the POST (Power On Self-Test) at the bottom-left corner of the screen, below the copyright message. Two additional BIOS ID strings (ID Strings 2 and 3) can be displayed by the AMI Hi-Flex BIOS by pressing the Insert key during POST. These additional ID strings display the options that are installed in the BIOS.

The general BIOS ID String 1 format for older AMI BIOS versions is shown in Table 4.1.

Table 4.1	ABBB-NNNN-mmddyy-KK
Position	**Description**
A	BIOS Options: D = Diagnostics built-in. S = Setup built-in. E = Extended Setup built-in.
BBB	Chipset or Motherboard Identifier: C&T = Chips & Technologies chipset. NET = C&T NEAT 286 chipset. 286 = Standard 286 motherboard.

(continues)

Table 4.1 Continued

Position	Description
	SUN = Suntac chipset.
	PAQ = Compaq motherboard.
	INT = Intel motherboard.
	AMI = AMI motherboard.
	G23 = G2 chipset 386 motherboard.
NNNN	The manufacturer license code reference number.
mmddyy	The BIOS release date, mm/dd/yy.
KK	The AMI keyboard BIOS version number.

The BIOS ID String 1 format for AMI Hi-Flex BIOS versions is shown in Table 4.2.

Table 4.2 AB-CCcc-DDDDDD-EFGHIJKL-mmddyy-MMMMMMMM-N

Position	Description
A	Processor Type:
	0 = 8086 or 8088.
	2 = 286.
	3 = 386.
	4 = 486.
	5 = Pentium.
	6 = Pentium Pro.
B	Size of BIOS:
	0 = 64K BIOS.
	1 = 128K BIOS.
CCcc	Major and Minor BIOS version number.
DDDDDD	Manufacturer license code reference number.
	0036xx = AMI 386 motherboard, xx = Series #.
	0046xx = AMI 486 motherboard, xx = Series #.
	0056xx = AMI Pentium motherboard, xx = Series #.
	0066xx = AMI Pentium Pro motherboard, xx = Series #.
E	1 = Halt on Post Error.
F	1 = Initialize CMOS every boot.
G	1 = Block pins 22 and 23 of the keyboard controller.
H	1 = Mouse support in BIOS/keyboard controller.
I	1 = Wait for <F1> key on POST errors.
J	1 = Display floppy error during POST.
K	1 = Display video error during POST.
L	1 = Display keyboard error during POST.
mmddyy	BIOS Date, mm/dd/yy.
MMMMMMMM	Chipset identifier or BIOS name.
N	Keyboard controller version number.

Knowing What to Look For (Selection Criteria)

AMI Hi-Flex BIOS ID String 2 is shown in Table 4.3.

Table 4.3 AAB-C-DDDD-EE-FF-GGGG-HH-II-JJJ

Position	Description
AA	Keyboard controller pin number for clock switching.
B	Keyboard controller clock switching pin function: H = High signal switches clock to high speed. L = High signal switches clock to low speed.
C	Clock switching through chip set registers: 0 = Disable. 1 = Enable.
DDDD	Port address to switch clock high.
EE	Data value to switch clock high.
FF	Mask value to switch clock high.
GGGG	Port Address to switch clock low.
HH	Data value to switch clock low.
II	Mask value to switch clock low.
JJJ	Pin number for Turbo Switch Input.

AMI Hi-Flex BIOS ID String 3 is shown in Table 4.4.

Table 4.4 AAB-C-DDD-EE-FF-GGGG-HH-II-JJ-K-L

Position	Description
AA	Keyboard controller pin number for cache control.
B	Keyboard controller cache control pin function: H = High signal enables the cache. L = High signal disables the cache.
C	1 = High signal is used on the keyboard controller pin.
DDD	Cache control through Chipset registers: 0 = Cache control off. 1 = Cache control on.
EE	Port address to enable cache.
FF	Data value to enable cache.
GGGG	Mask value to enable cache.
HH	Port address to disable cache.
II	Data value to disable cache.
JJ	Mask value to disable cache.
K	Pin number for resetting the 82335 memory controller.
L	BIOS Modification Flag: 0 = The BIOS has not been modified. 1–9, A–Z = Number of times the BIOS has been modified.

The AMI BIOS has many features, including a built-in setup program activated by pressing the Delete or Esc key in the first few seconds of booting up your computer. The BIOS will prompt you briefly as to which key to press and when to press it. The AMI BIOS offers user-definable hard disk types, essential for optimal use of many IDE or ESDI drives. The newer BIOS versions also support Enhanced IDE drives and will auto-configure the drive parameters.

A unique AMI BIOS feature is that, in addition to the setup, it has a built-in, menu-driven, diagnostics package—essentially a very limited version of the stand-alone AMIDIAG product. The internal diagnostics are not a replacement for more comprehensive disk-based programs, but they can help in a pinch. The menu-driven diagnostics does not do extensive memory testing, for example, and the hard disk low-level formatter works only at the BIOS level rather than at the controller register level. These limitations often have prevented it from being capable of formatting severely damaged disks.

The AMI BIOS is sold through distributors, a list of which is available at **http://www.ami.com/distributor.html**. You may also contact Washburn and Co., listed in the vendor list in Appendix A. However, keep in mind that you cannot buy upgrades and replacements direct from AMI.

Award. Award is unique among BIOS manufacturers because it sells its BIOS code to the OEM and allows the OEM to customize the BIOS. Of course, then the BIOS no longer is Award BIOS, but rather a highly customized version. AST uses this approach on its systems, as do other manufacturers, for total control over the BIOS code, without having to write it from scratch. Although AMI and Phoenix customize the ROM code for a particular system, they do not sell the ROM's source code to the OEM. Some OEMs that seem to have developed their own ROM code started with a base of source code licensed to them by Award or some other company.

The Award BIOS has all the normal features you expect, including a built-in setup program activated by pressing Ctrl+Alt+Esc. This setup offers user-definable drive types, required in order to fully use IDE or ESDI hard disks. The POST is good, and Award runs technical support on its Web site at **http://www.award.com**. They also run a BBS whose number is listed in the vendor list in Appendix A.

In all, the Award BIOS is high quality, has minimal compatibility problems, and offers a high level of support.

Phoenix. The Phoenix BIOS for many years has been a standard of compatibility by which others are judged. It was one of the first third-party companies to legally reverse-engineer the IBM BIOS using a "clean room" approach. In this approach, a group of engineers studied the IBM BIOS and wrote a specification for how that BIOS should work and what features should be incorporated. This information then was passed to a second group of engineers who had never seen the IBM BIOS. They could then legally write a new BIOS to the specifications set forth by the first group. This work would then be unique and not a copy of IBM's BIOS; however, it would function the same way. This code has been refined over the years and has very few compatibility problems compared to some of the other BIOS vendors.

The Phoenix BIOS excels in two areas that put it high on my list of recommendations. One is that the POST is excellent. The BIOS outputs an extensive set of beep codes that can be used to diagnose severe motherboard problems which would prevent normal operation of the system. In fact, this POST can isolate memory failures in Bank 0 right down to the individual chip with beep codes alone. The Phoenix BIOS also has an excellent setup program free from unnecessary frills, but that offers all the features one would expect, such as user-definable drive types, and so on. The built-in setup is activated by pressing either Ctrl+Alt+S or Ctrl+Alt+Esc, depending on the version of BIOS you have.

The second area in which Phoenix excels is the documentation. Not only are the manuals that you get with the system detailed, but also Phoenix has written a set of BIOS technical-reference manuals that are a standard in the industry. The set consists of three books, titled *System BIOS for IBM PC/XT/AT Computers and Compatibles*, *CBIOS for IBM PS/2 Computers and Compatibles*, and *ABIOS for IBM PS/2 Computers and Compatibles*. Phoenix is one of few vendors who has done extensive research on the PS/2 BIOS and produced virtually all the ROMs in the PS/2 Micro Channel clones on the market. In addition to being an excellent reference for the Phoenix BIOS, these books serve as an outstanding overall reference to any company's IBM-compatible BIOS. Even if you never have a system with a Phoenix BIOS, I highly recommend these books.

Micronics motherboards have always used the Phoenix BIOS, and these motherboards are used in many of the popular name-brand compatible systems. Phoenix has been one of the largest OEMs of Microsoft MS-DOS. If you have MS-DOS, you also have the Phoenix OEM version. Phoenix licenses its DOS to other computer manufacturers so long as they use the Phoenix BIOS. Because of its close relationship with Microsoft, it has had access to the DOS source code, which helps in eliminating compatibility problems.

Although Phoenix does not operate a technical support service by itself, their largest nationwide distributor does, which is Micro Firmware Inc. Online information is available at **http://www.firmware.com**, or check the phone numbers listed in the vendor list in Appendix B. Micro Firmware offers upgrades to many systems with a Phoenix BIOS, including many Packard Bell, Gateway 2000 (with Micronics motherboards), Micron Technologies, and other systems.

Unless the ROM BIOS is a truly compatible, custom OEM version such as Compaq's, you might want to install in the system the ROM BIOS from one of the known quantities, such as AMI, Award, or Phoenix. These companies' products are established as ROM BIOS standards in the industry, and frequent updates and improvements ensure that a system containing these ROMs will have a long life of upgrades and service.

A good source of online information about BIOS basics can be found at:

http://www.lemig.umontreal.ca/bios/bios_sg.htm

Using Correct Speed-Rated Parts
Some compatible vendors use substandard parts in their systems to save money. Because the CPU is one of the most expensive components on the motherboard, and many

motherboards are sold to system assemblers without the CPU installed, it is tempting for the assembler to install a CPU rated for less than the actual operating speed. A system could be sold as a 100MHz system, for example, but when you look "under the hood," you may find a CPU rated for only 90MHz. The system does appear to work correctly, but for how long? If the company that manufactures the CPU chip installed in this system had tested the chip to run reliably at 100MHz, it would have labeled the part accordingly. After all, the company could sell the chip for more money if it worked at the higher clock speed.

When a chip is run at a speed higher than it is rated for, it will run hotter than it would normally. This may cause the chip to overheat occasionally, which would appear as random lockups, glitches, and frustration. I highly recommend that you avoid systems whose operation speed exceeds the design of the respective parts.

This practice is easy to fall into because the faster rated chips cost more money, and Intel and other chip manufacturers usually rate their chips very conservatively. I have taken several 25MHz 486 processors and run them at 33MHz, and they seemed to work fine. The Pentium 90 chips I have tested seem to run fine at 100MHz. Although I might purchase a Pentium 90 system and make a decision to run it at 100MHz, if I were to experience lockups or glitches in operation, I would immediately return it to 90MHz and retest. If I purchase a 100MHz system from a vendor, I fully expect it to have 100MHz parts, not 90MHz parts running past their rated speed! These days, many chips will have some form of heat sink on them, which helps to prevent overheating, but which can also sometimes cover up for a "pushed" chip. If the price is too good to be true, ask before you buy: "Are the parts really manufacturer-rated for the system speed?"

To determine the rated speed of a CPU chip, look at the writing on the chip. Most of the time, the part number will end in a suffix of *–xxx* where the *xxx* is a number indicating the maximum speed. For example, –100 indicates that the chip is rated for 100MHz operation.

> **Caution**
> Be careful when running software to detect processor speed. Such programs can only tell you what speed the chip is currently running at, not what the true rating is. Also ignore the speed indicator lights on the front of some cases. These digital displays can literally be set via jumpers to read any speed you desire! They have no true relation to actual system speed.

Motherboard Form Factors

There are several compatible form factors used for motherboards. The form factor refers to the physical dimensions and size of the board, and dictates what type of case the board will fit into. The types of motherboard form factors generally available are the following:

- Backplane Systems
- Full-size AT
- Baby-AT
- LPX
- ATX
- NLX

Backplane Systems

Not all systems have a motherboard in the true sense of the word. In some systems, the components normally found on a motherboard are located instead on an expansion adapter card plugged into a slot. In these systems, the board with the slots is called a *backplane*, rather than a motherboard. Systems using this type of construction are called *backplane systems*.

Backplane systems come in two main types: *passive* and *active*. A passive backplane means the main backplane board does not contain any circuitry at all except for the bus connectors and maybe some buffer and driver circuits. All the circuitry found on a conventional motherboard is contained on one or more expansion cards installed in slots on the backplane. Some backplane systems use a passive design that incorporates the entire system circuitry into a single mothercard. The mothercard is essentially a complete motherboard that is designed to plug into a slot in the passive backplane. The passive backplane/mothercard concept allows the entire system to be easily upgraded by changing one or more cards. Because of the expense of the high function mothercard, this type of system design is rarely found in PC systems. The passive backplane design does enjoy popularity in industrial systems, which are often rack-mounted. Some high-end file servers also feature this design.

An active backplane means the main backplane board contains bus control and usually other circuitry as well. Most active backplane systems contain all the circuitry found on a typical motherboard except for the processor complex. The *processor complex* is the name of the circuit board that contains the main system processor and any other circuitry directly related to it, such as clock control, cache, and so forth. The processor complex design allows the user to easily upgrade the system later to a new processor type by changing one card. In effect, it amounts to a modular motherboard with a replaceable processor section. Most modern PC systems that use a backplane design use an active backplane/processor complex. Both IBM and Compaq have used this type of design in some of their high-end (server class) systems, for example. This allows an easier and generally more affordable upgrade than the passive backplane/mothercard design since the processor complex board is usually much cheaper than a mothercard. Unfortunately, because there are no standards for the processor complex interface to the system, these boards are proprietary and can only be purchased from the system manufacturer. This limited market and availability causes the prices of these boards to be higher than most complete motherboards from other manufacturers.

The motherboard system design and the backplane system design have both advantages and disadvantages. Most original personal computers were designed as backplanes in the late 1970s. Apple and IBM shifted the market to the now traditional motherboard with a slot-type design because this type of system generally is cheaper to mass-produce than one with the backplane design. The theoretical advantage of a backplane system, however, is that you can upgrade it easily to a new processor and new level of performance by changing a single card. For example, you can upgrade a system's processor just by changing the card. In a motherboard-design system, you often must change the motherboard itself, a seemingly more formidable task. Unfortunately, the reality of the situation is that a backplane design is often much more expensive to upgrade, and because the bus remains fixed on the backplane, the backplane design precludes more comprehensive upgrades that involve adding local bus slots, for example.

Another nail in the coffin of backplane designs is the upgradable processor. Intel has designed all 486, Pentium, Pentium MMX, and Pentium Pro processors to be upgradable to faster (sometimes called *OverDrive*) processors in the future by simply swapping (or adding) the new processor chip. Changing only the processor chip for a faster one is the easiest and generally most cost-effective way to upgrade without changing the entire motherboard.

Because of the limited availability of the processor complex boards or mothercards, they usually end up being more expensive than a complete new motherboard that uses an industry standard form factor. Intel recently announced the new NLX form factor for the Pentium II, and it shares some traits with traditional backplane systems. The NLX has been promised considerable industry support, so we may well see affordable backplane systems in the near future.

Full-Size AT
The full-size AT motherboard is so named because it matches the original IBM AT motherboard design. This allows for a very large board of up to 12 inches wide by 13.8 inches deep. The keyboard connector and slot connectors must conform to specific placement requirements to fit the holes in the case. This type of board will fit into full-size AT or Tower cases only. Because these motherboards will not fit into the popular Baby-AT or Mini-Tower cases, and because of advances in component miniaturization, they are no longer being produced by most motherboard manufacturers.

Baby-AT
The Baby-AT form factor is essentially the same as the original IBM XT motherboard, with modifications in screw hole positions to fit into an AT-style case (see Figure 4.1). These motherboards also have specific placement of the keyboard connector and slot connectors to match the holes in the case. Note that virtually all full-size AT and Baby-AT motherboards use the standard 5-pin DIN type connector for the keyboard. Baby-AT motherboards will fit into every type of case except the Low Profile or Slimline cases. Because of their flexibility, this is now the most popular motherboard form factor. Figure 4.1 shows the dimensions and layout of a Baby-AT motherboard.

Motherboard Form Factors

FIG. 4.1 Baby-AT motherboard form factor.

LPX

Another popular form factor used in motherboards today is the LPX and Mini-LPX form factors. This form factor was first developed by Western Digital for some of their motherboards. Although they no longer produce PC motherboards, the form factor lives on and has been duplicated by many other motherboard manufacturers. These are used in the Low Profile or Slimline case systems sold widely today. These are often lower-cost systems like those sold at retail electronics superstores. It should be noted that systems using LPX boards may have other differences which can cause compatibility problems similar to those of proprietary systems.

The LPX boards are characterized by several distinctive features. The most noticeable is that the expansion slots are mounted on a bus riser card that plugs into the motherboard. Expansion cards must plug sideways into the riser card. This sideways placement allows for the low profile case design. Slots are located on one or both sides of the riser card depending on the system and case design.

Another distinguishing feature of the LPX design is the standard placement of connectors on the back of the board. An LPX board has a row of connectors for video (VGA 15-pin), parallel (25-pin), two serial ports (9-pin each), and mini-DIN PS/2 style Mouse and

Keyboard connectors. All of these connectors are mounted across the rear of the motherboard and protrude through a slot in the case. Some LPX motherboards may have additional connectors for other internal ports such as Network or SCSI adapters. Figure 4.2 shows the standard form factors for the LPX and Mini-LPX motherboards used in many systems today.

FIG. 4.2 LPX and Mini-LPX motherboard form factors.

ATX

The ATX form factor is a recent evolution in motherboard form factors. ATX is a combination of the best features of the Baby-AT and LPX motherboard designs, with many new enhancements and features thrown in. The ATX form factor is essentially a Baby-AT motherboard turned sideways in the chassis, along with a modified power supply location and connector. The most important thing to know initially about the ATX form factor is that it is physically incompatible with either the previous Baby-AT or LPX designs. In other words, a different case and power supply are required to match the ATX motherboard. These new case and power supply designs have become common, and can be found in many new systems.

The official ATX specification was released by Intel in July 1995, and has been written as an open specification for the industry. The latest revision of the specification is Version 2.01, published in February 1997. Intel has published detailed specifications so other manufacturers can use the ATX design in their systems.

ATX improves on the Baby-AT and LPX motherboard designs in several major areas:

- *Built-in double high external I/O connector panel.* The rear portion of the motherboard includes a stacked I/O connector area, which is 6.25 inches wide by 1.75 inches tall. This allows external connectors to be located directly on the board and negates the need for cables running from internal connectors to the back of the case as with Baby-AT designs.

- *Single keyed internal power supply connector.* This is a boon for the average end user, who always had to worry about interchanging the Baby-AT power supply connectors and subsequently blowing the motherboard! The ATX specification includes a single keyed and shrouded power connector that is easy to plug in, and which cannot be installed incorrectly. This connector also features pins for supplying 3.3v to the motherboard, which means that ATX motherboards will not require built-in voltage regulators that are susceptible to failure.

- *Relocated CPU and memory.* The CPU and memory modules are relocated so they cannot interfere with any bus expansion cards, and they can easily be accessed for upgrade without removing any of the installed bus adapters. The CPU and memory are relocated next to the power supply, which has a single fan blowing air across them, thus eliminating the need for inefficient and failure-prone CPU cooling fans. There is room for a large passive heat sink above the CPU as well.

- *Relocated internal I/O connectors.* The internal I/O connectors for the floppy and hard disk drives are relocated to be near the drive bays and out from under the expansion board slot and drive bay areas. This means that internal cables to the drives can be much shorter, and accessing the connectors will not require card or drive removal.

- *Improved cooling.* The CPU and main memory are cooled directly by the power supply fan, eliminating the need for separate case or CPU cooling fans. Also, the ATX power supply fan blows *into* the system chassis, thus pressurizing it which greatly minimizes dust and dirt intrusion into the system. If desired, an air filter can be easily added to the air intake vents on the power supply, creating a system that is even more immune to dirt or dust in the environment.

- *Lower cost to manufacture.* The ATX specifications eliminate the need for the rats nest of cables to external port connectors found on Baby-AT motherboards, eliminates the need for additional CPU or chassis cooling fans, eliminates the need for on-board 3.3v voltage regulators, uses a single power supply connector, and allows for shorter internal drive cables. These all conspire to greatly reduce not only the cost of the motherboard, but also significantly reduces the cost of a complete system including the case and power supply.

Figure 4.3 shows the new ATX system layout and chassis features. Notice how the entire motherboard is virtually clear of the drive bays, and how the devices like CPU, memory, and internal drive connectors are easy to access and do not interfere with the bus slots. Also notice the power supply orientation and the single power supply fan that blows into the case directly over the high heat, generating items like the CPU and memory.

FIG. 4.3 ATX system chassis layout and features.

The ATX motherboard is basically a Baby-AT design rotated sideways. The expansion slots are now parallel to the shorter side dimension and do not interfere with the CPU, memory, or I/O connector sockets. In addition to a full-sized ATX layout, Intel also has specified a mini-ATX design as well, which will fit into the same case. Although the case holes are similar to the Baby-AT case, cases for the two formats are generally not compatible. The power supplies would require a connector adapter to be interchangeable, but the basic ATX power supply design is similar to the standard Slimline power supply. The ATX and mini-ATX motherboard dimensions are shown in Figure 4.4.

FIG. 4.4 ATX and Mini-ATX motherboard form factors.

http://www.quecorp.com

Clearly, the advantages of the ATX form factor make it a good choice for high-end systems. For backwards compatibility, Baby-AT is still hard to beat, and there are still more Baby-AT motherboards, cases, and power supplies on the market than the ATX versions. With the coming of NLX motherboards and the support that form factor is receiving from the industry, it seems unlikely that ATX will be the all encompassing wave of the future.

For complete specifications, check out the ATX Motherboard Specification page at

http://www.teleport.com/~atx/

On the Web

NLX

NLX is the latest development in desktop motherboard technology, and may prove to be the form factor of choice in the near future. It is a low-profile form factor similar in appearance to LPX, but with a number of improvements designed to allow full integration of the latest technologies. Whereas the primary limitation of LPX boards includes an inability to handle the physical size of newer processors, as well as their higher thermal characteristics, the NLX form factor has been designed specifically to address these problems.

Specific advantages of the NLX form factor include:

- *Support for current processor technologies.* This is especially important in Pentium II systems because the size of the Single Edge Contact cartridge this processor uses can limit its use on existing Baby-AT and LPX motherboards. Although a few motherboard manufacturers currently offer ATX-based Pentium II systems, they generally only have room for two 72-pin SIMM sockets!

- *Flexibility in the face of rapidly changing processor technologies.* Backplane-like flexibility has been built into the form by allowing a new motherboard to be easily and quickly installed without tearing your entire system to pieces. But unlike traditional backplane systems, many industry leaders are putting their support behind NLX, including AST, Digital, Gateway, Hewlett-Packard, IBM, Micron, NEC, and others.

- *Support for other emerging technologies.* This includes Accelerated Graphics Port (AGP) high-performance graphic solutions, Universal Serial Bus (USB), and tall memory modules and DIMM technology. Furthermore, with the emerging importance of multimedia applications, connectivity support for such things as video playback, enhanced graphics, and extended audio have been built into the motherboard. This should represent a good cost savings over expensive daughterboard arrangements, which have been necessary for many advanced multimedia uses in the past.

Figure 4.5 shows the basic NLX system layout. Notice that, like ATX, the system is clear of the drive bays and other chassis-mounted components. Also, the motherboard and I/O cards (which, like the LPX form factor, are mounted parallel to the motherboard) can easily be slid in and out of the side of the chassis, leaving the riser card and other cards in place. The processor itself can be easily accessed and enjoys greater cooling than in a more closed in layout.

Chapter 4—Motherboards

FIG. 4.5 NLX system chassis layout and features.

As you can see, the NLX form factor has been designed for maximum flexibility and space efficiency. Even extremely long I/O cards will fit easily, without fouling on other system components as has been such a problem with Baby-AT form factor systems.

Complete design specifications and information on NLX boards can be found online at the official NLX Motherboard Specification page, located at:

http://www.teleport.com/~nlx/

ATX and NLX form factors will probably be used in most future systems. I usually do not recommend LPX style systems if upgradability is a factor because it is not only difficult to locate a new motherboard that will fit, but LPX systems are also limited in expansion slots and drive bays as well. Baby-AT systems still offer a great deal of flexibility at present, but for future systems, ATX and NLX configurations are the way to go.

Motherboard Interface Connectors

There are a variety of different connectors on a modern motherboard. Tables 4.5 through 4.14 contain the pinouts of most of the different interface and I/O connectors you will find.

Table 4.5 ATX Motherboard Power Connector

Pin	Signal Name	Pin	Signal Name
1	+3.3 V	11	+3.3 V
2	+3.3 V	12	-12 V
3	Ground	13	Ground

Pin	Signal Name	Pin	Signal Name
4	+5 V	14	PS-ON# (Power Supply Remote On/Off Control)
5	Ground	15	Ground
6	+5 V	16	Ground
7	Ground	17	Ground
8	PWRGD (Power Good)	18	-5 V
9	+5 VSB (Standby)	19	+5 V
10	+12 V	20	+5 V

Table 4.6 Baby-AT Motherboard Power Connectors

Pin	Name	Pin	Name
1	PWRGD (Power Good)	7	Ground
2	+5 V	8	Ground
3	+12 V	9	-5 V
4	-12 V	10	+5 V
5	Ground	11	+5 V
6	Ground	12	+5 V

Table 4.7 Serial Port Pin-Header Connectors

Pin	Signal Name	Pin	Signal Name
1	DCD	6	CTS
2	DSR	7	DTR
3	Serial In - (SIN)	8	RI
4	RTS	9	GND
5	Serial Out - (SOUT)	10	Not Connected

Table 4.8 Parallel Port Pin-Header Connector

Signal Name	Pin	Pin	Signal Name
STROBE-	1	2	AUTO FEED-
Data Bit 0	3	4	ERROR-
Data Bit 1	5	6	INIT-
Data Bit 2	7	8	SLCT IN-
Data Bit 3	9	10	Ground
Data Bit 4	11	12	Ground
Data Bit 5	13	14	Ground
Data Bit 6	15	16	Ground
Data Bit 7	17	18	Ground
ACJ-	19	20	Ground
BUSY	21	22	Ground
PE (Paper End)	23	24	Ground
SLCT	25	26	N/C

Table 4.9 Motherboard Mouse Pin-Header Connector

Pin	Signal	Pin	Signal
1	Gnd	5	CLK
2	Data	6	KEY
3	N/C	7	KEY
4	Vcc	8	N/C

Table 4.10 Infrared Data (IrDA) Pin-Header Connector

Pin	Signal Name	Pin	Signal Name
1	+5 V	4	Ground
2	Key	5	IrTX
3	IrRX	6	CONIR (Consumer IR)

Table 4.11 Battery Connector

Pin	Signal	Pin	Signal
1	Gnd	3	KEY
2	Unused	4	+6v

Table 4.12 LED and Keylock Connector

Pin	Signal	Pin	Signal
1	LED Power (+5v)	4	Keyboard Inhibit
2	KEY	5	Gnd
3	Gnd		

Table 4.13 Speaker Connector

Pin	Signal	Pin	Signal
1	Ground	3	Board-Mounted Speaker
2	KEY	4	Speaker Output

Table 4.14 Microprocessor Fan Power Connector

Pin	Signal Name
1	Ground
2	+12V
3	Sense tachometer

Caution

Do not place a jumper on this connector; serious board damage will result if the 12v is shorted to ground.

Note that some boards have a board mounted piezo speaker. It is enabled by placing a jumper over pins 3 and 4, which routes the speaker output to the board mounted speaker. Removing the jumper allows a conventional speaker to be plugged in.

Motherboard CMOS RAM Addresses

Table 4.15 shows the information maintained in the 64-byte standard CMOS RAM module. This information controls the configuration of the system and is read and written by the system Setup program.

In the original AT system, a Motorola 146818 chip was used. Modern systems incorporate the CMOS into the chipset, Super I/O chip, or use a special battery and NVRAM (Non-Volatile RAM) module from companies like Dallas or Benchmarq. The standard format of the information stored in the CMOS RAM is shown in Table 4.15.

Table 4.15 AT CMOS RAM Addresses

Offset Hex	Offset Dec	Field Size	Function
00h	0	1 byte	Current second in binary coded decimal (BCD)
01h	1	1 byte	Alarm second in BCD
02h	2	1 byte	Current minute in BCD
03h	3	1 byte	Alarm minute in BCD
04h	4	1 byte	Current hour in BCD
05h	5	1 byte	Alarm hour in BCD
06h	6	1 byte	Current day of week in BCD
07h	7	1 byte	Current day in BCD
08h	8	1 byte	Current month in BCD
09h	9	1 byte	Current year in BCD

0Ah	10	1 byte	Status register A
			Bit 7 = Update in progress
			  0 = Date and time can be read
			  1 = Time update in progress
			Bits 6–4 = Time frequency divider
			  010 = 32.768KHz
			Bits 3–0 = Rate selection frequency
			  0110 = 1.024KHz square wave frequency

0Bh	11	1 byte	Status register B
			Bit 7 = Clock update cycle
			  0 = Update normally
			  1 = Abort update in progress
			Bit 6 = Periodic interrupt
			  0 = Disable interrupt (default)
			  1 = Enable interrupt
			Bit 5 = Alarm interrupt
			  0 = Disable interrupt (default)
			  0 = Disable interrupt (default)
			  1 = Enable interrupt
			Bit 4 = Update-ended interrupt

(continues)

Chapter 4—Motherboards

Table 4.15 Continued			
Offset Hex	**Offset Dec**	**Field Size**	**Function**
			0 = Disable interrupt (default)
			1 = Enable interrupt
			Bit 3 = Status register A square wave frequency
			0 = Disable square wave (default)
			1 = Enable square wave
			Bit 2 = Date format
			0 = Calendar in BCD format (default)
			1 = Calendar in binary format
			Bit 1 = 24-hour clock
			0 = 24-hour mode (default)
			1 = 12-hour mode
			Bit 0 = Daylight Savings Time
			0 = Disable Daylight Savings (default)
			1 = Enable Daylight Savings
0Ch	12	1 byte	Status register C
			Bit 7 = IRQF flag
			Bit 6 = PF flag
			Bit 5 = AF flag
			Bit 4 = UF flag
			Bits 3-0 = Reserved
0Dh	13	1 byte	Status register D
			Bit 7 = Valid CMOS RAM bit
			0 = CMOS battery dead
			1 = CMOS battery power good
			Bits 6–0 = Reserved
0Eh	14	1 byte	Diagnostic status
			Bit 7 = Real-time clock power status
			0 = CMOS *has not* lost power
			1 = CMOS *has* lost power
			Bit 6 = CMOS checksum status
			0 = Checksum is good
			1 = Checksum is bad
			Bit 5 = POST configuration information status
			0 = Configuration information is valid
			1 = Configuration information is invalid
			Bit 4 = Memory size compare during POST
			0 = POST memory equals configuration
			1 = POST memory *not equal* to configuration
			Bit 3 = Fixed disk/adapter initialization
			0 = Initialization good
			1 = Initialization failed
			Bit 2 = CMOS time status indicator
			0 = Time is valid
			1 = Time is Invalid
			Bits 1-0 = Reserved
0Fh	15	1 byte	Shutdown code
			00h = Power on or soft reset
			01h = Memory size pass

Offset Hex	Offset Dec	Field Size	Function
			02h = Memory test pass
			03h = Memory test fail
			04h = POST end; boot system
			05h = JMP double word pointer with EOI
			06h = Protected mode tests pass
			07h = Protected mode tests fail
			07h = Protected mode tests fail
			08h = Memory size fail
			09h = Int 15h block move
			0Ah = JMP double word pointer without EOI
			0Bh – used by 80386
10h	16	1 byte	Floppy disk drive types
			Bits 7-4 = Drive 0 type
			Bits 3-0 = Drive 1 type
			0000 = None
			0001 = 360K
			0010 = 1.2M
			0011 = 720K
			0100 = 1.44M
11h	17	1 byte	Reserved
12h	18	1 byte	Hard disk types
			Bits 7–4 = Hard disk 0 type (0–15)
			Bits 3–0 = Hard disk 1 type (0–15)
13h	19	1 byte	Reserved
14h	20	1 byte	Installed equipment
			Bits 7–6 = Number of floppy disk drives
			00 = 1 floppy disk drive
			01 = 2 floppy disk drives
			Bits 5–4 = Primary display
			00 = Use display adapter BIOS
			01 = CGA 40-column
			10 = CGA 80-column
			11 = Monochrome Display Adapter
			Bits 3–2 = Reserved
			Bit 1 = Math coprocessor present
			Bit 0 = Floppy disk drive present
15h	21	1 byte	Base memory low-order byte
16h	22	1 byte	Base memory high-order byte
17h	23	1 byte	Extended memory low-order byte
18h	24	1 byte	Extended memory high-order byte
19h	25	1 byte	Hard Disk 0 Extended Type (0–255)
1Ah	26	1 byte	Hard Disk 1 Extended Type (0–255)
1Bh	27	9 bytes	Reserved
2Eh	46	1 byte	CMOS checksum high-order byte
2Fh	47	1 byte	CMOS checksum low-order byte
30h	48	1 byte	Actual extended memory low-order byte

(continues)

Table 4.15 Continued

Offset Hex	Offset Dec	Field Size	Function
31h	49	1 byte	Actual extended memory high-order byte
32h	50	1 byte	Date century in BCD

33h	51	1 byte	POST information flag
			Bit 7 = Top 128K base memory status
			    0 = Top 128K base memory not installed
			    1 = Top 128K base memory installed
			Bit 6 = Setup program flag
			    0 = Normal (default)
			    1 = Put out first user message
			Bits 5–0 = Reserved

34h	52	2 bytes	Reserved

Table 4.16 shows the values that may be stored by your system BIOS in a special CMOS byte called the *diagnostics status byte*. By examining this location with a diagnostics program, you can determine whether your system has set *trouble codes*, which indicate that a problem has occurred previously.

Table 4.16 CMOS RAM (AT and PS/2) Diagnostic Status Byte Codes

Bit Number 7 6 5 4 3 2 1 0	Hex	Function
1	80	Real-time clock (RTC) chip lost power
. 1	40	CMOS RAM checksum is bad
. . 1	20	Invalid configuration information found at POST
. . . 1	10	Memory size compare error at POST
. . . . 1 . . .	08	Fixed disk or adapter failed initialization
. . . . . 1 . .	04	Real-time clock (RTC) time found invalid
. . . . . . 1 .	02	Adapters do not match configuration
. . . . 1	01	Time-out reading an adapter ID
. . . .	00	No errors found (Normal)

If the Diagnostic status byte is any value other than zero, you will normally get a CMOS configuration error on bootup. These types of errors can be cleared by re-running the Setup program.

Chapter 5

Bus Slots and I/O Cards

At the heart of every system is the motherboard; you learned about various motherboards in Chapter 4, "Motherboards." A motherboard is made up of components. The major component that determines how the motherboard actually works is called the bus. In this chapter, you learn about system buses.

What Is a Bus?

A *bus* is nothing but a common pathway across which data can travel within a computer. This pathway is used for communication and can be established between two or more computer elements. A PC has many kinds of buses, including the following:

- Processor bus
- Memory bus
- Address bus
- I/O bus

If you hear someone talking about the bus in a PC, chances are good that he or she is referring to the *I/O bus*, which also is called the *expansion slot bus*. Whatever name it goes by, this bus is the main system bus and the one over which most data flows. The I/O bus is the highway for most data in your system. Anything that goes to or from any device—including your video system, disk drives, and printer—travels over this bus. The busiest I/O pathway typically is to and from your video card.

Because the I/O bus is the primary bus in your computer system, it is the main focus of discussion in this chapter. The other buses deserve some attention, however, and they are covered in the following sections.

The Processor Bus

The *processor bus* is the communication pathway between the CPU and immediate support chips. These support chips are usually called the *chipset* in modern systems. This bus is used to transfer data between the CPU and the main system bus, for example, or between the CPU and an external memory cache. Figure 5.1 shows how this bus fits into a typical PC system.

Chapter 5—Bus Slots and I/O Cards

FIG. 5.1 The processor bus.

Most systems have an external cache for the CPU; these caches have typically been employed in all systems that use the Pentium, Pentium MMX, Pentium Pro, and Pentium II chips.

Because the purpose of the processor bus is to get information to and from the CPU at the fastest possible speed, this bus operates at a much faster rate than any other bus in your system; no bottleneck exists here. The bus consists of electrical circuits for data, for addresses (the address bus, which is discussed in the following section), and for control purposes. In a Pentium-based system, the processor bus has 64 data lines, 32 address lines, and associated control lines. The Pentium Pro and Pentium II have 36 address lines, but otherwise are the same as the Pentium and Pentium MMX.

The processor bus operates at the same base clock rate as the CPU does externally. This can be misleading as most CPUs these days run internally at a higher clock rate than they do externally. For example, a Pentium 100 system has a Pentium CPU running at 100MHz internally, but only 66.6MHz externally. A Pentium 133, Pentium 166, and even a Pentium Pro 200 also run the processor external bus at 66.6MHz. In most newer systems, the actual processor speed is some multiple (1.5x, 2x, 2.5x, 3x, and so on) of the processor bus. For more information on this, see "Processor Speed Ratings" in Chapter 6, "Microprocessor Types and Specifications."

The processor bus is tied to the external processor pin connections and can transfer one bit of data per data line every one or two clock cycles. Thus, a Pentium, Pentium Pro, or Pentium II can transfer 64 bits of data at a time.

To determine the transfer rate for the processor bus, you multiply the data width (64 bits for a Pentium, Pentium Pro, or Pentium II) by the clock speed of the bus (the same as the base or unmultiplied clock speed of the CPU). If you are using a Pentium, Pentium MMX, Pentium Pro, or Pentium II chip that runs at a 66MHz motherboard speed, and it can transfer a bit of data each clock cycle on each data line, you have a maximum instantaneous transfer rate of 528M/sec. You get this result by using the following formula:

$$66\text{MHz} \times 64 \text{ bits} = 4{,}224\text{Mbit/sec}$$

$$4{,}224\text{Mbit/sec} \div 8 = 528\text{M/sec}$$

This transfer rate, often called the *bandwidth* of the bus, represents a maximum. Like all maximums, this rate does not represent the normal operating bandwidth; you should expect much lower average throughput. Other limiting factors such as chipset design, memory design and speed, and so on, conspire to lower the effective average throughput.

The Memory Bus

The *memory bus* is used to transfer information between the CPU and main memory—the RAM in your system. This bus is either a part of the processor bus itself, or in most cases is implemented separately by a dedicated chipset that is responsible for transferring information between the processor bus and the memory bus. Systems that run at motherboard clock speeds of 16MHz or faster cycle at rates that exceed the capabilities of standard Dynamic RAM chips. In virtually all systems that are 16MHz or faster, there will be a special memory controller chipset that controls the interface between the faster processor bus and the slower main memory. This chipset typically is the same chipset that is responsible for managing the I/O bus. Figure 5.2 shows how the memory bus fits into your PC.

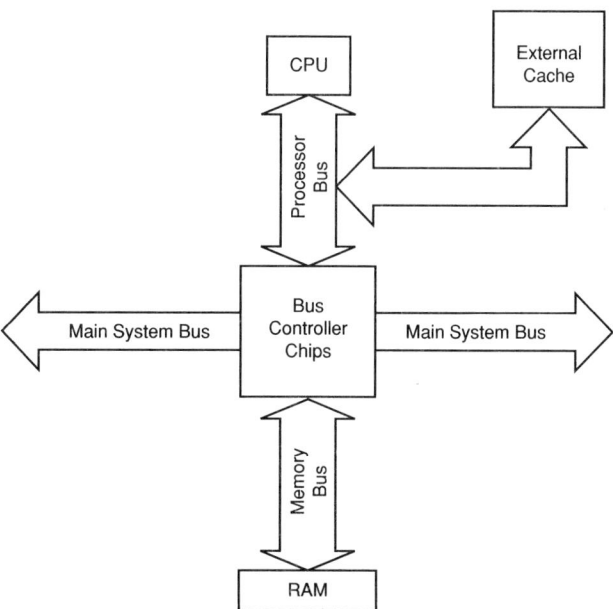

FIG. 5.2 The memory bus.

The information that travels over the memory bus is transferred at a much slower rate than the information on the processor bus. The chip sockets or the slots for memory SIMMs/DIMMs (Dual Inline Memory Modules) are connected to the memory bus in much the same way that expansion slots are connected to the I/O bus.

> **Caution**
>
> Notice that the main memory bus is always the same width as the processor bus. This means that in a 64-bit system, such as the various Pentium CPUs, you will have a 64-bit memory bus. This will define the size of what is called a "bank" of memory. For example, a 486DX4 processor has a 32-bit bus, so the memory in that system must be added 32 bits at a time for each bank. If you are using 30-pin (8-bit) SIMMs, then four will be required per bank; if the system uses 72-pin (32-bit) SIMMs, then only one has to be added at a time to make up a bank. Pentium systems are 64-bit and always require two 72-pin (32 bits each) SIMMs to be added at a time. Some newer systems use 168-pin DIMMs, which are 64 bits each. These compose a single bank in a 64-bit system.

The Address Bus

The *address bus* actually is a subset of the processor and memory buses. In our discussion of the processor bus, you learned that a Pentium system bus consists of 64 data lines, 32 address lines (36 in a Pentium Pro or Pentium II), and a few control lines. These address lines constitute the address bus; in most block diagrams, this bus is actually considered a part of the processor and memory buses.

The address bus is used to indicate what address in memory or what address on the system bus are to be used in a data transfer operation. The address bus indicates precisely where the next bus transfer or memory transfer will occur. The size of the memory bus also controls the amount of memory that the CPU can address directly.

The Need for Expansion Slots

The I/O bus or expansion slots are what enables your CPU to communicate with peripheral devices. The bus and its associated expansion slots are needed because basic systems cannot possibly satisfy all the needs of all the people who buy them. The I/O bus enables you to add devices to your computer to expand its capabilities. The most basic computer components, such as sound cards and video cards, can be plugged into expansion slots; you also can plug in more specialized devices, such as network interface cards, SCSI host adapters, and others.

> **Note**
>
> In most modern PC systems, a variety of basic peripheral devices are built into the motherboard. Most systems today have at least dual (primary and secondary) IDE controllers, a floppy controller, two serial ports, and a parallel port directly built into the motherboard. This is normally contained on a single chip called a *Super I/O chip*. Many will even add more items such as an integrated mouse port, video adapter, SCSI host adapter, or network interface also built into the motherboard; in such a system, an expansion slot on the I/O bus is probably not even needed. Nevertheless, these built-in controllers and ports still use the I/O bus to communicate with the CPU. In essence, even though they are built in, they act as if they are cards plugged into the system's bus slots.

Although some PC systems provide only a single expansion slot, most provide up to eight slots on the motherboard. This slot typically is called a *riser card slot*. The riser card that plugs into it in turn has expansion slots on its sides. Standard adapter cards are installed in the riser card, meaning that the adapter cards end up being parallel to the motherboard rather than perpendicular to it.

Riser cards are used when a vendor wants to produce a computer that is shorter in height than normal. These computers usually are called *Slimline, Low Profile,* or sometimes even *pizza-box* systems. Even though this type of configuration may seem to be odd, the actual bus used in these systems is the same kind used in normal computer systems; the only difference is the use of the riser card.

I usually recommend avoiding the Low Profile or Slimline systems that have what is called an *LPX form factor*. This refers to the shape of the board. Replacement LPX motherboards with riser cards that match the case for a given system are difficult to find. However, a newer form factor recently developed by Intel called *NLX* incorporates a Low Profile design, while at the same time enjoying growing industry support.

Bus Mastering

Newer bus types use a technology called *bus mastering* to speed up the system. In essence, a *bus master* is an adapter with its own processor that can execute operations independently of the CPU. To work properly, bus-mastering technology relies on an arbitration unit, most often called an *integrated system peripheral (ISP) chip*. The ISP enables a bus-mastered board to temporarily take exclusive control of the system, as though the board were the entire system. Because the board has exclusive control of the system, it can perform operations very quickly. A bus-mastering hard drive controller, for example, achieves much greater data throughput with a fast drive than can controller cards that are not bus-mastered.

The ISP determines which device gains control by using a four-level order of priority:

- System-memory refresh
- DMA transfers
- The CPU itself
- Bus masters

A bus-mastering adapter board notifies the ISP when it wants control of the system. At the earliest possible time (after the higher priorities have been satisfied), the ISP hands control over to the bus-mastered board. The board, in turn, has built-in circuitry to keep it from taking over the system for periods of time that would interfere with first-priority operations, such as memory refresh.

Types of I/O Buses

Since the introduction of the first PC, many I/O buses have been introduced. The reason is quite simple: Faster I/O speeds are necessary for better system performance. This need for higher performance involves three main areas:

- Faster CPUs
- Increasing software demands
- Greater multimedia requirements

Each of these areas requires the I/O bus to be as fast as possible. Surprisingly, virtually all PC systems shipped today still incorporate the same basic bus architecture as the 1984 vintage IBM PC/AT. However, most of these systems now also include a second high-speed local I/O bus such as VL-Bus or PCI, which offer much greater performance for adapters that need it.

One of the primary reasons why new I/O-bus structures have been slow in coming is compatibility—that old Catch-22 that anchors much of the PC industry to the past. One of the hallmarks of the PC's success is its standardization. This standardization spawned thousands of third-party I/O cards, each originally built for the early bus specifications of the PC. If a new high-performance bus system is introduced, it often has to be compatible with the older bus systems so that the older I/O cards do not become obsolete. Therefore, bus technologies seem to evolve rather than make quantum leaps forward.

You can identify different types of I/O buses by their architecture. The main types of I/O architecture are:

- ISA
- Micro Channel Architecture (MCA)
- EISA
- VESA Local Bus (VL-Bus)
- PCI Local Bus
- PC Card (formerly PCMCIA)
- FireWire (IEEE-1394)
- Universal Serial Bus (USB)

The differences among these buses consist primarily of the amount of data that they can transfer at one time and the speed at which they can do it. Each bus architecture is implemented by a chipset that is connected to the processor bus. Typically, this chipset also controls the memory bus (refer to Figure 5.2). The following sections describe the different types of PC buses.

The ISA Bus

ISA, which is an acronym for *Industry Standard Architecture*, is the bus architecture that was introduced as an 8-bit bus with the original IBM PC in 1981 and later expanded to 16 bits with the IBM PC/AT in 1984. ISA is the basis of the modern personal computer and the primary architecture used in the vast majority of PC systems on the market today. It may seem amazing that such a seemingly antiquated architecture is used in today's high-performance systems, but this is true for reasons of reliability, affordability, and compatibility, plus this old bus is still faster than many of the peripherals that we connect to it!

Two versions of the ISA bus exist, based on the number of data bits that can be transferred on the bus at a time. The older version is an 8-bit bus; the newer version is a 16-bit bus. The original 8-bit version ran at 4.77MHz in the PC and XT. The 16-bit version used in the AT ran at 6MHz and then 8MHz. Later, the industry as a whole agreed on an 8.33MHz maximum standard speed for 8- and 16-bit versions of the ISA bus for backward compatibility. Some systems have the ability to run the ISA bus faster than this, but some adapter cards will not function properly at higher speeds. ISA data transfers require anywhere from two to eight cycles. Therefore, the theoretical maximum data rate of the ISA bus is about 8M/sec, as the following formula shows:

8MHz × 16 bits = 128Mbit/sec

128Mbit/sec ÷ 2 cycles = 64Mbit/sec

64Mbit/sec ÷ 8 = 8M/sec

The bandwidth of the 8-bit bus would be half this figure (4M/sec). Remember, however, that these figures are theoretical maximums; because of I/O bus protocols, the effective bandwidth is much lower—typically by almost half. Even so, at 8M/sec, the ISA bus is still faster than many of the peripherals we connect to it.

The 8-Bit ISA Bus. This bus architecture is used in the original IBM PC computers. Although virtually nonexistent in new systems today, this architecture still exists in hundreds of thousands of PC systems in the field.

Physically, the 8-bit ISA expansion slot resembles the tongue-and-groove system that furniture makers once used to hold two pieces of wood together. It is specifically called a *Card/Edge connector*. An adapter card with 62 contacts on its bottom edge plugs into a slot on the motherboard that has 62 matching contacts. Electronically, this slot provides eight data lines and 20 addressing lines, enabling the slot to handle 1M of memory.

Figure 5.3 describes the pinouts for the 8-bit ISA bus.

Signal	Pin	Pin	Signal
Ground	B1	A1	-I/O CH CHK
RESET DRV	B2	A2	Data Bit 7
+5 Vdc	B3	A3	Data Bit 6
IRQ 2	B4	A4	Data Bit 5
-5 Vdc	B5	A5	Data Bit 4
DRQ 2	B6	A6	Data Bit 3
-12 Vdc	B7	A7	Data Bit 2
-CARD SLCTD	B8	A8	Data Bit 1
+12 Vdc	B9	A9	Data Bit 0
Ground	B10	A10	-I/O CH RDY
-SMEMW	B11	A11	AEN
-SMEMR	B12	A12	Address 19
-IOW	B13	A13	Address 18
-IOR	B14	A14	Address 17
-DACK 3	B15	A15	Address 16
DRQ 3	B16	A16	Address 15
-DACK 1	B17	A17	Address 14
DRQ 1	B18	A18	Address 13
-Refresh	B19	A19	Address 12
CLK(4.77MHz)	B20	A20	Address 11
IRQ 7	B21	A21	Address 10
IRQ 6	B22	A22	Address 9
IRQ 5	B23	A23	Address 8
IRQ 4	B24	A24	Address 7
IRQ 3	B25	A25	Address 6
-DACK 2	B26	A26	Address 5
T/C	B27	A27	Address 4
BALE	B28	A28	Address 3
+5 Vdc	B29	A29	Address 2
OSC(14.3MHz)	B30	A30	Address 1
Ground	B31	A31	Address 0

FIG. 5.3 Pinouts for the 8-bit ISA bus.

Figure 5.4 shows how these pins are oriented in the expansion slot.

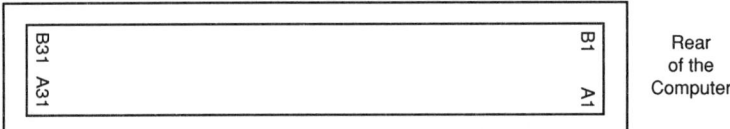

FIG. 5.4 The 8-bit ISA bus connector.

Although the design of the bus is simple, IBM waited until 1987 to publish full specifications for the timings of the data and address lines, so in the early days of PC compatibles, manufacturers had to do their best to figure out how to make adapter boards. This problem was solved, however, as PC-compatible personal computers became more widely accepted as the industry standard and manufacturers had more time and incentive to build adapter boards that worked correctly with the bus.

The dimensions of 8-bit ISA adapter cards are as follows:

4.2 inches (106.68mm) high

13.13 inches (333.5mm) long

0.5 inch (12.7mm) wide

The 16-Bit ISA Bus. IBM threw a bombshell on the PC world when it introduced the AT with the 286 processor in 1984. This processor had a 16-bit data bus, which meant that communications between the processor and the motherboard as well as memory would now be 16 bits wide instead of only 8 bits wide. Although this processor could have been installed on a motherboard with only an 8-bit I/O bus, that would have meant a huge sacrifice in the performance of any adapter cards or other devices installed on the bus.

The introduction of the 286 chip posed a problem for IBM in relation to its next generation of PCs. Should the company create a new I/O bus and associated expansion slots, or should it try to come up with a system that could support both 8- and 16-bit cards? IBM opted for the latter solution, and the PC/AT was introduced with a set of expansion slots with 16-bit extension connectors. You can plug an 8-bit card into the forward part of the slot or a 16-bit card into both parts of the slot.

> **Note**
>
> The expansion slots for the 16-bit ISA bus also introduced access keys to the PC environment. An *access key* is a cutout or notch in an adapter card that fits over a corresponding tab in the connector into which the adapter card is inserted. Access keys typically are used to keep adapter cards from being inserted into a connector improperly.

The extension connector in each 16-bit expansion slot adds 36 connector pins to carry the extra signals necessary to implement the wider data path. In addition, two of the pins in the 8-bit portion of the connector were changed. These two minor changes do not alter the function of 8-bit cards.

Figure 5.5 describes the pinouts for the full 16-bit ISA expansion slot.

Signal	Pin	Pin	Signal
Ground	B1	A1	-I/O CH CHK
RESET DRV	B2	A2	Data Bit 7
+5 Vdc	B3	A3	Data Bit 6
IRQ 9	B4	A4	Data Bit 5
-5 Vdc	B5	A5	Data Bit 4
DRQ 2	B6	A6	Data Bit 3
-12 Vdc	B7	A7	Data Bit 2
-0 WAIT	B8	A8	Data Bit 1
+12 Vdc	B9	A9	Data Bit 0
Ground	B10	A10	-I/O CH RDY
-SMEMW	B11	A11	AEN
-SMEMR	B12	A12	Address 19
-IOW	B13	A13	Address 18
-IOR	B14	A14	Address 17
-DACK 3	B15	A15	Address 16
DRQ 3	B16	A16	Address 15
-DACK 1	B17	A17	Address 14
DRQ 1	B18	A18	Address 13
-Refresh	B19	A19	Address 12
CLK(8.33MHz)	B20	A20	Address 11
IRQ 7	B21	A21	Address 10
IRQ 6	B22	A22	Address 9
IRQ 5	B23	A23	Address 8
IRQ 4	B24	A24	Address 7
IRQ 3	B25	A25	Address 6
-DACK 2	B26	A26	Address 5
T/C	B27	A27	Address 4
BALE	B28	A28	Address 3
+5 Vdc	B29	A29	Address 2
OSC(14.3MHz)	B30	A30	Address 1
Ground	B31	A31	Address 0

Signal	Pin	Pin	Signal
-MEM CS16	D1	C1	-SBHE
-I/O CS16	D2	C2	Latch Address 23
IRQ 10	D3	C3	Latch Address 22
IRQ 11	D4	C4	Latch Address 21
IRQ 12	D5	C5	Latch Address 20
IRQ 15	D6	C6	Latch Address 19
IRQ 14	D7	C7	Latch Address 18
-DACK 0	D8	C8	Latch Address 17
DRQ 0	D9	C9	-MEMR
-DACK 5	D10	C10	-MEMW
DRQ5	D11	C11	Data Bit 8
-DACK 6	D12	C12	Data Bit 9
DRQ 6	D13	C13	Data Bit 10
-DACK 7	D14	C14	Data Bit 11
DRQ 7	D15	C15	Data Bit 12
+5 Vdc	D16	C16	Data Bit 13
-Master	D17	C17	Data Bit 14
Ground	D18	C18	Data Bit 15

FIG. 5.5 Pinouts for the 16-bit ISA bus.

Figure 5.6 shows the orientation and relation of 8-bit and 16-bit ISA bus slots.

8/16-bit ISA Bus Pinouts.

8-bit PC/XT Connector:

Signal	Pin Numbers		Signal
GROUND	B1	A1	-I/O CHK
RESET DRV	B2	A2	DATA 7
+5 Vdc	B3	A3	DATA 6
IRQ 2	B4	A4	DATA 5
-5 Vdc	B5	A5	DATA 4
DRQ 2	B6	A6	DATA 3
-12 Vdc	B7	A7	DATA 2
-CARD SLCT	B8	A8	DATA 1
+12 Vdc	B9	A9	DATA 0
GROUND	B10	A10	-I/O RDY
-SMEMW	B11	A11	AEN
-SMEMR	B12	A12	ADDR 19
-IOW	B13	A13	ADDR 18
-IOR	B14	A14	ADDR 17
-DACK 3	B15	A15	ADDR 16
DRQ 3	B16	A16	ADDR 15
-DACK 1	B17	A17	ADDR 14
DRQ 1	B18	A18	ADDR 13
-REFRESH	B19	A19	ADDR 12
CLK (4.77MHz)	B20	A20	ADDR 11
IRQ 7	B21	A21	ADDR 10
IRQ 6	B22	A22	ADDR 9
IRQ 5	B23	A23	ADDR 8
IRQ 4	B24	A24	ADDR 7
IRQ 3	B25	A25	ADDR 6
-DACK 2	B26	A26	ADDR 5
T/C	B27	A27	ADDR 4
BALE	B28	A28	ADDR 3
+5 Vdc	B29	A29	ADDR 2
OSC (14.3MHz)	B30	A30	ADDR 1
GROUND	B31	A31	ADDR 0

16-bit AT Connector:

Signal	Pin Numbers		Signal
GROUND	B1	A1	-I/O CHK
RESET DRV	B2	A2	DATA 7
+5 Vdc	B3	A3	DATA 6
IRQ 9	B4	A4	DATA 5
-5 Vdc	B5	A5	DATA 4
DRQ 2	B6	A6	DATA 3
-12 Vdc	B7	A7	DATA 2
-OWS	B8	A8	DATA 1
+12 Vdc	B9	A9	DATA 0
GROUND	B10	A10	-I/O RDY
-SMEMW	B11	A11	AEN
-SMEMR	B12	A12	ADDR 19
-IOW	B13	A13	ADDR 18
-IOR	B14	A14	ADDR 17
-DACK 3	B15	A15	ADDR 16
DRQ 3	B16	A16	ADDR 15
-DACK 1	B17	A17	ADDR 14
DRQ 1	B18	A18	ADDR 13
-REFRESH	B19	A19	ADDR 12
CLK (8.33MHz)	B20	A20	ADDR 11
IRQ 7	B21	A21	ADDR 10
IRQ 6	B22	A22	ADDR 9
IRQ 5	B23	A23	ADDR 8
IRQ 4	B24	A24	ADDR 7
IRQ 3	B25	A25	ADDR 6
-DACK 2	B26	A26	ADDR 5
T/C	B27	A27	ADDR 4
BALE	B28	A28	ADDR 3
+5 Vdc	B29	A29	ADDR 2
OSC (14.3MHz)	B30	A30	ADDR 1
GROUND	B31	A31	ADDR 0
-MEM CS16	D1	C1	-SBHE
-I/O CS16	D2	C2	LADDR 23
IRQ 10	D3	C3	LADDR 22
IRQ 11	D4	C4	LADDR 21
IRQ 12	D5	C5	LADDR 20
IRQ 15	D6	C6	LADDR 19
IRQ 14	D7	C7	LADDR 18
-DACK 0	D8	C8	LADDR 17
DRQ 0	D9	C9	-MEMR
-DACK 5	D10	C10	-MEMW
DRQ 5	D11	C11	DATA 8
-DACK 6	D12	C12	DATA 9
DRQ 6	D13	C13	DATA 10
-DACK 7	D14	C14	DATA 11
DRQ 7	D15	C15	DATA 12
+5 Vdc	D16	C16	DATA 13
-MASTER	D17	C17	DATA 14
GROUND	D18	C18	DATA 15

FIG. 5.6 The 8-bit and 16-bit ISA bus connectors.

The extended 16-bit slots physically interfere with some 8-bit adapter cards that have a *skirt*—an extended area of the card that drops down toward the motherboard just after the connector. To handle these cards, IBM left two expansion ports in the PC/AT without the 16-bit extensions. These slots, which are identical to the expansion slots in earlier systems, can handle any skirted PC or XT expansion card. This is not a problem today, as no skirted 8-bit cards have been manufactured for years.

> **Note**
>
> 16-bit ISA expansion slots were introduced in 1984. Since then, virtually every manufacturer of 8-bit expansion cards have designed them without drop-down skirts so that they fit properly in 16-bit slots. Most new systems do not have any 8-bit only slots, because a properly designed 8-bit card will work in any 16-bit slot.

The dimensions of a typical AT expansion board are as follows:

4.8 inches (121.92mm) high

13.13 inches (333.5mm) long

0.5 inch (12.7mm) wide

Two heights actually are available for cards that are commonly used in AT systems: 4.8 inches and 4.2 inches (the height of older PC-XT cards). The shorter cards became an issue when IBM introduced the XT Model 286. Because this model has an AT motherboard in an XT case, it needs AT-type boards with the 4.2-inch maximum height. Most board makers trimmed the height of their boards; many manufacturers now make only 4.2-inch tall (or less) boards so that they will work in systems with either profile.

32-Bit Buses. After 32-bit CPUs became available, it was some time before 32-bit bus standards became available. Before MCA and EISA specs were released, some vendors began creating their own proprietary 32-bit buses, which were extensions of the ISA bus. Although the proprietary buses were few and far between, they do still exist.

The expanded portions of the bus typically are used for proprietary memory expansion or video cards. Because the systems are proprietary (meaning that they are nonstandard), pinouts and specifications are not available.

The Micro Channel Bus

The introduction of 32-bit chips meant that the ISA bus could not handle the power of another new generation of CPUs. The 386DX chips can transfer 32 bits of data at a time, but the ISA bus can handle a maximum 16 bits. Rather than extend the ISA bus again, IBM decided to build a new bus; the result was the MCA bus. *MCA* (an acronym for *Micro Channel Architecture*) is completely different from the ISA bus and is technically superior in every way.

IBM not only wanted to replace the old ISA standard but also to receive royalties on it; the company required vendors that licensed the new MCA bus to pay IBM royalties for using the ISA bus in all previous systems. This requirement led to the development of the competing EISA bus (see the next section on the EISA Bus) and hindered acceptance of the MCA bus. Another reason why MCA has not been adopted universally for systems with 32-bit slots is that adapter cards designed for ISA systems do not work in MCA systems.

> **Note**
>
> The MCA bus is not compatible with the older ISA bus, so cards designed for the ISA bus do not work in an MCA system.

MCA runs asynchronously with the main processor, meaning that fewer possibilities exist for timing problems among adapter cards plugged into the bus.

MCA systems produced a new level of ease of use, as anyone who has set up one of these systems can tell you. An MCA system has no jumpers and switches—neither on the motherboard nor on any expansion adapter. You don't need an electrical engineering degree to plug a card into a PC.

The MCA bus also supports bus mastering. Through implementing bus mastering, the MCA bus provides significant performance improvements over the older ISA buses. (Bus mastering is also implemented in the EISA bus. In the MCA bus mastering implementation, any bus mastering devices can request unobstructed use of the bus in order to communicate with another device on the bus. The request is made through a device known as the *Central Arbitration Control Point (CACP)*. This device arbitrates the competition for the bus, making sure all devices have access and that no single device monopolizes the bus.

Each device is given a priority code to ensure that order is preserved within the system. The main CPU is given the lowest priority code. Memory refresh has the highest priority, followed by the DMA channels, and then the bus masters installed in the I/O slots. One exception to this is when an NMI (non-maskable interrupt) occurs. In this instance, control returns to the CPU immediately.

The MCA specification provides for four adapter sizes, which are described in Table 5.1.

Table 5.1 Physical Sizes of MCA Adapter Cards

Adapter Type	Height (in Inches)	Length (in Inches)
Type 3	3.475	12.3
Type 3 half	3.475	6.35
Type 5	4.825	13.1
Type 9	9.0	13.1

Four types of slots are involved in the MCA design:

- 16-bit
- 16-bit with video extensions
- 16-bit with memory-matched extensions
- 32-bit

The sixth edition of this book, included on the CD-ROM, has detailed information about each of these cards and what systems they can be found in. IBM still has all of the technical reference manuals for MCA available; however, development has stopped for MCA devices due to the other faster and more feature-rich buses available today.

The EISA Bus

EISA is an acronym for *Extended Industry Standard Architecture*. This standard was announced in September 1988 as a response to IBM's introduction of the MCA bus—more specifically, to the way that IBM wanted to handle licensing of the MCA bus. Vendors did not feel obligated to pay retroactive royalties on the ISA bus, so they turned their backs on IBM and created their own buses.

The EISA standard was developed primarily by Compaq, and was intended as being their way of taking over future development of the PC bus away from IBM. Compaq knew that nobody would clone their bus if they were the only company that had it, so they essentially gave the design away to other leading manufacturers. They formed the EISA Committee, a non-profit organization designed specifically to control development of the EISA bus. Very few EISA adapters were ever developed. Those that were developed centered mainly around disk array controllers and server type network cards.

The EISA bus provides 32-bit slots for use with 386DX or higher systems. The EISA slot enables manufacturers to design adapter cards that have many of the capabilities of MCA adapters, but the bus also supports adapter cards created for the older ISA standard. EISA provides markedly faster hard drive throughput when used with devices such as SCSI bus-mastering hard drive controllers. Compared with 16-bit ISA system architecture, EISA permits greater system expansion with fewer adapter conflicts.

The EISA bus adds 90 new connections (55 new signals) without increasing the physical connector size of the 16-bit ISA bus. At first glance, the 32-bit EISA slot looks much like the 16-bit ISA slot. The EISA adapter, however, has two rows of connectors. The first row is the same kind used in 16-bit ISA cards; the other, thinner row extends from the 16-bit connectors. This means that ISA cards can still be used in EISA bus slots. Although this compatability was not enough to ensure the popularity of EISA buses, it is a feature that was carried over into the newer VL-bus standard. The physical specifications of an EISA card are as follows:

- 5 inches (127mm) high
- 13.13 inches (333.5mm) long
- 0.5 inches (12.7mm) wide

The EISA bus can handle up to 32 bits of data at an 8.33MHz cycle rate. Most data transfers require a minimum of two cycles, although faster cycle rates are possible if an adapter card provides tight timing specifications. The maximum bandwidth on the bus is 33M/sec, as the following formula shows:

$8.33\text{MHz} \times 32 \text{ bits} = 266.56\text{Mbit/sec}$

$266.56\text{Mbit/sec} \div 8 = 33.32\text{M/sec}$

Chapter 5—Bus Slots and I/O Cards

Data transfers through an 8- or 16-bit expansion card across the bus would be reduced appropriately. Remember, however, that these figures represent theoretical maximums. Wait states, interrupts, and other protocol factors can reduce the effective bandwidth—typically, by half.

Figure 5.7 describes the pinouts for the EISA bus.

Lower Signal	Upper Signal	Pin	Pin	Upper Signal	Lower Signal
Ground	Ground	B1	A1	-I/O CH CHK	-CMD
+5 Vdc	RESET DRV	B2	A2	Data Bit 7	-START
+5 Vdc	+5 Vdc	B3	A3	Data Bit 6	EXRDY
Reserved	IRQ 9	B4	A4	Data Bit 5	-EX32
Reserved	-5 Vdc	B5	A5	Data Bit 4	Ground
KEY	DRQ 2	B6	A6	Data Bit 3	KEY
Reserved	-12 Vdc	B7	A7	Data Bit 2	-EX16
Reserved	-0 WAIT	B8	A8	Data Bit 1	-SLBURST
+12 Vdc	+12 Vdc	B9	A9	Data Bit 0	-MSBURST
M-IO	Ground	B10	A10	-I/O CH RDY	W-R
-LOCK	-SMEMW	B11	A11	AEN	Ground
Reserved	-SMEMR	B12	A12	Address 19	Reserved
Ground	-IOW	B13	A13	Address 18	Reserved
Reserved	-IOR	B14	A14	Address 17	Reserved
-BE 3	-DACK 3	B15	A15	Address 16	Ground
KEY	DRQ 3	B16	A16	Address 15	KEY
-BE 2	-DACK 1	B17	A17	Address 14	-BE 1
-BE 0	DRQ 1	B18	A18	Address 13	Latch Address 31
Ground	-Refresh	B19	A19	Address 12	Ground
+5 Vdc	CLK(8.33MHz)	B20	A20	Address 11	-Latch Address 30
Latch Address 29	IRQ 7	B21	A21	Address 10	-Latch Address 28
Ground	IRQ 6	B22	A22	Address 9	-Latch Address 27
Latch Address 26	IRQ 5	B23	A23	Address 8	-Latch Address 25
Latch Address 24	IRQ 4	B24	A24	Address 7	Ground
KEY	IRQ 3	B25	A25	Address 6	KEY
Latch Address 16	-DACK 2	B26	A26	Address 5	Latch Address 15
Latch Address 14	T/C	B27	A27	Address 4	Latch Address 13
+5 Vdc	BALE	B28	A28	Address 3	Latch Address 12
+5 Vdc	+5 Vdc	B29	A29	Address 2	Latch Address 11
Ground	OSC(14.3MHz)	B30	A30	Address 1	Ground
Latch Address 10	Ground	B31	A31	Address 0	Latch Address 9
Latch Address 8	-MEM CS16	D1	C1	-SBHE	Latch Address 7
Latch Address 6	-I/O CS16	D2	C2	Latch Address 23	Ground
Latch Address 5	IRQ 10	D3	C3	Latch Address 22	Latch Address 4
+5 Vdc	IRQ 11	D4	C4	Latch Address 21	Latch Address 3
Latch Address 4	IRQ 12	D5	C5	Latch Address 20	Ground
KEY	IRQ 15	D6	C6	Latch Address 19	KEY
Data Bit 16	IRQ 14	D7	C7	Latch Address 18	Data Bit 17
Data Bit 18	-DACK 0	D8	C8	Latch Address 17	Data Bit 19
Ground	DRQ 0	D9	C9	-MEMR	Data Bit 20
Data Bit 21	-DACK 5	D10	C10	-MEMW	Data Bit 22
Data Bit 23	DRQ5	D11	C11	Data Bit 8	Ground
Data Bit 24	-DACK 6	D12	C12	Data Bit 9	Data Bit 25
Ground	DRQ 6	D13	C13	Data Bit 10	Data Bit 26
Data Bit 27	-DACK 7	D14	C14	Data Bit 11	Data Bit 28
KEY	DRQ 7	D15	C15	Data Bit 12	KEY
Data Bit 29	+5 Vdc	D16	C16	Data Bit 13	Ground
+5 Vdc	-Master	D17	C17	Data Bit 14	Data Bit 30
+5 Vdc	Ground	D18	C18	Data Bit 15	Data Bit 31
-MAKx		D19	C19		-MREQx

FIG. 5.7 Pinouts for the EISA bus.

Figure 5.8 shows the locations of the pins.

FIG. 5.8 The card connector for the EISA bus.

Automated Setup

EISA systems also use an automated setup to deal with adapter-board interrupts and addressing issues. These issues often cause problems when several different adapter boards are installed in an ISA system. EISA setup software recognizes potential conflicts and automatically configures the system to avoid them. EISA does, however, enable you to do your own troubleshooting, as well as to configure the boards through jumpers and switches. This concept was not new to EISA; IBM's MCA bus also supported configuration via software. Another new feature of EISA systems is IRQ sharing, meaning that multiple bus cards can share a single interrupt. This feature has also been implemented in PCI bus cards.

> **Note**
>
> Although automated setup traditionally has not been available in ISA systems, it is now available with Plug and Play (PnP) systems and components. PnP systems are discussed toward the end of this chapter in the section "Plug and Play Systems."

Local Buses

The I/O buses discussed so far (ISA, MCA, and EISA) have one thing in common: relatively slow speed. This speed limitation is a carryover from the days of the original PC, when the I/O bus operated at the same speed as the processor bus. As the speed of the processor bus increased, the I/O bus realized only nominal speed improvements, primarily from an increase in the bandwidth of the bus. The I/O bus had to remain at a slower speed, because the huge installed base of adapter cards could operate only at slower speeds.

Figure 5.9 shows a conceptual block diagram of the buses in a computer system.

FIG. 5.9 Bus layout in a traditional PC.

The thought of a computer system running slower than it could is very bothersome to some computer users. Even so, the slow speed of the I/O bus is nothing more than a nuisance in most cases. You don't need blazing speed to communicate with a keyboard or a mouse, for example; you gain nothing in performance. The real problem occurs in subsystems in which you need the speed, such as video and disk controllers.

The speed problem became acute when graphical user interfaces (such as Windows) became prevalent. These systems required the processing of so much video data that the I/O bus became a literal bottleneck for the entire computer system. In other words, it did little good to have a CPU that was capable of 66MHz speed if you could put data through the I/O bus at a rate of only 8MHz.

An obvious solution to this problem is to move some of the slotted I/O to an area where it could access the faster speeds of the processor bus—much the same way as the external cache. Figure 5.10 shows this arrangement.

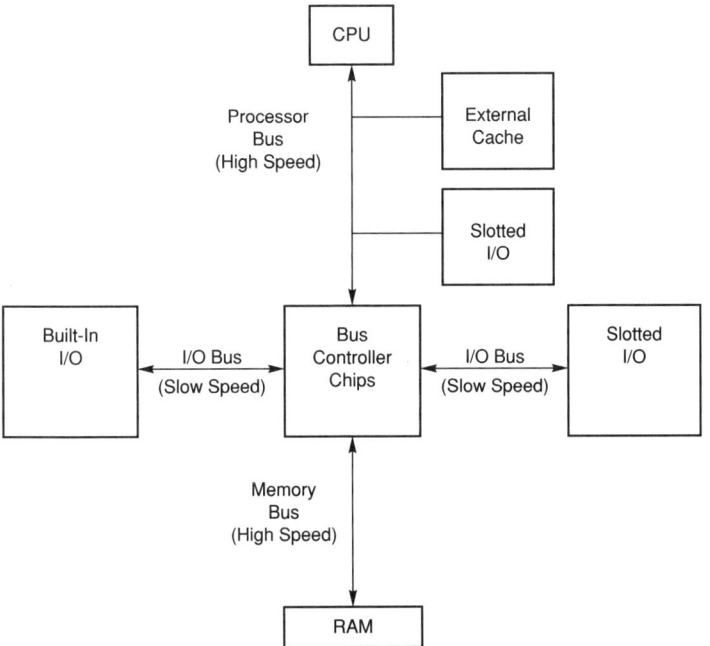

FIG. 5.10 How a local bus works.

This arrangement became known as *local bus*, because external devices (adapter cards) now could access the part of the bus that was local to the CPU—the processor bus. Physically, the slots provided to tap this new configuration would need to be different from existing bus slots, to prevent adapter cards designed for slower buses from being plugged into the higher bus speeds that this design made accessible.

It is interesting to note that the very first 8-bit and 16-bit ISA buses were a form of Local Bus architecture. These systems had the processor bus as the main bus, and everything ran at full processor speeds. When ISA systems ran faster than 8MHz, the main ISA bus had to be decoupled from the processor bus since expansion cards, memory, and so on could not keep up. In 1992, an extension to the ISA bus called the *VESA Local Bus* started showing up on PC systems, indicating a return to Local Bus architecture.

> **Note**
>
> A system does not have to have a local-bus expansion slot to incorporate local-bus technology; instead, the local-bus device can be built directly into the motherboard. (In such a case, the local-bus-slotted I/O shown in Figure 5.11 would in fact be built-in I/O.) This built-in approach to local bus is the way the first local-bus systems were designed.

Local-bus solutions do not replace earlier standards, such as ISA; they are designed as an extension to existing standards. Therefore, a typical system is based on ISA or EISA and has one or more local-bus slots available as well. Older cards still are compatible with the system, but high-speed adapter cards can also take advantage of the local-bus slots.

Local-bus systems are especially popular with users of Windows and OS/2, because these slots are used for special 32-bit video accelerator cards that greatly speed the repainting of the graphics screens used in those operating systems. The performance of Windows and OS/2 suffers greatly from bottlenecks in even the best VGA cards connected to an ISA or EISA bus.

VESA Local Bus. The VESA Local Bus was the most popular local bus design from its debut in August 1992 through 1994. It was created by the VESA committee, a non-profit organization founded by NEC to further develop video display and bus standards. In a similar fashion to how EISA evolved, NEC had done most of the work on the VL-bus (as it would be called) and, after founding the non-profit VESA committee, they turned over future development to VESA. At first, the local-bus slot seemed primarily designed to be used for video cards. Improving video performance was a top priority at NEC to help sell their high-end displays as well as their own PC systems. By 1991, video performance had become a real bottleneck in most PC systems.

The Video Electronics Standards Association (VESA) developed a standardized local-bus specification known as *VESA Local Bus* or simply *VL-Bus*. As in earlier local-bus implementations, the VL-Bus slot offers direct access to system memory at the speed of the processor itself. The VL-Bus can move data 32 bits at a time, enabling data to flow between the CPU and a compatible video subsystem or hard drive at the full 32-bit data width of the 486 chip. The maximum rated throughput of the VL-Bus is 128M to 132M/sec. In other words, local bus went a long way toward removing the major bottlenecks that existed in earlier bus configurations.

Additionally, VL-Bus offers manufacturers of hard-drive interface cards an opportunity to overcome another traditional bottleneck: the rate at which data can flow between the hard drive and the CPU. The average 16-bit IDE drive and interface can achieve throughput of up to 5M/sec, whereas VL-Bus hard drive adapters for IDE drives are touted as providing throughput of as much as 8M/sec. In real-world situations, the true throughput of VL-Bus hard drive adapters is somewhat less than 8M/sec, but VL-Bus still provides a substantial boost in hard-drive performance.

Despite all the benefits of the VL-Bus (and, by extension, of all local buses), this technology has a few drawbacks, which are described in the following list:

- *Dependence on a 486 CPU*. The VL-Bus inherently is tied to the 486 processor bus. This bus is quite different from that used by Pentium processors (and probably from those that will be used by future CPUs). A VL-Bus that operates at the full-rated speed of a Pentium has not been developed, although stopgap measures (such as stepping down speed or developing bus bridges) are available. Unfortunately, these result in poor performance. Some systems have been developed with both VL-Bus and PCI slots, but because of design compromises, performance often suffers.

- *Speed limitations*. The VL-Bus specification provides for speeds of up to 66MHz on the bus, but the electrical characteristics of the VL-Bus connector limit an adapter card to no more than 40 to 50MHz. In practice, running the VL-Bus at speeds over 33MHz causes many problems, so 33MHz has become the acceptable speed limit. Systems that use faster processor bus speeds must buffer and step down the clock on the VL-Bus or add wait states. Note that if the main CPU uses a clock modifier (such as the kind that doubles clock speeds), the VL-Bus uses the unmodified CPU clock speed as its bus speed.

- *Electrical limitations*. The processor bus has very tight timing rules, which may vary from CPU to CPU. These timing rules were designed for limited loading on the bus, meaning that the only elements originally intended to be connected to the local bus are elements such as the external cache and the bus controller chips. As you add more circuitry, you increase the electrical load. If the local bus is not implemented correctly, the additional load can lead to problems such as loss of data integrity and timing problems between the CPU and the VL-Bus cards.

- *Card limitations*. Depending on the electrical loading of a system, the number of VL-Bus cards is limited. Although the VL-Bus specification provides for as many as three cards, this can be achieved only at clock rates of up to 40MHz with an otherwise low system-board load. As the system-board load increases and the clock rate increases, the number of cards supported decreases. Only one VL-Bus card can be supported at 50MHz with a high system-board load. In practice, these limits could not usually be reached without problems.

The VL-Bus did not seem to be a well-engineered concept. The design was simple indeed—just take the pins from the 486 processor and run them out to a card connector socket. In other words, the VL-Bus is essentially the raw 486 processor bus. This allowed a very inexpensive design, since no additional chipsets or interface chips were required. A motherboard designer could add VL-Bus slots to their 486 motherboards very easily and at a very low cost. This is why these slots appeared on virtually all 486 system designs overnight.

Unfortunately, the 486 processor bus was not designed to have multiple devices (called *loads*) plugged into it at one time. Problems arose with timing glitches caused by the capacitance introduced into the circuit by different cards. Since the VL-Bus ran at the same speed as the processor bus, different processor speeds meant different bus speeds, and full compatibility was difficult to achieve. Although the VL-Bus could be adapted to other processors, including the 386 or even the Pentium, it was designed for the 486, and worked best as a 486 solution only. Despite the low cost, after a new bus called *PCI (Peripheral Component Interconnect)* appeared, VL-Bus fell into disfavor very quickly. It never did catch on with Pentium systems, and there is little or no further development of the VL-Bus in the PC industry. I would not recommend purchasing VL-Bus cards or systems today.

For a used system, or as an inexpensive upgrade for an older system, VL-Bus might be appropriate and can provide an acceptable solution for high-speed computing.

Physically, the VL-Bus slot is an extension of the slots used for whatever type of base system you have. If you have an ISA system, the VL-Bus is positioned as an extension of your existing 16-bit ISA slots. Likewise, if you have an EISA system or MCA system, the VL-Bus slots are extensions of those existing slots. Figure 5.11 shows how the VL-Bus slots could be situated in an ISA system. The VESA extension has 112 contacts and uses the same physical connector as the MCA bus.

The VL-Bus adds a total 116 pin locations to the bus connectors that your system already has. Table 5.2 lists the pinouts for only the VL-Bus connector portion of the total connector. (For pins for which two purposes are listed, the second purpose applies when the card is in 64-bit transfer mode.)

Table 5.2 Pinouts for the VL-Bus

Pin	Signal Name	Pin	Signal Name
B1	Data 0	A1	Data 1
B2	Data 2	A2	Data 3
B3	Data 4	A3	Ground
B4	Data 6	A4	Data 5
B5	Data 8	A5	Data 7
B6	Ground	A6	Data 9
B7	Data 10	A7	Data 11
B8	Data 12	A8	Data 13
B9	VCC	A9	Data 15
B10	Data 14	A10	Ground
B11	Data 16	A11	Data 17
B12	Data 18	A12	VCC
B13	Data 20	A13	Data 19
B14	Ground	A14	Data 21

Types of I/O Buses

Pin	Signal Name	Pin	Signal Name
B15	Data 22	A15	Data 23
B16	Data 24	A16	Data 25
B17	Data 26	A17	Ground
B18	Data 28	A18	Data 27
B19	Data 30	A19	Data 29
B20	VCC	A20	Data 31
B21	Address 31 or Data 63	A21	Address 30 or Data 62
B22	Ground	A22	Address 28 or Data 60
B23	Address 29 or Data 61	A23	Address 26 or Data 58
B24	Address 27 or Data 59	A24	Ground
B25	Address 25 or Data 57	A25	Address 24 or Data 56
B26	Address 23 or Data 55	A26	Address 22 or Data 54
B27	Address 21 or Data 53	A27	VCC
B28	Address 19 or Data 51	A28	Address 20 or Data 52
B29	Ground	A29	Address 18 or Data 50
B30	Address 17 or Data 49	A30	Address 16 or Data 48
B31	Address 15 or Data 47	A31	Address 14 or Data 46
B32	VCC	A32	Address 12 or Data 44
B33	Address 13 or Data 45	A33	Address 10 or Data 42
B34	Address 11 or Data 43	A34	Address 8 or Data 40
B35	Address 9 or Data 41	A35	Ground
B36	Address 7 or Data 39	A36	Address 6 or Data 38
B37	Address 5 or Data 37	A37	Address 4 or Data 36
B38	Ground	A38	Write Back
B39	Address 3 or Data 35	A39	Byte Enable 0 or 4
B40	Address 2 or Data 34	A40	VCC
B41	Unused or LBS64#	A41	Byte Enable 1 or 5
B42	Reset	A42	Byte Enable 2 or 6
B43	Data/Code Status	A43	Ground
B44	Memory-I/O Status or Data 33	A44	Byte Enable 3 or 7
B45	Write/Read Status or Data 32	A45	Address Data Strobe
B46	Access key	A46	Access key
B47	Access key	A47	Access key
B48	Ready Return	A48	Local Ready
B49	Ground	A49	Local Device
B50	IRQ 9	A50	Local Request
B51	Burst Ready	A51	Ground
B52	Burst Last	A52	Local Bus Grant
B53	ID0	A53	VCC
B54	ID1	A54	ID2

(continues)

126 Chapter 5—Bus Slots and I/O Cards

Table 5.2 Continued

Pin	Signal Name	Pin	Signal Name
B55	Ground	A55	ID3
B56	Local Clock	A56	ID4 or ACK64#
B57	VCC	A57	Unused
B58	Local Bus Size 16	A58	Loc/Ext Address Data Strobe

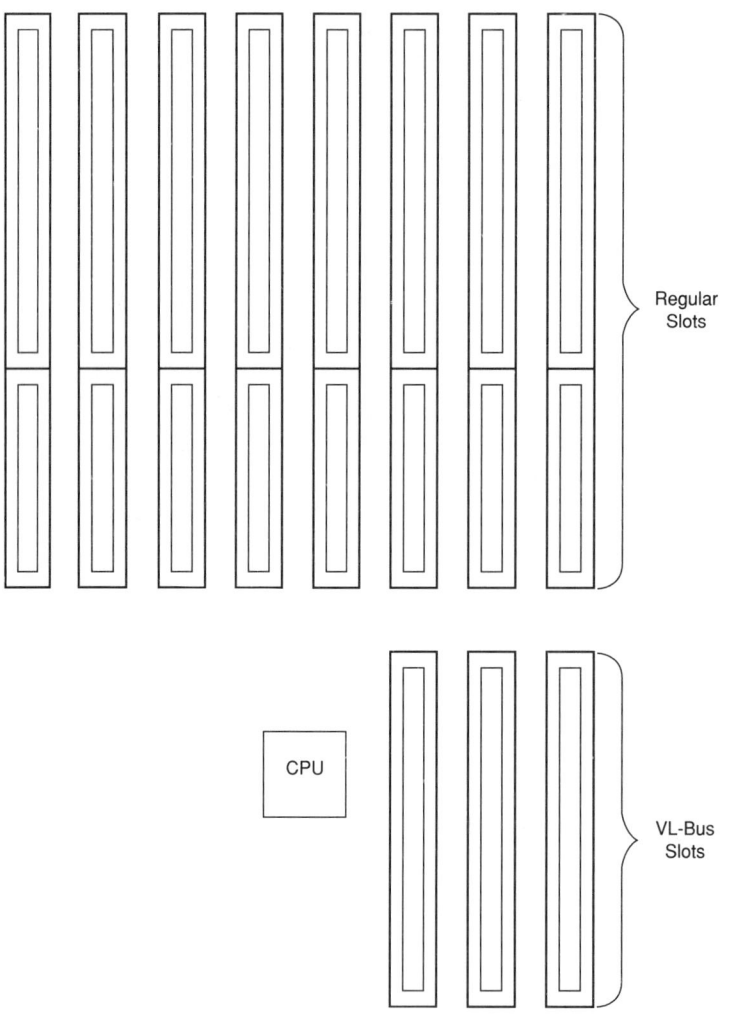

FIG. 5.11 An example of VL-Bus slots in an ISA system.

Figure 5.12 shows the locations of the pins.

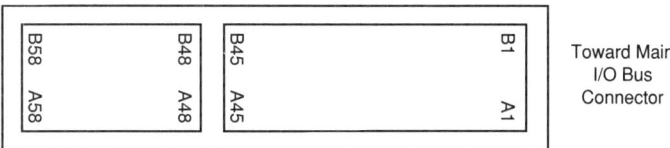

FIG. 5.12 The card connector for the VL-Bus.

The PCI Bus. In early 1992, Intel spearheaded the creation of another industry group. It was formed with the same goals as the VESA group in relation to the PC bus. Recognizing the need to overcome weaknesses in the ISA and EISA buses, the *PCI Special Interest Group* was formed.

PCI is an acronym for *Peripheral Component Interconnect*. The PCI bus specification, released in June 1992 and updated in April 1993, redesigned the traditional PC bus by inserting another bus between the CPU and the native I/O bus by means of bridges. Rather than tap directly into the processor bus, with its delicate electrical timing (as was done in the VL-Bus), a new set of controller chips was developed to extend the bus, as shown in Figure 5.13.

The PCI bus often is called a *mezzanine bus* because it adds another layer to the traditional bus configuration. PCI bypasses the standard I/O bus; it uses the system bus to increase the bus clock speed and take full advantage of the CPU's data path. Systems that integrate the PCI bus became available in mid 1993 and have since become the mainstay high-end systems.

Information is transferred across the PCI bus at 33MHz, at the full data width of the CPU. When the bus is used in conjunction with a 32-bit CPU, the bandwidth is 132M per second, as the following formula shows:

$$33\text{MHz} \times 32 \text{ bits} = 1{,}056\text{Mbit/sec}$$

$$1{,}056\text{Mbit/sec} \div 8 = 132\text{M/sec}$$

When the bus is used in future 64-bit implementations, the bandwidth doubles, meaning that you can transfer data at speeds up to 264M/sec. Real-life data transfer speeds necessarily will be lower, but still much faster than anything else that is currently available. Part of the reason for this faster real-life throughput is the fact that the PCI bus can operate concurrently with the processor bus; it does not supplant it. The CPU can be processing data in an external cache while the PCI bus is busy transferring information between other parts of the system—a major design benefit of the PCI bus.

A PCI adapter card uses its own unique connector. This connector can be identified within a computer system because it typically is offset from the normal ISA, MCA, or EISA connectors. See Figure 5.14 for an example. The size of a PCI card can be the same as that of the cards used in the system's normal I/O bus.

128 Chapter 5—Bus Slots and I/O Cards

FIG. 5.13 Conceptual diagram of the PCI bus.

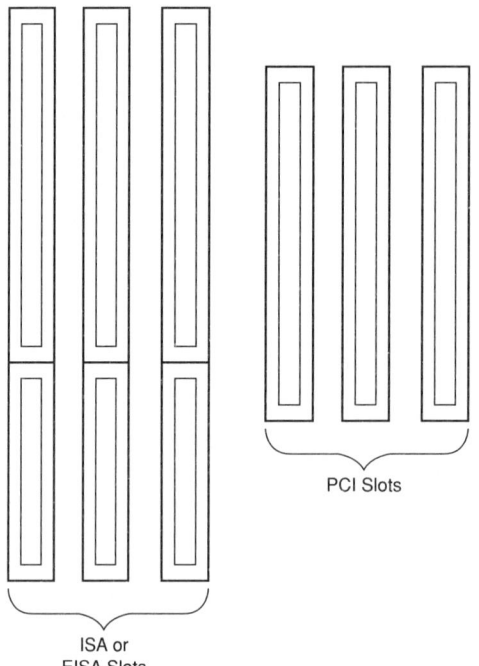

FIG. 5.14 Possible configuration of PCI slots in relation to ISA or EISA slots.

The PCI specification identifies three board configurations, each designed for a specific type of system with specific power requirements. The 5v specification is for stationary computer systems, the 3.3v specification is for portable machines, and the universal specification is for motherboards and cards that work in either type of system.

Table 5.3 shows the 5v PCI pinouts, and Figure 5.15 shows the pin locations. Table 5.4 shows the 3.3v PCI pinouts; the pin locations are indicated in Figure 5.16. Finally, Table 5.5 shows the pinouts, and Figure 5.17 shows the pin locations for a universal PCI slot and card. Notice that each figure shows both the 32-bit and 64-bit variations on the respective specifications.

> **Note**
>
> If the PCI card supports only 32 data bits, it needs only pins B1/A1 through B62/A62. Pins B63/A63 through B94/A94 are used only if the card supports 64 data bits.

Table 5.3 Pinouts for a 5v PCI Bus

Pin	Signal Name	Pin	Signal Name
B1	–12v	A1	Test Reset
B2	Test Clock	A2	+12v
B3	Ground	A3	Test Mode Select
B4	Test Data Output	A4	Test Data Input
B5	+5v	A5	+5v
B6	+5v	A6	Interrupt A
B7	Interrupt B	A7	Interrupt C
B8	Interrupt D	A8	+5v
B9	PRSNT1#	A9	Reserved
B10	Reserved	A10	+5v I/O
B11	PRSNT2#	A11	Reserved
B12	Ground	A12	Ground
B13	Ground	A13	Ground
B14	Reserved	A14	Reserved
B15	Ground	A15	Reset
B16	Clock	A16	+5v I/O
B17	Ground	A17	Grant
B18	Request	A18	Ground
B19	+5v I/O	A19	Reserved
B20	Address 31	A20	Address 30
B21	Address 29	A21	+3.3v
B22	Ground	A22	Address 28
B23	Address 27	A23	Address 26
B24	Address 25	A24	Ground

(continues)

Table 5.3 Continued

Pin	Signal Name	Pin	Signal Name
B25	+3.3v	A25	Address 24
B26	C/BE 3	A26	Init Device Select
B27	Address 23	A27	+3.3v
B28	Ground	A28	Address 22
B29	Address 21	A29	Address 20
B30	Address 19	A30	Ground
B31	+3.3v	A31	Address 18
B32	Address 17	A32	Address 16
B33	C/BE 2	A33	+3.3v
B34	Ground	A34	Cycle Frame
B35	Initiator Ready	A35	Ground
B36	+3.3v	A36	Target Ready
B37	Device Select	A37	Ground
B38	Ground	A38	Stop
B39	Lock	A39	+3.3v
B40	Parity Error	A40	Snoop Done
B41	+3.3v	A41	Snoop Backoff
B42	System Error	A42	Ground
B43	+3.3v	A43	PAR
B44	C/BE 1	A44	Address 15
B45	Address 14	A45	+3.3v
B46	Ground	A46	Address 13
B47	Address 12	A47	Address 11
B48	Address 10	A48	Ground
B49	Ground	A49	Address 9
B50	Access key	A50	Access key
B51	Access key	A51	Access key
B52	Address 8	A52	C/BE 0
B53	Address 7	A53	+3.3v
B54	+3.3v	A54	Address 6
B55	Address 5	A55	Address 4
B56	Address 3	A56	Ground
B57	Ground	A57	Address 2
B58	Address 1	A58	Address 0
B59	+5v I/O	A59	+5v I/O

Types of I/O Buses

Pin	Signal Name	Pin	Signal Name
B60	Acknowledge 64-bit	A60	Request 64-bit
B61	+5v	A61	+5v
B62	+5v Access key	A62	+5v Access key
B63	Reserved	A63	Ground
B64	Ground	A64	C/BE 7
B65	C/BE 6	A65	C/BE 5
B66	C/BE 4	A66	+5v I/O
B67	Ground	A67	Parity 64-bit
B68	Address 63	A68	Address 62
B69	Address 61	A69	Ground
B70	+5v I/O	A70	Address 60
B71	Address 59	A71	Address 58
B72	Address 57	A72	Ground
B73	Ground	A73	Address 56
B74	Address 55	A74	Address 54
B75	Address 53	A75	+5v I/O
B76	Ground	A76	Address 52
B77	Address 51	A77	Address 50
B78	Address 49	A78	Ground
B79	+5v I/O	A79	Address 48
B80	Address 47	A80	Address 46
B81	Address 45	A81	Ground
B82	Ground	A82	Address 44
B83	Address 43	A83	Address 42
B84	Address 41	A84	+5v I/O
B85	Ground	A85	Address 40
B86	Address 39	A86	Address 38
B87	Address 37	A87	Ground
B88	+5v I/O	A88	Address 36
B89	Address 35	A89	Address 34
B90	Address 33	A90	Ground
B91	Ground	A91	Address 32
B92	Reserved	A92	Reserved
B93	Reserved	A93	Ground
B94	Ground	A94	Reserved

132 Chapter 5—Bus Slots and I/O Cards

FIG. 5.15 The 5v PCI slot and card configuration.

Table 5.4 Pinouts for a 3.3v PCI Bus

Pin	Signal Name	Pin	Signal Name
B1	–12v	A1	Test Reset
B2	Test Clock	A2	+12v
B3	Ground	A3	Test Mode Select
B4	Test Data Output	A4	Test Data Input
B5	+5v	A5	+5v
B6	+5v	A6	Interrupt A
B7	Interrupt B	A7	Interrupt C
B8	Interrupt D	A8	+5v
B9	PRSNT1#	A9	Reserved
B10	Reserved	A10	+3.3v
B11	PRSNT2#	A11	Reserved
B12	Access key	A12	Access key
B13	Access key	A13	Access key
B14	Reserved	A14	Reserved
B15	Ground	A15	Reset
B16	Clock	A16	+3.3v
B17	Ground	A17	Grant
B18	Request	A18	Ground
B19	+3.3v	A19	Reserved
B20	Address 31	A20	Address 30
B21	Address 29	A21	+3.3v
B22	Ground	A22	Address 28
B23	Address 27	A23	Address 26
B24	Address 25	A24	Ground
B25	+3.3v	A25	Address 24

Pin	Signal Name	Pin	Signal Name
B26	C/BE 3	A26	Init Device Select
B27	Address 23	A27	+3.3v
B28	Ground	A28	Address 22
B29	Address 21	A29	Address 20
B30	Address 19	A30	Ground
B31	+3.3v	A31	Address 18
B32	Address 17	A32	Address 16
B33	C/BE 2	A33	+3.3v
B34	Ground	A34	Cycle Frame
B35	Initiator Ready	A35	Ground
B36	+3.3v	A36	Target Ready
B37	Device Select	A37	Ground
B38	Ground	A38	Stop
B39	Lock	A39	+3.3v
B40	Parity Error	A40	Snoop Done
B41	+3.3v	A41	Snoop Backoff
B42	System Error	A42	Ground
B43	+3.3v	A43	PAR
B44	C/BE 1	A44	Address 15
B45	Address 14	A45	+3.3v
B46	Ground	A46	Address 13
B47	Address 12	A47	Address 11
B48	Address 10	A48	Ground
B49	Ground	A49	Address 9
B50	Ground	A50	Ground
B51	Ground	A51	Ground
B52	Address 8	A52	C/BE 0
B53	Address 7	A53	+3.3v
B54	+3.3v	A54	Address 6
B55	Address 5	A55	Address 4
B56	Address 3	A56	Ground
B57	Ground	A57	Address 2
B58	Address 1	A58	Address 0
B59	+3.3v	A59	+3.3v
B60	Acknowledge 64-bit	A60	Request 64-bit
B61	+5v	A61	+5v
B62	+5v Access key	A62	+5v Access key
B63	Reserved	A63	Ground
B64	Ground	A64	C/BE 7

(continues)

Table 5.4 Continued

Pin	Signal Name	Pin	Signal Name
B65	C/BE 6	A65	C/BE 5
B66	C/BE 4	A66	+3.3v
B67	Ground	A67	Parity 64-bit
B68	Address 63	A68	Address 62
B69	Address 61	A69	Ground
B70	+3.3v	A70	Address 60
B71	Address 59	A71	Address 58
B72	Address 57	A72	Ground
B73	Ground	A73	Address 56
B74	Address 55	A74	Address 54
B75	Address 53	A75	+3.3v
B76	Ground	A76	Address 52
B77	Address 51	A77	Address 50
B78	Address 49	A78	Ground
B79	+3.3v	A79	Address 48
B80	Address 47	A80	Address 46
B81	Address 45	A81	Ground
B82	Ground	A82	Address 44
B83	Address 43	A83	Address 42
B84	Address 41	A84	+3.3v
B85	Ground	A85	Address 40
B86	Address 39	A86	Address 38
B87	Address 37	A87	Ground
B88	+3.3v	A88	Address 36
B89	Address 35	A89	Address 34
B90	Address 33	A90	Ground
B91	Ground	A91	Address 32
B92	Reserved	A92	Reserved
B93	Reserved	A93	Ground
B94	Ground	A94	Reserved

http://www.quecorp.com

Types of I/O Buses

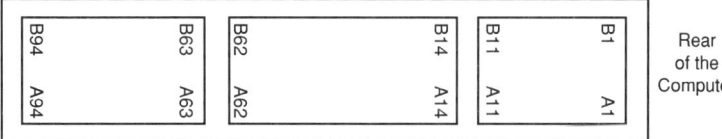

FIG. 5.16 The 3.3v PCI slot and card configuration.

Table 5.5 Pinouts for a Universal PCI Bus

Pin	Signal Name	Pin	Signal Name
B1	–12v	A1	Test Reset
B2	Test Clock	A2	+12v
B3	Ground	A3	Test Mode Select
B4	Test Data Output	A4	Test Data Input
B5	+5v	A5	+5v
B6	+5v	A6	Interrupt A
B7	Interrupt B	A7	Interrupt C
B8	Interrupt D	A8	+5v
B9	PRSNT1#	A9	Reserved
B10	Reserved	A10	+v I/O
B11	PRSNT2#	A11	Reserved
B12	Access key	A12	Access key
B13	Access key	A13	Access key
B14	Reserved	A14	Reserved
B15	Ground	A15	Reset
B16	Clock	A16	+v I/O
B17	Ground	A17	Grant
B18	Request	A18	Ground
B19	+v I/O	A19	Reserved
B20	Address 31	A20	Address 30
B21	Address 29	A21	+3.3v
B22	Ground	A22	Address 28
B23	Address 27	A23	Address 26
B24	Address 25	A24	Ground

(continues)

Table 5.5 Continued

Pin	Signal Name	Pin	Signal Name
B25	+3.3v	A25	Address 24
B26	C/BE 3	A26	Init Device Select
B27	Address 23	A27	+3.3v
B28	Ground	A28	Address 22
B29	Address 21	A29	Address 20
B30	Address 19	A30	Ground
B31	+3.3v	A31	Address 18
B32	Address 17	A32	Address 16
B33	C/BE 2	A33	+3.3v
B34	Ground	A34	Cycle Frame
B35	Initiator Ready	A35	Ground
B36	+3.3v	A36	Target Ready
B37	Device Select	A37	Ground
B38	Ground	A38	Stop
B39	Lock	A39	+3.3v
B40	Parity Error	A40	Snoop Done
B41	+3.3v	A41	Snoop Backoff
B42	System Error	A42	Ground
B43	+3.3v	A43	PAR
B44	C/BE 1	A44	Address 15
B45	Address 14	A45	+3.3v
B46	Ground	A46	Address 13
B47	Address 12	A47	Address 11
B48	Address 10	A48	Ground
B49	Ground	A49	Address 9
B50	Access key	A50	Access key
B51	Access key	A51	Access key
B52	Address 8	A52	C/BE 0
B53	Address 7	A53	+3.3v
B54	+3.3v	A54	Address 6
B55	Address 5	A55	Address 4
B56	Address 3	A56	Ground
B57	Ground	A57	Address 2
B58	Address 1	A58	Address 0
B59	+5 I/O	A59	+v I/O
B60	Acknowledge 64-bit	A60	Request 64-bit
B61	+5v	A61	+5v

http://www.quecorp.com

Pin	Signal Name	Pin	Signal Name
B62	+5v Access key	A62	+5v Access key
B63	Reserved	A63	Ground
B64	Ground	A64	C/BE 7
B65	C/BE 6	A65	C/BE 5
B66	C/BE 4	A66	+v I/O
B67	Ground	A67	Parity 64-bit
B68	Address 63	A68	Address 62
B69	Address 61	A69	Ground
B70	+v I/O	A70	Address 60
B71	Address 59	A71	Address 58
B72	Address 57	A72	Ground
B73	Ground	A73	Address 56
B74	Address 55	A74	Address 54
B75	Address 53	A75	+v I/O
B76	Ground	A76	Address 52
B77	Address 51	A77	Address 50
B78	Address 49	A78	Ground
B79	+v I/O	A79	Address 48
B80	Address 47	A80	Address 46
B81	Address 45	A81	Ground
B82	Ground	A82	Address 44
B83	Address 43	A83	Address 42
B84	Address 41	A84	+v I/O
B85	Ground	A85	Address 40
B86	Address 39	A86	Address 38
B87	Address 37	A87	Ground
B88	+v I/O	A88	Address 36
B89	Address 35	A89	Address 34
B90	Address 33	A90	Ground
B91	Ground	A91	Address 32
B92	Reserved	A92	Reserved
B93	Reserved	A93	Ground
B94	Ground	A94	Reserved

Notice that the universal PCI board specifications effectively combine the 5v and 3.3v specifications. For pins for which the voltage is different, the universal specification labels the pin simply V I/O. This type of pin represents a special power pin for defining and driving the PCI signaling rail.

FIG. 5.17 The universal PCI slot and card configuration.

Another important feature of PCI is the fact that it was the model for the Intel PnP specification. This means that PCI cards do not have jumpers and switches, and are instead configured through software. True PnP systems are able to automatically configure the adapters, while non-PnP systems with ISA slots have to configure the adapters through a program that is usually a part of the system CMOS configuration. Starting in late 1995, most PC-compatible systems have included a PnP BIOS that allows the automatic PnP configuration.

For online information about PCI bus technology, try

http://www.us.pc.ibm.com/infobrf/ibpci.html

FireWire (IEEE-1394)

FireWire is a relatively new bus technology; it is the result of the large data-moving demands of today's audio and video multimedia devices. It is extremely fast, with data transfer rates up to an incredible 400M/sec, and even faster speeds are being developed. The IEEE-1394 (as it is officially known) specification was published by the IEEE Standards Board in late 1995.

The IEEE-1394 standard currently exists with three different signaling rates: 100M/sec, 200M/sec, and 400M/sec. Most PC adapter cards support the 200M/sec rate, even though current devices generally only operate at 100M/sec. A maximum of 63 devices can be connected to a single IEEE-1394 adapter card by daisy chaining. Cables for IEEE-1394 devices use GameBoy-derived connectors and consist of six conductors; four wires are used for data transmission, and two conduct power. Connection with the motherboard is made either by a dedicated IEEE-1394 interface or by a PCI adapter card.

As of this writing, devices which conform to the IEEE-1394 standard are limited primarily to camcorders and VCRs with digital video (DV) capability. Sony was among the first to release such devices, although their products have a unique four-wire connector that requires an adapter cord to be used with IEEE-1394 PC cards. DV products are also available from Panasonic and Matsushita, and future IEEE-1394 applications should include DV conferencing devices, satellite audio and video data streams, audio synthesizers, DVD, and other high-speed disc drives.

Because of the current DV emphasis for IEEE-1394 peripherals, most PC cards currently offered by Adaptec, FAST Multimedia, Matrox, and others involve DV capturing and editing. If you're willing to spend $1,000 or more on DV equipment, these items should provide substantial video editing and dubbing capabilities on your PC. Of course, you will need IEEE-1394 I/O connectivity, which is still a rarity on current motherboards. Fortunately, Adaptec and Texas Instruments both offer PCI adapter cards which support IEEE-1394.

IEEE-1394 stands to offer unprecedented multimedia capabilities to current and future PC users. Current peripherals—particularly DV devices—are expensive, but as with any emerging technology, prices should come down in the future, opening the door wide for new PC uses both in the home and office. A great number of people would gain the ability to do advanced audio and video editing. If you anticipate having multimedia needs on your PC in the future, IEEE-1394 connectivity is a must.

Get more information about IEEE-1394 at

http://www.adaptec.com/firewire/1394wire.html

On the Web

Universal Serial Bus (USB)
Like IEEE-1394, the *Universal Serial Bus (USB)* is a new and promising bus technology that is rapidly gaining popularity among high-end manufacturers. Essentially, USB is a cable that allows for connection of up to 127 devices through the use of daisy chaining. While it is not as fast at data transfer as FireWire, at 12M/sec it is still more than adequate for most peripherals. The USB specification was published in 1996 by a consortium comprised of representatives from Compaq, Digital, IBM, Intel, Microsoft, NEC, and Northern Telecom.

Another benefit of the USB specification is self-identifying peripherals, a feature that should greatly ease installations. This feature is fully compatible with PnP systems and provides an industry standard for future connectivity. Also, USB devices can be "hot" plugged or unplugged, meaning that you should not have to turn off your computer every time you want to connect or disconnect a peripheral. As of this writing, USB-compatible devices are still hard to find, although most newer motherboards are being made to support them. One thing to keep in mind before purchasing USB peripherals is that your operating system must offer USB support. Whereas the original Windows 95 upgrade and NT 4.0 do not support USB, the later OSR-2 (OEM Service Release 2) release of Windows 95 does. Future versions of Windows and NT 5.0 will fully support USB. Because the USB standard shows promise, it should become an important bus technology in the years to come.

Get more information about USB online at

http://www.usb.org

System Resources

System resources are the communications channels, addresses, and other signals used by hardware devices to communicate on the bus. At their lowest level, these resources typically include the following:

- Memory addresses
- IRQ (Interrupt ReQuest) channels
- DMA (Direct Memory Access) channels
- I/O Port addresses

I have listed these roughly in the order you would experience problems with them. Memory conflicts are perhaps the most troublesome of these, certainly the most difficult to fully explain and overcome. These are discussed in Chapter 7, "Memory," which focuses on the others listed here in the order you will likely have problems with them. IRQs cause more problems than DMA because they are in much higher demand; therefore, virtually all cards will use IRQ channels. There are fewer problems with DMA channels because few cards use them, and there are usually more than enough channels to go around. I/O ports are used by all hardware devices on the bus, but there are technically 64K of them, which means plenty to go around. With all of these resources, you have to make sure that a unique card or hardware function uses each resource; they cannot or should not be shared.

These resources are required and used by many different components of your system. Adapter cards need these resources to communicate with your system and to accomplish their purposes. Not all adapter cards have the same resource requirements. A serial communications port, for example, needs an IRQ channel and I/O port address, whereas a sound board needs these resources and at least one DMA channel as well. Most network cards use a 16K block of memory addresses, an IRQ channel, and an I/O port address.

As your system increases in complexity, the chance for resource conflicts increases dramatically. Modern systems with sound cards and network cards can really push the envelope and can become a configuration nightmare for the uninitiated. So that you can resolve conflicts, most adapter cards allow you to modify resource assignments by setting jumpers or switches on the cards. Fortunately, in almost all cases there is a logical way to configure the system—once you know the rules.

Interrupts (IRQs)

Interrupt request channels (IRQs), or hardware interrupts, are used by various hardware devices to signal the motherboard that a request must be fulfilled. This procedure is the same as a student raising his hand to indicate that he needs attention.

These interrupt channels are represented by wires on the motherboard and in the slot connectors. When a particular interrupt is invoked, a special routine takes over the system, which first saves all the CPU register contents in a stack and then directs the system to the interrupt vector table. This vector table contains a list of memory addresses that correspond to the interrupt channels. Depending on which interrupt was invoked, the program corresponding to that channel is run.

The pointers in the vector table point to the address of whatever software driver is used to service the card that generated the interrupt. For a network card, for example, the vector may point to the address of the network drivers that have been loaded to operate the card; for a hard disk controller, the vector may point to the BIOS code that operates the controller.

After the particular software routine finishes performing whatever function the card needed, the interrupt-control software returns the stack contents to the CPU registers, and the system then resumes whatever it was doing before the interrupt occurred.

Through the use of interrupts, your system can respond to external events in a timely fashion. Each time that a serial port presents a byte to your system, an interrupt is generated to ensure that the system reads that byte before another comes in. Keep in mind that in some cases a port device—in particular, a modem with a 16550 or higher UART chip—may incorporate a byte buffer that allows multiple characters to be stored before an interrupt is generated.

Hardware interrupts are generally prioritized by their numbers; with some exceptions, the highest-priority interrupts have the lowest numbers. Higher-priority interrupts take precedence over lower-priority interrupts by interrupting them. As a result, several interrupts can occur in your system concurrently, each interrupt nesting within another.

If you overload the system—in this case, by running out of stack resources (too many interrupts were generated too quickly)—an internal stack overflow error occurs and your system halts. If you experience this type of system error and run DOS, you can compensate for it by using the STACKS parameter in your CONFIG.SYS file to increase the available stack resources. Most people will not see this error in Windows 95 or Windows NT.

The ISA bus uses edge-triggered *interrupt sensing*, in which an interrupt is sensed by a signal sent on a particular wire located in the slot connector. A different wire corresponds to each possible hardware interrupt. Because the motherboard cannot recognize which slot contains the card that used an interrupt line and therefore generated the interrupt, confusion would result if more than one card were set to use a particular interrupt. Each interrupt, therefore, usually is designated for a single hardware device, and most of the time, interrupts cannot be shared.

A device can be designed to share interrupts, and a few devices allow this; most cannot, however, because of the way interrupts are signaled in the ISA bus. Systems with the MCA bus use level-sensitive interrupts, which allow complete interrupt sharing to occur. In fact, in an MCA system, all boards can be set to the same interrupt with no conflicts or problems. The EISA bus can optionally use level-sensitive interrupts which allow sharing, but only for true EISA cards. For maximum performance, however, interrupts should be staggered as much as possible.

External hardware interrupts often are referred to as *maskable interrupts*, which simply means that the interrupts can be masked or turned off for a short time while the CPU is used for other critical operations. It is up to the programmer to manage interrupts properly and efficiently for the best system performance.

Because interrupts usually cannot be shared in an ISA bus system, you often run into conflicts and can even run out of interrupts when you are adding boards to a system. If two boards use the same IRQ to signal the system, the resulting conflict prevents either board from operating properly. The following sections discuss the IRQs that any standard devices use, as well as what may be free in your system.

8-Bit ISA Bus Interrupts. The PC and XT (the systems based on the 8-bit 8086 CPU) provide for eight different external hardware interrupts. Table 5.6 shows the typical uses for these interrupts, which are numbered 0 through 7.

Table 5.6 8-Bit ISA Bus Default Interrupt Assignments

IRQ	Function	Bus Slot
0	System Timer	No
1	Keyboard Controller	No
2	Available	Yes (8-bit)
3	Serial Port 2 (COM2:)	Yes (8-bit)
4	Serial Port 1 (COM1:)	Yes (8-bit)
5	Hard Disk Controller	Yes (8-bit)
6	Floppy Disk Controller	Yes (8-bit)
7	Parallel Port 1 (LPT1:)	Yes (8-bit)

If you have a system that has one of the original 8-bit ISA buses, you will find that the IRQ resources provided by the system present a severe limitation. Installing several devices that need the services of system IRQs in a PC/XT-type system can be a study in frustration, because the only way to resolve the interrupt-shortage problem is to remove the adapter board that you need the least.

16-Bit ISA, EISA, and MCA Bus Interrupts. The introduction of the AT, based on the 286 processor, was accompanied by an increase in the number of external hardware interrupts that the bus would support. The number of interrupts was doubled to 16 by using two Intel 8259 interrupt controllers, piping the interrupts generated by the second one through the unused IRQ 2 in the first controller. This arrangement effectively means that only 15 IRQ assignments are available, and IRQ 2 effectively became inaccessible.

By routing all of the interrupts from the second IRQ controller through IRQ 2 on the first, all of these new interrupts are assigned a nested priority level between IRQ 1 and IRQ 3. Thus, IRQ 15 ends up having a higher priority than IRQ 3. Figure 5.18 shows how the two 8259 chips were wired to create the cascade through IRQ 2 on the first chip.

System Resources

FIG. 5.18 Interrupt controller cascade wiring.

To prevent problems with boards set to use IRQ 2, the AT system designers routed one of the new interrupts (IRQ 9) to fill the slot position left open after removing IRQ 2. This means that any card you install in a modern system that claims to use IRQ 2 is really using IRQ 9 instead. Some cards now label this selection as IRQ 2/9, while others may only call it IRQ 2 or IRQ 9. No matter what the labeling says, you must never set two cards to use that interrupt!

Table 5.7 shows the typical uses for interrupts in the 16-bit ISA, EISA, and MCA buses, and lists them in priority order from highest to lowest.

Table 5.7 16-Bit ISA, EISA, and MCA Default Interrupt Assignments

IRQ	Standard Function	Bus Slot	Card Type
0	System Timer	No	-
1	Keyboard Controller	No	-
2	2nd IRQ Controller Cascade	No	-
8	Real-Time Clock	No	-
9	Network/Available (appears as IRQ 2)	Yes	8/16-bit
10	Available	Yes	16-bit
11	SCSI/Available	Yes	16-bit
12	Motherboard Mouse Port/Available	Yes	16-bit
13	Math Coprocessor	No	-
14	Primary IDE	Yes	16-bit
15	Secondary IDE/Available	Yes	16-bit
3	Serial Port 2 (COM2:)	Yes	8/16-bit
4	Serial Port 1 (COM1:)	Yes	8/16-bit
5	Sound/Parallel Port 2 (LPT2:)	Yes	8/16-bit
6	Floppy Disk Controller	Yes	8/16-bit
7	Parallel Port 1 (LPT1:)	Yes	8/16-bit

Because IRQ 2 now is used directly by the motherboard, the wire for IRQ 9 has been rerouted to the same position in the slot that IRQ 2 normally would occupy. Therefore, any board you install that is set to IRQ 2 actually is using IRQ 9. The interrupt vector table has been adjusted accordingly to enable this deception to work. This adjustment to the system provides greater compatibility with the PC interrupt structure and enables cards that are set to IRQ 2 to work properly.

Notice that interrupts 0, 1, 2, 8, and 13 are not on the bus connectors and are not accessible to adapter cards. Interrupts 8, 10, 11, 12, 13, 14, and 15 are from the second interrupt controller and are accessible only by boards that use the 16-bit extension connector, because this is where these wires are located. IRQ 9 is rewired to the 8-bit slot connector in place of IRQ 2, which means that IRQ 9 replaces IRQ 2 and therefore is available to 8-bit cards, which treat it as though it were IRQ 2.

> **Note**
>
> Although the 16-bit ISA bus has twice as many interrupts as systems that have the 8-bit ISA bus, you still may run out of available interrupts, because only 16-bit adapters can use most of the newly available interrupts.

The extra IRQ lines in a 16-bit ISA system are of little help unless the adapter boards that you plan to use enable you to configure them for one of the unused IRQs. Some devices are hard-wired so that they can use only a particular IRQ. If you have a device that already uses that IRQ, you must resolve the conflict before installing the second adapter. If neither adapter enables you to reconfigure its IRQ use, chances are that you cannot use the two devices in the same system.

IRQ Conflicts. One of the most common areas of IRQ conflict involves serial (COM) ports. You may have noticed in the preceding two sections that two IRQs are set aside for two COM ports. IRQ 3 is used for COM2:, and IRQ 4 is used for COM1:. The problem occurs when you have more than two serial ports in a system—a situation that is entirely possible, because a PC can support up to four COM ports.

The problems arise here because most people purchase poorly designed COM port boards that do not allow IRQ settings other than 3 or 4. What happens is that they end up setting COM3: to IRQ 4 (sharing it with COM1:), and COM4: to IRQ 3 (sharing it with COM2:). This is not acceptable, as it will prevent you from using the two COM ports on any one of the interrupt channels simultaneously. This was somewhat acceptable under plain DOS, because single-tasking (running only one program at a time) was the order of the day, but is totally unacceptable with Windows and OS/2. If you must share IRQs, you can usually get away with sharing devices on the same IRQ as long as they use different COM ports. For instance, a scanner and an internal modem could share an IRQ, although if the two devices are used simultaneously a conflict will result.

The best solution is to purchase a multiport serial I/O card that will allow interrupt sharing among COM ports. As a side note, also make sure that the COM board you purchase uses a buffered 16550A or higher type UART (Universal Asynchronous Receiver

Transmitter) chip rather than the slow, unbuffered 16450 types. One company providing specialized high quality COM boards is Byte Runner Technologies (see the vendor list in Appendix A).

For more information on COM boards and ports, see

http://www.byterunner.com
http://comminfo.com

On the Web

If a device listed in the table is not present, such as the motherboard mouse port (IRQ 12) or parallel port 2 (IRQ 5), then you can consider those interrupts as available. For example, a second parallel port is a rarity, and most systems will have a sound card installed and set for IRQ 5. Also, on most systems IRQ 15 is assigned to a secondary IDE controller. If you do not have a second IDE hard drive, you could disable the secondary IDE controller to free up that IRQ for another device.

DMA Channels

DMA (Direct Memory Access) channels are used by high-speed communications devices that must send and receive information at high speed. A serial or parallel port does not use a DMA channel, but a sound card or SCSI adapter often does. DMA channels sometimes can be shared if the devices are not of the type that would need them simultaneously. For example, you can have a network adapter and a tape backup adapter sharing DMA channel 1, but you cannot back up while the network is running. To back up during network operation, you must ensure that each adapter uses a unique DMA channel.

8-Bit ISA Bus DMA Channels. In the 8-bit ISA bus, four DMA channels support high-speed data transfers between I/O devices and memory. Three of the channels are available to the expansion slots. Table 5.8 shows the typical uses of these DMA channels.

Table 5.8 8-Bit ISA Default DMA-Channel Assignments		
DMA	**Standard Function**	**Bus Slot**
0	Dynamic RAM Refresh	No
1	Available	Yes (8-bit)
2	Floppy disk controller	Yes (8-bit)
3	Hard disk controller	Yes (8-bit)

Because most systems typically have both a floppy and hard disk drive, only one DMA channel is available in 8-bit ISA systems.

16-Bit ISA DMA Channels. Since the introduction of the 286 CPU, the ISA bus has supported eight DMA channels, with seven channels available to the expansion slots. Like the expanded IRQ lines described earlier in this chapter, the added DMA channels were created by cascading a second DMA controller to the first one. DMA channel 4 is used to cascade channels 0 through 3 to the microprocessor. Channels 0 through 3 are available for 8-bit transfers, and channels 5 through 7 are for 16-bit transfers only. Table 5.9 shows the typical uses for the DMA channels.

Table 5.9 16-Bit ISA, EISA, and MCA Default DMA-Channel Assignments

DMA	Standard Function	Bus Slot	Card Type	Transfer
0	Available	Yes	16-bit	8-bit
1	Sound/Available	Yes	8/16-bit	8-bit
2	Floppy Disk Controller	Yes	8/16-bit	8-bit
3	ECP Parallel/Available	Yes	8/16-bit	8-bit
4	1st DMA Controller	No	-	16-bit Cascade
5	Sound/Available	Yes	16-bit	16-bit
6	SCSI/Available	Yes	16-bit	16-bit
7	Available	Yes	16-bit	16-bit

The only standard DMA channel used in all systems is DMA 2, which is universally used by the floppy controller. DMA 4 is not usable, and does not appear in the bus slots. DMA channels 1 and 5 are most commonly used by sound cards such as the Sound Blaster 16. These cards use both an 8- and a 16-bit DMA channel for high-speed transfers.

> **Note**
>
> Although DMA channel 0 appears in a 16-bit slot connector extension and therefore can only be used by a 16-bit card, it only does 8-bit transfers! Because of this, you will generally not see DMA 0 as a choice on 16-bit cards. Most 16-bit cards (like SCSI host adapters) that use DMA channels have their choices limited to DMA 5 through 7.

EISA. Realizing the shortcomings inherent in the way DMA channels are implemented in the ISA bus, the creators of the EISA specification created a specific DMA controller for their new bus. They increased the number of address lines to include the entire address bus, thus allowing transfers anywhere within the address space of the system. Each DMA channel can be set to run either 8-, 16-, or 32-bit transfers. In addition, each DMA channel can be separately programmed to run any of four types of bus cycles when transferring data:

- *Compatible*. This transfer method is included to match the same DMA timing as used in the ISA bus. This is done for compatibility reasons; all ISA cards can operate in an EISA system in this transfer mode.

- *Type A*. This transfer type compresses the DMA timing by 25 percent over the Compatible method. It was designed to run with most (but not all) ISA cards and still yield a speed increase.

- *Type B*. This transfer type compresses timing by 50 percent over the Compatible method. Using this method, most EISA cards function properly, but only a few ISA cards will be problem-free.

- *Type C*. This transfer method compresses timing by 87.5 percent over the Compatible method; it is the fastest DMA transfer method available under the EISA specification. No ISA cards will work using this transfer method.

EISA DMA also allows for special reading and writing operations referred to as *scatter write* and *gather read*. Scattered writes are done by reading a contiguous block of data and writing it to more than one area of memory at the same time. Gathered reads involve reading from more than one place in memory and writing to a device. These functions are often referred to as *Buffered Chaining*, and they increase the throughput of DMA operations.

MCA. It might be assumed that because MCA is a complete rebuilding of the PC bus structure that DMA in an MCA environment would be better constructed. This is not so. Quite to the contrary, DMA in MCA systems were for the most part all designed around one DMA controller with the following issues:

- It can only connect to two 8-bit data paths. This can only transfer 1 or 2 bytes per bus cycle.
- It is only connected to A0:A23 on the address bus. This means it can only make use of the lower 16M of memory.
- Runs at 10MHz.

The inability of the DMA controller to address more than 2 bytes per transfer severely cripples this otherwise powerful bus.

I/O Port Addresses

Your computer's I/O ports enable you to attach a large number of important devices to your system to expand its capabilities. A printer attached to one of your system's LPT (parallel) ports enables you to make a printout of the work on your system. A modem attached to one of your system's COM (serial) ports enables you to use telephone lines to communicate with computers thousands of miles away. A scanner attached to an LPT port or a SCSI host adapter enables you to convert graphics or text to images and type that you can use with the software installed on your computer.

Most systems come configured with at least two COM (serial) ports and one LPT (parallel printer) ports. The two serial ports are configured as COM1: and COM2:, and the parallel port as LPT1. The basic architecture of the PC provides for as many as four COM ports (1 through 4) and three LPT ports (1 through 3). If you use more than two COM ports, make sure that COM3: and COM4: have unique IRQ settings and do not share those with COM1: and COM2:. In general, on most machines both COM1: and COM3: use IRQ 4; and both COM2: and COM4: use IRQ 3.

> **Caution**
>
> Theoretically, each of the four COM ports in a system can be used to attach a device, such as a mouse or modem, but doing so may lead to resource conflicts. For more information, see the discussion of resolving IRQ conflicts in "IRQ Conflicts" earlier in this chapter.

Every I/O port in your system uses an I/O address for communication. This address, which is in the lower memory ranges, is reserved for communication between the I/O device and the operating system. If your system has multiple I/O cards, each card must use a different I/O address; if not, your system will not be able to communicate with the devices reliably.

The I/O addresses that your ports use depend on the type of ports. Table 5.10 shows the I/O addresses expected by the various standard ports in a PC system.

Table 5.10 Standard I/O Addresses for Serial and Parallel Ports	
Port	**Base I/O Address**
COM1	3F8h
COM2	2F8h
COM3	3E8h
COM4	2E8h
LPT1	378h
LPT2	278h

Besides your serial and parallel ports, other adapters in your system use I/O addresses. Quite truthfully, the I/O addresses for the serial and parallel ports are fairly standard; it is unlikely that you will run into problems with them. The I/O addresses used by other adapters are not standardized, however, and you may have problems finding a mix of port addresses that works reliably. In the next section, you learn some of the techniques that you can use to solve this problem.

Resolving Resource Conflicts

The resources in a system are limited. Unfortunately, the demands on those resources seem to be unlimited. As you add more and more adapter cards to your system, you will find that the potential for resource conflicts increases. If your system is fully PnP-compatible, then potential conflicts should be resolved automatically. If your system does not have a bus that resolves conflicts for you (such as an MCA or EISA bus), you need to resolve the conflicts manually.

How do you know whether you have a resource conflict? Typically, one of the devices in your system stops working. Resource conflicts can exhibit themselves in other ways, though. Any of the following events could be diagnosed as a resource conflict:

- A device transfers data inaccurately.
- Your system frequently locks up.
- Your sound card doesn't sound quite right.
- Your mouse doesn't work.
- Garbage appears on your video screen for no apparent reason.
- Your printer prints gibberish.
- You cannot format a floppy disk.
- The PC starts in Safe Mode (Windows 95).

In the following sections, you learn some of the steps that you can take to head off resource conflicts or to track them down when they occur.

A good source of information online regarding resource conflicts can be found at:

http://www.atipa.com/InfoSheets/IRQs.shtml

On the Web

> **Caution**
>
> Be careful in diagnosing resource conflicts; a problem may not be a resource conflict at all, but a computer virus. Many computer viruses are designed to exhibit themselves as glitches or as periodic problems. If you suspect a resource conflict, it may be worthwhile to run a virus check first to ensure that the system is clean. This procedure could save you hours of work and frustration.

Resolving Conflicts Manually

Unfortunately, the only way to resolve conflicts manually is to take the cover off your system and start changing switches or jumper settings on your adapter cards. Each of these changes then must be accompanied by a system reboot, which implies that they take a great deal of time. This situation brings us to the first rule of resolving conflicts: When you set about ridding your system of resource conflicts, make sure that you allow a good deal of uninterrupted time.

Also make sure that you write down your current system settings before you start making changes. That way, you will know where you began and can go back to the original configuration (if necessary).

Finally, dig out the manuals for all your adapter boards; you will need them. If you cannot find the manuals, contact the manufacturers to determine what the various jumper positions and switch settings mean. Additionally, you could look for more current information online at the manufacturers' Web sites.

Now you are ready to begin your detective work. As you try various switch settings and jumper positions, keep the following questions in mind; the answers will help you narrow down the conflict areas:

- *When did the conflict first become apparent?* If the conflict occurred after you installed a new adapter card, that new card probably is causing the conflict. If the conflict occurred after you started using new software, chances are good that the software uses a device that is taxing your system's resources in a new way.

- *Are there two similar devices in your system that do not work?* For example, if your modem and mouse—devices that use a COM port—do not work, chances are good that these devices are conflicting with each other.

- *Have other people had the same problem, and if so, how did they resolve it?* Public forums—such as those on CompuServe, Internet newsgroups, and America Online—are great places to find other users who may be able to help you solve the conflict.

Whenever you make changes in your system, reboot and see whether the problem persists. When you believe that you have solved the problem, make sure that you test all your software. Fixing one problem often seems to causes another to crop up. The only way to make sure that all problems are resolved is to test everything in your system.

As you attempt to resolve your resource conflicts, you should work with and update a system-configuration template, as discussed in the following section.

Using a System-Configuration Template

A *system-configuration template* is helpful, simply because it is easier to remember something that is written down than it is to keep it in your head. To create a configuration template, all you need to do is start writing down what resources are used by which parts of your system. Then, when you need to make a change or add an adapter, you can quickly determine where conflicts may arise.

I like to use a worksheet split into three main areas—one for interrupts, another for DMA channels, and a middle area for devices that do not use interrupts. Each section lists the IRQ or DMA channel on the left and the I/O port device range on the right. This way, you get the clearest picture of what resources are used and which ones are available in a given system.

Here is the system-configuration template I have developed over the years and still use almost daily. This type of configuration sheet is resource-based instead of component-based. Each row in the template represents a different resource, and lists the component using the resource as well as the resources used. The chart has pre-entered all of the fixed items in a modern PC, whose configuration cannot be changed.

To fill out this type of chart, you would perform the following steps:

1. Enter the default resources used by standard components, such as serial and parallel ports, disk controllers, and video. You can use the filled out example I have provided to see how most standard devices are configured.

2. Enter the default resources used by additional add-on components such as sound cards, SCSI cards, network cards, proprietary cards, and so on.

3. Change any configuration items that are in conflict. Try to leave built-in devices at their default settings, as well as sound cards. Other installed adapters may have their settings changed, but be sure to document the changes.

Of course a template like this is best used when first installing components, not after. Once you have it completely filled out to match your system, you can label it and keep it with the system. When you add any more devices, the template will be your guide as to how any new devices should be configured.

The following example is the same template filled out for a typical modern PC system:

System Resource Worksheet

PC Make and Model: _____

Serial Number: _____

Date of Last Revision: _____

System Interrupts:

0 - Timer Circuits..
1 - Keyboard Controller..
2 - Second 8259 IRQ Controller............................
8 - Real-Time Clock / CMOS RAM.......................
9 - _____
10 - _____
11 - _____
12 - _____
13 - Math Coprocessor (N/A in Bus Slot)..............
14 - _____
15 - _____
3 - _____
4 - _____
5 - _____
6 - _____
7 - _____

I/O Port Addresses:

040-05F.......................
060 & 064....................
0A0-0BF.......................
070-07F........................
_____
_____
_____
_____
0F0-0FF........................
_____
_____
_____
_____
_____
_____
_____

Devices not Using Interrupts:

Mono/EGA/VGA Standard Ports.............................
EGA/VGA Standard Ports..
CGA/EGA/VGA Standard Ports..............................
_____
_____
_____
_____

I/O Port Addresses:

3B0-3BB.........................
3C0-3CF.........................
3D0-3DF.........................
_____
_____
_____
_____

DMA Channels:

0 - _____
1 - _____
2 - _____
3 - _____
4 - Cascade DMA Channels 0-3 (N/A in Bus Slot)...
5 - _____
6 - _____
7 - _____

System Resource Worksheet
         PC Make and Model: Intel Advanced ZP _____
             Serial Number: 100000 _____
     Date of Last Revision: 7/5/95 _____

System Interrupts: _____   I/O Port Addresses: _____

 0 - Timer Circuits..   040-05F...............................
 1 - Keyboard Controller..   060 & 064...........................
 2 - Second 8259 IRQ Controller...............................   0A0-0BF...............................
 8 - Real-Time Clock / CMOS RAM...........................   070-07F...............................
 9 - SMC EtherEZ Ethernet card*_____   340-35F_____
10 - _____   _____
11 - Adaptec 1542CF SCSI adapter (scanner, tape)   334-337*_____
12 - _____   _____
13 - Math Coprocessor (N/A in Bus Slot)   0F0-0FF.............
14 - Primary IDE (Hard Disk 1 and 2)_____   1F0-1F7_____
15 - Secondary IDE (IDE CD-ROM drive)_____   170-177_____
 3 - Serial Port 2 (COM2: Serial Mouse)_____   3F8-3FF_____
 4 - Serial Port 1 (COM1: External Modem)_____   2F8-2FF_____
 5 - Sound Blaster 16 Audio_____   220-233_____
 6 - Floppy Controller_____   3F0-3F7_____
 7 - Parallel Port 1 (LPT1: used by Printer)_____   378-37F_____

Devices not Using Interrupts: _____   I/O Port Addresses: _____
Mono/EGA/VGA Standard Ports....................................   3B0-3BB...............................
EGA/VGA Standard Ports..   3C0-3CF...............................
CGA/EGA/VGA Standard Ports....................................   3D0-3DF...............................
ATI Mach 64 SVGA Additional Ports_____   102,1CE,1CF,2EC-2EF____
Sound Blaster 16 MIDI Port_____   330-331_____
Sound Blaster 16 Game Port (Joystick connector)_____   200-207_____
Sound Blaster 16 FM Synthesizer (Music)_____   388-38B_____
                                                                                                    _____

DMA Channels: _____
 0 - _____
 1 - Sound Blaster 16 (Low DMA)_____
 2 - Floppy Controller_____
 3 - Parallel Port 1 (EPP/ECP mode)_____
 4 - Cascade DMA Channels 0-3 (N/A in Bus Slot)
 5 - Sound Blaster 16 (High DMA)_____
 6 - Adaptec 1542CF SCSI adapter*_____
 7 - _____

*Represents a resource setting that had to be changed to avoid a conflict.

As you can see from this template, only two IRQs and two DMA channels remain available. In this example configuration, the primary and secondary IDE connectors were built into the motherboard:

- Floppy controller
- Two serial ports
- One parallel port

Whether these devices are built into the motherboard or on a separate card makes no difference because the resource allocations are the same in either case. All default settings are normally used for these devices, and are indicated in the completed configuration. Next, the accessory cards were configured. In this example, the following cards were installed:

- SVGA video card (ATI Mach 64)
- Sound card (Creative Labs Sound Blaster 16)
- SCSI host adapter (Adaptec AHA-1542CF)
- Network interface card (SMC EtherEZ)

It helps to install the cards in this order. Start with the video card; next, add the sound card. Due to problems with software that must be configured to the sound card, it is best to install it early and make sure only default settings are used. It is better to change settings on other cards than the sound card.

After the sound card, the SCSI adapter was installed; however, the default I/O Port addresses (330-331) and DMA channel (DMA 5) used were in conflict with other cards (mainly the sound card). These settings were changed to their next logical settings which did not cause a conflict.

Finally, the network card was installed, which also had default settings that conflicted with other cards. In this case, the Ethernet card came pre-configured to IRQ 3, which was already in use by COM2:. The solution was to change the setting, and IRQ 9 was the next logical choice in the card's configuration settings.

Even though this is a fully loaded configuration, only three individual items among all of the cards had to be changed to achieve an optimum system configuration. As you can see, using a configuration template like the one shown can make what would otherwise be a jumble of settings lay out in an easy-to-follow manner. The only real problems you will run into once you work with these templates are cards that do not allow for enough adjustment in their settings, or cards which are lacking in documentation. As you can imagine, you will need the documentation for each adapter card, as well as the motherboard, in order to accurately complete a configuration table like the one shown.

Chapter 5—Bus Slots and I/O Cards

> **Tip**
>
> Do not rely too much on software diagnostics such as MSD.EXE that claim to be able to show hardware settings like IRQ and I/O port settings. While they can be helpful in certain situations, they are often wrong with respect to at least some of the information they are displaying about your system. One or two items shown incorrectly can be very troublesome if you believe the incorrect information and configure your system based on it!
>
> Unless your system fully supports PnP, then there is simply no standard way for software to determine resource usage in a PC system. In a non-PnP system, these programs will instead guess at how things are configured, and display these guesses with confidence, even though they may be incorrect.

Heading Off Problems: Special Boards

A number of devices that you may want to install in a computer system require IRQ lines or DMA channels, which means that a world of conflict could be waiting in the box that the device comes in. As mentioned in the preceding section, you can save yourself problems if you use a system-configuration template to keep track of the way that your system is configured.

You also can save yourself trouble by carefully reading the documentation for a new adapter board before you attempt to install it. The documentation details the IRQ lines that the board can use, as well as its DMA-channel requirements. In addition, the documentation will detail the adapter's upper-memory needs for ROM and adapter.

The following sections describe some of the conflicts that you may encounter when you install today's most popular adapter boards. Although the list of adapter boards covered in these sections is far from comprehensive, the sections serve as a guide to installing complex hardware with minimum hassle. Included are tips on sound boards, SCSI host adapters, and network adapters.

Sound cards. Sound cards are probably the biggest single resource hog in your system. They usually use at least one IRQ, two DMA channels, and multiple I/O port address ranges. This is because a sound card is actually several different pieces of hardware all on one board. Most sound cards are similar to the Sound Blaster 16 from Creative Labs.

Figure 5.19 shows the default resources used by the components on a typical Sound Blaster 16 card.

Device	Interrupt	I/O Ports	16-bit DMA	8-bit DMA
Audio	IRQ5	220h-233h	DMA 5	DMA 1

Device	Interrupt
MIDI Port	330h-331h
FM Synthesizer	388h-38Bh
Game Port	200h-207h

FIG. 5.19 Default resources for Sound Blaster 16 card.

As you can see, these cards use quite a few resources. If you take the time to read your sound board's documentation and determine its communications-channel needs, compare those needs to the IRQ lines and DMA channels that already are in use in your system, and then change the settings of the other adapters to avoid conflicts with the sound card, your installation will go quickly and smoothly.

> **Tip**
>
> The greatest single piece of advice I can give you for installing a sound card is to put the sound card in before all other cards except for video. In other words, let the sound card retain all of its default settings; never change a resource setting to prevent a conflict. Instead, always change the settings of other adapters when a conflict with the sound card arises. The problem here is that many educational and game programs that use sound are very poorly written with respect to supporting alternate resource settings on sound cards. Save yourself some grief and let the sound card have its way!

One example of a potential sound-board conflict is the combination of a Sound Blaster 16 and an Adaptec SCSI adapter. The Sound and SCSI adapters will conflict on DMA 5 as well as on I/O ports 330-331. Rather than changing the settings of the sound card, it is best to alter the SCSI adapter to the next available settings that will not conflict with the sound card or anything else. The final settings were shown in the previous configuration template.

The cards in question (Sound Blaster 16 and AHA-1542CF) are not singled out here because there is something wrong with them, but instead because they happen to be the most popular cards of their respective types, and as such will often be paired together.

SCSI Adapter Boards. SCSI adapter boards use more resources than just about any other type of add-in device except perhaps a sound card. They will often use resources that are in conflict with sound cards or network cards. A typical SCSI host adapter requires an IRQ line, a DMA channel, a range of I/O port addresses, plus a 16K range of unused upper memory for its ROM and possible scratch-pad RAM use. Fortunately, the typical SCSI adapter is also easy to reconfigure, and changing any of these settings should not affect performance or software operation.

Before installing a SCSI adapter, be sure to read the documentation for the card, and make sure that any IRQ lines, DMA channels, I/O ports, and upper memory that the card needs are available. If the system resources that the card needs are already in use, use your system-configuration template to determine how you can alter the settings on the SCSI card or other cards to prevent any resource conflicts before you attempt to plug in the adapter card.

Network Interface Cards (NICs). Networks are becoming more and more popular all the time. A typical network adapter does not require as many resources as some of the other cards discussed here, but will require at least a range of I/O port addresses and an interrupt. Most NICs will also require a 16K range of free upper memory to be used for the RAM transfer buffer on the network card. As with any other cards, make sure that all of these resources are unique to the card, and are not shared with any other devices.

Multiple-COM-Port Adapters. A serial port adapter usually has two or more ports on-board. These COM ports require an interrupt and a range of I/O ports each. There aren't too many problems with the I/O port addresses, because the ranges used by up to four COM ports in a system are fairly well defined. The real problem is with the interrupts. Most older installations of more than two serial ports have any additional ones sharing the same interrupts as the first two. This is incorrect, and will cause nothing but problems with software that runs under Windows or OS/2. With these older boards, make sure that each serial port in your system has a unique I/O port address range, and more importantly, a unique interrupt setting.

Because COM ports are required for so many peripherals that connect to the modern PC, and because the number of COM ports that can be used is strictly limited by the IRQ setup in the basic IBM system design, special COM-port cards are available that enable you to assign a unique IRQ to each of the COM ports on the card. For example, you can use such a card to leave COM1: and COM2: configured for IRQ 4 and IRQ 3, respectively, but to configure COM3: for IRQ 10 and COM4: for IRQ 12 (provided you do not have a motherboard-based mouse port in your system).

Many newer multiport adapter cards—such as those offered by Byte Runner Technologies—allow "intelligent" interrupt sharing among ports. In some cases, you can have up to 12 COM port settings without conflict problems. Check with your adapter card's manufacturer to determine if it allows for automatic or "intelligent" interrupt sharing.

Although most people have problems incorrectly trying to share interrupts when installing more than two serial ports in a system, there is a fairly common problem with the I/O port addressing that should be mentioned. Many of the newer high-performance SVGA (Super VGA) chipsets, such as those from S3 Inc. and ATI, use some additional I/O port addresses that will conflict with the standard I/O port addresses used by COM4:.

In the example system-configuration just covered, you can see that the ATI video card uses some additional I/O port addresses, specifically 2EC-2EF. This is a problem as COM4: is normally configured as 2E8-2EF, which overlaps with the video card. The video cards that use these addresses are not normally adjustable for this setting, so you will either have to change the address of COM4: to a nonstandard setting, or simply disable COM4: and restrict yourself to using only three serial ports in the system. If you do have a serial adapter that supports nonstandard I/O address settings for the serial ports, you must ensure that those settings are not used by other cards, and you must inform any software or drivers, such as those in Windows, of your nonstandard settings.

With a multiple-COM-port adapter card installed and properly configured for your system, you can have devices hooked to numerous COM ports, and up to four devices can be functioning at the same time. For example, you can use a mouse, modem, plotter, and serial printer at the same time.

Plug and Play Systems

Plug and Play (PnP) represents a major revolution in recent interface technology. PnP first came on the market in 1995, and most new systems come ready to take advantage of it. In the past, PC users have been forced to muddle through a nightmare of DIP switches and jumpers every time they wanted to add new devices to their systems. The results, all too often, were system resource conflicts and non-functioning cards.

PnP is not an entirely new concept. It was a key design feature of MCA and EISA interfaces, but the limited appeal of MCA and EISA meant that they never became industry standards. Therefore, mainstream PC users still worry about I/O addresses, DMA channels, and IRQ settings. But now that PnP specifications are available for ISA-, PCI-, SCSI-, IDE-, and PCMCIA-based systems, worry-free hardware setup is within the grasp of all new computer buyers.

Of course, PnP may well be within your grasp, but that does not necessarily mean you are ready to take advantage of it. For PnP to work, the following components are required:

- PnP hardware
- PnP BIOS
- PnP operating system (optional)

Each of these components needs to be PnP-compatible, meaning that it complies with the PnP specifications.

The Hardware Component. The *hardware component* refers to both computer systems and adapter cards. The term does not mean, however, that you cannot use your older ISA adapter cards (referred to as *legacy cards*) in a PnP system. You can use these cards; in fact, your PnP BIOS automatically re-assigns PnP-compatible cards around existing legacy components.

PnP adapter cards communicate with the system BIOS and the operating system to convey information about what system resources are needed. The BIOS and operating system, in turn, resolve conflicts (wherever possible) and inform the adapter cards which specific resources it should use. The adapter card then can modify its configuration to use the specified resources.

The BIOS Component. The BIOS component means that most users of older PCs need to update their BIOSes or purchase new machines that have PnP BIOSes. For a BIOS to be compatible, it must support 13 additional system function calls, which can be used by the OS component of a PnP system. The PnP BIOS specification was developed jointly by Compaq, Intel, and Phoenix Technologies.

The PnP features of the BIOS are implemented through an expanded POST. The BIOS is responsible for identification, isolation, and possible configuration of PnP adapter cards. The BIOS accomplishes these tasks by performing the following steps:

1. Disable any configurable devices on the motherboard or on adapter cards.
2. Identify any PnP PCI or ISA devices.
3. Compile an initial resource-allocation map for ports, IRQs, DMAs, and memory.

4. Enable I/O devices.

5. Scan the ROMs of ISA devices.

6. Configure initial-program-load (IPL) devices, which are used later to boot the system.

7. Enable configurable devices by informing them which resources have been assigned to them.

8. Start the bootstrap loader.

9. Transfer control to the operating system.

The Operating-System Component. The operating-system component can be implemented by most newer systems, such as OS/2, Windows 95, or DOS extensions. Extensions of this type should be familiar to most DOS users; extensions have been used for years to provide support for CD-ROM drives. Extension software is available now for existing operating systems, and you can expect all new PC operating systems to have PnP support built in. If you are using Windows NT 4.0, PnP drivers may or may not have been loaded automatically. If not, the driver can be found on the Windows NT 4.0 CD in the DRVLIB\PNPISA\ directory. Open the correct subdirectory for your chipset and install the file PNPISA.INF.

It is the responsibility of the operating system to inform users of conflicts that cannot be resolved by the BIOS. Depending on the sophistication of the operating system, the user then could configure the offending cards manually (on-screen) or turn the system off and set switches on the physical cards. When the system is restarted, the system is checked for remaining (or new) conflicts, any of which are brought to the user's attention. Through this repetitive process, all system conflicts are resolved.

> **Note**
>
> Plug and Play is still going through some revisions. Windows 95 requires at least version 1.0a of the ISA PnP BIOS. If your system does not have the most current BIOS, I suggest that you install a BIOS upgrade. With the Flash ROM used in most PnP systems, you can just download the new BIOS image from the system vendor or manufacturer and run the supplied BIOS update program.

Chapter 6

Microprocessor Types and Specifications

The brain of the PC is the processor, or *Central Processing Unit (CPU)*. The CPU performs the system's calculating and processing—except for special math-intensive processing in systems that have a math coprocessing unit chip. The processor is easily the most expensive chip in the system. All the PC-compatibles use processors that are compatible with the Intel family of chips, although the processors themselves may have been manufactured or designed by various companies, including AMD, IBM, Cyrix, and others.

The following sections cover the processor chips that have been used in personal computers since the first PC was introduced almost two decades ago. These sections provide a great deal of technical detail about these chips and explain why one type of CPU chip can do more work than another in a given period of time. First, however, you learn about two important components of the processor: the data bus and the address bus.

Processor Specifications

Many confusing specifications often are quoted in discussions of processors. The following sections discuss some of these specifications, including the data bus, address bus, and speed. The next section includes a table that lists the specifications of virtually all PC processors.

Data Bus

One of the most common ways to describe a processor is by the size of the processor's data bus and address bus. A *bus* is simply a series of connections that carry common signals. Imagine running a pair of wires from one end of a building to another. If you connect a 110v AC power generator to the two wires at any point and place outlets at convenient locations along the wires, you have constructed a power bus. No matter which outlet you plug the wires into, you have access to the same signal, which in this example is 110v AC power.

Any transmission medium that has more than one outlet at each end can be called a bus. A typical computer system has several buses, and a typical processor has two important buses for carrying data and memory—addressing information: the data bus and the address bus.

The processor bus discussed most often is the *data bus*—the bundle of wires (or pins) used to send and receive data. The more signals that can be sent at the same time, the more data can be transmitted in a specified interval and, therefore, the faster the bus.

Data in a computer is sent as digital information consisting of a time interval in which a single wire carries 5v to signal a 1 data bit, or 0v to signal a 0 data bit. The more wires you have, the more individual bits you can send in the same time interval. A chip such as the 286, which has 16 wires for transmitting and receiving such data, has a 16-bit data bus. A 32-bit chip, such as the 486, has twice as many wires dedicated to simultaneous data transmission as a 16-bit chip and can send twice as much information in the same time interval as a 16-bit chip.

A good way to understand this flow of information is to consider a highway and the traffic it carries. If a highway has only one lane for each direction of travel, only one car

Table 6.1 Intel Processor Specifications

Processor	CPU Clock	Std. Voltage	Internal Register Size	Data-Bus Width	Address-Bus Width	Maximum Memory
8088	1x	5v	16-bit	8-bit	20-bit	1M
8086	1x	5v	16-bit	16-bit	20-bit	1M
286	1x	5v	16-bit	16-bit	24-bit	16M
386SX	1x	5v	32-bit	16-bit	24-bit	16M
386SL	1x	3.3v	32-bit	16-bit	24-bit	16M
386DX	1x	5v	32-bit	32-bit	32-bit	4G
486SX	1x	5v	32-bit	32-bit	32-bit	4G
486SX2	2x	5v	32-bit	32-bit	32-bit	4G
487SX	1x	5v	32-bit	32-bit	32-bit	4G
486DX	1x	5v	32-bit	32-bit	32-bit	4G
486SL**	1x	3.3v	32-bit	32-bit	32-bit	4G
486DX2	2x	5v	32-bit	32-bit	32-bit	4G
486DX4	2-3x	3.3v	32-bit	32-bit	32-bit	4G
Pentium OD	2.5x	5v	32-bit	32-bit	32-bit	4G
Pentium 60/66	1x	5v	32-bit	64-bit	32-bit	4G
Pentium 75+	1.5-3x	3.3v***	32-bit	64-bit	32-bit	4G
Pentium Pro	2-3x	2.9v	32-bit	64-bit	36-bit	64G

*The 386SL contains an integral-cache controller, but the cache memory must be provided outside the chip.
**There are several different voltage variations of Pentium processors, including what Intel calls VRE (3.465v), and VR (3.3v).
***These figures do not include the optional 256K or 512K Level 2 cache built-in to the CPU packages. The L2 cache contains an additional 15.5 million or 31 million transistors!

at a time can move in a certain direction. If you want to increase traffic flow, you can add another lane so that twice as many cars pass in a specified time. You can think of an 8-bit chip as being a single-lane highway because with this chip, one byte flows through at a time. (One byte equals eight individual bits.) The 16-bit chip, with two bytes flowing at a time, resembles a two-lane highway. To move a large number of automobiles, you may have four lanes in each direction. This structure corresponds to a 32-bit data bus, which has the capability to move four bytes of information at a time.

Just as you can describe a highway by its lane width, you can describe a chip by the width of its data bus. When you read an advertisement that describes a computer system as being a 16-bit or 32-bit system, the ad usually is referring to the data bus of the CPU. This number provides a rough idea of the performance potential of the chip (and, therefore, the system).

Table 6.1 lists the specifications, including the data-bus sizes, for the Intel family of processors used in IBM and compatible PCs.

Integral Cache	Cache Type	Burst Mode	Integral FPU	No. of Transistors	Date Introduced
No	-	No	No	29,000	June '79
No	-	No	No	29,000	June '78
No	-	No	No	134,000	Feb. '82
No	-	No	No	275,000	June '88
0K*	WT	No	No	855,000	Oct. '90
No	-	No	No	275,000	Oct. '85
8K	WT	Yes	No	1,185,000	April '91
8K	WT	Yes	No	1,185,000	April '94
8K	WT	Yes	Yes	1,200,000	April '91
8K	WT	Yes	Yes	1,200,000	April '89
8K	WT	Yes	Optional	1,400,000	Nov. '92
8K	WT	Yes	Yes	1,100,000	March '92
16K	WT	Yes	Yes	1,600,000	Feb. '94
2×16K	WB	Yes	Yes	3,100,000	Jan. '95
2×8K	WB	Yes	Yes	3,100,000	March '93
2×8K	WB	Yes	Yes	3,300,000	March '94
2×8K	WB	Yes	Yes	5,500,000	Sept. '95

FPU = Floating-Point Unit (math coprocessor)
WT = Write-Through cache (caches reads only)
WB = Write-Back cache (caches both reads and writes)
Note that the Pentium Pro processor includes 256K of L2 cache in a separate die within the chip.

Internal Registers

The size of the internal register is a good indication of how much information the processor can operate on at one time. Most advanced processors today—all the chips from the 386 to the Pentium—use 32-bit internal registers.

Some processors have an internal data bus (made up of data paths and of storage units called *registers*) that is different from the external data bus. The 8088 and 386SX are examples of this structure. Each chip has an internal data bus twice the width of the external bus. These designs, which sometimes are called hybrid designs, usually are low-cost versions of a "pure" chip. The 386SX, for example, can pass data around internally with a full 32-bit register size; for communications with the outside world, however, the chip is restricted to a 16-bit-wide data path. This design enables a systems designer to build a lower-cost motherboard with a 16-bit bus design and still maintain compatibility with the full 32-bit 386.

Internal registers often are larger than the data bus, which means that the chip requires two cycles to fill a register before the register can be operated on. For example, both the 386SX and 386DX have internal 32-bit registers, but the 386SX has to "inhale" twice (figuratively) to fill them, whereas the 386DX can do the job in one "breath." The same thing would happen when the data is passed from the registers back out to the system bus.

The Pentium is an example of the opposite situation. This chip has a 64-bit data bus but only 32-bit registers—a structure that may seem to be a problem until you understand that the Pentium has two internal 32-bit pipelines for processing information. In many ways, the Pentium is like two 32-bit chips in one. The 64-bit data bus provides for very efficient filling of these multiple registers.

Address Bus

The *address bus* is the set of wires that carry the addressing information used to describe the memory location to which the data is being sent, or from which the data is being retrieved. As with the data bus, each wire in an address bus carries a single bit of information. This single bit is a single digit in the address. The more wires (digits) used in calculating these addresses, the greater the total number of address locations. The size (or width) of the address bus indicates the maximum amount of RAM that a chip can address.

The highway analogy can be used to show how the address bus fits in. If the data bus is the highway, and if the size of the data bus is equivalent to the number of lanes, the address bus relates to the house number or street address. The size of the address bus is equivalent to the number of digits in the house address number. For example, if you live on a street in which the address is limited to a two-digit (base 10) number, no more than 100 distinct addresses (00 to 99) can exist for that street (10 to the power of 2). Add another digit, and the number of available addresses increases to 1,000 (000 to 999), or 10 to the third power.

Computers use the binary (base 2) numbering system, so a two-digit number provides only four unique addresses (00, 01, 10, and 11) calculated as 2 to the power of 2; and a three-digit number provides only eight addresses (000 to 111) which is 2 to the 3rd power. For example, the 8086 and 8088 processors use a 20-bit address bus that calculates as a maximum of 2 to the 20th power or 1,048,576 bytes (1M) of address locations. Table 6.2 describes the memory-addressing capabilities of Intel processors.

Table 6.2 Intel Processor Memory-Addressing Capabilities

Processor Family	Address Bus	Bytes	Kilobytes	Megabytes	Gigabytes
8088/8086	20-bit	1,048,576	1,024	1	none
286/386SX	24-bit	16,777,216	16,384	16	none
386DX-Pentium Pro	32-bit	4,294,967,296	4,194,304	4,096	4
Pentium II	36-bit	68,719,476,736	67,108,864	65,536	64

The data bus and address bus are independent, and chip designers can use whatever size they want for each. Usually, however, chips with larger data buses have larger address buses. The sizes of the buses can provide important information about a chip's relative power, measured in two important ways. The size of the data bus is an indication of the information-moving capability of the chip, and the size of the address bus tells you how much memory the chip can handle.

Processor Speed Ratings

A common misunderstanding about processors is their different speed ratings. This section covers processor speed in general and then provides more specific information about Intel processors.

A computer system's clock speed is measured as a frequency, usually expressed as a number of cycles per second. A crystal oscillator controls clock speeds, using a sliver of quartz in a small tin container. As voltage is applied to the quartz, it begins to vibrate (oscillate) at a harmonic rate dictated by the shape and size of the crystal (sliver). The oscillations emanate from the crystal in the form of a current that alternates at the harmonic rate of the crystal. This alternating current is the clock signal. A typical computer system runs millions of these cycles per second, so speed is measured in megahertz (MHz). (One hertz is equal to one cycle per second.)

> **Note**
>
> The hertz was named for the German physicist Heinrich Rudolph Hertz. In 1885, Hertz confirmed through experimentation the electromagnetic theory, which states that light is a form of electromagnetic radiation and is propagated as waves.

A single cycle is the smallest element of time for the processor. Every action requires at least one cycle and usually multiple cycles. To transfer data to and from memory, for example, an 8086 chip needs four cycles plus wait states. (A *wait state* is a clock tick in which nothing happens to ensure that the processor isn't getting ahead of the rest of the computer.) A 286 needs only two cycles plus any wait states for the same transfer.

The time required to execute instructions also varies. The original 8086 and 8088 processors take an average of 12 cycles to execute a single instruction. The 286 and 386 processors improve this rate to about 4.5 cycles per instruction; the 486 drops the rate further to two cycles per instruction. The Pentium includes twin instruction pipelines and other improvements that provide for operation at 1 cycle per average instruction.

Different instruction execution times (in cycles) make it difficult to compare systems based purely on clock speed, or number of cycles per second. One reason the 486 is so fast is that it has an average instruction-execution time of 2 clock cycles. Therefore, a 100MHz Pentium is about equal to a 200MHz 486, which is about equal to a 400MHz 386 or 286, which is about equal to a 1,000MHz 8088. As you can see, you have to be careful in comparing systems based on pure MHz alone; many other factors affect system performance.

How can two processors that run at the same clock rate perform differently, with one running "faster" than the other? The answer is simple: efficiency.

Intel has devised a specific series of benchmarks that can be run against Intel chips to produce a relative gauge of performance. It has recently been updated to reflect performance on 32-bit systems, and is called the iCOMP 2.0 (intel COmparative Microprocessor Performance) index. Table 6.3 shows the relative power, or iCOMP 2.0 index, for several processors.

Table 6.3 Intel iCOMP 2.0 Index Ratings

Processor	iCOMP 2.0 Index
Pentium 75	67
Pentium 100	90
Pentium 120	100
Pentium 133	111
Pentium 150	114
Pentium 166	127
Pentium 200	142
Pentium-MMX 166	160
Pentium-MMX 200	182
Pentium-MMX 233	203
Pentium Pro 180	197
Pentium Pro 200	220
Pentium II 233	267
Pentium II 266	303
Pentium II 300	N/A*

As of this writing, the Pentium II 300 has not yet been rated.

The iCOMP 2.0 index is derived from several independent benchmarks and is a stable indication of relative processor performance. The benchmarks balance integer with floating point and multimedia performance.

Modern systems use a variable frequency synthesizer circuit usually found in the main motherboard chipset to control the motherboard speed and CPU speed. Most Pentium motherboards will have 3 or 4 speed settings. The processors used today are available in a variety of versions that run at different frequencies based on a given motherboard speed. For example, most of the Pentium chips run at a speed that is some multiple of the true motherboard speed. For example, Pentium processors and motherboards run at the speeds shown in Table 6.4.

Table 6.4 Intel Processor and Motherboard Speeds

CPU Type/Speed	CPU Clock	Motherboard Speed
Pentium 60	1x	60
Pentium 66	1x	66
Pentium 75	1.5x	50
Pentium 90	1.5x	60
Pentium 100	1.5x	66
Pentium 120	2x	60
Pentium 133	2x	66
Pentium 150	2.5x	60
Pentium/Pentium Pro/MMX 166	2.5x	66
Pentium/Pentium Pro 180	3x	60
Pentium/Pentium Pro/MMX 200	3x	66
Pentium-MMX/Pentium II 233	3.5x	66
Pentium II 266	4x	66
Pentium II 300	4.5x	66

If all other variables are equal—including the type of processor, the number of wait states (empty cycles) added to different types of memory accesses, and the width of the data bus—you can compare two systems by their respective clock rates. However, the construction and design of the memory subsystem can have an enormous effect on a system's final execution speed.

In building a processor, a manufacturer tests it at different speeds, temperatures, and pressures. After the processor is tested, it receives a stamp indicating the maximum safe speed at which the unit will operate under the wide variation of temperatures and pressures encountered in normal operation. The rating system usually is simple. For example, the top of the processor in one of my systems is marked like this:

A80486DX2-66

The A is Intel's indicator that this chip has a Ceramic Pin Grid Array form factor, or an indication of the physical packaging of the chip. The 80486DX2 is the part number, which identifies this processor as a clock-doubled 486DX processor. The -66 at the end indicates that this chip is rated to run at a maximum speed of 66MHz. Because of the clock doubling, the maximum motherboard speed is 33MHz. This chip would be acceptable for any application in which the chip runs at 66MHz or slower. For example, you could use this processor in a system with a 25MHz motherboard, in which case the processor would happily run at 50MHz.

Most 486 motherboards also have a 40MHz setting, in which case the DX2 would run at 80MHz internally. Because this is 14MHz beyond its rated speed, many would not work; or if they worked at all, it would only be for a short time. On the other hand, I have found that most of the newer chips marked with -66 ratings seem to run fine (albeit somewhat hotter!) at the 40/80MHz settings. This is called *overclocking*, and can end up being a simple, cost-effective way to speed up your system. However, I would not recommend this for mission-critical applications where the system reliability is of the utmost importance, because a system pushed beyond specification like this can often exhibit erratic behavior under stress.

On the Web

One good source of online overclocking information is located at

http://www.sysopt.com/overc.html

It includes, among other things, fairly thorough overclocking FAQs, and an ongoing survey of users that have successfully (and sometimes unsuccessfully) overclocked their CPUs.

Sometimes, however, the markings don't seem to indicate the speed directly. In the older 8086, for example, –3 translates to 6MHz operation. This marking scheme is more common in some of the older chips manufactured before some of the marking standards used today were standardized.

A manufacturer sometimes places the CPU under a heat sink, which prevents you from reading the rating printed on the chip. (A *heat sink* is a metal device that draws heat away from an electronic device.) Most of the processors running at 50MHz and higher should have a heat sink installed to prevent the processor from overheating.

Intel Processors

PC-compatible computers use processors manufactured primarily by Intel. Some other companies, such as Cyrix and AMD, have reverse-engineered the Intel processors and made their own compatible versions. IBM also manufactures processors for some of its own systems as well as for installation in boards and modules sold to others. The x86 series of IBM microprocessors was developed in conjunction with Cyrix, and is essentially identical to that company's popular 6x86 units.

Knowing the processors used in a system can be very helpful in understanding the capabilities of the system, as well as in servicing it. To fully understand the capabilities of a system and perform any type of servicing, you must know at least the type of processor that the system uses.

8088 and 8086 Processors

The original IBM PC used an Intel CPU chip called the 8088. The original 8088 CPU chip ran at 4.77MHz, which means that the computer's circuitry drove the CPU at a rate of 4,770,000 ticks, or computer heartbeats, per second. Each tick represents a small amount of work—the CPU executing an instruction or part of an instruction—rather than a period of elapsed time.

Computer users sometimes wonder why a 640K conventional-memory barrier exists if the 8088 chip can address 1M of memory. The conventional-memory barrier exists because IBM reserved 384K of the upper portion of the 1,024K (1M) address space of the 8088 for use by adapter cards and system BIOS (a computer program permanently "burned into" the ROM chips in the PC). The lower 640K is the conventional memory in which DOS and software applications execute.

In 1976, before the 8088 chip, Intel made a slightly faster chip named the 8086. The 8086, which was one of the first 16-bit chips on the market, addressed 1M of RAM. The design failed to catch on, however, because both the chip and a motherboard designed for the chip were costly. The cost was high because the system needed a 16-bit data bus rather than the less expensive 8-bit bus. Systems available at that time were 8-bit, and users apparently weren't willing to pay for the extra performance of the full 16-bit design. Therefore, Intel introduced the 8088 in 1978. Both the 8086 and the 8088 CPU chips are quite slow by today's standards.

80186 and 80188 Processors
After Intel produced the 8086 and 8088 chips, it turned its sights toward producing a more powerful chip with an increased instruction set. The company's first efforts along this line—the 80186 and 80188—were unsuccessful. But incorporating system components into the CPU chip was an important idea for Intel, because it led to faster, better chips, such as the 286.

The relationship between the 80186 and 80188 is the same as that of the 8086 and 8088; one is a slightly more advanced version of the other. Compared CPU to CPU, the 80186 is almost the same as the 8088 and has a full 16-bit design. The 80188 (like the 8088) is a hybrid chip that compromises the 16-bit design with an 8-bit external communications interface. The advantage of the 80186 and 80188 is that they combine on a single chip 15 to 20 of the 8086–8088 series system components, a fact that can greatly reduce the number of components in a computer design. The 80186 and 80188 chips are used for highly intelligent peripheral adapter cards, such as network adapters.

286 Processors
The Intel 80286 (normally abbreviated as 286) processor did not suffer from the compatibility problems that damned the 80186 and 80188. The 286 chip, introduced in 1981, is the CPU behind the IBM AT. Other computer makers manufactured what came to be known as IBM clones, many of these manufacturers calling their systems AT-compatible or AT-class computers.

When IBM developed the AT, it selected the 286 as the basis for the new system because the chip provided compatibility with the 8088 used in the PC and the XT, which means that software written for those chips should run on the 286. The 286 chip is many times faster than the 8088 used in the XT, and it offered a major performance boost to PCs used in businesses. The processing speed, or throughput, of the original AT (which ran at 6 MHz) was five times greater than that of the PC running at 4.77 MHz.

For several reasons, 286 systems are faster than their predecessors. The main reason is that 286 processors are much more efficient in executing instructions. An average instruction takes 12 clock cycles on the 8086 or 8088, but an average 4.5 cycles on the 286 processor. Additionally, the 286 chip can handle up to 16 bits of data at a time through an external data bus twice the size of the 8088.

The 286 chip has two modes of operation: real mode and protected mode. The two modes are distinct enough to make the 286 resemble two chips in one. In real mode, a 286 acts essentially the same as an 8086 chip and is fully object-code compatible with the 8086 and 8088. (A processor with object-code compatibility can run programs written for another processor without modification and execute every system instruction in the same manner.)

In the protected mode of operation, the 286 was truly something new. In this mode, a program designed to take advantage of the chip's capabilities believes that it has access to 1G of memory (including virtual memory). The 286 chip, however, can address only 16M of hardware memory. A significant failing of the 286 chip is that it cannot switch from protected mode to real mode without a hardware reset (a warm reboot) of the system. (It can, however, switch from real mode to protected mode without a reset.) A major improvement of the 386 over the 286 is that software can switch the 386 from real mode to protected mode, and vice versa.

Only a small amount of software that took advantage of the 286 chip was sold until Windows 3.0 offered Standard Mode for 286 compatibility; and by that time, the hottest-selling chip was the 386. Still, the 286 was Intel's first attempt to produce a CPU chip that supported multitasking, in which multiple programs run at the same time. The 286 is designed so that if one program locks up or fails, the entire system doesn't need a warm boot (reset) or cold boot (power off or on). Theoretically, what happens in one area of memory doesn't affect other programs. Before multitasked programs are "safe" from one another, however, the 286 chip (and subsequent chips) needs an operating system that works cooperatively with the chip to provide such protection.

386 Processors

The Intel 80386 (normally abbreviated as 386) caused quite a stir in the PC industry because of the vastly improved performance that it brought to the personal computer. Compared with 8088 and 286 systems, the 386 chip offers greater performance in almost all areas of operation.

The 386 is a full 32-bit processor optimized for high-speed operation and multitasking operating systems. Intel introduced the chip in 1985, but the 386 appeared in the first systems in late 1986 and early 1987. The Compaq Deskpro 386 and systems made by several other manufacturers introduced the chip; somewhat later, IBM used the chip in its PS/2 Model 80. For several years, the 386 chip rose in popularity, which peaked around 1991. Since then, the popularity of the 386 has waned to the point that it is virtually nonexistent on the market today.

The 386 can execute the real-mode instructions of an 8086 or 8088, but in fewer clock cycles. The 386 was as efficient as the 286 in executing instructions, which means that the average instruction takes about 4.5 clock cycles. In raw performance, therefore, the 286 and 386 actually seemed to be about at equal clock rates. Many 286 system manufacturers were touting their 16MHz and 20 MHz 286 systems as being just as fast as 16MHz and 20MHz 386 systems, and they were right! The 386 offered greater performance in other ways, mainly due to additional software capability (modes) and a greatly enhanced Memory Management Unit (MMU).

The 386 can switch to and from protected mode under software control without a system reset, a capability that makes using protected mode more practical. In addition, the 386 has a new mode, called virtual real mode, which enables several real-mode sessions to run simultaneously under protected mode.

Other than raw speed, probably the most important feature of this chip is its available modes of operation, which are:

- Real mode
- Protected mode
- Virtual real mode (sometimes called virtual 86 mode)

Real mode on a 386 chip, as on a 286 chip, is 8086-compatible mode. In real mode, the 386 essentially is a much faster "turbo PC" with 640K of conventional memory, just like systems based on the 8088 chip. DOS and any software written to run under DOS requires this mode to run.

The protected mode of the 386 is fully compatible with the protected mode of the 286. The protected mode for both chips often is called their native mode of operation, because these chips are designed for advanced operating systems such as OS/2 and Windows NT, which run only in protected mode. Intel extended the memory-addressing capabilities of 386 protected mode with a new MMU that provides advanced memory paging and program switching. These features are extensions of the 286 type of MMU, so the 386 remains fully compatible with the 286 at the system-code level.

The 386 chip's virtual real mode is new. In virtual real mode, the processor can run with hardware memory protection while simulating an 8086's real-mode operation. Multiple copies of DOS and other operating systems, therefore, can run simultaneously on this processor, each in a protected area of memory. If the programs in one segment crash, the rest of the system is protected. Software commands can reboot the blown partition.

Numerous variations of the 386 chip exist, some of which are less powerful and some of which are less power-hungry. The following sections cover the members of the 386-chip family and their differences.

386DX Processors

The 386DX chip was the first of the 386-family members that Intel introduced. The 386 is a full 32-bit processor with 32-bit internal registers, a 32-bit internal data bus, and a 32-bit external data bus. The 386 contains 275,000 transistors in a VLSI (Very Large Scale Integration) circuit. The chip comes in a 132-pin package and draws approximately 400 milliamperes (ma), which is less power than even the 8086 requires. The 386 has a smaller power requirement because it is made of CMOS (Complementary Metal Oxide Semiconductor) materials. The CMOS design enables devices to consume extremely low levels of power.

The Intel 386 chip was available in clock speeds ranging from 16MHz to 33MHz; other manufacturers, primarily AMD and Cyrix, offered comparable versions with speeds up to 40MHz. In general, these "clones" were fully functional with Intel chips, meaning that they could run any software designed for the Intel 386 chips.

The 386DX can address 4G of physical memory. Its built-in virtual memory manager enables software designed to take advantage of enormous amounts of memory to act as though a system has 64T of memory. (A *terabyte (T)* is 1,099,511,627,776 bytes of memory.)

386SX Processors

The 386SX, code-named the P9 chip during its development, was designed for systems designers who were looking for 386 capabilities at 286-system prices. Like the 286, the 386SX is restricted to only 16 bits when communicating with other system components such as memory. Internally, however, the 386SX is identical to the DX chip; the 386SX has 32-bit internal registers, and can therefore run 32-bit software. The 386SX uses a 24-bit memory-addressing scheme like that of the 286, rather than the full 32-bit memory address bus of the standard 386. The 386SX, therefore, can address a maximum 16M of physical memory rather than the 4G of physical memory that the 386DX can address. Before it was discontinued, the 386SX was available in clock speeds ranging from 16 to 33MHz.

The 386SX signaled the end of the 286 because of the 386SX chip's superior MMU and the addition of the virtual real mode. Under a software manager such as Windows or OS/2, the 386SX can run numerous DOS programs at the same time. The capability to run 386-specific software is another important advantage of the 386SX over any 286 or older design. For example, Windows 3.1 runs nearly as well on a 386SX as it does on a 386DX.

> **Note**
>
> One common fallacy about the 386SX is that you can plug one into a 286 system and give the system 386 capabilities. This is not true; the 386SX chip is not pin-compatible with the 286 and does not plug into the same socket. Several upgrade products, however, have been designed to adapt the chip to a 286 system. In terms of raw speed, converting a 286 system to a 386 CPU chip results in little performance gain because 286 motherboards are built with a restricted 16-bit interface to memory and peripherals. A 16MHz 386SX is not markedly faster than a 16MHz 286, but it does offer improved memory-management capabilities on a motherboard designed for it, as well as the capability to run 386-specific software.

386SL Processors

Another variation on the 386 chip is the 386SL. This low-power CPU has the same capabilities as the 386SX, but it is designed for laptop systems in which low power consumption is needed. The SL chips offer special power-management features that are important to systems that run on batteries. The SL chip offers several sleep modes that conserve power.

The chip includes an extended architecture that includes a *System Management Interrupt (SMI)*, which provides access to the power-management features. Also included in the SL chip is special support for LIM (Lotus Intel Microsoft) expanded memory functions and a cache controller. The cache controller is designed to control a 16–64K external processor cache.

These extra functions account for the higher transistor count in the SL chips (855,000) compared with even the 386DX processor (275,000). The 386SL is available in 25MHz clock speed.

Intel offered a companion to the 386SL chip for laptops called the 82360SL I/O subsystem. The 82360SL provides many common peripheral functions, such as serial and parallel ports, a direct memory access (DMA) controller, an interrupt controller, and power-management logic for the 386SL processor. This chip subsystem works with the processor to provide an ideal solution for the small size and low power-consumption requirements of portable and laptop systems.

486 Processors

In the race for more speed, the Intel 80486 (normally abbreviated as 486) was another major leap forward. The additional power available in the 486 fueled tremendous growth in the software industry. Tens of millions of copies of Windows, and millions of copies of OS/2, have been sold largely because the 486 finally made the graphical user interface (GUI) of Windows and OS/2 a realistic option for people who work on their computers every day.

Four main features make a given 486 processor roughly twice as fast as an equivalent MHz 386 chip. These features are:

- *Reduced instruction-execution time.* Instructions in the 486 take an average of only two clock cycles to complete, compared with an average of more than four cycles on the 386.

- *Internal (Level 1) cache.* The built-in cache has a hit ratio of 90 to 95 percent, which describes how often zero-wait-state read operations will occur. External caches can improve this ratio further.

- *Burst-mode memory cycles.* A standard 32-bit (4-byte) memory transfer takes two clock cycles. After a standard 32-bit transfer, more data up to the next 12 bytes (or three transfers) can be transferred with only one cycle used for each 32-bit (4-byte) transfer. Thus, up to 16 bytes of contiguous, sequential memory data can be transferred in as little as five cycles instead of eight cycles or more. This effect can be even greater when the transfers are only 8 bits or 16 bits each.

- *Built-in (synchronous) enhanced math coprocessor (some versions).* The math coprocessor runs synchronously with the main processor and executes math instructions in fewer cycles than previous designs did. On average, the math coprocessor built into the DX-series chips provides two to three times greater math performance than an external 387 chip.

The 486 chip is about twice as fast as the 386, which means that a 386DX-40 is about as fast as a 486SX-20. This made the 486 a much more desirable option, primarily because it could more easily be upgraded to a DX2 or DX4 processor at a later time. You can see why the arrival of the 486 rapidly killed off the 386 in the marketplace.

Before the 486, many people avoided GUIs because they didn't have time to sit around waiting for the hourglass, which indicates that the system is performing behind-the-scenes operations that the user cannot interrupt. The 486 changed that situation. Many people believe that the 486 CPU chip spawned the widespread acceptance of GUIs.

With the release of its faster Pentium CPU chip, Intel began to cut the price of the 486 line to entice the industry to shift over to the 486 as the mainstream system. Intel later did the same thing with its Pentium chips, spelling the end of the 486 line. The 486 is now offered by Intel only for use in embedded microprocessor applications, used primarily in expansion cards.

Most of the 486 chips were offered in a variety of maximum speed ratings, varying from 16MHz all the way up to 120MHz. Additionally, 486 processors have slight differences in overall pin configurations. The DX, DX2, and SX processors have a virtually identical 168-pin configuration, whereas the OverDrive chips have either the standard 168-pin configuration or a specially modified 169-pin OverDrive (sometimes also called 487SX) configuration. If your motherboard has two sockets, the primary one likely supports the standard 168-pin configuration, and the secondary (OverDrive) socket supports the 169-pin OverDrive configuration. Most newer motherboards with a single ZIF (Zero Insertion Force) socket support any of the 486 processors except the DX4. The DX4 is different because it requires 3.3v to operate instead of 5v, like most other chips up to that time.

A processor rated for a given speed always functions at any of the lower speeds. A 100MHz-rated 486DX4 chip, for example, runs at 75MHz if it is plugged into a 25MHz motherboard. Note that the DX2/OverDrive processors operate internally at two times the motherboard clock rate, whereas the DX4 processors operate at two, two-and-a-half, or three times the motherboard clock rate. Table 6.5 shows the different speed combinations that can result from using the DX2 or DX4 processors with different motherboard clock speeds.

Table 6.5 Intel DX2 and DX4 Operating Speeds versus Motherboard Clock Speeds

Motherboard Clock Speed	16MHz	20MHz	25MHz	33MHz	40MHz	50MHz
DX2 processor speed	32MHz	40MHz	50MHz	66MHz	80MHz	N/A
DX4 (2× mode) speed	32MHz	40MHz	50MHz	66MHz	80MHz	100MHz
DX4 (2.5× mode) speed	40MHz	50MHz	63MHz	83MHz	100MHz	N/A
DX4 (3× mode) speed	48MHz	60MHz	75MHz	100MHz	120MHz	N/A

The internal core speed of the DX4 processor is controlled by the CLKMUL (Clock Multiplier) signal at pin R-17 (socket 1) or S-18 (socket 2, 3, or 6). The CLKMUL input is sampled only during a reset of the CPU, and defines the ratio of the internal clock to the external bus frequency CLK signal at pin C-3 (socket 1) or D-4 (socket 2, 3, or 6). If CLKMUL is sampled low, the internal core speed will be two times the external bus frequency. If driven high or left floating (most motherboards would leave it floating), triple speed mode is selected. If the CLKMUL signal is connected to the BREQ (Bus Request) output signal at pin Q-15 (socket 1) or R-16 (socket 2, 3, or 6), the CPU internal core speed will be 2.5 times the CLK speed. To summarize, here is how the socket has to be wired for each DX4 speed selection:

CPU Speed	CLKMUL (Sampled Only at CPU Reset)
2x	Low
2.5x	Connected to BREQ
3x	High or Floating

You will have to determine how your particular motherboard is wired and if it can be changed to alter the CPU core speed in relation to the CLK signal. In most cases, there would be one or two jumpers on the board near the processor socket. The motherboard documentation should cover these settings if they can be changed.

One interesting capability here is to run the DX4-100 chip in a doubled mode with a 50MHz motherboard speed. This would give you a very fast memory bus, along with the same 100MHz processor speed as if you were running the chip in a 33/100MHz tripled mode.

Note

One caveat is that if your motherboard has VL-Bus slots, they will have to be slowed down to 33 or 40MHz to operate properly.

Many of the newer VL-Bus motherboards can run the VL-Bus slots in a buffered mode, add wait states, or even selectively change the clock only for the VL-Bus slots to keep them compatible. In most cases, they will not run properly at 50MHz. Consult your motherboard—or even better, your chipset documentation—to see how your board is set up.

Caution

If you are upgrading an existing system, be sure that your socket will support the chip that you are installing. In particular, if you are putting a DX4 processor in an older system, you need some type of adapter to regulate the voltage down to 3.3v. If you put the DX4 in a 5v socket, you will destroy the chip!

The 486-processor family is designed for high performance because it integrates formerly external devices, such as cache controllers, cache memory, and math coprocessors. Also, 486 systems are designed for upgradability. Most 486 systems can be upgraded by simple processor additions or swaps that can effectively double the speed of the system.

Internal (Level 1) Cache. All members of the 486 family include as a standard feature an integrated (Level 1) cache controller with either 8K or 16K of cache memory. This cache basically is an area of very fast memory built into the processor that is used to hold some of the current working set of code and data. Cache memory can be accessed with no wait states because it can fully keep up with the processor.

Using cache memory reduces a traditional system bottleneck because system RAM often is much slower than the CPU. This prevents the processor from having to wait for code and data from much slower main memory, therefore improving performance. Without the cache, a 486 frequently would be forced to wait until system memory caught up. If the data that the 486 chip wants is already in the internal cache, the CPU does not have to wait. If the data is not in the cache, the CPU must fetch it from the secondary processor cache or (in less sophisticated system designs) from the system bus.

The organization of the cache memory in the 486 family technically is called a *4-way set associative cache*, which means that the cache memory is split into four blocks. Each block also is organized as 128 or 256 lines of 16 bytes each.

To understand how a 4-way set associative cache works, consider a simple example. In the simplest cache design, the cache is set up as a single block into which you can load the contents of a corresponding block of main memory. This procedure is similar to using a bookmark to locate the current page of a book that you are reading. If main memory equates to all the pages in the book, the bookmark indicates which pages are held in cache memory. This procedure works if the required data is located within the pages marked with the bookmark, but it does not work if you need to refer to a previously read page. In that case, the bookmark is of no use.

An alternative approach is to maintain multiple bookmarks to mark several parts of the book simultaneously. Additional hardware overhead is associated with having multiple bookmarks, and you also have to take time to check all the bookmarks to see which one marks the pages of data that you need. Each additional bookmark adds to the overhead, but also increases your chance of finding the desired pages.

If you settle on marking four areas in the book to limit the overhead involved, you have essentially constructed a 4-way set associative cache. This technique splits the available cache memory into four blocks, each of which stores different lines of main memory. Multitasking environments, such as OS/2 and Windows, are good examples of environments in which the processor needs to operate on different areas of memory simultaneously and in which a four-way cache would improve performance greatly.

The contents of the cache must always be in sync with the contents of main memory to ensure that the processor is working with current data. For this reason, the internal cache in the 486 family is a *Write-Through cache*. Write-Through means that when the processor writes information out to the cache, that information is automatically written through to main memory as well.

By comparison, the Pentium and higher chips have an internal *Write-Back cache*, which means that both reads and writes are cached, further improving performance. Even though the internal 486 cache is Write-Through, the system still can employ an external Write-Back cache for increased performance. In addition, the 486 can buffer up to 4 bytes before actually storing the data in RAM, improving efficiency in case the memory bus is busy.

The cache controller built into the processor also is responsible for watching the memory bus when alternate processors, known as Bus Masters, are in control of the system. This process of watching the bus is referred to as *Bus Snooping*. If a Bus Master device writes to an area of memory that also is stored in the processor cache currently, the cache contents and memory no longer agree. The cache controller then marks this data as invalid and reloads the cache during the next memory access, preserving the integrity of the system.

An external secondary cache (Level 2) of extremely fast Static RAM (SRAM) chips also is used in most 486-based systems to further reduce the amount of time that the CPU must spend waiting for data from system memory. The function of the secondary processor cache is similar to that of the 486 chip's on-board cache. The secondary processor cache holds information that is moving to the CPU, thereby reducing the time that the CPU spends waiting and increasing the time that the CPU spends performing calculations. Fetching information from the secondary processor cache rather than from system memory is much faster because of the extremely fast speed of the SRAM chips—20 nanoseconds (ns) or less.

The following sections discuss the technical specifications and differences of the various members of the 486-processor family in more detail.

486DX Processors. The original Intel 486DX processor was introduced on April 10, 1989, and systems using this chip first appeared during 1990. The first chips had a maximum speed rating of 25MHz; later versions of the 486DX were available in 33MHz- and 50MHz-rated versions. The 486DX originally was available only in a 5v, 168-pin PGA (Pin Grid Array) version, but now is also available in 5v, 196-pin PQFP (Plastic Quad Flat Pack), and 3.3v, 208-pin SQFP (Small Quad Flat Pack) as well. These latter form factors are available in SL Enhanced versions, which are intended primarily for portable or laptop applications in which saving power is important.

Two main features separate the 486 processor from older processors such as the 386 or 286: integration and upgradability. The 486DX integrates functions such as the math coprocessor, cache controller, and cache memory into the chip. The 486 also was designed with upgradability in mind; double-speed OverDrive are upgrades available for most systems.

The 486DX processor is fabricated with low-power CMOS (Complimentary Metal Oxide Semiconductor) technology. The chip has a 32-bit internal register size, a 32-bit external data bus, and a 32-bit address bus. These dimensions are equal to those of the 386DX processor. The internal register size is where the "32-bit" designation used in advertisements comes from. The 486DX chip contains 1.2 million transistors on a piece of silicon no larger than your thumbnail. This figure is more than four times the number of components on 386 processors and should give you a good indication of the 486 chip's relative power.

The standard 486DX contains a processing unit, a Floating-Point Unit (math coprocessor), a memory-management unit, and a cache controller with 8K of internal-cache RAM. Due to the internal cache and a more efficient internal processing unit, the 486 family of processors can execute individual instructions in an average of only two processor cycles. Compare this figure with the 286 and 386 families, both of which execute an average 4.5 cycles per instruction, or with the original 8086 and 8088 processors, which execute an average 12 cycles per instruction. At a given clock rate (MHz), therefore, a 486 processor is roughly twice as efficient as a 386 processor; a 16MHz 486SX is roughly equal to a 33 MHz 386DX system; and a 20MHz 486SX is equal to a 40MHz 386DX system. Any of the faster 486s are way beyond the 386 in performance.

The 486 is fully instruction-set–compatible with previous Intel processors, such as the 386, but offers several additional instructions (most of which have to do with controlling the internal cache).

Like the 386DX, the 486 can address 4G of physical memory and manage as much as 64T of virtual memory. The 486 fully supports the three operating modes introduced in the 386: real mode, protected mode, and virtual real mode. In real mode, the 486 (like the 386) runs unmodified 8086-type software. In protected mode, the 486 (like the 386) offers sophisticated memory paging and program switching. In virtual real mode, the 486 (like the 386) can run multiple copies of DOS or other operating systems while simulating an 8086's real-mode operation. Under an operating system such as Windows or OS/2, therefore, both 16-bit and 32-bit programs can run simultaneously on this processor with hardware memory protection. If one program crashes, the rest of the system is protected, and you can reboot the blown portion through various means depending on the operating software.

The 486DX series has a built-in math coprocessor that sometimes is called an MCP (math coprocessor) or FPU (Floating-Point Unit). This series is unlike previous Intel CPU chips, which required you to add a math coprocessor if you needed faster calculations for complex mathematics. The FPU in the 486DX series is 100 percent software-compatible with the external 387 math coprocessor used with the 386: but, it delivers more than twice the performance because it runs in synchronization with the main processor and executes most instructions in half as many cycles as the 386.

486SL. The 486SL was a short-lived, stand-alone chip. The SL enhancements and features became available in virtually all the 486 processors (SX, DX, and DX2) in what are called SL Enhanced versions. *SL Enhancement* refers to a special design that incorporates special power-saving features.

The SL Enhanced chips originally were designed to be installed in laptop or notebook systems that run on batteries, but they are finding their way into desktop systems as well. The SL Enhanced chips feature special power-management techniques, such as sleep mode and clock throttling, to reduce power consumption when necessary. These chips are available in 3.3v versions as well.

Intel has designed a power-management architecture called *System Management Mode (SMM)*. This new mode of operation is totally isolated and independent from other CPU hardware and software. SMM provides hardware resources such as timers, registers, and other I/O logic that can control and power down mobile-computer components without interfering with any of the other system resources. SMM executes in a dedicated memory space called System Management Memory, which is not visible and does not interfere with operating-system and application software. SMM has an interrupt called *System Management Interrupt (SMI)*, which services power-management events, and which is independent from, and higher-priority than, any of the other interrupts.

SMM provides power management with flexibility and security that were not available previously. For example, when an application program tries to access a peripheral device that is powered down for battery savings, a SMI occurs, powering up the peripheral device and reexecuting the I/O instruction automatically.

Intel also has designed a feature called suspend/resume in the SL processor. The system manufacturer can use this feature to provide the portable-computer user with instant-on-and-off capability. An SL system typically can resume (instant on) in one second from the suspend state (instant off) to exactly where it left off. You do not need to reboot, load the operating system, load the application program, and then load the application data. Simply push the suspend/resume button, and the system is ready to go.

The SL CPU was designed to consume almost no power in the suspend state. This feature means that the system can stay in the suspend state possibly for weeks and yet start up instantly right where it left off. While it is in the suspend state, an SL system can keep working data in normal RAM memory safe for a long time, but saving to a disk still is prudent.

486SX. The 486SX, introduced in April 1991, was designed to be sold as a lower-cost version of the 486. The 486SX is virtually identical to the full DX processor, but the chip does not incorporate the FPU or math coprocessor portion.

As you read earlier in this chapter, the 386SX was a scaled-down (some people would say crippled) 16-bit version of the full-blown 32-bit 386DX. The 386SX even had a completely different pinout and was not interchangeable with the more powerful DX version. The 486SX, however, is a different story. The 486SX is in fact a full-blown 32-bit 486 processor that is basically pin-compatible with the DX. A few pin functions are different or rearranged, but each pin fits into the same socket.

The 486SX chip is more a marketing quirk than new technology. Early versions of the 486SX chip actually were DX chips that showed defects in the math-coprocessor section. Instead of being scrapped, the chips simply were packaged with the FPU section disabled and sold as SX chips. This arrangement lasted for only a short time; thereafter, SX chips got their own mask, which is different from the DX mask. (A *mask* is the photographic blueprint of the processor and is used to etch the intricate signal pathways into a silicon chip.) The transistor count dropped to 1.185 million (from 1.2 million) to reflect this new mask.

The 486SX chip is twice as fast as a 386DX with the same clock speed. Intel marketed the 486SX as being the ideal chip for new computer buyers, because not much entry-level software uses the math-coprocessor functions.

The 486SX was normally available in 16, 20, 25, and 33MHz-rated speeds, and there was also a 486 SX/2 that ran at up to 50 or 66MHz. The 486SX normally comes in a 168-pin version, although other surface-mount versions are available in SL Enhanced models.

Despite what Intel's marketing and sales information implies, no provision exists technically for adding a separate math coprocessor to a 486SX system; neither is a separate math coprocessor chip available to plug in. Instead, Intel wanted you to add a new 486 processor with a built-in math unit and disable the SX CPU that already is on the motherboard. If this situation sounds confusing, read on, because this topic brings you to the most important aspect of 486 design: upgradability.

487SX. The 487SX math coprocessor, as Intel calls it, really is a complete 25MHz 486DX CPU with an extra pin added and some other pins rearranged. When the 487SX is installed in the extra socket provided in a 486SX-CPU-based system, the 487SX turns off the existing 486SX via a new signal on one of the pins. The extra key pin actually carries no signal itself and exists only to prevent improper orientation when the chip is installed in a socket.

The 487SX takes over all CPU functions from the 486SX and also provides math coprocessor functionality in the system. At first glance, this setup seems rather strange and wasteful, so perhaps further explanation is in order. Fortunately, the 487SX turned out simply to be a stopgap measure while Intel prepared its real surprise: the OverDrive processor. The DX2/OverDrive speed-doubling chips, which are designed for the 487SX 169-pin socket, have the same pinout as the 487SX. These upgrade chips are installed in exactly the same way as the 487SX; therefore, any system that supports the 487SX also supports the DX2/OverDrive chips.

Although in most cases you can upgrade a system by removing the 486SX CPU and replacing it with a 487SX (or even a DX or DX2/OverDrive), Intel originally discouraged this procedure. Instead, Intel recommended that PC manufacturers include a dedicated upgrade (OverDrive) socket in their systems, because several risks were involved in removing the original CPU from a standard socket. (The following section elaborates on those risks.) Now, Intel recommends—or even insists on—the use of a single processor socket of a ZIF design, which makes upgrading an easy task physically.

DX2/OverDrive and DX4 Processors. On March 3, 1992, Intel introduced the DX2 speed-doubling processors. On May 26, 1992, Intel announced that the DX2 processors also would be available in a retail version called OverDrive. Originally, the OverDrive versions of the DX2 were available only in 169-pin versions, which meant that they could be used only with 486SX systems that had sockets configured to support the rearranged pin configuration.

On September 14, 1992, Intel introduced 168-pin OverDrive versions for upgrading 486DX systems. These processors could be added to existing 486 (SX or DX) systems as an upgrade, even if those systems did not support the 169-pin configuration. When you use this processor as an upgrade, you simply install the new chip in your system, which subsequently runs twice as fast.

The DX2/OverDrive processors run internally at twice the clock rate of the host system. If the motherboard clock is 25MHz, for example, the DX2/OverDrive chip runs internally at 50MHz; likewise, if the motherboard is a 33MHz design, the DX2/OverDrive runs at 66MHz. The DX2/OverDrive speed doubling has no effect on the rest of the system; all components on the motherboard run the same as they do with a standard 486 processor. Therefore, you do not have to change other components (such as memory) to accommodate the double-speed chip. The DX2/OverDrive chips have been available in several speeds. Three different speed-rated versions have been offered:

- 40MHz DX2/OverDrive for 16MHz or 20MHz systems
- 50MHz DX2/OverDrive for 25MHz systems
- 66MHz DX2/OverDrive for 33MHz systems

Notice that these ratings indicate the maximum speed at which the chip is capable of running. You could use a 66MHz-rated chip in place of the 50MHz- or 40MHz-rated parts with no problem, although the chip will run only at the slower speeds. The actual speed of the chip is double the motherboard clock frequency. When the 40MHz DX2/OverDrive chip is installed in a 16MHz 486SX system, for example, the chip will function only at 32MHz—exactly double the motherboard speed. Intel originally stated that no 100MHz DX2/OverDrive chip would be available for 50MHz systems—which technically has not been true because the DX4 could be set to run in a clock-doubled mode and used in a 50MHz motherboard (see our discussion of the DX4 processor in this section).

The only part of the DX2 chip that doesn't run at double speed is the bus interface unit, a region of the chip that handles I/O between the CPU and the outside world. By translating between the differing internal and external clock speeds, the bus interface unit makes speed doubling transparent to the rest of the system. The DX2 appears to the rest of the system to be a regular 486DX chip, but one that seems to execute instructions twice as fast.

DX2/OverDrive chips are based on the 0.8-micron circuit technology that was first used in the 50MHz 486DX. The DX2 contains 1.1 million transistors in a three-layer form. The internal 8K cache, integer, and Floating-Point Units all run at double speed. External communication with the PC runs at normal speed to maintain compatibility.

Besides upgrading existing systems, one of the best parts of the DX2 concept was the fact that system designers could introduce very fast systems by using cheaper motherboard designs, rather than the more costly designs that would support a straight high-speed clock. This means that a 50MHz 486DX2 system was much less expensive than a straight 50MHz 486DX system. In a 486DX-50 system, the system board operates at a true 50MHz. In a 486DX2-50 system, the 486DX2 CPU operates internally at 50MHz, but the motherboard operates at only 25MHz.

You may be thinking that a true 50MHz DX-processor–based system still would be faster than a speed-doubled 25MHz system, and this generally is true, but the differences in speed actually are very slight—a real testament to the integration of the 486 processor and especially to the cache design.

When the processor has to go to system memory for data or instructions, for example, it has to do so at the slower motherboard operating frequency, such as 25MHz. Because the 8K internal cache of the 486DX2 has a hit rate of 90 to 95 percent, however, the CPU has to access system memory only 5 to 10 percent of the time for memory reads. Therefore, the performance of the DX2 system can come very close to that of a true 50MHz DX system and cost much less. Even though the motherboard runs only at 33.33MHz, a system with a DX2 66MHz processor ends up being faster than a true 50MHz DX system, especially if the DX2 system has a good Level-2 cache.

Many 486 motherboard designs also include a secondary cache that is external to the cache integrated into the 486 chip. This external cache allows for much faster access when the 486 chip calls for external-memory access. The size of this external cache can vary anywhere from 16K to 512K or more. When you add a DX2 processor, an external cache is even more important for achieving the greatest performance gain, because this cache greatly reduces the wait states that the processor will have to add when writing to system memory or when a read causes an internal-cache miss. For this reason, some systems perform better with the DX2/OverDrive processors than others, usually depending on the size and efficiency of the external-memory cache system on the motherboard. Systems that have no external cache will still enjoy a near-doubling of CPU performance, but operations that involve a great deal of memory access will be slower.

This brings us to the DX4 processor. Although the standard DX4 technically was not sold as a retail part, it could be purchased from several vendors, along with the 3.3v voltage adapter needed to install the chip in a 5v socket. These adapters have jumpers that enable you to select the DX4 clock multiplier and set it to 2x, 2.5x, or 3x mode. In a 50MHz DX system, you could install a DX4/voltage-regulator combination set in 2x mode for a motherboard speed of 50MHz and a processor speed of 100MHz! Although you may not be able to take advantage of the latest local bus peripherals, you will in any case have one of the fastest 486-class PCs available.

Intel also sold a special DX4 OverDrive processor that included a built-in voltage regulator and heat sink that is specifically designed for the retail market. The DX4 OverDrive chip is essentially the same as the standard 3.3v DX4 with the main exception that it runs on 5v because it includes an on-chip regulator. Also, the DX4 OverDrive chip will only run in the tripled speed mode, and not the 2x or 2.5x modes of the standard DX4 processor.

> **Note**
>
> As of this writing, Intel has discontinued all 486 and DX2/DX4/OverDrive processors. However, the Pentium OverDrive Processor is still being offered for certain 486 systems. See the "OverDrive Processor Installation" section later in this chapter.

Vacancy. Perhaps you saw the Intel advertisements—both print and television—that featured a 486SX system with a neon Vacancy sign pointing to an empty socket next to the CPU chip. Unfortunately, these ads were not very informative, and they made it seem that only systems with the extra socket could be upgraded. When I first saw these ads, I was worried because I had just purchased a 486DX system, and the advertisements implied that only 486SX systems with the empty OverDrive socket were upgradable. This, of course, was not true, but the Intel advertisements surely did not communicate that fact very well.

I later found out that upgradability does not depend on having an extra OverDrive socket in the system and that virtually any 486SX or DX system can be upgraded. The secondary OverDrive socket was designed simply to make upgrading easier and more convenient. Even in systems that have the second socket, you can actually remove the primary SX or DX CPU and plug the OverDrive processor directly into the main CPU socket, rather than into the secondary OverDrive socket.

In that case, you would have an upgraded system with a single-functioning CPU installed; you could remove the old CPU from the system and sell it or trade it in for a refund. Unfortunately, Intel does not offer a trade-in or core-charge policy; it simply does not want your old chip. For this reason, some people saw the OverDrive socket as being a way for Intel to sell more CPUs. Some valid reasons exist, however, to use the OverDrive socket and leave the original CPU installed.

One reason is that many PC manufacturers void the system warranty if the CPU has been removed from the system. Also, when systems are serviced, most manufacturers require that the system be returned with only the original parts; you must remove all add-in cards, memory modules, upgrade chips, and similar items before sending the system in for servicing. If you replace the original CPU when you install the upgrade, returning the system to its original condition will be much more difficult.

Another reason for using the upgrade socket is that if the main CPU socket is damaged when you remove the original CPU or install the upgrade processor, the system will not function. By contrast, if a secondary upgrade socket is damaged, the system still should work with the original CPU.

> **Note**
>
> If you think that damaging the socket or chip is not a valid concern, you should know that it typically takes 100 pounds of insertion force to install a chip in a standard 169-pin screw machine socket. With this much force involved, you easily could damage either the chip or socket during the removal or reinstallation process.

Many motherboard manufacturers began using Low Insertion Force (LIF) sockets, which typically require only 60 pounds of insertion force for a 169-pin chip. With the LIF or standard socket, I usually advise removing the motherboard so that you can support the board from behind when you insert the chip. Pressing down on the motherboard with 60 to 100 pounds of force can crack the board if it is not supported properly. A special tool is also required to remove a chip from one of these sockets.

These days, nearly all motherboard manufacturers are using ZIF sockets. These sockets almost eliminate the risk involved in upgrading because no insertion force is necessary to install the chip. Most ZIF sockets are handle-actuated; you simply lift the handle, drop the chip into the socket, and then close the handle. This design makes replacing the original processor with the upgrade processor an easy task. Because it is so simple to perform the upgrade with a ZIF socket, most motherboards that use such a socket have only one processor socket rather than two. This arrangement is a bonus: the unnecessary second socket does not waste the additional motherboard space, and you are forced to remove the otherwise-dormant original processor, which you then can sell or keep as a spare.

OverDrive Processors and Sockets

Intel has stated that all its future processors will have OverDrive versions available for upgrading at a later date. As a result, Intel has developed a series of socket designs that will accommodate not only the original processor with which a system is shipped, but also the future OverDrive processor.

In many cases, the future OverDrive unit will be much more than just the same type of processor running at a higher clock rate. Although the original OverDrive series of processors for the 486SX and 486DX chip simply were clock-doubled versions of essentially the same chips, Intel has since developed OverDrive upgrades that go beyond this level. For example, the company currently has Pentium OverDrive-style single-chip upgrades for some 486 systems, and Pentium-MMX upgrades for existing Pentium systems.

These new processors generally require a larger socket than the original processors they replace; additional pins are reserved for new processors when they are ready. Intel has made available the pin specifications and some functions of the new processors so that motherboard designers can install the proper sockets. Then, all the end user has to do is purchase it and install the new chip in place of the original one. To make the process easy, Intel now requires that all these sockets be of ZIF design.

Intel has created a set of socket designs, named Socket 1 through Socket 8. Each socket is designed to support a different range of original and upgrade processors. Table 6.6 shows the specifications of these sockets.

The original OverDrive socket, now officially called Socket 1, is a 169-pin PGA socket. Motherboards that have this socket can support any of the 486SX, DX, and DX2 processors, as well as the DX2/OverDrive versions. This type of socket is found on most 486 systems that originally were designed for OverDrive upgrades. Figure 6.1 shows the pinout of Socket 1.

The original DX processor draws a maximum 0.9 amps of 5v power in 33MHz form (4.5 watts) and a maximum 1 amp in 50MHz form (5 watts). The DX2 processor or OverDrive processor draws a maximum 1.2 amps at 66MHz (6 watts). This minor increase in power requires only a passive heat sink consisting of aluminum fins that are glued to the processor with thermal transfer epoxy. OverDrive processors rated at 40MHz or less do not have heat sinks.

When the DX2 processor was released, Intel already was working on the new Pentium processor. The company wanted to offer a 32-bit, scaled-down version of the Pentium as an upgrade for systems that originally came with a DX2 processor. Rather than just increasing the clock rate, Intel created an all new chip with enhanced capabilities derived from the Pentium.

Intel Processors **183**

Table 6.6 Intel 486/Pentium CPU Socket Types and Specifications

Socket Number	No. of Pins	Pin Layout	Voltage	Supported Processors
Socket 1	169	17×17 PGA	5v	SX/SX2, DX/DX2*, DX4 OverDrive
Socket 2	238	19×19 PGA	5v	SX/SX2, DX/DX2*, DX4 OverDrive, 486 Pentium OverDrive
Socket 3	237	19×19 PGA	5v/3.3v	SX/SX2, DX/DX2, DX4, 486 Pentium OverDrive
Socket 4	273	21×21 PGA	5v	Pentium 60/66, Pentium 60/66 OverDrive
Socket 5	320	37×37 SPGA	3.3v	Pentium 75-133, Pentium 75+ OverDrive
Socket 6**	235	19×19 PGA	3.3v	DX4, 486 Pentium OverDrive
Socket 7	321	37×37 SPGA	VRM	Pentium 75-200, Pentium 75+ OverDrive
Socket 8	387	dual-pattern SPGA	VRM	Pentium Pro

*DX4 also can be supported with the addition of an aftermarket 3.3v voltage-regulator adapter.
**Socket 6 was a paper standard only and was never actually implemented in any systems.
PGA = Pin Grid Array
SPGA = Staggered Pin Grid Array
VRM = Voltage Regulator Module

FIG. 6.1 Intel Socket 1 pinout.

Chapter 6—Microprocessor Types and Specifications

The chip, called the Pentium OverDrive Processor, plugs into a processor socket with the Socket 2 or Socket 3 design. These sockets will hold any 486 SX, DX, or DX2 processor, as well as the Pentium OverDrive. Because this chip is essentially a 32-bit version of the (normally 64-bit) Pentium chip, many have taken to calling it a *Pentium-SX*. It is available in 25/63MHz and 33/83MHz versions. The first number indicates the base motherboard speed, while the second number indicates the actual operating speed of the Pentium OverDrive chip itself. As you can see, it is a clock multiplied chip that runs at 2.5 times the motherboard speed. Figure 6.2 shows the pinout configuration of the official Socket 2 design.

FIG. 6.2 238-pin Intel Socket 2 configuration.

Notice that although the new chip for Socket 2 is called Pentium OverDrive, it is not a full-scale (64-bit) Pentium. Intel released the design of Socket 2 a little prematurely and found that the chip ran too hot for many systems. The company solved this problem by adding a special active heat sink to the Pentium OverDrive processor. This active heat sink is a combination of a standard heat sink with a built-in electric fan. Unlike the aftermarket glue-on or clip-on fans for processors that you may have seen, this one actually draws 5v power directly from the socket to drive the fan. No external connection to disk drive cables or the power supply is required. The fan/heat sink assembly clips and plugs directly into the processor, providing for easy replacement should the fan ever fail.

Another requirement of the active heat sink is additional clearance—no obstructions for an area about 1.4 inches off the base of the existing socket to allow for heat-sink clearance. In systems that were not designed with this feature, the Pentium OverDrive upgrade will be difficult or impossible.

Another problem with this particular upgrade is power consumption. The 5v Pentium OverDrive processor will draw up to 2.5 amps at 5v (including the fan) or 12.5 watts, which is more than double the 1.2 amps (6 watts) drawn by the DX2 66 processor. Intel did not provide this information when it established the socket design, so the company set up a testing facility to certify systems for thermal and mechanical compatibility with the Pentium OverDrive upgrade. For the greatest peace of mind, ensure that your system is certified compatible before you attempt this upgrade.

Intel's Web site contains a comprehensive list of certified OverDrive compatible systems, available at

http://www.intel.com

On the Web

Figure 6.3 shows the dimensions of the Pentium OverDrive processor and the active heat sink/fan assembly.

FIG. 6.3 The physical dimensions of the Intel Pentium OverDrive processor and active heat sink.

Because of problems with the original Socket 2 specification and the enormous heat the 5v version of the Pentium OverDrive processor generates, Intel came up with an improved design. The new processor is the same as the previous Pentium OverDrive processor, with the exception that it runs on 3.3v and draws a maximum 3.0 amps of 3.3v (9.9 watts) and 0.2 amp of 5v (1 watt) to run the fan, for a total 10.9 watts. This configuration provides a slight margin over the 5v version of this processor. The fan will be easy to remove from the OverDrive processor for replacement, should it ever fail.

To support both the DX4 processor, which runs on 3.3v, and the 3.3v Pentium OverDrive processor, Intel had to create a new socket. In addition to the new 3.3v chips, this new socket supports the older 5v SX, DX, DX2, and even the 5v Pentium OverDrive chip. The design, called Socket 3, is the most flexible upgradable 486 design. Figure 6.4 shows the pinout specification of Socket 3.

Chapter 6—Microprocessor Types and Specifications

FIG. 6.4 237-pin Intel Socket 3 configuration.

Notice that Socket 3 has one additional pin and several others plugged compared with Socket 2. Socket 3 provides for better keying, which prevents an end user from accidentally installing the processor in an improper orientation. One serious problem exists, however: This socket cannot automatically determine the type of voltage that will be provided to it. A jumper is likely to be added on the motherboard near the socket to enable the user to select 5v or 3.3v operation.

> **Caution**
>
> Because this jumper must be manually set, however, a user could install a 3.3v processor in this socket when it is configured for 5v operation. This installation will instantly destroy a very expensive chip when the system is powered on. It will be up to the end user to make sure that this socket is properly configured for voltage, depending on which type of processor is installed. If the jumper is set in 3.3v configuration and a 5v processor is installed, no harm will occur, but the system will not operate properly unless the jumper is reset for 5v.

The original Pentium processor 60MHz and 66MHz versions had 273 pins and would plug into a 273-pin Pentium processor socket—a 5v-only socket, because all the original Pentium processors run on 5v. This socket will accept the original Pentium 60MHz or 66MHz processor, as well as the OverDrive processor. Figure 6.5 shows the pinout specification of Socket 4.

FIG. 6.5 273-pin Intel Socket 4 configuration.

Somewhat amazingly, the original Pentium 66MHz processor consumes up to 3.2 amps of 5v power (16 watts), not including power for a standard active heat sink (fan), whereas the 66 MHz OverDrive processor that replaced it consumes a maximum 2.7 amps (13.5 watts), including about 1 watt to drive the fan. Even the original 60MHz Pentium processor consumes up to 2.91 amps at 5v (14.55 watts). It may seem strange that the replacement processor, which is twice as fast, consumes less power than the original, but this has to do with the manufacturing processes used for the original and OverDrive processors.

Although both processors will run on 5v, the original Pentium processor was created with a circuit size of 0.8 micron, making that processor much more power-hungry than the newer 0.6-micron circuits used in the OverDrive and the other Pentium processors. Shrinking the circuit size is one of the best ways to decrease power consumption. Although the OverDrive processor for Pentium-based systems will indeed draw less power than the original processor, additional clearance may have to be allowed for the active heat sink (fan) assembly that is mounted on top. As in other OverDrive processors with built-in fans, the power to run the fan will be drawn directly from the chip socket, so no separate power-supply connection is required. Also, the fan will be easy to replace should it ever fail.

When Intel redesigned the Pentium processor to run at 75, 90, and 100MHz, the company went to a 0.6-micron manufacturing process as well as 3.3v operation. This change resulted in lower power consumption: only 3.25 amps at 3.3v (10.725 watts). Therefore, the 100MHz Pentium processor can use far less power than even the original 60MHz version. The newest 120 and higher Pentium, Pentium Pro and Pentium II chips use an even smaller die 0.35-micron process. This results in even lower power consumption and allows the extremely high clock rates without overheating.

The Pentium 75 and higher processors actually have 296 pins, although they plug into the official Intel Socket 5 design, which calls for a total 320 pins. The additional pins are used by the Pentium OverDrive for Pentium Processors. This socket has the 320 pins configured in a Staggered Pin Grid Array, in which the individual pins are staggered for tighter clearance.

Several OverDrive processors for existing Pentiums are currently available. If you have a first generation Pentium 60 or 66 with a Socket 4, you can purchase a standard Pentium OverDrive chip that effectively doubles the speed of your old processor. For second-generation 75MHz, 90MHz, and 100MHz Pentiums using Socket 5 or Socket 7, an OverDrive chip with MMX technology is available. Processor speeds after upgrade are 125MHz for the Pentium 75, 150MHz for the Pentium 90, and 166MHz for the Pentium 100. MMX greatly enhances processor performance, particularly under multimedia applications, and is discussed in the section "Pentium-MMX Processors" in this chapter.

Figure 6.6 shows the standard pinout for Socket 5.

The Pentium OverDrive for Pentium Processors has an active heat sink (fan) assembly that draws power directly from the chip socket. The chip requires a maximum 4.33 amps of 3.3v to run the chip (14.289 watts) and 0.2 amp of 5v power to run the fan (1 watt), which means total power consumption of 15.289 watts. This amount is less power than the original 66MHz Pentium processor requires, yet it runs a chip that is as much as four times faster!

The last 486 socket was created especially for the DX4 and the 486 Pentium OverDrive Processor. Socket 6 basically is a slightly redesigned version of Socket 3, which has an additional two pins plugged for proper chip keying. Socket 6 has 235 pins and will accept only 3.3v 486 or OverDrive processors. This means that Socket 6 will accept only the DX4 and the 486 Pentium OverDrive Processor. Because this socket provides only 3.3v, and because the only processors that plug into it are designed to operate on 3.3v, no chance exists that potentially damaging problems will occur, like those with the Socket 3 design. In practice, Socket 6 has seen very limited use. Figure 6.7 shows the Socket 6 pinout.

Socket 7 is essentially the same as Socket 5 with one additional key pin in the opposite inside corner of the existing key pin. Socket 7 therefore has 321 pins total in a 21×21 SPGA (Staggered Pin Grid Array) arrangement. The real difference with Socket 7 is not the socket itself, but with the companion VRM (Voltage Regulator Module) that must accompany it.

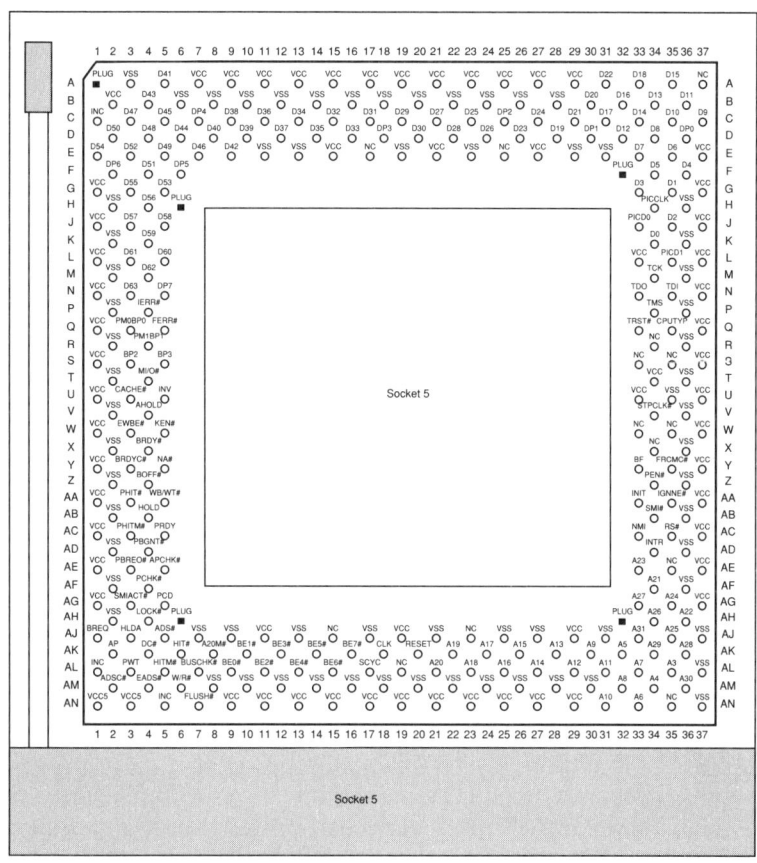

FIG. 6.6 320-pin Intel Socket 5 configuration.

The *VRM* is a small circuit board that contains all the voltage regulation circuitry used to drop the 5v power supply signal to the correct voltage for the processor. The VRM was implemented for several good reasons. One is that voltage regulators tend to run hot and are very failure-prone. By soldering these circuits on the motherboard, as has been done with the Pentium Socket 5 design, you make it very likely that a failure of the regulator will require a complete motherboard replacement. Although technically the regulator could be replaced, many of them are surface-mount soldered, which would make the whole procedure very time-consuming and expensive. Besides, in this day and age, when the top-of-the-line motherboards are only worth $250 (less the processor and any memory), it is just not cost-effective to service them. Having a replaceable VRM plugged into a socket will make it easy to replace the regulators should they ever fail.

Although replaceability is nice, the main reason behind the VRM design is that Intel is building new Pentium processors to run on a variety of voltages. Intel has several different versions of the Pentium, Pentium-MMX, Pentium Pro, and Pentium II processors that run on 3.3v (called *VR*), 3.465v (called *VRE*), as well as 3.1v, 2.8v, and 2.45v.

FIG. 6.7 235-pin Intel Socket 6 configuration.

In other words, if you want to purchase a Pentium board that can be upgraded to the next generation of even higher-speed processors—as well as be easily repairable should the voltage regulators fail—look for a system with a Socket 7 and VRM.

OverDrive Processor Installation. You can upgrade many systems with an OverDrive processor. The most difficult aspect of the installation is simply having the correct OverDrive processor for your system. Currently, 486 Pentium OverDrive processors are available for replacing 486SX and 486DX processors. Pentium and Pentium-MMX OverDrive processors are also available for some Pentium processors. Unfortunately, Intel no longer offers upgrade chips for 168-pin socket boards. The following table lists the current OverDrive processors offered by Intel:

Processor Designation	Replaces	Socket	Heat Sink
486 Pentium OverDrive	486SX/DX/SX2/DX2	Socket 2 or 3	Active
60/66 Pentium OverDrive	Pentium 60/66	Socket 4	Active
Pentium OverDrive with MMX	Pentium 75/90/100	Socket 5/7	Active

Upgrades that use the newer OverDrive chips for Sockets 2 through 7 are likely to be much easier because these chips almost always go into a ZIF socket and therefore require no tools. In most cases, special configuration pins in the socket and on the new OverDrive chips take care of any jumper settings for you. In some cases, however, you may have to set some jumpers on the motherboard to configure the socket for the new processor. If you have an SX system, you also will have to run your system's Setup program because you must inform the CMOS memory that a math coprocessor is present. (Some DX systems also require you to run the setup program.) Intel provides a utility disk that includes a test program to verify that the new chip is installed and functioning correctly.

After verifying that the installation functions correctly, you have nothing more to do. You do not need to reconfigure any of the software on your system for the new chip. The only difference that you should notice is that everything works nearly twice as fast as it did before the upgrade.

OverDrive Compatibility Problems. Although you can upgrade many older 486SX or 486DX systems with the OverDrive processors, some exceptions exist. Four factors can make an OverDrive upgrade difficult or impossible:

- BIOS routines that use CPU-dependent timing loops
- Lack of clearance for the OverDrive heat sink (25MHz and faster)
- Inadequate system cooling
- A 486 CPU that is soldered in rather than socketed

In some rare cases, problems may occur in systems that should be upgradable but are not. One of these problems is related to the ROM BIOS. A few 486 systems have a BIOS that regulates hardware operations by using timing loops based on how long it takes the CPU to execute a series of instructions. When the CPU suddenly is running twice as fast, the prescribed timing interval is too short, resulting in improper system operation or even hardware lockups. Fortunately, you usually can solve this problem by upgrading the system's BIOS, and Intel offers BIOS updates with the OverDrive processors it sells.

Another problem is related to physical clearance. All OverDrive chips have heat sinks glued or fastened to the top of the chip. The heat sink can add 0.25 to 1.2 inches to the top of the chip. This extra height can interfere with other components in the system, especially in small desktop systems and portables. Solutions to this problem must be determined on a case-by-case basis. You can sometimes relocate an expansion card or disk drive, or even modify the chassis slightly to increase clearance. In some cases, the interference cannot be resolved, leaving you only the option of running the chip without the heat sink. Needless to say, removing the glued-on heat sink will at best void the warranty provided by Intel and will at worst damage the chip or the system due to overheating. I do not recommend removing the heat sink.

The OverDrive chips can generate up to twice the heat of the chips that they replace. Even with the active heat sink/fan built into the faster OverDrive chips, some systems do not have enough airflow or cooling capability to keep the OverDrive chip within the prescribed safe operating-temperature range. Small desktop systems or portables are most likely to have cooling problems. Unfortunately, only proper testing can indicate whether a system will have a heat problem. For this reason, Intel has been running an extensive test program to certify systems that are properly designed to handle an OverDrive upgrade.

Finally, some systems have the 486SX or DX chip soldered directly into the motherboard rather than in a socket. This method is used sometimes for cost reasons because leaving out the socket is cheaper; in most cases, however, the reason is clearance. The IBM P75 portable, for example, has a credit card-size CPU board that plugs into the motherboard. Because the CPU card is close to one of the expansion slots, to allow for clearance between the 486 chip and heat sink, IBM soldered the CPU directly into the small card, making an OverDrive upgrade nearly impossible unless IBM offers its own upgrade via a new CPU card with the OverDrive chip already installed.

On the Web

To clarify which systems are tested to be upgradable without problems, Intel has compiled an extensive list of compatible systems. To determine whether a PC is upgradable with an OverDrive processor, contact Intel via its FAXBack system (see the vendor list in Appendix A) and ask for the OverDrive Processor Compatibility Data documents. The information is also available on Intel's Web site, located at **http://www.intel.com/overdrive/upgrade/index.htm**. These documents list the systems that have been tested with the OverDrive processors and indicate which other changes you may have to make for the upgrade to work (for example, a newer ROM BIOS or Setup program).

> **Note**
>
> If your system is not on the list, the warranty on the OverDrive processor is void. Intel recommends OverDrive upgrades only for systems that are in the compatibility list. The list also includes notes about systems that may require a ROM upgrade, a jumper change, or perhaps a new setup disk.

Pentium OverDrive for 486SX2 and DX2 Systems. In 1995, the Pentium OverDrive Processor became available. An OverDrive chip for 486DX4 systems had been planned, but poor marketplace performance of the SX2/DX2 chip meant that it never saw the light of day. One thing to keep in mind about the 486 Pentium OverDrive chip is that although it is intended primarily for SX2 and DX2 systems, it should work in any upgradable 486SX or DX system that has a Socket 2 or Socket 3. If in doubt, check Intel's online upgrade guide for compatibility.

The Pentium OverDrive Processor is designed for systems that have a processor socket that follows the Intel Socket 2 specification. This processor also will work in systems that have a Socket 3 design, although you should ensure that the voltage is set for 5v rather than 3.3v. The Pentium OverDrive chip includes a 32K internal Level 1 cache, and the same superscalar (multiple instruction path) architecture of the real Pentium chip. Besides a 32-bit Pentium core, these processors feature increased clock-speed operation due to internal clock multiplication, and incorporate an internal Write-Back cache (standard with the Pentium). If the motherboard supports the Write-Back cache function, increased performance will be realized. Unfortunately, most motherboards out there, especially older ones with the Socket 2 design, only support Write-Through cache.

Most of the tests of these OverDrive chips show them to be only slightly ahead of the DX4-100 and behind the DX4-120, as well as the true Pentium 60, 66, or 75. Unfortunately, these are the only solutions still offered by Intel for upgrading the 486. Based on the relative affordability today of low-end "real" Pentiums, it seems hard not to justify making the step up to a more modern system. I would not recommend the 486 Pentium OverDrive chips as a viable solution for the future.

Pentium

On October 19, 1992, Intel announced that the fifth generation of its compatible microprocessor line (code-named P5) would be named the Pentium processor rather than the 586, as everybody had been assuming. Calling the new chip the 586 would have been natural, but Intel discovered that it could not trademark a number designation, and the company wanted to prevent other manufacturers from using the same name for any clone chips that they might develop. The actual Pentium chip shipped on March 22, 1993. Systems that use these chips were only a few months behind.

The Pentium is fully compatible with previous Intel processors, but it also differs from them in many ways. At least one of these differences is revolutionary: The Pentium features twin data pipelines, which enable it to execute two instructions at the same time. The 486 and all preceding chips can perform only a single instruction at a time. Intel calls the capability to execute two instructions at the same time *superscalar technology*. This technology provides additional performance compared with the 486.

The standard 486 chip can execute a single instruction in an average of two clock cycles—cut to an average of one clock cycle with the advent of internal clock multiplication used in the DX2 and DX4 processors. With superscalar technology, the Pentium can execute many instructions at a rate of two instructions per cycle. Superscalar architecture usually is associated with high-output RISC (Reduced Instruction Set Computer) chips. The Pentium is one of the first CISC (Complex Instruction Set Computer) chips to be considered to be superscalar. The Pentium is almost like having two 486 chips under the hood. Table 6.7 shows the Pentium processor specifications.

Table 6.7 Pentium Processor Specifications

Introduced:	March 22, 1993 (first generation); March 7, 1994 (second generation)
Maximum rated speeds:	60, 66MHz (first generation); 75, 90, 100, 120, 133, 150, 166, 200MHz (second generation)
CPU clock multiplier:	1x (first generation), 1.5x–3x (second generation)
Register size:	32-bit
External data bus:	64-bit
Memory address bus:	32-bit
Maximum memory:	4G
Integral-cache size:	8K code, 8K data
Integral-cache type:	Two-Way Set Associative, Write-Back Data
Burst-mode transfers:	Yes
Number of transistors:	3.1 million
Circuit size:	0.8 micron (60/66MHz), 0.6 micron (75–100MHz), 0.35 micron (120MHz and up)
External package:	273-pin PGA, 296-pin SPGA, Tape Carrier
Math coprocessor:	Built-in FPU (Floating-Point Unit)
Power management:	SMM (System Management Mode), enhanced in second generation
Operating voltage:	5v (first generation), 3.465v, 3.3v, 3.1v, 2.9v (second generation)

PGA = Pin Grid Array
SPGA = Staggered Pin Grid Array

The two instruction pipelines within the chip are called the u- and v-pipes. The *u-pipe*, which is the primary pipe, can execute all integer and floating-point instructions. The *v-pipe* is a secondary pipe that can execute only simple integer instructions and certain floating-point instructions. The process of operating on two instructions simultaneously in the different pipes is called *pairing*. Not all sequentially executing instructions can be paired, and when pairing is not possible, only the u-pipe is used. To optimize the Pentium's efficiency, you can recompile software to allow more instructions to be paired.

The Pentium is 100 percent software-compatible with the 386 and 486, and although all current software will run much faster on the Pentium, many software manufacturers want to recompile their applications to exploit even more of the Pentium's true power. Intel has developed new compilers that will take full advantage of the chip; the company will license the technology to compiler firms so that software developers can take advantage of the superscalar (parallel processing) capability of the Pentium. This optimization is starting to appear in some of the newest software on the market. Optimized software should improve performance by allowing more instructions to execute simultaneously in both pipes.

To minimize stalls in one or more of the pipes caused by delays in fetching instructions that branch to nonlinear memory locations, the Pentium processor has a Branch Target Buffer (BTB) that employs a technique called *branch prediction*. The BTB attempts to predict whether a program branch will be taken or not and then fetches the appropriate next instructions. The use of branch prediction enables the Pentium to keep both pipelines operating at full speed. Figure 6.8 shows the internal architecture of the Pentium processor.

The Pentium has a 32-bit address bus width, giving it the same 4G memory-addressing capabilities as the 386DX and 486 processors. But the Pentium expands the data bus to 64 bits, which means that it can move twice as much data into or out of the CPU compared with a 486 of the same clock speed. The 64-bit data bus requires that system memory be accessed 64 bits wide, which means that each bank of memory is 64 bits.

On most motherboards, memory is installed via SIMMs (Single In-Line Memory Modules), and SIMMs are available in 9-bit-wide and 36-bit-wide versions. Most Pentium systems use the 36-bit-wide (32 data bits plus 4 parity bits) SIMMs—two of these SIMMs per bank of memory. Most Pentium motherboards have at least four of these 36-bit SIMM sockets, providing for a total of two banks of memory.

Even though the Pentium has a 64-bit data bus that transfers information 64 bits at a time into and out of the processor, the Pentium has only 32-bit internal registers. As instructions are being processed internally, they are broken down into 32-bit instructions and data elements, and processed in much the same way as in the 486. Some people thought that Intel was misleading them by calling the Pentium a 64-bit processor, but 64-bit transfers do indeed take place. Internally, however, the Pentium has 32-bit registers that are fully compatible with the 486.

The Pentium has two separate internal 8K caches, compared with a single 8K or 16K cache in the 486. The cache-controller circuitry and the cache memory are embedded in the CPU chip. The cache mirrors the information in normal RAM by keeping a copy of the data and code from different memory locations. The Pentium cache also can hold information to be written to memory when the load on the CPU and other system components is less. (The 486 makes all memory writes immediately.)

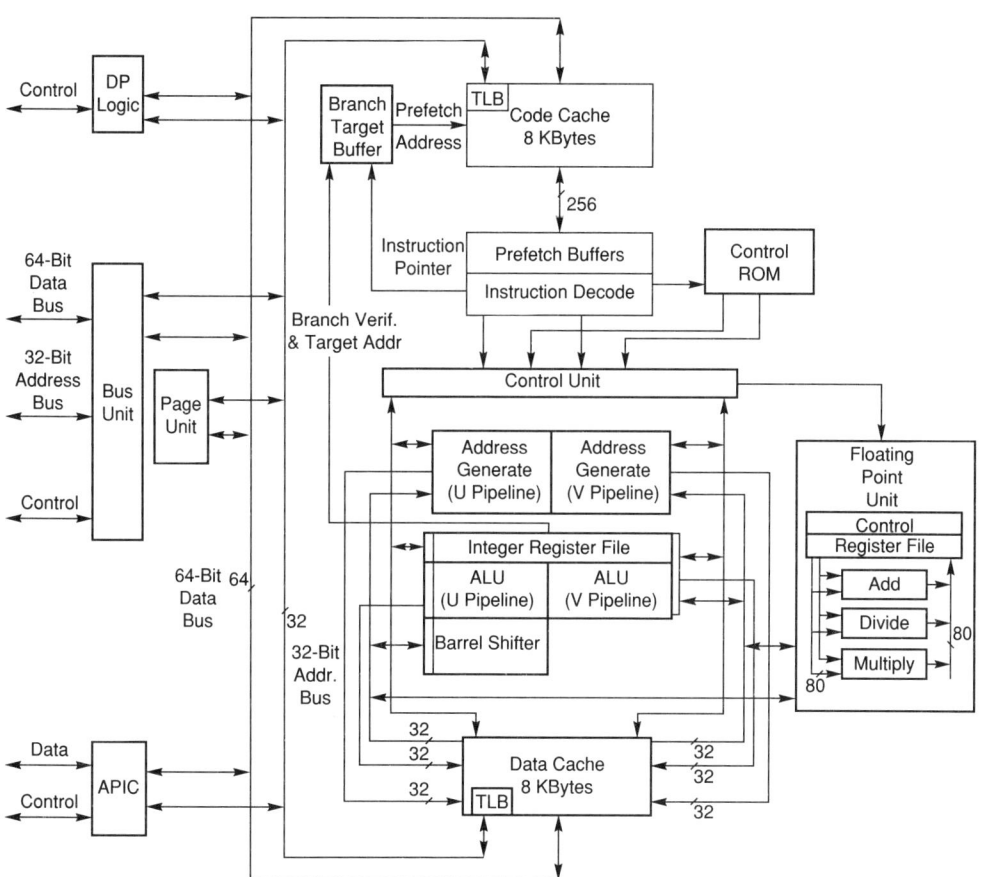

FIG. 6.8 Pentium processor internal architecture.

The separate code and data caches are organized in a two-way set associative fashion, with each set split into lines of 32 bytes each. Each cache has a dedicated Translation Lookaside Buffer (TLB), which translates linear addresses to physical addresses. You can configure the data cache as Write-Back or Write-Through on a line-by-line basis. When you use the Write-Back capability, the cache can store write operations as well as reads, further improving performance over read-only Write-Through mode. Using Write-Back mode results in less activity between the CPU and system memory—an important improvement, because CPU access to system memory is a bottleneck on fast systems. The code cache is an inherently write-protected cache because it contains only execution instructions and not data, which is updated. Because burst cycles are used, the cache data can be read or written very quickly.

Systems based on the Pentium can benefit greatly from secondary processor caches (Level 2), which usually consist of up to 512K or more of extremely fast (15 ns or less) Static RAM (SRAM) chips. When the CPU fetches data that is not already available in its internal processor (Level 1) cache, wait states slow the CPU. If the data already is in the secondary processor cache, however, the CPU can go ahead with its work without pausing for wait states.

The Pentium uses a BiCMOS (Bipolar Complementary Metal Oxide Semiconductor) process and superscalar architecture to achieve the high level of performance expected from the chip. BiCMOS adds about 10 percent to the complexity of the chip design, but adds about 30 to 35 percent better performance without a size or power penalty.

All Pentium processors are SL Enhanced, meaning that they incorporate the SMM to provide full control of power-management features, which helps reduce power consumption. The second-generation Pentium processors (75MHz and faster) incorporate a more advanced form of SMM that includes processor clock control. This enables you to throttle the processor up or down to control power use. With these more advanced Pentium processors, you can even stop the clock, putting the processor in a state of suspension that requires very little power. The second-generation Pentium processors run on 3.3v power (instead of 5v), reducing power requirements and heat generation even further.

Many current motherboards supply either 3.465v or 3.3v. The 3.465v setting is called *VRE (Voltage Reduced Extended)* by Intel and is required by some versions of the Pentium, particularly some of the 100MHz versions. The standard 3.3v setting is called *STD (Standard)*, which most of the second-generation Pentiums use. STD voltage means anything in a range from 3.135v to 3.465v with 3.3v nominal. There is also a special 3.3v setting called *VR (Voltage Reduced)*, which reduces the range from 3.300v to 3.465v with 3.38v nominal. Some of the processors require this narrower specification, which most motherboards provide. Here is a summary:

Voltage Specification	**Nominal**	**Tolerance**	**Minimum**	**Maximum**
STD (Standard)	3.30v	±0.165	3.135v	3.465v
VR (Voltage Reduced)	3.38v	±0.083	3.300v	3.465v
VRE (VR Extended)	3.50v	±0.100	3.400v	3.600v

For even lower power consumption, Intel has introduced special Pentium processors with Voltage Reduction Technology in the 75//100/120/133/150MHz family intended for mobile computer applications. These do not use a conventional chip package and are instead mounted using a new format called *Tape Carrier Packaging (TCP)*. The tape carrier packaging does not encase the chip in ceramic or plastic as with a conventional chip package, but instead covers the actual processor die directly with a thin, protective plastic coating. The entire processor is less than 1mm thick, or about half the thickness of a dime, and weighs less than 1 gram. They are sold to system manufacturers in a roll that looks very much like a filmstrip. The TCP processor is directly affixed (soldered) to the motherboard by a special machine, resulting in a smaller package, lower height, better thermal transfer, and lower power consumption. Special solder plugs on the circuit board located directly under the processor draw heat away and provide better cooling in the tight confines of a typical notebook or laptop system, and no cooling fans are required.

The Pentium, like the 486, contains an internal math coprocessor or Floating-Point Unit (FPU). The FPU in the Pentium has been rewritten and performs significantly better than the FPU in the 486, yet it is fully compatible with the 486 and 387 math coprocessor. The Pentium FPU is estimated to be two to as much as 10 times faster than the FPU in the 486. In addition, the two standard instruction pipelines in the Pentium provide two units to handle standard integer math. (The math coprocessor handles only more complex calculations.) Other processors, such as the 486, have only a single standard execution pipe and one integer-math unit. Interestingly, the Pentium FPU contains a flaw that received widespread publicity. See our discussion in the section "Pentium Defects" later in this chapter.

First-Generation Pentium Processor. The Pentium has been offered in two basic designs, each with several versions. The first-generation design, which is no longer available, came in 60 and 66MHz processor speeds. This design used a 273-pin PGA form factor and ran on 5v power. In this design, the processor ran at the same speed as the motherboard—in other words, a 1x clock is used.

The first-generation Pentium was created through an 0.8-micron BiCMOS process. Unfortunately, this process, combined with the 3.1 million transistor count, resulted in a die that was overly large and complicated to manufacture. As a result, reduced yields kept the chip in short supply; Intel could not make them fast enough. The 0.8-micron process was criticized by other manufacturers, including Motorola and IBM, which had been using 0.6-micron technology for their most advanced chips. The huge die and 5v operating voltage caused the 66MHz versions to consume up to an incredible 3.2 amps or 16 watts of power, resulting in a tremendous amount of heat—and problems in some systems that did not employ conservative design techniques. Often, the system required a separate fan to blow on the processor to keep it cool.

Much of the criticism leveled at Intel for the first-generation Pentium was justified. Some people realized that the first-generation design was just that; they knew that new Pentium versions, made in a more advanced manufacturing process, were coming. Many of those people advised against purchasing any Pentium system until the second-generation version became available.

> **Tip**
>
> A cardinal rule of computing is never to buy the first generation of any processor. Although you can wait forever because something better always will be on the horizon, a little waiting is worthwhile in some cases.

If you do have one of these first-generation Pentiums, do not despair. As with previous 486 systems, Intel offers OverDrive upgrade chips that effectively double the processor speed of your Pentium 60 or 66. These are a single chip upgrade, meaning they replace your existing CPU. Because subsequent Pentiums are incompatible with the Pentium

60/66 Socket 4 arrangement, these OverDrive chips are the only viable way to upgrade an existing first-generation Pentium without replacing the motherboard.

Second-Generation Pentium Processor. Intel announced the second-generation Pentium on March 7, 1994. This new processor was introduced in 90 and 100MHz versions, with a 75MHz version not far behind. Eventually, 120, 133, 150, 166, and 200MHz versions were also introduced. The second-generation Pentium uses 0.6-micron (75/90/100MHz) BiCMOS technology to shrink the die and reduce power consumption. The newer, faster 120 and higher MHz second-generation versions incorporate an even smaller die built on a 0.35-micron BiCMOS process. These smaller dies are not changed from the 0.6-micron versions, they are basically a photographic reduction of the P54C die. Additionally, these new processors run on 3.3v power. The 100MHz version consumes a maximum 3.25 amps of 3.3v power, which equals only 10.725 watts. Farther up the scale, the 150MHz chip uses 3.5 amps of 3.3v power (11.6 watts); the 166MHz unit draws 4.4 amps (14.5 watts); and the 200MHz processor uses 4.7 amps (15.5 watts).

The second-generation Pentium processors come in a 296-pin SPGA (Staggered Pin Grid Array) form factor that is physically incompatible with the first-generation versions. The only way to upgrade from the first generation to the second is to replace the motherboard. The second-generation Pentium processors also have 3.3 million transistors—more than the earlier chips. The extra transistors exist because additional clock-control SL enhancements were added, as were an on-chip Advanced Programmable Interrupt Controller (APIC) and dual-processor interface.

The APIC and dual-processor interface are responsible for orchestrating dual-processor configurations in which two second-generation Pentium chips can process on the same motherboard simultaneously. Many of the new Pentium motherboards come with dual Socket 7 specification sockets, which fully support the multiprocessing capability of the new chips. Already, software support for what usually is called Symmetric Multi-Processing (SMP) is being integrated into operating systems such as Windows NT and OS/2.

The second-generation Pentium processors use clock-multiplier circuitry to run the processor at speeds faster than the bus. The 150MHz Pentium processor, for example, can run at 2.5 times the bus frequency, which normally is 60MHz. The 200MHz Pentium processor can run at a 3x clock in a system using a 66MHz bus speed.

> **Note**
>
> Currently, running the motherboard faster than 66MHz is impractical because of memory and local-bus performance constraints.

Virtually all Pentium motherboards have three speed settings: 50, 60, and 66MHz. Pentium chips are available with a variety of different internal clock multipliers that cause the processor to operate at various multiples of these motherboard speeds. The following table lists the speeds of currently available Pentium processors and motherboards.

CPU Type/Speed	CPU Clock	Motherboard Speed
Pentium 75	1.5x	50
Pentium 90	1.5x	60
Pentium 100	1.5x	66
Pentium 120	2x	60
Pentium 133	2x	66
Pentium 150	2.5x	60
Pentium 166	2.5x	66
Pentium 200	3x	66

The Core-to-Bus frequency ratio or clock multiplier is controlled in a Pentium processor by two pins on the chip labeled BF1 and BF2. The following table shows how the state of the BFx pins will affect the clock multiplication in the Pentium processor.

BF1	BF2	Clock Multiplier	Bus Speed (MHz)	Core Speed (MHz)
0	1	3x	66	200
0	1	3x	60	180
0	1	3x	50	150
0	0	2.5x	66	166
0	0	2.5x	60	150
0	0	2.5x	50	125
1	0	2x	66	133
1	0	2x	60	120
1	0	2x	50	100
1	1	1.5x	66	100
1	1	1.5x	60	90
1	1	1.5x	50	75

Not all chips support the Bus Frequency (BF) pins. In other words, some of the Pentium processors will operate only at specific combinations of these settings, or maybe even fixed at one particular setting. Many of the newer motherboards have jumpers or switches that enable you to control the BF pins and therefore alter the clock multiplier ratio within the chip. In theory, you could run a 75MHz-rated Pentium chip at 133MHz by simply changing jumpers on the motherboard. This is called *overclocking*, and is discussed in the "Processor Speed Ratings" section of this chapter.

Now that the second-generation Pentium processors have become the industry standard, and the newer Pentium Pro, Pentium-MMX, and Pentium II processors are hitting the market at the high end, the time is right to economically purchase Pentium systems. The ideal system today uses the second-generation 133/166/200MHz processor with a 66MHz motherboard bus speed.

A single chip OverDrive upgrade is currently offered for second-generation Pentiums running at 75, 90, and 100MHz. These OverDrive chips replace the existing Socket 5 or 7

CPU, and increase processor speed by a factor of 1.66x. Simply stated, this means that a Pentium 75 system equipped with the OverDrive chip will have a processor speed of 125MHz, while a Pentium 100 system is upgradable to 166MHz. Perhaps the best feature of these Pentium OverDrive chips is that they incorporate MMX technology. MMX provides greatly enhanced performance while running the multimedia applications that are becoming so popular today. At present, OverDrive chips are not available for any of the faster Pentium chips, although Intel claims that the others (except the 200MHz chip) will be OverDrive-upgradable eventually.

Pentium-MMX Processors. A third generation of Pentium processors (code-named P55C) was released in January 1997, which incorporates what Intel calls *MMX technology* into the second-generation Pentium design. These Pentium-MMX processors are available in clock rates of 66/166MHz, 66/200MHz, and 66/233MHz. The MMX processors share much in common with other second-generation Pentiums, including superscalar architecture, multi-processor support, on-chip local APIC controller, and power management features. New features include a pipelined MMX unit, 16K code and Write-Back cache (versus 8K in earlier Pentiums), and 4.5 million transistors. Pentium-MMX chips are produced on an enhanced 0.35-micron CMOS silicon process which allows for a lower 2.8v voltage level.

In order to use the Pentium-MMX, the motherboard must be able to supply the lower 2.8v these processors use. To allow a more universal motherboard solution with respect to these changing voltages, Intel has come up with the Socket 7 with VRM. The VRM is a socketed module that plugs in next to the processor and supplies the correct voltage. Because the module is easily replaced, it is easy to reconfigure a motherboard to support any of the voltages required by the newer Pentium processors.

Of course, lower voltage is nice, but MMX is what this chip is really all about. MMX technology was developed by Intel as a direct response to the growing importance and increasing demands of multimedia and communication applications. Many such applications run repetitive loops of instructions that consume vast amounts of time to execute. As a result, MMX incorporates a process Intel calls *Single Instruction Multiple Data (SIMD)* that allows one instruction to perform the same function on many pieces of data. Furthermore, 57 new instructions have been added to the chip that are designed specifically to handle video, audio, and graphics data.

If you want maximum future upgradability to the MMX Pentiums, make sure that your Pentium motherboard includes 321-pin processor sockets that fully meet the Intel Socket 7 specification. These would also include the VRM (Voltage Regulator Module) socket. If you have dual sockets, you can add a second Pentium processor to take advantage of SMP (Symmetric Multi-Processing) support in some newer operating systems.

Also, make sure that any Pentium motherboard you buy can be jumpered or reconfigured for both 60 and 66MHz operation. This will enable you to take advantage of future Pentium OverDrive processors that will support the higher motherboard clock speeds. These simple recommendations will enable you to perform several dramatic upgrades without changing the entire motherboard.

Pentium Pro Processor

Intel's successor to the Pentium is called the *Pentium Pro*. The Pentium Pro was introduced in September of 1995, and became widely available in 1996. The chip itself is a 387-pin unit that resides in Socket 8, so it is not pin-compatible with earlier Pentiums. The new chip is unique among processors as it is constructed in a Multi-Chip Module (MCM) physical format, which Intel is calling a *Dual Cavity PGA (Pin Grid Array)* package. Inside the 387-pin chip carrier are two dies, one containing the actual Pentium Pro processor, and the other a 256K or 512K L2 cache. The processor die contains 5.5 million transistors, the 256K cache die contains 15.5 million transistors, and the 512K cache die has 31 million transistors, for a potential total of 36.5 million transistors in a complete 512K module!

The architecture of the Pentium Pro includes three internal instruction pipes, which can execute multiple instructions in one cycle. The main processor die includes a 16K split L1 cache with an 8K two-way set associative cache for primary instructions, and an 8K four-way set associative cache for data. The Pentium Pro can execute instructions out of order and has dynamic branch prediction and speculative execution capabilities. These techniques are collectively referred to by Intel as *Dynamic Execution*. Table 6.8 shows Pentium Pro processor specifications.

Table 6.8 Pentium Pro Processor Specifications

Introduced:	September 1995
Maximum rated speeds:	150, 166, 180, 200MHz
CPU clock multiplier:	2.5x–3x
Register size:	32-bit
External data bus:	64-bit
Integrated-cache bus:	64-bit
Memory address bus:	32-bit
Maximum memory:	4G
Integral-cache size:	8K code, 8K data
Integral-cache type:	non-blocking, L1 cache
Number of transistors:	5.5 million
Transistors in L2 cache:	15.5 million (256K cache), 31 million (512K cache)
Circuit size:	0.35 micron
External package:	387-pin Dual Cavity PGA (Pin Grid Array)
Math coprocessor:	Built-in FPU (Floating-Point Unit)
Power management:	SMM (System Management Mode)
Operating voltage:	3.3v

In many ways, the Pentium Pro seems to be more of an evolutionary design compared to the Pentium rather than something totally new. The core of the chip is very RISC (Reduced Instruction Set Computer)-like, while the external instruction interface is classic Intel CISC (Complex Instruction Set Computer). By breaking down the CISC instructions into several different RISC instructions and running them down parallel execution pipelines, the overall performance is increased.

Compared to the Pentium, the Pentium Pro is faster—as long as you're running 32-bit software. The Pro's Dynamic Execution is maximized for performance primarily when running 32-bit software such as Windows NT. If you are using 16-bit software, such as Windows 95 (which operates part-time in a 16-bit environment) and most older applications, the Pentium Pro will not provide a marked performance improvement over similarly speed rated Pentium and Pentium-MMX processors. Because of this, Windows NT is often regarded as the mandatory operating system for use with Pentium Pros. Although this is not exactly true (a Pentium Pro will run just fine under Windows 95), it is the only way to truly take advantage of the Pro's capabilities.

As we saw in Table 6.3, performance comparisons on the iCOMP 2.0 Index rate a classic Pentium 200MHz at 142, whereas a Pentium Pro 200MHz scores an impressive 220. Just for comparison, note that a Pentium MMX 200MHz falls right about in the middle performance-wise at 182. Keep in mind that using a Pentium Pro with Windows 95 or other 16-bit software will nullify much of the performance gain shown by the iCOMP 2.0 rating. The following table lists speeds for Pentium Pro processors and motherboards:

CPU Type/Speed	**CPU Clock**	**Motherboard Speed**
Pentium Pro 150	2.5x	60
Pentium Pro 166	2.5x	66
Pentium Pro 180	3x	60
Pentium Pro 200	3x	66

The integrated L2 cache is one of the really outstanding features of the Pentium Pro. By building the L2 cache into the CPU and getting it off the motherboard, they can now run the cache at full processor speed rather than the slower 60 or 66MHz motherboard bus speeds. In fact, the L2 cache features its own internal 64-bit backside bus, which does not share time with the external 64-bit frontside bus used by the CPU. The internal registers and data paths are still 32-bit as with the Pentium. By building the L2 cache into the system, motherboards can be cheaper because they no longer require separate cache memory. Some boards may still try to include cache memory in their design, but the general consensus is that Level 3 cache (as it would be called) would offer less improvement with the Pentium Pro than with the Pentium.

One of the features of the built-in L2 cache is that multiprocessing is greatly improved. Rather than just SMP, as with the Pentium, the Pentium Pro supports a new type of multiprocessor configuration called the *Multiprocessor Specification (MPS 1.1)*. The Pentium Pro with MPS allows configurations of up to four processors running together. Unlike other multiprocessor configurations, the Pentium Pro avoids cache coherency problems because each chip maintains a separate L1 and L2 cache internally.

Pentium Pro-based motherboards are pretty much exclusively PCI and ISA bus based, and Intel is producing their own chipsets for these motherboards. The first chipset was called Orion, while the newest version is called Natoma. Along with the new chipsets, Intel created a motherboard form factor change for Pentium Pro boards. The new form factor is called ATX, and is different from the Baby-AT form factor used by most

PC-compatibles in the past. The ATX form factor is about the same 9×13-inch size as the Baby-AT, but the board is turned 90 degrees from the way the Baby-AT boards mount. In other words, the long side is now against the back of the case, and the expansion slots will be parallel with the short side of the board. The main reason for the new form factor is to move the CPU to an area where expansion cards will not be located, which should allow much better cooling. Baby-AT based systems with the CPU under the slots can have problems in this area, sometimes preventing one from using all the available bus slots.

Another benefit of the ATX form factor is that the long edge of the board is against the back of the case, allowing room for many built-in connectors. ATX boards are highly integrated, featuring built-in dual serial ports, a parallel port, floppy controller, dual enhanced IDE ports, integrated sound, SVGA video, and optional SCSI and networking interfaces. Of course, this new motherboard form factor requires re-tooled cases, although Baby-AT power supplies can still be used. Intel is sharing the specifications of the new ATX form factor, and many other motherboard manufacturers already have designs ready. ATX boards have begun to show up on non-Pentium Pro systems, although the new NLX form factor may displace the emerging popularity of the ATX in the near future.

Some Pentium Pro system manufacturers have been tempted to stick with the Baby-AT form factor. The big problem with the standard Baby-AT form factor is keeping the CPU properly cooled. The massive Pentium Pro processor consumes more than 25 watts and generates an appreciable amount of heat.

Pentium II

Intel revealed its latest processor in May 1997 when it pulled the wraps off the Pentium II. Prior to its official unveiling, the Pentium II processor was popularly referred to by its code name "Klamath," and was surrounded by much speculation throughout the industry. From a physical standpoint, it is truly something new. The chip is characterized by its Single Edge Contact (SEC) cartridge and large heat sink. The processor mounts to its own little board—along with the L2 cache—which is then plugged into the motherboard through an edge connector, much like a PCI I/O card. Intel developed the new NLX motherboard form factor to go along with the Pentium II. Several manufacturers currently offer Pentium II motherboards that are based on the ATX form factor, but I would not recommend buying them because of space limitations. The ones I have seen only have two SIMM sockets, which is not acceptable. At present, Intel is offering Pentium II processors with the following speeds:

CPU Type/Speed	CPU Clock	Motherboard Speed
Pentium II 233	3.5x	66
Pentium II 266	4x	66
Pentium II 300	4.5x	66

These are some very fast processors, at least for now. As Table 6.3 shows, the iCOMP 2.0 Index rating for the Pentium II 266MHz chip is more than twice as fast as a classic Pentium 200MHz. Aside from speed, one way to think of the Pentium II is as a Pentium

Pro with MMX technology instructions. It has the same multiprocessor scalability as the Pentium Pro, as well as the integrated L2 cache. Also included are the 57 new multi-media-related instructions carried over from the MMX processors, and the ability to process repetitive loop commands more efficiently.

All Pentium II processors are still manufactured with the 0.35 micron process. Some have speculated about the possibility of 0.25 micron manufacturing techniques being put into use soon, but it has yet to materialize publicly. Maximum current draw for the 233MHz CPU is 11.8 amps; the 266MHz chip draws 12.7 amps; and the 300MHz unit takes 14.2 amps. At the 2.8v CPU voltage all Pentium II processors run on, wattage is in excess of 30 watts for all Pentium IIs. Table 6.9 shows Pentium II processor specifications.

Table 6.9 Pentium II Processor Specifications

Introduced:	May 1997
Maximum rated speeds:	233, 266, 300MHz
CPU clock multiplier:	3.5x, 4x–4.5x
Internal bus width:	300-bit
External data bus:	64-bit
Integrated-cache bus:	64-bit
Memory address bus:	32-bit
Maximum memory:	64G
Integral-cache size:	16K code, 16K data
Integral-cache type:	non-blocking, L1 cache
Number of transistors:	7.5 million
L2 cache size:	512K
Transistors in L2 cache:	31 million
Circuit size:	0.35 micron
External package:	242-pin Single Edge Cartridge
Math coprocessor:	Built-in FPU (Floating-Point Unit)
Power management:	SMM (System Management Mode)
Operating voltage:	2.8v

As you can see from the table, the Pentium II can handle up to 64G of physical memory. In addition, the CPU incorporates Dual Independent Bus architecture. This means the chip has two independent buses: one for accessing the L2 cache, the other for accessing main memory. These dual buses can operate simultaneously, greatly accelerating the flow of data within the system. Intel claims that this architecture allows up to three times the bandwidth of normal single bus processors. At any rate, the Pentium II looks to be the new industry standard—for now.

Intel-Compatible Processors

Several companies—mainly AMD and Cyrix—have developed processors that are compatible with Intel processors. These chips are fully Intel-compatible, which means that they emulate every processor instruction in the Intel chips. Most of the chips are pin-compatible, which means that they can be used in any system designed to accept an Intel processor; others require a custom motherboard design. Any hardware or software that works on Intel-based PCs will work on PCs made with these third-party CPU chips. There are a number of companies that currently offer Intel-compatible chips, and we will discuss some of the most popular ones here.

AMD Processors

Advanced Micro Designs (AMD) has become a major player in the Pentium-compatible chip market with their own line of Intel-compatible processors. AMD ran into trouble with Intel several years ago because their 486-clone chips used actual Intel microcode. These differences have been settled and AMD now has a five-year cross license agreement with Intel. In 1996, AMD finalized a deal to absorb NexGen, another maker of Intel-compatible CPUs. AMD currently offers a wide variety of CPUs, from 486 upgrades to the MMX capable K6. The following table lists the basic processors offered by AMD and their Intel socket:

CPU	Clock Speed	Socket
Am486DX4-100	100	Socket 1,2,3
Am486DX4-120	120	Socket 1,2,3
Am5x86	75	Socket 1,2,3
K5 PR75	75	Socket 5,7
K5 PR90	90	Socket 5,7
K5 PR100	100	Socket 5,7
K5 PR120	90	Socket 5,7
K5 PR133	100	Socket 5,7
K5 PR166	116.66	Socket 5,7
K6-166 MMX	166	Socket 7
K6-200 MMX	200	Socket 7
K6-233 MMX	233	Socket 7

Notice in the table that for the K5 PR120 through PR166 the model designation does not match the CPU clock speed. The later K5 chips benefit from improved design, so they run faster at a given clock speed. The model designations are meant to represent performance comparable with an equivalent Pentium-based system. AMD chips, particularly the new K6, have typically fared well in performance comparisons, and usually have a much lower cost.

You can get complete product information from AMD's Web page at

http://www.amd.com

On the Web

Cyrix

Like Intel, Cyrix has begun to limit its selection of available CPUs to only the latest technology. Cyrix is currently focusing on the Pentium market with the M1 (6x86 and 6x86MX) and M2 processors. The M1 has 3.3 million transistors and was initially manufactured on a 0.65-micron process. The 6x86 has dual internal pipelines and a single unified 16K internal cache. It offers speculative and out of order instruction execution, much like the Intel Pentium Pro processor. The 6x86MX adds MMX technology to the CPU. The chip is Socket 7-compatible, but some require modified chipsets and new motherboard designs. The following table lists Cyrix M1 processors and bus speeds:

CPU Type/Speed	Clock Speed	CPU Clock	Motherboard Speed
6x86-PR120	100	2x	50
6x86-PR133	110	2x	55*
6x86-PR150	120	2x	60
6x86-PR166	133	2x	66
6x86-PR200	150	2x	75**
6x86MX-PR166	150	2.5x	60
6x86MX-PR200	166	2.5x	66
6x86MX-PR233	188	2.5x	75**

*Not all motherboards support a 55MHz bus speed.
**This 75MHz bus speed requires a special motherboard and chipset.

Cyrix recently announced its latest chip, the M2. The M2 features 64K of unified L1 cache and more than double the performance of 6x86 CPUs. The M2 will be offered in clock speeds ranging from 180 to 225MHz, and like M1 chips it is Socket 7-compatible. All Cyrix chips are manufactured by IBM, who also markets the clone chips under its own name.

Math Coprocessors

The next several sections cover the math coprocessor. Older central processing units designed by Intel (and cloned by other companies) can use a math-coprocessor chip. However, when Intel introduced the 486DX they included a built-in math coprocessor, and every processor built by Intel (and AMD and Cyrix for that matter) since then includes a math coprocessor. Coprocessors provide hardware for floating-point math, which otherwise would create an excessive drain on the main CPU. Math chips speed your computer's operation only when you are running software designed to take advantage of the coprocessor.

Math chips (as coprocessors sometimes are called) can perform high-level mathematical operations—long division, trigonometric functions, roots, and logarithms, for example—at 10 to 100 times the speed of the corresponding main processor. The integer units in the primary CPU work with real numbers, so they perform addition, subtraction, and multiplication operations. The primary CPU is designed to handle such computations; these operations are not offloaded to the math chip.

The instruction set of the math chip is different from that of the primary CPU. A program must detect the existence of the coprocessor and then execute instructions written explicitly for that coprocessor; otherwise, the math coprocessor draws power and does nothing else. Fortunately, most modern programs that can benefit from the use of the coprocessor correctly detect and use the coprocessor. These programs usually are math-intensive programs: spreadsheet programs, database applications, statistical programs, and graphics programs, such as computer-aided design (CAD) software. Word processing programs do not benefit from a math chip and therefore are not designed to use one. Table 6.10 summarizes the coprocessors available for the Intel family of processors.

Table 6.10 Math Coprocessor Summary

Processor	Coprocessor
8086	8087
8088	8087
80286	80287
80386SX	80387SX
80386SL	80387SX
80386SLC	80387SX
80486SLC	80387SX
80486SLC2	80387SX
80386DX	80387DX
80486SX	80487SX, DX2/OverDrive*
80487SX*	Built-in FPU
80486SX2	DX2/OverDrive**
80486DX	Built-in FPU
80486DX2	Built-in FPU
80486DX4	Built-in FPU
Pentium/Pentium-MMX	Built-in FPU
Pentium Pro	Built-in FPU
Pentium II	Built-in FPU

FPU = Floating-Point Unit
*The 487SX chip is a modified pinout 486DX chip with the math coprocessor enabled. When you plug in a 487SX chip, it disables the 486SX main processor and takes over all processing.
**The DX2/OverDrive is equivalent to the SX2 with the addition of a functional FPU.

Within each 8087 group, the maximum speed of the math chips varies. A suffix digit after the main number, as shown in Table 6.11, indicates the maximum speed at which a system can run a math chip.

Table 6.11 Maximum Math Chip Speeds

Part	Speed	Part	Speed
8087	5MHz	80287	6MHz
8087-3	5MHz	80287-6	6MHz
8087-2	8MHz	80287-8	8MHz
8087-1	10MHz	80287-10	10MHz

The 387 math coprocessors, as well as the 486 or 487 and Pentium processors, always indicate their maximum speed rating in MHz in the part-number suffix. A 486DX2-66, for example, is rated to run at 66MHz. Some processors incorporate clock multiplication, which means that they may run at different speeds compared with the rest of the system.

> **Tip**
>
> The performance increase in programs that use the math chip can be dramatic—usually, a geometric increase in speed occurs. If the primary applications that you use can take advantage of a math coprocessor, you should upgrade your system to include one.

Most systems that use the 386 or earlier processors are socketed for a math coprocessor as an option, but they do not include a coprocessor as standard equipment. A few systems on the market don't even have a socket for the coprocessor because of cost and size considerations. Usually, these systems are low-cost or portable systems, such as older laptops, the IBM PS/1, and the PCjr. For more specific information about math coprocessors, see the discussions of the specific chips—8087, 287, 387, and 487SX—in the following sections. Table 6.12 shows some of the specifications of the various math coprocessors.

Table 6.12 Intel Math Coprocessor Specifications

Name	Power Consumption	Case Min. Temp.	Case Max. Temp.	No. of Transistors	Date Introduced
8087	3 watts	0°C, 32°F	85°C, 185°F	45,000	1980
287	3 watts	0°C, 32°F	85°C, 185°F	45,000	1982
287XL	1.5 watts	0°C, 32°F	85°C, 185°F	40,000	1990
387SX	1.5 watts	0°C, 32°F	85°C, 185°F	120,000	1988
387DX	1.5 watts	0°C, 32°F	85°C, 185°F	120,000	1987

Most often, you can learn what CPU and math coprocessor are installed in a particular system by checking the system documentation. The following sections examine the Intel family of CPUs and math coprocessors in more detail.

8087 Coprocessor

Intel introduced the 8086 processor in 1976. The math coprocessor that was paired with the chip—the 8087—often was called the numeric data processor (NDP), the math coprocessor, or simply the math chip. The 8087 is designed to perform high-level math operations at many times the speed and accuracy of the main processor. The primary advantage of using this chip is the increased execution speed in number-crunching programs, such as spreadsheet applications. Using the 8087 has several minor disadvantages, however, including software support, cost, power consumption, and heat production.

The primary disadvantage of installing the 8087 chip is that you notice an increase in speed only in programs written to use this coprocessor—and then not in all operations. Only math-intensive programs such as spreadsheet programs, statistical programs, CAD software, and engineering software support the chip. Even then, the effects vary from application to application, and support is limited to specific areas. For example, versions of Lotus 1-2-3 that support the coprocessor do not use the coprocessor for common operations, such as addition, subtraction, multiplication, and division.

Applications that usually do not use the 8087 at all include word processing programs, telecommunications software, and database programs.

80287 Coprocessor

The 80287, internally, is the same math chip as the 8087, although the pins used to plug them into the motherboard are different. Both the 80287 and the 8087 operate as though they were identical.

In most systems, the 80286 internally divides the system clock by 2 to derive the processor clock. The 80287 internally divides the system-clock frequency by 3. For this reason, most AT-type computers run the 80287 at one-third the system clock rate, which also is two-thirds the clock speed of the 80286. Because the 286 and 287 chips are asynchronous, the interface between the 286 and 287 chips is not as efficient as with the 8088 and 8087.

In summary, the 80287 and the 8087 chips perform about the same at equal clock rates. The original 80287 is not better than the 8087 in any real way—unlike the 80286, which is superior to the 8086 and 8088. In most AT systems, the performance gain that you realize by adding the coprocessor is much less substantial than the same type of upgrade for PC- or XT-type systems, or for the 80386.

80387 Coprocessor

Although the 80387 chips run asynchronously, 386 systems are designed so that the math chip runs at the same clock speed as the main CPU. Unlike the 80287 coprocessor, which was merely an 8087 with different pins to plug into the AT motherboard, the 80387 coprocessor is a high-performance math chip designed specifically to work with the 386.

All 387 chips use a low-power-consumption CMOS design. The 387 coprocessor has two basic designs: the 387DX coprocessor, which is designed to work with the 386DX processor; and the 387SX coprocessor, which is designed to work with the 386SX, SL, or SLC processors.

Intel originally offered several speeds for the 387DX coprocessor. But when the company designed the 33MHz version, a smaller mask was required to reduce the lengths of the signal pathways in the chip. This increased the performance of the chip by roughly 20 percent.

> **Note**
>
> Because Intel lagged in developing the 387 coprocessor, some early 386 systems were designed with a socket for a 287 coprocessor. Performance levels associated with that union, however, leave much to be desired.

Installing a 387DX is easy, but you must be careful to orient the chip in its socket properly; otherwise, the chip will be destroyed. The most common cause of burned pins on the 387DX is incorrect installation. In many systems, the 387DX is oriented differently from other large chips. Follow the manufacturer's installation instructions carefully to avoid damaging the 387DX; Intel's warranty does not cover chips that are installed incorrectly.

Several manufacturers have developed their own versions of the Intel 387 coprocessors, some of which are touted as being faster than the original Intel chips. The general compatibility record of these chips is very good.

Weitek Coprocessors

In 1981, several Intel engineers formed Weitek Corporation. Weitek has developed math coprocessors for several systems, including those based on Motorola processor designs. Intel originally contracted Weitek to develop a math coprocessor for the Intel 386 CPU, because Intel was behind in its own development of the 387 math coprocessor. The result was the Weitek 1167, a custom math coprocessor that uses a proprietary Weitek instruction set, which is incompatible with the Intel 387.

Weitek introduced the 4167 coprocessor chip for 486 systems in November 1989. To use the Weitek coprocessor, your system must have the required additional socket. Before purchasing one of the Weitek coprocessors, you should determine whether your software supports it. Then you should contact the software company to determine whether the Weitek has a performance advantage over the Intel coprocessor.

80487 Upgrade

The Intel 80486 processor was introduced in late 1989, and systems using this chip appeared during 1990. The 486DX integrated the math coprocessor into the chip.

The 486SX began life as a full-fledged 486DX chip, but Intel actually disabled the built-in math coprocessor before shipping the chip. As part of this marketing scheme, Intel marketed what it called a 487SX math coprocessor. Motherboard manufacturers installed an Intel-designed socket for this so-called 487 chip. In reality, however, the 487SX math chip was a special 486DX chip with the math coprocessor enabled. When you plugged this chip into your motherboard, it disabled the 486SX chip and gave you the functional equivalent of a full-fledged 486DX system.

Processor Tests

The processor is easily the most expensive chip in the system. Processor manufacturers use specialized equipment to test their own processors, but you have to settle for a little less. The best processor-testing device to which you have access is a system that you know is functional; you then can use the diagnostics available from IBM and other system manufacturers to test the motherboard and processor functions. Most systems mount processors in a socket for easy replacement.

Landmark offers specialized diagnostics software called Service Diagnostics to test various processors. Special versions are available for each processor in the Intel family. If you don't want to purchase this kind of software, you can perform a quick-and-dirty processor evaluation by using the normal diagnostics program supplied with your system.

Because the processor is the brain of a system, most systems don't function with a defective one. If a system seems to have a dead motherboard, try replacing the processor with one from a functioning motherboard that uses the same CPU chip. You may find that the processor in the original board is the culprit. If the system continues to play dead, however, the problem is elsewhere.

Known Defective Chips

A few system problems are built-in at the factory, although these bugs or design defects are rare. By learning to recognize these problems, you may avoid unnecessary repairs or replacements. This section describes several known defects in system processors.

Early 80386s. Some early 16MHz Intel 386DX processors had a small bug that you may have encountered in troubleshooting what seems to be a software problem. The bug, which apparently is in the chip's 32-bit multiply routine, manifests itself only when you run true 32-bit code in a program such as OS/2 2.x, UNIX/386, or Windows in Enhanced mode. Some specialized 386 memory-management software systems also may invoke this subtle bug, but 16-bit operating systems (such as DOS and OS/2 1.x) probably will not.

The bug usually causes the system to lock up. Diagnosing this problem can be difficult because the problem generally is intermittent and software-related. Running tests to find the bug is difficult; only Intel, with proper test equipment, can determine whether your chip has a bug. Some programs can diagnose the problem and identify a defective chip, but they cannot identify all defective chips. If a program indicates a bad chip, you certainly have a defective one; if the program passes the chip, you still may have a defective one.

Intel requested that its 386 customers return possibly defective chips for screening, but many vendors did not return them. Intel tested returned chips and replaced defective ones. The defective chips later were sold to bargain liquidators or systems houses that wanted chips that would not run 32-bit code. The defective chips were stamped with a 16-bit SW Only logo, indicating that they were authorized to run only 16-bit software.

Chips that passed the test, and all subsequent chips produced as bug-free, were marked with a double-sigma code (ΣΣ), which indicates a good chip. 386DX chips that are not marked with either of these designations have not been tested by Intel and may be defective.

The following marking indicates that a chip has not yet been screened for the defect; it may be either good or bad. Return a chip of this kind to the system manufacturer, which will return the chip for a free replacement.

    80386-16

The following marking indicates that the chip has been tested and has the 32-bit multiply bug. The chip works with 16-bit software (such as DOS) but not with 32-bit, 386-specific software (such as Windows or OS/2).

80386-16

16-bit SW Only

The following mark on a chip indicates that it has been tested as defect-free. This chip fulfills all the capabilities promised for the 80386.

80386-16

ΣΣ

This problem was discovered and corrected before Intel officially added DX to the part number. So if you have a chip labeled as 80386DX or 386DX, it does not have this problem.

Another problem with the 386DX can be stated more specifically. When 386-based versions of XENIX or other UNIX implementations are run on a computer that contains a 387DX math coprocessor, the computer locks up under certain conditions. The problem does not occur in the DOS environment, however. For the lockup to occur, all the following conditions must be in effect:

- Demand page virtual memory must be active.
- A 387DX must be installed and in use.
- DMA (direct memory access) must occur.
- The 386 must be in a wait state.

When all these conditions are true at the same instant, the 386DX ends up waiting for the 387DX, and vice versa. Both processors will continue to wait for each other indefinitely. The problem is in certain versions of the 386DX, not in the 387DX math coprocessor.

Intel published this problem (Errata 21) immediately after it was discovered to inform its OEM customers. At that point, it became the responsibility of each manufacturer to implement a fix in its hardware or software product. Some manufacturers, such as Compaq and IBM, responded by modifying their motherboards to prevent these lockups from occurring.

The Errata 21 problem occurs only in the B Stepping version of the 386DX and not in the later D Stepping version. You can identify the D Stepping version of the 386DX by the letters DX in the part number (for example, 386DX-20). If DX is part of the chip's part number, the chip does not have this problem.

Pentium Defects. Probably the most famous processor bug in history is the now legendary flaw in the Pentium *Floating-Point Unit (FPU)*. It has often been called the FDIV bug, because it affects primarily the FDIV (Floating-Point Divide) instruction, although several other instructions that use division are also affected. Intel officially refers to this problem as Errata No. 23, titled "Slight precision loss for floating point divides on specific operand pairs." The bug has been fixed in the D1 or later steppings of the 60/66MHz Pentium processors, as well as the B5 and later steppings of the 75/90/100MHz processors. The 120MHz and higher processors are manufactured from later steppings, which do not include this problem.

This bug caused a tremendous fervor when it first was reported on the Internet by a mathematician in October, 1994. Within a few days news of the defect had spread nationwide, and even people who did not have computers had heard about it. Using certain combinations of numbers, the Pentium would incorrectly perform floating point division calculations, with errors anywhere from the third digit on up.

By the time the bug was publicly discovered outside of Intel, they had already incorporated the fix into the next stepping of both the 60/66MHz and the 75/90/100MHz Pentium processor, along with the other corrections they had made.

After the bug was made public and Intel admitted to already knowing about it, a fury erupted. As people began checking their spreadsheets and other math calculations, many discovered that they had also encountered this problem and did not know it. Others who had not really encountered the problem had their faith in the core of their PCs very shaken. People had come to put so much trust in the PC that they had a hard time coming to terms with the fact that it might not even be able to do math correctly!

One interesting result of the fervor surrounding this defect is that people are less likely to implicitly trust their PCs, and are therefore doing more testing and evaluating of important results. The bottom line is that if your information and calculations are important enough, you should implement some program of checking your results. In looking for problems with math, several programs were found to have problems. For example, a bug was discovered in the yield function of Excel 5.0 that some were attributing to the Pentium processor. In this case, the problem turned out to be the software, which has been corrected in later versions (5.0c and later).

Intel finally decided that in the best interest of the consumer as well as their public image, they would begin a lifetime replacement warranty on the affected processors. This means that if you ever encounter one of the Pentium processors with the Errata 23 Floating-Point bug, they will replace the processor with an equivalent one without this problem. Normally, all you have to do is to call Intel and ask for the replacement. They will ship you a new part matching the ratings of the one you are replacing in an overnight shipping box. The replacement is free, including all shipping charges. You merely remove your old processor, replace it with the new one, and then put the old one back in the box. Then you call the overnight service who will pick it up and send it back. Intel will take a credit card number when you first call for the replacement only to ensure that the original defective chip is returned. As long as they get the original CPU back within a specified amount of time, there will be no charges to you. Intel has indicated that these defective processors will be destroyed and will not be remarketed or resold in another form.

Testing for the FPU Bug. Testing a Pentium for this bug is relatively easy. All you have to do is to execute one of the test division cases cited here and see if your answer compares to the correct result.

The division calculation can be done in a spreadsheet (such as Lotus 1-2-3, Microsoft Excel, or any other), in the Microsoft Windows built-in calculator, or in any other calculating program that uses the FPU. Make sure that for the purposes of this test the FPU has not been disabled. That would normally require some special command or setting specific to the application, and would of course ensure that the test came out correct no matter if the chip is flawed or not.

The most severe Pentium floating point errors occur as early as the third significant digit of the result. Here is an example of one of the more severe instances of the problem:

962,306,957,033 / 11,010,046 = 87,402.6282027341 (correct answer)

962,306,957,033 / 11,010,046 = 87,399.5805831329 (flawed Pentium)

Note that your particular calculator program may not show the answer to the number of digits shown here. Most spreadsheet programs limit displayed results to 13 or 15 significant digits.

As you can see, in the previous case the error turns up in the third most significant digit of the result. In an examination of over 5,000 integer pairs in the 5 to 15 digit range found to produce Pentium floating point division errors, errors beginning in the sixth significant digit were the most likely to occur, although errors occurred anywhere from the third digit on up.

Here is another division problem that will come out incorrectly on a Pentium with this flaw:

4,195,835 / 3,145,727 = 1.33382044913624100 (correct answer)

4,195,835 / 3,145,727 = 1.33373906890203759 (flawed Pentium)

This one shows an error in the fifth significant digit. A variation on the previous calculation can be performed as follows:

x = 4,195,835

y = 3,145,727

z = x − (x/y)*y

4,195,835 − (4,195,835 / 3,145,727) * 3,145,727 = 0 (correct answer)

4,195,835 − (4,195,835 / 3,145,727) * 3,145,727 = 256 (flawed Pentium)

With an exact computation, the answer here should be zero. In fact, you will get zero on most machines, including those using Intel 286, 386, and 486 chips. But, on the Pentium, the answer is 256!

Here is one more calculation you can try:

5,505,001 / 294,911 = 18.66665197 (correct answer)

5,505,001 / 294,911 = 18.66600093 (flawed Pentium)

This one represents an error in the sixth significant digit.

There are several workarounds for this bug, but they extract a performance penalty. Because Intel has agreed to replace any Pentium processor with this flaw under a lifetime warranty replacement program, if you have a chip with this defect, the best workaround is a free replacement!

Power Management Bugs. Starting with the second-generation Pentium processors, Intel added functions that allow these CPUs to be installed in energy efficient systems. These are usually called Energy Star systems because they meet the specifications imposed by the EPA Energy Star program, but they are also unofficially called "Green PCs" by many users.

Unfortunately, there have been several bugs with respect to these functions, causing them to either fail or be disabled. These bugs are in some of the functions in the power management capabilities accessed through SMM. These problems are only applicable to the second generation 75/90/100MHz processors, because the first generation 60/66MHz processors do not have SMM or power management capabilities, and all higher speed (120MHz and up) processors have the bugs fixed.

Most of the problems are related to the STPCLK# pin and the HALT instruction. If this condition is invoked by the chipset, the system will hang. For most systems, the only workaround for this problem is to simply disable the power-saving modes, such as suspend or sleep. Unfortunately, this means that your green PC won't be so green anymore! The best way to repair the problem is to replace the processor with a later stepping version that does not have the bug. These bugs affect the B1 stepping version of the 75/90/100MHz Pentiums, and were fixed in the B3 and later stepping versions.

Pentium Processor Models and Steppings

It is a sort of dirty little secret in the business that no processor is truly ever perfect. From time to time, the manufacturers will gather up what problems they have found and put into production a new *stepping*, which consists of a new set of masks that incorporate the corrections. Each subsequent stepping is better and more refined than the previous ones. Although no microprocessor is ever perfect, they come closer to perfection with each stepping. In the life of a typical microprocessor, a manufacturer may go through half a dozen or more such steppings.

The following table shows all the versions of the Pentium processor Model 1 (60/66MHz version) indicating the various steppings that have been available.

Type	Family	Model	Stepping	Mfg. Stepping	Speed	Spec. Number	Comments
0	5	1	3	B1	50	Q0399	ES
0	5	1	3	B1	60	Q0352	
0	5	1	3	B1	60	Q0400	ES
0	5	1	3	B1	60	Q0394	ES,HS
0	5	1	3	B1	66	Q0353	5v1
0	5	1	3	B1	66	Q0395	ES,HS,5v1
0	5	1	3	B1	60	Q0412	
0	5	1	3	B1	60	SX753	

(continues)

(continued)

Type	Family	Model	Stepping	Mfg. Stepping	Speed	Spec. Number	Comments
0	5	1	3	B1	66	Q0413	5v2
0	5	1	3	B1	66	SX754	5v2
0	5	1	5	C1	60	Q0466	HS
0	5	1	5	C1	60	SX835	HS
0	5	1	5	C1	60	SZ949	HS,BOX
0	5	1	5	C1	66	Q0467	HS,5v2
0	5	1	5	C1	66	SX837	HS,5v2
0	5	1	5	C1	66	SZ950	HS,BOX,5v2
0	5	1	7	D1	60	Q0625	HS
0	5	1	7	D1	60	SX948	HS
0	5	1	7	D1	60	SX974	HS,5v3
0	5	1	7	D1	60	-*	HS,BOX
0	5	1	7	D1	66	Q0626	HS,5v2
0	5	1	7	D1	66	SX950	HS,5v2
0	5	1	7	D1	66	Q0627	HS,5v3
0	5	1	7	D1	66	SX949	HS,5v3
0	5	1	7	D1	66	-*	HS,BOX,5v2

The following table shows all the versions of the Pentium processor Model 2 and higher (75+ MHz versions) indicating the various steppings that have been available:

Type	Family	Model	Stepping	Mfg. Stepping	Speed	Spec. Number	Comments
0	5	2	1	B1	75	Q0540	ES,HS
2	5	2	1	B1	75	Q0541	ES,HS
0	5	2	1	B1	90	Q0542	HS
0	5	2	1	B1	90	Q0613	VR,HS
2	5	2	1	B1	90	Q0543	DP,HS
0	5	2	1	B1	100	Q0563	HS
0	5	2	1	B1	100	Q0587	VR,HS
0	5	2	1	B1	100	Q0614	VR,HS
0	5	2	1	B1	75	Q0601	TCP
0	5	2	1	B1	90	SX879	HS
0	5	2	1	B1	90	SX885	MD,HS
0	5	2	1	B1	90	SX909	VR,HS
2	5	2	1	B1	90	SX874	DP,HS
0	5	2	1	B1	100	SX886	MD,HS
0	5	2	1	B1	100	SX910	VR,MD,HS

Type	Family	Model	Stepping	Mfg. Stepping	Speed	Spec. Number	Comments
0	5	2	2	B3	90	Q0628	HS
0/2	5	2	2	B3	90	Q0611	HS
0/2	5	2	2	B3	90	Q0612	VR,HS
0	5	2	2	B3	100	Q0677	VRE,MD,HS
0	5	2	2	B3	75	Q0606	TCP
0	5	2	2	B3	75	SX951	TCP
0	5	2	2	B3	90	SX923	HS
0	5	2	2	B3	90	SX922	VR,HS
0	5	2	2	B3	90	SX921	MD,HS
2	5	2	2	B3	90	SX942	DP,HS
2	5	2	2	B3	90	SX943	DP,VR,HS
2	5	2	2	B3	90	SX944	DP,MD,HS
0	5	2	2	B3	90	SZ951	BOX
0	5	2	2	B3	100	SX960	VRE,MD,HS
0/2	5	2	4	B5	75	Q0704	TCP
0/2	5	2	4	B5	75	Q0666	HS
0/2	5	2	4	B5	90	Q0653	HS
0/2	5	2	4	B5	90	Q0654	VR,HS
0/2	5	2	4	B5	90	Q0655	MD,HS
0/2	5	2	4	B5	100	Q0656	MD,HS
0/2	5	2	4	B5	100	Q0657	VR,MD,HS
0/2	5	2	4	B5	100	Q0658	VRE,MD,HS
0	5	2	4	B5	120	Q0707	VRE,MD,HS
0	5	2	4	B5	120	Q0708	HS
0	5	2	4	B5	75	SX975	TCP
0/2	5	2	4	B5	75	SX961	HS
0/2	5	2	4	B5	75	SZ977	HS,BOX
0/2	5	2	4	B5	90	SX957	HS
0/2	5	2	4	B5	90	SX958	VR,HS
0/2	5	2	4	B5	90	SX959	MD,HS
0/2	5	2	4	B5	90	SZ978	HS,BOX
0/2	5	2	4	B5	100	SX962	VRE,MD,HS
0	5	2	5	C2	75	Q0725	TCP
0/2	5	2	5	C2	75	Q0700	
0/2	5	2	5	C2	75	Q0749	MD
0/2	5	2	5	C2	90	Q0699	
0/2	5	2	5	C2	100	Q0698	VRE,MD
0/2	5	2	5	C2	100	Q0697	
0	5	2	5	C2	120	Q0711	VRE,MD

(continues)

Chapter 6—Microprocessor Types and Specifications

(continued)

Type	Family	Model	Stepping	Mfg. Stepping	Speed	Spec. Number	Comments
0	5	2	5	C2	120	Q0732	VRE,MD
0	5	2	5	C2	133	Q0733	MD
0	5	2	5	C2	133	Q0751	MD
0	5	2	5	C2	133	Q0775	VRE,MD
0	5	2	5	C2	75	SK079	TCP
0/2	5	2	5	C2	75	SX969	
0/2	5	2	5	C2	75	SX998	MD
0/2	5	2	5	C2	75	SZ994	BOX
0/2	5	2	5	C2	75	SU070	BOXF
0/2	5	2	5	C2	90	SX968	
0/2	5	2	5	C2	90	SZ995	BOX
0/2	5	2	5	C2	90	SU031	BOXF
0/2	5	2	5	C2	100	SX970	VRE,MD
0/2	5	2	5	C2	100	SX963	
0/2	5	2	5	C2	100	SZ996	BOX
0/2	5	2	5	C2	100	SU032	BOXF
0	5	2	5	C2	120	SK086	VRE,MD
0	5	2	5	C2	120	SX994	VRE,MD
0	5	2	5	C2	120	SU033	VRE,MD,BOXF
0	5	2	5	C2	133	SK098	MD
0	5	2	5	mA1	75	Q0686	VRT,TCP
0	5	2	5	mA1	75	Q0689	VRT
0	5	2	5	mA1	90	Q0694	VRT,TCP
0	5	2	5	mA1	90	Q0695	VRT
0	5	2	5	mA1	75	SK089	VRT,TCP
0	5	2	5	mA1	75	SK091	VRT
0	5	2	5	mA1	90	SK090	VRT,TCP
0	5	2	5	mA1	90	SK092	VRT
0/2	5	2	B	cB1	120	Q0776	
0/2	5	2	B	cB1	133	Q0772	
0/2	5	2	B	cB1	133	Q0773	
0/2	5	2	B	cB1	133	Q0774	VRE,MD
0/2	5	2	B	cB1	120	SK110	
0/2	5	2	B	cB1	133	SK106	
0/2	5	2	B	cB1	133	S106J	
0/2	5	2	B	cB1	133	SK107	
0/2	5	2	B	cB1	133	SU038	BOXF
0	5	2	B	mcB1	100	Q0884	VRT,TCP
0	5	2	B	mcB1	120	Q0779	VRT,TCP

Processor Tests

Type	Family	Model	Stepping	Mfg. Stepping	Speed	Spec. Number	Comments
0	5	2	B	mcB1	120	Q0808	
0	5	2	B	mcB1	100	SY029	VRT,TCP
0	5	2	B	mcB1	120	SK113	VRT,TCP
0	5	2	B	mcB1	120	SK118	VRT,TCP
0	5	2	B	mcB1	120	SX999	
0/2	5	2	C	cC0	150	Q0835	
0/2	5	2	C	cC0	150	Q0878	PPGA
0/2	5	2	C	cC0	166	Q0836	VRE
0/2	5	2	C	cC0	166	Q0841	VRE
0/2	5	2	C	cC0	166	Q0886	VRE,PPGA
0/2	5	2	C	cC0	166	Q0890	VRE,PPGA
0	5	2	C	cC0	166	Q0949	VRE,PPGA
0/2	5	2	C	cC0	150	SY015	
0/2	5	2	C	cC0	150	SU071	BOXF
0/2	5	2	C	cC0	166	SY016	VRE
0/2	5	2	C	cC0	166	SY017	VRE
0/2	5	2	C	cC0	166	SU072	VRE,BOXF
0	5	2	C	cC0	166	SY037	VRE,PPGA
0	5	7	0	mA4	75	Q0848	VRT,TCP
0	5	7	0	mA4	75	Q0851	VRT
0	5	7	0	mA4	90	Q0849	VRT,TCP
0	5	7	0	mA4	90	Q0852	VRT
0	5	7	0	mA4	100	Q0850	VRT,TCP
0	5	7	0	mA4	100	Q0853	VRT
0	5	7	0	mA4	75	SK119	VRT,TCP
0	5	7	0	mA4	75	SK122	VRT
0	5	7	0	mA4	90	SK120	VRT,TCP
0	5	7	0	mA4	90	SK123	VRT
0	5	7	0	mA4	100	SK121	VRT,TCP
0	5	7	0	mA4	100	SK124	VRT
0	5	2	C	mcC0	120	Q0879	VRT,TCP
0	5	2	C	mcC0	120	Q0880	3.1v
0	5	2	C	mcC0	133	Q0881	VRT,TCP
0	5	2	C	mcC0	133	Q0882	3.1v
0	5	2	C	mcC0	120	SY021	VRT,TCP
0	5	2	C	mcC0	120	SY027	3.1v
0	5	2	C	mcC0	120	SY030	
0	5	2	C	mcC0	133	SY019	VRT,TCP
0	5	2	C	mcC0	133	SY028	3.1v

(continues)

(continued)

Type	Family	Model	Stepping	Mfg. Stepping	Speed	Spec. Number	Comments
0	5	2	6	E0	75	Q0846	TCP
0/2	5	2	6	E0	75	Q0837	
0/2	5	2	6	E0	90	Q0783	
0/2	5	2	6	E0	100	Q0784	
0/2	5	2	6	E0	120	Q0785	VRE
0	5	2	6	E0	75	SY009	TCP
0/2	5	2	6	E0	75	SY005	
0/2	5	2	6	E0	90	SY006	
0/2	5	2	6	E0	100	SY007	
0/2	5	2	6	E0	120	SY033	

The following table shows all the versions of the Pentium OverDrive processors indicating the various steppings that have been available. Note that the Type 1 chips in this table are 486 Pentium OverDrive processors, which are designed to replace 486 chips in systems with Socket 2 or 3. The other OverDrive processors are designed to replace existing Pentium processors in socket 4 or 5/7.

Type	Family	Model	Stepping	Mfg. Stepping	Speed (MHz)	Spec. Number	Product Code	Version
1	5	3	1	B1	63	SZ953	PODP5v63	1.0
1	5	3	1	B2	63	SZ990	PODP5v63	1.1
1	5	3	2	C0	83	SU014	PODP5v83	2.1
0	5	1	A	tA0	133	SU082	PODP5v133	1.0
0	5	2	C	aC0	125	SU081	PODP3v125	1.0
0	5	2	C	aC0	150	SU083	PODP3v150	1.0
0	5	2	C	aC0	166	SU084	PODP3v166	1.0

ES = Engineering Sample. These chips were not sold through normal channels but were designed for development and testing purposes.
HS = Heat Spreader Package. This indicates a chip with a metal plate on the top, which is used to spread heat away from the center part of the chip. The heat spreader helps the chip run cooler; however, most later chips use a smaller, more powerful, more efficient die, and Intel has been able to eliminate the heat spreader from these.
DP = Dual Processor version where Type 0 is Primary only, Type 2 is Secondary only, and Type 0 or 2 is either.
MD = Minimum Delay timing restrictions on several processor signals.
VR = Voltage Reduced (3.300v to 3.465v).
VRE = VR and Extended (3.45v to 3.60v).
VRT = Voltage Reduction Technology: The processor I/O voltage is 3.3v, but the processor core runs on 2.9v.
TCP = Tape Carrier Package (Mobile Pentium). This is a filmstrip-type package intended mainly for laptop or notebook system use. This version is soldered rather than installed in a socket like the others.
BOX = A retail boxed processor with a standard passive heat sink.
BOXF = A retail boxed processor with an active (fan cooled) heat sink.
* = These chips have no Specification number.

In these tables, the processor Type heading refers to the dual processor capabilities of the Pentium. Versions indicated with a Type 0 can only be used as a primary processor, while those marked as Type 2 can only be used as the secondary processor in a pair. If the processor is marked as Type 0/2, that means it can serve as either the primary or secondary processor, or both.

The Family designation for all Pentiums is 5 (for 586), while the Model indicates the particular revision. Model 1 indicates the first-generation 60/66MHz version, while Model 2 or later indicates the second-generation 75+MHz version. The stepping number is the actual revision of the particular model. The family, model, and stepping number can be read by software such as the Intel CPUID program. These also correspond to a particular Manufacturer Stepping code, which is how Intel designates the chips in-house. These are usually an alphanumeric code. For example, stepping 5 of the Model 2 Pentium is also known as the C2 stepping inside Intel.

Manufacturing stepping codes that begin with an "m" indicate a Mobile processor, or one that is designed for laptop or portable systems. These often come in a Tape Carrier Package (TCP), which is a sort of filmstrip package where the raw chip is actually taped and soldered directly to the circuit board. Most Pentium processors come in a standard Ceramic Pin Grid Array (CPGA) package; however, the mobile processors also use the Tape Carrier Package (TCP). Now there is also a Plastic Pin Grid Array (PPGA) package being used to reduce cost.

The Specification Number is a code that is stamped or printed on the top and often bottom of the chip. This code is the only way externally that you can tell exactly which chip you have. In most systems, there will be a heat sink on the chip that will have to be removed to see the markings on the top; however, most Pentium processors are now marked on the bottom as well. If you cannot easily remove the heat sink, flip the chip over because the Specification code may be printed on the bottom, as well.

One interesting item to note is that there are several subtly different voltages required by different Pentium processors. The following table summarizes the different Processors and their required voltages:

Model	Stepping	Voltage Spec.	Voltage Range
1	-	Std.	4.75–5.25v
1	-	5v1	4.90–5.25v
1	-	5v2	4.90–5.40v
1	-	5v3	5.15–5.40v
2+	B1–B5	Std.	3.135–3.465v
2+	C2+	Std.	3.135–3.600v
2+	-	VR	3.300–3.465v
2+	B1–B5	VRE	3.45–3.60v
2+	C2+	VRE	3.40–3.60v

Many of the newer Pentium motherboards have jumpers that allow for adjustments to the different voltage ranges. If you are having problems with a particular processor, it may not be matched correctly to your motherboard voltage output.

Many of the Mobile Pentium processors use Voltage Reduction Technology (VRT), which means that they draw the standard 3.3v from the motherboard, but internally they operate on only 2.9v. Because the core of the CPU is operating on this lower voltage, it dramatically reduces overall power consumption and heat production, which is ideal for portable or notebook systems where battery life is important. In addition to VRT, some of the Mobile Pentium processors are now designed to run on 3.1v from the system instead of the standard 3.3v.

If I were purchasing a Pentium system today, I would recommend using only Model 2 (second generation) or later version processors that are available in 75MHz or faster speeds. I would definitely want stepping C2 or later. Virtually all of the important bugs and problems were fixed in the C2 and later releases.

Other Processor Problems

Some other problems with processors and math coprocessors are worth noting.

After you remove a math coprocessor from an AT-type system, you must rerun your computer's Setup program. Some AT-compatible SETUP programs do not properly unset the math-coprocessor bit. If you receive a Power-On Self Test (POST) error message because the computer cannot find the math chip, you may have to unplug the battery from the system board temporarily. All SETUP information will be lost, so be sure to write down the hard drive type, floppy drive type, and memory and video configurations before unplugging the battery. This information is critical in reconfiguring your computer correctly.

Another strange problem occurs in some IBM PS/2 Model 80 systems when a 387DX is installed. In the following computers, you may hear crackling or beeping noises from the speaker while the computer is running:

- 8580 Model 111, with serial numbers below 6019000
- 8850 Model 311, with serial numbers below 6502022

If you are experiencing this problem, contact IBM for a motherboard replacement.

Heating and Cooling Problems

Heat can be a problem in any high-performance 486, Pentium, or Pentium Pro system. The higher-speed processors normally consume more power and therefore generate more heat. If your system is based on any of the 66MHz or faster processors, you must dissipate the extra thermal energy; the fan inside your computer case may not be able to handle the load.

To cool a system in which processor heat is a problem, you can buy (for less than $5 in most cases) a special attachment for the CPU chip called a heat sink, which draws heat away from the CPU chip. Many applications may need only a larger standard heat sink with additional or longer fins for a larger cooling area. Several heat-sink manufacturers are listed in the vendor list. See also the section "OverDrive Processors and Sockets" earlier in the chapter.

Chapter 7

Memory

This chapter looks at memory from both a physical and logical point of view. We will discuss the physical chips and memory modules that you can purchase and install. The chapter also looks at the logical layout of memory, as well as defines the different areas and uses of these areas from the system's point of view. Because the logical layout and uses are within the "mind" of the processor, memory remains as perhaps the most difficult subject to grasp in the PC universe. This chapter contains much useful information that removes the mysteries associated with memory and enables you to get the most out of your system.

The System Logical Memory Layout

The original PC had a total of 1M of addressable memory, and the top 384K of that was reserved for use by the system. Placing this reserved space at the top (between 640K and 1024K instead of at the bottom, between 0K and 640K) led to what today is often called the *conventional memory barrier*. The constant pressures on system and peripheral manufacturers to maintain compatibility by never breaking from the original memory scheme of the first PC has resulted in a system memory structure that is (to put it kindly) a mess. Almost two decades after the first PC was introduced, even the newest Pentium II-based systems are limited in many important ways by the memory map of the first PCs.

Someone who wants to become knowledgeable about personal computers must at one time or another come to terms with the types of memory installed on their system—the small and large pieces of different kinds of memory, some accessible by software application programs, and some not. The following sections detail the different kinds of memory installed on a modern PC. The kinds of memory covered in the following sections include the following:

- Conventional (Base) memory
- Upper Memory Area (UMA)

- High Memory Area (HMA)
- Extended memory (XMS)
- Expanded memory (obsolete)
- Video RAM memory (part of UMA)
- Adapter ROM and Special-Purpose RAM (part of UMA)
- Motherboard ROM BIOS (part of UMA)

Subsequent sections also cover preventing memory conflicts and overlap, using memory managers to optimize your system's memory, and making better use of memory. In an AT system, the memory map extends beyond the 1M boundary and can continue to 16M on a system based on the 286 or higher processor, 4G (4,096M) on a 386DX or higher, or as much as 64G (65,536M) on a Pentium II. Any memory past 1M is called *extended memory*.

Figure 7.1 shows the logical address locations for a PC-compatible system. If the processor is running in real mode, only the first megabyte is accessible. If the processor is in protected mode, the full 16; 4,096; or 65,536M are accessible. Each symbol is equal to 1K of memory; each line or segment is 64K; and this map shows the first two megabytes of system memory.

> **Note**
> To save space, this map is ended after the end of the second megabyte. In reality, this map continues to the maximum of addressable memory.

Conventional (Base) Memory

The original PC/XT-type system was designed to use 1M of memory workspace, sometimes called *RAM (random access memory)*. This 1M of RAM is divided into several sections, some of which have special uses. DOS can read and write to the entire megabyte, but can manage the loading of programs only in the portion of RAM space called *conventional memory*, which at the time the first PC was introduced was 512K. The other 512K was reserved for use by the system itself, including the motherboard and adapter boards plugged into the system slots.

IBM decided after introducing the system that only 384K was needed for these reserved uses, and the company began marketing PCs with 640K of user memory. Thus, 640K became the standard for memory that can be used by DOS for running programs, and is often termed the *640K memory barrier*. The remaining memory after 640K was reserved for use by the graphics boards, other adapters, and the motherboard ROM BIOS.

Upper Memory Area (UMA)

The term *Upper Memory Area (UMA)* describes the reserved 384K at the top of the first megabyte of system memory on a PC/XT and the first megabyte on an AT-type system.

The System Logical Memory Layout

```
. = Program-accessible memory (standard RAM)
G = Graphics Mode Video RAM
M = Monochrome Text Mode Video RAM
C = Color Text Mode Video RAM
V = Video ROM BIOS (would be "a" in PS/2)
a = Adapter board ROM and special-purpose RAM (free UMA space)
r = Additional PS/2 Motherboard ROM BIOS (free UMA in non-PS/2 systems)
R = Motherboard ROM BIOS
b = IBM Cassette BASIC ROM (would be "R" in IBM compatibles)
h = High Memory Area (HMA), if HIMEM.SYS is loaded.

Conventional (Base) Memory:

        : 0---1---2---3---4---5---6---7---8---9---A---B---C---D---E---F---
000000: ................................................................
010000: ................................................................
020000: ................................................................
030000: ................................................................
040000: ................................................................
050000: ................................................................
060000: ................................................................
070000: ................................................................
080000: ................................................................
090000: ................................................................

Upper Memory Area (UMA):

        : 0---1---2---3---4---5---6---7---8---9---A---B---C---D---E---F---
0A0000: GGGGGGGGGGGGGGGGGGGGGGGGGGGGGGGGGGGGGGGGGGGGGGGGGGGGGGGGGGGGGGGG
0B0000: MMMMMMMMMMMMMMMMMMMMMMMMMMMMMMMMCCCCCCCCCCCCCCCCCCCCCCCCCCCCCCCC
        : 0---1---2---3---4---5---6---7---8---9---A---B---C---D---E---F---
0C0000: VVVVVVVVVVVVVVVVVVVVVVVVVVVVVVVVaaaaaaaaaaaaaaaaaaaaaaaaaaaaaaaa
0D0000: aaaaaaaaaaaaaaaaaaaaaaaaaaaaaaaaaaaaaaaaaaaaaaaaaaaaaaaaaaaaaaaa
        : 0---1---2---3---4---5---6---7---8---9---A---B---C---D---E---F---
0E0000: rrrrrrrrrrrrrrrrrrrrrrrrrrrrrrrrrrrrrrrrrrrrrrrrrrrrrrrrrrrrrrrr
0F0000: RRRRRRRRRRRRRRRRRRRRRRRRRRRRbbbbbbbbbbbbbbbbbbbbbbbbbbbbRRRRRRRR

Extended Memory:

        : 0---1---2---3---4---5---6---7---8---9---A---B---C---D---E---F---
100000: hhhhhhhhhhhhhhhhhhhhhhhhhhhhhhhhhhhhhhhhhhhhhhhhhhhhhhhhhhhhhhhh

Extended Memory Specification (XMS) Memory:

110000: ................................................................
120000: ................................................................
130000: ................................................................
140000: ................................................................
150000: ................................................................
160000: ................................................................
170000: ................................................................
180000: ................................................................
190000: ................................................................
1A0000: ................................................................
1B0000: ................................................................
1C0000: ................................................................
1D0000: ................................................................
1E0000: ................................................................
1F0000: ................................................................
```

FIG. 7.1 The logical memory map of the first 2M.

This memory has the addresses from A0000 through FFFFF. The way the 384K of upper memory is used breaks down as follows:

- The first 128K after conventional memory is called *Video RAM*. It is reserved for use by video adapters. When text and graphics are displayed on-screen, the electronic impulses that contain their images reside in this space. Video RAM is allotted the address range from A0000-BFFFF.

- The next 128K is reserved for the adapter BIOS that resides in read-only memory chips on some adapter boards plugged into the bus slots. Most VGA-compatible video adapters use the first 32K of this area for their on-board BIOS. The rest can be used by any other adapters installed. Many network adapters also use this area for special purpose RAM called Shared Memory. Adapter ROM and special purpose RAM is allotted the address range from C0000-DFFFF.

- The last 128K of memory is reserved for motherboard BIOS, (the basic input/output system, which is stored in read-only RAM chips or ROM). The POST (Power-On Self Test) and bootstrap loader, which handles your system at bootup until the operating system takes over, also reside in this space. Most systems only use the last 64K (or less) of this space, leaving the first 64K or more free for remapping with memory managers. Some systems also include the CMOS Setup program in this area. The motherboard BIOS is allotted the address range from E0000-FFFFF.

Not all the 384K of reserved memory is fully used on most AT-type systems. For example, according to IBM's definition of the PC standard, reserved video RAM begins at address A0000, which is right at the 640K boundary. Normally, this is used for VGA graphics modes, while the monochrome and color text modes use B0000-B7FFF and B8000-BFFFF, respectively. Older non-VGA adapters only used memory in the B0000 segment. Different video adapters use varying amounts of RAM for their operations depending mainly on the mode they are in. However, to the processor it always appears as the same 128K area no matter how much RAM is really on the video card. This is managed by bank switching areas of memory on the card in and out of the A0000-BFFFF segments.

Although the top 384K of the first megabyte was originally termed *reserved memory*, it is possible to use previously unused regions of this memory to load device drivers (like ANSI.SYS) and memory-resident programs (like MOUSE.COM), which frees up the conventional memory they would otherwise require. The amount of free UMA space varies from system to system depending on the adapter cards installed on the system. For example, most SCSI adapters and network adapters require some of this area for built-in ROMs or special-purpose RAM use.

Segment Addresses and Linear Addresses. One thing that can be confusing is the difference between a segment address and a full linear address. The use of segmented address numbers comes from the internal structure of the Intel processors, and is used primarily by older, 16-bit operating systems. They use a separate register for the segment information and another for the offset. The concept is very simple. For example, assume that I am staying in a hotel room, and somebody asks for my room number. The hotel has 10 floors, numbered from zero through nine; each floor has 100 rooms, numbered from 00 to 99. A segment is defined as any group of 100 rooms starting at a multiple of 10, and indicated by a two-digit number. So, a segment address of 54 would indicate the actual room 540, and you could have an offset of 00 to 99 rooms from there.

Thus in this hotel example, each segment is specified as a two-digit number from 00 to 99, and an offset can be specified from any segment starting with a number from 00 to 99 as well.

As an example, let's say I am staying in room 541. If the person needs this information in segment:offset form, and each number is two digits, I could say that I am staying at a room segment starting address of 54 (room 540), and an offset of 01 from the start of that segment. I could also say that I am in room segment 50 (room 500), and an offset of 41. You could even come up with other answers, such as I am at segment 45 (room 450) offset 91 (450+91=541). Here is an example of how this adds up:

Segment	Offset	Total
54	01	541
50	41	541
45	91	541

As you can see, although the particular segment and offset are different, they all add up to the same room address. In the Intel x86 processors, a similar scheme is used where a segment and offset are added internally to produce the actual address. It can be somewhat confusing, especially if you are writing assembly language or machine language software!

This is exactly how segmented memory in an Intel processor works. Notice that the segment and offset numbers essentially overlap on all digits except the first and last. By adding them together with the proper alignment, you can see the linear address total.

With 32-bit operating systems, segment addresses are not an issue. A linear address is one without segment:offset boundaries, such as saying room 541. It is a single number and not comprised of two numbers added together. For example, a SCSI host adapter might have 16K ROM on the card addressed from D4000 to D7FFF. These numbers expressed in segment:offset form are D400:0000 to D700:0FFF. The segment portion is composed of the most significant four digits, and the offset portion is composed of the least significant four digits. Because each portion overlaps by one digit, the ending address of its ROM can be expressed in four different ways, as follows:

```
D000:7FFF =   D000    segment        D7F0:00FF =   D7F0    segment
            + 7FFF    offset                     + 00FF    offset
              ----                                 ----
            = D7FFF   total                      = D7FFF   total

D700:0FFF =   D700    segment        D7FF:000F =   D7FF    segment
            + 0FFF    offset                     + 000F    offset
              ----                                 ----
            = D7FFF   total                      = D7FFF   total
```

As you can see in each case, although the segment and offset differ slightly, the total ends up being the same. Adding together the segment and offset numbers makes possible even more combinations, as in the following examples:

```
D500:2FFF =   D500   segment
            + 2FFF   offset
            ──────
            = D7FFF  total

D6EE:111F =   D6EE   segment
            + 111F   offset
            ──────
            = D7FFF  total
```

As you can see, several combinations are possible. The correct and generally accepted way to write this address as a linear address is D7FFF, whereas most would write the segment:offset address as D000:7FFF. Keeping the segment mostly zeros makes the segment:offset relationship easier to understand and the number easier to comprehend. If you understand the segment:offset relationship to the linear address, you know why when a linear address number is discussed it is five digits, whereas a segment number is only four.

Another important concept with newer 32-bit operating systems is their capability to map RAM from adapter cards into system memory using linear addressing. There is no 64K limit to the amount of memory that can be mapped here, as there is in the UMA.

Video RAM Memory. A video adapter installed in your system uses some of your system's memory to hold graphics or character information for display. Some adapters, like the VGA, also have on-board BIOS mapped into the system's space reserved for such types of adapters. Generally, the higher the resolution and color capabilities of the video adapter, the more system memory the video adapter uses. It is important to note that most VGA or Super VGA adapters have additional on-board memory used to handle the information currently displayed on-screen and to speed screen refresh.

▶▶ See "Video Memory," p. 412

In the standard system-memory map, a total of 128K is reserved for use by the video card to store currently displayed information. The reserved video memory is located in segments A000 and B000. The video adapter ROM uses additional upper memory space in segment C000.

The location of video adapter RAM is responsible for the 640K DOS *conventional memory barrier*. DOS can use all available contiguous memory in the first megabyte of memory until the video adapter RAM is encountered. The use of adapters such as the MDA and CGA allows DOS access to more than 640K of system memory. The video memory *wall* begins at A0000 for the EGA, MCGA, and VGA systems, but the MDA and CGA do not use as much video RAM, which leaves some space that can be used by DOS and programs. The previous segment and offset examples show that the MDA adapter enables DOS to use an additional 64K of memory (all of segment A000), bringing the total for

DOS program space to 704K. Similarly, the CGA enables a total of 736K of possible contiguous memory. The EGA, VGA, or MCGA is limited to the normal maximum of 640K of contiguous memory because of the larger amount used by video RAM. The maximum DOS-program memory workspace, therefore, depends on which video adapter is installed. Table 7.1 shows the maximum amount of memory available to DOS using the referenced video card.

Table 7.1 DOS Memory Limitations Based on Video Adapter Type

Video Adapter Type	Maximum DOS Memory
Monochrome Display Adapter (MDA)	704K
Color Graphics Adapter (CGA)	736K
Enhanced Graphics Adapter (EGA)	640K
Video Graphics Array (VGA)	640K
Super VGA (SVGA)	640K
eXtended Graphics Array (XGA)	640K

Using this memory to 736K might be possible depending on the video adapter, the types of memory boards installed, ROM programs on the motherboard, and the type of system. You can use some of this memory if your system has a 386 or higher processor. With memory manager software, such as EMM386 that comes with DOS, which can operate the 386+ Memory Management Unit (MMU), you can remap extended memory into this space.

The following sections examine how standard video adapters use the system's memory. Figures show where in a system the monochrome, EGA, VGA, and IBM PS/2 adapters use memory. This map is important because it may be possible to recognize some of this as unused in some systems, which may free up more space for software drivers to be loaded.

Monochrome Display Adapter Memory (MDA). Figure 7.2 shows where the original Monochrome Display Adapter (MDA) uses the system's memory. This adapter uses only a 4K portion of the reserved video RAM from B0000-B0FFF. Because the ROM code used to operate this adapter is actually a portion of the motherboard ROM, no additional ROM space is used in segment C000.

```
    . = Empty Addresses
    M = Original Monochrome Adapter RAM
    m = Additional Memory used in VGA Monochrome Text Mode

        : 0---1---2---3---4---5---6---7---8---9---A---B---C---D---E---F---
0A0000: ................................................................
0B0000: MMMMmmmmmmmmmmmmmmmmmmmmmmmmmmmm................................
```

FIG. 7.2 The Monochrome Display Adapter memory map.

Note that although the original Monochrome Display Adapter only used 4K of memory starting at B0000, a VGA adapter running in Monochrome emulation mode (Mono Text Mode) activates 32K of RAM at this address. A true Monochrome Display Adapter has no on-board BIOS, and instead is operated by driver programs found in the primary motherboard BIOS.

Color Graphics Adapter (CGA) Memory. Figure 7.3 shows where the Color Graphics Adapter (CGA) uses the system's memory. The CGA uses a 16K portion of the reserved video RAM from B8000-BBFFF. Because the ROM code used to operate this adapter is a portion of the motherboard ROM, no additional ROM space is used in segment C000.

```
. = Empty Addresses
C = Original Color Graphics Adapter (CGA) RAM
c = Additional Memory used in VGA Color Text Mode

       : 0---1---2---3---4---5---6---7---8---9---A---B---C---D---E---F---
0A0000: ................................................................
0B0000: ................................CCCCCCCCCCCCCCCCcccccccccccccccc
```

FIG. 7.3 The Color Graphics Adapter (CGA) memory map.

The CGA card leaves memory from A0000-B7FFF free, which can be used by memory managers for additional DOS memory space. However, this precludes using any graphics mode software such as Windows. The original CGA card only used 16K of space starting at B8000, whereas a VGA adapter running in CGA emulation (Color Text) mode can activate 32K of RAM at this address. The original CGA card has no on-board BIOS and is instead operated by driver programs found in the primary motherboard BIOS.

Enhanced Graphics Adapter (EGA) Memory. Figure 7.4 shows where the Enhanced Graphics Adapter (EGA) uses the system's memory. This adapter uses all 128K of the video RAM from A0000-BFFFF. The ROM code used to operate this adapter is on the adapter itself and consumes 16K of memory from C0000-C3FFF.

```
. = Empty Addresses
G = Enhanced Graphics Adapter (EGA) Graphics Mode Video RAM
M = EGA Monochrome Text Mode Video RAM
C = EGA Color Text Mode Video RAM
V = Standard EGA Video ROM BIOS
R = Standard Motherboard ROM BIOS

       : 0---1---2---3---4---5---6---7---8---9---A---B---C---D---E---F---
0A0000: GGGGGGGGGGGGGGGGGGGGGGGGGGGGGGGGGGGGGGGGGGGGGGGGGGGGGGGGGGGGGGGG
0B0000: MMMMMMMMMMMMMMMMMMMMMMMMMMMMMMMMCCCCCCCCCCCCCCCCCCCCCCCCCCCCCCCC
       : 0---1---2---3---4---5---6---7---8---9---A---B---C---D---E---F---
0C0000: VVVVVVVVVVVVVVVV................................................
0D0000: ................................................................
       : 0---1---2---3---4---5---6---7---8---9---A---B---C---D---E---F---
0E0000: ................................................................
0F0000: RRRRRRRRRRRRRRRRRRRRRRRRRRRRRRRRRRRRRRRRRRRRRRRRRRRRRRRRRRRRRRRR
```

FIG. 7.4 The Enhanced Graphics Adapter (EGA) memory map.

The original IBM EGA card only used 16K of ROM space at C0000. Aftermarket compatible EGA adapters can use additional ROM space up to 32K total. The most interesting thing to note about EGA (and this applies to VGA adapters as well) is that segments A000 and B000 are not all used at all times. For example, if the card is in a graphics mode, only segment A000 would appear to have RAM installed, whereas segment B000 would appear completely empty. If you switched the mode of the adapter (through software) into Color Text mode, segment A000 would instantly appear empty, and the last half of segment B000 would suddenly "blink on." The monochrome text mode RAM area would practically never be used on a modern system, because little or no software would ever need to switch the adapter into that mode. Figure 7.4 also shows the standard motherboard ROM BIOS as well so that you can get a picture of the entire UMA.

The EGA card became somewhat popular after it appeared, but this was quickly overshadowed by the VGA card that followed. Most of the VGA characteristics with regard to memory are the same as the EGA because the VGA is backward-compatible with EGA.

Video Graphics Array (VGA) Memory. All VGA-compatible cards, including Super VGA cards, are almost identical to the EGA in terms of memory use. Just as with the EGA, they use all 128K of the video RAM from A0000-BFFFF, but not all at once. Again, the video RAM area is split into three distinct regions, and each of these regions is used only when the adapter is in the corresponding mode. One minor difference with the EGA cards is that virtually all VGA cards use the full 32K allotted to them for on-board ROM (C0000 to C7FFF). Figure 7.5 shows the VGA adapter memory map.

```
       . = Empty Addresses
       G = Video Graphics Array (VGA) Adapter Graphics Mode Video RAM
       M = VGA Monochrome Text Mode Video RAM
       C = VGA Color Text Mode Video RAM
       V = Standard VGA Video ROM BIOS
       R = Standard Motherboard ROM BIOS

        : 0---1---2---3---4---5---6---7---8---9---A---B---C---D---E---F---
0A0000: GGGGGGGGGGGGGGGGGGGGGGGGGGGGGGGGGGGGGGGGGGGGGGGGGGGGGGGGGGGGGGGG
0B0000: MMMMMMMMMMMMMMMMMMMMMMMMMMMMMMMMCCCCCCCCCCCCCCCCCCCCCCCCCCCCCCCC
        : 0---1---2---3---4---5---6---7---8---9---A---B---C---D---E---F---
0C0000: VVVVVVVVVVVVVVVVVVVVVVVVVVVVVVVV................................
0D0000: ................................................................
        : 0---1---2---3---4---5---6---7---8---9---A---B---C---D---E---F---
0E0000: ................................................................
0F0000: RRRRRRRRRRRRRRRRRRRRRRRRRRRRRRRRRRRRRRRRRRRRRRRRRRRRRRRRRRRRRRRR
```

FIG. 7.5 The VGA (and Super VGA) adapter memory map.

You can see that the typical VGA card uses a full 32K of space for the on-board ROM containing driver code. Some VGA cards may use slightly less, but this is rare. Just as with the EGA card, the video RAM areas are only active when the adapter is in the particular mode designated. In other words, when a VGA adapter is in graphics mode, only segment A000 is used; and when it is in color text mode, only the last half of segment B000 is used. Because the VGA adapter is almost never run in monochrome text mode, the first half of segment B000 remains unused (B0000-B7FFF). Figure 7.5 also shows the standard motherboard ROM BIOS so that you can get a picture of how the entire UMA is laid out with this adapter.

Systems that use the LPX (Low Profile) motherboard design in an LPX- or Slimline-type case incorporate the video adapter into the motherboard. In these systems, even though the video BIOS and motherboard BIOS may be from the same manufacturer, they are always set up to emulate a standard VGA-type adapter card. In other words, the video BIOS appears in the first 32K of segment C000 just as if a stand-alone VGA-type card were plugged into a slot. The built-in video circuit in these systems can be easily disabled via a switch or jumper, which then allows a conventional VGA-type card to be plugged in. By having the built-in VGA act exactly as if it were a separate card, disabling it allows a new adapter to be installed without the compatibility problems that might arise if the video drivers had been incorporated into the motherboard BIOS.

If you were involved with the PC industry in 1987, you might remember how long it took for clone video card manufacturers to accurately copy the IBM VGA circuits. It took nearly two years (almost until 1989) before you could buy an aftermarket VGA card and expect it to run everything an IBM VGA system would with no problems. Some of my associates who bought some of the early cards inadvertently became members of the video card manufacturer's "ROM of the week" club! They were constantly finding problems with the operation of these cards, and many updated and patched ROMs were sent to try to fix the problems. Not wanting to pay for the privilege of beta testing the latest attempts at VGA compatibility, I bit the bullet and took the easy way out. I bought the IBM VGA card (PS/2 Display Adapter) for $595. That is still about as much as you would pay for the best Local Bus Super VGA cards on the market today.

Although the card worked very well, and although I never did find any compatibility problems, I did later run into some interesting problems with the memory use of this card. This was my first introduction to what I call *scratch pad memory* use by an adapter. I found that many different types of adapters may use some areas in the UMA for mapping scratch pad memory. This refers to memory on the card that stores status information, configuration data, or any other temporary type of information of a variable nature. Most cards keep this scratch pad memory to themselves and do not attempt to map it into the processor's address space. But some cards do place this type of memory in the address space so that the driver programs for the card can use it. Figure 7.6 shows the memory map of the IBM PS/2 Display Adapter (IBM's VGA card).

There is no difference between this VGA card and any other with respect to the Video RAM area. What is different is that the ROM code that operates this adapter only consumes 24K of memory from C0000-C5FFF. Also strange is the 2K "hole" at C6000, and the 6K of scratch pad memory starting at C6800, as well as the additional 2K of scratch pad memory at CA000. In particular, the 2K "straggler" area really caught me off guard when I installed a SCSI host adapter in this system that had a 16K on-board BIOS with a default starting address of C8000. I immediately ran into a conflict that completely disabled the system. In fact, it would not boot, had no display at all, and could only beep out error codes that indicated that the video card had failed. I first thought that I had somehow "fried" the card, but removing the new SCSI adapter made everything function normally. I also could get the system to work with the SCSI adapter and an old CGA card substituted for the VGA card, so I immediately knew a conflict was underfoot. This

http://www.quecorp.com

```
        . = Empty Addresses
        G = Video Graphics Array (VGA) Adapter Graphics Mode Video RAM
        M = VGA Monochrome Text Mode Video RAM
        C = VGA Color Text Mode Video RAM
        V = IBM VGA Video ROM BIOS
        v = IBM VGA Scratch Pad memory (used by the card)
        R = Standard Motherboard ROM BIOS

           : 0---1---2---3---4---5---6---7---8---9---A---B---C---D---E---F---
    0A0000 : GGGGGGGGGGGGGGGGGGGGGGGGGGGGGGGGGGGGGGGGGGGGGGGGGGGGGGGGGGGGGGGG
    0B0000 : MMMMMMMMMMMMMMMMMMMMMMMMMMMMMMMMCCCCCCCCCCCCCCCCCCCCCCCCCCCCCCCC
           : 0---1---2---3---4---5---6---7---8---9---A---B---C---D---E---F---
    0C0000 : VVVVVVVVVVVVVVVVVVVVVVV..vvvvvv........vv.......................
    0D0000 : ................................................................
           : 0---1---2---3---4---5---6---7---8---9---A---B---C---D---E---F---
    0E0000 : ................................................................
    0F0000 : RRRRRRRRRRRRRRRRRRRRRRRRRRRRRRRRRRRRRRRRRRRRRRRRRRRRRRRRRRRRRRRR
```

FIG. 7.6 IBM's ISA-bus VGA card (PS/2 Display Adapter) memory map.

scratch pad memory use was not documented clearly in the technical-reference information for the adapter, so it was something that I had to find out by trial and error. If you have ever had the IBM VGA card and had conflicts with other adapters, now you know why!

Needless to say, nothing could be done about this 2K of scratch pad memory hanging out there. I had to work around it as long as I had this card in the system. I solved my SCSI adapter problem by merely moving the SCSI adapter BIOS to a different address.

> **Note**
>
> I have seen other VGA-type video adapters use scratch pad memory, but they have all kept it within the C0000-C7FFF 32K region allotted normally for the video ROM BIOS. By using a 24K BIOS, I have seen other cards with up to 8K of scratch pad area, but none—except for IBM's—in which the scratch pad memory goes beyond C8000.

Adapter ROM and Special Purpose RAM Memory. The second 128K of upper memory beginning at segment C000 is reserved for the software programs, or BIOS (basic input/output system), on the adapter boards plugged into the system slots. These BIOS programs are stored on special chips known as read-only memory (ROM), which have fused circuits so that the PC cannot alter them. ROM is useful for permanent programs that always must be present while the system is running. Graphics boards, hard disk controllers, communications boards, and expanded memory boards, for example, are adapter boards that might use some of this memory.

On systems based on the 386 CPU chip or higher, memory managers like the MS DOS 6 MEMMAKER, IBM DOS RAMBOOST, or aftermarket programs like QEMM by Quarterdeck, can load device drivers and memory-resident programs into unused regions in the UMA.

To actually move the RAM usage on any given adapter requires that you consult the documentation for the card. Most older cards require that specific switches or jumpers be changed, and the settings will probably not be obvious without the manual. Most newer cards, especially those that are Plug and Play, allow these settings to be changed by software that either comes with the card itself, or the Configuration Manager program that goes with some of the newer operating systems like Windows 95 or OS/2.

Video Adapter BIOS. The video adapter BIOS handles communication between the video chipset and the video RAM. Although 128K of upper memory beginning at segment C000 is reserved for use by the video adapter BIOS, not all this space is used by various video adapters commonly found on PCs. Table 7.2 details the amount of space used by the BIOS on each type of common video adapter card.

Table 7.2 Memory Used by Different Video Cards

Type of Adapter	Adapter BIOS Memory Used
Monochrome Display Adapter (MDA)	None - Drivers in Motherboard BIOS
Color Graphics Adapter (CGA)	None - Drivers in Motherboard BIOS
Enhanced Graphics Adapter (EGA)	16K on-board (C0000-C3FFF)
Video Graphics Array (VGA)	32K on-board (C0000-C7FFF)
Super VGA (SVGA)	32K on-board (C0000-C7FFF)

Some more advanced graphics accelerator cards on the market do use most or all of the 128K of upper memory beginning at segment C000 to speed the repainting of graphics displays in Windows, OS/2, or other graphical user interfaces (GUIs). In addition, these graphics cards may contain up to 4M or more of on-board memory in which to store currently displayed data and more quickly fetch new screen data as it is sent to the display by the CPU.

Hard Disk Controller and SCSI Host Adapter BIOS. The upper memory addresses C0000 to DFFFF also are used for the BIOS contained on many hard drive controllers. Table 7.3 details the amount of memory and the addresses commonly used by the BIOS contained on hard drive adapter cards.

Table 7.3 Memory Addresses Used by Different Hard Drive Adapter Cards

Disk Adapter Type	On-Board BIOS Size	BIOS Address Range
IBM XT 10M Controller	8K	C8000-C9FFF
IBM XT 20M Controller	4K	C8000-C8FFF
Most XT Compatible Controllers	8K	C8000-C9FFF
Most AT Controllers	None	Drivers in Motherboard BIOS
Most IDE Adapters	None	Drivers in Motherboard BIOS
Most ESDI Controllers	16K	C8000-CBFFF
Most SCSI Host Adapters	16K	C8000-CBFFF

The hard drive or SCSI adapter card used on a particular system may use a different amount of memory, but it is most likely to use the memory segment beginning at C800 because this address is considered part of the IBM standard for personal computers.

Virtually all the disk controller or SCSI adapters today that have an on-board BIOS allow the BIOS starting address to be easily moved in the C000 and D000 segments. The locations listed in Table 7.3 are only the default addresses that most of these cards use. If the default address is already in use by another card, you have to consult the documentation for the new card to see how to change the BIOS starting address to avoid any conflicts.

Figure 7.7 shows an example memory map for an Adaptec AHA-1542CF SCSI adapter.

```
        . = Empty Addresses
        G = Video Graphics Array (VGA) Adapter Graphics Mode Video RAM
        M = VGA Monochrome Text Mode Video RAM
        C = VGA Color Text Mode Video RAM
        V = Standard VGA Video ROM BIOS
        S = SCSI Host Adapter ROM BIOS
        R = Standard Motherboard ROM BIOS

         : 0---1---2---3---4---5---6---7---8---9---A---B---C---D---E---F---
 0A0000: GGGGGGGGGGGGGGGGGGGGGGGGGGGGGGGGGGGGGGGGGGGGGGGGGGGGGGGGGGGGGGGG
 0B0000: MMMMMMMMMMMMMMMMMMMMMMMMMMMMMMMMCCCCCCCCCCCCCCCCCCCCCCCCCCCCCCCC
         : 0---1---2---3---4---5---6---7---8---9---A---B---C---D---E---F---
 0C0000: VVVVVVVVVVVVVVVVVVVVVVVVVVVVVVVV................................
 0D0000: ........................................SSSSSSSSSSSSSSSS
         : 0---1---2---3---4---5---6---7---8---9---A---B---C---D---E---F---
 0E0000: ................................................................
 0F0000: RRRRRRRRRRRRRRRRRRRRRRRRRRRRRRRRRRRRRRRRRRRRRRRRRRRRRRRRRRRRRRRR
```

FIG. 7.7 Adaptec AHA-1542CF SCSI adapter default memory use.

Note how this SCSI adapter fits in here. Although no conflicts are in the UMA memory, the free regions have been fragmented by the placement of the SCSI BIOS. Because most systems do not have any BIOS in segment E000, that remains as a free 64K region. With no other adapters using memory, this example shows another free UMB (Upper Memory Block) starting at C8000 and continuing through DBFFF, which represents an 80K free region. Using the EMM386 driver that comes with DOS, memory can be mapped into these two regions for loading memory-resident drivers and programs. Unfortunately, because programs cannot be split across regions, the largest program you could load is 80K, which is the size of the largest free region. It would be much better if you could move the SCSI adapter BIOS so that it is next to the VGA BIOS, as this would bring the free UMB space to a single region of 144K. It is much easier and more efficient to use a single 144K region than two regions of 80K and 64K, respectively.

Fortunately, it is possible to move this particular SCSI adapter, although doing so requires that several switches be reset on the card itself. One great thing about this Adaptec card is that a sticker is placed directly on the card detailing all the switch settings, or the settings are screened into the card! This means that you don't have to go hunting for a manual that may not be nearby. More adapter card manufacturers should place this information right on the card.

After changing the appropriate switches to move the SCSI adapter BIOS to start at C8000, the optimized map would look like Figure 7.8.

```
         . = Empty Addresses
         G = Video Graphics Array (VGA) Adapter Graphics Mode Video RAM
         M = VGA Monochrome Text Mode Video RAM
         C = VGA Color Text Mode Video RAM
         V = Standard VGA Video ROM BIOS
         S = SCSI Host Adapter ROM BIOS
         R = Standard Motherboard ROM BIOS

                : 0---1---2---3---4---5---6---7---8---9---A---B---C---D---E---F---
         0A0000: GGGGGGGGGGGGGGGGGGGGGGGGGGGGGGGGGGGGGGGGGGGGGGGGGGGGGGGGGGGGGGGG
         0B0000: MMMMMMMMMMMMMMMMMMMMMMMMMMMMMMMMCCCCCCCCCCCCCCCCCCCCCCCCCCCCCCCC
                : 0---1---2---3---4---5---6---7---8---9---A---B---C---D---E---F---
         0C0000: VVVVVVVVVVVVVVVVVVVVVVVVVVVVVVVVSSSSSSSSSSSSSSSS................
         0D0000: ................................................................
                : 0---1---2---3---4---5---6---7---8---9---A---B---C---D---E---F---
         0E0000: ................................................................
         0F0000: RRRRRRRRRRRRRRRRRRRRRRRRRRRRRRRRRRRRRRRRRRRRRRRRRRRRRRRRRRRRRRRR
```

FIG. 7.8 Adaptec AHA-1542CF SCSI adapter with optimized memory use.

Notice how the free space is now a single contiguous block of 144K. This represents a far more optimum setup than the default settings.

Network Adapters. Network adapter cards also can use upper memory in segments C000 and D000. The exact amount of memory used and the starting address for each network card varies with the type and manufacturer of the card. Some network cards do not use any memory at all. A network card might have two primary uses for memory. They are as follows:

- IPL (Initial Program Load or Boot) ROM
- Shared Memory (RAM)

An *IPL ROM* is usually an 8K ROM that contains a bootstrap loader program that allows the system to boot directly from a file server on the network. This allows the removal of all disk drives from the PC, creating a diskless workstation. Because no floppy or hard disk would be in the system to boot from, the IPL ROM gives the system the instructions necessary to locate an image of the operating system on the file server and load it as if it were on an internal drive. If you are not using your system as a diskless workstation, it would be beneficial to disable any IPL ROM or IPL ROM Socket on the adapter card. Note that many network adapters do not allow this socket to be disabled, which means that you lose the 8K of address space for other hardware even if the ROM chip is removed from the socket!

Shared memory refers to a small portion of RAM contained on the network card that is mapped into the PC's Upper Memory Area. This region is used as a memory window onto the network and offers very fast data transfer from the network card to the system. IBM pioneered the use of shared memory for its first Token-Ring Network adapters, and now shared memory is in common use among other companies' network adapters today. Shared memory was first devised by IBM because they found that transfers using the DMA channels were not fast enough in most systems. This had mainly to do with some quirks in the DMA controller and bus design, which especially affected 16-bit ISA bus systems. Network adapters that do not use shared memory will either use DMA or Programmed I/O (PIO) transfers to move data to and from the network adapter.

Although shared memory is faster than either DMA or PIO for ISA systems, it does require 16K of UMA space to work. Most standard performance network adapters use PIO because this makes them easier to configure, and they require no free UMA space, whereas most high performance adapters will use shared memory. The shared memory region on most network adapters that use one is usually 16K in size and may be located at any user-selected 4K increment of memory in segments C000 or D000.

Figure 7.9 shows the default memory addresses for the IPL ROM and shared memory of an IBM Token-Ring Network adapter, although other network adapters such as Ethernet adapters would be similar.

```
        . = Empty Addresses
        G = Video Graphics Array (VGA) Adapter Graphics Mode Video RAM
        M = VGA Monochrome Text Mode Video RAM
        C = VGA Color Text Mode Video RAM
        V = Standard VGA Video ROM BIOS
        I = Token Ring Network Adapter IPL ROM
        N = Token Ring Network Adapter Shared RAM
        R = Standard Motherboard ROM BIOS

              : 0---1---2---3---4---5---6---7---8---9---A---B---C---D---E---F---
        0A0000: GGGGGGGGGGGGGGGGGGGGGGGGGGGGGGGGGGGGGGGGGGGGGGGGGGGGGGGGGGGGGGGG
        0B0000: MMMMMMMMMMMMMMMMMMMMMMMMMMMMMMMMCCCCCCCCCCCCCCCCCCCCCCCCCCCCCCCC
              : 0---1---2---3---4---5---6---7---8---9---A---B---C---D---E---F---
        0C0000: VVVVVVVVVVVVVVVVVVVVVVVVVVVVVVVV................IIIIIIII........
        0D0000: ................................NNNNNNNNNNNNNNNN................
              : 0---1---2---3---4---5---6---7---8---9---A---B---C---D---E---F---
        0E0000: ................................................................
        0F0000: RRRRRRRRRRRRRRRRRRRRRRRRRRRRRRRRRRRRRRRRRRRRRRRRRRRRRRRRRRRRRRRR
```

FIG. 7.9 Network adapter default memory map.

I have also included the standard VGA video BIOS in Figure 7.9 because nearly every system would have a VGA-type video adapter as well. Note that these default addresses for the IPL ROM and the shared memory can easily be changed by reconfiguring the adapter. Most other network adapters are similar in that they also would have an IPL ROM and a shared memory address, although the sizes of these areas and the default addresses may be different. Most network adapters that incorporate an IPL ROM option can disable the ROM and socket such that those addresses are not needed at all. This helps to conserve UMA space and prevent possible future conflicts if you are never going to use the function.

Notice in this case that the SCSI adapter used in Figure 7.9 would fit both at its default BIOS address of DC000, as well as the optimum address of C8000. The Token-Ring shared memory location is not optimum and causes the UMB space to be fragmented. By adjusting the location of the shared memory, this setup can be greatly improved. Figure

7.10 shows an optimum setup with both the Token-Ring adapter and the SCSI adapter in the same machine.

```
       . = Empty Addresses
       G = Video Graphics Array (VGA) Adapter Graphics Mode Video RAM
       M = VGA Monochrome Text Mode Video RAM
       C = VGA Color Text Mode Video RAM
       V = Standard VGA Video ROM BIOS
       S = SCSI Host Adapter ROM BIOS
       I = Token Ring Network Adapter IPL ROM
       N = Token Ring Network Adapter Shared RAM
       R = Standard Motherboard ROM BIOS

            : 0---1---2---3---4---5---6---7---8---9---A---B---C---D---E---F---
      0A0000: GGGGGGGGGGGGGGGGGGGGGGGGGGGGGGGGGGGGGGGGGGGGGGGGGGGGGGGGGGGGGGGG
      0B0000: MMMMMMMMMMMMMMMMMMMMMMMMMMMMMMMMCCCCCCCCCCCCCCCCCCCCCCCCCCCCCCCC
            : 0---1---2---3---4---5---6---7---8---9---A---B---C---D---E---F---
      0C0000: VVVVVVVVVVVVVVVVVVVVVVVVVVVVVVVVSSSSSSSSSSSSSSSSNNNNNNNNNNNNNNNN
      0D0000: IIIIIIII........................................................
            : 0---1---2---3---4---5---6---7---8---9---A---B---C---D---E---F---
      0E0000: ................................................................
      0F0000: RRRRRRRRRRRRRRRRRRRRRRRRRRRRRRRRRRRRRRRRRRRRRRRRRRRRRRRRRRRRRRRR
```

FIG. 7.10 Adaptec AHA-1542CF SCSI adapter and Network adapter with optimized memory use.

This configuration allows a single 120K UMB that can very efficiently be used to load software drivers. Notice that the IPL ROM was moved to D0000, which places it as the last item installed before the free memory space. This is because if the IPL function is not needed, it can be disabled and the UMB space would increase to 128K and still be contiguous. If the default settings are used for both the SCSI and network adapters, the UMB memory would be fragmented into three regions of 16K, 40K, and 64K. The memory would still function, but it is hardly an optimum situation.

Other ROMs in the Upper Memory Area. In addition to the BIOS for hard drive controllers, SCSI adapters, and network cards, upper memory segments C000 and D000 are used by some terminal emulators, security adapters, memory boards, and various other devices and adapter boards. Some adapters may require memory only for BIOS information, and others may require RAM in these upper memory segments. For information on a specific adapter, consult the manufacturer's documentation.

Motherboard BIOS Memory. The last 128K of reserved memory is used by the motherboard BIOS. The BIOS programs in ROM control the system during the bootup procedure and remain as drivers for various hardware in the system during normal operation. Because these programs must be available immediately, they cannot be loaded from a device like a disk drive. The main functions of the programs stored in the motherboard ROM are as follows:

- *Power-On Self Test*, the POST, is a set of routines that tests the motherboard, memory, disk controllers, video adapters, keyboard, and other primary system components. This routine is useful when you troubleshoot system failures or problems.

- The *bootstrap loader* routine initiates a search for an operating system on a floppy disk or hard disk. If an operating system is found, it is loaded into memory and given control of the system.

- The *BIOS* is the software interface, or master control program, to all the hardware in the system. With the BIOS, a program easily can access features in the system by calling on a standard BIOS program module instead of talking directly to the device.

Both segments E000 and F000 in the memory map are considered reserved for the motherboard BIOS, but only some AT-type systems actually use this entire area. PC/XT-type systems require only segment F000 and enable adapter card ROM or RAM to use segment E000. Most AT systems use all of F000 for the BIOS, and may decode but not use any of segment E000. By decoding an area, the AT motherboard essentially grabs control of the addresses, which precludes installing any other hardware in this region. In other words, it is not possible to install any other adapters to use this area. That is why you will find that most adapters that use memory simply do not allow any choices for memory use in segment E000. Although this may seem like a waste of 64K of memory space, any 386 or higher system can use the powerful MMU in the processor to map RAM from extended memory into segment E000 as an Upper Memory Block, and subsequently use it for loading software. This is a nice solution to what otherwise would be wasted memory. Under DOS, the EMM386 driver controls the MMU remapping functions.

Many different ROM-interface programs are in the IBM motherboards, but the location of these programs is mostly consistent. Information on PC/XT System BIOS memory usage can be found in the sixth edition of this book, included on the CD.

Figure 7.11 shows the motherboard ROM BIOS memory use of most AT-compatible systems. These systems lack the IBM Cassette BASIC, but do usually include a built-in Setup program.

```
    . = Empty Addresses
    R = Standard Motherboard ROM BIOS

        : 0---1---2---3---4---5---6---7---8---9---A---B---C---D---E---F---
0E0000: ................................................................
0F0000: RRRRRRRRRRRRRRRRRRRRRRRRRRRRRRRRRRRRRRRRRRRRRRRRRRRRRRRRRRRRRRRR
```

FIG. 7.11 Motherboard ROM BIOS memory use of most AT-compatible systems.

Note that the standard AT-compatible system BIOS uses only segment F000 (64K). In almost every case, the remainder of the BIOS area (segment E000) is completely free and can be used as UMB space.

BIOS Error Messages. The ROM maps of most IBM compatibles equal the IBM system with which they are compatible—with the exception of the Cassette BASIC portion (also called *ROM BASIC*). It may come as a surprise to some personal computer users, but the original IBM PC actually had a jack on the rear of the system for connecting a cassette tape recorder. This was to be used for loading programs and data to or from a cassette tape. Tapes were used at the time because floppy drives were very costly, and hard disks were not even an option yet. Floppy drives came down in price quickly at the time, and the cassette port never appeared on any subsequent IBM systems. The cassette port also never appeared on any compatible system.

The original PC came standard with only 16K of memory in the base configuration. No floppy drives were included, so you could not load or save files from disks. Most computer users at the time would either write their own programs in the BASIC (Beginner's All-Purpose Symbolic Instruction Code) language or run programs written by others. A BASIC language interpreter was built into the ROM BIOS of these early IBMs, and was designed to access the cassette port on the back of the system.

What is really strange is that IBM kept this ROM BASIC relationship all the way through most of the PS/2 systems! The portable 486 PS/2 system (IBM P75 Portable) I was using until recently came standard with a built-in SCSI adapter and currently has a 4G SCSI drive installed. Yet this system still has the ROM BASIC wasting 32K of space! I liken this to humans having an appendix. The ROM BASIC in the IBM systems is a sort of vestigial organ—a leftover that had some use in prehistoric ancestors, but that has no function today.

You can catch a glimpse of this ROM BASIC on IBM systems that have it by disabling all the disk drives in the system. In that case, with nothing to boot from, most IBM systems unceremoniously dump you into the strange (vintage 1981) ROM BASIC screen. When this occurs, the message looks like this:

```
The IBM Personal Computer Basic
Version C1.10 Copyright IBM Corp 1981
62940 Bytes free
Ok
```

Many people used to dread seeing this because it usually meant that your hard disk had failed to be recognized! Because no compatible systems ever had the Cassette BASIC interpreter in ROM, they had to come up with different messages to display for the same situations in which an IBM system would invoke this BASIC. Compatibles that have an AMI BIOS in fact display a confusing message, as follows:

```
NO ROM BASIC - SYSTEM HALTED
```

This message is a BIOS error message that is displayed by the AMI BIOS when the same situations occur that would cause an IBM system to dump into Cassette BASIC, which of course is not present in an AMI BIOS (or any other compatible BIOS for that matter). Other BIOS versions display different messages. For example, under the same circumstances, a Compaq BIOS displays the following:

```
Non-System disk or disk error
replace and strike any key when ready
```

This is somewhat confusing on Compaq's part because this very same (or similar) error message is contained in the DOS Boot Sector, and would normally be displayed if the system files were missing or corrupted.

In the same situations that you would see Cassette BASIC on an IBM system, a system with an Award BIOS would display the following:

```
DISK BOOT FAILURE, INSERT SYSTEM DISK AND PRESS ENTER
```

Phoenix BIOS systems will display either:

```
No boot device available -
strike F1 to retry boot, F2 for setup utility
```

or

```
No boot sector on fixed disk -
strike F1 to retry boot, F2 for setup utility
```

The first or second Phoenix message displays depending on exactly which error actually occurred.

Although the message displayed varies from BIOS to BIOS, the cause is the same for all of them. Two things can generally cause any of these messages to be displayed, and they both relate to specific bytes in the Master Boot Record, which is the first sector of a hard disk at the physical location Cylinder 0, Head 0, Sector 1.

The first problem relates to a disk that has either never been partitioned, or has had the Master Boot Sector corrupted. During the boot process, the BIOS checks the last two bytes in the Master Boot Record (the first sector of the drive) for a "signature" value of 55AAh. If the last two bytes are not 55AAh, an Interrupt 18h is invoked. This calls the subroutine that displays the message you received, as well as the others indicated, or on an IBM system invokes Cassette (ROM) BASIC itself.

The Master Boot Sector (including the signature bytes) is written to the hard disk by the DOS FDISK program. Immediately after you low level format a hard disk, all the sectors are initialized with a pattern of bytes, and the first sector does *not* contain the 55AAh signature. In other words, these ROM error messages are exactly what you see if you attempt to boot from a hard disk that has been low level formatted, but has not yet been partitioned.

Now consider the second situation that can cause these messages. If the signature bytes are correct, the BIOS executes the Master Partition Boot Record code, which performs a test of the Boot Indicator Bytes in each of the four partition table entries. These bytes are at offset 446 (1BEh), 462 (1CEh), 478 (1DEh), and 494 (1EEh), respectively. They are used to indicate which of the four possible partition table entries contain an active (bootable) partition. A value of 80h in any of these byte offsets indicates that table contains the active partition, whereas all other values must be 00h. If more than one of these bytes is 80h (indicating multiple active partitions), or any of the byte values is anything other than 80h or 00h, you see the following error message:

```
Invalid partition table
```

If all four of these Boot Indicator Bytes are 00h, indicating no active (bootable) partitions, then you also see Cassette BASIC on an IBM system, or the other messages indicated earlier depending on which BIOS you have. This is exactly what occurs if you were to remove the existing partitions from a drive using FDISK, but had not created new partitions on the drive, or had failed to make one of the partitions Active (bootable) with FDISK before rebooting your system.

Extended Memory

As mentioned previously in this chapter, the memory map on a system based on the 286 or higher processor can extend beyond the 1M boundary that exists when the processor is in real mode. On a 286 or 386SX system, the extended memory limit is 16M; on a 386DX, 486, Pentium, Pentium MMX, or Pentium Pro system, the extended memory limit is 4G (4,096M). Systems based on the new Pentium II processor have a limit of 64G (65,536M).

For an AT system to address memory beyond the first megabyte, the processor must be in *protected mode*—the native mode of these newer processors. On a 286, only programs designed to run in protected mode can take advantage of extended memory. 386 and higher processors offer another mode, called *virtual real mode*, which enables extended memory to be, in effect, chopped into 1M pieces (each its own real mode session). Virtual real mode also allows for several of these sessions to be running simultaneously in protected areas of memory. Although several DOS programs can be running at once, each still is limited to a maximum of 640K of memory because each session simulates a real mode environment, right down to the BIOS and Upper Memory Area. Running several programs at once in virtual real mode, called *multitasking*, requires software that can manage each program and keep them from crashing into one another. OS/2, Windows 95, and Windows NT all do this.

The 286 and higher CPU chips also run in what is termed *real mode*, which enables full compatibility with the 8088 CPU chip installed on the PC/XT-type computer. Real mode enables you to run DOS programs one at a time on an AT-type system just like you would on a PC/XT. However, an AT-type system running in real mode, particularly a 386-, 486-, Pentium-, Pentium Pro-, or Pentium II-based system, is really functioning as little more than a turbo PC. In real mode, these processors can emulate the 8086 or 8088, but they cannot operate in protected mode at the same time. For that reason the 386 and above also provide a virtual real mode that operates under protected mode. This allows for the execution of real mode programs under the control of a protected mode operating system like OS/2 or Windows NT.

> **Note**
>
> Extended memory is basically all memory past the first megabyte, which can only be accessed while the processor is in protected mode.

XMS Memory. The extended memory specification (XMS) was developed in 1987 by Microsoft, Intel, AST Corp., and Lotus Development to specify how programs would use extended memory. The XMS specification functions on systems based on the 286 or higher and allows real mode programs (those designed to run in DOS) to use extended memory and another block of memory usually out of the reach of DOS.

Before XMS, there was no way to ensure cooperation between programs that switched the processor into protected mode and used extended memory. There was no way for one program to know what another had been doing with the extended memory because none of them could see that memory while in real mode. HIMEM.SYS becomes an arbitrator of sorts that first grabs all the extended memory for itself and then doles it out to programs that know the XMS protocols. In this manner, several programs that use XMS memory can operate together under DOS on the same system, switching the processor into and out of protected mode to access the memory. XMS rules prevent one program from accessing memory that another has in use. Because Windows 3.x is a program manager that switches the system to and from protected mode in running several programs at once, it has been set up to require XMS memory to function. Windows 95 operates mostly in protected mode, but still calls on real mode for access to many system components. Windows NT is a true protected mode operating system, as is OS/2.

Extended memory can be made to conform to the XMS specification by installing a device driver in the CONFIG.SYS file. The most common XMS driver is HIMEM.SYS, which is included with Windows 3.x and later versions of DOS, starting with 4.0 and up. Other memory managers, like QEMM, also convert extended memory into XMS-specification memory when you add its device drivers to CONFIG.SYS.

High Memory Area (HMA) and the A20 line. The High Memory Area (HMA) is an area of memory 16 bytes short of 64K in size, starting at the beginning of the first megabyte of extended memory. It can be used to load device drivers and memory-resident programs to free up conventional memory for use by real mode programs. Only one device driver or memory-resident program can be loaded into HMA at one time, no matter what its size. Originally this could be any program, but Microsoft decided that DOS could get there first, and built capability into DOS 5 and newer versions.

The HMA area is extremely important to those who use DOS 5 or higher because these DOS versions can move their own kernel (about 45K of program instructions) into this area. This is accomplished simply by first loading an XMS driver (such as HIMEM.SYS) and adding the line **DOS=HIGH** to your CONFIG.SYS file. Taking advantage of this DOS capability frees another 45K or so of conventional memory for use by real-mode programs by essentially moving 45K of program code into the first segment of extended memory. Although this memory was supposed to be accessible in protected mode only, it turns out that a defect in the design of the original 286 (which fortunately has been propagated forward to the more recent processors as a "feature") accidentally allows access to most of the first segment of extended memory while still in real mode.

The use of the HMA is controlled by the HIMEM.SYS or equivalent driver. The origins of this memory usage are interesting because they are based on a bug in the original 286 processor carried forward through even the new Pentium II.

The problem started from the fact that memory addresses in Intel processors are dictated by an overlapping segment and offset address. By setting the segment address to FFFF, which itself specifies an actual address of FFFF0 that is 16 bytes from the end of the first megabyte, and then specifying an offset of FFFF, which is equal to 64K, you can create a memory address as follows:

```
      FFFF  segment
+     FFFF  offset
    ───────
=  10FFEF  total
```

This type of address is impossible on a 8088 or 8086 system that has only 20 address lines and therefore cannot calculate an address that large. By leaving off the leading digit, these processors interpret the address as 0FFEF, in essence causing the address to "wrap around" and end up 16 bytes from the end of the first 64K segment of the first megabyte. The problem with the 286 and higher was that when they were in real mode, they were supposed to operate the same way, and the address should wrap around to the beginning of the first megabyte also. Unfortunately, a "bug" in the chip left the 21st address line active (called the A20 line), which allowed the address to end up 16 bytes from the end of the first 64K segment in the second megabyte. This memory was supposed to be addressable only in protected mode, but this bug allowed all but 16 bytes of the first 64K of extended memory to be addressable in real mode.

Because this bug caused problems with many real mode programs that relied on the wrap to take place, when IBM engineers designed the AT, they had to find a way to disable the A20 line while in real mode, but then re-enable it when in protected mode. They did this by using some unused pins on the 8042 keyboard controller chip on the motherboard. The 8042 keyboard controller was designed to accept scan codes from the keyboard and transmit them to the processor, but there were unused pins not needed strictly for this function. So IBM came up with a way to command the keyboard controller to turn on and off the A20 line, thus enabling the "defective" 286 to truly emulate an 8088 and 8086 while in real mode.

Microsoft realized that you could command the 8042 keyboard controller to turn back on the A20 line strictly for the purpose of using this "bug" as a feature that enabled you to access the first 64K of extended memory (less 16 bytes) without having to go through the lengthy and complicated process of switching to protected mode. Thus HIMEM.SYS and the High Memory Area was born! HIMEM.SYS has to watch the system to see if the A20 line should be off for compatibility, or on to enable access to the HMA or while in protected mode. In essence, HIMEM becomes a control program that manipulates the A20 line through the 8042 keyboard controller chip.

Expanded Memory

Some older programs can use a type of memory called *Expanded Memory Specification* or EMS memory. Unlike conventional (the first megabyte) or extended (the second through 16th or 4,096th megabytes) memory, expanded memory is *not* directly addressable by the processor. Instead, it can only be accessed through a 64K window and small 16K pages established in the UMA. Expanded memory is a segment or bank-switching scheme in which a custom memory adapter has a large number of 64K segments on-board, combined with special switching and mapping hardware. The system uses a free segment in the UMA as the home address for the EMS board. After this 64K is filled with data, the board rotates the filled segment out and a new, empty segment appears to take its place. In this fashion, you have a board that can keep on rotating in new segments to be filled with data. Because only one segment can be seen or operated on at one time, EMS is very inefficient for program code and is normally only used for data.

Figure 7.12 shows how expanded memory fits with conventional and extended memory.

FIG. 7.12 Conventional, extended, and expanded memory.

Intel originally created a custom-purpose memory board that had the necessary EMS bank-switching hardware. They called these boards *Above Boards*, and they were sold widely many years ago. EMS was designed with 8-bit systems in mind and was appropriate for them because they had no capability to access extended memory. 286 and newer systems, however, have the capability to have 15 or more megabytes of extended memory, which is much more efficient than the goofy (and slow) bank-switching EMS scheme. The Above Boards are no longer being manufactured, and EMS memory—as a concept as well as functionally—is extremely obsolete.

If you have any antique software that still requires EMS memory, you are advised to upgrade to newer versions that can use extended memory directly. It is also possible to use the powerful MMU of the 386 and higher processors to convert extended memory to function like LIM EMS, but this should only be done if there is no way to use the extended memory directly. EMM386 can convert extended to expanded, and in fact was originally designed for this purpose, although today it is more likely being used to map extended memory into the UMA for the purposes of loading drivers and not for EMS. The EMM386 driver is included with DOS versions 5 and newer as well as with Windows. If you have several versions on hand, as a rule, always use the newest one.

Preventing ROM BIOS Memory Conflicts and Overlap

As detailed in previous sections, C000 and D000 are reserved for use by adapter-board ROM and RAM. If two adapters have overlapping ROM or RAM addresses, usually neither board operates properly. Each board functions if you remove or disable the other one, but they do not work together.

With many adapter boards, you can change the actual memory locations to be used with jumpers, switches, or driver software, which might be necessary to allow two boards to coexist in one system. This type of conflict can cause problems for troubleshooters. You must read the documentation for each adapter to find out what memory addresses the adapter uses and how to change the addresses to allow coexistence with another adapter. Most of the time, you can work around these problems by reconfiguring the board or changing jumpers, switch settings, or software-driver parameters. This change enables the two boards to coexist and stay out of each other's way.

Additionally, you must ensure that adapter boards do not use the same IRQ (Interrupt Request Line), DMA (direct memory access) channel, or I/O Port address. You can easily avoid adapter board memory, IRQ, DMA channel, and I/O Port conflicts by creating a chart or template to mock up the system configuration by penciling on the template the resources already used by each installed adapter. You end up with a picture of the system resources and the relationship of each adapter to the others. This procedure helps you anticipate conflicts and ensures that you configure each adapter board correctly the first time. The template also becomes important documentation when you consider new adapter purchases. New adapters must be configurable to use the available resources in your system.

If your system has Plug and Play capabilities, and you use PnP adapters, it will be able to resolve conflicts between the adapters by moving the memory usage on any conflict. Unfortunately, this routine is not intelligent and still requires human intervention, that is, manual specification of addresses in order to achieve the most optimum location for the adapter memory.

ROM Shadowing

Computers based on the 386 or higher CPU chip, which provides memory access on a 32- or 64-bit path, often use a 16-bit data path for system ROM BIOS information. In addition, adapter cards with on-board BIOS may use an 8-bit path to system memory. On these high-end computers, using a 16- or 8-bit path to memory is a significant bottleneck to system performance. In addition to these problems of width, most actual ROM chips are available in maximum speeds far less than what is available for the system's dynamic RAM. For example, the fastest ROMs available are generally 150ns to 200ns, whereas the RAM in a modern system is rated at 60ns.

Because of the fact that ROM is so slow, any system accesses to programs or data in ROM cause many additional wait states to be inserted. These wait states can slow the entire system down tremendously, especially considering that many of the driver programs used constantly by DOS reside in the BIOS chips found on the motherboard and many of the installed adapters. Fortunately, a way was found to transfer the contents of the slow 8- or 16-bit ROM chips into much faster 32-bit main memory. This is called *shadowing the ROMs*.

Virtually all 386 and higher systems enable you to use what is termed *shadow memory* for the motherboard and possibly some adapter ROMs as well. Shadowing essentially moves the programming code from slow ROM chips into fast 32-bit system memory. Shadowing slower ROMs by copying their contents into RAM can greatly speed up these BIOS routines—sometimes making them four to five times faster.

The shadowing is accomplished by using the powerful MMU in the 386 and higher processors. With the appropriate instructions, the MMU can take a copy of the ROM code, place it in RAM, and enable the RAM such that it appears to the system in exactly the same addresses in which it was originally located. This actually disables the ROM chips themselves, which are essentially shut down. The system RAM that is now masquerading as ROM is fully write-protected so that it acts in every way just like the real ROM, with the exception of being much faster, of course! Most systems have an option in the system Setup to enable shadowing for the motherboard BIOS (usually segment F000) and the video BIOS (usually the first 32K of segment C000). Some systems will go further and offer you the capability to enable or disable shadowing in (usually 16K) increments throughout the remainder of the C000 and D000 segments.

> **Note**
>
> The important thing to note about shadowing is that if you enable shadowing for a given set of addresses, anything found there when the system is booting will be copied to RAM and locked in place. If you were to do this to a memory range that had a network adapter's shared memory mapped into it, the network card would cease to function. You must only shadow ranges that contain true ROM and no RAM.

Some systems do not offer shadowing for areas other than the motherboard and video BIOS. In these systems, you can use a memory manager such as EMM386 (which comes with DOS and Windows) to enable shadowing for any range you specify. It is preferable to use the system's own internal shadowing capabilities first because the system shadowing uses memory that would otherwise be discarded. Using an external memory manager such as EMM386 for shadowing costs you a small amount of extended memory, equal to the amount of space you are shadowing.

If you enable shadowing for a range of addresses and one or more adapters or the system in general no longer works properly, you may have scratch pad memory or other RAM within the shadowed area, which is not accessible as long as the shadowing remains active. In this case, you should disable the shadowing for the system to operate properly. If you can figure out precisely which addresses are ROM and which are RAM within the Upper Memory Area, you can selectively shadow only the ROM for maximum system performance.

Total Installed Memory versus Total Usable Memory

One thing that most people don't realize is that not all the SIMM or other RAM memory you purchase and install in a system will be available. Because of some quirks in system design, the system usually has to "throw away" up to 384K of RAM to make way for the Upper Memory Area.

For example, most systems with 4M of RAM (which is 4,096K) installed show a total of only 3,712K installed during the POST or when running Setup. This indicates that 4,096K–3,712K = 384K of missing memory! Some systems may show 3,968K with the same 4M installed, which works out to 4,096K–3,968K = 128K missing.

If you run your Setup program and check out your base and extended memory values, you will find more information than just the single figure for the total shown during the POST. In most systems with 4,096K (4M), you have 640K base and 3,072K extended. In some systems, Setup reports 640K base and 3,328K extended memory, which is a bonus. In other words, most systems come up 384K short, but some come up only 128K short.

This shortfall is not easy to explain, but it is consistent from system to system. Say that you have a 486 system with two installed 72-pin (36-bit) 1M SIMMs. This results in a total installed memory of 2M in two separate banks because the processor has a 32-bit data bus, and one parity bit is required for every eight data bits. Each SIMM is a single bank in this system. Note that most cheaper 486 systems use the 30-pin (9-bit) SIMMs of which four are required to make a single bank. The first bank (or SIMM in this case) starts at address 000000 (the first megabyte), and the second starts at 100000 (the second megabyte).

One of the cardinal rules of memory is that you absolutely cannot have two hardware devices wired to the same address. This means that 384K of the first memory bank in this system would be in direct conflict with the Video RAM (segments A000 and B000), any adapter card ROMs (segments C000 and D000), and of course the motherboard ROM (segments E000 and F000). This means that all SIMM RAM that occupies these addresses must be shut off or the system will not function! Actually, a motherboard designer can do three things with the SIMM memory that would overlap from A0000-FFFFF:

- Use the faster RAM to hold a copy of any slow ROMs (shadowing), disabling the ROM in the process.
- Turn off any RAM not used for shadowing, eliminating any UMA conflicts.
- Remap any RAM not used for shadowing, adding to the stack of currently installed extended memory.

Most systems shadow the motherboard ROM (usually 64K), the video ROM (32K), and simply turn off the rest. Some motherboard ROMs allow additional shadowing to be selected between C8000-DFFFF, usually in 16K increments.

> **Note**
>
> You can only shadow ROM, never RAM, so if any card (such as a network card for example) has a RAM buffer in the C8000-DFFFF area, you must not shadow the RAM buffer addresses or the card does not function. For the same reason, you cannot shadow the A0000-BFFFF area because this is the video adapter RAM buffer.

Most motherboards do not do any remapping, which means that any of the 384K not shadowed is simply turned off. That is why enabling shadowing does not seem to use any memory. The memory used for shadowing would otherwise be discarded in most systems. These systems would appear to be short by 384K compared to what is physically installed in the system. In my example system with 2M, no remapping would result in 640K of base memory and 1,024K of extended memory, for a total of 1,664K of usable RAM—384K short of the total (2,048K–384K).

More advanced systems shadow what they can and then remap any segments that do not have shadowing into extended memory so as not to waste the non-shadowed RAM. PS/2 systems, for example, shadow the motherboard BIOS area (E0000-FFFFF or 128K in these systems) and remap the rest of the first bank of SIMM memory (256K from A0000-DFFFF) to whatever address follows the last installed bank.

> **Note**
>
> Note that PS/2 systems have the video BIOS integrated with the motherboard BIOS in E0000-FFFFF, so no separate video BIOS exists to shadow as compared to other systems.

In my example system with two 1M 36-bit SIMMs, the 256K not used for shadowing would be remapped to 200000-23FFFF, which is the start of the third megabyte. This affects diagnostics because if you had any memory error reported in those addresses (200000-23FFFF), it would indicate a failure in the first SIMM, even though the addresses point to the end of installed extended memory. The addresses from 100000-1FFFFF would be in the second SIMM, and the 640K base memory 000000-09FFFF would be back in the first SIMM. As you can see, figuring out how the SIMMs are mapped into the system is not easy.

Most systems that do remapping can only remap an entire segment if no shadowing is going on within it. The video RAM area in segments A000 and B000 can never contain shadowing, so at least 128K can be remapped to the top of installed extended memory in any system that supports remapping. Because most systems shadow in segments F000 (motherboard ROM) and C000 (Video ROM), these two segments cannot be remapped. This leaves 256K maximum for remapping. Any system remapping the full 384K must not be shadowing at all, which would slow down the system and is not recommended. Shadowing is always preferred over remapping, and remapping what is not shadowed is definitely preferred to simply turning off the RAM.

Systems that have 384K of "missing" memory do not do remapping. If you want to determine if your system has any missing memory, all you need to know are three things. One is the total physical memory actually installed. The other two items can be discovered by running your Setup program. You want to know the total base and extended memory numbers recognized by the system. Then simply subtract the base and extended memory from the total installed to determine the missing memory. You will usually find that your system is "missing" 384K, but may be lucky and have a system that remaps 256K of what is missing and thus shows only 128K of memory missing.

Virtually all systems use some of the missing memory for shadowing ROMs, especially the motherboard and video BIOS. So what is missing is not completely wasted. Systems "missing" 128K will find that it is being used to shadow your motherboard BIOS (64K from F0000-FFFFF) and video BIOS (32K from C0000-C8000). The remainder of segment C0000 (32K from C8000-CFFFF) is simply being turned off. All other segments (128K from A0000-BFFFF and 128K from D0000-EFFFF) are being remapped to the start of the fifth megabyte (400000-43FFFF). Most systems simply disable these remaining segments rather than take the trouble to remap them. Remapping requires additional logic and BIOS routines, and many motherboard designers do not feel that it is worth the effort to reclaim 256K.

> **Note**
>
> If your system is doing remapping, any errors reported near the end of installed extended memory are likely to be in the first bank of memory because that is where they are remapped from. The first bank in a 32-bit system would be constructed of either four 30-pin (9-bit) SIMMs or one 72-pin (36-bit) SIMM.

Adapter Memory Configuration and Optimization

Ideally, all adapter boards would be PnP devices that require you to merely plug the adapter into a motherboard slot and then use it. With the new PnP specification, we are moving towards that goal. However, sometimes it almost seems that adapter boards are designed as if they were the only adapter likely to be present on a system. They usually require you to know the upper memory addresses and IRQ and DMA channels already on your system, as well as how to configure the new adapter so that it does not conflict with your already-installed adapters.

Adapter boards use upper memory for their BIOS and as working RAM. If two boards attempt to use the same BIOS area or RAM area of upper memory, a conflict occurs that can keep your system from booting. The following sections cover ways to avoid these potential conflicts and how to troubleshoot them if they do occur. In addition, these sections discuss moving adapter memory to resolve conflicts and provide some ideas on optimizing adapter memory use.

Adding adapters to EISA and MCA systems is somewhat easier because these system architectures feature *auto-configure adapter boards*. In other words, EISA and MCA systems work with adapters to determine available upper memory addresses, IRQs, and DMA channels and automatically configure all adapters to work optimally together.

How to Determine What Adapters Occupy the UMA. You can determine what adapters are using space in upper memory in the following two ways:

- Study the documentation for each adapter on your system to determine the memory addresses they use.

- Use a software utility that can quickly determine what upper memory areas your adapters are using.

The simplest way (although by no means always the most foolproof) is to use a software utility to determine the upper memory areas used by the adapters installed on your system. One such utility, Microsoft Diagnostics (MSD), comes with Windows 3.x and DOS 6 or higher versions. The Device Manager under System in the Windows 95 Control Panel also provides this information. These utilities examine your system configuration and determine not only the upper memory used by your adapters, but also the IRQs used by each of these adapters.

After you run MSD, Device Manager, or another utility to determine your system's upper memory configuration, make a printout of the memory addresses used. Thereafter, you can quickly refer to the printout when you are adding a new adapter to ensure that the new board does not conflict with any devices already installed on your system.

Moving Adapter Memory to Resolve Conflicts. After you identify a conflict or potential conflict by studying the documentation for the adapter boards installed on your system or using a software diagnostic utility to determine the upper memory addresses used by your adapter boards, you may have to reconfigure one or more of your adapters to move the upper memory space used by a problem adapter.

Most adapter boards make moving adapter memory a somewhat simple process, enabling you to change a few jumpers or switches to reconfigure the board. The following steps help you resolve most conflicts that arise because adapter boards conflict with one another.

1. Determine the upper memory addresses currently used by your adapter boards and write them down.

2. Determine if any of these addresses are overlapping, which results in a conflict.

3. Consult the documentation for your adapter boards to determine which boards can be reconfigured so that all adapters have access to unique memory addresses.

4. Configure the affected adapter boards so that no conflict in memory addresses occurs.

For example, if one adapter uses the upper memory range C8000-CBFFF and another adapter uses the range CA000-CCFFF, you have a potential address conflict. One of these must be changed.

Optimizing Adapter Memory Use. On an ideal PC, adapter boards would always come configured so that the upper memory addresses they use immediately follow the upper memory addresses used by the previous adapter, with no overlap that would cause conflicts. Such an upper memory arrangement would not only be "clean," but would make it much more simple to use available upper memory for loading device drivers and memory-resident programs. However, this is not the case. Adapter boards often leave gaps of unused memory between one another, which is, of course, preferable to an overlap, but still is not the best use of upper memory.

Someone who wanted to make the most of their upper memory might consider studying the documentation for each adapter board installed on his or her system to determine a way to compact the upper memory used by each of these devices. For example, if it were possible on a particular system using the adapters installed on it, the use of upper memory could be more simple if you configured your adapter boards so that the blocks of memory they use fit together like bricks in a wall, rather than like a slice of Swiss cheese, as is the case on most systems. The more you can reduce your free upper memory to as few contiguous chunks as possible, the more completely and efficiently you can take advantage of the UMA.

Taking Advantage of Unused Upper Memory

On systems using an older 16-bit operating system such as Windows 3.1 or DOS, memory-resident programs and device drivers can be moved into the UMA by using a memory manager like the MEMMAKER utility or Quarterdeck's QEMM. These memory management utilities examine the memory-resident programs and device drivers installed on your system, determine their memory needs, and then calculate the best way to move these drivers and programs into upper memory, thus freeing the conventional memory they used.

Using MEMMAKER and QEMM is quite simple. Make a backup of your CONFIG.SYS and AUTOEXEC.BAT files so that you have usable copies if you need them to restore your system configuration. Then run either MEMMAKER from the DOS prompt or use the installation program on the QEMM disk. Both programs install required device drivers in your CONFIG.SYS file, and then begin optimizing your memory configuration. Both do an outstanding job of freeing up conventional memory, although QEMM can free more conventional memory automatically than most other utilities. With careful fine-tuning, an individual can perform feats of memory management using only the raw DOS HIMEM.SYS and EMM386.EXE drivers that no automatic program can do.

Only driver programs that run in the processor's real mode must be loaded within the first megabyte of memory. Because real mode drivers are made up of 16-bit real mode program code, they cannot reside in extended memory, as only the first megabyte (base memory) is accessible when in real mode. DOS and Windows 3.x are 16-bit programs and utilize drivers that run in real mode, hence the need for the base memory optimization. With the number of drivers that people are using today, it can be difficult to fit them all in the available UMA space while leaving enough base memory free to run applications.

Things are changing with the newer operating systems. Windows 95, for example, uses primarily 32-bit protected mode drivers and program code, although there is still a large amount of 16-bit real mode program code left. Windows NT and OS/2 are full 32-bit operating systems, and all their drivers and applications are made up of 32-bit protected mode instruction code. If you are using all 32-bit programs, then virtually no memory optimization is necessary in the first megabyte, as 32-bit programs are free to run in extended memory.

The following sections cover using memory management software to optimize conventional memory, as well as additional ways to configure your system memory to make your system run as efficiently as possible. It is important to note that the DOS HIMEM.SYS and EMM386.EXE play an integral role in MEMMAKER's capability to move device drivers and memory-resident programs into upper memory. The next two sections describe using HIMEM.SYS and EMM386.EXE to configure extended and expanded memory.

> **Note**
>
> If you are running older 16-bit DOS applications under Windows 95, Windows NT, or OS/2, then you still need to know about base memory optimization. In these cases, you will be running the application in a DOS window, which, using the virtual real mode of the processor, can emulate the first megabyte of real mode workspace. Using these 32-bit operating systems, you can customize how the application running in the DOS window sees the system, and how the system memory appears to be organized.

Using HIMEM.SYS (DOS). The DOS device driver HIMEM.SYS, which has been included with Windows as well as DOS 4.0 and higher, is used to configure extended memory to the XMS specification, as well as to enable the use of the first 64K of extended memory as the high memory area (HMA). HIMEM.SYS is installed by adding a line invoking the device driver to your CONFIG.SYS file.

The XMS extended memory specification was developed by Microsoft, Intel, AST Corp., and Lotus Development in 1987 and specifies how programs can use memory beyond the first megabyte on systems based on the 286 CPU chip or higher. The XMS specification also allows real mode programs (those designed to run in DOS) to use extended memory in several different ways.

Using EMM386.EXE (DOS). The program EMM386.EXE, which is included with DOS 5.0 and higher, is used primarily to map XMS memory (extended memory managed by HIMEM.SYS) into unused regions of the UMA. This allows programs to be loaded into these regions for use under DOS. EMM386 also has a secondary function of using XMS memory to emulate EMS version 4 memory, which can then be used by programs that need expanded memory. For more information on using EMM386.EXE, refer to Que's *Using MS-DOS 6* or your DOS manual.

MS-DOS 6.x MEMMAKER. You can increase the amount of conventional memory available to software applications on systems based on the 386 chip and above by running the MS DOS 6.x utility MEMMAKER. DOS 5 had the capability, using EMM386, to map extended memory into the UMA so that DOS could load memory-resident programs and drivers into the UMA. Unfortunately, this required an extensive knowledge of the upper memory configuration of a particular system, as well as trial and error to see what programs could fit into the available free regions. This process was difficult enough that many people were not effectively using their memory under DOS (and Windows).

To make things easier, when DOS 6 was released, Microsoft included a menu-driven program called MEMMAKER that determines the system configuration, automatically creates the proper EMM386 statements, and inserts them into the CONFIG.SYS file. By manipulating the UMA manually or through MEMMAKER and loading device drivers and memory-resident programs into upper memory, you can have more than 600K of free conventional memory.

Over the course of months or years of use, the installation programs for various software utilities often install so many memory-resident programs and device drivers in your AUTOEXEC.BAT and CONFIG.SYS files that you have too little conventional memory left to start all the programs you want to run. You may want to use MEMMAKER to free up more conventional memory for your programs. You can get help on MEMMAKER by typing **HELP MEMMAKER** at the DOS prompt. When you run the MEMMAKER utility, it automatically performs the following functions:

- Moves a portion of the DOS kernel into the HMA.
- Maps free XMS memory into unused regions in the UMA as UMBs, into which DOS can then load device drivers and memory-resident programs to free up the conventional memory these drivers and programs otherwise use.
- Modifies CONFIG.SYS and AUTOEXEC.BAT to cause DOS to load memory-resident programs and device drivers into UMBs.

Before running MEMMAKER, carefully examine your CONFIG.SYS and AUTOEXEC.BAT files to identify unnecessary device drivers and memory-resident programs. For example, the DOS device driver ANSI.SYS is often loaded in CONFIG.SYS to enable you to use color and other attributes at the DOS prompt as well as to remap the keys on your keyboard. If you are primarily a Windows user and do not spend much time at the DOS prompt, you can eliminate ANSI.SYS from your CONFIG.SYS file to free up the memory the driver is using.

> **Tip**
>
> SETVER is another often loaded driver that most people don't need. If you don't run utilities or programs that require a specific version of DOS, you can remove SETVER from your CONFIG.SYS file.

After you strip down CONFIG.SYS and AUTOEXEC.BAT to their bare essentials (it is advisable to make backup copies first), you are ready to run MEMMAKER to optimize your system memory. To run MEMMAKER, follow these steps:

1. Exit from any other programs you are running.
2. Start your network or any memory-resident programs and device drivers you absolutely need.
3. At the DOS prompt, type **MEMMAKER**.

The MEMMAKER setup runs in two modes—Express and Custom. Express setup is preferable for users who want to enable MEMMAKER to load device drivers and memory-resident programs into high memory with the minimum amount of user input, unless they have an EGA or VGA (but not a Super VGA) monitor. If you have an EGA or VGA monitor, choose Custom Setup and answer Yes in the advanced options screen where it asks whether MEMMAKER should use monochrome region (B0000-B7FFF) for running programs. Use the defaults for the rest of the options in Custom setup unless you are sure that one of the defaults is not correct for your system. Custom setup is probably not a good idea unless you are knowledgeable about optimizing system memory, particular device drivers, and memory-resident programs on the system.

When MEMMAKER finishes optimizing the system memory, the following three lines are added to CONFIG.SYS:

```
DEVICE=C:\DOS\HIMEM.SYS
DEVICE=C:\DOS\EMM386.EXE NOEMS
DOS=HIGH,UMB
```

In addition, MEMMAKER modifies each line in CONFIG.SYS and AUTOEXEC.BAT that loads a device driver or memory-resident program now being loaded into UMBs. Various `DEVICE=` lines in your CONFIG.SYS are changed to `DEVICEHIGH=`, and various lines in your AUTOEXEC.BAT have the `LH` (LoadHigh) command inserted in front of them. For example, the line `DEVICE=ANSI.SYS` is changed to `DEVICEHIGH=ANSI.SYS`. In your AUTOEXEC.BAT, lines like `C:\DOS\DOSKEY` are changed to `LH C:\DOS\DOSKEY`. The `DEVICEHIGH` and `LH` commands load the device drivers and memory-resident programs into UMBs. MEMMAKER also adds codes to specify where in upper memory each program will be loaded. For example, after you run MEMMAKER, a statement like this might be added to your AUTOEXEC.BAT:

```
LH /L:1 C:\DOS\DOSKEY
```

The `/L:1` causes the resident program DOSKEY to load into the first UMB region. On many systems, MEMMAKER configures the system to free up 620K of conventional memory.

Quarterdeck QEMM. Although MEMMAKER does a good job of freeing-up conventional memory on most systems, memory management utilities like Quarterdeck's QEMM can do a better job on many systems with more complex configurations, and therefore, numerous memory-resident programs and device drivers. The following section provides information about QEMM. If you are running Windows 95 or Windows NT, be aware that many products are available in new versions that are specifically designed for those operating systems.

One of the strengths of QEMM is how simple it is to install and use. Before running the QEMM INSTALL program, make a backup of your CONFIG.SYS and AUTOEXEC.BAT files so that you have usable copies if you need them to restore your system configuration.

   1. Exit any program you are running.

2. At the DOS prompt, log in to the drive where the QEMM install disk is located and run the INSTALL program. QEMM copies its files to the C:\QEMM directory (or another directory, if you want).

   The INSTALL program loads the Optimize utility, which calculates the upper memory needed for your memory-resident programs and device drivers, and determines the proper region of upper memory for each. During this process, your system is rebooted several times (or when prompted, you may have to turn off your system and then restart it).

3. When Optimize is finished, type **MEM** at the DOS prompt to find out how much free conventional memory your system has.

After QEMM is installed and running on your system, each time you add a memory-resident program or device driver, or any time you add or remove an adapter board (which might change the configuration of upper memory), you need to again run OPTIMIZE. For additional information on installing and running QEMM, and for troubleshooting help, consult your QEMM user manual.

One of the best features of QEMM is that it comes with a system configuration diagnostic utility called MANIFEST. This program is much like MSD, but offers more information and detail in many areas.

Physical Memory

The CPU and motherboard architecture dictates a computer's physical memory capacity. The 8088 and 8086, with 20 address lines, can use as much as 1M (1024K) of RAM. The 286 and 386SX CPUs have 24 address lines; they can keep track of as much as 16M of memory. The 386DX, 486, Pentium, Pentium-MMX, and Pentium Pro CPUs have a full set of 32 address lines; they can keep track of 4G of memory, while the Pentium II with 36 address lines can manage an impressive 64G!

When the 286 and higher chips emulate the 8088 chip (as they do when running a single DOS program), they implement a hardware operating mode called *real mode*. Real mode is the only mode available on the 8086 and 8088 chips used in PC and XT systems. In real mode, all Intel processors—even the mighty Pentium—are restricted to using only 1M of memory, just as their 8086 and 8088 ancestors, and the system design reserves 384K of that amount. Only in protected mode can the 286 or better chips use their maximum potential for memory addressing.

Pentium-based systems can address as much as 4G of memory, and Pentium II systems can address 64G. To put these memory-addressing capabilities into perspective, 64G (65,536M) of memory costing the going rate of about $5 per megabyte for fast (60 ns or less) RAM chips would total $327,680. Of course, you could probably negotiate a much better price with a chip vendor if you planned to buy 64G of memory. Even if you could afford all this memory, the largest memory modules available today are 168-pin DIMMs with 128M capacity. Most Pentium motherboards only have four to eight SIMM sockets, and maybe one or two DIMM sockets, which allows a maximum of 256M to 512M if all sockets are filled. Boards that support 1G or more are becoming available, but they are still the exception and not the norm. Not all systems accept all SIMMs, and many do not accept DIMMs, so you might have a limitation of less than this amount for many older systems.

On many systems, accessing RAM chips installed directly on a motherboard is faster than accessing memory through an expansion slot. Even without considering this speed advantage, you have the advantage of saving slots. The more memory chips you can get on the motherboard, the fewer adapter slots you need to use. A system that does not have a memory expansion slot faces a large reduction in speed if you use a memory expansion board made for a standard 16-bit slot.

Some 386 and 486 motherboards may have problems addressing memory past 16M due to DMA (Direct Memory Access) controller problems. If you install an ISA adapter that uses a DMA channel and you have more than 16M of memory, you have the potential for problems because the ISA bus only allows DMA access to 16M. Attempted transfers beyond 16M cause the system to crash. This should not be an issue with newer 32-bit operating systems.

Because the PC hardware design reserves the top 384K of the first megabyte of system memory for use by the system itself, you have access to 640K for your programs and data. The use of 384K by the system results in the 640K conventional memory limit. The amount of conventional memory you can actually use for programs depends on the memory used by device drivers (such as ANSI.SYS) and memory-resident programs (such as MOUSE.COM) you load in your CONFIG.SYS and AUTOEXEC.BAT files. Device drivers and memory-resident programs usually use conventional memory.

RAM Chips

A *RAM chip* temporarily stores programs when they are running and the data being used by those programs. RAM chips are sometimes termed *volatile storage* because when you turn off your computer or an electrical outage occurs, whatever is stored in RAM is lost unless you saved it to your hard drive. Because of the volatile nature of RAM, many computer users make it a habit to save their work frequently. (Some software applications can do timed backups automatically.)

Launching a computer program brings files into RAM, and as long as they are running, computer programs reside in RAM. The CPU executes programmed instructions in RAM. RAM stores your keystrokes when you use a word processor. RAM stores numbers used in calculations. The CPU also stores results in RAM. Telling a program to save your data instructs the program to store RAM contents on your hard drive as a file.

If you decide to purchase more RAM, you need the information on RAM chips and their speeds presented in the following sections to help ensure that you don't slow down your computer when you add memory.

Physical Storage and Organization

RAM chips can be physically integrated into the motherboard or adapter board in several forms. Older systems used individual memory chips, called *dual in-line package (DIP)* chips, that were plugged into sockets or soldered directly to a board. Most modern systems use a 30- or 72-pin memory package called a *single in-line memory module (SIMM)*. In addition, many newer motherboards use a 168-pin package called *dual in-line memory module (DIMM)*. These modules combine several chips on a small circuit board plugged into a retaining socket. A *SIPP*, or *single in-line pinned package*, is similar to a SIMM, but it uses pins rather than an edge connector to connect to the motherboard. It would be possible to convert a SIPP to a SIMM by cutting off the pins, or to convert a SIMM to a SIPP by soldering pins on. Also, some companies have made SIPP to SIMM converters that allow the SIPPs to be plugged into 30-pin SIMM sockets.

Several types of memory chips have been used in PC system motherboards. Most of these chips are single-bit-wide chips, available in several capacities. The following table lists available RAM chips and their capacities:

RAM Chip	Capacity
16K by 1 bit	These devices were used in the original IBM PC with a Type 1 motherboard.
64K by 1 bit	These chips were used in the standard IBM PC Type 2 motherboard and in the XT Type 1 and 2 motherboards. Many memory adapters of the era, such as the popular vintage AST 6-pack boards, used these chips also.
128K by 1 bit	These chips, used in the IBM AT Type 1 motherboard, often were a strange physical combination of two 64K chips stacked on top of one another and soldered together. Single-chip versions were used also for storing the parity bits in the IBM XT 286.
256K by 1 bit (or 64K by 4 bits)	These chips once were very popular in motherboards and memory cards. The IBM XT Type 2 and IBM AT Type 2 motherboards, as well as most compatible systems of that era used these chips.
1M by 1 bit (or 256K by 4 bits)	1M chips were very popular for a number of years and were most often used in 256K to 8M SIMMs.
4M by 1 bit (or 1M by 4 bits)	4M chips are used primarily in SIMMs from 1M to 16M in capacity. They are used primarily in 4M and 8M SIMMs and generally are not sold as individual chips.
16M by 1 bit (or 4M by 4 bits)	16M chips are often used in 72-pin SIMMs of 16M to 32M capacity.
64M by 1 bit (or 16M by 4 bits)	64M chips are popular in high capacity 16M or larger memory modules, especially for notebook systems.
256M by 1 bit (or 64M by 4 bits)	256M chips are the most recent on the market. These chips allow enormous SIMM capacities of 128M or larger! Because of the high expense and limited availability of these chips, you see them only in the most expensive and highest capacity modules on the market.

Figure 7.13 shows a typical memory chip. Each marking on the chip is significant.

```
     F          MB81256-10

                8609 B04 BC
    USA
```

FIG. 7.13 The markings on a typical memory chip.

The -10 on the chip corresponds to its speed in nanoseconds (a 100-nanosecond rating). MB81256 is the chip's part number, which usually contains a clue about the chip's capacity. The key digits are 1256, which indicate that this chip is 1-bit wide, and has a depth of 256K. The 1 means that to make a full byte with parity, you need nine of these single-bit-wide chips. A chip with a part number KM4164B-10 indicates a 64K-by-1-bit chip at a speed of 100 ns. The following list matches common chips with their part numbers:

Part Number	Chip
4164	64K by 1 bit
4464	64K by 4 bits
41128	128K by 1 bit
44128	128K by 4 bits
41256	256K by 1 bit
44256	256K by 4 bits
41000	1M by 1 bit
44000	1M by 4 bits

Chips wider than 1 bit are used to construct banks of less than 9, 18, or 36 chips (depending on the system architecture). For example, in the IBM XT 286, which is an AT-type 16-bit system, the last 128K bytes of memory on the motherboard consist of a bank with only six chips; four are 64K-by-4 bits wide, and two parity chips are 1 bit wide, storing 18 bits.

In Figure 7.13, the "F" symbol centered between two lines is the manufacturer's logo for Fujitsu Microelectronics. The 8609 indicates the date of manufacture (ninth week of 1986). Some manufacturers, however, use a Julian date code. To decode the chip further, contact the manufacturer if you can tell who that is, or perhaps a memory chip vendor.

Memory Banks

Memory chips (DIPs, SIMMs, SIPPs, and DIMMs) are organized in *banks* on motherboards and memory cards. You should know the memory bank layout and position on the motherboard and memory cards.

You need to know the bank layout when adding memory to the system. In addition, memory diagnostics report error locations by byte and bit addresses, and you must use these numbers to locate which bank in your system contains the problem.

The banks usually correspond to the data bus capacity of the system's microprocessor. Table 7.4 shows the widths of individual banks based on the type of PC.

The number of bits for each bank can be made up of single chips, SIMMs, or DIMMs. For example, in a 286 system that would use an 18-bit bank, you could make up a bank of 18 individual 1-bit-wide chips, or you could use four individual 4-bit-wide chips to make up the data bits, and two individual 1-bit-wide chips for the parity bits.

Table 7.4 Memory Bank Widths on Different Systems

Processor	Data Bus	Memory Bank Size (No Parity)	Memory Bank Size (Parity)	30-pin SIMMs Per Bank	72-pin SIMMs Per Bank	168-pin SIMMs Per Bank
8088	8-bit	8-bits	9-bits	1	<1*	<1*
8086	16-bit	16-bits	18-bits	2	<1*	<1*
286	16-bit	16-bits	18-bits	2	<1*	<1*
386SX, SL, SLC	16-bit	16-bits	18-bits	2	<1*	<1*
386DX	32-bit	32-bits	36-bits	4	1	<1*
486SLC, SLC2	16-bit	16-bits	18-bits	2	<1*	<1*
486SX, DX, DX2, DX4	32-bit	32-bits	36-bits	4	1	<1*
Pentium, MMX	64-bit	64-bits	72-bits	8	2	1
Pentium Pro, II	64-bit	64-bits	72-bits	8	2	1

In these cases, a single SIMM or DIMM constitutes multiple banks of memory.

Most modern systems do not use chips, but instead use SIMMs. If the system has an 18-bit bank, it likely would use 30-pin SIMMs and have two SIMMs per bank. All the SIMMs in a single bank must be the same size and type. As you can see, the 30-pin SIMMs are less than ideal for 64-bit systems because you must use them in increments of eight per bank! Because these SIMMs are available in 1M and 4M capacities today, this means that a single bank has to be 8M or 32M of memory, with no in-between amounts. Using 30-pin SIMMs in 32- and 64-bit systems artificially constricts memory configurations and such systems are not recommended. If a 32-bit system uses 72-pin SIMMs, each SIMM represents a separate bank, and the SIMMs can be added or removed on an individual basis rather than in groups of four. This makes memory configuration much easier and more flexible. In modern 64-bit systems, two 72-pin SIMMs are required per bank.

Many newer systems now use the 168-pin DIMM devices. These are 64 bits without parity, and 72 bits each with parity. The devices function as a single bank in Pentium and higher systems.

Older systems often used individual chips. For example, the IBM PC Type 2 and XT Type 1 motherboards contain four banks of memory labeled Bank 0, 1, 2, and 3. Each bank uses nine 64K×1-bit chips. The total number of chips present is 4×9, or 36 chips.

This layout is used in many older 8-bit motherboards, including the Type 1 and 2 PC motherboards and the Type 1 and 2 XT motherboards. Most PC or XT clones also followed this scheme.

The physical orientation used on a motherboard or memory card is arbitrary and determined by the board's designers. Documentation covering your system or card comes in very handy. You can determine the layout of a motherboard or adapter card through testing, but this takes time and may be difficult, particularly after you have a problem with a system.

Parity Checking

One standard IBM set for the industry is that the memory chips in a bank of nine each handle one bit of data: eight bits per character plus one extra bit called the *parity bit*. The parity bit enables memory-control circuitry to keep tabs on the other eight bits—a built-in cross-check for the integrity of each byte in the system. If the circuitry detects an error, the computer stops and displays a message informing you of the malfunction. If you are running a newer operating system such as Windows or OS/2, a parity error will generally manifest itself as a locked system. When you reboot, the BIOS should detect the error and display the appropriate error message.

SIMMs are available both with and without parity bits. Until recently, all IBM-compatible systems used parity-checked memory to ensure accuracy. Other non-IBM-compatible systems like the Apple Macintosh have never used parity-checked memory. For example, Apple computers use the same 30-pin or 72-pin SIMMs as IBM systems, but Apple computers as a rule do not have parity-checking circuitry, so they can use slightly cheaper 30-pin SIMMs that are only 8 bits wide instead of 9 bits, as is required on many IBM-compatible systems. They also can use 72-pin SIMMs that are only 32-bits wide rather than 36-bits (32 data bits plus 4 parity bits) as is required on most IBM compatibles. You can use the parity SIMMs in Apple systems, they will simply ignore the extra bits. If you use non-parity SIMMs in an IBM compatible that requires parity-checked memory, you instantly get memory errors, and the system cannot operate. If you service both IBM and Apple systems, you could simply stock only parity SIMMs because they can be used in either system.

Recently, a disturbing trend has developed in the IBM-compatible marketplace. Some of the larger vendors have been shipping systems with parity checking disabled! These systems can use slightly cheaper non-parity SIMMs like the Apple systems. The savings amounts to about $10 per 4M SIMM, which can result in a savings to the manufacturer of about $20 for a typical 8M configuration.

Because several of the big names have started selling systems without parity, most of the others have been forced to follow to remain price competitive. Because nobody wants to announce this information, it has remained as a sort of dirty little secret within the industry. What is amazing is that the 386 and higher processors all contain the parity circuitry within them, so no additional circuits are needed on the motherboard. It is solely the cost of the parity chips on the SIMMs that is being saved.

IBM established the *odd parity* standard for error checking. The following explanation may help you understand what is meant by odd parity. As the eight individual bits in a byte are stored in memory, a parity generator/checker, which is either part of the CPU or located in a special chip on the motherboard, evaluates the data bits by counting the number of 1s in the byte. If an even number of 1s is in the byte, the parity generator/checker creates a 1 and stores it as the ninth bit (parity bit) in the parity memory chip. That makes the total sum for all nine bits an odd number. If the original sum of the eight data bits is an odd number, the parity bit created is 0, keeping the 9-bit sum an odd number. The value of the parity bit is always chosen so that the sum of all nine bits (eight data bits plus one parity bit) is an odd number. Remember that the eight data bits in a byte are numbered 0 1 2 3 4 5 6 7. The following examples may make it easier to understand:

Data bit number: 0 1 2 3 4 5 6 7   Parity bit

Data bit value: 1 0 1 1 0 0 1 1   0

In this example, because the total number of data bits with a value of 1 is an odd number (5), the parity bit must have a value of 0 to ensure an odd sum for all nine bits.

The following is another example:

Data bit number: 0 1 2 3 4 5 6 7   Parity bit

Data bit value: 0 0 1 1 0 0 1 1   1

In this example, because the total number of data bits with a value of 1 is an even number (4), the parity bit must have a value of 1 to create an odd sum for all nine bits.

When the system reads memory back from storage, it checks the parity information. If a (9-bit) byte has an even number of bits with a parity bit value of 1, that byte must have an error. The system cannot tell which bit has changed, or if only a single bit has changed. If three bits changed, for example, the byte still flags a parity-check error; if two bits changed, however, the bad byte may pass unnoticed. The following examples show parity-check messages for three types of systems:

```
For the IBM PC:                    PARITY CHECK x
For the IBM XT:                    PARITY CHECK x    yyyyy (z)
For the IBM AT and late model XT:  PARITY CHECK x    yyyyy
```

Where *x* is 1 or 2:

1 = Error occurred on the motherboard

2 = Error occurred in an expansion slot

yyyy represents a number from 00000 through FFFFF that indicates, in hexadecimal notation, the byte in which the error has occurred.

Where *(z)* is (S) or (e):

(S) = Parity error occurred in the system unit

(e)= Parity error occurred in the expansion chassis

> **Note**
>
> An expansion chassis was an option IBM sold for the original PC and XT systems to add more expansion slots. This unit consisted of a backplane motherboard with eight slots, one of which contained a special extender/receiver card cabled to a similar extender/receiver card placed in the main system. Due to the extender/receiver cards in the main system and the expansion chassis, the net gain was six slots.

When a parity-check error is detected, the motherboard parity-checking circuits generate a *non-maskable interrupt* (NMI), which halts processing and diverts the system's attention to the error. The NMI causes a routine in the ROM to be executed. The routine clears the screen and then displays a message in the upper-left corner of the screen. The message differs depending on the type of computer system. On some older IBM systems, the ROM parity-check routine halts the CPU. In such a case, the system locks up, and you must perform a hardware reset or a power-off/power-on cycle to restart the system. Unfortunately, all unsaved work is lost in the process.

Most systems do not halt the CPU when a parity error is detected; instead, they offer you a choice of either rebooting the system or continuing as though nothing happened. Additionally, these systems may display the parity error message in a different format from IBM, although the information presented is basically the same. For example, many systems with a Phoenix BIOS display these messages:

```
Memory parity interrupt at xxxx:xxxx
Type (S)hut off NMI, Type (R)eboot, other keys to continue
```

or

```
I/O card parity interrupt at xxxx:xxxx
Type (S)hut off NMI, Type (R)eboot, other keys to continue
```

The first of these two messages indicates a motherboard parity error (Parity Check 1), and the second indicates an expansion-slot parity error (Parity Check 2). Notice that the address given in the form `xxxx:xxxx` for the memory error is in a segment:offset form rather than a straight linear address such as with IBM's error messages. The segment:offset address form still gives you the location of the error to a resolution of a single byte.

You have three ways to proceed after viewing this error message.

- You can press S, which shuts off parity checking and resumes system operation at the point where the parity check first occurred.
- Pressing R forces the system to reboot, losing any unsaved work.
- Pressing any other key causes the system to resume operation with parity checking still enabled.

If the problem recurs, it is likely to cause another parity-check interruption. In most cases, it is most prudent to press S, which disables the parity checking so that you can then save your work. It would be best in this case to save your work to a floppy disk to prevent the possible corruption of a hard disk. You should also avoid overwriting any previous (still good) versions of whatever file you are saving, because in fact you may be saving a bad file due to the memory corruption. Because parity checking is now disabled, your save operations will not be interrupted. Then you should power the system off, restart it, and run whatever memory diagnostics software you have to try and track down the error. In some cases, the POST finds the error on the next restart, but in most cases you need to run a more sophisticated diagnostics program, perhaps in a continuous mode, to locate the error.

The AMI BIOS displays the parity error messages in the following forms:

```
ON BOARD PARITY ERROR ADDR (HEX) = (xxxxx)
```

or

```
OFF BOARD PARITY ERROR ADDR (HEX) = (xxxxx)
```

These messages indicate that an error in memory has occurred during the POST, and the failure is located at the address indicated. The first one indicates the error occurred on the motherboard, whereas the second message indicates an error in an expansion slot adapter card. The AMI BIOS also can display memory errors in the following manner:

```
Memory Parity Error at xxxxx
```

or

```
I/O Card Parity Error at xxxxx
```

These messages indicate that an error in memory has occurred at the indicated address during normal operation. The first one indicates a motherboard memory error, and the second indicates an expansion slot adapter memory error.

Although many systems enable you to continue processing after a parity error, and even allow for the disabling of further parity checking, continuing to use your system after a parity error is detected can be dangerous. The idea behind letting you continue using either method is to give you time to save any unsaved work before you diagnose and service the computer, but be careful how you do this.

> **Caution**
>
> When you are notified of a memory parity error, remember the parity check is telling you that memory has been corrupted. Do you want to save potentially corrupted data over the good file from the *last* time you saved? Definitely not! Make sure that you save your work to a different file name. In addition, after a parity error, save only to a floppy disk if possible and avoid writing to the hard disk; there is a slight chance that the hard drive could become corrupted if you save the contents of corrupted memory.

After saving your work, determine the cause of the parity error and repair the system. You may be tempted to use an option to shut off further parity checking and simply continue using the system as if nothing were wrong. Doing so resembles unscrewing the oil pressure warning indicator bulb on a car with an oil leak so that the oil pressure light won't bother you anymore!

SIMMs and DIMMs

For memory storage, most modern systems have adopted the single in-line memory module (SIMM) or dual in-line memory module (DIMM) as an alternative to individual memory chips. These small boards plug into special connectors on a motherboard or memory card. The individual memory chips are soldered to the SIMM/DIMM, so removing and replacing individual memory chips is impossible. Instead, you must replace the entire module if any part of it fails. The SIMM/DIMM is treated as though it were one large memory chip.

IBM compatibles have two main physical types of SIMMs—30-pin (9 bits) and 72-pin (36 bits)—with various capacities and other specifications. The 30-pin SIMMs are smaller than the 72-pin versions, and may have chips on either one or both sides. 30-pin SIMMs are on the wane, primarily because 64-bit systems—which would require eight 30-pin SIMMs per bank—are now the industry standard. DIMMs, which have become popular on Pentium-MMX and Pentium Pro-based systems, are 168-pin units with 64-bit (non-parity) or 72-bit (parity) data paths.

Figures 7.14 and 7.15 show typical 30-pin (9-bit) and 72-pin (36-bit) SIMMs, respectively. The pins are numbered from left to right and are connected through to both sides of the module. Note that all dimensions are in both inches and millimeters (in parentheses).

FIG. 7.14 A typical 30-pin (9-bit) SIMM.

FIG. 7.15 A typical 72-pin (36-bit) SIMM.

A SIMM is extremely compact considering the amount of memory it holds. SIMMs are available in several capacities, depending on the version. Table 7.5 lists the different capacities available for both the 30-pin and 72-pin SIMMs, as well as 168-pin DIMMs.

Table 7.5 SIMM and DIMM Capacities

30-Pin SIMM Capacities

Capacity	Parity SIMM	Non-Parity SIMM
256K	256K×9	256K×8
1M	1M×9	1M×8
4M	4M×9	4M×8
16M	16M×9	16M×8

72-Pin SIMM Capacities

Capacity	Parity SIMM	Non-Parity SIMM
1M	256K×36	256K×32
2M	512K×36	512K×32
4M	1M×36	1M×32
8M	2M×36	2M×32
16M	4M×36	4M×32
32M	8M×36	8M×32
64M	16M×36	16M×32

168-Pin DIMM Capacities

Capacity	Parity DIMM	Non-Parity DIMM
8M	1M×72	1M×64
16M	2M×72	2M×64
32M	4M×72	4M×64
64M	8M×72	8M×64
128M	16M×72	16M×64

Dynamic RAM (DRAM) SIMMs of each type and capacity are available in different speed ratings. These ratings are expressed in nanoseconds (billionths of a second, abbreviated ns). SIMMs have been available in many different speed ratings ranging from 120ns for some of the slowest, to 50ns for some of the fastest available. Many of the first systems to use SIMMs used versions rated at 120ns. These were quickly replaced in the market by 100ns and even faster versions. Today, you can generally purchase SIMMs rated at 70ns or 60ns. Both faster and slower ones are available, but they are not frequently required and are difficult to obtain.

If a system requires a specific speed, you can almost always substitute faster speeds if the one specified is not available. There are no problems in mixing SIMM speeds, as long as you use SIMMs equal or faster than what the system requires. Because often very little price difference exists between the different speed versions, I usually buy faster SIMMs than are needed for a particular application, as this may make them more usable in a future system that may require the faster speed.

> **Note**
>
> Most DIMMs are Synchronous DRAM (SDRAM) memory, which means they deliver data in very high speed bursts using a clocked interface. SDRAM supports bus speeds of up to 100MHz, and possibly more in the future.

Several variations on the 30-pin SIMMs can affect how they work (if at all) in a particular system. First, there are actually two variations on the pinout configurations. Most systems use a *generic* type of SIMM, which has an industry standard pin configuration. Many older IBM systems used a slightly modified 30-pin SIMM, starting with the XT-286 introduced in 1986 through the PS/2 Model 25, 30, 50, and 60. These systems require a SIMM with different signals on five of the pins. These are known as *IBM-style* 30-pin SIMMs. You can modify a generic 30-pin SIMM to work in the IBM systems and vice versa, but purchasing a SIMM with the correct pinouts is much easier. Be sure you tell the SIMM vendor if you need the specific IBM-style versions.

Another issue with respect to the 30-pin SIMMs relates to the chip count. The SIMM itself acts as if it were a single chip of 9-bits wide (with parity), and it really does not matter how this total is derived. Older SIMMs were constructed with nine individual 1-bit-wide chips to make up the total, whereas many newer SIMMs use two 4-bit-wide chips and one 1-bit-wide chip for parity, making a total of three chips on the SIMM. Accessing the 3-chip SIMMs can require adjustments to the refresh timing circuits on the motherboard, and many older motherboards could not cope. Most newer motherboards automatically handle the slightly different refresh timing of both the 3-chip or 9-chip SIMMs, and in this case the 3-chip versions are more reliable, use less power, and generally cost less as well. If you have an older system, most likely it will also work with the 3-chip SIMMs, but some do not. Unfortunately, the only way to know is to try them. To prevent the additional time required to change them for 9-chip versions should the 3-chip versions not work in an older system, it seems wise to stick with the 9-chip variety in any older systems.

The 72-pin SIMMs do not have different pinouts and are differentiated only by capacity and speed. These SIMMs are not affected by the number of chips on them. The 72-pin SIMMs are ideal for 32-bit systems like 486 machines because they comprise an entire bank of memory (32 data bits plus 4 parity bits). When you configure a 32-bit system that uses a 72-pin SIMM, you can usually add or remove memory in single SIMM modules (except on systems that use interleaved memory schemes to reduce wait states).

In 64-bit systems—which includes any Pentium or newer processor—72-pin SIMMs must be used in pairs to fill a single bank. A few motherboard manufacturers offer so-called "SIMM-saver" motherboards that are designed for newer Pentium processors, but have both 72- and 30-pin SIMM sockets. Although this is not the most desirable arrangement, it allows users on a budget to re-use their old 30-pin SIMMs. In this situation, eight 30-pin SIMMs can be used at a time to fill one bank. Alternatively, you could pair four

30-pin SIMMs with one 72-pin SIMM to create one bank. This really is not a very efficient setup because it consumes large amounts of space on the motherboard.

Other options are SIMM stackers and converters. These items allow you to use 30-pin SIMMs in 72-pin sockets, thereby saving you the expense of having to scrap all those old 30-pin SIMMs you have lying around. Again, such adapters can cause problems—especially if overhead clearance is tight—so investigate carefully before you buy. With the falling prices of SIMMs today, you are probably better off staying with 72-pin SIMMs and 168-pin DIMMs.

Remember that some 486 systems (such as the PS/2 90 and 95 systems) use interleaved memory to reduce wait states. This requires a multiple of two 36-bit SIMMs because interleaved memory access is alternated between the SIMMs to improve performance.

> **Note**
>
> A *bank* is the smallest amount of memory that can be addressed by the processor at one time and usually corresponds to the data bus width of the processor. If the memory is interleaved, a virtual bank may be twice the absolute data bus width of the processor.

You cannot always replace a SIMM with a greater-capacity unit and expect it to work. For example, the IBM PS/2 Model 70-Axx and Bxx systems accept 72-pin SIMMs of 1M or 2M capacity, which are 80ns or faster. Although an 80ns 4M SIMM is available, it does not work in these systems. The PS/2 Model 55 SX and 65 SX, however, accept 1M, 2M, or 4M 72-pin SIMMs. A larger-capacity SIMM works only if the motherboard is designed to accept it in the first place. Consult your system documentation to determine the correct capacity and speed to use.

SIMMs were designed to eliminate chip creep, which plagues systems with memory chips installed in sockets. *Chip creep* occurs when a chip works its way out of its socket, caused by the normal thermal expansion and contraction from powering a system on and off. Eventually, chip creep leads to poor contact between the chip leads and the socket, and memory errors and problems begin.

The original solution for chip creep was to solder all the memory chips to the printed circuit board. This approach, however, was impractical. Memory chips fail more frequently than most other types of chips, and soldering chips to the board made the units difficult to service.

The SIMM/DIMM incorporates the best compromise between socketed and soldered chips. The chips are soldered to the module, but you can replace the socketed module easily. In addition, the SIMM/DIMM is held tight to the motherboard by a locking mechanism that does not work loose from contraction and expansion, but is easy for you to loosen. This solution is a good one, but it can increase repair costs. You must replace what amounts to, in some cases, an entire bank rather than one defective chip.

All systems on the market today use SIMMs, and many use DIMMs. Even Apple Macintosh systems use SIMMs and DIMMs. The SIMM/DIMM is not a proprietary memory system but rather an industry-standard device. As mentioned, some SIMMs have slightly different pinouts and specifications other than speed and capacity, so be sure that you obtain the correct SIMMs for your system.

SIMM Pinouts

Tables 7.6 and 7.7 show the interface connector pinouts for both 30-pin SIMM varieties, as well as the standard 72-pin version. Also included is a special presence detect table that shows the configuration of the presence detect pins on various 72-pin SIMMs. The presence detect pins are used by the motherboard to detect exactly what size and speed SIMM is installed. Industry-standard 30-pin SIMMs do not have a presence detect feature, but IBM did add this capability to their modified 30-pin configuration.

Table 7.6 Industry-Standard and IBM 30-Pin SIMM Pinouts

Pin	Standard SIMM Signal Names	IBM SIMM Signal Names
1	+5 Vdc	+5 Vdc
2	Column Address Strobe	Column Address Strobe
3	Data Bit 0	Data Bit 0
4	Address Bit 0	Address Bit 0
5	Address Bit 1	Address Bit 1
6	Data Bit 1	Data Bit 1
7	Address Bit 2	Address Bit 2
8	Address Bit 3	Address Bit 3
9	Ground	Ground
10	Data Bit 2	Data Bit 2
11	Address Bit 4	Address Bit 4
12	Address Bit 5	Address Bit 5
13	Data Bit 3	Data Bit 3
14	Address Bit 6	Address Bit 6
15	Address Bit 7	Address Bit 7
16	Data Bit 4	Data Bit 4
17	Address Bit 8	Address Bit 8
18	Address Bit 9	Address Bit 9
19	Address Bit 10	Row Address Strobe 1
20	Data Bit 5	Data Bit 5
21	Write Enable	Write Enable
22	Ground	Ground
23	Data Bit 6	Data Bit 6
24	No Connection	Presence Detect (Ground)
25	Data Bit 7	Data Bit 7
26	Data Bit 8 (Parity) Out	Presence Detect (1M = Ground)
27	Row Address Strobe	Row Address Strobe
28	Column Address Strobe Parity	No Connection
29	Data Bit 8 (Parity) In	Data Bit 8 (Parity) I/O
30	+5 Vdc	+5 Vdc

Table 7.7 Standard 72-Pin SIMM Pinout

Pin	SIMM Signal Name	Pin	SIMM Signal Name
1	Ground	37	Parity Data Bit 1
2	Data Bit 0	38	Parity Data Bit 3
3	Data Bit 16	39	Ground
4	Data Bit 1	40	Column Address Strobe 0
5	Data Bit 17	41	Column Address Strobe 2
6	Data Bit 2	42	Column Address Strobe 3
7	Data Bit 18	43	Column Address Strobe 1
8	Data Bit 3	44	Row Address Strobe 0
9	Data Bit 18	45	Row Address Strobe 1
10	+5 Vdc	46	Block Select 1
11	Column Address Strobe Parity	47	Write Enable
12	Address Bit 0	48	Reserved
13	Address Bit 1	49	Data Bit 8
14	Address Bit 2	50	Data Bit 24
15	Address Bit 3	51	Data Bit 9
16	Address Bit 4	52	Data Bit 25
17	Address Bit 5	53	Data Bit 10
18	Address Bit 6	54	Data Bit 26
19	Reserved	55	Data Bit 11
20	Data Bit 4	56	Data Bit 27
21	Data Bit 20	57	Data Bit 12
22	Data Bit 5	58	Data Bit 28
23	Data Bit 21	59	+5 Vdc
24	Data Bit 6	60	Data Bit 29
25	Data Bit 22	61	Data Bit 13
26	Data Bit 7	62	Data Bit 30
27	Data Bit 23	63	Data Bit 14
28	Address Bit 7	64	Data Bit 31
29	Block Select 0	65	Data Bit 15
30	+5 Vdc	66	Block Select 2
31	Address Bit 8	67	Presence Detect Bit 0
32	Address Bit 9	68	Presence Detect Bit 1
33	Row Address Strobe 3	69	Presence Detect Bit 2
34	Row Address Strobe 2	70	Presence Detect Bit 3
35	Parity Data Bit 2	71	Block Select 3
36	Parity Data Bit 0	72	Ground

Notice that the 72-pin SIMMs employ a set of four pins to indicate the type of SIMM to the motherboard. These presence detect pins are either grounded or not connected to indicate the type of SIMM to the motherboard. This is very similar to the industry-standard DX code used on modern 35mm film rolls to indicate the ASA (speed) rating of the film to the camera. Unfortunately, unlike the film standards, the presence detect signaling is not a standard throughout the PC industry. Different system manufacturers sometimes use different configurations for what is expected on these 4 pins. Table 7.8 shows how IBM defines these pins.

Table 7.8 72-Pin SIMM Presence Detect Pins

70	69	68	67	SIMM Type	IBM Part Number
-	-	-	-	Not a valid SIMM	N/A
-	-	-	Gnd	1M 120ns	N/A
-	-	Gnd	-	2M 120ns	N/A
-	-	Gnd	Gnd	2M 70ns	92F0102
-	Gnd	-	-	8M 70ns	64F3606
-	Gnd	-	Gnd	Reserved	N/A
-	Gnd	Gnd	-	2M 80ns	92F0103
-	Gnd	Gnd	Gnd	8M 80ns	64F3607
Gnd	-	-	-	Reserved	N/A
Gnd	-	-	Gnd	1M 85ns	90X8624
Gnd	-	Gnd	-	2M 85ns	92F0104
Gnd	-	Gnd	Gnd	4M 70ns	92F0105
Gnd	Gnd	-	-	4M 85ns	79F1003 (square notch) L40-SX
Gnd	Gnd	-	Gnd	1M 100ns	N/A
Gnd	Gnd	-	Gnd	8M 80ns	79F1004 (square notch) L40-SX
Gnd	Gnd	Gnd	-	2M 100ns	N/A
Gnd	Gnd	Gnd	Gnd	4M 80ns	87F9980
Gnd	Gnd	Gnd	Gnd	2M 85ns	79F1003 (square notch) L40SX

- = No Connection (open)
Gnd = Ground
Pin 67 = Presence detect bit 0
Pin 68 = Presence detect bit 1
Pin 69 = Presence detect bit 2
Pin 70 = Presence detect bit 3

RAM Chip Speed

Memory-chip speed is reported in nanoseconds (ns). (One nanosecond is the time that light takes to travel 11.72 inches.) PC memory speeds vary from about 10ns to 200ns. When you replace a failed memory module, you must install a module of the same type and speed as the failed module. You can substitute a chip with a different speed only if the speed of the replacement chip is equal to or faster than that of the failed chip.

Some people have had problems when "mixing" chips because they used a chip that did not meet the minimum required specifications (for example, refresh timing

Chapter 7—Memory

specifications) or was incompatible in pinout, depth, width, or design. Chip access time always can be less (that is, faster) as long as your chip is the correct type and meets all other specifications.

Substituting faster memory usually doesn't provide improved performance because the system still operates the memory at the same speed. In systems not engineered with a great deal of "forgiveness" in the timing between memory and system, however, substituting faster memory chips might improve reliability.

The same common symptoms result when the system memory has failed or is simply not fast enough for the system's timing. The usual symptoms are frequent parity check errors or a system that does not operate at all. The POST also might report errors. If you're unsure of what chips to buy for your system, contact the system manufacturer or a reputable chip supplier.

EDO RAM

There is a newer type of memory being offered for Pentium systems called *EDO (Extended Data Out) RAM*. These are 72-pin SIMMs and 168-pin DIMMs with specially manufactured chips that allow for a timing overlap between successive accesses. EDO RAM has a dual-pipeline architecture that allows the unit to simultaneously read new data while discharging the old. This allows for a tighter coupled access cycle and a performance improvement of 20 percent or so over regular non-EDO SIMMs. EDO RAM is ideal for systems with bus speeds of up to 66MHz, which fits perfectly with the current and future Pentium and higher processor architectures. Unfortunately, all EDO RAM offered today is non-parity, and it is incapable of supporting systems with a bus speed higher than 66MHz.

To actually utilize EDO memory, your motherboard chipset must support it. Current chipsets like the Intel Triton and Opti Viper offer support for EDO. Because these chips cost the same to manufacture as standard chips, the market has jumped on the EDO bandwagon, and virtually all newer chipsets support it. A pleasant surprise in the last year or so has been a steady drop in EDO RAM prices, to the point that EDO SIMMs and DIMMs generally cost about the same as—or sometimes even less than—non-parity, non-EDO SIMMs.

A variation of EDO is *Burst Extended-Data-Out Dynamic Random Access Memory (BEDO DRAM)*. BEDO is basically EDO memory with burst features for speedier data transfer. Intel's 440FX Natoma and 440LX chipsets offer support for BEDO memory, which is used only in Pentium Pro and Pentium II systems.

Get more information on EDO RAM online at:

http://www.corsairmicro.com/EDOECCBrief.htm

SDRAM

SDRAM is similar to EDO RAM in that it has a dual-stage pipeline structure. SDRAM delivers information in very high speed bursts using a high-speed, clocked interface. Like EDO RAM, your chipset must support this type of memory. Intel's 430TX and 430VX

Triton II chipsets fully support SDRAM. Performance of SDRAM is similar to EDO RAM, with the exception that SDRAM supports bus speeds of up to 100MHz. It is anticipated that in the near future this figure will be pushed to 200MHz in order to keep up with faster systems of the future. SDRAM is limited primarily to DIMMs at this point, but prices are not appreciably higher than for other types of memory.

Upgrading by Increasing System Memory

Adding memory to a system is one of the most useful upgrades that you can perform and also one of the least expensive, especially when you consider the increased capabilities of Windows 95, Windows NT, and OS/2 when you give them access to more memory. In some cases, doubling the memory can virtually double the speed of a computer.

Memory chips come in different shapes and sizes, yet all memory chips in which you are interested are called *DRAM*, or *dynamic random-access memory*. DRAM chips are the most common type of memory. These chips are considered to be dynamic because they need to be energized hundreds of times per second to hold information. If you shut off the power, the information is lost.

This section discusses adding memory, including selecting memory chips, installing memory chips, and testing the installation.

Upgrade Strategies

Adding memory can be an inexpensive solution; at this writing, the cost of memory has fallen to less than $5 per megabyte. A small dose can give your computer's performance a big boost.

How do you add memory to your PC? You have three options, listed in order of convenience and cost:

- Adding memory in vacant slots on your motherboard.
- Replacing your current motherboard's memory with higher-capacity memory.
- Purchasing a memory expansion card.

Adding expanded memory to PC- or XT-type systems is not a good idea, mainly because an expanded memory board with a couple of megabytes of expanded memory installed can cost more than the entire system is worth. Also, this memory does not function for Windows, and a PC- or XT-class system cannot run OS/2. Instead, purchase a more powerful system—for example, an inexpensive Pentium 100—with greater expansion capabilities.

If you decide to upgrade to a more powerful computer system, you normally cannot salvage the memory from a PC or XT system. The 8-bit memory boards are useless in AT and Micro Channel systems, and the speed of the memory chips usually is inadequate for newer systems. Many new systems use high-speed SIMM modules rather than chips. A pile of 150ns, 64K, or 256K chips is useless if your next system is a high-speed system that uses SIMMs or memory devices faster than 70ns.

Be sure to weigh carefully your future needs for computing speed and for a multitasking operating system (OS/2, for example) with the amount of money that you spend to upgrade current equipment.

Adding Motherboard Memory

This section discusses *motherboard memory*—the memory actually installed on the motherboard—rather than the memory that resides on adapter boards. The first part of this section presents recommendations on selecting and installing chips. The last part of the section provides instructions for modifying an IBM XT Type 1 motherboard. This modification enables you to place a full 640K of memory on the motherboard, eliminating the need for memory expansion boards. IBM's more recent XT Type 2 motherboards already include this modification.

Selecting and Installing Memory Chips, SIMMs, or DIMMs

If you are upgrading a motherboard by adding memory, follow the manufacturer's guidelines on which memory chips or modules to purchase. As you learned earlier, memory comes in various form factors, including individual chips known as DIP memory chips, SIMMs (single in-line memory modules), SIPPs, and DIMMs. Your computer may use one or possibly a mixture of these form factors.

The maker of your computer's motherboard determines what type of memory chips are used. The following list describes each chip or module type:

- *DIPs*. Early computers used DIP memory chips. A DIP memory chip is a rectangular chip that has 16 metal legs, eight on each side. To install such a memory chip, you must plug it in place. DIP chips are installed in multiples of nine. For example, you must install 36 separate 256Kbit chips to acquire 1M of memory. Sometimes, the DIPs are permanently soldered to your motherboard.

- *SIMMs*. Single inline memory modules are like small circuit boards with chips soldered on them. Different numbers of chips can be mounted on the SIMM, and the chips can be mounted on one or both sides of the SIMM. A SIMM has a row of contacts on one edge of the board. The contacts can be tin- or gold-plated. SIMMs are retained in the system by special sockets with positive latching mechanisms that lock the SIMMs in place. SIMM connectors use a high-force wiping contact that is extremely resistant to corrosion.

    SIMMs are available in two types: 30-pin and 72-pin. The 30-pin modules come in 9-bit form with parity or 8-bit form for systems that lack parity checking. The 72-pin SIMMs are 36 bits wide with parity (32 data bits and 4 parity bits), or 32 bits wide without parity. Notice that the 9-bit and 36-bit SIMMs with parity always can be used in systems that lack parity checking. The nonparity SIMMs cannot be used in normal systems that require parity bits.

- *SIPPs*. Single in-line pinned packages, sometimes called SIP, really are SIMMs with pins rather than contacts. The pins are designed to be installed in a long connector socket that is much cheaper than the standard SIMM socket. SIPPs are inferior to

SIMMs because they lack the positive latching mechanism that retains the module, and the connector lacks the high-force wiping contacts that resist corrosion. SIPPs are rarely used today.

- *DIMMs.* Dual inline memory modules are 168-pin modules designed to work singly with today's 64-bit systems. DIMMs must be inserted carefully because they have different contacts on each side. Like SIMMs, DIMMs are held in place by a locking mechanism to prevent chip creep. Non-parity DIMMs are 64-bits wide, while parity DIMMs (which are nearly impossible to find) are 72-bits wide.

No matter what type of memory chips you have, the chips are installed in memory banks. A *memory bank* is a collection of memory chips that make up a block of memory. Each bank of memory is read by your processor in one pass. A memory bank does not work unless it is filled with memory chips.

286 computers usually can take four banks of 256Kbit chips to make 1,024K (1M). Some 286 computers can handle up to 4M on the motherboard, using 1M chips. In 386SX-based computers, four memory banks are used, requiring 18 chips (16 plus 2 for parity), or in most cases two 30-pin (8- or 9-bit) SIMMs each. 386DX, and 486 computers often have between two and four memory banks, each bank using four 30-pin (8- or 9-bit) SIMMs or one 72-pin (32- or 36-bit) SIMM. Pentium, Pentium Pro, and Pentium II computers also normally have between two and four banks of memory, but each bank usually requires two 72-pin (32- or 36-bit) SIMMs or one 168-pin DIMM.

Installing extra memory on your motherboard is an easy way to add memory to your computer. Most systems have at least one vacant memory bank in which you can install extra memory at a later time and speed your computer.

RAM-Chip Type (Capacity). Individual RAM chips come in different capacities. The capacity determines the number of data bits that can be stored in a chip of a particular size. For example, RAM chips for the original IBM PC store 16Kbits of data; these RAM chips are the smallest used in any IBM-compatible system. The RAM chips for the original version of the IBM XT store 64Kbits of data. The standard chip for Pentium-based systems today is the 4M bit or 16M bit chip (usually found in SIMMs).

Before you add RAM to a system (or replace defective RAM chips), you must determine the memory chips required for your system. Your system documentation contains this information.

If you need to replace a defective RAM chip and do not have the system documentation, you can determine the correct chip for your system by inspecting the chips that are already installed. Each chip has markings that indicate the chip's capacity and speed. The following table lists the markings on individual 1M chips produced by various companies:

Markings	Manufacturer
TMS4C1024N/DJ	Texas Instruments
HM511000AP/AJP/AZP	Hitachi
MB81C1000P/PJ/PSZ	Fujitsu

If you do not have the documentation for your system and the manufacturer does not offer technical support, open your system case and carefully write down the markings that appear on your memory chips. Then contact a local computer store or mail-order chip vendor for help in determining the proper RAM chips for your system. Adding the wrong RAM chips to a system can make it as unreliable as leaving a defective chip on the motherboard and trying to use the system in that condition.

RAM-Chip Speed. RAM chips also come in various speeds. For example, 80ns or slower chips are used in older systems, and 60 or 70ns chips are used in 486 and higher systems.

The motherboard manufacturer determines the correct speed of the memory chips installed in each system. IBM, for example, specifies different speed memory for different systems. Table 7.9 lists the required RAM-chip speeds and wait states for IBM motherboards.

System	CPU	Clock Speed (MHz)	Memory-Wait States	Access Time (ns)	Notes
PC	8088	4.77	1	200	
XT	8088	4.77	1	200	
AT	286	6	1	150	
AT	286	8	1	150	
XT-286	286	6	0	150	Zero wait
PS/1	286	10	1	120	
25	8086	8	0	150	Zero wait
30	8086	8	0	150	Zero wait
25-286	286	10	1	120	
30-286	286	10	1	120	
35 SX	386SX	20	0-2	85	Paged memory
40 SX	386SX	20	0-2	85	Paged memory
L40	386SX	20	0-2	80	Paged memory
50	286	10	1	150	
50Z	286	10	0	85	Zero wait
53486SLC2	486SLC2	50	0-2	70	Interleaved memory, internal 16K cache
55 SX	386SX	16	0-2	100	Paged memory
56 486SLC3	486SLC3	75	0-2	70	Interleaved memory, internal 16K cache
57 SX	386SX	20	0-2	70	Paged memory
57 486SLC3	486SLC3	75	0-2	70	Interleaved memory, internal 16K cache
60	286	10	1	150	
65	386SX	16	0-2	100	Paged memory
70	386DX	16	0-2	85	Paged memory

Adding Motherboard Memory

System	CPU	Clock Speed (MHz)	Memory-Wait States	Access Time (ns)	Notes
70	386DX	20	0-2	85	Paged memory
70	386DX	25	0-5	80	External 64K cache
70	486DX	25	0-5	80	Internal 8K cache
P70	386DX	16	0-2	85	Paged memory
P70	386DX	20	0-2	85	Paged memory
P75	486DX	33	0-5	70	Internal 8K cache
76	486DX2	66	0-2	70	Interleaved memory, internal 8K cache
76	486SX	33	0-2	70	Interleaved memory, internal 8K cache
76	486DX4	100	0-2	70	Interleaved memory, internal 16K cache
77	486DX2	66	0-2	70	Interleaved memory, internal 8K cache
77	486SX	33	0-2	70	Interleaved memory, internal 8K cache
77	486DX4	100	0-2	70	Interleaved memory, internal 16K cache
80	386DX	16	0-2	80	Paged memory
80	386DX	20	0-2	80	Paged memory
80	386DX	25	0-5	80	External 64K cache
90	486SX	20	0-5	70	Interleaved memory, internal 8K cache
90	486SX	25	0-5	70	Interleaved memory, internal 8K cache
90	486DX	25	0-5	70	Interleaved memory, internal 8K cache, optional external 256K cache
90	486DX	33	0-5	70	Interleaved memory, internal 8K cache, optional external 256K cache
90	486DX	50	0-5	70	Interleaved memory, internal 8K cache, optional external 256K cache
95	486SX	20	0-5	70	Interleaved memory, internal 8K cache
95	486SX	25	0-5	70	Interleaved memory, internal 8K cache
95	486DX	25	0-5	70	Interleaved memory, internal 8K cache, optional external 256K cache
95	486DX	33	0-5	70	Interleaved memory, internal 8K cache, optional external 256K cache
95	486DX	50	0-5	70	Interleaved memory, internal 8K cache, optional external 256K cache

> **Note**
>
> In general, non-IBM systems should use memory similar to their IBM counterparts listed previously. Memory slower than 70ns (60ns is better) should not be used in Pentium or higher systems.

It won't hurt to install chips that are faster than required for your motherboard or memory card; buying faster memory chips can be a benefit if you intend to transplant them to a faster computer in the future. Unfortunately, the faster memory won't speed your computer; your computer's design anticipates working at a certain speed and no faster.

The speed of a memory chip is printed on the surface of the chip. On the memory chips—whether they are the DIP, SIPP, or SIMM type—you will find an identifying number. The last two digits after the dash (—) are especially important, because they indicate the speed of your memory.

In some systems, the motherboard memory speed can be controlled. Systems with adjustable wait-state settings enable you to choose optimal performance by purchasing the proper high-speed memory, or to choose lower performance by purchasing cheaper memory. Many compatibles offer a wait-state jumper or configuration option, which controls whether the motherboard runs with wait states. Running with zero wait states may require faster-access-speed memory.

Systems that use 72-pin SIMMs can detect both the speed and capacity of the installed SIMMs through four special contacts called *presence detect pins*. The motherboard can use these pins to determine the installed SIMM's rated speed and capacity, in much the same way that many cameras can tell what speed film you have loaded by "reading" a series of contacts on the film canister. Installing memory that is too slow for the system may cause an error message to appear on startup.

Systems with 16MHz or faster clock speeds require extremely fast memory to keep up with the processor. In fact, the speeds that are required are so excessive that standard DRAM typically would be replaced by faster and more expensive static RAM (SRAM). One alternative—adding wait states to reduce the memory-speed requirements—greatly decreases performance, which is not what you want in a fast system.

RAM-Chip Architecture. Some special memory-architecture schemes have been devised to reduce the number of wait states required, boost overall system performance, and keep costs down. The following architecture schemes are most commonly used to increase memory performance:

- Paged memory
- Interleaved memory
- Memory caching

Paged memory is a simple scheme for improving memory performance that divides memory into pages ranging from 512 bytes to a few kilobytes long. The paging circuitry then enables memory locations within a page to be accessed with zero wait states. If the desired memory location is outside the current page, one or more wait states are added while the system selects the new page.

Interleaved memory offers greater performance than paged memory. This higher-performance scheme combines two banks of memory into one, organized as even and odd bytes. With this combination, an access cycle can begin in the second bank while the first is already processing a previous access, and vice versa. By alternating access to even and odd banks, you can request data from one bank, and while the request is pending, the system can move to the next bank to process another request. The first request becomes available while the second request is still pending, and so on. By interleaving access to memory in this manner, a system can effectively double memory-access performance without using faster memory chips.

Many of the highest-performance systems use interleaved memory to achieve increased performance. Some systems that offer interleaved memory can use the interleaving function only if you install banks in matched-capacity pairs, which usually means adding two 36-bit SIMMs of equal capacity at a time. If you add only a single bank or add two banks of different capacity, the system still functions, but memory interleaving is disabled, and you pay a considerable performance penalty. Consult your system's technical-reference manual for more information.

Memory caching is the most popular and usually the most effective scheme for improving memory performance. This technique relies on a small amount (8K to 512K) of raw, high-speed memory fast enough to keep up with the processor with zero wait states. This small bank of cache memory often is rated at *15ns or less* in access speed. Because this rate is faster than normal DRAM components can handle, a special type of memory is used. This memory is called SRAM. SRAM devices do not need the constant refresh signals that DRAM devices require. This feature, combined with other design properties, results in extremely fast access times and very high costs.

Memory Caching. As mentioned in the previous section, memory caching is one of the most effective means of improving memory performance. Although SRAM chips are expensive, only a small number of SRAM chips are required in a caching scheme. SRAM is used by a special cache-controller circuit that stores frequently accessed RAM locations and also is preloaded with the RAM values that the cache controller expects to be accessed next. The cache acts as an intelligent buffer between the CPU and slower dynamic RAM.

A *cache hit* means that the particular data the CPU wanted was available in the cache RAM and that no additional wait states are available for retrieving this data. A *cache miss* means that the data the CPU wanted had not been loaded into the cache RAM and that wait states must be inserted while the data is retrieved. A good cache controller has a hit ratio of 95 percent or more (the system runs with zero wait states 95 percent of the time). The net effect is that the system acts as though nearly all the memory is 15ns or less in speed, although most of the memory really is much slower (and, therefore, much less costly).

Systems based on the 486SX, SL, or DX processors include a cache controller and 8K of internal-cache RAM in the CPU that makes them much faster than earlier systems. The 486SLC CPU has a 1K internal cache; 486DX4 processors have a 16K internal cache; and the 486SLC2 and 486SLC3 processors have a 16K cache. Systems with 386SX or DX processors must use an external-cache controller with externally provided cache RAM; these systems have no internal cache. The Pentium and Pentium Pro CPUs include two 8K internal caches: one for code and the other for data. This dual-cache architecture is carried over in the Pentium-MMX and Pentium II CPUs, which both have separate 16K code and write-back data caches.

A CPU internal cache is called a primary or Level 1 (L1) cache, and an external cache is called a secondary or Level 2 (L2) cache. Typically, the larger the memory cache, the better the performance. A larger secondary processor cache, however, is no guarantee; you may find that the system with the least cache RAM can outperform a system with a greater amount of cache RAM. Actual performance depends on the efficiency of the cache controller and the system design. For example, a cache integrated into a CPU can far outperform an external cache. Adding the 256K L2 cache RAM option to a PS/2 Model 90 or 95 with a 486DX processor offers only a small increase in performance relative to the 8K of L1 cache memory built into the 486 CPU chip. This is because the L1 cache integrated into the CPU can outperform an external (L2) cache. Also, adding cache RAM does not result in a proportional increase in performance. You often gain the best performance by using the middle amount of secondary cache that your computer can accept. A PC that can accommodate a 256K or 512K secondary cache provides the most bang for the buck.

To get maximum system performance and reliability, the best recommendation for adding chips, SIMMs, or DIMMs to a motherboard is to use memory rated at the speeds recommended by the manufacturer. Faster memory is likely to work in the system, but it creates no performance benefit and therefore is a waste of money.

The minimum access-time specification for motherboard memory in a specific system is listed in the system's technical-reference manual. If you have an IBM-compatible system that lacks proper documentation, you can refer to other similar system documentation as a guide, because most compatibles follow the same requirements. Because of the variety of system designs on the market, however, you should try to acquire the proper documentation from the manufacturer.

Adding Adapter Boards

Memory expansion boards typically are a last-resort way to add memory. For many systems (such as older models from Compaq) with proprietary local bus memory-expansion connectors, you must purchase all memory-expansion boards from that company. Similarly, IBM used proprietary memory connectors in the PS/2 Model 80 systems. For other industry-standard systems that use nonproprietary memory expansion (such as the IBM PC, XT, and AT) and most IBM-compatible systems, as well as most PS/2 systems, you can purchase memory-expansion boards that plug into the standard bus slots from hundreds of vendors.

Unfortunately, any memory expansion that plugs into a standard bus slot runs at bus speed rather than at full system speed. For this reason, most systems today provide standard SIMM-connector sockets directly on the motherboard so that the memory can be plugged directly into the system's local bus. Using memory adapter cards in these systems only slows them down. Other systems use proprietary local bus connectors for memory-expansion adapters, which can cause additional problems and expense when you have to add or service memory.

In some cases, an adapter board can use slower memory than would be required on the system motherboard. (Memory adapters for PS/2 Models 50 and 60, for example, use 120ns memory chips.) Many systems run memory-expansion slots at a fixed slower speed—8MHz for most ISA bus systems—so that installed adapters function properly. The PS/2 system memory adapters may be able to run more slowly than main memory because of the Micro Channel Architecture (MCA) interface's higher level of controls and capabilities. The MCA's asynchronous design enables adapters to remain independent of the processor's speed and to request additional wait states, as required, to accommodate the slower adapters.

Installing Memory

This section discusses installing memory chips—specifically, new RAM chips or memory modules. The section also covers the problems that you are most likely to encounter and how to avoid them. You will also get information on configuring your system to use new memory.

When you install or remove memory, you are most likely to encounter the following problems:

- Electrostatic discharge
- Broken or bent pins
- Incorrect switch and jumper settings

To prevent electrostatic discharge (ESD) when you install sensitive memory chips or boards, do not wear synthetic-fiber clothing or leather-soled shoes. Remove any static charge that you are carrying by touching the system chassis before you begin, or better yet, wear a good commercial grounding strap on your wrist. You can order one from an electronics parts store or mail-order house. A grounding strap consists of a conductive wristband grounded at the other end by a wire clipped to the system chassis. Leave the system unit plugged in but turned off to keep it grounded.

> **Caution**
>
> Be sure to use a properly designed commercial grounding strap; *do not make one yourself.* Commercial units have a one-megohm resistor that serves as protection if you accidentally touch live power. The resistor ensures that you do not become the path of least resistance to the ground and therefore become electrocuted. An improperly designed strap can cause the power to conduct through you to the ground, possibly killing you.

Broken or bent leads are another potential problem associated with installing individual memory chips (DIPs) or SIPP modules. Sometimes, the pins on new chips are bent into a V, making them difficult to align with the socket holes. If you notice this problem on a DIP chip, place the chip on its side on a table, and press gently to bend the pins so that they are at a 90-degree angle to the chip. For a SIPP module, you may want to use needle-nose pliers to carefully straighten the pins so that they protrude directly down from the edge of the module, with equal amounts of space between pins. Then you should install the chips in the sockets one at a time.

> **Caution**
>
> Straightening the pins on a DIP chip or SIPP module is not difficult work, but if you are not careful, you could easily break off one of the pins, rendering the chip or memory module useless. Use great care when you straighten the bent pins on any memory chip or module. You can use chip-insertion and pin-straightening devices to ensure that the pins are straight and aligned with the socket holes; these inexpensive tools can save you a great deal of time.

Each memory chip or module must be installed to point in a certain direction. Each chip has a polarity marking on one end. This marking may be a polarity notch, a circular indentation, or both. The chip socket may have a corresponding notch. Otherwise, the motherboard may have a printed legend that indicates the orientation of the chip. If the socket is not marked, you should use other chips as a guide. The orientation of the notch indicates the location of Pin 1 on the chip. Aligning this notch correctly with the others on the board ensures that you do not install the chip backward. Gently set each chip into a socket, ensuring that every pin is properly aligned with the connector into which it fits. Then push the chip in firmly with both thumbs until the chip is fully seated.

SIMM and DIMM memory is oriented by a notch on one side of the module that is not present on the other side. The socket has a protrusion that must fit into this notched area on one side of the module. This protrusion makes it impossible to install a SIMM or DIMM backward unless you break the connector. SIPP modules, however, do not plug into a keyed socket; you have to orient them properly. The system documentation can be helpful if the motherboard has no marks to guide you. You also can use existing SIPP modules as a guide.

Before installing memory, make sure that the system power is off. Then remove the PC cover and any installed cards. SIMMs snap easily into place, but chips can be more difficult to install. A chip-installation tool is not required, but it can make inserting the chips into sockets much easier. To remove chips, use a chip extractor or small screwdriver. Never try removing a RAM chip with your fingers, because you can bend the chip's pins or poke a hole in your finger with one of the pins. You remove SIMMs by releasing the locking tabs and either pulling or rolling them out of their sockets.

After adding the memory chips and putting the system back together, you may have to alter motherboard switches or jumper settings. The original PC includes two switch blocks with eight switches per block. Switch positions 1 through 4 of a PC's second switch block must be set to reflect the total installed memory. The XT has only one switch block, which is set to reflect the number of memory banks installed on the system board but not the expansion-card memory. Appendix A provides more detailed information about the PC and XT motherboard switch settings.

IBM AT and compatible systems have no switches or jumpers for memory. Rather, you must run a setup program to inform the system of the total amount of memory installed. IBM-compatible AT-type systems usually have a setup program built into the system ROM BIOS, and you must run this program after installing new memory to configure the system properly.

> **Note**
>
> Information on installing memory on older memory-expansion cards can be found in Chapter 7 of the sixth edition of *Upgrading and Repairing PCs* on the CD accompanying this book.

After configuring your system to work properly with the additional memory, you should run a memory-diagnostics program to ensure the proper operation of the new memory. At least two and sometimes three memory-diagnostic programs are available for all systems. In order of accuracy, these programs are:

- POST (Power-On Self Test)
- User diagnostics disk
- Advanced diagnostics disk
- Aftermarket diagnostics software

The POST is used every time you power up the system; you can press Ctrl+A at the opening menu to access the advanced diagnostics on the reference disk.

Many additional diagnostics programs are available from aftermarket utility software companies. More information on aftermarket testing facilities can be found in Chapter 21, "Software and Hardware Diagnostic Tools."

> **Note**
>
> Information on installing 640K of RAM in an XT motherboard can be found on the CD accompanying this book.

Upgrading the ROM BIOS

In this section, you learn that ROM BIOS upgrades can improve a system in many ways. You also learn that the upgrades can be difficult and may require much more than plugging in a generic set of ROM chips.

The *ROM BIOS*, or read-only memory basic input/output system, provides the crude brains that get your computer's components working together. A simple $30–$90 BIOS replacement can give your computer faster performance and more features.

The BIOS is the reason why DOS can operate on virtually any IBM-compatible system despite hardware differences. Because the BIOS communicates with the hardware, the BIOS must be specific to the hardware and match it completely. Instead of creating their own BIOSes, many computer makers buy a BIOS from specialists such as American Megatrends Inc. (AMI), Award Software, Microid Research, or Phoenix Technologies Ltd. A hardware manufacturer that wants to license a BIOS must undergo a lengthy process of working with the BIOS company to tailor the BIOS code to the hardware. This process is what makes upgrading a BIOS so difficult; BIOS usually resides on ROM chips on the motherboard.

The BIOS is a collection of small computer programs embedded in an *EPROM* (erasable programmable read-only memory) chip or chips, depending on the design of your computer. That collection of programs is the first thing loaded when you start your computer, even before the operating system. Simply put, the BIOS has three main functions:

- It tests your computer's components when it is turned on. This test is called the Power-On Self Test, or POST. The POST tests your computer's memory, motherboard, video adapter, disk controller, keyboard, and other crucial components.

- It finds the operating system and loads, or boots, it. This operation is called the bootstrap loader routine. If an operating system is found, it is loaded and given control of your computer.

- After an operating system is loaded, the BIOS works with your processor to give software programs easy access to your computer's specific features. For example, the BIOS tells your computer how to work with your video card and hard disk when a software program requires these devices.

In older systems, you often must upgrade the BIOS to take advantage of some other upgrade. To install some of the newer IDE (Integrated Drive Electronics) hard drives and 1.44M or 2.88M floppy drives in older machines, for example, you may need a BIOS upgrade. Machines still are being sold with older BIOSes that do not support the user-definable drive-type feature required for easy installation of an IDE drive, or that may have timing problems associated with IDE drives.

The following list shows the primary functions of a ROM BIOS upgrade:

- Adding 720K, 1.44M, or 2.88M 3 1/2-inch floppy drive support to a system

- Eliminating controller- or device-driver-based hard disk parameter translation for MFM, RLL, IDE, or ESDI drives with 1,024 or fewer cylinders by using a user-definable hard drive type matched to the drive

- Adding support for block-mode Programmed I/O (PIO) transfers for a Fast-ATA (AT Attachment Interface) (Enhanced-IDE) hard disk.

- Adding 101-key Enhanced Keyboard support

- Adding compatibility for Novell networks

- Adding compatibility for SVGA displays
- Adding support for additional serial (COM) ports and printer ports
- Adding password protection
- Adding virus protection
- Adding support for additional disk drives
- Correcting known bugs or compatibility problems with certain hardware and software
- Adding PnP compatibility to the system
- Upgrading the CPU

Because of the variety of motherboard designs on the market, ordering a BIOS upgrade often is more difficult than it sounds initially. If you have a name-brand system with a well-known design, the process can be simple. For many lesser-known compatible systems, however, you must give the BIOS vendor information about the system, such as the type of manufacturer's chipset that the motherboard uses.

For most BIOS upgrades, you must obtain the following information:

- The make and model of the system unit
- The type of CPU (for example, 286, 386DX, 386SX, 486DX, 486SX, Pentium 100, and so on)
- The make and version of the existing BIOS
- The part numbers of the existing ROM chips (you may have to peel back the labels to read this information)
- The make, model, or part numbers of integrated motherboard chipsets, if used (for example, Intel, ALI, Chips & Technologies, VLSI, OPTI, UMC, and others)

An *integrated chipset* is a group of chips on the original AT motherboard that can perform the functions of hundreds of discrete chips. Many chipsets offer customizable features that are available only if you have the correct BIOS. Most differences among systems today lie in the variety of integrated chipsets that are now used to manufacture PCs, and in the special initialization required to operate these chips.

The BIOS also must support variations in keyboard-controller programming and in the way that nonstandard features such as speed switching are handled. A computer that uses the Chips & Technologies NEAT chipset, for example, must have a BIOS specifically made for it. The BIOS must initialize the NEAT chipset registers properly; otherwise, the machine does not even boot. The BIOS also must have support for this chipset's special features. Each of the more popular chipsets for 286, 386, 486, Pentium, Pentium-MMX, Pentium Pro, and Pentium II machines requires specific BIOS support for proper operation. A generic BIOS may boot some systems, but certain features, such as shifting to and from protected mode and speed switching, may not be possible without the correct BIOS.

Keyboard-Controller Chips

Besides the main system ROM, AT-class computers also have a keyboard controller or keyboard ROM, which is a keyboard-controller microprocessor with its own built-in ROM. The keyboard controller usually is an Intel 8042 microcontroller, which incorporates a microprocessor, RAM, ROM, and I/O ports. The keyboard controller usually is a 40-pin chip, often with a label that has a copyright notice identifying the BIOS code programmed into the chip.

The keyboard controller controls the reset and A20 lines and also deciphers the keyboard scan codes. The A20 line is used in extended memory and other protected-mode operations. In many systems, one of the unused ports is used to select the CPU clock speed. Because of the tie-in with the keyboard controller and protected-mode operation, many problems with keyboard controllers become evident when you use either Windows or OS/2. If you experience lockups or keyboard problems with either Windows or OS/2 software—or with any software that runs in protected mode, such as Lotus 1-2-3 Release 3.x—get a replacement from your BIOS vendor or system-board vendor.

IBM systems do not need a replacement of the keyboard controller for upgrade purposes. (Replacement is difficult because the chip normally is soldered in.) Most manufacturers of IBM-compatible systems install the keyboard-controller chip in a socket so that you can upgrade or replace it easily. If you upgrade the BIOS in your system, the BIOS vendor often includes a compatible keyboard controller as well. You usually do not have to buy the controller unless your old keyboard controller has a problem with the new BIOS.

BIOS Manufacturers and Vendors

Several BIOS manufacturers have developed ROM BIOS software for use in upgrading IBM or IBM-compatible systems. The following companies are the largest manufacturers of ROM BIOS software:

- Phoenix
- American Megatrends International (AMI)
- Award

Phoenix pioneered the IBM-compatible BIOS and the legal means to develop a product that is fully compatible with IBM's BIOS without infringing on the corporation's copyright. Phoenix first introduced many new features, such as user-defined hard drive types and 1.44M drive support. The Phoenix BIOS has a very good Power-On Self Test; this thorough POST presents a complete set of failure codes for diagnosing problems, especially the ones that occur when a system seems to be dead. (Appendix A contains a complete list of Phoenix BIOS POST error codes.)

The Phoenix BIOS documentation, a complete three-volume reference package, is one of the product's most useful features. This documentation includes *System BIOS for IBM PC/XT/AT Computers and Compatibles*, *CBIOS for IBM PS/2 Computers and Compatibles*, and *ABIOS for IBM PS/2 Computers and Compatibles*. I recommend these excellent reference works, published by Addison-Wesley, even if you do not have the Phoenix BIOS (although some of its specific information does not apply to other systems).

The BIOS produced by AMI is very popular and surpasses even Phoenix in new system installations. The AMI BIOS offers a less comprehensive POST than the Phoenix BIOS, but it has an extensive diagnostics program in ROM. You even can purchase the program separately, as AMIDIAG. The in-ROM version, however, lacks the capability to test memory—a crucial capability if the failure is in the first bank. On the other hand, the BIOS is very compatible with the PC standard, available for several different chipsets and motherboards, and has been handled responsibly from the support level. When problems have occurred, AMI has fixed them, earning this program full compatibility with OS/2 and other difficult environments.

Because AMI manufactures its own motherboards, it has a distinct advantage over other BIOS companies. If the motherboard and BIOS are made by the same source, the single vendor probably can resolve any interaction problems between the BIOS and motherboard quickly, without shifting blame for the problem to another party. I recommend buying AMI's motherboards, because you generally don't have to worry about compatibility problems between the AMI BIOS and the AMI motherboard. Even if problems occur, AMI corrects them.

Award, the third-largest manufacturer of BIOS software, has made a name for itself with many system vendors, because it licenses the BIOS code to them for further modification. AST, for example, purchased the rights to the Award BIOS for its own systems and now can modify the BIOS internally, as though it created the BIOS from scratch. In a sense, AST could develop its own custom BIOS, using the Award code as a starting point. Award also provides precustomized BIOS code for manufacturers. Although Award's BIOS is not yet as popular as the Phoenix and AMI BIOSes, it is very popular, and compatibility even in tough environments, such as OS/2, is ensured.

If you want to replace or upgrade your BIOS, you can obtain replacement chips directly from the BIOS manufacturer or from the following recommended distributors:

- *Micro Firmware Inc.* Micro Firmware offers an extensive line of Phoenix BIOS upgrades, with more than 50 common 8088, 286, 386, 486, Pentium, and higher versions available. This company develops BIOS upgrades for specific hardware platforms, even when the original motherboard manufacturer is no longer in business. Many other BIOS vendors sell BIOSes developed by Micro Firmware for specific platforms.

- *Washburn & Company Distributors.* This licensed AMI distributor deals exclusively with AMI BIOS upgrades. Washburn has complete AMI motherboard and BIOS packages. A primary distributor for AMI, Washburn has great expertise in dealing with BIOS upgrade problems. The company also sells Second Nature, a disk drive support product that may eliminate the need for a BIOS if all you want is additional hard disk or floppy drive support.

Special ROM BIOS-Related Problems

Some known problems exist in certain ROM BIOS versions as well as in some systems sold during the past few years. Several of these problems have the potential to affect a large number of people, either because the problem is severe or many systems have the problem. This section describes some of the most important known BIOS- and system-interaction problems and also provides solutions for those problems.

Some systems with BIOSes even as recent as 1992 or 1993 may not start after you upgrade to DOS 6.x. Some of the older BIOSes came online when DOS 3.3 or earlier was the current operating system. As a result, those older BIOSes often cannot take advantage of the advanced features of DOS 6.x.

If you use an AT&T 6300 system, you will want to use BIOS Version 1.43, which is the most recent one made for the system. This version solves many problems with older 6300 systems and also provides support for a 720K floppy disk drive. You can order BIOS Version 1.43 for about $35 from the AT&T National Parts Sales Center (see Appendix A) under part number 105203780.

Some systems with the AMI BIOS have had problems with IDE hard disk drives. IDE (Integrated Drive Electronics) drives have been touted as being fully port-compatible with existing ST-506/412 (MFM or RLL) and ESDI drives. Some IDE drives, however, take somewhat longer than they should after certain commands to present valid data at their ports. In late 1989, AMI received many reports of problems with IDE drives, especially Conner and Toshiba drives. Because of these timing problems, AMI BIOS versions dated earlier than April 9, 1990 are not recommended for use with IDE drives, and data loss can result if earlier versions are used. You may experience `Drive C not ready` errors with certain IDE drives, such as those from Conner Peripherals. If you have a computer with an IDE drive and an AMI BIOS dated earlier than 04/09/90, you should get a newer BIOS from the system vendor.

To make sure that you have the correct AMI BIOS version, look for this figure in the lower-left corner of the screen when you boot your computer:

`xxxx-zzzz-040990`

The `040990` indicates a BIOS date of April 9, 1990—the minimum version to use. Older versions are okay only if you are *not* using IDE drives. The `xxxx-zzzz` indicates the BIOS type code and an OEM (original equipment manufacturer) ID number. For AMI-manufactured motherboards, for example, the BIOS type code is DAMI-[*model code*].

Changes to an Existing BIOS

If you have access to the correct tools and knowledge, you can perform some interesting modifications or upgrades to your system by altering your existing ROM BIOS. This section discusses several modifications that I have performed on my own systems. (These modifications have worked *for me*, and I am not necessarily recommending that anyone else perform them.) If nothing else, the research and development of these modifications taught me much about the way some things work in an IBM-compatible system, and I know that many of you are interested in some of this information.

> **Note**
>
> BIOS modifications are for readers who are especially technically astute or extremely adventurous; they are not recommended for everyone, especially for readers for whom system reliability is of crucial importance. But the following information should prove to be interesting even for readers of this book who do not attempt these operations on their systems.

> **Note**
>
> More information on BIOS, including removing the POST Speed Check, making a backup of your BIOS, modifying the hard disk parameter tables, and changing the hard disk controller head step rate can be found on the CD that accompanies this book. They can also be found in Chapter 7 of the sixth edition of *Upgrading and Repairing PCs*.

Using a Flash BIOS. Flash ROM is a type of EEPROM chip that is included in most systems today. *EEPROM (electrically erasable programmable read-only memory)* is a type of ROM chip that you can erase and reprogram directly in the system without using ultraviolet light and an EPROM programmer device. Using Flash ROM enables a manufacturer to send out ROM upgrades on disk; you then can load the upgrade into the Flash ROM chip on the motherboard without removing and replacing the chip. Often these upgrades can be downloaded from the manufacturer's Web site. This method saves time and money for both the system manufacturer and the end user.

Sometimes, the Flash ROM in a system is write-protected, and you must disable the protection before performing an update, usually by means of a jumper or switch that controls the lock on the ROM update. Without the lock, any program that knows the right instructions can rewrite the ROM in your system—not a comforting thought. Without the write protection, it is conceivable that virus programs could be written that copy themselves directly into the ROM BIOS code in your system!

One potential drawback to Flash ROM equipped systems is their dependence on battery power. If the battery dies, so does the BIOS. Obviously, this presents an inconvenience beyond simply having to reset the clock every time you power up. In any case, it is a good idea to back up your BIOS. Several BIOS backup programs are available, and the manufacturers themselves generally provide some sort of provision to protect you in the event of a battery failure.

Most manufacturers that use the Flash BIOS system notify their customers when they upgrade the BIOS for a particular system line. Usually, the cost of the upgrade is nominal; if your system is new enough, the upgrade may even be free.

Using IML System Partition BIOS. IBM used a scheme similar to a Flash ROM called *Initial Microcode Load (IML)*. IML is a technique in which the BIOS code is installed on the hard disk in a special hidden system partition and is loaded every time the system is powered up. Of course, the system still has a core BIOS on the motherboard, but all that BIOS does is locate and load updated BIOS code from the system partition. This technique enabled IBM to distribute ROM updates on disk for installation in the system partition. The IML BIOS is loaded every time the system is reset or powered on.

Along with the system BIOS code, the system partition contains a complete copy of the Reference Disk, which provides the option of running the setup and system-configuration software at any time during a reboot operation. This option eliminates the need to boot from the Reference Disk to reconfigure the system, and gives the impression that the entire Reference Disk is contained in ROM.

One drawback to this technique is that the BIOS code is installed on the (SCSI) hard disk; the system cannot function properly without the correctly set-up hard disk connected. You always can boot from the Reference Disk floppy, should the hard disk fail or become disconnected, but you cannot boot from a standard floppy disk.

Chapter 8

The Power Supply

The power supply is a critical component in a PC, as it supplies electrical power to every component in the system. In my experiences, it is also one of the most failure-prone components in any computer system. Because of its importance to proper and reliable system operation, you should understand both the function and limitations of a power supply, as well as its potential problems and their solutions.

Power Supply Function and Operation

The basic function of the power supply is to convert the type of electrical power available at the wall socket to that which is usable by the computer circuitry. The power supply in a conventional desktop system is designed to convert the 120-volt, 60Hz, AC current into something the computer can use—specifically, +5- and +12v DC current, and +3.3v as well on some systems. Usually, the digital electronic components and circuits in the system (motherboard, adapter cards, and disk drive logic boards) use the 3.3v or +5v power, and the motors (disk drive motors and any fans) use the +12v power. The power supply must ensure a good, steady supply of DC current so that the system can operate properly.

If you look at a specification sheet for a typical PC power supply, you see that the supply generates not only +5v and +12v, but also –5v and –12v. Because it would seem that the +5v and +12v signals power everything in the system (logic and motors), what are the negative voltages used for? The answer is, not much! In fact, these additional negative voltages are not used at all in many modern systems, although they are still required for backwards compatibility.

Although –5v and –12v are supplied to the motherboard via the power supply connectors, the motherboard itself uses only the +5v. The –5v signal is simply routed to the ISA bus on pin B5 and is not used in any way by the motherboard. It was originally used by the analog data separator circuits found in older floppy controllers, which is why it was supplied to the bus. Because modern controllers do not need the –5v, it is no longer used but is still required because it is part of the ISA Bus standard.

> **Note**
>
> Power supplies in systems with a Micro Channel Architecture (MCA) Bus do not have –5v. This power signal was never needed in these systems, as they always used a more modern floppy controller design.

Both the +12v and –12v signals also are not used by the motherboard logic, and instead are simply routed to pins B9 and B7 of the ISA bus (respectively). These voltages can be used by any adapter card on the bus, but most notably they are used by serial port driver/receiver circuits. If the motherboard has serial ports built in, the +12v and –12v signals can sometimes be used for those ports.

> **Note**
>
> The load placed on these voltages by a serial port would be very small. For example, the PS/2 Dual Async adapter uses only 35mA of +12v and 35mA of –12v (0.035 amps each) to operate two ports.

Most newer serial port circuits no longer use 12v driver/receiver circuits, but instead now use circuits that run on only 5v or even 3.3v. If you have one of these modern design ports in your system, the –12v signal from your power supply is likely to be totally unused by anything in the system.

The main function of the +12v power is to run disk drive motors. Usually a large amount of current is available, especially in systems with a large number of drive bays, such as in a tower configuration. Besides disk drive motors, the +12v supply is used by any cooling fans in the system, which, of course, should always be running. A single cooling fan can draw between 100mA to 250mA (0.1 to 0.25 amps); however, most newer ones use the lower 100mA figure. Note that although most fans in desktop systems run on +12v, most portable systems use fans that run on +5v or even 3.3v instead.

In addition to supplying power to run the system, the power supply also ensures that the system does not run unless the power being supplied is sufficient to operate the system properly. In other words, the power supply actually prevents the computer from starting up or operating until all the correct power levels are present.

Each power supply completes internal checks and tests before allowing the system to start. The power supply sends to the motherboard a special signal, called *Power_Good*. If this signal is not present, the computer does not run. The effect of this setup is that when the AC voltage dips and the power supply becomes over-stressed or overheated, the Power_Good signal goes down and forces a system reset or complete shutdown. If your system has ever seemed dead when the power switch is on and the fan and hard disks are running, you know the effects of losing the Power_Good signal.

IBM originally used this conservative design with the view that if the power goes low or the supply is overheated or over-stressed, causing output power to falter, the computer should not be allowed to operate. You even can use the Power_Good feature as a method of designing and implementing a reset switch for the PC. The Power_Good line is wired to the clock generator circuit (an 8284 or 82284 chip in the original PC/XT and AT systems), which controls the clock and reset lines to the microprocessor. When you ground the Power_Good line with a switch, the chip and related circuitry stop the processor by killing the clock signal and then reset the processor when the Power_Good signal appears after you release the switch. The result is a full hardware reset of the system. Instructions for installing such a switch in a system not already equipped can be found later in this chapter.

Newer systems with ATX or LPX form factor motherboards include a special signal called *PS_ON* which can be used to turn the power supply (and thus the system) off via software; this is sometimes called the *soft-off feature*. This is most evident in Windows 95 when you select the Shut Down the Computer option. If the power supply soft-offs, Windows will automatically shut down the computer rather than display a message that it's safe to shut down the computer.

Power Supply Form Factors

The shape and general physical layout of a component is called the *form factor*, and items that share form factors are generally interchangeable. When a system is designed, the designers can choose to use one of the popular standard form factors, or they can "roll their own." Choosing the former means that a virtually inexhaustible supply of inexpensive replacements is available in a variety of quality and power output levels. Going the custom route means that the supply will be unique to the system and available only from the original manufacturer in only the model(s) they produce. If you cannot tell already, I am a fan of the industry-standard form factors!

The form factor of the power supply that a particular system uses is based on the case design. Six popular case and power supply types can be called *industry standard*. The different types are:

    PC/XT style   Baby AT style

    AT/Desk style   Slim style

    AT/Tower style   ATX style

Each of these supplies are available in numerous different configurations and power output levels. Of these standard types, the Slim style and ATX style are found in most modern systems, while the others are largely obsolete.

PC/XT Style. When IBM introduced the XT, it used the same basic power supply shape as the original PC, except that the new XT supply had more than double the power output capability (see Figure 8.1). Because they were identical in both external appearance and the type of connectors used, you could easily install the better XT supply as an upgrade for a PC system. Because of the tremendous popularity of the original PC and XT design, a number of manufacturers began building systems that mimicked their shape and layout. These *clones*, as they have been called, could interchange virtually all components with the IBM systems, including the power supply. Numerous manufacturers have since begun producing these components, and nearly all follow the form factor of one or more IBM systems.

FIG. 8.1 PC/XT-form factor power supply.

AT/Desk Style. When IBM later introduced the AT desktop system, it created a larger power supply that had a form factor different from the original PC/XT. This system was rapidly cloned as well, and to this day still represents the basis for most IBM-compatible designs. The power supply used in these systems is called the *AT/Desktop style power supply* (see Figure 8.2). Hundreds of manufacturers now make motherboards, power supplies, cases, and so on that are physically interchangeable with the original IBM AT. If you are buying a compatible system, I recommend those that have form factors that are compatible with the IBM AT, because you will have numerous motherboards and power supplies from which to choose.

AT/Tower Style. The compatible market has come up with a couple of other variations on the AT theme that are popular today. Besides the standard AT/Desktop type power supply, we also have the *AT/Tower configuration*, which is basically a full-sized AT-style desktop system running on its side. The power supply and motherboard form factors are basically the same in the Tower system as in the Desktop. The tower configuration is not new; in fact, even IBM's original AT had a specially mounted logo that could be rotated when you ran the system on its side in the tower configuration.

The type of power supply used in a tower system is identical to that used in a desktop system, except for the power switch location. Most AT/Desktop systems required that the power switch be located right on the power supply itself, while most AT/Tower systems use an external switch attached to the power supply through a short 4-wire cable. A full sized AT power supply with a remote switch is now called an *AT/Tower form-factor supply* (see Figure 8.3).

FIG. 8.2 AT/Desktop form factor power supply.

FIG. 8.3 AT/Tower form-factor power supply.

Baby-AT Style. Another type of AT-based form factor that has been developed is the so called *Baby-AT*, which is simply a shortened version of the full-sized AT system. The power supply in these systems is shortened on one dimension; however, it matches the AT design in all other respects. These Baby-AT style power supplies can be used in both Baby-AT chassis and the larger AT-style chassis; however, the full size AT/Tower power supply does not fit in the Baby-AT chassis (see Figure 8.4).

FIG. 8.4 Baby-AT form factor power supply.

Slim Style. The fifth type of form factor that has developed is the *Slimline* (see Figure 8.5). These systems use a different motherboard configuration that mounts the slots on a "riser" card that plugs into the motherboard. The expansion cards plug into this riser and are mounted sideways in the system. These types of systems are very low in height, hence the name *Slimline*. A new power supply was specifically developed for these systems and allows interchangeability between different manufacturers' systems. Some problems with motherboard interchanges occur because of the riser cards, but the Slimline power supply has become a standard in its own right.

The slimline power supply is by far the most popular power supply design in use today. Despite how it might sound, even most full-sized AT Desktop and Tower cases today are designed to accept the slimline form factor power supply.

Power Supply Function and Operation

5.9"x5.5"x3.4"

FIG. 8.5 Slimline/Low Profile form factor power supply.

ATX Style. The newest standard on the market today is the *ATX form factor* (see Figure 8.6). This describes a new motherboard shape, as well as a new case and power supply form factor. The ATX supply is based on the slimline or low-profile design, but has several differences worth noting.

One difference is that the fan is now mounted along the inner side of the supply, blowing air across the motherboard and drawing it in from the outside at the rear. This flow is the opposite of most standard supplies, which blow air out the back of the supply and also have the fan positioned at the back. The reverse flow cooling used in the ATX supply forces air over the hottest components of the board, such as the CPU, SIMMs, and expansion slots. This eliminates the need for the notoriously unreliable CPU fans that have unfortunately become common today.

Another benefit of the reverse flow cooling is that the system will remain cleaner and free from dust and dirt. The case is essentially pressurized, so air will push out of the cracks in the case, the opposite of what happens in non-ATX systems. For example, if you held a lit cigarette in front of your floppy drive on a normal system, the smoke would be inhaled through the front of the drive and contaminate the heads! On an ATX system with reverse flow cooling, the smoke would be blown away from the drive because the only air intake is the single fan vent on the power supply at the rear. Those who use systems that operate in extremely harsh environments could add a filter to the fan intake vent, which would ensure even further that all air entering the system is clean and dust free.

Chapter 8—The Power Supply

FIG. 8.6 ATX form factor power supply.

The ATX system format was designed by Intel in 1995, but became popular in the new Pentium Pro-based PCs in 1996. The ATX form factor takes care of several problems with the Baby-AT or Slimline form factors. Where the power supply is concerned, this covers two main problems. One problem is that the traditional PC power supply has two connectors that plug into the motherboard. The problem is that if you insert these connectors backwards or out of their normal sequence, you will fry the motherboard! Most responsible system manufacturers will have the motherboard and power supply connectors keyed so they cannot be installed backwards or out of sequence, but many of the cheaper system vendors do not feature this keying on the boards or supplies they use.

To solve the potential for disaster that awaits those who might plug in their power supply connectors incorrectly, the ATX form factor includes a new power plug for the motherboard. This new connector features 20 pins, and is a single-keyed connector. It is virtually impossible to plug it in backwards, and because there is only one connector instead of two nearly identical ones, it is impossible to plug them in out of sequence. The new connector also can optionally supply 3.3v, eliminating the need for voltage regulators on the motherboard to power the CPU and other 3.3v circuits. Although the 3.3v signals are labeled as optional in the ATX specification, they should be considered mandatory in any ATX form factor power supply you purchase. Many systems will require this in the future.

Besides the new 3.3v signals, there is one other set of signals that will be found on the ATX supply not normally seen on standard supplies. They are the *Power_On* and *5v_Standby* signals, which are also called *Soft Power*. Power_On is a motherboard signal that can be used with operating systems like Windows 95 or Windows NT, which support the ability to power the system down with software. This will also allow the optional use of the keyboard to power the system back on, exactly like the Apple Macintosh systems. The 5v_Standby signal is always active, giving the motherboard a limited source of power even when off.

Power Supply Function and Operation **299**

The other problem solved by the ATX form factor power supply is that of system cooling. Most of the high-end Pentium and Pentium Pro systems have active heat sinks on the processor, which means there is a small fan on the CPU designed to cool it. These small fans are notoriously unreliable, not to mention expensive when compared to standard passive heat sinks. In the ATX design, the CPU fan is eliminated, and the CPU is mounted in a socket right next to the ATX power supply, which has a reverse flow fan blowing onto the CPU.

You will find it easy to locate supplies that fit these industry-standard form factors. Several vendors who manufacture PC power supplies in all these form factors are listed later in this chapter. For proprietary units, you will likely have to go back to the manufacturer.

Power Supply Connectors

Table 8.1 shows the pinouts for most standard AT or PC/XT-compatible systems. Some systems may have more or fewer drive connectors. For example, IBM's AT system power supplies have only three disk drive power connectors, although most of the currently available AT/Tower type power supplies have four drive connectors. If you are adding drives and need additional disk drive power connectors, "Y" splitter cables are available from many electronics supply houses (including Radio Shack) that can adapt a single power connector to serve two drives. As a precaution, make sure that your total power supply output is capable of supplying the additional power.

Table 8.1 Typical PC/XT and AT Power Supply Connections

Connector	AT Type	PC/XT Type
P8-1	Power_Good (+5v)	Power_Good (+5v)
P8-2	+5v	Key (No connect)
P8-3	+12v	+12v
P8-4	–12v	–12v
P8-5	Ground (0)	Ground (0)
P8-6	Ground (0)	Ground (0)
P9-1	Ground (0)	Ground (0)
P9-2	Ground (0)	Ground (0)
P9-3	–5v	–5v
P9-4	+5v	+5v
P9-5	+5v	+5v
P9-6	+5v	+5v
P10-1	+12v	+12v
P10-2	Ground (0)	Ground (0)
P10-3	Ground (0)	Ground (0)
P10-4	+5v	+5v
P11-1	+12v	+12v
P11-2	Ground (0)	Ground (0)

(continues)

Table 8.1 Continued

Connector	AT Type	PC/XT Type
P11-3	Ground (0)	Ground (0)
P11-4	+5v	+5v
P12-1	+12v	—
P12-2	Ground (0)	—
P12-3	Ground (0)	—
P12-4	+5v	—
P13-1	+12v	—
P13-2	Ground (0)	—
P13-3	Ground (0)	—
P13-4	+5v	—

Notice that the Baby-AT and Slimline power supplies also use the AT/Desktop or Tower pin configuration. The only other type of industry standard power supply connector is found on the new ATX form factor power supply. This is a 20-pin keyed connector with pins configured as shown in Table 8.2.

Table 8.2 ATX Power Supply Connections

Signal	Pin	Pin	Signal
3.3v*	11	1	3.3v*
–12v	12	2	3.3v*
GND	13	3	GND
Pwr_On	14	4	5v
GND	15	5	GND
GND	16	6	5v
GND	17	7	GND
–5v	18	8	Power_Good
5v	19	9	5v_Standby
5v	20	10	12v

* = Optional signal

> **Note**
>
> The ATX supply features several signals not seen before, such as the 3.3v, Power_On, and 5v_Standby signals. Because of this, it will be difficult to adapt a standard slimline or low-profile form factor supply to work properly in an ATX system, although the shapes are virtually identical.

Although the PC/XT power supplies do not have any signal on pin P8-2, you can still use them on AT-type motherboards, or vice versa. The presence or absence of the +5v signal on that pin has little or no effect on system operation. If you are measuring voltages for testing purposes, anything within 10 percent is considered acceptable, although most manufacturers of high-quality power supplies specify a tighter 5 percent tolerance. I prefer to go by the 5 percent tolerance, which is a tougher test to pass.

Desired Voltage	Loose Tolerance Min. (−10%)	Max. (+8%)	Tight Tolerance Min. (−5%)	Max. (+5%)
+/−5.0v	4.5v	5.4v	4.75	5.25
+/−12.0v	10.8v	12.9v	11.4	12.6

The Power_Good signal has tolerances different from the other signals, although it is nominally a +5v signal in most systems. The trigger point for Power_Good is about +2.5v, but most systems require the signal voltage to be within about 3v to 6v.

A power supply should be replaced if the voltages are out of these ranges.

Power Switch Connectors. The AT/Tower and Slimline power supplies use a remote power switch. This switch is mounted in the front of the system case and is connected to the power supply through a standard type of 4-wire cable. The ends of the cable are fitted with spade connector lugs, which plug into the spade connectors on the power switch itself. The switch is usually a part of the case, so the power supply comes with the cable and no switch.

The cable from the power supply to the switch in the case contains four color-coded wires. There may also be a fifth wire supplying a ground connection to the case as well.

> **Caution**
>
> The remote power switch leads carry 110v AC current at all times. You could be electrocuted if you touch the ends of these wires with the power supply plugged in! Always make sure the power supply is unplugged before connecting or disconnecting the remote power switch.

The four or five wires are color-coded as follows:

- The brown and blue wires are the live and neutral feed wires from the 110v power cord to the power supply itself. These wires are always hot when the power supply is plugged in.

- The black and white wires carry the AC feed from the switch back to the power supply itself. These leads should only be hot when the power supply is plugged in and the switch is turned on.

- A green wire or a green wire with a yellow stripe is the ground lead. It should be connected somewhere to the PC case, and helps to ground the power supply to the case.

On the switch itself, the tabs for the leads are usually color-coded; if not, they can still be easily connected. If there is no color coding on the switch, then plug the blue and brown wires onto the tabs that are parallel to each other, and the black and white wires to the tabs that are angled away from each other. See Figure 8.7 for a guide.

302 Chapter 8—The Power Supply

FIG. 8.7 Power supply remote switch connections.

As long as the blue and brown wires are on the one set of tabs, and the black and white leads are on the other, the switch and supply will work properly. If you incorrectly mix the leads, you can create a direct short circuit, and you will likely blow the circuit breaker for the wall socket.

Disk Drive Power Connectors. The disk drive connectors are fairly universal with regard to pin configuration and even wire color. Table 8.3 shows the standard disk drive power connector pinout and wire colors.

Table 8.3	Disk Drive Power Connector Pinout	
Pin	**Wire Color**	**Signal**
1	Yellow	+12v
2	Black	Gnd
3	Black	Gnd
4	Red	+5v

This information applies whether the drive connector is the larger Molex version or the smaller mini-version used on most 3 1/2-inch floppy drives. In each case, the pinouts and wire colors are the same. To determine the location of pin 1, look at the connector carefully. It is usually embossed in the plastic connector body; however, it is often tiny and difficult to read. Fortunately, these connectors are keyed and therefore are difficult to insert incorrectly. Figure 8.8 shows the keying with respect to pin numbers on the larger drive power connector.

FIG. 8.8 A disk drive female power supply cable connector.

Notice that some drive connectors may supply only two wires—usually the +5v and a single ground (pins 3 and 4)—because the floppy drives in most newer systems run on only +5v and do not use the +12v at all.

Physical Connector Part Numbers. The physical connectors used in industry-standard PC power supplies were originally specified by IBM for the supplies used in the original PC/XT/AT systems. They used a specific type of connector between the power supply and the motherboard (the P8 and P9 connectors), as well as specific connectors for the disk drives. The motherboard connectors used in all the industry-standard power supplies have not changed since 1981 when the IBM PC appeared. With the advent of 3 1/2-inch floppy drives in 1986, however, a new smaller type of drive power connector appeared on the scene for these drives. Table 8.4 lists the standard connectors used for motherboard and disk drive power.

Table 8.4 Physical Power Connectors

Connector Description	Female (on Power Cable)	Male (on Component)
Motherboard P8/P9	Burndy GTC6P-1	Burndy GTC 6RI
Disk Drive (large style)	AMP 1-480424-0	AMP 1-480426-0
Disk Drive (small style)	AMP 171822-4	AMP 171826-4

You can get these raw connectors through electronics supply houses (Allied, Newark, Digi-Key, and so on) found in the vendor list. You also can get complete cable assemblies including drive adapters from the large to small connectors, disk drive "Y" splitter cables, and motherboard power extension cables from a number of the cable and miscellaneous supply houses such as Cables To Go, the Cable Connection, Ci Design, and Key Power.

The Power_Good Signal

The Power_Good signal is a +5v signal (+3.0 through +6.0 is generally considered acceptable) generated in the power supply when it has passed its internal self tests and the outputs have stabilized. This normally takes anywhere from 0.1 to 0.5 seconds after you turn on the power supply switch. This signal is sent to the motherboard, where it is received by the processor timer chip, which controls the reset line to the processor.

In the absence of Power_Good, the timer chip continuously resets the processor, which prevents the system from running under bad or unstable power conditions. When the timer chip sees Power_Good, it stops resetting the processor and the processor begins executing whatever code is at address FFFF:0000 (usually the ROM BIOS).

If the power supply cannot maintain proper outputs (such as when a brownout occurs), the Power_Good signal is withdrawn, and the processor is automatically reset. When proper output is restored, the Power_Good signal is regenerated and the system again begins operation (as if you just powered on). By withdrawing Power_Good, the system never "sees" the bad power because it is "stopped" quickly (reset) rather than allowed to operate on unstable or improper power levels, which can cause parity errors and other problems.

In most systems, the Power_Good connection is made via connector P8-1 (P8 Pin 1) from the power supply to the motherboard.

A well-designed power supply delays the arrival of the Power_Good signal until all voltages stabilize after you turn the system on. Badly designed power supplies, which are found in *many* low-cost compatibles, often do not delay the Power_Good signal properly and enable the processor to start too soon. The normal Power_Good delay is from 0.1 to 0.5 seconds. Improper Power_Good timing also causes CMOS memory corruption in some systems. If you find that a system does not boot up properly the first time you turn on the switch but subsequently boots up if you press the reset or Ctrl+Alt+Delete warm boot command, you likely have a problem with Power_Good. This happens because the Power_Good signal is tied to the timer chip that generates the reset signal to the processor. What you must do in these cases is find a new high-quality power supply and see whether it solves the problem.

Many cheaper power supplies do not have proper Power_Good circuitry and often just tie any +5v line to that signal. Some motherboards are more sensitive to an improperly designed or improperly functioning Power_Good signal than others. Intermittent startup problems are often caused by improper Power_Good signal timing. A common example occurs when somebody replaces a motherboard in a system and then finds that the system intermittently fails to start properly when the power is turned on. This ends up being very difficult to diagnose, especially for the inexperienced technician, because the problem appears to be caused by the new motherboard. Although it seems that the new motherboard might be defective, it usually turns out to be that the original power supply is poorly designed and either cannot produce stable enough power to properly operate the new board, or more likely has an improperly wired or timed Power_Good signal. In these situations, replacing the supply with a high-quality unit is the proper solution.

Power Supply Loading

PC power supplies are of a switching rather than a linear design. The switching type of design uses a high speed oscillator circuit to generate different output voltages, and is very efficient in size, weight, and energy compared to the standard linear design, which uses a large internal transformer to generate different outputs.

One characteristic of all switching type power supplies is that they do not run without a load. This means that you must have the supply plugged into something drawing +5v and +12v or the supply does not work. If you simply have the supply on a bench with nothing plugged into it, the supply burns up or protection circuitry shuts it down. Most power supplies are protected from no-load operation and will shut down. Some of the cheap clone supplies, however, lack the protection circuit and relay and are destroyed after a few seconds of no-load operation. A few power supplies have their own built-in load resistors, so that they can run even though no normal load is plugged in.

According to IBM specifications for the standard 192-watt power supply used in the original AT, a minimum load of 7.0 amps was required at +5v and a minimum load of 2.5 amps was required at +12v for the supply to work properly. Because floppy drives present no +12v load unless they are spinning, systems without a hard disk drive often do not operate properly. Most power supplies have a minimum load requirement for both the +5v and +12v sides, and if you fail to meet this minimum load, the supply shuts down.

Because of this characteristic, when IBM used to ship AT systems without a hard disk, they had the hard disk drive power cable plugged into a large 5-ohm 50-watt sandbar resistor mounted in a little metal cage assembly where the drive would have been. The AT case had screw holes on top of where the hard disk would go, specifically designed to mount this resistor cage. Several computer stores I knew in the mid-1980s would order the diskless AT and install their own 20M or 30M drives, which they could get more cheaply from sources other than IBM. They were throwing away the load resistors by the hundreds! I managed to grab a couple at the time, which is how I know the type of resistor they used.

This resistor would be connected between pin 1 (+12v) and pin 2 (Ground) on the hard disk power connector. This placed a 2.4-amp load on the supply's 12-volt output, drawing 28.8 watts of power—it would get hot!—thus enabling the supply to operate normally. Note that the cooling fan in most power supplies draws approximately 0.1 to 0.25 amps, bringing the total load to 2.5 amps or more. If the load resistor was missing, the system would intermittently fail to start up or operate properly. The motherboard draws +5v at all times, but +12v is normally used only by motors, and the floppy drive motors are off most of the time.

Most of the 200-watt power supplies in use today do not require as much of a load as the original IBM AT power supply. In most cases, a minimum load of 2.0 to 4.0 amps at +5v and a minimum load of 0.5 to 1.0 amps at +12v are considered acceptable. Most motherboards will easily draw the minimum +5v current by themselves. The standard power supply cooling fan draws only 0.1 to 0.25 amps, so the +12v minimum load may still be a problem for a diskless workstation. Generally the higher the rating on the supply, the more minimum load is required; however, there are exceptions, so this is a specification you want to check into.

Some high-quality switching power supplies, like the Astec units used by IBM in all the PS/2 systems, have built-in load resistors and can run under a no-load situation because the supply loads itself. Most of the cheaper clone supplies do not have built-in load resistors, so they must have both +5v and +12v loads to work.

If you want to bench test a power supply, make sure that loads are placed on both the +5v and +12v outputs. This is one reason why it is best to test the supply while it is installed in the system instead of separately on the bench. For impromptu bench testing, you can use a spare motherboard and hard disk drive to load the +5v and +12v outputs, respectively.

Power-Supply Ratings

Most system manufacturers will provide you with the technical specifications of each of their system-unit power supplies. This type of information is usually found in the system's technical-reference manual and also on stickers attached directly to the power supply. Power supply manufacturers can supply this data, which is preferable if you can identify the manufacturer and contact them directly.

Tables 8.5 and 8.6 list power-supply specifications for several of IBM's units, from which most of the compatibles are derived. The PC-system power supplies are the original units that most compatible power supplies have duplicated. The input specifications are listed as voltages, and the output specifications are listed as amps at several voltage levels. IBM reports output wattage level as "specified output wattage." If your manufacturer does not list the total wattage, you can convert amperage to wattage by using the following simple formula:

$$\text{Wattage} = \text{Voltage} \times \text{Amperage}$$

By multiplying the voltage by the amperage available at each output and then adding them up, you can calculate the total capable output wattage of the supply.

Table 8.5 Power Supply Output Ratings for IBM "Classic" Systems

	PC	Port-PC	XT	XT-286	AT
Minimum Input Voltage	104	90	90	90	90
Maximum Input Voltage	127	137	137	137	137
110/220v Switching	No	Yes	No	Auto	Yes
Output Current (amps):+5v	7.0	11.2	15.0	20.0	19.8
–5v	0.3	0.3	0.3	0.3	0.3
+12v	2.0	4.4	4.2	4.2	7.3
–12v	0.25	0.25	0.25	0.25	0.3
Calculated output wattage	63.5	113.3	129.9	154.9	191.7
Specified output wattage	63.5	114.0	130.0	157.0	192.0

Table 8.6 shows the standard power supply output levels available in industry-standard form factors. Most manufacturers that offer power have supplies with different ratings. Supplies are available with ratings from 100 watts to 450 watts or more. Table 8.6 shows the rated outputs at each of the voltage levels for supplies with different manufacturer-specified output ratings. To compile the table, I referred to the specification sheets for supplies from Astec Standard Power and PC Power and Cooling. As you can see, although most of the ratings are accurate, they are somewhat misleading for the higher wattage units.

Table 8.6 Typical Compatible Power Supply Output Ratings

Specified Output Wattage	100W	150W	200W	250W	300W	375W	450W
Output Current (amps):+5v	10.0	15.0	20.0	25.0	32.0	35.0	45.0
–5v	0.3	0.3	0.3	0.5	1.0	0.5	0.5
+12v	3.5	5.5	8.0	10.0	10.0	13.0	15.0
–12v	0.3	0.3	0.3	0.5	1.0	0.5	1.0
Calculated output wattage	97.1	146.1	201.1	253.5	297.0	339.5	419.5

Most compatible power supplies have ratings between 150 to 250 watts output. Although lesser ratings are not usually desirable, it is possible to purchase heavy-duty power supplies for most compatibles that have outputs as high as 500 watts.

The 300-watt and larger units are excellent for enthusiasts who are building a fully optioned desktop or tower system. These supplies run any combination of motherboard and expansion card, as well as a large number of disk drives. In most cases, you cannot exceed the ratings on these power supplies—the system will be out of room for additional items first!

Most power supplies are considered to be *universal,* or *worldwide.* That is, they run on the 220v, 50-cycle current used in Europe and many other parts of the world. Most power supplies that can switch to 220v input are automatic, but a few require that you set a switch on the back of the power supply to indicate which type of power you will access. (The automatic units sense the current and switch automatically.)

If your supply does not autoswitch, make sure the voltage setting is correct. If you plug the power supply into a 110v outlet while set in the 220v setting, there will be no damage, but it will certainly not operate properly until you correct the setting. On the other hand, if you are in a foreign country with a 220v outlet and have the switch set for 110v, you may cause some damage.

Power Supply Specifications

In addition to power output, many other specifications and features go into making a high-quality power supply. I have had many systems over the years. My experience has been that if a brownout occurs in a room with several systems running, the systems with higher-quality power supplies and higher output ratings always make it over power disturbances, whereas others choke. I would not give $5 for many of the cheap, junky power supplies that come in some of the low-end clone systems.

High-quality power supplies also help to protect your systems. A power supply from a vendor like Astec or PC Power and Cooling will not be damaged if any of the following conditions occur:

- A 100 percent power outage of any duration
- A brownout of any kind
- A spike of up to 2,500v applied directly to the AC input (for example, a lightning strike or a lightning simulation test)

Decent power supplies have an extremely low current leakage to ground of less than 500 microamps. This safety feature is important if your outlet has a missing or improperly wired ground line.

As you can see, these specifications are fairly tough and are certainly representative of a high-quality power supply. Make sure that your supply can meet these specifications. The vendors recommended in this chapter produce supplies that meet or exceed these specifications.

Power-Use Calculations

One way to see whether your system is capable of expansion is to calculate the levels of power drain in the different system components and deduct the total from the maximum power supplied. This calculation might help you decide when to upgrade the power supply to a more capable unit. Unfortunately, these calculations can be difficult to make because many manufacturers do not publish power consumption data for their products.

It is difficult to get power consumption data for most +5v devices, including motherboards and adapter cards. Motherboards can consume different power levels, depending on numerous factors. Most 486DX2 motherboards consume about 5 amps or so, but if you can get data on the one you are using, so much the better. For adapter cards, if you can find the actual specifications for the card, use those figures. To be on the conservative side, however, I usually go by the maximum available power levels as set forth in the respective bus standards.

For example, consider the typical power consumption figures for components in a modern PC system. Most standard desktop or slimline PC systems today come with a 200-watt power supply rated for 20 amps at +5v and 8 amps at +12v. The ISA specification calls for a maximum of 2.0 amps of +5v and 0.175 amps of +12v power for each slot in the system. Most systems have eight slots, and you can assume that four of them are filled for the purposes of calculating power draw. The following calculation shows what happens when you subtract the amount of power necessary to run the different system components:

5v Power:	20.0 Amps
Less:	Motherboard −5.0 4 slots filled at 2.0 each −8.0 3 1/2 and 5 1/4-inch floppy drives −1.5 3 1/2-inch hard disk drive −0.5 CD-ROM drive −1.0
Remaining power:	4.0 amps

12v Power:	8.0 Amps
Less:	4 slots filled at 0.175 each−0.7 3 1/2-inch hard disk drive −1.0 3 1/2 and 5 1/4-inch Floppy drives −1.0 Cooling fan −0.1 CD-ROM drive −1.0
Remaining power:	4.2 amps

In the preceding example, everything seems alright for now. With half the slots filled, two floppy drives, and one hard disk, the system still has room for more. There might be trouble if this system were expanded to the extreme. With every slot filled and two or more hard disks, there definitely will be problems with the +5v. However, the +12v does seem to have room to spare. You could add a CD-ROM drive or a second hard disk without worrying too much about the +12v power, but the +5v power will be strained.

If you anticipate loading up a system to the extreme—as in a high-end multimedia system, for example—you may want to invest in the insurance of a higher output supply. For example, a 250-watt supply usually has 25-amps of +5v and 10-amps of +5v current, whereas a 300-watt unit has 32-amps of +5v power. These supplies would permit a fully expanded system and are likely to be found in full-sized desktop or tower case configurations in which this capability can be fully used.

Motherboards can draw anywhere from 4 to 15 amps or more of +5v power to run. In fact, a single Pentium 66MHz CPU draws up to 3.2 amps of +5v power all by itself. Considering that dual 100MHz Pentium processor systems are now becoming available, you could have 6.4 amps or more drawn by the processors alone. A motherboard like this with 64M of RAM might draw 15 amps or more all by itself. Most 486DX2 motherboards draw approximately 5 to 7 amps of +5v. Bus slots are allotted maximum power in amps, as shown in Table 8.7.

Table 8.7 Maximum Power Consumption in Amps per Bus Slot

Bus Type	+5v Power	+12v Power	+3.3v Power
ISA	2.0	0.175	N/A
EISA	4.5	1.5	N/A
VL-Bus	2.0	N/A	N/A
16-Bit MCA	1.6	0.175	N/A
32-Bit MCA	2.0	0.175	N/A
PCI	5	0.5	7.6

As you can see from the table, ISA slots are allotted 2.0 amps of +5v and 0.175 amps of +12v power. Note that these are maximum figures and not all cards draw this much power. If the slot has a VL-Bus extension connector, an additional 2.0 amps of +5v power is allowed for the VL-Bus.

Floppy drives can vary in power consumption, but most of the newer 3 1/2-inch drives have motors that run off +5v in addition to the logic circuits. These drives usually draw 1.0 amp of +5v power and use no +12v at all. Most 5 1/4-inch drives use standard +12v motors that draw about 1.0 amp. These drives also require about 0.5 amps of +5v for the logic circuits. Most cooling fans draw about 0.1 amps of +12v power, which is negligible.

Typical 3 1/2-inch hard disks today draw about 1 amp of +12v power to run the motors and only about 0.5 amps of +5v power for the logic. The 5 1/4-inch hard disks, especially those that are full-height, draw much more power. A typical full-height hard drive draws 2.0 amps of +12v power and 1.0 amps of +5v power.

Another problem with hard disks is that they require much more power during the spinup phase of operation than during normal operation. In most cases, the drive draws double the +12v power during spinup, which can be 4.0 amps or more for the full-height drives. This tapers off to normal after the drive is spinning.

The figures most manufacturers report for maximum power supply output are full duty-cycle figures, which means that these levels of power can be supplied continuously. You usually can expect a unit that continuously supplies some level of power to supply more power for some noncontinuous amount of time. A supply usually can offer 50 percent greater output than the continuous figure indicates for as long as one minute. This cushion is often used to supply the necessary power to start spinning a hard disk. After the drive has spun to full speed, the power draw drops to a value within the system's continuous supply capabilities. Drawing anything over the rated continuous figure for any long length of time causes the power supply to run hot and fail early, and it can prompt several nasty symptoms in the system.

> **Tip**
>
> If you are using internal SCSI hard drives, you can ease the startup load on your power supply. The key is to enable the Remote Start option on the SCSI drive, which causes the drive to start spinning only when it receives a startup command over the SCSI bus. The effect is such that the drive remains stationary (drawing very little power) until the very end of the POST and spins up right when the SCSI portion of the POST is begun.
>
> If you have multiple SCSI drives, they all spin up sequentially based on their SCSI ID setting. This is designed so that only one drive is spinning up at any one time, and that no drives start spinning until the rest of the system has had time to start. This greatly eases the load on the power supply when you first power the system on.
>
> This tip is essential when dealing with portable type systems in which power is at a premium. I burned up a supply in one of my portable systems before resetting the internal drive to Remote Start.

The biggest causes of overload problems are filling up the slots and adding more drives. Multiple hard drives, CD-ROM drives, floppy drives, and so on can place quite a drain on the system power supply. Make sure that you have enough +12v power to run all the drives you are going to install. Tower systems can be a problem here because they have so many drive bays. Make sure that you have enough +5v power to run all your expansion cards, especially if you are using VL-Bus or EISA cards. It pays to be conservative, but remember that most cards draw less than the maximum allowed.

Many people wait until an existing unit fails before they replace it with an upgraded version. If you are on a tight budget, this "if it ain't broke, don't fix it" attitude works. Power supplies, however, often do not just fail; they can fail in an intermittent fashion or allow fluctuating power levels to reach the system, which results in an unstable operation. You might be blaming system lockups on software bugs when the culprit is an overloaded power supply. If you have been running with your original power supply for a long time, you should expect some problems.

Leave It On or Turn It Off?

A frequent question that relates to the discussion of power supplies concerns whether you should turn off a system when it is not in use. You should understand some facts about electrical components and what makes them fail. Combine this knowledge with information on power consumption and cost, not to mention safety, and perhaps you can come to your own conclusion. Because circumstances can vary, the best answer for your own situation might be different depending on your particular needs and application.

Frequently, powering a system on and off does cause deterioration and damage to the components. This seems logical, and the reason is simple but not obvious to most. Many people believe that flipping system power on and off frequently is harmful because it electrically "shocks" the system. The real problem, however, is temperature. In other words, it is not so much electrical shock as thermal shock that damages a system. As the system warms up, the components expand; and as it cools off, the components contract. This alone stresses everything. In addition, various materials in the system have different thermal expansion coefficients, which means that they expand and contract at different rates. Over time, thermal shock causes deterioration in many areas of a system.

From a pure system-reliability point, it is desirable to insulate the system from thermal shock as much as possible. When a system is turned on, the components go from ambient (room) temperature to as high as 185 degrees F (85 degrees C) within 30 minutes or less. When you turn the system off, the same thing happens in reverse, and the components cool back to ambient temperature in a short period of time. Each component expands and contracts at slightly different rates, which causes the system an enormous amount of stress.

Thermal expansion and contraction remains the single largest cause of component failure. Chip cases can split, allowing moisture to enter and contaminate them. Delicate internal wires and contacts can break, and circuit boards can develop stress cracks. Surface-mounted components expand and contract at different rates from the circuit board they are mounted on, which causes enormous stress at the solder joints. Solder joints can fail due to the metal hardening from the repeated stress causing cracks in the joint. Components that use heat sinks such as processors, transistors, or voltage regulators can overheat and fail because the thermal cycling causes heat sink adhesives to deteriorate, breaking the thermally conductive bond between the device and the heat sink. Thermal cycling also causes socketed devices and connections to "creep," which can cause a variety of intermittent contact failures.

Thermal expansion and contraction affects not only chips and circuit boards, but also things like hard disk drives. Most hard drives today have sophisticated thermal compensation routines that make adjustments in head position relative to the expanding and contracting platters. Most drives perform this thermal compensation routine once every five minutes for the first 30 minutes the drive is running, and then every 30 minutes thereafter. In many drives, this procedure can be heard as a rapid "tick-tick-tick-tick" sound.

In essence, anything you can do to keep the system at a constant temperature prolongs the life of the system, and the best way to accomplish this is to leave the system either permanently on or off. Of course, if the system is never turned on in the first place, it should last a long time indeed!

Now, although it seems like I am saying that you should leave all systems on 24 hours a day, that is not necessarily true. A system powered on and left unattended can be a fire hazard (I have had monitors spontaneously catch fire—luckily I was there at the time), is a data security risk (cleaning crews, other nocturnal visitors, and so on), can be easily damaged if moved while running, and simply wastes electrical energy.

I currently pay $0.11 for a kilowatt-hour of electricity. A typical desktop style PC with display consumes at least 300 watts (0.3 kilowatts) of electricity (and that is a conservative estimate). This means that it would cost 3.3 cents to run this typical PC for an hour. Multiplying by 168 hours in a week means that it would cost $5.54 per week to run this PC continuously. If the PC were turned on at 9 a.m. and off at 5 p.m., it would only be on 40 hours per week and would cost only $1.32—a savings of $4.22 per week! Multiply this savings by 100 systems, and you are saving $422 per week; multiply this by 1,000 systems, and you are saving $4,220 per week! Using systems certified under the new EPA Energy Star program (that is, "Green" PCs) would account for an additional savings of around $1 per system per week, or $1,000 per week for 1,000 systems. The great thing about Energy Star systems is that the savings are even greater if the systems are left on for long periods of time because the power management routines are automatic.

Based on these facts, my recommendations are that you power the systems on at the beginning of the work day, and off at the end of the work day. Do not power the systems off for lunch, breaks, or any other short duration of time. Servers and the like of course should be left on continuously. This seems to be the best compromise of system longevity with pure economics.

Energy Star Systems

The EPA has started a certification program for energy-efficient PCs and peripherals. To be a member of this program, the PC or display must drop to a power draw at the outlet of 30 watts or less during periods of inactivity. Systems that conform to this specification get to wear the Energy Star logo. This is a voluntary program, meaning there are no requirements to meet the specification; however, many PC manufacturers are finding that it helps to sell their systems if they can advertise them as energy-efficient.

One problem with this type of system is that the motherboard and disk drives literally can *go to sleep*, which means they can enter a standby or sleep mode where they draw very little power. This causes havoc with some of the older power supplies, because the low power draw does not provide enough of a load for them to function properly. Most of the newer supplies on the market are designed to work with these systems, and have a very low minimum load specification. I suggest that if you are purchasing a power supply upgrade for a system, ensure that the minimum load will be provided by the equipment in your system; otherwise, when the PC goes to sleep, it may take a power switch cycle to wake it up again! This problem would be most noticeable if you invest in a very high output supply and use it in a system that draws very little power to begin with.

Power Supply Problems

A weak or inadequate power supply can put a damper on your ideas for system expansion. Some systems are designed with beefy power supplies, as if to anticipate a great deal of system add-on or expansion components. Most desktop or tower systems are built in this manner. Some systems have inadequate power supplies from the start, however, and cannot accept the number and types of power-hungry options you might want to add.

In particular, portable systems often have power supply problems because they are designed to fit into a small space. Likewise, many older systems had inadequate power supply capacity for system expansion. For example, the original PC's 63.5-watt supply was inadequate for all but the most basic system. Add a graphics board, hard disk, math coprocessor (8087) chip, and 640K of memory, and you would kill the supply in no time. The total power draw of all the items in the system determines the adequacy of the power supply.

The wattage rating can sometimes be very misleading. Not all 200-watt supplies are created the same. Those who are into high-end audio systems know that some watts are better than others. Cheap power supplies may in fact put out the rated power, but what about noise and distortion? Some of the supplies are under-engineered to meet their specifications just barely, whereas others may greatly exceed their specifications. Many of the cheaper supplies output noisy or unstable power, which can cause numerous problems with the system. Another problem with under-engineered power supplies is that they run hot and force the system to do so as well. The repeated heating and cooling of solid-state components eventually causes a computer system to fail, and engineering principles dictate that the hotter a PC's temperature, the shorter its life. Many people recommend replacing the original supply in a system with a heavier duty model, which solves the problem. Because power supplies come in common form factors, finding a heavy duty replacement for most systems is easy.

Some of the available replacement supplies have higher capacity cooling fans than the originals, which can greatly prolong system life and minimize overheating problems, especially with some of the newer high-powered processors. If noise is a problem, models with special fans can run quieter than the standard models. These types often use larger diameter fans that spin slower, so that they run quiet while moving the same amount of air as the smaller fans. A company called PC Power and Cooling specializes in heavy-duty and quiet supplies. Another company called Astec has several heavy-duty models as well. Astec supplies are found as original equipment in many high-end systems, such as those from IBM and Hewlett-Packard.

Ventilation in a system can be important. You must ensure adequate air flow to cool the hotter items in the system. Most processors have heat sinks today that require a steady stream of air to cool the processor. If the processor heat sink has its own fan, this is not much of a concern. If you have free slots, space out the boards in your system to allow air flow between them. Place the hottest running boards nearest the fan or ventilation holes in the system. Make sure that there is adequate air flow around the hard disk drive, especially those that spin at higher rates of speed. Some hard disks can generate quite a bit of heat during operation. If the hard disks overheat, data is lost.

Always make sure that you run with the lid on, especially if you have a loaded system. Removing the lid can actually cause a system to overheat. With the lid off, the power supply fan no longer draws air through the system. Instead, the fan ends up cooling the supply only, and the rest of the system must be cooled by simple convection. Although most systems do not immediately overheat because of this, several of my own systems, especially those that are fully expanded, have overheated within 15 to 30 minutes when run with the case lid off.

If you experience intermittent problems that you suspect are related to overheating, a higher capacity replacement power supply is usually the best cure. Specially designed supplies with additional cooling fan capacity also can help. At least one company sells a device called a *fan card,* but I am not convinced that it is a good idea. Unless the fan is positioned to draw air to or from outside the case, all the fan does is blow hot air around inside the system and provide a spot cooling effect for anything it is blowing on. In fact, adding fans in this manner contributes to the overall heat inside the system because each fan consumes power and generates heat.

The CPU-mounted fans are an exception to this because they are designed only for spot cooling of the CPU. Many of the newer processors run so much hotter than the other components in the system that a conventional finned aluminum heat sink cannot do the job. In this case, a small fan placed directly over the processor can provide a spot cooling effect that keeps the processor temperatures down. One drawback to these active processor cooling fans is that if they fail, the processor overheats instantly and can even be damaged. Whenever possible, I try to use the biggest passive (finned aluminum) heat sink and stay away from more fans.

Tip

If you seal the ventilation holes on the bottom of the original IBM PC chassis, starting from where the disk drive bays begin and all the way to the right side of the PC, you drop the interior temperature some 10 to 20 degrees F—not bad for two cents' worth of electrical tape. IBM "factory-applied" this tape on every XT and XT-286 it sold. The result is greatly improved interior aerodynamics and airflow over the heat-generating components.

For other PC-compatible systems, this may not apply because their case designs may be different.

No matter what system you have, be sure that any empty slot positions have the filler brackets installed. If you leave these brackets off after removing a card, the resultant hole will disrupt the internal airflow and may cause higher internal temperatures.

Power Supply Troubleshooting

Troubleshooting the power supply basically means isolating the supply as the cause of problems within a system. Rarely is it recommended to go inside the power supply to make repairs because of the dangerous high voltages present. Such internal repairs are beyond the scope of this book and are specifically not recommended unless the technician knows what he or she is doing.

Many symptoms would lead me to suspect that the power supply in a system is failing. This can sometimes be difficult for an inexperienced technician to see, because at times little connection appears between the symptom and the cause—the power supply.

For example, in many cases a "parity check" type of error message or problem indicates a problem with the supply. This may seem strange because the parity check message itself specifically refers to memory that has failed. The connection is that the power supply is what powers the memory, and memory with inadequate power fails.

It takes some experience to know when these failures are not caused by the memory and are in fact power-related. One clue is the repeatability of the problem. If the parity check message (or other problem) appears frequently and identifies the same memory location each time, I suspect defective memory as the problem. However, if the problem seems random, or the memory location given as failed seems random or wandering, I suspect improper power as the culprit. The following is a list of PC problems that often are power supply-related:

- Any power-on or system startup failures or lockups.
- Spontaneous rebooting or intermittent lockups during normal operation.
- Intermittent parity check or other memory type errors.
- Hard disk and fan simultaneously fail to spin (no +12v).
- Overheating due to fan failure.
- Small brownouts cause the system to reset.
- Electric shocks felt on the system case or connectors.
- Slight static discharges disrupt system operation.

In fact, just about any intermittent system problem can be caused by the power supply. I always suspect the supply when flaky system operation is a symptom. Of course, the following fairly obvious symptoms point right to the power supply as a possible cause:

- System is completely dead (no fan, no cursor)
- Smoke
- Blown circuit breakers

If you suspect a power supply problem, some simple measurements as well as more sophisticated tests outlined in this section can help you determine whether the power supply is at fault. Because these measurements may not detect some intermittent failures, you might have to use a spare power supply for a long-term evaluation. If the symptoms and problems disappear when a "known good" spare unit is installed, you have found the source of your problem.

Digital Multi-Meters

A simple test that can be performed to a power supply is to check the output voltage. This shows if a power supply is operating correctly and whether the output voltages are within the correct tolerance range. Note that all voltage measurements must be made with the power supply connected to a proper load, which usually means testing while the power supply is still installed in the system.

Selecting a Meter. You need a simple *Digital Multi-Meter (DMM)* or *Digital Volt-Ohm Meter (DVOM)* to make voltage and resistance checks in electronic circuits (see Figure 8.9). You should use only a DMM rather than the older needle type multi-meters because the older meters work by injecting a 9v signal into the circuit when measuring resistance. This will damage most computer circuits.

A DMM uses a much smaller voltage (usually 1.5v) when making resistance measurements, which is safe for electronic equipment. You can get a good DMM from many sources and with many different features. I prefer the small pocket-sized meters for computer work because they are easy to carry around.

FIG. 8.9 A typical Digital Multi-Meter.

Some features to look for in a good DMM are:

- *Pocket size.* This is self-explanatory, but small meters are available that have many if not all the features of larger ones. The elaborate features found on some of the larger meters are not really needed for computer work.

- *Overload protection.* This means that if you plug the meter into a voltage or current beyond the capability of the meter's measurements, the meter protects itself from damage. Cheaper meters lack this protection and can be easily damaged by reading current or voltage values that are too high.

- *Autoranging.* This means that the meter automatically selects the proper voltage or resistance range when making measurements. This is preferable to the manual range selection; however, really good meters offer both an autoranging capability and a manual range override.

- *Detachable probe leads.* The leads can be easily damaged, and sometimes a variety of differently shaped probes are required for different tests. Cheaper meters have the leads permanently attached, which means that they cannot easily be replaced. Look for a meter with detachable leads.

- *Audible continuity test.* Although you can use the ohm scale for testing continuity (0 ohms indicates continuity), a continuity test function causes a beep noise to be heard when continuity exists between the meter test leads. By using the sound, you can more quickly test cable assemblies and other items for continuity. After you use this feature, you will never want to use the ohms display for this purpose again.

- *Automatic power off.* These meters run on batteries, and the batteries can easily be worn down if the meter is accidentally left on. Good meters have an automatic shutoff that turns off the meter if no readings are sensed for a predetermined period of time.

- *Automatic display hold.* This feature enables the last stable reading to be held on the display even after the reading is taken. This is especially useful if you are trying to work in a difficult-to-reach area single-handedly.

- *Minimum and maximum trap.* This feature enables the lowest and highest readings to be trapped in memory and held for later display. This is especially useful if you have readings that are fluctuating too quickly to see on the display.

Although you can get a basic pocket DMM for about $30, one with all these features is priced in the $200 range. Radio Shack carries some nice inexpensive units, whereas the high-end models can be purchased from electronics supply houses like Allied, Newark, or Digi-Key.

Measuring Voltage. When making measurements on a system that is operating, you must use a technique called *back probing* the connectors. This is because you cannot disconnect any of the connectors while the system is running and instead must measure with everything connected. Nearly all the connectors you need to probe have openings in the back where the wires enter the connector. The meter probes are narrow enough to fit into the connector alongside the wire and make contact with the metal terminal inside. This technique is called *back probing* because you are probing the connector from the back. Virtually all the following measurements must be made using this back probing technique.

To test a power supply for proper output, check the voltage at the Power_Good pin (P8-1 on most IBM-compatible supplies) for +3v to +6v. If the measurement is not within this range, the system never sees the Power_Good signal and, therefore, does not start or run properly. In most cases, the supply is bad and must be replaced.

Continue by measuring the voltage ranges of the pins on the motherboard and drive power connectors:

Desired Voltage	Loose Tolerance		Tight Tolerance	
	Min. (−10%)	Max. (+8%)	Min. (−5%)	Max. (+5%)
+/−5.0v	4.5v	5.4v	4.75	5.25
+/−12.0v	10.8v	12.9v	11.4	12.6

The Power_Good signal has tolerances that are different from the other signals, although it is nominally a +5v signal in most systems. The trigger point for Power_Good is about +2.5v, but most systems require the signal voltage to be within the tolerances listed:

Signal	Minimum	Maximum
Power_Good (+5v)	3.0v	6.0v

Replace the power supply if the voltages you measure are out of these ranges. Again, it is worth noting that any and all power supply tests and measurements must be made with the power supply properly loaded, which usually means it must be installed in a system and the system must be running.

Specialized Test Equipment

You can use several types of specialized test gear to test power supplies more effectively. Because the power supply is perhaps the most failure-prone item in PCs today, if you service many PC systems, it is wise to have many of these specialized items.

Load Resistors for Bench Testing a Power Supply. Bench testing a power supply requires some special setup because all PC power supplies require a load to operate. Information on how to construct your own load resistor network can be found on the CD accompanying this book.

Variable Voltage Transformer. In testing power supplies, it is desirable to simulate different voltage conditions at the wall socket to observe how the supply reacts. A *variable voltage transformer* is a useful test device for checking power supplies because it enables you to have control over the AC line voltage used as input for the power supply (see Figure 8.10). This device consists of a large transformer mounted in a housing with a dial indicator to control the output voltage. You plug the line cord from the transformer into the wall socket and plug the PC power cord into the socket provided on the transformer. The knob on the transformer can be used to adjust the AC line voltage seen by the PC.

Most variable transformers can adjust their AC output from 0v to 140v no matter what the AC input (wall socket) voltage is. Some can even cover a range from 0v to 280v as well. You can use the transformer to simulate brownout conditions, enabling you to observe the PC's response. Thus, among other things you can check for proper Power_Good signal operation.

FIG. 8.10 A variable voltage transformer.

By running the PC and dropping the voltage until the PC shuts down, you can see how much "reserve" is in the power supply for handling a brownout or other voltage fluctuations. If your transformer can output voltages in the 200v range, you can test the capability of the power supply to run on foreign voltage levels as well. A properly functioning supply should operate between 90v to 137v but shut down cleanly if the voltage is outside that range.

An indication of a problem is seeing "parity check" type error messages when you drop the voltage to 80v. This indicates that the Power_Good signal is not being withdrawn before the power supply output to the PC fails. The PC should simply stop operating as the Power_Good signal is withdrawn, causing the system to enter a continuous reset loop.

Variable voltage transformers are sold by a number of electronic parts supply houses such as Allied, Newark, and Digi-Key. You should expect to pay anywhere from $100 to $300 for these devices.

Repairing the Power Supply

Actually repairing a power supply is rarely performed anymore, primarily because it is usually cheaper simply to replace the supply with a new one. Even high-quality power supplies are not that expensive relative to the labor required to repair them.

Defective power supplies are usually discarded unless they happen to be one of the higher quality or more expensive units. In that case, it is usually wise to send the supply out to a company that specializes in repairing power supplies and other components. These companies provide what is called *depot repair*, which means you send the supply to them; they repair it and return it to you. If time is of the essence, most of the depot repair companies immediately send you a functional equivalent to your defective supply and take yours in as a core charge. Depot repair is the recommended way to service many PC components such as power supplies, monitors, and printers. If you take your PC in to a conventional service outlet, they often diagnose the problem to the major component and send it out to be depot repaired. You can do that yourself and save the markup that the repair shop normally charges in such cases.

For those with experience around high voltages, it might be possible to repair a failing supply with two relatively simple operations; however, these require opening the supply. I do not recommend this; I mention it only as an alternative to replacement in some cases.

Most manufacturers try to prevent you from entering the supply by sealing it with special tamper-proof Torx screws. These screws use the familiar Torx star driver, but also have a tamper-prevention pin in the center that prevents a standard driver from working. Most tool companies such as Jensen or Specialized sell sets of *TT (tamperproof Torx) bits*, which remove the tamper-resistant screws. Other manufacturers rivet the power supply case shut, which means you must drill out the rivets to gain access. Again, the manufacturers place these obstacles there for a reason—to prevent entry by those who are inexperienced around high voltage. Consider yourself warned!

Most power supplies have an internal fuse that is part of the overload protection. If this fuse is blown, the supply does not operate. It is possible to replace this fuse if you open the supply. Be aware that in most cases in which an internal power supply problem causes the fuse to blow, replacing it does nothing but cause it to blow again until the root cause of the problem is repaired. In this case, you are better off sending the unit to a professional depot repair company. The vendor list lists several companies that do depot repair on power supplies and other components.

PC power supplies have a voltage adjustment internal to the supply that is calibrated and set when the supply is manufactured. Over time, the values of some of the components in the supply can change, thus altering the output voltages. If this is the case, you often can access the adjustment control and tweak it to bring the voltages back to where they should be.

Several adjustable items are in the supply—usually small variable resistors that can be turned with a screwdriver. You should use a nonconductive tool such as a fiberglass or plastic screwdriver designed for this purpose. If you were to drop a metal tool into an operating supply, dangerous sparks or fire could result, not to mention danger of electrocution and damage to the supply.

You also have to figure out which of the adjustments are for voltage and which ones are for each voltage signal. This requires some trial and error testing. You can mark the current positions of all the resistors, begin measuring a single voltage signal, and try moving each adjuster slightly until you see the voltage change. If you move an adjuster and nothing changes, put it back to the original position you marked. Through this process, you can locate and adjust each of the voltages to the standard 5v and 12v levels.

Obtaining Replacement Units

There may be times when it is simply easier, safer, or less expensive (considering time and materials) to replace the power supply rather than repair it. As mentioned earlier, replacement power supplies are available from many manufacturers. Before you can shop for a supplier, however, you should consider other purchasing factors.

Deciding on a Power Supply

When looking at getting a new power supply, you should take several things into account. First, consider the power supply's shape, or form factor. For example, the power supply used in the IBM AT differs physically from the one used in the PC or XT. Therefore, AT and PC/XT supplies are not interchangeable.

Differences exist in the size, shape, screw-hole positions, connector type, number of connectors, and switch position in these and other power supplies. Systems that use the same form factor supply can easily interchange. The compatible manufacturers realized this and most began designing systems that mimicked the shape of IBM's AT with regard to motherboard and power supply configuration and mounting. As the clone market evolved, four standard form factors for power supplies became popular: AT/Tower, Baby-AT, Slimline, and PC/XT. You can easily interchange any supply with another one of the same form factor. Earlier, this chapter gave complete descriptions of these form factors. When ordering a replacement supply, you need to know which form factor your system requires.

Many systems use proprietary-designed power supplies, which makes replacement difficult. IBM uses a number of designs for the PS/2 systems, and little interchangeability exists between different systems. Some of the supplies do interchange, especially between any that have the same or similar cases, such as the Model 60, 65, and 80. Several different output level power supplies are available for these systems, including 207-, 225-, 242-, and 250-watt versions. The most powerful 250-watt unit was supplied originally for the Model 65 SX and later version Model 80 systems, although it fits perfectly in any Model 60, 65, or 80 system.

One risk with some of the non-standard compatibles is that they might not use one of the industry-standard form factor supplies. If a system uses one of the common form factor power supplies, replacement units are available from hundreds of vendors. An unfortunate user of a system with a nonstandard form factor supply does not have this kind of choice and must get a replacement from the original manufacturer of the system—and usually pay through the nose for the unit. Although you can find slim-style units for as little as $50, the proprietary units from some manufacturers run as high as $400 or more. PC buyers often overlook this and discover too late the consequences of having nonstandard components in a system.

An example of IBM-compatible systems with proprietary power supply designs are those from Compaq. None of its systems use the same form factor supply as the IBM systems, which means that Compaq usually is the only place from which you can get a replacement. If the power supply in your Compaq Deskpro system "goes south," you can expect to pay $395 for a replacement, and the replacement unit will be no better or quieter than the one you are replacing. You have little choice in the matter because almost no one offers Compaq form factor power supplies except Compaq. One exception is that PC Power and Cooling offers excellent replacement power supplies for the earlier Compaq Portable systems and for the Deskpro series. These replacement power supplies have higher-output power levels than the original supplies from Compaq and cost much less.

Sources for Replacement Power Supplies

Because one of the most failure-prone items in PC systems is the power supply, I am often called on to recommend a replacement. Literally hundreds of companies manufacture PC power supplies, and I certainly have not tested them all. I can, however, recommend some companies whose products I have come to know and trust.

Although other high-quality manufacturers are out there, at this time I recommend power supplies from either Astec Standard Power or PC Power and Cooling.

Astec makes the power supplies used in most of the high-end systems by IBM, Hewlett-Packard, Apple, and many other name brand systems. They have power supplies available in a number of standard form factors (AT/Tower, Baby-AT, and Slimline) and a variety of output levels. They have power supplies with ratings of up to 300 watts and power supplies especially designed for "green" PCs that meet the EPA Energy Star requirements for low power consumption. Their "green" power supplies are specifically designed to achieve high efficiency at low load conditions. Be aware that high output supplies from other manufacturers may have problems with very low loads. Astec also makes a number of power supplies for laptop and notebook PC systems and has numerous non-PC type supplies.

PC Power and Cooling has the most complete line of power supplies for PC systems. They make supplies in all the standard PC form factors used today (AT/Tower, Baby-AT, PC/XT, and Slimline). Versions are available in a variety of different quality and output levels, from inexpensive replacements to very high-quality high-output models with ratings up to 450 watts. They even have versions with built-in battery backup systems and a series of special models with high-volume low-speed (quiet) fan assemblies. Their quiet models are especially welcome to people who cannot take the fan noise that some power supplies emanate.

PC Power and Cooling also has units available to fit some of Compaq's proprietary designs. This can be a real boon if you have to service or repair Compaq systems because the PC Power and Cooling units are available in higher output ratings than Compaq's own. They also cost much less than Compaq and bolt in as a direct replacement.

The support offered by PC Power and Cooling is excellent also, and they have been in business a long time, which is sometimes rare in this industry. Besides just power supplies, they have an excellent line of cases as well.

A high-quality power supply from either of these vendors is one of the best cures for intermittent system problems and goes a long way toward ensuring trouble-free operation in the future.

Using Power-Protection Systems

Power-protection systems do just what the name implies: They protect your equipment from the effects of power surges and power failures. In particular, power surges and spikes can damage computer equipment, and a loss of power can result in lost data. In this section, you learn about the four primary types of power-protection devices available and under what circumstances you should use them.

Before considering any further levels of power protection, you should know that the power supply in your system (if your system is well-made) already affords you a substantial amount of protection. High-end power supplies from the vendors I recommend are designed to provide protection from higher-than-normal voltages and currents, and provide a limited amount of power-line noise filtering. Some of the inexpensive aftermarket power supplies probably do not have this sort of protection; be careful if you have an inexpensive clone system. In those cases, further protecting your system might be wise.

> **Caution**
>
> All of the power protection features in this chapter and the protection features in the power supply inside your computer expect and require that a ground be connected.
>
> Many older homes do not have three-prong (grounded) outlets to accommodate grounded devices.
>
> Do not use a three-prong adapter to plug in a surge suppresser, computer, or UPS. They don't necessarily provide a good ground and can hamper the capability for the power protection devices to protect your system.

Power supplies should stay within operating specifications and continue to run a system if any of these power line disturbances occur:

- Voltage drop to 80v for up to 2 seconds
- Voltage drop to 70v for up to .5 seconds
- Voltage surge of up to 143v for up to 1 second

IBM also states that neither their power supplies nor systems will be damaged by the following occurrences:

- Full power outage
- Any voltage drop (brownout)
- A spike of up to 2,500v

For example, because of the high-quality power supply design that IBM uses, they state in their documentation that external surge suppressers are not needed for PS/2 systems. Most other high-quality name brand manufacturers also use high-quality power supply designs. Companies like Astec, PC Power and Cooling, and others make very high-quality units.

To verify the levels of protection built into the existing power supply in a computer system, an independent laboratory subjected several unprotected PC systems to various spikes and surges of up to 6,000v—considered the maximum level of surge that can be transmitted to a system by an electrical outlet. Any higher voltage would cause the power to arc to ground within the outlet itself. Note that none of the systems sustained permanent damage in these tests; the worst thing that happened was that some of the systems rebooted or shut down if the surge was more than 2,000v. Each system restarted when the power switch was toggled after a shutdown.

I do not use any real form of power protection on my systems, and they have survived near-direct lightning strikes and powerful surges. The most recent incident, only 50 feet from my office, was a direct lightning strike to a brick chimney that blew the top of the chimney apart. None of my systems (which were running at the time) were damaged in any way from this incident; they just shut themselves down. I was able to restart each system by toggling the power switches. An alarm system located in the same office, however, was destroyed by this strike. I am not saying that lightning strikes or even much milder spikes and surges cannot damage computer systems—another nearby lightning strike did destroy a modem and serial adapter installed in one of my systems. I was just lucky that the destruction did not include the motherboard.

This discussion points out an important oversight in some power-protection strategies: You may elect to protect your systems from electrical power disturbances, but do not forget to provide similar protection also from spikes and surges on the phone line.

The automatic shutdown of a computer during power disturbances is a built-in function of most high-quality power supplies. You can reset the power supply by flipping the power switch from on to off and back on again. Some power supplies, such as those in most of the PS/2 systems, have an auto-restart function. This type of power supply acts the same as others in a massive surge or spike situation: It shuts down the system. The difference is that after normal power resumes, the power supply waits for a specified delay of three to six seconds and then resets itself and powers the system back up. Because no manual switch resetting is required, this feature is desirable in systems functioning as a network file server or in a system in a remote location.

The first time I witnessed a large surge cause an immediate shutdown of all my systems, I was extremely surprised. All the systems were silent, but the monitor and modem lights were still on. My first thought was that everything was blown, but a simple toggle of each system-unit power switch caused the power supplies to reset, and the units powered up with no problem. Since that first time, this type of shutdown has happened to me several times, always without further problems.

The following types of power-protection devices are explained in the sections that follow:

- Surge suppressers
- Line conditioners
- Standby power supplies (SPS)
- Uninterruptible power supplies (UPS)

Surge Suppressers (Protectors)

The simplest form of power protection is any of the commercially available surge protectors; that is, devices inserted between the system and the power line. These devices, which cost between $20 and $200, can absorb the high-voltage transients produced by nearby lightning strikes and power equipment. Some surge protectors can be effective for certain types of power problems, but they offer only very limited protection.

Surge protectors use several devices, usually *metal-oxide varistors (MOVs)*, that can clamp and shunt away all voltages above a certain level. MOVs are designed to accept voltages as high as 6,000v and divert any power above 200v to ground. MOVs can handle normal surges, but powerful surges such as a direct lightning strike can blow right through them. MOVs are not designed to handle a very high level of power, and self-destruct while shunting a large surge. These devices therefore cease to function after either a single large surge or a series of smaller ones. The real problem is that you cannot easily tell when they no longer are functional; the only way to test them is to subject the MOVs to a surge, which destroys them. Therefore, you never really know if your so-called surge protector is protecting your system.

Some surge protectors have status lights that let you know when a surge large enough to blow the MOVs has occurred. A surge suppresser without this status indicator light is useless because you never know when it has stopped protecting.

Underwriters Laboratories has produced an excellent standard that governs surge suppressers, called *UL 1449*. Any surge suppresser that meets this standard is a very good one, and definitely offers an additional line of protection beyond what the power supply in your PC already does. The only types of surge suppressers worth buying, therefore, should have two features:

- Conformance to the UL 1449 standard
- A status light indicating when the MOVs are blown

Units that meet the UL 1449 specification say so on the packaging or directly on the unit. If this standard is not mentioned, it does not conform, and you should avoid it.

Another good feature to have in a surge suppresser is a built-in circuit breaker that can be reset rather than a fuse. The breaker protects your system if it or a peripheral develops a short. These better surge suppressers usually cost about $40.

Phone Line Surge Protectors

In addition to protecting the power lines, it is critical to provide protection to your systems from any phone lines that are connected. If you are using a modem or fax board that is plugged into the phone system, any surges or spikes that travel the phone line can potentially damage your system. In many areas, the phone lines are especially susceptible to lightning strikes, which is the largest cause of fried modems and any computer equipment attached to them.

Several companies manufacture or sell simple surge protectors that plug between your modem and the phone line. These inexpensive devices can be purchased from most electronics supply houses. Most of the cable and communication products vendors listed in Appendix A sell these phone line surge protectors.

Line Conditioners

In addition to high-voltage and current conditions, other problems can occur with incoming power. The voltage might dip below the level needed to run the system and result in a brownout. Other forms of electrical noise other than simple voltage surges or spikes might be on the power line, such as radio-frequency interference or electrical noise caused by motors or other inductive loads.

Remember two things when you wire together digital devices (such as computers and their peripherals):

- Any wire can act as an antenna and will have voltage induced in it by nearby electromagnetic fields, which can come from other wires, telephones, CRTs, motors, fluorescent fixtures, static discharge, and, of course, radio transmitters.

- Digital circuitry also responds with surprising efficiency to noise of even a volt or two, making those induced voltages particularly troublesome. The electrical wiring in your building can act as an antenna and pick up all kinds of noise and disturbances.

A line conditioner can handle many of these types of problems. A *line conditioner* is designed to remedy a variety of problems. It filters the power, bridges brownouts, suppresses high-voltage and current conditions, and generally acts as a buffer between the power line and the system. A line conditioner does the job of a surge suppresser, and much more. It is more of an active device functioning continuously rather than a passive device that activates only when a surge is present. A line conditioner provides true power conditioning and can handle a myriad of problems. It contains transformers, capacitors, and other circuitry that temporarily can bridge a brownout or low-voltage situation. These units usually cost a few hundred dollars, depending on the power-handling capacity of the unit.

Backup Power

The next level of power protection includes *backup power-protection devices*. These units can provide power in case of a complete blackout, which provides the time needed for an orderly system shutdown. Two types are available: the *standby power supply (SPS)* and the *uninterruptible power supply (UPS)*. The UPS is a special device because it does much more than just provide backup power: It is also the best kind of line conditioner you can buy.

Standby Power Supplies (SPS). A standby power supply is known as an *offline device*: It functions only when normal power is disrupted. An SPS system uses a special circuit that can sense the AC line current. If the sensor detects a loss of power on the line, the system quickly switches over to a standby battery and power inverter. The power inverter converts the battery power to 110-volt AC power, which then is supplied to the system.

SPS systems do work, but sometimes a problem occurs with the switch to battery power. If the switch is not fast enough, the computer system unit shuts down or reboots anyway, which defeats the purpose of having the backup power supply. A truly outstanding SPS adds to the circuit a *ferroresonant transformer*, a large transformer with the capability to store a small amount of power and deliver it during the switch time. Having this device is similar to having on the power line a buffer that you add to an SPS to give it almost truly uninterruptible capability.

SPS units also may or may not have internal line conditioning of their own; most cheaper units place your system directly on the regular power line under normal circumstances and offer no conditioning. The addition of a ferroresonant transformer to an SPS gives it additional regulation and protection capabilities due to the buffer effect of the transformer. SPS devices without the ferroresonant transformer still require the use of a line conditioner for full protection. SPS systems usually cost from $200 to several thousands of dollars, depending on the quality and power-output capacity.

Uninterruptible Power Supplies (UPS). Perhaps the best overall solution to any power problem is to provide a power source that is both conditioned and that also cannot be interrupted—which describes an uninterruptible power supply. UPSs are known as *online systems* because they continuously function and supply power to your computer systems. Because some companies advertise ferroresonant SPS devices as though they were UPS devices, many now use the term *true UPS* to describe a truly online system. A true UPS system is constructed much the same as an SPS system; however, because you always are operating from the battery, there is no switching circuit.

In a true UPS, your system always operates from the battery, with a voltage inverter to convert from 12v DC to 110v AC. You essentially have your own private power system that generates power independently of the AC line. A battery charger connected to the line or wall current keeps the battery charged at a rate equal to or greater than the rate at which power is consumed.

When power is disconnected, the true UPS continues functioning undisturbed because the battery-charging function is all that is lost. Because you already were running off the battery, no switch takes place, and no power disruption is possible. The battery then begins discharging at a rate dictated by the amount of load your system places on the unit, which (based on the size of the battery) gives you plenty of time to execute an orderly system shutdown. Based on an appropriately scaled storage battery, the UPS functions continuously, generating power and preventing unpleasant surprises. When the line power returns, the battery charger begins recharging the battery, again with no interruption.

UPS cost is a direct function of both the length of time it can continue to provide power after a line current failure, and how much power it can provide; therefore, purchasing a

UPS that gives you enough power to run your system and peripherals as well as enough time to close files and provide an orderly shutdown would be sufficient. In most PC applications, this solution is the most cost-effective because the batteries and charger portion of the system must be much larger than the SPS type of device, and will be more costly.

Many SPS systems are advertised as though they were true UPS systems. The giveaway is the unit's *switch time*. If a specification for switch time exists, the unit cannot be a true UPS because UPS units never switch. Understand, however, that a good SPS with a ferroresonant transformer can virtually equal the performance of a true UPS at a lower cost.

Because of a UPS's almost total isolation from the line current, it is unmatched as a line conditioner and surge suppresser. The best UPS systems add a ferroresonant transformer for even greater power conditioning and protection capability. This type of UPS is the best form of power protection available. The price, however, can be very high. A true UPS costs from $1 to $2 per watt of power supplied. To find out just how much power your system requires, look at the UL sticker on the back of the unit. This sticker lists the maximum power draw in watts, or sometimes in just volts and amperes. If only voltage and amperage are listed, multiply the two figures to calculate a wattage figure.

As an example, the back of an IBM PC AT Model 339 indicates that the system can require as much as 110v at a maximum current draw of 5 amps. The maximum power this AT can draw is about 550 watts. This wattage is for a system with every slot full, two hard disks, and one floppy—in other words, the maximum possible level of expansion. The system should never draw any more power than that; if it does, a 5-ampere fuse in the power supply blows. This type of system normally draws an average 300 watts; to be safe when you make calculations for UPS capacity, however, be conservative and use the 550-watt figure. Adding a monitor that draws 100 watts brings the total to 650 watts or more. To run two fully loaded AT systems, you need an 1100-watt UPS. Don't forget two monitors, each drawing 100 watts; the total, therefore, is 1,300 watts. Using the $1 to $2 per watt figure, a UPS of at least that capacity or greater will cost from $1,300 to $2,600—expensive, but unfortunately what the best level of protection costs. Most companies can justify this type of expense for only a critical-use PC, such as a network file server.

> **Note**
>
> 1,400 watts is about the highest size UPS that will be sold for a conventional 15-amp outlet. Any higher, and you risk tripping a 15-amp circuit when the battery is charging heavily and the inverter is drawing maximum current.

In addition to the total available output power (wattage), several other factors can differentiate one UPS from another. The addition of a ferroresonant transformer improves a unit's power conditioning and buffering capabilities. Good units have also an inverter that produces a true sine wave output; the cheaper ones may generate a square wave. A *square wave* is an approximation of a sine wave with abrupt up-and-down voltage transitions. The abrupt transitions of a square wave signal are not compatible with some computer equipment power supplies. Be sure that the UPS you purchase produces a signal compatible with your computer equipment. Every unit has a specification for how long it can sustain output at the rated level. If your systems draw less than the rated level, you have some additional time.

> **Caution**
>
> Be careful, though: Most UPS systems are not designed for you to sit and compute for hours through an electrical blackout. They are designed to provide power to whatever is needed, to remain operating long enough to allow for an orderly shutdown. You pay a large amount for units that provide power for more than 15 minutes or so. At some point, it becomes more cost effective to buy a generator than to keep investing in extended life for a UPS.

There are many sources of power protection equipment, but several include APC, Best Power, Tripp Lite, Liebert, and others. These companies sell a variety of UPS, SPS, line, and surge protectors. They are listed in Appendix A.

> **Caution**
>
> Don't connect a laser printer to any SPS or UPS unit. They are both "electrically noisy" and have widely varying current draws. This can be hard on the inverter in a SPS or UPS and frequently causes the inverter to fail, or detect an overload and shut down. Either case means that your system will lose power, too.
>
> Printers are normally non-critical since whatever is being printed can be reprinted. Don't connect them to a UPS unless there's a good business need to do so.

RTC/NVRAM Batteries

All 16-bit and higher systems have a special type of chip in them that combines a Real-Time Clock (RTC) with at least 64 bytes (including the clock data) of Non-Volatile RAM (NVRAM) memory. This chip is officially called the *RTC/NVRAM chip*, but is often referred to as the *CMOS chip* or *CMOS RAM*, because the type of chip used is produced using a CMOS (Complimentary Metal Oxide Semiconductor) process. CMOS design chips are known for very low power consumption, and this special RTC/NVRAM chip is designed to run off of a battery for several years.

The original chip of this type used in the original IBM AT was the Motorola 146818 chip. Although the ones used today have different manufacturers and part numbers, they are all designed to be compatible with this original Motorola part.

These chips include a real-time clock, and the function there is obvious. The clock is used so that software can read the date and time, and so that the date and time will be preserved even though the system is powered off or unplugged.

The NVRAM portion of the chip has another function. It is designed to store the basic system configuration, including the amount of memory installed, types of floppy and hard disk drives, and other information as well. Some of the more modern motherboards use extended NVRAM chips with as much as 2K or more of space to hold this configuration information. This is especially true for the new breed of Plug and Play systems, where the configuration of not only the motherboard but also of adapter cards is stored. This information can then be read every time the system is powered on.

These chips are normally powered by some type of battery while the system is off to preserve the information in the NVRAM and to power the clock. Most often a lithium type battery is used, because they have a very long life, especially at the low power draw from the typical RTC/NVRAM chip.

Most of the higher-quality modern systems sold today have a new type of chip that has the battery embedded within it. These are made by several companies including Dallas Semiconductor and Benchmarq. These are notable for their long life. Under normal conditions, the battery within these chips will last for 10 years, which is of course longer than the useful life of the system. If your system uses one of the Dallas or Benchmarq modules, the battery and chip must be replaced as a unit because they are integrated. Most of the time these chip/battery combinations will be installed in a socket on the motherboard just in case there is a problem requiring an early replacement. You can get new modules for $18 or less direct from the manufacturers, which is often less than the cost of the older separate battery alone.

Some systems do not use a battery at all. Hewlett-Packard, for example includes a special capacitor in many of their systems that is automatically recharged any time the system is plugged in. Note that the system does not have to be running for the capacitor to charge; it only has to be plugged in. If the system is unplugged, the capacitor will power the RTC/NVRAM chip for up to a week or more. If the system remains unplugged for a duration longer than that, the NVRAM information will be lost. In that case, these systems can reload the NVRAM from a backup kept in a special Flash ROM chip contained on the motherboard. The only information that will actually be missing when you re-power the system is the date and time, which will have to be re-entered. By using the capacitor combined with a NVRAM backup in Flash ROM, they have a very reliable system that will last indefinitely.

Many systems use only a conventional battery, which may be either directly soldered into the motherboard or plugged in via a battery connector. For those systems with the battery soldered in, should it ever fail, they will normally have a spare battery connector on the motherboard where a conventional plug in battery can be used. In most cases, you would never have to replace the motherboard battery, even if it were completely dead.

Conventional-type batteries come in many forms. The best are of a lithium design because they will last from two to five years or more. I have seen systems with conventional alkaline batteries mounted in a holder; these are much less desirable as they fail more frequently and do not last as long. Also, they can be prone to leak, and if a battery leaks on the motherboard, the motherboard may be severely damaged.

Besides the different battery types, there are several different voltages used. The batteries used in PCs are normally either 3.6v, 4.5v, or 6v. If you are replacing the battery, make sure that your replacement is the same voltage as the one you removed from the system. Some motherboards can use batteries of several different voltages, and will have a jumper or switch to select the different settings. If you suspect your motherboard has this capability, consult the documentation for instructions on how to change the settings. Of course, the easiest thing to do is to replace the existing battery with another of the same type, in which case the settings would not have to be changed.

> **Caution**
>
> When you replace a PC battery, be sure that you get the polarity correct, or you will damage the RTC/NVRAM (CMOS) chip. Because these are soldered into most motherboards, this will be an expensive mistake! The battery connector on the motherboard as well as the battery itself are normally keyed to prevent a backwards connection. The pinout of this connector should be listed in your system documentation.

When you replace a battery, in most cases the existing data stored in the NVRAM will be lost. Often the data will remain for several minutes (I have observed NVRAM retain information with no power for an hour or more), so if you make the swap quickly, the information in the NVRAM will be retained. Just to be sure, it is recommended that you record all the system configuration settings stored in the NVRAM by your system Setup program. In most cases, you would want to run the BIOS Setup program and print out all the screens showing the different settings. Some Setup programs offer the capability to save the NVRAM data to a file for later restoration if necessary. That would be a good idea if it is an option in your system.

After replacing a battery, power up the system and use the Setup program to check the date and time setting as well as any other data that was stored in the NVRAM.

Part III

Input/Ouput Hardware

9 Input Devices

10 Video Display Hardware

11 Communications and Networking

12 Audio Hardware

Chapter 9

Input Devices

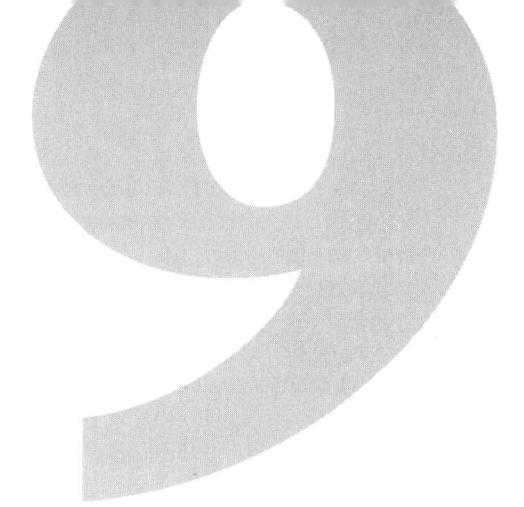

This chapter discusses input devices—the devices used to communicate with the computer. The most common input device is, of course, the keyboard, and this chapter discusses keyboards in depth. It also discusses mice and other pointing device alternatives because they are now a standard requirement for operating a modern PC with a GUI (graphical user interface) such as Windows or OS/2. Finally, this chapter also discusses the game or joystick interface, which is used to input signals from a joystick, paddles, or other game devices.

Keyboards

One of the most basic system components is your keyboard. The *keyboard* is the primary input device. It is used for entering commands and data into the system. This section looks at the keyboards available for PC-compatible systems. It examines the different types of keyboards, how the keyboard functions, the keyboard-to-system interface, and keyboard troubleshooting and repair.

Types of Keyboards

Over the years since the introduction of the original IBM PC, IBM has created three different keyboard designs for PC systems, and Microsoft has augmented one of them. They have become standards in the industry and are shared by virtually all of the PC-compatible manufacturers. More recently with the introduction of Windows 95, a modified version of the 101-key design (created by Microsoft) has appeared. The primary keyboard types are:

- 83-key PC and XT keyboard
- 84-key AT keyboard
- 101-key enhanced keyboard
- 104-key enhanced Windows keyboard

This section discusses each keyboard type, and shows their layout and physical appearance. Because most systems use keyboards based on the 101- and 104-key enhanced keyboard designs, these versions are emphasized.

83-Key PC and XT Keyboard. When the original PC was first introduced, it had something that few other personal computers had at the time: an external detachable keyboard. Most other small personal computers of the time had the keyboard built in, like the Apple II. Although the external design was a good move on IBM's part, the keyboard design was not without its drawbacks. One of the most criticized components of the original 83-key keyboard is the awkward layout (see Figure 9.1). The Shift keys are small and in the wrong place on the left side. The Enter key is also too small. These oversights were especially irritating at the time because IBM had produced the Selectric typewriter, perceived as a standard for good keyboard layout.

FIG. 9.1 PC and XT 83-key keyboard layout.

This keyboard has a built-in processor that communicates with the motherboard via a special serial data link. The communication is one-way, which means that the motherboard cannot send commands or data back to the keyboard. For this reason, IBM 83-key keyboards have no Light Emmiting Diode (LED) indicator lights. Because the status of the Caps Lock, Num Lock, and Scroll Lock are maintained by the motherboard, there is no way to make sure that any LED indicator lights remain in sync with the actual status of the function.

Many aftermarket (non-IBM) PC keyboards added the lights, and the keyboard attempted to keep track of the three functions independently of the motherboard. This worked in most situations, but it was entirely possible to see the LEDs become out of sync with the actual function status. Rebooting corrected this temporary problem, but it was annoying nonetheless.

The original 83-key PC/XT keyboard is no longer used and is not electrically compatible with AT-compatible motherboards, although some aftermarket units may be compatible by moving an XT/AT switch usually found on the bottom of the keyboard.

84-Key AT Keyboard. When the AT was introduced in 1984, it included a new keyboard—the 84-key unit (see Figure 9.2). This keyboard corrected many problems of the original PC and XT keyboards. The position and arrangement of the numeric keypad was modified. The Enter key was made much larger, like that of a Selectric typewriter. The Shift key positions and sizes were corrected. IBM also finally added LED indicators for the status of the Caps Lock, Scroll Lock, and Num Lock toggles.

FIG. 9.2 AT 84-key keyboard layout.

These keyboards use a slightly modified interface protocol that is bi-directional. This means that the processor built into the keyboard can talk to another processor (called the 8042 *keyboard controller chip*) built into the motherboard. The keyboard controller on the motherboard can send commands and data to the keyboard, which allows functions such as changing the keyboard typematic (or repeat) rate as well as the delay before repeating begins. The keyboard controller on the motherboard also performs *scan code translation*, which allow a much easier integration of foreign language keyboards into the system. *Scan codes* are the names for the hexadecimal codes actually sent by the keyboard to the motherboard. The bi-directional interface can be used to control the LED indicators on the keyboard, thus ensuring that the status of a particular function and the corresponding indicator are always in sync.

The 84-key unit that came with the original AT system is no longer used, although its electrical design is compatible with newer systems. It lacks some of the keys found in the newer keyboards and does not have as nice a numeric keypad section, but many users prefer the more Selectric-style layout of the alphanumeric keys. Likewise, some users prefer to have the 10 function keys arranged on the left-hand side as opposed to the enhanced arrangement in which 12 function keys are lined up along the top.

Enhanced 101-Key (or 102-Key) Keyboard. In 1986, IBM introduced the "corporate" enhanced 101-key keyboard for the newer XT and AT models (see Figure 9.3). I use the word "corporate" because this unit first appeared in IBM's RT PC, which is a *RISC (Reduced Instruction Set Computer)* system designed for scientific and engineering applications; keyboards with this design are now supplied with virtually every type of system and terminal that IBM sells. Other companies quickly copied this design, and it has been the standard in PC-compatible systems ever since.

This universal keyboard has a further improved layout over that of the 84-key unit, with perhaps the exception of the Enter key, which reverted to a smaller size. The 101-key enhanced keyboard was designed to conform to international regulations and specifications for keyboards. In fact, other companies such as Digital Equipment Corporation (DEC) and Texas Instruments (TI) had already been using designs similar to the IBM 101-key unit. The IBM 101-key units originally came in versions with and without the status indicator LEDs, depending on whether the unit was sold with an XT or AT system. Now there are many other variations to choose from, including some with integrated pointing devices.

Chapter 9—Input Devices

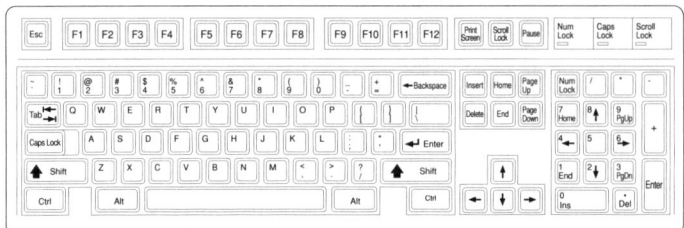

FIG. 9.3 101-key enhanced keyboard layout.

The enhanced keyboard is available in several different variations, but all are basically the same electrically and can be interchanged. IBM and its Lexmark keyboard and printer subsidiary have produced a number of versions, including keyboards with built-in pointing devices and new ergonomic layouts. Most of the enhanced keyboards attach to the system via the standard 5-pin DIN (Deutsche Industrie Norm) connector, but many others come with cables for the 6-pin mini-DIN connector found on many newer systems, including the IBM PS/2s and most Slimline compatibles. Although the connectors may be physically different, the keyboards are not, and you can either interchange the cables or use a cable adapter to plug one type into the other.

The 101-key keyboard layout can be divided into the following four sections:

- Typing area
- Numeric keypad
- Cursor and screen controls
- Function keys

The 101-key arrangement is similar to the Selectric keyboard layout with the exception of the Enter key. The Tab, Caps Lock, Shift, and Backspace keys have a larger striking area and are located in the familiar Selectric locations. Ctrl and Alt keys are on each side of the space bar. The typing area and numeric keypad have home-row identifiers for touch typing.

The cursor and screen-control keys have been separated from the numeric keypad, which is reserved for numeric input. (As with other PC keyboards, you can use the numeric keypad for cursor and screen control when the keyboard is not in Num Lock mode.) A division-sign key and an additional Enter key have been added to the numeric keypad.

The cursor-control keys are arranged in the inverted T format. The Insert, Delete, Home, End, Page Up, and Page Down keys, located above the dedicated cursor-control keys, are separate from the numeric keypad. The function keys, spaced in groups of four, are located across the top of the keyboard. The keyboard has two additional function keys: F11 and F12. The Esc key is isolated in the upper-left corner of the keyboard. Dedicated Print Screen/Sys Req, Scroll Lock, and Pause/Break keys are provided for commonly used functions.

Foreign language versions of the enhanced keyboard include 102-keys and a slightly different layout from the 101-key U.S. versions.

One of the many useful features of the enhanced keyboard is removable keycaps. With clear keycaps and paper inserts, you can customize the keyboard. Keyboard templates are also available to provide specific operator instructions.

The enhanced keyboard will probably come with any PC-compatible desktop system for quite some time. It is currently the most popular design and does not show any signs of being replaced in the future. Because most compatible systems use this same type of keyboard, it is relatively easy to move from one system to another without relearning the layout.

104-Key Windows Keyboard. If you are a touch typist like I am, then you really hate to take your hands off of the keyboard to use a mouse. Windows 95 makes this even more of a problem, because it exploits both mouse buttons. Many new keyboards, especially those in portable computers, include a variation of the IBM Trackpoint or the Alps Glidepoint (both of which are discussed later in this chapter), which allow touch typists to keep their hands on the keyboard even while moving the pointer, but there is still another alternative that can help. Microsoft has come up with a specification that calls for three new Windows-specific keys to be added to the keyboard. These new keys help with functions that would otherwise require multiple keystrokes or mouse clicks.

Microsoft has released a Windows keyboard specification that outlines a set of new keys and key combinations. The familiar 101-key layout grows to 104 keys, with the addition of left and right Windows keys and an Application key. These keys will be used for operating-system and application-level keyboard combinations, similar to today's Ctrl and Alt combinations. You don't need the new keys to use Windows 95 or NT, but software vendors are starting to add specific functions to their Windows products that will use the new Application key (which is the same as the right mouse button). Figure 9.4 shows the standard Windows keyboard layout including the three new keys.

FIG. 9.4 104-key Windows keyboard layout.

The recommended Windows keyboard layout calls for the Left and Right Windows keys (called *WIN keys*) to flank the Alt keys on each side of the space bar, and an Application key on the right of the Right Windows key. Note that the exact placement of these keys is up to the keyboard designer, so you will see variations from keyboard to keyboard.

The WIN keys open the Start menu, which then can be navigated with the arrow keys. The Application key simulates the right mouse button; in most applications, it brings up context-sensitive pop-up menus. Several WIN key combinations offer preset macro commands as well. For example, you press WIN+E to bring up the Windows Explorer. The following table shows a list of all the new Windows 95 key combinations:

Key Combination	*Action*
WIN+R	Displays the Run dialog box.
WIN+M	Minimizes All.
Shift+WIN+M	Undoes Minimize All.
WIN+F1	Starts Help.
WIN+E	Starts Windows Explorer.
WIN+F	Finds files or folders.
Ctrl+WIN+F	Finds the computer.
WIN+Tab	Cycles through taskbar buttons.
WIN+Break	Displays the System properties dialog box.

The Windows keyboard specification requires that keyboard makers increase the number of trilograms in their keyboard designs. A *trilogram* is a combination of three rapidly pressed keys that perform a special function, such as Ctrl+Alt+Delete. Designing a keyboard so that the switch matrix will correctly register trilograms is expensive, and this plus the additional Windows keys themselves will cause the price of these keyboards to rise. Volume sales should keep the price reasonable, as well as the natural market competition.

Virtually every keyboard manufacturer is now producing keyboards with these Windows-specific keys. Some are also combining these new keys with other features. For example, besides the new Windows keys, the *Microsoft Natural Keyboard* includes ergonomic features, such as split keypads that are rotated out from the middle to encourage a straight wrist position. It takes some getting used to. Unfortunately, this keyboard (made by Keytronics for Microsoft) does not have nearly the feel of the mechanical switch designs like Alps, Lite-On, or NMB, or the extremely high-quality feel of the Lexmark keyboards.

In addition to the Windows keys, other companies like Lexmark, NMB, and Alps have licensed a new space bar design called *Erase-Ease* from Keyboard Enhancements, Inc. This new design splits the space bar into two parts, using the shorter left (or optionally the right) half as an additional Backspace key. If you see a keyboard advertising 105-keys, then it probably has both the three additional Windows keys plus the extra Backspace key next to the space bar.

Although the new Windows keys are not mandatory when running Windows, and certainly not everybody will have them, I do expect more and more new PC systems to include keyboards with these extra keys. They can make it easier for both experienced touch typists as well as novice users to access some of the functions of Windows and their applications.

Compatibility. The 83-key PC/XT type is different from all the others and normally plugs into only 8-bit PC/XT systems that do not use the motherboard-based 8042-type keyboard controller chip. This is definitely true for IBM's keyboards and also is true for many compatible units. Some compatibles may be switchable to work with an AT-type motherboard via an XT/AT switch.

The 84-key unit from IBM works on only AT-type 16-bit (or greater) motherboards and does not work at all with PC/XT systems. Again, some aftermarket designs may have an XT/AT switch to allow for compatibility with PC/XT-type systems. If you have the keyboard set in the wrong mode, it will not work, but no damage will occur.

The enhanced keyboards from IBM are universal and *auto-switching*, which means that they work in virtually any system from the XT to the PS/2 or any PC-compatible by simply plugging them in. Some may require that a switch be moved on the keyboard to make it compatible with PC/XT systems that do not have the 8042-type keyboard controller on the motherboard. In some cases, you may also need to switch to a different cable with the proper system end connector, or use an adapter.

Although the enhanced keyboard is electrically compatible with any AT-type motherboard and even most PC/XT-type motherboards, many older systems will have software problems using these keyboards. IBM changed the ROM on the systems to support the new keyboard properly, and the compatible vendors followed suit. Very old (1986 or earlier) machines may require a ROM upgrade to use properly some of the features on the 101-key enhanced keyboards, such as the F11 and F12 keys. If the individual system ROM BIOS is not capable of operating the 101-key keyboard correctly, the 101-key keyboard may not work at all (as with all three ROM versions of the IBM PC); the additional keys (F11 and F12 function keys) may not work; or you may have problems with keyboard operation in general. In some cases, these compatibility problems cause improper characters to appear when keys are typed (causing the system to beep), and general keyboard operation is a problem. These problems can often be solved by a ROM upgrade to a newer version with proper support for the enhanced keyboard.

If you have an older IBM system, you can tell whether your system has complete ROM BIOS support for the 101-key unit: When you plug in the keyboard and turn on the system unit, the Num Lock light automatically comes on and the numeric keypad portion of the keyboard is enabled. This method of detection is not 100 percent accurate, but if the light goes on, your BIOS generally supports the keyboard. A notable exception is the IBM AT BIOS dated 06/10/85; it turns on the Num Lock light, but still does not properly support the enhanced keyboard. All IBM BIOS versions dated since 11/15/85 have proper support for the enhanced keyboards.

In IBM systems that support the enhanced keyboard, if it is detected on power up, Num Lock is enabled and the light goes on. If one of the older 84-key AT-type keyboards is detected, the Num Lock function is not enabled because these keyboards do not have arrow keys separate from the numeric keypad. When the enhanced keyboards first appeared in 1986, many users (including me) were irritated on finding that the numeric keypad was automatically enabled every time the system boots. Most compatibles began integrating a function into the system setup that allowed specification of the Num Lock status on boot.

Some thought that the automatic enabling of Num Lock was a function of the enhanced keyboard because none of the earlier keyboards seemed to operate this way. Remember that this function is not really a keyboard function; it is a function of the motherboard ROM BIOS, which identifies an enhanced 101-key unit and turns on the Num Lock as a "favor." In systems that cannot disable the automatic numeric keypad enable feature, you can use the DOS 6.0 or higher version NUMLOCK= parameter in CONFIG.SYS to turn Num Lock on or off as desired. If you are running a version of DOS earlier than 6.0, you can use one of the many public domain programs available for turning off the Num Lock function. Inserting the program to disable Num Lock in the AUTOEXEC.BAT file turns off the numeric keypad whenever the system reboots.

In an informal test, I plugged the new keyboard into an earlier XT. The keyboard seemed to work well. None of the keys that did not exist previously, such as F11 and F12, were operable, but the new arrow keys and the numeric keypad worked. The enhanced keyboard seems to work on XT or AT systems, but it does not function on the original PC systems because of BIOS and electrical interface problems. Many compatible versions of the 101-key enhanced keyboards have a manual XT/AT switch on the bottom that may allow the keyboard to work in an original PC system.

Keyboard Technology

The technology that makes up a typical PC keyboard is very interesting. This section focuses on all aspects of keyboard technology and design, including the key switches, the interface between the keyboard and the system, scan codes, and the keyboard connectors.

Key Switch Design. Several types of switches are used in keyboards today. Most keyboards use one of several variations on a mechanical key switch. A *mechanical key switch* relies on a mechanical momentary contact type switch to make electrical contact in a circuit. Some high-end keyboard designs use a totally different nonmechanical design that relies on capacitive switches. This section discusses these switches and the highlights of each design.

The most common type of key switch is the mechanical type, available in the following variations:

- Pure mechanical
- Foam element
- Rubber dome
- Membrane

The *pure mechanical* type is just that—a simple mechanical switch that features metal contacts in a momentary contact arrangement. Often a *tactile feedback mechanism*—consisting of a clip and spring arrangement to give a "clicky" feel to the keyboard and offer some resistance to pressing the key—is built in. Several companies, including Alps Electric, Lite-On, and NMB Technologies, manufacture this type of keyboard using switches primarily from Alps Electric. Mechanical switches are very durable, usually have self-cleaning contacts, and normally are rated for 20 million keystrokes, which is second only to the capacitive switch. They also offer excellent tactile feedback.

Foam element mechanical switches were a very popular design in some older keyboards. Most of the older compatible keyboards, including those made by Keytronics and many others, use this technology. These switches are characterized by a foam element with an electrical contact on the bottom that is mounted on the bottom of a plunger attached to the key itself (see Figure 9.5).

FIG. 9.5 Typical foam element mechanical key switch.

When the switch is pressed, a foil conductor on the bottom of the foam element closes a circuit on the printed circuit board below. A return spring pushes the key back up when the pressure is released. The foam dampens the contact, helping to prevent bounce, but unfortunately gives these keyboards a "mushy" feel. The big problem with this type of key switch design is that there is often little in the way of tactile feedback, and systems with these keyboards often resort to tricks such as clicking the PC's speaker to signify that contact has been made. Compaq has used keyboards of this type (made by Keytronics) in many of their systems, but perhaps the most popular user today is Packard Bell. Preferences in keyboard feel are somewhat subjective; I personally do not favor the foam element switch design.

Another problem with this type of design is that it is prone to corrosion on the foil conductor and the circuit board traces below. When this happens, the key strikes may become intermittent, which can be frustrating. Fortunately, these keyboards are among the easiest to clean. By disassembling this type of keyboard completely, you can usually remove the circuit board portion without removing each foam pad separately, and expose the bottoms of all the pads. Then you can easily wipe the corrosion and dirt off the bottom of the foam pads and the circuit board, thus restoring the keyboard to a "like-new" condition. Unfortunately, over time the corrosion problem will occur again. I recommend using some Stabilant 22a from D.W. Electrochemicals to improve the switch contact action and to prevent future corrosion. Because of problems like this, the foam element design is not used much anymore and has been superseded in popularity by the rubber dome design.

Rubber dome switches are mechanical switches that are similar to the foam element-type but are improved in many ways. Instead of a spring, these switches use a rubber dome that has a carbon button contact on the underside. As you press a key, the key plunger presses on the rubber dome, causing it to resist and then collapse all at once, much like the top of an oil can. As the rubber dome collapses, the user feels the tactile feedback, and the carbon button makes contact between the circuit board traces below. When the key is released, the rubber dome re-forms and pushes the key back up.

The rubber eliminates the need for a spring and provides a reasonable amount of tactile feedback without any special clips or other parts. A carbon button is used because it is resistant to corrosion and also has a self-cleaning action on the metal contacts below. The rubber domes are formed into a sheet that completely protects the contacts below from dirt, dust, and even minor spills. This type of design is the simplest, using the fewest parts. These things make this type of keyswitch very reliable and help make rubber dome-type keyboards the most popular in service today.

If rubber dome keyboards have a drawback at all, it is that the tactile feedback is not as good as many users would like. Although it is reasonable for most, some users prefer more tactile feedback than rubber dome keyboards normally provide.

The *membrane* keyboard is a variation on the rubber dome type in which the keys themselves are no longer separate, but are formed together in a sheet that sits on the rubber dome sheet. This severely limits key travel, and membrane keyboards are not considered usable for normal touch typing because of this. They are ideal in extremely harsh environments. Because the sheets can be bonded together and sealed from the elements, membrane keyboards can be used in situations in which no other type could survive. Many industrial applications use membrane keyboards especially for terminals that do not require extensive data entry but are used to operate equipment such as cash registers.

Capacitive switches are the only nonmechanical type of switch in use today (see Figure 9.6). These are the Cadillac of key switches. They are much more expensive than the more common mechanical rubber dome, but they also are more resistant to dirt and corrosion and offer the highest-quality tactile feedback of any type of switch.

A capacitive switch does not work by making contact between conductors. Instead, two plates usually made of plastic are connected in a switch matrix designed to detect changes in the capacitance of the circuit.

When the key is pressed, the plunger moves the top plate relative to the fixed bottom plate. Usually a mechanism provides for a distinct over-center tactile feedback with a resounding "click." As the top plate moves, the capacitance between the two plates changes and is detected by the comparator circuitry in the keyboard.

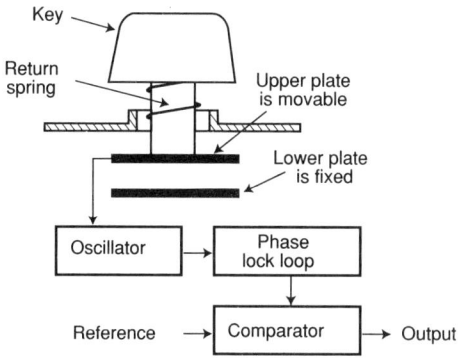

FIG. 9.6 A capacitive key switch.

Because this type of switch does not rely on metal contacts, it is nearly immune to corrosion and dirt. These switches are very resistant to key bounce problems that result in multiple characters appearing from a single strike. They are also the most durable in the industry—rated for 25 million or more keystrokes, as opposed to 10 to 20 million for other designs. The tactile feedback is unsurpassed because a relatively loud click and strong over-center feel normally are provided. The only drawback to this design is the cost. Capacitive switch keyboards are among the most expensive designs, but the quality of the feel and their durability are worth it.

Traditionally, the only vendors of capacitive key switch keyboards have been IBM and its keyboard division, Lexmark, which is why these keyboards have always seemed to stand out as superior from the rest.

The Keyboard Interface. A keyboard consists of a set of switches mounted in a grid or array called the *key matrix*. When a switch is pressed, a processor in the keyboard itself identifies which key is pressed by identifying which grid location in the matrix shows continuity. The keyboard processor also interprets how long the key is pressed and can even handle multiple keypresses at the same time. A 16-byte hardware buffer in the keyboard can handle rapid or multiple keypresses, passing each one in succession to the system.

When you press a key, in most cases the contact actually bounces slightly, meaning that there are several rapid on-off cycles just as the switch makes contact. This is called *bounce*, and the processor in the keyboard is designed to filter this, or *debounce* the keystroke. The keyboard processor must distinguish bounce from a double keystrike actually intended by the keyboard operator. This is fairly easy because the bouncing is much more rapid than a person could simulate by striking a key quickly several times.

The keyboard in an PC-compatible system is actually a computer itself. It communicates with the main system through a special serial data link that transmits and receives data in 11-bit packets of information consisting of 8 data bits in addition to framing and control bits. Although it is indeed a serial link (the data flows on one wire), it is not compatible with the standard RS-232 serial port commonly used to connect modems.

The processor in the original PC keyboard was an Intel 8048 microcontroller chip. Newer keyboards often use an 8049 version that has built-in ROM or other microcontroller chips compatible with the 8048 or 8049. For example, in its enhanced keyboards, IBM has always used a custom version of the Motorola 6805 processor, which is compatible with the Intel chips. The keyboard's built-in processor reads the key matrix, debounces the keypress signals, converts the keypress to the appropriate scan code, and transmits the code to the motherboard. The processors built into the keyboard contain their own RAM, possibly some ROM, and a built-in serial interface.

In the original PC/XT design, the keyboard serial interface is connected to an 8255 Programmable Peripheral Interface (PPI) chip on the motherboard of the PC/XT. This chip is connected to the interrupt controller IRQ1 line, which is used to signal that keyboard data is available. The data itself is sent from the 8255 to the processor via I/O port address 60h. The IRQ1 signal causes the main system processor to run a subroutine (INT 9h) that interprets the keyboard scan code data and decides what to do.

In an AT-type keyboard design, the keyboard serial interface is connected to a special keyboard controller on the motherboard. This is an Intel 8042 Universal Peripheral Interface (UPI) slave microcontroller chip in the original AT design. This microcontroller is essentially another processor that has its own 2K of ROM and 128 bytes of RAM. An 8742 version that uses *EPROM (Erasable Programmable Read Only Memory)* can be erased and reprogrammed. Often when you get a motherboard ROM upgrade from a motherboard manufacturer, it includes a new keyboard controller chip because it has somewhat dependent and updated ROM code in it as well. Some systems may use the 8041 or 8741 chips, which differ only in the amount of ROM or RAM built in, whereas other systems now have the keyboard controller built into the main system chipset.

In an AT system, the (8048-type) microcontroller in the keyboard sends data to the (8042-type) motherboard keyboard controller on the motherboard. The motherboard-based controller can also send data back to the keyboard. When the keyboard controller on the motherboard receives data from the keyboard, it signals the motherboard with an IRQ1 and sends the data to the main motherboard processor via I/O port address 60h, just as in the PC/XT. Acting as an agent between the keyboard and the main system processor, the 8042-type keyboard controller can translate scan codes and perform several other functions as well. Data also can be sent to the 8042 keyboard controller via port 60h, which is then passed on to the keyboard. Additionally, when the system needs to send commands to or read the status of the keyboard controller on the motherboard, it reads or writes through I/O port 64h. These commands are also usually followed by data sent back and forth via port 60h.

In most older systems the 8042 keyboard controller is also used by the system to control the A20 memory address line, which controls access to system memory greater than 1M. More modern motherboards usually incorporate this functionality directly in the motherboard chipset. This aspect of the keyboard controller is discussed in Chapter 7, "Memory," in the section that covers the High Memory Area (HMA).

Typematic Functions. If a key on the keyboard is held down, it becomes *typematic*, which means that the keyboard repeatedly sends the keypress code to the motherboard. In the AT-style keyboards, the typematic rate is adjustable by sending the keyboard processor the appropriate commands. This is not possible for the earlier PC/XT keyboard types because the keyboard interface is not bi-directional.

AT-style keyboards have a programmable typematic repeat rate and delay parameter. The DOS MODE command in versions 4.0 and later enables you to set the keyboard typematic (repeat) rate as well as the delay before typematic action begins. The default value for the RATE parameter (*r*) is 20 for PC-compatible systems and 21 for IBM PS/2 systems. The default value for the DELAY parameter is 2. Thus for most systems, the standard keyboard typematic speed is 10cps (characters per second), and the delay before typematic action occurs is 0.5 seconds.

To use the DOS MODE command to reset the keyboard typematic rate and delay, use the following command:

```
MODE CON[:] [RATE=r DELAY=d]
```

The acceptable values for the rate *r* and the resultant typematic rate in cps are shown in Table 9.1.

Table 9.1   DOS 4.0+ *MODE* Command Keyboard Typematic Rate Parameters

Rate No.	Rate ± 20%	Rate No.	Rate ± 20%
32	30.0cps	16	7.5cps
31	26.7cps	15	6.7cps
30	24.0cps	14	6.0cps
29	21.8cps	13	5.5cps
28	20.0cps	12	5.0cps
27	18.5cps	11	4.6cps
26	17.1cps	10	4.3cps
25	16.0cps	9	4.0cps
24	15.0cps	8	3.7cps
23	13.3cps	7	3.3cps
22	12.0cps	6	3.0cps
21	10.9cps	5	2.7cps
20	10.0cps	4	2.5cps
19	9.2cps	3	2.3cps
18	8.6cps	2	2.1cps
17	8.0cps	1	2.0cps

Table 9.2 shows the values for DELAY and the resultant delay time in seconds.

Table 9.2 DOS *MODE* Command Keyboard Typematic Delay Parameters

DELAY No.	Delay Time
1	0.25sec
2	0.50sec
3	0.75sec
4	1.00sec

For example, I always place the following command in my AUTOEXEC.BAT file:

```
MODE CON: RATE=32 DELAY=1
```

This command sets the typematic rate to the maximum speed possible, or 30cps. It also trims the delay to the minimum of 0.25 seconds before repeating begins. This command "turbocharges" the keyboard and makes operations requiring repeated keystrokes work much faster, such as moving within a file using arrow keys. The quick typematic action and short delay can sometimes be disconcerting to ham-fisted keyboard operators. In that case, slow typists might want to leave their keyboard speed at the default until they become more proficient.

> **Note**
>
> If you have an older system or keyboard, you may receive the following message:
>
> ```
> Function not supported on this computer
> ```
>
> This indicates that your system, keyboard, or both do not support the bi-directional interface or commands required to change the typematic rate and delay. Upgrading the BIOS or the keyboard may enable this function, but it is probably not cost-effective to do this on an older system.

> **Note**
>
> Many BIOS versions feature keyboard speed selection capability; however, not all of them allow full control over the speed and delay.

Windows maintains its own independent settings for the keyboard typematic rate and delay. This means that even if you use the MODE command to set them in DOS, when Windows is loaded it will override any previous settings. Fortunately, the keyboard typematic rate and delay can easily be viewed or changed from within Windows. To do this, first open the Control Panel, then select the Keyboard icon where you will see the repeat rate and delay settings. If you want to adjust the typematic rate, drag the Repeat Rate slider to the desired setting. If you want to adjust the time delay before repeating occurs, drag the Repeat Delay slider to the desired setting. You can test the repeat delay and repeat rate by clicking the box below the sliders and then holding down a key.

Keyboard Key Numbers and Scan Codes. When you press a key on the keyboard, the processor built into the keyboard (8048- or 6805-type) reads the keyswitch location in the keyboard matrix. The processor then sends to the motherboard a serial packet of data that contains the scan code for the key that was pressed. In AT-type motherboards that use an 8042-type keyboard controller, the 8042 chip translates the actual keyboard scan code into one of up to three different sets of system scan codes, which are sent to the main processor. It can be useful in some cases to know what these scan codes are, especially when troubleshooting keyboard problems or when reading the keyboard or system scan codes directly in software.

When a keyswitch on the keyboard sticks or otherwise fails, the scan code of the failed keyswitch is usually reported by diagnostics software, including the *POST (Power On Self-Test)*, as well as conventional disk-based diagnostics. This means that you have to identify the particular key by its scan code. Tables 9.3 through 9.7 list all the scan codes for every key on the 83-, 84-, and 101-key keyboards. By looking up the reported scan code on these charts, you can determine which keyswitch is defective or needs to be cleaned.

> **Note**
>
> 101-key enhanced keyboards are capable of three different scan code sets. Set 1 is the default. Some systems, including some of the PS/2 machines, use one of the other scan code sets during the POST. For example, the IBM P75 I have uses Scan Code Set 2 during the POST but switches to Set 1 during normal operation. This is rare and really threw me off in diagnosing a stuck key problem at one time, but it is useful to know if you are having difficulty interpreting the Scan Code number.

IBM also assigns each key a unique key number to distinguish it from the others. This is important when you are trying to identify keys on foreign keyboards, which may use different symbols or characters from the U.S. models. In the case of the enhanced keyboard, most foreign models are missing one of the keys (key 29) found on the U.S. version and have two other additional keys (keys 42 and 45) as well. This accounts for the 102-key total rather than the 101-keys found on the U.S. version.

Figure 9.7 shows the keyboard numbering and character locations for the original 83-key PC keyboard. Table 9.3 shows the scan codes for each key relative to the key number and character.

FIG. 9.7 83-key PC keyboard key number and character locations.

Table 9.3 83-Key (PC/XT) Keyboard Key Numbers and Scan Codes

Key Number	Scan Code	Key	Key Number	Scan Code	Key
1	01	Esc	39	27	;
2	02	1	40	28	'
3	03	2	41	29	'
4	04	3	42	2A	Left Shift
5	05	4	43	2B	\
6	06	5	44	2C	z
7	07	6	45	2D	x
8	08	7	46	2E	c
9	09	8	47	2F	v
10	0A	9	48	30	b
11	0B	0	49	31	n
12	0C	-	50	32	m
13	0D	=	51	33	,
14	0E	Backspace	52	34	.
15	0F	Tab	53	35	/
16	10	q	54	36	Right Shift
17	11	w	55	37	*
18	12	e	56	38	Alt
19	13	r	57	39	Space bar
20	14	t	58	3A	Caps Lock
21	15	y	59	3B	F1
22	16	u	60	3C	F2
23	17	i	61	3D	F3
24	18	o	62	3E	F4
25	19	p	63	3F	F5
26	1A	[	64	40	F6
27	1B	]	65	41	F7
28	1C	Enter	66	42	F8
29	1D	Ctrl	67	43	F9
30	1E	a	68	44	F10
31	1F	s	69	45	Num Lock
32	20	d	70	46	Scroll Lock
33	21	f	71	47	Keypad 7 (Home)
34	22	g	72	48	Keypad 8 (Up arrow)
35	23	h	73	49	Keypad 9 (PgUp)
36	24	j	74	4A	Keypad -
37	25	k	75	4B	Keypad 4 (Left arrow)
38	26	l	76	4C	Keypad 5

Key Number	Scan Code	Key	Key Number	Scan Code	Key
77	4D	Keypad 6 (Right arrow)	81	51	Keypad 3 (PgDn)
78	4E	Keypad +	82	52	Keypad 0 (Ins)
79	4F	Keypad 1 (End)	83	53	Keypad . (Del)
80	50	Keypad 2 (Down arrow)			

Figure 9.8 shows the keyboard numbering and character locations for the original 84-key AT keyboard. Table 9.4 shows the scan codes for each key relative to the key number and character.

FIG. 9.8 84-key AT keyboard key number and character locations.

Table 9.4 84-Key AT Keyboard Key Numbers and Scan Codes

Key Number	Scan Code	Key	Key Number	Scan Code	Key
1	29	`	21	14	t
2	02	1	22	15	y
3	03	2	23	16	u
4	04	3	24	17	i
5	05	4	25	18	o
6	06	5	26	19	p
7	07	6	27	1A	[
8	08	7	28	1B	]
9	09	8	30	1D	Ctrl
10	0A	9	31	1E	a
11	0B	0	32	1F	s
12	0C	-	33	20	d
13	0D	=	34	21	f
14	2B	\	35	22	g
15	0E	Backspace	36	23	h
16	0F	Tab	37	24	j
17	10	q	38	25	k
18	11	w	39	26	l
19	12	e	40	27	;
20	13	r	41	28	'

(continues)

Table 9.4 Continued

Key Number	Scan Code	Key	Key Number	Scan Code	Key
43	1C	Enter	71	3D	F3
44	2A	Left Shift	72	3F	F5
46	2C	z	73	41	F7
47	2D	x	74	43	F9
48	2E	c	90	01	Escape
49	2F	v	91	47	Keypad 7 (Home)
50	30	b	92	4B	Keypad 4 (Left arrow)
51	31	n	93	4F	Keypad 1 (End)
52	32	m	95	45	Num Lock
53	33	,	96	48	Keypad 8 (Up arrow)
54	34	.	97	4C	Keypad 5
55	35	/	98	50	Keypad 2 (Down arrow)
57	36	Right Shift	99	52	Keypad 0 (Ins)
58	38	Alt	100	46	Scroll Lock
61	39	Space bar	101	49	Keypad 9 (PgUp)
64	3A	Caps Lock	102	4D	Keypad 6 (Right arrow)
65	3C	F2	103	51	Keypad 3 (PgDn)
66	3E	F4	104	53	Keypad . (Del)
67	40	F6	105	54	SysRq
68	42	F8	106	37	Keypad *
69	44	F10	107	4A	Keypad -
70	3B	F1	108	4E	Keypad +

Figure 9.9 shows the keyboard numbering and character locations for the 101-key enhanced keyboard. Tables 9.5 through 9.8 show each of the three scan code sets for each key relative to the key number and character. Scan Code Set 1 is the default; the other two are rarely used. Figure 9.10 shows the layout of a typical foreign language 102-key version of the enhanced keyboard—in this case, a U.K. version.

FIG. 9.9 101-key enhanced keyboard key number and character locations (U.S. version).

FIG. 9.10 102-key enhanced keyboard key number and character locations (U.K. English version).

Table 9.5 101/102-Key (Enhanced) Keyboard Key Numbers and Scan Codes (Set 1)

Key Number	Scan Code	Key	Key Number	Scan Code	Key
1	29	`	29	2B	\ (101-key only)
2	02	1	30	3A	Caps Lock
3	03	2	31	1E	a
4	04	3	32	1F	s
5	05	4	33	20	d
6	06	5	34	21	f
7	07	6	35	22	g
8	08	7	36	23	h
9	09	8	37	24	j
10	0A	9	38	25	k
11	0B	0	39	26	l
12	0C	-	40	27	;
13	0D	=	41	28	'
15	0E	Backspace	42	2B	# (102-key only)
16	0F	Tab	43	1C	Enter
17	10	q	44	2A	Left Shift
18	11	w	45	56	\ (102-key only)
19	12	e	46	2C	z
20	13	r	47	2D	x
21	14	t	48	2E	c
22	15	y	49	2F	v
23	16	u	50	30	b
24	17	i	51	31	n
25	18	o	52	32	m
26	19	p	53	33	,
27	1A	[	54	34	.
28	1B	]	55	35	/

(continues)

Table 9.5 Continued

Key Number	Scan Code	Key	Key Number	Scan Code	Key
57	36	Right Shift	99	52	Keypad 0 (Ins)
58	1D	Left Ctrl	100	37	Keypad *
60	38	Left Alt	101	49	Keypad 9 (PgUp)
61	39	Space bar	102	4D	Keypad 6 (Left arrow)
62	E0,38	Right Alt			
64	E0,1D	Right Ctrl	103	51	Keypad 3 (PgDn)
75	E0,52	Insert	104	53	Keypad . (Del)
76	E0,53	Delete	105	4A	Keypad -
79	E0,4B	Left arrow	106	4E	Keypad +
80	E0,47	Home	108	E0,1C	Keypad Enter
81	E0,4F	End	110	01	Escape
83	E0,48	Up arrow	112	3B	F1
84	E0,50	Down arrow	113	3C	F2
85	E0,49	Page Up	114	3D	F3
86	E0,51	Page Down	115	3E	F4
89	E0,4D	Right arrow	116	3F	F5
90	45	Num Lock	117	40	F6
91	47	Keypad 7 (Home)	118	41	F7
92	4B	Keypad 4 (Left arrow)	119	42	F8
			120	43	F9
93	4F	Keypad 1 (End)	121	44	F10
95	E0,35	Keypad /	122	57	F11
96	48	Keypad 8 (Up arrow)	123	58	F12
			124	E0,2A, E0,37	Print Screen
97	4C	Keypad 5			
98	50	Keypad 2 (Down arrow)	125	46	Scroll Lock
			126	E1,1D,45, E1,9D,C5	Pause

Table 9.6 101/102-Key (Enhanced) Keyboard Key Numbers and Scan Codes (Set 2)

Key Number	Scan Code	Key	Key Number	Scan Code	Key
1	0E	`	7	36	6
2	16	1	8	3D	7
3	1E	2	9	3E	8
4	26	3	10	46	9
5	25	4	11	45	0
6	2E	5	12	4E	-

Key Number	Scan Code	Key	Key Number	Scan Code	Key
13	55	=	53	41	,
15	66	Backspace	54	49	.
16	0D	Tab	55	4A	/
17	15	q	57	59	Right Shift
18	1D	w	58	14	Left Ctrl
19	24	e	60	11	Left Alt
20	2D	r	61	29	Space bar
21	2C	t	62	E0,11	Right Alt
22	35	y	64	E0,14	Right Ctrl
23	3C	u	75	E0,70	Insert
24	43	i	76	E0,71	Delete
25	44	o	79	E0,6B	Left arrow
26	4D	p	80	E0,6C	Home
27	54	[	81	E0,69	End
28	5B	]	83	E0,75	Up arrow
29	5D	\ (101-key only)	84	E0,72	Down arrow
30	58	Caps Lock	85	E0,7D	Page Up
31	1C	a	86	E0,7A	Page Down
32	1B	s	89	E0,74	Right arrow
33	23	d	90	77	Num Lock
34	2B	f	91	6C	Keypad 7 (Home)
35	34	g	92	6B	Keypad 4 (Left arrow)
36	33	h	93	69	Keypad 1 (End)
37	3B	j	95	E0,4A	Keypad /
38	42	k	96	75	Keypad 8 (Up arrow)
39	4B	l	97	73	Keypad 5
40	4C	;	98	72	Keypad 2 (Down arrow)
41	52	'	99	70	Keypad 0 (Ins)
42	5D	# (102-key only)	100	7C	Keypad *
43	5A	Enter	101	7D	Keypad 9 (PgUp)
44	12	Left Shift	102	74	Keypad 6 (Left arrow)
45	61	\ (102-key only)	103	7A	Keypad 3 (PgDn)
46	1A	z	104	71	Keypad . (Del)
47	22	x	105	7B	Keypad -
48	21	c			
49	2A	v			
50	32	b			
51	31	n			
52	3A	m			

(continues)

Table 9.6 Continued

Key Number	Scan Code	Key	Key Number	Scan Code	Key
106	E0,5A	Keypad +	118	83	F7
108	E0,5A	Keypad Enter	119	0A	F8
110	76	Escape	120	01	F9
112	05	F1	121	09	F10
113	06	F2	122	78	F11
114	04	F3	123	07	F12
115	0C	F4	124	E0,12,E0,7C	Print Screen
116	03	F5	125	7E	Scroll Lock
117	0B	F6	126	E1,14,77,E1,F0,14,F0,77	Pause

Table 9.7 101/102-Key (Enhanced) Keyboard Key Numbers and Scan Codes (Set 3)

Key Number	Scan Code	Key	Key Number	Scan Code	Key
1	0E	`	20	2D	r
2	16	1	21	2C	t
3	1E	2	22	35	y
4	26	3	23	3C	u
5	25	4	24	43	i
6	2E	5	25	44	o
7	36	6	26	4D	p
8	3D	7	27	54	[
9	3E	8	28	5B	]
10	46	9	29	5C	\ (101-key only)
11	45	0	30	14	Caps Lock
12	4E	-	31	1C	a
13	55	=	32	1B	s
15	66	Backspace	33	23	d
16	0D	Tab	34	2B	f
17	15	q	35	34	g
18	1D	w	36	33	h
19	24	e	37	3B	j

Keyboards

Key Number	Scan Code	Key	Key Number	Scan Code	Key
38	42	k	91	6C	Keypad 7 (Home)
39	4B	l	92	6B	Keypad 4 (Left arrow)
40	4C	;	93	69	Keypad 1 (End)
41	52	'	95	77	Keypad /
42	53	# (102-key only)	96	75	Keypad 8 (Up arrow)
43	5A	Enter	97	73	Keypad 5
44	12	Left Shift	98	72	Keypad 2 (Down arrow)
45	13	\ (102-key only)	99	70	Keypad 0 (Ins)
46	1A	z	100	7E	Keypad *
47	22	x	101	7D	Keypad 9 (PgUp)
48	21	c	102	74	Keypad 6 (Left arrow)
49	2A	v	103	7A	Keypad 3 (PgDn)
50	32	b	104	71	Keypad . (Del)
51	31	n	105	84	Keypad -
52	3A	m	106	7C	Keypad +
53	41	,	108	79	Keypad Enter
54	49	.	110	08	Escape
55	4A	/	112	07	F1
57	59	Right Shift	113	0F	F2
58	11	Left Ctrl	114	17	F3
60	19	Left Alt	115	1F	F4
61	29	Space bar	116	27	F5
62	39	Right Alt	117	2F	F6
64	58	Right Ctrl	118	37	F7
75	67	Insert	119	3F	F8
76	64	Delete	120	47	F9
79	61	Left arrow	121	4F	F10
80	6E	Home	122	56	F11
81	65	End	123	5E	F12
83	63	Up arrow	124	57	Print Screen
84	60	Down arrow	125	5F	Scroll Lock
85	6F	Page Up	126	62	Pause
86	6D	Page Down			
89	6A	Right arrow			
90	76	Num Lock			

The new keys found on a 104-key Windows keyboard have their own unique scan codes. Table 9.8 shows the scan codes for the new keys.

Table 9.8 104-Key Windows Keyboard New Key Scan Codes

New Key	Scan Code Set 1	Scan Code Set 2	Scan Code Set 3
Left Windows	E0,5B	E0,1F	8B
Right Windows	E0,5C	E0,27	8C
Application	E0,5D	E0,2F	8D

Knowing these key number figures and scan codes is useful when you are troubleshooting stuck or failed keys on a keyboard. Diagnostics can report the defective keyswitch by the scan code, which varies from keyboard to keyboard as to the character it represents and its location.

Keyboard/Mouse Interface Connectors. Keyboards have a cable available with one of two primary types of connectors at the system end. Most aftermarket keyboards have a cable connected inside the keyboard case on the keyboard end and require that you open up the keyboard case to disconnect or test. Actual IBM enhanced keyboards use a unique cable assembly that plugs into both the keyboard as well as the system unit. This makes cable interchange or replacement an easy plug-in affair. A special connector called an *SDL (Shielded Data Link)* is used at the keyboard end and the appropriate DIN connector at the PC end. Any IBM keyboard or cable can be ordered separately as a spare part. The newer enhanced keyboards come with an externally detachable keyboard cable that plugs into the keyboard port with a special connector, much like a telephone connector. The other end of the cable is one of the following two types:

- *5-pin DIN connector.* Used on most PC-compatible systems with Baby-AT form factor motherboards.

- *6-pin mini-DIN connector.* Used on PS/2 systems and most Low Profile (LPX motherboard) PC compatibles.

Figure 9.11 and Table 9.9 show the physical layout and pinouts of all the respective keyboard connector plugs and sockets.

Table 9.9 Keyboard Connector Signals

Signal Name	5-Pin DIN	6-Pin Mini-DIN	6-Pin SDL
Keyboard Data	2	1	B
Ground	4	3	C
+5v	5	4	E
Keyboard Clock	1	5	D
Not Connected	—	2	A

Signal Name	5-Pin DIN	6-Pin Mini-DIN	6-Pin SDL
Not Connected	—	6	F
Not Connected	3	—	—

DIN = German Industrial Norm (Deutsche Industrie Norm), a committee that sets German dimensional standards

SDL = Shielded Data Link, a type of shielded connector created by AMP and used by IBM and others for keyboard cables

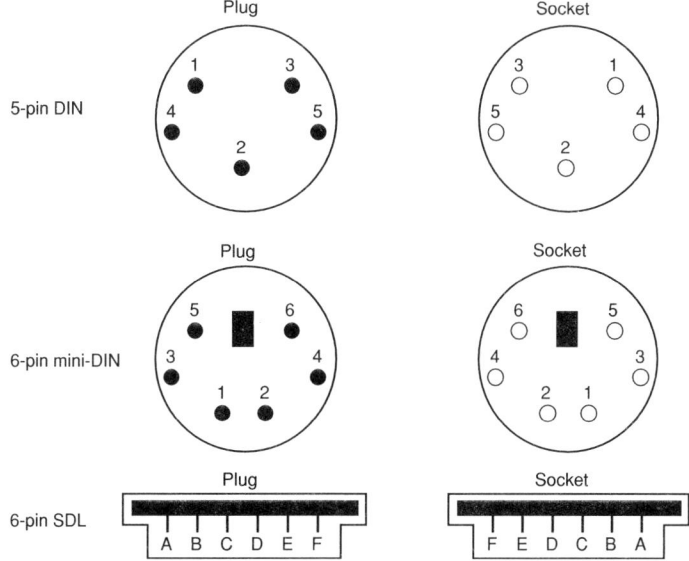

FIG. 9.11 Keyboard and mouse connectors.

Motherboard mouse connectors use the 6-pin mini-DIN connector and have the same pinout and signal descriptions as the keyboard connector; however, the data packets are incompatible. This means that you can easily plug a motherboard mouse (PS/2 style) into a mini-DIN keyboard connector, or plug the mini-DIN type keyboard connector into a motherboard mouse port; however, neither one would work properly in this situation.

Keyboards with Special Features. There are a number of keyboards on the market that have special features not found in the standard designs. These additional features can be simple things such as built-in calculators and clocks, to more complicated features such as integrated pointing devices, special character layouts, shapes, and even programmable keys.

Over the years, many have attempted to change the design of the standard keyboard in an attempt to improve typing speed and ergonomics. Around 1936, August Dvorak and William L. Dealy developed a modified character layout for the keyboard, which replaced the QWERTY layout we are all familiar with today.

The Dvorak-Dealy keyboard design is normally just called the Dvorak design for short. It featured different character positions on the keys designed to promote the alternation of hands during typing. The characters are arranged so that the vowels are in the home row under the left hand, while the consonants used most frequently are placed in the home row under the right hand. The theory was that this would dramatically improve typing speed; however, most tests show fairly modest improvements. The public being resistant to change, the Dvorak keyboard design has not achieved widespread popularity, and the familiar QWERTY layout is still by far the most common design.

A more recent trend is to change the shape of the keyboard instead of altering the character layout. This has resulted in a number of different so-called ergonomic designs. The goal is to shape the keyboard to better fit the human hand. The most common of these designs split the keyboard in the center, bending the sides back. Some allow the angle between the sides to be adjusted, such as with the Lexmark Select-Ease design, while others are fixed, such as the Microsoft Natural keyboard. These split or bent designs more easily conform to the natural angle of the hands while typing. They can improve productivity and typing speed, as well as help prevent medical problems such as Carpal Tunnel Syndrome (tendon inflammation).

Virtually every keyboard company now has some form of similar ergonometric keyboard, and the same things apply with respect to quality and feel as with the standard keyboard designs. The Microsoft Natural Keyboard is manufactured for Microsoft by Keytronics, and uses the inexpensive light-touch keyswitches they are known for. For those who prefer a more rugged keyboard with higher quality switches, I recommend the Lexmark Select-Ease, Alps, NMB Technologies, or Lite-On keyboards. These keyboards are available with very high quality mechanical switches with a positive tactile feel to them. The Lexmark design, in particular, allows you to adjust the angle between the two sides of the keyboard from fully closed like a standard keyboard, to split at virtually any angle. You can even separate the two halves completely. It also features built-in palm rests, an oversized space bar, and cursor keys on both sides of the keyboard.

Although these ergonometric keyboards sound like a good idea, people are resistant to change, and none of these designs has yet to significantly displace the standard keyboard layout.

Several companies including Maxi-Switch have introduced a keyboard that features keys that are programmable. You can assign different keystrokes to keys, or even reprogram the entire keyboard layout. This type of keyboard has been supplied in the past by some of the PC compatible vendors such as Gateway. At one time I used a number of these keyboards in the seminars I teach, and unfortunately I found the programming functions to be difficult to remember; accidentally pressing the programming control keys would often put the keyboard into an altered state requiring it to be reset. One other problem was that the extra keys added width to the keyboard, making it wider than most other standard designs. I quickly decided that the programming functions were so rarely used that they were simply not worth the hassle, and specified standard keyboards for future purchases.

Keyboard Troubleshooting and Repair

Keyboard errors are usually caused by two simple problems. Other more difficult intermittent problems can arise, but they are also much less likely. The most common problems are:

- Defective cables
- Stuck keys

Defective cables are easy to spot if the failure is not intermittent. If the keyboard stops working altogether or every keystroke results in an error or incorrect character, the cable is likely the culprit. Troubleshooting is simple, especially if you have a spare cable on hand. Simply replace the suspected cable with one from a known working keyboard, and verify whether the problem still exists. If it does, the problem must be elsewhere. You also can test the cable for continuity with it removed from the keyboard by using a *DMM (Digital Multi-Meter)*. DMMs that have an audible continuity tester built in make this procedure much easier to perform. Wiggle the ends of the cable as you check each wire to make sure that there are no intermittent connections. If you discover a problem with the continuity in one of the wires, replace the cable or the entire keyboard, if that is cheaper. Because replacement keyboards are so inexpensive, sometimes it can be cheaper to replace the entire unit than to get a new cable.

Many times you first discover a problem with a keyboard because the system has an error during the POST. Most systems use error codes in a 3xx numeric format to distinguish the keyboard. If you have any such errors during the POST, write them down. Some BIOS versions do not use cryptic numeric error codes and simply state something like the following:

```
Keyboard stuck key failure
```

This message normally would be displayed by a system with a Phoenix BIOS if a key were stuck. Unfortunately, that message does not identify which key it is!

If your 3xx (keyboard) error is preceded by a two-digit hexadecimal number, this number is the scan code of a failing or stuck keyswitch. Look up the scan code in the tables provided in this section to determine which keyswitch is the culprit. These charts tell you to which key the scan code refers. By removing the keycap of the offending key and cleaning the switch, you can often solve the problem.

For a simple test of the motherboard keyboard connector, you can check voltages on some of the pins. Use Figure 9.10 in the preceding section as a guide, and measure the voltages on various pins of the keyboard connector. To prevent possible damage to the system or keyboard, first turn off the power before disconnecting the keyboard. Then unplug the keyboard, and turn the power back on. Make measurements between the ground pin and the other pins according to Table 9.10. If the voltages are within these specifications, the motherboard keyboard circuitry is probably okay.

Chapter 9—Input Devices

Table 9.10 Keyboard Connector Specifications

DIN Connector Pin	Mini-DIN Connector Pin	Signal	Voltage
1	5	Keyboard Clock	+2.0v to +5.5v
2	1	Keyboard Data	+4.8v to +5.5v
3	-	Reserved	—
4	3	Ground	—
5	4	+5v Power	+2.0v to +5.5v

If your measurements do not match these voltages, the motherboard might be defective. Otherwise, the keyboard cable or keyboard might be defective. If you suspect that the cable is the problem, the easiest thing to do is to replace the keyboard cable with a known good one. If the system still does not work normally, you may have to replace either the entire keyboard or the motherboard.

In many newer systems, the motherboard keyboard and mouse connectors are protected by a fuse that can be replaced. Look for any type of fuse on the motherboard in the vicinity of the keyboard or mouse connectors. Other systems may have a socketed keyboard controller chip (8042-type). In that case, it may be possible to repair the motherboard keyboard circuit by replacing this chip. Because these chips have ROM code in them, it is best to get the replacement from the motherboard or BIOS manufacturer.

Here is a list of standard POST and diagnostics keyboard error codes:

Error Code	Description
3xx	Keyboard errors.
301	Keyboard reset or stuck-key failure (XX 301, XX = scan code in hex).
302	System unit keylock switch is locked.
302	User-indicated keyboard test error.
303	Keyboard or system-board error; keyboard controller failure.
304	Keyboard or system-board error; keyboard clock high.
305	Keyboard +5v error; PS/2 keyboard fuse (on motherboard) blown.
341	Keyboard error.
342	Keyboard cable error.
343	Keyboard LED card or cable failure.
365	Keyboard LED card or cable failure.
366	Keyboard interface cable failure.
367	Keyboard LED card or cable failure.

Disassembly Procedures and Cautions. Repairing and cleaning a keyboard often requires you to take it apart. When performing this task, you must know when to stop! Some keyboards literally come apart into hundreds of little pieces that are almost impossible to reassemble if you go too far. An IBM keyboard generally has these four major parts:

- Cable
- Case
- Keypad assembly
- Keycaps

You easily can break down a keyboard to these major components and replace any of them, but don't disassemble the keypad assembly or you will be showered with hundreds of tiny springs, clips, and keycaps. Finding all these parts—several hundred of them—and piecing the unit back together is not a fun way to spend your time. You also may not be able to reassemble the keyboard properly. Figure 9.12 shows a typical keyboard with the case opened.

FIG. 9.12 Typical keyboard components.

Another problem is that you cannot purchase the smaller parts separately, such as contact clips and springs. The only way to obtain these parts is from another keyboard. If you ever have a keyboard that is beyond repair, keep it around for these parts. They might come in handy some day.

Most repair operations are limited to changing the cable or cleaning some component of the keyboard, from the cable contact ends to the key contact points. The keyboard cable takes quite a lot of abuse and, therefore, can fail easily. The ends are stretched, tugged, pulled, and generally handled roughly. The cable uses strain reliefs, but you still might have problems with the connectors making proper contact at each end or even with wires that have broken inside the cable. You might want to carry a spare cable for every type of keyboard you have.

All keyboard cables plug into the keyboard and PC with connectors, and you can change the cables easily without having to splice wires or solder connections. With the earlier 83-key PC and 84-key AT keyboards, you must open the case to access the connector to which the cable attaches. On the newer 101-key enhanced keyboards from IBM and Lexmark, the cable plugs into the keyboard from the outside of the case, using a modular jack and plug similar to a telephone jack. This design also makes the IBM/Lexmark keyboards universally usable on nearly any system (except the original PC) by easily switching the cable.

The only difference, for example, between the enhanced keyboards for an IBM AT and an IBM PS/2 system is the attached cable. PS/2 systems use a tan cable with a smaller plug on the computer side. The AT cable is black and has the larger DIN-type plug on the computer side. You can interchange the enhanced keyboards as long as you use the correct cable for the system.

The only feasible way to repair a keyboard is to replace the cable and to clean the individual keyswitch assemblies, the entire keypad, or the cable contact ends. The individual spring and keyswitch assemblies are not available as a separate part, and disassembling the unit to that level is not advisable because of the difficulty in reassembling it. Other than cleaning a keyboard, the only thing that you can do is replace the entire keypad assembly (virtually the entire keyboard) or the cable.

Cleaning a Keyboard. One of the best ways to maintain a keyboard in top condition is periodic cleaning. As preventive maintenance, you should vacuum the keyboard weekly or at least monthly. You can also use canned compressed air (available at electronics supply houses) to blow the dust and dirt out instead of using a vacuum. Before you dust a keyboard with the compressed air, turn the keyboard upside down so that the particles of dirt and dust collected inside can fall out.

On all keyboards, each keycap is removable, which can be handy if a key sticks or acts erratically. For example, a common problem is a key that does not work every time you press it. This problem usually results from dirt collecting under the key. An excellent tool for removing keycaps on most any keyboard is the U-shaped chip-puller tool. Simply slip the hooked ends of the tool under the keycap, squeeze the ends together to grip the underside of the keycap, and lift up. IBM sells a tool designed specifically for removing keycaps from its keyboards, but the chip puller works even better. After removing the cap, spray some compressed air into the space under the cap to dislodge the dirt. Then replace the cap and check the action of the key.

> **Caution**
>
> When you remove the keycaps, be careful not to remove the space bar on the original 83-key PC and 84-key AT-type keyboards. This bar is very difficult to reinstall. The newer 101-key units use a different wire support that can be removed and replaced much more easily.

Spills also can be a problem. If you tip a soft drink or cup of coffee into a keyboard, you do not necessarily have a disaster. You should immediately (or as soon as possible) flush out the keyboard with distilled water. Partially disassemble the keyboard and use the water to wash the components. (See the following section for disassembly instructions.) If the spilled liquid has dried, soak the keyboard in some of the water for a while. When you are sure that the keyboard is clean, pour another gallon or so of distilled water over it and through the key switches to wash away any residual dirt. After the unit dries completely, it should be perfectly functional. You may be surprised to know that you can drench your keyboard with water, and it will not harm the components. Just make sure that you use distilled water, which is free from residue or mineral content. Also make sure that the keyboard is fully dry before you attempt to use it, or some of the components might short out.

Replacement Keyboards. In most cases, it is cheaper or more cost-effective to replace a keyboard rather than to repair it. This is especially true if the keyboard has an internal malfunction or if one of the keyswitches is defective. Replacement parts for keyboards are almost impossible to procure, and in most cases the installation of any repair part is difficult. In addition, many of the keyboards supplied with lower cost compatible machines leave much to be desired. They often have a mushy feel, with little or no tactile feedback. A poor keyboard can make using a system a frustrating experience, especially if you are a touch typist. For all these reasons, it is often a good idea to replace an existing keyboard with something better.

Perhaps the highest quality keyboards in the entire computer industry are those made by IBM, or more accurately Lexmark. Several years ago, IBM spun off its keyboard and printer divisions as a separate company called Lexmark. Lexmark used to manufacturer most IBM brand keyboards and printers and sells them not only to IBM but also to compatible vendors and end users. This means that if you are lucky, your compatible system comes with a Lexmark keyboard, but if not you can purchase one separately on your own.

Table 9.11 shows the part numbers of all IBM-labeled keyboards and cables. These numbers can serve as a reference when you are seeking a replacement IBM keyboard from IBM directly or from third-party companies. Many third-party companies sell IBM label keyboards for much less than IBM, in both new and refurbished form. Remember that you can also purchase these same keyboards through Lexmark, although they do not come with an IBM label.

Table 9.11 IBM Keyboard and Cable Part Numbers

Description	Part Number
83-key U.S. PC Keyboard assembly with cable	8529297
Cable assembly for 83-key PC Keyboard	8529168

(continues)

Table 9.11 Continued

Description	Part Number
84-key U.S. AT Keyboard assembly with cable	8286165
Cable assembly for 84-key keyboard	8286146
101-key U.S. Keyboard without LED panel	1390290
101-key U.S. Keyboard with LED panel	6447033
101-key U.S. Keyboard with LED panel (PS/2 logo)	1392090
6-foot cable for enhanced keyboard (DIN plug)	6447051
6-foot cable for enhanced keyboard (mini-DIN plug)	61X8898
6-foot cable for enhanced keyboard (shielded mini-DIN plug)	27F4984
10-foot cable for enhanced keyboard (mini-DIN plug)	72X8537

Notice that the original 83/84-key IBM keyboards are sold with a cable that has the larger, 5-pin DIN connector already attached. IBM enhanced keyboards are always sold (at least by IBM) without a cable. You must order the proper cable as a separate item. Cables are available to connect the keyboards to either the older system units that use the larger DIN connector or to PS/2 systems (and many compatibles) that use the smaller mini-DIN connector.

Recently, IBM has started selling complete keyboard assemblies under a program called *IBM Options*. This program is designed to sell these components in the retail channel to end users of both IBM and compatible systems from other vendors. Items under the IBM Options program are sold through normal retail channels such as CompUSA, Elek Tek, and Computer Discount Warehouse (CDW). These items are also priced much cheaper than items purchased as spare parts. They include a full warranty and are sold as complete packages including cables. Table 9.12 lists some of the IBM Options keyboards and part numbers.

Table 9.12 IBM Options Keyboards (Sold Retail)

Description	Part Number
IBM enhanced keyboard (cable w/DIN plug)	92G7454
IBM enhanced keyboard (cable w/mini-DIN plug)	92G7453
IBM enhanced keyboard, built-in trackball (cable w/DIN plug)	92G7456
IBM enhanced keyboard, built-in trackball (cable w/mini-DIN plug)	92G7455
IBM enhanced keyboard, integrated trackpoint II (cables w/mini-DIN plugs)	92G7461

The IBM/Lexmark keyboards use *capacitive keyswitches*, which are the most durable and lowest maintenance. These switches have no electrical contacts and, instead, rely on changing capacitance to signal a keypress within the switch matrix. This type of design does not have wear points, like a mechanical switch, and has no metal electrical contacts, which makes it virtually immune to the dirt and corrosion problems that plague other designs.

The extremely positive tactile feedback of the IBM/Lexmark design is also a benchmark of comparison for the rest of the industry. Although keyboard feel is an issue of personal preference, I have never used a keyboard that feels better than the IBM/Lexmark designs. I now equip every system I use with a Lexmark keyboard, including the many clone or compatible systems I use. You can purchase these keyboards through Lexmark or a Lexmark distributor for very reasonable prices. You can find IBM-labeled models available from advertisers in *Processor* or *Computer Hotline* magazines selling for less than $60.

IBM/Lexmark sells other versions for very reasonable prices as well. Many different models are available, including some with a built-in trackball or even the revolutionary Trackpoint pointing device. *Trackpoint* refers to a small stick mounted between the G, H, and B keys. This device is an IBM/Lexmark exclusive and was first featured on the IBM Thinkpad laptop systems, although the keyboards are now sold for use on compatibles, and the technology is being licensed to other firms, including Toshiba. Note that this keyboard comes only with the mini-DIN type connectors for both the keyboard and Trackpoint portions, and it works only with a motherboard (PS/2 type) mouse port.

Other high-quality keyboards are available. Several companies, such as Alps, Lite-On, or NMB Technologies, manufacture keyboards similar in feel to the IBM/Lexmark units. They have excellent tactile feedback with a positive click sound. They are my second choice, after a Lexmark unit. Maxi-Switch also makes a high-quality aftermarket keyboard used by a number of compatible manufacturers, including Gateway 2000. These also have a good feel and are recommended. Many of these companies can make their keyboards with your own company logo on them (such as the Maxi-Switch models used by Gateway), which is ideal for clone manufacturers looking for name-brand recognition.

Reference Material

If you are interested in more details about keyboard design or interfacing, a company called Annabooks publishes a book/disk package called *PC Keyboard Design*. This document defines the protocol between the keyboard and computer for both XT and AT types and includes schematics and keyboard controller source code. The kit includes a license to use the source code and costs $249.

Other excellent sources of information are the various technical reference manuals put out by IBM. The vendor list contains a list of the important IBM reference manuals in which you can find much valuable information. This information is especially valuable to compatible system manufacturers, because they often do not put out the same level of technical information as IBM, and compatible systems are in many ways similar or even identical to one or more IBM systems. After all, that is why they are called IBM-compatible. Much of my personal knowledge and expertise comes from pouring over the various IBM technical reference manuals.

Mice

The mouse was invented in 1964 by Douglas Englebart, who at the time was working at the Stanford Research Institute (SRI), a think tank sponsored by Stanford University. The mouse was officially called an *X-Y Position Indicator for a Display System*. Xerox later applied the mouse to its revolutionary Alto computer system in 1973. At the time, unfortunately, these systems were experimental and used purely for research.

In 1979, several people from Apple, including Steve Jobs, were invited to see the Alto and the software that ran the system. Steve Jobs was blown away by what he saw as the future of computing, which included the use of the mouse as a pointing device and the GUI it operated. Apple promptly incorporated these features into what was to become the Lisa computer and lured away 15 to 20 Xerox scientists to work on the Apple system.

Although Xerox released the Star 8010 computer that used this technology in 1981, it was expensive, poorly marketed, and perhaps way ahead of its time. Apple released the Lisa computer, which was its first system that used the mouse, in 1983. It also was not a runaway success, largely because of its $10,000 list price, but by then Jobs already had Apple working on the low-cost successor to the Lisa, the Macintosh. The Apple Macintosh was introduced in 1984; although it was not an immediate hit, the Macintosh has grown in popularity since that time.

Many credit the Macintosh with inventing the mouse and GUI, but as you can see, this technology was actually borrowed from others, including SRI and Xerox. Certainly the Macintosh, and now Microsoft Windows and OS/2, have gone on to popularize this interface and bring it to the legion of PC-compatible systems.

Although the mouse did not catch on quickly in the PC-compatible marketplace, today the GUIs for PC systems such as Windows and OS/2 virtually demand the use of a mouse. Because of this, it is common for a mouse to be sold with nearly every new system on the market.

Mice come in many shapes and sizes from many different manufacturers. Some have taken the standard mouse design and turned it upside down, creating the *trackball*. In the trackball devices, you move the ball with your hand directly rather than the unit itself. IBM even produced a very cool mouse/trackball convertible device called the *trackpoint* (p/n 1397040). The trackpoint could be used as either a mouse (ball side down), or as a track ball (ball side up). In most cases, the dedicated trackballs have a much larger ball than would be found on a standard mouse. Other than the orientation and perhaps the size of the ball, a trackball is identical to a mouse in design, basic function, and electrical interface.

The largest manufacturers of mice are Microsoft and Logitech. Even though mice may come in different varieties, their actual use and care differ very little. The standard mouse consists of several components:

- A housing that you hold in your hand and move around on your desktop
- A roller ball that signals movement to the system
- Buttons (usually two) for making selections
- A cable for connecting the mouse to the system
- An interface connector to attach the mouse to the system

The housing is made of plastic and consists of very few moving parts. On top of the housing, where your fingers normally reside, are buttons. There may be any number of buttons, but in the PC world there are typically only two. If additional buttons are on your mouse, specialized software is required for them to operate. On the bottom of the housing is a small rubber ball that rotates as you move the mouse across the tabletop. The movements of this rubber ball are translated into electrical signals transmitted to the computer across the cable. Some mice use a special optical sensor that detects movement over a grid. These optical mice have fallen into disfavor because they work only if you use a special grid pad underneath them.

The cable can be any length, but is typically between four and six feet long.

> **Tip**
>
> If you have a choice on the length of cable to purchase, go for a longer one. This allows easier placement of the mouse in relation to your computer.

The connector used with your mouse depends on the type of interface you are using. Three basic interfaces are used, with a fourth combination device possible as well.

After the mouse is connected to your computer, it communicates with your system through the use of a *device driver*, which can be either separately loaded or built into the system software. For example, no separate drivers are needed to use a mouse with Windows or OS/2, but using the mouse with most DOS-based programs requires a separate driver to be loaded. Regardless of whether it is built in, the driver translates the electrical signals sent from the mouse into positional information and information that indicates the status of the buttons.

Internally, a mouse is very simple as well. The ball usually rests against two rollers, one for translating the X-axis movement and the other for the Y-axis. These rollers are usually connected to small disks with shutters that alternately block and allow the passage of light. Small optical sensors detect movement of the wheels by watching an internal infrared light blink on and off as the shutter wheel rotates and "chops" the light. These blinks are translated into movement along the axes. This type of setup is called an *opto-mechanical mechanism* and is by far the most popular in use today (see Figure 9.13).

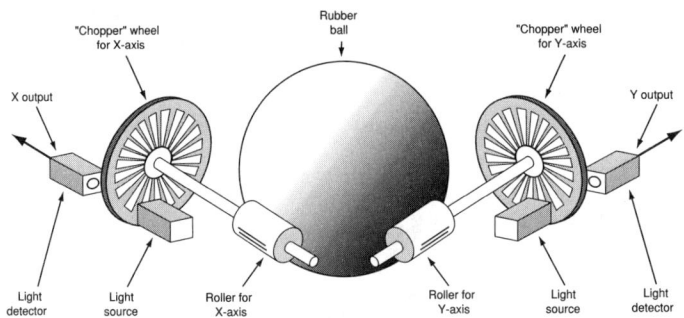

FIG. 9.13 Typical opto-mechanical mouse mechanism.

Microsoft IntelliMouse

Late in 1996, Microsoft introduced a new variation of its popular mouse, called the *IntelliMouse*. This device looks exactly like the standard Microsoft mouse except for a miniature gray wheel rising up between the left and right buttons. This wheel represents the only major change in mouse design for many years.

The wheel has two main functions. The primary function is to act as a scrolling device, allowing one to scroll through documents or Web pages by merely pulling down or pushing up with your index finger. It can also function as a third mouse button when you press it.

Although there have been three-button mice available for years, the scrolling function is a real breakthrough. No longer do you have to move the mouse pointer to click the scroll bar on the right hand side of your screen or take your right hand off of the mouse to use the arrow keys on the keyboard; instead, all you have to do is push up or pull down on the wheel! This is a major convenience, especially when browsing Web pages or working with word processing documents or spreadsheets. Also, unlike three-button mice from other vendors, the IntelliMouse's wheel-button doesn't seem to get in the way, and you are less likely to click it by mistake.

One drawback to the IntelliMouse is that the new wheel will only function in software that is rewritten to support it. At the time the IntelliMouse debuted, Microsoft Internet Explorer was already modified to use the new wheel, and all of the applications in Office 97 support it as well. For example, besides just the scrolling capability, most Office 97 applications also allow you to hold down the Ctrl key while turning the wheel to zoom in and out. The wheel and Shift key can also be used to expand and collapse outlines as well. As new and updated versions of other software comes out, you can expect that they will also support the new wheel functions.

The IntelliMouse 2.0 driver combines features from earlier versions of Microsoft's mouse driver with some interesting new functions. A feature called *ClickLock* allows you to drag items without holding down the left mouse button. You can customize this feature by specifying how long you have to hold the button down to activate ClickLock. The wheel can also be set to scroll a specified number of lines or a screen with each click of the wheel.

You can also set the driver software so that the wheel-button ignores all such application-specific actions and instead performs one of four preset functions in all Windows applications. The four choices are:

- Double-left-click
- Opening an application's help file
- Switching to Windows Explorer
- Bringing up the Start menu

Other driver features retained from earlier versions include a Snap To feature, which moves the pointer to the default button of a dialog box, and a function that adds trails when the pointer moves and also makes the pointer disappear when you start typing.

Mouse Interface Types

Mice can be connected to your computer through the following three interfaces:

- Serial interface
- Dedicated motherboard mouse port
- Bus-card interface

Serial. A popular method of connecting a mouse to most older PC-compatible computers is through a *serial* interface. As with other serial devices, the connector on the end of the mouse cable is either a 9-pin or 25-pin male connector. Only a couple of pins in the DB-9 or DB-25 connectors are used for communications between the mouse and the device driver, but the mouse connector typically has all 9 or 25 pins present.

Because most PCs come with two serial ports, a serial mouse can be plugged into either COM1: or COM2:. The device driver, when initializing, searches the ports to determine the one to which the mouse is connected.

Because a serial mouse does not connect to the system directly, it does not use system resources by itself. Instead, the resources used are those used by the serial port to which it is connected. For example, if you have a mouse connected to COM2, it most likely uses IRQ3 and I/O port addresses 2F8h-2FFh.

Motherboard Mouse Port (PS/2). Most newer computers now come with a dedicated mouse port built into the motherboard. This was started by IBM with the PS/2 systems in 1987, so this interface is often referred to as a *PS/2 mouse interface*. This term does not imply that such a mouse can work only with a PS/2; instead, it means that the mouse can connect to any system that has a dedicated mouse port on the motherboard.

A motherboard mouse connector usually is exactly the same as the mini-DIN connector used for newer keyboards. In fact, the motherboard mouse port is connected to the 8042-type keyboard controller found on the motherboard. All the PS/2 computers include mini-DIN keyboard and mouse port connectors on the back. Most compatible Slimline computers also have these same connectors for space reasons. Other motherboards have a pin-header type connector for the mouse port because most standard cases do not have a provision for the mini-DIN mouse connector. In that case, an adapter cable is usually supplied with the system that adapts the pin-header connector on the motherboard to the standard mini-DIN type connector used for the motherboard mouse.

Connecting a mouse to the built-in mouse port is the best method of connection because you do not lose any interface slots or any serial ports, and the performance is not limited by the serial port circuitry. The standard resource usage for a motherboard (or PS/2) mouse port is IRQ 12 and I/O port addresses 60h and 64h. Because the motherboard mouse port uses the 8042-type keyboard controller chip, the port addresses are those of this chip. IRQ 12 is an interrupt that is usually free on most systems and, of course, must remain free on any ISA bus systems that have a motherboard mouse port because interrupt sharing is not allowed with the ISA bus.

Serial and Motherboard Mouse Port (PS/2). A hybrid type of mouse can plug into both a serial port or a motherboard mouse port connection. This combination serial-PS/2 mouse is the most popular type because it is more flexible than the single design types. Circuitry in this mouse automatically detects the type of port to which it is connected and configures the mouse automatically. These mice usually come with a mini-DIN connector on the end of their cable and also include an adapter between the mini-DIN to a 9- or 25-pin serial port connector.

Sometimes people use adapters to try to connect a serial mouse to a motherboard mouse port, or a motherboard mouse to a serial port. This does not work and is not the fault of the adapter. If the mouse does not explicitly state that it is both a serial-PS/2 type mouse, it does not work on either interface but instead works only on the single interface for which it was designed. Most of the time, you find the designation for what type of mouse you have printed on the bottom of it.

Bus. A *bus* mouse is typically used in systems that do not have a motherboard mouse port or any available serial ports. The name *bus mouse* is derived from the fact that the mouse requires a special bus interface board that occupies a slot in your computer and communicates with the device driver across the main motherboard bus. Although the use of a bus mouse is transparent to the user (there is no operational difference between a bus mouse and other types of mice), many people view a bus mouse as less desirable than other types because it occupies a slot that could be used for other peripherals.

Another drawback to the bus mouse is that it is electrically incompatible with the other types of mice. Because it is not very popular, a bus mouse can be hard to find in a pinch. Likewise, the bus adapters are typically available only for ISA slots; because they are always 8-bit cards, you are limited in the choice of nonconflicting hardware interrupts. A bus mouse can also be dangerous because it uses a mini-DIN connector just like the motherboard (PS/2)-type mouse, although they are totally incompatible. I have even heard of people damaging motherboards by plugging a bus mouse into a motherboard mouse connector.

Bus mouse adapter cards usually have a selectable interrupt and I/O port address setting, but the IRQ selection is limited to only 8-bit interrupts. This usually means that you must choose IRQ 5 in most systems that already have two serial ports because all the other 8-bit interrupts will be used. If you also are using another 8-bit-only card that needs an interrupt, like some of the sound cards, you will not be able to run both devices in the same system without conflicts. All in all, I do not recommend bus mice and think they should be avoided.

> **Note**
>
> Microsoft sometimes calls a bus mouse an *inport mouse*, which is its proprietary name for a bus mouse connection.

Mouse Troubleshooting

If you are experiencing problems with your mouse, you need to look in only two general places—hardware or software. Because mice are basically simple devices, looking at the hardware takes very little time. Detecting and correcting software problems can take a bit longer, however.

Hardware Problems. Two types of hardware problems can crop up when you are using a mouse. The most common is a dirty mouse, which is fixed by doing some "mouse cleaning." The other relates to interrupt conflicts and is more difficult to solve.

Cleaning Your Mouse. If you notice that the mouse pointer moves across the screen in a jerky fashion, it may be time to clean your mouse. This jerkiness is caused when dirt and dust get trapped around the mouse's ball and roller assembly, thereby restricting its free movement.

From a hardware perspective, the mouse is a simple device, and cleaning it is also very simple. The first step is to turn the mouse housing over so that you can see the ball on the bottom. Notice that surrounding the ball is an access panel that you can open. There may even be some instructions that indicate how the panel is to be opened. (Some off-brand mice may require you to remove some screws to get at the roller ball.) Remove the panel, and you can see more of the roller ball and the socket in which it rests.

If you turn the mouse back over, the rubber roller ball should fall into your hand. Take a look at the ball. It may be gray or black, but it should have no visible dirt or other contamination. If it does, wash it in soapy water or a mild solvent such as contact cleaner solution or alcohol and dry it off.

Now take a look at the socket in which the roller ball normally rests. You will see two or three small wheels or bars against which the ball normally rolls. If you see dust or dirt on or around these wheels or bars, you need to clean them. The best way is to use a compressed air duster can to blow out any dust or dirt. You also can use some electrical contact cleaner to clean the rollers. Remember, any remaining dirt or dust impedes the movement of the roller ball and means that the mouse will not work as it should.

Put the mouse back together by inserting the roller ball into the socket and then securely attaching the cover panel. The mouse should look just like it did before you removed the panel except that it will be noticeably cleaner.

Chapter 9—Input Devices

Interrupt Conflicts. *Interrupts* are internal signals used by your computer to indicate when something needs to happen. With a mouse, an interrupt is used whenever the mouse has information to send to the mouse driver. If a conflict occurs and the same interrupt used by the mouse is used by a different device, the mouse will not work properly, if at all.

Interrupt conflicts do not normally occur if your system uses a mouse port, but they can occur with the other types of mouse interfaces. Mouse ports built into modern motherboards are almost always set to IRQ 12. If your system has a motherboard mouse port, be sure that that you don't set any other adapter cards to IRQ 12 or a conflict will result.

If you are using a serial mouse, interrupt conflicts typically occur if you add a third and fourth serial port. This is because in ISA bus systems, odd-numbered serial ports (1 and 3) are often improperly configured to use the same interrupts as the even-numbered ports (2 and 4). Thus, if your mouse is connected to COM2: and an internal modem uses COM4:, they both may use the same interrupt, and you cannot use them at the same time. You may be able to use the mouse and modem at the same time by moving one of them to a different serial port. For instance, if your mouse uses COM1: and the modem still uses COM4:, you can use them both at once because odd and even ports use different interrupts.

The best way around these interrupt conflicts is to make sure that no two devices use the same interrupt. Serial port adapters are available for adding COM3: and COM4: serial ports that do not share the interrupts used by COM1: and COM2:. These boards enable the new COM ports to use other normally available interrupts, such as IRQs 10, 11, 12, 15, or 5. I never recommend configuring a system with shared interrupts; it is a sure way to run into problems later.

If you suspect an interrupt problem with a bus-type mouse, you can use the Device Manager built into Windows 95 or even a program such as Microsoft's MicroSoft Diagnostics (MSD) to help you identify what interrupt the mouse is set to. You get MSD free with Windows 3.0 or higher as well as MS-DOS 6.0 or higher. If you use OS/2 and/or PC DOS, you can still get MSD for free by downloading it from the Microsoft BBS (see the vendor list).

Beware that programs like MSD that attempt to identify IRQ usage are not always 100 percent accurate—in fact they are inaccurate in many cases—and usually require that the device driver for the particular device be loaded to work at all.

The Device Manager in Windows 95 is part of the Plug and Play (PnP) software for the system, and is usually 100 percent accurate on PnP hardware. Although some of these interrupt-reporting programs can have problems, most will easily identify the mouse IRQ if the mouse driver has been loaded. After the IRQ is identified, you may need to change the IRQ setting of the bus mouse adapter or one or more other devices in your system so that everything works together properly.

If your driver refuses to recognize the mouse at all, regardless of its type, try using a different mouse that you know works. Replacing a defective mouse with a known good one may be the only way to identify if the problem is indeed caused by a bad mouse.

I have had problems in which a bad mouse caused the system to lock just as the driver loaded or even when diagnostics such as MSD attempted to access the mouse. You can easily ferret out this type of problem by loading MSD with the /I option, which causes MSD to bypass its initial hardware detection. Then run each of the tests separately, including the mouse test, to see whether the system locks. If the system locks during the mouse test, you have found a problem with either the mouse or the mouse port. Try replacing the mouse to see whether that helps. If does not, you may need to replace the serial port or bus mouse adapter. If a motherboard-based mouse port goes bad, you can replace the entire motherboard—usually expensive—or you can just disable the motherboard mouse port via jumpers or the system setup program and install a serial or bus mouse instead. This enables you to continue using the system without having to replace the motherboard.

Software Problems. Software problems can be a little trickier than hardware problems. Software problems generally manifest themselves as the mouse "just not working." In such instances, you need to check the driver and your software applications before assuming that the mouse itself has gone bad.

Driver Software. To function properly, the mouse requires the installation of a device driver. Under DOS, you have to load the driver manually through your CONFIG.SYS or AUTOEXEC.BAT file, but under Windows the driver is automatically loaded. I normally recommend using the default drivers built into the Windows or OS/2 operating environments, meaning in those environments no additional external driver is necessary. The only reason for loading an external driver (via CONFIG.SYS) is if you want the mouse to work with DOS applications.

If you need the mouse to work under standard DOS—in other words, outside Windows or OS/2—you must load a device driver through either your CONFIG.SYS file or your AUTOEXEC.BAT file. This driver, if loaded in the CONFIG.SYS file, is typically called MOUSE.SYS. The version that loads in the AUTOEXEC.BAT file is called MOUSE.COM. (It is possible that your mouse drivers have different names, depending on who manufactured your mouse.) Again, remember that if you only use a mouse under Windows or OS/2, no external drivers are required because the mouse driver is built in.

The first step is to make sure that the proper command to load the driver is in your CONFIG.SYS or AUTOEXEC.BAT file. If it is not, add the proper line, according to the information supplied with your mouse. For instance, the proper command to load the mouse driver through the CONFIG.SYS file for a Microsoft mouse is as follows:

```
DEVICEHIGH=\DOS\MOUSE.SYS
```

The actual working or syntax of the command may vary, depending on whether you are loading the device into upper memory and where the device driver is located on your disk.

One of the biggest problems with the separate mouse driver is getting it loaded into an Upper Memory Block (UMB). The older drivers—9.0 and earlier—require a very large block of 40K to 56K UMB to load into, and upon loading they shrink down to less than 20K. Even though they only take 20K or less after loading, you still need a very large area to get them "in the door."

The best tip I can give you with respect to these separate drivers is to use the newest 9.01 or higher drivers from Microsoft. This new driver is included with the newer Microsoft mice, and is also sold separately as an upgrade. The Microsoft driver works with any type of Microsoft-compatible mouse, which basically means just about any mouse at all. Microsoft requires that you pay about $50 for an upgrade to the newer versions of the mouse driver. You can also get the new driver with a new mouse for $35 or less, which makes the driver-only purchase not very cost-effective. Microsoft still includes only the older driver with DOS 6.22 or earlier. IBM included the new driver with PC DOS 6.3 but switched back to the 8.2 driver in PC DOS 7.0.

If you use version 9.01 or later, it will require less memory than previous versions and will automatically load itself into high memory as well. One of the best features is that it first loads itself into low memory, shrinks down to about 24K, and then moves into upper memory automatically. Not only that, but the driver seeks out the smallest UMB that can hold it, instead of trying only the largest, as would happen if you use the DEVICEHIGH, LOADHIGH, or LH commands to load the driver. Previous versions of the driver could not fit into an upper memory block unless that block was at least 40K to 56K or larger in size, and would certainly not do it automatically. The enhanced self-loading capability of the mouse driver 9.01 and higher can save much memory space and is very much worth having. I hope that this type of self-loading and self-optimizing technique will be used in other device drivers. It will make memory management much easier than it currently is.

After placing the proper driver load command in your CONFIG.SYS or AUTOEXEC.BAT file, reboot the system with the mouse connected and observe that the driver loads properly. If the proper command is in place and the driver is not loading, watch your video screen as your system boots. At some point, you should see a message from the mouse driver indicating that it is loaded. If instead you see a message indicating that the loading was not done, you must determine why. For example, the driver may not be able to load because not enough memory is available. After you determine why it is not loading, you need to rectify the situation and make sure that the driver loads. Again, the new 9.01 or higher driver versions help greatly with memory problems.

It is also possible that some software requires a certain mouse device driver. If you are using an older mouse driver and your application software requires a newer-version mouse driver, the mouse may not work properly. In such cases, contact your mouse vendor directly and request a mouse driver update. Often you can get these through the vendor's BBS or on CompuServe; however, Microsoft charges for its new drivers and does not make them available on its BBS. In that case, it is cheaper to purchase an entire new mouse, which includes the new driver, rather than just the driver upgrade.

Application Software. If your mouse does not work with a specific piece of application software, check the setup information or configuration section of the program. Make sure that you indicated to the program (if necessary) that you are using a mouse. If it still does not work and the mouse works with other software you are using, contact the technical support department of the application software company.

Trackpoint II/III

On October 20, 1992, IBM introduced a revolutionary new pointing device called *TrackPoint II* as an integrated feature of its new ThinkPad 700 and 700C computers. Often referred to as a *pointing stick* device, it consists primarily of a small rubber cap that appears on the keyboard right above the B key, between the G and H keys. This was the first significant new pointing device since the mouse had been invented nearly 30 years earlier!

This device occupies no space on a desk, does not have to be adjusted for left-handed or right-handed use, has no moving parts to fail or become dirty, and—most important—does not require you to move your hands from the home row to use. This is an absolute boon for anybody who is a good typist.

I was fortunate enough to meet the actual creator and designer of this device in early 1992 at the spring COMDEX/Windows World in Chicago. He was in a small corner of the IBM booth showing off his custom-made keyboards with a small silicone rubber nub in the middle. In fact, the devices he had were hand-built prototypes installed in standard desktop keyboards, and he was there trying to get public reaction and feedback on his invention.

I was invited to play with one of the keyboards, which was connected to a demonstration system. By pressing on the stick with my index finger, I could move the mouse pointer on the screen. The stick itself did not move and as such is not a joystick. Instead it had a silicone rubber cap that was connected to pressure transducers that measured the amount of force my finger was applying and the direction of the force and moved the mouse pointer accordingly. The harder I pressed, the faster the pointer moved. I could move the pointer in any direction smoothly, by slightly changing the direction of push or pull. The silicone rubber gripped my finger even though I had been sweating from dashing about the show. After playing around with it for just a few minutes, the movements became automatic—almost as if I could just "think" about where I wanted the pointer to go.

After reflecting on this for a minute, it really hit me: This had to be the most revolutionary pointing device since the mouse itself! Not only would this be a natural replacement for a mouse, but it would also be a boon for touch typists like me who don't like to take their hands off of the keyboard.

The gentleman at the booth turned out to be Ted Selker, the primary inventor of the device. He and Joseph Rutledge created this integrated pointing device at the IBM T.J. Watson Research Center. When I asked him when such keyboards would become available, he could not answer. At the time, there were apparently no plans for production, and he was only trying to test user reaction to the device.

Just over six months later, IBM announced the *Thinkpad 700*, which included this revolutionary device, then called the Trackpoint II Integrated Pointing Device. Since the original version came out, an enhanced version with greater control and sensitivity called the *Trackpoint III* has become available.

> **Note**
>
> The reason the device was called trackpoint II is that IBM had previously been selling a convertible mouse/trackball device called the trackpoint. No relationship exists between the original trackpoint mouse/trackball, which has since been discontinued, and the trackpoint II integrated device. Since the original Trackpoint II came out, an improved version called Trackpoint III is now available. It is basically an improved version of the same thing. In the interest of simplicity, I will refer to all of the Trackpoint II, III, and successive devices as just trackpoint.

In final production form, the trackpoint consisted of a small red silicone rubber knob nestled between the G, H, and B keys on the keyboard. Two buttons are placed below the space bar to emulate the LH and RH mouse buttons for making selections. These buttons also can be easily reached by your thumbs without taking your hand off the keyboard.

IBM studies conducted by Selker found that the act of removing your hand from the keyboard, reaching for a mouse, and replacing the hand on the keyboard takes approximately 1.75 seconds. If you type 60 wpm, that can equal nearly two lost words, plus in that time you can lose your train of thought. Almost all this time can be saved each time the trackpoint is used to either move the pointer or make a selection (click or double-click). The combination of the buttons and the positioning knob also enable drag and drop functions to be performed easily as well.

IBM's research also found that people can get up to 20 percent more work accomplished using the trackpoint instead of a mouse, especially where the application involves a mix of typing and pointing activities such as with word processing, spreadsheets, and other typical office applications. In usability tests with the Trackpoint III, IBM gave a number of them to desktop computer users, along with a mouse. After two weeks, 80 percent of the users had unplugged their mice and switched solely to the trackpoint device. Selker is convinced (as am I) that the trackpoint is the best pointing solution for both laptop and desktop systems as well.

Another feature of the trackpoint is that a mouse can be connected to the system to allow for dual-pointer use. In this case, a single mouse pointer would still be on the screen; however, both the Trackpoint and the simultaneously connected mouse could move the pointer. This allows not only the use of both devices by a single person, but in fact two people can use both the Trackpoint and the mouse simultaneously to move the pointer on the screen. The first pointing device that moves takes precedence and retains control over the mouse pointer on the screen until it completes a movement action. The second pointing device is automatically locked out until the primary device is stationary. This enables both devices to be used, but prevents each one from interfering with the other.

Recognizing the significance of the Trackpoint especially for portable systems, several other manufacturers of laptop and notebook portable computers such as Toshiba and TI have licensed the trackpoint pointing device from IBM. Often they will give it a different name, although the technology and operation is the same. For example Toshiba calls it Accupoint on its systems.

I have compared the trackpoint device to other pointing devices for notebooks, such as the trackballs and even the capacitive touch pads, and nothing compares for accuracy, control, and of course the fact that you don't have to take your hands off of the keyboard!

Unfortunately, many of the lower-end portable system manufacturers have chosen not to license the IBM trackpoint technology, but instead have attempted to copy it using inferior transducers and control software. The major drawback to these non-licensed trackpoint type devices is that they simply do not perform as well as the official versions licensed from IBM. They are usually slow to respond, sluggish in operation, and lack the sensitivity and accuracy found in the IBM designed versions.

One way of telling that the trackpoint device is licensed from IBM and uses the IBM technology is that it will accept IBM Trackpoint II or III rubber caps. These have a square hole in them and will properly lock on to any of the licensed versions such as those found in Toshiba systems.

IBM recently upgraded this system and now calls it Trackpoint III. There are two main differences in the III system over the II, but the one that is directly noticeable is the rubber cap itself. IBM always uses red caps in their Trackpoint device while other companies use different colors (Toshiba uses green or gray), although the color itself is unimportant. In any case, the main difference in the new Trackpoint III caps is in the rubber composition, not the color.

The IBM Trackpoint II and Toshiba Accupoint caps are made out of silicone rubber, which is grippy and works well in most situations. However, if the user has greasy fingers, the textured surface of the rubber can absorb some of the grease and become slippery. Cleaning the cap (and the user's hands) solves the problem, but it can be annoying at times. The new Trackpoint III caps are made out of a different type of rubber, which Selker calls "plastic sandpaper." This type of cap is much more grippy, and does not require cleaning except for cosmetic purposes. I have used both types of caps and can say for certain that the Trackpoint III cap is superior!

> **Note**
>
> Since the Accupoint device used in the Toshiba notebooks is licensed from IBM, it uses the same hardware (a pressure transducer called a strain gauge) and takes the same physical caps as IBM's product. What I did was order a set of the new Trackpoint III caps and install them on my Toshiba portable systems, which dramatically improved the grip. You can get these caps by ordering them from IBM Parts directly or from others who sell IBM parts such as DakTech under IBM part number 84G6536; the cost is approximately $9 for a set of two "plastic sandpaper" red caps.

Replacing the cap is easy—simply grab the existing cap with your fingers and pull straight up; it will pop right off. Then push on the new red IBM Trackpoint III cap in its place. You will thank me when you feel how you can grip the new IBM cap much more easily than compared to the designs used by others.

The other difference between the Trackpoint II and III from IBM is in the control software. IBM added routines that implement a subtle technique Selker calls "negative inertia," but which is marketed under the term *QuickStop response*. This software not only takes into account how far you push the pointer in any direction, but also how quickly you push or release it. Selker found that this improved software (and the sandpaper cap) allows people to make selections up to 8 percent faster.

The trackpoint is obviously an ideal pointing device for a laptop system where lugging around an external mouse or trackball can be a pain. The trackballs and mini-trackballs built into some laptop keyboards are also very difficult to use and usually require removing your hands from the home row. Mouse and trackball devices are notorious for becoming "sticky" as the ball picks up dirt that affects the internal roller motion. This is especially aggravated with the smaller mini-trackball devices.

Many newer notebook systems include a touch pad, which although it seems like a good idea at first, pales in comparison to the trackpoint. The touch pads work on a capacitive effect, and pointer operation can become erratic if your skin is either too dry or too moist. Their biggest drawback is that they are positioned on the keyboard below the spacebar, which means you either have to remove your hand from the home row to place your index finger on the pad, or try to use the pad with your thumb, which has too wide a contact area for precise movement and control.

The bottom line is that anybody who touch types should strongly consider only notebook systems which include an IBM-licensed trackpoint device (such as Toshiba). trackpointers are far superior to other pointing devices such as the touch pads, because the trackpoint is faster to use (you don't have to take your hands off of the home row on the keyboard), easier to adapt to (especially for speedy touch typists), and far more precise.

But the benefits of the trackpoint are not limited to laptop systems. Because I use a notebook so often and have found the Trackpoint system so fast and easy to use, I also wanted to use it on my desktop systems as well. For desktop systems I use a Lexmark keyboard with the IBM-licensed trackpoint device built-in. This makes for a more consistent interface between desktop and notebook use because I can use the same pointing device in both environments. One drawback for some older systems is that the Track-point device in these keyboards works only with systems that used a PS/2- or motherboard-type mouse connector; no serial version is available. I list the part number for the IBM enhanced keyboard with the trackpoint in the section "Replacement Keyboards" earlier in this chapter. You can also purchase these keyboards directly from Lexmark.

The trackpoint probably stands as the most important and revolutionary new pointing device since the original invention of the mouse. As IBM licenses this technology to other manufacturers, you will see this device show up in many different systems. It is already available built into keyboards, which can upgrade many existing systems, and companies such as Toshiba are using this IBM-developed technology in their own systems.

Glidepoint

In response to the trackpoint, other companies have adopted new pointing device technology as well. For example, Alps Electric has introduced a touch pad pointing device called the *glidepoint*. The glidepoint uses a flat square pad, which senses finger position through body capacitance. This is similar to the capacitance-sensitive elevator button controls you sometimes encounter in office buildings or hotels. Instead of sitting in between the keys, the glidepoint is mounted below the space bar, and detects pressure applied by your thumbs or fingers. Transducers under the pad convert finger movement into pointer movement. Several laptop and notebook manufacturers have licensed this technology from Alps and are incorporating it into their portable systems. Apple was one of the first to adopt it in its portable systems.

Although it seems to have gained wide acceptance, this technology has a number of drawbacks. Operation of the device can be erratic depending on skin resistance and moisture content. The biggest drawback is that to operate the touch pad, users have to remove their hands from the home row on the keyboard, which dramatically slows them down. In addition, the operation of the touch pad can be imprecise depending on how pointy your finger or thumb is!

On the other hand, if you're not touch typist, then removing your hands from the keyboard to operate the touch pad may be easier than using a trackpointer. Even with its drawbacks, touch pad type pointing devices are still vastly preferred for portable systems over using a trackball or a cumbersome external mouse.

Game Adapter (Joystick) Interface

The *game control* or *joystick* adapter is a special input device that enables up to four paddles or two joysticks to be attached to a PC system. The term *paddle* is used to refer to a knob that can be rotated to move an object on the screen, and was named after the first popular videogame called Pong, where the knob moved the game paddles.

The game adapter function can be found on a dedicated ISA or MCA bus adapter card, or can be combined with other functions in a multifunction card. The game connector on the card is a female 15-pin D-Shell type socket (see Figure 9.14).

The game adapter can recognize up to four switches (called *buttons*) and four resistive inputs. Each paddle normally has one button and one knob that controls a variable resistor, whereas a joystick normally has two buttons and a central stick that controls two variable resistors. In a joystick, the variable resistors are tied to the central stick. One indicates the relative vertical position (or x-coordinate) of the stick, and the other indicates its relative horizontal position (or y-coordinate).

Resistor inputs are variable from 0 to 100K ohms. The adapter converts the resistive value to a digital pulse with a duration proportional to the resistive load. Software can time these pulses to determine the relative resistance value. The game adapter does not use much in the way of system resources. The card does not use an IRQ, DMA channel, or memory and requires only a single I/O address (port) 201h. The adapter is controlled by reading and writing data to and from port 201h.

FIG. 9.14 Typical game adapter and 15-pin connector.

Note that joystick resistance is read by polling the adapter; the game port interface is not interrupt driven. This means that a program has to scan the device by sending an I/O command for input rather than by receiving an interrupt as with other (such as serial) devices.

Table 9.13 shows the interface connector pinout specification for a PC-compatible game adapter.

Table 9.13	PC-Compatible Game Adapter Connector		
Pin	**Signal**	**Function**	**I/O**
1	+5v	Paddle 1, Joystick A	Out
2	Button 4	Paddle 1 button, Joystick A button #1	In
3	Position 0	Paddle 1 position, Joystick A x-coordinate	In
4	Ground	—	—
5	Ground	—	—
6	Position 1	Paddle 2 position, Joystick A y-coordinate	In

Pin	Signal	Function	I/O
7	Button 5	Paddle 2 button, Joystick A button #2	In
8	+5v	Paddle 2	Out
9	+5v	Paddle 3 and Joystick B	Out
10	Button 6	Paddle 3 button, Joystick B button #1	In
11	Position 2	Paddle 3 position, Joystick B x-coordinate	In
12	Ground	—	—
13	Position 3	Paddle 4 position, Joystick B y-coordinate	In
14	Button 7	Paddle 4 button, Joystick B button #2	In
15	+5v	Paddle 4	Out

Because this adapter actually reads resistance and can be easily manipulated with standard programming languages, the game adapter serves as a poor man's data acquisition board or real-time interface card. With it, you can hook up to four sensors and four switches and easily read the data in the PC.

Game adapters are available for ISA and MCA bus systems from a number of vendors. Consult the vendor list for some companies that may offer these types of adapters. Generally, the best place to look is one of the larger mail order system and peripheral vendors.

Some manufacturers have produced specialized joysticks that really don't look like joysticks at all. Perhaps the best known of these are the steering wheel and pedal control sets sold for use with driving and flight simulator games. These are really exactly the same as the standard joystick and paddles as far as your system is concerned. Instead of paddle knobs, they have steering wheels and pedals controlling the variable resistors in the circuit. There are a number of these devices on the market for the popular driving and flight simulator games, and they can make these games much more realistic. Because the different controls can be connected to different paddle inputs on the game adapters, make sure that your software will support the particular control device you select.

Chapter 10

Video Display Hardware

Your monitor provides the link between you and your computer. Although you can possibly get rid of your printer, disk drives, and expansion cards, you cannot sacrifice the monitor. Without it, you would be operating blind; you could not see the results of your calculations or the mistyped words on-screen.

The first microcomputers were small boxes that lacked displays. Instead, users observed the information contained in system registers via banks of flashing LEDs and waited for the final output to be printed. All interaction with the system was normally done through a typewriter terminal. When the CRT (cathode ray tube) terminal or monitor was finally added as an interface, the computer became more attractive to a wider audience. This visual trend in user interface technology continues today with the adoption of graphical user interfaces such as Windows over text-based systems like DOS.

The video subsystem of a PC consists of two main components:

- Monitor (or video display)
- Video adapter (also called the video card or graphics card)

This chapter explores the range of available PC-compatible video adapters and the displays that work with them.

Monitors

The *monitor* is, of course, the display located on top of, near, or inside your computer. Like any computer device, a monitor requires a source of input. The signals that run to your monitor come from video circuitry inside or plugged into your computer. Some computers—such as those that use the low profile (LPX) or new low profile (NLX) motherboard form factor—usually contain this circuitry on the motherboard. Most systems, though, use Baby-AT or ATX style motherboards and normally incorporate the video on a separate circuit board that is plugged into an expansion or bus slot. The expansion cards that produce video signals are called *video cards*, *video adapters*, or *graphics cards*. Whether the video circuit is built into the motherboard or on a separate card, the circuitry operates the same way and uses generally the same components.

Display Technologies

A monitor may use one of several display technologies. By far the most popular is cathode ray tube (CRT) technology, the same technology used in television sets. CRTs consist of a vacuum tube enclosed in glass. One end of the tube contains an electron gun; the other end contains a screen with a phosphorous coating.

When heated, the electron gun emits a stream of high-speed electrons that are attracted to the other end of the tube. Along the way, a focus control and deflection coil steer the beam to a specific point on the phosphorous screen. When struck by the beam, the phosphor glows. This light is what you see when you watch TV or your computer screen.

The phosphor chemical has a quality called *persistence*, which indicates how long this glow will remain on-screen. You should have a good match between persistence and scanning frequency so that the image has less flicker (if the persistence is too low) and no ghosts (if the persistence is too high).

The electron beam moves very quickly, sweeping the screen from left to right in lines from top to bottom, in a pattern called a *raster*. The *horizontal scan rate* refers to the speed at which the electron beam moves across the screen.

During its sweep, the beam strikes the phosphor wherever an image should appear on-screen. The beam also varies by intensity in order to produce different levels of brightness. Because the glow fades almost immediately, the electron beam must continue to sweep the screen to maintain an image—a practice called *redrawing* or *refreshing* the screen.

Most displays have an ideal *refresh rate* (also called a *vertical scan frequency*) of about 70 hertz (Hz), meaning that the screen is refreshed 70 times a second. Low refresh rates cause the screen to flicker, contributing to eye strain. The higher the refresh rate, the better for your eyes.

It is important that the scan rates expected by your monitor match those produced by your video card. If you have mismatched rates, you cannot see an image and may actually damage your monitor.

Some monitors have a fixed refresh rate. Other monitors may support a range of frequencies; this support provides built-in compatibility with future video standards (described in the "Video Cards" section later in this chapter). A monitor that supports many video standards is called a *multiple-frequency monitor*. Most monitors today are multiple-frequency monitors, which means that they support operation with a variety of popular video signal standards. Different vendors call their multiple-frequency monitors by different names, including multisync, multifrequency, multiscan, autosynchronous, and autotracking.

Phosphor-based screens come in two styles—*curved* and *flat*. The typical display screen is curved, meaning that it bulges outward from the middle of the screen. This design is consistent with the vast majority of CRT designs (the same as the tube in your television set).

The traditional screen is curved both vertically and horizontally. Some models use the *Trinitron design*, which is curved only horizontally and is flat vertically. Many people prefer this flatter screen because it results in less glare and a higher-quality, more accurate image. The disadvantage is that the technology required to produce flat-screen displays is more expensive, resulting in higher prices for the monitors.

Alternative display designs are available. Borrowing technology from laptop manufacturers, some companies provide LCD (liquid-crystal display) displays. LCDs have low-glare flat screens and low power requirements (5 watts versus nearly 100 watts for an ordinary monitor). The color quality of an active-matrix LCD panel actually exceeds that of most CRT displays. At this point, however, LCD screens usually are more limited in resolution than typical CRTs and are much more expensive; for example, a 12.1-inch screen costs several thousand dollars. There are three basic LCD choices: passive-matrix monochrome, passive-matrix color, and active-matrix color. The passive-matrix designs are also available in single- and dual-scan versions.

In an LCD, a polarizing filter creates two separate light waves. In a color LCD, there is an additional filter that has three cells per each pixel—one each for displaying red, green, and blue.

The light wave passes through a liquid-crystal cell, with each color segment having its own cell. The liquid crystals are rod-shaped molecules that flow like a liquid. They enable light to pass straight through, but an electrical charge alters their orientation, as well as the orientation of light passing through them. Although monochrome LCDs do not have color filters, they can have multiple cells per pixel for controlling shades of gray.

In a passive-matrix LCD, each cell is controlled by electrical charges transmitted by transistors according to row and column positions on the screen's edge. As the cell reacts to the pulsing charge, it twists the light wave, with stronger charges twisting the light wave more. *Supertwist* refers to the orientation of the liquid crystals, comparing on mode to off mode—the greater the twist, the higher the contrast.

Charges in passive-matrix LCDs are pulsed, so the displays lack the brilliance of active-matrix, which provides a constant charge to each cell. To increase the brilliance, some vendors have turned to a new technique called *double-scan LCD*, which splits passive-matrix screens into a top half and bottom half, cutting the time between each pulse. Besides increasing the brightness, dual-scan designs also increase the response time or speed of the display, making this type more usable for video or other applications where the displayed information changes rapidly.

In an active-matrix LCD, each cell has its own transistor to charge it and twist the light wave. This provides a brighter image than passive-matrix displays because the cell can maintain a constant, rather than momentary, charge. However, active-matrix technology uses more energy than passive-matrix. With a dedicated transistor for every cell, active-matrix displays are more difficult and expensive to produce.

In both active- and passive-matrix LCDs, the second polarizing filter controls how much light passes through each cell. Cells twist the wavelength of light to closely match the filter's allowable wavelength. The more light that passes through the filter at each cell, the brighter the pixel.

Monochrome LCDs achieve gray scales (up to 64) by varying the brightness of a cell or dithering cells in an on-and-off pattern. Color LCDs, on the other hand, dither the three-color cells and control their brilliance to achieve different colors on the screen. Double-scan passive-matrix LCDs have recently gained in popularity because they approach the quality of active-matrix displays but do not cost much more to produce than other passive-matrix displays.

The big problem with active-matrix LCDs is that the manufacturing yields are low, forcing higher prices. This means that many of the panels produced have more than a certain maximum number of failed transistors. The resulting low yields limit the production capacity and incur higher prices.

In the past, several hot CRTs were needed to light an LCD screen, but portable computer manufacturers now use a single tube the size of a cigarette. Light emitted from a tube gets spread evenly across an entire display using fiber-optic technology.

Thanks to supertwist and triple-supertwist LCDs, today's screens enable you to see the screen clearly from more angles with better contrast and lighting. To improve readability, especially in dim light, some laptops include *backlighting* or *edgelighting* (also called *sidelighting*). Backlit screens provide light from a panel behind the LCD. Edgelit screens get their light from the small fluorescent tubes mounted along the sides of the screen. Some older laptops excluded such lighting systems to lengthen battery life. Most modern laptops enable you to run the backlight at a reduced power setting that dims the display but allows for longer battery life.

The best color displays are *active-matrix* or *thin-film transistor (TFT)* panels, in which each pixel is controlled by three transistors (for red, green, and blue). Active-matrix–screen refreshes and redraws are immediate and accurate, with much less ghosting and blurring than in passive-matrix LCDs (which control pixels via rows and columns of transistors along the edges of the screen). Active-matrix displays are also much brighter and can easily be read at an angle.

An alternative to LCD screens is gas-plasma technology, typically known for its black and orange screens in some of the older Toshiba notebook computers. Some companies are incorporating gas-plasma technology for desktop screens and possibly color high-definition television (HDTV) flat-panel screens.

Monochrome versus Color

During the early years of the IBM PC and compatibles, owners had only two video choices—color using a CGA display adapter and monochrome using an MDA display adapter. Since then, many adapter and display options have hit the market.

Monochrome monitors produce images of one color. The most popular is amber, followed by white and green. The color of the monitor is determined by the color of the phosphors on the CRT screen. Some monochrome monitors with white phosphors can support many shades of gray.

Color monitors use more sophisticated technology than monochrome monitors, which accounts for their higher prices. Whereas a monochrome picture tube contains one electron gun, a color tube contains three guns arranged in a triangular shape referred to as a *delta configuration*. Instead of amber, white, or green phosphors, the monitor screen contains phosphor triads, which consist of one red phosphor, one green phosphor, and one blue phosphor arranged in the same pattern as the electron guns. These three primary colors can be mixed to produce all other colors.

The Right Size

Monitors come in different sizes, ranging from 9-inch to 42-inch diagonal measure. The larger the monitor, the higher the price tag. The most common monitor sizes are 14, 15, 17, and 21 inches. These diagonal measurements, unfortunately, represent not the actual screen that will be displayed but the size of the tube. As a result, comparing one company's 15-inch monitor to that of another may be unfair unless you actually measure the active screen area. This area can vary slightly from monitor to monitor, so one company's 17-inch monitor may display a 15.0-inch image, and another company's 17-inch monitor may present a 15.5-inch image.

The following table shows the advertised monitor diagonal size along with the approximate diagonal measure of the actual active viewing area for the most common display sizes:

Monitor Size (in Inches)	Viewing Area (in Inches)
12	10.5
14	12.5
15	13.5
16	14.5
17	15.5
18	16.5
19	17.5
20	18.5
21	19.5

The size of the actual viewable area varies slightly from manufacturer to manufacturer, but these figures are representative of most monitors. As you can see, the viewable area of a monitor is normally about 1.5 inches less than the advertised specification. The viewing area refers to the diagonal measure of the lighted area on the screen. In other words, if you are running Windows, the viewing area is the actual diagonal measure of the desktop.

In most cases, the 17-inch monitor is currently the best bargain in the industry. A 17-inch monitor is most often recommended for new systems and is not much more expensive than a 15-inch display. I recommend a 17-inch monitor as the minimum you should consider for most normal applications. Low-end applications can still get away with a 15-inch display, but resolution will suffer. 18- to 21-inch or larger displays are recommended for high-end systems, especially where graphics applications are the major focus.

Larger monitors are handy for applications such as desktop publishing, in which the smallest details must be clearly visible. With a 17-inch or larger display, you can see nearly an entire 8 1/2×11-inch page in 100 percent view—in other words, what you see on-screen virtually matches the page that will be printed. This feature is called *WYSIWYG*—short for "what you see is what you get." If you can see the entire page at its actual size, you can save yourself the trouble of printing several drafts before you get it right.

With the popularity of the Internet, monitor size and resolution becomes even more of an issue. Many Web pages are being designed for 1,024×768 resolution, which requires a 17-inch CRT display as a minimum to handle without eye strain and inadequate focus. Because of their much tighter dot pitch, LCD displays in laptop computers can handle that resolution easily on 13.3- or even 12.1-inch displays. Using 1,024×768 resolution means you will be able to view most Web pages without scrolling sideways, which is a major convenience.

Monitor Resolution

Resolution is the amount of detail that a monitor can render. This quantity is expressed in the number of horizontal and vertical picture elements, or *pixels*, contained in the screen. The greater the number of pixels, the more detailed the images. The resolution required depends on the application. Character-based applications (such as word processing) require little resolution, whereas graphics-intensive applications (such as desktop publishing and Windows software) require a great deal.

There are several standard resolutions available in PC graphics adapters. The following table lists the standard resolutions used in PC video adapters and the term used to commonly describe them:

Resolution	Acronym	Standard Designation
640×480	VGA	Video Graphics Array
800×600	SVGA	Super VGA
1,024×768	XGA	eXtended Graphics Array
1,280×1,024	UVGA	Ultra VGA

In a monochrome monitor, the picture element is a screen phosphor, but in a color monitor, the picture element is a phosphor triad. This difference raises another consideration called *dot pitch*, which applies only to color monitors. Dot pitch is the distance, in millimeters, between phosphor triads. Screens with a small dot pitch contain less distance between the phosphor triads; as a result, the picture elements are closer together, producing a sharper picture. Conversely, screens with a large dot pitch tend to produce images that are less clear.

Another consideration of resolution is the dot pitch of the monitor. Smaller pitch values allow the monitor to produce sharper images. The original IBM PC color monitor had a dot pitch of 0.43mm, which is considered to be poor by almost any standard. The state-of-the-art displays marketed today have a dot pitch of 0.25mm or less; I would not recommend more than 0.28mm in most cases. While you can save money by picking a smaller monitor or one with a higher dot pitch, the trade-off is not usually worth it.

Interlaced versus Noninterlaced

Monitors and video adapters may support interlaced or noninterlaced resolution. In *noninterlaced* (conventional) mode, the electron beam sweeps the screen in lines from top to bottom, one line after the other, completing the screen in one pass. In *interlaced* mode, the electron beam also sweeps the screen from top to bottom, but it does so in two passes—sweeping the odd lines first and the even lines second. Each pass takes half the time of a full pass in noninterlaced mode. Therefore, both modes refresh the entire screen in the same amount of time. This technique redraws the screen faster and provides more stable images.

Monitors that use interlacing can use lower refresh rates, lessening their cost. The drawback is that interlacing depends on the ability of the eye to combine two nearly identical lines, separated by a gap, into one solid line. If you are looking for high-quality video, however, you want to get a video adapter and monitor that support high-resolution, noninterlaced displays.

Energy and Safety

A properly selected monitor can save energy. Many PC manufacturers are trying to meet the Environmental Protection Agency's Energy Star requirements. Any PC-and-monitor combination that consumes less than 60 watts (30 watts apiece) during idle periods can use the Energy Star logo. Some research shows that such "green" PCs can save each user about $70 per year in electricity costs.

Monitors, being one of the most power-hungry computer components, can contribute to those savings. Perhaps the best-known energy-saving standard for monitors is VESA's Display Power-Management Signaling (DPMS) spec, which defines the signals that a computer sends to a monitor to indicate idle times. The computer or video card decides when to send these signals.

If you buy a DPMS monitor, you can take advantage of energy savings without remodeling your entire system. If you do not have a DPMS-compatible video adapter, some cards can be upgraded to DPMS with a software utility typically available at no cost. Similarly, some energy-saving monitors include software that works with almost any graphics card to supply DPMS signals.

Another trend in green monitor design is to minimize the user's exposure to potentially harmful electromagnetic fields. Several medical studies indicate that these electromagnetic emissions may cause health problems, such as miscarriages, birth defects, and cancer. The risk may be low, but if you spend a third of your day (or more) in front of a computer monitor, that risk is increased.

The concern is that VLF (very low frequency) and ELF (extremely low frequency) emissions might affect the body. These two emissions come in two forms: *electric* and *magnetic*. Some research indicates that ELF magnetic emissions are more threatening than VLF emissions, because they interact with the natural electric activity of body cells. Monitors are not the only culprits; significant ELF emissions also come from electric blankets and power lines.

> **Note**
>
> ELF and VLF are a form of electromagnetic radiation; they consist of radio frequencies below those used for normal radio broadcasting.

These two frequencies are covered by the new Swedish monitor-emission standard called *SWEDAC*, named after the Swedish regulatory agency. In many European countries, government agencies and businesses buy only low-emission monitors. The degree to which emissions are reduced varies from monitor to monitor. The Swedish government's MPR I standard, which dates back to 1987, is the least restrictive. MPR II, established in 1990, is significantly stronger (adding maximums for ELF as well as VLF emissions) and is the level that you will most likely find in low-emission monitors today.

A more stringent 1992 standard called *TCO* further tightens the MPR II requirements. In addition, it is a more broad-based environmental standard that includes power-saving requirements and emission limits. Nanao is one of the few manufacturers currently offering monitors that meet the TCO standard.

A low-emission monitor costs about $20 to $100 more than similar regular-emission monitors. When you shop for a low-emission monitor, don't just ask for a low-emission monitor; also find out whether the monitor limits specific types of emission. Use as your guideline the three electromagnetic-emission standards described in this section.

If you decide not to buy a low-emission monitor, you can take other steps to protect yourself. The most important is to stay at arm's length (about 28 inches) from the front of your monitor. When you move a couple of feet away, ELF magnetic emission levels usually drop to those of a typical office with fluorescent lights. Likewise, monitor emissions are weakest at the front of a monitor, so stay at least 3 feet from the sides and backs of nearby monitors and 5 feet from any photocopiers, which are also strong sources of ELF.

Electromagnetic emissions should not be your only concern; you also should be concerned about screen glare. In fact, some antiglare screens not only reduce eye strain but also cut ELF and VLF emissions.

Monitor Buying Criteria

A monitor may account for as much as 50 percent of the price of a computer system. What should you look for when you shop for a monitor?

The trick is to pick a monitor that works with your selected video card. You can save money by purchasing a single-standard (fixed-frequency) monitor and a matching video card; for example, you can order a VGA monitor and a VGA video card. For greatest flexibility, get a multisync monitor that accommodates a range of standards, including those that are not yet standardized.

With multisync monitors, you must match the range of horizontal and vertical frequencies the monitor accepts with those generated by your video card. The wider the range of signals, the more expensive—and more versatile—the monitor. Your video card's vertical and horizontal frequencies must fall within the ranges supported by your monitor. The *vertical frequency* (or refresh/frame rate) determines how stable your image will be. The higher the vertical frequency, the better. Typical vertical frequencies range from 50 to 90Hz. The *horizontal frequency* (or line rate) ranges between 31.5KHz to 60KHz or more.

To keep the horizontal frequency low, some video cards use interlaced signals, alternately displaying half the lines of the total image. On most monitors, interlacing produces a pronounced flicker in the display, unless the phosphor is designed with a very long persistence. For this reason, you should avoid using interlaced video modes if possible. Some older cards and displays used interlacing as an inexpensive way to attain a higher resolution than otherwise would be possible. For example, the original IBM XGA adapters and monitors used an interlaced vertical frame rate of 43.5Hz in 1,024×768 mode, instead of the 60Hz or higher frame rate that most other adapters and displays use at that resolution.

In my experience, a 60Hz vertical scan frequency (frame rate) is the minimum anybody should use, and even at this frequency a flicker will be noticed by most people. Especially on a larger display, this can cause eye strain and fatigue. If you can select a frame rate (vertical scan frequency) of 72Hz or higher, most people will not be able to discern any flicker. Most modern displays easily handle vertical frequencies of up to 85Hz or more, which greatly reduces the flicker seen by the user. Note that increasing the frame rate can slow down the video hardware, because it now needs to display each image more times per second. In general, I recommend you set the lowest frame rate you are comfortable with.

When you shop for a VGA monitor, make sure that the monitor supports a horizontal frequency of at least 31.5KHz—the minimum that a VGA card needs to paint a 640×480 screen. The VESA Super VGA (800×600) or SVGA standard requires a 72Hz vertical frequency and a horizontal frequency of at least 48KHz. The sharper 1,024×768 image requires a vertical frequency of 60Hz and a horizontal frequency of 58KHz. If the vertical frequency increases to 72Hz, the horizontal frequency must be 58KHz. For a super-crisp display, look for available vertical frequencies of 75Hz or higher and horizontal frequencies of up to 90KHz or more.

Most of the analog monitors produced today are, to one extent or another, multisync. Because literally hundreds of manufacturers produce thousands of monitor models, it is impractical to discuss the technical aspects of each monitor model in detail. Suffice it to say that before investing in a monitor, you should check the technical specifications to make sure that the monitor meets your needs. If you are looking for a place to start, check out some of the different magazines, which periodically feature reviews of monitors. If you cannot wait for a magazine review, investigate monitors at the Web sites run by any of the following vendors:

IBM	Sony	NEC
Mitsubishi	Viewsonic	

Each of these manufacturers creates monitors that set the standards by which other monitors can be judged. Although you typically pay a bit more for these manufacturers' monitors, they offer a known high level of quality and compatibility as well as service and support.

Many inexpensive monitors are curved because it is easier to send an electron beam across them. Flat-screen monitors, which are a bit more expensive, look better to most people. As a general rule, the less curvature a monitor has, the less glare it will reflect.

Consider the size of your desk before you think about a monitor 16 inches or larger. A 16-inch monitor typically is at least 1 1/2 feet deep, and a 20-inch monitor takes up 2 square feet. Typical 14-inch monitors are 16 to 18 inches deep.

You also should check the dot pitch of the monitor. Smaller pitch values indicate sharper images. Most monitors have a dot pitch between 0.25 and 0.52mm. To avoid grainy images, look for a dot pitch of 0.26mm or smaller. Be wary of monitors with anything larger than a 0.28mm dot pitch; they lack clarity for fine text and graphics.

What resolution do you want for your display? Generally, the higher the resolution, the larger the display you will want. If you are operating at 640×480 resolution, for example, you should find a 15-inch monitor to be comfortable. At 1,024×768, you probably will find that the display of a 15-inch monitor is too small and therefore will prefer to use a larger one, such as a 17-inch monitor.

Here are the minimum monitor sizes I recommend to properly display popular VGA and SVGA resolutions:

Resolution	Minimum Recommended Monitor
640×480	13-inch
800×600	15-inch
1,024×768	17-inch
1,280×1,024	21-inch

The minimum recommended display size is the advertised diagonal display dimension of the monitor. Note that this is not what the monitor may be capable of, but is what I recommend. In other words, most 15-inch monitors will display resolutions at least up to 1,024×768, but the characters, icons, and displayed information will be too small and will cause eye strain if you try to run beyond the 800×600 recommended. In other words, if you plan on spending a lot of time in front of your PC, and you want to run 1,024×768 resolution, I absolutely recommend a 17-inch display. Anything smaller is not considered proper ergonomics, and eye strain, headaches, and fatigue can result.

One exception to this rule is with the laptop and notebook displays. These are usually an LCD-type display, which is always crisp and perfectly focused by nature. Also, the dimensions advertised for the LCD screens are exactly what you get for display, unlike conventional CRT-based monitors. So the 12.1-inch LCD panels found on many laptop systems today actually have a viewable area that is 12.1-inch diagonal. In other words, 12.1-inch is the size of the Windows desktop or functional area of the screen. This measurement compares to a 14-inch or even 15-inch conventional display in most cases. Not only that, but the LCD is so crisp that you can easily handle resolutions that are higher than otherwise would be acceptable on a CRT. For example, many of the high-end laptop systems now use 13.3-inch LCD panels that feature 1,024×768 resolution. Although this resolution is unacceptable on a 14-inch or 15-inch CRT display, it works well on the 13.3-inch LCD panel due to the crystal clear image.

> **Tip**
>
> Get a monitor with positioning and image controls that are easy to reach. Look for more than just basic contrast and brightness controls; some monitors also enable you to adjust the width and height of your screen images. A tilt-swivel stand should be included with your monitor, enabling you to move the monitor to the best angle for your use.

Most of the newer monitors now use digital controls instead of analog controls. This has nothing to do with the signals sent to the monitor, but the controls (or lack of them) on the front panel. Monitors with digital controls have a built-in menu system that allows you to set things like brightness, contrast, screen size, vertical and horizontal shifts, and even focus. The menu is brought up on the screen by a button, and you use controls to make menu selections and vary the settings. When completed, the monitor saves your settings in NVRAM (Non-Volatile RAM) in the monitor. These settings are permanently stored using no battery, and can be altered at any time in the future. Digital controls give a much higher level of control over the monitor, and are highly recommended.

A monitor is such an important part of your computer that it is not enough to know just its technical specifications. Knowing a monitor has a 0.28mm dot pitch does not necessarily tell you that it is ideal for you. It is best to "kick the tires" of your new monitor at a showroom or (with a liberal return policy) in the privacy of your office. To test your monitor:

- Draw a circle with a graphics program. If the result is an oval, not a circle, this monitor will not serve you well with graphics or design software.

- Type some words in 8- or 10-point type (1 point equals 1/72 inch). If the words are fuzzy, or if the black characters are fringed with color, select another monitor.

- Turn the brightness up and down while examining the corner of the screen's image. If the image blooms or swells, it is likely to lose focus at high brightness levels.

- Load Microsoft Windows to check for uniform focus. Are the corner icons as sharp as the rest of the screen? Are the lines in the title bar curved or wavy? Monitors usually are sharply focused at the center, but seriously blurred corners indicate a poor design. Bowed lines may be the result of a poor graphics card, so don't dismiss a monitor that shows those lines without using another card to double-check the effect.

A good monitor will be calibrated so that rays of red, green, and blue light hit their targets (individual phosphor dots) precisely. If they don't, you have bad convergence. This is apparent when edges of lines appear to illuminate with a specific color. If you have good convergence, the colors will be crisp, clear, and true, provided that there is not a predominant tint in the phosphor.

Video Cards

A *video card* provides signals that operate your monitor. With the PS/2 systems introduced in 1987, IBM developed new video standards that have overtaken the older display standards in popularity and support.

Most video cards follow one of several industry standards:

MDA (Monochrome Display Adapter)   VGA (Video Graphics Array)

CGA (Color Graphics Adapter)   SVGA (Super VGA)

EGA (Enhanced Graphics Adapter)   XGA (eXtended Graphics Array)

These adapters and video standards are supported by virtually every program that runs on IBM or compatible equipment. Other systems are developing into de facto standards as well. For example, SVGA offers different resolutions from different vendors, but 1,024×768 resolution is becoming a standard resolution for doing detailed work.

Most microcomputer monitors support at least one video standard, enabling you to operate them with video cards and software that are compatible with that standard. For example, a monitor that supports VGA may operate with VGA video cards and VGA software.

Obsolete Display Adapters

Although many types of display systems are considered to be standards, not all systems are considered to be viable standards for today's hardware and software. For example, the CGA standard works but is unacceptable for running the graphics-intensive programs on which many users rely. In fact, Microsoft Windows 3.1 does not work with any PC that has less-than-EGA resolution, and Windows 95 and Windows NT require VGA as an absolute minimum. The next several sections discuss the display adapters that are viewed as being obsolete in today's market.

Monochrome Display Adapter (MDA) and Display. The simplest (and first available) display type is the IBM *Monochrome Display Adapter (MDA)*. It was introduced along with the IBM PC itself in 1981. The MDA video card can display text only at a 720×350 resolution. One interesting point is that the MDA card also incorporated a printer port and was the first multi-function adapter card available.

A character-only system, the display has no inherent graphics capabilities. The display originally was a top-selling option because it is fairly cost-effective. As a bonus, the MDA provides a printer interface, conserving an expansion slot.

The display is known for clarity and high resolution, making it ideal for business use—especially for businesses that use DOS-based word processing or spreadsheet programs.

Figure 10.1 shows the MDA pinouts.

FIG. 10.1 Monochrome Display Adapter pinouts.

Because the monochrome display is a character-only display, you cannot use it with software that requires graphics. Originally, that drawback only kept the user from playing games on a monochrome display, but today even the most serious business software uses graphics and color to great advantage. With the 9×14 dot character box (*matrix*), the IBM monochrome monitor displays attractive characters.

Table 10.1 summarizes the features of the MDA's single mode of operation.

Table 10.1 IBM Monochrome Display Adapter (MDA) Specifications

Resolution	Colors	Mode Type	BIOS Mode	Character Format	Character Box	Vertical (Hz)	Horizontal (KHz)
720×350	4	Text	07h	80×25	9×14	50	18.432

Later, a company named Hercules released a video card called the *Hercules Graphics Card (HGC)*. This card displays sharper text and can handle graphics, such as bar charts.

Color Graphics Adapter (CGA) and Display. The *Color Graphics Adapter (CGA)* was introduced along with the IBM PC itself in 1981 and for many years was the most common video card. Of course, by today's standards, its capabilities now leave much to be desired. This adapter has two basic modes of operation: alphanumeric (A/N) or all points addressable (APA). In *A/N mode*, the card operates in 40-column by 25-line mode or 80-column by 25-line mode with 16 colors. In APA and A/N modes, the character set is formed with a resolution of 8×8 pixels. In *APA* mode, two resolutions are available: medium-resolution color mode (320×200), with four colors available from a palette of 16; and two-color high-resolution mode (640×200).

Figures 10.2 and 10.3 show the pinouts for the CGA.

Most of the monitors sold for the CGA are RGBs, not composite monitors. The color signal of a composite monitor contains a mixture of colors that must be decoded or separated. RGB monitors receive red, green, and blue separately, and combine the colors in different proportions to generate other colors. RGB monitors offer better resolution than composite monitors, and they do a much better job of displaying 80-column text.

One drawback of a CGA video card is the fact that it produces flicker and snow. *Flicker* is the annoying tendency of the text to flash as you move the image up or down. *Snow* is the flurry of bright dots that can appear anywhere on the screen.

Most companies that sold CGA-type adapters have long since discontinued those products. When many VGA cards cost less than $100, recommending a CGA makes little sense.

Table 10.2 lists the specifications for all CGA modes of operation.

Table 10.2 IBM Color Graphics Adapter (CGA) Specifications

Resolution	Colors	Mode Type	BIOS Mode	Character Format	Character Box	Vertical (Hz)	Horizontal (KHz)
320×200	16	Text	00/01h	40×25	8×8	60	15.75
640×200	16	Text	02/03h	80×25	8×8	60	15.75
160×200	16	APA	—	—	—	60	15.75

Resolution	Colors	Mode Type	BIOS Mode	Character Format	Character Box	Vertical (Hz)	Horizontal (KHz)
320×200	4	APA	04/05h	40×25	8×8	60	15.75
640×200	2	APA	06h	80×25	8×8	60	15.75

APA = All points addressable (graphics)
— = Not supported

FIG. 10.2 CGA display connector specifications.

FIG. 10.3 CGA RF modulator and light-pen connector specifications.

Enhanced Graphics Adapter (EGA) and Display. The IBM *Enhanced Graphics Adapter* was introduced in 1984, just after the IBM AT system. It was discontinued when the PS/2 systems were introduced in April 1987. It consists of a graphics board, a graphics memory-expansion board, a graphics memory-module kit, and a high-resolution color monitor. The whole package originally cost about $1,800! The aftermarket gave IBM a great deal of competition in this area; it was possible to put together a similar system from non-IBM vendors for much less money. One advantage of EGA, however, is that you can build your system in modular steps. Because the card works with any of the monitors IBM produced at the time, you can use it with the IBM Monochrome Display, the earlier IBM Color Display, or the IBM Enhanced Color Display.

With the EGA card, the IBM color monitor displays 16 colors in 320×200 or 640×200 mode, and the IBM monochrome monitor shows a resolution of 640×350 with a 9×14 character box (text mode).

Figures 10.4 and 10.5 show the pinouts and P-2 connector of the EGA.

With the EGA card, the IBM Enhanced Color Display is capable of displaying 640×350 pixels in 16 colors from a palette of 64. The character box for text is 8×14, compared with 8×8 for the earlier CGA board and monitor. The 8×8 character box can be used,

FIG. 10.4 EGA display connector specifications.

FIG. 10.5 EGA light-pen connector specifications.

however, to display 43 lines of text. Through software, the character box can be manipulated up to the size of 8×32.

You can enlarge a RAM-resident, 256-member character set to 512 characters by using the IBM memory expansion card. A 1,024-character set is added with the IBM graphics memory-module kit. These character sets are loaded from programs.

All this memory fits in the unused space between the end of RAM user memory and the current display-adapter memory. The EGA has a maximum 128K of memory that maps into the RAM space just above the 640K boundary. If you install more than 640K, you will probably lose the extra memory after installing the EGA. The graphics memory-expansion card adds 64K to the standard 64K, for a total 128K. The IBM graphics memory-module kit adds another 128K, for a total 256K. This second 128K of memory is only on the card and does not consume any of the PC's memory space. (Because almost every aftermarket EGA card comes configured with the full 256K of memory, expansion options are not necessary.)

The VGA system supersedes the EGA in many respects. The EGA has problems emulating the earlier CGA or MDA adapters, and some software that works with the earlier cards will not run on the EGA until the programs are modified.

Table 10.3 shows the modes supported by the EGA adapter.

Table 10.3 IBM Enhanced Graphics Adapter (EGA) Specifications

Resolution	Colors	Mode Type	BIOS Mode	Character Format	Character Box	Vertical (Hz)	Horizontal (KHz)
320×350	16	Text	00/01h	40×25	8×14	60	21.85
640×350	16	Text	02/03h	80×25	8×14	60	21.85
720×350	4	Text	07h	80×25	9×14	50	18.432
320×200	16	APA	0Dh	40×25	8×8	60	15.75
640×200	16	APA	0Eh	80×25	8×8	60	15.75
640×350	4	APA	0Fh	80×25	8×14	50	18.432
640×350	16	APA	10h	80×25	8×14	60	21.85

APA = All points addressable (graphics)

Professional Color Display and Adapter. The *Professional Graphics Display System* is a video display product that IBM introduced in 1984. At $4,290, the system was too expensive to become a mainstream product and never achieved any popularity. It was the first processor-based video adapter for PCs; it actually incorporated an 8088 processor on the card itself.

The system consists of a Professional Graphics Monitor and a Professional Graphics Card Set. When fully expanded, this card set uses three slots in an XT or AT system—a high price to pay, but the features are impressive. The Professional Graphics Adapter (PGA) offers three-dimensional rotation and clipping as a built-in hardware function. The adapter can run 60 frames of animation per second because the PGA uses a built-in dedicated microcomputer.

The Professional Graphics card and monitor targeted engineering and scientific applications rather than financial or business applications. This system, which was discontinued when the PS/2 was introduced, has been replaced by the VGA and other higher-resolution graphics standards for these newer systems.

Table 10.4 lists all supported PGA modes.

Table 10.4 IBM Professional Graphics Adapter (PGA) Specifications

Resolution	Colors	Mode Type	BIOS Mode	Character Format	Character Box	Vertical (Hz)	Horizontal (KHz)
320×200	16	Text	00/01	40×25	8×8	60	15.75
640×200	16	Text	02/03	80×25	8×8	60	15.75
320×200	4	APA	04/05	40×25	8×8	60	15.75
640×200	2	APA	06	80×25	8×8	60	15.75
640×480	256	APA	—	—	—	60	30.48

APA = All points addressable (graphics)
— = Not supported

8514/A Display Adapter. The PS/2 *8514/A Display Adapter*, introduced in 1987 along with the PS/2 systems, offers higher resolution and more colors than the standard VGA. This adapter, designed to use the PS/2 Color Display 8514, plugs into a Micro Channel slot in any PS/2 model so equipped.

All operation modes of the built-in VGA continue to be available. An IBM 8514 memory-expansion kit is available for the 8514/A. This kit provides increased color and grayscale support.

To take full advantage of this adapter, you should use the 8514 display because it is matched to the capabilities of the adapter. Notice that IBM has discontinued the 8514/A adapter and specifies the XGA in its place.

Table 10.5 shows all 8514 modes.

Table 10.5 IBM 8514/A Display Adapter Specifications

Resolution	Colors	Mode Type	BIOS Mode	Character Format	Character Box	Vertical (Hz)	Horizontal (KHz)
1024×768	256	APA*	H-0h	85×38	12×20	43.48	35.52
640×480	256	APA	H-1h	80×34	8×14	60	31.5
1024×768	256	APA*	H-3h	146×51	7×15	43.48	35.52

APA = All points addressable (graphics)
* = Interlaced

MultiColor Graphics Array (MCGA). The *MultiColor Graphics Array (MCGA)* is a graphics adapter that is integrated into the motherboard of the PS/2 Models 25 and 30. The MCGA supports all CGA modes when an IBM analog display is attached, but any previous IBM display is not compatible. In addition to providing existing CGA mode support, the MCGA includes four additional modes.

The MCGA uses as many as 64 shades of gray in converting color modes for display on monochrome monitors, so that users who prefer a monochrome display still can execute color-based applications.

Table 10.6 lists the MCGA display modes.

Table 10.6 IBM MultiColor Graphics Array (MCGA) Specifications

Resolution	Colors	Mode Type	BIOS Mode	Character Format	Character Box	Vertical (Hz)	Horizontal (KHz)
320×400	16	Text	00/01h	40×25	8×16	70	31.5
640×400	16	Text	02/03h	80×25	8×16	70	31.5
320×200	4	APA	04/05h	40×25	8×8	70	31.5
640×200	2	APA	06h	80×25	8×8	70	31.5
640×480	2	APA	11h	80×30	8×16	60	31.5
320×200	256	APA	13h	40×25	8×8	70	31.5

APA = All points addressable (graphics)

VGA Adapters and Displays

When IBM introduced the PS/2 systems on April 2, 1987, it also introduced the *Video Graphics Array (VGA)* display. On that day, in fact, IBM also introduced the lower-resolution MultiColor Graphics Array (MCGA) and higher-resolution 8514 adapters. The MCGA and 8514 adapters did not become popular standards like the VGA, and both were discontinued.

Digital Versus Analog Signals. Unlike earlier video standards, which are digital, the VGA is an analog system. Why are displays going from digital to analog when most other electronic systems are going digital? Compact-disc players (digital) have replaced most turntables (analog), and newer VCRs and camcorders have digital picture storage for smooth slow-motion and freeze-frame capability. With a digital television set, you can watch several channels on a single screen by splitting the screen or placing a picture within another picture.

Why, then, did IBM decide to change the video to analog? The answer is color.

Most personal-computer displays introduced before the PS/2 are digital. This type of display generates different colors by firing the RGB electron beams in on-or-off mode. You can display up to eight colors (2 to the third power). In the IBM displays and adapters, another signal intensity doubles the number of color combinations from 8 to 16 by displaying each color at one of two intensity levels. This digital display is easy to manufacture and offers simplicity with consistent color combinations from system to system. The real drawback of the digital display system is the limited number of possible colors.

In the PS/2 systems, IBM went to an analog display circuit. Analog displays work like the digital displays that use RGB electron beams to construct various colors, but each color in the analog display system can be displayed at varying levels of intensity—64 levels, in the case of the VGA. This versatility provides 262,144 possible colors (64^3). For realistic computer graphics, color often is more important than high resolution, because the human eye perceives a picture that has more colors as being more realistic. IBM moved graphics into analog form to enhance the color capabilities.

Video Graphics Array (VGA). PS/2 systems contain the primary display adapter circuits on the motherboard. The circuits, or VGA, are implemented by a single custom VLSI chip designed and manufactured by IBM. To adapt this new graphics standard to the earlier systems, IBM introduced the PS/2 Display Adapter. Also called a VGA card, this adapter contains the complete VGA circuit on a full-length adapter board with an 8-bit interface. IBM has since discontinued its VGA card, but many third-party units are available.

The VGA *BIOS (Basic Input/Output System)* is the control software residing in the system ROM for controlling VGA circuits. With the BIOS, software can initiate commands and functions without having to manipulate the VGA directly. Programs become somewhat hardware-independent and can call a consistent set of commands and functions built into the system's ROM-control software.

Future implementations of the VGA will be different in hardware but will respond to the same BIOS calls and functions. New features will be added as a superset of the existing functions. The VGA, therefore, will be compatible with the graphics and text BIOS functions that were built into the PC systems from the beginning. The VGA can run almost any software that originally was written for the MDA, CGA, or EGA.

In a perfect world, software programmers would write to the BIOS interface rather than directly to the hardware and would promote software interchanges between different types of hardware. More frequently, however, programmers want the software to perform better, so they write the programs to control the hardware directly. As a result, these programmers achieve higher-performance applications that are dependent on the hardware for which they were first written.

When bypassing the BIOS, a programmer must ensure that the hardware is 100 percent compatible with the standard so that software written to a standard piece of hardware runs on the system. Just because a manufacturer claims this register level of compatibility does not mean that the product is 100 percent compatible or that all software runs as it would on a true IBM VGA. Most manufacturers have "cloned" the VGA system at the register level, which means that even applications that write directly to the video registers will function correctly. Also, the VGA circuits themselves emulate the older adapters even to the register level and have an amazing level of compatibility with these earlier standards. This compatibility makes the VGA a truly universal standard.

The VGA displays up to 256 colors on screen, from a palette of 262,144 (256K) colors. Because the VGA outputs an analog signal, you must have a monitor that accepts an analog input.

VGA displays come not only in color but also in monochrome VGA models, using color summing. With *color summing*, 64 gray shades are displayed instead of colors; the translation is performed in the ROM BIOS. The summing routine is initiated if the BIOS detects the monochrome display when the system is booted. This routine uses a formula that takes the desired color and rewrites the formula to involve all three color guns, producing varying intensities of gray. The color that would be displayed, for example, is converted to 30 percent red plus 59 percent green plus 11 percent blue to achieve the desired gray. Users who prefer a monochrome display, therefore, can execute color-based applications.

Table 10.7 lists the VGA display modes.

Table 10.7 IBM Video Graphics Array (VGA) Specifications

Resolution	Colors	Mode Type	BIOS Mode	Character Format	Character Box	Vertical (Hz)	Horizontal (KHz)
360×400	16	Text	00/01h	40×25	9×16	70	31.5
720×400	16	Text	02/03h	80×25	9×16	70	31.5
320×200	4	APA	04/05h	40×25	8×8	70	31.5
640×200	2	APA	06h	80×25	8×8	70	31.5
720×400	16	Text	07h	80×25	9×16	70	31.5
320×200	16	APA	0Dh	40×25	8×8	70	31.5
640×200	16	APA	0Eh	80×25	8×8	70	31.5
640×350	4	APA	0Fh	80×25	8×14	70	31.5
640×350	16	APA	10h	80×25	8×14	70	31.5
640×480	2	APA	11h	80×30	8×16	60	31.5
640×480	16	APA	12h	80×30	8×16	60	31.5
320×200	256	APA	13h	40×25	8×8	70	31.5

APA = All points addressable (graphics)

XGA and XGA-2. IBM announced the PS/2 XGA Display Adapter/A on October 30, 1990, and the XGA-2 in September 1992. Both adapters are high-performance, 32-bit bus-master adapters for Micro Channel-based systems. These video subsystems, evolved from the VGA, provide greater resolution, more colors, and much better performance. Combine fast VGA, more colors, higher resolution, a graphics coprocessor, and bus-mastering, and you have XGA. Being a bus-master adapter means that the XGA can take control of the system as though it were the motherboard. In essence, a bus master is an adapter with its own processor that can execute operations independent of the motherboard.

The XGA was introduced as the default graphics-display platform with the Model 90 XP 486 and the Model 95 XP 486. In the desktop Model 90, the XGA is on the motherboard; in the Model 95 (a tower unit), it is located on a separate add-in board. This board—the XGA Display Adapter/A—also is available for other 386- and 486-based Micro Channel systems. The XGA adapter can be installed in any MCA systems that have 80386, 80386SX, 80386SLC, 486SLC2, 486SLC3, or 80486 processors, including PS/2 Models 53, 55, 57, 65, 70, and 80.

The XGA comes standard with 512K of graphics memory, which can be upgraded to 1M with an optional video-memory expansion.

In addition to all VGA modes, the XGA adapter offers several new modes of operation, which are listed in Table 10.8.

Table 10.8 XGA Unique Modes of Operation

Maximum Resolution	Maximum Colors	Required VRAM
1,024×768	256 colors	1M
1,024×768	64 gray shades	1M
1,024×768	16 colors	512K
1,024×768	16 gray shades	512K
640×480	65,536 colors	1M
640×480	64 gray shades	512K

The reasons for the different memory requirements are explained in the next section. The 65,536-color mode provides almost photographic output. The 16-bit pixel is laid out as 5 bits of red, 6 bits of green, and 5 bits of blue (5-6-5)—in other words, 32 shades of blue, 64 shades of green, and 32 shades of blue. (The eye notices more variations in green than in red or blue.) One major drawback of the current XGA implementation is the interlacing that occurs in the higher-resolution modes. With interlacing, you can use a less expensive monitor, but the display updates more slowly, resulting in a slight flicker.

The XGA-2 improves on the performance of the XGA in several ways. To begin with, the XGA-2 increases the number of colors supported at 1,024×768 resolution to 64K. In addition, because of the circuitry of the XGA-2, it can process data at twice the speed of the XGA. The XGA-2 also works in noninterlaced mode, so it produces less flicker than the XGA does.

Both the XGA and XGA-2 support all existing VGA and 8514/A video modes. A large number of popular applications have been developed to support the 8514/A high-resolution 1,024×768 mode. These applications are written to the *8514/A Adapter interface*, which is a software interface between the application and the 8514/A hardware. The XGA's extended graphics function maintains compatibility at the same level. Because of the power of the XGA and XGA-2, current VGA or 8514/A applications run much faster.

Much of the speed of the XGA and XGA-2 also can be attributed to its *video RAM (VRAM)*, a type of dual-ported RAM designed for graphics-display systems. This memory can be accessed by both the processor on the graphics adapter and the system CPU simultaneously, providing almost instant data transfer. The XGA VRAM is mapped into the system's address space. The VRAM normally is located in the top addresses of the 386's 4G address space. Because no other cards normally use this area, conflicts are rare. The adapters also have an 8K ROM BIOS extension that must be mapped somewhere in segments C000 or D000. (The motherboard implementation of the XGA does not require its own ROM, because the motherboard BIOS contains all the necessary code.)

Table 10.9 summarizes the XGA modes.

Table 10.9 IBM eXtended Graphics Array (XGA) Specifications

Resolution	Colors	Mode Type	BIOS Mode	Character Format	Character Box	Vertical (Hz)	Horizontal (KHz)
360×400	16	Text	00/01h	40×25	9×16	70	31.5
720×400	16	Text	02/03h	80×25	9×16	70	31.5
320×200	4	APA	04/05h	40×25	8×8	70	31.5
640×200	2	APA	06h	80×25	8×8	70	31.5
720×400	16	Text	07h	80×25	9×16	70	31.5
320×200	16	APA	0Dh	40×25	8×8	70	31.5
640×200	16	APA	0Eh	80×25	8×8	70	31.5
640×350	4	APA	0Fh	80×25	8×14	70	31.5
640×350	16	APA	10h	80×25	8×14	70	31.5
640×480	2	APA	11h	80×30	8×16	60	31.5
640×480	16	APA	12h	80×30	8×16	60	31.5
320×200	256	APA	13h	40×25	8×8	70	31.5
1,056×400	16	Text	14h	132×25	8×16	70	31.5
1,056×400	16	Text	14h	132×43	8×9	70	31.5
1,056×400	16	Text	14h	132×56	8×8	70	31.5
1,056×400	16	Text	14h	132×60	8×6	70	31.5
1,024×768	256	APA*	14h	85×38	12×20	43.48	35.52
640×480	65,536	APA	14h	80×34	8×14	60	31.5
1,024×768	256	APA*	14h	128×54	8×14	43.48	35.52
1,024×768	256	APA*	14h	146×51	7×15	43.48	35.52

APA = All points addressable (graphics)
* = Interlaced

Super VGA (SVGA). When IBM's XGA and 8514/A video cards were introduced, competing manufacturers chose not to clone these incremental improvements on VGA. Instead, they began producing lower-cost adapters that offered even higher resolutions. These video cards fall into a category loosely known as *Super VGA (SVGA)*.

SVGA provides capabilities that surpass those offered by the VGA adapter. Unlike the display adapters discussed so far, SVGA refers not to a card that meets a particular specification but to a group of cards that have different capabilities.

For example, one card may offer several resolutions (such as 800×600 and 1,024×768) that are greater than those achieved with a regular VGA, whereas another card may offer the same or even greater resolutions but also provide more color choices at each resolution. These cards have different capabilities; nonetheless, both are classified as SVGA.

The SVGA cards look much like their VGA counterparts. They have the same connectors, including the feature adapter shown in Figure 10.6.

Video Cards

FIG. 10.6 The IBM PS/2 Feature Adapter (VGA card).

Because the technical specifications from different SVGA vendors vary tremendously, it is impossible to provide a definitive technical overview in this book. The pinouts for the standard VGA and SVGA video card connector are shown in the following table:

Pin	Function	Direction
1	Red	Out
2	Green	Out
3	Blue	Out
4	Monitor ID 2	In
5	Digital Ground (monitor self-test)	—
6	Red Analog Ground	—
7	Green Analog Ground	—
8	Blue Analog Ground	—
9	Key (Plugged Hole)	—
10	Sync Ground	—
11	Monitor ID 0	In
12	Monitor ID 1	In
13	Horizontal Sync	Out
14	Vertical Sync	Out
15	Monitor ID 3	In

VESA SVGA Standards

The Video Electronics Standards Association (VESA) includes members from various companies associated with PC and computer video products. In October 1989, recognizing that programming for the many SVGA cards on the market was virtually impossible, VESA proposed a standard for a uniform programmer's interface for SVGA cards.

The SVGA standard is called the *VESA BIOS Extension*. If a video card incorporates this standard, a program easily can determine the capabilities of the card and access them. The benefit of the VESA BIOS Extension is that a programmer needs to worry about only one routine or driver to support SVGA. Different cards from different manufacturers are accessible through the common VESA interface.

When first proposed, this concept met with limited acceptance. Several major SVGA manufacturers started supplying the VESA BIOS Extension as a separate memory-resident program that you could load when you booted your computer. Over the years, however, other vendors started supplying the VESA BIOS Extension as an integral part of their SVGA BIOS. Obviously, from a user's perspective, support for VESA in BIOS is a better solution. You do not have to worry about loading a driver or other memory-resident program whenever you want to use a program that expects the VESA extensions to be present.

Today, most SVGA cards support the VESA BIOS Extensions in one way or another. When you shop for a SVGA card, make sure that it supports the extensions in BIOS. Also, if you are interested in finding out more about programming for the VESA BIOS Extensions, contact the Video Electronics Standards Association for a copy of the VESA Programmer's Toolkit.

The current VESA SVGA standard covers just about every video resolution and color-depth combination currently available, up to 1,280×1,024 with 16,777,216 (24-bit) colors. Even if a SVGA video adapter claims to be VESA-compatible, however, it still may not work with a particular driver, such as the 800×600, 256-color, SVGA driver that comes with Microsoft Windows. In practice, however, manufacturers continue to provide their own driver software.

Table 10.10 lists the video modes of the Chips and Technologies 65554 SVGA graphics accelerator, a typical chipset used today.

Table 10.10 Chips and Technologies 65554 Graphics Accelerator Chipset Video Modes

BIOS Mode	Mode Type	Resolution	Character	Colors	Scan Freq (Hor/Vert)
0, 1	VGA Text	40×25 char	9×16	16/256K	31.5KHz/70Hz
2, 3	VGA Text	80×25 char	9×16	16/256K	31.5KHz/70Hz
4, 5	VGA Graph	320×200 pels	8×8	4/256K	31.5KHz/70Hz
6	VGA Graph	640×200 pels	8×8	2/256K	31.5KHz/70Hz
7	VGA Text	80×25 char	9×16	Mono	31.5KHz/70Hz

Video Cards

BIOS Mode	Mode Type	Resolution	Character	Colors	Scan Freq (Hor/Vert)
D	VGA Graph	320×200 pels	8×8	16/256K	31.5KHz/70Hz
E	VGA Graph	640×200 pels	8×8	16/256K	31.5KHz/70Hz
F	VGA Graph	640×350 pels	8×14	Mono	31.5KHz/70Hz
10	VGA Graph	640×350 pels	8×14	16/256K	31.5KHz/70Hz
11	VGA Graph	640×480 pels	8×16	2/256K	31.5KHz/60Hz
12	VGA Graph	640×480 pels	8×16	16/256K	31.5KHz/60Hz
13	VGA Graph	320×200 pels	8×8	256/256K	31.5KHz/70Hz
20	SVGA Graph	640×480 pels	8×16	16/256K	31.5KHz/60Hz
					37.6KHz/75Hz
					43.2KHz/85Hz
22	SVGA Graph	800×600 pels	8×8	16/256K	37.9KHz/60Hz
					46.9KHz/75Hz
					53.7KHz/85Hz
24	SVGA Graph	1024×768 pels	8×16	16/256K	35.5KHz/87Hz*
					48.5KHz/60Hz
					60.0KHz/75Hz
					68.8KHz/85Hz
28	SVGA Graph	1280×1024 pels	8×16	16/256K	35.5KHz/87Hz*
					35.5KHz/60Hz
30	SVGA Graph	640×480 pels	8×16	256/256K	31.5KHz/60Hz
					37.6KHz/75Hz
					43.2KHz/85Hz
32	SVGA Graph	800×600 pels	8×16	256/256K	37.9KHz/60Hz
					46.9KHz/75Hz
					53.7KHz/85Hz
34	SVGA Graph	1024×768 pels	8×16	256/256K	35.5KHz/87Hz*
					48.5KHz/60Hz
					60.0KHz/75Hz
					68.8KHz/85Hz
38	SVGA Graph	1280×1024 pels	8×16	256/256K	35.5KHz/87Hz*
					35.5KHz/60Hz
40	SVGA Graph	640×480 pels	8×16	32K/32K	31.5KHz/60Hz
					37.6KHz/75Hz
					43.2KHz/85Hz
41	SVGA Graph	640×480 pels	8×16	64K/64K	31.5KHz/60Hz
					37.6KHz/75Hz
					43.2KHz/85Hz
42	SVGA Graph	800×600 pels	8×16	32K/32K	37.9KHz/60Hz
					46.9KHz/75Hz

(continues)

Table 10.10 Continued

BIOS Mode	Mode Type	Resolution	Character	Colors	Scan Freq (Hor/Vert)
43	SVGA Graph	800×600 pels	8×16	64K/64K	53.7KHz/85Hz 37.9KHz/60Hz 46.9KHz/75Hz
44	SVGA Graph	1024×768 pels	8×16	32K/32K	53.7KHz/85Hz 48.5KHz/60Hz
45	SVGA Graph	1024×768 pels	8×16	64K/64K	48.5KHz/60Hz
50	SVGA Graph	640×480 pels	8×16	16M/16M	31.5KHz/60Hz
52	SVGA Graph	800×600 pels	8×16	16M/16M	37.9KHz/60Hz

* = *interlaced*

Video Memory

A video card relies on memory in drawing your screen. You can often select how much memory you want on your video card—for example, 256K, 512K, 1M, 2M, 4M, 6M, or 8M are common choices today. Most cards today come with at least 1M and usually have 2M. Adding more memory does not speed up your video card; instead, it enables the card to generate more colors and/or higher resolutions.

The amount of memory needed by a video adapter to display a particular resolution and color depth is a mathematical equation. There has to be a memory location used to display every dot (or pixel) on the screen, and the number of total dots is determined by the resolution. For example 1,024×768 resolution represents 786,432 dots on the screen.

If you were to display that resolution with only two colors, you would only need 1 bit to represent each dot. If the bit were a 0, the dot would be black, and if it were a 1, the dot would be white. If you used 4 bits to control each dot, you could display 16 colors, since there are 16 combinations possible with a four-digit binary number (2 to the 4th power equals 16). If you multiplied the number of dots times the number of bits required to represent each dot, you have the amount of memory required to display that resolution. Here is how the calculation would work:

$$1{,}024 \times 768 = 786{,}432 \text{ dots} \times 4 \text{ bits per dot}$$

$$= 3{,}145{,}728 \text{ bits}$$

$$= 393{,}216 \text{ bytes}$$

$$= 384K$$

As you can see, to display only 16 colors at 1,024×768 resolution would require exactly 384K of RAM on the video card. Because most cards would normally support only memory amounts of 256K, 512K, 1M, 2M, or 4M, you would have to install 512K to run that resolution. Upping the color depth to 8 bits per pixel results in 256 possible colors, and a memory requirement of 786,432 bytes or 768K. Again, since no video card can install that exact amount, you would have to install an actual 1M on the video card.

In order to use the higher resolution modes and greater numbers of colors in SVGA cards, such cards will need more memory than the 256K found on a standard VGA adapter. Table 10.11 shows some of the requirements for SVGA cards based on resolution and color depth.

Table 10.11	Display Adapter Minimum Memory Requirements			
Resolution	**Color Depth**	**Colors**	**Video**	**Memory Required**
640×480	4-bit	16	256K	153,600 bytes
640×480	8-bit	256	512K	307,200 bytes
640×480	16-bit	65,536	1M	614,400 bytes
640×480	24-bit	16,777,216	1M	921,600 bytes
800×600	4-bit	16	256K	240,000 bytes
800×600	8-bit	256	512K	480,000 bytes
800×600	16-bit	65,536	1M	960,000 bytes
800×600	24-bit	16,777,216	2M	1,440,000 bytes
1,024×768	4-bit	16	512K	393,216 bytes
1,024×768	8-bit	256	1M	786,432 bytes
1,024×768	16-bit	65,536	2M	1,572,864 bytes
1,024×768	24-bit	16,777,216	4M	2,359,296 bytes
1,280×1,024	4-bit	16	1M	655,360 bytes
1,280×1,024	8-bit	256	2M	1,310,720 bytes
1,280×1,024	16-bit	65,536	4M	2,621,440 bytes
1,280×1,024	24-bit	16,777,216	4M	3,932,160 bytes

From this table, you can see that a video adapter with 2M can display 65,536 colors in 1,024×768 resolution mode, but for a true color (16.8M colors) display, you would need to upgrade to 4M. In most cases, unless you are doing photo-realistic editing requiring 24-bit (16.8M color) support, 2M is all you need on your video adapter.

A 24-bit (or true-color) video card can display photographic images by using 16.8 million colors. If you spend a lot of time working with graphics, you may want to invest in a 24-bit video card with up to 4M of RAM. Many of the cards today can easily handle 24-bit color, but you may need to upgrade from 2M to 4M of RAM to get that capability in the higher-resolution modes.

Another issue with respect to memory on the graphics adapter is how wide the access is between the graphics chipset and the memory on the adapter. The *graphics chipset* is usually a single large chip on the card that contains virtually all of the adapter's functions. It is wired directly to the memory on the card through a local bus. Most of the high-end adapters use an internal 64-bit or even 128-bit wide memory bus. This jargon is confusing, because this does not refer to the kind of bus slot the card plugs into. In other words, when you read about a 64-bit graphics adapter, it is really a 32-bit (PCI or VLB) card that has a 64-bit local memory bus on the card itself.

Improving Video Speed

Many efforts have been made recently to improve the speed of video adapters because of the complexity and sheer data of the high-resolution displays used by today's software. The improvements in video speed are occurring along three fronts:

- Processor
- RAM
- Bus

The combination of these three is reducing the video bottleneck caused by the demands of graphical user interface software, such as Microsoft Windows.

The Video Processor. Three types of processors, or *chipsets*, can be used in creating a video card. The chipset used is, for the most part, independent of which video specification (VGA, SVGA, or XGA) the adapter follows.

The oldest technology used in creating a video adapter is known as *frame-buffer technology*. In this scheme, the video card is responsible for displaying individual frames of an image. Each frame is maintained by the video card, but the computing necessary to create the frame comes from the CPU of your computer. This arrangement places a heavy burden on the CPU, which could be busy doing other program-related computing.

At the other end of the spectrum is a chip technology known as *coprocessing*. In this scheme, the video card includes its own processor, which performs all video-related computations. This arrangement frees the main CPU to perform other tasks. Short of integrating video functions directly into the CPU, this chipset provides the fastest overall system throughput.

Between these two arrangements is a middle ground: a fixed-function *accelerator chip*. In this scheme, used in many of the graphics accelerator boards on the market today, the circuitry on the video card does many of the more time-consuming video tasks (such as drawing lines, circles, and other objects), but the main CPU still directs the card by passing graphics-primitive commands from applications, such as an instruction to draw a rectangle of a given size and color.

The Video RAM. Historically, most video adapters have used regular *dynamic RAM (DRAM)* to store video images. This type of RAM, although inexpensive, is rather slow. The slowness can be attributed to the need constantly to refresh the information contained within the RAM, as well as to the fact that DRAM cannot be read at the same time it is being written.

Modern PC graphics cards need extremely high data transfer rates to and from the video memory. At a resolution of 1,024×768 and a standard refresh rate of 72Hz, the Digital to Analog Converter (DAC) on the card needs to read the contents of the video memory frame buffer 72 times per second. In true color (24-bits per pixel) mode, this means that the video memory must be read at the rate of about 170M/sec, which is just about the maximum rate available from a conventional DRAM design. Because of the high bandwidth required, a number of competing memory technologies have emerged over the past several years to meet the performance needs of high-end video memory.

One of the more recent memory designs to be incorporated into video cards is *EDO (Extended Data Out)* RAM. EDO provides a wider effective bandwidth by offloading memory precharging to separate circuits, so that the next access can essentially begin before the last access has finished. As a result, EDO offers a 10 percent speed boost over DRAM, at a similar cost. EDO RAM was introduced by Micron Technologies. It was originally designed for use in main memories, but it is now also being used in video card applications. EDO chips are constructed using the same dies as conventional DRAM chips, and they differ from DRAMs only in how they are wired in final production. This method enables EDO chips to be made on the same manufacturing lines and at the same relative costs as DRAM.

VRAM (Video RAM) is a popular type of memory that has been used in video cards for some time now. VRAM is designed to be *dual-ported*, which allows the processor or accelerator chip on the graphics card as well as the DAC or even the PC's own processor to access the RAM simultaneously. This allows for much greater performance than standard DRAM or even EDO, but it comes at a higher price.

WRAM, or *Window RAM,* is a modified VRAM-type dual-ported memory technology developed by Samsung that is aimed specifically at graphics cards. WRAM offers marginally better performance than standard VRAM at a lower cost. WRAM is now being used in many high-end graphics cards as a replacement for VRAM.

MDRAM (Multibank DRAM) is a new type of memory that is explicitly aimed at graphics and video applications. Developed by MoSys Inc., MDRAMs are constructed of a large number of small (32K) banks. Traditionally, DRAM or VRAM is logically organized as a single, monolithic bank. Being organized into small banks allows MDRAMs to be installed in any size that is an integral multiple of 32K, instead of restricting the size to the traditional binary multiple sizes found in many video cards. This is a significant advantage for the cost-sensitive PC marketplace.

For example, a 1,024×768 true color (24-bit) graphics system requires 2.3M for the frame buffer plus some extra memory for off-screen storage. If 256K×16 DRAMs and a 64-bit bus are used, the only workable memory size that accommodates this frame buffer is 4M, constructed of two banks of four chips each. However, with MDRAM, a memory system of 2.5M can be constructed of only two or three individual chips. This eliminates the waste of an extra 1.5M, and the total memory cost can be significantly reduced.

In addition to the better memory sizing, MDRAM organizes its internal banks off a narrow central bus, which allows access to each bank individually. As such, this design can complete a burst to or from one bank and then begin a burst to or from another, all in a single clock cycle, offering much higher performance than VRAM or WRAM.

SGRAM, or *Synchronous Graphics RAM,* is a high-end solution for very fast video card designs. This type of memory can operate at 66MHz or faster and will likely be used in PCI cards when the 66MHz version of PCI begins appearing on PC motherboards. It offers up to four times the speed of conventional DRAM and can run at speeds up to 80MHz. Currently SGRAM is expensive, and until the PCI bus steps up from 33 to 66MHz, you won't see it in many applications.

The Bus. You learned that certain video cards are designed for certain buses. For example, the VGA was designed for use with an MCA bus, and the XGA and XGA-2 are still intended for use with the MCA. The bus system that you use in your computer (ISA, EISA, or MCA) affects the speed at which your system processes video information. The ISA offers a 16-bit data path at speeds of 8.33MHz. The EISA or MCA buses can process 32 bits of data at a time, but they also run at speeds up to 10MHz. (Don't confuse the bus speed with the CPU speed. Even though the CPU currently runs at speeds up to 100MHz, the bus still can handle only a limited level of speed.)

One improvement on this frontier was the *VESA local bus (VL-Bus)* standard. The VL-Bus standard typically is an addition to an existing bus technology. For example, you might have an ISA system that also contains a VL-Bus slot. Even if it is used in an ISA system, the VL-Bus processes 32 bits of data at a time and at the full-rated speed of the CPU, up to 40MHz. Thus, you can achieve blinding speed by using a well implemented VL-Bus in your system.

In July 1992, Intel Corporation introduced Peripheral Component Interconnect (PCI) as a blueprint for directly connecting microprocessors and support circuitry; it then extended the design to a full expansion bus with Release 2 in 1993. Popularly termed a *mezzanine bus,* PCI combines the speed of a local bus with microprocessor independence. PCI video cards, like VL-Bus video cards, can increase video performance dramatically. PCI video cards, by their design, are meant to be *Plug and Play (PnP)*, meaning that they require little configuration. The PCI standard has virtually replaced the older VL-Bus standard overnight. From here on, I recommend only PCI-based systems for new purchases and VL-Bus only for upgrading older systems that already have these slots.

VL-Bus and PCI have some important differences, as Table 10.12 shows.

Table 10.12 Local Bus Specifications

Feature	VL-Bus	PCI
Theoretical maximum throughput	132M/sec	528M/sec*
Slots**	3 (typical)	4/5 (typical)
Plug and Play support	No	Yes
Cost	Inexpensive	Slightly higher
Ideal use	Low cost 486	High-end 486, Pentium, P6

*At the maximum 66MHz bus speed and 64-bits
**More slots are possible through the use of PCI bridge chips.

The Fastest Speed Possible. Fortunately, you can choose the best of each area—chipset, RAM, and bus—to achieve the fastest speed possible. The faster you want your card to perform, the more money you must spend. It is not unusual to find high-performance video cards that cost more than $1,000. This price does not include the cost of a new motherboard, if you want to implement PCI.

The trick to choosing a video subsystem is making an early decision. As you research specifications for your entire system, you should pay attention to the video and make sure that it performs the way you want it to. The best speeds can be achieved by a PCI card that uses a coprocessor and VRAM.

Video Card Buying Criteria

One trend is to display higher-resolution images on larger and larger monitors. The growth of multimedia also has encouraged users to invest in 24-bit video cards for photographic-quality images. Both of these trends mean that you may want your video card to produce its 16 million colors at high resolution—at least 1,024×768 pixels.

Better cards can produce high color (or 64K colors) at even finer resolutions of 1,280×1,024 and 256 colors at very high resolutions of 1,600×1,280. To avoid bothersome flickering images, make sure that your card supports at least 72Hz vertical refresh rates at all resolutions; 76Hz is even better. To accomplish such tasks, you need at least 2M of VRAM, although 4M is preferable.

True-color cards now appear in both VL-Bus and PCI versions. If you have an older system, plenty of ISA and MCA 24-bit cards are still available.

Whichever card you buy, make sure that it also has on-board VGA support so that you do not need an extra VGA card. Drivers for your particular operating system should be included, as well as a utility for switching resolutions. Look for extras that better cards now include: auto-installation and mode-switching utilities. A Microsoft Windows utility should be provided to ease switching resolutions and colors. Many of these utilities now allow for video mode switching on-the-fly without having to leave the Windows environment. This capability for changing resolutions is standard in Windows 95 and was available for Windows 3.1 by using a utility program.

If you are shopping for a video card to provide SVGA resolutions, you need special software drivers for each of your software programs to take advantage of this resolution; otherwise, your video card will act as a typical VGA card. When you shop for a higher-resolution video card, make sure that it has drivers that support the software packages you own.

Chipsets

It is important to note that a video card essentially consists of four major components:

- Chipset
- DAC (Digital to Analog Converter)
- Video memory
- BIOS (Basic Input/Output System)

The chipset is the heart of any video card and essentially defines the card and its functions. Any two video cards built using the same chipset can have the same relative performance and capabilities. Also, when you install drivers, they are normally written by the chipset manufacturer and installed for your particular chipset rather than the card itself. Of course, cards built using the same chipset can differ in the amount and type of memory installed, so performance may vary.

When you inspect video cards for purchase, you should inquire about which chipset is used on the card; that will give you a much better basis for comparing that card against others. Also, knowing the chipset manufacturer of your card enables you to contact that manufacturer directly (via the Web, for example) so you can download the latest drivers in case of problems.

The vendor list in Appendix A has information on most of the popular video chipset manufacturers, including how to contact them.

Video Cards for Multimedia

Multimedia is the result of several different media working together. Video is just one, albeit an important, element. Topics not yet discussed include animation, full-motion video (playback and capture), still images, and graphics processing. Still images and video provide dazzling slides, and animation and full-motion video breathe life into any presentation.

A computer can mathematically animate sequences between keyframes. A *keyframe* identifies specific points. A bouncing ball, for example, can have three keyframes: up, down, and up. Using these frames as a reference point, the computer can create all the images in between. This creates a smooth bouncing ball.

More people are realizing the benefits of 3-D animation. Prices are dropping, and technology once available only to high-end workstations is now available on PCs. 3-D graphics accelerator cards incorporate a chipset that is capable of on-board rendering. This enables smooth, photo-realistic 3-D images to be performed on a PC level at speeds exceeding those of low-end workstations.

Video Feature Connector (VFC). Since IBM first developed the VGA standard in 1987, one often overlooked part of the standard was the *Video Feature Connector*, or *VFC*. This was a 26-pin connector that allowed other video cards to connect to a VGA adapter directly. Unfortunately, this standard was poorly documented by IBM and poorly implemented by most VGA adapter manufacturers. In fact, many VGA cards did not implement this connector at all, basically ignoring the need. That may have been fine in the early days of VGA, because there were few multimedia products that would need to tap into the VGA signal. Today, however, there are many types of multimedia add-on boards that have features such as motion video, video capture, television tuners, and so on that need the services of this connector to do their job.

Unfortunately, there was another problem with the VFC besides it not being there or being implemented incorrectly. The problem was one of performance. The original VGA adapter was designed as an 8-bit bus adapter, and worked at a resolution of only 640×480 pixels. Thus, the VFC had these same limitations, which put a damper on the type of video signal that could be transferred directly from one card to another. In November 1983, these problems were solved by the Video Electronics Standards Association's (VESA) announcement of the VESA Advanced Feature Connector (VAFC) and the VESA

Media Channel (VMC) video bus standards. These new standards should bring about compatibility and performance for interconnected multimedia adapters and video adapters. These standards will ensure rapid growth in the adoption of new applications such as interactive video, video presentation, video conferencing, and desktop video editing.

The *VESA Advanced Feature Connector (VAFC)* provides a low cost extension of the industry standard VFC found on many graphics boards. VAFC meets high bandwidth requirements by widening the current feature connector data path from 8 to 16/32-bits and adding additional signals, which provide more reliable operation. The VAFC delivers 75M/sec throughput in its 16-bit baseline configuration, and up to 150M/sec in the 32-bit configuration. Other features include multiple pixels per clock, color space data, genlocking, and asynchronous video input.

The VAFC overcomes the current 640×480 pixel 256-color resolution limitations of most video overlay products. New video capture, overlay, compression, and playback products will use the VAFC interface to transfer video pixel data from board to board. This will allow video playback in a window to become a standard feature on PC systems.

The *VESA Media Channel (VMC)* is a dedicated multimedia bus that provides an independent path for the simultaneous processing of several high bandwidth video streams. The VMC directly addresses the current limitations of running video across a computer's system bus. This design solves the universal bandwidth bottleneck and latency issues that exist in all system or processor bus architectures including ISA, EISA, MicroChannel, VL-Bus, and PCI.

To correct these problems, the *VESA Media Channel* is designed to allow the transparent integration of video and graphics without the interference of processor interrupts or bus contention. The VESA Media Channel provides the option for a 68-pin multi-drop cable, allowing multiple devices to be combined in a modular fashion. For example, a graphics system supporting the VESA Media Channel can easily and cost-effectively be configured as a capture, decode-only, encode-only, or a full encode/decode video system. This is important in applications such as video teleconferencing, and provides flexible cost effective engineering of a particular system.

> **Tip**
>
> For any high performance video adapter, make sure that it supports at least the 80-pin VAFC connector or the 68-pin VMC connector. If you see only a 26-pin connector on the card, then the card would not be recommended as that is the standard VFC. Most of the higher-quality multimedia adapters will require a VAFC connection for high-performance video signal transfer.

If you will be using your system for video editing or other functions where connecting to the video card is important, make sure that your card is compatible. There are some cards out there that do not conform to the standard VAFC specifications.

Video Output Devices. When video technology was first introduced, it was based upon television. There is a difference between the signals a television uses and the signals used by a computer. In the United States, color TV standards were established in 1953 by the National Television System Committee (NTSC). Some countries, such as Japan, followed this standard. Many countries in Europe developed more sophisticated standards, including Phase Alternate Line (PAL) and SEquential Couleur Avec Memoire (SECAM). Table 10.13 shows the differences among these standards.

Table 10.13 Television versus Computer Monitors

Standard	Year Est.	Country	Lines	Rate
Television				
NTSC	1953 (color)	U.S., Japan	525	60Hz
	1941 (b&w)			
PAL	1941	Europe*	625	50Hz
SECAM	1962	France	625	25Hz
Computer				
VGA	1987	U.S.	640×480**	72Hz

*England, Holland, West Germany
**VGA is based upon more lines and uses pixels (480) versus lines; "genlocking" is used to lock pixels into lines and synchronize computers with TV standards.

A video-output (or VGA-to-NTSC) adapter enables you to show computer screens on a TV set or record them onto videotape for easy distribution. These products fall into two categories: those with *genlocking* (which enables the board to synchronize signals from multiple video sources or video with PC graphics) and those without. Genlocking provides the signal stability needed to obtain adequate results when recording to tape but is not necessary for simply using a video display.

VGA-to-NTSC converters come as both internal boards or external boxes that you can port along with your laptop-based presentation. These latter devices do not replace your VGA adapter but instead connect to your video adapter via an external cable that works with any type of VGA card. In addition to VGA input and output ports, a video-output board has a video output interface for S-Video and composite video.

VGA-to-TV converters support the standard NTSC television format and may also support the European PAL format. The resolution shown on a TV set or recorded on videotape is often limited to straight VGA at 640×480 pixels. Such boards may contain an "anti-flicker" circuit to help stabilize the picture, which often suffers from a case of the jitters in VGA-to-TV products.

Still-Image Video Capture Cards. Like a Polaroid camera, you can capture individual screen images for later editing and playback. Some plug into a PC's parallel port. These units capture still images from NTSC video sources like camcorders or VCRs. Although image quality is limited by the input signal, the results are still good enough for presentations and desktop publishing applications. These devices work with 8-, 16-, and 24-bit VGA cards and usually accept video input from VHS, Super VHS, and Hi-8 devices. As you might expect, though, Super VHS and Hi-8 video sources give better results, as do Super VGA modes with more than 256 colors.

You may want to invest in image-processing applications that offer features such as image editing, file conversion, screen capture, and graphics file management.

Desktop Video (DTV) Boards. You can also capture NTSC (television) signals to your computer system for display or editing. When capturing video, you should think in terms of digital versus analog. The biggest convenience of an analog TV signal is efficiency; it is a compact way to transmit video information through a low-bandwidth pipeline. The disadvantage is that while you can control how the video is displayed, you cannot edit it.

Actually capturing and recording video from external sources and saving the files onto your PC requires special technology. What is needed is a *video capture board,* which is also referred to as a *video digitizer* or *video grabber.*

One of the most common uses for analog video is with interactive Computer-Based Training (CBT) programs in which your application sends start, stop, and search commands to a laserdisc player that plays disks you have mastered. The software controls the player via an interface that also converts the laserdisc's NTSC signal into a VGA-compatible signal for display on your computer's monitor. These types of applications require NTSC-to-VGA conversion hardware.

Whereas a computer can display up to 16 million colors, the NTSC standard allows for only approximately 32,000 colors. Affordable video is the Achilles' heel of multimedia. The images are often jerky or less than full-screen. The reason is because full-motion video, such as you see on TV, requires 30 images or frames per second (fps).

The typical computer screen was designed to display mainly static images. The storing and retrieving of these images requires managing huge files. Consider this: A single, full-screen color image requires almost 2M of disk space; a one-second video would require 45M. Likewise, any video transmission that you want to capture for use on your PC must be converted from an analog NTSC signal to a digital signal that your computer can use. On top of that, the video signal must be moved inside your computer at 10 times the speed of the conventional ISA bus structure. You need not only a superior video card and monitor but also an excellent expansion bus, such as VL-Bus or PCI.

Considering the fact that full-motion video can consume massive quantities of disk space (0.5 seconds equals 15M), it becomes apparent that compression is needed. Compression and decompression (or *codec*) applies to both video and audio. Not only does a compressed file take up less space, it also performs better; there is simply less data to process. When you are ready to replay the video/audio, you simply decompress the file during playback. In any case, ensure your hard drive is large enough and has enough performance to handle the huge files that can result in storing video capture files. I would recommend a minimum of a 1 or 2G drive with either an enhanced IDE or SCSI-2 interface.

There are two types of codecs: *hardware-dependent codecs* and *software* (or *hardware-independent*) *codecs*. Hardware codecs are typically better; however, they require additional hardware. Software codes do not require hardware for compression or playback, but they typically do not deliver the same quality or compression ratio. Two of the major codec algorithms are:

- *JPEG (Joint Photographic Experts Group)*. Originally developed for still images, JPEG can be compressed and decompressed at rates acceptable for nearly full-motion video (30 fps). JPEG still uses a series of still images, which is easier for editing. JPEG is typically lossy, but it can also be lossless. It eliminates redundant data for each individual image (intraframe). Compression efficiency is approximately 30:1 (20:1–40:1).

- *MPEG (Motion Pictures Expert Group)*. Because MPEG can compress up to 200:1 at high-quality levels, it results in better, faster videos that require less space. MPEG is an interframe compressor. Because MPEG stores only incremental changes, it is not used during editing phases. MPEG decoding can be performed in software on high-performance Pentium systems.

If you will be capturing, compressing, and playing video, you will need Microsoft Video for Windows (VFW) or QuickTime. Codecs are provided along with VFW:

- *Cinepak*. Although Cinepak can take longer to compress, it can produce better quality and higher compression than Indeo. It is also referred to as *Compact Video Coded (CVC)*.

- *Indeo*. Indeo can outperform Cinepak and is capable of real-time compression. An Intel Smart Video board is required for real-time compression.

- *Microsoft Video 1*. Developed by MediaVision (MotiVE) and renamed MS Video 1, this codec is a DCT-based post-processor. A file is compressed after capture.

To play or record video on your multimedia PC (MPC), you will need some extra hardware and software:

- Video system software, such as Apple's QuickTime for Windows or Microsoft's Video for Windows.

- A compression/digitization video card that enables you to digitize and play large video files.

- An NTSC-to-VGA adapter that combines TV signals with computer video signals for output to a VCR. Video can come from a variety of sources: TV, VCR, video camera, or laserdisc player. When an animation file is recorded, it can be saved in a variety of different file formats: AVI (Audio Video Interleave), FLI (a 320×200 pixel animation file), or FLC (an animation file of any size).

You can incorporate these files into a multimedia presentation by using authoring software such as Icon Author from AIMTECH, or you can include the animated files as OLE objects to be used with Microsoft Word, Excel, Access, or other OLE-compliant applications.

http://www.quecorp.com

When you connect video devices, use the S-Video (S-VHS) connector whenever available. This cable provides the best signal because separate signals are used for color (*chroma*) and brightness (*luma*). Otherwise, you will have to use *composite video*, which mixes luma and chroma. This results in a lower-quality signal. The better your signal, the better your video quality will be.

You can get devices that just display NTSC signals on your computer. Soon, you will not know whether you are using a computer screen or a television. Digital video, in-screen filling, and full-motion color has arrived on desktop platforms with titles, playback boards, and encoding equipment. Soon, MPEG movie clip libraries will be the next form of clip art on CD-ROM. Hardware advances such as the MMX instructions incorporated into the Pentium architecture are helping to make motion video more of a useful reality rather than just a novelty.

3-D Graphics Accelerators. A three-dimensional—or 3-D—image can contain an immense amount of detail. To manage that detail, 3-D application programs usually store and work with abstractions of the images, rather than the actual images themselves. Up until recently, 3-D applications had to rely on support from software routines to convert these abstractions into live images. This heavily burdens the CPU in your PC, which significantly impacts the performance not only of the visual display but also of any other applications which may be running. Now there is a new breed of video accelerator chipset found on many new video adapters which can take on the job of rendering 3-D images, greatly lessening the load on your CPU and therefore greatly improving overall system performance.

The basic function of 3-D software is to convert image abstractions into what is seen on the video display. These abstractions generally consist of:

- *Vertices*. Locations in 3-D space, described in terms of their X, Y, and Z coordinates.
- *Primitives*. Simple geometric objects, described in terms of the relative locations of their vertices.
- *Textures*. Two-dimensional images or surfaces designed to be mapped onto primitives.

These abstract image descriptions must then be *rendered*, which means to be converted to visible form. Rendering depends on fairly standardized functions to convert the abstractions into the image that is displayed on-screen. The standard functions performed in rendering are:

- *Geometry*. Sizing, orienting, and moving primitives in space and calculating the effects of light sources.
- *Rasterization*. Converting primitives into pixels on the video display by filling the primitives with properly illuminated shading, textures, or a combination of the two.

A modern video card which is based on a chipset capable of 3-D video acceleration will have special built-in hardware that can perform the rasterization much faster than if done by software alone. Most chipsets with 3-D acceleration perform the following rasterization functions:

- *Scan conversion.* Determining which on-screen pixels are covered by each primitive.
- *Shading.* Filling pixels with colors that flow smoothly between the vertices.
- *Texturing.* Filling pixels with images from a 2-D picture or surface image.
- *Visible surface determination.* Identifying which pixels in a scene are obscured by objects closest to the viewer.
- *Animation.* Switching rapidly and cleanly to successive frames of motion sequences.

Hardware-accelerated rendering gives better image quality and faster animation than with software alone. Using special drivers, these cards can take over the intensive calculations formerly done by software to render a 3-D graphics image. This is especially useful if you are working with 3-D images, or if you are into the many modern games that rely extensively on 3-D displays.

System Video Information

There's more to video cards and monitors than just resolutions. You also have to know how the video card communicates to the monitor, and vice versa. The following sections describe how information is communicated to the monitor and back.

Monitor ID Pins

Table 10.14 shows the settings used for the monitor ID bits for several different IBM displays. By sensing which of these four pins are grounded, the video adapter can determine what type of display is attached. This is used especially with monochrome or color display detection. In this manner, the VGA or XGA circuitry can properly select the color mapping and image size to suit the display.

Table 10.14 IBM Display Monitor ID Settings

Display	Size	Type	ID0	ID1	ID2	ID3
8503	12-inch	Mono	No Pin	Ground	No Pin	No Pin
8512	13-inch	Color	Ground	No Pin	No Pin	No Pin
8513	12-inch	Color	Ground	No Pin	No Pin	No Pin
8514	15-inch	Color	Ground	No Pin	Ground	No Pin
8515	14-inch	Color	No Pin	No Pin	Ground	No Pin
9515	14-inch	Color	No Pin	No Pin	Ground	No Pin
9517	17-inch	Color	Ground	No Pin	Ground	Ground
9518	14-inch	Color	Ground	No Pin	Ground	No Pin

Advanced Power Management (APM)

APM is a specification created by Microsoft and Intel that allows the system BIOS to manage the power consumption of the system and various system devices.

For displays, power management is implemented by a standard called *DPMS (Display Power Management Signalling)*. This standard defines a method for signalling the monitor to enter into the various APM modes. The basis of the DPMS standard is the condition of the synchronization signals being sent to the display. By altering these signals, a DPMS-compatible monitor can be forced into the various APM modes.

The defined monitor states in DPMS are as follows:

- *On*. Refers to the state of the display when it is in full operation.

- *Stand-By*. Defines an optional operating state of minimal power reduction with the shortest recovery time.

- *Suspend*. Refers to a level of power management in which substantial power reduction is achieved by the display. The display can have a longer recovery time from this state than from the Stand-By state.

- *Off*. Indicates that the display is consuming the lowest level of power and is non-operational. Recovery from this state may optionally require the user to manually power on the monitor.

Table 10.15 summarizes the DPMS modes.

Table 10.15 Display Power Management Signaling

State	Horizontal	Vertical	Video	Power Savings	Recovery Time
On	Pulses	Pulses	Active	None	Not Applicable
Stand-by	No Pulses	Pulses	Blanked	Minimal	Short
Suspend	Pulses	No Pulses	Blanked	Substantial	Longer
Off	No Pulses	No Pulses	Blanked	Maximum	System Dependent

Adapter and Display Troubleshooting

Solving most graphics adapter and monitor problems is fairly simple, although costly, because replacing the adapter or display is the usual procedure. A defective or dysfunctional adapter or display usually is replaced as a single unit, rather than repaired. Most of today's cards cost more to service than to replace, and the documentation required to service the adapters or displays properly is not always available. You cannot get schematic diagrams, parts lists, wiring diagrams, and so on for most of the adapters or monitors. Many adapters now are constructed with surface-mount technology that requires a substantial investment in a rework station before you can remove and replace these components by hand. You cannot use a $25 pencil-type soldering iron on these boards!

Servicing monitors is a slightly different proposition. Although a display often is replaced as a whole unit, many displays are simply too expensive to replace. Your best bet is to either contact the company from which you purchased the display, or to contact one of the companies that specializes in monitor depot repair.

Depot repair means that you would send in your display to depot repair specialists who would either fix your particular unit or return an identical unit they have already repaired. This is normally accomplished for a flat-rate fee; in other words, the price is the same no matter what they have done to repair your actual unit.

Because you will usually get a different (but identical) unit in return, they can ship out your repaired display immediately on receiving the one you sent in, or even in advance in some cases. This way you have the least down time and can receive a repaired display as quickly as possible. In some cases, if your particular monitor is unique or one they don't have in stock, then you will have to wait while they repair your specific unit.

Troubleshooting a failed monitor is relatively simple. If your display goes out, for example, a swap with another monitor can confirm that the display is the problem. If the problem disappears when you change the display, then the problem was almost certainly in the original display; if the problem remains, then it is likely in the video card or PC itself.

After you narrow down the problem to the display, call the display manufacturer for the location of the nearest factory repair depot. There are also alternative third-party depot repair service companies that can repair most displays; their prices often are much lower than factory service. Check the vendor list in Appendix A for several companies who do depot repair of computer monitors and displays.

> **Caution**
>
> You should not attempt to repair a display yourself. Touching the wrong item can be fatal. The display circuits sometimes hold extremely high voltages for hours, days, or even weeks after the power is shut off. A qualified service person should discharge the cathode ray tube and power capacitors before proceeding.

For most displays, you are limited to making simple adjustments. For color displays, the adjustments can be quite formidable if you lack experience. Even factory service technicians often lack proper documentation and service information for newer models; they usually exchange your unit for another and repair the defective one later. Never buy a display for which no local factory repair depot is available.

If you have a problem with a display or adapter, it pays to call the manufacturer who might know about the problem and make repairs available, as occurred with the IBM 8513 display. Large numbers of the IBM 8513 color displays were manufactured with components whose values change over time and may exhibit text or graphics out of focus. I discovered that IBM replaced these displays at no cost when focusing is a problem. As the 8513 has been out of production for some time, replacements are no longer available.

Remember that most of the problems you have with modern video adapters and displays will be related to the drivers that control these devices rather than the hardware itself. Contact the manufacturers to ensure that you have the latest and proper drivers; there may be a solution that you are unaware of.

DisplayMate

DisplayMate is a unique diagnostic and testing program that is designed to thoroughly test your video adapter and display. It is somewhat unique in that most conventional PC hardware diagnostics programs do not emphasize video testing as this program does.

I find it useful not only in testing if a video adapter is functioning properly, but also in checking out video displays. You can easily test the image quality of a display, which allows you to make focus, centering, brightness and contrast, color level, and other adjustments much more accurately than before. If you are purchasing a new display, you can use Display Mate to evaluate the sharpness and linearity of the display, and to have a consistent way of checking each one you are considering. If you use projection systems for presentations as I do in my PC hardware seminars, you will find it invaluable for setting up and adjusting the projector.

DisplayMate can also test a video adapter thoroughly. It will set the video circuits into each possible video mode, and you can test what modes your card is capable of. It will also help you determine the performance level of your card, both with respect to resolution and colors as well as to speed. The program can be used to benchmark the performance of the display, which enables you to compare one type of video adapter system to another.

See the vendor list in Appendix A for more information on Sonera Technologies, the manufacturer and distributor of DisplayMate.

Chapter 11

Communications and Networking

Most computer-to-computer connections occur through a serial port, a parallel port, or a network adapter. In this chapter, you explore ways to connect your PC to other computers. Such connections enable you to transfer and share files, send electronic mail, access software on other computers, and generally make two or more computers behave as a team.

> **Note**
>
> For a much more detailed account of how to upgrade and repair networks, refer to Que's *Upgrading and Repairing Networks*, ISBN 0-7897-0181-2.

Using Communications Ports and Devices

The basic communications ports in any PC system are the serial and parallel ports. The serial ports are used primarily for devices that must communicate bidirectionally with the system. Such devices include modems, mice, scanners, digitizers, and any other devices that "talk to" and receive information from the PC.

Several companies also manufacture communications programs that perform high-speed transfers between PC systems using serial or parallel ports. Several products are currently on the market that make nontraditional use of the parallel port. You can purchase network adapters, floppy disk drives, CD-ROM drives, or tape backup units that attach to the parallel port, for example.

Serial Ports

The *asynchronous serial interface* is the primary system-to-system communications port. *Asynchronous* means that no synchronization or clocking signal is present, so characters may be sent with any arbitrary time spacing.

Each character sent over a serial connection is framed by a standard start and stop signal. A single 0 bit, called the *start bit*, precedes each character to tell the receiving system that the next 8 bits constitute a byte of data. One or two stop bits follow the character to signal that the character has been sent. At the receiving end of the communication, characters are recognized by the start and stop signals instead of by the timing of their arrival. The asynchronous interface is character-oriented and has about a 20 percent overhead for the extra information needed to identify each character.

Serial refers to data sent over a single wire, with each bit lining up in a series as the bits are sent. This type of communication is used over the phone system, because this system provides one wire for data in each direction. Add-on serial ports for the PC are available from many manufacturers. You usually can find these ports on one of the multifunction boards available or on a board with at least a parallel port. Figure 11.1 shows the standard 9-pin AT-style serial port, and Figure 11.2 shows the 25-pin version.

Serial ports may connect to a variety of devices such as modems, plotters, printers, other computers, bar code readers, scales, and device control circuits. Basically, anything that needs a two-way connection to the PC uses the industry-standard Reference Standard number 232 revision c (RS-232c) serial port. This device enables data transfer between otherwise incompatible devices. Tables 11.1, 11.2, and 11.3 show the pinouts of the 9-pin (AT-style), 25-pin, and 9-pin-to-25-pin serial connectors.

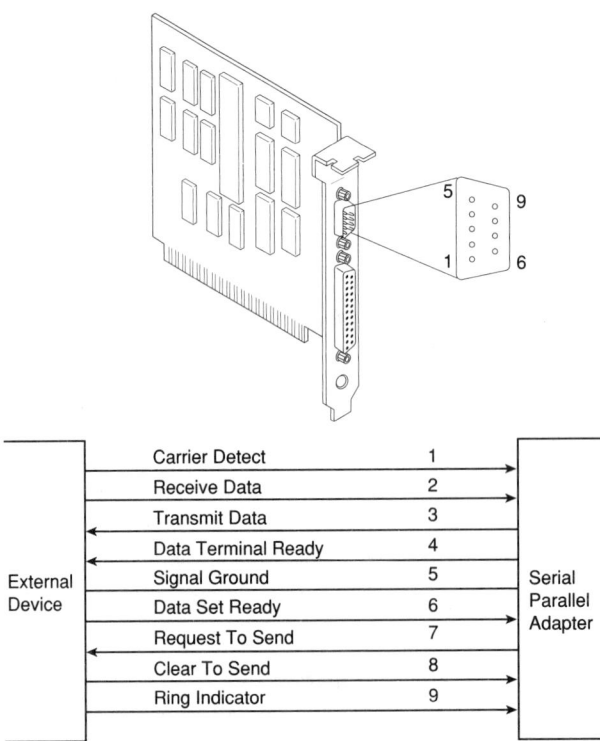

FIG. 11.1 AT-style 9-pin serialport connector specifications.

Using Communications Ports and Devices   **431**

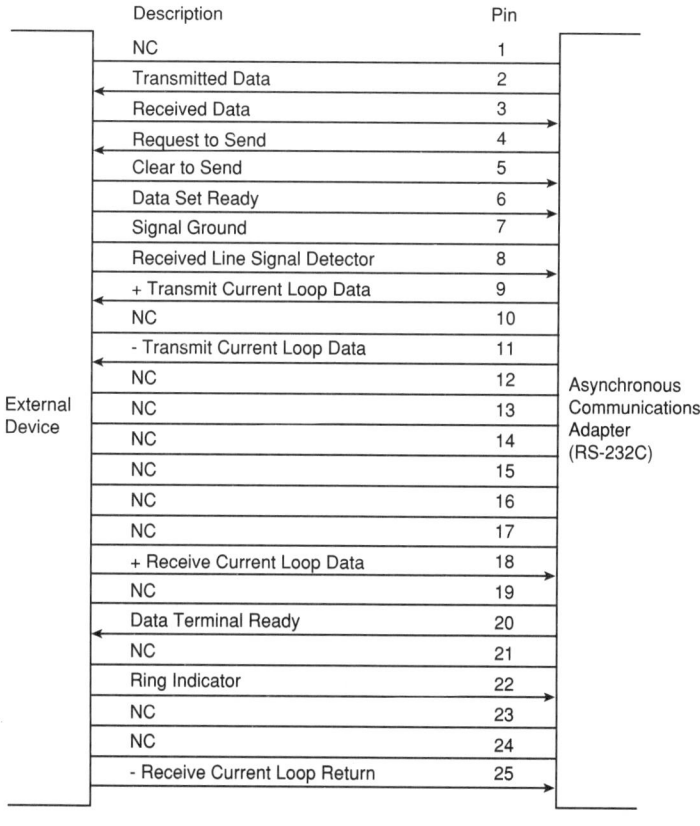

FIG. 11.2 Standard 25-pin serialport connector specifications.

Table 11.1 9-Pin (AT) Serial Port Connector

Pin	Signal	Description	I/O
1	CD	Carrier detect	In
2	RD	Receive data	In
3	TD	Transmit data	Out
4	DTR	Data terminal ready	Out
5	SG	Signal ground	—
6	DSR	Data set ready	In
7	RTS	Request to send	Out
8	CTS	Clear to send	In
9	RI	Ring indicator	In

Table 11.2 25-Pin (PC, XT, and PS/2) Serial Port Connector

Pin	Signal	Description	I/O
1	—	Chassis ground	—
2	TD	Transmit data	Out
3	RD	Receive data	In
4	RTS	Request to send	Out
5	CTS	Clear to send	In
6	DSR	Data set ready	In
7	SG	Signal ground	—
8	CD	Carrier detect	In
9	—	+Transmit current loop return	Out
11	—	-Transmit current loop data	Out
18	—	+Receive current loop data	In
20	DTR	Data terminal ready	Out
22	RI	Ring indicator	In
25	—	-Receive current loop return	In

Table 11.3 9-Pin to 25-Pin Serial Cable Adapter Connections

9-Pin	25-Pin	Signal	Description
1	8	CD	Carrier detect
2	3	RD	Receive data
3	2	TD	Transmit data
4	20	DTR	Data terminal ready
5	7	SG	Signal ground
6	6	DSR	Data set ready
7	4	RTS	Request to send
8	5	CTS	Clear to send
9	22	RI	Ring indicator

> **Note**
>
> Macintosh systems use a similar serial interface defined as RS-422. Most external modems in use today can interface with either RS-232 or RS-422, but it is safest to make sure that the external modem you get for your PC is designed for a PC, not a Macintosh.

The heart of any serial port is the *Universal Asynchronous Receiver/Transmitter (UART) chip*. This chip completely controls the process of breaking the native parallel data within the PC into serial format, and later converting serial data back into the parallel format.

There are several types of UART chips on the market. The original PC and XT used the 8250 UART, which is still used in many low-price serial cards on the market. In the PC/AT (or other systems based on at least an 80286 processor), the 16450 UART is used. The only difference between these chips is their suitability for high-speed communications. The 16450 is better suited for high-speed communications than the 8250; otherwise, both chips appear identical to most software.

The 16550 UART was the first serial chip used in the PS/2 line. This chip could function as the earlier 16450 and 8250 chips, but it also included a 16-byte buffer that aided in faster communications. This is sometimes referred to as a *FIFO (first in/first out) buffer*. Unfortunately, the 16550 also had a few bugs, particularly in the buffer area. These bugs were corrected with the release of the 16550A UART, which is used in all high-performance serial ports.

> **Tip**
>
> The 16550 UART chip is pin-for-pin compatible with the 16450 UART. If your 16450 UART is socketed, it is a cheap and easy way to improve serial performance to install a 16550 UART chip in the socket.

Because the 16550A is a faster, more reliable chip than its predecessors, it is best to look for serial ports that use it. If you are in doubt about which chip you have in your system, you can use the Microsoft MSD program (provided with Windows, MS DOS 6.x, and Windows 95) to determine the type of UART you have.

Another way to tell if you have a 16650 UART in Windows 95 is to right-click My Computer, and then click Properties. This brings up the System Properties dialog box. Choose the Device Manager tab, Ports, and then the communications port that you want to check. Choose the Port Settings tab and then click the Advanced button. This will bring up the Advanced Port Settings box. If you have a 16650 UART, there will be a check mark in the use FIFO Buffers option.

The original designer of these UARTs is National Semiconductor (NS). Many other manufacturers are producing clones of these UARTs, such that you probably don't have an actual NS brand part in your system. Even so, the part you have will be compatible with one of the NS parts, hopefully the 16550. In other words, you should check to see that whatever UART chip you do have does indeed feature the 16-byte FIFO buffer as found in the NS 16550 part.

Chapter 11—Communications and Networking

Some manufacturers have also begun making integrated chips which take on the functions of multiple chips. Boca Research, for instance, sells serial and parallel cards with little more than one Integrated Circuit (IC) on them. Most of these integrated chips function as a 16550 would; however, you should make sure that they have 16550 compatibility before purchasing them.

Table 11.4 lists the standard UART chips used in IBM and compatible systems.

Table 11.4 UART Chips in PC or AT Systems

Chip	Description
8250	IBM used this original chip in the PC serial port card. The chip has several bugs, none of which are serious. The PC and XT ROM BIOS are written to anticipate at least one of the bugs. This chip was replaced by the 8250B.
8250A	Do not use the second version of the 8250 in any system. This upgraded chip fixes several bugs in the 8250, including one in the interrupt enable register, but because the PC and XT ROM BIOS expect the bug, this chip does not work properly with those systems. The 8250A should work in an AT system that does not expect the bug, but does not work adequately at 9600 bps.
8250B	The last version of the 8250 fixes bugs from the previous two versions. The interrupt enable bug in the original 8250, expected by the PC and XT ROM BIOS software, has been put back into this chip, making the 8250B the most desirable chip for any non-AT serial port application. The 8250B chip may work in an AT under DOS, but does not run properly at 9600 bps.
16450	IBM selected the higher-speed version of the 8250 for the AT. Because this chip has fixed the interrupt enable bug mentioned earlier, the 16450 does not operate properly in many PC or XT systems, because they expect this bug to be present. OS/2 requires this chip as a minimum, or the serial ports do not function properly. It also adds a scratch-pad register as the highest register. The 16450 is used primarily in AT systems because of its increase in throughput over the 8250B.
16550	This newer UART improves on the 16450. This chip cannot be used in a FIFO buffering mode because of problems with the design, but it does enable a programmer to use multiple DMA channels and thus increase throughput on an AT or higher class computer system. I highly recommend replacing the 16550 UART with the 16550A.
16550A	This chip is a faster 16450 with a built-in 16-character Transmit and Receive FIFO buffer that works. It also allows multiple DMA channel access. You should install this chip in your AT system serial port cards if you do any serious communications at 9600 bps or higher. If your communications program makes use of the FIFO, which most do today, it can greatly increase communications speed and eliminate lost characters and data at the higher speeds.

On the Web

If you want more information on various chips, check out:

http://www.civil.mtu.edu/chipdir/chipdir.html

High-Speed Serial Ports

Some modem manufacturers have gone a step further on improving serial data transfer by introducing *Enhanced Serial Ports (ESP)* or *Super High Speed Serial Ports*. These ports enable a 28,800 bps modem to communicate with the computer at data rates up to 921,600 bps. The extra speed on these ports is generated by increasing the buffer size. These ports are usually based on a 16550AF UART or a 16550AF UART emulator with dual 1,024-byte buffers and on-board data flow control, and can provide great benefit in an environment where both your computer and the "receiving" computer are equipped

Using Communications Ports and Devices

with these ports. Otherwise, just one of the computers having an ESP doesn't yield any benefit.

As the need for additional serial devices continues to increase, users are beginning to need more than the two com ports that are standard in PCs. As a result, *multi-port serial cards* were created. These cards generally have 2–32 ports on them. Often they also provide higher baud rates than can be achieved on a standard serial port.

Most of the multiport serial cards on the market use standard 16550 UARTs with a processor (typically an 80×86 based processor) and some memory. These cards can improve performance slightly because the processor is dedicated to handling serial information. However, it's not always the best method for high-performance applications.

Some of the better multiport serial cards have broken the model of the 16550 UART in favor of a single integrated circuit. These cards have the advantage of higher sustainable throughput without loss. One such card is the Rocketport by Comtrol. It comes in ISA and PCI versions with up to 32 ports. Each port is capable of 232K baud sustained.

Various manufacturers make versions of the 16550A; National Semiconductor was the first. Its full part number for the 40-pin DIP is NS16550AN or NS16550AFN. Make sure that the part you get is the 16550A, and not the older 16550. You can contact Fry's Electronics or Jameco Electronics to obtain the NS16550AN, for example.

Serial Port Configuration

Each time a character is received by a serial port, it has to get the attention of the computer by raising an *Interrupt Request Line (IRQ)*. Eight-bit ISA bus systems have eight of these lines, and systems with a 16-bit ISA bus have 16 lines. The 8259 interrupt controller chip usually handles these requests for attention. In a standard configuration, COM1 uses IRQ4, and COM2 uses IRQ3.

When a serial port is installed in a system, it must be configured to use specific I/O addresses (called *ports*), and interrupts (called *IRQs* for Interrupt ReQuest). The best plan is to follow the existing standards for how these devices should be set up. For configuring serial ports, you should use the addresses and interrupts indicated in Table 11.5.

Table 11.5 Standard Serial I/O Port Addresses and Interrupts

System	COMx	Port	IRQ
All	COM1	3F8h	IRQ4
All	COM2	2F8h	IRQ3
ISA bus	COM3	3E8h	IRQ4*
ISA bus	COM4	2E8h	IRQ3*

*Note that although many serial ports can be set up to share IRQ 3 and 4 with COM1 and COM2, it is not recommended. The best recommendation is setting COM3 to IRQ 5. If ports above COM3 are required, it is recommended that you purchase a multiport serial board.

You should ensure that if you are adding more than the standard COM1 and COM2 serial ports, they use unique and nonconflicting interrupts. If you purchase a serialport adapter card and intend to use it to supply ports beyond the standard COM1 and COM2, be sure that it can use interrupts other than IRQ3 and IRQ4.

Another problem is that IBM never built BIOS support for COM3 and COM4 into its original ISA bus systems. Therefore, the DOS MODE command cannot work with serial ports above COM2 because DOS gets its I/O information from the BIOS, which finds out what is installed in your system and where during the POST. The POST in these older systems checks only for the first two installed ports. PS/2 systems have an improved BIOS that checks for as many as eight serial ports, although DOS is limited to handling only four of them.

To get around this problem, most communications software and some serial peripherals (such as mice) support higher COM ports by addressing them directly, rather than making DOS function calls. The communications program Procomm, for example, supports the additional ports even if your BIOS or DOS does not. Of course, if your system or software does not support these extra ports or you need to redirect data using the MODE command, trouble arises.

On the Web

Datastorm, the maker of Procomm, can be found at:

http://www.datastorm.com/

Windows 95 has added the support for up to 128 serial ports. This allows for the use of multiport boards in the system. *Multiport boards* give your system the ability to collect or share data with multiple devices, while using only one slot and one interrupt.

A couple of utilities enable you to append your COM port information to the BIOS, making the ports DOS-accessible. A program called Port Finder is one of the best, and is available in the "general hardware" data library of the **PCHW** forum on CompuServe.

Port Finder activates the extra ports by giving the BIOS the addresses and providing utilities for swapping the addresses among the different ports. Address swapping enables programs that don't support COM3 and COM4 to access them. Software that already directly addresses these additional ports usually is unaffected.

> **Caution**
>
> Sharing interrupts between COM ports or any devices can function some times and not others. It is recommended that you *never* share interrupts. It will cause you hours of frustration trying to track down drivers, patches, and updates to allow this to work successfully—if it's even possible in your system.

Modem Standards

Bell Labs and the CCITT have set standards for modem protocols. *CCITT* is an acronym for a French term that translates into English as the *Consultative Committee on International Telephone and Telegraph*. The organization was renamed the International Telecommunications Union (ITU) in the early 1990s, but the protocols developed under the old name are often referred to as such. Newly developed protocols are referred to as ITU-T standards. A *protocol* is a method by which two different entities agree to communicate. Bell Labs no longer sets new standards for modems, although several of its older standards are still used. Most modems built in the last few years conform to the CCITT standards.

The *ITU* is an international body of technical experts responsible for developing data communications standards for the world. The group falls under the organizational umbrella of the United Nations, and its members include representatives from major modem manufacturers, common carriers (such as AT&T), and governmental bodies. The ITU establishes communications standards and protocols in many areas, so one modem often adheres to several different standards, depending on its various features and capabilities. Modem standards can be grouped into the following three areas:

- Modulation standards

Bell 103	CCITT V.29
Bell 212A	CCITT V.32
CCITT V.21	CCITT V.32bis
CCITT V.22bis	CCITT V.34

- Error-correction standards

  CCITT V.42

- Data-compression standards

  V.42bis

Other standards have been developed by different companies (not Bell Labs or the ITU). These are sometimes called *proprietary standards*, even though most of these companies publish the full specifications of their protocols so that other manufacturers can develop modems to work with them. The following list shows some of the proprietary standards that have become fairly popular:

- Modulation

  HST

  PEP

  DIS

- Error correction

  MNP 1-4

  Hayes V-series

- Data compression

  MNP 5

  CSP

> ### 56K Modems
>
> At the time of this writing, two competing factions have developed for the development of so-called 56K modems. U.S. Robotics, one of today's leaders in modem technology, has developed a "standard" which they call X2. Rockwell and others have proposed a 56KFlex "standard."
>
> It remains to be seen if one or the other of these technologies will become "the standard" or if the ITU will decide to develop a third option which is the standard.

Almost all modems today claim to be *Hayes-compatible*, a phrase which has come to be as meaningless as IBM-compatible when referring to PCs. It does not refer to any communication protocol, but instead to the commands required to operate the modem. Because almost every modem uses the Hayes command set, this compatibility is a given and should not really affect your purchasing decisions about modems.

Not all modems that function at the same speed have the same functionality. Many modem manufacturers produce modems that have different feature sets at different price points. The more expensive modem usually supports such features as distinctive ring support and caller ID. When purchasing a modem, be sure that it supports all the features that you need.

On the Web

The following are the Web sites for U.S. Robotics, Hayes, Microcom, and Megahertz, respectively:

http://www.usrobotics.com/

http://www.hayes.com/

http://www.microcom.com/

http://www.megahertz.com/

The basic modem commands don't vary from modem manufacturer to manufacturer as much as they did. Some modems, most notably U.S. Robotics, allow you to query the command set by simply sending **AT$** to the modem.

A list of the basic commands can be found in Table 11.6 of the sixth edition of this book, which is included on the CD-ROM. However, the best sources of modem commands are the manuals that came with the modem.

Baud Versus Bits Per Second (bps). Baud rate and bit rate often are confused in discussions about modems. *Baud rate* is the rate at which a signal between two devices changes in one second. If a signal between two modems can change frequency or phase at a rate of 300 times per second, for example, that device is said to communicate at 300 baud.

Sometimes a single modulation change is used to carry a single bit. In that case, 300 baud also equals 300 bits per second (bps). If the modem could signal two bit values for each signal change, the bps rate would be twice the baud rate, or 600 bps at 300 baud. Most modems transmit several bits per baud, so that the actual baud rate is much slower than the bps rate. In fact, people usually use the term *baud* incorrectly. We normally are not interested in the raw baud rate, but in the bps rate, which is the true gauge of communications speed.

Modulation Standards. Modems start with *modulation*, which is the electronic signaling method used by the modem (from modulator to demodulator). Modems must use the same modulation method to understand each other. Each data rate uses a different modulation method, and sometimes more than one method exists for a particular rate.

The three most popular modulation methods are:

- *Frequency-shift keying (FSK).* A form of frequency modulation, otherwise known as *FM*. By causing and monitoring frequency changes in a signal sent over the phone line, two modems can send information.

- *Phase-shift keying (PSK).* A form of phase modulation, in which the timing of the carrier signal wave is altered and the frequency stays the same.

- *Quadrature-amplitude modulation (QAM).* A modulation technique that combines phase changes with signal-amplitude variations, resulting in a signal that can carry more information than the other methods.

Bell 103. Bell 103 is a U.S. and Canadian 300 bps modulation standard. It uses FSK modulation at 300 baud to transmit 1 bit per baud. Most higher-speed modems will still communicate using this protocol, even though it is obsolete.

Bell 212A. Bell 212A is the U.S. and Canadian 1200 bps modulation standard. It uses differential phase-shift keying (DPSK) at 600 baud to transmit 2 bits per baud.

V.21. V.21 is an international data-transmission standard for 300 bps communications, similar to Bell 103. Because of some differences in the frequencies used, Bell 103 modems are not compatible with V.21 modems. This standard is used primarily outside the United States.

V.22. V.22 is an international 1200 bps data-transmission standard. This standard is similar to the Bell 212A standard, but is incompatible in some areas, especially in answering a call. This standard was used primarily outside the United States.

V.22bis. V.22bis is a data-transmission standard for 2400 bps communications. *Bis* is derived from the Latin meaning *second*, indicating that this data transmission is an improvement to or follows V.22. This data transmission is an international standard for 2,400 bps and is used inside and outside the United States. V.22bis uses QAM at 600 baud and transmits 4 bits per baud to achieve 2,400 bps.

V.23. V.23 is a split data-transmission standard, operating at 1,200 bps in one direction and 75 bps in the reverse direction. Therefore, the modem is only *pseudo-full-duplex*, meaning that it can transmit data in both directions simultaneously, but not at the maximum data rate. This standard was developed to lower the cost of 1200 bps modem technology, which was expensive in the early 1980s. This standard was used primarily in Europe.

V.29. V.29 is a data-transmission standard at 9,600 bps, which defines a half duplex (one-way) modulation technique. This standard generally is used in Group III facsimile (fax) transmissions, and only rarely in modems. Because V.29 is a half-duplex method, it is substantially easier to implement this high-speed standard than to implement a high-speed full-duplex standard. As a modem standard, V.29 has not been fully defined, so V.29 modems of different brands seldom can communicate with each other. This does not affect fax machines, which have a fully defined standard.

V.32. V.32 is a full-duplex (two-way) data transmission standard that runs at 9,600 bps. It is a full modem standard, and also includes forward error-correcting and negotiation standards. V.32 uses *TCQAM (trellis-coded quadrature amplitude modulation)* at 2,400 baud to transmit 4 bits per baud, resulting in the 9,600 bps transmission speed.

The trellis coding is a special forward error-correction technique that creates an additional bit for each packet of 4. This extra check bit is used to allow on-the-fly error correction to take place at the other end. It also greatly increases the resistance of V.32 to noise on the line.

In the past, V.32 has been expensive to implement because the technology it requires is complex. Because a one-way, 9600 bps stream uses almost the entire bandwidth of the phone line, V.32 modems implement echo cancellation, meaning that they cancel out the overlapping signal that their own modems transmit and just listen to the other modem's signal. This procedure is complicated and was at one time costly. Advances in lower-cost chipsets then made these modems inexpensive, and they were the de facto 9,600 bps standard for some time.

V.32bis. V.32bis is a 14,400 bps extension to V.32. This protocol uses TCQAM modulation at 2,400 baud to transmit 6 bits per baud, for an effective rate of 14,400 bps. The trellis coding makes the connection more reliable. This protocol is also a full-duplex modulation protocol, with a fallback to V.32 if the phone line is impaired. It is the communications standard for dialup lines because of its excellent performance and resistance to noise. I recommend the V.32bis-type modem.

V.32fast. V.32fast, or V.FC (Fast Class) as it is also called, was a new standard being proposed to the CCITT. V.32fast is an extension to V.32 and V.32bis, but offers a transmission speed of 28,800 bps. It has been superseded by V.34.

V.34. V.34 is the latest in the world of modem standards. It has superseded all the other 28.8Kbps standards, and is the current state of the art in analog modem communications. It has been proven as the most reliable standard of communication at 28.8Kbps. A recent annex to the V.34 standard also defines optional higher speeds of 31.2 and 33.6Kbps, which most of the newer V.34 modems will be capable of. Many existing V.34 modems designed using sophisticated Digital Signal Processors (DSPs) can be upgraded to support the new 33.6Kbps speeds by merely installing a software upgrade in the modem. This is accomplished by downloading the Modem ROM upgrade from the manufacturer, and then running a program they supply to "flash" the modem's ROM with the new code.

V.34 is the fastest communication now possible over an analog serial connection. It is also the fastest that analog communications are likely to get. Looming on the horizon is the fact that the phone system eventually will be digital. All further development on analog transmission schemes will end, and new digital modems will be developed.

Error-Correction Protocols. *Error correction* refers to the capability of some modems to identify errors during a transmission, and to automatically resend data that appears to have been damaged in transit. For error correction to work, both modems must adhere to the same correction standard. Fortunately, most modem manufacturers adhere to the same error-correction standards.

MNP 1-4. This is a proprietary standard that was developed by Microcom which provides basic error correction. The Microcom networking Protocol (MNP) is covered in more detail in the "Proprietary Standards" section.

V.42. V.42 is an error-correction protocol, with fallback to MNP 4, and version 4 is an error-correction protocol as well. Because the V.42 standard includes MNP compatibility through Class 4, all MNP 4-compatible modems can establish error-controlled connections with V.42 modems.

This standard uses a protocol called *LAPM (Link Access Procedure for Modems)*. LAPM, like MNP, copes with phone-line impairments by automatically retransmitting data corrupted during transmission, assuring that only error-free data passes between the modems. V.42 is considered to be better than MNP 4 because it offers about a 20 percent higher transfer rate due to its more intelligent algorithms.

Data-Compression Standards. *Data compression* refers to a built-in capability in some modems to compress the data they're sending, thus saving time and money for long-distance modem users. Depending on the type of files that are sent, data can be compressed to one-fourth its original size, effectively quadrupling the speed of the modem. For example, a 14,400 modem with compression can yield transmission rates of up to 57,600 bps, and a 28,800 modem can yield up to 115,200 bps.

MNP 5. Microcom continued the development of its MNP protocols to include a compression protocol named MNP 5. This protocol is discussed more fully in the section "Proprietary Protocols."

V.42bis. V.42bis is a CCITT data-compression standard similar to MNP Class 5 but providing about 35 percent better compression. V.42bis is not actually compatible with MNP Class 5, but nearly all V.42bis modems include the MNP 5 data-compression capability as well.

This protocol can sometimes quadruple throughput, depending on the compression technique used. This fact has led to some mildly false advertising; for example, a 2400 bps V.42bis modem might advertise "9600 bps throughput" by including V.42bis as well, but this would be possible in only extremely optimistic cases, such as in sending text files that are very loosely packed. In the same manner, many 9600 bps V.42bis makers now advertise "up to 38.4K bps throughput" by virtue of the compression. Just make sure that you see the truth behind such claims.

V.42bis is superior to MNP 5 because it analyzes the data first, and then determines whether compression would be useful. V.42bis only compresses data that needs compression. Files found on bulletin board systems often are compressed already (using PKZIP or a similar program). Further attempts at compressing already compressed data can increase the size of the file and slow things down. MNP 5 always attempts to compress the data, which slows down throughput on previously compressed files. V.42bis, however, compresses only data that will benefit from the compression.

To negotiate a standard connection using V.42bis, V.42 also must be present. Therefore, a modem with V.42bis data compression is assumed to include V.42 error correction. These two protocols, when combined, result in an error-free connection that has the maximum data compression possible.

Proprietary Standards. In addition to the industry-standard protocols for modulation, error correction, and data compression that generally are set forth or approved by the ITU-T, several protocols in these areas were invented by various companies and included in their products without any official endorsement by any standards body. Some of these protocols have been quite popular at times and became pseudo-standards of their own.

The most successful proprietary protocols are the MNP (Microcom Networking Protocols) that were developed by Microcom. These error-correction and data-compression protocols are supported widely by other modem manufacturers as well.

Another company that has been successful in establishing proprietary protocols as limited standards is U.S. Robotics, with its HST (high-speed technology) modulation protocols. Because of an aggressive marketing campaign with BBS operators, it captured a large portion of the market with its products in the 1980s.

This section examines these and other proprietary modem protocols.

HST. The HST is a 14,400 bps and 9,600 bps modified half-duplex proprietary modulation protocol used by U.S. Robotics. Although common in BBSes, the HST is now all but extinct, due to V.32 modems having become more competitive in price. HST modems run at 9,600 bps or 14,400 bps in one direction, and 300 or 450 bps in the other direction. This is an ideal protocol for interactive sessions. Because echo-cancellation circuitry is not required, costs are lower.

U.S. Robotics also marketed modems that used the standard protocols as well as their proprietary standard. These dual standard modems incorporated both V.32bis and HST protocols, giving you the best of the standard and proprietary worlds and enabling you to connect to virtually any other system at the maximum communications rate. They were at one time among the best modems available; I used and recommended them for many years.

DIS. The DIS is a 9,600 bps proprietary modulation protocol by CompuCom, which uses *dynamic impedance stabilization (DIS)*, with claimed superiority in noise rejection over V.32. Implementation appears to be very inexpensive, but like HST, only one company makes modems with the DIS standard. Because of the lower costs of V.32 and V.32bis, this proprietary standard will likely disappear.

MNP. MNP offers end-to-end error correction, meaning that the modems are capable of detecting transmission errors and requesting retransmission of corrupted data. Some levels of MNP also provide data compression.

As MNP evolved, different classes of the standard were defined, describing the extent to which a given MNP implementation supports the protocol. Most current implementations support Classes 1 through 5. Higher classes usually are unique to modems manufactured by Microcom, Inc., because they are proprietary.

MNP generally is used for its error-correction capabilities, but MNP Classes 4 and 5 also provide performance increases, with Class 5 offering real-time data compression. The lower classes of MNP usually are not important to you as a modem user, but they are included in the following list for the sake of completeness:

- *MNP Class 1 (block mode)* uses asynchronous, byte-oriented, half-duplex (one-way) transmission. This method provides about 70 percent efficiency and error correction only, so it's rarely used today.

- *MNP Class 2 (stream mode)* uses asynchronous, byte-oriented, full-duplex (two-way) transmission. This class also provides error correction only. Because of protocol overhead (the time it takes to establish the protocol and operate it), throughput at Class 2 is only about 84 percent of that for a connection without MNP, delivering about 202 cps (characters per second) at 2,400 bps (240 cps is the theoretical maximum). Class 2 is used rarely today.

- *MNP Class 3* incorporates Class 2 and is more efficient. It uses a synchronous, bit-oriented, full-duplex method. The improved procedure yields throughput about 108 percent of that of a modem without MNP, delivering about 254 cps at 2,400 bps.

- *MNP Class 4* is a performance-enhancement class that uses Adaptive Packet Assembly and Optimized Data Phase techniques. Class 4 improves throughput and performance by about 5 percent, although actual increases depend on the type of call and connection, and can be as high as 25 to 50 percent.

- *MNP Class 5* is a data-compression protocol that uses a real-time adaptive algorithm. It can increase throughput up to 50 percent, but the actual performance of Class 5 depends on the type of data being sent. Raw text files allow the highest increase, although program files cannot be compressed as much and the increase is smaller. On precompressed data (files already compressed with ARC, PKZIP, and so on), MNP 5 decreases performance, and therefore is often disabled on BBS systems.

V-Series. The Hayes V-series is a proprietary error-correction protocol by Hayes that was used in some of its modems. Since the advent of lower-cost V.32 and V.32bis modems (even from Hayes), the V-series has all but become extinct. These modems used a modified V.29 protocol, which is sometimes called a *ping-pong protocol* because it has one high-speed channel and one low-speed channel that alternate back and forth.

CSP. The *CSP (CompuCom Speed Protocol)* is an error-correction and data-compression protocol available on CompuCom DIS modems.

FAXModem Standards. Facsimile technology is a science unto itself, although it has many similarities to data communications. These similarities have led to the combination of data and faxes into the same modem. You now can purchase a single board that will send and receive both data and faxes. All of the major modem manufacturers have models that support this capability.

Over the years, the CCITT has set international standards for fax transmission. This has led to the grouping of faxes into one of four groups. Each group (I through IV) uses different technology and standards for transmitting and receiving faxes. Groups I and II are relatively slow and provide results that are unacceptable by today's standards. Group III is the standard in use today by virtually all fax machines, including those combined with modems. Whereas Groups I through III are analog in nature (similar to modems), Group IV is digital and designed for use with ISDN or other digital networks. Because the telephone system has not been converted to a fully digital network yet, there are very few Group IV fax systems available.

Group III Fax. There are two general subdivisions within the Group III fax standard—Class 1 and Class 2. Many times you will hear about a FAXModem supporting Group III, Class 1 fax communications. This simply indicates which protocols the board is able to send and receive. If your FAXModem does this, it can communicate with most of the other fax machines in the world. In FAXModems, the Class 1 specification is implemented by an additional group of modem commands that the modem translates and acts upon.

Earlier you learned about the V.29 modulation standard. As stated in that section, this standard is used for Group III fax transmissions.

Modem Recommendations. Today the cost of 33.6K-bps modems has dropped to between $100 and $200, on average, including fax capabilities. I would normally recommend that you purchase an internal modem if your computer has space for it; however, I prefer external modems myself, due to the additional troubleshooting capabilities possible by watching the LEDs that indicate the modem's status. Internal modems usually ship with a high-speed UART on the modem card, thus eliminating the need to upgrade any older, slower UARTs you may have in your PC. If you don't have an internal slot for a modem, be sure that you have the appropriate UART. Today, most modems come with multiple forms of error correction or data compression.

Integrated Services Digital Network (ISDN)

ISDN modems are the next step in telecommunications. ISDN modems make the break from the old technology of analog data transfer to the newer digital data transfer. Digital technology allows you to send voice, data, images, and faxes simultaneously over the same pair of wires at up to 128Kbps. ISDN modems required an ISDN service for connection, which is more readily available today. Prices for ISDN service vary widely, depending on your location. U.S. prices—on average—are approximately $130 to $150 for the initial installation and $50 to $100 a month. There is usually a connect-time charge as well that can range from 1 to 6 cents a minute. These are all line charges paid to the telephone company. You will also have to purchase an ISDN modem, and there will also be an additional charge from your service provider for Internet Access at ISDN speeds.

> **Caution**
>
> When purchasing an ISDN modem, you will almost always want to purchase an internal version. An ISDN modem with compression can easily exceed a serial port's ability to reliably send and receive data. Consider that even a moderate 2:1 compression ratio exceeds the maximum rated speed of 232Kbps that most high-speed COM ports support.

ISDN has become extremely popular in Europe, where leased lines are often prohibitively expensive. ISDN modems have also dropped considerably in price; what was once a $1,500 to $2,000 device can now be purchased for as little as $400. As demands for more bandwidth increase, and conventional asynchronous modem standards become more inadequate, ISDN should gain in popularity, causing prices to drop further. ISDN modems are far more complex than standard analog modems.

ISDN modems have three separate channels. Two of the channels are called B channels; these are the data-carrying channels and are 64Kbps each. The third channel is the D channel, which is 16Kbps. The slower D channel is used for routing and handling information. It is this technology that is making it possible for more and more people to participate in video conferencing.

To be technically precise, ISDN devices are not "modems." Modems modulate digital signals so they can be transmitted over an analog phone line and then demodulate the signal back to digital form for the computer. ISDN runs over an entirely digital telephone network (most of the telephone infrastructure in the United States is now digital), so there is no need for the modulation and demodulation processes. The most common type of ISDN device for a PC is called a *terminal adapter*. ISDN can be implemented as either a serial device or as a network interface. Using a network type interface eliminates the bottleneck at the computer's serial port. This type of ISDN terminal adapter may be the preferred solution for reasons of performance, even if you have only one computer and don't need the other services provided by a network.

ISDN requires additional telephone wiring and service from the telephone company. You will first need to check with your local telephone company to see if ISDN service is available in your area. (It is now available in most parts of the U.S.) In many cases, this can be the most difficult part of the installation. ISDN service, although available for many years, is only beginning to become a popular item. Often, the first hurdle to overcome is finding someone at a telephone company who knows what ISDN is. Then, you will find that prices can vary widely, depending on the distance between your location and the nearest phone company POP (point of presence). You can have the telephone company install the wiring and jacks or install them yourself, if you are so inclined. Que's *Special Edition Using ISDN* has excellent detailed coverage of the wiring process for the ISDN do-it-yourselfer.

56K Modems

In the ever-continuing quest for speed, a new breed of modems is coming to market. These modems allow for downstream communications—those going from the host to the client—up to 56Kbits/sec. This doubles 28.8K and not quite doubles the preceding standard of 33.6K/sec.

> **Note**
>
> New technologies, which require central office (CO) upgrades, promise to bring multimegabyte speeds to the same telephone wiring that is already run to your home. However, these technologies are still being tested and are not widely deployed yet.

To understand how this additional speed was captured, you need to understand a few basic principles of modem technology. In a traditional modem, circuit information is converted from digital form to analog, so it can travel over the Public Switched Telephone Network (PSTN), and finally back to a digital signal.

This conversion from digital to analog and back causes some speed loss. Even though the phone line is capable of carrying about 56K of information over it, the effective maximum speed because of conversions is about 33.6Kbits. A man by the name of Shannon came up with a law (Shannon's Law) which states that the maximum speed over an analog phone circuit is 33.6K.

However, Shannon's Law assumes that the telephone network is entirely analog. That is not the case in most of the United States today. In urban areas, most circuits are digital until they reach the CO which your phone line is connected to. The CO converts the digital signal into an analog signal before sending it to your home.

Considering the fact that the phone system is largely digital, you can—in some cases—remove the first step of translating the information from digital form to analog form for transmission over the digital PSTN.

The result is that you can, if you connect the host modem digitally, eliminate the restriction of 33.6K shown in Shannon's Law. The result is that data can be transmitted at the full 56K capacity of the phone line in one direction. The other direction, from your computer to the host, will still operate at the 33.6K speed.

When looking to purchase an 56K modem, you may be surprised to know that you may not be able to use these modems at their top speed based on the PSTN between you and the host system.

There are some very specific requirements to make 56K modems work. They are:

- *There can be only one digital-to-analog conversion in the network*. This means that the connections between your CO and the CO which services the host must be all digital.

- *The host must be connected digitally*. One end of the connection must be connected to the PSTN.

- *Both modems must support the 56K technology*. Both modems must support the same 56K technology.

Parallel Ports

A *parallel port* has eight lines for sending all the bits that comprise 1 byte of data simultaneously across eight wires. This interface is fast and has traditionally been used for printers. However, programs to transfer data between systems have always used the parallel port as an option for transmitting data because it can do so 4 bits at a time rather than 1 bit at a time with a serial interface.

In the following section, we'll look at how these programs transfer data between parallel ports. The only problem with parallel ports is that their cables cannot be extended for any great length without amplifying the signal, or errors occur in the data. Table 11.6 shows the pinout for a standard PC parallel port.

Table 11.6 25-Pin PC-Compatible Parallel Port Connector

Pin	Description	I/O
1	-Strobe	Out
2	+Data Bit 0	Out
3	+Data Bit 1	Out
4	+Data Bit 2	Out
5	+Data Bit 3	Out
6	+Data Bit 4	Out
7	+Data Bit 5	Out
8	+Data Bit 6	Out
9	+Data Bit 7	Out
10	-Acknowledge	In
11	+Busy	In
12	+Paper End	In
13	+Select	In
14	-Auto Feed	Out
15	-Error	In
16	-Initialize Printer	Out
17	-Select Input	Out
18	-Data Bit 0 Return (GND)	In
19	-Data Bit 1 Return (GND)	In
20	-Data Bit 2 Return (GND)	In
21	-Data Bit 3 Return (GND)	In
22	-Data Bit 4 Return (GND)	In
23	-Data Bit 5 Return (GND)	In
24	-Data Bit 6 Return (GND)	In
25	-Data Bit 7 Return (GND)	In

Over the years, several types of parallel ports have evolved. Some of them are IBM-specific, while others can be found in any PC-compatible system. Here are the primary types of parallel ports found in systems today:

- Unidirectional (4-bit)
- Bidirectional (8-bit)
- Type 1 (standard)
- DMA Type 3 (IBM specific)
- Enhanced Parallel Port (EPP)
- Enhanced Capabilities Port (ECP)

The following sections discuss each of these types of parallel ports.

Unidirectional (4-bit). The original IBM PC did not have different types of parallel ports available. The only port available was the parallel port used to send information from the computer to a device, such as a printer. This is not to say that bidirectional parallel ports were not available; indeed, they were common in other computers on the market and in hobbyist computers at the time.

The unidirectional nature of the original PC parallel port is consistent with its primary use—that is, of sending data to a printer. There were times, however, when it was desirable to have a bidirectional port—for example, when you need feedback from a printer, which is common with PostScript printers. This could not be done with the original unidirectional ports.

Although it was never intended to be used for input, a clever scheme was devised where four of the signal lines could be used as a 4-bit input connection. Thus these ports can do 8-bit byte output and 4-bit (nibble) input. This is still very common on low-end desktop systems. Systems built after 1993 are likely to have more capable parallel ports, such as 8-bit, EPP, or ECP.

Four-bit ports are capable of effective transfer rates of about 40–60K/sec with typical devices and can be pushed to upwards of 140K/sec with certain design tricks.

Bidirectional (8-bit) Type 1. With the introduction of the PS/2 in 1987, IBM introduced the bidirectional parallel port. These are commonly found in PC-compatible systems today, and may be designated "PS/2 type," "bidirectional," or "extended" parallel port. This port design opened the way for true communications between the computer and the peripheral across the parallel port. This was done by defining a few of the previously unused pins in the parallel connector, and defining a status bit to indicate in which direction information was traveling across the channel.

In IBM documentation, this original PS/2 port became known as a *Type 1 parallel port.* Other vendors also introduced third-party ports that were compatible with the Type 1 port. These ports can usually be configured in both standard and bidirectional modes, and unless you specifically configure the port for bidirectional use, it will function just like the original unidirectional port. This configuration is normally done with the CMOS SETUP or configuration program that accompanies your system. Most systems built since 1991 have this capability, although many do not enable it as a default setting.

These ports can do both 8-bit input and output using the standard eight data lines, and are considerably faster than the 4-bit ports when used with external devices. 8-bit ports are capable of speeds ranging from 80–300K/sec, depending on the speed of the attached device, the quality of the driver software, and the port's electrical characteristics.

These ports are also largely not supported by software because they were almost universally installed in PS/2 machines and not standard PC-compatible machines.

Bidirectional (8-bit DMA) Type 3. With the introduction of the PS/2 Models 57, 90, and 95, IBM introduced the Type 3 parallel port. This was a special bidirectional port that featured greater throughput through the use of DMA techniques. This port was specifically used in IBM systems only, and was not found in other PC compatibles.

You may be wondering why IBM skipped from Type 1 to Type 3. In reality, they did not. There is a Type 2 parallel port, and it served as a predecessor to the Type 3. It is only slightly less capable, but was never used widely in any IBM systems.

The Type 3 bidirectional parallel port also never gained enough industry acceptance to obtain good driver or software support.

Enhanced Parallel Port (EPP). EPP is a newer specification sometimes referred to as the *Fast Mode parallel port.* The EPP was developed by Intel, Xircom, and Zenith Data Systems and announced in October 1991. The first products to offer EPP were ZDS laptops, Xircom Pocket LAN Adapters, and the Intel 82360 SL I/O chip.

EPP operates almost at ISA bus speed, and offers a 10-fold increase in the raw throughput capability over a conventional parallel port. EPP is especially designed for parallel port peripherals such as LAN adapters, disk drives, and tape backups. EPP has been included in the new IEEE 1284 Parallel Port standard. Transfer rates of 1 to 2M/sec are possible with EPP.

Since the original Intel 82360 SL I/O chip in 1992, other major chip vendors (such as National Semiconductor, SMC, Western Digital, and VLSI) have also produced I/O chipsets offering some form of EPP capability. One problem is that the procedure for enabling EPP across the various chips differs widely from vendor to vendor, and many vendors offer more than one I/O chip.

EPP version 1.7 (March 1992) identifies the first popular version of the hardware specification. With minor changes, this has since been abandoned and folded into the IEEE 1284 standard. Some technical reference materials have erroneously made reference to "EPP specification version 1.9," causing confusion about the EPP standard. Note that "EPP version 1.9" does not exist, and any EPP specification after the original version 1.7 is technically a part of the IEEE 1284 specification.

Unfortunately, this has resulted in two somewhat incompatible standards for EPP parallel ports: the original EPP Standards Committee version 1.7 standard, and the IEEE 1284 Committee standard. The two standards are sufficiently similar that new peripherals may be designed in such a way as to support both standards, but existing EPP 1.7 peripherals may not operate with EPP 1284 ports.

EPP ports were more common with IBM machines than with other hardware manufacturers who seemed to stay away from the printer port issue until the Enhanced Capabilities Port (ECP) was introduced by Microsoft and Hewlett-Packard (HP). However, because the EPP port is defined in the IEEE 1284 standard, it has gained software and driver support, including support in Windows NT.

Enhanced Capabilities Port (ECP). Another type of high-speed parallel port called the *ECP (Enhanced Capabilities Port)* was jointly developed by Microsoft and Hewlett-Packard and formally announced in 1992. Like EPP, ECP offers improved performance for the parallel port and requires special hardware logic.

Since the original announcement, ECP is included in IEEE 1284 just like EPP. Unlike EPP, ECP is not tailored to support portable PC's parallel port peripherals; its purpose is to support an inexpensive attachment to a very high-performance printer. Further, ECP mode requires the use of a DMA channel, which EPP did not define, and which can cause troublesome conflicts with other devices that use DMA. Most PCs with newer "super I/O" chips will be able to support either EPP or ECP mode.

Most new systems are being delivered with ECP ports which support high throughput communications. In most cases, the ECP ports can be turned into EPP, or standard unidirectional parallel ports via BIOS. However, it's recommended that the port be placed in ECP mode for the best throughput.

IEEE 1284. The IEEE 1284 standard called "Standard Signaling Method for a Bidirectional Parallel Peripheral Interface for Personal Computers" was approved for final release in March 1994. This standard defines the physical characteristics of the parallel port, including data transfer modes and physical and electrical specifications.

IEEE 1284 defines the electrical signaling behavior external to the PC for a multimodal parallel port which may support 4-bit and modes of operation. Not all modes are required by the 1284 specification, and the standard makes some provision for additional modes.

The IEEE 1284 specification is targeted at standardizing the behavior between a PC and an attached device, most specifically attached printers, although the specification is of interest to vendors of parallel port peripherals (disks, LAN adapters, and so on).

IEEE 1284 is a hardware and line control-only standard and does not define how software should talk to the port. An offshoot of the original 1284 standard has been created to define the software interface. The IEEE 1284.3 committee was formed to develop a standard for software used with IEEE 1284-compliant hardware. This standard, designed to address the disparity among providers of parallel port chips, contains a specification for supporting EPP mode via the PC's system BIOS.

IEEE 1284 allows for much higher throughput in a connection between a computer and a printer, or two computers. The result is that the printer cable is no longer the standard printer cable. The IEEE 1284 printer cable uses twisted-pair technology, the same technology that allows Category 5 cabling to carry speeds up to 100Mbps.

IEEE 1284 also defined a new port, which most people aren't familiar with. A type A connector in the IEEE 1284 standard is defined as a DB25 pin connector. A type B connector is defined as a Centronics 36 connector. The new connector, referred to as type C, is a high-density connector, which is already beginning to be installed in HP's printer line. The three connectors are shown in Figure 11.3.

Upgrading to EPP/ECP Ports. If you are purchasing a system today, I would recommend one that has a so called "Super I/O" chip that supports both EPP and ECP operation. If you want to test the parallel ports in a system, especially to determine what type they are, I highly recommend a utility called *Parallel*. This is a handy parallel port information utility that examines your system's parallel ports and reports the Port Type, IO address, IRQ level, BIOS name, and an assortment of informative notes and warnings in a compact and easy-to-read display. The output may be redirected to a file for tech support purposes. Parallel uses very sophisticated techniques for port and IRQ detection, and is aware of a broad range of quirky port features. You can get it from Parallel Technologies (see the vendor list in Appendix A).

FIG. 11.3 The three different IEEE 1284 connectors.

If you have an older system that does not include an EPP/ECP port and you would like to upgrade, there are several companies now offering boards with the correct Super I/O chips that implement these features. I recommend you check with Farpoint Communications and Byterunner Technologies; they are listed in the vendor list in Appendix A.

The following are the Web sites for Byte Runner Technologies and Farpoint Communications, respectively:

On the Web

http://www.byterunner.com/

http://www.fapo.com/

Parallel-Port Configuration

Parallel-port configuration is not as complicated as it is for serial ports. Even the original IBM PC has BIOS support for three LPT ports, and DOS has always had this support as well. Table 11.7 shows the standard I/O address and interrupt settings for parallel port use.

Table 11.7 Parallel Interface I/O Port Addresses and Interrupts

System	LPTx Std.	LPTx Alt	I/O Port	IRQ
8/16-bit ISA	LPT1	—	3BCh	IRQ7
8/16-bit ISA	LPT1	LPT2	378h	IRQ5
8/16-bit ISA	LPT2	LPT3	278h	None

Because the BIOS and DOS always have provided three definitions for parallel ports, problems with older systems are infrequent. Problems can arise, however, from the lack of available interrupt-driven ports for ISA bus systems. Normally, an interrupt-driven port is not absolutely required for printing operations; in fact, many programs do not use the interrupt-driven capability. Many programs do use the interrupt, however, such as network print programs and other types of background or spooler-type printer programs.

Also, high-speed, laser-printer utility programs often use the interrupt capabilities to allow for printing. If you use these types of applications on a port that is not interrupt driven, you see the printing slow to a crawl, if it works at all. The only solution is to use an interrupt-driven port. MS-DOS and Windows 95 now support up to 128 parallel ports.

To configure parallel ports in ISA bus systems, you probably will have to set jumpers and switches. Because each board on the market is different, you always should consult the OEM manual for that particular card if you need to know how the card should be configured.

Parallel Port Devices. The original IBM PC designers envisioned that the parallel port would be used only for communicating with a printer. Over the years, the number of devices that can be used with a parallel port has increased tremendously. You now can find everything from tape backup units to LAN adapters to CD-ROMs that connect through your parallel port. Some modem manufacturers now have modems that connect to the parallel port instead of the serial port for faster data transfer.

Perhaps one of the most common uses for bidirectional parallel ports is to transfer data between your system and another, such as a laptop computer. If both systems use an EPP/ECP port, you can actually communicate at rates of up to 2M/sec, which rivals the speed of some hard disk drives. This capability has led to an increase in software to serve this niche of the market. If you are interested in such software (and the parallel ports necessary to facilitate the software), you should refer to the reviews that periodically appear in sources such as *PC Magazine*.

Connecting two computers with standard unidirectional parallel ports requires a special cable. Most programs sell or provide these cables with their software. However, if you need to make one for yourself, Table 11.8 provides the wiring diagram you need.

Table 11.8 Parallel Port Interlink/Lap Link Cable Wiring

25-pin	Signal Descriptions			25-pin
pin 2	Data Bit 0	<-->	-Error	pin 15
pin 3	Data Bit 1	<-->	Select	pin 13
pin 4	Data Bit 2	<-->	Paper End	pin 12
pin 5	Data Bit 3	<-->	-Acknowledge	pin 10
pin 6	Data Bit 4	<-->	Busy	pin 11
pin 15	-Error	<-->	Data Bit 0	pin 2
pin 13	Select	<-->	Data Bit 1	pin 3
pin 12	Paper End	<-->	Data Bit 2	pin 4
pin 10	-Acknowledge	<-->	Data Bit 3	pin 5
pin 11	Busy	<-->	Data Bit 4	pin 6
pin 25	Ground	<-->	Ground	pin 25

> **Tip**
>
> Even though cables are most often provided for data transfer programs, notebook users may want to look for an adapter that makes the appropriate changes to a standard parallel cable. This can make traveling lighter by preventing the need for additional cables. Most of the time, these adapters attach to the centronics end of the cable, and provide a standard DB25 connection on the other end. They're sold under a variety of names; however, Laplink adapter or Laplink converter are the most common.

While the wiring configuration and premade interlink cables given in Table 11.9 will work for connecting two machines with ECP/EPP ports, they won't be able to take advantage of the advanced transfer rates of these ports. Special cables are needed to communicate between ECP/EPP ports. Parallel Technologies is a company that sells ECP/EPP cables for connecting to other ECP/EPP computers, and also sells a universal cable for connecting any two parallel ports together to use the highest speed. Connect Air is listed in Appendix A.

Testing Serial Ports

You can perform several tests on serial and parallel ports. The two most common types of tests involve software only, or both hardware and software. The software-only tests are done with diagnostic programs such as Microsoft's MSD, while the hardware and software tests involve using a wrap plug to perform loopback testing.

Microsoft Diagnostics (MSD). MSD is a diagnostic program supplied with MS-DOS 6.x, Microsoft Windows, or Windows 95. Early versions of the program also were shipped with some Microsoft applications such as Microsoft Word for DOS.

To use MSD, switch to the directory in which it is located. This is not necessary, of course, if the directory containing the program is in your search path—which is often the case with the DOS 6.x or Windows-provided versions of MSD. Then, simply type **MSD** at the DOS prompt and press Enter. Soon you see the MSD screen.

Chapter 11—Communications and Networking

Choose the Serial Ports option. Notice that you are provided information about what type of serial chip you have in your system, as well as information about what ports are available. If any of the ports are in use (for example, a mouse), that information is provided as well.

MSD is helpful in at least determining whether your serial ports are responding. If MSD cannot determine the existence of a port, it does not provide the report indicating that the port exists. This sort of "look-and-see" test is the first action I usually take to determine why a port is not responding.

Windows 95 also shows whether or not your ports are functioning. To check your ports, right-click Your Computer and choose Properties. Choose the Device Manager tab. On the Device Manager screen, if a device is not working properly there will be an exclamation point in a yellow circle next to the device on the list. You can also double-click Ports (COM & LPT), and then double-click the desired port to see whether Windows 95 says that the port is functioning or not. In many cases, it tells you what is conflicting with that specific port.

Advanced Diagnostics Using Loopback Testing. One of the most useful tests is the *loopback test*, which can be used to ensure the correct function of the serial port, as well as any attached cables. Loopback tests basically are internal (digital), or external (analog). Internal tests can be run simply by unplugging any cables from the port and executing the test via a diagnostics program.

The external loopback test is more effective. This test requires that a special loopback connector or wrap plug be attached to the port in question. When the test is run, the port is used to send data out to the loopback plug, which simply routes the data back into the port's receive pins so that the port is transmitting and receiving at the same time. A loopback or wrap plug is nothing more than a cable doubled back on itself. Most diagnostics programs that run this type of test include the loopback plug, and if not, these types of plugs can be purchased easily or even built.

The wiring that is needed to construct your own loopback or wrap plugs is as follows:

- IBM 25-Pin Serial (Female DB25S) Loopback Connector (Wrap Plug). Connect these pins:

    | 1 to 7 | 6 to 11 to 20 to 22 |
    | 2 to 3 | 15 to 17 to 23 |
    | 4 to 5 to 8 | 18 to 25 |

- IBM 9-Pin Serial (Female DB9S) Loopback Connector (Wrap Plug). Connect these pins:

    1 to 7 to 8

    2 to 3

    4 to 6 to 9

If you need to test serial ports further, refer to Chapters 21 and 22, which describe third-party testing software and operating system–based testing procedures, respectively.

Testing Parallel Ports

Testing parallel ports is, in most cases, simpler than testing serial ports. The procedures you use are effectively the same as those used for serial ports, except that when you use the diagnostics software, you choose the obvious choices for parallel ports rather than serial ports.

Not only are the software tests similar, but the hardware tests require the proper plugs for the loopback tests on the parallel port. To create an IBM 25-Pin Parallel (Male DB25P) Loopback Connector (Wrap Plug), connect these pins:

    1 to 13   10 to 16
    2 to 15   11 to 17

Future Serial and Parallel Port Replacements

Two new high-speed serial-bus architectures for desktop and portable are becoming available, called the *Universal Serial Bus (USB)* and *IEEE 1394*. These are high-speed communications ports that far outstrip the capabilities of the standard serial and parallel ports most systems contain today, and may be used as an alternative to SCSI for high-speed peripheral connections. In addition to performance, these new ports will offer I/O device consolidation, meaning all types of external peripherals will connect to these ports.

The recent trend in high-performance peripheral bus design is to use a serial architecture, where one bit is sent at a time down a wire. Parallel architecture uses 8, 16, or more wires to send bits simultaneously. At the same clock speed, the parallel bus is faster; however, it is much easier to increase the clock speed of a serial connection than a parallel one.

Parallel connections suffer from several problems, the biggest being signal skew and jitter. Skew and jitter are the reasons that high-speed parallel busses like SCSI are limited to short distances of three meters or less. The problem is that although the 8 or 16 bits of data are fired from the transmitter at the same time, by the time they reach the receiver, propagation delays have conspired to allow some bits to arrive before the others. The longer the cable, the longer the time between the arrival of the first and last bits at the other end! This *signal skew*, as it is called, either prevents you from running a high-speed transfer rate, a longer cable, or both. *Jitter* is the tendency for the signal to reach its target voltage and float above and below for a short period of time.

With a serial bus, the data is sent one bit at a time. Because there is no worry about when each bit will arrive, the clocking rate can be increased dramatically.

With a high clock rate, parallel signals tend to interfere with each other. Serial again has an advantage in that with only one or two signal wires, crosstalk and interference between the wires in the cable is negligible.

Parallel cables are very expensive. In addition to the many additional wires needed to carry the multiple bits in parallel, the cable also needs to be specially constructed to prevent crosstalk and interference between adjacent data lines. This is one reason external SCSI cables are so expensive. Serial cables, on the other hand, are very inexpensive. For one thing, they have very few wires, plus the shielding requirements are far simpler, even at very high speeds.

It is for these reasons, plus the need for new Plug and Play external peripheral interfaces, as well as the elimination of the physical port crowding on portable computers, that these new high-performance serial busses have been developed. Both USB and 1394 are available on desktop and portable PCs today.

USB (Universal Serial Bus)

The USB was designed as a convenient method to connect a variety of different peripherals to a system. Intel has been the primary proponent of USB, and most of their new PC chipsets, starting with the Triton II (82430HX and VX), will include USB support as standard. Six other companies have worked with Intel in co-developing the USB, including Compaq, Digital, IBM, Microsoft, NEC, and Northern Telecom. Together these companies have established the USB Implementers Forum to develop, support, and promote the USB architecture.

On the Web

For more information on this group, you can contact them at their Web site:

http://www.teleport.com/~usb

The USB is a 12Mbit/sec (1.5M/sec) interface over a simple four-wire connection. The bus supports up to 127 devices and uses a tiered star topology built on expansion hubs that can reside in the PC, any USB peripheral, or even stand-alone hub boxes. For low-performance peripherals such as pointing devices and keyboards, the USB also has a slower 1.5Mbit/sec subchannel.

USB also conforms to Intel's Plug and Play (PnP) specification, including *hot plugging*, which means that devices can be plugged in dynamically without powering down or rebooting the system. Simply plug in the device, and the USB controller in the PC will detect the device and automatically determine and allocate the resources and drivers required. Microsoft has USB drivers developed and has included them in existing versions of Windows 95 and NT. USB support will also be required in the BIOS, which will be included in newer systems with USB ports built in.

Aftermarket USB boards will be available for adding USB to an existing system. Such boards will likely have ROM on-board, which will allow the USB peripherals to function under DOS, while Windows built-in drivers will take care of the USB function under Windows.

USB peripherals will include modems, telephones, joysticks, keyboards, and pointing devices such as mice and trackballs.

One interesting feature of USB is that all attached devices will be powered by the USB bus itself. The PnP aspects of USB allow the system to query the attached peripherals as to their power requirements and issue a warning if available power levels are being exceeded. This will be important for USB when used in portable systems, because battery power to run the external peripherals may be limited.

IEEE 1394

IEEE 1394 is a high-speed local serial bus. 1394 supports speeds of 100, 200, and 400Mbits/sec (12.5, 25, 50M/sec), with gigabit per second versions in the works! This bus was derived from the "Firewire" bus originally developed by Apple and Texas Instruments, and is also a part of the new Serial SCSI standard.

1394 uses a simple six-wire cable with two differential pairs of clock and data lines plus two power lines. Just as with USB, 1394 is fully PnP, including the ability for hot plugging (insertion and removal of components without powering down). Unlike the much more complicated parallel SCSI bus, 1394 does not require complicated termination, and devices connected to the bus can draw up to 1.5 amps of electrical power. 1394 offers equal or greater performance compared to Ultra-Wide SCSI, with a much less expensive and less complicated connection.

1394 is built on a daisy-chained and branched topology and allows up to 63 nodes with a chain of up to 16 devices on each node. If this is not enough, the standard also calls for up to 1,023 bridged busses, which can interconnect more than 64,000 nodes! Additionally, 1394 can support devices with different data rates on the same bus, just as with SCSI.

The types of devices that will be connected to the PC via 1394 include practically anything that might use SCSI today. This includes all forms of disk drives, including hard disk, optical, floppy, CD-ROM, and the new DVD (Digital Video Disc) drives. Also digital cameras, tape drives, and many other high-speed peripherals featuring 1394 interfaces built in. Expect the 1394 bus to be implemented in both desktop as well as portable computers as a replacement for other external high-speed busses like SCSI.

1394 already includes a list of more than 200 companies that are members of the 1394 Trade Association. For more information on the 1394 bus or the 1394 Trade Association, you can contact them on the Web at:

On the Web

http://www.firewire.org

Chipsets and PCI adapters for the 1394 bus are already available. Microsoft has developed drivers to support 1394 in Windows 95 and Windows NT.

Understanding the Components of a LAN

A local area network (LAN) enables you to share files, applications, printers, disk space, modems, faxes, and CD-ROM drives; use client/server software products; send electronic mail; and otherwise make a collection of computers work as a team.

In today's world, there are many ways to construct a LAN. A LAN can be as simple as two computers connected together via either their serial or parallel ports. This is the simplest and probably the most common LAN today. Many users connect their laptop to their desktop computer for access to a printer or to transfer files. This type of connection is usually called a *direct cable connection*, in which one computer is designated as the host computer. The *host computer* is the machine with the resources you want to access. The *guest computer* wants to use the resources of the host. You can purchase software that allows you to connect two computers in this manner, but some operating systems such as DOS and Windows 95 have direct cable connection support built in. Although the term *network* is not often used for this sort of arrangement, it does satisfy the definition.

Peer-to-peer networks have become more popular as the software became more reliable and personal computers became more powerful. *Peer-to-peer* means computer to computer. In a peer-to-peer network, any computer can access any other computer to which it is connected and has been granted access rights. Essentially, every computer functions as both a server and a client. Peer-to-peer networks can be as small as two computers, or as large as hundreds of units, and they may or may not use a LAN card or network interface card (NIC). For more than two stations, or when higher data transfer speeds are desired, NICs should be used.

Peer-to-peer networks are more common in small offices or within a department in a larger organization. The advantage of a peer-to-peer network is that you don't have to dedicate a computer to be a file server. Most peer-to-peer networks allow you to share practically any device attached to any computer. The potential disadvantages to a peer-to-peer network are that there is typically less security and less control.

Windows 95 has peer-to-peer networking built in. With Windows 95, setting up a peer-to-peer LAN can be accomplished in two ways. The first method is to install the dial-up networking modules. Dial-up networking requires a Windows 95-compatible server, such as Windows 95 dial-up server in the Plus! package, or Windows NT. Dial-Up Networking allows the remote system (the one dialing in) to access the server and any peripherals attached to the server to which the remote user has been given rights. These peripherals can be CD-ROM drives, tape drives, removable media drives, hard drives, and even another network as long as it is an IPX/SPX or NetBEUI network. IPX/SPX are the network transport protocols used in NetWare and other networks. NetBEUI is the NetBIOS (Network Basic Input Output System) Extended User Interface; it is the native protocol of Microsoft Windows networks.

The other method of peer-to-peer networking is much like that with which we all became familiar in Windows for Workgroups, but it is much easier to set up in Windows 95. With the new PnP technology incorporated into the operating system, most NICs are automatically detected. Supported NIC manufacturers include 3COM, Digital Equipment Corporation, IBM, Intel, Madge, Novell, Proteon, Racal, SMC, and Thomas-Conrad. Once the NIC is detected, Windows 95 asks for a computer name and a workgroup name. Once this is accomplished, your Windows 95 network workstation is ready to go.

A LAN is a combination of computers, LAN cables (usually), network adapter cards, network operating system software, and LAN application software. (You sometimes see network operating system abbreviated as *NOS*.) On a LAN, each personal computer is called a *workstation*, except for one or more computers designated as network servers. Each workstation and server contains a network adapter card. LAN cables connect all the workstations and servers, except in less frequent cases when infrared, radio, or microwaves are used.

A network in which the workstations connect only to servers (as opposed to each other, as in a peer-to-peer) is called a *client/server network*. In addition to its local operating system (usually DOS or one of the Windows operating systems), each workstation runs network software (*client* software) that enables the workstation to communicate with the servers. Windows 95 itself contains the client software necessary to connect to Novell NetWare 3.12 and 4.x, IBM OS/2 LAN Server, and Windows NT networks. In turn, the servers run network software (*server* software) that communicates with the workstations and serves up files and other services to those workstations. LAN-aware application software runs at each workstation, communicating with the server when it needs to read and write files. Figure 11.4 illustrates the components that make up a LAN.

FIG. 11.4 The components of a LAN.

Workstations

A LAN is made up of computers. You will usually find two kinds of computers on a LAN: the *workstations*, usually manned by people on their individual desktops, and the *servers*, usually located in a secured area, like a separate room or closet. The workstation is used only by the person sitting in front of it, whereas a server allows many people to share its resources. Workstations usually are at least intermediate-speed AT-class machines with an 80286 or better CPU, and they may have 1M to 4M of RAM. Workstations often have good-quality color or grayscale VGA monitors, as well as high-quality keyboards, but these are characteristics that make them easy to use; they are not required to make the LAN work.

A workstation also usually has a relatively inexpensive slow small hard disk. When constructing a new LAN today, the minimum recommended workstation, for either a client/server or peer-to-peer network, is at least a 486DX2/66 with 8M of RAM and a 500M hard drive. The preferred system is a Pentium 75 or greater with 16M or more of RAM and a 500M or larger hard drive. As a matter of fact, most of the major suppliers of PCs to the corporate world no longer even carry 486-based machines.

Many existing networks operate very well with older machines, however. Some sites even continue to use diskless workstations—that is, computers that do not have a disk drive of their own. Such workstations rely completely on the LAN for their file access. A diskless workstation requires a NIC with an autoboot PROM. This type of ROM causes the workstation to boot from files stored on a network server.

The advantages to this type of workstation are lower cost for hardware and greater security, which is increased by not having any drives at the local workstation with which to copy files to or from the server. The primary disadvantage is that today's high-performance operating systems will not run efficiently from a network drive. The sheer number of program files opened and closed, as well as the need for frequent swapping of memory to hard disk space, make the practice prohibitive.

File Servers

All the workstations on a peer-to-peer LAN can function as file servers, in that any drive on any peer workstation can be shared with (or served to) other users.

On a client/server network, however, a *file server* is a computer that serves all the workstations—primarily by storing and retrieving data from files shared on its disks. Servers usually are fast 486 Pentium- or Pentium Pro-based computers, running at 66MHz or faster and with 16M or more of RAM. Most servers usually have inexpensive monitors and keyboards, because people do not use the file server console as heavily as that of a workstation. The server normally operates unattended, and almost always has one or more fast, expensive, large hard disks, however.

Servers must be high-quality, heavy-duty machines because, in serving the whole network, they do many times the work of an ordinary workstation computer. In particular, the file server's hard disk(s) need to be durable and reliable, and geared to the task of serving multiple users simultaneously. For this reason, SCSI hard drives are usually preferred over IDE drives in today's servers (see Chapter 15, "Hard Disk Interfaces," for more information on IDE versus SCSI).

You will most often see a computer wholly dedicated to the task of being a server. Sometimes, on smaller LANs, the server doubles as a workstation, depending on the network operating system being used. Serving an entire network is a big job that does not leave much spare horsepower to handle workstation duties, however, and if a user locks up the workstation that also serves as the file server, your network also locks up.

Under a heavy load, if there are 20 workstations and one server, each workstation can use only 1/20th of the server's resources. In practice, though, most workstations are idle most of the time—at least from a network disk-file-access point of view. As long as no other workstation is using the server, your workstation can use 100 percent of the server's resources.

Evaluating File Server Hardware

A typical file server consists of a personal computer that you dedicate to the task of sharing disk space, files, and possibly printers. On a larger network, you may use a personal computer especially built for file server work (a superserver), but the basic components are the same as those of a desktop PC. No matter what sort of computer you choose as a server, it communicates with the workstations through its network adapter cards the LAN cables.

A file server does many times the work of an ordinary workstation. You may type on the server's keyboard only a couple of times a day, and you may glance at its monitor only infrequently. The server's CPU and hard disk drives, however, take the brunt of responding to the file-service requests of all the workstations on the LAN.

If you consider your LAN an important part of your investment in your business (and it is hard to imagine otherwise), you will want to get the highest quality computer you can afford for the file server. If you're going to be running on the Intel platform, the processor should be a Pentium, Pentium Pro, or Pentium II, and it should be one of the faster models. The hard disk drives should be large and fast, although in some cases the highest capacity drive available is not necessarily the best choice. When you consider that the server will be processing the file requests of many users simultaneously, it can be more efficient to have, for example, nine 1G SCSI hard drives rather than one 9G drive. That way, the requests can be spread across several different units, rather than queued up waiting for one device.

Performance is important, of course, but the most crucial consideration in purchasing a server is that the CPU, the motherboard on which the CPU is mounted, and the hard disk drives should be rugged and reliable. Do not skimp on these components.

Downtime (periods when the network is not operating) can be expensive because people cannot access their shared files to get their work done. Higher-quality components will keep the LAN running without failure for longer periods of time.

It is very important that you configure your LAN properly. Be sure that you have enough slots for all your present adapters and any future adapters that you can anticipate. It is also very important that you follow the RAM and hard drive sizing guidelines for your network operating system.

In the same vein, you will want to set up a regular maintenance schedule for your file server. Over the course of a few weeks, the fans within the computer can move great volumes of air through the machine to keep it cool. The air may contain dust and dirt, which accumulates inside the computer. You should clean out the "dust bunnies" in the server every month or two. Chapter 3, "System Teardown and Inspection," discusses how to clean out the "dust bunnies" without harming your system. Many larger network sites house their servers in rooms or closets designed to maintain low dust and static levels as well as constant temperatures.

You do not replace components in the server as part of your regular preventive maintenance, but you will want to know whether a part is beginning to fail. You may want to acquire diagnostic software or hardware products to periodically check the health of your file server. (Chapter 19, "Building a System," discusses the tools you can use to keep your file server fit and trim.)

The electricity the file server gets from the wall outlet may, from time to time, vary considerably in voltage (resulting in sags and spikes). To make your file server as reliable as possible, you should install an uninterruptable power supply (UPS) between the electric power source and your server. The UPS not only provides electricity in case of a power failure, but also conditions the line to protect the server from voltage fluctuations.

In general, you want to do whatever you can to make your network reliable, including placing the server away from public access areas.

Evaluating the File Server Hard Disk. The hard disk drives are the most important components of a file server. The *hard disks* are where the people who use the LAN store their files. To a large extent, the reliability, access speed, and capacity of a server's hard disks determine whether people will be happy with the LAN and will be able to use it productively. The most common bottleneck in the average LAN is disk I/O time at the file server. And the most common complaint voiced by people on the average LAN is that the file server has run out of free disk space. Make sure that your file server's disk drives and hard disk controller are high-performance components, and that you always have plenty of free disk space on your server's drives.

Evaluating the File Server CPU. The *file server CPU* tells the hard disk drives what to store and retrieve. The CPU is the next most important file server component after the hard disks. Unless your LAN will have only a few users and will never grow, a file server with a fast Pentium, Pentium Pro, or Pentium II CPU and plenty of RAM is a wise investment. The next section discusses server RAM.

The CPU chip in a computer executes the instructions given to it by the software you run. If you run an application, that application runs more quickly if the CPU is fast. Likewise, if you run a network operating system, that NOS runs more quickly if the CPU is fast.

Some NOSes absolutely require certain types of CPU chips. NetWare version 2, for example, required at least a 286 CPU. NetWare versions 3 and 4 require at least a 386. IBM LAN Server version 2 and Microsoft LAN Manager version 2 require that OS/2 1.3 be running on the server computer; OS/2 1.3 requires an 80286 or later CPU. LAN Server 3.0 requires that the file server use OS/2 2.x, which runs only on 386 or later CPUs. Microsoft Windows NT Advanced Server 3.51 requires a 386DX25 or later CPU and 16M of RAM. These are, of course, the absolute minimum CPU requirements. Exceeding them is a practice that is highly recommended, for any of these products.

Evaluating Server RAM. The network operating system loads into the computer's RAM, just like any other application. You need to have enough RAM in the computer for the NOS to load and run properly. On a peer LAN, the recommended amount of RAM would be whatever it takes to run your applications, whereas on a client/server LAN, you might install 32M, 64M, or more in your file server. Windows 95 in a peer-to-peer environment should have a minimum of 16M of RAM. Windows NT should have more. The proper amount of RAM for a server-based LAN operating system like NetWare is calculated using a formula that accounts for the software you will be running and the capacity and configuration of your disk drives. Be sure to follow the operating system manufacturer's RAM recommendations carefully, or severe performance problems may result.

You can realize significant performance gains in a NetWare server with a faster CPU and extra RAM because of a process called *file caching*. If the server has sufficient memory installed, it can "remember" those portions of the hard disk that it has accessed previously. When the next user asks for the same file represented by those portions of the hard disk, the server can send it to the next user without having to actually access the hard disk. Because the file server is able to avoid waiting for the hard disk to rotate into position, the server can do its job more quickly. The NOS merely needs to look in the computer's RAM for the file data that a workstation has requested. Thus, you can be assured that any extra memory installed in your server will be put to beneficial use.

Note that the NOS's caching of file data is distinct from (and in addition to) any caching that might occur due to the hard disk or hard disk controller card having on-board memory.

Evaluating the Network Adapter Card. The server's *network adapter card* is its link to all the workstations on the LAN. All file requests and other network communications enter and leave the server through the network adapter. Figure 11.5 shows a network adapter you might install in a file server. As you can imagine, the network adapter in a server is a very busy component.

FIG. 11.5 The file server's network adapter sends and receives messages to and from all the workstations on the LAN.

All the network adapters on the LAN use Ethernet, Token Ring, ARCnet, or some other low-level protocol. You can find network adapters for each of these protocols, however, that perform better than others. A network adapter may be faster at processing messages because it has a large amount of on-board memory (RAM), because it contains its own microprocessor, or perhaps because the adapter uses a 16-bit or a 32-bit slot instead of an 8-bit slot and thus can transfer more data to and from the CPU at one time. 32-bit slots in server computers could be EISA, VLB, or PCI. PCI is currently the most commonly found 32-bit bus type in the Pentium class machine. A faster, more capable network adapter is an ideal candidate for installation in a file server, but be sure to check its compatibility with the network adapters installed in your workstations.

Evaluating the Server's Power Supply. In a file server, the power supply is an important but often overlooked item. Power supply failures and malfunctions can cause problems elsewhere in the computer that are difficult to diagnose. Your file server may display a message indicating that a RAM chip has failed, and then stop; the cause of the problem may indeed be a failed RAM chip, or the problem may be in the power supply.

The fan(s) in the power supply sometimes stop working or become obstructed with dust and dirt. The computer overheats and fails completely or acts strangely. Cleaning the fan(s)—after unplugging the computer from the wall outlet, of course—should be a part of the regular maintenance of your file server.

Evaluating the Keyboard, Monitor, and Mouse. The keyboard, monitor, and mouse (if any) are usually not significant components on a file server computer, because they receive far less use than their workstation counterparts. Often you can use lower-quality, less-expensive components here. A typical file server runs unattended and may go for hours or days without interaction from you. You can power off the monitor for these long periods.

> **Caution**
>
> Tuck the server keyboard away so that falling objects (pencils or coffee mugs, for example) do not harm your network's file server.

Your network server may also have external shared CD-ROM drives, either single or multiple disk and or a network tape drive. If your server has any of these devices, be sure they are easily accessible. When the backup of the server is complete, be sure to remove the tape and store it in a safe place.

Network Interface Cards (NICs)

A *network interface card*, or *NIC*, fits into a slot in each workstation and file server. (Some computers now ship with network interface hardware embedded on the motherboard, but most network administrators prefer to select their own.) Your workstation sends requests through the network adapter to the server. The workstation then receives responses through the network adapter when the server delivers all or a portion of a file to that workstation. The sending and receiving of these requests and responses is the LAN equivalent of reading and writing files on your PC's local hard disk. If you're like most people, you probably think of reading and writing files in terms of loading or saving your work.

A typical LAN consists of only a single data channel connecting its various computers. This is called a *baseband network*. As a result of this, only two network adapters can communicate with each other at the same time. If one person's workstation is currently accessing the file server (processing the requests and responses that deliver a file to the workstation), then other users' workstations must wait their turn. Fortunately, such delays are usually not noticeable. The LAN gives the appearance of many workstations accessing the file server simultaneously.

Ethernet adapters have a single BNC connector (for Thinnet), a D-shaped 15-pin connector called a DB15 (for Thicknet), a connector that looks like a large telephone jack called an RJ45 (for 10BaseT), or sometimes a combination of all three. Token Ring adapters can have a 9-pin connector called a DB9 or sometimes an RJ45 telephone jack outlet. Figure 11.6 shows a high-performance Token Ring adapter with both kinds of connectors.

FIG. 11.6 The Thomas-Conrad 16/4 Token Ring adapter (with a 9-pin connector and a telephone wire connector).

Cards with two or more connectors enable you to choose from a wider variety of LAN cables. A Token Ring card with two connectors, for example, enables you to use shielded twisted pair (STP) or unshielded twisted pair (UTP) cable. You cannot use both connectors at the same time, however, except on special adapters designed specifically for this purpose.

> ### Shielded versus Unshielded Twisted Pair
>
> When cabling was being developed for use with computers, it was first thought that shielding the cable from external interference was the best way to reduce interference and allow for greater transmission speeds. However, it was discovered that twisting the pairs of wires is a more effective way to prevent interference from disrupting transmissions. As a result, earlier cabling scenarios relied on shielded cables rather than the unshielded cables more commonly in use today.
>
> Shielded cables also have some special grounding concerns because one—and only one—end of a shielded cable should be connected to an earth ground; issues arose where people inadvertently caused grounding loops to occur by connecting both ends, or caused the shield to act as an antenna because it wasn't grounded.
>
> *Grounding loops* are situations where two different grounds are tied together. This is a bad situation because each ground can have a slightly different potential. This results in a circuit that has very low voltage but infinite amperage. This causes undue stress on electrical components and can be a fire hazard.

The LAN adapter card in your PC receives all the traffic going by on the network cable, accepts only the messages destined for your workstation, and passes on the rest to the next machine. The adapter hands these messages over to your workstation when the workstation is ready to attend to them. When the workstation wants to send a request to a server, the adapter card waits for the appropriate time (according to the network type), and inserts your message into the data stream. The workstation is also notified as to whether the message arrived intact, and resends the message if it was garbled.

Network adapters range in price from less than $100 to much more than $1,000. What do you get for your money? Primarily, speed. The faster adapters can push data faster onto the cable, which means that the file server receives a request more quickly and sends back a response more quickly.

> ### Data-Transfer Speeds on a LAN
>
> Electrical engineers and technical people measure the speed of a network in megabits per second (Mbps). Because a byte of information consists of 8 bits, you can divide the Mbps rating by 8 to find out how many millions of characters (bytes) per second the network can handle theoretically.
>
> Suppose that you want to transfer an entire 3 1/2-inch 720K floppy disk's worth of information across a LAN. The rated speed of the LAN is 4Mbit/sec. Dividing 4Mbps by 8 tells you that the LAN theoretically can transmit 500K of data per second. This is equivalent to an average hard disk's transfer rate. The data transfer rate for a floppy drive is 500Kbit/sec. The data from the 720K floppy disk takes at least a few seconds to transfer, as you can see from these rough calculations.
>
> In practice, a LAN is slower than its rated speed. In fact, a LAN is no faster than its slowest component. If you were to transfer 720K of data from one workstation's hard disk to the file server, the

> elapsed time would include not only the transmission time but also the workstation hard disk retrieval time, the workstation processing time, and the file server's hard disk and server CPU processing times. The transfer rate of your hard disk, which in this case is probably the slowest component involved in the copying of the data to the server, governs the rate at which data flows to the file server. Other people's requests interleave with your requests on the LAN, and the total transfer time may be longer because the other people are using the LAN at the same time you are.
>
> If you transfer the data from a 720K floppy disk to the file server, you see that it takes even longer. Floppy disk drives, as you know, are slower than hard disks. Your workstation uses the network in small bursts as it reads the data from the floppy disk. The workstation cannot send data across the LAN in this case any faster than it can read the data from the disk.

ARCnet Adapters. *ARCnet* is one of the oldest types of LAN hardware. It originally was a proprietary scheme of the Datapoint Corporation, but today many companies make ARCnet-compatible cards. By modern standards, ARCnet is very slow, but it is forgiving of minor errors in installation. It is known for solid reliability, and ARCnet cable/adapter problems are easy to diagnose. ARCnet generally costs less than Ethernet, but hardware prices for Ethernet adapters have plummeted so much in recent years that the difference in price between the two is no longer that great an issue. ARCnet operates something like Token Ring, but at the slower rate of 2.5Mbps. The section "Token Ring Adapters" later in this chapter explains the basic principles on which ARCnet and Token Ring work.

Ethernet Adapters. The most widely used type of network adapter is *Ethernet*. Ethernet-based LANs allow you to interconnect a wide variety of equipment, including UNIX workstations, Apple computers, IBM PCs, and IBM clones. You can buy Ethernet cards from dozens of competing manufacturers. Ethernet comes in three varieties (Thinnet, UTP, and Thicknet), depending on the type of cabling you use. Thicknet cables can span a greater distance, but they are much more expensive. Ethernet traditionally operates at a rate of 10Mbps, but there are now Ethernet adapters available that operate at a rate of 100Mbps. These "Fast Ethernet" adapters are manufactured by Intel, Thomas-Conrad, and others.

There are even models that run at both 10 and 100Mbps speeds, allowing you to gradually upgrade your network by installing new NICs and hubs over an extended period of time. 100Mbps adapters only function at that speed when communicating through a high-speed hub to another 100 Mbps adapter.

Between data transfers (requests and responses to and from the file server), Ethernet LANs remain quiet. After a workstation sends a request across the LAN cable, the cable falls silent again. What happens when two or more workstations (and/or file servers) attempt to use the LAN at the same time?

Suppose that one of the workstations wants to request something from the file server, just as the server is sending a response to another workstation. A collision occurs. (Remember that only two computers can communicate through the cable at a given moment.) Both computers—the file server and the workstation—back off and try again. Ethernet network adapters use an algorithm called *Carrier Sense, Multiple Access with*

Collision Detection (CSMA/CD) to deal with collisions, causing each computer to back off for a random amount of time. This method effectively enables one computer to go first. A certain number of collisions are therefore normal and expected on an Ethernet network, but with higher amounts of traffic, the frequency of collisions rises higher and higher, and response times become worse and worse. A saturated Ethernet network actually can spend more time recovering from collisions than it does sending data. IBM and Texas Instruments, recognizing Ethernet's traffic limitations, designed the Token-Ring network to solve the problem.

Token-Ring Adapters. Except for fiber-optic and some of the new high-speed technologies, Token Ring is the most expensive type of LAN. Token Ring can use STP or UTP cable. Token Ring's cost is justified, however, when you have a great deal of traffic generated by workstations because under normal conditions collisions are all but eliminated. You often find Token Ring in large corporations with large LANs, especially if the LANs are attached to mainframe computers. Token Ring can operate at 4 or 16Mbps.

Workstations on a Token-Ring LAN continuously pass an electronic token among themselves. The *token* is just a short message indicating that the workstation or server possessing it is allowed to transmit. If a workstation has nothing to send, as soon as it receives the token, it passes it on to the next downstream workstation. Only when a workstation receives the token can it transmit data onto the LAN. After transmitting, the token is again passed down the line. If the LAN is busy, and you want your workstation to send a message to another workstation or server, you must wait patiently for the token to come around. Only then can your workstation send its message. The message circulates through all the workstations and file servers on the LAN, and eventually winds its way back to you, the sender. The sender then generates a new token, releasing control of the network to the next workstation. During the circulation of the message around the ring, the workstations or server that is the designated recipient recognizes that the message is addressed to it and begins processing that message, but still passes it on to the next workstation.

Token Ring is not as wasteful of LAN resources as this description makes it sound. An unclaimed token takes almost no time at all to circulate through a LAN, even with 100 or 200 workstations. It is also possible to assign priorities to certain workstations and file servers so that they get more frequent access to the LAN. And, of course, the token-passing scheme is much more tolerant of high traffic levels on the LAN than the collision-prone Ethernet.

Early Token Release

On a momentarily idle Token-Ring LAN, workstations circulate a token. The LAN becomes busy (carries information) when a workstation receives a token and turns it into a data frame targeted at another computer on the network. After receipt by the target node, the data frame continues circulating around the LAN until it is returned to its source node. The source node turns the data frame back into a token that circulates until a downstream node needs it. So far, so good—these are just standard Token Ring concepts.

> When a workstation sends a file request to a server, it consists of only a few bytes, far fewer than the transmission that actually returns the file to the workstation. If the request packet must go into and out of many workstations to circulate the ring, and if the data frame is small, latency occurs. *Latency* is the unproductive delay that occurs while the source node waits for its upstream neighbor to return its data frame.
>
> During the latency period, the source node appends idle characters onto the LAN following the data frame until the frame circulates the entire LAN and arrives back at the source node. The typical latency period of a 4Mbps ring will result in the transmission of about 50 to 100 idle characters. On a 16Mbps ring, latency may reach 400 or more bytes worth of LAN time.
>
> Early Token Release, available only on 16Mbps networks, is a feature that allows the originating workstation to transmit a new token immediately after sending its data frame. Downstream nodes pass along the data frame and then receive an opportunity to transmit data themselves—the new token. If you were to perform a protocol analysis of a network using Early Token Release, you would see tokens and other data frames immediately following the file request, instead of a long trail of idle characters.

Sometimes a station fumbles and "drops" the token. LAN stations monitor each other and use a complex procedure called *beaconing* to detect the location of the problem and regenerate a lost token. Token Ring is quite a bit more complicated than Ethernet, and the hardware is correspondingly more expensive.

ARCnet and Token Ring are not compatible with one another, but ARCnet uses a similar token-passing scheme to control workstation and server access to the LAN.

Adapter Functions. As mentioned in the "Network Interface Card (NIC)" section earlier, network adapters generally are collision-sensing or token-passing. A network adapter's design ties it to one of the low-level protocols—Ethernet, Token Ring, FDDI, ARCnet, or some other protocol.

Collision-sensing and token-passing adapters contain sufficient on-board logic to know when it is permissible to send a frame and to recognize frames intended for the adapters. With the adapter support software, both types of cards perform seven major steps during the process of sending or receiving a frame. When sending data out from the card, the steps are performed in the order presented in the following list. When receiving data in, however, the steps are reversed. Here are the steps:

1. *Data transfer.* Data is transferred from PC memory (RAM) to the adapter card or from the adapter card to PC memory via DMA, shared memory, or programmed I/O.

2. *Buffering.* While being processed by the network adapter card, data is held in a buffer. The buffer gives the card access to an entire frame at once, and the buffer enables the card to manage the difference between the data rate of the network and the rate at which the PC can process data.

3. *Frame formation.* The network adapter has to break up the data into manageable chunks (or, on reception, reassemble it). On an Ethernet network, these chunks are about 1,500 bytes. Token-Ring networks generally use a frame size of about 4K. The

adapter prefixes the data packet with a frame header and appends a frame trailer to it. The header and trailer are the Physical layer's envelope. At this point, a complete, ready-for-transmission frame exists. (Inbound, on reception, the adapter removes the header and trailer at this stage.)

4. *Cable access.* In a CSMA/CD network such as Ethernet, the network adapter ensures that the line is quiet before sending its data (or retransmits its data if a collision occurs). In a token-passing network, the adapter waits until it gets a token it can claim. (These steps are not significant to receiving a message, of course.)

5. *Parallel/serial conversion.* The bytes of data in the buffer are sent or received through the cables in serial fashion, with one bit following the next. The adapter card does this conversion in the split second before transmission (or after reception).

6. *Encoding/decoding.* The electrical signals that represent the data being sent or received are formed. Ethernet adapters use a technique called *Manchester encoding*, while Token-Ring adapters use a slightly different scheme called *Differential Manchester*. These techniques have the advantage of incorporating timing information into the data through the use of bit periods. Instead of representing a 0 as the absence of electricity and a 1 as its presence, the 0s and 1s are represented by changes in polarity as they occur in relation to very small time periods.

7. *Sending/receiving impulses.* The electrically encoded impulses making up the data (frame) are amplified and sent through the wire. (On reception, the impulses are handed up to the decoding step.)

Of course, the execution of all of these steps takes only a fraction of a second. While you were reading about these steps, thousands of frames could have been sent across the LAN.

Network adapter cards and the support software recognize and handle errors, which occur when electrical interference, collisions (in CSMA/CD networks), or malfunctioning equipment cause some portion of a frame to be corrupted. Errors generally are detected through the use of a *cyclic redundancy check (CRC)* data item in the frame. The CRC is checked by the receiver; if its own calculated CRC doesn't match the value of the CRC in the frame, the receiver tells the sender about the error and requests retransmission of the frame in error. Several products exist that perform network diagnostic and analysis functions on the different types of LANs, should you find yourself in need of such troubleshooting.

The different types of network adapters vary not only in access method and protocol, but also in the following elements:

- Transmission speed
- Amount of on-board memory for buffering frames and data
- Bus design (8-bit, 16-bit, or Micro Channel)
- Bus speed (some fail when run at high speeds)

- Compatibility with various CPU chipsets
- DMA usage
- IRQ and I/O port addressing
- Intelligence (some use an on-board CPU, such as the 80186)
- Connector design

LAN Cables

Generally speaking, the cabling systems described in the next few sections use one of three distinct cable types. These are twisted pair, shielded and unshielded (also known as STP and UTP or 10BaseT), coaxial cable, thin and thick (also known as 10Base2 and 10Base5, respectively), and fiber-optic cable.

The kind of cable you use depends mostly on the kind of network layout you select, the conditions at the network site, and of course your budget.

Using Twisted Pair Cable

Twisted pair cable is just what its name implies: insulated wires within a protective casing, with a specified number of twists per foot. Twisting the wires reduces the effect of electromagnetic interference on the signals being transmitted. *Shielded twisted pair (STP)* refers to the amount of insulation around the cluster of wires and therefore its noise immunity. You are familiar with *unshielded twisted pair (UTP)*; it is often used for telephone wiring. Figure 11.7 shows unshielded twisted pair cable; Figure 11.8 illustrates shielded twisted pair cable.

FIG. 11.7 An unshielded twisted pair cable.

Using Coaxial Cable

Coaxial cable is fairly prevalent in your everyday life; you often find it connected to the backs of television sets and audio equipment. Thin and thick, of course, refer to the diameter of the coaxial cable. Standard Ethernet cable (Thick Ethernet) is as thick as your thumb. Thin Ethernet (sometimes called Thinnet or CheaperNet) cable is slightly narrower than your little finger. The thick cable has a greater degree of noise immunity, is more difficult to damage, and requires a *vampire tap* (a connector with teeth that pierce the tough outer insulation) and a drop cable to connect to a workstation. Although thin cable carries the signal over shorter distances than the thick cable, Thinnet uses a simple BNC (Bayonet-Neill-Concelman) connector (a bayonet-locking connector for thin coaxial cables), is lower in cost, and was at one time the standard in office coaxial cable. Thinnet is wired directly to the back of each computer on the network, and generally installs much more easily than Thicknet, but it is more prone to signal interference and physical connection problems.

FIG. 11.8   A shielded twisted pair cable.

Figure 11.9 shows an Ethernet BNC coaxial T-connector, and Figure 11.10 illustrates the design of coaxial cable.

FIG. 11.9   An Ethernet coaxial cable T-connector.

FIG. 11.10 Coaxial cable.

Using Fiber-Optic Cable

Fiber-optic cable uses pulses of light rather than electricity to carry information. It is therefore completely resistant to the electromagnetic interference that limits the length of copper cables. *Attenuation* (the weakening of a signal as it traverses the cable) is also less of a problem, allowing fiber to send data over huge distances at high speeds. It is, however, very expensive and difficult to work with. Splicing the cable, installing connectors, and using the few available diagnostic tools for finding cable faults are skills that very few people have.

> **Tip**
>
> Fiber-optic cable is sometimes needed to connect buildings together in a campus network environment for two very important reasons. One is that fiber can travel approximately 2.2 km, whereas copper-based technologies are significantly more restricted. The other reason is because fiber, by its design, eliminates the problems with differing ground sources.

Fiber-optic cable is simply designed, but unforgiving of bad connections. Fiber cable usually consists of a core of glass thread, with a diameter measured in microns, surrounded by a solid glass cladding. This, in turn, is covered by a protective sheath. The first fiber-optic cables were made of glass, but plastic fibers also have been developed. The light source for fiber-optic cable is a light-emitting diode (LED); information usually is encoded by varying the intensity of the light. A detector at the other end of the cable converts the received signal back into electrical impulses. Two types of fiber cable exist: single mode and multimode. *Single mode* has a smaller diameter, is more expensive, and can carry signals over a greater distance.

Figure 11.11 illustrates fiber-optic cables and their connectors.

FIG. 11.11 Fiber-optic cables use light to carry LAN messages. The ST connector is commonly used with fiber-optic cables.

Network Topologies

Each workstation on the network is connected with cable (or some other medium) to the other workstations and to one or more servers. Sometimes a single piece of cable winds from station to station, visiting all the servers and workstations along the way. This cabling arrangement is called a *bus topology*, as shown in Figure 11.12. (A *topology* is simply a description of the way the workstations and servers are physically connected.) The potential disadvantage to this type of wiring is that if a workstation has a problem, it can cause all of the stations beyond it on the bus to lose their network connections.

Sometimes separate cables run from a central wiring nexus, often called a *hub* or a *concentrator*, to each workstation. Figure 11.13 shows this arrangement, called a *star topology*. Sometimes the cables branch out repeatedly from a root location, forming the star-wired tree shown in Figure 11.14. Bus cabling schemes use the least amount of cable but are the hardest to diagnose or bypass when problems occur.

The other topology often listed in discussions of this type is a *ring*, in which each workstation is connected to the next, and the last workstation is connected to the first again (essentially a bus topology with the two ends connected). Data travels around a Token-Ring network in this fashion, for example. However, the ring is not physically evident in the cabling layout for the network. In fact, the ring exists only within the hub (called a *multistation access unit* or *MSAU* on a Token-Ring network). Signals generated from one workstation travel back to the hub, are sent out to the next workstation, and then back to the hub again. The data is then passed to each workstation in turn until it arrives back at the computer that originated it, where it is removed from the network. Therefore, although the wiring topology is a star, the data path is theoretically a ring. This is called a *logical ring*.

FIG. 11.12 The linear bus topology, attaching all network devices to a common cable.

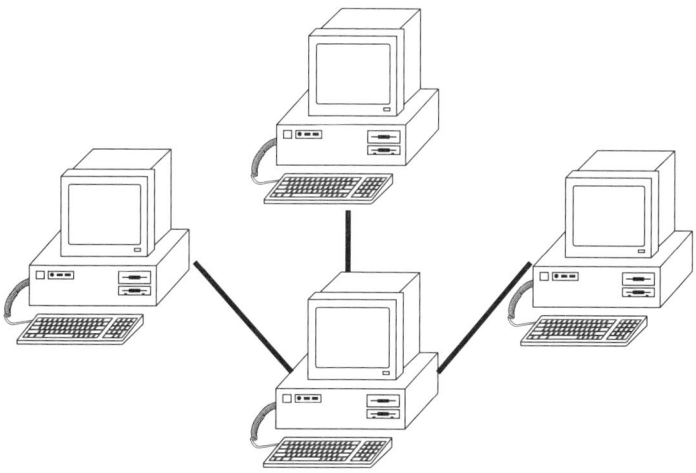

FIG. 11.13 The star topology, connecting the LAN's computers and devices with cables that radiate outward, usually from a file server.

If you have to run cables (of any type) through walls and ceilings, the cable installation can be the most expensive part of setting up a LAN. At every branching point, special fittings connect the intersecting wires. Sometimes you also need various additional components along the way, such as hubs, repeaters, or access units.

A few companies, such as Motorola, are working on LANs that do not require cables at all. Wireless LANs use infrared or radio waves to carry network signals from computer to computer, but have not yet achieved the speed and reliability needed for today's applications.

Planning the cabling layout, cutting the cable, attaching connectors, and installing the cables and fittings are jobs usually best left to experienced workers. If the fittings are not perfect, you may get electronic echoes on the network, which cause transmission errors.

FIG. 11.14 The star-wired tree topology, linking the LAN's computers and devices to one or more central hubs, or access units.

There are also a great many physical specifications for each network type that must be observed if the network is to function properly. Coaxial cable costs about 15 cents per foot, whereas STP costs about 25 cents per foot. This may sound like a moderate expense, even for a large LAN, but the cost of installing cable, at about $45 per hour, overshadows the cost of the cable itself. The moral of this story is to have the installer run much more cable than you initially need so that you won't have to have them come back and install more. The only time that you might consider installing LAN cable yourself is when you have a group of computers located on adjacent desks and you do not have to pull cable through the walls or ceiling.

Building codes almost always require you to use fireproof plenum cables. Plenum cables are more fire-resistant than some other cables. A professional cable installer should be familiar with the building codes in your area. You would be very upset if you installed ordinary cable yourself and were later told by the building inspector to rip out the cable and start over again with the proper kind.

Selecting the Proper Cable

As the demands of network users for ever increasing amounts of bandwidth continue, and new networking systems are developed to accommodate them, it soon becomes necessary to examine the capabilities of the most fundamental part of the network infrastructure: the cable itself. Ethernet over UTP cable, or 10BaseT, is the medium of choice in the majority of LAN installations today.

The cable used for such networks has traditionally been the same as that used for business telephone wiring. This is known as *Category 3*, or *voice grade UTP cable*, measured according to a scale that quantifies the cable's data transmission capabilities. The cable itself is 24 AWG (American Wire Gauge, a standard for measuring the diameter of a wire), copper tinned, with solid conductors, 100–105 ohm characteristic impedance, and a minimum of two twists per foot. Category 3 cable is adequate for networks running at up to 16Mbps.

Newer, faster network types require greater performance levels, however. Fast Ethernet technologies that run at 100Mbps using the same number of wires as standard Ethernet need a greater resistance to signal crosstalk and attenuation, and so the use of Category 5 cabling is essential. If, when you are building a LAN, you can use Category 3 wiring that is already in place, by all means do so. If, however, you are pulling new cable for your network, the use of Category 5 cable is recommended. Even if you are not running a high-speed network today, you will probably want to consider it in the future.

In a token-passing network, the cables from the workstations (or from the wall faceplates) connect centrally to a MSAU. The MSAU keeps track of which workstations on the LAN are neighbors and which neighbor is upstream or downstream. It is an easy job; the MSAU usually does not even need to be plugged into an electrical power outlet. The exceptions to this need for external power are MSAUs that support longer cable distances, or the use of UTP (Type 3) cable in high-speed LANs. The externally powered MSAU helps the signal along by regenerating it.

An IBM MSAU has eight ports for connecting one to eight Token-Ring devices. Each connection is made with a genderless data connector (as specified in the IBM cabling system). The MSAU has two additional ports, labeled RI (Ring-In) and RO (Ring-Out), that daisy-chain several MSAUs together when you have more than eight workstations on the LAN.

It takes several seconds to open the adapter connection on a Token-Ring LAN (something you may have noticed). During this time, the MSAU and your Token-Ring adapter card perform a small diagnostic check, after which the MSAU establishes you as a new neighbor on the ring. After being established as an active workstation, your computer is linked on both sides to your upstream and downstream neighbors (as defined by your position on the MSAU). In its turn, your Token-Ring adapter card accepts the token or frame, regenerates its electrical signals, and gives the token or frame a swift kick to send it through the MSAU in the direction of your downstream neighbor.

In an Ethernet network, the number of connections (taps) and their intervening distances are the network's limiting factors. Repeaters regenerate the signal every 500 meters or so. If repeaters were not used, standing waves (additive signal reflections) would distort the signal and cause errors. Because collision detection is highly dependent on timing, only five 500-meter segments and four repeaters can be placed in series before the propagation delay becomes longer than the maximum allowed period for the detection of a collision. Otherwise, the workstations farthest from the sender would be unable to determine whether a collision had occurred.

The people who design computer systems love to find ways to circumvent limitations. Manufacturers of Ethernet products have made it possible to create Ethernet networks in star, branch, and tree designs that overcome the basic limitations already mentioned. You can have thousands of workstations on a complex Ethernet network.

LANs are local because the network adapters and other hardware components cannot send LAN messages more than about a few hundred feet. Table 11.9 reveals the distance limitations of different kinds of LAN cable. In addition to the limitations shown in the table, keep in mind that you cannot connect more than 30 computers on a single Thinnet Ethernet segment, more than 100 computers on a Thicknet Ethernet segment, more than 72 computers on a UTP Token-Ring cable, or more than 260 computers on an STP Token-Ring cable.

Table 11.9 Network Distance Limitations

Network Adapter	Cable Type	Maximum	Minimum
Ethernet	Thin	607 ft.	20 in.
	Thick (drop cable)	164 ft.	8 ft.
	Thick (backbone)	1,640 ft.	8 ft.
	UTP	328 ft.	8 ft.
Token Ring	STP	328 ft.	8 ft.
	UTP	148 ft.	8 ft.
ARCnet (passive hub)		393 ft.	Depends on cable
ARCnet (active hub)		1,988 ft.	Depends on cable

Examining Protocols, Frames, and Communications

The network adapter sends and receives messages among the LAN computers, and the network cable carries the messages. It is the less tangible elements, however—the layers of networking protocols in each computer—that turn the individual machines into a local area network.

At the lowest level, networked computers communicate with one another by using message packets, often called *frames*. These frames, so-called because they surround and encapsulate that actual information to be transmitted, are the foundation on which all LAN activity is based. The network adapter, along with its support software, sends and receives these frames. Each computer on the LAN is identified by a unique address to which frames can be sent.

Frames are sent over the network for many different purposes, including the following:

- Opening a communications session with another adapter
- Sending data (perhaps a record from a file) to a PC
- Acknowledging the receipt of a data frame

- Broadcasting a message to all other adapters
- Closing a communications session

Figure 11.15 shows what a typical frame looks like. Different network implementations define frames in very different, highly specific ways, but the following data items are common to all implementations:

- The sender's unique network address
- The destination's unique network address
- An identification of the contents of the frame
- A data record or message
- A checksum or CRC for error-detection purposes

These items are used to perform fundamental tasks that underlie every network transmission: to take the needed information, send it to the proper destination, and ensure that it is received successfully.

| Sender ID | Destination ID | Frame Type | Data/Message | CRC |

FIG. 11.15 The basic layout of a frame.

Using Frames that Contain Other Frames

The layering of networking protocols within a single frame is a powerful concept that makes network communication possible. The lowest layer knows how to tell the network adapter to send a message, but that layer is ignorant of file servers and file redirection. The highest layer understands file servers and redirection but knows nothing about Ethernet or Token Ring. Together, though, the layers give you the full functionality of a local area network. Frames always are layered (see Figure 11.16).

When a higher-level file redirection protocol gives a message to a midlevel protocol (such as the Network Basic Input Output System, or NetBIOS, for example), it asks that the message be sent to another PC on the network (probably a file server). The midlevel protocol then puts an envelope around the message packet and hands it to the lowest level protocol, implemented as the network support software and the network adapter card. This lowest layer in turns wraps the (NetBIOS) envelope in an envelope of its own and sends it out across the network. On receipt, the network support software on the receiving computer removes the outer envelope and hands the result upward to the next higher-level protocol. The midlevel protocol running on the receiver's computer removes its envelope and gives the message—now an exact copy of the sender's message—to the receiving computer's highest-level protocol.

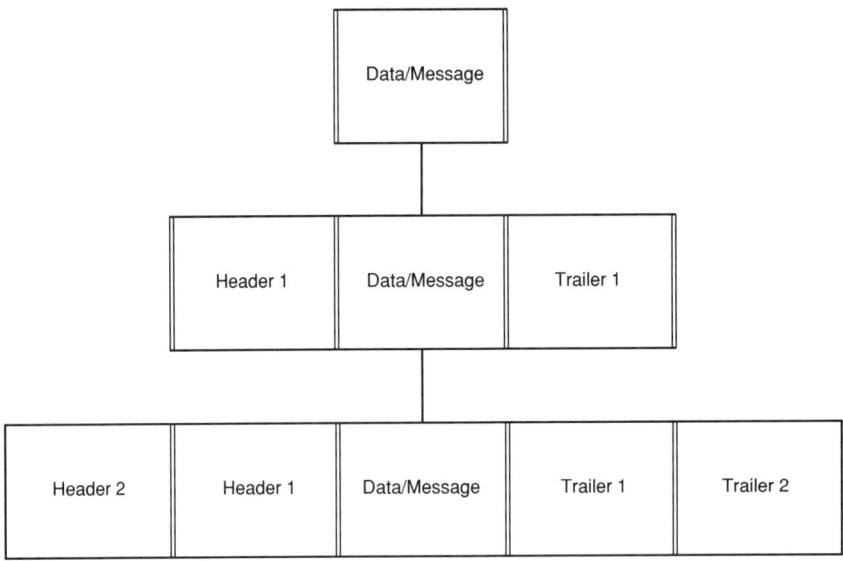

FIG. 11.16 Frame layers.

The primary reason for splitting the networking functionality into layers in this manner is that the different hardware and software components of the network are manufactured by different companies. If a single vendor produced every product used on your network, from applications to operating systems to network adapters to cabling, then they could arrange the communications however they wanted, and still be assured of the interoperability of the different parts.

This is not the case, however. Different vendors may split the LAN communications functions in slightly different ways, but they all have to rely on a common diagram of the overall process to ensure that their products will successfully interact with all of the others used on a typical LAN. One such diagram is called the OSI Reference Model.

Using the OSI Reference Model

The International Organization for Standardization (cryptically abbreviated as the ISO), has published a document called the *Open System Interconnection (OSI) model*. Most vendors of LAN products endorse the OSI standard but few or none implement it fully. The OSI model divides LAN communications into seven layers. Most NOS vendors use three or four layers of protocols, overlapping various OSI layers to span the same distance.

The OSI model describes how communications between two computers should occur. It calls for seven layers and specifies that each layer be insulated from the others by a well-defined interface. Figure 11.17 shows the seven layers. Various development projects over the years have attempted to create a networking system that is fully compliant with the OSI architecture, but no practical product has emerged. The OSI model remains a popular reference tool, however, and is a ubiquitous part of the education of any networking professional.

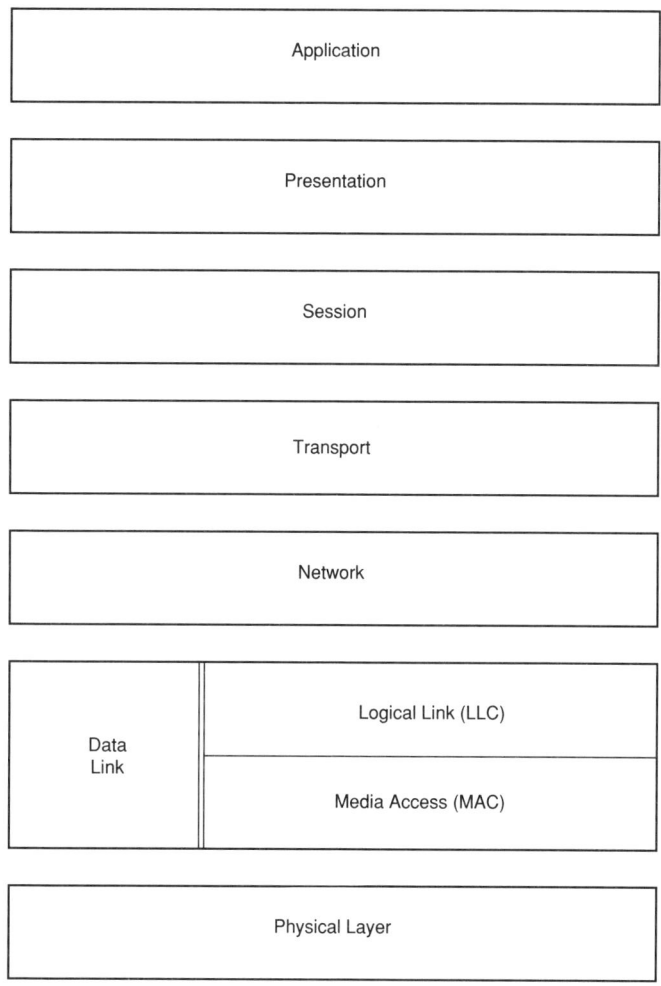

FIG. 11.17 The OSI model.

Descriptions of the seven layers follow:

- *Physical.* This part of the OSI model specifies the physical and electrical characteristics of the connections that make up the network (twisted pair cables, fiber-optic cables, coaxial cables, connectors, repeaters, and so on). You can think of this layer as the hardware layer. Although the rest of the layers may be implemented as chip-level functions rather than as actual software, the other layers are software in relation to this first layer.

- *Data Link.* At this stage of processing, the electrical impulses enter or leave the network cable. The network's electrical representation of your data (bit patterns, encoding methods, and tokens) is known to this layer and only to this layer. It is at this point that most errors are detected and corrected (by requesting retransmissions of corrupted packets). Because of its complexity, the Data Link layer often is subdivided into a Media Access Control (MAC) layer and a Logical Link Control (LLC) layer. The MAC layer deals with network access (token-passing or collision-sensing) and network control. The LLC layer, operating at a higher level than the MAC layer, is concerned with sending and receiving the user data messages. Ethernet and Token Ring are Data Link Layer protocols.

- *Network.* This layer switches and routes the packets as necessary to get them to their destinations. This layer is responsible for addressing and delivering message packets. While the Data Link layer is conscious only of the immediately adjacent computers on the network, the Network layer is responsible for the entire route of a packet, from source to destination. IPX and IP are examples of Network layer protocols.

- *Transport.* When more than one packet is in process at any time, such as when a large file must be split into multiple packets for transmission, the Transport layer controls the sequencing of the message components and regulates inbound traffic flow. If a duplicate packet arrives, this layer recognizes it as a duplicate and discards it. SPX and TCP are Transport layer protocols.

- *Session.* The functions in this layer enable applications running at two workstations to coordinate their communications into a single session (which you can think of in terms of a highly structured dialog). The Session layer supports the creation of the session, the management of the packets sent back and forth during the session, and the termination of the session.

- *Presentation.* When IBM, Apple, DEC, NeXT, and Burroughs computers want to talk to one another, obviously a certain amount of translation and byte reordering needs to be done. The Presentation layer converts data into (or from) a machine's native internal numeric format.

- *Application.* This is the layer of the OSI model seen by an application program. A message to be sent across the network enters the OSI model at this point, travels downward toward Layer 1 (the Physical layer), zips across to the other workstation, and then travels back up the layers until the message reaches the application on the other computer through its own Application layer.

One of the factors that makes the NOS of each vendor proprietary (as opposed to having an open architecture) is the vendor's degree and method of noncompliance with the OSI model. Sufficient protocol standardization has been implemented to allow all Ethernet products to function interchangeably (for example), but these standards do not directly comply with the OSI model document.

Using Low-Level Protocols

The MAC method for most LANs (part of the Data Link layer functionality discussed above) works in one of two basic ways: collision-sensing or token-passing. Ethernet is an example of a collision-sensing network; Token Ring is an example of a token-passing network.

The Institute of Electrical and Electronic Engineers (IEEE) has defined and documented a set of standards for the physical characteristics of both collision-sensing and token-passing networks. These standards are known as IEEE 802.3 (Ethernet) and IEEE 802.5 (Token Ring). Be aware, though, that the colloquial names Ethernet and Token Ring actually refer to earlier versions of these protocols, upon which the IEEE standards were based. There are minor differences between the frame definitions for true Ethernet and true IEEE 802.3. In terms of the standards, IBM's 16Mbps Token-Ring adapter card is an 802.5 Token-Ring extension. You learn the definitions and layout of Ethernet and Token Ring frames in the sections "Using Ethernet" and "Using Token Ring" later in this chapter.

Some LANs don't conform to IEEE 802.3 or IEEE 802.5, of course. The most well-known of these is ARCnet, available from such vendors as Datapoint Corporation, Standard Microsystems, and Thomas-Conrad. Other types of LANs include StarLan (from AT&T), VistaLan (from Allen-Bradley), LANtastic (from Artisoft), Omninet (from Corvus), PC Net (from IBM), and ProNet (from Proteon). All of these architectures can be considered archaic, however, and are almost never used in the construction of new LANs anymore.

The following sites list the different adapters by some of the major NIC vendors:

On the Web

http://www.3com.com/0files/products/bguide/index.html
http://www.networks.digital.com/html/products_guide/cat_toc.html
http://www.intel.com/comm-net/sns/showcase/speed/
http://www.proteon.com/products/client-server.html
http://www.smc.com/network/network.html

Fiber Distributed Data Interface (FDDI) is a new physical-layer LAN standard. FDDI uses fiber-optic cable and a token-passing scheme similar to IEEE 802.5 to transmit data frames at a snappy 100Mbps. There are also new standards now on the market designed to upgrade Ethernet networks to 100Mbps. Some of these, such as 100VG AnyLAN, can no longer be considered as Ethernet and use brand new methods for gaining media access. Some of these new standards are covered in the following section.

Evaluating High-Speed Networking Technologies

If you have fast workstations and a fast file server, you will want a fast network as well. Even the 16Mbps supplied by Token Ring may be too slow if your applications are data-intensive. The explosive growth of multimedia, groupware, and other technologies that require enormous amounts of data has forced network administrators to consider the need for high-speed network connections to individual desktop workstations.

Networking at speeds above 16Mbps has been around for several years, but it has primarily been limited to high-speed backbone connections between servers, due to its additional expense. Several new technologies are available today, however, that are designed to deliver data at high speeds—up to 100Mbps and more—to standard user workstations. Real-time data feeds from financial services, videoconferencing, video editing, and high-color graphics processing are just some of the tasks now being performed on PCs that would benefit greatly from an increase in network transmission speed.

Using the Fiber Distributed Data Interface

FDDI has been available for several years, but it is still a much newer protocol than Ethernet or Token Ring. Designed by the X3T9.5 Task Group of ANSI (the American National Standards Institute), FDDI passes tokens and data frames around a ring of optical fiber at a rate of 100Mbps. FDDI was designed to be as much like the IEEE 802.5 Token-Ring standard as possible, above the Physical layer. Differences occur only where necessary to support the faster speeds and longer transmission distances of FDDI.

If FDDI were to use the same bit-encoding scheme used by Token Ring, every bit would require two optical signals: a pulse of light and then a pause of darkness. This means that FDDI would need to send 200 million signals per second to have a 100 Mbps transmission rate. Instead, the scheme used by FDDI—called NRZI 4B/5B—encodes 4 bits of data into 5 bits for transmission so that fewer signals are needed to send a byte of information. The 5-bit codes (symbols) were chosen carefully to ensure that network timing requirements are met. The 4B/5B scheme, at a 100Mbps transmission rate, actually causes 125 million signals per second to occur (this is 125 megabaud). Also, because each carefully selected light pattern symbol represents 4 bits (a half byte, or nibble), FDDI hardware can operate at the nibble and byte level rather than at the bit level, making it easier to achieve the high data rate.

Two major differences in the way the token is managed by FDDI and IEEE 802.5 Token Ring exist. In traditional Token Ring, a new token is circulated only after a sending workstation gets back the frame that it sent. In FDDI, a new token is circulated immediately by the sending workstation after it finishes transmitting a frame, a technique that has since been adapted for use in Token-Ring networks and called *Early Token Release*. FDDI classifies attached workstations as *asynchronous* (workstations that are not rigid about the time periods that occur between network accesses) and *synchronous* (workstations having very stringent requirements regarding the timing between transmissions). FDDI uses a complex algorithm to allocate network access to the two classes of devices.

Although it provides superior performance, FDDI's acceptance as a desktop network has been hampered by its extremely high installation and maintenance costs (see "Using Fiber-Optic Cable" earlier in this chapter).

Using 100Mbps Ethernet

One of the largest barriers to the implementation of high-speed networking has been the need for a complete replacement of the networking infrastructure. Most companies cannot afford the down time needed to rewire the entire network, replace all the hubs and NICs, and then configure everything to operate properly. As a result of this, some of the new 100Mbps technologies are designed to make the upgrade process easier in several ways. First, they can often use the network cable that is already in place, and second, they are compatible enough with the existing installation to allow a gradual changeover to the new technology, workstation by workstation. Obviously, these factors also serve to minimize the expense associated with such an upgrade.

The two systems that take this approach are *100BaseT*, first developed by the Grand Junction Corp., and *100VG AnyLAN*, advocated by Hewlett-Packard and AT&T. Both of these systems run at 100Mbps over standard UTP cable, but that is where the similarities end. In fact, of the two, only 100BaseT can truly be called an Ethernet network. 100BaseT uses the same CSMA/CD media access protocol and the same frame layout defined in the IEEE 802.3 standard. In fact, 100BaseT as been ratified as an extension to that standard, called *802.3u*.

To accommodate existing cable installations, the 802.3u document defines four different cabling standards, as shown in Table 11.10.

Table 11.10 100BaseT Cabling Standards

Standard	Cable Type	Segment Length
100BaseTX	Category 5 (2 pairs)	100 meters
100BaseT4	Category 3, 4, or 5 (4 pairs)	100 meters
100BaseFX	62.6 micrometer Multimode fiber (2 strands)	400 meters

Sites with Category 3 cable already installed can therefore use the system without the need for rewiring, as long as the full four pairs in a typical run are available.

> **Note**
>
> Despite the apparent wastefulness, in most cases it is not recommended that that data and voice traffic be mixed within the same cable, even if sufficient wire pairs are available. Digital phone traffic could possibly coexist, but normal analog voice lines will definitely inhibit the performance of the data network.

100BaseT also requires the installation of new hubs and new NICs, but because the frame type used by the new system is identical to that of the old, this replacement can be done gradually, to spread the labor and expense over a protracted period of time. You could replace one hub with a 100BaseT model, and then switch workstations over to it, one at a time, as the users need and the networking staff's time permits. You can even purchase NICs that can operate at both 10 and 100Mbps speeds to make the changeover even easier.

100VG (voice grade) AnyLAN also runs at 100Mbps, and is specifically designed to use existing Category 3 UTP cabling. Like 100BaseT4, it requires four pairs of cable strands to affect its communications. There are no separate Category 5 or fiber-optic options in the standard. Beyond the cabling, 100VG AnyLAN is quite different from 100BaseT and indeed from Ethernet.

While 10 and 100BaseT networks both reserve one pair of wires for collision detection, 100VG AnyLAN is able to transmit over all four pairs simultaneously. This technique is called *quartet signaling*. A different signal encoding scheme called 5B/6B NRZ is also used, sending 2.5 times more bits per cycle than an Ethernet network's Manchester encoding scheme. Multiplied by the four pairs of wires (as compared to 10BaseT's one), you have a tenfold increase in transmission speed.

The fourth pair is made available for transmission because there is no need for collision detection on a 100VG AnyLAN network. Instead of the CSMA/CD media access system that defines an Ethernet network, 100VG AnyLAN uses a brand new technique called *demand priority*. Individual network computers have to request and be granted permission to transmit by the hub before they can send their data.

100VG AnyLAN also used the 802.3 frame type, so its traffic can coexist on a LAN with regular Ethernet. Like 100BaseT, combination 10/100 NICs are available, and the installation can be gradually migrated to the new technology.

Support for 100VG AnyLAN has almost completely disappeared from the market due to the cost of the adapters and the popularity of 10/100Mbps Ethernet adapters.

Using ATM

Asynchronous Transfer Mode is one of the newest of the high-speed technologies. It has been in an "emerging" state for some time now, without having developed into its full potential. ATM defines a Physical layer protocol in which a standard-size 53-byte packet (called a *cell*) can be used to transmit voice, data and real-time video over the same cable, simultaneously. The cells contain identification information that allow high-speed ATM switches (*wiring hubs*) to separate the data types and ensure that the cells are reassembled in the right order.

The basic ATM standard runs at 155Mbps, but some implementations can go as high as 660Mbps. Work is also progressing on an ATM desktop standard that runs at 25Mbps, but this doesn't seem to be enough of a gain over Token Ring's 16Mbps to be worth the adoption of an entirely new networking technology.

ATM is a radically different concept, and there are no convenient upgrade paths as there are with the 100Mbps standards described earlier. All the networking hardware must be replaced, and the ATM products currently on the market are still riding the wave of extremely high prices that are common to any new technology. For this reason, ATM is being used primarily for WAN links at this time. When the delivery of real-time video over the network becomes more of a practical reality than it is now, ATM might find its rightful place. For now, it remains a niche technology with very good potential.

TCP/IP and the Internet

TCP/IP stands for *Transmission Control Protocol/Internet Protocol*. It is the colloquial name given to the suite of networking protocols used by the Internet, as well as by most UNIX operating systems. TCP is primarily the Transport layer protocol in the suite, and IP defines the Network layer protocol that transmits blocks of data to the host.

TCP/IP is an extensive collection of Internet protocol applications and transport protocols, and includes File Transfer Protocol (FTP), Terminal Emulation (Telnet), and the Simple Mail Transfer Protocol (SMTP). TCP/IP was originally developed by the U.S. Department of Defense in the 1970s as platform and hardware-independent medium for communication over what was to become known as the Internet. A good example of this independence is the capability of DOS, Windows, or Windows 95 workstations to access information and transfer files on the Internet, which is a mixed platform environment. The primary advantages of TCP/IP are:

- *Platform Independence.* TCP/IP is not designed for use in any single hardware or software environment. It can and has been used on networks of all types.

- *Absolute Addressing.* TCP/IP provides a means of uniquely identifying every machine on the Internet.

- *Open Standards.* The TCP/IP specifications are publicly available to users and developers alike. Suggestions for changes to the standard can be submitted by anyone.

- *Application Protocols.* TCP/IP allows dissimilar environments to communicate. High-level protocols like FTP and Telnet have become ubiquitous in TCP/IP environments on all platforms.

Although it has been the protocol of choice on UNIX networks for many years, the explosive growth of the Internet has brought the protocols onto all kinds of LANs as well. Many network administrators are finding that they can adapt their current NOSes to use TCP/IP, and thus lessen the network traffic problems that can be caused by running several different sets of protocols on the same network.

Connecting to the Internet

You can connect a computer to the Internet through virtually any of the access ports discussed in this chapter thus far. Individual computers can use modems to connect to an Internet Service Provider (ISP), or a network connection can be established through which all of the users on the LAN gain access. Depending on your organization's degree of Internet involvement, any one of the following access options can be selected.

Asynchronous Modem Connections. Individual computers can use normal asynchronous modems attached to a serial port to connect to the Internet, through the services of an ISP. ISPs provide dial-in capabilities using either the PPP (Point-to-Point Protocol) or the SLIP (Serial Line Internet Protocol). Both of these protocols are part of the TCP/IP suite, and are now provided by virtually all of the third-party TCP/IP stacks available for DOS and Windows 3.1. Windows 95 and Windows NT include support for both protocols as part of the operating system. Whichever protocol you use must be supported by the TCP/IP stack on the remote computer, as well as the system to which you are connecting. Your service provider will be able to tell you what protocols are supported by the host system.

SLIP. The SLIP is an extremely simple protocol that provides a mechanism for the packets generated by IP (called *datagrams*) to be transmitted over a serial connection. It sends each datagram sequentially, separating them with a single byte known as the SLIP END character to signify the end of a packet. SLIP provides no means of error correction or data compression, and was eventually superseded by the PPP.

PPP. The PPP improves the reliability of serial TCP/IP communications with a three-layer protocol that provides the means for implementing the error correction and compression that SLIP lacks. Most TCP/IP stacks provide PPP support, as do most of the ISPs operating today. When given a choice, you should always select PPP over SLIP; it provides superior throughput and reliability.

ISDN Connections. An increasingly popular option for Internet connectivity is the ISDN connection. Providing speeds of 128Kbps (when both B channels are combined), it is more than four times faster than a 28.8Kbps modem connection. ISDN can be used to provide Internet access to a network or to an individual computer. The basics of ISDN communications are covered in the "Integrated Services Digital Network" section earlier in this chapter.

For basic e-mail connectivity and modest use, an ISDN connection could support 10 to 20 users on a network nicely. Giving users a taste of the Internet often leads to a substantial habit, however, and you may find that World Wide Web browsing and FTP transfers cause you to quickly outgrow an ISDN link.

T-1 Connections. For networks that must support a large number of Internet users, and especially for organizations that will be hosting their own Internet services, a T-1 connection to your service provider may be the wise investment. A *T-1* is a digital connection running at 1.55 Mbps. This is more than 10 times faster than an ISDN link. A T-1 may be split (or *fractioned*), depending on how it is to be used. It can be split into 24 individual 64K lines, or left as a single high-capacity pipeline. Some service providers allow you to lease any portion of a T-1 connection that you want (in 64K increments).

T-1 links in the United States usually cost several thousand dollars per month, plus a substantial installation fee, but for a large organization that is heavily committed to the Internet, it can be more economical to install a higher capacity service and grow into it, rather than constantly upgrade the link.

T-3 Connections. Equivalent in throughput to approximately 30 T-1 lines, a T-3 connection runs at 45Mbps, and is suitable for use by very large networks, university campuses, and the like. Pricing information falls into the "if you have to ask, you can't afford it" category.

Chapter 12
Audio Hardware

One of the problems with the PC standard is that when it was first created, it did not include audio capabilities other than rudimentary beeping or tone generation. Part of this was due to the fact that the PC standard originated in 1981, and other computers of that time had similar rudimentary capabilities. Systems that were designed later, such as the Macintosh which debuted in 1984, did include high-quality audio capabilities as an integral part of the system hardware and software. Although there still is no universal audio hardware and software standard for PC-compatible systems, the inherent expandability of the PC platform allows audio capability to be easily added, and at least one de facto standard has emerged. This chapter focuses on these products and how they are installed and operated.

Sound Card Applications

At first, consumer sound cards were used only for games. Several companies including AdLib, Roland, and Creative Labs had introduced products by the late 1980s. In 1989, Creative Labs introduced the Game Blaster, which provided stereo sound to a handful of computer games. The question for many buyers was, "Why spend $100 for a card that adds sound to a $50 game?" More importantly, because no sound standards existed at the time, a sound card might be useless with other games.

> **Note**
>
> About the same time, the Musical Instrument Digital Interface (MIDI) interfaces became available for the PC, but were used in very specialized recording applications.

A few months after releasing the Game Blaster, Creative Labs announced the Sound Blaster sound card. The Sound Blaster was compatible with the AdLib sound card and Creative Labs' own Game Blaster card. It included a built-in microphone jack and a MIDI (Musical Instrument Digital Interface) for connecting the PC to a musical synthesizer. Finally, the sound card had uses other than games.

Unfortunately, there is no single standard for PC-compatible sound cards. As in other aspects of the computer industry, standards are often developed by the market leader in a particular segment of the marketplace. These are called *de facto standards*. For example, Hewlett-Packard printers use a command language and graphics language that has become a de facto standard simply because many of their printers have been sold and most software supports them. Other printer manufacturers then strive to make their printers emulate the Hewlett-Packard printers so they don't require unique commands and they can use the same commands and drivers as a Hewlett-Packard printer. This is how a de facto standard is born. It is essentially based on popularity. While other printer command standards exist, the Hewlett-Packard standard is supported by most PC-compatible printers.

Over the last few years, several sound card manufacturers have fought for dominance, and there are several popular brands. Although several different companies make audio boards, the ones from Creative Labs have dominated the marketplace and have become the de facto standard. Thus, most audio boards from other companies emulate the Creative Labs Sound Blaster boards. Like the Hewlett-Packard printer standard, the Creative Labs Sound Blaster interface is the one that most hardware products emulate, and the one that most drivers are written for.

A sound card has many uses, including the following:

- Adding stereo sound to entertainment (game) software
- Increasing the effectiveness of educational software, particularly for young children
- Adding sound effects to business presentations and training software
- Creating music by using MIDI hardware and software
- Adding voice notes to files
- Adding sound effects to operating system events
- Enabling a PC to read
- Enabling PC use by handicapped individuals
- Playing audio CDs

Games

The sound card was originally designed to play games. In fact, many sound cards include a *game adapter interface*, which is a connector for adding a game control device (usually a joystick or control paddles). This is a potential area of conflict because other cards such as the multi-I/O type cards used in many PCs that have serial ports, parallel ports, and so on also have a game interface. This will result in an I/O Port address conflict since all game interfaces use the same I/O Port addresses. In these cases, it is usually best to use the game adapter interface on the sound card and disable any other in your system.

By adding a sound card, the game playing takes on a new dimension. The sounds add a level of realism that would otherwise be impossible, even with the best graphics. For example, some games use digitized human voices and dialog. In addition to realistic sounds and effects, games can have musical scores, which add to the excitement and entertainment.

Multimedia

A sound card is a prerequisite if you want to turn your PC into a *Multimedia PC (MPC)*. What is multimedia? The term embraces a number of PC technologies, but primarily deals with video, sound, and storage. Basically, multimedia means the ability to merge images, data, and sound on a computer. In a practical sense, multimedia simply means adding a sound card and a CD-ROM drive to your system.

An organization called the Multimedia PC Marketing Council was originally formed by Microsoft to generate standards for MPCs. The council created several MPC standards and license its logo and trademark to manufacturers whose hardware and software conform to these standards. This allows compatible hardware and software to be developed for multimedia operation on PC-compatible systems.

More recently, the MPC Marketing Council has formally transferred responsibility for its standards to the Software Publishers Association's Multimedia PC Working Group. This group includes many of the same members as the original MPC, and will now be the body governing the MPC specifications. The first thing this group has done is create a new MPC standard.

The MPC Marketing Council originally developed two primary standards for multimedia. They are called the *MPC Level 1* and *MPC Level 2* standards. Now under the direction of the Software Publishers Association (SPA), these first two standards have been augmented by a third standard called *MPC Level 3*, which was introduced in June 1995. These standards define the minimum capabilities for an MPC. Table 12.1 shows these standards.

Table 12.1   Multimedia Standards

	MPC Level 1	MPC Level 2	MPC Level 3
Processor	16MHz 386SX	25MHz 486SX	75MHz Pentium
RAM	2M	4M	8M
Hard Disk	30M	160M	540M
Floppy Disk	1.44M 3 1/2-inch	1.44M 3 1/2-inch	1.44M 3 1/2-inch
CD-ROM Drive	Single-Speed	Double-Speed	Quad-Speed
Audio	8-bit	16-bit	16-bit
VGA Video Resolution	640×480; 16 colors	640×480; 64K colors	640×0; 64K colors
Other I/O	Serial, Parallel, MIDI, Game	Serial, Parallel, MIDI, Game	Serial, Parallel, MIDI, Game
Software	Microsoft Windows 3.1	Microsoft Windows 3.1	Microsoft Windows 3.1
Date Introduced	1990	May 1993	June 1995

The MPC-3 specifications should be considered the bare minimums for any multimedia system today. In fact, I would normally recommend a system that exceeds the Level 3 standards in several areas, such as CPU, RAM, hard disk size, and video capability. Note that although speakers are technically not a part of the MPC specification, they are certainly required for sound reproduction!

MIDI

If you're musically inclined, you'll enjoy *MIDI (Musical Instrument Digital Interface)*. Developed in the early 1980s, MIDI essentially is a powerful programming language that lets your computer store and edit or play back music in tandem with a MIDI-compatible electronic musical instrument, typically a keyboard synthesizer.

The MPC specs mentioned earlier call for MIDI support. With MIDI, you can compose and edit music for presentations, learn about music theory, or turn your PC into a one-stop music mixing studio.

MIDI makes a musical note sound as though it comes from any of a wide array of instruments. The MPC specifications require a sound card to contain an FM MIDI synthesizer chip and be able to play at least six notes simultaneously.

To connect a MIDI device to a PC, you need a sound card that has two round serial ports in back—a MIDI input port and a MIDI output port. In addition to a keyboard, you'll need sequencing software to modify the tempo, sound, and volume of your recordings, or to cut and paste together various prerecorded music sequences.

Unlike other sound files, MIDI messages require little disk space. An hour of stereo music stored in MIDI requires less than 500K. (To contrast, a Microsoft Windows digital sound WAV file consumes more than 1,000 times that space.) Many games use MIDI sounds to conserve on disk space.

The quality of sound reproduction from MIDI files can vary greatly from card to card. This depends largely on whether your card uses wavetable synthesis or FM synthesis for MIDI reproduction.

Most sound boards generate sounds by using *FM synthesis*, a technology first pioneered in 1976. By using one sine wave operator to modify another, FM synthesis creates an artificial sound that mimics an instrument. Over the years, the technology has progressed (some FM synthesizers now use four operators) to a point where FM synthesis sounds good, but it still sounds artificial.

More realistic, inexpensive sound was pioneered by Ensoniq Corp., the makers of professional keyboards, in 1984. Using a technology that had been theorized at about the same time as FM synthesis, Ensoniq found a way to sample any instrument—including pianos, violins, guitars, flutes, trumpets, and drums—and to store the digitized sound in a wavetable. Stored either in ROM chips or on disk, the wavetable supplies an actual digitized sound of an instrument when called by the application. Soon after Ensoniq's discovery, other keyboard makers replaced their FM synthesizers with wavetable synthesis.

Wavetable synthesis won't make every sound on your PC more realistic—only the MIDI sounds, which are often used in games. Windows WAV files are actual stored sounds and don't benefit from wavetable synthesis.

Presentations

Businesses are discovering that combining graphics, animation, and sound is more impressive, and often less expensive, than a slide show. A sound card adds impact to any presentation or classroom.

A variety of business-presentation software and high-end training and authoring packages already exist. And you don't have to be a programmer to get your own show on the road. Even such popular software packages as CorelDRAW! and PowerPoint now include sound and animation features for their presentation files.

Some presentation software, such as PowerPoint and Corel Presents!, packages support WAV, AVI, and MIDI files. With these products, you can synchronize sounds with objects. When a picture of a new product is displayed, for example, you can play a roaring round of applause. You can even pull in audio from a CD in your CD-ROM drive. Such presentation software programs often include clip-media libraries.

A sound card can make tasks (such as learning how to use software) easier. PC software manufacturers have taken an early lead in this area. Many publishers are shipping special CD-ROM versions of some of their products. These versions often include animated online help, replete with music.

You can even take your show on the road. Many laptop and notebook computers today include sound capability and even have built-in CD-ROM drives and speakers. There are also external sound cards and even CD-ROM drives that attach to a laptop computer's parallel port to provide multimedia on the go. Finally, there are also several PC Card (PCMCIA)-based sound cards and CD-ROM drives on the market.

Recording

Virtually all sound cards have an audio input jack. With a microphone, you can record your voice. Using the Microsoft Windows Sound Recorder, you can play, edit, or record a sound file. These files are saved as *WAV files*, a type of file format. In the Windows Control Panel, you can assign certain Windows events a specific WAV file (see Figure 12.1). I always get a laugh when I exit Windows and hear the sound of a flushing toilet!

By recording your own sounds, you can create your own WAV files. Then you can use them for certain events. These are some of the standard events:

- Start Windows
- Exit Windows
- Open Program
- Close Program
- Minimize
- Menu Command
- Default Sound
- Asterisk
- Critical Stop
- Program Error
- Menu Pop-up
- Exclamation
- Maximize
- Question

FIG. 12.1 The Sounds section of the Windows 95 Control Panel adds sound to different Windows events.

Through the same audio input jack, you can attach your stereo system and record a song to a WAV file. You can also purchase prepackaged WAV files. Prerecorded WAV files can also be found on your local electronic bulletin board or online services such as CompuServe and America Online.

On the Web

You can find audio files, particularly WAV files, at several locations such as:

- The Wav Emporium, **http//wav-emporium.forsite.net/**
- Wav Central, **http://www.wavecentral.com/**
- Ruger's Wav Repository, **http://rand.nidlink.com/~ruger/wavs1.html**

Voice Annotation

By using WAV files, you can record messages into your Windows documents and spreadsheets. For example, a business executive could pick up a microphone and, by embedding a message in a contract, give his or her secretary explicit instructions. This message is called a *voice annotation*. I like to think of it as a verbal Post-It note.

With voice annotation, you can embed voice messages, suggestions, or questions in a document and send it to a colleague. To leave such messages, your Windows application must support Windows' Object Linking and Embedding (OLE).

Imagine that you're editing a worksheet in Excel and want to insert a voice note next to a total that looks questionable. Place the cursor in the cell next to the total, then select Edit, Insert, Object, Sound to call up Windows' Sound Recorder. Click the Record button and begin speaking.

Voice Recognition

Some sound cards are capable of voice recognition. You can also get voice recognition for your current sound card in the form of add-on software. Voice-recognition technology is unfortunately still in its infancy, and you will need a fast computer, such as a Pentium, for quick response times.

Voice Recognition is still sensitive to changes in a person's voice, with both illness and stress changing a person's voice enough to throw off most of the "consumer" voice recognition products. Advances in this technology may develop to a point where we'll be able to use continuous speech to control our computer, rather than typing.

Proofreading

Sound cards can be used also as inexpensive proofreaders. Text-to-speech utilities can read back to you a list of numbers or text. This software is included with some sound cards and can be used to read back highlighted words or even an entire file.

This will allow you to more easily spot forgotten words or awkward phrases when you hear a note read back to you. Accountants can double-check numbers, and busy executives can listen to their e-mail while they are doing paperwork.

Audio CDs

One entertaining use of a CD-ROM drive is to play audio CDs while you are working on something else. The music can be piped not only through a pair of speakers but also through a headphone set plugged into the front of your CD-ROM drive. Most sound cards include a CD-player utility, although free versions are available on online services such as CompuServe. These programs usually present a visual display similar to an audio CD player. You operate the controls with a mouse or the keyboard, and can listen to audio CDs while you work on other things.

Sound Mixer

Any time you have multiple sources of sound that you want to play through a single set of speakers, a mixer is necessary. Most mixers are the kind that you see in music videos, or in use by your local DJ.

Most sound cards have a built-in mixer to allow all of the different audio sources, MIDI, WAV, Line IN, and the CD to be played out of the single Line Out. Normally, software is included with the sound card that displays visual sliders like you would see on a standard mixer. This allows you to control the relative volume of each of the sound sources.

Sound Card Concepts and Terms

To understand sound cards, you need to understand various concepts and terms. Terms like *16-bit*, *CD quality*, and *MIDI port* are just a few. Concepts such as *sampling* and *digital-to-audio conversion (DAC)* are often sprinkled throughout stories about new sound products. The following sections describe some common sound card terms and concepts.

The Nature of Sound

To understand a sound card, you need to understand sound itself. Every sound is produced by vibrations that compress air or other substances. These sound waves travel in all directions, expanding in balloon-like fashion from the source of the sound. When these waves reach your ear, they cause vibrations that you perceive as sound.

The two basic properties of any sound are its pitch and its intensity.

Pitch is simply the rate at which vibrations are produced. It is measured in the number of *hertz (Hz)*, or cycles per second. One cycle is a complete vibration back and forth. The number of Hz is the frequency of the tone; the higher the frequency, the higher the pitch. You cannot hear all possible frequencies. Very few people can hear any fewer than 16Hz or any more than about 20KHz (kilohertz; 1KHz equals 1,000Hz). In fact, the lowest note on a piano has a frequency of 27Hz, the highest note, a little more than 4KHz. And frequency-modulation (FM) radio stations broadcast notes up to 15KHz.

The intensity of a sound is called its *amplitude*. This intensity depends upon the strength of the vibrations producing the sound. A piano string, for example, vibrates gently when the key is struck softly. The string swings back and forth in a narrow arc, and the tone it sends out is soft. If the key is struck forcefully, however, the string swings back and forth in a wider arc. The loudness of sounds is measured in *decibels (db)*. The rustle of leaves is rated at 20db, average street noise at 70db, and nearby thunder at 120db.

Game Standards

Most sound cards support both of the current entertainment audio standards: AdLib and Sound Blaster. The *Sound Blaster* is a family of sound cards sold by Creative Labs; *AdLib* sells their own cards as well. To play most games, you must tell your game which of these sound card standards your sound card supports. Sticking with a popular sound card product (like the Sound Blaster line from Creative Labs) will ensure that you always have software support. Most software supports the Sound Blaster or AdLib cards, and because of this, now most other brands' sound cards will emulate one of these popular ones. If you have some off-the-wall brand sound card and it does not emulate either the Sound Blaster or AdLib cards, then you may find many software products that do not specifically support your card.

> **Note**
> More and more games are being developed for Windows 95. Games that are written for Windows 95 do not require specific compatibility with any sound card. They will work even if your sound card is not Sound Blaster- or AdLib-compatible.

Frequency Response

The quality of a sound card is often measured by two criteria: frequency response (or range) and total harmonic distortion.

The *frequency response* of a sound card is the range in which an audio system can record or play at a constant and audible amplitude level. Many cards support 30Hz to 20KHz. The wider the spread, the better the sound card.

The *total harmonic distortion* measures a sound card's *linearity*, the straightness of a frequency response curve. In layman's terms, the harmonic distortion is a measure of accurate sound reproduction. Any nonlinear elements cause distortion in the form of harmonics. The smaller the percentage of distortion, the better.

Sampling

With a sound card, a PC can record Waveform audio. *Waveform audio* (also known as *sampled* or *digitized sound*) uses the PC as a tape recorder. Small computer chips built into a sound card, called *analog-to-digital converters (ADCs)*, convert analog sound waves into digital bits the computer can understand. Likewise, *digital-to-analog converters (DACs)* convert the recorded sounds to something audible.

Sampling is the process of turning the original analog sound waves (see Figure 12.2) into digital (on/off) signals that can be saved and later replayed. Snapshots of the analog sounds are taken and saved. For example, at time X the sound may be measured with an amplitude of Y. The higher (or more frequent) the sample rate, the more accurate the digital sound is to its real-life source.

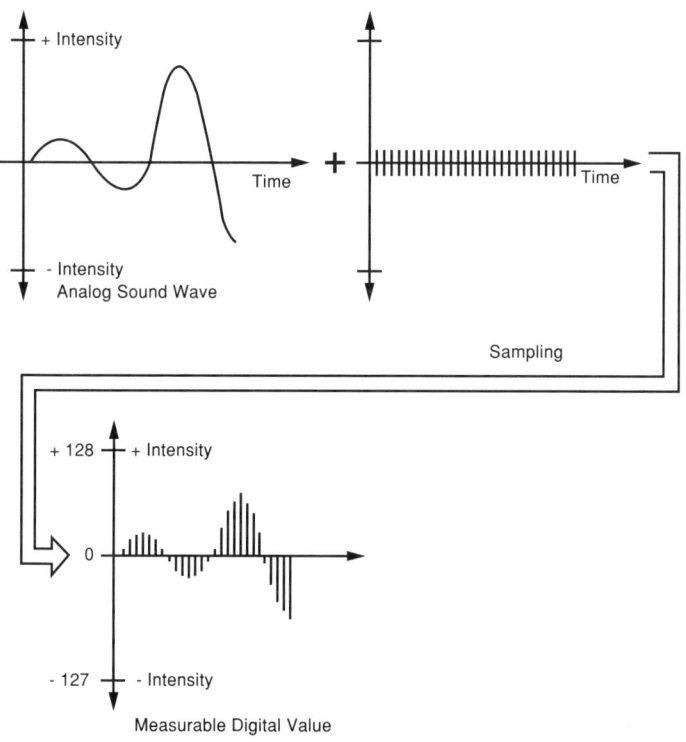

FIG. 12.2 Sampling turns a changing sound wave into measurable digital values.

8-Bit versus 16-Bit

The original MPC specifications required 8-bit sound. This doesn't mean the sound card must fit into an 8-bit instead of a 16-bit expansion slot. Rather, *8-bit audio* means that the sound card uses 8 bits to digitize each sound sample. This translates into 256 possible digital values to which the sample can be pegged (less quality than the 65,536 values possible with a 16-bit sound card). Generally , 8-bit audio is adequate for recorded speech, whereas 16-bit sound is best for the demands of music. Figure 12.3 shows the difference between 8- and 16-bit sound.

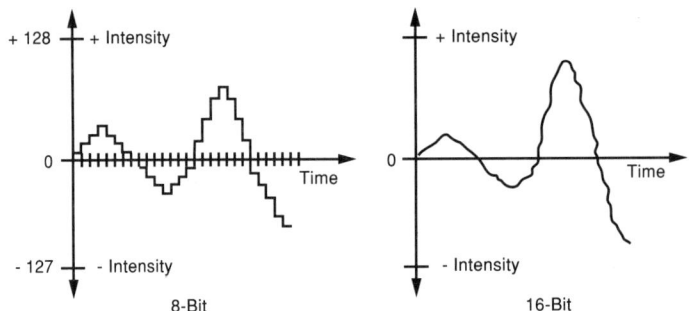

FIG. 12.3 16-bit resolution allows more accurate sound reproduction than 8-bit resolution.

Many of the older sound cards did 8-bit sound reproduction only. Today, I would not recommend anything less than a 16-bit card, which offers very high resolution.

Besides resolution, the sampling rate or frequency determines how often the sound card measures the level of the sound being recorded or played back. Basically, you have to sample at about two times the highest frequency you want to produce, plus an extra 10 percent to keep out unwanted signals. Humans can hear up to 20,000 cycles per second, or 20KHz. If you double this number and add 10 percent, you get a 44.1KHz sampling rate, the same sampling rate used by high-fidelity audio CDs.

Sound recorded at 11KHz (capturing 11,000 samples per second) is fuzzier than sound sampled at 22KHz. A sound sampled in 16-bit stereo (two channel) at 44KHz (CD-audio quality) requires as much as 10.5M per minute of disk space! The same sound sample in 8-bit mono (single channel) at 11KHz takes 1/16th the space. If you were to add a one-minute hi-fi voice annotation to your spreadsheet, you'd find a spreadsheet whose size had increased by more than 10M.

The CD-ROM Connection

In addition to a sound card, the other foundation of multimedia is a CD-ROM (compact disk read-only memory) drive.

CD-ROM drives provide access to a wealth of text, graphics, sound, video, and animation. Like a sound card, a CD-ROM drive is essential for any multimedia PC.

Many sound cards double as a CD-ROM controller, or interface, card. Some sound cards, however, use a proprietary connection that accommodates only certain proprietary interface CD-ROM drives. For a wider selection of drives, consider a sound card that includes an IDE (Integrated Drive Electronics) or SCSI-2 (Small Computer Systems Interface-2) connector. If you are also going to attach other SCSI devices such as hard disks, tape drives, or scanners, then I recommend staying with a separate stand-alone SCSI-2 adapter. The software driver support and performance will be much better than on the Sound/SCSI combo cards.

For more information on CD-ROM drives, see Chapter 17 "CD-ROM Drives."

Sound File Formats

There are several file formats for storing and editing digitized sound. The most notable is the *WAV format* supported by Windows. (*WAV* is short for *waveform audio*.) One audio minute saved to a WAV file requires 2.5M to 10M or more of disk space, depending on the recording options you select. Windows 95 offers recordings at several different rates and bit depths.

Sound Reproduction

As mentioned previously, there are two methods for sound reproduction. The older, cheaper, and less desirable method called Frequency Modulation is losing favor as people move to wavetable sound. When looking for a card today, look for wavetable-based sound.

Compression/Decompression

Because one minute of stereo audio can consume up to 11M of disk space, several sound card makers use *Adaptive Differential Pulse Code Modulation (ADPCM) compression* to reduce file size by more than 50 percent. However, a simple fact of audio life is that when you use such compression, you lose sound quality.

Because the sound quality can be degraded, there is no ADPCM standard. Creative Labs uses a proprietary hardware approach, while Microsoft is pushing the Business Audio ADPCM design developed with Compaq.

The most popular compression standard is the *Motion Pictures Experts Group (MPEG) standard*, which works with both audio and video compression and is gaining support in the non-PC world from products like the Philips CD-I player. MPEG sports a potential compression ratio of 12:1, and due to this, several full-motion-video MPEG CD-ROM titles are now available.

Sound Card Characteristics

What are some key features to consider in a sound card? Although some aspects are subjective, the following sections describe some key buying points.

Compatibility

Although there are no official sound card standards, the popular Sound Blaster card has become a de facto standard. The Sound Blaster—the first widely distributed sound card—is supported by the greatest number of software programs. A sound card advertised as Sound Blaster-compatible should run virtually any application that supports sound. Many sound cards also support the MPC Level 2 or Level 3 specifications, allowing you to play sound files in Windows and more. Some sound cards, by excluding a MIDI interface, barely fall short of the MPC specs. Other compatibility standards to look for are AdLib and Pro AudioSpectrum.

> **Caution**
> Beware of sound cards that require special drivers to be Sound Blaster-compatible. These drivers can cause problems and will take up additional memory that otherwise would be available.

Sampling

The most important sound card quality is its sampling capability. The rate at which the card samples (measured in KHz) and the size of its sample (expressed in bits) determine the quality of the sound. The standard sampling rates for sound cards are 11.025KHz, 22.050KHz, and 44.1KHz; sample sizes are 8, 12, and 16 bits.

Inexpensive monophonic cards generally sample at 8 bits up to speeds of 22.050KHz, which is fine for recording voice messages. Some stereo-capable cards sample at 8 bits and run at speeds of 22.050KHz in stereo and up to 44.1KHz in mono. Other cards can sample 8 bits at 44.1KHz speeds in both stereo and mono. The latest generation of cards do it all; they can record CD-quality audio of 16 bits at 44.1KHz.

If you do buy a card that supports 16-bit sampling and plan on doing any recording, make sure you have plenty of hard disk space. The higher the resolution of sampling, the more hard disk space needed to store the file. The sampling rate also affects file size; sampling at the next higher rate doubles the file size.

Stereo versus Mono

You'll also have to consider buying a monophonic or stereophonic sound card. Inexpensive sound cards are *monophonic*, producing sound from a single source. Still, monophonic cards produce better sound than your PC's speaker.

Stereophonic cards produce many voices, or sounds, concurrently and from two different sources. The more voices a card has, the higher the sound fidelity. Each stereo chip in a sound card is capable of 11 or more voices. To get 20 or more voices, manufacturers had to resort to two FM synthesizer chips. Today, a single chip produces 20 voices, providing truer stereo sound.

The number of voices a stereo card has is especially important for music files because the voices correspond to the individual instruments the card can play.

Most cheaper sound cards use FM synthesis to imitate the musical instruments played. Most use synthesizer chips developed by Yamaha. The least expensive sound cards use the monophonic 11-voice YM3812 or OPL2 chip. Better sound cards use the stereophonic 20-voice YMF262 or OPL3 chip.

Imitated musical instruments are not as impressive as the real thing. Wavetable sound cards often use digital recordings of real instruments and sound effects. Often, several megabytes of these sound clips are embedded in ROM chips on the card. For example, some sound cards use the Ensoniq chip set (a type of circuit design) that does wavetable synthesis of musical instruments. Instead of pretending to play a trombone D flat, the Ensoniq chip set has a little digitized recording of an actual instrument playing that note.

If your primary interest in a sound card is for entertainment or for use in educational or business settings, FM synthesis quality may be good enough.

Stereo sound cards vary in sampling rates and sizes. Some stereo cards do not work in mono mode. Also, moving from mono to stereo sound means an increase in the size of the sound files. As with 16-bit resolution, stereo sound is not supported by most software applications. However, a stereo card playing mono software does generate better sound than a mono card.

Another consideration when buying the more expensive stereo cards is that they generally come with additional interfaces, such as connections to a SCSI device (such as a CD-ROM drive) or a MIDI device (such as a keyboard). In most cases, you will get better performance from a CD-ROM drive by connecting it to a motherboard IDE port or a separate high-performance SCSI host adapter.

CD-ROM Connector

Most stereo sound cards not only provide great sound but also can operate your CD-ROM drive. Although many cards come with a SCSI port for any SCSI device, such as a CD-ROM drive, others support only a proprietary CD-ROM interface, such as Mitsumi or Sony CD-ROM interfaces. If you own a CD-ROM drive, make sure it's compatible with the sound card you plan to buy. If you plan to add a CD-ROM drive or expect to upgrade your drive, keep in mind that a proprietary interface will limit your choices, perhaps to a single CD-ROM brand.

If you're seeking to add both a sound card and a CD-ROM drive, consider multimedia upgrade kits. These kits bundle a sound card, CD-ROM drive, CD-ROM titles, software, and cables in an attractively priced package. By buying a multimedia upgrade kit rather than disparate components, you may save some money. And you'll know that the components will work together, especially if the kit includes proper documentation.

Data Compression

Most sound cards today can easily produce CD-quality audio, which is sampled at 44.1KHz. At this rate, recorded files (even of your own voice) can consume as many as 11M for every minute of recording. To counter this demand for disk space, many sound cards include a data-compression capability. For example, the Sound Blaster ASP 16 includes on-the-fly compression of sound in ratios of 2:1, 3:1, or 4:1.

MIDI Interface

The *Musical Instrument Digital Interface (MIDI)* is a standard for connecting musical instruments to PCs. Many stereo cards come with MIDI, synthesizer, and sequencing software for composing music. Some cards include only a MIDI interface; you have to purchase the hardware separately to hook up other MIDI devices. Other sound cards may exclude the MIDI.

MIDI allows your computer to store, edit, and play back music through a MIDI instrument such as a keyboard synthesizer. MIDI is more like a networking programming language, allowing you to add more instruments, including drum machines and special sound effects generators.

Bundled Software

Sound cards usually include several sound utilities so that you can begin using your sound card right away. Most of this software is DOS-based, but Windows-based versions are available with some cards. The possibilities include:

- Text-to-speech conversion programs
- Programs for playing, editing, and recording audio files
- Sequencer software, which helps you compose music (generally included with cards with MIDI)
- Various sound clips

Multi-Purpose Digital Signal Processors

One recent addition to many sound boards is the *digital signal processor (DSP)*. DSPs add intelligence to your sound card, freeing your computer from work-intensive tasks, such as filtering noise from recordings or compressing audio on-the-fly.

About half of most general-purpose sound cards use DSPs. The Cardinal Technologies Sound Pro 16 and Sound Pro 16 Plus, for example, use the Analog Devices ADSP2115 digital signal processor. The Sound Blaster AWE32's programmable DSP features compression algorithms for processing text-to-speech data and enables the card's QSound surround-sound 3-D audio, along with reverb and chorus effects. DSPs allow a sound card to be a multi-purpose device. IBM uses its DSP to add a 14.4Kbit/sec modem, 9.6Kbps fax, and a digital answering machine to its WindSurfer Communications Adapter.

Are DSPs worth the extra price? On low-powered PCs (those less powerful than a 486SX/25) or in true multitasking environments like Windows 95, Windows NT, or OS/2 Warp, a DSP can make real-time compression possible—a feature valuable for voice annotation. Note that many cards can be purchased without the DSP chip and can have it added later as an upgrade.

Sound Drivers

Most sound cards include universal drivers for DOS and Windows applications. Find out what drivers are included with your card. Windows 95 already includes drivers for the most popular sound cards, such as Sound Blaster. Other drivers are available on a separate driver disk available from Microsoft or from Microsoft's Product Support download service.

Connectors

Most sound cards have the same connectors. These 1/8-inch minijack connectors provide ways to pass sound from the sound card to speakers, headphones, and stereo systems and to receive sound from a microphone, CD player, tape player, or stereo. The four types of connectors your sound card typically could or should have are shown in Figure 12.4:

Sound Card Characteristics   503

FIG. 12.4 The basic features most sound cards have in common.

- *Stereo line, or audio, out connector.* The line out is used to send sound signals from the sound card to a device outside the computer. The cables from the line out connector can be hooked up to stereo speakers, a headphone set, or your stereo system. If you hook up your stereo system, you can have amplified sound. Some sound cards, such as the Microsoft Windows Sound System, provide two jacks for line out. One is for the left channel of the stereo signal; the other is for the right channel.

- *Stereo line, or audio, in connector.* The line in connector is used to record, or mix, sound signals to the computer's hard disk.

- *Speaker/headphone connector.* The speaker/headphone connector is not always provided on a sound card. Instead, the line out (described earlier) doubles as a way to send stereo signals from the sound card to your stereo system or speakers. When both speaker/headphone and line out connectors are provided, the speaker/headphone connector provides an amplified signal that can power your headphones or small bookshelf speakers. Most sound cards can provide up to 4 watts of power to drive your speakers. Conversely, signals sent through the line out connector are not amplified. Using the line out connector provides the best sound reproduction because the stereo system or amplified speakers will amplify the sounds.

Notice that most sound cards have a special pin type connector that plugs directly into an internal CD-ROM drive to allow sound to be played from the drive through the speakers attached to the sound card.

- *Microphone, or mono, in connector.* You connect a microphone to this 1/8-inch minijack to record your voice or other sounds to disk. This microphone jack records in mono, not in stereo. Many sound cards use *Automatic Gain Control (AGC)* to improve recordings. This feature adjusts the recording levels on-the-fly. A 600 to 10K ohm dynamic or condenser microphone works best with this jack. Some inexpensive sound cards use the line in connector instead of a separate microphone jack.

- *Joystick/MIDI connector.* The joystick connector is a 15-pin, D-shaped connector. Two of the pins are used to control a MIDI device, such as a keyboard. Many sound card makers offer an optional MIDI connector.

Sometimes the joystick port can accommodate two joysticks if you order the optional Y-adapter. To use this connector as MIDI, you'll need to buy the optional MIDI cable. Some sound cards do not provide MIDI. If you're not interested in making music (and spending a few hundred dollars more for the MIDI keyboard), you may want to consider these models. And don't worry about the lack of a joystick port. These are already found in some PCs as a part of a Multi-I/O card; otherwise, you can buy a separate stand-alone game card.

Volume Control

A thumbwheel volume control is provided on some sound cards, although sophisticated sound cards have no room for such a control. Instead, a combination of keys or a visual slider control can be used to adjust the sound. By pressing these key combinations, you adjust the volume from within a game, Windows program, or any other application.

Sound Card Options

You'll seldom buy just a sound card. You'll need—or want—other accessories that raise the cost of your PC sound system. At the very least, you'll have to invest in a set of speakers or headphones. At most, you may want to purchase a MIDI synthesizer keyboard.

Speakers

Successful business presentations, multimedia applications, and MIDI work demand external high-fidelity stereo speakers. Although you can use standard stereo speakers, they are too big to fit on or near your desk. Smaller bookshelf speakers are better.

Sound cards offer little or no power to drive external speakers. Although some sound cards have small 4-watt amplifiers, they are not powerful enough to drive quality speakers. Also, conventional speakers sitting near your display may create magnetic interference, which can distort colors and objects on-screen or jumble the data recorded on your nearby floppy disks.

To solve these problems, computer speakers need to be small, efficient, and self-powered. Also, you need to provide magnetic shielding, either in the form of added layers of insulation in the speaker cabinet or by electronically canceling out the magnetic distortion.

> **Caution**
>
> Although most computer speakers are magnetically shielded, do not leave recorded tapes, watches, personal credit cards, or floppy disks in front of the speakers for long periods of time.

Quality sound depends on quality speakers. A 16-bit sound card may provide better sound to computer speakers, but even an 8-bit sound card sounds good from a good speaker. Conversely, an inexpensive speaker makes both 8-bit and 16-bit sound cards sound tinny.

The dozens of models on the market range from less expensive minispeakers from Sony and Koss to larger self-powered models from companies such as Bose. To evaluate speakers, you need to know the lingo. Speakers are measured by three criteria:

- *Frequency response.* A measurement of the range of high and low sounds a speaker can reproduce. The ideal range is from 20Hz to 20KHz, the range of human hearing. No speaker system reproduces this range perfectly. In fact, few people hear sounds above 18KHz. An exceptional speaker may cover a range of 30Hz to 23,000KHz. Lesser models may cover only 100Hz to 20,000Hz. Frequency response is the most deceptive specification, because identically rated speakers can sound completely different.

- *Total Harmonic Distortion (THD).* An expression of the amount of distortion or noise created by amplifying the signal. Simply put, distortion is the difference between the sound sent to the speaker and the sound you hear. The amount of distortion is measured in percentages. An acceptable level of distortion is below .1 percent (one-tenth of 1 percent). For some CD-quality recording equipment, a common standard is .05 percent. Some speakers have a distortion of 10 percent or more. Headphones often have a distortion of about 2 percent or less.

- *Watts.* Usually stated as *watts per channel*, the amount of amplification available to drive the speakers. Check that the company means "per channel" (or RMS) and not total power. Many sound cards have built-in amplifiers, providing up to 8 watts per channel. (Most provide 4 watts.) The wattage is not enough to provide rich sound, however, which is why many speakers have built-in amplifiers. With the flick of a switch or the press of a button, such speakers amplify the signals they receive from the sound card. If you do not want to amplify the sound, you typically leave the speaker switch set to "direct." In most cases, you'll want to amplify the signal.

Two or four C batteries are often used to power computer speakers. Because these speakers require so much power, you may want to invest in an AC adapter, although more-expensive speakers include one. With an AC adapter, you won't have to buy new batteries every few weeks. If your speakers didn't come with an AC adapter, you can pick one up from your local Radio Shack or hardware store. Be sure that the adapter you purchase matches your speakers in voltage and polarity.

You can control your speakers in various ways, depending on their complexity and cost. Typically, each speaker has a volume knob, although some share one volume control. If one speaker is farther away than the other, you may want to adjust the volume accordingly. Many computer speakers include a *dynamic bass boost (DBB) switch*. This button provides a more powerful bass and clearer treble, regardless of the volume setting. Other speakers have separate bass and treble boost switches or a three-band equalizer to control low, middle, and high frequencies. When you rely on your sound card's power rather than your speaker's built-in amplifier, the volume and dynamic bass boost controls have no effect. Your speakers are at the mercy of the sound card's power.

A 1/8-inch stereo minijack connects from the sound card output jack to one of the speakers. The signal is then split and fed through a separate cable from the first speaker to the second one.

Before purchasing a set of speakers, check that the cables between the speakers are long enough for your computer setup. For example, a tower case sitting alongside one's desk may require longer speaker wires than a desktop computer.

Beware of speakers that have a tardy built-in "sleep" feature. Such speakers, which save electricity by turning themselves off when they are not in use, may have the annoying habit of clipping the first part of a sound after a period of inactivity.

Headphones are an option when you can't afford a premium set of speakers. Headphones also provide privacy and allow you to play your sound card as loud as you like.

Microphone

Some sound cards do not include a microphone. You'll need one to record your voice to a WAV file. Selecting a microphone is quite simple. You need one that has a 1/8-inch minijack to plug into your sound card's microphone, or audio in, jack. Most have an on/off switch.

Like speakers, microphones are measured by their frequency range. This is not an important buying factor, however, because the human voice has a limited range. If you are recording only voices, consider an inexpensive microphone that covers a limited range of frequencies. An expensive microphone's recording capabilities extend to frequencies outside the voice's range. Why pay for something you won't be needing?

If you are recording music, invest in an expensive microphone, although an 8-bit sound card can record music just as well with an inexpensive microphone.

Your biggest decision is to select a microphone that suits your recording style. If you work in a noisy office, you may want a unidirectional microphone that will prevent extraneous noises from being recorded. An omnidirectional mike is best for recording a group conversation.

Most higher-priced sound cards include a microphone of some type. This can be a small lapel microphone, a hand-held microphone, or one with a desktop stand. If you want to leave your hands free, you may want to shun the traditional hand-held microphone for a lapel model. If your sound card does not come with a microphone, see your local stereo or electronics parts store. Be sure that any microphone you purchase has the correct impedance to match the sound card input.

Joysticks

Many sound cards include a joystick, or game, port. (This joystick port often doubles as a connection to a MIDI device.) A joystick is ideally meant for game playing, such as simulating flying a Cessna aircraft. Joysticks, like speakers, are best chosen through hands-on experience.

A joystick has a fire button on top of a center wand you move in any of eight directions, with a second button or pair of buttons located on the base.

Good joysticks have resistance that increases the further you move the center wand from dead center. Some joysticks include suction cups that mount the unit on your desk. If you're short on desk space, you may prefer a smaller joystick that fits in your hand. If you are left-handed, look for an ambidextrous joystick, not one that is contoured for right-handers.

Some joysticks are meant especially for flight-simulation or driving games. These simulate an aircraft control yoke, or an automobile steering wheel. They often include pedals for other functions as well.

MIDI Connector

If you are interested in MIDI to create synthesized music, you'll need to connect your musical keyboard or other MIDI device to your sound card. The joystick port on sound cards has unused pins that can be used to send and receive MIDI data. By connecting a MIDI cable to the joystick port, you can connect your PC to a MIDI device. The cable has three connectors: a joystick connector, and MIDI In and Out connectors.

Synthesizer

If you are considering MIDI, you will want to get a MIDI keyboard synthesizer if you intend on composing or playing music, although you can play back MIDI scores without one. To make MIDI scores, you also need sequencer software to record, edit, and play back MIDI files. (Some sound cards include sequencing software.) A MIDI file contains up to 16 channels of music data, so you can record many different instruments and play them back. By using the keyboard, you can enter the notes for various instruments.

To enhance MIDI sounds for the Sound Blaster cards, Creative Labs offers the *Wave Blaster*. The Wave Blaster plugs into the Sound Blaster card. When MIDI music is played, it looks to the Wave Blaster for any of 213 CD-quality digitally recorded musical instrument sounds. Without the Wave Blaster, the Sound Blaster would imitate these sounds through FM synthesis. With the Wave Blaster, music sounds as though it's being played by real instruments—because it is. Many sound cards are available with built-in full MIDI and wavetable support.

Several MIDI keyboards are available from companies such as Roland, Yamaha, Casio, or others. These keyboards range in price from $100 or less to many thousands of dollars.

Some sound cards have optional memory that can be added to store more sound samples.

Sound Card Installation

Installing a sound card is no more intimidating than installing an internal modem or a VGA card. Typically, you follow these steps to install a sound card:

1. Open your computer.
2. Configure your sound card.
3. Install the sound card and attach the CD-ROM drive, if present.

4. Close your computer.

5. Install the sound card software.

6. Attach your speakers and other sound accessories.

Installing the Sound Card

Once your computer is open, you can install the sound card. Your sound card may be either an 8-bit or 16-bit expansion card. Select a slot that matches the type of card you have. You don't want to put a 16-bit card (one with dual edge connectors) into an 8-bit slot (one with a single edge connector). An 8-bit card, however, can fit into either an 8-bit or 16-bit slot.

If you have several empty slots from which to choose, you may want to place the new card in one as far away as possible from the others. This reduces any possible electromagnetic interference; that is, it reduces stray radio signals from one card that might affect the sound card.

Next, you must remove the screw that holds the metal cover over the empty expansion slot you've chosen. Remove your sound card from its protective packaging. When you open this bag, carefully grab the card by its metal bracket and edges. Do not touch any of the components on the card. Any static electricity you may transmit can damage the card. And do not touch the gold edge connectors. You may want to invest in a grounding wrist strap, which continually drains you of static build-up as you work on your computer.

You may have to set jumpers or DIP switches to configure your sound card to work best with your computer, although most newer Plug and Play (PnP) sound cards don't have any jumpers or switches and are set by software instead. For example, you may want to turn off your sound card's joystick port because your joystick is already connected elsewhere to your PC. See the instructions that came with your sound card.

If an internal CD-ROM drive is to be connected to the sound card, attach its cables. Attach your CD-ROM's striped ribbon cable to your sound card, placing the red edge of the CD-ROM cable on the side of the connector on which "0" or "1" is printed. The cable must be placed this way for the CD-ROM drive to work.

The CD-ROM drive also may have an audio cable. Connect this cable to the audio connector on the sound card. This connector is keyed so that you can't insert it improperly. Note that there is no true standard for this audio cable, so be sure that you get the right one that matches your drive and sound card.

Next, insert the card in the edge connector. First touch a metal object, such as the inside of the computer's cover, to drain yourself of static electricity. Then, holding the card by its metal bracket and edges, place it in the expansion slot. Attach the screw to hold the expansion card and then reassemble your computer.

You can connect small speakers to the speaker jack. Typically, sound cards provide 4 watts of power per channel to drive bookshelf speakers. If you are using speakers rated for less than 4 watts, do not turn up the volume on your sound card to the maximum; your speakers may burn out from the overload. You'll get better results if you plug your sound card into powered speakers—that is, speakers with built-in amplifiers.

Using Your Stereo Instead of Speakers

Another alternative is to patch your sound card into your stereo system for greatly amplified sound. Check the plugs and jacks at both ends of the connection. Most stereos use *pin plugs*—also called *RCA* or *phono plugs*—for input. Although pin plugs are standard on some sound cards, most use miniature 1/8-inch phono plugs, which require an adapter when connecting to your stereo system. From Radio Shack, for example, you can purchase an audio cable that provides a stereo 1/8-inch miniplug on one end and a phono plug on the other (Cat. No. 42-2481A).

Make sure that you get stereo, not mono, plugs, unless your sound card supports mono only. To ensure that you have enough cable to reach from the back of your PC to your stereo system, get a six-foot long cable.

Hooking up your stereo to a sound card is simply a matter of sliding the plugs into jacks. If your sound card gives you a choice of outputs—speaker/headphone and stereo line out—choose the stereo line out jack for the connection. Choosing it will give you the best sound quality because the signals from the stereo line out jack are not amplified. The amplification is best left to your stereo system.

Connect this output to the auxiliary input of your stereo receiver, preamp, or integrated amplifier. If your stereo doesn't have an auxiliary input, other input options include—in order of preference—tuner, CD, or Tape 2. (Do not use phono inputs, however, because the level of the signals will be uneven.) You can connect the cable's single stereo miniplug to the sound card's Stereo Line Out jack, for example, and then connect the two RCA phono plugs to the stereo's Tape/VCR 2 Playback jacks.

The first time you use your sound card with a stereo system, turn down the volume on your receiver to prevent blown speakers. Barely turn up the volume control and then select the proper input (such as Tape/VCR 2) on your stereo receiver. Finally, start your PC. Never increase the volume to more than three-fourths of the way up. Any higher and the sound may become distorted.

Tricks for Using the Tape Monitor Circuit of Your Stereo

Your receiver is probably equipped with something called a *tape monitor*. This outputs the sound coming from the tuner, tape, or CD to the tape out port on the back, and then expects the sound to come back in on the tape in port. These ports, in conjunction with the line in and line out ports on your sound card, allow you to play computer sound and the radio through the same set of speakers.

Here's how you do it:

1. Turn off the tape monitor circuit on your receiver.

(continues)

> (continued)
>
> 2. Turn down all of the controls on the sound card's mixer application.
>
> 3. Connect the receiver's tape out ports to the sound card's line in port.
>
> 4. Connect the sound card's line out port to the receiver's tape in ports.
>
> 5. Turn on the receiver, select some music, and set the volume to a medium level.
>
> 6. Turn on the tape monitor circuit.
>
> 7. Slowly adjust the line in and main out sliders in the sound card mixer application until the sound level is about the same as before.
>
> 8. Disengage and reengage the tape monitor circuit while adjusting the output of the sound card so that the sound level is the same, whether the tape monitor circuit is engaged or not.
>
> 9. Start playing a WAV file.
>
> 10. Slowly adjust up the volume slider for the WAV file in the sound card's mixer application until it plays at a level (slightly above, or below the receiver) that is comfortable.
>
> Now you can get sounds from your computer, as well as the radio, through the receiver's speakers.

Troubleshooting Sound Card Problems

To install a sound card, you need to select IRQ numbers, a base I/O address, or DMA channels that don't conflict with other devices. Most cards come already configured to use an otherwise idle set of ports, but problems occasionally arise. Troubleshooting may mean that you have to change board jumpers or switches, or even reconfigure your other cards. No one said life was fair.

Hardware (Resource) Conflicts

The most common problem for sound cards is that they fight with other devices installed in your PC. You may notice that your sound card simply doesn't work (no sound effects or music), repeats the same sounds over and over, or causes your PC to freeze. This situation is called a *device*, or *hardware*, *conflict*. What are they fighting over? Mainly the same bus signal lines or channels (called *resources*) used for talking to your PC. The sources of conflict in sound card installations are generally threefold:

- *Interrupt ReQuests (IRQs)*. IRQs are used to "interrupt" your PC and get its attention.

- *Direct Memory Access (DMA) channels*. DMA channels are the way to move information directly to your PC's memory, bypassing your PC's processor. DMA channels allow sound to play while your PC is doing other work.

- *Input/Output (I/O) Port addresses*. An I/O Port address in your PC is used to channel information between the hardware devices on your sound card and your PC. The addresses usually mentioned in a sound card manual are the starting or base addresses. A sound card has several devices on it, and each one will use a range of addresses starting with a particular base.

Most sound cards include installation software that analyzes your PC and attempts to notify you should any of the standard settings be in use by other devices. Although fairly reliable, unless a device is operating during the analysis it may not always be detectable.

Table 12.2 shows the default resources used by the components on a typical Sound Blaster 16 card.

Table 12.2 Default Sound Blaster Resource Assignments				
Device	**Interrupt**	**I/O Ports**	**16-bit DMA**	**8-bit DMA**
Audio	IRQ 5	220h-233h	DMA 5	DMA 1
MIDI Port	—	330h-331h	—	—
FM Synthesizer	—	388h-38Bh	—	—
Game Port	—	200h-207h	—	—

All these resources are used by a *single* sound card in your system. No wonder many people have conflicts and problems with sound card installations! In reality, working out these conflicts is not all that hard, as we shall see. Most of these resources used can be changed to alternate settings, should there be conflicts with other devices, or even better, you can change the settings of the other device to eliminate the conflict. Note that some devices on the sound card like the MIDI Port, FM Synthesizer, and Game Port do not use resources like IRQs or DMA channels.

It is always best to install a sound card using the default settings where possible. This is mainly because of poorly written software that cannot work properly with alternate settings, even it they do not cause conflicts. In other words, if you are having a conflict with another type of adapter, move the settings on the other adapter rather than the sound card. Take this from experience; otherwise, you will have to explain to your five-year-old why the new Dinosaur program you just installed does not make any sounds!

If your system is PnP, you can use the Device Manager in Windows 95 to assist with the configuration of the devices in your system.

Resolving Resource Conflicts. The audio portion of a sound card has a default IRQ setting, but also supports any of several alternate interrupts. As was just stated, you should endeavor to leave the sound card at the default setting (usually IRQ 5) and change other adapters where possible.

If your sound card is set to the same IRQ as another item in your system, you may see symptoms such as skipping, jerky sound, or system lockups.

A typical sound card requires *two* simultaneous DMA channels to be used. These are usually split into a requirement for an 8-bit DMA as well as a 16-bit DMA channel. Most cards will use DMA 1 for 8-bit sound (Creative Labs calls this *Low DMA*), and DMA 5 for 16-bit sound (*High DMA*). The primary symptom of a DMA conflict is that you hear no sound at all.

Due to inflexibly written software, it is recommended that you stick with the default settings wherever possible in all sound card installations.

Solving Hardware Conflicts. The best way to find a hardware conflict is to locate all of the documentation for your PC and its various devices, such as a tape backup interface card, CD-ROM drive, and so on. This topic is discussed more completely in Chapter 5, "Bus Slots and I/O Cards."

The most common causes of system resource conflicts are the following:

- SCSI host adapters
- Network interface cards
- Bus Mouse adapter cards
- Serial Port adapter cards for COM3: or COM4:
- Parallel Port adapter cards for LPT2:
- Internal modems
- Tape drive interface cards
- Scanner interface cards

One easy way to find which device is conflicting with your sound card is to temporarily remove all of your expansion cards except the sound card and other essential cards (such as the video card). Then add each of the cards you removed, one at a time, until your sound card no longer works. The last card you added is the troublemaker.

Having found the card that's causing the conflict, you can either switch the settings for the device that is conflicting with your sound card or change the settings of the sound card. In either case, you will have to change the IRQ, DMA, or I/O address. To do this, you must set jumpers or DIP switches, or use your sound card's setup software to change its settings.

If you are running Windows 95 and have a PnP system, you can use the built-in Device Manager to help locate and resolve conflicts.

Other Sound Card Problems

Like the common cold, sound card problems have common symptoms. Use the following sections to diagnose your problem.

No Sound. If you don't hear anything from your sound card, consider these solutions:

- Make sure that the sound card is set to use all default resources, and that other devices using these resources are either changed or removed.
- Are the speakers connected? Check that the speakers are plugged into the sound card's Stereo Line Out or speaker jack.
- If you're using amplified speakers, are they powered on? Check the strength of the batteries or the adapter's connection to the electrical outlet.

- Are the speakers stereo? Check that the plug inserted into the jack is a stereo plug, not mono.

- Are mixer settings high enough? Many sound cards include a mixer control for DOS and/or Microsoft Windows. The mixer controls the settings for various sound devices, such as a microphone or CD player. There may be controls for both recording and playback. Increase the master volume or speaker volume when you are in the play mode. In DOS, you can adjust the setting by either modifying your AUTOEXEC.BAT file or pressing keys.

- Use your sound card's setup or diagnostic software to test and adjust the volume of the sound card. Such software usually includes sample sounds that play.

- Turn off your computer for one minute and then turn it back on. Such a hard reset (as opposed to pressing the Reset button or pressing Ctrl+Alt+Delete) may clear the problem.

- If your computer game lacks sound, check that it works with your sound card. For example, some games may require the exact settings of IRQ 7, DMA 1, and address 220 to be Sound Blaster-compatible.

One-Sided Sound. If you hear sound coming from only one speaker, check out these possible causes:

- Are you using a mono plug in the stereo jack? A common mistake is to place a mono plug into the sound card's speaker or stereo out jacks. Seen from the side, a stereo connector has two darker stripes. A mono connector has only one stripe.

- Is the driver loaded? Some sound cards provide only left-channel sound if the driver is not loaded in the CONFIG.SYS file. Again, run your sound card's setup software.

Volume Is Low. If you can barely hear your sound card, try these solutions:

- Are the speakers plugged into the proper jack? Speakers require a higher level of drive signal than headphones. Again, adjust the volume level in your DOS or Windows mixer. If your sound card uses keystrokes to adjust the volume, use them.

- Are the mixer settings too low? Again, adjust the volume level in your DOS or Windows mixer. If your sound card uses keystrokes to adjust the volume, use them.

- Is the initial volume too low? Some sound cards provide volume settings as part of the line in CONFIG.SYS that loads the sound card driver. The number for the volume may be set too low.

- Are the speakers too weak? Some speakers may need more power than your sound card can produce. Try other speakers or put a stereo amplifier between your sound card and speakers.

Scratchy Sound. Scratchy or staticy sound can be caused by several different things. Improving the sound may be as simple as rearranging things a little. The following lists suggests possible solutions to the problem of scratchy sound:

- Is your sound card near other expansion cards? The sound card may be picking up electrical interference from other expansion cards inside the PC. Move the sound card to an expansion slot as far away as possible from other cards.

- Are your speakers too close to your monitor? The speakers may pick up electrical noise from your monitor. Move them farther away.

- Are you using a cheaper FM synthesis sound card? Most of the cards that use FM synthesis instead of wavetable sound generation have very poor quality output. Many people have been fooled into thinking they had a defective sound card, when in reality it was just a poor quality FM synthesis card that simply does not sound good. I recommend upgrading to a card that does wavetable synthesis so you can get the full benefit of high quality sound.

Your Computer Won't Start. If your computer won't start at all, you may not have inserted the sound card completely into its slot. Turn off the PC and then press firmly on the card until it is seated correctly.

Parity Errors or Other Lockups. Your computer may display a memory parity error message or simply "crash." This is normally caused by resource conflicts in one of the following areas:

- IRQ (Interrupt ReQuest)
- DMA (Direct Memory Access)
- I/O (Input/Output) Ports

If other devices in your system are using the same resources as your sound card, crashes, lockups, or parity errors can result. You must ensure that multiple devices in your system do not share these resources. Usually it is better to leave the sound card at its default settings and change the other devices to eliminate the conflict. Consult the documentation that comes with all of your other devices to determine which resources they use and how to change them if necessary.

Joystick Troubleshooting. If your joystick won't work, consider the following list of cures:

- Are you using two game ports? If you already have a game port installed in your PC, the game or joystick port provided on your sound card may conflict with it. Usually it is best to disable any other game ports and use the one on the sound card. Many of the Multi-I/O or Super-I/O adapters that come in PC-compatible systems feature game ports that should be disabled when a sound card is installed.

- Is your computer too fast? Some fast computers get confused by the inexpensive game ports. During the heat of battle, for example, you may find yourself flying upside down or spiraling out of control. This is one sign that your game port is inadequate. Most of the game adapters built into the sound cards work better than the ones on the Multi-I/O adapters. There are also dedicated game cards available, which can work with faster computers. Such game cards include software to calibrate your joystick and dual ports so that you can enjoy a game with a friend. Another solution is to run your computer at a slower speed, which is usually done by pressing some type of "de-turbo" button on your PC.

Other Problems. Sometimes sound problems can be difficult to solve. Due to quirks and problems with the way DMA is implemented in some motherboard chipsets, there can be problems interacting with certain cards or drivers. Sometimes altering the Chipset Setup options in your CMOS settings can resolve problems. These kinds of problems can take a lot of trial and error to solve.

The PC "standard" is based loosely on the cooperation among a handful of companies. Something as simple as one vendor's BIOS or motherboard design can make the standard nonstandard.

Part IV

Mass Storage

13 Floppy Disk Drives

14 Hard Disk Drives

15 Hard Disk Interfaces

16 Hard Disk Drive Installation

17 CD-ROM Drives

18 Tape and Other Mass Storage Drives

Chapter 13

Floppy Disk Drives

This chapter examines in detail floppy disk drives and disks. It explores how floppy disk drives and disks function, how DOS uses a disk, what types of disk drives and disks are available, and how to properly install and service drives and disks.

Development of the Floppy Disk Drive

Alan Shugart is generally credited with inventing the floppy drive while working for IBM in the late 1960s. In 1967, he headed the disk drive development team at IBM's San Jose lab, when and where the floppy drive was created. One of Shugart's senior engineers, David Noble, actually proposed the flexible media (then 8 inches in diameter) and the protective jacket with the fabric lining. Shugart left IBM in 1969, and took more than 100 IBM engineers with him to Memorex. He was nicknamed "The Pied Piper" because of the loyalty exhibited by the many staff members who followed him. In 1973, he left Memorex, again taking with him a number of associates, and started Shugart Associates to develop and manufacture floppy drives. The floppy interface developed by Shugart is still the basis of all PC floppy drives. IBM used this interface in the PC, enabling them to use off-the-shelf third-party drives instead of custom building their own solutions.

Shugart wanted to incorporate processors and floppy drives into complete microcomputer systems at that time, but the financial backers of the new Shugart Associates wanted him to concentrate on floppy drives only. He quit (or was forced to quit) Shugart Associates in 1974, right before they introduced the mini-floppy (5 1/4-inch) diskette drive, which of course became the standard eventually used by personal computers, rapidly replacing the 8-inch drives. Shugart Associates also introduced the Shugart Associates System Interface (SASI), which was later renamed Small Computer Systems Interface (SCSI) when it was formally approved by the ANSI committee in 1986. After being forced to leave, Shugart attempted to legally force Shugart Associates to remove his name from the company, but failed. The remnants of Shugart Associates still operates today as Shugart Corporation.

For the next few years, Shugart took time off, ran a bar, and even dabbled in commercial fishing. In 1979, Finis Conner approached Shugart to create and market 5 1/4-inch hard disk drives. Together they founded Seagate Technology and by the end of 1979 had announced the ST-506 (6M unformatted, 5M formatted capacity) drive and interface. This drive is known as the father of all PC hard disk drives. Seagate then introduced the ST-412 (12M unformatted, 10M formatted capacity) drive, which was adopted by IBM for the original XT in 1983. IBM was Seagate's largest customer for many years. Today, Seagate Technology is the largest disk drive manufacturer in the world.

When you stop to think about it, Alan Shugart has had a tremendous effect on the PC industry. He (or his companies) has created the floppy, hard disk, and SCSI drive and controller interfaces still used today. All PC floppy drives are still based on (and compatible with) the original Shugart designs. The ST-506/412 interface was the de facto hard disk interface standard for many years and served as the basis for the ESDI and IDE interfaces as well. Shugart also created the SCSI interface, used in both IBM and Apple systems today.

As a side note, in the late 80s Finis Conner left Seagate and founded Conner Peripherals, originally wholly owned and funded by Compaq. Conner became Compaq's exclusive drive supplier, and gradually began selling drives to other system manufacturers as well. Compaq eventually cut Conner Peripherals free, selling off most (if not all) of their ownership of the company. In late 1996, Seagate bought Conner Peripherals, and has fully incorporated all of the Conner products into the Seagate line.

Drive Components

This section describes the components that make up a typical floppy drive and examines how these components operate together to read and write data—the physical operation of the drive. All floppy drives, regardless of type, consist of several basic common components. To properly install and service a disk drive, you must be able to identify these components and understand their function (see Figure 13.1).

Read/Write Heads

A floppy disk drive normally has two read/write heads, making the modern floppy disk drive a double-sided drive. A head exists for each side of the disk, and both heads are used for reading and writing on their respective disk sides. At one time, single-sided drives were available for PC systems (the original PC had such drives), but today single-sided drives are a fading memory (see Figure 13.2).

> **Note**
>
> Many people do not realize that the first head is the bottom one. Single-sided drives, in fact, use only the bottom head; the top head is replaced by a felt pressure pad (refer to Figure 13.2). Another bit of disk trivia is that the top head (Head 1) is not directly over the bottom head—the top head is located either four or eight tracks inward from the bottom head, depending on the drive type.

FIG. 13.1 A typical full-height disk drive.

The head mechanism is moved by a motor called a *head actuator*. The heads can move in and out over the surface of the disk in a straight line to position themselves over various tracks. The heads move in and out tangentially to the tracks that they record on the disk. Because the top and bottom heads are mounted on the same rack, or mechanism, they move in unison and cannot move independently of each other. The heads are made of soft ferrous (iron) compounds with electromagnetic coils. Each head is a composite design, with a read/write head centered within two tunnel-erase heads in the same physical assembly (see Figure 13.3).

The recording method is called *tunnel erasure*; as the track is laid down, the trailing tunnel erase heads erase the outer bands of the track, trimming it cleanly on the disk. The heads force the data to be present only within a specified narrow "tunnel" on each track. This process prevents the signal from one track from being confused with the signals from adjacent tracks. If the signal were allowed to "taper off" to each side, problems would occur. The forcibly trimmed track prevents this problem.

FIG. 13.2 Single- and double-sided drive head assemblies.

Alignment is the placement of the heads with respect to the tracks they must read and write. Head alignment can be checked only against some sort of reference-standard disk recorded by a perfectly aligned machine. These types of disks are available, and you can use one to check your drive's alignment. Unfortunately, that is not practical because one calibrated analog alignment disk costs more than three new drives today!

The two heads are spring-loaded and physically grip the disk with a small amount of pressure, which means that they are in direct contact with the disk surface while reading and writing to the disk. Because PC-compatible floppy disk drives spin at only 300 or 360 RPM, this pressure does not present an excessive friction problem. Some newer disks are specially coated with Teflon or other compounds to further reduce friction and enable the disk to slide more easily under the heads. Because of the contact between the heads and the disk, a buildup of the oxide material from the disk eventually forms on the heads. The buildup periodically can be cleaned off the heads as part of a preventive-maintenance or normal service program.

Drive Components

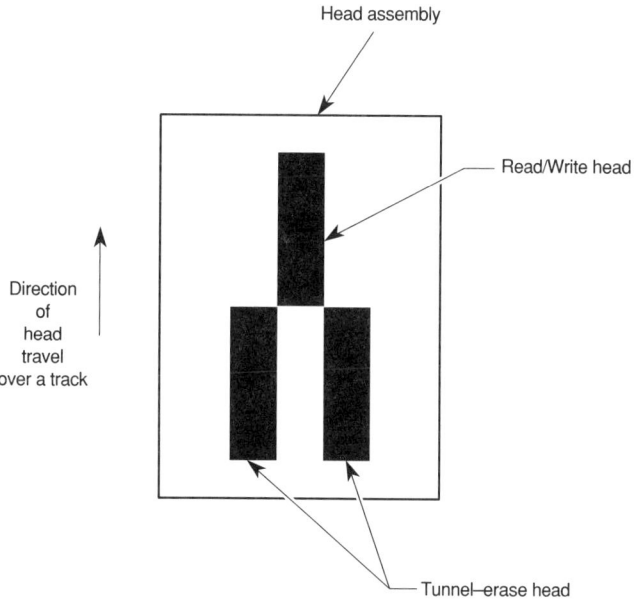

FIG. 13.3 Composite construction of a typical floppy drive head.

To read and write to the disk properly, the heads must be in direct contact with the media. Very small particles of loose oxide, dust, dirt, smoke, fingerprints, or hair can cause problems with reading and writing the disk. Disk and drive manufacturer's tests have found that a spacing as little as .000032 inches (32 millionths of an inch) between the heads and the media can cause read/write errors. You now can understand why it is important to handle disks carefully and avoid touching or contaminating the surface of the disk media in any way. The rigid jacket and protective shutter for the head access aperture on the 3 1/2-inch disks is excellent for preventing problems with media contamination. 5 1/4-inch disks do not have the same protective elements; therefore, more care must be exercised in their handling.

The Head Actuator

The *head actuator* is a mechanical motor device that causes the heads to move in and out over the surface of a disk. These mechanisms for floppy disk drives universally use a special kind of motor, a *stepper motor*, that moves in both directions in an increment called a *step*. This type of motor does not spin around continuously; rather, the motor turns a precise specified distance and stops. Stepper motors move in fixed increments, or *detents*, and must stop at a particular detent position. Stepper motors are not infinitely variable in their positioning. Each increment of motion, or a multiple thereof, defines each track on the disk. The motor can be commanded by the disk controller to position itself according to any relative increment within the range of its travel. To position the heads at track 25, for example, the motor is commanded to go to the 25th detent position.

The stepper motor usually is linked to the head rack by a coiled, split steel band. The band winds and unwinds around the spindle of the stepper motor, translating the rotary motion into linear motion. Some drives use a worm gear arrangement rather than a band. With this type, the head assembly rests on a worm gear driven directly off the stepper motor shaft. Because this arrangement is more compact, you normally find worm gear actuators on the smaller 3 1/2-inch drives.

Most stepper motors used in floppy drives can step in specific increments that relate to the track spacing on the disk. Most 48 Track Per Inch (TPI) drives have a motor that steps in increments of 3.6° (degrees). This means that each 3.6° of stepper motor rotation moves the heads from one track (or cylinder) to the next. Most 96 or 135 TPI drives have a stepper motor that moves in 1.8° increments, which is exactly half of what the 48 TPI drives use. Sometimes you see this information actually printed or stamped right on the stepper motor itself, which is useful if you are trying to figure out what type of drive you have. 5 1/4-inch 360K drives are the only 48 TPI drives available and use the 3.6° increment stepper motor. All other drive types normally use the 1.8° stepper motor. On most drives, the stepper motor is a small cylindrical object near one corner of the drive.

A stepper motor usually has a full travel time of about 1/5 of a second—about 200ms. On average, a half-stroke is 100ms, and a one-third stroke is 66ms. The timing of a one-half or one-third stroke of the head-actuator mechanism often is used to determine the reported average-access time for a disk drive. *Average-access time* is the normal amount of time the heads spend moving at random from one track to another.

The Spindle Motor

The *spindle motor* spins the disk. The normal speed of rotation is either 300 or 360 RPM, depending on the type of drive. The 5 1/4-inch high-density (HD) drive is the only drive that spins at 360 RPM; all others, including the 5 1/4-inch double-density (DD), 3 1/2-inch DD, 3 1/2-inch HD, and 3 1/2-inch extra-high density (ED) drives, spin at 300 RPM.

Most earlier drives used a mechanism on which the spindle motor physically turned the disk spindle with a belt, but all modern drives use a direct-drive system with no belts. The direct-drive systems are more reliable and less expensive to manufacture, as well as smaller in size. The earlier belt-driven systems did have more rotational torque available to turn a sticky disk because of the torque multiplication factor of the belt system. Most newer direct-drive systems use an automatic torque-compensation capability that automatically sets the disk-rotation speed to a fixed 300 or 360 RPM, and compensates with additional torque for sticky disks or less torque for slippery ones. This type of drive eliminates the need to adjust the rotational speed of the drive.

Most newer direct-drive systems use this automatic-speed feature, but many earlier systems require that you periodically adjust the speed. Looking at the spindle provides you with one clue to the type of drive you have. If the spindle contains strobe marks for 50Hz and 60Hz strobe lights (fluorescent lights), the drive probably has an adjustment for speed somewhere on the drive. Drives without the strobe marks almost always include an automatic tachometer-control circuit that eliminates the need for adjustment.

The technique for setting the speed involves operating the drive under fluorescent lighting and adjusting the rotational speed until the strobe marks appear motionless, much like the "wagon wheel effect" you see in old Western movies. The procedure is described later in this chapter in the "Setting the Floppy Drive Speed Adjustment" section.

Circuit Boards

A disk drive always incorporates one or more *logic boards*, which are circuit boards that contain the circuitry used to control the head actuator, read/write heads, spindle motor, disk sensors, and any other components on the drive. The logic board represents the drive's interface to the controller board in the system unit.

The standard interface used by all PC types of floppy disk drives is the Shugart Associates SA-400 interface, which is based on the NEC 765 controller chip. The interface, invented by Shugart in the 1970s, has been the basis of most floppy disk interfacing. The selection of this industry-standard interface is the reason that you can purchase "off-the-shelf" drives (raw, or bare, drives) that can plug directly into your controller.

> **Tip**
>
> Logic boards for a drive can fail and usually are difficult to obtain as a spare part. One board often costs more than replacing the entire drive. I recommend keeping failed or misaligned drives that might otherwise be discarded so that they can be used for their remaining good parts—such as logic boards. The parts can be used to restore a failing drive very cost-effectively.

The Faceplate

The *faceplate*, or *bezel*, is the plastic piece that comprises the front of the drive. These pieces, usually removable, come in different colors and configurations.

Most drives use a bezel slightly wider than the drive. These types of drives must be installed from the front of a system because the faceplate is slightly wider than the hole in the system-unit case. Other drive faceplates are the same width as the drive's chassis; these drives can be installed from the rear—an advantage in some cases. In the later-version XT systems, for example, IBM uses this design in its drives so that two half-height drives can be bolted together as a unit and then slid in from the rear to clear the mounting-bracket and screw hardware. On occasion, I have filed the edges of a drive faceplate to install the drive from the rear of a system—which sometimes can make installation much easier.

Connectors

Nearly all disk drives have at least two connectors—one for power to run the drive, and the other to carry the control and data signals to and from the drive. These connectors are fairly standardized in the computer industry; a four-pin in-line connector (called Mate-N-Lock, by AMP), in both a large and small style is used for power (see Figure 13.4); and a 34-pin connector in both edge and pin header designs is used for the data and control signals. 5 1/4-inch drives normally use the large style power connector and the 34-pin edge type connector, whereas most 3 1/2-inch drives use the smaller version of the power connector and the 34-pin header type logic connector. The drive controller and logic connectors and pinouts are detailed later in this chapter as well as in Appendix A, "Vendor List."

FIG. 13.4 A disk drive female power supply cable connector.

Both the large and small power connectors from the power supply are female plugs. They plug into the male portion, which is attached to the drive itself. One common problem with upgrading an older system with 3 1/2-inch drives is that your power supply only has the large style connectors, whereas the drive has the small style. An adapter cable is available from Radio Shack (Cat. No. 278-765) and other sources that converts the large style power connector to the proper small style used on most 3 1/2-inch drives.

The following chart shows the definition of the pins on the drive power-cable connectors:

Large Power Connector	Small Power Connector	Signal	Wire Color
Pin 1	Pin 4	+12 Vdc	Yellow
Pin 2	Pin 3	Ground	Black
Pin 3	Pin 2	Ground	Black
Pin 4	Pin 1	+5 Vdc	Red

> **Note**
>
> Note that the pin designations are reversed between the large- and small-style power connectors. Also, it is important to know that not all manufacturers follow the wire color coding properly. I have seen instances in which all the wires are a single color (for example, black), or the wire colors are actually reversed from normal! For example, I once purchased the Radio Shack power connector adapter cables just mentioned that had all the wire colors backwards. This was not really a problem as the adapter cable was wired correctly from end to end, but it was disconcerting to see the red wire in the power supply connector attach to a yellow wire in the adapter (and vice versa)!

Not all drives use the standard separate power and signal connectors. IBM, for example, uses either a single 34-pin or single 40-pin header connector for both power and floppy controller connections in most of the PS/2 systems. In some older PS/2 systems, for example, IBM used a special version of a Mitsubishi 3 1/2-inch 1.44M drive called the MF-355W-99, which has a single 40-pin power/signal connector. Other PS/2 systems use a Mitsubishi 3 1/2-inch 2.88M drive called the MF356C-799MA, which uses a single 34-pin header connector for both power and signal connections.

Most standard PC compatible systems use 3 1/2-inch drives with a 34-pin signal connector and a separate small style power connector. For older systems, many drive manufacturers also sell 3 1/2-inch drives installed in a 5 1/4-inch frame assembly and have a special adapter built in that allows the larger power connector and standard edge type signal connectors to be used. These drives included an adapter that enables the standard large style power connector, 34-pin edge type control, and data connector to be used. Because no cable adapters are required and they install in a 5 1/4-inch half-height bay, these types of drives are ideal for upgrading earlier systems. Most 3 1/2-inch drive-upgrade kits sold today are similar and include the drive, appropriate adapters for the power and control and data cables, a 5 1/4-inch frame adapter and faceplate, and rails for AT installations. The frame adapter and faceplate enable the drive to be installed where a 5 1/4-inch half-height drive normally would go.

Drive-Configuration Devices

Most floppy drives come properly configured for PC installation. In some cases, if the drive is used or not properly configured to begin with, you will have to check or change the configuration yourself. Most drives have a stable of jumpers and switches, and many drives are different from each other. You will find no standards for what these jumpers and switches are called, where they should be located, or how they should be implemented. There are some general guidelines to follow, but in order to set up a specific drive correctly and know all the options available, you must have information from the drive's manufacturer, normally found in the original equipment manufacturer's (OEM) manual. The manual is a "must-have" item when you purchase a disk drive.

Many drives have the following configuration settings:

- Drive select jumper
- Disk changeline jumper
- Terminating resistor
- Media sensor jumper

Drive Select

Floppy drives are connected by a cabling arrangement called a *daisy chain*. The name is descriptive because the cable is strung from controller to drive to drive in a single chain. All drives have a drive select (sometimes called *DS*) jumper that must be set to indicate a certain drive's physical drive number. Some drives allow four settings, as that was what the original SA-400 floppy interface called for, but the controllers used in PC systems support only two drives on a single daisy-chain cable. Some controllers support four drives but only on two separate cables—each one a daisy chain with a maximum of two drives.

Every drive on a particular cable must be set to have unique drive select settings. In a normal configuration, the drive you want to respond as the first drive (A:) is set to the first drive select position, and the drive you want to respond as the second drive (B:) is set to the second drive-select position. On some drives, the usable DS jumper positions are labeled DS0 and DS1; other drives use the numbers DS1 and DS2 for the same settings. For some drives then, a setting of DS0 is drive A:. For others, however, DS1 indicates drive A:.

> **Note**
>
> If you have incorrect DS settings, both drives respond simultaneously (both lights come on at the same time) or neither drive responds at all.

The type of cable you use controls the drive select configuration. Most systems have a special twist in the floppy cable that electrically changes the DS configuration of the drive plugged in after the twist. This twist causes a drive physically set to the second DS position (B:) to appear to the controller to be set to the first DS position (A:) and vice versa. With such a cable, both drives have to be set to the same DS setting for them to work. Normally, both drives should be set to the second DS position. The drive plugged into the connector farthest from the controller, which is after the twist in the cable, then would have the physical second-DS-position setting appear to be changed to a first-DS-position setting. Then the system would see this drive as A:, and the drive plugged into the middle cable connector still would appear as B:. A typical daisy-chain drive cable with this included "twist" is connected as shown in Figure 13.5.

FIG. 13.5 A floppy controller cable showing the location of the twist in lines 10-16.

An IBM-style floppy cable is a 34-pin cable with lines 10–16 sliced out and cross-wired (twisted) between the drive connectors (refer to Figure 13.5). This twisting "cross-wires" the first and second drive-select and motor-enable signals, and therefore inverts the DS setting of the drive following the twist. All the drives in a system using this type of cable, therefore—whether you want them to be A: or B:—are physically jumpered the same way; installation and configuration are simplified because both floppies can be preset to the second DS position. Some drives used by IBM, in fact, have had the DS "jumper" setting permanently soldered into the drive logic board.

Most drives you purchase have the DS jumper already set to the second position, which is correct for the majority of systems that use a cable with the twisted lines. Although this setting is correct for the majority of systems, if you are using a cable with only a single floppy drive and no provisions for adding a second one (in other words, with only one drive connector attached, and no twist in lines 10–16), then the DS setting you make on the drive is exactly what the controller sees. You can attach only one drive, and it should appear to the system as A:—therefore, set the drive to the first DS position.

Terminating Resistors

Any signal carrying electronic media or cable with multiple connections can be thought of as an *electrical bus*. In almost all cases, a bus must be terminated properly at each end with terminating resistors to allow signals to travel along the bus error free. Terminating resistors are designed to absorb any signals that reach the end of a cabling system or bus so that no reflection of the signal echoes, or bounces, back down the line in the opposite direction. Engineers sometimes call this effect *signal ringing*. Simply put, noise and distortion can disrupt the original signal and prevent proper communications between the drive and controller. Another function of proper termination is to place the proper resistive load on the output drivers in the controller and drive.

Most older 5-1/4 inch drives use a terminating resistor in the drive plugged into the physical end of a cable. The function of this resistor is to prevent reflections or echoes of signals from reaching the end of the cable. Most removable terminating resistors used in 5-1/4 inch drives have resistance values of 150 to 330 ohms.

In a typical cabling arrangement with two 5 1/4-inch floppies, for example, the terminating resistor is installed in drive A: (at the end of the cable), and this resistor is removed from the other floppy drive on the same cable (B:). The letter to which the drive responds is not important in relation to terminator settings; the important issue is that the drive at the end of the cable has the resistor installed and functioning, and that other drives on the same cable have the resistor disabled or removed.

Most 3 1/2-inch drives have permanently installed, non-configurable terminating resistors. This is the best possible setup because you never have to remove or install them, and there are never any TR jumpers to set. Although some call this automatic termination, technically the 3 1/2-inch drives use a technique called *distributed termination*. With distributed termination, each 3 1/2-inch drive has a much higher value (1,000 to 1,500 ohm) terminating resistor permanently installed, and therefore carries a part of the termination load. These terminating resistors are fixed permanently to the drive and never have to be removed or adjusted.

When you mix 5 1/4-inch and 3 1/2-inch drives, you should enable or disable the terminators on the 5 1/4-inch drives appropriately, according to their position on the cable, and ignore the non-changeable settings on the 3 1/2-inch drives.

A terminating resistor usually looks like a memory chip—a 16-pin dual inline package (DIP) device. The device is actually a group of eight resistors physically wired in parallel with each other to terminate separately each of the eight data lines in the interface subsystem. Normally, this "chip" is a different color from other black chips on the drive. Orange, yellow, blue, or white are common colors for a terminating resistor. Some drives use a resistor network in a single inline pin (SIP) package, which looks like a slender device with eight or more pins in a line. IBM always labels the resistor with a T-RES sticker for easy identification on their drives. On some systems, the resistor is a built-in device enabled or disabled by a jumper or series of switches (often labeled TM or TR).

> **Caution**
>
> Be aware that not all drives use the same type of terminating resistor, however, and it might be physically located in different places on different manufacturer's drive models. The OEM manual for the drive comes in handy in this situation because it shows the location, physical appearance, enabling and disabling instructions, and even the precise value required for the resistors.
>
> Do not lose the terminator if you remove it from a drive; you might need to reinstall it later if you relocate the drive to a different position in a system or even to a different system.

Figure 13.6 shows the location and appearance of the terminating resistor or switches on a typical floppy drive. Because most 3 1/2-inch drives have a form of automatic termination, there is no termination to configure.

You don't have to worry about the controller end of the cable because a terminating resistor network is built into the controller to properly terminate that end of the bus.

Note that in many cases, even if the termination is improper a system seems to work fine, although the likelihood of read and write errors may be increased. In older systems with only 5-1/2 inch drives, the drives do not work properly at all unless termination is properly configured.

Diskette Changeline

The standard PC floppy controller and drive use a special signal on pin 34 called *Diskette Changeline* to determine whether the disk has been changed, or more accurately, whether the same disk loaded during the previous disk access is still in the drive. *Disk Change* is a pulsed signal that changes a status register in the controller to let the system know that a disk has been either inserted or ejected. This register is set to indicate that a disk has been inserted or removed (changed) by default. The register is cleared when the controller sends a step pulse to the drive and the drive responds, acknowledging that the heads have moved. At this point, the system knows that a specific disk is in the drive. If the disk change signal is not received before the next access, the system can assume that the same disk is still in the drive. Any information read into memory during the previous access can therefore be reused without rereading the disk.

FIG. 13.6 A typical floppy drive terminating resistor, or termination switches.

Because of this process, systems can buffer or cache the contents of the file allocation table (FAT) or directory structure of a disk in the system's memory. By eliminating unnecessary rereads of these areas of the disk, the apparent speed of the drive is increased. If you move the door lever or eject button on a drive that supports the disk change signal, the DC pulse is sent to the controller, thus resetting the register and indicating that the disk has been changed. This procedure causes the system to purge buffered or cached data that had been read from the disk because the system then cannot be sure that the same disk is still in the drive.

AT-class systems use the DC signal to increase significantly the speed of the floppy interface. Because the AT can detect whether you have changed the disk, the AT can keep a copy of the disk's directory and FAT information in RAM buffers. On every subsequent disk access, the operations are much faster because the information does not have to be reread from the disk in every individual access. If the DC signal has been reset (has a value of 1), the AT knows that the disk has been changed and appropriately rereads the information from the disk.

You can observe the effects of the DC signal by trying a simple experiment. Boot DOS on an AT-class system and place a formatted floppy disk with data on it in drive A:. Drive A: can be any type of drive except 5 1/4-inch double-density, although the disk you use can be anything the drive can read, including a double-density 360K disk, if you want. Then type the following command:

DIR A:

The disk drive lights up, and the directory is displayed. Note the amount of time spent reading the disk before the directory is displayed on-screen. Without touching the drive, enter the **DIR A:** command again, and watch the drive-access light and screen. Note again the amount of time that passes before the directory is displayed. The drive A: directory should appear almost instantly the second time because virtually no time is spent actually reading the disk. The directory information was simply read back from RAM buffers or cache rather than read again from the disk. Now eject and re-insert the disk. Type the **DIR A:** command again. The disk again takes some time reading the directory before displaying anything because the system "thinks" that you changed the disk.

Older PC and XT low-density controllers (and systems) are not affected by the status of the DC signal. These systems "don't care" about signals on pin 34. The PC and XT systems always operate under the assumption that the disk is changed before every access, and they reread the disk directory and FAT each time—one reason why these systems are slower in using the floppy disk drives.

One interesting problem can occur when certain drives are installed in a 16-bit or greater system. As mentioned, some drives use pin 34 for a "Ready" (RDY) signal. The RDY signal is sent whenever a disk is installed and rotating in the drive. If you install a drive that has pin 34 set to send RDY, the system "thinks" that it is continuously receiving a disk change signal, which causes problems. Usually the drive fails with a `Drive not ready` error and is inoperable. The only reason that the RDY signal exists on some drives is that it happens to be a part of the standard Shugart SA-400 disk interface; however, it has never been used in PC systems.

The biggest problem occurs if the drive is not sending the DC signal on pin 34, and it should. If a system is told (through CMOS setup) that the drive is any other type than a 360K (which cannot ever send the DC signal), the system expects the drive to send DC whenever a disk has been ejected. If the drive is not configured properly to send the signal, the system never recognizes that a disk has been changed. Therefore, even if you do change the disk, the AT still acts as though the first disk is in the drive and holds the first disk's directory and FAT information in RAM. This can be dangerous because the FAT and directory information from the first disk can be partially written to any subsequent disks written to in the drive.

> **Caution**
>
> If you ever have seen an AT-class system with a floppy drive that shows "phantom directories" of the previously installed disk, even after you have changed or removed it, you have experienced this problem firsthand. The negative side effect is that all disks after the first one you place in this system are in extreme danger. You likely will overwrite the directories and FATs of many disks with information from the first disk.
>
> If even possible at all, data recovery from such a catastrophe can require quite a bit of work with utility programs such as Norton Utilities. These problems with Disk Change most often are traced to an incorrectly configured drive. This problem will be covered in more detail in the section "Phantom Directory (Disk Change) Problems" later in this chapter.

If the drive is a 5 1/4-inch 360K drive, set the status of pin 34 to Open (disconnected) regardless of the type of system in which you are installing the drive. The only other option normally found for pin 34 on 360K drives is RDY, which is incorrect. If you are using only a low-density controller, as in a PC or XT, pin 34 is ignored no matter what is sent on it.

If the drive you are installing is a 5 1/4-inch 1.2M or 3 1/2-inch 720K, 1.44M, or 2.88M drive, be sure to set pin 34 to send the Disk Change (DC) signal. The basic rule is simple:

> For 360K drives only, pin 34 = Open (disconnected)
>
> For any other drive, pin 34 = Disk Change

Media Sensor

This configuration item exists only on the 3 1/2-inch 1.44M or 2.88M drives. The jumper selection, called the *media sensor (MS) jumper*, must be set to enable a special media sensor in the disk drive, which senses a media sensor hole found only in the 1.44M HD and the 2.88M ED floppy disks. The labeling of this jumper (or jumpers) varies greatly between different drives. In many drives, the jumpers are permanently set (enabled) and cannot be changed.

The three types of configurations with regards to media sensing are as follows:

- No media sense (sensor disabled or no sensor present)
- Passive media sense (sensor enabled)
- Active or intelligent media sense (sensor supported by Controller/BIOS)

Most systems use a passive media sensor arrangement. The passive media sensor setup enables the drive to determine the level of recording strength to use and is required for most installations of these drives, because of a bug in the design of the Western Digital hard disk and floppy controllers used by IBM in the AT systems. This bug prevents the controller from properly instructing the drive to switch to double-density mode when you write or format DD disks. With the media sensor enabled, the drive no longer depends on the controller for density mode switching and relies only on the drive's media sensor. Unless you are sure that your disk controller does not have this flaw, make sure that your HD drive includes a media sensor (some older or manufacturer-specific drives do not), and that it is properly enabled.

The 2.88M drives universally rely on media sensors to determine the proper mode of operation. The 2.88M drives, in fact, have two separate media sensors because the ED disks include a media sensor hole in a different position than the HD disks.

With only a few exceptions, HD 3 1/2-inch drives installed in most PC-compatible systems do not operate properly in double-density mode unless the drive has control over the write current (recording level) via an installed and enabled media sensor. Exceptions are found primarily in systems with floppy controllers integrated on the motherboard, including most older IBM PS/2 and Compaq systems as well as most laptop or notebook systems from other manufacturers. These systems have floppy controllers without the bug referred to earlier, and can correctly switch the mode of the drive without the aid of the media sensor.

In these systems, it technically does not matter whether you enable the media sensor. If the media sensor is enabled, the drive mode is controlled by the disk you insert, as is the case with most PC-compatible systems. If the media sensor is not enabled, the drive mode is controlled by the floppy controller, which in turn is controlled by DOS.

If a disk is already formatted correctly, DOS reads the volume boot sector to determine the current disk format, and the controller then switches the drive to the appropriate mode. If the disk has not been formatted yet, DOS has no idea what type of disk it is, and the drive remains in its native HD or ED mode.

When you format a disk in systems without an enabled media sensor (such as most PS/2s), the mode of the drive depends entirely on the FORMAT command issued by the user, regardless of the type of disk inserted. For example, if you insert a DD disk into an HD drive in an IBM PS/2 Model 70 and format the disk by entering **FORMAT A:**, the disk is formatted as though it is an HD disk because you did not issue the correct parameters (/F:720) to cause the FORMAT command to specify a DD format. On a system with the media sensor enabled, this type of incorrect format fails, and you see the Invalid media or Track 0 bad error message from FORMAT. In this case, the media sensor prevents an incorrect format from occurring on the disk, a safety feature most older IBM PS/2 systems lack.

Most of the newer PS/2 systems—including all those that come standard with the 2.88M drives—have what is called an *active* or *intelligent media sensor setup*. This means that the sensor not only detects what type of disk is in the drive and changes modes appropriately, but also the drive informs the controller (and the BIOS) about what type of disk is in the drive. Systems with an intelligent media sensor do not need to use the disk type parameters in the FORMAT command. In these systems, the FORMAT command automatically "knows" what type of disk is in the drive and formats it properly. With an intelligent media sensor, you never have to know what the correct format parameters are for a particular type of disk; the system figures it out for you automatically. Many high-end systems such as the newer PS/2 systems as well as high-end Hewlett-Packard PCs have this type of intelligent media sensor arrangement.

The Floppy Disk Controller

The *floppy disk controller* consists of the circuitry either on a separate adapter card or integrated on the motherboard, which acts as the interface between the floppy drives and the system. Most PC- and XT-class systems use a separate controller card that occupied a slot in the system. The AT systems normally have the floppy controller and hard disk controller built into the same adapter card and also plugged into a slot. In most of the more modern systems built since then, the controller is integrated on the motherboard. In any case, the electrical interface to the drives has remained largely static, with only a few exceptions.

The original IBM PC and XT system floppy controller was a 3/4-length card that could drive as many as four floppy disk drives. Two drives could be connected to a cable plugged into a 34-pin edge connector on the card, and two more drives could be plugged into a cable connected to the 37-pin connector on the bracket of this card. Figures 13.7 and 13.8 show these connectors and the pinouts for the controller.

	At Standard TTL Levels	Land Number	
	Ground-Odd Numbers	1-33	
	Unused	2,4,6	
	Index	8	
	Motor Enable A	10	
	Drive Select B	12	
	Drive Select A	14	
	Motor Enable B	16	
External Drives	Direction (Stepper Motor)	18	Drive Adapter
	Step Pulse	20	
	Write Data	22	
	Write Enable	24	
	Track 0	26	
	Write Protect	28	
	Read Data	30	
	Select Head 1	32	
	Ground	34	

FIG. 13.7 A PC and XT floppy controller internal connector.

The AT used a board made by Western Digital, which included both the floppy and hard disk controllers in a single adapter. The connector location and pinout for the floppy controller portion of this card is shown in Figure 13.9.

IBM used two variations of this controller during the life of the AT system. The first one was a full 4.8 inches high, which used all the vertical height possible in the AT case. This board was a variation of the Western Digital WD1002-WA2 controller sold through distributors and dealers. The second-generation card was only 4.2 inches high, which enabled it to fit into the shorter case of the XT-286 as well as the taller AT cases. This card was equivalent to the Western Digital WD1003-WA2, also sold on the open market.

At Standard TTL Levels	Pin Number	
Unused	1-5	
Index	6	
Motor Enable C	7	
Drive Select D	8	
Drive Select C	9	
Motor Enable D	10	
Direction (Stepper Motor)	11	
Step Pulse	12	
Write Data	13	
Write Enable	14	
Track 0	15	
Write Protect	16	
Read Data	17	
Select Head 1	18	
Ground	20-37	

(External Drives ↔ Drive Adapter)

FIG. 13.8 A PC and XT floppy controller external connector.

Disk Physical Specifications and Operation

PC-compatible systems now use one of as many as five standard types of floppy drives. Also, five types of disks can be used in the drives. This section examines the physical specifications and operations of these drives and disks.

Drives and disks are divided into two classes: 5 1/4-inch and 3 1/2-inch. The physical dimensions and components of a typical 5 1/4-inch disk and a 3 1/2-inch disk are shown later in this chapter.

Disk Physical Specifications and Operation

FIG. 13.9 An AT floppy controller connector.

The physical operation of a disk drive is fairly simple to describe. The disk rotates in the drive at either 300 or 360 RPM. Most drives spin at 300 RPM; only the 5 1/4-inch 1.2M drives spin at 360 RPM (even when reading or writing 360K disks). With the disk spinning, the heads can move in and out approximately 1 inch and write either 40 or 80 tracks. The tracks are written on both sides of the disk and therefore sometimes are called *cylinders*. A single cylinder comprises the tracks on the top and bottom of the disk. The heads record by using a tunnel-erase procedure in which a track is written to a specified width, and then the edges of the track are erased to prevent interference with any adjacent tracks.

The tracks are recorded at different widths for different drives. Table 13.1 shows the track widths in both millimeters and inches for the five types of floppy drives supported in PC systems.

Table 13.1 Floppy Drive Track-Width Specifications

Drive Type	No. of Tracks	Track	Width
5 1/4-inch 360K	40 per side	0.300 mm	0.0118 in.
5 1/4-inch 1.2M	80 per side	0.155 mm	0.0061 in.
3 1/2-inch 720K	80 per side	0.115 mm	0.0045 in.
3 1/2-inch 1.44M	80 per side	0.115 mm	0.0045 in.
3 1/2-inch 2.88M	80 per side	0.115 mm	0.0045 in.

The differences in recorded track width can result in data-exchange problems between 5 1/4-inch drives. The 5 1/4-inch drives are affected because the DD drives record a track width nearly twice that of the HD drives. A problem occurs, therefore, if an HD drive is used to update a DD disk with previously recorded data on it.

Even in 360K mode, the HD drive cannot completely overwrite the track left by an actual 360K drive. A problem occurs when the disk is returned to the person with the 360K drive: That drive reads the new data as embedded within the remains of the previously written track. Because the drive cannot distinguish either signal, an `Abort`, `Retry`, `Ignore` error message appears on-screen. The problem does not occur if a new disk (one that never has had data recorded on it) is first formatted in a 1.2M drive with the `/4` option, which formats the disk as a 360K disk.

> **Note**
>
> You also can format a brand new 360K disk in a 1.2M drive with the `/N:9`, `/T:40`, or `/F:360` options, depending on the DOS version. The 1.2M drive can then be used to fill the brand new and newly formatted 360K disk to its capacity, and every file will be readable on the 40-track, 360K drive.

> **Note**
>
> I use this technique all the time to exchange data disks between AT systems that have only the 1.2M drive and XT or PC systems that have only the 360K drive. The key is to start with either a new disk or one wiped clean magnetically by a bulk eraser or degaussing tool. Just reformatting the disk does not work by itself because formatting does not actually erase a disk; instead it records data across the entire disk.

Disk Magnetic Properties

A subtle problem with the way a disk drive works magnetically is that the recording volume varies depending on the type of format you are trying to apply to a disk. The high-density formats use special disks that require a much higher volume level for the recording than do the DD disks. My classes nearly always are either stumped or incorrect (unless they have read ahead in the book) when they try to answer this question: "Which type of disk is magnetically more sensitive: a 1.2M disk or a 360K disk?" If you answer that the 1.2M disk is more sensitive, you are wrong! The HD disks are approximately half as sensitive magnetically as the DD disks.

The HD disks are called *high-coercivity disks* also because they require a magnetic field strength much higher than do the DD disks. Magnetic field strength is measured in *oersteds*. The 360K floppy disks require only a 300-oersted field strength to record, and the HD 1.2M disks require a 600-oersted field strength. Because the HD disks need double the magnetic field strength for recording, you should not attempt to format a 1.2M HD disk as though it were a 360K disk, or a 360K disk as though it were a 1.2M HD disk.

An interesting problem results from this type of improper formatting: You can imprint the 360K disk magnetically with an image that is difficult to remove. The HD format places on the disk a recording at twice the strength it should be. How do you remove this recording and correct the problem? If you attempt to reformat the disk in a 360K drive, the drive writes in a reduced write-current mode and in some cases cannot overwrite the higher-volume recorded image you mistakenly placed on the disk. If you attempt to reformat the disk in the high-density drive with the /4 (or equivalent) parameter, which indicates 360K mode, the HD drive uses a reduced write-current setting and again cannot overwrite the recording.

You can correct the problem in several ways. You can throw away the disk and write it off as a learning experience, or you can use a bulk eraser or degaussing tool to demagnetize the disk. These devices can randomize all the magnetic domains on a disk and return it to an essentially factory-new condition. You can purchase a bulk-erasing device at electronic supply stores for about $25.

The opposite problem with disk formatting is not as common, but some have tried it anyway: formatting an HD disk with a DD format. You should not (and normally cannot) format a 1.2M HD disk to a 360K capacity. If you attempt to use one, the drive changes to reduced write-current mode and does not create a magnetic field strong enough to record on the "insensitive" 1.2M disk. The result in this case is normally an immediate error message from the FORMAT command: Invalid media or Track 0 bad - disk unusable. Fortunately, the system usually does not allow this particular mistake to be made.

The 3 1/2-inch drives don't have the same problems as the 5 1/4-inch drives—at least for data interchange. Because both the HD and DD drives write the same number of tracks and these tracks are always the same width, no problem occurs when one type of drive is used to overwrite data written by another type of drive. A system manufacturer therefore doesn't need to offer a DD version of the 3 1/2-inch drive for systems equipped with the HD or ED drive. The HD and ED drives can perfectly emulate the operations of the 720K DD drive, and the ED drive can perfectly emulate the 1.44M HD drive.

The HD and ED drives can be trouble, however, for inexperienced users who try to format disks to incorrect capacities. Although an ED drive can read, write, and format DD, HD, and ED disks, a disk should be formatted and written at only its specified capacity. An ED disk therefore should be formatted only to 2.88M, and never to 1.44M or 720K. You must always use a disk at its designated format capacity. You are asking for serious problems if you place a 720K disk in the A: drive of a PS/2 Model 50, 60, 70, or 80 and enter **FORMAT A:**. This step causes a 1.44M format to be written on the 720K disk, which renders it unreliable at best and requires a bulk eraser to reformat it correctly. If you decide to use the resulting incorrectly formatted disk, you will eventually have massive data loss.

This particular problem could have been averted if IBM had used media sensor drives in all PS/2 systems. Drives that use the disk media-sensor hole to control the drive mode are prevented from incorrectly formatting a disk. The hardware causes the FORMAT command to fail with an appropriate error message if you attempt to format the disk to an incorrect capacity.

Logical Operation

Each type of drive can create disks with different numbers of sectors and tracks. This section examines how DOS sees a drive. It gives definitions of the drives according to DOS and the definitions of cylinders and clusters.

How the Operating System Uses a Disk. To the operating system, data on your PC disks is organized in tracks and sectors. *Tracks* are narrow, concentric circles on a disk. *Sectors* are pie-shaped slices of the disk. DOS versions 1.0 and 1.1 read and write 5 1/4-inch DD disks with 40 tracks (numbered 0–39) per side and eight sectors (numbered 1–8) per track. DOS versions 2.0 and higher automatically increase the track density from eight to nine sectors for greater capacity on the same disk. On an AT with a 1.2M disk drive, DOS V3.0 supports HD 5 1/4-inch drives that format 15 sectors per track and 80 tracks per side; DOS V3.2 supports 3 1/2-inch drives that format nine sectors per track and 80 tracks per side; DOS V3.3 supports 3 1/2-inch drives that format 18 sectors per track and 80 tracks per side. The distance between tracks and, therefore, the number of tracks on a disk, is a built-in mechanical and electronic function of the drive.

Tables 13.2 and 13.3 summarize the standard disk formats supported by DOS version 5.0 and higher.

Table 13.2 5 1/4-inch Floppy Disk Drive Formats

5 1/4-Inch Floppy Disks	Double Density 360K (DD)	High Density 1.2M (HD)
Bytes per Sector	512	512
Sectors per Track	9	15
Tracks per Side	40	80
Sides	2	2
Capacity (K)	360	1,200
Capacity (Megabytes)	0.352	1.172
Capacity (Million bytes)	0.369	1.229

Table 13.3 3 1/2-inch Floppy Disk Drive Formats

3 1/2-Inch Floppy Disks	Double Density 720K (DD)	High Density 1.44M (HD)	Extra-High Density 2.88M (ED)
Bytes per Sector	512	512	512
Sectors per Track	9	18	36
Tracks per Side	80	80	80
Sides	2	2	2
Capacity (K)	720	1,440	2,880
Capacity (Megabytes)	0.703	1.406	2.813
Capacity (Million bytes)	0.737	1.475	2.949

You can calculate the capacity differences between different formats by multiplying the sectors per track by the number of tracks per side together with the constants of two sides and 512 bytes per sector.

Note that the disk capacity can actually be expressed in different ways. The most common method is to refer to the capacity of a floppy by the number of kilobytes (1,024 bytes equals 1K). This works fine for 360K and 720K disks, but is strange when applied to the 1.44M and 2.88M disks. As you can see, a 1.44M disk is really 1,440K, and not actually 1.44 megabytes. Because a megabyte is 1,024K, what we call a 1.44M disk is actually 1.406M in capacity.

Another way of expressing disk capacity is in millions of bytes. In that case, the 1.44M disk has 1.475 million bytes of capacity. To add to the confusion over capacity expression, both megabyte and millions of bytes are abbreviated as MB or M. No universally accepted standard for the definition of M or MB exists, so throughout this book I use M.

Like blank sheets of paper, new disks contain no information. Formatting a disk is similar to adding lines to the paper so that you can write straight across. Formatting places on the disk the information DOS needs to maintain a directory and file table of contents. Using the /S (system) option in the FORMAT command resembles making the paper a title page. FORMAT places on the disk the portions of DOS required to boot the system.

The operating system reserves the track nearest to the outside edge of a disk (track 0) almost entirely for its purposes. Track 0, Sector 1 contains the *DOS Boot Record (DBR)*, or Boot Sector, the system needs to begin operation. The next few sectors contain the FATs, which act as the disk "room reservation clerk" that keeps records of which clusters or allocation units (rooms) on the disk have file information and which are empty. Finally, the next few sectors contain the root directory, in which DOS stores information about the names and starting locations of the files on the disk; you see most of this information when you use the DIR command.

In computer-industry jargon, this process is "transparent to the user," which means that you don't have to (and generally cannot) decide where information is stored on disks. That this process is "transparent," however, doesn't necessarily mean that you shouldn't be aware of the decisions DOS makes for you.

When DOS writes data, it always begins by attempting to use the earliest available data sectors on the disk. Because the file might be larger than the particular block of available sectors selected, DOS then writes the remainder of the file in the next available block of free sectors. In this manner, files can become fragmented as they are written to fill a hole on the disk created by the deletion of some smaller file. The larger file completely fills the hole; then DOS continues to look for more free space across the disk, from the outermost tracks to the innermost tracks. The rest of the file is deposited in the next available free space.

This procedure continues until eventually all the files on your disk are intertwined. This situation is not really a problem for DOS because it was designed to manage files in this way. The problem is a physical one: Retrieving a fragmented file that occupies 50 or 100 separate places across the disk takes much longer than if the file were in one piece. Also, if the files were in one piece, recovering data in the case of a disaster would be much easier. Consider unfragmenting a disk periodically simply because it can make recovery from a disk disaster much easier; many people, however, unfragment disks for the performance benefit in loading and saving files that are in one piece.

How do you unfragment a disk? DOS 6.0 and higher versions include a command called DEFRAG. This utility is actually a limited version of the Norton Utilities Speedisk program. It does not have some of the options of the more powerful Norton version and is not as fast, but it does work well in most cases. Earlier versions of DOS do not provide any easy method for unfragmenting a disk, although by backing up and restoring files, you can accomplish the goal. To unfragment a floppy disk for example, you can copy all the files one by one to an empty disk, delete the original files from the first disk, and then recopy the files. With a hard disk, you can back up all the files, reformat the disk, and restore the files. This procedure is time-consuming, to say the least.

Windows 95 also includes a Disk Defragmenter utility that not only works under the Windows graphical environment, but also operates in the background while other applications are running.

Because DOS versions earlier than 6.0 did not provide a good way to unfragment a disk, many software companies have produced utility programs that can easily unfragment disks in a clean and efficient manner. These programs can restore file contiguity without reformat and restore operations. My favorite for an extremely safe, easy, and fast unfragmenting program is the Vopt utility by Golden Bow. In my opinion, no other unfragmenting utility even comes close to this amazing $50 package. Golden Bow's address and phone number are in Appendix B, "Glossary."

If you are using Windows 95 with long file names, be aware that many of the older defragmenter programs do not preserve these file name entries, which can cause many problems. Contact the manufacturer of any disk defragmenting utilities to ensure that they are safe to use on a Windows 95 formatted disk. Many of these programs will require updated versions to work properly.

> **Caution**
>
> Before using an unfragmenting program, make sure that you have a good backup. What shape do you think your disk would be in if the power failed during an unfragmenting session? Also, some programs have bugs or are incompatible with new releases of DOS or Windows.

Cylinders. The term *cylinder* usually is used in place of *track*. A *cylinder* is all the tracks under read/write heads on a drive at one time. For floppy drives, because a disk cannot have more than two sides and the drive has two heads, normally there are two tracks per cylinder. Hard disks can have many disk platters, each with two (or more) heads, for many tracks per single cylinder.

Clusters or Allocation Units. A *cluster* also is called an *allocation unit* in DOS version 4.0 and higher. The term is appropriate because a single cluster is the smallest unit of the disk that DOS can allocate when it writes a file. A cluster or allocation unit consists of one or more sectors—usually two or more. Having more than one sector per cluster reduces the FAT size and enables DOS to run faster because it has fewer individual allocation units of the disk with which to work. The tradeoff is in some wasted disk space. Because DOS can manage space only in the cluster size unit, every file consumes space on the disk in increments of one cluster.

Table 13.4 lists the default cluster sizes used by DOS for different floppy disk formats. Chapter 14, "Hard Disk Drives," discusses hard disk cluster or allocation unit sizes.

Table 13.4 DOS Default Cluster and Allocation Unit Sizes

Floppy Disk Capacity	Cluster/Allocation	FAT Type	Unit Size
5 1/4-inch, 360K	2 sectors	1,024 bytes	12-bit
5 1/4-inch, 1.2M	1 sector	512 bytes	12-bit
3 1/2-inch, 720K	2 sectors	1,024 bytes	12-bit
3 1/2-inch, 1.44M	1 sector	512 bytes	12-bit
3 1/2-inch, 2.88M	2 sectors	1,024 bytes	12-bit

K = 1,024 bytes
M = 1,048,576 bytes

The HD disks normally have smaller cluster sizes, which seems strange because these disks have many more individual sectors than do DD disks. The probable reason is that because these HD disks are faster than their DD counterparts, IBM and Microsoft thought that the decrease in wasted disk space cluster size and speed would be welcome. You learn later that the cluster size on hard disks can vary much more between different versions of DOS/Windows and different disk sizes.

Types of Floppy Drives

Five types of standard floppy drives are available for a PC-compatible system. The drives can be summarized most easily by their formatting specifications (refer to Tables 13.2 and 13.3).

Most drive types can format multiple types of disks. For example, the 3 1/2-inch ED drive can format and write on any 3 1/2-inch disk. The 5 1/4-inch HD drive also can format and write on any 5 1/4-inch disk (although, as mentioned, sometimes track-width problems occur). This drive can even create some older obsolete formats, including single-sided disks and disks with eight sectors per track.

As you can see from Table 13.5, the different disk capacities are determined by several parameters, some of which seem to remain constant on all drives, whereas others change from drive to drive. For example, all drives use 512-byte physical sectors, which remains true for hard disks as well. Note, however, that DOS treats the sector size as though it could be a changeable parameter, although the BIOS does not.

> **Note**
>
> Note also that now all standard floppy drives are double-sided. IBM has not shipped PC systems with single-sided drives since 1982; these drives are definitely considered obsolete. Also, IBM has never used any form of single-sided 3 1/2-inch drives, although that type of drive appeared in the first Apple Macintosh systems in 1984. IBM officially began selling and supporting 3 1/2-inch drives in 1986 and has used only double-sided versions of these drives.

Table 13.5 Floppy Disk Logical DOS-Format Parameters

	Current Formats					Obsolete Formats		
Disk Size (in.)	3 1/2"	3 1/2"	3 1/2"	5 1/4"	5 1/4"	5 1/4"	5 1/4"	5 1/4"
Disk Capacity (K)	2,880	1,440	720	1,200	360	320	180	160
Media Descriptor Byte	F0h	F0h	F9h	F9h	FDh	FFh	FCh	FEh
Sides (Heads)	2	2	2	2	2	2	1	1
Tracks per Side	80	80	80	80	40	40	40	40
Sectors per Track	36	18	9	15	9	8	9	8
Bytes per Sector	512	512	512	512	512	512	512	512
Sectors per Cluster	2	1	2	1	2	2	1	1
FAT Length (Sectors)	9	9	3	7	2	1	2	1
Number of FATs	2	2	2	2	2	2	2	2
Root Dir. Length (Sectors)	15	14	7	14	7	7	4	4
Maximum Root Entries	240	224	112	224	112	112	64	64
Total Sectors per Disk	5,760	2,880	1,440	2,400	720	640	360	320
Total Available Sectors	5,726	2,847	1,426	2,371	708	630	351	313
Total Available Clusters	2,863	2,847	713	2,371	354	315	351	313

The 360K 5 1/4-Inch Drive

The 5 1/4-inch low-density drive is designed to create a standard-format disk with 360K capacity. Although I persistently call these *low-density drives*, the industry term is *double-density*. I use *low-density* because I find the term *double-density* to be somewhat misleading, especially when I am trying to define these drives in juxtaposition to the high-density drives.

The term *double-density* arose from the use of the term *single density* to indicate a type of drive that used frequency modulation (FM) encoding to store approximately 90K on a disk. This type of obsolete drive never was used in any PC-compatible systems, but was used in some older systems such as the original Osborne-1 portable computer. When drive manufacturers changed the drives to use Modified Frequency Modulation (MFM) encoding, they began using the term *double-density* to indicate it, as well as the (approximately doubled) increase in recording capacity realized from this encoding method. All modern floppy disk drives use MFM encoding, including all types listed in this section. Encoding methods such as FM, MFM, and RLL (Run Length Limited) variants are discussed in Chapter 14, "Hard Disk Drives."

The 360K 5 1/4-inch drives spin at 300 RPM, which equals exactly five revolutions per second, or 200 ms per revolution. All standard floppy controllers support a 1:1 interleave, in which each sector on a specific track is numbered (and read) consecutively. To read and write to a disk at full speed, a controller sends data at a rate of 250,000 bps. Because all low-density controllers can support this data rate, virtually any controller supports this type of drive, depending on ROM BIOS code that supports these drives.

All standard PC-compatible systems include ROM BIOS support for these drives; therefore, you usually do not need special software or driver programs to use them. This statement might exclude some aftermarket (non-IBM) 360K drives for PS/2 systems that might require some type of driver in order to work. The IBM-offered units use the built-in ROM support to enable these drives to work. The only requirement usually is to run the Setup program for the machine to enable it to properly recognize these drives.

The 1.2M 5 1/4-Inch Drive

The 1.2M high-density floppy drive first appeared in the IBM AT system introduced in August 1984. The drive required the use of a new type of disk to achieve the 1.2M format capacity, but it still could read and write (although not always reliably) the lower-density 360K disks.

The 1.2M 5 1/4-inch drive normally recorded 80 cylinders of two tracks each, starting with cylinder 0, at the outside of the disk. This situation differs from the low-density 5 1/4-inch drive in its capability to record twice as many cylinders in approximately the same space on the disk. This capability alone suggests that the recording capacity for a disk would double, but that is not all. Each track normally is recorded with 15 sectors of 512 bytes each, increasing the storage capacity even more. In fact, these drives store nearly four times the data of the 360K disks. The density increase for each track required the use of special disks with a modified media designed to handle this type of recording.

Because these disks initially were expensive and difficult to obtain, many users attempted incorrectly to use the low-density disks in the 1.2M 5 1/4-inch drives and format them to the higher 1.2M-density format, which results in data loss and unnecessary data-recovery operations.

A compatibility problem with the 360K drives stems from the 1.2M drive's capability to write twice as many cylinders in the same space as the 360K drives. The 1.2M drives position their heads over the same 40 cylinder positions used by the 360K drives through *double stepping*, a procedure in which the heads are moved every two cylinders to arrive at the correct positions for reading and writing the 40 cylinders on the 360K disks. The problem is that because the 1.2M drive normally has to write 80 cylinders in the same space in which the 360K drive writes 40, the heads of the 1.2M units had to be made dimensionally smaller. These narrow heads can have problems overwriting tracks produced by a 360K drive that has a wider head because the narrower heads on the 1.2M drive cannot "cover" the entire track area written by the 360K drive.

The 1.2M 5 1/4-inch drives spin at 360 RPM, or six revolutions per second, or 166.67ms per revolution. The drives spin at this rate no matter what type of disk is inserted—either low- or high-density. To send or receive 15 sectors (plus required overhead) six times per second, a controller must use a data-transmission rate of 500,000 bps (500KHz). All standard high- and low-density controllers support this data rate and, therefore, these drives.

This support of course depends also on proper ROM BIOS support of the controller in this mode of operation. When a standard 360K disk is running in an HD drive, it also is spinning at 360 RPM; a data rate of 300,000 bps (300KHz) therefore is required in order to work properly. All standard AT-style low- and high-density controllers support the 250KHz, 300KHz, and 500KHz data rates. The 300KHz rate is used only for HD 5 1/4-inch drives reading or writing to low-density 5 1/4-inch disks.

Virtually all standard AT-style systems have a ROM BIOS that supports the controller's operation of the 1.2M drive, including the 300KHz data rate.

The 720K 3 1/2-Inch Drive

The 720K, 3 1/2-inch, DD drives first appeared in an IBM system with the IBM Convertible laptop system introduced in 1986. In fact, all IBM systems introduced since that time have 3 1/2-inch drives as the standard supplied drives. This type of drive also is offered by IBM as an internal or external drive for the AT or XT systems.

> **Note**
>
> Outside the PC-compatible world, other computer-system vendors (Apple, Hewlett-Packard, and so on) offered 3 1/2-inch drives for their systems well before the PC-compatible world "caught on."

The 720K, 3 1/2-inch, DD drive normally records 80 cylinders of two tracks each, with nine sectors per track, resulting in the formatted capacity of 720K.

It is interesting to note that many disk manufacturers label these disks as 1.0M disks, which is true. The difference between the actual 1.0M of capacity and the usable 720K after formatting is that some space on each track is occupied by the header and trailer of each sector, the inter-sector gaps, and the index gap at the start of each track before the first sector. These spaces are not usable for data storage, and account for the differences between the unformatted and formatted capacities. Most manufacturers report the unformatted capacities because they do not know on which type of system you will format the disk. Apple Macintosh systems, for example, can store 800K of data on the same disk because of a different formatting technique.

Note also that the 720K of usable space does not account for the disk areas DOS reserves for managing the disk (boot sectors, FATs, directories, and so on) and that because of these areas, only 713K remains for file data storage.

PC-compatible systems have used 720K, 3 1/2-inch, DD drives primarily in XT-class systems because the drives operate from any low-density controller. The drives spin at 300 RPM, and therefore require only a 250KHz data rate from the controller to operate properly. This data rate is the same as the 360K disk drives, which means that any controller that supports a 360K drive also supports the 720K drives.

The only issue to consider in installing a 720K, 3 1/2-inch drive is whether the ROM BIOS offers the necessary support. An IBM system with a ROM BIOS date of 06/10/85 or later has built-in support for 720K drives and requires no driver in order to use them. If your system has an earlier ROM BIOS date, the DRIVER.SYS program from DOS V3.2 or higher—as well as the DRIVPARM CONFIG.SYS command in some OEM DOS versions—is all you need to provide the necessary software support to operate these drives. Of course, a ROM BIOS upgrade to a later version negates the need for "funny" driver software and is usually the preferred option when you add one of these drives to an older system.

The 1.44M 3 1/2-Inch Drive

The 1.44M, 3 1/2-inch, HD drives first appeared from IBM in the PS/2 product line introduced in 1987. Although IBM has not officially offered this type of drive for any of its older systems, most compatible vendors started offering the drives as options in systems immediately after IBM introduced the PS/2 system.

The drives record 80 cylinders consisting of two tracks each with 18 sectors per track, resulting in the formatted capacity of 1.44M. Most disk manufacturers label these disks as 2.0M disks, and the difference between this unformatted capacity and the formatted usable result is lost during the format. Note that the 1,440K of total formatted capacity does not account for the areas DOS reserves for file management, leaving only 1423.5K of actual file-storage area.

These drives spin at 300 RPM, and in fact must spin at that speed to operate properly with your existing high- and low-density controllers. To use the 500KHz data rate, the maximum from most standard high- and low-density floppy controllers, these drives could spin at only 300 RPM. If the drives spun at the faster 360 RPM rate of the 5 1/4-inch drives, they would have to reduce the total number of sectors per track to 15, or else the controller could not keep up. In short, the 1.44M 3 1/2-inch drives store 1.2 times the data of the 5 1/4-inch 1.2M drives, and the 1.2M drives spin exactly 1.2 times faster than the 1.44M drives. The data rates used by both HD drives are identical and compatible with the same controllers. In fact, because these 3 1/2-inch HD drives can run at the 500KHz data rate, a controller that can support a 1.2M 5 1/4-inch drive can support the 1.44M drives also. If you are using a low-density disk in the 3 1/2-inch HD drive, the data rate is reduced to 250KHz, and the disk capacity is 720K.

The primary issue in a particular system using a 1.44M 3 1/2-inch drive is one of ROM BIOS support. An IBM system with a ROM BIOS date of 11/15/85 or later has built-in support for these drives, and no external driver support program is needed. You might need a generic AT setup program because IBM's Setup program doesn't offer the 1.44M drive as an option. Another problem relates to the controller and the way it signals the HD drive to write to a low-density disk. The problem is discussed in detail in the following section.

The 2.88M 3 1/2-Inch Drive

The new 2.88M drive was developed by Toshiba Corporation in the 1980s, and was officially announced in 1987. Toshiba began production manufacturing of the drives and disks in 1989, and then several vendors began selling the drives as upgrades for systems. IBM officially adopted these drives in the PS/2 systems in 1991, and virtually all PS/2s sold since then have these drives as standard equipment. Because a 2.88M drive can fully read and write 1.44M and 720K disks, the change was an easy one. DOS version 5.0 or higher is required to support the 2.88M drives.

A number of manufacturers are making these drives, including Toshiba, Mitsubishi, Sony, and Panasonic. Unfortunately due to high media costs, these drives have not caught on, although virtually all systems today have built-in support for them.

The 2.88M ED drive uses a technique called *vertical recording* to achieve its great linear density of 36 sectors per track. This technique increases density by magnetizing the domains perpendicular to the recording surface. By essentially placing the magnetic domains on their ends and stacking them side-by-side, density increases enormously.

The technology for producing heads that can perform a vertical or perpendicular recording has been around a while. It is not the heads or even the drives that represent the major breakthrough in technology; rather, it is the media that is special. Standard disks have magnetic particles shaped like tiny needles that lie on the surface of the disk. Orienting these acicular particles in a perpendicular manner to enable vertical recording is very difficult. The particles on a barium-ferrite floppy disk are shaped like tiny, flat, hexagonal platelets that easily can be arranged to have their axes of magnetization perpendicular to the plane of recording. Although barium ferrite has been used as a material in the construction of permanent magnets, no one has been able to reduce the grain size of the platelets enough for HD recordings.

Toshiba has perfected a glass-crystallization process for manufacturing the ultra-fine platelets used in coating the barium-ferrite disks. This technology, patented by Toshiba, is being licensed to a number of disk manufacturers, all of whom are producing barium-ferrite disks using Toshiba's process. Toshiba also made certain modifications to the design of standard disk drive heads to enable them to read and write the new barium-ferrite disks, as well as standard cobalt or ferrite disks. This technology is being used not only in floppy drives but also is appearing in a variety of tape drive formats.

The disks are called *4M disks* in reference to their unformatted capacity. Actual formatted capacity is 2,880K, or 2.88M. Because of space lost in the formatting process, as well as space occupied by the volume boot sector, FATs, and root directory, the total usable storage space is 2,863K.

To support the 2.88M drive, modifications to the disk controller circuitry were required because these drives spin at the same 300 RPM but have an astonishing 36 sectors per track. Because all floppy disks are formatted with consecutively numbered sectors (1:1 interleave), these 36 sectors have to be read and written in the same time it takes a 1.44M drive to read and write 18 sectors. This requires that the controller support a much higher data transmission rate of 1MHz (1 million bps). Most of the older floppy controllers either found on an adapter card or built into the motherboard support only the maximum of 500KHz data rate used by the 1.44M drives. To upgrade to 2.88M drives would require that the controller be changed to one that supports the higher 1MHz data rate.

An additional support issue is the ROM BIOS. The BIOS must have support for the controller and the capability to specify and accept the 2.88M drive as a CMOS setting. Newer motherboard BIOS sets from companies like Phoenix, AMI, and Award have support for the new ED controllers.

In addition to the newer IBM PS/2 systems, most newer IBM clone and compatible systems now have built-in floppy controllers and ROM BIOS software that fully supports the 2.88M drives. Adding or upgrading to a 2.88M drive in these systems is as easy as plugging in the drive and running the CMOS Setup program. For those systems that do not have this built-in support, this type of upgrade is much more difficult. Several companies offer new controllers and BIOS upgrades as well as the 2.88M drives specifically for upgrading older systems.

Although the 2.88M drives themselves are not much more expensive than the 1.44M drives they replace, the disk media is currently still very expensive. Although you can purchase 1.44M disks for around (or under) 50 cents each, the 2.88M disks can cost more than $2 per disk! This drive never really took off because it didn't help the problem much; even 2.88M is not enough for some Word docs these days.

Handling Recording Problems with 1.44M 3 1/2-Inch Drives

A serious problem awaits many users who use the 1.44M 3 1/2-inch drives: If the drive is installed improperly, any write or format operations performed incorrectly on 720K disks can end up trashing data on low-density disks. The problem is caused by the controller's incapability to signal the HD drive that a low-density recording will take place.

HD disks require a higher write-current or signal strength when they record than do the low-density disks. A low-density drive can record at only the lower write-current, which is correct for the low-density disks; the HD drive, however, needs to record at both high and low write-currents depending on which type of disk is inserted in the drive. If a signal is not sent to the HD drive telling it to lower or reduce the write-current level, the drive stays in its normal high write-current default mode, even when it records on a low-density disk. The signal normally should be sent to the drive by the controller, but many controllers do not provide this signal properly for the 1.44M drives.

The Western Digital controller used by IBM enables the *reduced write-current (RWC) signal* only if the controller also is sending data at the 300KHz data rate, indicating the special case of a low-density disk in a HD drive. The RWC signal is required to tell the HD drive to lower the head-writing signal strength to be proper for the low-density disks. If the signal is not sent, the drive defaults to the higher write-current, which should be used for only HD disks. If the controller is transmitting the 250KHz data rate, the controller knows that the drive must be a low-density drive and therefore no RWC signal is necessary because the low-density drives can write only with reduced current.

This situation presented a serious problem for owners of 1.44M drives using 720K disks because the drives spin the disks at 300 RPM, and in writing to a low-density disk use the 250KHz data rate—not the 300KHz rate. This setup "fools" the controller into thinking that it is sending data to a low-density drive, which causes the controller to fail to send the required RWC signal. Without the RWC signal, the drive records improperly on the disk, possibly trashing any data being written or any data already present. Because virtually all compatibles use controllers based on the design of the IBM AT floppy disk controller, most share the same problem as the IBM AT.

Drive and disk manufacturers devised the perfect solution for this problem, short of using a redesigned controller. They built into the drives a media sensor which, when it is enabled, can override the controller's RWC signal (or lack of it) and properly change the head-current levels within the drive. Essentially, the drive chooses the write-current level independently from the controller when the media sensor is operational.

The sensor is a small, physical or optical sensor designed to feel, or "see," the small hole on the HD 3 1/2-inch disks located opposite the write-enable hole. The extra hole on these HD or ED disks is the media sensor's cue that the full write-current should be used in recording. If an ED disk is detected, the ED drive enables the vertical recording heads. Low-density disks do not have these extra holes; therefore, when the sensor cannot see a media-sensor hole, it causes the drive to record in the proper reduced write-current mode for a DD disk.

Some people override the function of these sensors by punching an extra hole in a low-density disk to fool the drive's sensor into acting as though an actual HD disk has been inserted. Several unscrupulous companies have made a fast buck by selling media sensor hole-punchers. These disk-punch vendors try to mislead you into believing that no difference exists between the low- and high-density disks except for the hole, and that punching the extra hole makes the low-density disk a legitimate HD disk. This, of course, is absolutely untrue: The HD disks are different from low-density disks. The differences between the disks are explained in more detail in section "Floppy Disk Media Types and Specifications" later in this chapter.

Many systems, including the IBM PS/2 series, do not need 1.44M drives with media sensors. Their controllers have been fixed to allow the RWC signal to be sent to the drive even when the controller is sending the 250KHz data rate. This setup allows for proper operation no matter what type of disk or drive is used, as long as the user formats properly. Because these systems do not have a media sensor policing users, they easily can format low-density disks as HD disks, regardless of what holes are on the disk. This has caused problems for users of the older PS/2 systems who have accidentally formatted 720K disks as 1.44M disks. When passed to a system that has an enabled media sensor, the system refuses to read the disks at all because it is not correctly formatted. If you are having disk interchange problems, make sure that you are formatting your disks correctly.

The newer PS/2 and other high-end systems from other manufacturers (Hewlett-Packard, for example) use an active media sensor setup in which the user no longer has to enter the correct FORMAT command parameters to format the disk. In these systems, the media sensor information is passed through the controller to the BIOS, which properly informs the FORMAT command about which disk is in the drive. With these systems, it is impossible for a user to accidentally format a disk incorrectly, and it eliminates the user from having to know anything about the different disk media types.

Analyzing Floppy Disk Construction

The 5 1/4-inch and 3 1/2-inch disks each have unique construction and physical properties.

The flexible (or floppy) disk is contained within a plastic jacket. The 3 1/2-inch disks are covered by a more rigid jacket than are the 5 1/4-inch disks; the disks within the jackets, however, are virtually identical except, of course, for the size.

Differences and similarities exist between these two different-sized disks. This section looks at the physical properties and construction of each disk type.

When you look at a typical 5 1/4-inch floppy disk, you see several things (see Figure 13.10). Most prominent is the large round hole in the center. When you close the disk drive's "door," a cone-shaped clamp grabs and centers the disk through the center hole. Many disks come with *hub-ring reinforcements*—thin, plastic rings like those used to reinforce three-ring notebook paper—intended to help the disk withstand the mechanical forces of the clamping mechanism. The HD disks usually lack these reinforcements because the difficulty in accurately placing them on the disk means they will cause alignment problems.

On the right side, just below the center of the hub hole, is a smaller round hole called the *index hole*. If you carefully turn the disk within its protective jacket, you see a small hole in the disk. The drive uses the index hole as the starting point for all the sectors on the disk—sort of the "prime meridian" for the disk sectors. A disk with a single index hole is a soft-sectored disk; the software (operating system) decides the actual number of sectors on the disk. Some older equipment, such as Wang word processors, use hard-sectored disks, which have an index hole to demarcate individual sectors. Do not use hard-sectored disks in a PC.

FIG. 13.10 Construction of a 5 1/4-inch floppy disk.

Below the hub hole is a slot shaped somewhat like a long racetrack through which you can see the disk surface. Through this media-access hole, the disk drive heads read and write information to the disk surface.

At the right side, about 1 inch from the top, is a rectangular punch from the side of the disk cover. If this write-enable notch is present, writing to the disk has been enabled. Disks without this notch (or with the notch taped over) are write-protected disks. The notch might not be on all disks, particularly those purchased with programs on them.

On the rear of the disk jacket at the bottom, two very small oval notches flank the head slot. The notches relieve stress on the disk and help prevent it from warping. The drive might use these notches also to assist in keeping the disk in the proper position in the drive.

Because the 3 1/2-inch disks use a much more rigid plastic case, which helps stabilize the disk, these disks can record at track and data densities greater than the 5 1/4-inch disks (see Figure 13.11). A metal shutter protects the media-access hole. The shutter is manipulated by the drive and remains closed whenever the disk is not in a drive. The media then is insulated from the environment and from your fingers. The shutter also obviates the need for a disk jacket.

Because the shutter is not necessary for the disk to work, it can be removed from the plastic case if it becomes bent or damaged. Simply pry it off the disk case; it will pop off with a snap. The spring that pushes it closed should come off as well. After the damaged shutter is removed, it would be a good idea to copy the data from the disk to a new one.

FIG. 13.11 Construction of a 3 1/2-inch floppy disk.

Rather than an index hole in the disk, the 3 1/2-inch disks use a metal center hub with an alignment hole. The drive "grasps" the metal hub, and the hole in the hub enables the drive to position the disk properly.

On the lower-left part of the disk is a hole with a plastic slider, called the *write-protect/-enable hole* (refer to Figure 13.9). When the slider is positioned so that the hole is visible, the disk is write-protected; the drive is prevented from recording on the disk. When the slider is positioned to cover the hole, writing is enabled, and you can record on the disk. For more permanent write-protection, some commercial software programs are supplied on disks with the slider removed so that you cannot easily enable recording on the disk, which is exactly opposite of a 5 1/4-inch floppy where Covered equals Write Protect, not Write Enable.

On the other (right) side of the disk from the write-protect hole, there might be in the disk jacket another hole called the *media-density-selector hole*. If this hole is present, the disk is constructed of a special media and is therefore an HD or ED disk. If the media-sensor hole is exactly opposite the write-protect hole, it indicates a 1.44M HD disk. If the media-sensor hole is located more toward the top of the disk (the metal shutter is at the top of the disk), it indicates an ED disk. No hole on the right side means that the disk is a low-density disk. Most 3 1/2-inch drives have a media sensor that controls recording capability based on the existence or absence of these holes.

Both the 3 1/2-inch and 5 1/4-inch disks are constructed of the same basic materials. They use a plastic base (usually Mylar) coated with a magnetic compound. The compound is usually a ferric-oxide-based compound for the standard density versions; a cobalt-ferric compound usually is used in the higher-coercivity (higher density) disks. Extended density disks use a barium-ferric media compound. The rigid jacket material on the 3 1/2-inch disks often causes people to believe incorrectly that these disks are some sort of "hard disk" and not really a floppy disk. The disk "cookie" inside the 3 1/2-inch case is just as floppy as the 5 1/4-inch variety.

Floppy Disk Media Types and Specifications

This section examines all the types of disks you can purchase for your system. Especially interesting are the technical specifications that can separate one type of disk from another, as Table 13.6 shows. This section defines all the specifications used to describe a typical disk.

Table 13.6 Floppy Disk Media Specifications

	5 1/4-Inch			3 1/2-Inch		
Media Parameters	Double Density (DD)	Quad Density (QD)	High Density (HD)	Double Density (DD)	High Density (HD)	Extra-High Density (ED)
Tracks Per Inch (TPI)	48	96	96	135	135	135
Bits Per Inch (BPI)	5,876	5,876	9,646	8,717	17,434	34,868
Media Formulation	Ferrite	Ferrite	Cobalt	Cobalt	Cobalt	Barium
Coercivity (Oersteds)	300	300	600	600	720	750
Thickness (Micro-In.)	100	100	50	70	40	100
Recording Polarity	Horiz.	Horiz.	Horiz.	Horiz.	Horiz.	Vert.

Density. *Density*, in simplest terms, is a measure of the amount of information that can be packed reliably into a specific area of a recording surface. The keyword here is *reliably*.

Disks have two types of densities: longitudinal density and linear density. *Longitudinal density* is indicated by how many tracks can be recorded on the disk, often expressed as a number of tracks per inch (TPI). *Linear density* is the capability of an individual track to store data, often indicated as a number of bits per inch (BPI). Unfortunately, both types of densities often are interchanged incorrectly in discussing different disks and drives. Table 13.6 provides a rundown of each available type of disk.

> **Note**
>
> IBM skipped the quad-density disk type—that is, no IBM system uses a quad-density drive or requires quad-density disks. Don't purchase a quad-density disk unless you just want a better-quality DD disk.

Both the quad- and DD disks store the same linear data on each track. They use the same formula for the magnetic coating on the disk, but the quad-density versions represent a more rigorously tested, higher-quality disk. The HD disks are entirely different, however. To store the increased linear density, an entirely different magnetic coating was required.

In both the 5 1/4-inch and 3 1/2-inch HD disks, a high-coercivity coating is used to allow the tremendous bit density for each track. A HD disk never can be substituted for a double- or quad-density disk because the write-current must be different for these very different media formulations and thicknesses.

The ED 3 1/2-inch disk in the chart is newly available in some systems. This type of disk, invented by Toshiba, is available from several other vendors as well. The ED disks enables a vertical recording technique to be used. In vertical recording, the magnetic domains are recorded vertically rather than flat. The higher density results from their capability to be stacked much more closely together. These types of drives can read and write the other 3 1/2-inch disks because of their similar track dimensions on all formats.

Media Coercivity and Thickness. The coercivity specification of a disk refers to the magnetic-field strength required to make a proper recording on a disk. *Coercivity*, measured in oersteds, is a value indicating magnetic strength. A disk with a higher coercivity rating requires a stronger magnetic field to make a recording on that disk. With lower ratings, the disk can be recorded with a weaker magnetic field. In other words, the lower the coercivity rating, the more sensitive the disk.

HD media demands higher coercivity ratings so that the adjacent magnetic domains don't interfere with each other. For this reason, HD media is actually less sensitive and requires a stronger recording signal strength.

Another factor is the thickness of the disk. The thinner the disk, the less influence a region of the disk has on another adjacent region. The thinner disks therefore can accept many more bits per inch without eventually degrading the recording.

Formatting Disks. One basic rule that applies to all drives (except 2.88M) is that a drive always formats in its native mode unless specifically instructed otherwise through the FORMAT command parameters. Therefore, if you insert a 1.44M HD disk in a 1.44M HD A: drive, you can format that disk by simply entering **FORMAT A:**—no optional parameters are necessary in that case. If you insert any other type of disk (DD, for example), you absolutely must enter the appropriate parameters in the FORMAT command to change the format mode from the default 1.44M mode to the mode appropriate for the inserted disk. Even though the drive might have a media sensor that can detect which type of disk is inserted in the drive, in most cases the sensor does not communicate to the controller or DOS, which does not know which disk it is.

An exception to this is the 2.88M drive installations that support active media sense. Most 2.88M drive installations support this advanced feature, which means that the media sensor will communicate the type of the inserted disk to the controller and DOS. In this case, no parameters are ever needed when formatting disks, no matter what type is inserted. The FORMAT command will automatically default to the proper type as indicated by the active sensors on the 2.88M drive. I have even seen 1.44M drive installations with active media sensing (certain Hewlett-Packard systems, for example), but this is rare.

Chapter 13—Floppy Disk Drives

In most cases of 1.44M drive installations, the media sensor in the drive is passive, and in effect all the sensor does is force the FORMAT command to fail if you do not enter the correct parameters for the inserted disk type.

Table 13.7 shows the proper format command for all possible variations in drive and disk types. It also shows which DOS versions support the various combinations of drives, disks, and FORMAT parameters. To use this table, just look up the drive type and disk type you have. You then can see the proper FORMAT command parameters to use, as well as the DOS versions that support the combination you want.

Table 13.7 Proper Disk Formatting

Drive Type	Disk Type	DOS Version	Proper FORMAT Command
5 1/4-inch 360K	DD 360K	DOS 2.0+	FORMAT d:
5 1/4-inch 1.2M	HD 1.2M	DOS 3.0+	FORMAT d:
5 1/4-inch 1.2M	DD 360K	DOS 3.0+	FORMAT d: /4
5 1/4-inch 1.2M	DD 360K	DOS 3.2+	FORMAT d: /N:9 /T:40
5 1/4-inch 1.2M	DD 360K	DOS 4.0+	FORMAT d: /F:360
3 1/2-inch 720K	DD 720K	DOS 3.2+	FORMAT d:
3 1/2-inch 1.44M	HD 1.44M	DOS 3.3+	FORMAT d:
3 1/2-inch 1.44M	DD 720K	DOS 3.3+	FORMAT d: /N:9 /T:80
3 1/2-inch 1.44M	DD 720K	DOS 4.0+	FORMAT d: /F:720
3 1/2-inch 2.88M	ED 2.88M	DOS 5.0+	FORMAT d:
3 1/2-inch 2.88M	HD 1.44M	DOS 5.0+	FORMAT d: /F:1.44
3 1/2-inch 2.88M	DD 720K	DOS 5.0+	FORMAT d: /F:720

+ = *Includes all higher versions*
d: = *Specifies drive to format*
DD = *double-density*
HD = *high-density*
ED = *extra-high density*

> **Note**
>
> If the drive and installation you are using supports active (intelligent) media sensing, no disk type parameters are required. The drive will automatically communicate the type of the installed disk to the FORMAT program. This is normal for most 2.88M drive installations.

Caring for and Handling Floppy Disks and Drives

Most computer users know the basics of disk care. Disks can be damaged or destroyed easily by the following:

- Touching the recording surface with your fingers or anything else
- Writing on a disk label with a ball-point pen or pencil
- Bending the disk
- Spilling coffee or other substances on the disk
- Overheating a disk (leaving it in the hot sun or near a radiator, for example)
- Exposing a disk to stray magnetic fields

Despite all these cautions, disks are rather hardy storage devices; I can't say that I have ever destroyed one by just writing on it with a pen, because I do so all the time. I am careful, however, not to press too hard, which can put a crease in the disk. Also, simply touching a disk does not necessarily ruin it but rather gets the disk and your drive head dirty with oil and dust. The danger to your disks comes from magnetic fields that, because they are unseen, can sometimes be found in places you never dreamed of.

For example, all color monitors (and color TV sets) have around the face of the tube a degaussing coil used to demagnetize the shadow mask inside when the monitor is turned on. The coil is connected to the AC line and controlled by a thermistor that passes a gigantic surge of power to the coil when the tube is powered on, which then tapers off as the tube warms up. The degaussing coil is designed to remove any stray magnetism from the shadow mask at the front area of the tube. Residual magnetism in this mask can bend the electron beams so that the picture appears to have strange colors or be out of focus.

If you keep your disks anywhere near (within one foot) of the front of the color monitor, you expose them to a strong magnetic field every time you turn on the monitor. Keeping disks in this area is not a good idea because the field is designed to demagnetize objects, and indeed works well for demagnetizing disks. The effect is cumulative and irreversible.

Another major disk destructor is the telephone. The mechanical ringer in a typical telephone uses a powerful electromagnet to move the striker into the bell. The ringer circuit uses some 90 volts, and the electromagnetic fields have sufficient power to degauss a disk lying on the desk next to or partially underneath the phone. Keep disks away from the telephone. A telephone with an electronic ringer might not cause this type of damage to a disk, but there are also magnets in the handset, so be careful anyway.

Another source of powerful magnetic fields is an electric motor, found in vacuum cleaners, heaters or air conditioners, fans, electric pencil sharpeners, and so on. Do not place these devices near areas where you store disks.

Airport X-Ray Machines and Metal Detectors

People associate myths with things they cannot see, and we certainly cannot see data as it is stored on a disk, nor the magnetic fields that can alter the data.

One of my favorite myths to dispel is that the airport X-ray machine somehow damages disks. I have a great deal of experience in this area from having traveled around the country for the past 10 years or so with disks and portable computers in hand. I fly about 150,000 miles per year, and my portable computer equipment and disks have been through X-ray machines more than 100 times each year.

The biggest problem people have when they approach the airport X-ray machines with disks or computers is they don't pass the stuff through! Seriously, X-rays are in essence just a form of light, and disks and computers are just not affected by X-rays at anywhere near the levels found in these machines.

What can damage your magnetic media is the metal detector. Time and time again, someone with magnetic media or a portable computer approaches the security check. They freeze and say, "Oh no, I have disks and a computer—they have to be hand-inspected." The person then refuses to place the disk and computer on the X-ray belt, and either walks through the metal detector with disks and computer in hand or passes the items over to the security guard, in very close proximity to the metal detector.

Metal detectors work by monitoring disruptions in a weak magnetic field. A metal object inserted in the field area causes the field's shape to change, which the detector observes. This principle, which is the reason that the detectors are sensitive to metal objects, can be dangerous to your disks; the X-ray machine, however, is the safest area through which to pass either your disk or computer.

The X-ray machine is not dangerous to magnetic media because it merely exposes the media to electromagnetic radiation at a particular (very high) frequency. *Blue light* is an example of electromagnetic radiation of a different frequency. The only difference between X-rays and blue light is in the frequency, or wavelength, of the emission.

Some people worry about the effect of X-ray radiation on their system's *EPROM (Erasable Programmable Read-Only Memory) chips*. This concern might actually be more valid than worrying about disk damage because EPROMs are erased by certain forms of electromagnetic radiation. In reality, however, you do not need to worry about this effect, either. EPROMs are erased by direct exposure to very intense ultraviolet light. Specifically, to be erased, an EPROM must be exposed to a 12,000 uw/cm2 UV light source with a wavelength of 2,537 angstroms for 15 to 20 minutes, and at a distance of 1 inch. Increasing the power of the light source or decreasing the distance from the source can shorten the erasure time to a few minutes.

The airport X-ray machine is different by a factor of 10,000 in wavelength, and the field strength, duration, and distance from the emitter source are nowhere near what is necessary for EPROM erasure. Be aware that many circuit-board manufacturers use X-ray inspection on circuit boards (with components including EPROMs installed) to test and check quality control during manufacture.

In my own experiences, I passed one disk through different airport X-ray machines for two years, averaging two or three passes a week. The same disk still remains intact with all the original files and data, and never has been reformatted. I also have several portable computers with hard disks installed; one of them went through the X-ray machines safely every week for more than four years. I prefer to pass computers and disks through the X-ray machine because it offers the best shielding from the magnetic fields produced by the metal detector standing next to it. Doing so also used to lower the "hassle factor" with the security guards because if I had it X-rayed, they usually did not require that I unpack it and turn it on. Unfortunately, with the greater emphasis on airport security these days, even if it is X-rayed, most airlines require the system be demonstrated (turned on) anyway.

Now you may not want to take my word for it, but there has been published scientific research that corroborates what I have stated here. A few years ago, a study was published by two scientists, one of whom actually designs X-ray tubes for a major manufacturer. Their study was titled "Airport X-rays and floppy disks: no cause for concern," and was published in 1993 in the journal *Computer Methods and Programs in Biomedicine*. According to the abstract,

> A controlled study was done to test the possible effects of X-rays on the integrity of data stored on common sizes of floppy disks. Disks were exposed to doses of X-rays up to seven times that to be expected during airport examination of baggage. The readability of nearly 14 megabytes of data was unaltered by X-irradiation, indicating that floppy disks need not be given special handling during X-ray inspection of baggage.

In fact, the disks were re-tested after two years of storage, and there has still been no measurable degradation since the exposure.

Now although the X-rays themselves do not cause damage, I have heard reports that magnetic fields from the conveyor belt motors have damaged some disks. Personally, I have never seen this.

Drive-Installation Procedures

The procedure for installing floppy drives is simple. You install the drive in two phases. The first phase is to configure the drive for the installation, and the second is to perform the physical installation. Of these two steps, the first one usually is the most difficult to perform, depending on your knowledge of disk interfacing and whether you have access to the correct OEM drive manuals.

When you physically install a drive, you attach the drive to the chassis or case and then plug the power and signal cables into the drive. Some type of bracket and screws are normally required to attach the drive to the chassis. These are normally included with the chassis or case itself. Several companies listed in Appendix A specialize in cases, cables, brackets, screw hardware, and other items useful in assembling systems or installing drives.

When you connect a drive, make sure that the power cable is installed properly. The cable normally is keyed so that it cannot be plugged in backward. Also, install the data and control cable. If no key is in this cable, which allows only a correct orientation, use the colored wire in the cable as a guide to the position of pin 1. This cable is oriented correctly when you plug it in so that the colored wire is plugged into the disk drive connector toward the cut-out notch in the drive edge connector.

Troubleshooting and Correcting Problems

The majority of floppy drive problems are caused primarily by improper drive configuration, installation, or operation. Unfortunately, floppy drive configuration and installation is much more complicated than the average technician seems to realize. Even if you had your drive "professionally" installed, it still might have been done incorrectly.

"Phantom Directory" (Disk Change) Problems

One of the most common mistakes people make in installing a disk drive is incorrectly setting the signals sent by the drive on pin 34 of the cable to the controller. All drives except the 360K drive must be configured so that a Disk Change (DC) signal is sent along pin 34 to the controller.

If you do not enable the DC signal when the system expects you to, you might end up with trashed disks as a result. For example, a PC user with disk in hand might say to you, "Moments ago, this disk contained my document files, and now it seems as though my entire word processing program disk has mysteriously transferred to it. When I attempt to run the programs that now seem to be on this disk, they crash or lock up my system." Of course, in this case the disk has been damaged, and you will have to perform some data-recovery magic to recover the information for the user. A good thing about this particular kind of problem is that recovering most—if not all—the information on the disk is entirely possible.

You also can observe this installation defect manifested in the "phantom directory" problem. For example, you place a disk with files on it in the A: drive of your AT-compatible system and enter the **DIR A:** command. The drive starts spinning, the access light on the drive comes on, and after a few seconds of activity, the disk directory scrolls up the screen. Everything seems to be running well. Then you remove the disk and insert in drive A: a different disk with different files on it and repeat the **DIR A:** command. This time, however, the drive barely (if at all) spins before the disk directory scrolls up the screen. When you look at the directory listing that has appeared, you discover in amazement that it is the same listing as on the first disk you removed from the drive.

Understand that the disk you have inserted in the drive is in danger. If you write on this disk in any way, you will cause the FATs and root directory sectors from the first disk (which are stored in your system's memory) to be copied over to the second disk, thereby "blowing away" the information on the second disk. Most AT-compatible systems with high- or low-density controllers use a floppy disk caching system that buffers the FATs and directories from the floppy disk that was last read in system RAM. Because this data is kept in memory, these areas of the disk do not have to be reread as frequently. This system greatly speeds access to the disk.

Opening the door lever or pressing the eject button on a drive normally sends the DC signal to the controller, which in turn causes DOS to flush out the floppy cache. This action causes the next read of the disk drive to reread the FAT and directory areas. If this signal is not sent, the cache is not flushed when you change a disk, and the system acts as though the first disk still is present in the drive. Writing to this newly inserted disk writes not only the new data but also either a full or partial copy of the first disk's FAT and directory areas. Also, the data is written to what was considered free space on the first disk, which might not be free on the subsequent disk and results in damaged files and data.

This problem has several simple solutions. One is temporary; the other is permanent. For a quick, temporary solution, press Ctrl+Break or Ctrl+C immediately after changing any disk to force DOS to manually flush the floppy I/O buffers. This method is exactly how the old CP/M operating system used to work. After pressing Ctrl+Break or Ctrl+C, the next disk access rereads the FAT and directory areas of the disk and places fresh copies in memory. In other words, you must be sure that every time you change a disk, the buffer gets flushed. Because these commands work only from the DOS prompt (and not in Windows), you must not change a disk while working in an application.

A more permanent and correct solution to the problem is simple—just correct the drive installation. In my experience, incorrect installation is the root cause of this problem nine out of 10 times. Remember this simple rule: If a jumper block is on the disk drive labeled DC, you should install a jumper there. If you are absolutely certain that the installation was correct—for example, the drive has worked perfectly for some time, but then suddenly develops this problem—check the following list of items, all of which can prevent the DC signal from being sent:

- *Bad cable.* Check for continuity on pin 34.
- *Drive configuration/Setup.* Make sure that the DC jumper is enabled; check CMOS Setup for proper drive type.
- *Bad Disk Change sensor.* Clean sensor or replace drive and retest.
- *Bad drive logic board.* Replace drive and retest.
- *Bad controller.* Replace controller and retest.
- *Wrong DOS OEM version.*

The last of these checklist items can stump you because the hardware seems to be functioning correctly. As a rule, you should use only the DOS supplied by the same OEM as the computer system on the system. For example, use IBM DOS on IBM systems, Compaq DOS on Compaq systems, Zenith DOS on Zenith systems, Toshiba DOS on Toshiba systems, Tandy DOS on Tandy systems, and so on. This problem is most noticeable with some laptop systems that apparently have a modified floppy controller design, such as some Toshiba laptops. On many of these systems, you must use the correct (Toshiba, for example) OEM version of DOS.

Off-Center Disk Clamping

Clamping the disk off-center in the drive is a frequent cause of problems with floppy drives. Ejecting and reinserting the disk so that it is clamped properly usually makes the disk reading or booting problem disappear immediately. This step might solve the problem in most cases, but it is not much help if you have formatted or written a disk in an off-center position. In that case, all you can do is try to DISKCOPY the improperly written disk to another disk and attempt various data-recovery operations on both disks.

Repairing Floppy Drives

Attitudes about repairing floppy drives have changed over the years, primarily because of the decreasing cost of drives. When drives were more expensive, people often considered repairing the drive rather than replacing it. With the cost of drives decreasing every year, however, certain labor- or parts-intensive repair procedures have become almost as expensive as replacing the drive with a new one.

Because of cost considerations, repairing floppy drives usually is limited to cleaning the drive and heads and lubricating the mechanical mechanisms. On drives that have a speed adjustment, adjusting the speed to within the proper operating range also is common. Note that most newer half-height drives and virtually all 3 1/2-inch drives do not have an adjustment for speed. These drives use a circuit that automatically sets the speed at the required level and compensates for variations with a feedback loop. If such an auto-taching drive is off in speed, the reason usually is that the circuit failed. Replacement of the drive is usually necessary.

Cleaning Floppy Drives

Sometimes read and write problems are caused by dirty drive heads. Cleaning a drive is easy; you can proceed in two ways:

- Use one of the simple head-cleaning kits available from computer- or office-supply stores. These devices are easy to operate and don't require the system unit to be open for access to the drive.

- The manual method: Use a cleaning swab with a liquid such as pure alcohol or trichloroethane. With this method, you must open the system unit to expose the drive and, in many cases (especially in earlier full-height drives), also remove and partially disassemble the drive.

The manual method can result in a better overall job, but usually the work required is not worth the difference.

The cleaning kits come in two styles: The wet type uses a liquid squirted on a cleaning disk to wash off the heads; the dry kit relies on abrasive material on the cleaning disk to remove head deposits. I recommend that you never use the dry drive-cleaning kits. Always use a wet system in which a liquid solution is applied to the cleaning disk. The dry disks can prematurely wear the heads if used improperly or too often; wet systems are very safe to use.

The manual drive-cleaning method requires that you have physical access to the heads in order to swab them manually with a lint-free foam swab soaked in a cleaning solution. This method requires some level of expertise: Simply jabbing at the heads incorrectly with a cleaning swab might knock the drive heads out of alignment. You must use a careful in-and-out motion, and lightly swab the heads. No side-to-side motion (relative to the way the heads travel) should be used; this motion can snag a head and knock it out of alignment. Because of the difficulty and danger of this manual cleaning, for most applications I recommend a simple wet-disk cleaning kit because it is the easiest and safest method.

One question that comes up repeatedly in my seminars is "How often should you clean a disk drive?" Only you can answer that question. What type of environment is the system in? Do you smoke cigarettes near the system? If so, cleaning would be required more often. Usually, a safe rule of thumb is to clean drives about once a year if the system is in a clean office environment in which no smoke or other particulate matter is in the air. In a heavy-smoking environment, you might have to clean every six months or perhaps even more often. In dirty industrial environments, you might have to clean every month or so. Your own experience is your guide in this matter. If DOS reports drive errors in the system by displaying the familiar DOS `Abort, Retry, Ignore` prompt, you should clean your drive to try to solve the problem. If cleaning does solve the problem, you probably should step up the interval between preventive-maintenance cleanings.

In some cases, you might want to place a very small amount of lubricant on the door mechanism or other mechanical contact point inside the drive. Do not use oil; use a pure silicone lubricant. Oil collects dust rapidly after you apply it and usually causes the oiled mechanism to gum up later. Silicone does not attract dust in the same manner and can be used safely. Use very small amounts of silicone; do not drip or spray silicone inside the drive. You must make sure that the lubricant is applied only to the part that needs it. If the lubricant gets all over the inside of the drive, it may cause unnecessary problems.

Aligning Floppy Disk Drives

If your disk drives are misaligned, you will notice that other drives cannot read disks created in your drive, and you might not be able to read disks created in other drives. This situation can be dangerous if you allow it to progress unchecked. If the alignment is bad enough, you probably will notice it first in the incapability to read original application-program disks, while still being able to read your own created disks. The Drive Probe program from Accurite for checking the alignment and operation of floppy drives is discussed next.

To solve this problem, you can have the drive realigned. I don't recommend realigning drives because of the low cost of simply replacing the drive compared to aligning one. Also, an unforeseen circumstance catches many people off-guard: You might find that your newly aligned drive might not be able to read all your backup or data disks created while the drive was out of alignment. If you replace the misaligned drive with a new one and keep the misaligned drive, you can use it for `DISKCOPY` purposes to transfer the data to newly formatted disks in the new drive.

Aligning disk drives is usually no longer performed because of the high relative cost. To align a drive properly requires access to an oscilloscope (for about $500), a special analog-alignment disk ($75), and the OEM service manual for the drive; also, you must spend half an hour to an hour aligning the drive.

A new program, Drive Probe by Accurite, uses special test disks called *High-Resolution Diagnostic (HRD) disks*. These disks are as accurate as the analog alignment disks (AAD) and eliminate the need for an oscilloscope to align a drive. You cannot use any program that relies on the older Digital Diagnostic Disk (DDD) or Spiral format test disks because they are not accurate enough to use to align a drive. The Drive Probe and HRD system can make an alignment more cost-effective than before, but it is still a labor-intensive operation.

With the price of most types of floppy drives hovering at or below the $35 mark, aligning drives usually is not a cost-justified alternative to replacement. One exception exists. In a high-volume situation, drive alignment might pay off. Another alternative is to investigate local organizations that perform drive alignments, usually for $25 to $50. Weigh this cost against the replacement cost and age of the drive. I have purchased brand new 1.44M floppy drives for as low as $25. At these prices, alignment is no longer a viable option.

Floptical Drives

A special type of high capacity floppy drive has been developed called a *floptical drive*. A 21M as well as a 120M version have been available over the years, and the 21M version has become obsolete. The older 21M version was created by Insite Peripherals, and packed 21M of data on the same size disk as a 3 1/2-inch floppy. More recently, 3M and Matsushita have introduced a drive called the LS-120 that can store 120M on a single 3 1/2-inch floppy disk! In addition, all floptical drives can read and write 1.44M and 720K floppy disks (although they cannot handle 2.88M disks). Because of their greatly increased storage capacity and ability to use common floppy disks, the newer 120M flopticals are considered by many as the perfect replacement floppy disk drive.

The name "floptical" might suggest the use of laser beams to burn or etch data onto the disk or to excite the media in preparation for magnetic recording—as is the case with the CD-R and Write Once, Read Many (WORM). But this suggestion is erroneous. The read/write heads of a floptical drive use magnetic recording technology, much like that of floppy drives. The floptical disk itself is composed of the same ferrite materials common to floppy and hard disks. Floptical drives are capable of such increased capacity because many more tracks are packed on each disk, compared with a standard 1.44M floppy. Obviously, in order to fit so many tracks on the floptical disk, the tracks must be much more narrow than those on a floppy disk.

That's where optical technology comes into play. Flopticals use a special optical mechanism to properly position the drive read/write heads over the data tracks on the disk. The way this works, *servo information*, which specifically defines the location of each track, is embedded in the disk during the manufacturing process. Each track of servo information is actually etched or stamped on the disk and is never disturbed during the recording process. Each time the floptical drive writes to the disk, the recording mechanism (including the read/write heads) is guided by a laser beam precisely into place by this servo information. When the floptical drive reads the encoded data, this servo information again is used by the laser to guide the read/write heads precisely into place.

21M Floptical Drives

The original Insite 21M floptical disks used tracks formatted to 27 sectors of 512 bytes. The disks themselves revolved at 720 RPM. Flopticals are capable of nearly 10M per minute data throughput. These drives used a SCSI interface to the system.

Unfortunately, the 21M drives by Insite never really caught on due to several reasons. One is that no leading manufacturer has included these drives in a standard configuration with built-in BIOS drivers and support. Also, Microsoft, IBM, and Apple have not built support for these drives directly into their operating systems.

Iomega Zip Drives

Iomega introduces a proprietary drive based on the Bernoulli principle (see Chapter 18, "Tape and Other Mass-Storage Drives"). This drive took the market by storm. It is a portable external drive, usually connected to your PC via the parallel port. The media is the size of a 3 1/2-inch floppy (a little thicker), yet it holds 100M of data, has an access time (29ms) as fast as some early hard drives, and can transfer data at 1M/sec using a SCSI interface! With overwhelming support in the industry, Iomega has gotten a huge jump on its closest competitor, the LS-120 Drive.

LS-120 (120M) Floptical Drives

The LS-120 drive was designed to become the new standard floppy disk drive in the PC industry. This drive was developed by 3M and Matsushita-Kotobuki Electronics Industries, Ltd., and stores 120M of data, or about 80 times more data than current 1.44M floppy disks. In addition to storing more, these drives read and write up to five times the speed of standard floppy disk drives.

The LS-120 floppy drive can act as the PC's bootable A: drive, and is fully compatible with Windows NT and Windows 95. In addition to the new 120M floppy disks, the LS-120 drive accepts standard 720K and 1.44M floppy disks, and actually reads and writes those disks up to three times faster than standard floppy drives. Iomega Zip drives are not backwards-compatible and cannot use existing floppy disks; the proprietary Zip media stores less and is more expensive than the 3M LS-120 media. The LS-120 uses a standard IDE interface, which is already built into most existing systems. Zip drives usually use either the slower external parallel port as an interface or require the addition of a SCSI adapter, which adds to the expense, but Iomega has supplied OEM's with bootable IDE version we should start seeing on the streets soon.

The LS-120 drives are perfect for portable systems, providing a solution that not only replaces the existing floppy, but which can even be used in place of the floppy drive internally. Having one of these high-capacity drives in a portable will allow the use of the relatively inexpensive 120M removable disks while on the road. They are perfect for storing entire applications or datasets, which can be removed and secured when the portable system is not in use.

Compaq was the first PC maker to offer computers equipped with LS-120 drives. Other leading PC manufacturers are incorporating LS-120 drives in their products, making this the new standard for PC floppy drives. Besides coming in new systems, these drives are also available separately at a cost of about $200 in internal or external versions for upgrading older systems. The 120M floppy disks are available for about $15 or less per disk.

The 3M LS-120 disk has the same shape and size as a standard 1.44M 3 1/2-inch floppy disk; however, it uses a combination of magnetic and optical technology to enable greater capacity and performance. Named after the Laser Servo (LS) mechanism it employs, LS-120 technology places optical reference tracks on the disk that are both written and read by a laser system. The optical sensor in the drive allows the read-write head to be precisely positioned over the magnetic data tracks, enabling track densities of 2,490 TPI versus the 135 TPI for a 1.44M floppy disk.

On the Web

3M has recently moved its disk and tape drive division into an independent, publicly owned data storage and imaging company called Imation. If you want more information on the LS-120 drives or any of the 3M tape products, Imation can be reached on the Web at the following address:

http://www.imation.com

Unlike the previous Insite Floptical or Zip drives, the LS-120 is being endorsed by major PC manufacturers, starting with Compaq, and will be supported by the system BIOS. Microsoft and IBM are also building support for the LS-120 drives into Windows and OS/2, meaning that the LS-120 will probably be the next evolutionary standard for PC floppy drives.

Chapter 14

Hard Disk Drives

To most users, the hard disk drive is the most important, yet most mysterious, part of a computer system. A *hard disk drive* is a sealed unit that holds the data in a system. When the hard disk fails, the consequences usually are very serious. To maintain, service, and expand a PC system properly, you must fully understand the hard disk unit.

Most computer users want to know how hard disk drives work and what to do when a problem occurs. Few books about hard disks, however, cover the detail necessary for the PC technician or sophisticated user. This chapter corrects that situation.

This chapter thoroughly describes the hard disk drive from a physical, mechanical, and electrical point of view. In particular, this chapter examines the construction and operation of a hard disk drive in a practical sense.

Definition of a Hard Disk

A hard disk drive contains rigid, disk-shaped platters usually constructed of aluminum or glass. Unlike floppy disks, the platters cannot bend or flex—hence the term *hard disk*. In most hard disk drives, the platters cannot be removed; for that reason, IBM calls them *fixed disk drives*. Although a removable hard disk drive has been very popular of late, the Jaz drive by Iomega is unlike its smaller brother, the Zip drive, in that the Jaz drive's removable media is comprised of the same hard disks found in any fixed disk drive.

Hard disk drives used to be called *Winchester drives*. This term dates back to the 1960s, when IBM developed a high-speed hard disk drive that had 30M of fixed-platter storage and 30M of removable-platter storage. The drive had platters that spun at high speeds and heads that floated over the platters while they spun in a sealed environment. That drive, the *30-30 drive*, soon received the nickname *Winchester* after the famous Winchester 30-30 rifle. After that time, drives that used a high-speed spinning platter with a floating head also became known as *Winchester drives*. The term has no technical or scientific meaning; it is a slang term, and is considered synonymous with *hard disk*.

Capacity Measurements

To eliminate confusion in capacity measurements, I will be using the abbreviation M in this section. The true industry standard abbreviations for these figures are shown in Table 14.1.

Table 14.1 Standard Abbreviations and Meanings

Abbreviation	Description	Decimal Meaning	Binary Meaning
Kbit	Kilobit	1,000	1,024
K	Kilobyte	1,000	1,024
Mbit	Megabit	1,000,000	1,048,576
M	Megabyte	1,000,000	1,048,576
Gbit	Gigabit	1,000,000,000	1,073,741,824
G	Gigabyte	1,000,000,000	1,073,741,824
Tbit	Terabit	1,000,000,000,000	1,099,511,627,776
T	Terabyte	1,000,000,000,000	1,099,511,627,776

Unfortunately, there are no differences in the abbreviations when used to indicate metric verses binary values. In other words, M can be used to indicate both "millions of bytes" and megabytes. In general, memory values are always computed using the binary derived meanings, while disk capacity goes either way. Unfortunately, this often leads to confusion in reporting disk capacities.

Hard Drive Advancements

In the 15 or more years that hard disks have commonly been used in PC systems, they have undergone tremendous changes. To give you an idea of how far hard drives have come in that time, following are some of the most profound changes in PC hard disk storage:

- Maximum storage capacities have increased from the 10M 5 1/4-inch full-height drives available in 1982 to 10G or more for small 3 1/2-inch half-height drives, and 3G or more for notebook 2 1/2-inch drives.

- Data transfer rates from the media have increased from 85 to 102K/sec for the original IBM XT in 1983 to nearly 10M/sec for some of the fastest drives today.

- Average seek times have decreased from more than 85 ms (milliseconds) for the 10M XT hard disk in 1983 to fewer than 8 ms for some of the fastest drives today.

- In 1982, a 10M drive cost more than $1,500 ($150 per megabyte). Today, the cost of hard drives has dropped to 10 cents per megabyte or less.

Areal Density

Areal density has been used as a primary technology-growth-rate indicator for the hard disk drive industry. *Areal density* is defined as the product of the linear bits per inch (BPI), measured along the length of the tracks around the disk, multiplied by the number of tracks per inch (TPI) measured radially on the disk. The results are expressed in units of Mbit per square inch (Mbit/sq-inch) and are used as a measure of efficiency in drive recording technology. Current high-end 2.5-inch drives record at areal densities of about 1.5Gbit per square inch (Gbit/sq-inch). Prototype drives with densities as high as 10Gbit/sq-inch have been constructed, allowing for capacities of more than 20G on a single 2 1/2-inch platter for notebook drives.

Areal density (and, therefore, drive capacity) has been doubling approximately every two to three years, and production disk drives are likely to reach areal densities of 10+Gbit/sq-inch before the year 2000. A drive built with this technology would be capable of storing more than 10G of data on a single 2 1/2-inch platter, allowing 20 or 30G drives to be constructed that fit in the palm of your hand. New media and head technologies, such as ceramic or glass platters, MR (Magneto-Resistive) heads, pseudo-contact recording, and PRML (Partial Response Maximum Likelihood) electronics, are being developed to support these higher areal densities. The primary challenge in achieving higher densities is manufacturing drive heads and disks to operate at closer tolerances.

It seems almost incredible that computer technology improves by doubling performance or capacity every two to three years—if only other industries could match that growth and improvement rate!

Hard Disk Drive Operation

The basic physical operation of a hard disk drive is similar to that of a floppy disk drive: A hard drive uses spinning disks with heads that move over the disks and store data in tracks and sectors. A *track* is a concentric ring of information, which is divided into individual sectors that normally store 512 bytes each. In many other ways, however, hard disk drives are different from floppy disk drives.

Hard disks usually have multiple platters, each with two sides on which data can be stored. Most drives have at least two or three platters, resulting in four or six sides, and some drives have up to 11 or more platters. The identically positioned tracks on each side of every platter together make up a *cylinder*. A hard disk drive normally has one head per platter side, and all the heads are mounted on a common carrier device, or *rack*. The heads move in and out across the disk in unison; they cannot move independently because they are mounted on the same rack.

Hard disks operate much faster than floppy drives. Most hard disks originally spun at 3,600 RPM—approximately 10 times faster than a floppy drive. Until recently, 3,600 RPM was pretty much a constant among hard drives. Now, however, quite a few hard drives spin even faster. The Toshiba 3.3G drive in my notebook computer spins at 4,852 RPM; other drives spin as fast as 5,400, 5,600, 6,400, 7,200 and even 10,000 RPM. High rotational speed combined with a fast head-positioning mechanism and more sectors per track make one hard disk faster than another, and all these features combine to make hard drives much faster than floppy drives in storing and retrieving data.

The heads in most hard disks do not (and should not!) touch the platters during normal operation. When the heads are powered off, however, they land on the platters as they stop spinning. While the drive is on, a very thin cushion of air keeps each head suspended a short distance above or below the platter. If the air cushion is disturbed by a particle of dust or a shock, the head may come into contact with the platter spinning at full speed. When contact with the spinning platters is forceful enough to do damage, the event is called a *head crash*. The result of a head crash may be anything from a few lost bytes of data to a totally trashed drive. Most drives have special lubricants on the platters and hardened surfaces that can withstand the daily "takeoffs and landings" as well as more severe abuse.

Because the platter assemblies are sealed and non-removable, track densities can be very high. Many drives have 3,000 or more TPI of media. *Head Disk Assemblies (HDAs)*, which contain the platters, are assembled and sealed in clean rooms under absolutely sanitary conditions. Because few companies repair HDAs, repair or replacement of items inside a sealed HDA can be expensive. Every hard disk ever made will eventually fail. The only questions are when the hard disk will fail and whether your data is backed up.

Many PC users think that hard disks are fragile, and generally, they are one of the most fragile components in your PC. In my weekly PC Hardware and Troubleshooting or Data Recovery seminars, however, I have run various hard disks for days with the lids off, and have even removed and installed the covers while the drives were operating. Those drives continue to store data perfectly to this day with the lids either on or off. Of course, I do not recommend that you try this test with your own drives; neither would I use this test on my larger, more expensive drives.

The Ultimate Hard Disk Drive Analogy
I'm sure that you have heard the traditional analogy that compares the interaction of the head and media in a typical hard disk as being similar in scale to a 747 flying a few feet off the ground at cruising speed (500+ mph). I have heard this analogy used over and over again for years, and I've even used it in my seminars many times without checking to see whether the analogy is technically accurate with respect to modern hard drives.

One highly inaccurate aspect of the 747 analogy has always bothered me—the use of an airplane of any type to describe the head-and-platter interaction. This analogy implies that the heads fly very low over the surface of the disk—but technically, this is not true. The heads do not fly at all, in the traditional aerodynamic sense; instead, they float on a cushion of air that's dragged around by the platters.

A much better analogy would use a hovercraft instead of an airplane; the action of a hovercraft much more closely emulates the action of the heads in a hard disk drive. Like a hovercraft, the drive heads rely somewhat on the shape of the bottom of the head to capture and control the cushion of air that keeps them floating over the disk. By nature, the cushion of air on which the heads float forms only in very close proximity to the platter and is often called an *air bearing* by the disk drive industry.

I thought it was time to come up with a new analogy that more correctly describes the dimensions and speeds at which a hard disk operates today. I looked up the specifications on a specific hard disk drive, and then equally magnified and rescaled all the dimensions involved to make the head floating height equal to 1 inch. For my example, I used a Seagate model ST-12550N Barracuda 2 drive, which is a 2G (formatted capacity), 3 1/2-inch SCSI-2 drive. In fact, I originally intended to install this drive in the portable system on which I am writing this book, but the technology took another leap and I ended up installing an ST-15230N Hawk 4 drive (4G) instead! Table 14.2 shows the specifications of the Barracuda drive, as listed in the technical documentation.

Table 14.2. Seagate ST-12550N Barracuda 2, 3 1/2-inch, SCSI-2 Drive Specifications

Specification	Value	Unit of Measure
Linear density	52,187	Bits Per Inch (BPI)
Bit spacing	19.16	Micro-inches (u-in)
Track density	3,047	Tracks Per Inch (TPI)
Track spacing	328.19	Micro-inches (u-in)
Total tracks	2,707	Tracks
Rotational speed	7,200	Revolutions per minute(RPM)
Average head linear speed	53.55	Miles per hour (MPH)
Head slider length	0.08	Inches
Head slider height	0.02	Inches
Head floating height	5	Micro-inches (u-in)
Average seek time	8	Milliseconds (ms)

By interpreting these specifications, you can see that in this drive, the head sliders are about 0.08-inch long and 0.02-inch high. The heads float on a cushion of air about 5 u-in (millionths of an inch) from the surface of the disk while traveling at an average speed of 53.55 MPH (figuring an average track diameter of 2 1/2 inches). These heads read and write individual bits spaced only 19.16 u-in apart on tracks separated by only 328.19 u-in. The heads can move from one track to any other in only 8ms during an average seek operation.

To create my analogy, I simply magnified the scale to make the floating height equal to 1 inch. Because 1 inch is 200,000 times greater than 5 u-in, I scaled up everything else by the same amount.

The heads of this "typical" hard disk, magnified to such a scale, would be more than 1,300 feet long and 300 feet high (about the size of the Sears Tower, lying sideways!), traveling at a speed of more than 10.7 million MPH (2,975 miles per second!) only 1 inch above the ground, reading data bits spaced a mere 3.83 inches apart on tracks separated by only 5.47 feet.

Additionally, because the average seek of 8ms (.008 seconds) is defined as the time it takes to move the heads over one-third of the total tracks (about 902, in this case), each skyscraper-size head could move sideways to any track within a distance of 0.93 miles (902 tracks×5.47 feet) which results in an average sideways velocity of more than 420,000 MPH (116 miles per second)!

The forward speed of this imaginary head is difficult to comprehend, so I'll elaborate. The diameter of the Earth at the equator is 7,926 miles, which means a circumference of about 24,900 miles. At 2,975 miles per second, this imaginary head would circle the Earth about once every 8 seconds!

This analogy should give you a new appreciation of the technological marvel that the modern hard disk drive actually represents. It makes the 747 analogy look rather pathetic (not to mention totally inaccurate), doesn't it?

Magnetic Data Storage
Learning how magnetic data storage works will help you develop a feel for the way that your disk drives operate and can improve the way that you work with disk drives and disks.

Nearly all disk drives in personal computer systems operate on magnetic principles. Purely optical disk drives often are used as a secondary form of storage, but the computer to which they are connected is likely to use a magnetic storage medium for primary disk storage. Due to the high performance and density capabilities of magnetic storage, optical disk drives and media probably never will totally replace magnetic storage in PC systems.

Magnetic drives, such as floppy and hard disk drives, operate by using *electromagnetism*. This basic principle of physics states that as an electric current flows through a conductor, a magnetic field is generated around the conductor. This magnetic field then can influence magnetic material in the field. When the direction of the flow of electric current is reversed, the magnetic field's polarity also is reversed. An electric motor uses electromagnetism to exert pushing and pulling forces on magnets attached to a rotating shaft.

Another effect of electromagnetism is that if a conductor is passed through a changing magnetic field, an electrical current is generated. As the polarity of the magnetic field changes, so does the direction of the electric current flow. For example, a type of electrical generator used in automobiles, called an *alternator*, operates by rotating electromagnets past coils of wire conductors in which large amounts of electrical current can be induced. The two-way operation of electromagnetism makes it possible to record data on a disk and read that data back later.

The read/write heads in your disk drives (both floppy and hard disks) are U-shaped pieces of conductive material. This U-shaped object is wrapped with coils of wire, through which an electric current can flow. When the disk drive logic passes a current through these coils, it generates a magnetic field in the drive head. When the polarity of the electric current is reversed, the polarity of the field that is generated also changes. In essence, the heads are electromagnets whose voltage can be switched in polarity very quickly.

When a magnetic field is generated in the head, the field jumps the gap at the end of the U-shaped head. Because a magnetic field passes through a conductor much more easily than through the air, the field bends outward through the medium and actually uses the disk media directly below it as the path of least resistance to the other side of the gap. As the field passes through the media directly under the gap, it polarizes the magnetic particles through which it passes so that they are aligned with the field. The field's polarity—and, therefore, the polarity of the magnetic media—is based on the direction of the flow of electric current through the coils.

The disk consists of some form of substrate material (such as Mylar for floppy disks or aluminum or glass for hard disks) on which a layer of magnetizable material has been deposited. This material usually is a form of iron oxide with various other elements added. The polarities of the magnetic fields of the individual magnetic particles on an erased disk normally are in a state of random disarray. Because the fields of the individual particles point in random directions, each tiny magnetic field is canceled by one that points in the opposite direction, for a total effect of no observable or cumulative field polarity.

Particles in the area below the head gap are aligned in the same direction as the field emanating from the gap. When the individual magnetic domains are in alignment, they no longer cancel one another, and an observable magnetic field exists in that region of the disk. This local field is generated by the many magnetic particles that now are operating as a team to produce a detectable cumulative field with a unified direction.

The term *flux* describes a magnetic field that has a specific direction. As the disk surface rotates below the drive head, the head can lay a magnetic flux over a region of the disk. When the electric-current flowing through the coils in the head is reversed, so is the magnetic-field polarity in the head gap. This reversal also causes the polarity of the flux being placed on the disk to reverse.

The *flux reversal* or *flux transition* is a change in polarity of the alignment of magnetic particles on the disk surface. A drive head places flux reversals on a disk to record data. For each data bit (or bits) written, a pattern of flux reversals is placed on the disk in specific areas known as bit or transition cells. A *bit cell* or *transition cell* is a specific area of the disk controlled by the time and rotational speed in which flux reversals are placed by a drive head. The particular pattern of flux reversals within the transition cells used to store a given data bit or bits is called the *encoding method*. The drive logic or controller takes the data to be stored and encodes it as a series of flux reversals over a period of time, according to the encoding method used.

Modified Frequency Modulation (MFM) and *Run Length Limited (RLL)* are popular encoding methods. All floppy disk drives use the MFM scheme. Hard disks use MFM or several variations of RLL encoding methods. These encoding methods are described in more detail later in the section "MFM Encoding" later in this chapter.

During the write process, voltage is applied to the head, and as the polarity of this voltage changes, the polarity of the magnetic field being recorded also changes. The flux transitions are written precisely at the points where the recording polarity changes.

Strange as it may seem, during the read process, a head does not output exactly the same signal that was written; instead, the head generates a voltage pulse or spike only when it crosses a flux transition. When the transition changes from positive to negative, the pulse that the head would detect is negative voltage. When the transition changes from negative to positive, the pulse would be a positive voltage spike.

In essence, while reading the disk the head becomes a flux transition detector, emitting voltage pulses whenever it crosses a transition. Areas of no transition generate no pulse. Figure 14.1 shows the relationship between the read and write waveforms and the flux transitions recorded on a disk.

FIG. 14.1 Magnetic write and read processes.

You can think of the write pattern as being a square waveform that is at a positive or negative voltage level and that continuously polarizes the disk media in one direction or another. Where the waveform transitions go from positive to negative voltage, or vice versa, the magnetic flux on the disk also changes polarity. During a read, the head senses the flux transitions and outputs a pulsed waveform. In other words, the signal is zero volts unless a positive or negative transition is being detected, in which case there is a positive or negative pulse. Pulses appear only when the head is passing over flux transitions on the disk media. By knowing the clock timing used, the drive or controller circuitry can determine whether a pulse (and therefore a flux transition) falls within a given transition cell.

The electrical pulse currents generated in the head while it is passing over a disk in read mode are very weak and can contain significant noise. Sensitive electronics in the drive and controller assembly then can amplify the signal above the noise level and decode the train of weak pulse currents back into data that is (theoretically) identical to the data originally recorded.

So as you now can see, disks are both recorded and read by means of basic electromagnetic principles. Data is recorded on a disk by passing electrical currents through an electromagnet (the drive head) that generates a magnetic field stored on the disk. Data on a disk is read by passing the head back over the surface of the disk; as the head encounters changes in the stored magnetic field, it generates a weak electrical current that indicates the presence or absence of flux transitions in the originally recorded signal.

Data Encoding Schemes

Magnetic media essentially is an analog storage medium. The data that we store on it, however, is digital information—that is, ones and zeros. When digital information is applied to a magnetic recording head, the head creates magnetic domains on the disk media with specific polarities. When a positive current is applied to the write head, the magnetic domains are polarized in one direction; when negative voltage is applied, the magnetic domains are polarized in the opposite direction. When the digital waveform that is recorded switches from a positive to a negative voltage, the polarity of the magnetic domains is reversed.

During a readback, the head actually generates no voltage signal when it encounters a group of magnetic domains with the same polarity, but it generates a voltage pulse every time it detects a switch in polarity. Each *flux reversal* generates a voltage pulse in the read head; it is these pulses that the drive detects when reading data. A read head does not generate the same waveform that was written; instead, it generates a series of pulses, each pulse appearing where a magnetic flux transition has occurred.

To optimize the placement of pulses during magnetic storage, the raw digital input data is passed through a device called an *encoder/decoder (endec)*, which converts the raw binary information to a waveform that is more concerned with the optimum placement of the flux transitions (pulses). During a read operation, the endec reverses the process and decodes the pulse train back into the original binary data. Over the years, several different schemes for encoding data in this manner have been developed; some are better or more efficient than others.

In any consideration of binary information, the use of timing is important. When interpreting a read or write waveform, the timing of each voltage transition event is critical. If the timing is off, a given voltage transition may be recognized at the wrong time, and bits may be missed, added, or simply misinterpreted. To ensure that the timing is precise, the transmitting and receiving devices must be in sync. This synchronization can be accomplished by adding a separate line for timing, called a *clock signal*, between the two devices. The clock and data signals also can be combined and then transmitted on a single line. This combination of clock and data is used in most magnetic data encoding schemes.

When the clock information is added in with the data, timing accuracy in interpreting the individual bit cells is ensured between any two devices. Clock timing is used to determine the start and end of each bit cell. Each bit cell is bounded by two clock cells where the clock transitions can be sent. First there is a clock transition cell, and then the data transition cell, and finally the clock transition cell for the data that follows. By sending clock information along with the data, the clocks will remain in sync, even if a long string of 0 bits are transmitted. Unfortunately, all the transition cells that are used solely for clocking take up space on the media that otherwise could be used for data.

Because the number of flux transitions that can be recorded on a particular medium is limited by the disk media and head technology, disk drive engineers have been trying various ways of encoding the data into a minimum number of flux reversals, taking into consideration the fact that some flux reversals, used solely for clocking, are required. This method permits maximum use of a given drive hardware technology.

Although various encoding schemes have been tried, only a few are popular today. Over the years, these three basic types have been the most popular:

- Frequency Modulation (FM)
- Modified Frequency Modulation (MFM)
- Run Length Limited (RLL)

The following section examines these codes, discusses how they work, where they have been used, and any advantages or disadvantages that apply to them.

FM Encoding. One of the earliest techniques for encoding data for magnetic storage is called *Frequency Modulation (FM)* encoding. This encoding scheme, sometimes called *Single Density encoding*, was used in the earliest floppy disk drives that were installed in PC systems. The original Osborne portable computer, for example, used these Single Density floppy drives, which stored about 80K of data on a single disk. Although it was popular until the late 1970s, FM encoding no longer is used today.

MFM Encoding. *Modified Frequency Modulation (MFM)* encoding was devised to reduce the number of flux reversals used in the original FM encoding scheme and, therefore, to pack more data onto the disk. In MFM encoding, the use of the clock transition cells is minimized, leaving more room for the data. Clock transitions are recorded only if a stored 0 bit is preceded by another 0 bit; in all other cases, a clock transition is not required. Because the use of the clock transitions has been minimized, the actual clock frequency can be doubled from FM encoding, resulting in twice as many data bits being stored in the same number of flux transitions as in FM.

Because it is twice as efficient as FM encoding, MFM encoding also has been called *Double Density recording*. MFM is used in virtually all PC floppy drives today and was used in nearly all PC hard disks for a number of years. Today, most hard disks use RLL (Run Length Limited) encoding, which provides even greater efficiency than MFM.

Because MFM encoding places twice as many data bits in the same number of flux reversals as FM, the clock speed of the data is doubled, so that the drive actually sees the same number of total flux reversals as with FM. This means that data is read and written at twice the speed in MFM encoding, even though the drive sees the flux reversals arriving at the same frequency as in FM. This method allows existing drive technology to store twice the data and deliver it twice as fast.

The only caveat is that MFM encoding requires improved disk controller and drive circuitry, because the timing of the flux reversals must be more precise than in FM. As it turned out, these improvements were not difficult to achieve, and MFM encoding became the most popular encoding scheme for many years.

Table 14.3 shows the data bit to flux reversal translation in MFM encoding.

Table 14.3 MFM Data to Flux Transition Encoding

Data Bit Value	Flux Encoding
1	NT
0 preceded by 0	TN
0 preceded by 1	NN

T = Flux transition
N = No flux transition

RLL Encoding. Today's most popular encoding scheme for hard disks, called *RLL (Run Length Limited)*, packs up to 50 percent more information on a given disk than even MFM does and three times as much information as FM. In RLL encoding, groups of bits are taken as a unit and combined to generate specific patterns of flux reversals. By combining the clock and data in these patterns, the clock rate can be further increased while maintaining the same basic distance between the flux transitions on the disk.

IBM invented RLL encoding and first used the method in many of its mainframe disk drives. During the late 1980s, the PC hard disk industry began using RLL encoding schemes to increase the storage capabilities of PC hard disks. Today, virtually every drive on the market uses some form of RLL encoding.

Instead of encoding a single bit, RLL normally encodes a group of data bits at a time. The term *Run Length Limited* is derived from the two primary specifications of these codes, which is the minimum number (the run length) and maximum number (the run limit) of transition cells allowed between two actual flux transitions. Several schemes can be achieved by changing the length and limit parameters, but only two have achieved any real popularity: RLL 2,7 and RLL 1,7.

Even FM and MFM encoding can be expressed as a form of RLL. FM can be called RLL 0,1, because there can be as few as zero and as many as one transition cell separating two flux transitions. MFM can be called RLL 1,3, because as few as one and as many as three transition cells can separate two flux transitions. Although these codes can be expressed in RLL form, it is not common to do so.

RLL 2,7 initially was the most popular RLL variation because it offers a high-density ratio with a transition detection window that is the same relative size as that in MFM. This method allows for high storage density with fairly good reliability. In very high-capacity drives, however, RLL 2,7 did not prove to be reliable enough. Most of today's highest-capacity drives use RLL 1,7 encoding, which offers a density ratio 1.27 times that of MFM and a larger transition detection window relative to MFM. Because of the larger relative window size within which a transition can be detected, RLL 1,7 is a more forgiving and more reliable code; and, forgiveness and reliability are required when media and head technology are being pushed to their limits.

Another little-used RLL variation called *RLL 3,9*—sometimes called *ARLL (Advanced RLL)*—allowed an even higher density ratio than RLL 2,7. Unfortunately, reliability suffered too greatly under the RLL 3,9 scheme; the method was used by only a few controller companies that have all but disappeared.

It is difficult to understand how RLL codes work without looking at an example. Because RLL 2,7 was the most popular form of RLL encoding used with older controllers, I will use it as an example. Even within a given RLL variation such as RLL 2,7 or 1,7, many different flux transition encoding tables can be constructed to show what groups of bits are encoded as what sets of flux transitions. For RLL 2,7 specifically, thousands of different translation tables could be constructed, but for my examples, I will use the endec table used by IBM because it is the most popular variation used.

According to the IBM conversion tables, specific groups of data bits two, three, and four bits long are translated into strings of flux transitions four, six, and eight transition cells long, respectively. The selected transitions coded for a particular bit sequence are designed to ensure that flux transitions do not occur too close together or too far apart.

It is necessary to limit how close two flux transitions can be because of the basically fixed resolution capabilities of the head and disk media. Limiting how far apart these transitions can be ensures that the clocks in the devices remain in sync.

Table 14.4 shows the IBM-developed encoding scheme for 2,7 RLL.

Table 14.4 RLL 2,7 (IBM Endec) Data to Flux Transition Encoding

Data Bit Values	Flux Encoding
10	NTNN
11	TNNN
000	NNNTNN
010	TNNTNN
011	NNTNNN
0010	NNTNNTNN
0011	NNNNTNNN

T = Flux transition
N = No flux transition

In studying this table, you may think that encoding a byte such as 00000001b would be impossible because no combinations of data bit groups fit this byte. Encoding this type of byte is not a problem, however, because the controller does not transmit individual bytes; instead, the controller sends whole sectors, making it possible to encode such a byte simply by including some of the bits in the following byte. The only real problem occurs in the last byte of a sector if additional bits are needed to complete the final group sequence. In these cases, the endec in the controller simply adds excess bits to the end of the last byte. These excess bits are truncated during any reads so that the last byte always is decoded correctly.

Encoding Scheme Comparisons

Figure 14.2 shows an example of the waveform written to store an X ASCII character on a hard disk drive under three different encoding schemes.

FIG. 14.2 ASCII character "X" write waveforms using FM, MFM, and RLL 2,7 encoding.

In each of these encoding-scheme examples, the top line shows the individual data bits (01011000b) in their bit cells separated in time by the clock signal, which is shown as a period (.). Below that line is the actual write waveform, showing the positive and negative voltages as well as voltage transitions that result in the recording of flux transitions. The bottom line shows the transition cells, with T representing a transition cell that contains a flux transition and N representing a transition cell that is empty.

The FM encoding example is easy to explain. Each bit cell has two transition cells: one for the clock information and one for the data itself. All the clock transition cells contain flux transitions, and the data transition cells contain a flux transition only if the data is a 1 bit. No transition at all is used to represent a 0 bit. Starting from the left, the first data bit is 0, which decodes as a flux transition pattern of TN. The next bit is a 1, which decodes as TT. The next bit is 0, which decodes as TN, and so on. Using Table 14.2, you easily can trace the FM encoding pattern to the end of the byte.

The MFM encoding scheme also has clock and data transition cells for each data bit to be recorded. As you can see, however, the clock transition cells carry a flux transition only when a 0 bit is stored after another 0 bit. Starting from the left, the first bit is a 0, and the preceding bit is unknown (assume 0), so the flux transition pattern is TN for that bit. The next bit is a 1, which always decodes to a transition-cell pattern of NT. The next bit is 0, which was preceded by 1, so the pattern stored is NN. Using Table 14.3, you can easily trace the MFM encoding pattern to the end of the byte. You can see that the minimum and maximum number of transition cells between any two flux transitions is one and three, respectively; hence, MFM encoding also can be called RLL 1,3.

The RLL 2,7 pattern is more difficult to see because it relies on encoding groups of bits rather than encoding each bit individually. Starting from the left, the first group that matches the groups listed in Table 14.4 are the first three bits, 010. These bits are translated into a flux transition pattern of TNNTNN. The next two bits, 11, are translated as a group to TNNN; and the final group, 000 bits, is translated to NNNTNN to complete the byte. As you can see in this example, no additional bits were needed to finish the last group.

Notice that the minimum and maximum number of empty transition cells between any two flux transitions in this example are two and six, although a different example could show a maximum of seven empty transition cells. This is where the RLL 2,7 designation comes from. Because even fewer transitions are recorded than in MFM, the clock rate can be further increased to three times that of FM or 1.5 times that of MFM, allowing more data to be stored in the same space on the disk. Notice, however, that the resulting write waveform itself looks exactly like a typical FM or MFM waveform in terms of the number and separation of the flux transitions for a given physical portion of the disk. In other words, the physical minimum and maximum distances between any two flux transitions remain the same in all three of these encoding-scheme examples.

Another new feature in high-end drives involves the disk read circuitry. Read channel circuits using Partial-Response, Maximum-Likelihood (PRML) technology allow disk drive manufacturers to increase the amount of data that can be stored on a disk platter by up to 40 percent. PRML replaces the standard "detect one peak at a time" approach of traditional analog peak-detect read/write channels with digital signal processing. In digital signal processing, noise can be digitally filtered out, allowing flux change pulses to be placed closer together on the platter, achieving greater densities.

I hope that the examinations of these different encoding schemes and how they work have taken some of the mystery out of the way data is recorded on a drive. You can see that although schemes such as MFM and RLL can store more data on a drive, the actual density of the flux transitions remains the same as far as the drive is concerned.

Sectors

A disk track is too large to manage effectively as a single storage unit. Many disk tracks can store 50,000 or more bytes of data, which would be very inefficient for storing small files. For that reason, a disk track is divided into several numbered divisions known as *sectors*. These sectors represent slices of the track.

Different types of disk drives and disks split tracks into different numbers of sectors, depending on the density of the tracks. For example, floppy disk formats use 8 to 36 sectors per track, whereas hard disks usually store data at a higher density and can use 17 to 100 or more sectors per track. Sectors created by standard formatting procedures on PC systems have a capacity of 512 bytes, but this capacity may change in the future.

Sectors are numbered on a track starting with 1, unlike the heads or cylinders which are numbered starting with 0. For example, a 1.44M floppy disk contains 80 cylinders numbered from 0 to 79 and two heads numbered 0 and 1, and each track on each cylinder has 18 sectors numbered from 1 to 18.

When a disk is formatted, additional ID areas are created on the disk for the disk controller to use for sector numbering and identifying the start and end of each sector. These areas precede and follow each sector's data area, which accounts for the difference between a disk's unformatted and formatted capacities. These sector headers, inter-sector gaps, and so on are independent of the operating system, file system, or files stored on the drive. For example, a 4M floppy disk (3 1/2-inch) has a capacity of 2.88M when it is formatted, a 2M floppy has a formatted capacity of 1.44M, and an older 38M hard disk has a capacity of only 32M when it is formatted. Modern IDE and SCSI hard drives are preformatted, so the manufacturers now only advertise formatted capacity. Even so, nearly all drives use some reserved space for managing the data that can be stored on the drive.

Although I have stated that each disk sector is 512 bytes in size, this statement technically is false. Each sector does allow for the storage of 512 bytes of data, but the data area is only a portion of the sector. Each sector on a disk typically occupies 571 bytes of the disk, of which only 512 bytes are usable for user data. The actual number of bytes required for the sector header and trailer can vary from drive to drive, but this figure is typical. A few modern drives now use an ID-less recording which virtually eliminates the storage overhead of the sector header information. In an ID-less recording, virtually all of the space on the track is occupied by data.

You may find it helpful to think of each sector as being a page in a book. In a book, each page contains text, but the entire page is not filled with text; rather, each page has top, bottom, left, and right margins. Information such as chapter titles (track and cylinder numbers) and page numbers (sector numbers) is placed in the margins. The "margin" areas of a sector are created and written to during the disk-formatting process. Formatting also fills the data area of each sector with dummy values. After the disk is formatted, the data area can be altered by normal writing to the disk. The sector header and trailer information cannot be altered during normal write operations unless you reformat the disk.

Each sector on a disk has a *prefix portion*, or header, that identifies the start of the sector and a sector number, as well as a *suffix portion*, or trailer, that contains a *checksum* (which helps ensure the integrity of the data contents). Each sector also contains 512 bytes of data. The data bytes normally are set to some specific value, such as F6h (hex), when the disk is physically (or low-level) formatted. (The following section explains low-level formatting.)

In many cases, a specific pattern of bytes that are considered to be difficult to write are written so as to flush out any marginal sectors. In addition to the gaps within the sectors, gaps exist between sectors on each track and also between tracks; none of these gaps contain usable data space. The prefix, suffix, and gaps account for the lost space between the unformatted capacity of a disk and the formatted capacity.

Table 14.5 shows the format for each track and sector on a typical hard disk with 17 sectors per track.

Table 14.5 Typical 17-Sector/17-Track Disk Sector Format

Bytes	Name	Description
16	POST INDEX GAP	All 4Eh, at the track beginning after the Index mark.

The following sector data (shown between the lines in this table) is repeated 17 times for an MFM encoded track.

Bytes	Name	Description
13	ID VFO LOCK	All 00h; synchronizes the VFO for the sector ID.
1	SYNC BYTE	A1h; notifies the controller that data follows.
1	ADDRESS MARK	FEh; defines that ID field data follows.
2	CYLINDER NUMBER	A value that defines the actuator position.
1	HEAD NUMBER	A value that defines the head selected.
1	SECTOR NUMBER	A value that defines the sector.
2	CRC	Cyclic Redundancy Check to verify ID data.
3	WRITE TURN-ON GAP	00h written by format to isolate the ID from DATA.
13	DATA SYNC VFO LOCK	All 00h; synchronizes the VFO for the DATA.
1	SYNC BYTE	A1h; notifies the controller that data follows.
1	ADDRESS MARK	F8h; defines that user DATA field follows.
512	DATA	The area for user DATA.
2	CRC	Cyclic Redundancy Check to verify DATA.
3	WRITE TURN-OFF GAP	00h; written by DATA update to isolate DATA.
15	INTER-RECORD GAP	All 00h; a buffer for spindle speed variation.
693	PRE-INDEX GAP	All 4Eh, at track end before Index mark.

571 Total bytes per sector
512 Data bytes per sector
10,416 Total bytes per track
8,704 Data bytes per track

This table refers to a hard disk track with 17 sectors. Although this capacity was typical during the mid 1980s, modern hard disks place as many as 150 or more sectors per track, and the specific formats of those sectors may vary slightly from the example.

As you can see, the usable space on each track is about 16 percent less than the unformatted capacity. This example is true for most disks, although some may vary slightly.

The Post Index Gap provides a head-switching recovery period so that when switching from one track to another, sequential sectors can be read without waiting for an additional revolution of the disk. In some drives this time is not enough; additional time can be added by skewing the sectors on different tracks so that the arrival of the first sector is delayed.

The Sector ID data consists of the Cylinder, Head, and Sector Number fields, as well as a CRC field to allow for verification of the ID data. Most controllers use bit 7 of the Head Number field to mark the sector as bad during a low-level format or surface analysis. This system is not absolute, however; some controllers use other methods to indicate a marked bad sector. Usually, though, the mark involves one of the ID fields.

Write Turn on Gap follows the ID field CRC bytes and provides a pad to ensure a proper recording of the following user data area as well as to allow full recovery of the ID CRC.

The user Data field consists of all 512 bytes of data stored in the sector. This field is followed by a CRC field to verify the data. Although many controllers use two bytes of CRC here, the controller may implement a longer Error Correction Code (ECC) that requires more than two CRC bytes to store. The ECC data stored here provide the possibility of Data-field read correction as well as read error detection. The correction/detection capabilities depend on the ECC code chosen and on the controller implementation. A Write Turn-Off Gap is a pad to allow the ECC (CRC) bytes to be fully recovered.

The Inter-Record Gap provides a means to accommodate variances in drive spindle speeds. A track may have been formatted while the disk was running slower than normal and then write-updated while the disk was running faster than normal. In such cases, this gap prevents accidental overwriting of any information in the next sector. The actual size of this padding varies, depending on the speed of disk rotation when the track was formatted and each time the Data field is updated.

The Pre-Index Gap allows for speed tolerance over the entire track. This gap varies in size, depending on the variances in disk-rotation speed and write-frequency tolerance at the time of formatting.

This sector prefix information is extremely important, because it contains the numbering information that defines the cylinder, head, and sector. All this information except the Data field, Data CRC bytes, and Write Turn-Off Gap is written only during a low-level format. On a typical non-servo-guided (stepper-motor actuator) hard disk on which thermal gradients cause mistracking, the data updates that rewrite the 512-byte Data area and the CRC that follows may not be placed exactly in line with the sector header information. This situation eventually causes read or write failures of the Abort, Retry, Fail, Ignore variety. You can often correct this problem by redoing the Low Level Formatting (LLF) of the disk; this process rewrites the header and data information together at the current track positions. Then, when you restore the data to the disk, the Data areas are written in alignment with the new sector headers.

Disk Formatting. You usually have two types of formats to consider:

- Physical, or *low-level*
- Logical, or *high-level*

When you format a floppy disk, the DOS FORMAT command performs both kinds of formats simultaneously. To format a hard disk, however, you must perform the operations separately. Moreover, a hard disk requires a third step, between the two formats, in which the partitioning information is written to the disk. *Partitioning* is required because a hard disk is designed to be used with more than one operating system. Separating the physical format in a way that is always the same, regardless of the operating system being used and regardless of the high-level format (which would be different for each operating system), makes possible the use of multiple operating systems on one hard drive. The partitioning step allows more than one type of operating system to use a single hard disk or a single DOS to use the disk as several volumes or logical drives. A *volume* or *logical drive* is anything to which DOS assigns a drive letter.

Consequently, formatting a hard disk involves three steps:

1. Low-Level Formatting (LLF)
2. Partitioning
3. High-Level Formatting (HLF)

During a low-level format, the disk's tracks are divided into a specific number of sectors. The sector header and trailer information is recorded, as are intersector and intertrack gaps. Each sector's data area is filled with a dummy byte value or test pattern of values. For floppy disks, the number of sectors recorded on each track depends on the type of disk and drive; for hard disks, the number of sectors per track depends on the drive and controller interface.

The original ST-506/412 MFM controllers always placed 17 sectors per track on a disk. ST-506/412 controllers with RLL encoding increase the number of sectors on a drive to 25 or 26 sectors per track. ESDI drives can have 32 or more sectors per track. IDE drives simply are drives with built-in controllers, and depending on exactly what type of controller design is built in, the number of sectors per track can range from 17 to 100 or more. SCSI drives essentially are the same as IDE drives internally with an added SCSI Bus Adapter circuit, meaning that they also have some type of built-in controller; and like IDE drives, SCSI drives can have practically any number of sectors per track, depending on what controller design was used.

Virtually all IDE and SCSI drives use a technique called *Zoned Recording*, which writes a variable number of sectors per track. The outermost tracks hold more sectors than the inner tracks do, because they are longer. Because of limitations in the PC BIOS, these drives still have to act as though they have a fixed number of sectors per track. This situation is handled by translation algorithms that are implemented in the controller.

Multiple Zone Recording. One way to increase the capacity of a hard drive is to format more sectors on the outer cylinders than on the inner ones. Because they have a larger circumference, the outer cylinders can hold more data. Drives without Zoned Recording store the same amount of data on every cylinder, even though the outer cylinders may be twice as long as the inner cylinders. The result is wasted storage capacity, because the disk media must be capable of storing data reliably at the same density as on the inner cylinders. With older ST-506/412 and ESDI controllers, unfortunately, the number of sectors per track was fixed; drive capacity, therefore, was limited by the density capability of the innermost (shortest) track.

In a Zoned Recording, the cylinders are split into groups called *zones*, with each successive zone having more and more sectors per track as you move out from the inner radius of the disk. All the cylinders in a particular zone have the same number of sectors per track. The number of zones varies with specific drives, but most drives have 10 or more zones.

Another effect of Zoned Recording is that transfer speeds vary depending on what zone the heads are in. Because there are more sectors in the outer zones, and the rotational speed is always the same, the transfer rate will be highest.

Drives with separate controllers could not handle zoned recordings because there was no standard way to communicate information about the zones from the drive to the controller. With SCSI and IDE disks, it became possible to format individual tracks with different numbers of sectors, due to the fact that these drives have the disk controller built in. The built-in controllers on these drives can be made fully aware of the zoning that is used. These built-in controllers must then also translate the physical Cylinder, Head, and Sector numbers to logical Cylinder, Head, and Sector numbers so that the drive has the appearance of having the same number of sectors on each track. The PC BIOS was designed to handle only a single number of specific sectors per track throughout the entire drive, meaning that zoned drives always must run under a sector translation scheme.

The use of Zoned Recording has allowed drive manufacturers to increase the capacity of their hard drives by between 20 percent and 50 percent compared with a fixed-sector-per-track arrangement. Virtually all IDE and SCSI drives today use Zoned Recording.

Partitioning. Partitioning segments the drive into areas, called *partitions*, that can hold a particular operating system's file system. Today, PC operating systems use four common file systems:

- *FAT (File Allocation Table)*. The standard file system used by DOS, Windows 95 (Non-OSR2 release), OS/2, and Windows NT. FAT partitions support file names of 11 characters maximum (8+3 character extension) under DOS, and 255 characters under Windows 95 or NT 4.0 or later versions. Under the standard FAT system, 12-bit or 16-bit numbers are used to identify allocation units, resulting in a maximum volume size of 2G.

- *FAT32 (File Allocation Table, 32-bit)*. An optional file system used by Windows 95 OSR2 (also called OEM Service Release 2 or Windows 95B) or later versions. Under FAT32, file allocation units are stored as 32-bit numbers, allowing for a single volume of 2T or 2,048G in size. FAT-32 support will likely be added to Windows NT in the future.

- *HPFS (High Performance File System)*. A file system that's accessible only under OS/2 and Windows NT 3.51 or earlier. DOS applications running under OS/2 or Windows NT, or via a network, can access files in HPFS partitions, but straight DOS cannot. File names can be 256 characters long, and volume size is limited to 8G.

- *NTFS (Windows NT File System)*. A UNIX-like file system that's accessible only under Windows NT. DOS cannot access these partitions, but DOS applications running under Windows NT or accessing a Windows NT volume from the network can. File names can be 256 characters long, and volume size is limited to 8G.

Of these four file systems, the FAT file system still is by far the most popular (and recommended). The main problem with the original 16-bit FAT file system is that disk space is used in groups of sectors called *allocation units* or *clusters*. Because the total number of clusters is limited to 65,536 (the most that can be represented with a 16-bit number), larger drives required that the disk be broken into larger clusters. The larger cluster sizes required cause disk space to be used inefficiently. FAT-32 solves this problem by allowing the disk to be broken up into over 4 billion clusters, so the cluster sizes can be kept smaller. Most FAT-32 and NTFS volumes use 4K clusters.

The term *cluster* was changed to *allocation unit* in DOS 4.0 and later versions. The newer term is appropriate because a single cluster is the smallest unit of the disk that DOS can allocate when it writes a file. A cluster is equal to one or more sectors, and although a cluster can be a single sector in some cases (specifically 1.2M and 1.44M floppies), it is usually more than one. Having more than one sector per cluster reduces the size and processing overhead of the FAT and enables DOS to run faster because it has fewer individual units of the disk to manage. The tradeoff is in wasted disk space. Because DOS and Windows can manage space only in full cluster units, every file consumes space on the disk in increments of one cluster.

Smaller clusters generate less slack (space wasted between the actual end of each file and the end of the cluster). With larger clusters, the wasted space grows larger. For hard disks, the cluster size varies with the size of the partition. Table 14.6 shows the default cluster sizes FDISK selects for a particular partition volume size.

Table 14.6 Default Cluster Sizes

Hard Disk Partition Size	Cluster (Allocation Unit) Size	FAT Type
0–15M	8 sectors or 4,096 (4K) bytes	12-bit
16–128M	4 sectors or 2,048 (2K) bytes	16-bit
129–256M	8 sectors or 4,096 (4K) bytes	16-bit
257–512M	16 sectors or 8,192 (8K) bytes	16-bit
513–1,024M	32 sectors or 16,384 (16K) bytes	16-bit
1,025–2,048M	64 sectors or 32,768 (32K) bytes	16-bit
0–260M	1 sector or 512 bytes	32-bit
260M–8G	8 sectors or 4,096 (4K) bytes	32-bit
8–16G	16 sectors or 8,192 (8K) bytes	32-bit
16–32G	32 sectors or 16,384 (16K) bytes	32-bit
32–2,048G	64 sectors or 32,768 (32K) bytes	32-bit

In most cases, these cluster sizes, which are selected by the FORMAT command, are the minimum possible for a given partition size. Therefore, 8K clusters are the smallest possible for a partition size greater than 256M. Note that FDISK creates a FAT using 12-bit numbers if the partition is 16M or less, while all other FATs are created using 16-bit numbers, unless Large Disk Support is specifically enabled in Windows 95 OSR2 or later.

The effect of the larger cluster sizes on larger disk partitions can be substantial. There can be a significant amount of slack space in the leftover portions of larger clusters. On average the amount of slack space for a file is one half of the space of the last cluster the file uses. To calculate an estimate of slack space on an entire drive, use the following formula:

slack space = #_files * cluster_size / 2

A drive partition of over 1G and up to 2G using FAT16 (thus 32K clusters) containing 10,000 files wastes about 16K per file or 160,000K (160M) total [10000*32K/2]. If you were to repartition the drive into two separate partitions of less than or equal to 1G each, then the cluster size would be cut in half, as would the total wasted slack space. You would therefore gain 80M of disk space. The tradeoff is that managing multiple partitions is not as convenient as a single large partition. The only way you can control cluster or allocation unit sizing using FAT16 is by changing the sizes of the partitions.

If you were to reformat the drive using FAT32, then the wasted space would drop to only 2K per file or about 20M total! In other words, by converting to FAT32, you would end up with approximately 140M more disk space free in this example.

NTFS, HPFS, and FAT32 all dramatically reduce the slack space but also increase file management overhead because many more allocation units must be managed.

Despite the problem with slack space, the basic FAT file system is still often the most recommended for compatibility reasons. All the operating systems can access FAT volumes, and the file structures and data-recovery procedures are well known. Also note that data recovery can be difficult to impossible under the HPFS and NTFS systems; for those systems, good backups are imperative.

During partitioning, no matter what file system is specified, the partitioning software writes a special boot program and partition table to the first sector, called the Master Boot Sector (MBS). Because the term *record* sometimes is used to mean *sector*, this sector can also be called the Master Boot Record (MBR).

High-Level Format. During the high-level format, the operating system (such as DOS, OS/2, or Windows) writes the structures necessary for managing files and data. FAT partitions have a Volume Boot Sector (VBS), a file allocation table (FAT), and a root directory on each formatted logical drive. These data structures (discussed in detail in Chapter 22, "Operating Systems Software and Troubleshooting") enable the operating system to manage the space on the disk, keep track of files, and even manage defective areas so that they do not cause problems.

High-level formatting is not really formatting, but creating a table of contents for the disk. In low-level formatting, which is the real formatting, tracks and sectors are written on the disk. As mentioned, the DOS FORMAT command can perform both low-level and high-level format operations on a floppy disk, but it performs only the high-level format for a hard disk. Hard disk low-level formats require a special utility, usually supplied by the disk-controller manufacturer.

Basic Hard Disk Drive Components

Many types of hard disks are on the market, but nearly all drives share the same basic physical components. Some differences may exist in the implementation of these components (and in the quality of materials used to make them), but the operational characteristics of most drives are similar. Following are the components of a typical hard disk drive (see Figure 14.3):

- Disk platters
- Read/write heads
- Head actuator mechanism
- Spindle motor
- Logic board
- Cables and connectors
- Configuration items (such as jumpers or switches)
- Bezel (optional)

FIG. 14.3 Hard disk drive components.

The platters, spindle motor, heads, and head actuator mechanisms usually are contained in a sealed chamber called the *Head Disk Assembly (HDA)*. The HDA usually is treated as a single component; it rarely is opened. Other parts external to the drive's HDA—such as the logic boards, bezel, and other configuration or mounting hardware—can be disassembled from the drive.

Hard Disk Platters (Disks)

A typical hard disk has one or more platters, or *disks*. Hard disks for PC systems have been available in a number of form factors over the years. Normally, the physical size of a drive is expressed as the size of the platters. Following are the most common platter sizes used in PC hard disks today:

- 5 1/4-inch (actually 130mm, or 5.12 inches)
- 3 1/2-inch (actually 95mm, or 3.74 inches)
- 2 1/2-inch
- 1.8-inch

Larger hard drives that have 8-inch, 14-inch, or even larger platters are available, but these drives typically have not been associated with PC systems. Currently, the 3 1/2-inch drives are the most popular for desktop and some portable systems, whereas the 2 1/2-inch and smaller drives are very popular in portable or notebook systems. These little drives are fairly amazing, with current capacities of up to 1G or more, and capacities of 20G are expected by the year 2000. Imagine carrying a notebook computer around with a built-in 20G drive; it will happen sooner than you think! Due to their small size, these drives are extremely rugged; they can withstand rough treatment that would have destroyed most desktop drives a few years ago.

Most hard drives have two or more platters, although some of the smaller drives have only one. The number of platters that a drive can have is limited by the drive's physical size vertically. So far, the maximum number of platters that I have seen in any 3 1/2-inch drive is 11.

Platters traditionally have been made from an aluminum alloy, for strength and light weight. With manufacturers' desire for higher and higher densities and smaller drives, many drives now use platters made of glass (or, more technically, a glass-ceramic composite). One such material is called MemCor, which is produced by the Dow Corning Corporation. MemCor is composed of glass with ceramic implants, which resists cracking better than pure glass.

Glass platters offer greater rigidity and therefore can be machined to one-half the thickness of conventional aluminum disks, or less. Glass platters also are much more thermally stable than aluminum platters, which means that they do not change dimensions (expand or contract) very much with any changes in temperature. Several hard disks made by companies such as Seagate, Toshiba, Areal Technology, Maxtor, and Hewlett-Packard currently use glass or glass-ceramic platters. For most manufacturers, glass disks will replace the standard aluminum substrate over the next few years, especially in high-performance 2 1/2- and 3 1/2-inch drives.

Recording Media

No matter what substrate is used, the platters are covered with a thin layer of a magnetically retentive substance called *media* in which magnetic information is stored. Two popular types of media are used on hard disk platters:

- Oxide media
- Thin-film media

Oxide media is made of various compounds, containing iron oxide as the active ingredient. A magnetic layer is created by coating the aluminum platter with a syrup containing iron-oxide particles. This media is spread across the disk by spinning the platters at high speed; centrifugal force causes the material to flow from the center of the platter to the outside, creating an even coating of media material on the platter. The surface then is cured and polished. Finally, a layer of material that protects and lubricates the surface is added and burnished smooth. The oxide media coating normally is about 30 millionths of an inch thick. If you could peer into a drive with oxide-media-coated platters, you would see that the platters are brownish or amber.

As drive density increases, the media needs to be thinner and more perfectly formed. The capabilities of oxide coatings have been exceeded by most higher-capacity drives. Because oxide media is very soft, disks that use this type of media are subject to head-crash damage if the drive is jolted during operation. Most older drives, especially those sold as low-end models, have oxide media on the drive platters. Oxide media, which has been used since 1955, remained popular because of its relatively low cost and ease of application. Today, however, very few drives use oxide media.

Thin-film media is thinner, harder, and more perfectly formed than oxide media. Thin film was developed as a high-performance media that enabled a new generation of drives to have lower head floating heights, which in turn made possible increases in drive density. Originally, thin-film media was used only in higher-capacity or higher-quality drive systems, but today, virtually all drives have thin-film media.

Thin-film media is aptly named. The coating is much thinner than can be achieved by the oxide-coating method. Thin-film media also is known as *plated*, or *sputtered*, media because of the various processes used to place the thin film of media on the platters.

Thin-film plated media is manufactured by placing the media material on the disk with an electroplating mechanism, much the way chrome plating is placed on the bumper of a car. The aluminum platter then is immersed in a series of chemical baths that coat the platter with several layers of metallic film. The media layer is a cobalt alloy about 3 u-in thick.

Thin-film sputtered media is created by first coating the aluminum platters with a layer of nickel phosphorus and then applying the cobalt-alloy magnetic material in a continuous vacuum-deposition process called *sputtering*. During this process, magnetic layers as thin as 1 or 2 u-in are deposited on the disk, in a fashion similar to the way that silicon wafers are coated with metallic films in the semiconductor industry. The sputtering technique then is used again to lay down an extremely hard, 1 u-in protective carbon coating. The need for a near-perfect vacuum makes sputtering the most expensive of the processes described here.

The surface of a sputtered platter contains magnetic layers as thin as 1 u-in. Because this surface also is very smooth, the head can float closer to the disk surface than was possible previously; floating heights as small as 3 u-in above the surface are possible. When the head is closer to the platter, the density of the magnetic flux transitions can be increased to provide greater storage capacity. Additionally, the increased intensity of the magnetic field during a closer-proximity read provides the higher signal amplitudes needed for good signal-to-noise performance.

Both the sputtering and plating processes result in a very thin, very hard film of media on the platters. Because the thin-film media is so hard, it has a better chance of surviving contact with the heads at high speed. In fact, modern thin-film media is virtually uncrashable. Oxide coatings can be scratched or damaged much more easily. If you could open a drive to peek at the platters, you would see that the thin-film media platters look like the silver surfaces of mirrors.

The sputtering process results in the most perfect, thinnest, and hardest disk surface that can be produced commercially. The sputtering process has largely replaced plating as the method of creating thin-film media. Having a thin-film media surface on a drive results in increased storage capacity in a smaller area with fewer head crashes—and in a drive that will provide many years of trouble-free use.

Read/Write Heads

A hard disk drive usually has one read/write head for each platter side, and these heads are connected, or *ganged*, on a single movement mechanism. The heads, therefore, move across the platters in unison.

Mechanically, read/write heads are simple. Each head is on an actuator arm that is spring-loaded to force the head into a platter. Few people realize that each platter actually is "squeezed" by the heads above and below it. If you could open a drive safely and lift the top head with your finger, the head would snap back into the platter when you released it. If you could pull down on one of the heads below a platter, the spring tension would cause it to snap back up into the platter when you released it.

Figure 14.4 shows a typical hard disk head-actuator assembly from a voice coil drive.

FIG. 14.4 Read/write heads and rotary voice coil actuator assembly.

When the drive is at rest, the heads are forced into direct contact with the platters by spring tension, but when the drive is spinning at full speed, air pressure develops below the heads and lifts them off the surface of the platter. On a drive spinning at full speed, the distance between the heads and the platter can be anywhere from 3 to 20 u-in or more.

In the early 1960s, hard disk drive recording heads operated at floating heights as large as 200 to 300 u-in; today's drive heads are designed to float as low as 3 to 5 u-in above the surface of the disk. To support higher densities in future drives, the physical separation between the head and disk is expected to be as little as 0.5 u-in by the end of the century.

> **Caution**
>
> The small size of this gap is why the disk drive's HDA should never be opened except in a clean-room environment: Any particle of dust or dirt that gets into this mechanism could cause the heads to read improperly, or possibly even to strike the platters while the drive is running at full speed. The latter event could scratch the platter or the head.

To ensure the cleanliness of the interior of the drive, the HDA is assembled in a class-100 or better clean room. This specification is such that a cubic foot of air cannot contain more than 100 particles that measure up to 0.5 micron (19.7 u-in). A single person breathing while standing motionless spews out 500 such particles in a single minute! These rooms contain special air-filtration systems that continuously evacuate and refresh the air. A drive's HDA should not be opened unless it is inside such a room.

Although maintaining such an environment may seem to be expensive, many companies manufacture tabletop or bench-size clean rooms that sell for only a few thousand dollars. Some of these devices operate like a glove box; the operator first inserts the drive and any tools required, and then closes the box and turns on the filtration system. Inside the box, a clean-room environment is maintained, and a technician can use the built-in gloves to work on the drive.

In other clean-room variations, the operator stands at a bench where a forced-air curtain is used to maintain a clean environment on the bench top. The technician can walk in and out of the clean-room field simply by walking through the air curtain. This air curtain is much like the curtain of air used in some stores and warehouses to prevent heat from escaping in the winter while leaving a passage wide open.

Because the clean environment is expensive to produce, few companies except those that manufacture the drives are prepared to service hard disk drives.

Read/Write Head Designs

As disk drive technology has evolved, so has the design of the Read/Write head. The earliest heads were simple iron cores with coil windings (electromagnets). By today's standards, the original head designs were enormous in physical size and operated at very low recording densities. Over the years, many different head designs have evolved from the first simple Ferrite Core designs into several types and technologies available today. This section discusses the different types of heads found in PC-type hard disk drives, including the applications and relative strengths and weaknesses of each.

Four types of heads have been used in hard disk drives over the years:

- Ferrite
- Metal-In-Gap (MIG)
- Thin Film (TF)
- Magneto-Resistive (MR)

Ferrite. *Ferrite heads*, the traditional type of magnetic-head design, evolved from the original IBM Winchester drive. These heads have an iron-oxide core wrapped with electromagnetic coils. A magnetic field is produced by energizing the coils; a field also can be induced by passing a magnetic field near the coils. This process gives the heads full read and write capability. Ferrite heads are larger and heavier than thin-film heads and therefore require a larger floating height to prevent contact with the disk.

Many refinements have been made in the original (monolithic) ferrite head design. A type of ferrite head called a *composite ferrite head* has a smaller ferrite core bonded with glass in a ceramic housing. This design permits a smaller head gap, which allows higher track densities. These heads are less susceptible to stray magnetic fields than are heads in the older monolithic design.

During the 1980s, composite ferrite heads were popular in many low-end drives, such as the popular Seagate ST-225. As density demands grew, the competing MIG and thin-film head designs were used in place of ferrite heads, which are virtually obsolete today. Ferrite heads cannot write to the higher coercivity media needed for high-density designs and have poor frequency response with higher noise levels. The main advantage of ferrite heads is that they are the cheapest type available.

Metal-In-Gap. *Metal-In-Gap (MIG) heads* basically are a specially enhanced version of the composite ferrite design. In MIG heads, a metal substance is sputtered into the recording gap on the trailing edge of the head. This material offers increased resistance to magnetic saturation, allowing higher-density recording. MIG heads also produce a sharper gradient in the magnetic field for a better-defined magnetic pulse. These heads permit the use of higher-coercivity thin-film disks and can operate at lower floating heights.

Two versions of MIG heads are available: single-sided and double-sided. Single-sided MIG heads are designed with a layer of magnetic alloy placed along the trailing edge of the gap. Double-sided MIG designs apply the layer to both sides of the gap. The metal alloy is applied through a vacuum-deposition process called *sputtering*. This alloy has twice the magnetization capability of raw ferrite and allows writing to the higher-coercivity thin-film media needed at the higher densities. Double-sided MIG heads offer even higher coercivity capability than the single-sided designs do.

Because of these increases in capabilities through improved designs, MIG heads, for a time, were the most popular head used in all but very high-capacity drives. Due to market pressures that have demanded higher and higher densities, however, MIG heads have been largely displaced in favor of thin-film heads.

Thin Film. *Thin-film (TF) heads* are produced in much the same manner as a semiconductor chip—that is, through a photolithographic process. In this manner, many thousands of heads can be created on a single circular wafer. This manufacturing process also results in a very small high-quality product.

TF heads offer an extremely narrow and controlled head gap created by sputtering a hard aluminum material. Because this material completely encloses the gap, this area is very well protected, minimizing the chance of damage from contact with the media. The core is a combination of iron and nickel alloy that is two to four times more powerful magnetically than a ferrite head core.

TF heads produce a sharply defined magnetic pulse that allows extremely high densities to be written. Because they do not have a conventional coil, TF heads are more immune to variations in coil impedance. The small, lightweight heads can float at a much lower height than the ferrite and MIG heads; floating height has been reduced to 2 u-in or less in some designs. Because the reduced height enables a much stronger signal to be picked up and transmitted between the head and platters, the signal-to-noise ratio increases, which improves accuracy. At the high track and linear densities of some drives, a standard ferrite head would not be able to pick out the data signal from the background noise. When TF heads are used, their small size enables more platters to be stacked in a drive.

Until the past few years, TF heads were relatively expensive compared with older technologies, such as ferrite and MIG. Better manufacturing techniques and the need for higher densities, however, have driven the market to TF heads. The widespread use of these heads also has made them cost-competitive, if not cheaper, than MIG heads.

TF heads currently are used in most high-capacity drives, especially in the smaller form factors. They have displaced MIG heads as the most popular head design being used in drives today. The industry is working on ways to improve TF head efficiency, so TF heads are likely to remain popular for some time, especially in mainstream drives.

Magneto-Resistive. *Magneto-Resistive (MR) heads* are the latest technology. Invented and pioneered by IBM, MR heads currently are the superior head design, offering the highest performance available. Most 3 1/2-inch drives with capacities in excess of 1G currently use MR heads. As areal densities continue to increase, the MR head eventually will become the head of choice for nearly all hard drives, displacing the popular MIG and TF head designs.

MR heads rely on the fact that the resistance of a conductor changes slightly when an external magnetic field is present. Rather than put out a voltage by passing through a magnetic-field flux reversal, as a normal head would, the MR head senses the flux reversal and changes resistance. A small current flows through the heads, and the change in resistance is measured by this sense current. This design enables the output to be three or more times more powerful than a TF head during a read. In effect, MR heads are power-read heads, acting more like sensors than generators.

MR heads are more costly and complex to manufacture than other types of heads, because several special features or steps must be added. Among them:

- Additional wires must be run to and from the head to carry the sense current.
- Four to six more masking steps are required.

- Because MR heads are so sensitive, they are very susceptible to stray magnetic fields and must be shielded.

Because the MR principle can only read data and is not used for writing, MR heads really are two heads in one. A standard inductive TF head is used for writing, and an MR head is used for reading. Because two separate heads are built into one assembly, each head can be optimized for its task. Ferrite, MIG, and TF heads are known as *single-gap heads* because the same gap is used for both reading and writing, whereas the MR head uses a separate gap for each operation.

The problem with single-gap heads is that the gap length always is a compromise between what is best for reading and what is best for writing. The read function needs a thin gap for higher resolution; the write function needs a thicker gap for deeper flux penetration to switch the media. In a dual-gap MR head, the read and write gaps can be optimized for both functions independently. The write (TF) gap writes a wider track than the read (MR) gap does. The read head then is less likely to pick up stray magnetic information from adjacent tracks.

Drives with MR heads require better shielding from stray magnetic fields, which can affect these heads more easily than they do the other head designs. All in all, however, the drawback is minor compared with the advantages that the MR heads offer.

Head Sliders

The term *slider* is used to describe the body of material that supports the actual drive head itself. The slider is what actually floats or slides over the surface of the disk, carrying the head at the correct distance from the media for reading and writing. Most sliders resemble a catamaran, with two outboard pods that float along the surface of the disk media and a central "rudder" portion that actually carries the head and read/write gap.

The trend toward smaller and smaller form factor drives has forced a requirement for smaller and smaller sliders as well. The typical mini-Winchester slider design is about .160×.126×.034 inch in size. Most head manufacturers now are shifting to 50 percent smaller nanosliders, which have dimensions of about .08×.063×.017 inch. The nanoslider is being used in both high-capacity and small-form-factor drives. Smaller sliders reduce the mass carried at the end of the head actuator arms, allowing for increased acceleration and deceleration, and leading to faster seek times. The smaller sliders also require less area for a landing zone, thus increasing the usable area of the disk platters. Further, the smaller slider contact area reduces the slight wear on the media surface that occurs during normal startup and spindown of the drive platters.

The newer nanoslider designs also have specially modified surface patterns that are designed to maintain the same floating height above the disk surface, whether the slider is above the inner or outer cylinders. Conventional sliders increase or decrease their floating height considerably, according to the velocity of the disk surface traveling below them. Above the outer cylinders, the velocity and floating height are higher. This arrangement is undesirable in newer drives that use Zoned Recording, in which the same bit density is achieved on all the cylinders. Because the same bit density is maintained throughout the drive, the head floating height should be relatively constant as well for maximum performance. Special textured surface patterns and manufacturing techniques allow the nanosliders to float at a much more consistent height, making them ideal for Zoned Recording drives.

Head Actuator Mechanisms

Possibly more important than the heads themselves is the mechanical system that moves them: the *head actuator*. This mechanism moves the heads across the disk and positions them accurately above the desired cylinder. Many variations on head actuator mechanisms are in use, but all of them can be categorized as being one of two basic types:

- Stepper motor actuators
- Voice coil actuators

The use of one or the other type of positioner has profound effects on a drive's performance and reliability. The effect is not limited to speed; it also includes accuracy, sensitivity to temperature, position, vibration, and overall reliability. To put it bluntly, a drive equipped with a stepper motor actuator is much less reliable (by a large factor) than a drive equipped with a voice coil actuator.

The head actuator is the single most important specification in the drive. The type of head actuator mechanism in a drive tells you a great deal about the drive's performance and reliability characteristics. Table 14.7 shows the two types of hard disk drive head actuators and the affected performance parameters.

Table 14.7 Characteristics of Stepper Motor versus Voice Coil Drives

Characteristic	Stepper Motor	Voice Coil
Relative access speed	Slow	Fast
Temperature sensitive	Yes (very)	No
Positionally sensitive	Yes	No
Automatic head parking	Not usually	Yes
Preventive maintenance	Periodic format	None required
Relative reliability	Poor	Excellent

Generally, a stepper motor drive has a slow average access rating, is temperature-sensitive during read and write operations, is sensitive to physical orientation during read and write operations, does not automatically park its heads above a save zone during power-down, and usually requires annual or biannual reformats to realign the sector data with the sector header information due to mistracking. Overall, stepper motor drives are vastly inferior to drives that use voice coil actuators.

Some stepper motor drives feature automatic head parking at power-down. If you have a newer stepper motor drive, refer to the drive's technical reference manual to determine whether your drive has this feature. Sometimes, you hear a noise after power-down, but that can be deceptive; some drives use a solenoid-activated spindle brake, which makes a noise as the drive is powered off and does not involve head parking.

Floppy disk drives position their heads by using a stepper motor actuator. The accuracy of the stepper mechanism is suited to a floppy drive, because the track densities usually are nowhere near those of a hard disk. Many of the less expensive, low-capacity hard disks also use a stepper motor system. Most hard disks with capacities of more than 40M have voice coil actuators, as do all drives I have seen that have capacities of more than 100M, which means all drives being manufactured today.

This breakdown does not necessarily apply to other system manufacturers, but it is safe to say that hard disk drives with less than 80M capacity may have either type of actuator and that virtually all drives with more than 80M capacity have voice coil actuators. The cost difference between voice coil drives and stepper motor drives of equal capacity is marginal today, so there is little reason not to use a voice coil drive. No new stepper motor drives are being manufactured today.

Stepper Motor. A *stepper motor* is an electrical motor that can "step," or move from position to position, with mechanical detents or click stop positions. If you were to grip the spindle of one of these motors and spin it by hand, you would hear a clicking or buzzing sound as the motor passed each detent position with a soft click. The sensation is much like that of the volume control on some stereo systems which use a detented type control instead of something smooth and purely linear.

Stepper motors cannot position themselves between step positions; they can stop only at the predetermined detent positions. The motors are small (between 1 and 3 inches) and can be square, cylindrical, or flat. Stepper motors are outside the sealed HDA, although the spindle of the motor penetrates the HDA through a sealed hole. The stepper motor is located in one of the corners of the hard disk drive and usually is easy to see.

Mechanical Links. The stepper motor is mechanically linked to the head rack by a split-steel band coiled around the motor spindle or by a rack-and-pinion gear mechanism. As the motor steps, each detent, or click-stop position, represents the movement of one track through the mechanical linkage.

Some systems use several motor steps for each track. In positioning the heads, if the drive is told to move from track 0 to 100, the motor begins the stepping motion, proceeds to the 101st detent position, and stops, leaving the heads above the desired cylinder. The fatal flaw in this type of positioning system is that due to dimensional changes in the platter-to-head relationship over the life of a drive, the heads may not be precisely placed above the cylinder location. This type of positioning system is called a *blind system*, because the heads have no true way of determining the exact placement of a given cylinder.

Most stepper motor actuator systems use a *split-metal-band mechanism* to transmit the rotary stepping motion to the in-and-out motion of the head rack. The band is made of special alloys to limit thermal expansion and contraction as well as stretching of the thin band. One end of the band is coiled around the spindle of the stepper motor; the other is connected directly to the head rack. The band is inside the sealed HDA and is not visible from outside the drive.

Some drives use a *rack-and-pinion gear mechanism* to link the stepper motor to the head rack. This procedure involves a small pinion gear on the spindle of the stepper motor that moves a rack gear in and out. The rack gear is connected to the head rack, causing it to move. The rack-and-pinion mechanism is more durable than the split-metal-band mechanism and provides slightly greater physical and thermal stability. One problem, however, is *backlash*, or the amount of play in the gears. Backlash increases as the gears wear and eventually renders the mechanism useless.

Temperature Fluctuation Problems. Stepper motor mechanisms are affected by a variety of problems. The greatest problem is temperature. As the drive platters heat and cool, they expand and contract, respectively; the tracks then move in relation to a predetermined track position. The stepper mechanism does not allow the tracks to move in increments of less than a single track to correct for these temperature-induced errors. The drive positions the heads to a particular cylinder according to a predetermined number of steps from the stepper motor, with no room for nuance.

The low-level formatting of the drive places the initial track and sector marks on the platters at the positions where the heads currently are located, as commanded by the stepper motor. If all subsequent reading and writing occurs at the same temperature as the initial format, the heads always record precisely within the track and sector boundaries.

At different temperatures, however, the head position does not match the track position. When the platters are cold, the heads miss the track location because the platters have shrunk and the tracks have moved toward the center of the disk. When the platters are warmer than the formatted temperature, the platters will have grown larger and the track positions are located outward. Gradually, as the drive is used, the data is written inside, on top of, and outside the track and sector marks. Eventually, the drive fails to read one of these locations, and a DOS Abort, Retry, Ignore error message usually appears.

The temperature sensitivity of stepper motor drives also may cause the "Monday morning blues." When the system is powered up cold (on Monday, for example), a 1701, 1790, or 10490 Power-On Self Test (POST) error occurs. If you leave the system on for about 15 minutes, the drive can come up to operating temperature, and the system then may boot normally. This problem sometimes occurs in reverse when the drive gets particularly warm, such as when a system is in direct sunlight or during the afternoon, when room temperature is highest. In that case, the symptom is a DOS error message with the familiar Abort, Retry, Ignore prompt.

Temperature-induced mistracking problems can be solved by reformatting the drive and restoring the data. Then the information is placed on the drive at the current head positions for each cylinder. Over time, the mistracking recurs, necessitating another reformat-and-restore operation, which is a form of periodic preventive maintenance for stepper motor drives. An acceptable interval for this maintenance is once a year (or perhaps twice a year, if the drive is extremely temperature-sensitive).

Reformatting a hard drive, because it requires a complete backup-and-restore operation, is inconvenient and time-consuming. To help with these periodic reformats, most low-level format programs offer a special reformat option that copies the data for a specific track to a spare location, reformats the track, and then copies the data back to the original track. When this type of format operation is finished, you don't have to restore your data because the program took care of that chore for you, one track at a time.

> **Caution**
>
> Never use a so-called nondestructive format program without first making a complete backup. This type of program does wipe out the data as it operates. "Destructive-reconstructive" more accurately describes its operation. If a problem occurs with the power, the system, or the program (maybe a bug that stops the program from finishing), all the data will not be restored properly, and some tracks may be wiped clean. Although such programs save you from having to restore data manually when the format is complete, they do not remove your obligation to perform a backup first.

Voice Coil. A *voice coil actuator* is found in all higher-quality hard disk drives, including most drives with capacities greater than 40M and virtually all drives with capacities exceeding 80M. Unlike the blind stepper motor positioning system, a voice coil actuator uses a feedback signal from the drive to accurately determine the head positions and to adjust them, if necessary. This system allows for significantly greater performance, accuracy, and reliability than traditional stepper motor actuators offered.

A voice coil actuator works by pure electromagnetic force. The construction of this mechanism is similar to that of a typical audio speaker, from which the term *voice coil* is derived. An audio speaker uses a stationary magnet surrounded by a voice coil connected to the speaker's paper cone. Energizing the coil causes the coil to move relative to the stationary magnet, which produces sound from the speaker cone. In a typical hard disk voice coil system, the electromagnetic coil is attached to the end of the head rack and placed near a stationary magnet. No contact is made between the coil and the magnet. As the electromagnetic coils are energized, they attract or repulse the stationary magnet and move the head rack. Such systems are extremely quick and efficient, and usually much quieter than systems driven by stepper motors.

Unlike a stepper motor, a voice coil actuator has no click-stops, or detent positions; rather, a special guidance system stops the head rack above a particular cylinder. Because it has no detents, the voice coil actuator can slide the heads in and out smoothly to any position desired, much like the slide of a trombone. Voice coil actuators use a guidance mechanism called a *servo* to tell the actuator where the heads are in relation to the cylinders and to place the heads accurately at the desired positions. This positioning system often is called a *closed loop, servo-controlled mechanism*. *Closed loop* indicates that the index (or servo) signal is sent to the positioning electronics in a closed-loop system. This loop sometimes is called a *feedback loop*, because the feedback from this information is used to position the heads accurately. *Servo-controlled* refers to this index or the servo information that is used to dictate or control head-positioning accuracy.

A voice coil actuator with servo control is not affected by temperature changes, as a stepper motor is. When the temperature is cold and the platters have shrunk (or when the temperature is hot and the platters have expanded), the voice coil system compensates because it never positions the heads in predetermined track positions. Rather, the voice coil system searches for the specific track, guided by the prewritten servo information, and can position the head rack precisely above the desired track at that track's current position, regardless of the temperature. Because of the continuous feedback of servo information, the heads adjust to the current position of the track at all times. For example, as a drive warms up and the platters expand, the servo information allows the heads to "follow" the track. As a result, a voice coil actuator often is called a *track following system*.

Two main types of voice-coil positioner mechanisms are available:

- Linear voice-coil actuators
- Rotary voice-coil actuators

The types differ only in the physical arrangement of the magnets and coils.

A *linear actuator* (see Figure 14.5) moves the heads in and out over the platters in a straight line, much like a tangential-tracking turntable. The coil moves in and out on a track surrounded by the stationary magnets. The primary advantage of the linear design is that it eliminates the head azimuth variations that occur with rotary positioning systems. (*Azimuth* refers to the angular measurement of the head position relative to the tangent of a given cylinder.) A linear actuator does not rotate the head as it moves from one cylinder to another, thus eliminating this problem.

FIG. 14.5 A linear voice coil actuator.

Although the linear actuator seems to be a good design, it has one fatal flaw: The devices are much too heavy. As drive performance has increased, the desire for lightweight actuator mechanisms has become very important. The lighter the mechanism, the faster it can be accelerated and decelerated from one cylinder to another. Because they are much heavier than rotary actuators, linear actuators were popular only for a short time; they are virtually nonexistent in drives manufactured today.

Rotary actuators (refer to Figure 14.4) also use stationary magnets and a movable coil, but the coil is attached to the end of an actuator arm, much like that of a turntable's tone arm. As the coil is forced to move relative to the stationary magnet, it swings the head arms in and out over the surface of the disk. The primary advantage of this mechanism is light weight, which means that the heads can be accelerated and decelerated very quickly, resulting in very fast average seek times. Because of the lever effect on the head arm, the heads move faster than the actuator, which also helps to improve access times.

The disadvantage with a rotary system is that as the heads move from the outer to inner cylinders, they are rotated slightly with respect to the tangent of the cylinders. This rotation results in an azimuth error and is one reason why the area of the platter in which the cylinders are located is somewhat limited. By limiting the total motion of the actuator, the azimuth error can be contained to within reasonable specifications. Virtually all voice coil drives today use rotary actuator systems.

Servo Mechanisms. Three servo mechanism designs have been used to control voice coil positioners over the years:

- Wedge servo
- Embedded servo
- Dedicated servo

These designs are slightly different, but they accomplish the same basic task: They enable the head positioner to adjust continuously so that it is precisely placed above a given cylinder in the drive. The main difference among these servo designs is where the gray code information is actually written on the drive.

All servo mechanisms rely on special information that is only written to the disk when the disk is manufactured. This information usually is in the form of a special code called a gray code. A *gray code* is a special binary notational system in which any two adjacent numbers are represented by a code that differs in only one bit place or column position. This system makes it easy for the head to read the information and quickly determine its precise position. This guidance code can be written only when the drive is manufactured; the code is used over the life of the drive for accurate positional information.

The servo gray code is written at the time of manufacture by a special machine called a *servowriter*: Basically, a jig that mechanically moves the heads to a given reference position and then writes the servo information for that position. Many servowriters are themselves guided by a laser-beam reference that calculates its own position by calculating distances in wavelengths of light. Because the servowriter must be capable of moving the heads mechanically, this process is done with the lid of the drive off or through special access ports on the HDA. After the servowriting is complete, these ports usually are covered with sealing tape. You often see these tape-covered holes on the HDA, usually accompanied by warnings that you will void the warranty if you remove the tape. Because servowriting exposes the interior of the drive, it must be done in a clean-room environment.

A servowriter is an expensive piece of machinery, costing up to $50,000 or more, and often must be custom-made for a particular make or model of drive. Some drive-repair companies have *servowriting capability*, which means that they can rewrite the servo information on a drive if it becomes damaged. Lacking a servowriter, a drive with servo-code damage must be sent back to the drive manufacturer for the servo information to be rewritten.

Fortunately, it is impossible to damage the servo information through any normal reading and writing to a hard disk. Drives are designed so that servo information cannot be overwritten, even during low-level formatting of a drive. One myth that has been circulating (especially with respect to IDE drives) is that you can damage the servo information by improper low-level formatting. This is not true. An improper low-level format may compromise the performance of the drive, but the servo information is totally protected and cannot be overwritten.

The track-following capabilities of a servo-controlled voice coil actuator eliminates the positioning errors that occur over time with stepper motor drives. Voice coil drives simply are not affected by conditions such as thermal expansion and contraction of the platters. In fact, many voice coil drives today perform a special thermal-recalibration procedure at predetermined intervals while they run. This procedure usually involves seeking the heads from cylinder 0 to some other cylinder one time for every head on the drive. As this sequence occurs, the control circuitry in the drive monitors how much the track positions have moved since the last time the sequence was performed, and a thermal calibration adjustment is calculated and stored in the drive's memory. This information then is used every time the drive positions to ensure the most accurate positioning possible.

Most drives perform the thermal-recalibration sequence every five minutes for the first half-hour that the drive is powered on and then once every 25 minutes after that. With some drives (such as Quantum, for example), this thermal-calibration sequence is very noticeable; the drive essentially stops what it is doing, and you hear rapid ticking for a second or so. At this time, some people think that their drive is having a problem reading something and perhaps is conducting a read retry, but this is not true. Most of the newer intelligent drives (IDE and SCSI) employ this thermal-recalibration procedure for ultimate positioning accuracy.

As multimedia applications grew, thermal recalibration became a problem with some manufacturer's drives. The thermal recalibration sequence could interrupt a data transfer, which would make audio and video playback jitter. These companies released special A/V (Audio Visual) drives that would hide the thermal recalibration sequences and not let them ever interrupt a transfer. Most of the newer IDE and SCSI drives are A/V capable, which means the thermal recalibration sequences will not interrupt a transfer such as a video playback.

While we are on the subject of automatic drive functions, most of the drives that perform thermal-recalibration sequences also automatically perform a function called a *disk sweep*. This procedure is an automatic head seek that occurs after the drive has been idle for a period of time (for example, nine minutes). The disk-sweep function moves the heads to a random cylinder in the outer portion of the platters, which is considered to be the high float-height area because the head-to-platter velocity is highest. Then, if the drive continues to remain idle for another period, the heads move to another cylinder in this area, and the process continues indefinitely as long as the drive is powered on.

The disk-sweep function is designed to prevent the head from remaining stationary above one cylinder in the drive, where friction between the head and platter eventually would dig a trench in the media. Although the heads are not in direct contact with the media, they are so close that the constant air pressure from the head floating above a single cylinder causes friction and excessive wear.

Wedge Servo. Some early servo-controlled drives used a technique called a *wedge servo*. In these drives, the gray-code guidance information is contained in a "wedge" slice of the drive in each cylinder immediately preceding the index mark. The index mark indicates the beginning of each track, so the wedge-servo information was written in the Pre-Index Gap, which is at the end of each track. This area is provided for speed tolerance and normally is not used by the controller. Figure 14.6 shows the servo-wedge information on a drive.

Some controllers, such as the Xebec 1210 that IBM used in the XT, had to be notified that the drive was using a wedge servo so that they could shorten the sector timing to allow for the wedge-servo area. If they were not correctly configured, these controllers would not work properly with such drives. Many people believed—erroneously—that the wedge-servo information could be overwritten in such cases by an improper low-level format. This is not the case, however; all drives using a wedge servo disable any write commands and take control of the head select lines whenever the heads are above the wedge area. This procedure protects the servo from any possibility of being overwritten, no matter how hard you try. If the controller tried to write over this area, the drive would prevent the write, and the controller would be unable to complete the format. Most controllers simply do not write to the Pre-Index Gap area and do not need to be configured specially for wedge-servo drives.

The only way that the servo information normally could be damaged is by a powerful external magnetic field (or perhaps by a head crash or some other catastrophe). In such a case, the drive would have to be sent in for repair and re-servoing.

One problem is that the servo information appears only one time every revolution, which means that the drive often needs several revolutions before it can accurately determine and adjust the head position. Because of these problems, the wedge servo never was a popular design; it no longer is used in drives.

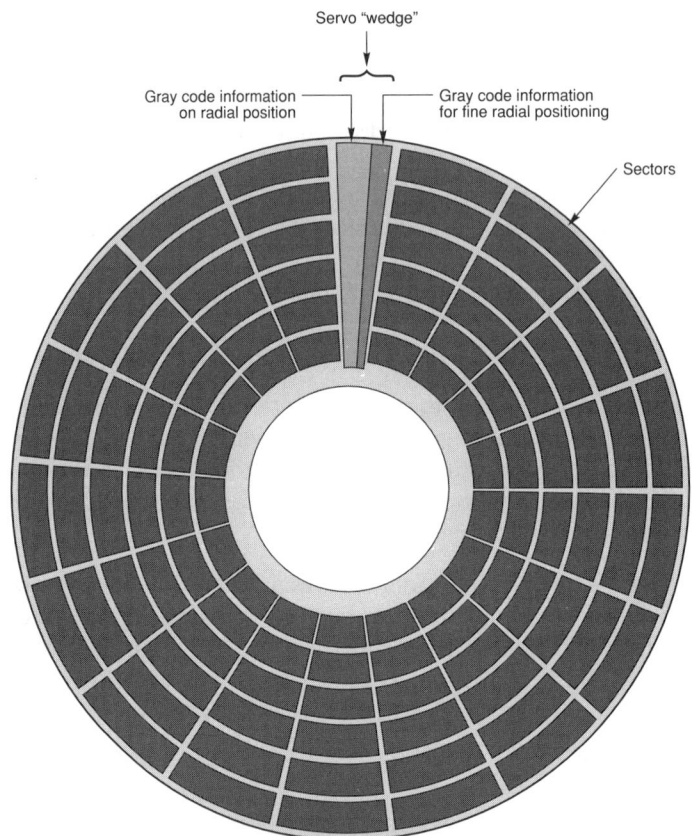

FIG. 14.6 A wedge servo.

Embedded Servo. An *embedded servo* (see Figure 14.7) is an enhancement of the wedge servo. Instead of placing the servo code before the beginning of each cylinder, an embedded servo design writes the servo information before the start of each sector. This arrangement enables the positioner circuits to receive feedback many times in a single revolution, making the head positioning much faster and more precise. Another advantage is that every track on the drive has this positioning information, so each head can quickly and efficiently adjust position to compensate for any changes in the platter or head dimensions, especially for changes due to thermal expansion or physical stress.

Most drives today use an embedded servo to control the positioning system. As in the wedge servo design, the embedded-servo information is protected by the drive circuits, and any write operations are blocked whenever the heads are above the servo information. Thus, it is impossible to overwrite the servo information with a low-level format, as many people incorrectly believed.

Although the embedded servo works much better than the wedge servo, because the feedback servo information is available several times in a single disk revolution, a system that offered continuous servo feedback information would be better.

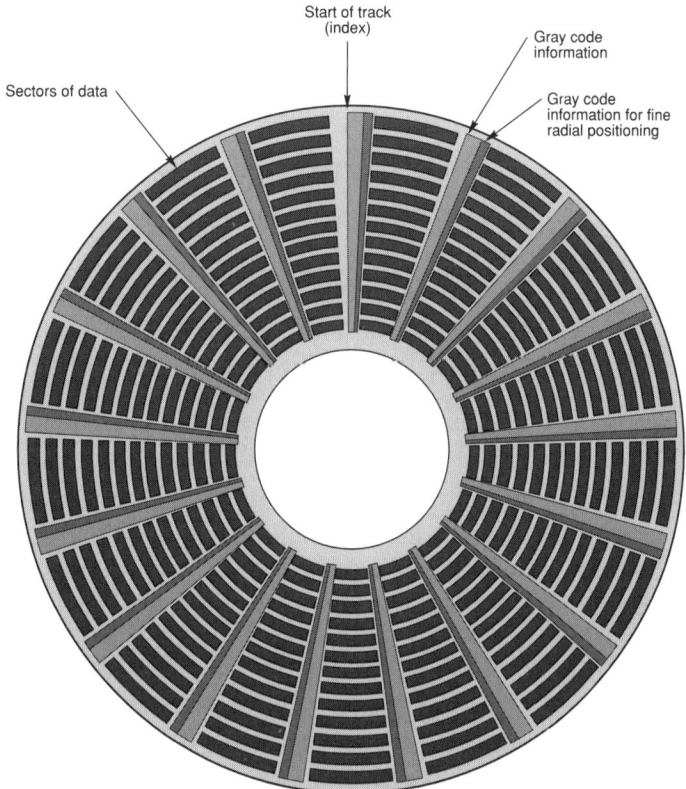

FIG. 14.7 An embedded servo.

Dedicated Servo. A *dedicated servo* is a design in which the servo information is written continuously throughout the entire track, rather than just one time per track or at the beginning of each sector. Unfortunately, if this procedure were performed on the entire drive, no room would be left for data. For this reason, a dedicated servo uses one side of one of the platters exclusively for the servo-positioning information. The term *dedicated* comes from the fact that this platter side is completely dedicated to the servo information and cannot contain any data. Although the dedicated-servo design may seem to be wasteful, none of the other platter sides carries any servo information, and you end up losing about the same amount of total disk real estate as with the embedded servo.

When a dedicated-servo drive is manufactured, one side of one platter is deducted from normal read/write usage; on this platter is recorded a special set of gray-code data that indicates proper track positions. Because the head that rests above this surface cannot be used for normal reading and writing, these marks can never be erased, and the servo information is protected, as in the other servo designs. No low-level format or other procedure can possibly overwrite the servo information.

When the drive is commanded to move the heads to a specific cylinder, the internal drive electronics use the signals received by the servo head to determine the position of the heads. As the heads are moved, the track counters are read from the dedicated servo surface. When the requested track is detected below the servo head, the actuator is stopped. The servo electronics then fine-tune the position so that before writing is allowed, the heads are positioned precisely above the desired cylinder. Although only one head is used for servo tracking, the other heads are attached to the same rigid rack so that if one head is above the desired cylinder, all the others will be as well.

One noticeable trait of dedicated servo drives is that they usually have an odd number of heads. For example, the Toshiba MK-538FB 1.2G drive on which I am saving this chapter has eight platters but only 15 read/write heads; the drive uses a dedicated-servo positioning system, and the 16th head is the servo head. You will find that virtually all high-end drives use a dedicated servo because such a design offers servo information continuously, no matter where the heads are located. This system offers the greatest possible positioning accuracy. Some drives even combine a dedicated servo with an embedded servo, but this type of hybrid design is rare.

Automatic Head Parking. When a hard disk drive is powered off, the spring tension in each head arm pulls the heads into contact with the platters. The drive is designed to sustain thousands of takeoffs and landings, but it is wise to ensure that the landing occurs at a spot on the platter that contains no data. Some amount of abrasion occurs during the landing and takeoff process, removing just a "micro puff" from the media; but if the drive is jarred during the landing or takeoff process, real damage can occur.

One benefit of using a voice coil actuator is *automatic head parking*. In a drive that has a voice coil actuator, the heads are positioned and held by magnetic force. When power is removed from the drive, the magnetic field that holds the heads stationary over a particular cylinder dissipates, enabling the head rack to skitter across the drive surface and potentially cause damage. In the voice coil design, therefore, the head rack is attached to a weak spring at one end and a head stop at the other end. When the system is powered on, the spring normally is overcome by the magnetic force of the positioner. When the drive is powered off, however, the spring gently drags the head rack to a park-and-lock position before the drive slows down and the heads land. On many drives, you can actually hear the "ting...ting...ting...ting" sound as the heads literally bounce-park themselves, driven by this spring.

On a drive with a voice coil actuator, you can activate the parking mechanism simply by turning off the system; you do not need to run a program to park or retract the heads. In the event of a power outage, the heads park themselves automatically. (The drives unpark automatically when the system is powered on.)

Some stepper motor drives (such as the Seagate ST-251 series drives) park their heads, but this function is rare among stepper motor drives. The stepper motor drives that do park their heads usually use an ingenious system whereby the spindle motor actually is used as a generator after the power to the drive is turned off. The back *EMF (Electro Motive Force)*, as it is called, is used to drive the stepper motor to park the heads.

Air Filters

Nearly all hard disk drives have two air filters. One filter is called the *recirculating filter*, and the other is called either a *barometric* or *breather filter*. These filters are permanently sealed inside the drive and are designed never to be changed for the life of the drive, unlike many older mainframe hard disks that had changeable filters. Many mainframe drives circulate air from outside the drive through a filter that must be changed periodically.

A hard disk on a PC system does not circulate air from inside to outside the HDA, or vice versa. The recirculating filter that is permanently installed inside the HDA is designed to filter only the small particles of media scraped off the platters during head takeoffs and landings (and possibly any other small particles dislodged inside the drive). Because PC hard disk drives are permanently sealed and do not circulate outside air, they can run in extremely dirty environments (see Figure 14.8).

FIG. 14.8 Air circulation in a hard disk.

The HDA in a hard disk is sealed but not airtight. The HDA is vented through a barometric or breather filter element that allows for pressure equalization (breathing) between the inside and outside of the drive. For this reason, most hard drives are rated by the drive's manufacturer to run in a specific range of altitudes, usually from –1,000 to +10,000 feet above sea level. In fact, some hard drives are not rated to exceed 7,000 feet while operating, because the air pressure would be too low inside the drive to float the heads properly. As the environmental air pressure changes, air bleeds into or out of the drive so that internal and external pressures are identical. Although air does bleed through a vent, contamination usually is not a concern, because the barometric filter on this vent is designed to filter out all particles larger than 0.3 micron (about 12 u-in) to meet the specifications for cleanliness inside the drive. You can see the vent holes on most drives, which are covered internally by this breather filter. Some drives use even finer-grade filter elements to keep out even smaller particles.

I conducted a seminar in Hawaii several years ago, and several of the students were from the Mauna Kea astronomical observatory. They indicated that virtually all hard disks they had tried to use at the observatory site had failed very quickly, if they worked at all. This was no surprise, because the observatory is at the 13,800-foot peak of the mountain, and at that altitude, even people don't function very well! At the time, it was suggested that the students investigate solid-state (RAM) disks, tape drives, or even floppy drives as their primary storage medium. Since that time, IBM's Adstar division (which produces all IBM hard drives) introduced a line of rugged 3 1/2-inch drives that are in fact hermetically sealed (airtight), although they do have air inside the HDA. Because they carry their own internal air under pressure, these drives can operate at any altitude, and also can withstand extremes of shock and temperature. The drives are designed for military and industrial applications, such as aboard aircraft and in extremely harsh environments.

Hard Disk Temperature Acclimation

To allow for pressure equalization, hard drives have a filtered port to bleed air into or out of the HDA as necessary.

This breathing also enables moisture to enter the drive, and after some period of time, it must be assumed that the humidity inside any hard disk is similar to that outside the drive. Humidity can become a serious problem if it is allowed to condense—and especially if the drive is powered up while this condensation is present. Most hard disk manufacturers have specified procedures for acclimating a hard drive to a new environment with different temperature and humidity ranges, especially for bringing a drive into a warmer environment in which condensation can form. This situation should be of special concern to users of laptop or portable systems with hard disks. If you leave a portable system in an automobile trunk during the winter, for example, it could be catastrophic to bring the machine inside and power it up without allowing it to acclimate to the temperature indoors.

The following text and Table 14.8 are taken from the factory packaging that Control Data Corporation (later Imprimis and eventually Seagate) used to ship its hard drives:

> If you have just received or removed this unit from a climate with temperatures at or below 50°F (10°C) do not open this container until the following conditions are met, otherwise condensation could occur and damage to the device and media may result. Place this package in the operating environment for the time duration according to the temperature chart.

Table 14.8 Hard Disk Drive Environmental Acclimation Table

Previous Climate Temp.	Acclimation Time
+40°F (+4°C)	13 hours
+30°F (−1°C)	15 hours
+20°F (−7°C)	16 hours
+10°F (−12°C)	17 hours
0°F (−18°C)	18 hours
−10°F (−23°C)	20 hours
−20°F (−29°C)	22 hours
−30°F (−34°C) or less	27 hours

As you can see from this table, a hard disk that has been stored in a colder-than-normal environment must be placed in the normal operating environment for a specified amount of time to allow for acclimation before it is powered on.

Spindle Motors

The motor that spins the platters is called the *spindle motor* because it is connected to the spindle around which the platters revolve. Spindle motors in hard disks always are connected directly; no belts or gears are used. The motors must be free of noise and vibration; otherwise, they transmit to the platters a rumble that could disrupt reading and writing operations.

The motors also must be precisely controlled for speed. The platters on hard disks revolve at speeds ranging from 3,600 to 7,200 RPM or more, and the motor has a control circuit with a feedback loop to monitor and control this speed precisely. Because this speed control must be automatic, hard drives do not have a motor-speed adjustment. Some diagnostics programs claim to measure hard drive rotation speed, but all that these programs do is estimate the rotational speed by the timing at which sectors arrive.

There actually is no way for a program to measure hard disk rotational speed; this measurement can be made only with sophisticated testing equipment. Don't be alarmed if some diagnostic program tells you that your drive is spinning at an incorrect speed; most likely the program is wrong, not the drive. Platter rotation and timing information is simply not provided through the hard disk controller interface. In the past, software could give approximate rotational speed estimates by performing multiple sector read requests and timing them, but this was valid only when all drives had the same number of sectors per track (17) and they all spun at 3,600 RPM. Zoned Recording—combined with a variety of different rotational speeds found in modern drives, not to mention built-in buffers and caches—means that these calculation estimates cannot be performed accurately.

On most drives, the spindle motor is on the bottom of the drive, just below the sealed HDA. Many drives today, however, have the spindle motor built directly into the platter hub inside the HDA. By using an internal hub spindle motor, the manufacturer can stack more platters in the drive, because the spindle motor takes up no vertical space. This method allows for more platters than would be possible if the motor were outside the HDA.

> **Note**
>
> Spindle motors, particularly on the larger form-factor drives, can consume a great deal of 12-volt power. Most drives require two to three times the normal operating power when the motor first spins the platters. This heavy draw lasts only a few seconds, or until the drive platters reach operating speed. If you have more than one drive, you should try to sequence the start of the spindle motors so that the power supply does not receive such a large load from all the drives at the same time. Most SCSI and IDE drives have a delayed spindle-motor start feature.

Spindle Ground Strap

Some drives have a special grounding strap attached to a ground on the drive and resting on the center spindle of the platter spindle motor. This device is the single most likely cause of excessive drive noise.

The *grounding strap* usually is made of copper and often has a carbon or graphite button that contacts the motor or platter spindle. The grounding strap dissipates static generated by the platters as they spin through the air inside the HDA. If the platters generate static due to friction with the air, and if no place exists for this electrical potential to bleed off, static may discharge through the heads or the internal bearings in the motor. When static discharges through the motor bearings, it can burn the lubricants inside the sealed bearings. If the static charge discharges through the read/write heads, the heads can be damaged or data can be corrupted. The grounding strap bleeds off this static buildup to prevent these problems.

Where the spindle of the motor contacts the carbon contact button (at the end of the ground strap) spinning at full speed, the button often wears, creating a flat spot. The flat spot causes the strap to vibrate and produce a high-pitched squeal or whine. The noise may come and go, depending on temperature and humidity. Sometimes, banging the side of the machine can jar the strap so that the noise changes or goes away, but this is not the way to fix the problem. *I am not suggesting that you bang on your system!* (Most people mistake this noise for something much more serious, such as a total drive-motor failure or bearing failure, which rarely occur.)

If the spindle grounding strap vibrates and causes noise, you can remedy the situation in several ways:

- Dampen the vibration of the strap by attaching some foam tape or rubber to it.
- Lubricate the contact point.
- Tear off the strap (not recommended!).

On some drives, the spindle motor strap is easily accessible. On other drives, you have to partially disassemble the drive by removing the logic board or other external items to get to the strap.

Of these suggested solutions, the first one is the best. The best way to correct this problem is to glue (or otherwise affix) some rubber or foam to the strap. This procedure changes the harmonics of the strap and usually dampens vibrations. Most manufacturers now use this technique on newly manufactured drives. An easy way to do this is to place some foam tape on the back side of the ground strap.

You also can use a dab of silicone RTV (room-temperature vulcanizing) rubber or caulk on the back of the strap. If you try this method, be sure to use low-volatile (noncorrosive) silicone RTV sealer, which commonly is sold at auto-parts stores. The noncorrosive silicone will be listed on the label as being safe for automotive oxygen sensors. This low-volatile silicone also is free from corrosive acids that can damage the copper strap and is described as low-odor because it does not have the vinegar odor usually associated with silicone RTV. Dab a small amount on the back side of the copper strap (do not interfere with the contact location), and the problem should be solved permanently.

Lubricating the strap is an acceptable, but often temporary, solution. You will want to use some sort of conducting lube, such as a graphite-based compound (the kind used on frozen car locks). Any conductive lubricant (such as moly or lithium) will work as long as it is conductive, but do not use standard oil or grease. Simply dab a small amount of lubricant onto the end of a toothpick, and place a small drop directly on the point of contact.

The last solution is not acceptable. Tearing off the strap eliminates the noise, but it has several possible ramifications. Although the drive will work (silently) without the strap, an engineer placed it there for a reason. Imagine those ungrounded static charges leaving the platters through the heads, perhaps in the form of a spark—possibly even damaging the TF heads. You should choose one of the other solutions.

I mention this last solution only because several people have told me that members of the tech-support staff of some of the hard drive vendors, and even of some manufacturers, told them to remove the strap, which—of course—I do not recommend.

Logic Boards

A disk drive, including a hard disk drive, has one or more logic boards mounted on it. The *logic boards* contain the electronics that control the drive's spindle and head actuator systems and that present data to the controller in some agreed-upon form. In some drives, the controller is located on the drive, which can save on a system's total chip count.

Many disk drive failures occur in the logic board, not in the mechanical assembly. (This statement does not seem logical, but it is true.) Therefore, you can repair many failed drives by replacing the logic board, not the entire drive. Replacing the logic board, moreover, enables you to regain access to the data on the failed drive—something that replacing the entire drive precludes.

Logic boards can be removed or replaced because they simply plug into the drive. These boards usually are mounted with standard screw hardware. If a drive is failing and you have a spare, you may be able to verify a logic-board failure by taking the board off the known good drive and mounting it on the bad one. If your suspicions are confirmed, you can order a new logic board from the drive manufacturer, but unless you have data you need to recover, it makes more sense to just buy a new drive, considering today's cost.

To reduce costs further, many third-party vendors also can supply replacement logic-board assemblies. These companies often charge much less than the drive manufacturers for the same components. (See the vendor list in Appendix B for vendors of drive components, including logic boards.)

Cables and Connectors

Most hard disk drives have several connectors for interfacing to the system, receiving power, and sometimes grounding to the system chassis. Most drives have at least these three types of connectors:

- Interface connector(s)
- Power connector
- Optional ground connector (tab)

Of these, the *interface connectors* are the most important, because they carry the data and command signals from the system to and from the drive. In many drive interfaces, the drive interface cables can be connected in a *daisy chain* or bus-type configuration. Most interfaces support at least two drives, and SCSI (Small Computer System Interface) supports up to seven in the chain. Some interfaces, such as ST-506/412 or ESDI (Enhanced Small Device Interface), use a separate cable for data and control signals. These drives have two cables from the controller interface to the drive. SCSI and IDE (Integrated Drive Electronics) drives usually have a single data and control connector. With these interfaces, the disk controller is built into the drive (see Figure 14.9).

(Rear view)

FIG. 14.9 Typical hard disk connections (ST-506/412 or ESDI shown).

The different interfaces and cable specifications are covered in the sections on drive interfaces later in this chapter. You also will find connector pinout specifications for virtually all drive interfaces and cable connections in Chapter 15, "Hard Disk Interfaces."

The *power connector* usually is the same type that is used in floppy drives, and the same power-supply connector plugs into it. Most hard disk drives use both 5v and 12v power, although some of the smaller drives designed for portable applications use only 5v power. In most cases, the 12v power runs the spindle motor and head actuator, and the 5v power runs the circuitry. Make sure that your power supply can provide adequate power for the hard disk drives installed in your system.

The 12v-power consumption of a drive usually varies with the physical size of the unit. The larger the drive is and the more platters there are to spin, the more power is required. Also, the faster the drive spins, the more power required. For example, most of the 3 1/2-inch drives on the market today use roughly one-half to one-fourth the power (in watts) of the full-size 5 1/4-inch drives. Some of the very small (2 1/2- or 1.8-inch) hard disks barely sip electrical power and actually use 1 watt or less!

Ensuring an adequate power supply is particularly important with some systems, such as the original IBM AT. These systems have a power supply with three disk drive power connectors, labeled P10, P11, and P12. The three power connectors may seem to be equal, but the technical-reference manual for these systems indicates that 2.8 amps of 12v current is available on P10 and P11, and that only 1 amp of 12v current is available on P12. Because most full-height hard drives draw much more power than 1 amp, especially at startup, the P12 connector can be used only by floppy drives or half-height hard drives. Some 5 1/2-inch drives draw as much as 4 amps of current during the first few seconds of startup. These drives also can draw as much as 2.5 amps during normal operation. Most PC-compatible systems have a power supply with four or more disk drive power connectors that provide equal power.

A *grounding tab* provides a positive ground connection between the drive and the system's chassis. In most systems, the hard disk drive is mounted directly to the chassis using screws so the ground wire is unnecessary. On some systems, the drives are installed on plastic or fiberglass rails, which do not provide proper grounding. These systems must provide a grounding wire plugged into the drive at this grounding tab. Failure to ground the drive may result in improper operation, intermittent failure, or general read and write errors.

Configuration Items

To configure a hard disk drive for installation in a system, several jumpers (and, possibly, terminating resistors) usually must be set or configured properly. These items will vary from interface to interface and often from drive to drive as well. A complete discussion of the configuration settings for each interface appears in the section "Hard Disk Installation Procedures" later in this chapter.

The Faceplate or Bezel

Many hard disk drives offer a front faceplate, or *bezel* (see Figure 14.10) as an option. A bezel usually is supplied as an option for the drive rather than as a standard item. In most cases today, the bezel is a part of the case and not the drive itself.

FIG. 14.10 A hard drive faceplate (bezel).

Older systems had the drive installed so that it was visible outside the system case. Covering the hole drives could be an optional bezel or faceplate. Bezels often come in several sizes and colors to match various PC systems. Many faceplate configurations for 3 1/2-inch drives are available, including bezels that fit 3 1/2-inch drive bays as well as 5 1/4-inch drive bays. You even have a choice of colors (usually, black, cream, or white).

Some bezels feature a light-emitting diode (LED) that flickers when your hard disk is in use. The LED is mounted in the bezel; the wire hanging off the back of the LED plugs into the drive or perhaps the controller. In some drives, the LED is permanently mounted on the drive, and the bezel has a clear or colored window so that you can see the LED flicker while the drive is accessed.

One type of LED problem occurs with some older hard disk installations: If the drive has an LED, the LED may remain on continuously, as though it were a "power-on" light rather than an access light. This problem happens because the controllers in those systems have a direct connection for the LED, thus altering the drive LED function. Some controllers have a jumper that enables the controller to run the drive in what is called latched or unlatched mode. *Latched mode* means that the drive is selected continuously and that the drive LED remains lighted; in *unlatched mode* (to which we are more accustomed), the LED lights only when the drive is accessed. Check to see whether your controller has a jumper for changing this function; if so, you may be able to control the way the LED operates.

In systems in which the hard disk is hidden by the unit's cover, a bezel is not needed. In fact, using a bezel may prevent the cover from resting on the chassis properly, in which case the bezel will have to be removed. If you are installing a drive that does not have a proper bezel, frame, or rails to attach to the system, check Appendix B of this book; several listed vendors offer these accessories for a variety of drives.

Hard Disk Features

To make the best decision in purchasing a hard disk for your system, or to understand what differentiates one brand of hard disk from another, you must consider many features. This section examines the issues that you should consider when you evaluate drives:

- Reliability
- Shock mounting
- Speed
- Cost

Reliability

When you shop for a drive, you may notice a feature called the *Mean Time Between Failures (MTBF)* described in the brochures. MTBF figures usually range from 20,000 hours to 500,000 hours or more. I usually ignore these figures, because they usually are just theoretical—not actual—statistical values. Most drives that boast these figures have not even been manufactured for that length of time. One year of five-day work weeks with eight-hour days equals 2,080 hours of operation. If you never turn off your system for 365 days and run the full 24 hours per day, you operate your system 8,760 hours each year; a drive with a 500,000-hour MTBF rating is supposed to last (on average) 57 years before failing! Obviously, that figure cannot be derived from actual statistics because the particular drive probably has been on the market for less than a year.

Statistically, for the MTBF figures to have real weight, you must take a sample of drives, measure the failure rate for at least twice the rated figure, and measure how many drives fail in that time. To be really accurate, you would have to wait until all the drives fail and record the operating hours at each failure. Then you would average the running time for all the test samples to arrive at the average time before a drive failure. For a reported MTBF of 500,000 hours (common today), the test sample should be run for at least 1 million hours (114 years) to be truly accurate, yet the drive carries this specification on the day that it is introduced.

The bottom line is that I do not really place much emphasis on MTBF figures. Some of the worst drives that I have used boasted high MTBF figures, and some of the best drives have lower ones. These figures do not necessarily translate to reliability in the field, and that is why I generally place no importance on them.

Performance

When you select a hard disk, an important feature to consider is the performance (speed) of the drive. Hard disks come in a wide range of performance capabilities. As is true of many things, one of the best indicators of a drive's relative performance is its price. An old saying from the automobile-racing industry is appropriate here: "Speed costs money. How fast do you want to go?"

You can measure the speed of a disk drive in two ways:

- Average seek time
- Transfer rate

Average seek time, normally measured in milliseconds (ms), is the average amount of time it takes to move the heads from one cylinder to another cylinder a random distance away. One way to measure this specification is to run many random track-seek operations and then divide the timed results by the number of seeks performed. This method provides an average time for a single seek.

The standard way to measure average seek time used by many drive manufacturers involves measuring the time that it takes the heads to move across one-third of the total cylinders. Average seek time depends only on the drive; the type of interface or controller has little effect on this specification. The rating is a gauge of the capabilities of the head actuator.

> **Tip**
>
> Be wary of benchmarks that claim to measure drive seek performance. Most IDE and SCSI drives use a scheme called *sector translation*, so any commands to the drive to move the heads to a specific cylinder do not actually cause the intended physical movement. This situation renders some benchmarks meaningless for those types of drives. SCSI drives also require an additional command, because the commands first must be sent to the drive over the SCSI bus. Even though these drives can have the fastest access times, because the command overhead is not factored in by most benchmarks, the benchmark programs produce poor performance figures for these drives.

A slightly different measurement, called *average access time*, involves another element, called latency. *Latency* is the average time (in milliseconds) that it takes for a sector to be available after the heads have reached a track. On average, this figure is half the time that it takes for the disk to rotate one time, which is 8.33 ms at 3,600 RPM. A drive that spins twice as fast would have half the latency. A measurement of average access time is the sum of the average seek time and latency. This number provides the average amount of time required before a randomly requested sector can be accessed.

Latency is a factor in disk read and write performance. Decreasing the latency increases the speed of access to data or files, accomplished only by spinning the drive platters faster. I have a drive that spins at 4,318 RPM, for a latency of 6.95 ms. Some drives spin at 7,200 RPM or faster, resulting in an even shorter latency time of only 4.17 ms. In addition to increasing performance where real-world access to data is concerned, spinning the platters faster also increases the data-transfer rate after the heads arrive at the desired sectors.

The transfer rate probably is more important to overall system performance than any other specification. *Transfer rate* is the rate at which the drive and controller can send data to the system. The transfer rate depends primarily on the drive's HDA and secondarily on the controller. Transfer rate used to be more bound to the limits of the controller, meaning that drives that were connected to newer controllers often outperformed those connected to older controllers. This situation is where the concept of interleaving sectors came from. *Interleaving* refers to the ordering of the sectors so that they are not sequential, enabling a slow controller to keep up without missing the next sector.

Modern drives with integrated controllers are fully capable of keeping up with the raw drive transfer rate. In other words, they no longer have to interleave the sectors to slow the data for the controller.

Another performance issue is the raw interface performance, which, in IDE or SCSI drives, usually is far higher than any of the drives themselves are able to sustain. Be wary of quoted transfer specifications for the interface, because the specifications may have little effect on what the drive can actually put out. The drive interface simply limits the maximum theoretical transfer rate; the actual drive and controller place the real limits on performance.

In older ST-506/412 interface drives, you could sometimes double or triple the transfer rate by changing the controller, because many of the older controllers could not support a 1:1 interleave. When you change the controller to one that does support this interleave, the transfer rate will be equal to the drive's true capability.

To calculate the true transfer rate of a drive, you need to know several important specifications. The two most important specifications are the true rotational speed of the drive (in RPM) and the average number of physical sectors on each track. I say "average" because most drives today use a Zoned Recording technique that places different numbers of sectors on the inner and outer cylinders. The transfer rate on Zoned Recording drives always is fastest in the outermost zone, where the sector per track count is highest. Also be aware that many drives (especially Zoned Recording drives) are configured with sector translation, so that the BIOS reported number of sectors per track has little to do with physical reality. You need to know the true physical parameters, rather than what the BIOS thinks.

When you know these figures, you can use the following formula to determine the maximum transfer rate in millions of bits per second (Mbps):

Maximum Data Transfer Rate (Mbps) = SPT $\times$ 512 bytes $\times$ RPM / 60 seconds / 1,000,000 bits

For example, the ST-12551N 2G 3 1/2-inch drive spins at 7,200 RPM and has an average of 81 sectors per track. The maximum transfer rate for this drive is figured as follows:

81 $\times$ 512 $\times$ 7,200 / 60 / 1,000,000 = 4.98Mbps

Using this formula, you can calculate the true maximum sustained transfer rate of any drive.

Cache Programs and Caching Controllers. At the software level, disk cache programs such as SMARTDRV (DOS) or VCACHE (Windows 95) can have a major effect on disk drive performance. These cache programs hook into the BIOS hard drive interrupt and then intercept the read and write calls to the disk BIOS from application programs and the device drivers of DOS.

When an application program wants to read data from a hard drive, the cache program intercepts the read request, passes the read request to the hard drive controller in the usual way, saves the data that was read in its cache buffer, and then passes the data back to the application program. Depending on the size of the cache buffer, numerous sectors are read into and saved in the buffer.

When the application wants to read more data, the cache program again intercepts the request and examines its buffers to see whether the data is still in the cache. If so, the data is passed back to the application immediately, without another hard drive operation. As you can imagine, this method speeds access tremendously and can greatly affect disk drive performance measurements.

Most controllers now have some form of built-in hardware buffer or cache that doesn't intercept or use any BIOS interrupts. Instead, the caching is performed at the hardware level and is invisible to normal performance-measurement software. Track read-ahead buffers originally were included in controllers to allow for 1:1 interleave performance. Some controllers have simply increased the sizes of these read-ahead buffers; others have added intelligence by making them a cache instead of a simple buffer.

Many IDE and SCSI drives have cache memory built directly into the drive. For example, the Seagate Hawk 4G drive on which I am saving this chapter has 512K of built-in cache memory. Other drives have even more built-in caches, such as the Seagate Barracuda 4G with 1M of integral cache memory. I remember when 640K was a lot of memory; now, tiny 3 1/2-inch hard disk drives have more than that built right in! These integral caches are part of the reason why most IDE and SCSI drives perform so well.

Although software and hardware caches can make a drive faster for routine transfer operations, a cache will not affect the true maximum transfer rate that the drive can sustain.

Interleave Selection. In a discussion of disk performance, the issue of interleave always comes up. Although traditionally this was more a controller performance issue than a drive issue, most modern hard disks now have built-in controllers (IDE and SCSI) that are fully capable of taking the drive data as fast as the drive can send it. In other words, virtually all modern IDE and SCSI drives are formatted with no interleave (sometimes expressed as a 1:1 interleave ratio).

Head and Cylinder Skewing. Most controllers today are capable of transferring data at a 1:1 sector interleave. This is especially true of controllers that are built in to IDE and SCSI drives. With a 1:1 interleave controller, the maximum data transfer rate can be maintained when reading and writing sectors to the disk. Although it would seem that there is no other way to further improve efficiency and the transfer rate, many people overlook two important factors that are similar to interleave: *head* and *cylinder skewing*.

When a drive is reading (or writing) data sequentially, first all of the sectors on a given track are read; then the drive must electronically switch to the next head in the cylinder to continue the operation. If the sectors are not skewed from head to head within the cylinder, no delay occurs after the last sector on one track and before the arrival of the first sector on the next track. Because all drives require some time (although a small amount) to switch from one head to another, and because the controller also adds some overhead to the operation, it is likely that by the time the drive is ready to read the sectors on the newly selected track, the first sector will already have passed by. By skewing the sectors from one head to another—that is, rotating their arrangement on the track so that the arrival of the first sector is delayed relative to the preceding track—you can ensure that no extra disk revolutions will be required when switching heads. This method provides the highest possible transfer rate when head switching is involved.

In a similar fashion, it takes considerable time for the heads to move from one cylinder to another. If the sectors on one cylinder were not skewed from those on the preceding adjacent cylinder, it is likely that by the time the heads arrive, the first sector will already have passed below them, requiring an additional revolution of the disk before reading of the new cylinder can begin. By skewing the sectors from one cylinder to the next, you can account for the cylinder-to-cylinder head-movement time and prevent any additional revolutions of the drive.

Head Skew. *Head skew* is the offset in logical sector numbering between the same physical sectors on two tracks below adjacent heads of the same cylinder. The number of sectors skewed when switching from head to head within a single cylinder is to compensate for head switching and controller overhead time. Think of it as the surface of each platter being rotated as you traverse from head to head. This method permits continuous read or write operation across head boundaries without missing any disk revolutions, thus maximizing system performance.

To understand head skew, you first need to know the order in which tracks and sectors are read from a disk. If you imagine a single-platter (two-head) drive with 10 cylinders and 17 sectors per track, the first sector that will be read on the entire drive is Cylinder 0, Head 0, Sector 1. Following that, all the remaining sectors on that first track (Cylinder 0, Head 0) will be read until Sector 17 is reached. After that, two things could take place:

- The heads could be moved so that the drive could continue reading the next track on the same side of the platter.

- The second head could be selected, and therefore another entire track could be read with no head movement.

Because head movement takes much longer than electronically selecting another head, all disk drives will select the subsequent heads on a cylinder before physically moving the heads to the next cylinder. Thus, the next sector to be read would be Cylinder 0, Head 1, Sector 1. Next, all the remaining sectors on that track are read (2 through 17), and then in our single platter example it is time to switch heads. This sequence continues until the last sector on the last track is read—in this example, Cylinder 9, Head 1, Sector 17.

If you could take the tracks off a cylinder in this example and lay them on top of one another, the tracks might look like this:

Cylinder 0, Head 0:   1- 2- 3- 4- 5- 6- 7- 8- 9-10-11-12-13-14-15-16-17

Cylinder 0, Head 1:   1- 2- 3- 4- 5- 6- 7- 8- 9-10-11-12-13-14-15-16-17

After reading all the sectors on head 0, the controller switches heads to head 1 and continues the read (looping around to the beginning of the track). In this example, the sectors were not skewed at all between the heads, which means that the sectors are directly above and below one another in a given cylinder.

Now the platters in this example are spinning at 3,600 RPM, so one sector is passing below a head once every 980 millionths of a second! This obviously is a very small timing window. It takes some time for the head switch to occur (usually, 15 millionths of a second), plus some overhead time for the controller to pass the head-switch command. By the time the head switch is complete and you are ready to read the new track, sector 1 has already gone by! This problem is similar to interleaving when the interleave is too low. The drive is forced to wait while the platter spins around another revolution so that it can begin to pick up the track, starting with Sector 1.

This problem is easy to solve: Simply offset the sector numbering on subsequent tracks from those that precede them sufficiently to account for the head-switching and controller overhead time. That way, when Head 0, Sector 17 finishes and the head switches, Head 1, Sector 1 arrives right on time. The result looks something like this:

Cylinder 0, Head 0:   1- 2- 3- 4- 5- 6- 7- 8- 9-10-11-12-13-14-15-16-17

Cylinder 0, Head 1:   16-17- 1- 2- 3- 4- 5- 6- 7- 8- 9-10-11-12-13-14-15

Shifting the second track by two sectors provides time to allow for the head-switching overhead and is the equivalent to a head-skew factor of 2. In normal use, a drive switches heads much more often than it switches physical cylinders, which makes head skew more important than cylinder skew. Throughput can rise dramatically when a proper head skew is in place. Different head skews can account for different transfer rates among drives that have the same number of sectors per track and the same interleave.

A nonskewed MFM drive, for example, may have a transfer rate of 380K/sec, whereas the transfer rate of a drive with a head skew of 2 could rise to 425K/sec. Notice that different controllers and drives have different amounts of overhead, so real-world results will be different in each case. In most cases, the head-switch time is very small compared with the controller overhead. As with interleaving, it is better to be on the conservative side to avoid additional disk revolutions.

Cylinder Skew. *Cylinder skew* is the offset in logical sector numbering between the same physical sectors on two adjacent tracks on two adjacent cylinders.

The number of sectors skewed when switching tracks from one cylinder to the next is to compensate for track to track seek time. In essence, all of the sectors on adjacent tracks are rotated with respect to each other. This method permits continuous read or write operations across cylinder boundaries without missing any disk revolutions, thus maximizing system performance.

Cylinder skew is a larger numerical factor than head skew because more overhead exists. It takes much longer to move the heads from one cylinder to another than simply to switch heads. Also, the controller overhead in changing cylinders is higher as well.

Following is a depiction of our example drive with a head-skew factor of 2 but no cylinder skew.

Cylinder 0, Head 0:	1- 2- 3- 4- 5- 6- 7- 8- 9-10-11-12-13-14-15-16-17
Cylinder 0, Head 1:	16-17- 1- 2- 3- 4- 5- 6- 7- 8- 9-10-11-12-13-14-15
Cylinder 1, Head 0:	8- 9-10-11-12-13-14-15-16-17- 1- 2- 3- 4- 5- 6- 7

In this example, the cylinder-skew factor is 8. Shifting the sectors on the subsequent cylinder by eight sectors gives the drive and controller time to be ready for sector 1 on the next cylinder and eliminates an extra revolution of the disk.

Calculating Skew Factors. You can derive the correct head-skew factor from the following information and formula:

Head skew = (head-switch time/rotational period) × SPT + 2

In other words, the head-switching time of a drive is divided by the time required for a single rotation. The result is multiplied by the number of sectors per track, and 2 is added for controller overhead. The result should then be rounded up to the next whole integer (for example, 2.3 = 2, 2.5 = 3).

You can derive the correct cylinder-skew factor from the following information and formula:

Cylinder skew = (track-to-track seek time/rotational period) × SPT + 4

In other words, the track-to-track seek time of a drive is divided by the time required for a single rotation. The result is multiplied by the number of sectors per track, and 4 is added for controller overhead. Round the result up to a whole integer (for example, 2.3 = 2, 2.5 = 3).

The following example uses typical figures for an ESDI drive and controller. If the head-switching time is 15 us (microseconds), the track-to-track seek is 3 ms, the rotational period is 16.67 ms (3,600 RPM), and the drive has 53 physical sectors per track:

Head skew = (0.015/16.67) × 53 +2 = 2 (rounded up)

Cylinder Skew = (3/16.67) × 53 + 4 = 14 (rounded up)

If you do not have the necessary information to make the calculations, contact the drive manufacturer for recommendations. Otherwise, you can make the calculations by using conservative figures for head-switch and track-to-track access times. If you are unsure, just as with interleaving, it is better to be on the conservative side, which minimizes the possibility of additional rotations when reading sequential information on the drive. In most cases, a default head skew of 2 and a cylinder skew of 16 work well.

Because factors such as controller overhead can vary from model to model, sometimes the only way to figure out the best value is to experiment. You can try different skew values and then run data-transfer rate tests to see which value results in the highest performance. Be careful with these tests, however; many disk benchmark programs will only read or write data from one track or one cylinder during testing, which totally eliminates the effect of skewing on the results. The best type of benchmark to use for this testing is one that reads and writes large files on the disk.

Most real (controller register level) low-level format programs are capable of setting skew factors. Those programs that are supplied by a particular controller or drive manufacturer usually are already optimized for their particular drives and controllers, and may not allow you to change the skew. One of the best general-purpose register-level formatters on the market that gives you this flexibility is the Disk Manager program by Ontrack. I highly recommend this program, which you will find listed in Appendix B.

I normally do not recommend programs such as Norton Calibrate and Gibson Spinrite for re-interleaving drives, because these programs work only through the BIOS INT 13h functions rather than directly with the disk controller hardware. Thus, these programs cannot set skew factors properly, and using them actually may slow a drive that already has optimum interleave and skew factors.

Notice that most IDE and SCSI drives have their interleave and skew factors set to their optimum values by the manufacturer. In most cases, you cannot even change these values; in the cases in which you can, the most likely result is a slower drive. For this reason, most IDE drive manufacturers recommend against low-level formatting their drives. With some IDE drives, unless you use the right software, you might alter the optimum skew settings and slow the drive. IDE drives that use Zoned Recording cannot ever have the interleave or skew factors changed, and as such, they are fully protected. No matter how you try to format these drives, the interleave and skew factors cannot be altered. The same can be said for SCSI drives.

Shock Mounting

Most hard disks manufactured today have a *shock-mounted* HDA, which means that a rubber cushion is placed between the disk drive body and the mounting chassis. Some drives use more rubber than others, but for the most part, a shock mount is a shock mount. Some drives do not have a shock-isolated HDA due to physical or cost constraints. Be sure that the drive you are using has adequate shock-isolation mounts for the HDA, especially if you are using the drive in a portable PC system or in a system in which environmental conditions are less favorable than in a normal office. I usually never recommend a drive that lacks at least some form of shock mounting.

Cost

The cost of hard disk storage recently has fallen to 10 cents per megabyte or less. You can purchase 4G drives for under $400. That places the value of the 10M drive that I bought in 1983 at about $1. (Too bad—I paid $1,800 for it at the time!)

Of course, the cost of drives continues to fall, and eventually, even 10 cents per megabyte will seem expensive. Because of the low costs of disk storage today, not many drives that are less than 1G are even being manufactured.

Capacity

Four figures commonly are used in advertising drive capacity:

- Unformatted capacity, in millions of bytes (M)
- Formatted capacity, in millions of bytes (M)
- Unformatted capacity, in megabytes (Meg)
- Formatted capacity, in megabytes (Meg)

Most manufacturers of IDE and SCSI drives now report only the formatted capacities, because these drives are delivered preformatted. Most of the time, advertisements refer to the unformatted or formatted capacity in millions of bytes, because these figures are larger than the same capacity expressed in megabytes. This situation generates a great deal of confusion when the user runs FDISK (which reports total drive capacity in megabytes) and wonders where the missing space is. This question ranks as one of the most common questions that I hear during my seminars. Fortunately, the answer is easy; it only involves a little math to figure it out.

Perhaps the most common questions I get are concerning "missing" drive capacity. Consider the following example: "I just installed a new Western Digital AC2200 drive, billed as 212M. When I entered the drive parameters (989 cylinders, 12 heads, 35 sectors per track), both the BIOS Setup routine and FDISK report the drive as only 203M! What happened to the other 9M?"

The answer is only a few calculations away. By multiplying the drive specification parameters, you get this result:

Cylinders:	989
Heads:	12
Sectors per track:	35
Bytes per sector:	512
Total bytes:	212.67M
Total megabytes:	202.82Meg

The result figures to a capacity of 212.67M or 202.82Meg. Drive manufacturers usually report drive capacity in millions of bytes, whereas your BIOS and FDISK usually report the capacity in megabytes. One megabyte equals 1,048,576 bytes (or 1,024K, wherein each kilobyte is 1,024 bytes). So the bottom line is that this 212.67M drive also is a 202.82Meg drive! What is really confusing is that there is no industry-wide accepted way of differentiating binary Megabytes from decimal ones. Officially they are both abbreviated as M, so it is often hard to figure which one is being reported. Usually drive manufacturers will always report metric megabytes, since they result in larger, more impressive sounding numbers! One additional item to note about this particular drive is that it is a Zoned Recording drive and that the actual physical parameters are different. Physically, this drive has 1,971 cylinders and four heads; however, the total number of sectors on the drive (and, therefore, the capacity) is the same no matter how you translate the parameters.

Although Western Digital does not report the unformatted capacity of this particular drive, unformatted capacity usually works out to be about 19 percent larger than a drive's formatted capacity. The Seagate ST-12550N Barracuda 2G drive, for example, is advertised as having the following capacities:

Unformatted capacity:	2,572.00M
Unformatted capacity:	2,452.85Meg
Formatted capacity:	2,139.00M
Formatted capacity:	2,039.91Meg

Each of these four figures is a correct answer to the question "What is the storage capacity of the drive?" As you can see, however, the numbers are very different. In fact, yet another number could be used. Divide the 2,039.91Meg by 1,024, and the drive's capacity is 1.99G! So when you are comparing or discussing drive capacities, make sure that you are working with a consistent unit of measure, or your comparisons will be meaningless.

Specific Recommendations

If you are going to add a hard disk to a system today, I can give you a few recommendations. For the drive interface, there really are only two types to consider:

- IDE (Integrated Drive Electronics)
- SCSI (Small Computer System Interface)

SCSI offers great expandability, cross-platform compatibility, high capacity, performance, and flexibility. IDE is less expensive than SCSI and also offers a very high-performance solution, but expansion, compatibility, capacity, and flexibility are more limited compared with SCSI. On the other hand, I usually recommend IDE for most people, because they will not be running more than two hard drives and may not need SCSI for other devices as well. SCSI offers some additional performance potential with a multithreaded OS like Windows NT or OS/2, but IDE offsets this with a lower overhead direct system bus attachment.

> **Note**
>
> Note that the current IDE standard is ATA-2 (AT Attachment), otherwise called Fast ATA-2 or Enhanced IDE. SCSI-2 is the current SCSI standard, with SCSI-3 still on the drawing board.

Chapter 15

Hard Disk Interfaces

This chapter describes the hard disk interface, from the drives to the cables and controllers that run them. You learn about the various disk interfaces you can select, and the shortcomings and strengths of each type.

Interfaces Choices

A variety of hard disk interfaces are available today. As time has passed, the number of choices has increased, and many of the older designs are no longer viable in newer systems. You need to know about all these interfaces, from the oldest to the newest designs, because you will encounter all of them whenever upgrading or repairing systems is necessary.

The interfaces have different cabling and configuration options, and the setup and format of drives will vary as well. Special problems may arise when you are trying to install more than one drive of a particular interface type or (especially) when you are mixing drives of different interface types in one system.

This section covers the different hard disk drive interfaces, giving you all the technical information you need to deal with them in any way— troubleshooting, servicing, upgrading, and even mixing the different types.

This section also examines the standard controllers and describes how you can work with these controllers, as well as replace them with much faster units. Also discussed are the different types of drive interfaces: ST-506/412, ESDI, IDE, and SCSI. Choosing the proper interface is important, because your choice also affects your disk drive purchase and the ultimate speed of the disk subsystem.

The primary job of the hard disk controller or interface is to transmit and receive data to and from the drive. The different interface types limit how fast data can be moved from the drive to the system and offer different levels of performance. If you are putting together a system in which performance is a primary concern, you need to know how these different interfaces affect performance and what you can expect from them. Many of the statistics that appear in technical literature are not indicative of the real performance figures that you will see in practice. I will separate the myths presented by some of these over-optimistic figures from the reality of what you will actually see.

With regard to disk drives, and especially hard disk drives, the specification on which people seem to focus the most is the drive's reported *average seek time*, the (average) time it takes for the heads to be positioned from one track to another. Unfortunately, the importance of this specification often is overstated, especially in relation to other specifications, such as the data transfer rate.

The transfer rate of data between the drive and the system is more important than access time, because most drives spend more time reading and writing information than they do simply moving the heads around. The speed at which a program or data file is loaded or read is affected most by the data transfer rate. Specialized operations such as sorting large files, which involve a lot of random access to individual records of the file (and, therefore, many seek operations), are helped greatly by a faster-seeking disk drive, so seeking performance is important in these cases. Most normal file load and save operations, however, are affected most by the rate at which data can be read and written to and from the drive. The data transfer rate depends on both the drive and the interface.

Several types of hard disk interfaces have been used in PC systems over the years:

- ST-506/412
- ESDI
- IDE
- SCSI

Of these interfaces, only ST-506/412 and ESDI are what you could call true disk-controller-to-drive interfaces. SCSI and IDE are system-level interfaces that usually incorporate a chipset-based variation of one of the other two types of disk controller interfaces internally. For example, most SCSI and IDE drives incorporate the same basic controller circuitry used in separate ESDI controllers. The SCSI interface adds another layer of interface that attaches the controller to the system bus, whereas IDE is a direct bus-attachment interface.

In data recovery, it helps to know the disk interface you are working with, because many data-recovery problems involve drive setup and installation problems. Each interface requires a slightly different method of installation and drive configuration. If the installation or configuration is incorrect or accidentally altered by the system user, it may prevent access to data on a drive. Accordingly, anyone who wants to become proficient in data recovery must be an expert on installing and configuring various types of hard disks and controllers.

IBM's reliance on industry-standard interfaces such as those listed here was a boon for everybody in the IBM-compatible industry. These standards allow a great deal of cross-system and cross-manufacturer compatibility. The use of these industry-standard interfaces allows you to pick up a mail-order catalog, purchase a hard disk for the lowest possible price, and be assured that it will work with your system. This Plug-and-Play capability results in affordable hard disk storage and a variety of options in capacities and speed.

The ST-506/412 Interface

The ST-506/412 interface was developed by Seagate Technologies around 1980. The interface originally appeared in the Seagate ST-506 drive, which was a 5M formatted (or 6M unformatted) drive in a full-height, 5 1/4-inch form factor. By today's standards, this drive is a tank! In 1981, Seagate introduced the ST-412 drive, which added a feature called *buffered seek* to the interface. This drive was a 10M formatted (12M unformatted) drive that also qualifies as a tank by today's standards. Besides the Seagate ST-412, IBM also used the Miniscribe 1012 as well the International Memories, Inc. (IMI) model 5012 drive in the XT. IMI and Miniscribe are long gone, but Seagate remains as one of the largest drive manufacturers. Since the original XT, Seagate has supplied drives for numerous systems made by many different manufacturers.

Most drive manufacturers that made hard disks for PC systems adopted the Seagate ST-506/412 standard, a situation that helped make this interface popular. One important feature is the interface's Plug-and-Play design. No custom cables or special modifications are needed for the drives, which means that virtually any ST-506/412 drive will work with any ST-506/412 controller. The only real compatibility issue with this interface is the level of BIOS support provided by the system.

When introduced to the PC industry by IBM in 1983, ROM BIOS support for this hard disk interface was provided by a BIOS chip on the controller. Contrary to what most believed, the PC and XT motherboard BIOS had no inherent hard disk support. When the AT system was introduced, IBM placed the ST-506/412 interface support in the motherboard BIOS and eliminated it from the controller. Since then, any system that is compatible with the IBM AT (which includes most systems on the market today) has an enhanced version of the same support in the motherboard BIOS as well. Because this support was somewhat limited, especially in the older BIOS versions, many disk controller manufacturers also placed additional BIOS support for their controllers directly on the controllers themselves. In some cases, you would use the controller BIOS and motherboard BIOS together; in other cases, you would disable the controller or motherboard BIOS and then use one or the other. These issues will be discussed more completely later in this chapter in the section "System Configuration."

The ST-506/412 interface does not quite make the grade in today's high-performance PC systems. This interface was designed for a 5M drive, and I have not seen any drives larger than 152M (Modified Frequency Modulation encoding) or 233M (Run-Length Limited encoding) available for this type of interface. Because the capacity, performance, and expandability of ST-506/412s are so limited, this interface is obsolete and generally unavailable in new systems. However, many older systems still use drives that have this interface.

Encoding Schemes and Problems

As indicated in Chapter 14 in the section "Data Encoding Schemes," *encoding schemes* are used in communications for converting digital data bits to various tones for transmission over a telephone line. For disk drives, the digital bits are converted, or *encoded*, in a pattern of magnetic impulses, or *flux transitions* (also called *flux reversals*), which are written on the disk. These flux transitions are decoded later when the data is read from the disk.

A device called an *endec (encoder/decoder)* accomplishes the conversion to flux transitions for writing on the media and the subsequent reconversion back to digital data during read operations. The function of the endec is very similar to that of a modem (modulator/demodulator) in that digital data is converted to an analog waveform, which then is converted back to digital data. Sometimes, the endec is called a *data separator*, because it is designed to separate data and clocking information from the flux-transition pulse stream read from the disk.

One of the biggest problems with ST-506/412 was the fact that this endec resided on the disk controller (rather than the drive), which resulted in the possibility of corruption of the analog data signal before it reached the media. This problem became especially pronounced when the ST-506/412 controllers switched to using RLL endecs to store 50 percent more data on the drive. With the RLL encoding scheme, the actual density of magnetic flux transitions on the disk media remains the same as with MFM encoding, but the timing between the transitions must be measured much more precisely.

In *RLL encoding*, the intervals between flux changes are approximately the same as with MFM, but the actual timing between them is much more critical. As a result, the transition cells in which signals must be recognized are much smaller and more precisely placed than with MFM. RLL encoding places more stringent demands on the timing of the controller and drive electronics. With RLL encoding, accurately reading the timing of the flux changes is paramount. Additionally, because RLL encodes variable-length groups of bits rather than single bits, a single error in one flux transition can corrupt two to four bits of data. For these reasons, an RLL controller usually has a more sophisticated error-detection and error-correction routine than an MFM controller.

Most of the cheaper disk drives on the market did not have data-channel circuits that were designed to be precise enough to handle RLL encoding without problems. RLL encoding is also much more susceptible to noise in the read signal, and conventional oxide media coatings did not have a sufficient signal-to-noise ratio for reliable RLL encoding. This problem often was compounded by the fact that many drives of the time used stepper motor head positioning systems, which are notoriously inaccurate, that further amplified the signal-to-noise ratio problem.

At this time, manufacturers are implementing RLL-certifying drives for use with RLL endec controllers. This stamp of approval essentially means that the drive has passed tests and is designed to handle the precise timing requirements that RLL encoding requires. In some cases, the drive electronics were upgraded between a manufacturer's MFM and RLL drive versions, but the drives are essentially the same. In fact, if any improvements were made in the so-called RLL-certified drives, the same upgrades usually also were applied to the MFM version.

The bottom line is that other than improved precision, there is no real difference between an ST-506/412 drive that is sold as an MFM model and one that is sold as an RLL model. If you want to use a drive that originally was sold as an MFM model with an RLL controller, I suggest that you do so only if the drive uses a voice coil head actuator and thin-film media. Virtually any ST-506/412 drive with these qualities is more than good enough to handle RLL encoding with no problems.

Using MFM encoding, a standard ST-506/412 format specifies that the drive will contain 17 sectors per track, with each sector containing 512 bytes of data. A controller that uses an RLL endec raises the number of sectors per track to 25 or 26.

The real solution to reliability problems with RLL encoding was to place the endec directly on the drive rather than on the controller. This method reduces the susceptibility to noise and interference that can plague an ST-506/412 drive system running RLL encoding. ESDI, IDE, and SCSI drives all have the endec (and, often, the entire controller) built into the drive by default. Because the endec is attached to the drive without cables and with an extremely short electrical distance, the propensity for timing- and noise-induced errors is greatly reduced or eliminated. This situation is analogous to a local telephone call between the endec and the disk platters. This local communication makes the ESDI, IDE, and SCSI interfaces much more reliable than the older ST-506/412 interface; they share none of the reliability problems that were once associated with RLL encoding over the ST-506/412 interface. Virtually all ESDI, IDE, and SCSI drives use RLL encoding today with tremendously increased reliability over even MFM ST-506/412 drives.

Historical Notes

The following sections list some information on the original ST-506/412 controllers used in the PC environment. These were the controllers that IBM supplied in the XT and AT systems. At the time of introduction, these controllers set standards that—especially in the case of the AT controller—we still live with today. In fact, the entire IDE interface standard is based on the controller that IBM designed and used in the AT. All of the conventions and standards for the hard disk interfaces that we currently use started with these controllers.

Original IBM 8-Bit Controllers

The first ST-506/412 controller standard sold for PC systems was the hard disk controller used in the original 10M IBM XT. This controller actually was made for IBM by Xebec Corporation and also was sold under the Xebec name as the Xebec 1210 controller. The Xebec 1210 is an ST-506/412 controller that uses MFM encoding to record data on a drive. This controller's ROM, produced by IBM, contains an 8K hard disk BIOS with an internal table that had entries for four different drives. Each drive was selected by jumpers on the controller, which actually were soldered in the early IBM units. If you purchased the controller from Xebec, you received a slightly different but completely compatible ROM, and the jumpers were not soldered, so you easily could select one of the four BIOS table entries. Xebec also allowed system integrators to copy its ROM to modify the built-in drive tables for a specific drive.

Later IBM XT systems with a 20M hard disk still used the Xebec 1210, but it had a new 4K ROM that contained different drive tables, as well as jumpers like those found on the versions also sold separately by Xebec. Xebec never sold an autoconfigure version of this controller, which would have made integrating different drives easier.

(continues)

(continued)

The Xebec 1210 is one of the slowest ST-506/412 controllers ever made, supporting at best a 5:1 interleave on a stock IBM PC or IBM XT system. If you use the IBM Advanced Diagnostics program for the IBM PC or IBM XT, the low-level formatter produces a standard 6:1 interleave, which results in a paltry 85K/sec data transfer rate. By changing the interleave to 5:1, you can wring 102K/sec from this controller—still unbelievably slow by today's standards.

Xebec also made a Model 1220 that combined a hard disk and floppy disk controller, was hardware-compatible with the 1210, and works with the IBM or standard Xebec ROM. The separate floppy controller then could be removed from the system, and you could save a slot.

I recommend replacing this controller with an autoconfigure controller whenever you get the chance. Most other controllers also are significantly faster than the Xebec.

Original IBM 16-Bit Controllers

For the AT, IBM used two controllers made by Western Digital (WD): the *WD1002-WA2* and the *WD1003A-WA2*. The WD1003 is an upgraded WD1002 with a much lower chip count. The WD1003 also was shorter than the WD1002 to fit into the IBM XT 286.

The WD1002 is used in the IBM AT as a combination hard disk and floppy disk controller. The WD1002 and the WD1003 are standard ST-506/412 controllers that supply MFM encoding to the drive. Neither controller contains a ROM BIOS; instead, BIOS support is built into the motherboard ROM. Both controllers support a 2:1 interleave, even on a standard 6MHz IBM AT system. The IBM Advanced Diagnostics low-level formatter can put down a 2:1 interleave, but the default is 3:1. Most users of these controllers can realize a performance gain if they simply reformat to the lower interleave.

The ESDI Interface

ESDI, or *Enhanced Small Device Interface*, is a specialized hard disk interface established as a standard in 1983, primarily by Maxtor Corporation. Maxtor led a consortium of drive manufacturers to adopt its proposed interface as a high-performance standard to succeed ST-506/412. ESDI later was adopted by the ANSI (American National Standards Institute) organization and published under the ANSI X3T9.2 Committee. The latest version of the ANSI ESDI document is known as X3.170a-1991. You can obtain this document, and other ANSI-standard documents, from ANSI itself or from Global Engineering Documents. These companies are listed in Appendix A.

Compared with ST-506/412, ESDI has provisions for increased reliability, such as building the endec into the drive. ESDI is a very-high-speed interface, capable of a maximum 24Mbit/sec transfer rate. Most drives running ESDI, however, are limited to a maximum 10 or 15Mbit/sec. Unfortunately, compatibility problems between different ESDI implementations combined with pressure from low-cost, high-performance IDE interface drives have served to make the ESDI interface obsolete. Few if any new systems today include ESDI drives, although ESDI became somewhat popular in high-end systems during the late 1980s.

Enhanced commands enabled some ESDI controllers to read a drive's capacity parameters directly from the drive, as well as to control defect mapping, but several manufacturers had different methods for writing this information on the drive. When you install an ESDI drive, in some cases the controller automatically reads the parameter and defect information directly from the drive. In other cases, however, you still have to enter this information manually, as with ST-506/412.

The ESDI's enhanced defect-mapping commands provide a standard way for the PC system to read a defect map from a drive, which means that the manufacturer's defect list can be written to the drive as a file. The defect-list file then can be read by the controller and low-level format software, eliminating the need for the installer to type these entries from the keyboard and enabling the format program to update the defect list with new entries if it finds new defects during the low-level format or the surface analysis.

Most ESDI implementations have drives formatted to 32 sectors per track or more (80 or more sectors per track are possible)—many more sectors per track than the standard ST-506/412 implementation of 17 to 26. The greater density results in two or more times the data-transfer rate, with a 1:1 interleave. Almost without exception, ESDI controllers support a 1:1 interleave, which allows for a transfer rate of 1M/sec or greater.

Because ESDI is much like the ST-506/412 interface, it can replace that interface without affecting software in the system. Most ESDI controllers are register-compatible with the older ST-506/412 controllers, which enables OS/2 and other non-DOS operating systems to run with few or no problems. The ROM BIOS interface to ESDI is similar to the ST-506/412 standard, and many low-level disk utilities that run on one interface will run on the other. To take advantage of ESDI defect mapping and other special features, however, use a low-level format and surface-analysis utility designed for ESDI (such as the ones usually built into the controller ROM BIOS and called by DEBUG).

During the late 1980s, most high-end systems from major manufacturers were equipped with ESDI controllers and drives. More recently, manufacturers have been equipping high-end systems with SCSI. The SCSI interface allows for much greater expandability, supports more types of devices than ESDI does, and offers equal or greater performance. I no longer recommend installing ESDI drives unless you are upgrading a system that already has an ESDI controller.

The IDE Interface

Integrated Drive Electronics (IDE) is a generic term applied to any drive with an integrated (built-in) disk controller. The IDE interface as we know it is officially called *ATA (AT Attachment)*, and is an ANSI standard; however, IDE can roughly apply to any disk drive with a built-in controller.

The first drives with integrated controllers were *hardcards*; today, a variety of drives with integrated controllers are available. In a drive with IDE, the disk controller is integrated into the drive, and this combination drive/controller assembly usually plugs into a bus connector on the motherboard or bus adapter card. Combining the drive and controller greatly simplifies installation, because there are no separate power or signal cables from the controller to the drive. Also, when the controller and the drive are assembled as a unit, the number of total components is reduced, signal paths are shorter, and the electrical connections are more noise-resistant, resulting in a more reliable design than is possible when a separate controller, connected to the drive by cables, is used.

Placing the controller (including endec) on the drive gives IDE drives an inherent reliability advantage over interfaces with separate controllers. Reliability is increased because the data encoding, from digital to analog, is performed directly on the drive in a tight noise-free environment; the timing-sensitive analog information does not have to travel along crude ribbon cables that are likely to pick up noise and insert propagation delays into the signals. The integrated configuration allows for increases in the clock rate of the encoder, as well as the storage density of the drive.

Integrating the controller and drive also frees the controller and drive engineers from having to adhere to the strict standards imposed by the earlier interface standards. Engineers can design what essentially are custom drive and controller implementations because no other controller would ever have to be connected to the drive. The resulting drive and controller combinations can offer higher performance than earlier stand-alone controller and drive setups. IDE drives sometimes are called drives with embedded controllers.

The IDE connector on motherboards in many systems is nothing more than a stripped-down bus slot. In ATA IDE installations, these connectors normally contain a 40-pin subset of the 98 pins that would be available in a standard 16-bit ISA bus slot. The pins used are only the signal pins required by a standard-type XT or AT hard disk controller. For example, because an AT-style disk controller uses only interrupt line 14, the motherboard AT IDE connector supplies only that interrupt line; no other interrupt lines are needed. The XT IDE motherboard connector supplies interrupt line 5 because that is what an XT controller would use.

> **Note**
>
> Many people who use systems with IDE connectors on the motherboard believe that a hard disk controller is built into their motherboard, but the controller really is in the drive. I do not know of any PC systems that have hard disk controllers built into the motherboard.

When IDE drives are discussed, the ATA IDE variety usually is the only kind mentioned because it is so popular. But other forms of IDE drives exist, based on other buses. For example, several PS/2 systems came with Micro-Channel (MCA) IDE drives which plug directly into a Micro-Channel Bus slot (through an angle adapter or interposer card). An 8-bit ISA form of IDE also existed but was never very popular. Most IBM-compatible systems with the ISA or EISA Bus use AT-Bus (16-bit) IDE drives. The ATA IDE interface is by far the most popular type of drive interface available.

The primary advantage of IDE drives is cost. Because the separate controller or host adapter is eliminated and the cable connections are simplified, IDE drives cost much less than a standard controller-and-drive combination. These drives also are more reliable, because the controller is built into the drive. Therefore, the endec or data separator (the converter between the digital and analog signals on the drive) stays close to the media. Because the drive has a short analog-signal path, it is less susceptible to external noise and interference.

Another advantage is performance. IDE drives are some of the highest-performance drives available—but they also are among the lowest-performance drives. This apparent contradiction is a result of the fact that all IDE drives are different. You cannot make a blanket statement about the performance of IDE drives because each drive is unique. The high-end models, however, offer performance that is equal or superior to that of any other type of drive on the market for a single-user, single-tasking operating system.

IDE Origins

Technically, the first IDE drives were hardcards. Companies such as the Plus Development division of Quantum took small 3 1/2-inch drives (either ST-506/412 or ESDI) and attached them directly to a standard controller. The assembly then was plugged into a bus slot as though it were a normal disk controller. Unfortunately, the mounting of a heavy, vibrating hard disk in an expansion slot with nothing but a single screw to hold it in place left a lot to be desired—not to mention the possible interference with adjacent cards due to the fact that many of these units were much thicker than a controller card alone.

Several companies got the idea that you could redesign the controller to replace the logic-board assembly on a standard hard disk and then mount it in a standard drive bay just like any other drive. Because the built-in controller in these drives still needed to plug directly into the expansion bus just like any other controller, a cable was run between the drive and one of the slots.

These connection problems were solved in different ways. Compaq was the first to incorporate a special bus adapter in its system to adapt the 98-pin AT bus edge connector on the motherboard to a smaller 40-pin header style connector that the drive would plug into. The 40-pin connectors were all that were needed, because it was known that a disk controller never would need more than 40 of the bus lines.

In 1987, IBM developed its own MCA IDE drives and connected them to the bus through a bus adapter device called an *interposer card*. These bus adapters (sometimes called *paddle boards*) needed only a few buffer chips and did not require any real circuitry because the drive-based controller was designed to plug directly into the bus. The paddle board nickname came from the fact that they resembled game paddle or joystick adapters, which do not have much circuitry on them. Another 8-bit variation of IDE appeared in 8-bit ISA systems such as the PS/2 Model 30. The XT IDE interface uses a 40-pin connector and cable that is similar to, but not compatible with, the 16-bit version.

IDE Bus Versions

Three main types of IDE interfaces are available, with the differences based on three different bus standards:

- AT Attachment (ATA) IDE (16-bit ISA)

- XT IDE (8-bit ISA)
- MCA IDE (16-bit Micro Channel)

> **Note**
>
> Many people are confused about 16- versus 32-bit bus connections and 16- versus 32-bit hard drive connections. A PCI connection allows for a 32-bit (and 64-bit in the future) bandwidth from the bus to the drive controller only. In an IDE (or EIDE) drive configuration, you are still getting only 16-bit bandwidth between the drive and the controller. This usually does not create a bottleneck, however, because one or two hard drives cannot supply the controller enough data to saturate even a 16-bit channel. Fast Wide SCSI-3 is the only device/controller combination that gives you 32 bits from the controller to the drive, primarily because you can hang 15 devices off a SCSI Wide chain and there is a good chance that many devices will saturate a 16-bit channel at some time.

The XT and ATA versions have standardized on 40-pin connectors and cables, but the connectors have slightly different pinouts, rendering them incompatible with one another. MCA IDE uses a completely different 72-pin connector and is designed for MCA bus systems only.

In most cases, you must use the type of IDE drive that matches your system bus. This situation means that XT IDE drives work only in XT-class 8-bit ISA slot systems, AT IDE drives work only in AT-class 16-bit ISA or EISA slot systems, and MCA IDE drives work only in Micro-Channel systems (such as the IBM PS/2 Model 50 or higher). A company called Silicon Valley offers adapter cards for XT systems that will run ATA IDE drives. Other companies, such as Arco Electronics and Sigma Data, have IDE adapters for Micro-Channel systems that allow ATA IDE drives to be used on these systems. (You can find these vendors in Appendix A.) These adapters are very useful for XT or PS/2 systems, because there is a very limited selection of XT or MCA IDE drives, whereas the selection of ATA drives is virtually unlimited.

In most modern ISA and EISA systems, you will find an ATA connector on the motherboard. If your motherboard does not have one of these connectors and you want to attach an AT IDE drive to your system, you can purchase an adapter card that changes your 98-pin slot connector to the 40-pin IDE connector. These adapter cards are nothing more than buffered cables; they are not really controllers. The controller is built into the drive. Some of the cards offer additional features, such as an on-board ROM BIOS or cache memory.

ATA IDE. CDC, Western Digital, and Compaq actually created what could be called the first ATA type IDE interface drive and were the first to establish the 40-pin IDE connector pinout. The first ATA IDE drives were 5 1/4-inch half-height CDC 40M units (I believe that they had a green activity LED) with integrated WD controllers sold in the first Compaq 386 systems in 1986. After that, Compaq helped found a company called Conner Peripherals to supply Compaq with IDE drives. Conner originally made drives only for Compaq, but later Compaq sold much of its ownership of Conner.

Eventually, the 40-pin IDE connector and drive interface method was placed before one of the ANSI standards committees which, in conjunction with drive manufacturers, ironed out some deficiencies, tied up some loose ends, and published what is known as the *CAM ATA (Common Access Method AT Attachment) interface*. The CAM Committee was formed in October 1988, and the first working document of the ATA interface was introduced in March 1989. Before the CAM ATA standard, many companies that followed CDC, such as Conner Peripherals, made proprietary changes to what had been done by CDC. As a result, many older ATA drives are very difficult to integrate into a dual-drive setup that has newer drives.

Some areas of the ATA standard have been left open for vendor-specific commands and functions. These vendor-specific commands and functions are the main reason why it is so difficult to low-level format IDE drives. To work properly, the formatter that you are using usually must know the specific vendor-unique commands for rewriting sector headers and remapping defects. Unfortunately, these and other specific drive commands differ from OEM to OEM, clouding the "standard" somewhat.

> **Note**
>
> It is important to note that only the ATA IDE interface has been standardized by the industry. The XT IDE and MCA IDE never were adopted as industry-wide standards and never became very popular. These interfaces are no longer in production, and no new systems of which I am aware come with these nonstandard IDE interfaces.

The ATA Specification. The ATA specification was introduced in March 1989 as an ANSI standard. ATA-1 was finally approved in 1994, and ATA-2 (also called *Enhanced IDE*) was approved in 1995. ATA-3 is currently in the works. You can obtain the current version of these standards from Global Engineering Documents, which is listed in Appendix A. The ATA standards have gone a long way toward eliminating incompatibilities and problems with interfacing IDE drives to ISA and EISA systems. The ATA specifications define the signals on the 40-pin connector, the functions and timings of these signals, cable specifications, and so on. The following section lists some of the elements and functions defined by the ATA specification.

Dual-Drive Configurations. Dual-drive ATA installations can be problematic because each drive has its own controller, and both controllers must function while being connected to the same bus. There has to be a way to ensure that only one of the two controllers will respond to a command at a time.

The ATA standard provides the option of operating on the AT Bus with two drives in a daisy-chained configuration. The primary drive (drive 0) is called the *master*, and the secondary drive (drive 1) is the *slave*. You designate a drive as being master or slave by setting a jumper or switch on the drive or by using a special line in the interface called the *Cable Select (CSEL) pin*.

When only one drive is installed, the controller responds to all commands from the system. When two drives (and, therefore, two controllers) are installed, all commands from the system are received by both controllers. Each controller then must be set up to respond only to commands for itself. In this situation, one controller then must be designated as the master and the other as the slave. When the system sends a command for a specific drive, the controller on the other drive must remain silent while the selected controller and drive are functioning. Setting the jumper to master or slave allows discrimination between the two controllers by setting a special bit (the *DRV bit*) in the Drive/Head Register of a command block.

ATA I/O Connector. The ATA interface connector is a 40-pin header-type connector that should be keyed to prevent the possibility of installing it upside down. A key is provided by the removal of pin 20, and the corresponding pin on the cable connector should be plugged in to prevent a backward installation. The use of keyed connectors and cables is highly recommended, because plugging an IDE cable in backward can damage both the drive and the bus adapter circuits (although I have done it myself many times with no smoked parts yet!).

Table 15.1 shows the ATA-IDE interface connector pinout.

Table 15.1 ATA Connector

Signal Name	Pin	Pin	Signal Name
-RESET	1	2	GROUND
Data Bit 7	3	4	Data Bit 8
Data Bit 6	5	6	Data Bit 9
Data Bit 5	7	8	Data Bit 10
Data Bit 4	9	10	Data Bit 11
Data Bit 3	11	12	Data Bit 12
Data Bit 2	13	14	Data Bit 13
Data Bit 1	15	16	Data Bit 14
Data Bit 0	17	18	Data Bit 15
GROUND	19	20	KEY (pin missing)
DRQ 3	21	22	GROUND
-IOW	23	24	GROUND
-IOR	25	26	GROUND
I/O CH RDY	27	28	SPSYNC:CSEL
-DACK 3	29	30	GROUND
IRQ 14	31	32	-IOCS16
Address Bit 1	33	34	-PDIAG
Address Bit 0	35	36	Address Bit 2
-CS1FX	37	38	-CS3FX
-DA/SP	39	40	GROUND
+5 Vdc (Logic)	41	42	+5 Vdc (Motor)
GROUND	43	44	-TYPE (0=ATA)

ATA I/O Cable. A 40-conductor ribbon cable is specified to carry signals between the bus adapter circuits and the drive (controller). To maximize signal integrity and to eliminate potential timing and noise problems, the cable should not be longer than 0.46 meters (18 inches).

ATA Signals. This section describes some of the most important signals in more detail.

Pin 20 is used as a key pin for cable orientation and is not connected through in the interface. This pin should be missing from any ATA connectors, and the cable should have the pin-20 hole in the connector plugged off to prevent the cable from being plugged in backward.

Pin 39 carries the *Drive Active/Slave Present (DASP) signal*, which is a dual-purpose, time-multiplexed signal. During power-on initialization, this signal indicates whether a slave drive is present on the interface. After that, each drive asserts the signal to indicate that it is active. Early drives could not multiplex these functions and required special jumper settings to work with other drives. Standardizing this function to allow for compatible dual-drive installations is one of the features of the ATA standard.

Pin 28 carries the *Cable Select* or *Spindle Synchronization signal (CSEL or SPSYNC)*, which is a dual-purpose conductor; a given installation, however, may use only one of the two functions. The CSEL function is the most widely used and is designed to control the designation of a drive as master (drive 0) or slave (drive 1) without requiring jumper settings on the drives. If a drive sees the CSEL as being grounded, the drive is a master; if CSEL is open, the drive is a slave.

You can install special cabling to ground CSEL selectively. This installation normally is accomplished through a Y-cable arrangement, with the IDE bus connector in the middle and each drive at opposite ends of the cable. One leg of the Y has the CSEL line connected through, indicating a master drive; the other leg has the CSEL line open (conductor interrupted or removed), making the drive at that end the slave.

ATA Commands. One of the best features of the ATA IDE interface is the enhanced command set. The ATA IDE interface was modeled after the WD1003 controller that IBM used in the original AT system. All ATA IDE drives must support the original WD command set (eight commands), with no exceptions, which is why IDE drives are so easy to install in systems today. All IBM-compatible systems have built-in ROM BIOS support for the WD1003, which means that essentially they support ATA IDE as well.

In addition to supporting all the WD1003 commands, the ATA specification added numerous other commands to enhance performance and capabilities. These commands are an optional part of the ATA interface, but several of them are used in most drives available today and are very important to the performance and use of ATA drives in general.

Perhaps the most important is the `Identify Drive` command. This command causes the drive to transmit a 512-byte block of data that provides all details about the drive. Through this command, any program (including the system BIOS) can find out exactly what type of drive is connected, including the drive manufacturer, model number, operating parameters, and even the serial number of the drive. Many modern BIOSes use this information to automatically receive and enter the drive's parameters into CMOS memory, eliminating the need for the user to enter these parameters manually during system configuration. This arrangement helps prevent mistakes that can later lead to data loss when the user no longer remembers what parameters he or she used during setup.

The Identify Drive data can tell you many things about your drive, including the following:

- Number of cylinders in the recommended (default) translation mode
- Number of heads in the recommended (default) translation mode
- Number of sectors per track in the recommended (default) translation mode
- Number of cylinders in the current translation mode
- Number of heads in the current translation mode
- Number of sectors per track in the current translation mode
- Manufacturer and model number
- Firmware revision
- Serial number
- Buffer type, indicating sector buffering or caching capabilities

Several public-domain programs can execute this command to the drive and report the information on-screen. I use the IDEINFO or IDEDIAG program. Phone numbers for these information services appear in Appendix A. I find these programs especially useful when I am trying to install IDE drives and need to know the correct parameters for a user-definable BIOS type. These programs get the information directly from the drive itself.

On the Web

You can get a copy of IDEINFO at

http://www.dc.ee/Files/Utils/IDEINFO.ARJ

You can pick up IDEDIAG at

http://www.pcorner.com/tpc/old/24-151.html

Two other very important commands are the Read Multiple and Write Multiple commands. These commands permit multiple-sector data transfers and, when combined with block-mode Programmed I/O (PIO) capabilities in the system, can result in incredible data-transfer rates many times faster than single-sector PIO transfers.

> **Tip**
>
> If you want the ultimate in IDE performance and installation ease, make sure that your motherboard BIOS and IDE adapter supports ATA-2 or EIDE. This support allows your BIOS to execute data transfers to and from the IDE drive several times faster than normal, and also makes installation and configuration easier because the BIOS will be able to detect the drive-parameter information automatically. High-speed PIO and automatic detection of the drive type are included in the latest versions of most PC BIOSes.

There are many other enhanced commands, including room for a given drive manufacturer to implement what are called *vendor-unique commands*. These commands often are used by a particular vendor for features unique to that vendor. Often, features such as low-level formatting and defect management are controlled by vendor-unique commands. This is why low-level format programs can be so specific to a particular manufacturer's IDE drives and why many manufacturers make their own LLF programs available.

ATA IDE Drive Categories. ATA-IDE drives can be divided into three main categories. These categories separate the drives by function (such as translation capabilities) and design (which can affect features such as low-level formatting):

- Non-Intelligent ATA-IDE drives
- Intelligent ATA-IDE drives
- Intelligent Zoned Recording ATA-IDE drives

Non-Intelligent IDE. As I stated earlier, the ATA standard requires that the built-in controller respond exactly as though it were a Western Digital WD1003 controller. This controller responds to a command set of eight commands. Early IDE drives supported these commands and had few, if any, other options. These early drives actually were more like regular ST-506/412 or ESDI controllers bolted directly into the drive than the more intelligent drives that we consider today to be IDE.

These drives were not considered to be intelligent IDE drives; an intelligent drive is supposed to have several capabilities that these early IDE drives lacked. The drives could not respond to any of the enhanced commands that were specified as (an optional) part of the ATA IDE specification, including the Identify Drive command. These drives also did not support *sector translation*, in which the physical parameters could be altered to appear as any set of logical cylinders, heads, and sectors. Enhanced commands and sector-translation support are what make an IDE drive an intelligent IDE drive, and these features were not available in the early IDE drives.

These drives could be low-level formatted in the same manner as any normal ST-506/412 or ESDI drive. They were universally low-level formatted at the factory, with factory-calculated optimum interleave (usually, 1:1) and head- and cylinder-skew factors. Also, factory defects were recorded in a special area on the drive; they no longer were written on a sticker pasted to the exterior. Unfortunately, this arrangement means that if you low-level format these drives in the field, you most likely will alter these settings (especially the skew factors) from what the factory set as optimum, as well as wipe out the factory-written defect table.

Some manufacturers released special low-level format routines that would reformat the drives while preserving these settings, but others did not make such programs available. Because they did not want you to overwrite the defect list or potentially slow the drive, most manufacturers stated that you should never low-level format their IDE drives.

This statement started a myth that the drives could somehow be damaged or rendered inoperable by such a format, which truly is not the case. One rumor was that the servo information could be overwritten, which would mean that you would have to send the drive back to the manufacturer for re-servoing. This also is not true; the servo information is protected and cannot be overwritten. The only consequence of an improper low-level format of these drives is the possible alteration of the skew factors and the potential loss of the factory defect maps.

The Disk Manager program by Ontrack is the best special-purpose format utility to use on these drives for formatting because it is aware of these types of drives and often can restore the skew factors and preserve the defect information. If you are working with a drive that already has had the defect map overwritten, Disk Manager can perform a very good surface analysis that will mark off any of these areas that it finds. Disk Manager allows you to specify the skew factors and to mark defects at the sector level so that they will not cause problems later. Other general-purpose diagnostics that work especially well with IDE drives such as this include the Microscope program by Micro 2000.

Intelligent IDE. Later IDE drives became known as *intelligent IDE drives*. These drives support enhanced ATA commands, such as the `Identify Drive` command, and sector-translation capabilities.

These drives can be configured in two ways: in raw physical mode or in translation mode. To configure the drive in raw physical mode, you simply enter the CMOS drive parameters during setup so that they match the true physical parameters of the drive. For example, if the drive physically has 800 cylinders, 6 heads, and 50 sectors per track, you enter these figures during setup. To configure the drive in translation mode, you simply enter any combination of cylinders, heads, and sectors that adds up to equal or less than the true number of sectors on the drive.

In the example I just used, the drive has a total of 240,000 sectors (800×6×50). All I have to do is figure out another set of parameters that adds up equal to or less than 240,000 sectors. The simplest way to do this is to cut the number of cylinders in half and double the number of heads. Thus, the new drive parameters become 400 cylinders, 12 heads, and 50 sectors per track. This method adds up to 240,000 sectors and enables the drive to work in translation mode.

When these drives are in translation mode, a low-level format cannot alter the interleave and skew factors, nor can it overwrite the factory defect-mapping information. A low-level format program can, however, perform additional defect mapping or sector sparing while in this mode.

If the drive is in true physical mode, a low-level format rewrites the sector headers and modifies the head and cylinder skewing. If performed incorrectly, the format can be repaired by a proper low-level format program that allows you to set the correct head and cylinder skew. This task can be accomplished automatically by the drive manufacturer's recommended low-level format program (if available) or by other programs, such as Disk Manager by Ontrack. When you use Disk Manager, you have to enter the skew values manually; otherwise, the program uses predetermined defaults. To obtain the correct skew values, it is best to contact the drive manufacturer's technical support department. You can calculate the skew values if the manufacturer cannot provide them.

To protect the skew factors and defect information on intelligent IDE drives, all you have to do is run them in translation mode. In translation mode, this information cannot be overwritten.

Intelligent Zoned Recording IDE. The last and most sophisticated IDE drives combine intelligence with Zoned Recording. With *Zoned Recording*, the drive has a variable number sectors per track in several zones across the surface of the drive. Because the PC BIOS can handle only a fixed number of sectors on all tracks, these drives always must run in translation mode. Because these drives are always in translation mode, you cannot alter the factory-set interleave and skew factors or wipe out the factory defect information.

You still can low-level format these drives, however, and use such a format to map or spare additional defective sectors that crop up during the life of the drive. To low-level format intelligent Zoned Recording drives, you need either a specific utility from the drive manufacturer or an IDE-aware program, such Disk Manager by Ontrack or Microscope by Micro 2000.

ATA-2 (Enhanced IDE). *ATA-2* is an extension of the original ATA (IDE) specification. The most important additions are performance enhancing features such as fast PIO and DMA modes. ATA-2 also features improvements in the Identify Drive command allowing a drive to tell the software exactly what its characteristics are; this is essential for both Plug and Play (PnP) and compatibility with future revisions of the standard.

ATA-2 is often called Enhanced IDE (or EIDE). EIDE is technically a marketing program from Western Digital. Fast-ATA and Fast-ATA-2 are similar Seagate-inspired marketing programs, which are also endorsed by Quantum. As far as the hard disk and BIOS are concerned, these are all different terms for basically the same thing.

There are four main areas where ATA-2 and EIDE have improved the original ATA/IDE interface:

- Increased maximum drive capacity
- Faster data transfer
- Secondary two-device channel
- ATAPI (ATA Program Interface)

The following section describes these improvements.

Increased Drive Capacity. ATA-2/EIDE allows for increased drive capacity over the original ATA/IDE specification. This is done through an Enhanced BIOS, which makes it possible to use hard disks exceeding the 504M barrier. The origin of this limit is the disk geometry (cylinders, heads, sectors) supported by the combination of an IDE drive and the BIOS' software interface. Both IDE and the BIOS are capable of supporting huge disks, but their combined limitations conspire to restrict the useful capacity to 504M.

An Enhanced BIOS circumvents this by using a different geometry when talking to the drive than when talking to the software. What happens in between is called *translation*.

For example, if your drive has 2,000 cylinders and 16 heads, a translating BIOS will make programs think that the drive has 1,000 cylinders and 32 heads.

You can usually tell if your BIOS is enhanced by the ability to specify more than 1,024 cylinders in the BIOS setup, although this is not conclusive. If you see drive-related settings like LBA, ECHS, or even Large, these are tell-tale signs of a BIOS with translation support. Most BIOSes with a date of 1994 or later are enhanced. If your system currently does not have an Enhanced BIOS, you may be able to get an upgrade.

There are roughly three ways today's BIOSes can handle translation: Standard CHS addressing, Extended CHS addressing, and LBA (Logical Block Addressing). They are summarized in the following table:

BIOS Mode	Operating System to BIOS	BIOS to Drive Ports
Standard CHS	Logical CHS Parameters	Logical CHS Parameters
Extended CHS	Translated CHS Parameters	Logical CHS Parameters
LBA	Translated CHS Parameters	LBA Parameters

In Standard CHS, there is only one possible translation step internal to the drive. The drive's actual, physical geometry is completely invisible from the outside with all zoned recorded ATA drives today. The Cylinders, Heads, and Sectors printed on the label for use in the BIOS setup are purely logical geometry, and do not represent the actual physical parameters. Standard CHS addressing is limited to 16 heads and 1,024 cylinders, which gives the us a limit of 504M.

This is often called "Normal" in the BIOS setup, and causes the BIOS to behave like an old-fashioned one without translation. Use this setting if your drive has fewer than 1,024 cylinders or if you want to use the drive with a non-DOS operating system that doesn't understand translation.

In Extended CHS, a translated logical geometry is used to communicate between the drive and the BIOS, while a different translated geometry is used to communicate between the BIOS and everything else. In other words, there are normally two translation steps. The drive still translates internally, but has logical parameters that exceed the 1,024 cylinder limitation of the standard BIOS. In this case, the drive's cylinder count is usually divided by 2, and the head count is multiplied by 2 to get the translated values from those actually stored in the CMOS Setup. This type of setting breaks the 504/528M barrier.

This is often called "Large" or "ECHS" in the BIOS setup, and tells the BIOS to use Extended CHS translation. It uses a different geometry (cylinders/heads/sectors) when talking to the drive than when talking to the BIOS. This type of translation should be used with drives that have more than 1,024 cylinders but that do not support LBA. Note that the geometry entered in your BIOS setup is the logical geometry, not the translated one.

LBA is a means of linearly addressing sector's addresses, beginning at Cylinder 0, Head 0, Sector 1 as LBA 0, and proceeding on to the last physical sector on the drive. This is new in ATA-2, but has always been the one and only addressing mode in SCSI.

With LBA, each sector on the drive is numbered starting from 0. The number is a 28-bit binary number internally, which translates to a sector number of from 0 to 268,435,456. Because each sector represents 512 bytes, this results in a maximum drive capacity of exactly 128G, or 137 billion bytes. Unfortunately, the operating system still needs to see a translated CHS, so the BIOS determines how many sectors there are, and comes up with Translated CHS to match. The BIOS CHS limits are 1,024 cylinders, 256 heads, and 63 sectors per track, which limits total drive capacity to just under 8G.

In other words, this breaks the 528M barrier in essentially the same way as Extended CHS does. Because it is somewhat simpler to use a single linear number to address a sector on the hard disk compared to a CHS type address, this is the preferred method if the drive supports LBA.

> **Caution**
>
> A word of warning with these BIOS translation settings: If you switch between Standard CHS, Extended CHS, or LBA, the BIOS may change the (translated) geometry. The same thing may happen if you transfer a disk that has been formatted on an old, non-LBA computer to a new one that uses LBA. This will cause the logical CHS geometry seen by the operating system to change, and will cause the date to appear in the wrong locations from where it actually is! This can cause you to lose access to your data if you are not careful. I always recommend recording the CMOS Setup screens associated with the hard disk configuration so that you can properly match the setup of a drive to the original settings.

Faster Data Transfer. ATA-2/EIDE defines several high-performance modes for transferring data to and from the drive. These faster modes are the main part of the new specifications and were the main reason they were initially developed. Most of the faster drives on the market today will support either PIO transfer Mode 3 or Mode 4, which results in a very fast transfer. The following section discusses these modes.

The PIO mode determines how fast data is transferred to and from the drive. In the slowest possible mode—PIO mode 0—the data cycle time cannot exceed 600 nanoseconds (ns). In a single cycle, 16 bits are transferred in or out of the drive making the theoretical transfer rate of PIO Mode 0 (600ns cycle time) 3.3M/sec. Most of the high-performance ATA-2 (EIDE) drives today support PIO Mode 4, which offers a 16.6M/sec transfer rate.

The following table shows the PIO modes, with their respective transfer rates:

PIO Mode	Cycle Time (ns)	Transfer Rate (M/sec)	Specification
0	600	3.3	ATA
1	383	5.2	ATA
2	240	8.3	ATA
3	180	11.1	ATA-2
4	120	16.6	ATA-2

To run in Mode 3 or 4 requires that the IDE port on the system be a local bus port. This means that it must operate through either a VL-Bus or PCI bus connection. Some newer motherboards with ATA-2/EIDE support have dual IDE connectors on the motherboard, with only the primary connector running through the system's PCI local bus. The secondary connector usually runs through the ISA bus, and therefore supports up to Mode 2 operation only. Make sure you get clarification of this before you purchase that new motherboard!

When interrogated with an `Identify Drive` command, a hard disk returns, among other things, information about the PIO and DMA modes it is capable of using. Most enhanced BIOSes will automatically set the correct mode to match the capabilities of the drive. If you set a mode faster than the drive can handle, data corruption will result.

ATA-2 drives also perform *Block Mode PIO*, which means that they use the `Read/Write Multiple` commands that greatly reduce the number of interrupts sent to host processor. This lowers the overhead, and the resulting transfers are even faster.

DMA Transfer Modes. Although it is not used by most operating system or BIOS software, ATA-2 drives also support Direct Memory Access transfers. DMA means that the data is transferred directly between drive and memory without using the CPU as an intermediary, as opposed to PIO.

There are two distinct types of direct memory access: *DMA* and *busmastering DMA*. Ordinary DMA relies on the DMA controller on the system's mainboard to perform the complex task of arbitration, grabbing the system bus and transferring the data. In the case of busmastering DMA, all this is done by logic on the interface card itself. Of course, this adds considerably to the complexity and the price of a busmastering interface.

Unfortunately, the DMA controller on ISA systems is ancient and slow, and out of the question for use with a modern hard disk. Today, proper software support for DMA is still rare.

ATAPI (ATA Packet Interface). *ATAPI* is a standard designed for devices such as CD-ROMs and tape drives that plug into an ordinary ATA (IDE) connector. The principal advantage of ATAPI hardware is that it's cheap and works on your current adapter. For CD-ROMs, it has a somewhat lower CPU usage compared to proprietary adapters, but there's no performance gain otherwise. For tape drives, ATAPI has potential for superior performance and reliability compared to the popular "floppy" tape devices.

While ATAPI CD-ROMs use the hard disk interface, this does not mean that they look like an ordinary hard disk; to the contrary, from a software point of view they are a completely different kind of animal. They actually most closely resemble a SCSI device.

> **Caution**
>
> Intelligent caching controllers that are not ATAPI-aware will *not* work with these devices. This means that, at present, you cannot boot from an ATAPI CD-ROM and you still must load a driver to use it under DOS or Windows. Windows 95/NT has native ATAPI support, and the first ATAPI-aware BIOS that will even allow booting from an ATAPI CD-ROM are now available.

IDE Drive Configuration. IDE drives can be both simple and troublesome to configure. Single-drive installations usually are very simple, with few if any special jumper settings to worry about. Multiple-drive configurations, however, can be a problem. Jumpers have to be set on both drives; the names, locations, and even functions of these jumpers can vary from drive to drive.

Because the CAM ATA IDE specification was ironed out only after many companies were already making and selling drives, many older IDE drives have problems in dual-drive installations, especially when the drives are from different manufacturers. In some cases, two particular drives may not function together at all. Fortunately, most of the newer drives follow the CAM ATA specification, which clears up this problem. Drives that follow the specification have no problems in dual-drive installations.

Cable Configuration. The cable connection to IDE drives usually is very simple. There is a single 40-pin cable that normally has three pin-header style connectors on it. One of the connectors plugs into the IDE interface connector; the other two plug into the primary and secondary drives. The cable normally runs from the IDE connector to both drives in a daisy-chain arrangement. On one end, this cable plugs into the IDE interface connector, which is located on the motherboard in many systems but also may be located on an IDE interface adapter card. The cable then connects to the secondary (D) and primary (C) drives in succession, with the primary drive usually (but not always) being at the end of the cable opposite the IDE interface connector.

There are no terminating resistors to set with IDE drives; instead, a distributed termination circuit is built into all IDE drives. The last drive on the cable need not be the primary drive, so you actually may find the primary or secondary drive at either connector. Jumpers on the drives themselves normally control whether a drive responds as primary or secondary.

> **Caution**
>
> You may see a different arrangement of cable connections in some IDE installations. In some installations, the middle connector is plugged into the motherboard, and the primary and secondary drives are at opposite ends of the cable in a Y arrangement. If you see this arrangement, be careful; in some of these Y-cable installations, the cable, rather than jumpers on the drives, actually controls which drive is primary and which is secondary.

Controlling master/slave selection via the cable rather than jumpers on the drive is performed via a special signal on the IDE interface called CSEL, which is on pin 28 of the interface. If the CSEL line is connected through from the drive to the IDE interface connector, the drive automatically is designated as primary. If the CSEL line is open between a drive and the IDE interface connector, that drive automatically is designated as secondary.

In the Y-cable approach, the IDE interface connector is in the middle of the cable, and a separate length of cable goes to each drive. Study this type of cable closely. If one of the ends of the Y has line 28 open (usually a hole in the cable through that wire), only the secondary drive can be plugged into that connector. HP Vectra PC systems use exactly this type of IDE cable arrangement. This type of setup eliminates the need to set jumpers on the IDE drives to configure them for primary or secondary operation, but the setup can be troublesome if you do not know about it.

IDE Drive Jumper Settings. Configuring IDE drives can be simple, as is the case with most single-drive installations, or troublesome, especially where it comes to mixing two drives from different manufacturers on a single cable.

Most IDE drives come in three configurations:

- Single-drive (master)
- Master (dual-drive)
- Slave (dual-drive)

Because each IDE drive has its own controller, you must specifically tell one drive to be the master and the other to be the slave. There's no functional difference between the two, except that the drive that's specified as the slave will assert the DASP signal after a system reset that informs the master that a slave drive is present in the system. The master drive then pays attention to the Drive Select line, which it otherwise ignores. Telling a drive that it's the slave also usually causes it to delay its spinup for several seconds to allow the master to get going and thus to lessen the load on the system's power supply.

Until the ATA IDE specification, no common implementation for drive configuration was in use. Some drive companies even used different master/slave methods for different models of drives. Because of these incompatibilities, some drives work together only in a specific master/slave or slave/master order. This situation affects mostly older IDE drives that were introduced before the ATA specification.

Most drives that fully follow the ATA specification now need only one jumper (Master/Slave) for configuration. A few also need a Slave Present jumper as well. Table 15.2 shows the jumper settings required by most ATA IDE drives.

Table 15.2 Jumper Settings for Most ATA IDE-Compatible Drives

Jumper Name	Single-Drive	Dual-Drive Master	Dual-Drive Slave
Master (M/S)	On	On	Off
Slave Present (SP)	Off	On	Off

The Master jumper indicates that the drive is a master or a slave. Some drives also require a Slave Present jumper, which is used only in a dual-drive setup and then installed only on the master drive, which is somewhat confusing. This jumper tells the master that a slave drive is attached. With many ATA IDE drives, the Master jumper is optional and may be left off. Installing this jumper doesn't hurt in these cases and may eliminate confusion, so I recommend that you install the jumpers listed here.

Conner Peripherals Drives. Because they were introduced before the ATA IDE specification was formalized, Conner Peripherals drives often are different in configuration from many other-brand drives. When you mix and match IDE hard drives from different manufacturers, the drives are not always fully compatible. Table 15.3 shows the jumper settings that are correct for most Conner IDE drive installations.

Table 15.3 Jumper Settings for Conner Peripherals IDE Drives			
Jumper Name	**Single Drive**	**Dual-Drive Master**	**Dual-Drive Slave**
Master or Slave (C/D)	On	On	Off
Drive Slave Present (DSP)	Off	On	Off
Host Slave Present (HSP)	Off	Off	On
Drive Active (ACT)	On	On	Off

The C/D jumper is used to determine whether the drive is a master (drive C) or a slave (drive D). The drive is configured as master when this jumper is on. The DSP jumper indicates that a slave drive is present. The HSP jumper causes the drive to send the Slave Present signal to the master drive. The ACT jumper enables the master drive to signal when it is active.

Some Conner drives are not set up to support the industry-standard CAM ATA interface by default. The problems show up when you attempt to connect another manufacturer's drive to some Conner drives in either a master or slave role. Fortunately, you can correct many of these situations by changing the configuration of the drive.

You can make this change in two ways. One way is to use a special program to semi-permanently change the mode of the drive. A special file available on the Conner BBS, called FEATURE.COM, contains a program that displays the current ISA/ATACAM setting and allows the setting to be changed. The change actually is stored in a feature byte in the firmware of the drive, and after this byte is changed, most other manufacturers' drives will work with the Conner drives. The program also can be used to reset the feature byte to its original configuration, which is best when you are connecting to other Conner drives.

The second method for changing this configuration is available on some Conner drives. These drives also have a special jumper called ATA/ISA. This jumper almost always should be installed in the ATA position to provide compatibility with the ATA standard. If you are using only Conner drives, you can leave this jumper in ISA mode if you want. Some Conner drives have a separate jumper (E1) that can delay startup of the drive to minimize the load on the power supply. This jumper should be enabled on any drive that is configured as a slave. Most other drives automatically delay startup of the slave drive for a few seconds.

Most Conner drives also have a special 12-pin connector that is used to drive an optional LED (pin 1, LED +5v; and pin 2, ground), as well as to connect to special factory equipment for low-level formatting and configuration. A company called TCE (see Appendix A) sells a device called *The Conner*, which connects to this port and permits full factory-level initialization, formatting, and testing of Conner drives. I consider this piece of gear to be essential to anybody who services or supports a large number of Conner Peripherals drives. Notice that Compaq uses Conner drives in most of its systems.

For more information on any specific Conner drive, you can use the company's FAXBack system (see the vendor list in Appendix A) at (800) 4CONNER. Through this system, you can get drive information and jumper settings that are specific to Conner drives.

XT-Bus (8-Bit) IDE

Many systems with XT ISA bus architecture used XT IDE hard drives. The IDE interface in these systems usually is built into the motherboard. The IBM PS/2 Model 25, 25-286, 30, and 30-286 systems used an 8-bit XT IDE interface. These 8-bit XT IDE drives are difficult to find; few manufacturers other than IBM, Western Digital, and Seagate made them; none of these drives were available in capacities beyond 40M.

Because the ATA IDE interface is a 16-bit design, it could not be used in 8-bit (XT type) systems, so some of the drive manufacturers standardized on an XT-Bus (8-bit) IDE interface for XT class systems. These drives were never very popular, and were usually only available in capacities from 20M to 40M. Table 15.4 shows the industry standard 8-bit IDE connector pinout.

Table 15.4 XT-Bus IDE Connector

Signal Name	Pin	Pin	Signal Name
-RESET	1	2	GROUND
Data Bit 7	3	4	GROUND
Data Bit 6	5	6	GROUND
Data Bit 5	7	8	GROUND
Data Bit 4	9	10	GROUND
Data Bit 3	11	12	GROUND
Data Bit 2	13	14	GROUND
Data Bit 1	15	16	GROUND
Data Bit 0	17	18	GROUND
GROUND	19	20	KEY (pin missing)
AEN	21	22	GROUND
-IOW	23	24	GROUND
-IOR	25	26	GROUND
-DACK 3	27	28	GROUND
DRQ 3	29	30	GROUND
IRQ 5	31	32	GROUND
Address Bit 1	33	34	GROUND
Address Bit 0	35	36	GROUND
-CS1FX	37	38	GROUND
-Drive Active	39	40	GROUND

Notice that IBM used a custom version of the XT-Bus IDE interface in the PS/2 Model 25 and Model 30 systems. The pinout for the custom IBM XT-Bus IDE connector is shown in Table 15.5.

Table 15.5 IBM Unique XT-Bus (PS/2 Model 25 and 30) IDE Connector

Signal Name	Pin	Pin	Signal Name
-RESET	1	2	-Disk Installed
Data Bit 0	3	4	GROUND
Data Bit 1	5	6	GROUND
Data Bit 2	7	8	GROUND
Data Bit 3	9	10	GROUND
Data Bit 4	11	12	GROUND
Data Bit 5	13	14	GROUND
Data Bit 6	15	16	GROUND
Data Bit 7	17	18	GROUND
-IOR	19	20	GROUND
-IOW	21	22	GROUND
-CS1FX	23	24	GROUND
Address Bit 0	25	26	GROUND
Address Bit 1	27	28	GROUND
Address Bit 2	29	30	+5v DC
RESERVED	31	32	+5 Vdc
-DACK 3	33	34	GROUND
DRQ 3	35	36	GROUND
IRQ 5	37	38	GROUND
I/O CH RDY	39	40	+12 Vdc
Spare	41	42	+12 Vdc
Spare	39	44	+12 Vdc

The newer PS/1, PS/Valuepoint, and PS/2 systems with 16-bit ISA architecture use ATA IDE drives. Because nearly all hard disk manufacturers make a multitude of drives with the ATA IDE interface, these systems are easy to upgrade or repair. ATA IDE drives are available in capacities up to and beyond 1G.

MCA IDE

The IBM PS/2 Models 50 and higher come with Micro-Channel Architecture (MCA) bus slots. Although most of these systems now use SCSI drives, for some time IBM used a type of MCA IDE drive in these systems. MCA IDE is a form of IDE interface, but it is designed for the MCA bus and is not compatible with the more industry-standard ATA IDE interface. Few companies other than IBM and Western Digital make replacement MCA IDE drives for these systems. I recommend replacing these drives with ATA IDE drives, using adapters from Arco Electronics or Sigma Data, or switching to SCSI drives instead. The IBM MCA IDE drives are expensive for the limited capacity that they offer.

The pinout of the MCA IDE connector is shown in Table 15.6.

Table 15.6 MCA IDE Connector

Signal Name	Pin	Pin	Signal Name
-CD SETUP	A1	B1	Address Bit 15
Address Bit 13	A2	B2	Address Bit 14
GROUND	A3	B3	GROUND
Address Bit 11	A4	B4	OSC (14.3 MHz)
Address Bit 10	A5	B5	GROUND
Address Bit 9	A6	B6	Address Bit 12
+5 Vdc	A7	B7	-CMD
Address Bit 8	A8	B8	-CD SFDBK
Address Bit 7	A9	B9	GROUND
Address Bit 6	A10	B10	Data Bit 1
+5 Vdc	A11	B11	Data Bit 3
Address Bit 5	A12	B12	Data Bit 4
Address Bit 4	A13	B13	GROUND
Address Bit 3	A14	B14	CHRESET
+5 Vdc	A15	B15	Data Bit 8
Address Bit 2	A16	B16	Data Bit 9
Address Bit 1	A17	B17	GROUND
Address Bit 0	A18	B18	Data Bit 12
+12 Vdc	A19	B19	Data Bit 14
-ADL	A20	B20	Data Bit 15
-PREEMPT	A21	B21	GROUND
-BURST	A22	B22	Data Bit 0
+5 Vdc	A23	B23	Data Bit 2
ARB 0	A24	B24	Data Bit 5
ARB 1	A25	B25	GROUND
ARB 2	A26	B26	Data Bit 6
+12 Vdc	A27	B27	Data Bit 7
ARB 3	A28	B28	Data Bit 10
+ARB/-GRANT	A29	B29	GROUND
-TC	A30	B30	Data Bit 11
+5 Vdc	A31	B31	Data Bit 13
-S0	A32	B32	-SBHE
-S1	A33	B33	GROUND
+M/-IO	A34	B34	-CD DS 16
GROUND	A35	B35	-IRQ 14
CD CHRDY	A36	B36	GROUND

Introduction to SCSI

SCSI (pronounced "scuzzy") stands for *Small Computer System Interface*. This interface has its roots in *SASI*, the *Shugart Associates System Interface*. SCSI is not a disk interface, but a systems-level interface. SCSI is not a type of controller, but a bus that supports as many as eight devices. One of these devices, the host adapter, functions as the gateway between the SCSI bus and the PC system bus. The SCSI bus itself does not talk directly with devices such as hard disks; instead, it talks to the controller that is built into the drive.

A single SCSI bus can support as many as eight physical units, usually called *SCSI IDs*. One of these units is the adapter card in your PC; the other seven can be other peripherals. You could have hard disks, tape drives, CD-ROM drives, a graphics scanner, or other devices (up to seven total) attached to a single SCSI host adapter. Most systems support up to four host adapters, each with seven devices, for a total 28 devices! Some of the newer SCSI implementations allow for 15 devices on each bus.

When you purchase a SCSI hard disk, you usually are purchasing the drive, controller, and SCSI adapter in one circuit. This type of drive usually is called an *embedded SCSI drive*; the SCSI interface is built into the drive. Most SCSI hard drives actually are IDE drives with SCSI bus adapter circuits added. You do not need to know what type of controller is inside the SCSI drive, because your system cannot talk directly to the controller as though it were plugged into the system bus, like a standard controller. Instead, communications go through the SCSI host adapter installed in the system bus. You can access the drive only with the SCSI protocols.

Apple originally rallied around SCSI as being an inexpensive way out of the bind in which it put itself with the Macintosh. When the engineers at Apple realized the problem in making the Macintosh a closed system (with no slots), they decided that the easiest way to gain expandability was to build a SCSI port into the system, which is how external peripherals can be added to the slotless Macs. Because PC systems always have been expandable, the push toward SCSI has not been as urgent. With eight bus slots supporting different devices and controllers in IBM and IBM-compatible systems, it seemed as though SCSI was not needed.

SCSI now is becoming popular in the IBM-based computer world because of the great expandability that it offers and the number of devices that are available with built-in SCSI. One block that stalled acceptance of SCSI in the PC marketplace was the lack of a real standard; the SCSI standard was designed primarily by a committee. No single manufacturer has led the way, at least in the IBM arena; each company has its own interpretation of how SCSI should be implemented, particularly at the host-adapter level.

SCSI is a standard, in much the same way that RS-232 is a standard. The SCSI standard (like the RS-232 standard), however, defines only the hardware connections, not the driver specifications required to communicate with the devices. Software ties the SCSI subsystem into your PC, but unfortunately, most of the driver programs work only for a specific device and a specific host adapter. For example, a graphics scanner comes with its own SCSI host adapter to connect to the system; a CD-ROM drive comes with another (different) SCSI host adapter and driver software that works only with that SCSI adapter.

On a system with those two SCSI adapters, you would need a third SCSI host adapter to run SCSI hard disk drives, because the host adapters supplied by the scanner and CD-ROM companies do not include a built-in, self-booting BIOS that supports hard disk drives.

SCSI has become something of a mess in the IBM world because of the lack of a host-adapter standard, a software interface standard, and standard ROM BIOS support for hard disk drives attached to the SCSI bus. Fortunately, some simple recommendations can keep you from living this compatibility nightmare!

In the beginning, SCSI lacked the capability to run hard disks off the SCSI bus. To boot from these drives and use a variety of operating systems was a problem that resulted from the lack of an interface standard. The standard IBM XT and AT ROM BIOS software was designed to talk to ST-506/412 hard disk controllers. The software easily was modified to work with ESDI because ESDI controllers are similar to ST-506/412 controllers at the register level. (This similarity at the register level enabled manufacturers to easily design self-booting, ROM-BIOS-supported ESDI drives.) The same can be said of IDE, which completely emulates the WD1003 ST-506/412 controller interface and works perfectly with the existing BIOS as well. SCSI is so different from these other standard disk interfaces that a new set of ROM BIOS routines are necessary to support the system so that it can self-boot. The newer IBM PS/2 systems that come with SCSI drives have this support built into the motherboard BIOS or as an extension BIOS on the SCSI host adapter.

Companies such as Adaptec and Future Domain have produced SCSI cards with built-in ROM BIOS support for several years, but these BIOS routines were limited to running the drives only under DOS. The BIOS would not run in the AT-protected mode, and other operating systems included drivers for only the standard ST-506/412 and ESDI controllers. Thus, running SCSI was impossible under many non-DOS operating systems. This situation has changed significantly, however; IBM now supports many third-party SCSI host adapters in OS/2, especially those from Adaptec and Future Domain. For compatibility reasons, I usually recommend using SCSI adapters from these two companies, or any other adapters that are fully hardware-compatible with the Adapted and Future Domain adapters.

Because of the lead taken by Apple in developing systems software (operating systems and ROM) support for SCSI, peripherals connect to Apple systems in fairly standard ways. Until recently, this kind of standard-setting leadership was lacking for SCSI in the IBM world. This situation changed on March 20, 1990, when IBM introduced several "standard" SCSI adapters and peripherals for the IBM PS/2 systems, with complete ROM BIOS and full operating-system support.

IBM has standardized on SCSI for nearly all its high-end systems. In these systems, a SCSI host adapter card is in one of the slots, or the system has a SCSI host adapter built into the motherboard. This arrangement is similar in appearance to the IDE interface, because a single cable runs from the motherboard to the SCSI drive, but SCSI supports as many as seven devices (some of which may not be hard disks), whereas IDE supports only four devices (two per controller), which must be either a hard disk, IDE-type CD-ROM drive, or a tape drive, or the new IDE Zip drive. PS/2 systems with SCSI drives are easy to upgrade, because virtually any third-party SCSI drive will plug in and function.

The example set by IBM is causing other manufacturers to supply systems with either SCSI host adapters or SCSI interfaces integrated into the motherboards. As SCSI becomes more and more popular in the PC world, SCSI peripheral integration will be easier due to better operating-system and device-driver support.

ANSI SCSI Standards. The SCSI standard defines the physical and electrical parameters of a parallel I/O bus used to connect computers and peripheral devices in daisy-chain fashion. The standard supports devices such as disk drives, tape drives, and CD-ROM drives. The original SCSI standard (ANSI X3.131-1986) was approved in 1986, SCSI-2 was approved in January 1994, and a new revision called SCSI-3 is being developed.

The SCSI interface is defined as a standard by ANSI. The X3 Task Group operates as an ASC (Accredited Standards Committee) under ANSI to develop Information Processing System standards. X3T9 is the I/O Interfaces group, and X3T9.2 specifically is in charge of low-level interfaces such as SCSI and ATA-IDE (among others). The original SCSI-1 standard was published by the X3T9 ANSI group in 1986, and is officially published by ANSI as X3.131-1986.

One problem with the original SCSI-1 document was that many of the commands and features were optional, and there was little or no guarantee that a particular peripheral would support the expected commands. This problem caused the industry as a whole to define a set of 18 basic SCSI commands called the *Common Command Set (CCS)*, which would become the minimum set of commands supported by all peripherals. CCS became the basis for what is now the SCSI-2 specification.

In addition to formal support for CCS, SCSI-2 provided additional definitions for commands to access CD-ROM drives (and their sound capabilities), tape drives, removable drives, optical drives, and several other peripherals. In addition, an optional higher speed called Fast SCSI-2 and a 16-bit version called Wide SCSI-2 were defined. Another feature of SCSI-2 is *command queuing*, which enables a device to accept multiple commands and execute them in the order that the device deems to be most efficient. This feature is most beneficial when you are using a multitasking operating system that could be sending several requests on the SCSI bus at the same time.

The X3T9 group approved the SCSI-2 standard as X3.131-1990 in August 1990, but the document was recalled in December 1990 for changes before final ANSI publication. Final approval for the SCSI-2 document was finally made in January 1994, although it has changed little from the original 1990 release. The SCSI-2 document is now called ANSI X3.131-1994. The official document is available from Global Engineering Documents or the ANSI committee, which are listed in Appendix A. You can also download working drafts of these documents from the NCR SCSI BBS, found in the vendor list under "NCR Microelectronics."

Most companies indicate that their host adapters follow both the ANSI X3.131-1986 (SCSI-1) as well as the x3.131-1994 (SCSI-2) standards. Note that because virtually all parts of SCSI-1 are supported in SCSI-2, virtually any SCSI-1 device is also considered SCSI-2 by default. Many manufacturers advertise that their devices are SCSI-2, but this does not mean that they support any of the additional optional features that were incorporated in the SCSI-2 revision.

For example, an optional part of the SCSI-2 specification includes a fast synchronous mode that doubles the standard synchronous transfer rate from 5M/sec to 10M/sec. This Fast SCSI transfer mode can be combined with 16-bit Wide SCSI for transfer rates of up to 20M/sec. There was an optional 32-bit version defined in SCSI-2, but component manufacturers have shunned this as too expensive. In essence, 32-bit SCSI was a stillborn specification. Most SCSI implementations are 8-bit standard SCSI or Fast/Wide SCSI. Even devices which support none of the Fast or Wide modes can still be considered SCSI-2.

The SCSI-3 standard is still being defined and is still a long way off from being approved. However, portions of this specification, although not final, are being sold in products today. One of these developments is the new Fast-20 mode, which is also called *Ultra-SCSI*. This essentially is quad-speed SCSI, and will run 20M/sec on an 8-bit standard SCSI bus, and 40M/sec on Wide (16-bit) SCSI.

Table 15.7 shows the maximum transfer rates for the SCSI bus at various speeds and widths, as well as the cable type required for the specific transfer widths.

Table 15.7 SCSI Data-Transfer Rates

Bus Width	Standard SCSI	Fast SCSI	Fast-20 (Ultra) SCSI	Cable Type
8-bit	5M/sec	10M/sec	20M/sec	A (50-pin)
16-bit (Wide)	10M/sec	20M/sec	40M/sec	P (68-pin)

Note

The A cable is the standard 50-pin SCSI cable, whereas the P cable is a 68-pin cable designed for 16-bit. Maximum cable length is 6m (about 20 feet) for standard speed SCSI, and only 3m (about 10 feet) for Fast or Fast-20 (Ultra) SCSI. Pinouts for these cable connections are listed in this chapter in Tables 15.13 through 15.21.

So-called SCSI-1 adapters have no problems with SCSI-2 peripherals. In fact, as was stated earlier, virtually any SCSI-1 device can also legitimately be called SCSI-2 (or even SCSI-3). You can't take advantage of Fast, Fast-20, or Wide transfer capabilities, but the extra commands defined in SCSI-2 can be sent by means of a SCSI-1 controller. In other words, nothing is different between SCSI-1 and SCSI-2 compliant hardware. For example, I am running a Seagate Barracuda 4G Fast SCSI-2 drive with my standard IBM SCSI-1 host adapter, and it runs fine. Most adapters are similar in that they actually are SCSI-2 compatible, even if they advertise only SCSI-1 support.

Because the SCSI-2 standard was not actually approved before January 1994, any devices that claimed to be SCSI-2 before that time were not officially in compliance with the standard. This is really not a problem, however, because the SCSI-2 document had not changed appreciably since it was nearly approved in 1990. The same thing is currently happening with advertisers listing devices as "SCSI-3." The SCSI-3 specification is not yet approved, although certain areas are being worked out.

SCSI Hard Disk Evolution and Construction. SCSI is not a disk interface, but a bus that supports SCSI bus interface adapters connected to disk and other device controllers. The first SCSI drives for PCs simply were standard ST-506/412 or ESDI drives with a separate SCSI bus interface adapter (sometimes called a *bridge controller*) that converted the ST-506/412 or ESDI interfaces to SCSI. This interface originally was in the form of a secondary logic board, and the entire assembly often was mounted in an external case.

The next step was to build the SCSI bus interface "converter" board directly into the drive's own logic board. Today, we call these drives *embedded SCSI drives*, because the SCSI interface is built in.

At that point, there was no need to conform to the absolute specifications of ST-506/412 or ESDI on the internal disk interface, because the only other device that the interface ever would have to talk to was built in as well. Thus, the disk-interface and controller-chipset manufacturers began to develop more customized chipsets that were based on the ST-506/412 or ESDI chipsets already available but offered more features and higher performance. Today, if you look at a typical SCSI drive, you often can identify the chip or chipset that serves as the disk controller on the drive as being exactly the same kind that would be used on an ST-506/412 or ESDI controller or as some evolutionary customized variation thereof.

Consider some examples. An ATA IDE drive must fully emulate the system-level disk-controller interface introduced with the Western Digital WD1003 controller series that IBM used in the AT. These drives must act as though they have a built-in ST-506/412 or ESDI controller; in fact, they actually do. Most of these built-in controllers have more capabilities than the original WD1003 series (usually in the form of additional commands), but they must at least respond to all the original commands that were used with the WD1003.

If you follow the hard drive market, you usually will see that drive manufacturers offer most of their newer drives in both ATA-IDE and SCSI versions. In other words, if a manufacturer makes a particular 500M IDE drive, you invariably will see that the company also makes a SCSI model with the same capacity and specifications, which uses the same HDA (Head Disk Assembly) and even looks the same as the IDE version. If you study these virtually identical drives, the only major difference you will find is the additional chip on the logic board of the SCSI version, called a *SCSI Bus Adapter Chip (SBIC)*.

Figures 15.1 and 15.2 show the logic-block diagrams of the WD-AP4200 (a 200M ATA-IDE drive) and WD-SP4200 (a 200M SCSI drive), respectively. These drives use the same HDA; they differ only in their logic boards, and even the logic boards are the same except for the addition of an SBIC on the SCSI drive's logic board.

658 Chapter 15—Hard Disk Interfaces

Notice that even the circuit designs of these two drives are almost identical. Both drives use an LSI (Large Scale Integrated circuit) chip called the WD42C22 Disk Controller and Buffer manager chip. In the ATA drive, this chip is connected through a DMA control chip directly to the AT bus. In the SCSI version, a WD33C93 SCSI bus interface controller chip is added to interface the disk-controller logic to the SCSI bus. In fact, the logic diagrams of these two drives differ only in the fact that the SCSI version has a complete subset of the ATA drive, with the SCSI bus interface controller logic added. This essentially is a very condensed version of the separate drive and bridge controller setups that were used in the early days of PC SCSI!

FIG. 15.1 WD-AP4200 200M ATA-IDE drive logic-board block diagram.

FIG. 15.2 WD-SP4200 200M SCSI drive logic-board block diagram.

To top off this example, study the following logic diagram for the WD 1006V-MM1, which is an ST-506/412 controller (see Figure 15.3).

You can clearly see that the main LSI chip on board is the same WD42C22 disk controller chip used in the IDE and SCSI drives. Here is what the technical reference literature says about that chip:

Chapter 15—Hard Disk Interfaces

FIG. 15.3 Western Digital WD1006V-MM1 ST-506/412 Disk Controller block diagram.

The WD42C22 integrates a high-performance, low-cost Winchester controller's architecture. The WD42C22 integrates the central elements of a Winchester controller subsystem such as the host interface, buffer manager, disk formatter/controller, encoder/decoder, CRC/ECC (Cyclic Redundancy Check/Error Correction Code) generator/checker, and drive interface into a single 84-pin PQFP (Plastic Quad Flat Pack) device.

The virtually identical design of ATA-IDE and SCSI drives is not unique to Western Digital. Most drive manufacturers design their ATA-IDE and SCSI drives the same way, often using these very same WD chips as well as disk controller and SCSI bus interface chips from other manufacturers. You now should be able to understand that most SCSI drives simply are "regular" ATA-IDE drives with SCSI bus logic added. This fact will come up again later in this chapter in the section "SCSI versus IDE," which discusses performance and other issues differentiating these interfaces.

For another example, I have several IBM 320M and 400M embedded SCSI-2 hard disks; each of these drives has on-board a WD-10C00 Programmable Disk Controller in the form of a 68-pin PLCC (Plastic Leaded Chip Carrier) chip. The technical literature states:

This chip supports ST412, ESDI, SMD, and Optical interfaces. It has 27Mbit/sec maximum transfer rate and an internal, fully programmable 48- or 32-bit ECC, 16-bit CRC-CCITT or external user defined ECC polynomial, fully programmable sector sizes, and 1.25 micron low power CMOS design.

In addition, these particular embedded SCSI drives include the 33C93 SCSI Bus Interface Controller chip, which also is used in the other SCSI drive that I mentioned. Again, there is a distinctly separate disk controller, and the SCSI interface is added on.

So again, most embedded SCSI drives have a built-in disk controller (usually based on previous ST-506/412 or ESDI designs) and additional logic to interface that controller to the SCSI bus (a built-in bridge controller, if you like). Now think about this from a performance standpoint. If virtually all SCSI drives really are ATA-IDE drives with a SCSI Bus Interface Controller chip added, what conclusions can you draw?

First, no drive can perform sustained data transfers faster than the data can actually be read from the disk platters. In other words, the HDA limits performance to whatever it is capable of achieving. Drives can transmit data in short bursts at very high speeds, because they often have built-in cache or read-ahead buffers that store data. Many of the newer high-performance SCSI and ATA-IDE drives have 1M or more of cache memory on-board! No matter how big or intelligent the cache is, however, sustained data transfer still will be limited by the HDA.

Data from the HDA must pass through the disk controller circuits, which, as you have seen, are virtually identical between similar SCSI and ATA-IDE drives. In the ATA-IDE drive, this data then is presented directly to the system bus. In the SCSI drive, however, the data must pass through a SCSI Bus Interface adapter on the drive, travel through the SCSI bus itself, and then pass through another SCSI Bus Interface controller in the SCSI host adapter card in your system. The longer route that a SCSI transfer must take makes this type of transfer slower than the much more direct ATA-IDE transfer.

The conventional wisdom has been that SCSI always is much faster than IDE; unfortunately, this wisdom usually is wrong! This incorrect conclusion was derived by looking at the raw SCSI and ISA bus performance capabilities. An 8-bit Fast SCSI-2 bus can transfer data at 10M/sec, whereas the 16-bit ISA bus used directly by IDE drives can transfer data at rates ranging from 2M to 8M/sec. Based on these raw transfer rates, SCSI seems to be faster, but the raw transfer rate of the bus is not the limiting factor. Instead, the actual HDA and disk-controller circuitry place the limits on performance. Another point to remember is that unless you are using a PCI, VL-Bus, EISA, or 32-bit MCA SCSI adapter, the SCSI data-transfer speeds will be limited by the host bus performance as well as by the drive performance.

However, modern operating systems are multitasking, and SCSI devices (with all their additional controller circuitry) function independent of each other, unlike IDE. Therefore, data can be read and written to any of the SCSI devices *simultaneously*. This allows for smoother multitasking and increased overall data throughput. The most advanced operating systems like Windows NT even allow drive striping. A *strip drive set* is two or more drives that appear to the user as one drive. Data is split between the drives equally, again increasing overall throughput.

On the Web

For more on stripe sets in Windows NT, search for

http://www.microsoft.com/kb/articles/q113/9/33.htm

Single-Ended or Differential SCSI. "Normal" SCSI also is called *single-ended SCSI*. For each signal that needs to be sent across the bus, a wire exists to carry it. With differential SCSI, for each signal that needs to be sent across the bus, a pair of wires exists to carry it. The first in this pair carries the same type of signal that the single-ended SCSI carries. The second in this pair, however, carries the logical inversion of the signal. The receiving device takes the difference of the pair (hence the name *differential*), which makes it less susceptible to noise and allows for greater cable length. Because of this, differential SCSI can be used with cable lengths up to 25m, whereas single-ended SCSI is good only for 6m with standard asynchronous or synchronous transfers or for only 3m for Fast SCSI.

You cannot mix single-ended and differential devices on a single SCSI bus; the result would be catastrophic. (That is to say, you probably will see smoke!) Notice that the cables and connectors are the same, so it's entirely possible to make this mistake. This usually is not a problem, however, because very few differential SCSI implementations exist. Especially with SCSI in the PC environment, single-ended is about all you will ever see. If, however, you to come upon a peripheral that you believe might be differential, there are a few ways to tell. One way is to look for a special symbol on the unit; the industry has adopted different universal symbols for single-ended and differential SCSI. Figure 15.4 shows these symbols.

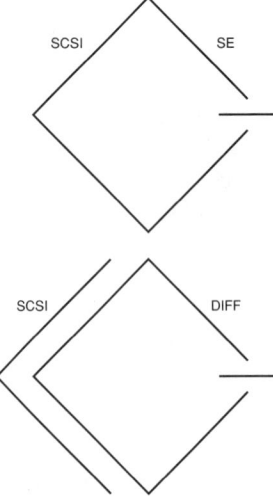

FIG. 15.4 Single-ended and differential SCSI universal symbols.

If you do not see such symbols, you can tell whether you have a differential device by using an ohmmeter to check the resistance between pins 21 and 22 on the device connector. On a single-ended system, the pins should be tied together and also tied to the ground. On a differential device, the pins should be open or have significant resistance between them. Again, this generally should not be a problem, because virtually all devices used in the PC environment are single-ended.

SCSI-1 and SCSI-2. The SCSI-2 specification essentially is an improved version of SCSI-1 with some parts of the specification tightened and with several new features and options added. Normally, SCSI-1 and SCSI-2 devices are compatible, but SCSI-1 devices ignore the additional features in SCSI-2.

Some of the changes in SCSI-2 are very minor. For example, SCSI-1 allowed SCSI Bus parity to be optional, whereas parity must be implemented in SCSI-2. Another requirement is that initiator devices, such as host adapters, provide terminator power to the interface; most devices already did so.

SCSI-2 also has several optional features:

- Fast SCSI
- Wide SCSI
- Command queuing
- High-density cable connectors
- Improved Active (Alternative 2) termination

These features are not required; they are optional under the SCSI-2 specification. If you connect a standard SCSI host adapter to a Fast SCSI drive, for example, the interface will work, but only at standard SCSI speeds.

SCSI-3. *SCSI-3* is a term used to describe a set of standards currently being developed. Simply put, it is the next generation of documents a product conforms to. See the section "New Commands" later in this chapter.

Fast and Fast-Wide SCSI. *Fast SCSI* refers to high-speed synchronous transfer capability. Fast SCSI achieves a 10M/sec transfer rate on the standard 8-bit SCSI cabling. When combined with a 16-bit Wide SCSI interface, this configuration results in data-transfer rates of 20M/sec (called *Fast/Wide*).

Fast-20 (Ultra) SCSI. *Fast-20* or *Ultra SCSI* refers to high-speed synchronous transfer capability that is twice as fast as Fast-SCSI. This has been introduced in the Draft (unfinished) SCSI-3 specification and has already been adopted by the marketplace, especially for high-speed hard disks. Ultra SCSI achieves a 20M/sec transfer rate on the standard 8-bit SCSI cabling. When combined with a 16-bit Wide SCSI interface, this configuration results in data-transfer rates of 40M/sec (called *Ultra/Wide*).

Fast-40 SCSI. Fast-40 SCSI is a future revision of SCSI-3 (mentioned earlier in the chapter) capable of achieving a 40M/sec transfer rate.

Wide SCSI. *Wide SCSI* allows for parallel data transfer at a bus width of 16 bits. The wider connection requires a new cable design. The standard 50-conductor 8-bit cable is called the *A cable*. SCSI-2 originally defined a special 68-conductor B cable that was supposed to be used in conjunction with the A cable for wide transfers, but the industry ignored this specification in favor of a newer 68-conductor P cable that was introduced as part of the SCSI-3 specification. The P cable superseded the A and B cable combination because the P cable can be used alone (without the A cable) for 16-bit Wide SCSI.

A 32-bit Wide SCSI version was originally defined on paper as a part of the SCSI-2 specification, but has not found popularity and probably never will in the PC environment. Theoretically, 32-bit SCSI implementations would require two cables: a 68-conductor P cable and a 68-conductor Q cable.

Fiber Channel SCSI. Fiber Channel SCSI is a specification for a serial interface using a fiber channel physical and protocol characteristic, with a SCSI command set. It can achieve 100M/sec over either fiber or coaxial cable.

Termination. The single-ended SCSI bus depends on very tight termination tolerances to function reliably. Unfortunately, the original 132-ohm passive termination defined in the SCSI-1 document was not designed for use at the higher synchronous speeds now possible. These passive terminators can cause signal reflections resulting in errors when transfer rates increase or when more devices are added to the bus. SCSI-2 defines an active (voltage-regulated) terminator that lowers termination impedance to 110 ohms and improves system integrity.

Command Queuing. In SCSI-1, an initiator device, such as a host adapter, was limited to sending one command per device. In SCSI-2, the host adapter can send as many as 256 commands to a single device, which will store and process those commands internally before responding on the SCSI bus. The target device even can resequence the commands to allow for the most efficient execution or performance possible. This feature is especially useful in multitasking environments, such as OS/2 and Windows NT, that can take advantage of this feature.

New Commands. SCSI-2 took the Common Command Set that was being used throughout the industry and made it an official part of the standard. The CCS was designed mainly for disk drives and did not include specific commands designed for other types of devices. In SCSI-2, many of the old commands are reworked, and several new commands have been added. New command sets have been added for CD-ROMs, optical drives, scanners, communications devices, and media changers (jukeboxes).

SCSI-3. Even though the SCSI-2 specification has only recently been approved (although it has remained stable for some time), the SCSI-3 specification is already being developed. SCSI-3 will have everything that SCSI-2 has and definitely will add new commands, features, and implementations. For example, SCSI-3 will provide support for up to 32 devices on the bus instead of only eight.

One of the most exciting things about SCSI-3 is the proposed *Serial SCSI*, a scheme that may use only a six-conductor cable and that will be able to transfer data at up to

100M/sec! The switch to serial instead of parallel is designed to control the delay, noise, and termination problems that have plagued SCSI-2, as well as to simplify the cable connection. Serial SCSI will be capable of transferring more data over six wires than 32-bit Fast Wide SCSI-2 can over 128 wires! The intention is that Serial SCSI be implemented on the motherboard of future systems, giving them incredible expansion and performance capabilities.

Although Serial SCSI may not make the older host adapters and cables obsolete overnight, it does make future cabling possibilities even more of a puzzle. Serial SCSI offers the possibility of longer cable lengths, less electromagnetic interference, and easier connections on laptops, notebooks, and docking stations. Expect SCSI-3 to offer almost pain-free installations with automatic PnP SCSI ID setup and termination schemes.

In any practical sense, SCSI-3 is still some ways away from being approved. Because the standard exists in draft documents before being officially approved, if the portions of the standard become stable, we may very well see products claiming SCSI-3 compatibility well before the standard truly exists. Because SCSI-3 actually incorporates all of what is in SCSI-2, technically anybody can call any SCSI-1 or SCSI-2 device a SCSI-3 device as well. Beware of product hype along these lines. Some of the new SCSI-3 features will likely be incompatible with previous SCSI implementations, and may take a while to appear on the market.

SCSI Cables and Connectors. The SCSI standards are very specific when it comes to cables and connectors. The most common connectors specified in this standard are the 50-position unshielded pin header connector for internal SCSI connections and the 50-position shielded Centronics latch-style connectors for external connections. The shielded Centronics style connector also is called *Alternative 2* in the official specification. Passive or Active termination (Active is preferred) is specified for both single-ended and differential buses. The 50-conductor bus configuration is defined in the SCSI-2 standard as the A-cabled.

The SCSI-2 revision added a high-density, 50-position, D-shell connector option for the A-cable connectors. This connector now is called *Alternative 1*. The Alternative 2 Centronics latch-style connector remains unchanged from SCSI-1. A 68-conductor B-cable specification was added to the SCSI-2 standard to provide for 16- and 32-bit data transfers; the connector, however, had to be used in parallel with an A cable. The industry did not widely accept the B cable option, which has been dropped from the SCSI-3 standard.

To replace the ill-fated B cable, a new 68-conductor P cable was developed as part of the SCSI-3 specification. Shielded and unshielded high-density D-shell connectors are specified for both the A cable and P cable. The shielded high-density connectors use a squeeze-to-release latch rather than the wire latch used on the Centronics-style connectors. Active termination for single-ended buses is specified, providing a high level of signal integrity.

SCSI Cable and Connector Pinouts. The following section details the pinouts of the various SCSI cables and connectors. There are two electrically different versions of SCSI, *single-ended* and *differential*. These two versions are electrically incompatible, and must not be interconnected or damage will result. Fortunately, there are very few differential SCSI applications available in the PC industry, so you will rarely (if ever) encounter it. Within each electrical type (single-ended or differential), there are basically three SCSI cable types:

- A Cable (Standard SCSI)
- P Cable (16- and 32-bit Wide SCSI)
- Q Cable (32-bit Wide SCSI)

The A cable is used in most SCSI-1 and SCSI-2 installations, and is the most common cable you will encounter. SCSI-2 Wide (16-bit) applications use a P cable instead, which completely replaces the A cable. You can intermix standard and Wide SCSI devices on a single SCSI bus by interconnecting A and P cables with special adapters. 32-bit wide SCSI-3 applications use both the P and Q cables in parallel to each 32-bit device. Today there are virtually no PC applications for 32-bit Wide SCSI-3, and because of the two-cable requirement, it is not likely to catch on.

The A cables can have Pin Header (Internal) type connectors or External Shielded connectors, each with a different pinout. The P and Q cables feature the same connector pinout on either Internal or External cable connections.

Single-Ended SCSI Cables and Connectors. The single-ended electrical interface is the most popular type for PC systems. Tables 15.8 and 15.9 show all the possible single-ended cable and connector pinouts. The A cable is available in both internal unshielded as well as external shielded configurations. A hyphen preceding a signal name indicates the signal is Active Low. The RESERVED lines have continuity from one end of the SCSI bus to the other. In an A cable bus, the RESERVED lines should be left open in SCSI devices (but may be connected to ground), and are connected to ground in the bus terminator assemblies. In the P and Q cables, the RESERVED lines are left open in SCSI devices as well as in the bus terminator assemblies.

Table 15.8   A Cable (Single-Ended) Internal Unshielded Header Connector

Signal Name	Pin	Pin	Signal Name
GROUND	1	2	-DB(0)
GROUND	3	4	-DB(1)
GROUND	5	6	-DB(2)
GROUND	7	8	-DB(3)
GROUND	9	10	-DB(4)
GROUND	11	12	-DB(5)
GROUND	13	14	-DB(6)
GROUND	15	16	-DB(7)
GROUND	17	18	-DB(Parity)
GROUND	19	20	GROUND
GROUND	21	22	GROUND

Signal Name	Pin	Pin	Signal Name
RESERVED	23	24	RESERVED
Open	25	26	TERMPWR
RESERVED	27	28	RESERVED
GROUND	29	30	GROUND
GROUND	31	32	-ATN
GROUND	33	34	GROUND
GROUND	35	36	-BSY
GROUND	37	38	-ACK
GROUND	39	40	-RST
GROUND	41	42	-MSG
GROUND	43	44	-SEL
GROUND	45	46	-C/D
GROUND	47	48	-REQ
GROUND	49	50	-I/O

Table 15.9 A-Cable (Single-Ended) External Shielded Connector

Signal Name	Pin	Pin	Signal Name
GROUND	1	26	-DB(0)
GROUND	2	27	-DB(1)
GROUND	3	28	-DB(2)
GROUND	4	29	-DB(3)
GROUND	5	30	-DB(4)
GROUND	6	31	-DB(5)
GROUND	7	32	-DB(6)
GROUND	8	33	-DB(7)
GROUND	9	34	-DB(Parity)
GROUND	10	35	GROUND
GROUND	11	36	GROUND
RESERVED	12	37	RESERVED
Open	13	38	TERMPWR
RESERVED	14	39	RESERVED
GROUND	15	40	GROUND
GROUND	16	41	-ATN
GROUND	17	42	GROUND
GROUND	18	43	-BSY
GROUND	19	44	-ACK
GROUND	20	45	-RST
GROUND	21	46	-MSG
GROUND	22	47	-SEL
GROUND	23	48	-C/D
GROUND	24	49	-REQ
GROUND	25	50	-I/O

Chapter 15—Hard Disk Interfaces

IBM has standardized on the SCSI interface for virtually all PS/2 systems introduced since 1990. These systems use a Micro-Channel SCSI adapter or have the SCSI Host Adapter built into the motherboard. In either case, IBM's SCSI interface uses a special 60-pin mini-Centronics type external shielded connector that is unique in the industry. A special IBM cable is required to adapt this connector to the standard 50-pin Centronics style connector used on most external SCSI devices. The pinout of the IBM 60-pin mini-Centronics style External Shielded connector is shown Table 15.10. Notice that although the pin arrangement is unique, the pin number to signal designations correspond with the standard unshielded internal pin header type of SCSI connector.

Table 15.10 IBM PS/2 SCSI External Shielded 60-Pin Connector

Signal Name	Pin	Pin	Signal Name
GROUND	1	60	Not Connected
-DB(0)	2	59	Not Connected
GROUND	3	58	Not Connected
-DB(1)	4	57	Not Connected
GROUND	5	56	Not Connected
-DB(2)	6	55	Not Connected
GROUND	7	54	Not Connected
-DB(3)	8	53	Not Connected
GROUND	9	52	Not Connected
-DB(4)	10	51	GROUND
GROUND	11	50	-I/O
-DB(5)	12	49	GROUND
GROUND	13	48	-REQ
-DB(6)	14	47	GROUND
GROUND	15	46	-C/D
-DB(7)	16	45	GROUND
GROUND	17	44	-SEL
-DB(Parity)	18	43	GROUND
GROUND	19	42	-MSG
GROUND	20	41	GROUND
GROUND	21	40	-RST
GROUND	22	39	GROUND
RESERVED	23	38	-ACK
RESERVED	24	37	GROUND
Open	25	36	-BSY
TERMPWR	26	35	GROUND
RESERVED	27	34	GROUND
RESERVED	28	33	GROUND
GROUND	29	32	-ATN
GROUND	30	31	GROUND

The P cable (single-ended) and connectors are used in 16-bit wide SCSI-2 applications (see Table 15.11 for the pinout).

Table 15.11 P Cable (Single-Ended) Internal or External Shielded Connector

Signal Name	Pin	Pin	Signal Name
GROUND	1	35	-DB(12)
GROUND	2	36	-DB(13)
GROUND	3	37	-DB(14)
GROUND	4	38	-DB(15)
GROUND	5	39	-DB(Parity 1)
GROUND	6	40	-DB(0)
GROUND	7	41	-DB(1)
GROUND	8	42	-DB(2)
GROUND	9	43	-DB(3)
GROUND	10	44	-DB(4)
GROUND	11	45	-DB(5)
GROUND	12	46	-DB(6)
GROUND	13	47	-DB(7)
GROUND	14	48	-DB(Parity 0)
GROUND	15	49	GROUND
GROUND	16	50	GROUND
TERMPWR	17	51	TERMPWR
TERMPWR	18	52	TERMPWR
RESERVED	19	53	RESERVED
GROUND	20	54	GROUND
GROUND	21	55	-ATN
GROUND	22	56	GROUND
GROUND	23	57	-BSY
GROUND	24	58	-ACK
GROUND	25	59	-RST
GROUND	26	60	-MSG
GROUND	27	61	-SEL
GROUND	28	62	-C/D
GROUND	29	63	-REQ
GROUND	30	64	-I/O
GROUND	31	65	-DB(8)
GROUND	32	66	-DB(9)
GROUND	33	67	-DB(10)
GROUND	34	68	-DB(11)

The Q Cable (single-ended) and connector is defined only for 32-bit SCSI implementations, which also require a P cable as well (see Table 15.12 for the pinout). 32-bit SCSI applications are rare to virtually nonexistent.

Table 15.12 Q Cable (Single-Ended) Internal or External Shielded Connector

Signal Name	Pin	Pin	Signal Name
GROUND	1	35	-DB(28)
GROUND	2	36	-DB(29)
GROUND	3	37	-DB(30)
GROUND	4	38	-DB(31)
GROUND	5	39	-DB(Parity 3)
GROUND	6	40	-DB(16)
GROUND	7	41	-DB(17)
GROUND	8	42	-DB(18)
GROUND	9	43	-DB(19)
GROUND	10	44	-DB(20)
GROUND	11	45	-DB(21)
GROUND	12	46	-DB(22)
GROUND	13	47	-DB(23)
GROUND	14	48	-DB(Parity 2)
GROUND	15	49	GROUND
GROUND	16	50	GROUND
TERMPWRQ	17	51	TERMPWRQ
TERMPWRQ	18	52	TERMPWRQ
RESERVED	19	53	RESERVED
GROUND	20	54	GROUND
GROUND	21	55	TERMINATED
GROUND	22	56	GROUND
GROUND	23	57	TERMINATED
GROUND	24	58	-ACKQ
GROUND	25	59	TERMINATED
GROUND	26	60	TERMINATED
GROUND	27	61	TERMINATED
GROUND	28	62	TERMINATED
GROUND	29	63	-REQQ
GROUND	30	64	TERMINATED
GROUND	31	65	-DB(24)
GROUND	32	66	-DB(25)
GROUND	33	67	-DB(26)
GROUND	34	68	-DB(27)

Differential SCSI Signals. Differential SCSI is not normally used in a PC environment, but is very popular with minicomputer installations due to the very long bus lengths that are allowed. Although not popular in PC systems, the interface connector specifications are show here for reference.

The A cable (differential) connector is available in both internal unshielded form as well as an external shielded form. Table 15.13 shows the pinout for the Internal cable, while Table 15.14 shows the pinout for the External cable.

Table 15.13 A Cable (Differential) Internal Unshielded Header Connector

Signal Name	Pin	Pin	Signal Name
-RESET	1	2	-Disk Installed
GROUND	1	2	GROUND
+DB(0)	3	4	-DB(0)
+DB(1)	5	6	-DB(1)
+DB(2)	7	8	-DB(2)
+DB(3)	9	10	-DB(3)
+DB(4)	11	12	-DB(4)
+DB(5)	13	14	-DB(5)
+DB(6)	15	16	-DB(6)
+DB(7)	17	18	-DB(7)
+DB(Parity)	19	20	-DP(Parity)
DIFFSENS	21	22	GROUND
RESERVED	23	24	RESERVED
TERMPWR	25	26	TERMPWR
RESERVED	27	28	RESERVED
+ATN	29	30	-ATN
GROUND	31	32	GROUND
+BSY	33	34	-BSY
+ACK	35	36	-ACK
+RST	37	38	-RST
+MSG	39	40	-MSG
+SEL	41	42	-SEL
+C/D	43	44	-C/D
+REQ	45	46	-REQ
+I/O	47	48	-I/O
GROUND	49	50	GROUND

Table 15.14 A Cable (Differential) External Shielded Connector

Signal Name	Pin	Pin	Signal Name
GROUND	1	26	GROUND
+DB(0)	2	27	-DB(0)
+DB(1)	3	28	-DB(1)
+DB(2)	4	29	-DB(2)
+DB(3)	5	30	-DB(3)
+DB(4)	6	31	-DB(4)

(continues)

Table 15.14 Continued

Signal Name	Pin	Pin	Signal Name
+DB(5)	7	32	-DB(5)
+DB(6)	8	33	-DB(6)
+DB(7)	9	34	-DB(7)
+DB(Parity)	10	35	-DP(Parity)
DIFFSENS	11	36	GROUND
RESERVED	12	37	RESERVED
TERMPWR	13	38	TERMPWR
RESERVED	14	39	RESERVED
+ATN	15	40	-ATN
GROUND	16	41	GROUND
+BSY	17	42	-BSY
+ACK	18	43	-ACK
+RST	18	44	-RST
+MSG	20	45	-MSG
+SEL	21	46	-SEL
+C/D	22	47	-C/D
+REQ	23	48	-REQ
+I/O	24	49	-I/O
GROUND	25	50	GROUND

The P cable (differential) and connector is used for 16-bit wide SCSI connections. Table 15.15 has the pinouts for the P cable (differential).

Table 15.15 P Cable (Differential) Internal or External Shielded Connector

Signal Name	Pin	Pin	Signal Name
+DB(12)	1	35	-DB(12)
+DB(13)	2	36	-DB(13)
+DB(14)	3	37	-DB(14)
+DB(15)	4	38	-DB(15)
+DB(Parity 1)	5	39	-DB(Parity 1)
GROUND	6	40	GROUND
+DB(0)	7	41	-DB(0)
+DB(1)	8	42	-DB(1)
+DB(2)	9	43	-DB(2)
+DB(3)	10	44	-DP(3)
+DB(4)	11	45	-DB(4)
+DB(5)	12	46	-DB(5)
+DB(6)	13	47	-DB(6)
+DB(7)	14	48	-DB(7)

Signal Name	Pin	Pin	Signal Name
+DB(Parity 0)	15	49	-DB(Parity 0)
DIFFSENS	16	50	GROUND
TERMPWR	17	51	TERMPWR
TERMPWR	18	52	TERMPWR
RESERVED	19	53	RESERVED
+ATN	20	54	-ATN
GROUND	21	55	GROUND
+BSY	22	56	-BSY
+ACK	23	57	-ACK
+RST	24	58	-RST
+MSG	25	59	-MSG
+SEL	26	60	-SEL
+C/D	27	61	-C/D
+REQ	28	62	-REQ
+I/O	29	63	-I/O
GROUND	30	64	GROUND
+DB(8)	31	65	-DB(8)
+DB(9)	32	66	-DB(9)
+DB(10)	33	67	-DB(10)
+DB(11)	34	68	-DB(11)

The Q cable (differential) and connector is used only with the proposed 32-bit wide SCSI implementations (which have not been implemented by the marketplace as of yet), and in that case would also require a 16-bit wide P cable. Table 15.16 shows the Q cable (differential) pinout.

Table 15.16 Q Cable (Differential) Internal or External Shielded Connector

Signal Name	Pin	Pin	Signal Name
-RESET	1	2	-Disk Installed
+DB(28)	1	35	-DB(28)
+DB(29)	2	36	-DB(29)
+DB(30)	3	37	-DB(30)
+DB(31)	4	38	-DB(31)
+DB(Parity 3)	5	39	-DB(Parity 3)
GROUND	6	40	GROUND
+DB(16)	7	41	-DB(16)
+DB(17)	8	42	-DB(17)
+DB(18)	9	43	-DB(18)
+DB(19)	10	44	-DP(19)
+DB(20)	11	45	-DB(20)

(continues)

Table 15.16 Continued

Signal Name	Pin	Pin	Signal Name
+DB(21)	12	46	-DB(21)
+DB(22)	13	47	-DB(22)
+DB(23)	14	48	-DB(23)
+DB(Parity 2)	15	49	-DB(Parity 2)
DIFFSENS	16	50	GROUND
TERMPWRQ	17	51	TERMPWRQ
TERMPWRQ	18	52	TERMPWRQ
RESERVED	19	53	RESERVED
TERMINATED	20	54	TERMINATED
GROUND	21	55	GROUND
TERMINATED	22	56	TERMINATED
+ACKQ	23	57	-ACKQ
TERMINATED	24	58	TERMINATED
TERMINATED	25	59	TERMINATED
TERMINATED	26	60	TERMINATED
TERMINATED	27	61	TERMINATED
+REQQ	28	62	-REQQ
TERMINATED	29	63	TERMINATED
GROUND	30	64	GROUND
+DB(24)	31	65	-DB(24)
+DB(25)	32	66	-DB(25)
+DB(26)	33	67	-DB(26)
+DB(27)	34	68	-DB(27)

Termination. All buses need to be electrically terminated at each end; the SCSI bus is no exception. Improper termination still is one of the most common problems in SCSI installations. Three types of terminators typically are available for the SCSI bus:

- Passive

- Active (also called Alternative 2)

- Forced Perfect Termination (FPT): FPT-3, FPT-18, and FPT-27

Typical passive terminators (a network of resistors) allow signal fluctuations in relation to the terminator power signal on the bus. Usually, passive terminating resistors suffice over short distances, such as 2 or 3 feet, but for longer distances, active termination is a real advantage. Active termination is required with Fast SCSI.

An active terminator actually has one or more voltage regulators to produce the termination voltage, rather than resistor voltage dividers. This arrangement helps ensure that the SCSI signals always are terminated to the correct voltage level. Active terminators will usually have some sort of LED indicating the termination activity. The SCSI-2 specification recommends active termination on both ends of the bus and requires active termination whenever Fast or Wide SCSI devices are used. Most high-performance host adapters have an "auto-termination" feature so if it is the end of a chain, it will terminate itself.

A variation on active termination is available: Forced Perfect Termination. *Forced Perfect Termination* is an even better form of active termination, in which diode clamps are added to eliminate signal overshoot and undershoot. The trick is that instead of clamping to +5 and Ground, these terminators clamp to the output of two regulated voltages. This arrangement enables the clamping diodes to eliminate signal overshoot and undershoot, especially at higher signaling speeds and over longer distances.

FPT terminators are available in several versions. FPT-3 and FPT-18 versions are available for 8-bit standard SCSI, while the FPT-27 is available for 16-bit (Wide) SCSI. The FPT-3 version forces perfect the three most highly active SCSI signals on the 8-bit SCSI bus, while the FPT-18 forces perfect all the SCSI signals on the 8-bit bus except grounds. FPT-27 also forces perfect all of the 16-bit Wide SCSI signals except grounds.

> **Note**
>
> Several companies make high-quality terminators for the SCSI bus, including Aeronics and the Data Mate division of Methode. Both of these companies make a variety of terminators, but Aeronics is well-noted for some unique FPT versions that are especially suited to problem configurations that require longer cable runs or higher signal integrity. One of the best investments that you can make in any SCSI installation is in high-quality cables and terminators.

SCSI Drive Configuration. SCSI drives are not too difficult to configure, especially compared with IDE drives. The SCSI standard controls the way that the drives must be set up. You need to set two or three items when you configure an SCSI drive:

- SCSI ID setting (0–7)
- Terminating resistors

The SCSI ID setting is very simple. Up to eight SCSI devices can be used on a single SCSI bus, and each device must have a unique SCSI ID address. The host adapter takes one address, so the rest are free for up to seven SCSI peripherals. Most SCSI host adapters are factory-set to ID 7, which is the highest-priority ID. All other devices must have unique IDs that do not conflict with one another. Some host adapters boot only from a hard disk set to a specific ID. In my system, for example, the IBM SCSI host adapter requires the boot drive to be set to ID 6. Newer IBM host adapters and systems enable you to boot from a hard disk at any SCSI ID. Older Adaptec host adapters required the boot hard disk to be ID 0; newer ones can boot from any ID.

Setting the ID usually involves changing jumpers on the drive itself. If the drive is installed in an external chassis, the chassis may have an ID selector switch that is accessible at the rear. This selector makes ID selection a simple matter of pressing a button or rotating a wheel until the desired ID number appears. If no external selector is present, you must open the external device chassis and set the ID via the jumpers on the drive.

Three jumpers are required to set the SCSI ID; the particular ID selected actually is derived from the binary representation of the jumpers themselves. For example, setting all three ID jumpers off results in a binary number of 000b, which translates to an ID of 0. A binary setting of 001b equals ID 1, 010b equals 2, 011b equals 3, and so on. (Notice that as I list these values, I append a lowercase b to indicate binary numbers.)

Unfortunately, the jumpers can appear either forward or backward on the drive, depending on how the manufacturer set them up. To keep things simple, I have recorded all the different ID jumper settings in the following tables. Table 15.17 shows the settings for drives that order the jumpers with the Most Significant Bit (MSB) to the left; Table 15.18 shows the settings for drives that have the jumpers ordered so that the MSB is to the right.

Table 15.17 SCSI ID Jumper Settings with the Most Significant Bit to the Left

SCSI	ID Jumper Settings		
0	0	0	0
1	0	0	1
2	0	1	0
3	0	1	1
4	1	0	0
5	1	0	1
6	1	1	0
7	1	1	1

1 = Jumper On, 0 = Jumper Off

Table 15.18 SCSI ID Jumper Settings with the Most Significant Bit to the Right

SCSI	ID Jumper Settings		
0	0	0	0
1	1	0	0
2	0	1	0
3	1	1	0
4	0	0	1
5	1	0	1
6	0	1	1
7	1	1	1

1 = Jumper On, 0 = Jumper Off

SCSI termination is very simple. Termination is required at both ends of the bus; there are no exceptions. If the host adapter is at one end of the bus, it must have termination enabled. If the host adapter is in the middle of the bus, and if both internal and external bus links are present, the host adapter must have its termination disabled, and the devices at each end of the bus must have terminators installed. Several types of terminators are available, differing both in quality and in appearance. Active terminators are the minimum recommended, and Forced Perfect Terminators (FPT) are considered the best available. For more information on the different types, see the previous section on terminators.

The rules are simple: Use the best terminators possible, and make sure that only the ends of the SCSI bus are terminated. The majority of problems that I see with SCSI installations are the result of improper termination. Some devices have built-in termination resistors that are enabled or disabled through a jumper or by being physically removed. Other devices do not have built-in terminating resistors; these devices instead rely on external terminator modules for termination.

When installing an external SCSI device, you will usually find the device in a storage enclosure with both input and output SCSI connectors, so that you can use the device in a daisy chain. If the enclosure is at the end of the SCSI bus, an external terminator module most likely will have to be plugged into the second (outgoing) SCSI port to provide proper termination at that end of the bus (see Figure 15.5).

FIG. 15.5 External SCSI device terminator.

External terminator modules are available in a variety of connector configurations, including pass-through designs, which are needed if only one port is available. Pass-through terminators also are commonly used in internal installations in which the device does not have built-in terminating resistors. Many hard drives use pass-through terminators for internal installations to save space on the logic-board assembly (see Figure 15.6).

The pass-through models are required when a device is at the end of the bus and only one SCSI connector is available.

FIG. 15.6 Internal pin-header connector pass-through SCSI terminator.

> **Tip**
>
> Remember to stick with high-quality active or Forced Perfect terminators at each end of the bus, and you will eliminate most common termination problems.

Other configuration items on a SCSI drive can be set via jumpers. Following are several of the most common additional settings that you will find:

- Start on Command (delayed start)
- SCSI Parity
- Terminator Power
- Synchronous Negotiation

These configuration items are described in the following sections.

Start On Command (Delayed Start). If you have multiple drives installed in a system, it is wise to set them up so that all the drives do not start to spin immediately when the system is powered on. A hard disk drive can consume three or four times more power during the first few seconds after power-on than during normal operation. The motor requires this additional power to get the platters spinning quickly. If several drives are drawing all this power at the same time, the power supply may be overloaded, which can cause the system to hang or to have intermittent startup problems.

Nearly all SCSI drives provide a way to delay drive spinning so that this problem does not occur. When most SCSI host adapters initialize the SCSI bus, they send out a command called Start Unit to each of the ID addresses in succession. By setting a jumper on the hard disk, you can prevent the disk from spinning until it receives the Start Unit command from the host adapter. Because the host adapter sends this command to all the

ID addresses in succession, from the highest-priority address (ID 7) to the lowest (ID 0), the higher-priority drives can be made to start first, with each lower-priority drive spinning up sequentially. Because some host adapters do not send the Start Unit command, some drives may simply delay spinup for a fixed number of seconds rather than wait for a command that never will arrive.

If drives are installed in external chassis with separate power supplies, you need not implement the delayed-start function. This function is best applied to internal drives that must be run from the same power supply that runs the system. For internal installations, I recommend setting Start on Command (delayed start) even if you have only one SCSI drive; this setting will ease the load on the power supply by spinning the drive up after the rest of the system has full power. This method is especially good for portable systems and other systems in which the power supply is limited.

SCSI Parity. SCSI Parity is a limited form of error checking that helps ensure that all data transfers are reliable. Virtually all host adapters support SCSI parity checking, so this option should be enabled on every device. The only reason why it exists as an option is that some older host adapters do not work with SCSI parity, so the parity must be turned off.

Terminator Power. The terminators at each end of the SCSI bus require power from at least one device on the bus. In most cases, the host adapter supplies this terminator power; in some cases, however, it does not. For example, parallel-port SCSI host adapters typically do not supply terminator power. It is not a problem if more than one device supplies terminator power because each source is diode-protected. For simplicity's sake, many will configure all devices to supply terminator power. If no device supplies terminator power, the bus will not be terminated correctly and will not function properly.

SCSI Synchronous Negotiation. The SCSI bus can run in two modes: *asynchronous* (the default) and *synchronous*. The bus actually switches modes during transfers through a protocol called *synchronous negotiation*. Before data is transferred across the SCSI bus, the sending device (called the *initiator*) and the receiving device (called the *target*) negotiate how the transfer will take place. If both devices support synchronous transfers, they will discover this fact through the negotiation, and the transfer will take place at the faster synchronous rate.

Unfortunately, some older devices do not respond to a request for synchronous transfer and can actually be disabled when such a request is made. For this reason, both host adapters and devices that support synchronous negotiation often have a jumper that can be used to disable this negotiation so that it can work with older devices. By default, all devices today should support synchronous negotiation, and this function should be enabled.

Plug and Play (PnP) SCSI. Plug and Play SCSI was originally released in April 1994. This specification allows SCSI device manufacturers to build PnP peripherals that will automatically configure when used with a PnP operating system. This will allow you to easily connect or reconfigure external peripherals, such as hard disk drives, backup tapes, and CD-ROMs.

To connect SCSI peripherals to the host PC, the specification requires a PnP SCSI host adapter such as PnP ISA or PCI. PnP add-in cards enable a PnP operating system to automatically configure software device drivers and system resources for the host bus interface.

The PnP SCSI specification version 1.0 includes these technical highlights:

- A single cable-connector configuration
- Automatic termination of the SCSI bus
- SCAM (SCSI Configured AutoMatically) automatic ID assignment
- Full backward compatibility of PnP SCSI devices with the installed base of SCSI systems.

This should go a long way in making SCSI easier to use for the normal user.

Each SCSI peripheral that you add to your SCSI bus (other than hard disk drives) requires an external driver to make the device work. Hard disks are the exception; driver support for them normally is provided as part of the SCSI host adapter BIOS. These external drivers are specific not only to a particular device, but also to the host adapter.

Recently, two types of standard host adapter interface drivers have become popular, greatly reducing this problem. By having a standard host adapter driver to write to, peripheral makers can more quickly create new drivers that support their devices and then talk to the universal host adapter driver. This arrangement eliminates dependence on one particular type of host adapter. These primary or universal drivers link the host adapter and the operating system.

The *Advanced SCSI Programming Interface (ASPI)* currently is the most popular universal driver, with most peripheral makers writing their drivers to talk to ASPI. The A in ASPI used to stand for Adaptec, the company that introduced it, but other SCSI device vendors have licensed the right to use ASPI with their products. DOS does not support ASPI directly, but it does when the ASPI driver is loaded. Windows 95, Windows NT, and OS/2 2.1 and later versions provide automatic ASPI support for several SCSI host adapters.

Future Domain and NCR have created another interface driver called the *Common Access Method (CAM)*. CAM is an ANSI-approved protocol that enables a single driver to control several host adapters. In addition to ASPI, OS/2 2.1 and later versions currently offer support for CAM. Future Domain also provides a CAM-to-ASPI converter in the utilities that go with its host adapters.

SCSI Configuration Tips. When you are installing a chain of devices on a single SCSI bus, the installation can get complicated very quickly. Here are some tips for getting your setup to function quickly and efficiently:

- *Start by adding one device at a time.* Rather than plug numerous peripherals into a single SCSI card and then try to configure them at the same time, start by installing the host adapter and a single hard disk. Then you can continue installing devices one at a time, checking to make sure that everything works before moving on.

- *Keep good documentation.* When you add a SCSI peripheral, write down the SCSI ID address as well as any other switch and jumper settings, such as SCSI Parity, Terminator Power, and Delayed and/or Remote Start. For the host adapter, record the BIOS addresses, Interrupt, DMA channel, and I/O Port addresses used by the adapter, as well as any other jumper or configuration settings (such as termination) that might be important to know later.

- *Use proper termination.* Each end of the bus must be terminated, preferably with active or Forced Perfect (FPT) terminators. If you are using any Fast SCSI-2 device, you must use active terminators rather than the cheaper passive types. Even with standard (slow) SCSI devices, active termination is highly recommended. If you have only internal or external devices on the bus, the host adapter and last device on the chain should be terminated. If you have external and internal devices on the chain, you generally will terminate the first and last of these devices but not the SCSI host adapter itself (which is in the middle of the bus).

- *Use high-quality shielded SCSI cables.* Make sure that your cable connectors match your devices. Use high-quality shielded cables, and observe the SCSI bus-length limitations. Use cables designed for SCSI use and, if possible, stick to the same brand of cable throughout a single SCSI bus. Different brands of cables have different impedance values; this situation sometimes causes problems, especially in long or high-speed SCSI implementations.

Following these simple tips will help minimize problems and leave you with a trouble-free SCSI installation.

IDE versus SCSI

When you compare the performance and capabilities of IDE and SCSI interfaced drives, you need to consider several factors. These two types of drives are the most popular drives used in PC systems today, and a single manufacturer may make identical drives in both interfaces. Deciding which drive type is best for your system is a difficult decision that depends on many factors.

In most cases, you will find that an IDE drive outperforms an equivalent SCSI drive at a given task or benchmark, and that IDE drives usually cost less than SCSI drives, thus offering better value. In some cases, however, SCSI drives have significant performance and value advantages over IDE drives.

Performance

ATA IDE drives currently are used in most PC configurations on the market today, because the cost of an IDE-drive implementation is low and the performance capabilities are high. In comparing any given IDE and SCSI drive for performance, you have to look at the capabilities of the HDAs that are involved.

To minimize the variables in this type of comparison, it is easiest to compare IDE and SCSI drives from the same manufacturer that also use the identical HDA. You will find that in most cases, a drive manufacturer makes a given drive available in both IDE and SCSI forms. For example, Seagate makes the ST-3600A (ATA-IDE) and ST-3600N (Fast SCSI-2) drives, both of which use identical HDAs and which differ only in the logic board. The IDE version has a logic board with a built-in disk controller and a direct AT Bus interface. The SCSI version has the same built-in disk controller and bus interface circuits, and also an SBIC chip. The SBIC chip is a SCSI adapter that places the drive on the SCSI bus. What you will find, in essence, is that virtually all SCSI drives actually are IDE drives with the SBIC chip added.

The HDAs in these example drives are capable of transferring data at a sustained rate of 2.38M to 4M/sec. Because the SCSI version always has the additional overhead of the SCSI bus to go through, in almost all cases the directly attached IDE version performs faster.

SCSI versus IDE: Advantages and Limitations

IDE drives have much less command overhead for a given sector transfer than do SCSI drives. In addition to the drive-to-controller command overhead that both IDE and SCSI must perform, a SCSI transfer involves negotiating for the SCSI bus; selecting the target drive; requesting data; terminating the transfer over the bus; and finally converting the logical data addresses to the required cylinder, head, and sector addresses. This arrangement gives IDE an advantage in sequential transfers handled by a single-tasking operating system. In a multitasking system that can take advantage of the extra intelligence of the SCSI bus, SCSI can have the performance advantage.

SCSI drives offer significant architectural advantages over IDE and other drives. Because each SCSI drive has its own embedded disk controller that can function independently from the system CPU, the computer can issue simultaneous commands to every drive in the system. Each drive can store these commands in a queue and then perform the commands simultaneously with other drives in the system. The data could be fully buffered on the drive and transferred at high speeds over the shared SCSI bus when a time slot was available.

Although IDE drives also have their own controllers, they do not operate simultaneously, and command queuing is not supported. In effect, the dual controllers in a dual-drive IDE installation work one at a time so as not to step on each other.

Although SCSI drives require an additional-cost host adapter card, more and more PCs require tape-backup, CD-ROM, or optical-drive support and thus must still be configured with a SCSI host bus adapter. This means that the incremental cost of supporting SCSI drives is virtually nil, because the SCSI host bus adapter is shared with other devices, such as tape and optical drives. In addition, all major operating systems today include software support for a wide range of SCSI devices.

What are the limitations of IDE?

- IDE does not support overlapped, multitasked I/O.
- IDE does not support command queuing.
- IDE does not support bus mastering.

As you can see, SCSI has some advantages over IDE, especially where expansion is concerned, and also with regard to support for multitasking operating systems. Unfortunately, it also costs more to implement.

Recommended Aftermarket Controllers and Host Adapters

Many companies manufacture disk controllers for IBM and IBM-compatible systems. Many newer systems include IDE drives, which have built-in controllers and offer a high level of performance at a low cost. Other systems are using SCSI drives because of the inherent flexibility of the SCSI bus in supporting many drives and other peripherals.

I recommend IDE drives for most standard installations because the connections are simple and the drives are inexpensive for the power. For higher-end systems, or for systems in which upgradability and flexibility are most important, I recommend SCSI drives.

Recommended SCSI Host Adapters

For SCSI host adapters, I normally recommend Adaptec. Their adapters work well and come with the necessary formatting and operating software. Windows 95, Windows NT, and OS/2 have built-in support for Adaptec SCSI adapters. This support is a consideration in many cases, because it frees you from having to deal with additional drivers.

Standard or Fast SCSI is adequately supported by the ISA bus, but if you are going to install a Fast-Wide SCSI bus, or especially an Ultra-Wide bus, then you should consider some form of local bus SCSI adapter, normally PCI. This is because the ISA bus supports a maximum transfer speed of about 8M/sec, while a Fast-Wide SCSI bus runs up to 20M/sec, and an Ultra-Wide SCSI bus runs up to a blazing 40M/sec! In most cases, a local bus SCSI adapter would be a PCI bus version, which is supported in most current PC systems.

One example of a popular SCSI adapter for the PCI bus is the Adaptec AHA-2940AU (see Figure 15.7) and 2940UW. The 2940AU is an Ultra-SCSI adapter and the 2940UW is Ultra-Wide. These adapters are most notable for their ease of installation and use. Virtually all functions on the card can be configured and set through software. No more digging through manuals or looking for Interrupt, DMA, I/O Port, and other jumper settings—everything is controlled by software and saved in a flash memory module on the card. Following are some of the features of this card:

- Complete configuration utility built into the adapter's ROM
- Software-configurable IRQ, ROM addresses, DMA, I/O Port addresses, SCSI Parity, SCSI ID, and other settings
- Software-selectable termination (no resistors to pull out!)
- Enhanced BIOS support for up to eight 7.88G drives
- No drivers required for more than two hard disks
- Drive spinup on a per-drive basis available
- Boots from any SCSI ID

FIG. 15.7 An Adaptec AHA-2940AU SCSI host adapter.

More recently, Adaptec has released full PnP versions of their SCSI adapters. These adapters will be automatically configured in any PC that supports the PnP specification, or they can be configured manually through supplied software in non-PnP systems. The PnP SCSI adapters are highly recommended because they can be configured without opening up the PC! All functions are set by software, and there are no jumpers or switches to attend to. Most peripheral manufacturers write drivers for Adaptec's cards first, so you will not have many compatibility or driver-support problems with any Adaptec card.

Disk Hardware and Software Limitations

By studying the capabilities of the different disk interfaces as well as the ROM BIOS and operating systems, it is possible to determine the limits on disk storage. The following section details the limits under the different interfaces and operating systems.

Disk Interface Capacity Limitations

Different disk interfaces have different limitations on the theoretical maximum drive capacities that they may support. These limitations are due to variations in the way that each interface operates at the hardware level. It is important to note that even though a particular interface may permit access to a given amount of disk real estate, the BIOS and DOS usually are much more limiting and end up being the true limits for system disk capacity.

ST-506/412, ESDI, and IDE. To determine the capacity limits for the ST-506/412, ESDI, or IDE interface, you first need to determine the limits on the maximum number of cylinders, heads, and sectors per track. To do so, look at the size of the registers that hold this data in the controller. All these interfaces have the same controller register specifications, so the capacity limits calculated here apply to all of them. As you will see, the interface capacity limits are quite high. The drive parameter limits are as follows:

   Cylinders (16 bits) = 65,536

   Heads (4 bits) = 16

   Sectors (8 bits) = 256

This calculates to a maximum theoretical drive size of:

65,536 cylinders × 16 heads × 256 sectors × 512 bytes = 137,438,953,472 bytes (128G)

Unfortunately, the maximum capacity—128G—is limited by the BIOS. There are two different BIOS types with regards to disk size limitations. The standard BIOS built into most systems is limited to 1,024 cylinders, 16 heads, and 63 sectors per track. If the BIOS is an enhanced version, it will be limited to 1,024 cylinders, 256 heads, and 63 sectors per track. Combining the BIOS and interface limits results in the following maximum capacities (assuming 512-byte sectors):

Limit with Standard BIOS: 1,024 cylinders × 16 heads × 63 sectors = 528,482,304 bytes (504M)

Limit with Enhanced BIOS: 1,024 cylinders × 256 heads × 63 sectors = 8,455,716,864 bytes (7.88G)

If you do not have enhanced BIOS support on your motherboard, you could add an IDE bus adapter that has an on-board enhanced BIOS. To get around such BIOS problems, some IDE drive implementations greater than 528 million bytes split the drive to act as two physical units. In this case, the drive would appear on the IDE bus connector as being both master and slave, and could be used only as two 504M maximum-size drives.

ATA-2 has defined LBA support for EIDE. This is a Logical Block Address mode where each sector on the drive is numbered from 0 to x. The limitations are that x is a 28-bit number that has a maximum value of 268,435,456. Using 512-byte sectors, this brings the maximum drive capacity to 137,438,953,472. That is coincidentally the same as the IDE internal limit has always been. The LBA is translated by the ATA-2/EIDE enhanced BIOS to the extended Cylinder, Head, and Sector (CHS) parameters which allow a maximum of 1,024 cylinders, 256 heads, and 63 sectors, respectively.

SCSI. According to the SCSI specification, drives are not addressed by cylinders, heads, and sectors but instead by what is called a Logical Block Address (LBA). This is a sector number in which all the sectors on the drive are numbered sequentially from start to finish. The LBA is specified by a 32-bit number and with 512-byte sectors, results in the following limitation:

4,294,967,296 LBAs (sectors) × 512 bytes = 2,199,023,255,552 bytes (2,048G or 2T)

As you can see, SCSI drive capacity limits are extremely high. However, because the SCSI drive must appear to the BIOS as being a given number of cylinders, heads, and sectors per track, the BIOS limits SCSI capacity. Virtually all SCSI adapters have an enhanced BIOS that supports a maximum drive capacity as follows (assuming 512-byte sectors):

SCSI with Enhanced BIOS: 1,024 cylinders × 256 heads × 63 sectors = 8,455,716,864 bytes (7.88G)

> **Tip**
>
> If you do not have enhanced BIOS support in your SCSI adapter or motherboard, in some cases you can load an external driver for your adapter to provide this support.

Most systems support up to four SCSI host adapters, each with up to seven hard disk drives, for a total 28 physically installed drives.

ROM BIOS Capacity Limitations

In addition to the capacity limit of 504M, the standard ROM BIOS is limited to supporting only two hard disk drives. The enhanced BIOS is limited to 128 drives maximum. Most SCSI and IDE adapters get around the two-drive standard BIOS limits by incorporating an enhanced BIOS on board that takes over the disk interface. Some of the newer adapter on-board BIOS versions support booting from CD-ROM drives as well.

Operating System Capacity Limitations

IBM and Microsoft officially say that DOS 5 and later versions will support up to eight physical hard disks. IBM says that OS/2 1.30.1 and later versions (including 2.x) support up to 24 physical hard disks, and because OS/2 includes DOS, that implies that DOS under OS/2 would support 24 physical drives as well. OS/2 HPFS (High Performance File System) also supports a maximum partition size of 8G and a maximum single-file size of 2G, whereas DOS and OS/2 FAT partitions have a maximum size of 2G and a maximum single-file size of 2G. As you have seen, BIOS limitations currently limit the maximum physical hard disk size to about 7.88G (or about 8.46 million bytes).

Chapter 16

Hard Disk Drive Installation

This chapter thoroughly describes hard disk installation. In particular, the chapter examines the configuration, physical installation, and formatting of a hard disk drive. This chapter also covers the basic procedures necessary to install a hard disk drive into a PC system.

Hard Disk Installation Procedures

To install a hard drive in an IBM-compatible system, you must perform several procedures:

- Configure the drive
- Configure the controller or interface
- Physically install the drive
- Configure the system
- Low-level format the drive (not required with IDE and SCSI)
- Partition the drive
- High-level format the drive

Drive configuration was discussed in Chapter 15, "Hard Disk Interfaces." For complete configuration information, consult the section that covers the type of drive that you are installing.

The following sections describe the other steps, which are simple to execute and, if done properly, result in the successful installation of a bootable hard disk. Special attention is given to issues of reliability and data integrity to ensure that the installation is long-lasting and trouble-free.

To begin the setup procedure, you need to know several details about the hard disk drive, controller or host adapter, and system ROM BIOS, as well as most of the other devices in the system. This information usually appears in the various OEM manuals that come with these devices. Make sure when you

Chapter 16—Hard Disk Drive Installation

purchase these items that the vendor includes these manuals. (Many vendors do not include the manuals unless you ask for them.) For most equipment sold today, you will get enough documentation from the vendor or reseller of the equipment to enable you to proceed.

If you are like me, however, and want all the technical documentation on the device, you will want to contact the original manufacturer of the device and order the technical specification manual. For example, if you purchase an IBM-compatible system that comes with a Western Digital IDE hard disk, the seller probably will give you some limited information on the drive, but not nearly the amount that the actual Western Digital technical specification manual provides. To get this documentation, you have to call Western Digital and order it. The same goes for any of the other components in most clones that are assembled rather than manufactured. I find the OEM technical manuals to be essential in providing the highest level of technical support possible.

On the Web

Here are a few of the major hard drive vendors' Web sites:

http://www.maxtor.com

http://www.micropolis.com

http://www.conner.com/toc.shtml

http://www.wdc.com/welcome.html

Controller Configuration

Configuring a disk controller involves setting the different system resources that the controller requires. Some controllers have these resources fixed, which means that they cannot be altered. Other controllers provide jumpers, switches, or even software that enable you to reconfigure or change the resources used. Controllers with adjustable resource settings often can be used in conjunction with other controllers in a system, but controllers with fixed resources usually cannot coexist with others.

All hard disk controllers and SCSI host adapters require one or more of the following system resources:

- ROM addresses
- Interrupt Request Channel (IRQ)
- DMA channel (DRQ)
- I/O port addresses

Not all adapters use every one of these resources, but some will use them all. In most cases, these resources must be configured so that they are unique and cannot be shared among several adapters. For example, if a disk controller is using I/O port addresses from 1F0–1F7h, no other device in the system can use those addresses.

When a conflict in resource use occurs, not all of the adapters involved may function. In the case of disk controllers, the controller will not function, and disk access will be impossible or corrupted. You need to identify which boards in the system have overlapping resources and then change the configuration of one or more of those boards to eliminate the conflict. Before installing a board, you should know which resources the board will require, and you should make sure that these resources are not being used by other boards.

In most systems, this is a manual procedure that requires you to know exactly what every adapter in the system is using. If your system supports Plug and Play (PnP), this will be much easier. On older MCA and EISA systems, the procedure is also under software control. PnP ISA, PCI, MCA, and EISA systems can automatically determine whether two adapters use the same resource and then change the configuration to eliminate the conflict.

For most systems, you need the documentation for every adapter in the system to ensure that no conflicts exist and to find out how to reconfigure a card to eliminate a conflict. Software included with your system, such as MSD (Microsoft Diagnostics, which comes with Windows 3.x and DOS 6.x) or the Device Manager in Windows 95, can help when documentation is not available or is limited. Aftermarket diagnostics and utility programs can also be helpful. Unless your system conforms to the PnP specification, software will normally not be able to identify direct conflicts, but if you install one board at a time, they can identify the addresses or resources that a given board is using.

Many system resources simply cannot be identified by software alone. Several companies, including AllMicro, Quarterdeck, Data Depot, and others manufacture cards that can be used to monitor interrupt and DMA channels. These boards are very helpful in identifying which of these resources are used in your system. These companies and others are listed in Appendix A.

> **Note**
>
> For more on software and hardware diagnostic tools, see Chapter 21, "Software and Hardware Diagnostic Tools." For additional information on interrupts and DMA channels, see also Chapter 5, "Bus Slots and I/O Cards."

ROM Addresses. Many disk controllers and SCSI host adapters require an on-board BIOS to function. An on-board BIOS can provide many functions, including:

- Low-level formatting
- Drive-type (parameter) control
- Adapter configuration
- Support for nonstandard I/O port addresses and interrupts

If the motherboard BIOS supports a hard disk controller, an on-board BIOS is not needed—and in fact is undesirable because it uses memory in the Upper Memory Area (UMA). Fortunately, the on-board BIOS usually can be disabled if it is not required.

Only controllers that meet certain standards can run off the motherboard BIOS, including ST-506/412 controllers, ESDI controllers, and IDE bus adapters. These standards include the use of I/O port addresses 170–17Fh and interrupt 14. If you are installing a controller that uses other I/O port addresses or interrupt settings (such as when adding a second controller to a system), the motherboard BIOS will not be able to support it, and an on-board BIOS will be required. XT controllers universally need an on-board BIOS because the motherboard BIOS has no hard disk support whatsoever.

SCSI adapters normally do not emulate the WD1003-type disk interface and almost always require an on-board BIOS to provide disk driver functions. This on-board BIOS supports any of the adapter's settings; in most cases, multiple SCSI host adapters can use the BIOS of the first adapter, in which case the BIOSes on all but the first adapter can be disabled.

If an on-board BIOS is required and enabled, it will use specific memory address space in the UMA. The UMA is the top 384K in the first megabyte of system memory. The UMA is divided into three areas of two 64K segments each, with the first and last areas being used by the video-adapter circuits and the motherboard BIOS, respectively. Segments C000h and D000h are reserved for use by adapter ROMs such as those found on disk controllers or SCSI host adapters.

> **Note**
>
> You need to ensure that any adapters using space in these segments do not overlap with another adapter that uses this space. No two adapters can share this memory space. Most adapters have jumpers, switches, or even software that can adjust the configuration of the board and change the addresses that are used to prevent conflict.

Interrupt Request Channel (IRQ). All disk controllers and SCSI host adapters require an interrupt line to gain the system's attention. These devices invoke a hardware interrupt to gain timely access to the system for data transfers and control. The original 8-bit ISA systems have only eight interrupt levels, with interrupts 2–7 available to any adapter. AT bus (16-bit ISA), EISA, and MCA systems have 16 interrupt levels, with interrupts 3–7, 9–12, and 14 and 15 available to any adapter cards. IRQs 10–12 and 14 and 15 are 16-bit interrupts available only to 16- or 32-bit adapters.

Tables 16.1 and 16.2 show the normally used and normally available interrupts in ISA, EISA, and MCA systems and in 8-bit ISA systems. The tables list the default use for each interrupt and indicate whether the interrupt is available in a bus slot.

Table 16.1 ISA, EISA, and MCA Default Interrupt Assignments

IRQ	Function	Bus Slot
0	System Timer	No
1	Keyboard Controller	No
2	Second IRQ Controller	No
8	Real-Time Clock	No
9	Network/Available (Redirected IRQ 2)	Yes (8-bit)
10	Available	Yes (16-bit)

IRQ	Function	Bus Slot
11	SCSI/Available	Yes (16-bit)
12	Motherboard Mouse Port	Yes (16-bit)
13	Math Coprocessor	No
14	Hard Disk Controller	Yes (16-bit)
15	Secondary IDE	Yes (16-bit)
3	Serial Port 2 (COM2:)	Yes (8-bit)
4	Serial Port 1 (COM1:)	Yes (8-bit)
5	Sound/Parallel Port 2 (LPT2:)	Yes (8-bit)
6	Floppy Disk Controller	Yes (8-bit)
7	Parallel Port 1 (LPT1:)	Yes (8-bit)

Table 16.2 XT-Bus (8-Bit ISA) Default Interrupt Assignments

IRQ	Function	Bus Slot
0	System Timer	No
1	Keyboard Controller	No
2	Network/Available	Yes (8-bit)
3	Serial Port 2 (COM2:)	Yes (8-bit)
4	Serial Port 1 (COM1:)	Yes (8-bit)
5	Hard Disk Controller	Yes (8-bit)
6	Floppy Disk Controller	Yes (8-bit)
7	Parallel Port 1 (LPT1:)	Yes (8-bit)

Notice that some of the interrupts are simply not available in slots; they are reserved for use only by the indicated system function. Any interrupt that is listed as being in use by an item that is not installed in your system would be available. For example, if your system does not have a motherboard mouse port, IRQ 12 would be available; if your system does not have a second serial port, IRQ 3 would be available.

You must discover which interrupts are currently in use and which are currently available in a system, and then configure any new cards to use only the available interrupts. In a standard configuration, the hard disk controller uses interrupt (IRQ) 14. Any secondary controllers would have to use other interrupts. The standard interrupt for a secondary controller is IRQ 15. If the system does not support EIDE (Enhanced IDE) in the motherboard BIOS, then any controllers that do not use IRQ 14 must have an on-board BIOS to function. The older motherboard BIOS supports disk controllers only at IRQ 14, whereas a BIOS with EIDE support will run IDE ports at both IRQ 14 and 15. Most newer systems have integral EIDE support and automatically include a secondary IDE port, which is at IRQ 15.

Standard IDE adapters come preconfigured for IRQ 14, which is fine if the adapter is the only disk adapter in the system. Many SCSI host adapters, such as the Adaptec 1540/1542C, come configured to one of the other available 16-bit interrupts, such as IRQ 11. Old XT (8-bit) hard disk controllers normally use IRQ 5.

DMA Channel. *Direct Memory Access (DMA)* is a technique for transferring blocks of data directly into system memory without the complete attention of the main processor. The motherboard has DMA control circuits that orchestrate and govern DMA transfers. In the original 8-bit XT bus, DMA was the highest-performance transfer method, and XT hard disk controllers universally used DMA channel 3 for high-speed transfers.

In AT-Bus (16-bit ISA) systems, most 16-bit disk controllers and SCSI host adapters do not use a DMA channel, partly because the performance of the AT Bus DMA circuitry turned out to be very poor. Therefore, most adapters use a technique called *Programmed I/O (PIO)*, which simply sends bytes of data through the I/O ports. PIO transfers are faster than DMA transfers in most cases, especially if the motherboard BIOS and device support block-mode PIO, such as with the new IDE drives. If an adapter does not use DMA, you can assume that PIO is used as the data-transfer method and that no DMA channel is required.

Some adapters have found a way around the poor performance of the ISA bus by becoming what is known as a bus master. A *bus master* actually takes control of the bus and can override the DMA controller circuitry of the motherboard to perform fast DMA transfers. These transfers can exceed the performance of a PIO transfer (even block-mode PIO), so you will find that many of the highest-performing controllers have bus-master capabilities.

You have to select a DMA channel for bus-master adapters to use. In an 8-bit ISA bus, normally only DMA channel 1 is available; in a 16-bit ISA bus, however, DMA channels 0–1, 3, and 5–7 are available. DMA channels 5–7 are 16-bit channels that most high-performance bus-master adapters would want to use. XT disk controllers always use DMA channel 3, whereas most 16-bit AT or IDE controllers do not use DMA at all. This is not a concern in the newer PCI bus systems.

Tables 16.3 and 16.4 show the normally used and normally available DMA channels. The tables list the default use for each DMA channel and indicate whether the DMA channel is available in a bus slot.

Table 16.3 16-Bit ISA Default DMA Channel Assignments

DMA	Function	Transfer	Bus Slot
0	Available	8-bit	Yes(16-bit)
1	Sound/Available	8-bit	Yes (8-bit)
2	Floppy Disk Controller	8-bit	Yes (8-bit)
3	ECP Parallel/Available	8-bit	Yes (8-bit)
4	First DMA Controller	N/A	No
5	Sound/Available	16-bit	Yes(16-bit)
6	SCSI/Available	16-bit	Yes(16-bit)
7	Available	16-bit	Yes(16-bit)

Table 16.4 8-Bit ISA Default DMA Channel Assignments

DMA	Function	Transfer	Bus Slot
0	Dynamic RAM Refresh	N/A	No
1	Sound/Available	8-bit	Yes (8-bit)
2	Floppy Disk Controller	8-bit	Yes (8-bit)
3	Hard Disk Controller	8-bit	Yes (8-bit)

Notice that some of the DMA channels simply are not available in slots; they are reserved for use only by the indicated system function. Any DMA channel that is listed as being in use by an item that is not installed in your system would be available. For example, if your 8-bit ISA bus system does not have a hard disk controller, DMA channel 3 would be available.

PCI and EISA bus systems have additional DMA capabilities that support even faster transfers without the performance problems associated with non-bus-master cards. The PCI and EISA buses also provide even better support for bus-master devices that offer even higher performance.

To configure an adapter that requires a DMA channel, you first must find out which DMA channels currently are in use and which channels are available in your system. Unless you have an PCI or EISA system, software techniques for determining this are very limited. Most programs that claim to be capable of discovering which DMA channels are being used are only reporting what any standard configuration would be. In standard ISA systems, the only way to know for sure is to check the documentation for each adapter or to use a special hardware device that monitors DMA transfers.

After determining what DMA channels are free, you can set your adapter to any of those free channels. DMA conflicts usually result in improper operation or corrupted data transfers, so if you made a mistake, you usually will know quickly.

PCI and EISA systems automatically set up the boards so that no DMA conflicts exist. This method works fully only in EISA systems with all EISA 32-bit adapters installed. PCI buses usually have at least two or more ISA slots that you still need to worry about.

I/O Port Addresses. *I/O port* addresses are like mailboxes through which data and commands are sent to and from an adapter. These addresses are different from memory addresses. I/O ports must be used exclusively and cannot be shared among different adapters. Each adapter usually uses a group of sequential port addresses for communication with the bus.

The standard I/O port addresses used by disk controllers are 1F0–1F7h. These are the only addresses that the motherboard BIOS supports, so if you have a disk controller at any other port address, it must have an on-board BIOS. Obviously, if you are adding a secondary controller to a system, that controller must use different I/O addresses and also must have an on-board BIOS. Most controllers use 170–177h as secondary I/O addresses, which would be used if another disk controller were in the system; however, you can use any I/O addresses that are free.

I/O port conflicts are rare unless you are installing multiple disk controllers in a system. In that case, each controller needs different I/O port address settings so as not to conflict with the others. To determine what I/O ports are currently in use, you normally have to refer to the documentation that comes with each device in your system. Software normally cannot identify all used I/O port addresses unless you have a PCI or EISA system. When port conflicts exist, the devices in conflict do not function, or they function improperly.

> **Multi-Function I/O Cards**
>
> Multi-function I/O cards are a combination floppy disk, hard disk, and serial and parallel port adapters all on one expansion card. Most newer motherboards have all these functions built right into the motherboard, but you may see a few of these multi-function boards in older PCI or VLB systems, and it is important to note that you will have to disable the hard disk controller on this board before installing a new controller.

Physical Installation

The procedure for physical installation of a hard disk is much the same as the procedure for installing a floppy drive. You must have the correct screws, brackets, and faceplates for the specific drive and system before you can install the drive.

Some AT or Baby-AT type computer cases require plastic rails that are secured to the sides of the drives so that they can slide into the proper place in the system (see Figure 16.1). Compaq uses a different type of rail, as does Hewlett-Packard, Packard Bell, and so on. When you purchase a drive, the vendor usually includes the "Standard-type" rails, so be sure to specify whether you need the special manufacturer type. IBM PC-type and XT-type systems do not need rails, but they may need a bracket to enable double-stacking of half-height drives. Several companies listed in Appendix B specialize in drive-mounting brackets, cables, and other hardware accessories. Also, many newer after market computer cases have eliminated the need for drive rails all together by making the expansion slot itself to the 3 1/2- or 5 1/4-inch drive specification, allowing you to bolt the new drive directly to the case itself.

> **Note**
>
> You should also note the length of the cable itself. In some cases, the drive cable is not long enough to reach the new drive location. You can try to reposition the original drive if you have the available expansion slots, or just get a longer cable.

Different faceplate, or bezel, options are available; make sure that you have the correct bezel for your application. Some systems, for example, do not need a bezel; if a bezel is on the drive, it must be removed. If you are installing a half-height drive in a full-height bay, you may need a blank half-height bezel to fill the hole, or you may want to order a half-height drive with a full-height bezel so that no hole is created. Several vendors listed in Appendix A sell a variety of drive mounting kits, hardware, rails, adapters, and cables.

FIG. 16.1 A full-height hard disk with AT mounting rails.

> **Caution**
>
> Make sure you use only the screws that come with your new drive. Many drives come with a special short-length screw that can have the same thread as other screws you might use in your system, but the shorter screws will not drive too far into the drive, which could cause problems.

System Configuration

When the drive is physically installed, you can begin configuring the system to the drive. You have to tell the system about the drive so that the system can boot from it when it powered on. How you set and store this information depends on the type of drive and system you have. Standard (IDE) setup procedures are used for most hard disks except SCSI drives. SCSI drives normally follow a custom setup procedure that varies depending on the host adapter that you are using. If you have SCSI drives, follow the instructions included with the host adapter to configure the drives.

Automatic Drive Typing. If the system is an AT type and you are using the motherboard BIOS to support the hard disks, you need to know some information about the BIOS, such as what drives are supported in the hard drive table. Many BIOS versions now have user-definable drive types that enable you to enter any set of parameters required to match your drive. For IDE drives, all new BIOS versions have automatic typing, which interrogates the drive and automatically enters the parameter information returned by the drive. This procedure eliminates errors or confusion in parameter selection.

If you are dealing with an older motherboard that does not support automatic typing, the information about the drive table appears in the technical manuals provided with the motherboard or the BIOS. Appendix A includes a list of drive types for many different BIOS versions. For systems that are not listed, you can find this information in the system's technical reference manual. Often, the BIOS setup program shows you all the available selections on-screen, enabling you to select the best choice interactively and eliminating the need to research this information.

Manual Drive Typing. After you collect the necessary information, the next step is to tell the system what kind of drive is attached so that the system can boot from the drive (eventually). This chapter discusses the installation of an example drive in an AT-type and ATX-type of system. With knowledge of drive interfacing, you can install just about any drive in any system.

First, you need to read the drive manual and locate the required information. The manual for this example contains the following drive-parameter information:

- 918 cylinders
- 15 heads
- 17 or 26 sectors per track (MFM or RLL encoding)
- No write precompensation required
- Seven defective tracks: (specific to each drive)

    | Cyl 188, Head 7 | Cyl 601, Head 13 |
    | Cyl 217, Head 5 | Cyl 798, Head 10 |
    | Cyl 218, Head 5 | Cyl 835, Head 5 |
    | Cyl 219, Head 5 | |

To install this drive in an AT-type case, I could simply use the original IDE drive; however, I would have to live with the relatively slow performance that this controller provides. A better choice is to upgrade the controller with an EIDE PIO mode 4 controller. This controller not only supports up to four IDE devices including CD-ROM, but will provide me with up to 16.6M/sec transfer rate.

> **Note**
>
> For more information on installation and configuration of drive controllers, see Chapter 15, "Hard Disk Interfaces."

The example controller uses PIO transfers and does not require a DMA channel for the hard disk controller portion. Because this controller also contains a floppy controller, some additional information specific to the floppy controller portion of the card is required:

- Interrupt Request Channel (IRQ) = 6
- DMA channel (DRQ) = 2
- I/O ports = 3F0–3F7

You need some of this information to ensure that the card is uniquely configured compared with other cards in the system. The system cannot have other cards using the same IRQ, DMA, ROM, or I/O ports as this card. Keep this information for future reference, and cross-check for conflicts when you add other cards to the system. The step pulse rates and interleave information are all that you need to complete the setup.

After you find the information about the drive and controller, you need to match the drive's parameters to one of the drive-table entries in the motherboard ROM. ROM drive tables for IBM and many other compatible systems are listed in Appendix A, which also includes a detailed list of a large number of hard disk drives with parameter specifications. The information in Appendix A saved me several times when the original manuals were nowhere to be found. However, most drive tables are now embedded in the CMOS of the motherboard, and usually you have to choose User Defined (if you don't have an Auto-Configure option) option anyway, and fill in your new drive's parameters because most new drives are *much* larger than any of the available drive type choices.

> **Tip**
>
> The landing-cylinder designation is superfluous because all new drives automatically park and lock their heads at power-down, although it would be used if you ever ran a correctly written head-parking program.

This type of drive-table information does not apply to IBM ESDI or SCSI hard disk controllers, host adapters, and drives. Because ESDI and SCSI controllers and host adapters query the drive directly for the required parameters, no table-entry selection is necessary. The table for ST-506/412 drives, however, still appears in the ROM BIOS of most PS/2 systems, even if the model came standard with the ESDI or SCSI disk subsystem.

The manufacturers of most compatibles have enhanced the motherboard ROM BIOS tables in three ways:

- *Additional types.* The first thing that the manufacturers did was add more drive types to the table. Because the table had room for 47 or more entries, many compatible BIOS versions simply filled out all the entries with values that matched the most popular drives on the market, generally making drive installations easier. IBM tables often were short of the maximum number of possible entries.

- *User-definable drive types.* Most makers of compatibles then added a user-definable type, which used unused areas of the CMOS memory to store all the drive-parameter information. This was an excellent solution, because during setup you can type a parameter that matches any drive on the market. The only drawback is that if the CMOS battery dies or the saved values are corrupted in some way, you would have to re-enter the information exactly as it was before to regain access to the drive. Many people did not write down the parameters that they used, or they used improper parameters that caused problems.

- *Automatic detection.* Most of the newer BIOS versions include a feature that is specific to IDE drives. Because most IDE drives are intelligent and will respond to a command called `Identify Drive`, the BIOS sends this command to the drive, which then responds with the correct parameters. This feature eliminates the need to type the parameters because the BIOS will accept what the drive tells it.

As mentioned earlier, most of the newer compatible BIOS versions have both the user-definable type feature and automatic determination for IDE drives.

ROM Replacement. One way around the drive-table limits is to purchase and install a new ROM BIOS. A Phoenix ROM BIOS set, for example, costs about $50. These ROMs include a user-definable drive-type setting, which is the most elegant solution to this problem. A new set of ROMs probably will give you additional features, such as a built-in setup program, support for HD or ED 3 1/2-inch floppy drives, and Enhanced Keyboard support.

RLL/ESDI System Configuration. RLL and ESDI drives usually are not represented in the internal drive tables of older BIOS versions. Consequently, the controllers for these drives often have an on-board ROM BIOS that either contains an internal list of choices for the interface or enables you to dynamically configure (define) the controller to the specific geometry of the drive.

If you have a motherboard BIOS with a user-defined drive type (recommended), you can simply enter the correct parameters and the drive will be supported. (Remember to write down the parameters that you use; if you lose them, you can lose access to the drive if you don't re-enter the parameters properly.) When using a user-definable type, you can disable the controller BIOS.

IDE System Configuration. Intelligent IDE drives can use the geometry that represents their true physical parameters, or they can translate to other drive geometries that have the same number of sectors or fewer. Simply select a type, or enter a user-definable type that is less than or equal to the total capacity of the drive.

SCSI System Configuration. Almost all SCSI drives use `DRIVE TYPE 0` or `NONE`, because the host adapter BIOS and the drive communicate to establish the drive geometry. The low-level formatting routines usually are accessed on the host adapter through a configuration, setup, and format program. All SCSI drives are low-level formatted at the factory.

Formatting and Software Installation

Proper setup and formatting are critical to a drive's performance and reliability. This section describes the procedures used to format a hard disk drive correctly. Use these procedures when you install a new drive in a system or immediately after you recover data from a hard disk that has been exhibiting problems.

Three major steps complete the formatting process for a hard disk drive subsystem:

- Low-level formatting
- Partitioning
- High-level formatting

Considerations Before Low-Level Formatting. In a *low-level format (LLF)*, which is a "real" format, the tracks and sectors of the disk are outlined and written. During the LLF, data is written across the entire disk. An improper LLF results in lost data and in many read and write failures. You need to consider several things before initiating an LLF.

Data Backup. Low-level formatting is the primary standard repair procedure for hard disk drives that are having problems. Because data values are copied to the drive at every possible location during an LLF, necessary data-recovery operations must be performed before an LLF operation.

> **Caution**
>
> After an LLF has been performed, you cannot recover any information previously written to the drive.

Because an LLF overwrites all the data on a drive, it is a good way to erase an entire drive if you are trying to ensure that nobody will be able to get data from it. Government standards for this type of procedure actually require the data to be overwritten several times with different patterns, but for most intents and purposes, if the drive is overwritten one time, nobody will be able to read any data that was on it.

System Temperature. Sector header and trailer information is written or updated only during the LLF operation. During normal read and write activity, only the 512 bytes plus the CRC (Cyclic Redundancy Check) bytes in the trailer are written in a sector. Temperature-induced dimensional changes in the drive platters during read and write operations can become a problem.

When a 5 1/4-inch platter drive is low-level formatted five minutes after powerup at a relatively cold platter temperature of 70° F, the sector headers and trailers and the 512-byte dummy data values are written to each track on each platter at specific locations.

Suppose that you save a file on a drive that has been running for several hours at a platter temperature of 140° F. The data areas of only several sectors are updated. But with the drive platters as much as 70° warmer than when the drive was formatted, each aluminum drive platter will have expanded in size by 2.5 thousandths of an inch (taking into account the coefficient of linear thermal expansion of aluminum). Each track, therefore, would have moved outward a distance of approximately 1.25 thousandths of an inch. Most 5 1/4-inch hard disks have track densities between 500 and 1,000 TPI (tracks per inch), with distances of only 1 to 2 thousandths of an inch between adjacent tracks. As a result, the thermal expansion of a typical 5 1/4-inch hard disk platter could cause the tracks to migrate from one-half to more than one full track of distance below the heads. If the drive head-movement mechanism does not compensate for these thermally induced dimensional changes in the platters, severe mistracking results.

When mistracking occurs, the data areas in each sector that have been updated at the higher temperature fail to line up with the sector header and trailer information. If the sector header and trailer information cannot be read properly, DOS usually issues an error message like this one:

```
Sector not found reading drive C
Abort, Retry, Ignore, Fail?
```

The data is misaligned with the sector boundaries on those tracks. This thermal effect also can work in reverse: If the drive is formatted and written to while it is extremely hot, it may not read properly while cold because of dimensional changes in the platters. This problem occurs with drives that have the "Monday-morning blues," in which they spin but cannot read data properly when they are first powered on, especially after being off for an extended period (over a weekend, for example). If you leave the power to the system on for some time so that the drive can warm up, the system then may boot and run normally.

If this happens, the next step is to back up the drive completely and initiate a new LLF at the proper operating temperature (described next). This procedure enables the drive to work normally again until temperature-induced mistracking becomes great enough to cause the problem again.

Knowing that temperature fluctuations can cause mistracking, you should understand the reasons for the following basic rules of disk use:

- Leave the system's power on for at least 30 minutes before performing an LLF on its hard disk. This step ensures that the platters are at a normal operating temperature and have stabilized dimensionally.

- If possible, allow a system some time to warm up after power-on before storing any data on the hard disk. This procedure is not required for voice coil drives.

If you have a cheap stepper motor drive that consistently exhibits temperature-related mistracking problems, you may want to consider running the drive constantly. Doing so would extend its trouble-free life span significantly because the temperature and dimensions of the platters would stay relatively constant.

These kinds of temperature-fluctuation problems are more of a problem with drives that have open-loop stepper motor actuators (which offer no thermal compensation) than with the closed-loop voice coil actuators (which follow temperature-induced track migration and compensate completely, resulting in no tracking errors even with large changes in platter dimensions).

Modern voice coil actuator drives do not exhibit these dimensional instabilities due to thermal expansion and contraction of the platters because they have a track-following servo mechanism. As the tracks move, the positioner automatically compensates. Many of these drives undergo a noticeable thermal compensation sequence every five minutes or so for the first 30 minutes after being powered on, and usually every 30 minutes after that. During these thermal-compensation routines, you hear the heads move back and forth as they measure and compensate for platter-dimension changes.

Drive Operating Position. Another consideration before formatting a drive is ensuring that the drive is formatted in the operating position it will have when it is installed in the system. Gravity can place on the head actuator different loads that can cause mistracking if the drive changes between a vertical and a horizontal position. This effect is minimized or even eliminated in most voice coil drives, but this procedure cannot hurt.

Additionally, drives that are not properly shock-mounted should be formatted only when they are installed in the system because the installation screws exert twisting forces on the drive's Head Disk Assembly (HDA), which can cause mistracking. If you format the drive with the mounting screws installed tightly, it may not read with the screws out, and vice versa. Be careful not to overtighten the mounting screws, because doing so can stress the HDA. This usually is not a problem if the drive's HDA is isolated from the frame by rubber bushings.

In summary, for a proper LLF, the drive should be

- At a normal operating temperature
- In a normal operating position
- Mounted in the host system (if the drive HDA is not shock-mounted or isolated from the drive frame by rubber bushings)

Because many different makes and models of controllers differ in the way that they write data to a drive, especially with respect to the encoding scheme, it is best to format the drive using the same make and model of controller as the controller that will be used in the host system. Some brands of controllers work exactly alike, however, so this is not an absolute requirement even if the interface is the same. This problem does not occur with IDE or SCSI drives, of course, because the controller is built into the drive. Usually, if the controller establishes the drive type by using its own on-board ROM rather than the system setup program, it will be incompatible with other controllers.

Low-Level Format. Of these procedures, the LLF is most important to ensure trouble-free operation of the drive. This format is the most critical of the operations and must be done correctly for the drive to work properly. The LLF includes several subprocedures:

- Scanning for existing defect mapping
- Selecting the interleave
- Formatting and marking (or remarking) manufacturer defects
- Running a surface analysis

On all new systems, these subprocedures are performed automatically by the system's LLF program and require no user intervention, and you need not continue in this section. On older systems, you must take the initiative, and should read on.

To perform the drive defect mapping, to select an interleave, and to complete a surface analysis of the drive, you need information about the drive, the controller, and possibly the system. This information usually is provided in separate manuals or documents for each item; therefore, be sure that you get the complete documentation for your drive and controller products when you purchase them. The specific information required depends on the type of system, controller, and LLF program that you are using.

Defect Mapping. Before formatting the disk, you need to know whether the drive has defects that have to be mapped out. Older drives came with a list of defects discovered by the manufacturer during the drive's final quality control testing. These defects were marked so that they are not used later to store programs or data.

Defect mapping was one of the most critical aspects of low-level formatting, now just a historical curiosity as low-level formatting is now done almost exclusively by the manufacturer. If you would like to understand the defect-mapping procedures, you first must understand what happens when a defect is mapped on a drive.

The manufacturer's defect list usually indicated defects by cylinder and track. When this information is entered, an LLF program marked these tracks with invalid checksum figures in the header of each of the sectors, ensuring that nothing can read or write to these locations. When DOS performed a high-level format of the disk, the DOS FORMAT program could not read these locations, and it marked the involved clusters in the File Allocation Table (FAT) so that they never will be used.

The list of defects that the manufacturer gives you probably is more extensive than what a program could determine from your system, because the manufacturer's test equipment is far more sensitive than a regular disk controller. The FORMAT program did not find the defects automatically; you probably had to enter them manually. The exceptions are new systems, in which the defect list is encoded in a special area of the drive that normal software cannot access. The LLF program (included in the motherboard BIOS program that comes with the systems) reads this special map, thereby eliminating the need to enter these locations manually.

> **Tip**
>
> If your motherboard BIOS does not have an LLF utility built in, you are probably better off not low-level formatting an IDE drive.

All new drives are low-level formatted by the manufacturer. If you bought a system with a drive already installed by the manufacturer or dealer, an LLF probably was done for you. Most manufacturers no longer recommend you LLF any IDE type drive.

Although an actual defect is technically different from a marked defect, these defects should correspond to one another if the drive is formatted properly. For example, I can enter the location of a good track into the LLF program as a defective track. The LLF program then corrupts the checksum values for the sectors on that track, rendering them unreadable and unwriteable. When the DOS FORMAT program encounters that track, it finds the track unreadable and marks the clusters occupying that track as being bad. After that, as the drive is used, DOS ensures that no data ever is written to that track. The drive stays in that condition until you redo the LLF of that track, indicate that the track is not to be marked defective, and redo the high-level format that no longer will find the track unreadable and therefore permit those clusters to be used. In general, unless an area is marked as defective in the LLF, it will not be found as defective by the high-level format, and DOS will subsequently use it for data storage.

Defect mapping becomes a problem when someone formats a hard disk and fails to enter the manufacturer's defect list, which contains actual defect locations, so that the LLF can establish these tracks or sectors as marked defects. Letting a defect go unmarked will cost you data when the area is used to store a file that you subsequently cannot retrieve.

Unfortunately, the LLF program does not automatically find and mark any areas on a disk that are defective. The manufacturer's defect list is produced by very sensitive test equipment that tests the drive at an analog level. Most manufacturers indicate areas as being defective even if they are just marginal. The problem is that a marginal area today may be totally unreadable in the future. You should avoid any area suspected as being defective by entering the location during the LLF so that the area is marked; then DOS is forced to avoid the area.

Currently Marked Defects Scan. Most LLF programs have the capability to perform a scan for previously marked defects on a drive. Some programs call this operation a *defect scan*; IBM calls it *Read Verify* in the IBM Advanced Diagnostics. This type of operation is nondestructive and reports by cylinder and head position all track locations marked bad. Do not mistake this for a true scan for defective tracks on a disk, which is a destructive operation normally called a surface analysis (discussed in the section "Surface Analysis" later in this chapter).

If a drive was low-level formatted previously, you should scan the disk for previously marked defects before running a fresh LLF for several reasons:

- *To ensure that the previous LLF correctly marked all manufacturer-listed defects.* Compare the report of the defect scan with the manufacturer's list, and note any discrepancies. Any defects on the manufacturer's list that were not found by the defect scan were not marked properly.

- *To look for tracks that are marked as defective but are not on the manufacturer's list.* These tracks may have been added by a previously run surface-analysis program (in which case they should be retained), or they may result from the previous formatter's typographical errors in marking the manufacturer's defect. One of my drive manufacturer's lists showed Cylinder 514 Head 14 as defective. A defect scan, however, showed that track as good but Cylinder 814, Head 14 as bad. Because the latter location was not on the manufacturer's list, and because typing **5** instead of **8** would be an easy mistake to make, I concluded that a typographical error was the cause and then reformatted the drive, marking Cylinder 514, Head 14 as bad and enabling Cylinder, 814 Head 14 to be formatted as a good track, thus "unmarking" it.

If you run a surface analysis and encounter defects in addition to those on the manufacturer's list, you can do one of two things:

- If the drive is under warranty, consider returning it.

- If the drive is out of warranty, grab a pen and write on the defect-list sticker, adding the bad tracks discovered by the surface-analysis program. (The low-level formatter built into the system BIOS performs a surface analysis immediately after the LLF; if it discovers additional defects, it automatically adds them to the defect list recorded on the drive.) Adding new defects to the sticker in this manner means that these areas are not forgotten when the drive is subsequently reformatted.

Manufacturer's Defect List. The manufacturer tests a new hard disk by using sophisticated analog test instruments that perform an extensive analysis of the surface of the platters. This kind of testing can indicate the functionality of an area of the disk with great accuracy, precisely measuring information such as the signal-to-noise ratio and recording accuracy.

Some manufacturers have more demanding standards than others about what they consider to be defects. Many people are bothered by the fact that when they purchase a new drive, it comes with a list of defective locations; some even demand that the seller install a defect-free drive. The seller can satisfy this request by substituting a drive made by a company with less-stringent quality control, but the drive will be of poorer quality. The manufacturer that produces drives with more listed defects usually has a higher-quality product because the number of listed defects depends on the level of quality control. What constitutes a defect depends on who is interpreting the test results.

To mark the manufacturer defects listed for the drive, consult the documentation for your LLF program. For most drives, the manufacturer's defect list shows the defects by cylinder and head; other lists locate the defect down to the bit on the track that is bad, starting with the index location.

> **Caution**
>
> Make sure that all manufacturer's defects have been entered before proceeding with the LLF.

Some systems automatically mark the manufacturer's defects, using a special defect file recorded on the drive by the manufacturer. For such a system, you need a special LLF program that knows how to find and read this file. Automatic defect-map entry is standard for IBM PS/2 systems and for most ESDI and all SCSI systems. Consult the drive or controller vendor for the proper LLF program and defect-handling procedures for your drive.

> **Note**
>
> Data recovery utilities such as ScanDisk (DOS/Windows) or Norton Utilities cannot mark the sectors or tracks at the physical format level. The bad cluster marks that they make are stored only in the FAT and are easily erased during the next high-level format operation. You should also use an LLF utility designed for your drive (contact the manufacturer), which will properly mark bad sectors and assign spares at the physical disk level.

Surface Analysis. A defect scan is a scan for marked defects; a *surface analysis* is a scan for actual defects. A surface analysis ignores tracks already marked defective by an LLF and tests the unmarked tracks. The surface-analysis program writes 512 bytes to each sector on the good tracks, reads the sectors back, and compares the data read to what was written. If the data does not verify, the program (like an LLF) marks the track bad by corrupting the checksum values for each sector on that track. A proper surface analysis is like an LLF program in that it should bypass the DOS and the BIOS so that it can turn off controller retry operations and also see when ECC (Error Correction Code) is invoked to correct soft errors.

Surface-analysis programs are destructive: They write over every sector except those that already are marked as bad. You should run a surface-analysis program immediately after running an LLF to determine whether defects have appeared in addition to the manufacturer's defects entered during the LLF. A defect scan after the LLF and the surface analysis shows the cumulative tracks that were marked bad by both programs.

If you have lost the manufacturer's defect list, you can use the surface-analysis program to indicate which tracks are bad, but this program never can duplicate the accuracy or sensitivity of the original manufacturer testing.

Although it is recommended if you have been experiencing any problems with a drive, on new drives I normally do not run a surface analysis after low-level formatting for several reasons:

- Compared with formatting, surface analysis takes a long time. Most surface-analysis programs take two to five times longer than an LLF. An LLF of a 120M drive takes about 15 minutes; a surface analysis of the same drive takes an hour or more. Moreover, if you increase the accuracy of the surface analysis by allowing multiple passes or multiple patterns, the surface analysis takes even longer.

- With high-quality drives, I never find defects beyond those that the manufacturer specified. In fact, the surface-analysis programs do not find all the manufacturer's defects if I do not enter them manually. Because the high-quality (voice coil) drives that I use have been tested by the manufacturer to a greater degree than a program can perform on my system, I simply mark all the defects from the manufacturer's list in the LLF. If I were using a low-quality (stepper motor) drive or installing a used and out-of-warranty drive, I would consider performing a surface analysis after the LLF.

Why Low-Level Format? Even though it generally is not necessary (or even recommended) to LLF IDE or SCSI drives, there are a few good reasons to consider an LLF. One reason is that an LLF will wipe out all the data on a drive, ensuring that other people will not be able to read or recover that data. This procedure is useful if you are selling a system and do not want your data to be readable by the purchaser. Another reason for wiping all the data from a drive is to remove corrupted or non-DOS operating-system partitions and even virus infections. The best reason is for defect management. As you may have noticed, most ATA-IDE drives appear to have no "bytes in bad sectors" under CHKDSK or any other software.

Any defects that were present on the drive after manufacturing were reallocated by the factory LLF. Essentially, any known bad sectors are replaced by spare sectors stored in different parts of the drive. If any new defects occur, such as from a minor head/platter contact or drive mishandling, a proper IDE-aware LLF program can map the new bad sectors to other spares, hiding them and restoring the drive to what appears to be defect-free status.

Because the IDE (ATA) specification is an extension of the IBM/WD ST-506/412 controller interface, the specification includes several new CCB commands that were not part of the original INT 13h/CCB support. Some of these new CCB commands are vendor-specific and are unique to each IDE drive manufacturer. Some manufacturers use these special CCB commands for tasks such as rewriting the sector headers to flag bad sectors, which in essence means LLF. When using these commands, the drive controller can rewrite the sector headers and data areas and then carefully step over any servo information (if the drive uses an embedded servo).

IDE drives can be low-level formatted, although some drives require special vendor-specific commands to activate certain LLF features and defect-management options. Seagate, Western Digital, Maxtor, IBM, and others make specific LLF and spare-sector defect-management software specific to their respective IDE drives. Conner drives are unique in that to actually LLF them, you need a special hardware device that attaches to a diagnostic port connector on the Conner IDE drive. A company called TCE (they are in the vendor list in Appendix A) sells such a device for $99. Coincidentally, this device is called The Conner. It includes software and the special adapter device that permits true low-level formatting (including rewriting all sectors and sector headers, as well as completely managing spare sector defects) at the factory level.

Other companies have developed LLF software that recognizes the particular IDE drive and uses the correct vendor-specific commands for the LLF and defect mapping. The best of these programs is Ontrack's Disk Manager. A general-purpose diagnostic program that also supports IDE-drive formatting is the MicroScope package by Micro 2000.

Intelligent IDE drives must be in *nontranslating*, or native, mode to LLF them. Zoned Recording drives can perform only a partial LLF, in which the defect map is updated and new defective sectors can be marked or spared, but the sector headers usually are rewritten only partially, and only for the purpose of defect mapping. In any case, you are writing to some of the sector headers in one form, and physical (sector-level) defect mapping and sector sparing can be performed. This procedure is, by any standard definition, an LLF.

On an embedded servo drive, all the servo data for a track is recorded at the same time by a specialized (usually laser-guided) servowriter. This servo information is used to update the head position continuously during drive function, so that the drive automatically compensates for thermal effects. As a result, all the individual servo bursts are in line on the track. Because the servo controls head position, there is no appreciable head-to-sector drift, as there could be on a nonservo drive.

This is why even though it is possible to LLF embedded servo drives, it rarely is necessary. The only purpose for performing an LLF on an embedded servo drive is to perform additional physical- (sector-) level defect mapping or sector sparing for the purpose of managing defects that occur after manufacture. Because no drift occurs, when a sector is found to contain a flaw, it should remain permanently marked bad; a physical flaw cannot be repaired by reformatting.

Most IDE drives have three to four spare sectors for each physical cylinder of the drive. These hundreds of spare sectors are more than enough to accommodate the original defects and any subsequent defects. If more sectors are required, the drive likely has serious physical problems that cannot be fixed by software.

Software for Low-Level Formatting. You often can choose among several types of LLF programs, but no single LLF program works on all drives or all systems. Because LLF programs must operate very closely with the controller, they often are specific to a controller or controller type. Therefore, ask the controller manufacturer for the formatting software it recommends.

If the controller manufacturer supplies an LLF program (usually in the controller's ROM), use that program, because it is the one most specifically designed for your system and controller. The manufacturer's program can take advantage of special defect-mapping features, for example. A different format program not only might fail to use a manufacturer-written defect map, but also might overwrite and destroy it.

For a general-purpose ST-506/412, ESDI, or IDE LLF program, I recommend the Disk Manager program by Ontrack. For the ST-506/412 interface only, I recommend the IBM Advanced Diagnostics or the HDtest program by Jim Bracking, a user-supported product found on many electronic bulletin boards, including CompuServe. (These companies are listed in the vendor list at the back of this book.) For SCSI systems and systems on which the other recommended programs do not work, you normally use will the format program supplied with the SCSI host adapter.

How Low-Level Format Software Works. There are several ways that a program can LLF a drive. The simplest way is to call the BIOS by using INT 13h functions such as the `INT 13h, function 05h (Format Track)` command. The BIOS then converts this command to what is called a CCB (Command Control Block) command: A block of bytes sent from the proper I/O ports directly to the disk controller. In this example, the BIOS would take `INT 13h, 05h` and convert it to a `CCB 50h (Format Track)` command, which would be sent through the Command Register Port (I/O address 1F7h for ST-506/412 or IDE). When the controller receives the CCB `Format Track` command, it may actually format the track or may simply fill the data areas of each sector on the track with a predetermined pattern.

The best way to LLF a drive is to bypass the ROM BIOS and send the CCB commands directly to the controller. Probably the greatest benefit in sending commands directly to the drive controller is being able to correctly flag defective sectors via the CCB `Format Track` command, including the capability to perform sector sparing. This is why IDE drives that are properly low-level formatted never show any bad sectors.

By using the CCB commands, you also gain the ability to read the Command Status and Error registers (which enable you to detect things such as ECC corrected data, which is masked by DOS INT 13h). You also can detect whether a sector was marked bad by the manufacturer or during a previous LLF and can maintain those marks in any subsequent Format Track commands, thereby preserving the defect list. I do not recommend unmarking a sector (returning it to "good" status), especially if the manufacturer previously marked it as bad.

When you use CCB commands, you can read and write sector(s) with automatic retries as well as ECC turned off. This capability is essential for any good surface analysis or LLF program, and this is why I recommend programs that use the CCB hardware interface rather than the DOS INT 13h interface.

Ontrack Disk Manager. For AT-type systems and other systems with controllers that do not have an autoconfigure routine, the Disk Manager program from Ontrack is excellent. It probably is the most sophisticated hard disk format tool available and has many capabilities that make it a desirable addition to your toolbox.

Disk Manager is a true register-level format program that goes around the BIOS and manipulates the disk controller directly. This direct controller access gives it powerful capabilities that simply are not possible in programs that work through the BIOS.

Some of these advanced features include the capability to set head- and cylinder-skew factors. Disk Manager also can detect intermittent (soft) errors much better than most other programs can, because it can turn off the automatic retries that most controllers perform. The program also can tell when ECC has been used to correct data, indicating that an error occurred, as well as directly manipulate the bytes that are used for ECC. Disk Manager has been written to handle most IDE drives and uses vendor-specific commands to unlock the capability to perform a true LLF on IDE drives.

All these capabilities make Disk Manager one of the most powerful and capable LLF programs available. Ontrack also offers an excellent package of hard disk diagnostic and data-recovery utilities called *DOS Utils*. Anybody who has to support, maintain, troubleshoot, repair, or upgrade PCs needs a powerful disk formatter such as Disk Manager.

HDtest. HDtest is an excellent BIOS-level format program that will function on virtually any drive that has an INT 13h ROM BIOS interface, which includes most drives. HDtest does not have some of the capabilities of true register-level format programs, but it can be used when the additional capabilities of a register-level program are not required. For example, you can use this program to do a quick wipe of all the data on a drive, no matter what the interface or controller type is. HDtest also is good for BIOS-level read and write testing, and has proved to be especially useful in verifying the functions of disk interface BIOS code.

HDtest, by Jim Bracking, is a user-supported software program. This program is distributed through electronic bulletin boards and public-domain software libraries. You also can obtain the program from the Public Software Library, listed in Appendix A. It costs $35, but you can try it for free.

HDtest has an easy-to-use interface and pull-down menu system. The program offers all functions that normally are associated with a standard LLF program, as well as some extras:

- Normal formatting
- Defect mapping
- Surface analysis
- Interleave test
- Nondestructive low-level reformat
- Hard disk tests (duplicate of the IBM Advanced Diagnostics hard disk tests), including tests for drive seek, head selection, and error detection and correction, as well as a read/write/verify of the diagnostics cylinder. This program also can run low-level ROM BIOS commands to the controller.

HDtest includes most of what you would want in a generic LLF program and hard disk diagnostics utility. Its real limitation is that it works only through the BIOS and cannot perform functions that a true register-level format program can. In some cases, the program cannot format a drive that a register-level program could format. Only register-level programs can perform defect mapping in most IDE and SCSI environments.

SCSI Low-Level Format Software. If you are using a SCSI drive, you must use the LLF program provided by the manufacturer of the SCSI host adapter. The design of these devices varies enough that a register-level program can work only if it is tailored to the individual controller. Fortunately, all SCSI host adapters include such format software, either in the host adapter's BIOS or in a separate disk-based program.

The interface to the SCSI drive is through the host adapter. SCSI is a standard, but there are no true standards for what a host adapter is supposed to look like. This means that any formatting or configuration software will be specific to a particular host adapter. For example, IBM supplies formatting and defect-management software that works with the IBM PS/2 SCSI host adapters directly on the PS/2 Reference disk. That software performs everything that needs to be done to a SCSI hard disk connected to an IBM host adapter. IBM has defined a standard interface to its adapter through an INT 13h and INT 4Bh BIOS interface in a ROM installed on the card. The IBM adapters also include a special ABIOS (Advanced BIOS) interface that runs in the processor's protected mode of operation (for use under protected-mode operating systems such as OS/2).

Other SCSI host adapters often include the complete setup, configuration, and formatting software in the host adapter's on-board ROM BIOS. Most of these adapters also include an INT 13h interface in the BIOS. The best example is the Adaptec 1540/1542C adapters, which include software in ROM that completely configures the card and all attached SCSI devices.

> **Note**
>
> Notice that SCSI format and configuration software is keyed to the host adapter and is not specific in any way to the particular SCSI hard disk drive that you are using.

IDE Low-Level Format Software. IDE drive manufacturers have defined extensions to the standard WD1002/1003 AT interface, which was further standardized for IDE drives as the ATA (AT Attachment) interface. The ATA specification provides for vendor-unique commands, which are manufacturer proprietary extensions to the standard. To prevent improper low-level formatting, many of these IDE drives have special codes that must be sent to the drive to unlock the format routines. These codes vary among manufacturers. If possible, you should obtain LLF and defect-management software from the drive manufacturer; this software usually is specific to that manufacturer's products.

The custom nature of the ATA interface drives is the source of some myths about IDE. Many people say, for example, that you cannot perform an LLF on an IDE drive, and that if you do, you will wreck the drive. This statement is untrue! What can happen is that in some drives, you may be able to set new head and sector skew factors that are not as optimal for the drive as the ones that the manufacturer set, and you also may be able to overwrite the defect-map information. This situation is not good, but you still can use the drive with no problems provided that you perform a proper surface analysis.

Most ATA IDE drives are protected from any alteration to the skew factors or defect map erasure because they are in a translated mode. Zoned Recording drives always are in translation mode and are fully protected. Most ATA drives have a custom command set that must be used in the format process; the standard format commands defined by the ATA specification usually do not work, especially with intelligent or Zoned Recording IDE drives. Without the proper manufacturer-specific format commands, you will not be able to perform the defect management by the manufacturer-specified method, in which bad sectors often can be spared.

Currently, the following manufacturers offer specific LLF and defect-management software for their own IDE drives:

- Seagate
- Western Digital
- Maxtor
- IBM

These utilities are available for downloading on the various BBSes run by these companies. The numbers appear in Appendix A.

Conner Peripherals drives are unique in that they cannot be low-level formatted through the standard interface; they must be formatted by a device that attaches to a special diagnostics and setup port on the drive. You see this device as a 12-pin connector on Conner drives. A company called TCE sells an inexpensive device that attaches your PC to this port through a serial port in your system, and includes special software that can perform sophisticated test, formatting, and surface-analysis operations. The product is called The Conner. (TCE is listed in Appendix A.)

For other drives, I recommend Disk Manager by Ontrack, as well as the MicroScope program by Micro 2000. These programs can format most IDE drives because they know the manufacturer-specific IDE format commands and routines. They also can perform defect-mapping and surface-analysis procedures.

Nondestructive Formatters. General-purpose, BIOS-level, nondestructive formatters such as Calibrate and SpinRite are not recommended in most situations for which a real LLF is required. These programs have several limitations and problems that limit their effectiveness; in some cases, they can even cause problems with the way defects are handled on a drive. These programs attempt to perform a track-by-track LLF by using BIOS functions, while backing up and restoring the track data as they go. These programs do not actually perform a complete LLF, because they do not even try to LLF the first track (Cylinder 0, Head 0) due to problems with some controller types that store hidden information on the first track.

These programs also do not perform defect mapping in the way that standard LLF programs do, and they can even remove the carefully applied sector header defect marks during a proper LLF. This situation potentially allows data to be stored in sectors that originally were marked defective and may actually void the manufacturer's warranty on some drives. Another problem is that these programs work only on drives that are already formatted and can format only drives that are formattable through BIOS functions.

A true LLF program bypasses the system BIOS and send commands directly to the disk controller hardware. For this reason, many LLF programs are specific to the disk controller hardware for which they are designed. It is virtually impossible to have a single format program that will run on all different types of controllers. Many hard drives have been incorrectly diagnosed as being defective because the wrong format program was used and the program did not operate properly.

Drive Partitioning. *Partitioning* a hard disk is the act of defining areas of the disk for an operating system to use as a volume. To DOS, a volume is an area of a disk denoted as a drive letter; for example, drive C is volume C, drive D is volume D, and so on. Some people think that you have to partition a disk only if you are going to divide it into more than one volume. This is a misunderstanding; a disk must be partitioned even if it will be the single volume C.

When a disk is partitioned, a master partition boot sector is written at cylinder 0, head 0, sector 1—the first sector on the hard disk. This sector contains data that describes the partitions by their starting and ending cylinder, head, and sector locations. The partition table also indicates to the ROM BIOS which of the partitions is bootable and, therefore, where to look for an operating system to load. A single hard disk can have 1 to 24 partitions. This number includes all the hard drives installed in the system, which means that you can have as many as 24 separate hard disks with one partition each, a single hard disk with 24 partitions, or a combination of disks and partitions such that the total number of partitions is no more than 24. If you have more than 24 drives or partitions, DOS does not recognize them, although other operating systems may. What limits DOS is that a letter is used to name a volume, and the Roman alphabet ends with Z—the 24th volume, when you begin with C.

FDISK. The DOS FDISK program is the accepted standard for partitioning hard disks. Partitioning prepares the boot sector of the disk in such a way that the DOS FORMAT program can operate correctly; it also enables different operating systems to coexist on a single hard disk.

Chapter 16—Hard Disk Drive Installation

If a disk is set up with two or more partitions, FDISK shows only two total DOS partitions: the primary partition and the extended partition. The extended partition then is divided into logical DOS volumes, which are partitions themselves. FDISK gives a false impression of how the partitioning is done. FDISK reports that a disk divided as C, D, E, and F is set up as two partitions, with a primary partition having a volume designator of C and a single extended partition containing logical DOS volumes D, E, and F. But in the real structure of the disk, each logical DOS volume is a separate partition with an extended partition boot sector describing it. Each drive volume constitutes a separate partition on the disk, and the partitions point to one another in a daisy-chain arrangement.

The minimum size for a partition in any version of DOS is one cylinder; however, FDISK in DOS 4 and later versions allocates partitions in megabytes, meaning that the minimum-size partition is 1M. DOS 4.x and later versions permit individual partitions or volumes to be as large as 2G, whereas versions of DOS earlier than 4.0 have a maximum partition size of 32M.

The current DOS (version 7 underlying Windows 95 OSR2) supports partition sizes of up to 2T using FAT 32.

FDISK Undocumented Functions. FDISK is a very powerful program, and in DOS 5 and later versions, it gained some additional capabilities. Unfortunately, these capabilities were never documented in the DOS manual and remain undocumented even in DOS 7. The most important undocumented parameter in FDISK is the /MBR (Master Boot Record) parameter, which causes FDISK to rewrite the Master Boot Sector code area, leaving the partition tables intact.

> **Caution**
>
> Beware: It will overwrite the partition tables if the two signature bytes at the end of the sector (55AAh) are damaged. This situation is highly unlikely, however. In fact, if these signature bytes were damaged, you would know; the system would not boot and would act as though there were no partitions at all.

The /MBR parameter seems to be tailor-made for eliminating boot-sector virus programs that infect the Master Partition Boot Sector (Cylinder 0, Head 0, Sector 1) of a hard disk. To use this feature, you simply enter

    FDISK /MBR

FDISK then rewrites the boot sector code, leaving the partition tables intact. This should not cause any problems on a normally functioning system, but just in case, I recommend backing up the partition table information to floppy disk before trying it. You can do this with the following command:

    MIRROR /PARTN

This procedure uses the MIRROR command to store partition-table information in a file called PARTNSAV.FIL, which should be stored on a floppy disk for safekeeping. To restore the complete partition-table information, including all the master and extended partition boot sectors, you would use the UNFORMAT command as follows:

    UNFORMAT /PARTN

This procedure causes the UNFORMAT command to ask for the floppy disk containing the PARTNSAV.FIL file and then to restore that file to the hard disk.

Note that if you are using Windows 95, the MIRROR and UNFORMAT programs have been eliminated, and you will have to purchase Norton Utilities instead.

FDISK also has three other undocumented parameters: /PRI:, /EXT:, and /LOG:. These parameters can be used to have FDISK create master and extended partitions, as well as logical DOS volumes in the extended partition, directly from the command line rather than through the FDISK menus. This feature was designed so that you can run FDISK in a batch file to partition drives automatically. Some system vendors probably use these parameters (if they know about them, that is!) when setting up systems on the production line. Other than that, these parameters have little use for a normal user, and in fact may be dangerous!

Other Partitioning Software. Since DOS 4, there has been little need for aftermarket disk partitioning utilities, except in special cases. If a system is having problems that cause you to consider using a partitioning utility, I recommend that you upgrade to a newer version of DOS instead. Using nonstandard partitioning programs to partition your disk jeopardizes the data in the partitions and makes recovery of data lost in these partitions extremely difficult.

The reason why disk partitioning utilities other than FDISK even existed is that the maximum partition size in older DOS versions was restricted: 16M for DOS 2.x and 32M for DOS 3.x. These limits are bothersome for people whose hard disks are much larger than 32M, because they must divide the hard disk into many partitions to use all of the disk. Versions of DOS before 3.3 cannot even create more than a single DOS-accessible partition on a hard disk. If you have a 120M hard disk and are using DOS 3.2 or an earlier version, you can access only 32M of that disk as a C partition.

To overcome this limitation, several software companies created enhanced partitioning programs which you can use rather than FDISK. These programs create multiple partitions and partitions larger than 32M on a disk that DOS can recognize. These partitioning programs include a high-level format program, because the FORMAT program in DOS 3.3 and earlier versions can format partitions only up to 32M.

Disk Manager by Ontrack is probably the best-known of the partitioning utilities. These programs include LLF capabilities, so you can use one of them as a single tool to set up a hard disk. The programs even include disk driver software that provides the capability to override the physical type selections in the system ROM BIOS, enabling a system to use all of a disk, even though the drive-type table in the system ROM BIOS does not have an entry that matches the hard disk.

Many drive vendors and integrators gave away these nonstandard partitioning and formatting programs, which makes some purchasers of such products feel that they must use those drivers to operate the drive. In most cases, however, better alternatives are available; nonstandard disk partitioning and formatting can cause more problems than it solves.

For example, Seagate shipped Ontrack Disk Manager with its drives larger than 32M. One purpose of the program is to perform low-level formatting of the drive, which Disk Manager does well, and I recommend it highly for this function. If possible, however, you should avoid the partitioning and high-level formatting functions and stick with FDISK and FORMAT.

When you use a program other than standard FDISK and FORMAT to partition and high-level (DOS) format a drive, the drive is set up in a nonstandard way, different from pure DOS. This difference can cause trouble with utilities—including disk cache programs, disk test and interleave check programs, and data recovery or retrieval programs—written to function with a standard DOS disk structure. In many situations that a standard format would avoid, a nonstandard disk format can cause data loss and also can make data recovery impossible.

> **Caution**
>
> You should use only standard DOS FDISK and FORMAT to partition or high-level format your hard disks. If you use aftermarket partitioning software to create a nonstandard disk system, some programs that bypass DOS for disk access will not understand the disk properly and may write in the wrong place. Windows is an example of a program that bypasses DOS when you turn on the Use 32-bit Disk Access option in the Control Panel.

It is especially dangerous to use these partitioning programs to override your ROM BIOS disk-table settings. Consider the following disaster scenario.

Suppose that you have a Seagate ST-4096 hard disk, which has 1,024 cylinders and nine heads, and requires that your controller never perform a data-write modification called write precompensation to cylinders of the disk. Some drives require this precompensation on the inner cylinders to compensate for the peak shifting that takes place because of the higher density of data on the (smaller) inner cylinders. The ST-4096 internally compensates for this effect and therefore needs no precompensation from the controller.

Now suppose that you install this drive in an IBM AT that does not have a ROM BIOS drive table that matches the drive. The best matching type you can select is type 18, which enables you to use only 977 cylinders and seven heads—56.77M of what should be a 76.5M hard disk. If your IBM AT is one of the older ones with a ROM BIOS dated 01/10/84, the situation is worse, because its drive-table ends with type 14. In that case, you would have to select type 12 as the best match, giving you access to 855 cylinders and seven heads, or only 49.68M of a 76.5M drive.

ROM BIOS drive tables are listed in Appendix A. Most IBM-compatibles have a more complete drive-type table and would have an exact table match for this drive, allowing you to use the full 76.5M with no problems. In most compatibles with a Phoenix ROM BIOS, for example, you would select type 35, which would support the drive entirely.

Now suppose that you are not content with using only 50M or 57M of this 76.5M drive. You invoke the SuperPartition aftermarket partitioning program that came with the drive and use it to LLF the drive. Then you use the aftermarket program to override the type 18 or type 12 settings in the drive table. The program instructs you to set up a very small C partition (of only 1M) and then partitions the remaining 75.5M of the disk as D. This partitioning overrides the DOS 3.3 32M partition limitation. (If you had an IBM-compatible system that did not require the drive-type override, you still would need to use the aftermarket partitioner to create partitions larger than the DOS 3.3 standard 32M.) Following that, you use the partitioner to high-level format the C and D partitions, because the DOS high-level format in DOS 3.3 works only on volumes of 32M or less.

Most aftermarket partitioners create a special driver file that they install in the CONFIG.SYS file through the `DEVICE` command. After the system boots from the C partition and loads the device driver, the 75.5M D partition is completely accessible.

Along comes an innocent user of the system who always boots from her own DOS floppy disk. After booting from the floppy, she tries to log into the D partition. No matter what version of DOS this user boots from on the floppy disk, the D partition seems to have vanished. An attempt to log into that partition results in an `Invalid drive specification` error message. No standard version of DOS can recognize that specially created D partition if the device driver is not loaded.

An attempt by this user to recover data on this drive with a utility program such as Norton or PC Tools results in failure, because these programs interpret the drive as having 977 cylinders and seven heads (type 18) or 855 cylinders and seven heads (type 12). In fact, when these programs attempt to correct what seems to be partition-table damage, data will be corrupted in the vanished D partition.

Thinking that there may be a physical problem with the disk, the innocent user boots and runs the Advanced Diagnostics software to test the hard disk. Because Advanced Diagnostics incorporates its own special boot code and does not use standard DOS, it does not examine partitioning but goes to the ROM BIOS drive-type table to determine the capacity of the hard disk. It sees the unit as having only 977 or 855 cylinders (indicated by the type 18 or 12 settings), as well as only seven heads. The user then runs the Advanced Diagnostics hard disk tests, which use the last cylinder of the disk as a test cylinder for diagnostic read and write tests. This cylinder subsequently is overwritten by the diagnostics tests, which the drive passes because there is no physical problem with the drive.

This innocent user has just wiped out the D-drive data that happened to be on cylinder 976 in the type-18 setup or on cylinder 854 in the type-12 setup. Had the drive been partitioned by FDISK, the last cylinder indicated by the ROM BIOS drive table would have been left out of any partitions, being reserved so that diagnostics tests could be performed on the drive without damaging data.

Beyond the kind of disaster scenario just described, other potential problems can be caused by nonstandard disk partitioning and formatting, such as the following:

- Problems in using the 32-bit Disk Access feature provided by Windows, which bypasses the BIOS for faster disk access in 386 Enhanced Mode.

- Data loss by using OS/2, UNIX, XENIX, Novell Advanced NetWare, or other non-DOS operating systems that do not recognize the disk or the nonstandard partitions.

- Difficulty in upgrading a system from one DOS version to another.

- Difficulty in installing a different operating system, such as OS/2, on the hard disk.

- Data loss by using an LLF utility to run an interleave test; the test area for the interleave test is the diagnostics cylinder, which contains data on disks formatted with Disk Manager.

- Data loss by accidentally deleting or overwriting the driver file and causing the D partition to disappear after the next boot.

- Data-recovery difficulty or failure because nonstandard partitions do not follow the rules and guidelines set by Microsoft and IBM, and no documentation on their structure exists. The sizes and locations of the FATs and root directory are not standard, and the detailed reference charts in this book (which are valid for an FDISK-created partition) are inaccurate for nonstandard partitions.

I could continue, but I think you get the idea. If these utility programs are used only for low-level formatting, they do not cause problems; it is the drive-type override, partitioning, and high-level format operations that cause difficulty. If you consider data integrity to be important, and you want to be able to perform data recovery, follow these disk support and partitioning rules:

- Every hard disk must be properly supported by system ROM BIOS, with no software overrides. If the system does not have a drive table that supports the full capacity of the drive, accept the table's limit, upgrade to a new ROM BIOS (preferably with a user-definable drive-type setting), or use a disk controller with an on-board ROM BIOS for drive support.

- Use only FDISK to partition a hard disk. If you want partitions larger than 32M, use DOS 4 or a later version.

High-Level (Operating-System) Format. The final step in the software preparation of a hard disk is the DOS high-level format. The primary function of the high-level format is to create a FAT and a directory system on the disk so that DOS can manage files.

Usually, you perform the high-level format with the standard DOS FORMAT program, using the following syntax:

```
FORMAT C: /S /V
```

This step high-level formats drive C (or volume C, in a multivolume drive), places the hidden operating-system files in the first part of this partition, and prompts for the entry of a volume label to be stored on the disk at completion.

The high-level format program performs the following functions and procedures:

1. Scans the disk (read only) for tracks and sectors marked as bad during the LLF, and notes these tracks as being unreadable.

2. Returns the drive heads to the first cylinder of the partition, and at that cylinder, head 1, sector 1, writes a DOS volume boot sector.

3. Writes a FAT at head 1, sector 2. Immediately after this FAT, it writes a second copy of the FAT. These FATs essentially are blank except for bad-cluster marks noting areas of the disk that were found to be unreadable during the marked-defect scan.

4. Writes a blank root directory.

5. If the /S parameter is specified, copies the system files (IBMBIO.COM and IBMDOS.COM or IO.SYS and MSDOS.SYS, depending on which DOS you run) and COMMAND.COM files to the disk (in that order).

6. If the /V parameter is specified, prompts the user for a volume label, which is written as the fourth file entry in the root directory.

Now DOS can use the disk for storing and retrieving files, and the disk is a bootable disk.

> **Note**
>
> The Format command can be run through the Windows Explorer within Windows 95 even on hard disks, as long as no files are open. You cannot format the drive where Windows 95 resides.

During the first phase of the high-level format, a marked defect scan is performed. Defects marked by the LLF operation show up during this scan as being unreadable tracks or sectors. When the high-level format encounters one of these areas, it automatically performs up to five retries to read these tracks or sectors. If the unreadable area was marked by the LLF, the read fails on all attempts.

After five retries, the DOS FORMAT program gives up on this track or sector and moves to the next. Areas that remain unreadable after the initial read and the five retries are noted in the FAT as being bad clusters. DOS 3.3 and earlier versions can mark only entire tracks bad in the FAT, even if only one sector was marked in the LLF. DOS 4 and later versions individually check each cluster on the track and recover clusters that do not involve the LLF marked-bad sectors. Because most LLF programs mark all the sectors on a track as bad, rather than the individual sector that contains the defect, the result of using DOS 3.3 or 4 is the same: all clusters involving sectors on that track are marked in the FAT as bad.

> **Note**
>
> Some LLF programs mark only the individual sector that is bad on a track, rather than the entire track. This is true of the IBM PS/2 low-level formatters on the IBM PS/2 Advanced Diagnostics or Reference disk. In this case, high-level formatting with DOS 4 or later versions results in fewer lost bytes in bad sectors, because only the clusters that contain the marked bad sectors are marked bad in the FAT. DOS 4 and later versions display the Attempting to recover allocation unit x message (in which x is the number of the cluster) in an attempt to determine whether a single cluster or all the clusters on the track should be marked bad in the FAT.

If the controller and LLF program together support sector and track sparing, the high-level format finds the entire disk defect-free, because all the defective sectors have been exchanged for spare good ones.

If a disk has been low-level formatted correctly, the number of bytes in bad sectors is the same before and after the high-level format. If the number does change after you repeat a high-level format (reporting fewer bytes or none), the LLF was not done correctly. The manufacturer's defects were not marked correctly; or Norton, Mace, PC Tools, or a similar utility was used to mark defective clusters on the disk. The utilities cannot mark the sectors or tracks at the LLF level; the bad-cluster marks that they make are stored only in the FAT and erased during the next high-level format operation. Defect marks made in the LLF consistently show up as bad bytes in the high-level format, no matter how many times you run the format.

Only an LLF or a surface-analysis tool can correctly mark defects on a disk; anything else makes only temporary bad-cluster marks in the FAT. This kind of marking may be acceptable temporarily, but when additional bad areas are found on a disk, you should run a new LLF of the disk and either mark the area manually or run a surface analysis to place a more permanent mark on the disk.

Hard Disk Drive Troubleshooting and Repair

If a hard disk drive has a problem inside its sealed HDA, repairing the drive usually is not feasible. If the failure is in the logic board, you can replace that assembly with a new or rebuilt assembly easily and at a much lower cost than replacing the entire drive.

Most hard disk problems really are not hardware problems; instead, they are soft problems that can be solved by a new LLF and defect-mapping session. *Soft problems* are characterized by a drive that sounds normal but produces various read and write errors.

Hard problems are mechanical, such as when the drive sounds as though it contains loose marbles. Constant scraping and grinding noises from the drive, with no reading or writing capability, also qualify as hard errors. In these cases, it is unlikely that an LLF will put the drive back into service. If a hardware problem is indicated, first replace the logic-board assembly. You can make this repair yourself and, if successful, you can recover the data from the drive.

If replacing the logic assembly does not solve the problem, contact the manufacturer or a specialized repair shop that has clean-room facilities for hard disk repair. (See Appendix B for a list of drive manufacturers and companies that specialize in hard disk drive repair.)

17xx, 104xx, and 210xxxx Hardware Error Codes

When a failure occurs in the hard disk subsystem at power-on, the *Power-On Self Test* *(POST)* finds the problem and reports it with an error message. The 17xx, 104xx, and 210xxxx errors during the POST or while running the Advanced Diagnostics indicate problems with hard disks, controllers, or cables. The 17xx codes apply to ST-506/412 interface drives and controllers; 104xx errors apply to ESDI drives and controllers; and 210xxxx errors apply to SCSI drives and host adapters.

Table 16.11 shows a breakdown of these error messages and their meanings.

Table 16.11 Hard Disk and Controller Diagnostic Error Codes

ST-506/412 Drive and Controller Error Codes

Error	Description
1701	Fixed disk general POST error
1702	Drive/controller time-out error
1703	Drive seek error
1704	Controller failed
1705	Drive sector not found error
1706	Write fault error
1707	Drive track 0 error
1708	Head select error
1709	Error Correction Code (ECC) error
1710	Sector buffer overrun
1711	Bad address mark
1712	Internal controller diagnostics failure
1713	Data compare error
1714	Drive not ready
1715	Track 0 indicator failure
1716	Diagnostics cylinder errors
1717	Surface read errors
1718	Hard drive type error
1720	Bad diagnostics cylinder
1726	Data compare error
1730	Controller error
1731	Controller error
1732	Controller error

(continues)

Table 16.11 Continued
ST-506/412 Drive and Controller Error Codes

Error	Description
1733	BIOS undefined error return
1735	Bad command error
1736	Data corrected error
1737	Bad track error
1738	Bad sector error
1739	Bad initialization error
1740	Bad sense error
1750	Drive verify failure
1751	Drive read failure
1752	Drive write failure
1753	Drive random read test failure
1754	Drive seek test failure
1755	Controller failure
1756	Controller Error Correction Code (ECC) test failure
1757	Controller head select failure
1780	Seek failure; drive 0
1781	Seek failure; drive 1
1782	Controller test failure
1790	Diagnostic cylinder read error; drive 0
1791	Diagnostic cylinder read error; drive 1

SCSI Drive and Host Adapter Error Codes

Error	Description
096xxxx	SCSI adapter with cache (32-bit) errors
112xxxx	SCSI adapter (16-bit without cache) errors
113xxxx	System board SCSI adapter (16-bit) errors
210xxxx	SCSI fixed disk errors

The first x *in* xxxx *is the SCSI ID number.*
The second x *in* xxxx *is the logical unit number (usually 0).*
The third x *in* xxxx *is the host adapter slot number.*
The fourth x *in* xxxx *is a letter code indicating drive capacity.*

Most of the time, a *seek failure* indicates that the drive is not responding to the controller. This failure usually is caused by one of the following problems:

- Incorrect drive-select jumper setting
- Loose, damaged, or backward control cable
- Loose or bad power cable
- Stiction between drive heads and platters
- Bad power supply

If a diagnostics cylinder read error occurs, the most likely problems are these:

- Incorrect drive-type setting
- Loose, damaged, or backward data cable
- Temperature-induced mistracking

The methods for correcting most of these problems are obvious. If the drive-select jumper setting is incorrect, for example, correct it. If a cable is loose, tighten it. If the power supply is bad, replace it. You get the idea.

If the problem is temperature-related, the drive usually will read data acceptably at the same temperature at which it was written. Let the drive warm up for a while and then attempt to reboot it, or let the drive cool and reread the disk if the drive has overheated.

Chapter 17

CD-ROM Drives

This chapter explains the technology behind CD-ROM drives, delineates the various recording formats used on PC CD-ROMs, and examines the performance characteristics of the typical CD-ROM drive. After showing you the process of selecting a good drive for a system upgrade, the chapter guides you through the installation of the CD-ROM interface card, the drive itself, and the software that must be added to your PC for the drive to communicate with the system. This chapter also focuses on the latest CD technology, including brief coverage of CD-R (CD-Recordable), CD-E (CD-Erasable), and the new DVD (Digital Versatile Disk) drives.

> **Note**
>
> Detailed CD-R coverage can be found in Chapter 18, "Tape and Other Mass-Storage Drives," because its primary use for the average user is as a convenient way to back up or store large amounts of data.

What Is a CD-ROM?

Within minutes of inserting a compact disc into your computer, you have access to information that might have taken you days, or even weeks, to find a few short years ago. Science, medicine, law, business profiles, and educational materials—every conceivable form of human endeavor or pursuit of knowledge—are making their way to aluminum-coated, five-inch plastic data discs called *CD-ROMs*, or *compact disc read-only memory*.

> **Note**
>
> The CD-ROM (compact disc read-only memory) is a read-only optical storage medium capable of holding up to 682M of data (approximately 333,000 pages of text), 74 minutes of high-fidelity audio, or some combination of the two. The CD-ROM is very similar to the familiar audio compact disc, and can, in fact,
>
> *(continues)*

> (continued)
>
> play in a normal audio player. The result would be noise unless audio accompanies the data on the CD-ROM (see the CD+ coverage later in this chapter). Accessing data from a CD-ROM is quite a bit faster than floppy disk but considerably slower than a modern hard drive. The term *CD-ROM* refers to both the discs themselves and the drive that reads them.

Although only a few dozen CD-ROM discs, or titles, were published for personal computer users in all of 1988, there are currently thousands of individual titles containing data and programs ranging from world-wide agricultural statistics to preschool learning games. Individual businesses, local and federal government offices, and small businesses also publish thousands of their own, limited-use titles.

CD-ROM, a Brief History

In 1978, Philips and Sony Corporations joined forces to produce the current audio CD. Philips had already developed commercial laser-disc players, whereas Sony had a decade of digital recording research under its belt. The two companies were poised for a battle—the introduction of potentially incompatible audio laser disc formats—when they came to terms on an agreement to formulate a single audio technology.

Sony pushed for a 12-inch platter. Philips wanted to investigate smaller sizes, especially when it became clear that they could pack an astonishing 12 hours of music on the 12-inch discs.

By 1982, the companies announced the standard, which included the specifications for recording, sampling, and—above all—the 4.72-inch format we live with today. To be specific, the discs are precisely 120mm in diameter, have a 15mm hole in the center, and are 1.2mm thick. This size was chosen (legend has it) because it could contain Beethoven's Ninth Symphony.

With the continued cooperation of Sony and Philips through the 1980s, additional specifications were announced concerning the use of CD technology for computer data. These recommendations evolved into the computer CD-ROM drives in use today. Where once engineers struggled to find the perfect fit between disc form-factor and the greatest symphony ever recorded, software developers and publishers are cramming these little discs with the world's information.

CD Technology

Although identical in appearance to audio CDs, computer CDs store data in addition to audio. The CD drives that read the data discs when attached to PCs also bear a strong resemblance to an audio CD. How you must handle the CDs (insert them into the CD drive and eject them when finished) is already familiar to anyone who has used an audio CD. Both forms of CD operate on the same general mechanical principles.

The disc itself, 120mm (nearly 4.75 inches in diameter), is made of a polycarbonate wafer. This wafer base is coated with a metallic film, usually an aluminum alloy. The aluminum film is the portion of the disc that the CD-ROM drive reads for information.

The aluminum film or *strata* is then covered by a plastic polycarbonate coating that protects the underlying data. A label is usually placed on the top of the disc, and all reading occurs from the bottom. CD-ROMs are single-sided.

> **Note**
>
> CD-ROM media should be handled with the same care afforded a photographic negative. The CD-ROM is an optical device and it degrades as its optical surface becomes dirty or scratched. If your drive uses a *caddy*—a container for the disc that does not require handling the disc itself—you should purchase a sufficient supply of these to reduce disc handling.

Mass-Producing CD-ROMs

Although a laser is used to etch data onto a master disc, this technique would be impractical for the reproduction of hundreds or thousands of copies. Each production of a master disc can take over one-half hour to encode. In addition, these master discs are made of materials that aren't as durable as a mass-produced disc for continued or prolonged use.

For limited run productions of CDs, an original master is coated with metal in a process similar to electroplating. After the metal is formed and separated from the master, the metal imprint of the original can be used to stamp copies, not unlike the reproduction of vinyl records. This process works effectively for small quantities; eventually the stamp wears out.

To produce a large volume of discs, the following three-step process is employed:

1. The master is, once again, plated and a stamp is produced.
2. This stamp is used to create a duplicate master made of a more resilient metal.
3. The duplicate master then can be used to produce numerous stamps.

This technique allows a great many production stamps to be made from the duplicate master, preserving the original integrity of the first encoding. It also allows for the mass production to be made from inexpensive materials. The CDs you buy are coated with aluminum after they are stamped into polycarbonate and then protected with a thin layer of plastic. The thin, aluminum layer that coats the etched pits, as well as smooth surfaces, enables the reading laser to determine the presence or absence of strongly relented light.

This mass manufacturing process is identical for both data and audio CDs.

Reading the information back is a matter of reflecting a lower-powered laser off the aluminum strata. A receiver or light receptor notes where light is strongly reflected or where it is absent or diffused. Diffused or absent light is caused by the pits etched in the CD. Strong reflection of the light indicates no pit—this is called a *land*. The light receptors within the player collect the reflected and diffused light as it is refracted from the surface. As the light sources are collected from the refraction, they are passed along to microprocessors that translate the light patterns back into data or sound.

Individual pits are 0.12 microns deep and about 0.6 microns wide. They are etched into a spiral track with a spacing of 1.6 microns between turns, corresponding to a track density of nearly 16,000 tracks per inch! The pits and lands run from 0.9 to 3.3 microns long.

The track starts at the inside of the disc and ends as close as 5mm from the edge of the disc. This single spiral track is nearly three miles long!

When a CD—audio or data—seeks out a bit of data on the disc, it looks up the address of the data from a table of contents and positions itself near the beginning of this data across the spiral, waiting for the right string of bits to flow past the laser beam.

CD-ROM data is recorded using a technique called *Constant Linear Velocity (CLV)*. This means that the track data is always moving past the read laser at the same linear speed. In other words, the disk must spin faster when reading the inner track area and slower when reading the outer track area. Because CDs were originally designed to record audio, the speed at which the data was read had to be a constant. Thus each disc is broken up into blocks, or sectors, which are stored at the rate of 75 blocks per second on a disc that can hold a total of 74 minutes of information, resulting in a maximum of 333,000 blocks (sectors).

New multispeed CD-ROM readers still read the same CLV recorded CDs, but they play them back at a *Constant Angular Velocity (CAV)*. This means that the track data is moving past the read laser at a different speed, depending on where the track is physically located on the CD (inner or outer track). Tracks at the edge of the disk are read faster than ones near the center, because the CD is rotating at a constant speed, similar to old record players. A combination of these two technologies is referred to as *P-CAV* or *Partial-CAV*.

In a CD-DA (Digital Audio) disc, each block stores 2,352 bytes. In a CD-ROM disc, 304 of these bytes are used for Sync (Synchronizing bits), ID (Identification bits), and ECC (Error Correcting Code) information, leaving 2,048 bytes for user data. Because these blocks are read at a constant speed of 75 per second, this results in a standard CD-ROM transfer rate of 153,600 bytes per second, which is exactly 150K/sec.

Because a disc can hold a maximum of 74 minutes of data, and each second contains 75 blocks of 2,048 bytes each, one can calculate the absolute maximum storage capacity of a CD-ROM at 681,984,000 bytes.

> **Note**
> Recordable CDs come in 74-minute and 63-minute versions.

Inside Data CDs

The microprocessor that decodes the electrical impulses is the key difference between music and data compact players. Audio CDs convert the digital information stored on the disc into analog signals for a stereo amplifier to process. In this scheme, some imprecision is acceptable, because it would be virtually impossible to hear in the music. CD-ROMs, however, cannot tolerate any imprecision. Each bit of data must be accurately read. For this reason, CD-ROM discs have a great deal of additional *ECC (Error Correcting Code)* information written to the disc. The ECC can be used to detect and correct most minor errors, improving the reliability and precision to levels that are acceptable for data storage.

CD-ROM drives operate in the following manner:

1. The *laser diode* (see Figure 17.1) emits a low-energy infrared beam toward a reflecting mirror.

2. The *servo motor*, on command from the microprocessor, positions the beam onto the correct track on the CD-ROM by moving the reflecting mirror.

3. When the beam hits the disc, its refracted light is gathered and focused through the first lens beneath the platter, bounced off the mirror, and sent toward the beam splitter.

4. The *beam splitter* directs the returning laser light toward another focusing lens.

5. The last lens directs the light beam to a photo detector that converts the light into electric impulses.

6. These incoming impulses are decoded by the microprocessor and sent along to the host computer as data.

FIG. 17.1 Typical components inside a CD-ROM drive.

The pits that are etched into the CD-ROM vary in length. The reflected light beam changes in intensity as it crosses over from a land to a pit area. The corresponding electrical signal from the photodetector varies with the reflected light intensity. Data bits are read as the transitions between high and low signals, which is physically recorded at the start and end of each pit area.

Because a single bit error can be disastrous in a program or data file, extensive error detection and correction algorithms are utilized. These routines allow for the probability of a nondetected error to be less than 1 in 10^{25}. In more physical terms, this means that there would be only one undetected error in 2 quadrillion discs (this would form a stack 1 billion miles high!).

Error correction alone requires 288 bytes for every 2,048 bytes of disc data. This allows for the correction of numerous bad bits, including bursts of bad data more than 1,000 bits long. This powerful error-correction capability is required because physical defects can cause errors, and because the CD media was originally designed for audio reproduction where minor errors or even missing data can be tolerated.

In the case of an audio CD, missing data can be *interpolated*—that is, the information follows a predictable pattern that allows the missing value to be guessed at. For example, if three values are stored on an audio disc, say 10, 13, and 20 appearing in a series, and the middle value is missing—due to damage or dirt on the CD's surface—you can interpolate a middle value of 15, which is midway between the 10 and 20 values. Although this is not exactly correct, in the case of audio recording, it will not be noticeable to the listener. If those same three values appear on a CD-ROM in an executable program, there is no way to guess at the correct value for the middle sample. Interpolation cannot work because executable program data follows no natural law; the data is a series of values. To guess 15 is not just slightly off, it is completely wrong.

Because of the need for such precision, CD-ROM drives for use on PCs were later to market than their audio counterparts. When first introduced, CD-ROM drives were too expensive for widespread adoption. In addition, drive manufacturers were slow in adopting standards, causing a lag time for the production of CD-ROM titles. Without a wide base of software to drive the industry, acceptance was slow.

What Types of Drives Are Available?

When purchasing a CD-ROM drive for your PC, consider three distinct sets of attributes of CD-ROM drives, as follows:

- The drive's performance specifications
- The interface it requires for connection to your PC
- The physical disc-handling system used

The variance in any of these categories is enormous; in fact, single vendors offer entire lines of drives that vary in performance specifications, disc-handling mechanisms, and type of adapters they can use to interface with your PC. For these reasons, drive prices vary widely. CD-DA (Compact Disc-Digital Audio) drives, for example, are very inexpensive because they don't require the precision in reproducing music that is required by a drive used for storing data. So before you buy, know the drive's characteristics.

All three drive characteristics are discussed in this section, giving you a better understanding of what type of drive you need to buy.

CD-ROM Drive Specifications

Drive specifications tell you the drive's performance capabilities. If you're shopping for a sports car, for example, and the dealer tells you the car can accelerate from a standing stop to 60 miles per hour in five seconds, you know you've got a hot car. The car's horsepower, weight, suspension design, and other specifications can be used to understand the vehicle's performance.

CD-ROM drive specifications tell the shopper much the same thing. Typical performance figures published by manufacturers are the data transfer rate, access time, internal cache or buffers (if any), and the interface used.

Data Transfer Rate. The data transfer rate tells you how much data the drive can read from a data CD and transfer to the host computer when reading one large, sequential chunk of data. The standard measurement in the industry is kilobytes per second, usually abbreviated as K/sec. If a manufacturer claims a drive can transfer data at 150K/sec, it means that a drive reading a sequential stream of data from the CD will achieve 150K/sec after it has come up to speed. Note that this is a sustained and sequential read, not access across the data disc from different portions of the platter. Obviously, the data transfer specification is meant to convey the drive's peak data-reading capabilities. A higher rate of transfer might be better, but a number of other factors come into play.

You can obtain a CD-ROM benchmark tool by visiting TestaCD Labs Web site at the following:

On the Web

http:/www.azstarnet.com/~gcs/

The standard CD format dictates that there are 75 blocks (or sectors) of data per second, with each block containing 2,048 bytes of data. This gives a transfer rate of exactly 150K/sec. This is the standard for CD-DA (Digital Audio) drives, and also is called *Single-speed* in CD-ROM drives. The term *Single-speed* is used to refer to the original 150K/sec drives, because CD discs are recorded in a *Constant Linear Velocity (CLV) format*, which means that the rotational speed of the disc will vary to keep the track speed a constant. A Double-speed drive (or 2x) simply attains a transfer rate of 300K/sec or two times the single-speed drive.

Because CD-ROM drives can read data that is not time-based like audio, it is possible to speed up the reading of these discs by spinning them at a higher linear velocity. There are currently several different speed drives available, all of which are multiples of the original Single-speed drives. Table 17.1 shows the speeds at which CD-ROM drives can operate.

Table 17.1 CD-ROM Drive Speeds and Data Transfer Rates

Drive Speed	Transfer Rate (bps)	Transfer Rate (K/sec)
Single-speed (1x)	153,600	150
Double-speed (2x)	307,200	300
Triple-speed (3x)	460,800	450
Quad-speed (4x)	614,400	600
Six-speed (6x)	921,600	900
Eight-speed (8x)	1,228,800	1,200
Ten-speed (10x)	1,536,000	1,500
Twelve-speed (12x)	1,843,200	1,800
Sixteen-speed (16x)	2,457,600	2,400
CAV drives (12x-24x)	1,843,200–3,686,400	1,800–3,600

bps = bytes per second
K/sec = kilobytes per second

The 10x and 12x drives currently are the most popular, and the 4x drives are the minimum recommended today which meet the new MPC-3 (Multimedia Personal Computer) standard. There are some 16x (sixteen-speed) drives on the market now, but they are already being overshadowed by the CAV 12/24x (multispeed) drives in popularity. Unless you are using a laptop system, the 16x drives are not recommended, as they cost more than 12x drives, yet do not offer a significant overall jump in performance to be worthwhile. For laptop multimedia computers with integrated CD-ROM drives, 8x drives are quite popular; however, for desktop systems, the 10x drives were quickly passed over by cheaper 12x drives, just as the 3x drives were passed over by cheaper 4x units. For an increase to be worthwhile, it should be double the previous standard. It remains to be seen how the CAV 12/24x drives will fare in the marketplace.

Even the fastest CD-ROM drives pale in comparison to hard disk drive transfer rates, which can obtain 16M or more per second. This means that the SCSI or ATA-IDE interfaces used by CD-ROM drives are more than up to-the-task. If you expect to run a variety of CD-based software on your system, you need a drive with a high data transfer rate. Applications that employ full-motion video, animation, and sound require high transfer rates, and you'll be disappointed in the results of a slower drive. The minimum recommended drive should be a Quad-speed drive, which means it can transfer data at a rate of 600K/sec.

Access Time. The access time for a CD-ROM drive is measured the same way for PC hard drives. In other words, the *access time* is the delay between the drive receiving the command to read, and its actual first reading of a bit of data. The time is recorded in milliseconds; a typical manufacturer's rating for a Quad-speed drive would be listed as 200ms. This is an *average access rate*; the *true access rate* depends entirely on where the data is located on the disc. Positioning the read mechanism to a portion of the disc near the narrower center of the disc gives you a faster access rate than positioning it at the wider outer perimeter. Access rates quoted by many manufacturers are an average taken by calculating a series of random reads from a disc.

Obviously, a faster average access rate is desirable, especially when you are relying on the drive to locate and pull up data quickly. Access times for CD-ROM drives are steadily improving, and the advancements are discussed later in this chapter. Note that these average times are significantly slower than PC hard drives, ranging from 500 to 100ms when compared to 8ms found on your typical hard disk. Most of the speed difference lies in the construction of the drive itself; hard drives have multiple read heads and range over a smaller surface area of media. CD-ROM drives have only one laser read beam, and it must be positioned over the entire range of the disc. In addition, the data on a CD is organized in a long spiral from the outer edge inward. When the drive positions its head to read a track, it must estimate the distance into the disc and skip forward or backward to the appropriate point in the spiral. Reading off the outer edge requires a longer access time than the inner segments, unless you have a CAV drive, which spins at a constant rate so outer tracks have equal access time to inner tracks.

Access times have been falling since the original Single-speed drives came out. With each subsequent boost in data transfer speed, we usually have also seen an increase in access time as well. As you can see in Table 17.2, any improvements here are much less significant, as you are seeing the physical limitation of the drive's single-read mechanism design.

Table 17.2 Typical CD-ROM Drive Access Times

Drive Speed	Access Time (ms)
Single-speed (1x)	400
Double-speed (2x)	300
Triple-speed (3x)	200
Quad-speed (4x)	150
Six-speed (6x)	150
Eight-speed (8x)	100
Ten-speed (8x)	100
Twelve-speed (12x)	100
Sixteen-speed (16x)	90
CAV (12/24x)	150–90

The times listed here are typical examples for good drives; within each speed category there will be drives that are faster and slower.

Buffer/Cache. Most drives are shipped with internal buffers or caches of memory installed on-board. These *buffers* are actual memory chips installed on the drive's board that enable data to be staged or stored in larger segments before they are sent to the PC. A typical buffer for a CD-ROM drive is 256K, although drives are available that have either more or less (more is usually better!). Generally, the faster drives come with more buffer to handle the higher transfer rates.

Having buffer or cache memory on the CD-ROM drive offers a number of advantages. Buffers can ensure that the PC receives data at a constant rate; when an application requests data from the CD-ROM disc, the data is probably scattered across different segments of the disc. Because the drive has a relatively slow access time, the pauses between data reads can cause a drive to send data to the PC sporadically. You might not notice this in typical text applications, but a slower access rate drive coupled with no data buffering is very noticeable, even irritating, in the display of video or some audio segments. In addition, a drive's buffer, when under control of sophisticated software, can read and have ready the disc's table of contents, making the first request for data faster to find on the disc platter. A minimum size of 256K for a built-in buffer or cache is recommended, which is standard on most Eight-speed drives.

Interface

A CD-ROM's *interface* is the physical connection of the drive to the PC's expansion bus. The interface is the pipeline of data from the drive to the computer, and its importance shouldn't be minimized. There are three different types of interfaces available for attaching a CD-ROM drive to your system. They are:

Chapter 17—CD-ROM Drives

- SCSI/ASPI (Small Computer System Interface, Advanced SCSI Programming Interface)
- IDE/ATAPI (Integrated Drive Electronics/AT Attachment Packet Interface)
- Proprietary

This next section examines these different interface choices.

SCSI/ASPI. *SCSI* (pronounced SKUH-zee), or the *Small Computer System Interface*, is a name given to a special interface bus that enables many different types of peripherals to communicate. The current implemented version of the standard is called *SCSI-2*. A standard software interface called *ASPI (Advanced SCSI Programming Interface)* is most commonly used to communicate between the CD-ROM drive (or other SCSI peripherals) and the host adapter. SCSI offers the greatest flexibility and performance of the interfaces available for CD-ROM drives and can be used to connect many other types of peripherals to your system as well.

The SCSI bus enables computer users to string a group of devices along a chain from one SCSI host adapter, avoiding the complication of inserting a different adapter card into the PC bus slots every time a new hardware device, such as a tape unit or additional CD-ROM drive, is added to the system. These traits make SCSI interfaces preferable for connecting peripherals such as your CD-ROM to your PC.

All SCSI adapters are not created equal, however. Although they may share a common command set, they can implement these commands differently, depending on how the adapter's manufacturer designed the hardware. To eliminate these incompatibilities, ASPI was created. ASPI stands for Advanced SCSI Programming Interface and was originally developed by Adaptec, Inc. (Adaptec SCSI Interface), a leader in the development of SCSI controller cards and adapters. ASPI consists of two main parts. The primary part is an ASPI-Manager program, which is a driver that is written to work between the particular operating system used and the specific SCSI host adapter. The ASPI-Manager sets up the ASPI interface to the SCSI bus.

The second part of an ASPI system is the individual ASPI device drivers. For example, you would get an ASPI driver for your SCSI CD-ROM drive. You also can get ASPI drivers for your other SCSI peripherals such as tape drives, scanners, and so on. The ASPI driver for the peripheral talks to the ASPI-Manager for the host adapter. This is what allows the devices to communicate together on the SCSI bus.

The bottom line is that if you are getting a SCSI interface CD-ROM, make sure that it includes an ASPI driver that runs under your particular operating system. Also, be sure that your SCSI host adapter has the corresponding ASPI-Manager driver as well.

On the Web

You can visit Adaptec's home page on the Web at:

http://www.adaptec.com

The SCSI interface offers the most powerful and flexible connection for CD-ROMs and other devices. It allows for higher performance, and up to seven or more drives can be connected to a single host adapter. The drawback is cost. If you do not need SCSI for other peripherals, and if you intend on connecting only one CD-ROM drive to the SCSI bus, then you will be spending a lot of money on unused potential. In that case, an IDE/ATAPI interface CD-ROM drive would be a more cost-effective choice.

IDE/ATAPI. The *IDE/ATAPI (Integrated Drive Electronics/AT Attachment Packet Interface)* is an extension of the same ATA (AT Attachment) interface most people connect their hard disk drives to. Specifically, ATAPI is an industry standard Enhanced IDE interface for CD-ROM drives. ATAPI is a software interface that adapts the SCSI/ASPI commands to the IDE/ATA interface. This has allowed drive manufacturers to take their high-end CD-ROM drive products and quickly adapt them to the IDE interface. This also allows the IDE CD-ROM drives to remain compatible with the MSCDEX (Microsoft CD-ROM Extensions) that are used to interface with DOS. With Windows 95, the CD-ROM extensions are contained in the CDFS (CD File System) VxD (virtual device) driver.

ATAPI drives are sometimes also called Enhanced IDE drives, because this is an extension of the original IDE (technically the ATA) interface. In most cases, an IDE/ATA CD-ROM drive will connect to the system via a second IDE interface connector and channel, leaving the primary one for hard disk drives only. This is done because IDE does not share the single channel well, and would cause the hard disk to wait for CD-ROM commands to complete and vice versa. SCSI does not have this problem because you can send commands to different devices without having to wait for each previous command to complete.

The IDE/ATAPI interface represents the most cost-effective, yet high performance interface for CD-ROM drives. Most new systems that include a CD-ROM drive have it connected through IDE/ATAPI. To prevent performance problems, be sure that your CD-ROM drive is connected on a secondary IDE channel that is separate from the primary channel used by your hard disk drive. Many sound cards now include an ATAPI interface driver and the requisite secondary IDE interface connector specifically for a CD-ROM drive. Up to two drives can be connected to the secondary IDE connector, but for more than that, SCSI would be a better choice.

Proprietary Interfaces. The last type of interface you might see for CD-ROM drives is the *proprietary* interfaces. These are often included in the very low cost CD-ROM drive kits that come with their own adapter card. These interfaces are nonstandard and although inexpensive, are not flexible and do not offer high performance. It is recommended that you stay away from any of the proprietary CD-ROM interfaces and only use drives that interface via SCSI or IDE/ATAPI.

Loading Mechanism

There are two distinctly different mechanisms for loading a CD into a CD-ROM drive. They are the *caddy* and the *tray*. Each one offers some benefits and features. Which type you select will have a major impact on your use of the drive because you will interact with this every time you load a disc.

There are some multiple disc drives on the market now that enable you to insert more than one disc at a time. Most of these use a special cartridge that you fill with discs, much like a multidisc player for automotive use.

Caddy. The *caddy system* is used on most high-end CD-ROM drives. This system requires that you place the CD itself into a special caddy, which is a sealed container with a metal shutter. The caddy has a hinged lid that enables you to open it for inserting the CD, but after that the lid remains shut. When you insert the caddy containing the CD into the drive, the drive will open a metal shutter on the caddy, allowing access to the CD by the laser.

The caddy is not the most convenient loading mechanism. Although, if all of your CDs are in their own caddies, then all you have to do is grab the caddy containing the disc you want and shove it into the drive. This makes the CD operate much like a 3 1/2-inch disk. You can handle the caddy without worrying about touching or contaminating the disc or the drive, making this the most accurate and durable mechanism as well. Young children can easily handle the caddies and don't have to touch the delicate CD discs themselves.

Because the caddy is sealed, the discs are protected from damage caused by handling. The only time the disc is actually handled is when it is first put into the caddy. The caddy loading system also ensures that the disc is properly located when inside the drive. This allows for more accurate laser head positioning mechanisms, and caddy drives generally have faster access times as well.

The real drawback to the caddy is the expense. You only get one caddy with the drive, so you need to buy many more. Otherwise, each time you insert a new disc into the drive, you first have to eject the caddy/disc, remove the disc from the caddy, put the disc back into the original jewel case, open the jewel case for the new disc, put the new disc into the caddy, and finally insert the caddy/disc back into the drive. Caddies cost about $3 each, and it is recommended that you have at least 20 or so on hand, or at least as many as you have discs that you regularly use. Of course this will add $60 or more to the cost of your CD-ROM drive, but that is the price you pay for convenience, durability, reliability, and higher performance.

After you have caddies for all of your discs, the disc swap procedure is much easier—simply eject the one in the drive, grab the new caddy/disc and shove it back in! The caddy essentially takes the place of the jewel case, and the disc should be left in the caddy permanently.

A final advantage of caddy-loaded drives is that they can be mounted in either a horizontal or vertical plane, meaning that the drive can be installed sideways. This cannot be done with the cheaper tray-loaded drives, but newer tray-loaded drives have small retaining tabs that allow both horizontal or vertical mounting.

Tray. Most drives use a *tray loading* mechanism. This is similar to the CD-DA (Digital Audio) drive used with your stereo system. Because you don't need to put each disc into a separate caddy, this mechanism is much less expensive overall. However, it also means that you have to handle each disc every time you insert or remove it.

Tray loading is more convenient than a caddy system, because you don't need a caddy. However, this can make it much more difficult for young children to use the discs without smudging or damaging them due to the excessive handling.

The tray loader itself also is subject to damage. The trays can be easily broken if they are bumped or if something is dropped on them while they are extended. Also, any contamination you place on the tray or disc is brought right into the drive when the tray is retracted. Tray-loaded drives should not be used in a harsh environment, such as a commercial or industrial establishment.

The tray mechanism also does not hold the disc as securely as the caddy. If you don't have the disc placed in the tray properly when it is retracted, then the disc or tray can be damaged. Some tray drives cannot be run in a vertical (sideways) position, as gravity would prevent proper loading and operation. Check to see if the drive tray has retaining clips on the outer edge of the CD seat, like the Hitachi drive I have in my HP Vectra. If so, you can run the drive in either horizontal or vertical position.

The real advantage to the tray mechanism over the caddy system is in cost, and that is a big factor. If you do not have young children and the drive will be run in a clean environment where careful handling and cleanliness can be assured, then the tray mechanism would be recommend due to its significantly lower cost.

Other Drive Features

Although drive specifications are of the utmost importance, other factors and features should be taken into consideration as well. Besides quality of construction, the following criteria bear scrutiny when making a purchase decision:

- Drive sealing
- Self-cleaning lenses
- Internal versus external drive

Drive Sealing. Dirt is your CD-ROM's biggest enemy. Dust or dirt, when it collects on the lens portion of the mechanism, can cause read errors or severe performance loss. Many manufacturers seal the lens and internal components in airtight enclosures from the drive bay. Other drives, although not sealed, have double dust doors—one external and one internal—to keep dust from the inside of the drive. All these features help prolong the life of your drive.

Caddy-loaded drives are inherently sealed better and are much more resistant to the external environment than tray-loaded drives. Always use a caddy-loaded drive in harsh industrial or commercial environments.

Self-Cleaning Lenses. If the laser lens gets dirty, so does your data. The drive will spend a great deal of time seeking and reseeking, or finally giving up. Lens cleaning discs are available, but built-in cleaning mechanisms are now included on virtually all good quality drives. This may be a feature you'll want to consider, particularly if you work in a less-than-pristine work environment, or you have trouble keeping your desk clean, let alone your CD-ROM drive lens.

Internal versus External Drives. When deciding whether you want an internal or external drive, think about where and how you're going to use your CD-ROM drive. What about the future expansion of your system? Both types of drives have advantages and disadvantages. The following lists some of the issues:

- *External Enclosure.* These tend to be rugged, portable, and large—in comparison to their internal versions. Buy an external one only if you lack the space inside the system. You might also consider an external if you want to move the drive from one PC to another easily. If each PC has its own SCSI adapter, all you need to do is unplug the drive from one adapter and plug it in to the other. Only SCSI CD-ROM drives can be external, so if you are looking for an IDE type interface, you must go internal.

- *Internal Enclosure.* Internal drives will clear off a portion of your desk. Buy an internal drive if you have a free drive bay, or plan on keeping the CD-ROM drive exclusively on one machine. All modern PCs should have a CD-ROM drive; it is no longer looked at as a peripheral. The internal drives are nice because you can connect the audio connector to your sound card and leave the external audio connectors free for other inputs. Internal drives can be IDE or SCSI.

CD-ROM Disc and Drive Formats

Compact discs are pitted to encode the binary bits of 0 and 1. Without this logical organization to this disc full of digits, the CD-ROM drive and PC would be at a loss to find any discernible data amid all those numbers. To this end, the data is encoded to conform to particular standards. When a drive encounters particular patterns, it—and the PC—can recognize the organization of the disc and find its way around the platter. Without standard data formats, the CD-ROM industry would be dead in the water; vendors of particular discs and disc drives would be producing incompatible software discs and drives, and thereby limiting the number of units that could be sold.

Formats are also needed to advance the technology. For example, hard rubber wheels and no suspension were just fine for the first automobiles as they cruised along at the break-neck speed of 30 miles an hour. But hitting a pothole at 60 mph could cause serious damage to the vehicle—and the riders. Inflatable tires and shock absorbers became necessary components of the modern car.

Similarly, the standards for disc formats evolved as well. The first compact data discs stored only text information, which was relatively easy to encode onto a disc. Graphics produced a greater challenge, and the standards evolved to incorporate them. The use of animation with synchronized sound, and then live-motion video, called for other expansions to the standards in which CDs store data.

It is extremely important to note that advanced CD-ROM standards are in the process of evolution right now. Multiple vendors are deploying a number of different techniques for expanding the capabilities of CD-ROM technology. They may be incompatible with each other or immature in their development, but acceptance of these newer standards by software vendors is essential to the widespread use of these standards. It is important that you are familiar with these issues before you purchase a drive; consider the formats it is capable of reading now—and in the future.

The majority of drives available today, however, do comply with earlier CD-ROM formats, ensuring that the vast library of CD-ROM applications available today can be used on these drives.

Data Standard: ISO 9660

Manufacturers of the first CD-ROM data discs produced their discs for one particular drive. In other words, a data disc produced for company A's drive could not be read by anyone who had purchased company B's CD-ROM drive—the disc needed to be formatted for each manufacturer's drive. Obviously, this stalled the development of the industry. Philips and Sony developed the "Yellow Book" specifications for data CD-ROMs.

When Philips and Sony first published the audio CD specifications, the material was released in a red binder and became known as the "Red Book." Subsequent CD-ROM specifications have been dubbed by color as well, such as the "Orange Book" and the "Green Book."

An extension of the way in which audio data was stored on disc, the Yellow Book specifications detail how data—rather than audio—can be organized on a disc for its later retrieval. The *International Standards Organization (ISO)* refined this specification (called ISO 9660) in such a way that every vendor's drive and disc would expect to find a table of contents for a data disc. This is known as a *Volume Table of Contents*, and it really is quite similar to a standard book's table of contents in theory. ISO 9660 did not completely solve compatibility problems, however. The incorporation of additional data to aid and refine the search for data on a disc, and even how to format the data blocks were still left to each separate vendor's design.

High Sierra Format

It was in all manufacturers' interests to resolve this issue. In a meeting in 1985 at the High Sierra Hotel and Casino in Lake Tahoe, California, leading manufacturers of CD-ROM drives and CD-ROM discs came together to resolve the differences in their implementation of the ISO 9660 format. The agreement has become known as the *High Sierra format* and is now a part of the ISO 9660 specification document. This expansion enabled all drives to read all ISO 9660-compliant discs, opening the way for the mass production of CD-ROM software publishing. Adoption of this standard also enabled disc publishers to provide cross-platform support for their software, easily manufacturing discs for DOS, UNIX, and other operating system formats. Without this agreement, the maturation of the CD-ROM marketplace would have taken years longer and stifled the production of available CD ROM-based information.

The exact and entire specifications for how to format the CD media are complex, strewn with jargon you may never need, and superfluous to your understanding of drive capabilities. You should know the basics, however, because it gives you a glimpse of the inner workings of retrieving data so quickly from such an enormous well.

To put the basic High Sierra format in perspective, the disc layout is roughly analogous to a floppy disk. A floppy has a system track that not only identifies itself as a floppy and its density and operating system, but also tells the computer how it's organized—into directories, which are made up of files.

Basic CD-ROM formats are much the same. The initial track of a data CD identifies itself as a CD and begins synchronization between the drive and the disc. Beyond the synchronization lies a system level that details how the entire disc is structured; as a part of the system area, the disc identifies the location of the volume area—where the actual data is held. The system also contains the directories of this volume, with pointers or addresses to various named areas, as illustrated in Figure 17.2. A significant difference between CD directory structures and that of DOS is that the system area also contains direct addresses of files within their subdirectories, allowing the CD to seek to a specific location on the spiral data track.

Because the CD data is all really on one, long, spiral track, when speaking of tracks in the context of a CD, we're talking about sectors or segments of data along the spiral.

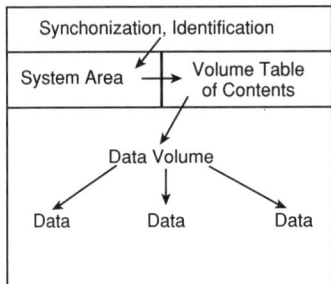

FIG. 17.2 A diagram of CD-ROM basic file organizational format.

CD-DA (Digital Audio)

Data drives that can read data and audio are called *CD-DA*. Virtually any data drive now being sold reads both types of discs. When you insert a disc, the drive reads the first track of the disc to determine what type you loaded. Most drives ship with audio CD software, which enables you to play music CDs from your PC. You can use headphones, or with an installed sound card, connect speakers to the system. Some external drives ship with standard Left/Right audio plugs; just plug them into any external amplifier.

CD+

Philips and Sony have recently introduced a new CD format called CD+. This is a new format that enables audio CD players and multimedia PCs to easily play the same compact discs. This new format allows both audio and data to be integrated on the same CD.

CD+ uses a new technology called *stamped multisession*, which solves the problem of trying to use a computer CD-ROM title in an audio player. Because the first track of a computer CD-ROM contains data and not music, the audio player attempts to play it and the result is static. If the volume is turned up, the speakers can be damaged.

The new CD+ format will allow a new type of CD to appear that contains not only music, but also data such as song lyrics, biographies, and any other text that is desired.

PhotoCD

First announced back in 1990, but not available until 1992, CD drives or players that display your own CD-ROM recorded photographs over your television are now being sold by Kodak. You merely drop off a roll of film at a participating Kodak developer; later you take home a PhotoCD and drop it into your Kodak PhotoCD compatible disc player. But what's a PhotoCD compatible player?

This is a home A/V (Audio Visual) entertainment system component that is designed to play your PhotoCDs and your audio CDs as well. Because virtually all data-ready CD drives also can interpret audio, it's no mean feat for the Kodak CD players to play audio discs. The player merely reads off the first track and determines what type of disc you've fed it. The real breakthrough is in the drive's capability to determine whether one, two, or dozens of individual photo "sessions" are on the data disc.

Remember from the High Sierra format discussion that each data disc holds a VTOC, or Volume Table of Contents, which tells the CD reader where—and how—the data is laid out on disc. CD data has, until this point, been single-session in its encoding. In other words, when a CD is mastered, all the data that will ever reside on the disc must be recorded in one session. The format, or the media, has no provision for returning later to append more information. The PhotoCD format—along with the XA and CD-I formats discussed later—not only allow for multiple sessions, but also allow multiple sessions to be read back on a fully PhotoCD-capable CD-ROM drive. However, the drive must be capable of finding the multiple VTOCs associated with the appended sessions.

And this is where some confusion now reigns. When Kodak first released the PhotoCD, the company maintained that a drive must be CD-ROM XA compliant to use PhotoCD. An explanation of the XA specifications follows in the section "CD-ROM-XA, or Extended Architecture." As of January 1992, however, Kodak has tested non-XA drives with new software drivers and approved them as single-session PhotoCD compatible. In other words, many of the drives shipping right now may be perfectly suited to reading PhotoCD discs that contain a single session of photos. The drive can only recognize the first session, and ignores any data or subsequent volume entries made after the initial session.

PC-based CD-ROM drives, if supplied with the proper device driver and Kodak-based software, can read single-session PhotoCD images. Kodak is licensing the "viewer" portion of its software so that it can be incorporated into existing software packages. Special filters—or decoders—will be added to desktop publishing, word processing, and PC paint software that will allow them to import PhotoCD images into their documents.

Kodak has future plans to incorporate synchronized audio and text to the existing photo format. For these capabilities, the drive that reads these advanced discs must be XA-compatible. In addition, drives must be XA-compatible to read any disc that has multiple recordings.

PhotoCD Production

When you drop off your roll of film, the Kodak developers produce prints, just as they normally do. After prints are made, however, the process goes high-tech. Using high-speed UNIX operating system-based SUN SparcStations, the prints are scanned into the SparcStation at a very high resolution using ultra-high resolution scanners. To give you an idea of the amount of information each

(continues)

(continued)

scan carries, one color photograph can take 15–20M of storage. When the image is stored on disc, it is compressed using Kodak's own custom software. The compressed, stored images are then encoded onto special writable CD discs. The finished product is packaged in a familiar CD case and shipped back to your local developer for pickup.

Even though these scanned images occupy an enormous amount of media space, the capacity of CD technology can easily carry 100 photos, at the highest possible resolution. Because existing television, and even most home computers, cannot use these ultra-high resolutions, the typical home or PC-based PhotoCD can hold hundreds of images. See Table 17.3 for more details. Because most of us rarely have that many photos developed at the same time, Kodak developed the system in conjunction with Philips so that multiple sessions can be recorded on one disc. You can have your Thanksgiving photos developed and recorded to disc in November, for example, and then bring the same disc back in late December to have your other holiday photos added to the remaining portion of the disc. Keep bringing the disc in until it fills up.

Table 17.3 PhotoCD Resolutions

Resolution	Description
256 lines×384	Fine for most conventional TVs
512×768	Good for S-VHS TVs and VGA PCs
1024×1536	Beyond current TV technology
2048×3072	Beyond TV or most PC capacities

As of this writing, Kodak PhotoCD discs run fine in single session mode in many current CD-ROM drives—in Philips CD-I home entertainment systems as well as the Kodak systems.

For multisession capabilities and the capability to use audio and text on a PhotoCD for the PC, you must have an XA-compatible CD-ROM drive.

CD-ROM-XA or Extended Architecture

CD-ROM XA, or *Extended Architecture*, is backwards compatible with the earlier High Sierra or ISO 9660 CD-ROMs. It adds another dimension to the world of CD-ROM technology.

Interleaving. CD-ROM XA drives employ a technique known as *interleaving*. The specification calls for the capability to encode on disc whether the data directly following an identification mark is graphics, sound, or text. Graphics can include standard graphics pictures, animation, or full-motion video. In addition, these blocks can be *interleaved*, or interspersed, with each other. For example, a frame of video may start a track followed by a segment of audio, which would accompany the video, followed by yet another frame of video. The drive picks up the audio and video sequentially, buffering the information in memory, and then sending it along to the PC for synchronization.

In short, the data is read off the disc in alternating pieces, and then synchronized at playback so that the result is a simultaneous presentation of the data.

Mode 1 and Mode 2, Form 1 and Form 2. To achieve this level of sophistication, the CD format is broken up so that the data types are layered. *Mode 1* is CD data with error correction. *Mode 2* is CD data without error correction. The Mode 2 track, however, allows what are called Form 1 and Form 2 tracks to exist one after the other on the Mode 2 track, thereby allowing the interleaving. These interleaved tracks may include their own error correction and can be any type of data. Figure 17.3 shows a visual representation of the breakdowns of Mode and Form structure.

FIG. 17.3 A diagrammatic view of Mode and Form format for CD-ROM XA.

For a drive to be truly XA-compatible, the Form 2 data encoded on the disc as audio must be *ADPCM (Adaptive Differential Pulse Code Modulation) audio*—specially compressed and encoded audio. This requires that the drive or the SCSI controller have a signal processor chip that can decompress the audio during the synchronization process.

What all this translates into is that drives currently available may be partially XA-compliant. They might be capable of the interleaving of data and reading of multisession discs, but may not have the ADPCM audio component on the disc or its controller.

Presently, the only drives with full XA compliance are produced by Sony and IBM. The Sony drive incorporates the ADPCM chip on its drive. The IBM XA drive is for IBM's proprietary Micro Channel bus and is designed for its high-end PS/2 Model computers.

Manufacturers may claim that their drives are "XA-ready," which means that they are capable of multisession and Mode 1 and Mode 2, Form 1 and Form 2 reading, but they do not incorporate the ADPCM chip. Software developers, including Kodak, have yet to produce many XA software titles. IBM has a few under its Multimedia program, but others have not yet hit the market.

If you get a drive that is fully mode and form compatible and is capable of reading multiple sessions, you may have the best available at this time. XA is a specification waiting for acceptance right now. Audio and video interleaving is possible without full XA compliance, as MPC (Multimedia PC) applications under Microsoft Windows demonstrate.

CD-R

Sometimes known as *CD-WORM* and *CD-WO, CD-R (CD-Recordable)* enables you to write your own CDs.

As with mastering any CD, your data must be laid out or formatted before recording it to the CD-R unit. Often this layout is performed on a PC with large hard disks or other magnetic and removable media.

The CD-R is not quite the CD you might expect, however. Instead of the recording beam burning pits into a metallic or glass strata, the CD-R media is coated with a dye that has the same reflective properties as a "virgin" CD —in other words, a CD reader would see an unrecorded CD-R disc as one long land. When the recording laser begins to burn data into the CD-R media, it heats the gold layer and the dye layer beneath. The result of heating these areas causes the dye and gold areas to diffuse light in exactly the same way that a pit would on a glass master disc or a mass-produced CD. The reader is fooled into thinking a pit exists; but there is no actual pit, just a spot of less-reflective disc caused by the chemical reaction of heating the dye and gold.

Many of the newer recordable CD-ROM drives support all the formats discussed—ISO 9660 all the way through CD-ROM XA. In addition, these drives read the formats as well, serving as a ROM reader. Prices have been falling steadily, and are now in the $700 area for a drive, and under $5 for the blank media. These drives are now affordable for small businesses, who can distribute databases easily on CD-ROM discs. After you make a master, it can cost less than $1 per disc to have duplicates made, bringing the price of distributing your data to a very reasonable figure.

CD-E

Although CD-R is a write once standard, it is now possible to purchase fully re-recordable CD drives. Philips Electronics and Ricoh have introduced erasable CD-ROMs (called CD-E). The CD-E standard has been developed and supported by more than 10 manufacturers, including IBM, Hewlett-Packard, Mitsubishi, Mitsumi, Matsushita, Sony, 3M, Olympus, Philips, and Ricoh.

The new medium has an archival life of more than 10 years, or roughly 10,000 access cycles, and will allow at least 1,000 overwrites to occur. As such it is not intended to replace magnetic media for primary online storage, but can supplement it for archival purposes. The media has a lower optical reflectability than standard CDs, requiring an increase of five times the read/write gain for the drive units.

This new technology is backward compatible with standard CD-ROM and CD-R technology, meaning that CD-E drives would read existing CD and CD-R discs. These new drives will initially be expensive, but if the price falls it may catch on as a viable backup and online storage solution.

DVD (Digital Versatile Disc)

The future of CD-ROM is called DVD (Digital Versatile Disc). This is a new standard that dramatically increases the storage capacity of, and therefore the useful applications for, CD-ROMs. The problem with current CD-ROM technology is that it is severely limited in storage capacity. A CD-ROM can only hold a maximum of about 680M of data, which may sound like a lot, but is simply not enough for many up and coming applications, especially where the use of video is concerned.

One of the primary applications envisioned for the new DVD standard is a replacement for video tapes. In the future, instead of renting a tape at your local video store, you will be able to rent or purchase a movie on a CD-ROM disc! As such, DVD will have applications not only in computers, but in the consumer entertainment market as well.

DVD had a somewhat confusing beginning. During 1995, two competing standards for high capacity CD-ROM drives emerged to compete with each other for future market share. A standard called Multimedia CD was introduced and backed by Sony and Philips Electronics, while a competing standard called the Super Density (SD) disk was introduced and backed by Toshiba, Time Warner, and several other companies. If both of these standards had hit the market as is, consumers as well as entertainment and software producers would have been in a quandary over which one to choose!

Fearing a repeat of the Beta/VHS situation, several organizations including the Hollywood Video Disc Advisory Group and the Computer Industry Technical Working Group banded together. They insisted on a single format and refused to endorse either competing proposal. With this incentive, both groups worked out an agreement on a single, new, high capacity CD-ROM in September of 1995. The new standard, called DVD (Digital Versatile Disc), combines elements of both previously proposed standards. The single DVD standard has avoided a confusing replay of the VHS/Betamax fiasco and has given the software, hardware, and movie industries a single unified standard to support.

DVD offers an initial storage capacity of 4.7G of digital information on a single-sided, single-layer disc the same diameter and half the thickness (0.6mm) of a current CD-ROM. With MPEG-2 (Motion Picture Experts Group) compression, that's enough to contain 135 minutes of video, enough for a full-length, full-screen, full-motion feature film—including three channels of CD-quality audio and four channels of subtitles. The initial capacity is no coincidence; the creation of DVD was driven by the film industry, which has long sought a storage medium cheaper and more durable than videotape.

Future plans for DVD include 9.4G double-layer discs as well as double-sided, double-layer discs that will store 18.8G (nearly 30 times the capacity of today's CD-ROMs). With advancements coming in blue light lasers, this capacity may be increased several fold in the future. DVD drives are also very fast compared to current CD-ROM technology. The standard transfer rate is 1.3M/sec, which is approximately equivalent to a 9X CD-ROM drive.

DVD drives will be fully backward compatible, and as such will be able to play today's CD-ROMs as well as audio CDs. When playing existing CDs, the performance will be equivalent to a standard 4x CD-ROM drive. As such, users who currently own 4x CD-ROM drives should probably consider waiting for DVD drives instead of upgrading to a 6x or faster drive. Any products that require faster than 4x speeds will likely come out in DVD form and not use current CD-ROM technology anyway.

If you want to take advantage of DVD's multimedia capabilities you will need a sound-and-video card that can handle MPEG-2 and the three DVD audio formats. This type of hardware is expected to be available along with the drives.

Multimedia CD-ROM

Multimedia is not a specific standard but a descriptive term. Any CD that incorporates text with graphics, sound, or video is by definition multimedia. Multimedia CDs exist for DOS, Macintosh System 7, Windows, OS/2, and UNIX operating systems and can be in many different formats.

A consortium of hardware and software manufacturers led by Microsoft Corporation announced the formation of the Multimedia PC Marketing Council at COMDEX in the fall of 1991. This council described the recommended platform for implementing multimedia on PC systems, and as more manufacturers joined the council, applications and hardware conformed to the prescribed specifications.

The MPC Council recommends minimum performance requirements for MPC-compatible CD-ROM drives, however. They are as follows:

Specification Transfer Rate	MPC Level 1 Single-Speed (1x)	MPC Level 2 Double-Speed (2x)	MPC Level 3 Quad-Speed (4x)
Average Access	1,000 ms	400 ms	200 ms

The minimum recommended specifications today are the MPC Level 3 standard. In other words, your drive should meet or exceed those performance standards.

Far from being an exact specification or format for data, MPC CD-ROM is a convention for storing audio, animation, video, and text for synchronization under the Microsoft Windows operating system from data received from an MPC-compliant CD-ROM. Microsoft has developed Windows Application Programmer's Interface software, which allows CD-ROM software manufacturers to organize the data on their CDs in such a way that information can be passed to Windows for processing.

Note that discs labeled as MPC only run under Microsoft Windows 3.0 or higher with the Microsoft Multimedia Extensions, or under OS/2 with MMPM. If a drive meets the minimum MPC Council recommendation for performance, it will run MPC CD-ROMs under Windows.

Audio drives deliver sound at a preset transfer rate to the amplifiers. Today's CD-ROM drives can spin at faster rates when retrieving data. The minimum recommended speed today would be the Quad-speed drive. Particular applications, such as live-motion video, especially benefit from this technology. Data is delivered in a constant stream, allowing the PC to process the video frames at a smoother rate. Some drives without high-speed technology, especially those that have no buffering capabilities, deliver video in a jerky and uneven manner.

Installing Your Drive

You decided on the drive you want. You ordered it. Now it has arrived at your doorstep. What next?

Installation of a CD-ROM drive is as difficult or as easy as you make it. If you plan ahead, the installation should go smoothly.

This section walks you through the installation of typical internal (applies to SCSI and IDE) and external (applies to IDE only) CD-ROM drives with tips that often aren't included in your manufacturer's installation manuals. Even after you install the hardware, it isn't always enough to just turn on the drive and toss in a CD (unless your drive is supported by Windows 95). Special software must be loaded onto your PC first.

Avoiding Conflict: Get Your Cards in Order

Regardless of your type of installation—internal or external drive—you need to check your CD-ROM drive's controller before installation. In most cases, you will be adding your CD-ROM drive to an existing IDE or SCSI controller. If that is so, the controller will have already been set up so as not to conflict with other devices in your system. All you need to do is add the CD-ROM to the chain. If not, then you will need to configure your new controller's:

- IRQ
- DMA channel
- I/O port address

Refer to Chapter 15, "Hard Disk Interfaces," for help with your particular IDE or SCSI controller.

Drive Configuration

Configuration of your new CD disk is paramount to its proper function. Examine your new drive (see Figure 17.4) and locate any jumpers. For an IDE drive, here are the typical ways to jumper the drive:

- As the primary (master) drive on the secondary IDE connection
- As the secondary (slave) drive to a current hard disk drive

FIG. 17.4 The rear connection interfaces of a typical IDE internal CD-ROM drive.

If the CD drive is to be the *only* one on your secondary EIDE interface, the factory settings are usually correct (see Figure 17.5). In this case, the jumper is not being used.

When you use the CD-ROM as a secondary drive—that is, the second drive on the same ribbon cable—make sure it is jumpered as the slave drive, and set the hard disk so that it is the master drive. In most cases, the CD-ROM will show up as the next logical drive, or D: drive.

FIG. 17.5 An embedded EIDE interface with a primary and secondary IDE connection.

SCSI drives are a bit easier to jumper because you need only to select the proper device ID for the drive. By convention, the boot disk (the C: drive) in a SCSI system is set as ID0, and the host adapter has the ID of 7. You are free to choose any other available ID. If your new SCSI drive falls at the end of a SCSI bus, you will also need to terminate the drive.

  ▶▶ See "Termination," p. 664 and 674

> **Note**
>
> IDE/EIDE disks and SCSI CD drives *can* co-exist in the same system. The CD drive will need its own controller or host adapter. Some sound cards have a SCSI interface built-in.

External (SCSI) CD-ROM Hook-Up

Unpack the CD-ROM carefully. With the purchase of an external drive, you should receive the following items:

- CD-ROM drive
- SCSI adapter cable
- SCSI adapter card (optional)

This is the bare minimum to get the drive up and running. You'll probably also find a CD caddy, a manual or pamphlet for the adapter card, and possibly a sampling of CDs to get you started.

Take a look at your work area and the SCSI cable that came with the drive. Where will the drive find a new home? You're limited by the length of the cable. Find a spot for the drive, and insert the power cable into the back of the unit. Make sure that you have an outlet, or preferably a free socket in a surge-suppressing power strip to plug in the new drive.

Plug one end of the supplied cable into the connector socket of the drive, and one into the SCSI connector on the adapter card. Most external drives have two connectors on the back—either connector can be hooked to the PC (see Figure 17.6). The following sections discuss the extra connector. Secure the cable with the guide hooks on both the drive and adapter connector, if provided. Some SCSI cables supplied with Future Domain 16-bit controllers have a micro-connector for the adapter end, and simply clip into place.

External CD SCSI Connectors

FIG. 17.6 Older Centronics-style External CD-ROM drive SCSI connectors.

Finally, your external CD-ROM drive should have a SCSI ID select switch on the back. This switch sets the identification number for the drive when hooked to the host adapter. The adapter, by most manufacturer's defaults, should be set for SCSI ID 7. Make sure that you set the SCSI ID for the CD-ROM drive to any other number—6, 5, or 4, for example. The only rule to follow is to make sure that you do not set the drive for an ID that is already occupied—by either the card or any other SCSI peripheral on the chain.

Internal Drive Installation

Unpack your internal drive kit. You should have the following pieces:

- The drive
- Power cord
- SCSI interface board (optional)
- Internal IDE/SCSI ribbon cable
- Internal CD-Audio cable

- Floppy disks/CD-ROM with device driver software and manual
- Drive rails and/or mounting screws

Your manufacturer also may have provided a *power cable splitter*—a bundle of wires with plastic connectors on each of three ends. A disc caddy and owner's manual may also be included.

Make sure that the PC is off and leave the cover off the PC for now. Before installing the card into the PC bus, however, connect the SCSI ribbon cable onto the adapter card (see Figure 17.7).

FIG. 17.7 Connecting a ribbon cable to a SCSI adapter.

Ribbon Cable and Card Edge Connector

The ribbon cable should be identical on both ends. You'll find a red stripe of dotted line down one side of the outermost edge of the cable. This stripe indicates a pin-1 designation, and ensures that the SCSI cable is connected properly into the card and into the drive. If you're lucky, the manufacturer supplied a cable with notches or keys along one edge of the connector. With such a key, you can insert the cable into the card and drive in only one way. Unkeyed cables must be hooked up according to the pin-1 designation.

Along one edge of your SCSI adapter, you'll find a double row of 50 brass-colored pins. This is the card edge connector. In small print along the base of this row of pins you should find at least two numbers next to the pins—1 and 50. Aligning the ribbon cable's marked edge over pin 1, carefully and evenly insert the ribbon cable connector. Now insert the adapter card, leaving the drive end of the cable loose for the time being.

Choose a slot in the front bay for your internal drive. Make sure that it's easily accessible and not blocked by other items on your desk. You'll be inserting the CDs here, and you'll need the elbow room.

Remove the drive bay cover. Inside the drive bay you should find a metal enclosure with screw holes for mounting the drive. If the drive has mounting holes along its side and fits snugly into the enclosure, you won't need mounting rails. If it's a loose fit, however, mount the rails along the sides of the drive with the rail screws, and then slide the drive into the bay. Secure the drive into the bay with four screws—two on each side. If the rails or drive don't line up evenly with four mounting holes, make sure that you use at least two—one mounting screw on each side. Because you'll be inserting and ejecting many CDs over the years, mounting the drive securely is a must.

Once again, find the striped side of the ribbon cable and align it with pin 1 on the drive's edge connector. Either a diagram in your owner's manual or designation on the connector itself tells you which is pin 1.

The back of the CD drive has a power connector outlet. Inside the case of your PC, at the back of your floppy or hard disk, are power cords—bundled red and yellow wires with plastic connectors on them. You may already have an open power connector laying open in the case. Take the open connector and plug it into the back of the power socket on the CD-ROM drive. These connectors only go in one way. If you do not have an open connector, use the splitter (see Figure 17.8). Disconnect a floppy drive power cord. Attach the splitter to the detached power cord. Plug one of the free ends into the floppy drive, the other into the CD-ROM drive.

FIG. 17.8 Power cord splitter and connector.

> **Note**
>
> It's best to "borrow" juice from the floppy drive connector in this way. Your hard drive may require more power or be more sensitive to sharing this line than the floppy is. If you have no choice—the splitter and ribbon cable won't reach, for example—you can split off any power cord that hasn't already been split. Check the power cable to ensure that you have a line not already overloaded with a split.

750   Chapter 17—CD-ROM Drives

Do *not* replace the PC cover yet—you need to make sure that everything is running perfectly before you seal the case. You're now ready to turn on the computer. For the drive to work, however, you need to install the software drivers.

SCSI Chains: Internal, External, a Little of Both

Remember, one of the primary reasons for using a SCSI controller for your CD-ROM drive is the capability to chain a string of peripherals from one adapter card, thus saving card slots inside the PC, and limiting the nightmare of tracking IRQs, DMAs, and I/O memory addresses.

You can add scanners, tape backup units, and other SCSI peripherals to this chain (see Figure 17.9). You must keep a few things in mind, chief among them is SCSI termination.

   ▶▶ See "Termination," p. 664 and 674

FIG. 17.9 A SCSI chain of devices on one adapter card.

Example One: All External SCSI Devices. Say that you installed your CD-ROM drive and added a tape device to the chain with the extra connector on the back of the CD-ROM drive. The first device in this SCSI chain is the adapter card itself. Most modern host adapters are *auto terminating*, meaning they will terminate themselves without your intervention if they are at the end of the SCSI chain.

From the card, you ran an external cable to the CD-ROM drive, and from the CD-ROM drive, you added another cable to the back of the tape unit. The tape unit must then be terminated as well. Most external units are terminated with a SCSI cap—a small connector that plugs into the unused external SCSI connector. These external drive connectors come in two varieties: a SCSI cap and a pass-through terminator. The cap is just that; it plugs over the open connector and covers it. The pass-through terminator, however, plugs into the connector and has an open end that you can use to plug the SCSI cable into. This type of connector is essential if your external drive has only one SCSI connector; you can plug the drive in and make sure that it's terminated—all with one connector.

Example Two: Internal Chain and Termination. The same rules apply—all the internal devices must have unique SCSI ID numbers, and the first and last devices must be terminated. In the case of internal devices, however, you must check for termination. Internal devices have terminator packs or resistors similar to the ones installed on your adapter card. If you install a tape unit as the last device on the chain, it must have resistors on its circuit board. If you place your CD-ROM drive in the middle of this chain, its resistors must be removed. The adapter card, at the end of the chain, keeps its resistors intact.

> **Note**
>
> Most internal SCSI devices ship with terminating resistors and/or DIP switches on board. Check your user's manuals for their locations. Any given device may have one, two, or even three such resistors.

Example Three: Internal and External SCSI Devices. If you mix and match external as well as internal devices, follow the rules. The example shown in Figure 17.10 has an internal CD-ROM drive, terminated and set for SCSI ID 6; the external tape unit also is terminated, and we assign it SCSI ID 5. The SCSI adapter itself is set for ID 7 and, most importantly, its terminating resistor packs have been removed.

FIG. 17.10 Examples of various SCSI termination scenarios.

> **Note**
>
> As with any adapter card, be careful when handling the card itself. Make sure that you ground yourself first. Chip pullers—specially made tweezers found in most computer tool kits—are especially useful in removing resistor packs from adapter cards and internal peripherals such as CD-ROM drives. The resistor packs have very thin teeth that are easily bent. Once bent, they're tough to straighten out and reinsert, so be careful when removing the packs.

CD-ROM Software on Your PC

After you configure the controller card, you're ready for the last step—installation of the CD-ROM software. The CD-ROM needs the following three software components for it to operate on a PC:

- A SCSI adapter driver (not needed for ATAPI IDE CD-ROM drives). Most popular SCSI adapter drivers are built-in to Windows 95.

- A SCSI driver for the specific CD-ROM drive you've installed. An ASPI driver is built into Windows 95, as is an ATAPI IDE CD-ROM driver.

- MSCDEX—Microsoft CD Extensions for DOS, which is built into Windows 95 as the CDFS VxD.

If you are still using DOS, you can have the first two drivers—the SCSI adapter driver and CD-ROM driver—load into your system at startup by placing command lines in your CONFIG.SYS file. The MSCDEX, or DOS extension, is an executable file added into your system through your AUTOEXEC.BAT file. This is not required in Windows 95 (unless you plan to run DOS games); it will auto-detect the drive upon startup and prompt you to install the correct drivers if it can't find them in its standard arsenal of device drivers.

Using Windows 95 along with a CD-ROM drive that conforms to the ATAPI (AT Attachment Packet Interface) IDE specification does not require you to do anything. All the driver support for these drives is built into Windows 95, including the ATAPI driver and the CDFS VxD driver.

If you are running a SCSI CD-ROM drive under Windows 95, you will still need the ASPI (Advanced SCSI Programming Interface) driver that goes with your drive. The ASPI driver for your drive normally will come from the drive manufacturer and is included with the drive in most cases. Windows 95 includes the corresponding ASPI driver for most SCSI host adapters, and also automatically runs the CDFS VxD virtual device driver.

DOS SCSI Adapter Driver. Each SCSI adapter model has a specific driver that allows communications between the PC and the SCSI interface. Normally, these drivers conform to the ASPI (Advanced SCSI Programming Interface). The ASPI driver that goes with the drive will connect with the ASPI driver that goes with the SCSI host adapter and allow the adapter and drive to communicate. An ASPI driver should have been provided with your SCSI drive and adapter kit. Documentation should also have been included that walks you through the installation of the software. You can manually add the SCSI device driver to your CONFIG.SYS file as follows:

At the front of the CONFIG.SYS file, add the name and path of the driver with the `DEVICE=` command:

    DEVICE=C:\DRIVERS\MYSCSI.SYS

C:\DRIVERS is the subdirectory in which you copied the SCSI ASPI device drivers. Some drivers have option switches or added commands that, for example, enable you to view the progress of the driver being loaded.

DOS CD-ROM Device Driver. This driver, as well, should be a part of your basic installation kit. If not, contact the drive's manufacturer for the proper device driver for your SCSI card.

The device driver should come with an installation program that prompts you for the memory I/O address for the SCSI adapter on which you installed your CD-ROM drive. This device driver allows communication with the drive through the SCSI bus to your PC. Installation programs add a line similar to the following to your CONFIG.SYS file:

    DEVICE=C:\DRIVERS\MYCDROM.SYS /D:mscd001

C:\DRIVERS is the subdirectory that contains the driver MYCDROM.SYS, the CD-ROM driver for your specific CD-ROM drive.

Note the `/D:mscd001` option after the preceding statement. This designates this CD-ROM driver as controlling the first (001), and only, CD-ROM drive on the system. This portion of the device driver statement is for the Microsoft DOS Extension driver, which designates CD-ROM drives in this fashion.

MSCDEX: Adding CDs to DOS. The Microsoft CD Extensions for DOS enable the DOS operating system to identify and use data from CD-ROMs attached to the system. The original DOS operating system had no provisions for this technology, so "hooks" or handling of this unique media are not a part of the basic operating environment. Using these extensions is convenient for all involved, however. As CD-ROM technology changes, the MSCDEX can be changed, independently of the DOS system. For example, most PhotoCD, multiple-session CD-ROM drives require MSCDEX.EXE version 2.21, which has been modified from earlier versions to accommodate the newer CD format.

MSCDEX.EXE should be in your software kit with your drive. If not, you can obtain the latest copy from Microsoft directly. The latest version of the DOS extension also is available on CompuServe in the Microsoft forum. If you are a registered user of the DOS operating system, the MSCDEX is free. Read the licensing agreement that appears on the disk or in your manual concerning the proper licensing of your MSCDEX files.

Your installation software should add a line similar to the following to your AUTOEXEC.BAT file:

    C:\WINDOWS\COMMAND\MSCDEX.EXE /d:mscd001

C:\WINDOWS\COMMAND is the directory in which the MSCDEX.EXE file is located by default. The `/d:mscd001` portion of the command line tells the MSCDEX extension the DOS name of the device defined in the CD-ROM device driver of your CONFIG.SYS file.

> **Note**
>
> The MSCDEX and CD-ROM device driver names must match. The defaults that most installations provide are used in this example. As long as the two names are the same, the drivers can find one another.

Sounds complicated? Don't worry. As long as you have these three drivers—the SCSI adapter driver, the CD-ROM driver, and the DOS CD extensions—loaded properly in your system, the CD-ROM drive will operate as transparently as any other drive in your system.

Table 17.5 lists the options MSCDEX.EXE has that you can add to its command line.

Table 17.5 MSCDEX Command Line Options

Switch	Function
/V	Called *Verbose*; lists information about memory allocation, buffers, drive letter assignments, and device driver names on your screen at boot up when this option is added to the command line.
/L: \<letter\>	Designates which DOS drive letter you will assign the drive. For example, /L:G assigns the drive letter G: to your CD-ROM drive. Two conditions apply: first, you must not have another drive assigned to that letter; and second, your lastdrive= statement in your CONFIG.SYS file must be equal to or greater than the drive letter you're assigning. LASTDRIVE=G would be fine. LASTDRIVE=F would cause an error if you attempt to assign the CD-ROM drive to the G: drive through the /L: switch.
/M: \<buffers\>	Enables you to buffer the data from the CD-ROM drive. This is useful if you want faster initial access to the drive's directory. Buffers of 10 to 15 are more than enough for most uses. Any more is overkill. Each buffer, however, is equal to 2K of memory. So a /M:10 buffer argument, for example, would take 20K of memory. Note that this does not significantly increase the overall performance of the drive, just DOS's initial access to the drive and the access of large data blocks when the drive is gulping down live-motion video, for example. You can't turn a 400ms drive into a speed demon by adding a 200K buffer. With no /M: argument added, MSCDEX will add, as a default, six buffers anyway. That may be fine for most PCs and CD-ROM drives.
/E	Loads the aforementioned buffers into DOS high memory, freeing up space in the conventional 640K. Early versions of MSCDEX—anything below version 2.1—does not load into extended memory. You must have DOS 5.0 for this option to load.
/K	Kanji (Japanese) support.
/S	Enables you to share your CD-ROM drive on a peer-to-peer network, such as Windows for Workgroups.

Note that Windows 95 uses a built-in CDFS (CD File System) driver that takes the place of MSCDEX. It is configured through the Registry in Windows 95.

Software Loading

As mentioned earlier, your drive should come with installation software that copies the device driver files to your hard drive. It should also add the necessary command lines to your CONFIG.SYS and AUTOEXEC.BAT files or to the SYSTEM.DAT Registry file for Windows 95. When this is accomplished, you can reboot your machine and look for signs that all went smoothly in the software installation.

Following is a series of sample portions of your boot up screens to give you an idea of what messages you'll receive when a given driver is properly loaded into the system. When you're sure that the software is loaded correctly, try out the drive by inserting a CD into the disc caddy and loading it into the CD-ROM drive. Then get a directory of the disc from the DOS prompt by issuing the following command:

`DIR/w G:`

This command gives you a directory of the CD you've inserted if your CD has been assigned the drive letter G.

You can log in to the CD-ROM drive, just as you would any DOS drive. The only DOS commands not possible on a CD-ROM drive are those that write to the drive. CDs, remember, are media that cannot be overwritten, erased, or formatted.

If you logged in to the CD-ROM and received a directory of a sample CD, you're all set.

Now you can power down the PC and replace the cover.

CD-ROM in Microsoft Windows 3.x

When your drive is added to your system, Windows already knows about it through the device drivers and DOS. The CD-ROM drive is accessible through File Manager by double-clicking its file cabinet icon. You see your CD-ROM drive among the drive icons across the top. Windows knows that the drive is a CD-ROM drive through the DOS extensions discussed earlier.

You can set your CD-ROM player to play audio CDs while you are working in Windows. You need to hook up your drive to a sound card and speakers, or connect the CD's audio ports to a stereo first. Go to Window's Control Panel and select Drivers. If you do not see `[MCI] CD Audio` among the files in the driver's list, choose Add. Insert the Windows installation disk that contains the CDAUDIO driver. When the driver appears on the list, exit the Drivers and Control Panel windows.

Double-click the Media Player icon. Under Devices, select CD. A listing of the track numbers on your audio CD appears along the bottom edge of the Media Player. The controls on Media Player are similar to those of an audio CD player, including track select, continuous play, and pause (see Figure 17.11).

Many drive manufacturers supply DOS-based CD audio players with their systems. Check your installation manual and software disks for these utilities.

CD-ROM in Windows 95 and Windows NT 4.0

As stated earlier, Windows 95/NT includes virtually all the drivers you will need to run your CD-ROM drive, making the software installation automatic. Windows automatically

FIG. 17.11 The Media Player with an audio CD loaded.

recognizes most IDE CD-ROM drives, and with the addition of the appropriate drive-specific ASPI driver, most SCSI CD-ROM drives as well.

There are several new capabilities with CDs in Windows 95/NT. The most dramatic is the Autoplay feature. Autoplay is a feature integrated into Windows 95 that enables you to simply insert a CD into the drive, and Windows will automatically run it without any user intervention. It will also detect whether that particular CD has already been installed on your system, and if not, it will automatically start the install program. If the disc has already been installed, it will start the application program on the disc.

The Autoplay feature is simple. When you insert a disc, Windows 95 automatically spins it and looks for a file called AUTORUN.INF. If this file exists, Windows 95 opens it and follows the instructions contained within. As you can see, this Autoplay feature will only work on new CDs that have this file. Most software companies are now shipping CD-ROM titles that incorporate the Autoplay feature.

Windows 95/NT includes a new version of the Media Player found in Windows 3.x called the CD-Player. This application enables you to play audio CDs in your drive while you work at the computer. The CD-Player features graphical controls that look like a standard audio CD-ROM drive, and even has advanced features found in audio drives such as random play, programmable playback order, and the capability to save play list programs.

Troubleshooting CD-ROMs

Some people believe that CD-ROM discs and drives are indestructible compared to their magnetic counterparts. Actually, the modern CD-ROM drive is far less reliable than the modern hard disk! Reliability is the bane of any removable media, and CD-ROMs are no exception.

By far the most common causes of problems with CDs or CD-ROM drives are scratches, dirt, or other contamination. Small scratches or fingerprints on the bottom of the disc should not affect performance because the laser focuses on a point inside the actual disk, but dirt or deep scratches can interfere with reading a disc.

To remedy this type of problem, you can clean the bottom surface of the CD with a soft cloth, but be careful not to scratch the surface in the process. The best technique is to wipe the disc in a radial fashion, using strokes that start from the center of the disc and emanate toward the outer edge. This way any scratches will be perpendicular to the tracks rather than parallel to them, minimizing the interference they might cause. You can use any type of solution on the cloth to clean the disc, so long as it will not damage plastic. Most window cleaners are excellent at removing fingerprints and other dirt from the disc and will not damage the plastic surface.

If there are deep scratches, they can often be buffed or polished out. A commercial plastic cleaner such as that sold in auto parts stores for cleaning plastic instrument cluster and tail lamp lenses is very good for removing these types of scratches. This type of plastic polish or cleaner has a very mild abrasive that serves to polish scratches out of a plastic surface. Products labeled as cleaners are usually designed for more serious scratches, while those labeled as a polish are usually milder and work well as a final buff after using the cleaner. Polishes can be used alone if the surface is not scratched very deeply.

Read errors can also occur when dust accumulates on the read lens of your CD-ROM drive. You can try to clean out the drive and lens with a blast of "canned air," or by using a CD drive cleaner (which can be purchased at most music stores that sell audio CDs).

If your discs and your drive are clean, but you still can't read a particular CD-ROM, then your trouble might be due to disc capacity. Early CD-ROM discs had a capacity of about 550M (equivalent to about 60 minutes of CD audio). More recently, the capacity of a standard CD has been pushed to 680M (74 minutes of CD audio). Many older CD-ROM drives are unreliable when they try to read the outermost tracks of newer discs where the last bits of data are stored. You're more likely to run into this problem with a CD that has lots of data—including some Microsoft multimedia titles such as Ancient Lands, Art Gallery, and Complete Baseball. If you have this problem, you may be able to solve it with a firmware or driver upgrade for your CD-ROM drive, but it's possible that the only solution will be to replace the drive.

Sometimes too little data on the disc can be problematic as well. Some older CD-ROM drives use an arbitrary point on the disc's surface to calibrate their read mechanism and if there happens to be no data at that point on the disc, the drive will have problems calibrating successfully. For example, some CD-ROM drives are not able to calibrate successfully with the Microsoft Flight Simulator 5.1 CD-ROM because that disc does not have very much data on it. Fortunately, this problem can usually be corrected by a firmware or driver upgrade for your CD-ROM drive.

Many older drives have had problems working under Windows 95. If you are having problems, contact your drive manufacturer to see if there is a firmware or software driver upgrade that may take care of your problem. With new Eight-speed drives approaching $50 in cost, it may not make sense to spend any time messing with an older drive that is having problems. It would be more cost-effective to simply upgrade to a new 8x or 12x drive instead!

If you are having problems with only one particular disc, and not the drive in general, then you may find that your difficulties are in fact caused by a defective disc. See if you can exchange the disc for another to determine if that is indeed the cause.

Chapter 18
Tape and Other Mass-Storage Drives

The data backup and archive needs on a personal computer can be overwhelming. People with large hard drives, numerous application programs installed, and those who generate a large amount of data should find it necessary to back up their computers on a weekly or even a daily basis.

In addition, a critical need on today's PCs is data storage space. Sometimes it seems the storage requirements of a PC can never be satisfied. On nearly any PC used for business, study, or even for fun, the amount of software installed can quickly overwhelm even a "jumbo" hard drive. Data used infrequently should be archived to another storage device to save space on the primary storage devices.

This chapter focuses on tape backup drives and removable media disk drives, which increasingly are used to solve the problems of the growing need for data storage space and the need for a fast and efficient way to back up many megabytes of data.

Tape Backup Drives

Any computer book worth reading warns repeatedly that you should back up your system regularly. Backups are necessary because at any time a major problem, or even some minor ones, can corrupt the important information and the programs stored on your computer's hard drive, rendering this information useless. A wide range of problems can damage the data on your hard drive. Here is a list of some of these data-damaging problems:

- Sudden fluctuations in the electricity that powers your computer (*power spikes*) resulting in data damage or corruption.

- Overwriting a file by mistake.

- Mistakenly formatting your hard disk when you meant to format a floppy.

- Hard drive failure resulting in loss of data that has not been backed up. Not only do you have to install a new drive but, because you have no backup, you also must reinstall your software programs, disk-by-disk.

- Catastrophic damage to your computer (storm, flood, lightning strike, fire, theft). A single lightning strike near your office or home can destroy the circuitry of your computer, including your hard drive. Theft of your computer, of course, is equally devastating. A recent, complete backup greatly simplifies the process of setting up a replacement computer.

- Loss of valuable data due to a computer-related virus. One single download could contain a virus that can damage valuable files and even your entire hard drive. With several hundred new viruses appearing each month, no anti-virus software program can keep you entirely safe. A recent backup of non-infected, critical files can help repair even the worst damage.

Backups are also the cure for such common headaches as a full hard drive and the need to transfer data between computers. By backing up data you rarely use, then deleting the original data from your hard drive, you free up the space once occupied by that data. If you later need a particular data file, you can retrieve that file from your backup. Sharing large amounts of data between computers—as when you send data from one city to another, for example—is more easily accomplished by backing up the data to a tape and sending the tape.

Regardless of how important regular backups are, many people avoid making them. A major reason for this lapse is that for many people, backing up their system is tedious work when they have to use their floppy disk drive. When you use your floppy drive, you may have to insert and remove hundreds of disks to back up all of the important programs and data, depending on whether your backup software includes *data compression*, the capability to specially encode backed-up data in less space than it takes to store the same data on your hard drive.

Tape backup drives are the most simple and efficient device for backing up your system. With a tape backup drive installed in your system, you simply insert a tape into the drive, start your backup software, and select the drive and files you want to back up. The backup software copies your selected files onto the tape while you attend to other business. Later, when you need to retrieve some or all of the files on the backup tape, you insert the tape in the drive, start your backup program, and select the files you want to restore. The tape backup drive takes care of the rest of the job.

This section examines the various types of tape backup drives on the market, describing the capacities of different drives as well as the system requirements for installation and use of a tape drive. The following topics are covered in this chapter:

- Common standards for tape backup drives, including QIC-40 and QIC-80 drives
- Common backup tape capacities
- Newer higher-capacity tape drives
- Common tape drive interfaces
- The QIC standards for tape backup drives
- Portable tape drives
- Tape backup software

The Origins of Tape Backup Standards

The evolution of tape backup standards is similar to that of standards for many computer components. Using tape to back up computer data became a common practice long before accepted tape backup standards existed. At first, reel-to-reel systems (somewhat similar to old reel-to-reel audio tape recorders) were used to store data. The most commonly used tape—*quarter-inch*—eventually developed into a de facto standard. But each tape system manufacturer used its own data-encoding specifications for backup tapes. Variations included not only the number of tracks and data density on the tape, but also the interface used to connect the drive to the computer.

In 1972, more than a decade before the introduction of the first IBM-PC, the 3M company introduced the first quarter-inch tape cartridge designed for data storage. The cartridge measured 6×4×5/8 inches. Inside this cartridge, the tape was threaded onto two reels. The tape was moved from one reel to another during the recording or read-back process by a drive belt. Because of the reliability of this tape cartridge, the demand for tape backup systems began to grow, despite the lack of established standards for storing data on these cartridges.

The result of this lack of standardization was that quarter-inch tapes written on one manufacturer's tape backup drive generally could not be read on another manufacturer's quarter-inch tape drive. One problem created by this situation was that the way particular manufacturers encoded data on a tape continued to change. If a particular model of tape drive became disabled and the manufacturer had discontinued that particular drive and no longer used its encoding format, the data stored on tapes written on the disabled drive could be unavailable until the drive had been sent for repairs. In the event the manufacturer could not repair the drive, the data was lost forever.

As with other computer components, such as hard drive interface cards, consumers were the force behind standardization. Consumers clamored for standardized tape drives that could read tapes created on different tape drives manufactured by different companies.

The QIC Standards

In response to this demand for standardization, the tape drive industry formed the Quarter-Inch Cartridge Drive Standards Inc., sometimes simply referred to as the *Quarter-Inch Committee (QIC)*. In 1983–84, the first tape drive based on a QIC standard was shipped: the *QIC-02*, which stored 60M of data encoded in nine data tracks on roughly 300 feet of tape.

As the technology improved, and because the 4×6×5/8-inch size of the first tape cartridges was difficult to adapt to the 5 1/2-inch drive bays in most IBM-compatible PCs, QIC adopted a second standard for tape cartridges roughly the size of an audio cassette. These mini-cartridges measure roughly 3 1/4×2 1/2×3/5 inches.

These two cartridge sizes are currently used in various QIC-standard tape drives. A two-letter code at the end of the QIC standard number designates whether the tape standard is based on the full-sized cartridge or the mini-cartridge. These two-letter codes are shown in the following:

- *DC* in a QIC standard number stands for *data cartridge*, the 4×6×5/8-inch cassette.

- *MC* in a QIC standard number stands for *mini-cartridge*, the 3 1/4×2 1/2×3/5-inch cassette.

The new QIC-5B-DC, for example, is a 5G-capacity tape based on the QIC standard for the full-sized cartridge. The new QIC-5010-MC, which has 13G capacity, is based on the mini-cartridge standard.

Table 18.1 shows the common QIC-standard tape formats and their technical specifications.

Table 18.1 Specifications of QIC-standard Quarter-inch Tape Cassettes and Minicartridges
QIC Minicartridge Tape Standards
DC-2000 QIC Tape Standards (Approximate Dimensions 3 1/4-by-2 1/2-by-3/5)

QIC Standard Number	Capacity (w/o Compression) (1)	Tracks	Data Transfer Rate (Approximate)
QIC-40	40MB/60MB	20	2MB-to-8MB minute
QIC-80	80MB/120MB	28	3MB-to-9MB minute
QIC-100 (obsolete)	20MB/40MB	12 or 24	—
QIC-128	86MB/128MB	32	—
QIC-3010	255MB	40	9MB minute
QIC-3020	500MB	40	9MB minute
QIC-3030	555MB	40	
QIC-3040	840MB (3)	42 or 52	
QIC-3050	750MB	40	
QIC-3060 (inactive)	875MB	38	
QIC-3070	4GB	144	
QIC-3080	1.6GB	50	
QIC-3110	2GB	48	
QIC-5010	13GB	144	

*Tape capacity may vary according to tape length.
**Tape lengths may vary by manufacturer.
***1GB with drives based on 0.315-inch tape cartridge.
****SCSI: Small Computer Systems Interface.

Unlike software whose version numbers (1.0, 1.1, 2.0, 2.1) tell you which version of the software is the most recent, the QIC number designation does not serve as an accurate guide to understanding which QIC-standard tape drives are the latest technology. The designations QIC-100 and QIC-128, for example, were used for tape drives marketed long before today's QIC-40 and QIC-80 drives. Furthermore, the QIC-standard version numbers frequently have no correlation with the capacity of the tape cassettes or mini-cartridges used with a drive bearing a QIC designation. For example, the QIC-40 tapes have a capacity of 60M; the QIC-80 tapes, a capacity of 120M.

QIC-standard backup tapes are magnetic media, primarily ferric oxide, and are recorded in a manner similar to the way data is encoded on your hard drive, using either modified frequency modulation (MFM) or run-length limited (RLL) technologies.

Data Density	Tape Length (2)	Encoding Method	Interface Type
10,000bpi	205 ft. /307.5 ft.	MFM	Floppy or optional adapter card
14,700bpi	205 ft./ 307.5 ft.	MFM	Floppy or optional adapter card
10,000bpi	—	MFM	SCSI (4) or QIC
16,000bpi	—	MFM	SCSI or QIC
22,000bpi	300 ft.	MFM	Floppy or IDE
42,000bpi	400 ft.	MFM	Floppy or IDE
51,000bpi	275 ft.	MFM	SCSI-2 or QIC
41,000bpi	400 ft.	RLL	SCSI-2 or QIC
—	295 ft.	RLL	SCSI-2 or QIC
—	295 ft.	RLL	—
68,000	295 ft.	RLL	SCSI-2 or QIC
60,000	—	RLL	SCSI-2 or QIC
—	—	RLL	SCSI-2 or QIC
—	—	RLL	SCSI-2 or QIC

Table 18.1 Continued
QIC Full-Sized Data Cartridge Standards

DC-300a/DC-600/DC-6000 QIC Tape Standards (Approximate Dimensions 4-by-6-by-5/8)			
QIC Standard Number	Capacity (w/o Compression)	Tracks	Max. Data Transfer Rate (Approximate)
QIC-11 (DC-300)	45MB	9	—
QIC-24	45MB/60MB	9	—
QIC-120	125MB	15	—
QIC-150	150MB/250MB	18	—
QIC-525	320MB/525MB	26	12MB minute
QIC-1000	1GB	30	18MB minute
QIC-1350	1.35GB	30	18MB minute
QIC-2100	2.1GB	30	18MB minute
QIC-2GB	2.0GB	42	18MB minute
QIC-5GB	5GB	44	18MB minute
QIC-5010	13GB	144	18MB minute

(1) Tape capacity may vary according to tape length.
(2) Tape lengths may vary by manufacturer.

Common QIC Tape Backup Types

The most common QIC-standard drives, QIC-40 and QIC-80, are based on mini-cartridges. Millions of drives based on the QIC-40 and QIC-80 standards are currently installed in computer systems. There are several reasons for the success of QIC-40 and QIC-80, not the least of which is that these two standards resulted in the first generation of economically attractive tape drives which stored data in a manner compatible from one manufacturer to another. In other words, QIC-40 and QIC-80 tape drives and tapes are quite affordable, and backups made on one QIC-40 or QIC-80 tape drive can be read in a tape drive built by another manufacturer.

In addition, the compact size of the mini-cartridge used for QIC-40 and QIC-80 tapes has resulted in drives made by numerous manufacturers that fit easily into both 5 1/2-inch half-height drive bays and 3 1/2×1-inch drive bays. Portable tape drives that read and write QIC-80 format tapes are quite common, but QIC-40 drives are near extinction. Unlike a drive that is installed in a computer's drive bay, portable drives can be used to back up any number of computers.

Another reason for the success of QIC-40 and QIC-80 tape drives is that the cost of tapes themselves is considerably lower per megabyte than the cost of a stack of floppy disks that can store the same amount of backup data. For example, a name brand QIC-80 tape

Data Density (1)	Tape Length (2)	Encoding Method	Interface Type
—	450 ft.	MFM	QIC-02
8,000	450 ft. 600 ft.	MFM	SCSI or QIC-02
10,000	600 ft.	MFM	SCSI or QIC-02
10,000bpi	600 ft. 1,000 ft.	MFM	SCSI or QIC-02
16,000bpi	1,000 ft.	MFM	SCSI or SCSI-2
36,000bpi	760 ft.	MFM	SCSI or SCSI-2
51,000bpi	760 ft.	RLL	SCSI-2
68,000bpi	875 ft.	RLL	SCSI-2
40,640bpi	900 ft.	MFM	SCSI-2
96,000bpi	1,200 ft.	RLL	SCSI-2
68,000bpi	—	RLL	SCSI-2

that can hold 250M of data (with data compression) costs between $14 and $25. The street price of 13 boxes (10 per box) name brand 1.44M 3 1/2-inch floppy disks, which hold roughly the same amount of compressed data, is about $90. The same number of generic, bulk floppy disks, which many people are hesitant to rely upon for backing up important data, costs nearly $50. Of course, the price difference doesn't include the valuable time spent swapping those disks or the relative cost of storing them.

Most of the QIC-80 drives on the market today have one major shortcoming—the use of the floppy drive interface, especially on an older PC, makes the tape drive performance extremely slow. Data transfers occur at roughly the same slow rate as when data is written to a floppy disk. Controllers that support only the Double Density (DD) floppy drives can only write data at 250Kbps, which is fewer than 2M (millions of bytes) per minute. A floppy controller that supports HD (High Density) drives can operate at 300 or 500Kbps, which is up to 3.75M per minute. The latest ED (Extra-high Density) controllers can operate at rates of up to 7.5M per minute, which is quite good (see Table 18.2). Note that these rates are the maximum raw throughput of the controller, and due to overhead you will never achieve these actual figures in practice.

Table 18.2 Floppy Controller Raw Data Transfer Rates

Controller Type	DD	HD	HD	ED
Transfer rate in kilobits per second (Kbps)	250.00	300.00	500.00	1,000.00
Transfer rate in kilobytes per second (K/sec)	31.25	37.50	62.50	125.00
Transfer rate in megabytes per second (M/sec)	1.88	2.25	3.75	7.50

Backup tapes, like floppy disks and hard drives, must be formatted before use. And one aspect of using a QIC-80 tape drive that has not been improved is the time it takes to format a tape. Formatting a 125M length QIC-80 tape can take more than three hours. It's almost impossible to find an unformatted tape because of these long format times. The industry has been preformatting tapes since 1994. Other tape formats have the ability to format on-the-fly, which means they don't require preformatted tapes.

Data is stored on QIC-40 and QIC-80 tapes in MFM format, the format used on floppy disks (and older hard drives). Another similarity between formatting a backup tape, floppy disks, or a hard drive is that the formatting process creates a record-keeping system. The record-keeping system used on QIC-40 and QIC-80 tapes is similar to that on a hard drive or floppy disk.

The QIC standard calls for a file allocation table (FAT) that keeps track of where data is stored on the tape and keeps bad sectors from being used for data storage. A QIC-40 tape is divided into 20 tracks, with each track divided into 68 segments of 29 sectors each. Each sector stores 1K (1,024 bytes). This record-keeping system and the error-correcting system that ensures reliably stored backup data use a total of 30 percent or more of each QIC-40 tape.

Despite the slow backup speeds of tape backup drives on some computers and the time it takes to format tapes, the ease of using a backup tape drive makes it easy to understand the popularity of QIC-40 and QIC-80 tape drives. And that popularity has its benefits. Prices of QIC-80 tape drives—the smallest-capacity tape drives anyone should consider—have plunged in recent years. Brand-name QIC-80 tape backup drives often cost less than $150; sometimes you can buy them for as little as $100 by shopping mail order.

QIC-40 Drives. The first tape backup drives to gain wide acceptance were based on the QIC-40 standard, adopted in 1986. Most early QIC-40 tape drives were built to fit a 5 1/2-inch drive bay. The QIC-40-standard drives use an internal power connector and send and receive data through a cable linked to the floppy controller generally. The first QIC-40 tapes, which had a *native capacity* of 40M (they could hold 40M of data without data compression), were soon followed by QIC-40 tapes capable of holding 60M without data compression.

One disadvantage of the first QIC-40 tape drives was that because a spare connector had to be used on the floppy drive cable, only one floppy drive could be used on a system in which a tape drive was installed. But with the use of a special cable, more recent QIC-40 drives are installed easily on systems with two floppy drives.

Although a major goal of the QIC organization was to achieve compatibility between tape backup systems, a tape created on one brand of tape drive could not necessarily be read in another brand. Manufacturers still clung to their individual arrangements for the physical placement of data on the tape. The goal of compatibility between tape backup systems became more of a reality with the introduction of QIC-80 drives.

QIC-80 Drives. The QIC-80 tape backup drive is the most popular tape backup drive on the market and the minimum any buyer should consider. QIC-80 tape drives generally are built to fit 3 1/2×1-inch bays, although they usually include a frame and faceplate that enable them to be used in a larger 5 1/2-inch bay. Like the QIC-40 drives, QIC-80 tape systems use an internal power connector. The data connection for a QIC-80 tape backup can be the same type of floppy disk controller connection used for QIC-40 drives, or a special high-speed interface installed in an available expansion slot on the motherboard. The use of a high-speed interface card greatly can increase the data transfer rate and decrease the amount of time needed for a backup.

Generally, a tape created on one brand of QIC-80 tape drive can be read and written to by another manufacturer's drive. This improved compatibility is due in large measure to the QIC-80 standard itself, which specifies not only the type of record-keeping system for each tape, but also the logical data structure of the tape. QIC-80-standard drives can read, but not write, QIC-40 tapes.

Portable Tape Drives. The *portable tape drive* is one of the most popular tape drive configurations because portables can be moved easily from system to system—desktops, laptops, a single system, or multisystem installations. Portable tape drives are particularly useful to people who use laptops (in which an internal tape backup drive will not fit) and those who want to back up a number of systems on a single tape backup drive. Portable tape drives are good also for people who want to use a tape backup drive for their desktop system but whose system has no available drive bay, as is often the case with small profile, or slimline, desktop systems.

Portable tape drives can meet so many needs because these drives are self-contained. The drive itself is contained in a rectangular box. The unit connects to the computer's parallel port and is powered by a transformer that plugs into a common AC socket.

To set up a portable tape drive, you simply plug the transformer cord into the system unit and an AC socket, connect the data cable to the computer's parallel port, and run the backup software. One limitation of portable units is availability of compatible backup software. Although portable tape drive manufacturers include software that operates the drive, some popular third-party backup software cannot be used with portable drives.

The most popular portable tape drives are available in QIC-80 standards. These models can achieve a data transfer rate of 3M to 6M per minute.

Newer High-Capacity QIC-Standard Drives

Using a QIC-80 tape drive to back up a network server's 4G drive or other large hard drive packed with data can be as frustrating as swapping floppies during a backup on a system with a more common 200M–500M drive. To back up a 4G network server hard drive with a QIC-40 tape drive without using data compression, for example, you need about 64 tapes. With data compression, the number of tapes drops to 32—but making the backup takes longer.

The solution to this tape-swapping problem is to use a larger-capacity tape drive system. QIC has established a number of standards for higher-capacity tape drive systems ranging from 86M to 13G. Generally, these larger-capacity systems pack data more densely on the tape, using as many as 144 tracks to pack 60,000 bits per inch (bpi) or more onto the tape (compared to the QIC-40's 20 tracks and 10,000 bpi). To achieve these higher capacities, QIC-standards call for tape media with a higher coercivity level of 1,300 oersted or more (compared to QIC-40 and QIC-80 tape media, which has a coercivity level of 550 oersted). High-capacity tapes are also longer. QIC-5010 tapes, for example, are 1,200 feet long (compared to QIC-40 and QIC-80 tapes, both of which are roughly 300 feet long).

> **Note**
>
> Just as the higher coercivity level of 1.44M floppy disks enables an HD drive to write more densely packed tracks than is possible with 720K floppy disks, higher-coercivity tape media enables higher densities as well.

Although tape systems based on the mini-cartridge dominate the market for lower-capacity tape drives (the QIC-40 60M and QIC-80 120M systems), high-capacity tape backup systems are based on both mini-cartridge-sized tapes and full-sized data cartridge tapes. For example, the QIC-525 standard, which has a capacity of 525M (without data compression), is based on the full-sized (4×6×5/8) cartridge. The QIC-5010 standard is based on a mini-cartridge (3 1/4×2 1/2×3/5).

QIC-Tape Compatibility

Although QIC-standard drives are based on the standard mini-cartridge and the full-sized data cartridge, it would be a mistake to assume that tapes based on the same cartridge standard are always compatible. For example, QIC-5010-standard tapes are incompatible with QIC-40 and QIC-80 tape backup systems, although both standards are based on the mini-cartridge. Similarly, QIC-525-standard tapes are incompatible with earlier standards based on the full-sized data cartridge. The lack of compatibility between tapes based on the same sized cartridge is due to differences in tape drive mechanisms, as well as the coercivity differences between tape standards. Table 18.3 shows the compatibility of common QIC-standard backup tapes.

Tape compatibility is an important issue to consider when you choose a tape backup system. For example, as you can see from Table 18.3, the 4G QIC-3070-standard drive can read only its own tapes and those that conform to the QIC-3030 standard. If you have many QIC-80 tapes containing data that you must be able to continue to access, a better choice might be a drive based on the 2G QIC-3010 standard. The QIC-3010 can read QIC-40 and QIC-80 tapes. This chapter's "Choosing a Tape Backup Type" section covers similar issues to be considered when you purchase a new tape backup drive.

Table 18.3 QIC-Tape-Standard Compatibility

QIC Mini-Cartridge Standard	Compatibility
QIC-40	N/A
QIC-80	QIC-40 (read-only)
QIC-100	N/A
QIC-128	QIC-100 (read-only)
QIC-3010	QIC-40 and QIC-80 (read only)
QIC-3030	QIC-3010 (read-only)
QIC-3070	QIC-3030 (read-only)

QIC Full-Sized Cartridge Standard	Compatibility
QIC-24	N/A
QIC-120	QIC-24 (read-only)
QIC-150	QIC-24 and QIC-120 (read-only)
QIC-525	QIC-24, QIC-120, and QIC-150 (read-only)
QIC-1000	QIC-120, QIC-150, and QIC-525 (read-only)
QIC-1350	QIC-525 and QIC-1000 (read-only)
QIC-2G	QIC-120, QIC-150, QIC-525, and QIC-1000 (read-only)
QIC-2100	QIC-525 and QIC-1000 (read-only)
QIC-5G	QIC-24, QIC-120, QIC-150, QIC-525, and QIC-1000 (read-only)
QIC-5010	QIC-150, QIC-525, and QIC-1000 (read-only)

Other High-Capacity Tape Drive Standards

Although ferric oxide QIC-standard tapes continue to be popular, two other types of tape backup systems are becoming increasingly popular for backing up networks and other systems with large amounts of data: 4mm digital audio tape (DAT) and 8mm videotape.

Sony, which introduced DAT tape, licenses DAT tape technologies to other manufacturers, in effect setting the standard for drives and tapes manufactured by those companies. There is only one company, Exabyte, which manufacturers 8mm tape drive assemblies. As a result, you're assured compatibility. Table 18.4 shows the basic specifications of the DAT and 8mm technology tapes.

Helical scan recording is similar in many ways to the way video images are recorded to videotape. As with QIC-standard tape drives, DAT and 8mm tapes move past the recording heads, which are mounted on a drum. These read/write heads rotate at a slight angle to the tape, writing a section of a *helix*, or spiral. The tape drive mechanism wraps the tape about halfway around the read/write heads, causing the heads to touch the tape at an angle. With helical scan technology, the entire surface of the tape is used to record data, unlike other technologies in which data tracks are separated by areas of unrecorded tape. This use of the entire tape surface enables helical scan backup drives to pack a much greater amount of data on a particular length of tape.

Table 18.4 DAT and 8mm Tape Specifications

Tape Standard	Capacity (w/o Compression)	Data Density	Tracks (Approximate)
DAT tape (4mm metal particle)	2G/4G	114Mbit	1,869
8mm video tape	14G	NA	NA

DDS: Digital data storage

The DAT Tape Drive Standard. *DAT (Digital Audio Tape)* is a tape standard that has primarily been developed and marketed by Hewlett-Packard. HP chairs the DDS (Digital Data Storage) Manufacturers Group and has led the development of the DDS standards.

The technology behind digital audio tape is similar in many ways to the techniques used to record music and encode it on musical compact discs (CDs). Data is not recorded on the tape in the MFM or RLL formats used by QIC-standard drives; rather, bits of data received by the tape drive are assigned numerical values, or digits. Then these digits are translated into a stream of electronic pulses that are placed in the tape. Later, when information is being restored to a computer system from the tape, the DAT tape drive translates these digits back into binary bits that can be stored on the computer.

DAT tapes can store up to 12G of uncompressed data, or about 24G compressed. Two types of data formats—DDS and DataDAT—are used for DAT tapes; however, DDS type drives are by far the most common. DDS drives are available in three types:

- *DDS-1 drives* store 2G of uncompressed data (4G compressed).
- *DDS-2 drives* can store 4G of data uncompressed (up to 8G with compression).
- *DDS-3 drives* have a native 12M capacity, or 24M compressed.

The new DDS-3 drives offer full read and write compatibility with all DDS-2 and DDS-1 drives. DDS-3 offers three times the capacity and double the data-transfer rates of current DDS-2 drives. DDS-3 drives are designed to provide reliable high-performance backup for medium to large networks at a substantially lower price than 8mm or DLT (digital linear tape) products with similar capacities.

The new HP DDS-3 drive (Model C1537A) has a native capacity of 12G with a transfer rate of 1M/sec. The DDS-3 drive typically can store 24G on a single 125m tape at a rate of 2M/sec using built-in hardware data compression. The new HP DDS-3 drive incorporates several innovations, including the use of a *Partial Response Maximum Likelihood* (*PRML*) data-channel detection scheme that enables the tape's read head to differentiate between bits of data picked up simultaneously.

A typical DDS-2 drive costs about $750, while DDS-3 drives are right around $1,000. DDS technology has an excellent track record and a reputation for reliability that has made it the technology of choice for workstation, end user, and network backup.

Tape Length	Recording Technology	Encoding Format	Interface
195 ft./300 ft.	Helical Scan DataDAT	DDS*	SCSI
120m	Helical Scan		

The 8mm Tape Drive. A single manufacturer, Exabyte, offers tape backup drives that take advantage of 8mm videotape cartridges. These drives are offered in several capacities—1.5G (3G with hardware data compression), 5G (10G with hardware compression), 7G (14G with hardware compression), and 20G (40G with hardware compression)

Although these drives use 8mm videotapes, video technology is not used in the process of recording computer data to these drives. Rather, Exabyte developed its own technology for encoding data on the tapes. The helical scan method is used to record data to the tape.

The 6M/sec data throughput rate of the Exabyte 8mm tape backup drive, compared with the 10M per minute throughput of the DAT drive, makes the 8mm tape drive a more attractive choice. The extraordinary speed and huge capacity of these 8mm tape drives makes them extremely attractive for backing up network servers and for backing up workstations from the server.

DLT (Digital Linear Tape). Over the last year, a new tape technology has taken off because of its capability to provide high-capacity, high-speed, and highly reliable backup. *Digital Linear Tape (DLT)* is now considered one of the hottest products in the high-end tape-backup market. DLT started as a proprietary technology belonging to Digital Equipment Corporation. The technology has been on the market since 1991, but in December 1994, Quantum purchased Digital's DLT and magneto-resistive drive technology.

DLT has a capacity of up to 35–70G compressed, and a data-transfer rate of 5–10M/sec or more. This is approximately the same speed as a high speed 8mm drive; however, 8mm has a slight performance advantage in real-world tests.

DLT segments the tape into parallel horizontal tracks and records data by streaming the tape across a single stationary head at 100–150 inches/sec during read/write operations. This is a dramatic contrast to traditional helical-scan technology, in which the data is recorded in diagonal stripes with a rotating drum head while a much slower tape motor draws the media past the recording head.

The result is a very durable drive and a robust medium. DLT drive heads have a minimum life expectancy of 15,000 hours under worst-case temperature and humidity conditions, and the tapes have a life expectancy of 500,000 passes. DLT drives are designed primarily for network server backup, and cost $6,000 to $8,000 or more depending on capacity. With automatic tape changers, DLT drives can be left unattended for many network backup tasks.

Travan Cartridge Tape. 3M has created an entirely new tape cartridge standard based on the QIC format called *Travan*. Tape drives based on Travan technology have had a significant impact on the tape market for PCs and workstations, and drives based on this technology should dominate this market over the next several years.

The Travan platform features a unique drive/mini-cartridge interface that is patented by 3M. The Travan platform fits in a 3 1/2-inch form factor, making it easy to install in a variety of systems and enclosures. Travan drives can accept current QIC and Travan mini-cartridges—a critical need for users, given the installed base of more than 200 million QIC-compatible mini-cartridges worldwide.

Travan cartridges contain 750 feet of .315-inch wide tape. There are currently several different levels of Travan cartridges and drives available called TR-1 through TR-4, each based on a particular QIC standard:

- The TR-1 mini-cartridge provides users with 400M of uncompressed storage, more than doubling the capacity of the industry's top-selling QIC-80 mini-cartridge (125M).

- The TR-2 mini-cartridge, a new modified QIC-3010 drive/cartridge, stores 800M of uncompressed data, which is significantly more than the 340M available in QIC-3010 form.

- The capacity of the TR-3 mini-cartridge, a new modified 3020 drive/cartridge, is 1.6G of uncompressed data (up from 670M in QIC-3020 form).

- The newest Travan cartridge, TR-4, stores 4G of uncompressed data! The Travan migration path for the new drive and mini-cartridge products should exceed 15G of uncompressed storage capacity by 1997, according to 3M.

Notice that virtually all Travan drives offer 2:1 data compression, which doubles the uncompressed native capacity. This means that a Travan TR-4 drive can store up to 8G on a single cartridge! A typical TR-4 based drive, such as those from Hewlett-Packard's Colorado Memory Systems Division, sell for under $400. Because Travan tapes sell in the $40 price range and are available through any of 3M's worldwide network of distributors and resellers, the low cost and high availability of these drives and cartridges make Travan one of the best backup solutions possible for most individuals.

The TR-1 through TR-3 drives usually interface to the system via the floppy controller or parallel port. I recommend using an EPP or ECP parallel port for ease of use and performance. The higher end TR-4 drives often use a SCSI-2 interface, which offers greater performance than either floppy or parallel port interfaces. A typical TR-4 system such as the HP T4000 drive operates at 514K/sec, which is approximately four times faster than floppy-interface systems, providing backup speeds up to 31M per minute native and up to 62M per minute with 2:1 data compression. Using a typical Pentium system, users can back up a 1G hard drive in about 30 minutes. If you are using the floppy controller or parallel port, you can expect backup times about four times longer or about two hours for a 1G drive.

Storage industry leaders such as 3M, HP/Colorado, Iomega, Conner Peripherals, Exabyte, Tandberg Data, AIWA, Pertec Memories, TEAC, Rexon, and Sony offer Travan drives and support future development of Travan drive and recording formats.

Choosing a Tape Backup Drive

Choosing a tape backup drive can be a simple job if you need to back up a single standalone system with a 500M (or smaller) hard drive. The decision becomes more complex if the system has a larger hard drive, or if you must back up not only a desktop system but also a laptop. Choosing a backup tape drive type can be an even more complex program if you must back up a network server's 4G hard drive and perhaps even back up the workstations from the server. As you ponder which backup tape drive type you should choose, consider the following factors:

- The amount of data you must back up
- The data throughput you need
- The tape standard that is best for your needs
- The cost of the drive and tapes
- The capabilities and compatibility of the included driver and backup software

By balancing the considerations of price, capacity, throughput, compatibility, and tape standard, you can find a tape drive that best meets your needs.

> **Note**
>
> When purchasing a tape backup drive, take the time to look through magazines where dealers or distributors advertise. Several publications specialize in PCs and carry advertising from many hardware and software distributors. I recommend publications such as the *Computer Reseller News*, *Computer Hotline*, *The Processor*, and *Computer Shopper*. These publications cater to people or companies willing to go around the middlemen and buy direct. By reading such publications, you can get an excellent idea of the drives available and the price you can expect to pay.
>
> While reading about drive capabilities and prices, don't neglect to read reviews of the software included with each drive. Verify that the software capabilities match your expectations and needs. This is especially important if you intend to use the drive on a non-Windows 95 system, because most backup software is tailored for Windows 95 systems.

Capacity. The first rule for choosing a tape backup drive is to buy a drive whose capacity is large enough for your needs, now and for the foreseeable future. The ideal is to buy a drive with enough capacity that you can start your backup software, insert a blank tape in the drive, walk away from the system (or go about other work), and find the backup completed when you return. You can safely store the tape and resume working.

Given that ideal, an internal QIC-80 drive might be just the ticket if you need to back up a single system with a hard drive of 250M or less. If you need to back up several systems, including laptops, with hard drives of 250M or less, a portable QIC-80 drive might be the solution.

If you must back up a large network server hard drive, relying on a QIC-80 tape drive with its 125M capacity (250M with software data compression) is a bad idea. A better choice would be one of the larger-capacity tape backup drive systems detailed earlier in "Other High-Capacity Tape Drive Standards."

Lately, no matter what the capacity needs for a workstation, I have been recommending either DAT drives or the newer Travan drives. These are simply the most cost-effective, highest-performing drives on the market today. The tapes are preformatted, which saves a lot of time, and can store up to 8G on a single Travan TR-4 tape or 24G on a single DDS-3 DAT tape.

You should always make sure that your tape backup media supports a capacity larger than your largest single drive or partition. This will make automated backups possible because you won't have to change a tape in the middle of a backup. Because the DAT drives normally interface via SCSI, you can use a parallel port SCSI adapter to connect the drive to a system's parallel port as well as an internal SCSI adapter. Of course, the internal adapter will perform better, but a portable DAT drive connected via the parallel port can be used to back up many different systems. The DAT media is also cheaper than any other media.

Tape Standards. The next most important consideration, after adequate capacity, is choosing a drive whose tapes meet a standard that is useful to you. For example, if you must be able to restore backup data using any of a number of different tape backup drives, you should ensure that all these drives can at least read the tapes. For this reason, if you have several systems to work with, you should choose a tape standard that will work in them all.

There is no quick, simple answer as to which standard is the best. Many people stick with QIC-standard drives because QIC created the first standards and continues to develop new standards for large-capacity tape backups. But if you need a large-capacity backup tape system, DAT or 8mm may be the correct choice.

If you need backward compatibility with tapes or tape drives you already have, you will need to buy drives that are the same standard or a higher compatible standard. For example, if you need a large-capacity tape drive that is backwardly compatible with your QIC-80 tapes, you should consider the 2G-capacity QIC-3010, which reads QIC-40 and QIC-80 tapes. If, on the other hand, you don't have to worry about data already stored on old tapes, the important considerations may be capacity and performance. Therefore, DAT or 8mm drives may be the best choice.

> **Tip**
>
> It is important that you make a choice you can live with. If you manage a large installation of computers, mixing QIC, Travan, DAT, and 8mm drives among systems is seldom a good idea.

Software Compatibility. Equally important to your consideration is the software required to operate each drive. Currently, most drives come with software that runs under the Windows 95 operating system. However, finding software that runs equally well under Windows NT or UNIX might be difficult.

Most operating systems have their own software for backing up data to a tape drive. If you intend to use this software, you should verify that the drive you purchase is supported by each piece of software on each system that you intend to use the drive with.

> **Note**
>
> For more information on tape drive software, see "Tape Drive Backup Software" later in this chapter.

Data Throughput. You should consider the 8mm or DLT drives if performance is more important to you than price or compatibility. These drives offer huge capacity and tremendous data throughput—as high as 6M/sec. Large-capacity drives based on newer QIC-standards are capable of 18M per minute throughput. DAT tape drives offer throughput of 10M per minute.

The low end of the tape backup drive performance spectrum is older QIC-80 standard drives. When linked to a floppy controller, these drives achieve 3M to 4M per minute throughput. Even with a dedicated interface card purchased at added cost, QIC-80 drives are lucky to achieve their advertised throughput of 9M per minute. Portable QIC-80 drives are advertised at 3M to 8M per minute, but 2M or 3M a minute is a more realistic figure.

The Cost of the Drive and Tapes. The price of tape drives varies considerably based upon where you buy, so it pays to shop enthusiastically for price after you have settled on the type of drive you want to buy.

The cost of backup tapes also varies widely, depending on where you buy. The same name-brand 12G DAT tape that costs as much as $14 from one vendor can cost $12 from another. The cost of a formatted name-brand QIC-80 (120M) tape can range from $15 to $26, depending on where you buy it. Because many computer retailers and direct channel vendors offer lower prices when you buy three or more tapes at a time, it pays to shop for price and buy the largest quantity of tapes you expect to need.

> **Tip**
>
> One point worth remembering when you evaluate whether to buy a tape drive is that the cost of the tapes and drive, taken as a whole, is nowhere near as high as the costs (in terms of frustration and lost productivity) of a single data-damaging hard drive problem. Considering that most people are more likely to back up their system if they have a tape drive installed than if they must use floppy disks for the backup, the cost of a drive and tapes is quite small, even on a stand-alone PC used mostly for fun.

Tape Drive Installation Issues

Each of the tape drive standards covered in this chapter provides a range of options for installation. These options include both internal and external installation. Whether to choose an internal or external drive, and which external drive to choose if that appears to be the best choice for you, is not always a cut-and-dried issue. If you must back up a single computer with a relatively small hard drive (500M or less), an internal QIC-80 drive might be your best choice. If you have to back up several computers with 500M hard drives, or if you must be able to share data between several computers, you might be able to make do with a QIC-80 portable. If your backup needs are not that simple, however, here are some additional considerations:

- If your computer has a large hard drive and you back up often, or if you administer a large number of systems and want to minimize the amount of work you must do and the number of tapes you have to store for each computer, installing large-capacity QIC, DAT, or 8mm tape drives in each computer might be what you need to do.

- If your best choice is a large capacity QIC, DAT, or 8mm tape drive and almost all the computers you administer have an available drive bay, you might choose a portable DAT or 8mm tape system, which can be moved from system-to-system.

> **Caution**
>
> Steer away from nonstandard tape backup drives. For example, some drives may not conform to QIC, DAT, or Exabyte standards. Because Exabyte is the only manufacturer of 8mm tape backup drives, you can be confident that tapes made on this manufacturer's drives can be read on their drives. I would avoid drives based on VHS videotape, for example, because these types of drives are not a true standard and are not very well-supported.

The following sections cover some important installation issues for internally- and externally-mounted drives.

Internal Installation. Virtually all internal tape backup drives available today are designed to be installed in a half-height drive bay. Many are designed to be installed in either half-height drive bays or the smaller drive bays generally used for 3 1/2-inch floppy drives. Drives that can be installed in 3 1/2-inch floppy drive bays generally are shipped in a *cage*, or frame, that enables them to be installed in a 5 1/4-inch bay. To install the drive in a 3 1/2-inch bay, you remove the cage and the 5 1/4-inch bay faceplate. Most tape drives are between about 5 and 9 inches deep; they require approximately 5–9 inches of clearance inside the system case. To mount tape drives inside the system, use the same rails or cage apparatus used for floppy drives, hard drives, and devices such as CD-ROM drives.

> **Note**
>
> Remember that the drive bay you select needs to have access to the outside of the machine!

> **Note**
>
> Half-height drive bays measure roughly 1.7 inches high by 5.9 inches wide. The smaller drive bays measure 1×4 inches.

Internal tape drives require a spare power connector, usually the larger connector used for hard drives, although some may require the smaller power connector common to 3 1/2-inch floppy drives. If a power connector is not available inside your system, you can buy a power splitter from a computer store or cable supply vendor. A *power splitter* looks like the letter Y and acts like an extension cord. You unplug the power connector from a device (such as a floppy drive) that's already installed. Then plug the bottom point of the Y into that power connector. The two arms of the Y then provide you with two power connectors.

> **Note**
>
> More information about power connections for drives is available in Chapter 17, "CD-ROM Drives."

Internal tape drives also require an interface to the system. QIC-40 and QIC-80 drives most often connect to the system through the floppy controller. On a system with only one floppy drive, you connect the tape drive to an unused connector on the floppy disk data cable. On systems with two floppy disk drives, you use a special cable linked to the floppy disk data cable—in effect, a splitter cable.

Internal drives other than QIC-40s and QIC-80s usually require a special adapter card, or they may link to a card already installed in your system. This card is usually one of the following: a QIC-standard adapter card, a Small Computer Systems Interface (SCSI) adapter, a SCSI-2 adapter card, or an Integrated Drive Electronics (IDE) card. When purchasing a drive, you must determine which interface you need; make sure that the drive kit includes the adapter card you need or that you purchase the correct card.

External Installation. If you want to move an external tape drive from computer to computer, you must install an adapter card in each system on which you want to use the tape drive. Portable tape backup drives such as the DAT portables have a SCSI-to-parallel port converter that uses the computer's parallel port connector. Adapter cards designed for use with external tape drives have a different connector, depending on the interface used, that is accessible from the back panel of the system unit. These cards are generally QIC-standard, SCSI, SCSI-2, or IDE.

When you buy an external tape backup drive that requires an adapter, you must ensure either that the drive includes the necessary adapter card or that you purchase the card at the same time you purchase the drive. In addition, if you plan to use the external tape drive to back up a number of systems, you must buy a card for each system on which you plan to use the drive.

Power is supplied to external units by a transformer that plugs into an ordinary 120v AC wall socket. Generally, the transformer connects to the external tape drive with a small connector. When you choose an external tape drive, be sure you have enough AC power sockets available for your computer, its peripherals, and the tape drive.

Tape Drive Backup Software

The most important decision you can make after you choose the tape standard and capacity of your backup tape drive is the backup software you will use with it. Most tape drives are shipped with backup software that generally is adequate for your basic backup needs.

Often, however, third-party software compatible with the drive you have chosen gives you greater flexibility and functionality. For example, some tape drives may be shipped with only DOS-based software. If you want to use one of these drives from within Windows, or on a system running OS/2 or UNIX, you may need to purchase third-party backup software. And if you will be backing up network workstations from a server, you must make sure that the drive is shipped with software capable of performing this function; otherwise, you will need to acquire third-party software.

One important issue with backup software is *data compression*, special programming that stores data on the backup tape in less space than is needed on the original source disk that is provided with most backup software. Some companies produce backup software that is well-known for especially efficient data compression. In other words, backup software produced by these companies does a better job of compressing large data files into a small amount of space.

> **Note**
>
> The backup software built into Windows 95 supports a variety of QIC 40, 80, and 3010 tape drives that are connected via the floppy controller card, as well as the Colorado Memory Systems QIC 40, 80, and 3010 drives attached via the parallel port. Unfortunately, the Windows 95 backup does *not* support the majority of tape drives currently on the market! For example, SCSI tape drives of any kind are not supported, and neither are the newer QIC-type drives such as 3020 or Travan. Fortunately, many superior backup programs are available from aftermarket sources. Most of the time, you will get this software with the drive itself. Check with your tape drive manufacturer to verify Windows 95 support.

You may want to take the time to read reviews on backup software in one of the many monthly computer magazines, such as *PC Magazine, Windows Magazine,* or *BYTE Magazine*. The reviews can help you determine which backup software does the best job of compressing data; they also provide information on how quickly backup software programs perform a typical backup. The speed of the backup software and its data-compression capabilities are important considerations. Also of great importance is whether the software is easy to use. If your backup software makes backing up more difficult than it has to be, chances are you won't back up as often as you should.

> **Tip**
>
> Some of the more recent software for tape drives include a "Disaster Recovery" feature. This feature creates a boot disk (floppy) that can be used to quickly reformat a drive and install a basic Windows 95 platform for use with the drive. Look for this feature when considering your purchase decision.

Bundled Software. Before you buy a backup tape drive, you should always check whether the drive includes software that will meet your needs and, if it doesn't, be sure to buy third-party software that does the job. Generally, the software bundled with most tape backup drives will do the job for you—provided that you don't plan to place great demands on the tape drive.

The software included with a QIC-80 drive, for example, generally cannot be used to back up network workstations from the server. If you want to use a QIC-80 drive for this task, you may need to buy special software compatible with your network and the tape backup drive. If you use Windows, Windows NT, OS/2, or UNIX, your backup software must be compatible with your operating system as well as the drive, and you must determine whether the software shipped with the drive will do the job for you.

Third-Party Software. A large number of companies manufacture backup software designed for different types of tape drives and different uses. For example, many manufacturers design their backup software to be compatible with most networks. Others specialize in DOS and Windows backup software. Some specialize in OS/2 software. Others are well-known among those whose computers run in UNIX. You may need to ask a trusted retailer or call the software company itself to determine whether a particular type of software is compatible not only with the tape drive you have chosen, but also with your network and operating environment.

Often, third-party software is easier to use than the software designed by a tape manufacturer. The tape manufacturer's software may have an unfamiliar interface or its commands may seem cryptic to you, even if you have used backup software for years. It is not uncommon for tape manufacturers to include inadequate or even incomplete documentation for the backup software included with the drive, although this is generally the case only with lower-cost models. In such a case, you may be able to solve the problem by purchasing third-party software.

Third-party software often does a better job of data compression than the software designed by a tape manufacturer. In addition, third-party software often includes capabilities not included with the software bundled with many drives. Some of the capabilities you might want to look for include the following:

- *Unattended backup scheduling*. Enables you to schedule a backup for a time when you won't need to use your computer.
- *Macro capability*. Use when selecting options and the files to back up.
- *A quick tape-erase capability*. Use when erasing the entire contents of a tape.
- *Partial tape-erase capability*. Use when erasing only part of a tape.
- *Tape unerase capability*. Use when recovering erased data.
- *Password-protect capability*. Enables you to protect backup data from access by unauthorized persons.

You can find backup software manufacturers by reading some of the many monthly computer magazines, paying particular attention to their usability reviews. Generally, if a backup software product gets good reviews, works on a system configuration such as yours, and has the features you need, it is worth the price you pay.

Removable Storage Drives

The reason for the shortage of storage space on today's PCs is easy enough to understand. Just take a look at the sheer number and size of the files stored in the two main directories used by Windows (usually C:\WINDOWS and C:\WINDOWS\SYSTEM). The amount of disk space used by the files in those two directories alone can quickly balloon to 80M or more after you also install a few Windows applications. The reason is simple: Nearly all Windows applications place files in one of the Windows directories that the application will use later. These files include those with extensions such as DLL, 386, VBX, DRV, TTF, and many others. Similarly, Windows NT, OS/2, and UNIX, as well as the software applications that run in these operating systems, can require enormous amounts of storage space.

The remainder of this chapter focuses on some of the more advanced data storage options on the market: removable media large-capacity storage drives. Some removable media drives use media as small as a 3 1/2-inch floppy disk, while others use media about the size of a 5 1/4-inch floppy.

These drives, whose capacities range from 35M to 1G or more, offer fairly speedy performance, the capability to store data or less frequently used programs on a removable disk, and the capability to easily transport huge data files—*Computer Aided Drawing (CAD)* files and graphics files, for example—from one computer to another. Or, you can use a removable media disk to remove sensitive data from your office so that you can lock it safely away from prying eyes.

> **Note**
>
> Removable media drives can also be used to back up critical data from a hard drive. However, the higher price of the media itself (disks or cartridges) makes this use somewhat prohibitive.

> **Tip**
>
> There are literally dozens of removable storage devices currently on the market. Be sure to compare your chosen solution against the competition before making a final purchase. Be especially wary of missing statistics in press releases and product packaging—manufacturers are apt to omit a specification if their drive doesn't measure up to the competition.

See Table 18.5 for a direct comparison of the most popular removable drive technologies.

Types of Removable Media Drives

There are two commonly used types of removable media drives: magnetic media and optical media, also called *magneto-optical media*. Magnetic media drives use much the same technology used on a floppy disk or hard drive to encode data for storage.

Magneto-optical media drives encode information on disk by using newer technology, which is a combination of traditional magnetic and laser technologies.

Magnetic media drives are considerably faster than magneto-optical drives and offer similar capacities. The Syquest magnetic media drives, for example, offer 14ms average access times, compared to the 30ms (or slower) access times of magneto-optical drives. Magneto-optical drives can be more than twice as expensive as magnetic media drives. If you have a great deal of data to store, however, the comparative cost of using a magneto-optical drive drops because magneto-optical media cartridges are considerably less expensive than magnetic media. For example, 10 270M Syquest cartridges can cost roughly $80 each, and 150M Bernoulli cartridges can cost about $90 apiece. The 128M magneto-optical cartridges can cost as little as $25 apiece.

There are also several connection options for the leading removable drives. Although SCSI has been, and continues to be, a popular solution, many drives today connect to the computer's parallel port. This option allows one drive to be easily shared between several different computers. Of course, internal SCSI and IDE solutions remain just as popular for the single machine installation.

> **Note**
>
> Connection or installation of removable media drives is very similar to connecting and installing other internal and external peripherals.
>
> The installation of external parallel port drives is generally straightforward, requiring a special cable that comes with the drive and installation of special software drivers. See the instructions that come with each drive for the specifics of its installation.

The following sections provide information on magnetic media and magneto-optical drive types.

Magnetic Media Drives

A small group of companies dominate the market for magnetic removable media drives. One company, Iomega, always tops the list because it developed the first popular large-capacity removable magnetic media drives, and because its disk cartridges are known as the most rugged in the industry. Two other leading names in removable magnetic media drives are Syquest and 3M.

Removable magnetic media drives are usually floppy or hard disk based. For example, the popular Zip drive is merely a 3 1/2-inch version of the original Bernoulli drive made by Iomega. The new 3M LS-120 drive stores 120M on a disk that looks exactly like a 1.44M floppy!

Both the Bernoulli and Syquest designs are their own de facto standard. Other manufacturers market drives based on the Bernoulli and Syquest designs (and some actually manufactured by Bernoulli or Syquest). For example, the Jaz drive from Iomega uses a hard disk cartridge similar to the Syquest. Generally these manufacturers' drives are somewhat less expensive than the Bernoulli and Syquest models. If you are considering one of these compatible drives, however, make sure that the drive you are buying has the same performance characteristics (average access speed, and so on) as the original, and that the drive manufacturer offers the same warranty as the original (Bernoulli, three years; Syquest/SyDOS, two years).

Bernoulli Removable Media Drives. The disk used in the Bernoulli drive is roughly the same size as a 5 1/4-inch floppy disk, although a large shutter, similar to the shutter on a 3 1/2-inch floppy disk, easily differentiates Bernoulli disks from floppy disks. Modern Bernoulli cartridges are available in 35M, 65M, 105M, and 150M capacities. The Iomega Bernoulli MultiDisk 150 drive, the company's newest model, reads and writes all of these drive capacities. In addition, the MultiDisk reads and writes to older Bernoulli 90M disks and reads older 40M disks. The MultiDisk is available in both internal and external models.

Bernoulli disks are widely known as the most durable of the removable media drive types. It is probably safer to mail a Bernoulli cartridge than another type of removable disk because the media is well-protected inside the cartridge. Bernoulli encases a magnetic-media-covered flexible disk (in effect, a floppy disk) in a rigid cartridge in the same way the thin disk of a 1.44M floppy is encased in a rigid plastic shell.

When it rotates in the drive, the disk is pulled by air pressure towards the drive heads. Many people do not think that there is head-to-disk contact in a Bernoulli drive, but indeed there is. As the disk spins, the airflow generated by the disk movement encounters what is called a *Bernoulli plate*, a stationary plate designed to control the air flow so that the disk is pulled toward the read/write head. At full speed, the head does touch the disk, which causes wear. Bernoulli drives have built-in random seek functions that prevent any single track on the disk from wearing excessively during periods of inactivity. Bernoulli disk cartridges should be replaced periodically because they can wear out. The disk itself spins at speeds approaching the 3,600 rpm of relatively slow hard drives. The drive has an average seek time of 18ms, not a great deal slower than today's medium-priced hard drives.

The Bernoulli MultiDisk 150 drive is available in an internal model, which requires a half-height drive bay, and an external model. The internal model connects to the IDE hard drive adapter already installed in your system. The external model requires a SCSI adapter card with an external connector. The external model is powered by a transformer that connects to a grounded AC wall plug.

Another form of Bernoulli drive from Iomega is the popular Zip drive. This device is available as a external or internal SCSI unit and is also available as an external parallel port device. The drive is capable of storing up to 100M of data on a small removable magnetic cartridge that resembles a 3 1/2-inch floppy disk, and has approximately a 29ms access time and a 1M/sec transfer rate when used with a SCSI connection. If the parallel connection is used, the drive's speed is often limited by the speed of the parallel port.

The Zip drives use a proprietary 3 1/2-inch disk made by Iomega. It is about twice as thick as a standard 3 1/2-inch floppy disk. The Zip drives do not accept standard 1.44M or 720K floppy disks, making this an unlikely candidate for a floppy drive replacement. Zip drives have become popular in use as an external drive for exchanging data between systems, but the major PC manufacturers have not recognized the proprietary format directly in the system BIOS or in the operating system. The popularity and functionality of the Zip drive has now been greatly exceeded by the new LS-120 "floptical" drive introduced by 3M and Matsushita, and supported by Compaq and other major PC manufacturers. More information about the revolutionary LS-120 drive follows in the next few sections.

Removable Media Hard Disk Drives. Syquest manufactures some drives that use 5 1/4-inch cartridges and others that use 3 1/2-inch cartridges. But the Syquest disks, like the Bernoulli cartridges, are easily differentiated from floppy disks. The 5 1/4-inch 44M and 88M cartridges used in some SyDOS drives are encased in clear plastic, as are the SyDOS 3 1/2-inch 105M and Syquest 270M cartridges. The disk spins inside the cartridge at several thousand rpm. Syquest claims a 14ms average access time for the drives it manufactures.

The disks for the Syquest and SyDOS drives are composed of a rigid platter inside a plastic cartridge but are not as well-protected as the disk in a Bernoulli cartridge. Some people consider these disks fragile. If the Syquest and SyDOS cartridges are not severely jostled or dropped, however, they can be transported safely. These cartridges must be carefully protected when they are mailed or shipped.

The Syquest/SyDOS drives are available in internal and external models. The internal models require a connection to the existing IDE hard drive interface card. The external models require a SCSI interface card with an external connector and are powered by a transformer that connects to a grounded AC wall plug.

Another type of removable hard disk drive is the *Jaz drive* from Iomega. This is physically and functionally identical to the Syquest drives in that it is a true removable cartridge hard disk, except the capacity of the cartridge has been increased to 1G. Unfortunately, the cartridges themselves cost about $100, which is about seven times the cost of a DAT (Digital Audio Tape) cartridge that stores four to eight times more data! The high cost of the media makes the Jaz drive unsuitable for backup compared to traditional tape media, but possibly useful as an add-on external SCSI hard disk.

Magneto-Optical Drives

Magneto-optical drives, which are manufactured by a large number of companies, use an ingenious combination of magnetic and laser technology to pack data on 5 1/4-inch and 3 1/2-inch disks contained in cartridges. The media itself and the construction of the platter are similar in ways to the media of a CD-ROM disc. An aluminum base is covered with clear plastic, then a layer of magnetic, optically active media particles—an alloy of cobalt, iron, and terbium. A clear plastic coating seals the disk, rendering it nearly impervious to shock, contamination, and damage.

Although the magneto-optical disks are similar to CD-ROM discs, there is a world of difference in the way data is stored. When manufacturers write CD-ROM discs, the laser actually burns pits into the media to represent the data. These pits are read by the laser and translated into the form of computer data. In the case of magneto-optical disks, the magnetically/optically active media is not burned or pitted. Instead, during the writing process a magneto-optical drive focuses a laser beam onto a very tight track—a much thinner track than could be used to store data on a purely magnetic media platter. The laser beam heats the track, and a weak magnetic signal is applied. The result is that only the thin track of heated media receives the magnetic signal and stores the data it contains.

Unlike a CD-ROM disc, a magneto-optical disk theoretically can be rewritten an infinite number of times because the media is never burned or pitted. When the time comes to erase data from or rewrite the disk, the disk is simply reheated with the laser and the old data is removed magnetically so that new data can be recorded. When the magneto-optical drive reads the disk, the drive functions optically—that is, the laser reads the data from the disk (without heating the media).

Because of the thin tracks on which data is written to magneto-optical disks, the data is packed extremely densely: Large amounts of data can be packed on a platter about the same size as common 3 1/2-inch and 5 1/4-inch floppy disks. The current maximum capacity of the 3 1/2-inch cartridges is 230M; the 5 1/2-inch cartridges can hold as much as 1G of data. It is important to note, however, that capacity ratings of magneto-optical disks can be misleading. Magneto-optical disks are double-sided, like floppy disks, but magneto-optical drives have only one read/write head. Therefore, to read or write to the second side, you must manually flip over the cartridge. So only half the disk capacity is available at any one time.

For many applications, magneto-optical drives are tediously slow, although some drives—using refinements of the basic magneto-optical technology—offer data-access speeds that are inching more closely to those of removable magnetic media drives. One reason that magneto-optical drives are slow is that they typically spin the disk at roughly 2,000 rpm—much slower than the 3,600 rpm of a relatively slow hard drive. Another reason for the slow speeds is that the read/write head mechanism, although optically and magnetically advanced, is mechanically a kludge. The massive mechanism of a magneto-optical drive's read/write heads takes much longer to move and settle than the read/write heads of a hard drive or even a removable magnetic media drive.

Magneto-optical drives typically are rated with average access speeds of about 30ms. However, these average access speed figures do not tell the entire story. The process of rewriting a disk can take nearly twice the time it takes to read the disk. Because of the way magneto-optical technology works, all the bias magnetic field of the area of the disk to be written must be oriented in a single direction during the write process. Because of this limitation, during the write process most magneto-optical drives must make a first pass over the disk to align the tracks of the disk that are to be rewritten. Then the drive makes a second pass over the disk to realign, or change the alignment of, the necessary areas. This alignment/realignment process is known as *two-pass recording.*

New magneto-optical technologies are emerging which use single pass recording of disks. If speed is an important factor in choosing a magneto-optical drive, you should be prepared to pay extra for a drive whose performance is not penalized by two-pass recording technology. In addition, several manufacturers are offering drives that spin the platter at speeds approaching the 3,600 rpm speeds of a hard drive. The performance boost offered by these drives is considerable, but this technology also boosts considerably the prices of these drives.

Most manufacturers adhere to the International Standards Organization (ISO) specifications for magneto-optical disks and drives. The ISO standard calls for all drives to use a SCSI host adapter to interface with the computer. Under the ISO standard, 5 1/4-inch drives must be able to read two different disk formats: disks with 512-byte sectors and disks with 1,024-byte sectors. The disks with 512-byte sectors have a capacity of roughly 600M; those 1,024-byte sectors hold 650M of data. Under the ISO standard, the 3 1/2-inch drives, which are quite popular among first-time purchasers, are required to read only the 128M disks.

Some manufacturers, in addition to designing their drives to meet ISO standards, also design their drives to use a proprietary data format that can increase the capacity of 5 1/4-inch disks to about 1.3G. Both 5 1/4-inch and 3 1/2-inch drives are available as internal and external units.

Comparing Removable Drives

Deciding on a removable drive is getting tougher with more than a dozen removable drives currently on the market. Iomega and Syquest lead the pack, but new entries from Exabyte and Avatar Peripherals provide their own proprietary drives as well.

Table 18.5 shows a direct comparison between the most popular removable drives on the market.

Table 18.5 Removable Drive Specifications

Drive Type	Drive Cost	Disk/Cartridge Cost	Disk/Cartridge Capacity	Average Seek Time	Data Transfer Rate
Iomega Zip Parallel	$149	$15	100M	29ms	1.4M/sec
Iomega Zip SCSI	$149	$15	100M	29ms	1.4M/sec
Imation LS-120 Internal	$179	$18	120M	70ms	4.0M/sec
Syquest 235 Parallel	$250	$30	235M	13.5ms	1.25M/sec
Avatar Shark 250 Parallel	$299	$30	250M	12ms	1.2 M/sec
Avatar Shark PCMCIA	$299	$30	250M	12ms	2.0M/sec
Syquest 235 SCSI/IDE	$299	$30	235M	13.5ms	2.4M/sec
Iomega Jaz (SCSI)	$399	$99	1G	12ms	5.4M/sec

(continues)

Table 18.5 Continued					
Drive Type	Drive Cost	Disk/ Cartridge Cost	Disk/ Cartridge Capacity	Average Seek Time	Data Transfer Rate
Avatar Shark iSeries IDE	$30	250M	12ms	2.5M/sec	
Syquest Syjet SCSI	$399	$99	1.5G	12ms	5.3M/sec
Syquest Syjet IDE	$399	$99	1.5G	12ms	5.3M/sec
CD-R Drives	$500–$1,000	$5	650M	<150ms	150K/sec-2.4M/sec

When shopping for a removable drive, keep the following in mind:

- *Price per megabyte of storage.* Take the cost of the drive's cartridge or disk and divide it by the storage capacity to see how much you are paying per megabyte of storage. This difference in price will become quite apparent as you buy more cartridges or disks for the drive. (Don't forget to factor in the cost of the drive itself!)

- *Access time versus need of access.* The access and data transfer speeds are only important if you need to access the data frequently or quickly. If your primary use is archiving data, a slower drive may be fine. However, if you plan on running programs off of the drive, choose a faster drive instead.

- *Compatibility and portability.* Opt for an external SCSI or parallel port solution if you will need to move the drive between various computers. Also verify that the drive has drivers available for each type of machine you want to connect the drive to.

Write-Once, Read Many (WORM) Drives

The removable media drive known as *write-once, read many (WORM)* is designed to serve as a nearly bulletproof data archival system. If you have extremely important data files that absolutely must remain in an unaltered state—perhaps accounting or database data—a WORM drive can provide the kind of security you are looking for. Data written to a WORM disk cannot be changed.

The WORM disk is encased in a high-impact cartridge with a sliding shutter similar to the shutter on a 3 1/2-inch floppy disk. The cartridge and the extremely durable nature of the disk inside make WORM disks worry free for data exchange. A WORM drive cartridge is very difficult to damage. The disk itself, with the media sandwiched in plastic, is not unlike a CD-ROM disc or a magneto-optical disk. The technology used to write a WORM disk, however, is more like the technology used for CD-ROM recording than that used for writing to magneto-optical disks. The WORM drive uses a laser to burn microscopic patches of darkness into the light-colored media.

A number of companies manufacture WORM drives but follow no single standard. Therefore, a WORM disk written on one manufacturer's drive is quite unlikely to be readable on another manufacturer's drive. Each manufacturer (sometimes small groups of manufacturers) uses its own proprietary data format and disk capacity, and many use a cartridge size only their drives can handle. For example, most WORM drives are designed for 5 1/4-inch cartridges but some WORM drives handle only 12-inch disks. In addition, although most WORM drives interface the computer via SCSI host adapter, others use different interfaces, some of them proprietary.

Certainly, at least in part because of these incompatibility problems, WORM drives are not big sellers. No more than several thousand are sold each year at prices soaring to the heights—some 5 1/4-inch drives cost several thousand dollars. The 5 1/4-inch-drive cartridges, which range in capacity from 650M to 1.3G, can cost more than $180.

The term *niche market* is used occasionally to describe a computer product or peripheral that lacks broad appeal or usefulness. Because of its cost and incompatibility problems, WORM drive technology is a niche market product. Unless you must be able to store massive amounts of data and ensure it can never be altered, you are better off buying a magneto-optical drive, or perhaps even a tape backup drive.

Compact Disc Recordable (CD-R) Drives

Note that a variation on WORM technology is also found in *CD-R (CD-Recordable) drives*. CD-R drives are indeed WORM; however, they use a special recordable CD-ROM disc that, once recorded, can be played back or read in any standard CD-ROM drive. CD-R drives are very useful for creating master CDs, which can be duplicated for distribution within a company.

CD-ROMs, as you will remember from Chapter 17, "CD-ROM Drives," work by reading the light reflected by a laser striking the surface of the disc. Light is either returned from the disc, or not. CD-R recorders work by using a laser to etch a pattern into the raw media, leaving places where light is reflected or not reflected.

> **Note**
>
> Because of the technical changes in the way the media is made, there can be some problems reading CDs made by CD-R devices in a standard CD-ROM player. Most of these problems just result in poor play performance as the CD-ROM tries to align itself to the CD. However, some very old CD-ROM players can't handle CD-R media.

CD-R Drive History. CD-R drives were originally used to pre-master CDs prior to production of massive quantities by a CD manufacturing facility. The CD-R drive was used to create a few (normally less than 20) CDs that would then be tested to make sure that the program worked or was installed correctly. Then three of the CDs would be sent to the manufacturing facility to be mastered and printed into thousands of CDs.

Writing a CD with a CD-R Drive. CD-R drives generally come in slower speeds than their CD-ROM reader counterparts. The fastest CD-R drives write at 4x normal speed—given the system performance to do so. However, some can read at up to 6x normal speed.

Whenever a CD-R is writing data, it is making one long spiral on the CD, alternating on and off to etch the pattern into the raw media. Because the CD-R can't realign itself like a hard drive, once you start writing, you must keep writing until you're finished with the track, or you will ruin the CD.

You'll recall from Chapter 17 that the normal speed for a CD is 150K/sec. When writing at a 4x speed, the computer must provide data to the CD-R drive at 600K/sec. If the computer isn't able to maintain that data rate, you'll receive a `Buffer under-run` message.

The `Buffer under-run` message indicates that the CD-R had to abort recording because it ran out of data in its buffer to write to the CD. This is the biggest problem that people have with CD-R devices. Providing a fast source to write from—usually a fast SCSI drive—on a system with plenty of RAM will generally help avoid buffer under-run.

CD-R Software. Another difficulty with CD-R devices is that they require special software to write them. Where most removable drives can be used immediately by built-in drives, the CD-R drive must have special CD-ROM burning software.

This software handles the differences between how data is stored on a CD and how it is stored on a hard drive. As you learned in Chapter 17, there are several CD-ROM standards for storing information. The CD-ROM burning software arranges the data into one of these formats so the CD can be read by a CD-ROM reader.

It used to be that CD-ROM burning software required that all of the files on the hard drive be arranged into a single file which was then written to the CD. The single file contained all of the sectors on the CD, which means every file, all of the directory information, plus the volume information. This single file took as much space as the files being placed on the CD. The result was that you had to have about 1.5G of storage to burn a single CD (650M/CD × 2 = 1.3G + overhead≈1.5G).

This is no longer a requirement as most software supports virtual images. The software assembles the directory information and burns it to the CD, then opens each file on the CD and provides the data directly from the original file. This works well, however, because the files are not sequentially located on the hard drive; it must seek track-to-track, which takes longer. As a result, some slower hard drives may not be able to keep up with writing at the maximum 4x rate supported by some drives.

Most software and CD-R drives support a simulate recording mode which performs the same actions as in a normal writing mode; however, the laser isn't powered up to a level to etch the disc. This is useful in testing the performance of your complete system, and if it can't handle the data rate, you don't waste a CD.

CD-R as Mass Storage. CD-R costs are unique when considering a form of mass storage. Most mass-storage mediums enable you to rewrite on the media over and over, and although there is a new breed of CD-R drives called *CD-RW* which support rewriting a CD, most don't.

Each CD-R CD can be found for less than $5 in quantities of 25 or above. Most other storage mediums have a much greater media cost. Even at deeply discounted pricing, your DAT, 8mm, QIC, or DLT tapes can cost between $20–$100. Removable media costs can range from $75–$300.

Even though tapes store more and their cost per megabyte is much smaller, accessing files on tape can be a time-consuming process. Removable media is generally more expensive and requires that the recipient have the same kind of drive, or the drive must be transported with you when trying to shuttle files from one place to another.

Compared with either tape or other removable media, using a CD-R to burn CDs can be very cost-effective and easy when transporting large files or making archival copies. Another benefit of the CD for making archival copies is that CDs have a much longer shelf life than tapes or removable media.

However, CD-R isn't a very effective backup medium because the CD can only be written once. Because you can't reformat and reuse the CDs, subsequent backups make previous discs disposable at best.

Part V

System Assembly Maintenance

19   Building a System

20   Portable Systems

Chapter 19

Building a System

In these days of commodity parts and component pricing, building your own system from scratch is no longer the daunting process it once was. Every component necessary to build a PC-compatible system is available off the shelf, and at very competitive pricing. In many cases, the system you build can use the same components as the top name-brand systems.

There are, however, some cautions. The main thing to note is that you rarely save money when building your own system compared to purchasing a complete system from a mail order vendor or mass merchandiser. The reasoning for this is simple: Most system vendors today who build systems to order use many if not all the same components you can when building your own. The difference is that they buy these components in quantity and receive a much larger discount than you can purchasing only one of a particular item.

There also is only one shipping or handling charge when you purchase a complete system instead of the individual shipping charges when you purchase separate components. In fact, the shipping, handling, and even phone charges from ordering all of the separate parts needed to build a PC often add up to $100 or more. This cost rises if you encounter problems with any of the components and have to make additional calls or send improper or malfunctioning parts back for replacement.

It is clear that the reasons for building a system from scratch often has less to do with saving money than with the experience and end result. In the end, you have a custom system that contains the exact components and features you have selected. The experience itself is also very rewarding. You know exactly how your system is constructed and configured because you have done it yourself. This makes future support and installation of additional accessories much easier.

It may be possible to save some money using components of your current system when building your new system. You might have recently upgraded your hard drive or memory in an attempt to extend the life of your current computer. You can take those components with you to the new system in most cases, if you plan appropriately. For example, if you used 30-pin SIMMs in your old system, you can buy a new motherboard that supports both 72- and 30-pin SIMMs, or buy a SIMM adapter to convert your 30-pin SIMMs to 72.

So if you are interested in a rewarding experience, want to have a custom system that is not exactly offered by any vendor, want to save some money by re-using some of the components from your current system, and you are not in a hurry, then building your own PC-compatible may be the way to go. On the other hand, if you are interested in getting a PC-compatible for the best price, want one-stop support for warranty claims, and need an operational system quickly, then building your own system should definitely be avoided!

This chapter details the components needed to assemble your own system, explains the assembly procedures, and lists some recommendations for components and their sources.

System Components

The components used in building a typical PC compatible are:

- Case and power supply
- Motherboard:

Processor	Parallel
Memory	IDE
Serial	Floppy

- Floppy disk drive
- Hard disk drive(s)
- CD-ROM drive
- Keyboard and pointing device (mouse)
- PCI video card and display
- Sound card and speakers
- Accessories:

Heat sinks/cooling fans	Hardware
Cables	Operating system software

Each of these components is discussed in the following sections.

Case and Power Supply

The case and power supply is usually sold as a unit. There are several designs to choose from, most of which will take a standard Baby-AT or the new ATX form factor motherboards. The size of the case, power supply, and even the motherboard are called the *form factor*. The most popular case form factors are as follows:

- Full Tower
- Mid-Tower
- Mini-Tower
- Desktop
- Low Profile (also called Slimline)

Out of these choices, it is recommended that you avoid the Low Profile systems. These cases require a special type of motherboard called a *Low Profile* or *LPX board*. LPX motherboards have virtually everything built in, even video, and do not have any normal adapter slots. Instead, all of the expansion slots are mounted on a "tree" board called a *riser card*, which plugs into a special slot on the motherboard. Adapter cards then plug sideways into the riser card, making expansion somewhat limited and difficult.

Most of the case designs other than the Low Profile (or Slimline) take a standard sized motherboard called a *Baby-AT* type. This designation refers to the form factor or shape of the motherboard, which is to say that it mimics the original IBM AT but is slightly smaller. Actually, the Baby-AT form factor is a kind of a cross between the IBM XT and AT motherboard sizes.

▶▶ See "Motherboard Form Factors," p. 90

Many of the newer cases accept the standard Baby-AT form factor motherboards as well as the ATX-style boards, but an older case designed for Baby-AT motherboards does *not* accept an ATX motherboard. The ATX form factor will eventually replace the Baby-AT style for most newer motherboards. So if you are interested in the most flexible type of case and power supply that will support future upgrades, look for a unit that conforms to the ATX and Baby-AT motherboard form factors.

Whether you choose a desktop or one of the tower cases is really a personal preference. Most feel that the tower systems are easier to work on, and the full-sized tower cases have lots of bays for different storage devices. Tower cases have enough bays to hold floppy drives, multiple hard disks, CD-ROM drives, tape drives, and anything else you might want to install. Some of the desktop cases also can have as much room as the towers, particularly the mini- or mid-tower models. In fact, a tower case can really be considered a desktop case turned sideways or vice versa. Some cases are convertible—that is, they can be used in either a desktop or tower orientation.

Motherboard

There are several compatible form factors used for motherboards. The form factor refers to the physical dimensions and size of the board, and dictates what type of case the board will fit into. The types of motherboard form factors generally available are the following:

- Full-size AT
- Baby-AT
- ATX
- LPX

The full-size AT motherboard is so named because it matches the original IBM AT motherboard design. This allows for a very large board of up to 12 inches wide by 13.8 inches deep. The keyboard connector and slot connectors must conform to specific placement requirements to fit the holes in the case. This type of board will fit into the tower or full-sized desktop cases only. Because the cases that will fit these boards are more limited in availability, and due to component miniaturization, the full-size AT boards are no longer being produced by most motherboard manufacturers.

The Baby-AT form factor is essentially the same as the original IBM XT motherboard, with modifications in screw hole positions to fit into an AT-style case (see Figure 19.1). These motherboards also have specific placement of the keyboard connector and slot connectors to match the holes in the case.

> **Note**
>
> Virtually all full size AT and Baby-AT motherboards use the standard 5-pin DIN type connector for the keyboard. Baby-AT motherboards will fit into every type of case except the Low Profile or Slimline cases. Because of their flexibility, this is now the most popular motherboard form factor. Figure 19.1 shows the dimensions and layout of a Baby-AT motherboard.

The newest form factor on the market today is the ATX form factor, which was released by Intel in July 1995 (see Figure 19.2). This motherboard design is featured on many new Pentium and Pentium Pro-based motherboards and should continue to be featured over the next few years, and it is destined to replace the Baby-AT form factor. ATX-shaped boards are the same basic dimensions as Baby-AT; however, they are rotated 90 degrees from the standard Baby-AT orientation. This places the slots parallel to the short side of the board, allowing more space for other components without interfering with expansion boards. Components that produce large amounts of heat, such as the CPU and memory, are located next to the power supply, which is redesigned to feature an internal fan blowing directly across the board.

The ATX-style power supply also features a redesigned single keyed (foolproof!) connector that cannot be plugged in backwards, and it also supplies the motherboard with 3.3v for many of the newer CPUs and other components.

Consider that if you don't purchase an ATX form factor motherboard this time, the next time you probably will! Virtually all motherboard manufacturers have committed to the new ATX design in the long run, as the ATX motherboard designs will be cheaper, easier to access for user serviceability, and more reliable.

Other form factors used in motherboards today are the LPX and Mini-LPX form factors. These form factors require the use of a Low Profile case and are normally not recommended when building your own system. This is due to the number of different variations on case and riser card designs. These types of form factors are popular with many of the PC systems sold through retail outlets and appliance stores.

System Components **797**

FIG. 19.1 Baby-AT motherboard form factor.

> **Tip**
>
> There can be some differences between systems with LPX motherboards, so it is possible to find interchangability problems between different motherboards and cases. I usually do not recommend LPX style systems if future upgradability is a factor; it is not only difficult to locate a new motherboard that will fit, but LPX systems are also limited in expansion slots and drive bays as well. Generally, the Baby-AT configuration is the most popular and the most flexible type of system to consider.

Besides the form factor, there are several other features you should consider in a motherboard. The primary considerations would be the processor type and chipset. Motherboards you should consider would have a socket for one of three different processor families:

- Pentium
- Pentium with MMX (MultiMedia eXtension)
- Pentium Pro
- Pentium II

798 Chapter 19—Building a System

FIG. 19.2 ATX motherboard form factor.

Pentium motherboards will normally have a Zero Insertion Force (ZIF) Socket 7 (321-pin), which is available in speeds from 120MHz to 233MHz. *MMX* is an extension of the Pentium line that includes additional instructions to handle and accelerate multimedia function calls, such as video and sound. The Pentium II is to the Pentium Pro as the Pentium with MMX is to the Pentium. The Pentium II processor is Intel's newest processor family and is becoming a popular alternative among the highest end systems that run full 32-bit OSes, for example, Windows NT.

 ▶▶ See "Intel Processors," p. 166

Depending on the exact processor version you install and the speed at which it is to be run, there may be jumpers on the motherboard to set. There may also be jumpers to control the voltage supplied to the processor; these should be carefully checked or the board and processor will not operate properly.

There are a few other items to consider when purchasing a motherboard. Besides the processor, the main component on the board would be the *chipset*. This is normally a set of one to five chips that contain the main motherboard circuits. These chipsets replace the 100 or more discrete components that were used in the original IBM AT systems, and allow a motherboard designer to easily create a functional system. The chipset will contain the local bus controller (usually PCI), the cache controller, main memory controller, DMA and Interrupt controllers, and several other circuits as well. The chipset used in a given motherboard will have a profound effect on the performance of the board, and will dictate performance parameters and limitations such as cache size and speed, main memory size and speed, processor types and speeds, and more.

Because chipsets are constantly being introduced and improved over time, I cannot possibly list all of them and their functions, but as an example, I will discuss some of the popular ones for Pentium-based systems. There are several very popular high performance chipsets designed for Pentium motherboards on the market today. The best of these offer support for EDO (Extended Data Out) RAM, pipeline burst cache SRAM (Static RAM), PCI local bus, and Advanced Power Management (APM), as well as other functions, such as IDE interfaces.

Here are several of the high-performance chipsets available for Pentium-based motherboards:

- *Intel Triton/Triton II*. The 82430FX PCIset (called Triton) and HX (called Triton II) are both four chipsets. The Triton chipset consists of the 82437FX Triton System Controller (TSC), two 82438FX Triton Data Paths (TDP), and the 82371FB PCI ISA IDE Xcelerator (PIIX). The TSC integrates the cache and main memory control functions and provides bus control for transfers between the CPU, cache, main memory, and the PCI Bus. The L2 cache controller in the TSC supports write-back cache for cache sizes of 256 and 512K, as well as lower cost cacheless designs. Cache memory can be implemented with either standard, burst, or pipeline burst SRAMs. The TSC and TDPs together support up to 128M of EDO or standard main memory. The PIIX acts as a PCI to ISA bridge, and includes the DMA controllers, interrupt controllers, timer/counter, power management support, and an Enhanced IDE interface with up to two IDE connectors for four IDE devices.

> **Note**
>
> The original (FX suffix) version Triton chipset unfortunately does *not* support parity-checked RAM. This means that any motherboard built with this chipset will not be able to detect memory errors during system operation. Even if you purchase parity SIMMs, the parity will not be used. Many system integrators will not use non-parity RAM in mission-critical systems, such as file servers. Because of market pressures demanding such support, Intel has released a second-generation (HX suffix) Triton II chipset that includes both parity and ECC (Error Correcting Code) memory support.

- *Opti Viper*. The 82C550 Viper-DP from Opti supports not only the Pentium, but the AMD K5 and Cyrix M1 processors as well, in both single and dual processor configurations. The Viper-DP chipset consists of three chips: the 82C556 Data Buffer

Controller (DBC), the 82C557 System Controller (SC), and the 82C558 Integrated Peripherals Controller (IPC). The SC is the main chip and contains the main memory controller, L2 cache controller, and the PCI and VL-Bus interfaces. The IPC contains the ISA bus controller, DMA and Interrupt controllers, and PCI to ISA bridge. The DBC buffers the CPU and main memory and contains the parity generation and checking circuits. Viper supports up to 512M of EDO or standard main memory with or without parity checking, and up to 2M of L2 write-back cache using either asynchronous, burst, or pipeline burst SRAMs.

- *ALI Aladdin.* The Aladdin M1510 chipset from Acer Laboratories Inc. also supports the Pentium, AMD K5, and Cyrix M1 series processors in both single and dual processor configurations. Aladdin M1510 is a four-chip set. It includes the M1511 Memory/Cache Controller that supports EDO RAM as well as standard RAM up to 768M with or without parity checking.

    This chip also supports up to 1M of L2 write-back cache, including support for standard burst and pipeline burst SRAMs. The M1513 System I/O Controller contains the PCI bus interface, DMA and Interrupt controllers, timer circuits, and PCI Enhanced IDE interface, as well as an integrated keyboard controller. Finally, two M1512 data buffers are used to serve as an intermediate between the CPU and main memory.

The choices for Pentium II motherboard chipsets are a little more restricted. As of this printing, only a couple of chipsets are available, including the Intel Orion and Natoma chipsets. Intel's original Pentium Pro (Pentium II without MMX support) chipset was code-named Orion and is technically known as the 82450GX or KX. This chipset is generally made up of seven individual chips and supports up to four Pentium Pro processors and two separate PCI buses in the GX server version. A desktop version of Orion, the 82450KX, supports two processors and a single PCI bus.

More recently, Intel released a less expensive and more efficient Natoma chipset for Pentium Pro machines. Natoma is technically called the 82440FX chipset and consists of only three chips rather than seven as with Orion. Natoma supports only two Pentium Pro processors and a single PCI bus, making it less suited to servers than the GX version of the Orion chipset. However, the greater internal efficiency of Natoma makes it a better performer overall than Orion.

 ▶▶ See "Knowing What to Look For (Selection Criteria)," p. 79

No matter what Pentium class chipset you look for, I would recommend looking for the following supported features:

- EDO RAM (main memory)
- Pipeline Burst (also called Synchronous) SRAM cache
- Parity generation and checking

- ECC memory support
- APM (Advanced Power Management) energy saving functions
- MMX support (if you plan to do any multimedia)
- PCI Local Bus

Most of the better Pentium chipsets on the market today should have these features. If you are buying a motherboard, I highly recommend you contact the chipset manufacturer and obtain the documentation (usually called the *Data Book*) for your particular chipset. This will explain how the memory and cache controllers, as well as many other devices in your system, operate. This documentation will also describe the Advanced Chipset Setup functions in your system's Setup program. With this information, you may be able to fine-tune the motherboard configuration by altering the chipset features. Because chipsets are discontinued and new ones are introduced all the time, don't wait too long to get the chipset documentation, as most manufacturers only make it available for chips currently in production.

> **Note**
>
> One interesting tidbit about the chipset is that in the volume that the motherboard manufacturers purchase them, the chipsets usually cost about $40 each. If you have an older motherboard and need repair, you normally cannot purchase the chipset because they are normally not stocked by the manufacturer after they are discontinued. The low-cost chipset is one of the reasons motherboards have become disposable items and are rarely, if ever, repaired.

Another feature on your motherboard will be the *BIOS (Basic Input/Output System)*. This is also called the *ROM BIOS* because the code is stored in a Read Only Memory (ROM) chip. There are several things to look for here. One is that the BIOS be supplied by one of the major BIOS manufacturers such as AMI (American Megatrends International), Phoenix, Award, or Microid Research. Also, make sure that the BIOS is contained in a special type of reprogrammable chip called a *Flash ROM* or *EEPROM (Electrically Erasable Programmable Read Only Memory)*. This will allow you to download BIOS updates from the manufacturer and, using a program they supply, easily update the code in your BIOS. If you do not have the Flash ROM or EEPROM type, you will have to physically replace the chip if an update is required.

Make sure that the motherboard and BIOS support the new Plug and Play (PnP) specification. This will make installing new cards, especially PnP cards, much easier. PnP automates the installation and uses special software that is both built in to the BIOS as well as the operating system (such as Windows 95) to automatically configure adapter cards and resolve adapter resource conflicts.

Processor. In most cases, your motherboard comes with the processor already installed. Most of the name-brand motherboard manufacturers like to install the processor and warranty the board and processor as a unit. This is not always the case, and it is definitely possible to purchase the motherboard and processor separately.

The processor normally is installed in a special ZIF socket on the motherboard. Make sure the jumpers on the board are set to match the correct processor type, speed, and voltage.

Memory. Your system will require memory for the Level 2 (secondary) cache as well as the main memory. The cache memory will be in the form of individual SRAM chips, or possibly in what is called *COAST (Cache On A Stick)* or *CELP (Card Edge Low Profile)*. COAST and CELP are different names for the same thing. This is a new standard for cache SIMMs. COAST/CELP SIMMs have a different number of pins and pinout from standard main memory SIMMs, and are not interchangeable with them.

Most Pentium motherboards support at least 256–512K of cache memory. The chips themselves are available in three basic cache types: standard asynchronous, burst, and pipeline burst. The latter offers the highest performance; choose it if your motherboard supports it. Most of the newer Pentium boards support the pipeline burst cache chips; most of the 486 boards didn't. This is because these faster cache chips are not really needed at the slower 33 to 40MHz memory bus speeds on the 486 compared to the 60 and 66MHz memory bus speeds in a Pentium system.

Main memory will normally be installed in the form of *SIMMs (Single Inline Memory Modules)* or in some cases the newer *DIMMs (Dual Inline Memory Modules)*. There are three different physical types of main memory modules used in PC systems today, with several variations of each. The three main types are as follows:

- 30-pin SIMMs
- 72-pin SIMMs
- 168-pin DIMMs

The 72-pin SIMMs are by far the most common type of memory module used today; however, just a few years ago most systems came with 30-pin modules. Many of the high-end systems use the DIMMs, because they are 64-bits wide and can be used as a single bank on a Pentium or Pentium Pro system. Depending on the type of processor, a different number of SIMMs must be installed to make a complete memory bank, and the 72-pin SIMMs are four times as dense as the 30-pin types.

For example, in a 486-based system, you would need four 30-pin SIMMs to make a single bank of memory, while only one 72-pin SIMM would be required for a single bank. This is because the 72-pin SIMMs hold data 32 bits wide, while the 30-pin SIMMs only hold data 8 bits wide. A 64-bit Pentium system, then, would require two 72-pin SIMMs or a single 168-pin DIMM to make a single bank.

Memory modules can include an extra bit for each eight to be used for parity checking. These are called *parity SIMMs* or *parity DIMMs* and are required by most older boards. Many newer motherboards do not employ parity checking, which means that you will not be able to use the slightly more expensive parity SIMMs. You can install them, but the extra parity bits will not function. I do not necessarily agree with this philosophy, but nevertheless, many newer motherboards (such as those based on the Intel Triton chipset) simply cannot use parity checking at all! Most other chipsets, including the newer Triton II, do support memory parity checking.

Another thing to watch out for is the type of metal on the memory module contacts. They are available with either tin- or gold-plated contacts. While it may seem that gold-plated contacts are better (they are), you should not use them in all systems. You should instead always match the type of plating on the module contacts to what is also used on the socket contacts. In other words, if the motherboard SIMM or DIMM sockets have tin-plated contacts, then you *must* use SIMMs or DIMMs with tin-plated contacts also.

If you mix dissimilar metals (tin with gold), there will be a rapidly accelerated corrosion occurring on the tin side, and also tiny electrical currents will be generated. The combination of the corrosion and tiny currents causes havoc, and all types of memory problems and errors occur. In some systems, I have observed that everything will seem fine for about a year, during which the corrosion develops. After that, random memory errors result. Removing and cleaning the memory module and socket contacts postpones the problem for another year, upon which the problems return again. How would you like this problem if you had 100 or more systems to support? Of course you can avoid these problems if you insist on using SIMMs with contacts whose metal matches the metal found in the sockets in which they will be installed.

Finally, some systems now use a special type of memory called *EDO (Extended Data Out)*. These memory chips are slightly redesigned and do not cost much more than standard non-EDO memory, but they can operate at increased efficiency in a motherboard designed for them. The actual speed increase varies but is usually not more than a couple of percentage points. Motherboards that use EDO memory also can use standard non-EDO memory, but they will not enjoy the increased performance. You also can install EDO memory in older systems that do not support it because EDO is backward-compatible with standard (called *fast page mode*) memory. Of course, installing the more expensive EDO modules in an older system will not improve performance.

▶▶ See "Adding Motherboard Memory," p. 274

I/O Ports

Most motherboards today have built-in I/O ports. If these ports are not built-in, then they will have to be supplied via a plug-in expansion board that unfortunately wastes a slot. The following ports should be included in any new system you assemble:

- Mouse port (so-called PS/2 type)
- Two local bus Enhanced IDE ports (primary and secondary)
- Floppy controller (2.88M capable)
- Two serial ports (16550A buffered type)
- Parallel port (EPP/ECP type)

The standard procedure is to include these ports directly on the motherboard. This is possible because there are several chip companies that have implemented all of these features except the mouse port (which uses the keyboard controller) on a single Super

I/O chip! These chips often cost less than $5 in quantities of 1,000 or more, so adding these items directly to the motherboard saves a more expensive board taking up an expansion slot.

If these devices are not present on the motherboard, then various Super or Multi-I/O boards are available that implement all of these ports. Again, most of the newer versions of these boards use a single chip implementation because it is cheaper and more reliable.

Floppy Disk Drive

Obviously, your system needs some type of floppy drive to load software. Usually, this is a 1.44M 3 1/2-inch drive, but I normally recommend a 2.88M drive these days. The 2.88M drives are superior to the 1.44M drives, and they are fully backward-compatible. Most current controllers and ROM BIOS fully support the 2.88M drives.

If you are interested in a 5 1/4-inch drive, most of the floppy drive manufacturers make combo drives that include both a 3 1/2-inch 1.44M and 5 1/4-inch 1.2M drive in a single unit, which installs in a half-height 5 1/4-inch bay. At least one company (Teac) offers a combo drive that combines a 1.44M floppy and a quad-speed CD-ROM drive in a single unit as well. One drawback of these combo units is that if one of the components fails, the entire combo drive has to be replaced. Also, no one seems to make these with the more desirable 2.88M floppy drives.

Hard Disk Drive

Your system also needs a hard disk. In most cases, a drive with a minimum capacity of 1.6G is recommended, although in some cases you can get away with less for a low-end configuration; you will be hard pressed to find one smaller. High-end systems should have drives of 2–4G or higher. The most popular interface is IDE, although SCSI is preferred for multitasking OSes. IDE generally offers greater performance for single installations, but SCSI is better for two or more drives or with multitasking operating systems like Windows 95 and NT. This is due to the greater intelligence in the SCSI interface, which relieves some of the I/O processing from the CPU in the system.

There are several brands of drives to choose from, but most of them offer similar performance within their price and capacity categories.

 ▶▶ See "Performance," p. 681

CD-ROM Drive

A CD-ROM drive should be considered a mandatory item in any PC you construct these days. This is because most software—particularly multimedia programs—is now being distributed on CD-ROM. Systems can now boot from CD-ROM drives (Windows NT 4.0, for example). There are several types of CD-ROM drives to consider these days, but mostly I recommend a minimum of a quad-speed drive interfaced via an IDE connection. This results in the best possible performance with the minimum amount of hassle. If you already have a SCSI adapter, go with a SCSI CD-ROM as well; you'll improve your multitasking performance and save money on an unneeded IDE controller.

Keyboard and Pointing Device (Mouse)

Obviously, your system needs a keyboard and some type of pointing device, such as a mouse. Different people prefer different types of keyboards, and the "feel" of one type can vary considerably from other types. I suggest that you try a variety of keyboards until you find what suits you best. I prefer a stiff action with tactile feedback myself, but others prefer a lighter, quieter touch.

Because there are two types of keyboard connectors found in systems today, make sure that the keyboard you purchase matches the connector on your motherboard. Most Baby-AT boards use the larger 5-pin DIN connector, and most ATX boards use the 6-pin, mini-DIN connector; however, the trend now seems to be changing to the mini-DIN connector for all boards. On some motherboards, you have an option of choosing either connector when you purchase the board. If you end up with a keyboard and motherboard that do not match, there are several companies that sell adapters to mate either type of keyboard to either type of motherboard connector.

The same concept applies to mice or other pointing devices; there are a number of different choices that suit different individuals. Try several before deciding on the type you want. If your motherboard includes a built-in mouse port, make sure that you get a mouse that is designed for that interface. This mouse is often called a *PS/2 type mouse* because the IBM PS/2 systems introduced this type of mouse port. Many systems use a serial mouse connected to a serial port, but having a motherboard-integrated mouse port would be better because you would have both serial ports free for other devices.

> **Tip**
>
> You might be tempted to skimp here to save a few dollars. *Don't*. You do all of your interacting with your new PC through these devices, and cheap ones make their presence known every time you use your system.

Video Card and Display

You need a PCI video adapter as well as a monitor or display to complete your system. There are numerous choices in this area, but the biggest piece of advice I have is to choose a good monitor. The display is your main view to the system and can be the cause of many hours of either pain or pleasure, depending on what monitor you choose.

I usually recommend a minimum of a 17-inch display these days. Anything smaller cannot acceptably display 1,024×768 pixel resolution. If you opt for a 15-inch or smaller display, you might find that the maximum tolerable resolution would be 800×600. This may be confusing, because most 15-inch monitors claim to be able to display 1,024×768 resolution or even higher, but the characters and features are so small on-screen at that resolution that excessive eyestrain and headaches will result. If you spend a lot of time in front of your system and want to display the higher resolution, a 17-inch display should be considered mandatory.

Your video card and monitor should be compatible in terms of refresh rate, and a minimum refresh rate for a solid, nonflickering display is 70–72Hz; the higher the better. If your new video card can display 16 million colors at a resolution of 1,024×768 and a refresh rate of 76Hz, your monitor's maximum refresh rate at 1,024×768 is 56Hz, and you can't use the video card to its maximum potential.

Sound Card and Speakers

You need a sound card and a set of external speakers for any system that is to be multimedia capable. The sound card should be compatible with the Creative Labs Sound Blaster cards, which have set the standards in this area. Getting a sound card with an upgradable memory (the same SIMMs you use for your main memory) enables you to download additional sound samples—speaker size and quality are up to you.

Accessories

Often you need various accessories to complete your system. These are the small parts that can make or break the assembly process.

Heat Sinks/Cooling Fans. Most of today's faster processors produce a lot of heat, and this heat has to be dissipated or your system will operate intermittently or even fail completely. Heat sinks are available in two main types: passive and active.

Passive heat sinks are simply finned chunks of metal (usually aluminum) that are clipped or glued to the top of the processor. They act as a radiator, and in effect give the processor more surface area to dissipate the heat. I normally recommend this passive design type of heat sink because there are no mechanical parts to fail. In some cases, you should use a thermal transfer grease or sticky tape to fill any air gaps between the heat sink and the processor. This allows for maximum heat transfer and the best efficiency.

An *active heat sink* includes a fan. These can offer greater cooling capacity than the passive types, but require power and are not known for reliability. They often use a cheap fan mechanism that fails after a year or so, thus allowing the processor to overheat and the system to fail. If you do use an active heat sink with a fan, stay away from cheaper units that may be more failure prone.

> **Note**
>
> Notice that the newer ATX form factor motherboards are designed to eliminate the troublesome and unreliable active heat sink (CPU fan). These systems feature a power supply with reverse flow cooling that blows air directly over the CPU, which is relocated in these systems to take advantage of this. Due to a superior design, the ATX motherboard form factor eliminates the need for any sort of cooling fan mounted directly to the CPU.

Cables. Any PC system needs a number of different cables to hook everything up. These can include power cables or adapters, disk drive cables, CD-ROM cables, and many others. Most of the time, the devices you purchase come with included cables, but in some cases they aren't supplied. The vendor list in Appendix A of this book has several cable and small parts suppliers listed that can get you the cables or other parts you need to complete your system.

Another advantage of the ATX motherboard form factor is that these boards feature externally accessible I/O connectors directly mounted to the rear of the board. This eliminates the "rat's nest" of cables found in the common Baby-AT form factor systems. This feature also makes the ATX system a little cheaper and more reliable as well.

Hardware. You need screws, standoffs, and other miscellaneous hardware to assemble your system. Most of this comes with the case, but in some situations you may need more. Again, you can consult the vendor list in Appendix A for suppliers of small parts and hardware needed to get your system operational.

Operating System Software. You need OS software such as DOS, Linux, or Windows to run your PC. Most software houses carry a selection of appropriate operating system software and any applications you need.

System Assembly

Actually assembling the system is easy after you have lined up all of the components! In fact, you may find the procurement phase the most lengthy and trying of the entire experience. Completing the system is simply a matter of screwing everything together, plugging in all of the cable and connectors, and configuring everything to operate properly together.

More explicit instructions for installing any of the system components can be found in the section of this book that covers that particular component. For example, to find out about configuring and installing the floppy drive, consult Chapter 13, "Floppy Disk Drives."

In short order, you will find out whether your system operates as you had planned, or whether there are some incompatibilities between some of the components. Be careful and pay attention to how you install all of your components. It is rare that a newly assembled system operates perfectly the first time, even for those who are somewhat experienced. It is easy to forget a jumper, switch, cable connection, and so on, which would cause problems in system operation. The first reaction if there are problems is to blame the problem on defective hardware, but that is usually not the case. Usually the problem can be traced to some missed step or error made in the assembly process.

Sources and Suppliers

One of the most valuable (to me anyway) parts of this book is the vendor list in Appendix A. Here you will find a number of vendors of different PC components, including addresses, phone numbers, and other information as it is available. These vendors are in this list usually because I recommend their products, or because they are an important company whose products are very popular. There are companies in the vendor list covering all of the components needed to build your system. In some cases, the manufacturers of the components listed will not sell direct to end users, and you may find yourself purchasing through a distributor instead. That is okay; I normally include the actual manufacturers in my list because they can best recommend a distributor for their own products, and of course they should support their own products as well.

Chapter 20
Portable Systems

Portable computers, like their desktop counterparts, have evolved enormously since the days when the word portable could mean as little as a case with a handle on it. Today, portable systems can rival the performance of their desktop counterparts in nearly every way, to the point at which many systems are now being marketed as "desktop replacements" that companies are providing to traveling employees as primary systems. This chapter examines the types of portable computers available and the technologies designed specifically for use in mobile systems.

Portables started out as suitcase-sized systems that differed from desktops mainly in that all of the components were installed into a single case. Compaq was among the first to market portable computers like these in the 1980s, and although their size, weight, and appearance were almost laughable when compared to today's portables, they were cutting-edge technology for the time. The components themselves were not very different from those in standard computers. Most portable systems are now built using the clamshell design that has become an industry standard (see Figure 20.1), with nearly every component developed specifically for use in mobile systems.

The computers have settled into a number of distinct roles that now determine the size and capabilities of the systems available. Traveling users have specific requirements of portable computers, and the added weight and expense incurred by additional features makes it less likely for a user to carry a system more powerful than is needed.

Form Factors

There are three basic form factors that describe most of the portable computers on the market today: laptops, notebooks, and subnotebooks. The definitions of the three types are fluid, however, with the options available on some systems causing particular models to ride the cusp of two categories. The categories are based primarily on size and weight, but these factors have a natural relationship to the capabilities of the system, because a larger case obviously can fit more into it. The three form factors are described in the following sections.

Laptops

As the original name coined for the clamshell-type portable computer, the laptop is the largest of the three basic form factors (see Figure 20.1). Typically, a laptop system weighs seven pounds or more, and is approximately 9×12×2 inches in size, although the larger screens now arriving on the market are causing all portable system sizes to increase. Originally the smallest possible size for a computer, laptops have today become the high-end machines, offering features and performance that are comparable to a desktop system.

FIG. 20.1 A laptop.

Indeed, many laptops are being positioned in the market either as desktop replacement or as multimedia systems suitable for delivering presentations on the road. Because of their weight, they are typically used by sales people and other travelers who require the features they provide, although many laptops are now being issued to users as their sole computer, even if they only travel from the office to the home. Large displays, 16M or more of RAM, and hard drives up to 2G in size are all but ubiquitous, with many systems now carrying CD-ROM drives, on-board speakers, and connectivity options that enable the use of external display, storage, and sound systems.

As a desktop replacement, many laptops can be equipped with a docking station that functions as the user's "home base," allowing connection to a network and the use of a full-size monitor and keyboard. For a person that travels frequently, this arrangement often works better than separate desktop and portable systems, on which data must continually be kept in sync. Naturally, you pay a premium for all of this functionality. Cutting-edge laptop systems can now cost as much as $6,000 to $7,000, more than three times the price of a comparable desktop.

Notebooks

A notebook system is designed to be somewhat smaller than a laptop in nearly every way: size, weight, features, and price. Weighing 5 to 7 pounds, notebooks typically have smaller and less capable displays and lack the high-end multimedia functions of laptops, but they need not be stripped-down machines. Many notebooks have hard drive and memory configurations comparable to laptops, and some are equipped with CD-ROM drives or sound capabilities.

Designed to function as an adjunct to a desktop system, rather than a replacement, a notebook probably won't impress your clients but can be a completely serviceable road machine. Notebooks typically have a wide array of options, as they are targeted at a wider audience, from the power user that can't quite afford the top-of-the-line laptop, to the bargain hunter that requires only basic services. Prices can range from less than $2,000 to more than $4,000.

Subnotebooks

Subnotebooks are substantially smaller than both notebooks and laptops, and are intended for users who must enter and work with data on the road, as well as connect to the office network. Weighing four to five pounds, and often less than an inch thick, the subnotebook is intended for the traveler that feels overburdened by the larger machines and doesn't need their high-end capabilities.

Usually, the first component omitted in a subnotebook design is the internal floppy drive, although some include external units. You also will not find CD-ROM drives and other bulky hardware components. However, many subnotebooks do include large high-quality displays, plenty of hard drive space, and a full-size keyboard (by portable standards).

As is common in the electronics world, devices become more inexpensive as they get smaller, but only up to a certain point, at which small size becomes a commodity and prices go up. Some subnotebooks are intended (and priced) for the high-end market, such as the executive that uses the system for little else but e-mail and scheduling, but wants a lightweight, elegant, and impressive-looking system. Subnotebooks can cost as much as $4,000. Others are much cheaper.

Portable System Designs

Obviously, portable systems are designed to be smaller and lighter than desktops, and much of the development work that has been done on desktop components has certainly contributed to this end. The 2 1/2-inch hard drives typically used in portables today are a direct extension of the size reductions that have occurred in all hard drives over the past few years. However, the other two issues that have created a need for the development of new technologies specifically for portables are power and heat.

Obviously, operating a computer from a battery imposes system limitations that designers of desktop systems have never had to consider. What's more, the demand for additional features like CD-ROM drives and ever faster processors has increased the power drain on the typical system enormously. The problem of conserving power and increasing the system's battery life is typically addressed in three ways:

- *Low power components.* Nearly all of the components in today's portable systems are specifically designed to use less power than their desktop counterparts.

- *Increased battery efficiency.* Newer battery technologies like lithium ion, while not keeping up with the power requirements of increasingly loaded systems, are making power supplies more consistent and reliable.

- *Power management.* Operating systems and utilities that turn off specific system components, such as disk drives when they are not in use, can greatly increase battery life.

Perhaps a more serious problem than battery life is heat. The moving parts in a computer, such as disk drives, generate heat through friction, which must somehow be dissipated. In desktop systems, this is usually accomplished by using fans to continuously ventilate the empty spaces inside the system.

The worst culprit by far, however, as far as heat is concerned, is the system processor. When they were first released, the amount of heat generated by Intel's 80486 and Pentium processors was a problem even in desktop systems. Heat sinks and tiny fans mounted on top of the chip became standard components in most systems.

Because many portable systems are now being designed as replacements for desktops, users are not willing to compromise on processing power, so the chips being manufactured for use in portables have all of the speed and capabilities of the desktop models. However, for reasons of power consumption, noise, and space, there are often no fans in portable computers and very little empty space within the case for ventilation.

To address this problem, Intel has created a special method for packaging its mobile processors that is designed to keep heat output to a minimum. Other components are also designed to withstand the heat within a portable computer, which is usually greater than that of a desktop, in any case.

Upgrading and Repairing Portables

The portable systems manufactured today are generally as upgradeable and repairable as traditional desktop systems. In fact, the process of replacing a device is often simpler than on a desktop, because portable systems use modular components with snap-in connectors that eliminate the need for ribbon cables, mounting rails, and separate electrical connections. Thus, common upgrades like adding memory and swapping out a hard drive can usually be accomplished in seconds.

The problem with replacing components in portables is that the hardware tends to be much less generic in portable systems than it is in desktops. Except for PC Cards, which are interchangeable by definition, and in some cases hard drives, purchasing a component that is not specifically intended for use in your exact system model can be risky.

In some cases, these compatibility problems are a matter of simple logistics. Portable system manufacturers jam a great deal of machinery into a very small case, and sometimes a new device just will not fit in the space left by the old one. This is particularly true of devices that must be accessible from the outside of the case, like CD-ROM and floppy drives. Keyboards and monitors, the most easily replaceable of desktop components, are so completely integrated into the case of a portable system that they may not be practically removed at all.

In other cases, your upgrade path may be deliberately limited by the options available in the system BIOS. For example, a manufacturer may limit the hard drive types supported by the system in order to force you to buy a replacement drive from them, and not a third party. This is something that you should check when shopping for a system by asking whether the BIOS is upgradeable and finding out how much the vendor charges for replacement components.

Most of the time, components for portable systems are sold by referencing the system model numbers, even when third parties are involved. If you look through a catalog for desktop memory, for example, you see parts listed generically by attributes like chip speed, form factor, and parity or non-parity. The memory listings for portable systems, on the other hand, will very likely consist of a series of systems manufacturers' names and model numbers, plus the amount of memory in the module.

There are always exceptions to the rule, of course. It is even possible to purchase a basic laptop case and populate it with individual components from various manufacturers. However, purchasing compatible components that fit together properly is certainly more of a challenge than it is for a desktop system.

> **Note**
>
> Generally speaking, purchasing a pre-assembled system from a reputable manufacturer is strongly recommended, as is purchasing only replacement components that are advertised as being specifically designed for your system.

Portable System Hardware

From a technical standpoint, some of the components used in portable systems are very similar to those in desktop computers, while others are completely different. The following sections examine the various subsystems found in portable computers and how they differ from their counterparts, discussed in the rest of this book.

Displays

Perhaps the most obvious difference between a portable system and a desktop is the display screen. Gone is the box with an emitter bombarding a concave glass tube with electrons, In its place is a flat screen, the whole assembly for which is more than half an inch thick. This is called an *LCD*, or *liquid crystal diode display*. Virtually all of the screens in portable systems today are color, although monochromes were at one point the industry standard, just as in standard monitors.

The display is usually the single most expensive component in a portable system, often costing the manufacturer $1,000 or more. In fact, it is sometimes more economical to replace the entire computer rather than have a broken display replaced. In the first laptops with color screens, the display was a poor replacement for a standard VGA monitor. Today's portable screens are much improved, and while not quite up to the standards of a good monitor, provide excellent performance, suitable even for graphic-intensive applications like bitmap editing and videoconferencing.

The LCD display in a portable system is designed to operate at a specific resolution. This is because the size of the pixels on an LCD panel cannot be changed. On a desktop system, the signal output from the video adapter can change the resolution on the monitor, thus changing the number of pixels created on the screen. Obviously, as you switch from a resolution of 640×480 to 800×600, the pixels must be smaller in order to fit into the same space.

An LCD panel, on the other hand, should be thought of as a grid ruled off to a specified resolution, with transistors controlling the color that is displayed by each individual pixel. The arrangement of the transistors defines the two major types of LCD displays used in portable systems today: dual scan and active matrix.

Dual Scan Displays. The *dual scan* display, sometimes called a *passive matrix* display, has an array of transistors running down the x- and y-axes of two sides of the screen. The number of transistors determines the screen's resolution. For example, a dual scan display with 640 transistors along the x-axis and 480 along the y creates a grid like that shown in Figure 20.2. Each pixel on the screen is controlled by the two transistors representing its coordinates on the x- and y-axes.

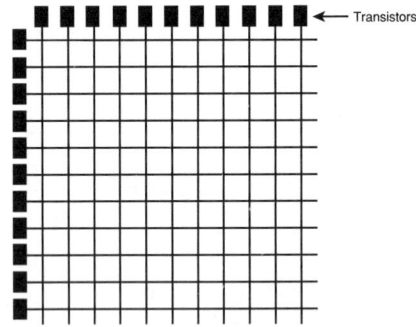

FIG. 20.2 Dual scan LCD displays use a combination of two transistors on intersecting axes to control the color of each pixel.

If a transistor in a dual scan display should fail, a whole line of pixels is disabled, causing a black line across the screen. There is no solution for this problem other than to replace the display or just live with it. The term *dual scan* comes from the fact that the processor redraws half of the screen at a time, which speeds up the refresh process somewhat.

Dual scan displays are decidedly inferior to active matrix screens. Dual scan displays tend to be dimmer, because the pixels work by modifying the properties of reflected light (either room light or, more likely, a white light source behind the screen), rather than generating their own. Dual scan panels are also prone to ghost images, and are difficult to view from an angle, making it hard for two or more people to share the same screen.

Of course, they are also far less expensive than active matrix screens. These drawbacks are most noticeable during video-intensive applications, such as presentations, full-color graphics, video, or fast-moving games. For computing tasks that consist largely of reading words on the screen, like word processing and e-mail, the display is quite serviceable, even for long periods of time.

The standard size for a dual scan display is 10 1/2 inches (measured diagonally), running at 640×480, but there are now some systems with 12.1-inch displays that run at 800×600 resolution. If you are familiar with the dual scan display of an older portable, you will find that today's models are greatly improved.

Active Matrix Displays. An active matrix display, also known as a *TFT (thin film transistor)* display, differs from a dual scan in that it contains a transistor for every pixel on the screen, rather than just at the edges. The transistors are arranged on a grid of conductive material, with each connected to a horizontal and a vertical member (see Figure 20.3). Selected voltages are applied by electrodes at the perimeter of the grid in order to address each pixel individually.

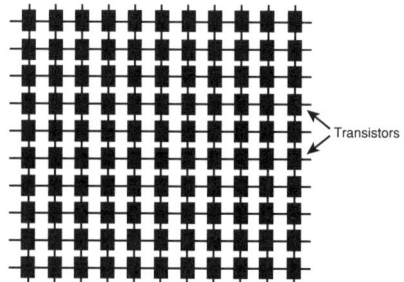

FIG. 20.3 Active matrix LCD displays contain a transistor for each pixel on the screen. The pixels generate their own light for a brighter display.

Because every pixel is individually powered, each one generates its own light of the appropriate color, creating a display that is much brighter and more vivid than a dual scan panel. The viewing angle is also greater, allowing multiple viewers to gather around the screen; and refreshes are faster and crisper, without the fuzziness of the dual scans, even in the case of games or full-motion video.

On the downside, it should be no surprise that, with 480,000 transistors rather than 1,400 (on a 800×600 screen), an active matrix display requires a lot more power than a dual scan. It also drains batteries faster, and costs a great deal more as well.

With all of these transistors, it is not uncommon for failures to occur, resulting in displays with one or more "dead pixels," due to malfunctioning transistors. Unlike a dual scan display, in which the failure of a single transistor causes an immediate and obvious flaw, a single black pixel is far less noticeable. However, many buyers feel (and rightly so) that a computer costing thousands of dollars should be perfect and have attempted to return systems to the manufacturer solely for this reason.

This has occurred often enough that many portable computer manufacturers refuse to accept returns of systems for less than a set number of bad pixels. This is another part of the vendor's purchasing policy that you should check before ordering a system with an active matrix display.

The 12.1-inch active matrix screen has become a standard on high-end laptops, running at a resolution of 800×600 or even 1,024×768. Many portable systems now also include PCI bus video adapters with 2M of RAM, providing extra speed, even at 16- or 24-bit color depths. These displays come very close to rivaling that of a quality monitor and video adapter in a desktop system.

Not to be accused of dragging their feet, however, manufacturers are now bringing new systems to market with 13- and even 14-inch TFT screens.

> **Note**
>
> Another flat screen technology, called the gas plasma display, has been used in large display screens and a few portables. Plasma displays provide a CRT-quality picture on a thin flat screen using two glass panes filled with a neon/xenon gas mixture. Unfortunately, the displays require far more power than LCDs and have never become a practical alternative for the portable computer market.

Screen Resolution. The screen resolution of a portable system's display can be an important factor in your purchasing decision. If you are accustomed to working on desktop systems running at 800×600 or 1,024×768 pixels or more, you will find a 640×480 laptop screen to be very restrictive. Remember that an LCD screen's resolution is determined as much by the screen hardware as by the drivers and the amount of video memory installed in the system.

Some portables can use a *virtual screen* arrangement to provide an 800×600 (or larger) display on a 640×480 pixel screen. The larger display is maintained in video memory while the actual screen displays only the portion that fits into a 640×480 window (see Figure 20.4). When you move the cursor to the edge of the screen, the image pans, moving the 640×480 window around within the 800×600 display. The effect is difficult to get used to, rather like a "scan and pan" video tape of a wide-screen movie. The most serious problem with this arrangement is that some manufacturers have advertised it as an 800×600 display, without being more clear about the actual nature of the display.

Color depth, on the other hand, is affected by video memory, just as in a desktop system. To operate any LCD screen in 16- or 24-bit color mode, you must have sufficient video memory available. Portables typically have the video adapter hardware permanently installed on the motherboard, leaving little hope for a video memory upgrade. There are, however, a few PC Card video adapters that you can use to connect to an external monitor and increase the system's video capabilities.

FIG. 20.4 A virtual screen lets you use a small display to view a portion of a larger screen.

Processors

As with desktop systems, the majority of portables use Intel multiprocessors, and the creation of chips designed specifically for portable systems is a major part of the company's development effort. The heat generated by Pentium processors has been a concern since the first chips were released. In desktop systems, the heat problem is addressed, to a great extent, by computer case manufacturers. The use of multiple cooling fans and better internal layout designs can keep air flowing through the system to cool the processor, which is usually also equipped with its own fan and heat sink.

For developers of portable systems, however, not as much can be accomplished with the case arrangement. So it was up to Intel to address the problem in the packaging of the chip itself. At the same time, users became increasingly unwilling to compromise on the clock speed of the processors in portable systems. Running a Pentium at 133 or 166MHz requires more power and generates even more heat than the 75MHz Pentiums that were originally designed for mobile use.

Tape Carrier Packaging. Intel's solution to the size and heat problems is the *tape carrier package (TCP)*, a method of packaging Pentium processors for use in portable systems that reduces the size, the power consumed, and the heat generated by the chip. A Pentium mounted onto a motherboard using TCP is much smaller and lighter than the standard PGA (pin grid array) processors used in desktop systems. The 49mm square of the PGA is reduced to 29mm in the TCP processor, the thickness to approximately 1mm, and the weight from 55 grams to under 1 gram.

Instead of metal pins inserted into a socket on the motherboard, a TCP processor is bonded to an oversized piece of polyimide film, not unlike photographic film, using a process called *tape automated bonding (TAB)*, the same process used to connect electrical connections to LCD panels. The film, called the *tape*, is laminated with copper foil that is etched to form the leads that will connect the processor to the motherboard (see Figure 20.5). This is similar to the way that electrical connections are photographically etched onto a printed circuit board. Once the leads are formed, they are plated with gold to guard against corrosion, bonded to the processor chip itself, and then the whole assembly is coated with a protective resin.

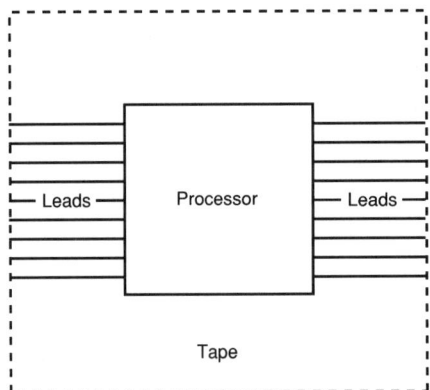

FIG. 20.5 A processor that is mounted using the tape carrier package is attached to a piece of copper-laminated film that replaces the pins used in standard desktop processors.

After testing, the processor ships to the motherboard manufacturer in this form. To mount the processor on a motherboard, the tape is cut to the proper size and the ends are folded into a modified gull wing shape that allows the leads to be soldered to the motherboard while the processor itself is suspended slightly above it (see Figure 20.6). Before the actual soldering takes place, a thermally conductive paste is added between the actual processor chip and the motherboard. Heat can therefore be dissipated through a sink on the underside of the motherboard itself while it is kept away from the soldered connections. Because TCP processors are soldered to the motherboard, they are not usually upgradeable.

It should be noted that there are manufacturers of portable systems who use standard desktop PGA processors, sometimes accompanied by fans. Apart from a greatly diminished battery life, systems like these can sometimes be too hot to touch comfortably. For this reason, it is a good idea to determine the exact model processor used in a system that you intend to purchase, and not just the speed.

FIG. 20.6 The tape keeps the processor's connections to the motherboard away from the chip itself and allows the underside of the processor to be thermally bonded to the motherboard.

Voltage Reduction. Intel has also taken measures to reduce the amount of power used by its mobile processors, which extends battery life and helps to reduce the output of heat. The pinouts of mobile Pentiums have operated at 3.3v since the original 75MHz chip, but the newer and faster models now incorporate a voltage reduction technology that uses only 2.9v for the chip's internal operations while retaining the 3.3v interface with the motherboard.

This results in processors that use up to 40 percent less power than their desktop counterparts without forcing systems manufacturers to modify the electrical standards that they use to design their machines.

Memory

Adding memory is one of the most common upgrades performed on computers, and portables are no exception. However, most portable systems are exceptional in the design of their memory chips. Unlike desktop systems, in which there are only three basic types of slots for additional RAM, there are literally dozens of different memory chip configurations that have been designed to shoehorn memory upgrades into the tightly packed cases of portable systems.

Some portables use extender boards like the SIMMs and DIMMs in desktop systems, while others use memory cartridges that look very much like PC Cards, but which plug into a dedicated IC (integrated circuit) memory socket. In any case, appearance is not a reliable measure of compatibility. It is strongly recommended that you install only memory modules that have been designed for your system, in the configurations specified by the manufacturer.

This recommendation does not necessarily limit you to purchasing memory upgrades only from the manufacturer. There are now many companies that manufacture memory upgrade modules for dozens of different portable systems, by reverse-engineering the original vendor's products. This adds a measure of competition to the market, usually making third-party modules much cheaper than those of a manufacturer that is far more interested in selling new computers for several thousand dollars rather than memory chips for a few hundred.

> **Note**
>
> Some companies have developed memory modules that exceed the original specifications of the system manufacturer, allowing you to install more memory than you could with the maker's own modules. Some manufacturers, such as IBM, have certification programs to signify their approval of these products. Otherwise, there is an element of risk involved in extending the system's capabilities in this way.

Inside the memory modules, the components are not very different from those of desktop systems. Portables use the same types of DRAM and SRAM as desktops, including the new memory technologies like EDO (Enhanced Data Out). At one time, portable systems tended not to have memory caches because the SRAM chips typically used for this purpose generate a lot of heat. Advances in thermal management have now made this less of an issue, however, and you expect a high-end system to include SRAM cache memory.

Hard Disk Drives

Hard disk drive technology is also largely unchanged in portable systems, except for the size of the disks and their packaging. Enhanced IDE drives are all but universal in portable computers, with the exception of Macintosh, which uses SCSI. Internal hard drives typically use 2 1/2-inch platters, and are 12.5mm or 19mm tall, depending on the size of the system.

As with memory modules, systems manufacturers have different ways of mounting hard drives in the system, which can cause upgrade compatibility problems. Some systems use a caddy to hold the drive and make the electrical and data connections to the system. This makes the physical part of an upgrade as easy as inserting a new drive into the caddy and then mounting it in the system. In other cases, you might have to purchase a drive that has been specifically designed for your system, with the proper connectors built into it.

In many portables, replacing a hard drive is much simpler than in a desktop system. Multiple users can share a single machine by snapping in their own hard drives, or you can use the same technique to load different operating systems on the same system.

The most important aspect of hard drive upgrades that you must be aware of is the drive support provided by the system's BIOS. The BIOS in some systems, and particularly older ones, may offer limited hard drive size options. This is particularly true if your system was manufactured before 1995 or so, when EIDE hard drives came into standard use. BIOSes made before this time support a maximum drive size of 508M. In some cases, flash BIOS upgrades may be available for your system, which provide support for additional drives.

Another option for extending hard drive space is PC Card hard drives. These are devices that fit into a type III PC Card slot that can provide as much as 450M of disk space in a remarkably tiny package (usually with a remarkably high price). You can also connect external drives to a portable PC, using a PC Card SCSI host adapter or specialized parallel port drive interface. This frees you from the size limitations imposed by the system's case, and you can use any size SCSI drive you want, without concern for BIOS limitations.

Removable Media

Apart from hard disk drives, portable systems are now being equipped with other types of storage media that can provide access to large amounts of data. CD-ROM drives are now available in many laptop and notebook systems while a few include removable cartridge drives, such as Iomega's Zip drive. This has been made possible by the Enhanced IDE specifications that let other types of devices share the same interface as the hard drive.

Another important issue is that of the floppy drive. Small subnotebook systems usually omit the floppy drive to save space, sometimes including an external unit. For certain types of users, this may or may not be an acceptable inconvenience. Many users of portables, especially those that frequently connect to networks, have little use for a floppy drive. This is becoming increasingly true even for the installation of applications, as more and more software now ships on CD-ROMs.

One of the features that is becoming increasingly common in laptop and notebook systems is swappable drive bays that you can use to hold any one of several types of components. This arrangement lets you customize the configuration of your system to suit your immediate needs. For example, when traveling you might remove the floppy drive and replace it with an extra battery, or install a second hard drive when your storage needs increase.

PC Cards

In an effort to give laptop and notebook computers the kind of expandability that users have grown used to in desktop systems, the Personal Computer Memory Card International Association (PCMCIA) has established several standards for credit card-size expansion boards that fit into a small slot on laptops and notebooks. The development of the PC Card interface is one of the few successful feats of hardware standardization in a market full of proprietary designs.

The PC Card standards, which were developed by a consortium of more than 300 manufacturers (including IBM, Toshiba, and Apple), have been touted as being a revolutionary advancement in mobile computing. PC Card laptop and notebook slots enable you to add memory expansion cards, fax/modems, SCSI adapters, network interface adapters, and many other types of devices. If your computer has PC Card slots that conform to the standard developed by the PCMCIA, you can insert any type of PC Card (built to the same standard) into your machine and expect it to be recognized and usable.

Detailed online information about the standard is available at

http://www.pccard.com

The promise of PC Card technology is enormous. There are not only memory expansion cards, tiny hard drives, and wireless modems, but also ISDN adapters, MPEG decoders, network interface adapters, sound cards, CD-ROM controllers, and even GPS systems that use global positioning satellites to locate your exact position on the earth.

Originally designed as a standard interface for memory cards, the PCMCIA document defines both the PC Card hardware and the software support architecture used to run it. The PC Cards defined in version 1 of the standard, called Type I, are credit card size (3.4×2.1 inches) and 3.3mm thick. The standard has since been revised to support cards with many other functions. The third version, called PC Card Specification—February 1995, defines three types of cards; the only difference between each one is their thickness. This was done to support the hardware for different card functions.

Most of the PC Cards on the market today, such as modems and network interface adapters, are 5mm thick Type II devices. Type III cards are 10.5mm thick and are typically used for PC Card hard drives. All of the card types are backwards compatible; you can insert a Type I card into a Type II or III slot. The standard PC Card slot configuration for portable computers is two Type II slots, with one on top of the other. This way, a single Type III card can be inserted, taking up both slots but using only one of the connectors.

> **Note**
>
> There is also a Type IV PC Card, thicker still than the Type III, that was designed for higher-capacity hard drives. This card type is not recognized by the PCMCIA, however, and is not included in the standard document. There is, therefore, no guarantee of compatibility between Type IV slots and devices, and they should probably be avoided.

The latest version of the standard, published in March 1997, includes many features designed to increase the speed and efficiency of the interface, such as:

- DMA (direct memory access) support
- 3.3v operation
- Support for APM (Advanced Power Management)
- Plug and Play support
- The PC Card ATA standard, which lets manufacturers use the AT Attachment protocols to implement PC CARD hard disk drives.
- Support for multiple functions on a single card (such as a modem and a network adapter)
- The Zoomed Video (ZV) interface, a direct video bus connection between the PC Card adapter and the system's VGA controller, allowing high-speed video displays for videoconferencing applications and MPEG decoders
- A thermal ratings system that can be used to warn users of excessive heat conditions
- CardBus, a 32-bit interface that runs at 33MHz and provides 32-bit data paths to the computer's I/O and memory systems, as well as a new shielded connector that prevents CardBus devices from being inserted into slots that do not support the latest version of the standard. The first PC Cards that use CardBus, in the form of network interface cards made by 3com and others, are just now being released to market. If you connect your portable computer to a 100Mbps network, CardBus will provide the high-speed interface that, in a desktop system, would use PCI.

The PC Card itself usually has a sturdy metal case, and is sealed except for the interface to the PCMCIA adapter in the computer at one end, which consists of 68 tiny pinholes. The other end of the card may contain a connector for a cable leading to a telephone line, a network, or some other external device.

The pinouts for the PC Card interface are shown in Table 20.1.

Table 20.1 Pinouts for a PCMCIA Card

Pin	Signal Name	Pin	Signal Name
1	Ground		
2	Data 3	8	Address 10
3	Data 4	9	–Output Enable
4	Data 5	10	Address 11
5	Data 6	11	Address 9
6	Data 7	12	Address 8
7	–Card Enable 1	13	Address 13

Pin	Signal Name	Pin	Signal Name
14	Address 14	42	–Card Enable 2
15	–Write Enable/–Program	43	Refresh
16	Ready/–Busy (IREQ)	44	RFU (–IOR)
17	+5V	45	RFU (–IOW)
18	Vpp1	46	Address 17
19	Address 16	47	Address 18
20	Address 15	48	Address 19
21	Address 12	49	Address 20
22	Address 7	50	Address 21
23	Address 6	51	+5V
24	Address 5	52	Vpp2
25	Address 4	53	Address 22
26	Address 3	54	Address 23
27	Address 2	55	Address 24
28	Address 1	56	Address 25
29	Address 0	57	RFU
30	Data 0	58	RESET
31	Data 1	59	–WAIT
32	Data 2	60	RFU (–INPACK)
33	Write Protect (–IOIS16)	61	–Register Select
34	Ground	62	Battery Voltage Detect 2 (–SPKR)
35	Ground	63	Battery Voltage Detect 1 (–STSCHG)
36	–Card Detect 1	64	Data 8
37	Data 11	65	Data 9
38	Data 12	66	Data 10
39	Data 13	67	–Card Detect 2
40	Data 14	68	Ground
41	Data 15		

PC Card Software Support. PC Cards are by definition *hot-swappable*, meaning that you can remove a card from a slot and replace it with a different one without having to reboot the system. If your PC Card devices and your operating system conform to the Plug and Play standard, simply inserting a new card into the slot causes the appropriate drivers for the device to be loaded and configured automatically.

To make this possible, two separate software layers are needed on the computer that provide the interface between the PCMCIA adapter (that controls the card slots) and the applications that use the services of the PC Card devices (see Figure 20.7). These two layers are called *Socket Services* and *Card Services*. A third module, called an *enable*, actually configures the settings of the PC Cards themselves.

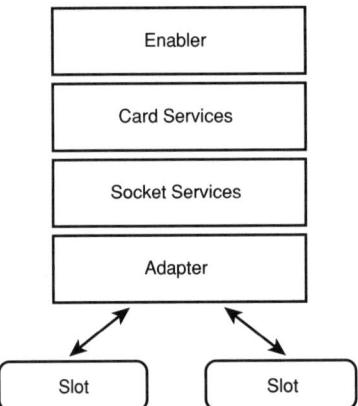

FIG. 20.7 The Card and Socket Services allow an operating system to recognize the PC Card inserted into a slot and configure the appropriate system hardware resources for the device.

Socket Services. The PCMCIA adapter that provides the interface between the card slots and the rest of the computer is one of the only parts of the PCMCIA architecture that is not standardized. There are many different adapters available to portable systems manufacturers and, as a result, an application or operating system cannot address the slot hardware directly, as it can a parallel or serial port.

Instead, there is a software layer called Socket Services that is designed to address a specific make of PCMCIA adapter hardware. The Socket Services software layer isolates the proprietary aspects of the adapter from all of the software operating above it. The communications between the driver and the adapter may be unique, but the other interface, between the Socket Services driver and the Card Services software, is defined by the PCMCIA standard.

Socket Services can take the form of a device driver, a TSR program run from the DOS prompt (or the AUTOEXEC.BAT file), or a service running on an operating system like Windows 95 or Windows NT. It is possible for a computer to have PC Card slots with different adapters, as in the case of a docking station that provides extra slots in addition to those in the portable computer itself. In this case, the computer can run multiple Socket Services drivers, all of which communicate with the same Card Services program.

Card Services. The Card Services software communicates with Socket Services and is responsible for assigning the appropriate hardware resources to PC Cards. PC Cards are no different from other types of bus expansion cards, in that they require access to specific hardware resources in order to communicate with the computer's processor and memory subsystems. If you have ever inserted an ISA network interface card into a desktop system, you know that you must specify a hardware interrupt, and maybe an I/O port or memory address in order for the card to operate.

A PC Card network adapter requires the same hardware resources, but you do not manually configure the device using jumpers or a software utility as you would an ISA card. The problem is also complicated by the fact that the PCMCIA standard requires that the computer be able to assign hardware resources to different devices as they are inserted into a slot. Card Services addresses this problem by maintaining a collection of various hardware resources that it allots to devices as needed, and reclaims as the devices are removed.

If, for example, you have a system with two PC Card slots, the Card Services software might be configured to use two hardware interrupts, two I/O ports, and two memory addresses, whether any cards are in the slots at boot time or not. No other devices in the computer can use those interrupts. When cards are inserted, Card Services assigns configuration values for the settings requested by the devices, ensuring that the settings allotted to each card are unique.

Card Services is not the equivalent of Plug and Play, although the two may seem similar. In fact, in Windows 95, Card Services obtains the hardware resources that it assigns to PC Cards using Plug and Play. For other operating systems, the resources may be allotted to the Card Services program using a text file or command-line switches. In a non-Plug and Play system, you must configure the hardware resources assigned to Card Services with the same case that you would configure an ISA board. Although Card Services won't allow two PC Cards to be assigned the same interrupt, there is nothing in the PCMCIA architecture to prevent conflicts between the resources assigned to Card Services and those of other devices in the system.

You can have multiple Socket Services drivers loaded on one system, but there can be only one Card Services program. Socket Services must always be loaded before Card Services.

Enablers. One of the oldest rules of PC configuration is that the software configuration must match that of the hardware. For example, if you configure a network interface card to use interrupt 10, then you must also configure the network driver to use the same interrupt, so that it can address the device. Today, this can be confusing because most hardware is configured not by physically manipulating jumpers or DIP switches, but by running a hardware configuration utility.

In spite of their other capabilities, neither Socket Services nor Card Services are capable of actually configuring the hardware settings of PC Cards. This job is left to a software module called an *enabler*. The enabler receives the configuration settings assigned by Card Services and actually communicates with the PC Card hardware itself to set the appropriate values.

Like Socket Services, the enabler must be designed to address the specific PC Card that is present in the slot. In most cases, a PCMCIA software implementation includes a *generic enabler*, that is, one that can address many different types of PC Cards. This, in most cases, lets you insert a completely new card into a slot and have it be recognized and configured by the software.

The problem with a generic enabler, and with the PCMCIA software architecture in general, is that it requires a significant amount of memory to run. Because it must support many different cards, a generic enabler can require 50K of RAM or more, plus another

50K for the Card and Socket Services. For systems running DOS (with or without Windows 3.1), this is a great deal of conventional memory, just to activate one or two devices. Once installed and configured, the PC Card devices may also require additional memory, for network, SCSI, or other device drivers.

> **Note**
>
> Windows 95 is definitely the preferred operating system for running PC Card devices. The combination of its advanced memory management, its Plug and Play capabilities, and the integration of the Card and Socket Services into the operating system makes the process of installing a PC Card usually as easy as inserting it into the slot.

When memory is scarce, there can be an alternative to the generic enabler. A *specific enabler* is designed to address only a single specific PC Card, and uses much less memory for that reason. Some PC Cards ship with specific enablers that you can use in place of a generic enabler. However, it is also possible to use a specific enabler when you have a PC Card that is not recognized by your generic enabler. You can load the specific enabler to address the unrecognized card, along with the generic enabler to address any other cards that you may use. This practice, of course, increases the memory requirements of the software.

Finally, you can avoid the overhead of generic enablers and the Card and Socket Services entirely, by using what is known as a *point enabler*. A point enabler is a software module that is included with some PC Cards that addresses the hardware directly, eliminating the need for Card and Socket Services. As a result, the point enabler removes the capability to hot swap PC Cards and have the system automatically recognize and configure them. If, however, you intend to use the same PC Cards all of the time, and have no need for hot swapping, point enablers can save you a tremendous amount of memory.

Keyboards

Unlike desktop systems, portables have keyboards that are integrated into the one-piece unit. This makes them difficult to repair or replace. The keyboard should also be an important element of your system purchasing decision, because manufacturers are forced to modify the standard 101-key desktop keyboard layout in order to fit in a smaller case.

The numeric keypad is always the first to go in a portable system's keyboard. Usually, its functionality is embedded into the alphanumeric keyboard and activated by a Function key combination. The Function (or Fn) key is an additional control key used on many systems to activate special features like the use of an alternate display or keyboard.

Most systems today have keyboards that approach the size and usability of desktop models. This is a vast improvement over some older designs in which keys were reduced to a point at which you could not comfortably type with both hands. Standard conventions like the "inverted T" cursor keys were modified, causing extreme user displeasure.

Some systems still have half-sized function keys, but one of the by-products of the larger screens found in many of today's portable systems is more room for the keyboard. Thus, many manufacturers are taking advantage of the extra space.

Pointing Devices

As with the layout and feel of the keyboard, pointing devices are a matter of personal taste. Most portable systems have pointing devices that conform to one of the three following types (see Figure 20.8):

- *Trackball.* A small ball (usually about 1/2-inch) embedded partially in the keyboard below the space bar, that is rolled by the user. While serviceable and accurate, trackballs have become unpopular, primarily due to their tendency to gather dust and dirt in the well that holds the ball, causing degraded performance.

- *Trackpoint.* Developed by IBM and adopted by many other manufacturers, the trackpoint is a small (about 1/4-inch) rubberized button located between the G, H, and B keys of the keyboard. It looks like a pencil eraser and can be nudged in any direction to move the cursor around the screen. The trackpoint is very convenient because you can manipulate it without taking your hands off of the keyboard. On some earlier models, the rubber cover tended to wear off after heavy use, and replacements were mysteriously unavailable. Newer versions are made of sturdier materials.

- *Trackpad.* The most recent development of the three, the trackpad is an electromagnetically sensitive pad, usually about 1×2 inches, that responds to the movement of a finger across its surface. Mouse clicks are simulated by tapping the pad. Trackpads have great potential, but tend to be overly sensitive to accidental touches, causing undesired cursor movements and especially unwanted mouse clicks. Trackpads are also sensitive to humidity and moist fingers, resulting in unpredictable performance.

FIG. 20.8 Portable systems are usually equipped with one (or two) of these three pointing devices.

The trackpad is still a relatively new innovation to the portable system market (although the technology has been around for years), and some systems allow users a choice by providing both a trackpoint and a trackpad. Unfortunately, on most of the systems that do this, the two devices use the same interrupt, forcing you to select one device or the other in the system BIOS, rather than letting you use both at the same time.

Another important part of the pointer arrangement is the location of the primary and secondary buttons. Some systems locate the buttons in peculiar configurations that require unnatural contortions to perform a click-and-drag operation. Pointing devices are definitely a feature of a portable system that you should test drive before you make a purchase. As an alternative, remember that nearly all portables have a serial port that you can use to attach an external mouse to the system, when your workspace permits.

Batteries

Battery life is one of the biggest complaints that users have about portable systems. Although a great deal has been done to improve the power management capabilities of today's portable computers, the average hardware configuration has grown enormously at the same time. The efficiency of a computer's power utilization may have doubled in the last two years, but the power required by the system in order to run a faster processor and a CD-ROM drive has also doubled, leaving the battery life the same as it was before.

Battery Types. The battery technology also has a role in the issue, of course. Most portable systems today use one of three battery types:

- *Nickel Cadmium (NiCad)*. As the oldest of the three technologies, nickel cadmium batteries are rarely used in portable systems today, because of their shorter life and their sensitivity to improper charging and discharging. NiCad batteries hold a charge well when not in use, but the life of the charge can be severely shortened if the battery is not fully discharged before recharging, or if it is overcharged.

- *Nickel Metal-Hydride (NiMH)*. More expensive than NiCads, NiMH batteries have a slightly longer life (about 50 percent), and are less sensitive to improper charging and discharging. They do not hold a charge as well as NiCad batteries when not used, and usually cannot be recharged as many times. NiMH batteries are still used in most portable systems, usually those in the lower end of the price range.

- *Lithium-Ion (Li-Ion)*. As the current industry standard, Li-Ion batteries are longer-lived than either of the other two technologies, cannot be overcharged, and hold a charge well when not in use. Li-Ion batteries can also support the heavy duty power requirements of today's high-end systems. Unlike NiCad and NiMH batteries, which can be used in the same system without modification to the circuitry, Li-Ion batteries can only be used in systems specifically designed for them. Inserting a Li-Ion battery into a system designed for a NiCad or NiMH can result in a fire. As the most expensive of the three technologies, Li-Ion batteries are usually found in high-end systems.

- *Lithium Polymer*. This is a fourth battery type that has been in development for several years, but which has not yet appeared on the market. Lithium polymer batteries can be formed into thin flat sheets and placed behind the LCD panel of a portable computer, thus providing a battery life 40 percent longer than that of Li-Ion batteries with far less weight. If this technology is implemented in portable systems, it will represent a sorely needed innovation in mobile computing.

> **Note**
>
> All of the battery types in use today function best when they are completely discharged before being recharged. Lithium Ion batteries are affected the least by incomplete discharging, but the effect on the life of future charges is still noticeable. When storing charged batteries, refrigerating them helps them to retain their charges for longer periods.

Unfortunately, buying a portable computer with a Li-Ion battery does not necessarily mean that you will realize a longer charge life. Power consumption depends on the components installed in the system, the power management capabilities provided by the system software, and the size of the battery itself. Some manufacturers, for example, when moving from NiMH to Li-Ion batteries, see this as an opportunity to save some space inside the computer. They decide that since they are using a more efficient power storage technology, they can make the battery smaller and still deliver the same performance.

Unfortunately, battery technology trails behind nearly all of the other subsystems found in a portable computer, as far as the development of new innovations is concerned. Power consumption in mobile systems has risen enormously in recent years, and power systems have barely been able to keep up. On a high-end laptop system, a battery life of two hours is very good, even with all of the system's power management features activated.

One other way that manufacturers are addressing the battery life problem is by designing systems that are capable of carrying two batteries. The inclusion of multipurpose bays within the system's case enables users to replace the floppy or CD-ROM drive with a second battery pack, effectively doubling the computer's power supply.

Power Management. There are various components in a computer that do not need to run continuously while the system is turned on. Mobile systems often conserve battery power by shutting down these components based on the activities of the user. If, for example, you open a text file in an editor, the entire file is read into memory and there is no need for the hard drive to spin while you are working on the file.

After a certain period of inactivity, a power management system can park the drive heads and stop the platters from spinning until you save the file to disk or issue any other call that requires its service. Other components, such as floppy and CD-ROM drives and PC Cards, can be powered down when not in use, resulting in a significant reduction of the power needed to run the system.

Most portables also have systemic power saver modes that suspend the operation of the entire system when it is not in use. The names assigned to these modes can differ, but there are usually two system states that differ in that one continues to power the sys-tem's RAM while one does not. Typically, a "suspend" mode shuts down virtually the entire system after a preset period of inactivity except for the memory. This requires only a small amount of power and allows the system to be re-awakened almost instantaneously.

Portable systems usually have a "hibernate" mode as well, which writes the current contents of the system's memory to a special file and then shuts down the system, erasing memory as well. When the computer is reactivated, the contents of the file are read back into memory and work can continue. The reactivation process takes a bit longer in this case, but the system conserves more power by shutting down the memory array.

> **Note**
>
> The memory swap file used for hibernate mode may, in some machines, be located in a special partition on the hard drive, dedicated to this purpose. If you inadvertently destroy this partition, you may need a special utility from the system manufacturer to re-create the file.

In most cases, these functions are defined by the APM (Advanced Power Management) standard, a document developed jointly by Intel and Microsoft that defines an interface between an operating system power management policy driver and the hardware-specific software that addresses devices with power management capabilities. This interface is usually implemented in the system BIOS.

However, as power management techniques continue to develop, it becomes increasingly difficult for the BIOS to maintain the complex information states needed to implement more advanced functions. There is, therefore, another standard under development by Intel, Microsoft, and Toshiba called *ACPI (the Advanced Configuration and Power Interface)*, which is designed to implement power management functions in the operating system.

Placing power management under the control of the OS allows for a greater interaction with applications. For example, a program can indicate to the operating system which of its activities are crucial, forcing an immediate activation of the hard drive, and which can be delayed until the next time that the drive is activated for some other reason.

Peripherals

There are a great many add-on devices available for use with portable systems, which provide functions that cannot practically or economically be included inside the system itself. Many of the most common uses for portable systems may require additional hardware, either because of the computer's location or the requirements of the function itself. The following sections discuss some of the most common peripherals used with portable systems.

External Displays

High-end laptop systems are often used to host presentations to audiences that can range in size from the boardroom to the auditorium. For all but the smallest groups of viewers, some means of enlarging the computer display is needed. Most portable systems are equipped with a standard VGA jack that allows the connection of an external monitor.

Systems typically allow the user to choose whether the display should be sent to the internal, the external, or both displays, as controlled by a keystroke combination or the system BIOS. Depending on the capabilities of the video display adapter in the computer, you may be able to use a greater display resolution on an external monitor than you would on the LCD panel.

For environments where the display of a standard monitor is not large enough, there are several alternatives, as discussed in the following sections.

Overhead LCD Display Panels. An LCD display panel is something like the LCD screen in your computer except that there is no back on it, making the display transparent. The display technologies and screen resolution options are the same as those for the LCD displays in portable systems, although most of the products on the market use active matrix displays.

You use an LCD panel by placing it on an ordinary overhead projector, causing the image on the panel to be projected onto a screen (or wall). Because they are not intended solely for use with portable systems, these devices typically include a pass-through cable arrangement, allowing a connection to a standard external monitor, as well as the panel.

While they are serviceable for training and internal use, overhead display panels do not usually deliver the depth and vibrancy of color that can add to the excitement of a sales presentation. The quality of the image is also dependent on the brightness of the lamp used to display it. While the panel itself is fairly small and lightweight, overhead projectors frequently are not. If a projector is already available at the presentation site, the LCD panel is a convenient way of enlarging your display. If, however, you are in a position where you must travel to a remote location and supply the overhead projector yourself, you are probably better off with a self-contained LCD projector.

Overhead display panels are not cheap. You will probably have to pay more for one than you paid for your computer. However, on a few models of the IBM ThinkPad, you can remove the top cover that serves as the back of the display and use the LCD screen as an overhead panel.

LCD Projectors. An *LCD projector* is essentially a self-contained unit that is a combination of a transparent display panel and a projector. The unit connects to a VGA jack like a regular monitor and frequently includes speakers that connect with a separate cable. Not all LCD projectors are portable; some are intended for permanent installations. The portable model varies in weight, display technologies, and the brightness of the lamp, which is measured in lumens.

A 16-pound unit delivering 300–400 lumens is usually satisfactory for a conference room environment; a larger room may require a projector delivering 500 lumens or more, weighing up to 25 pounds. LCD projectors tend to deliver images that are far superior to those of overhead panels; and they offer a one-piece solution to the image-enlargement problem. However, you have to pay dearly for the convenience. Prices of LCD projectors can range from $4,000 to well over $10,000, but if your business relies on your presentations, the cost may be justified.

TV-Out. One of the simplest display solutions is a feature that is being incorporated into many of the high-end laptop systems on the market today. It allows you to connect the computer to a standard television set. Called *TV-out*, various systems provide support for either the North American NTSC television standard, the European PAL standard, or both. Once connected, a software program lets you calibrate the picture on the TV screen.

TV-out is becoming a popular feature on high-end video adapters for desktop systems, as well as portables. There are also some manufacturers that are producing external boxes that plug into any computer's VGA port and a television set, to provide an external TV display solution. The products convert the digital VGA signal to an analog output that typically can be set to use the NTSC or PAL standard.

Obviously, TV-out is an extremely convenient solution, as it provides an image size that is limited only by the type of television available, costs virtually nothing, and adds no extra weight to the presenter's load (unless you have to bring the TV yourself). You can also connect your computer to a VCR and record your presentation on standard videotape. However, the display resolution of a television set does not approach that of a computer monitor, and the picture quality suffers as a result. This is particularly noticeable when displaying images that contain a lot of text, such as presentation slides and Web sites. It is recommended that you test the output carefully with various size television screens before using TV-out in a presentation environment.

Docking Stations

Now that many portable systems are being sold as replacements for standard desktop computers, docking stations are becoming increasingly popular. A docking station is a desktop unit to which you attach (or dock) your portable system when you are at your home or office. At the very least, a docking station provides an AC power connection, a full-size keyboard, a mouse, a complete set of input and output ports, and a VGA jack for a standard external monitor.

Once docked, the keyboard and display in the portable system are deactivated, but the other components, particularly the processor, memory, and hard drive, remain active. You are essentially running the same computer, but using a standard full-size desktop interface. Docking stations can also contain a wide array of other features, such as a network interface adapter, external speakers, additional hard disk or CD-ROM drives, additional PC Card slots, and a spare battery charger.

An operating system like Windows 95 can maintain multiple hardware profiles for a single machine. A hardware profile is a collection of configuration settings for the devices accessible to the system. To use a docking station, you create one profile for the portable system in its undocked state, and another that adds support for the additional hardware available while docked.

The use of a docking station eliminates much of the tedium involved in maintaining separate desktop and portable systems. With two machines, you must install your applications twice, and continually keep the data between the two systems synchronized. This is traditionally done using a network connection or the venerable null modem cable (a crossover cable used to transfer files between systems by connecting their parallel or serial ports). With a docking station and a suitably equipped portable, you can achieve the best of both worlds.

Docking stations are highly proprietary items that are designed for use with specific computer models. Prices vary widely depending on the additional hardware provided, but since a docking station lacks a CPU, memory, and a display, the cost is usually not excessive.

Connectivity

One of the primary uses for portable computers is to keep in touch with the home office while traveling by using a modem. Because of this, many hotels and airports are starting to provide telephone jacks for use with modems, but there are still many places where finding a place to plug into a phone line can be difficult. There are products on the market, however, that can help you to overcome these problems, even if you are traveling overseas.

Line Testers. Many hotels use digital PBXs for their telephone systems, which typically carry more current than standard analog lines. This power is needed to operate additional features on the telephone itself, such as message lights and LCD displays. This additional current can permanently damage your modem without warning, and unfortunately, the jacks used by these systems are the same standard RJ-11 connectors used by traditional telephones.

To avoid this problem, you can purchase a line-testing device for about $50 that plugs into a wall jack and measures the amount of current on the circuit. It then informs you whether or not it is safe to plug in your modem.

Acoustic Couplers. On those occasions when you cannot plug your modem into the phone jack, or when there is no jack available, such as at a pay phone, the last resort is an acoustic coupler. The acoustic coupler is an ancient telecommunications device that predates the system of modular jacks used to connect telephones today. To connect to a telephone line, the coupler plugs into your modem's RJ-11 jack at one end and clamps to a telephone handset at the other end. A speaker at the mouthpiece and a microphone at the earpiece allow the audible signals generated by the modem and the phone system to interact.

The acoustic coupler may be an annoying bit of extra baggage to have to carry with you, but it is the one foolproof method for connecting to any telephone line without having to worry about international standards, line current, or wiring.

Part VI

Troubleshooting and Diagnostics

21 Software and Hardware Diagnostic Tools

22 Operating Systems Software and Troubleshooting

23 IBM Personal Computer Family Hardware

24 A Final Word

Chapter 21

Software and Hardware Diagnostic Tools

Diagnostic software, the kind that comes with your computer as well as the types of available third-party software, is vitally important to you any time your computer malfunctions or you begin the process of upgrading a system component or adding a new device. Even when you attempt a simple procedure, such as adding a new adapter card, or begin the sometimes tedious process of troubleshooting a hardware problem that causes a system crash or lockup when you are working, you need to know more about your system than you can learn from the packing list sent with the system. Diagnostic software provides the portal through which you can examine your system hardware and the way your components are working.

This chapter describes three levels of diagnostic software (POST, system, and advanced) included with your computer or available from your computer manufacturer. The chapter describes how you can get the most from this software. It also details IBM's audio codes and error codes, which are similar to the error codes used by most computer manufacturers, and examines after-market diagnostics and public-domain diagnostic software.

Diagnostics Software

Several types of diagnostic software are available for PC-compatible systems. This software, some of which is included with the system when purchased, assists users in identifying many problems that can occur with a computer's components. In many cases, these programs can do most of the work in determining which PC component is defective. There are three programs that can help you locate a problem; each program is more complex and powerful than the one that precedes it. The diagnostic programs include the following:

- *POST.* The Power-On Self Test operates whenever any PC is powered up (switched on).

- *Manufacturer supplied diagnostics software.* Many of the larger manufacturers—especially high-end, name-brand manufacturers such as IBM, Compaq, Hewlett Packard, and others—make special diagnostics software that is expressly designed for their systems. This manufacturer-specific software normally consists of a suite of tests that thoroughly examines the system. IBM's diagnostics software is on the reference disk for the PS/2 systems, and on an advanced diagnostics disk for their other systems. Both Compaq and Hewlett- Packard also produce diagnostics that are designed for a technician to use in troubleshooting his or her respective systems. In some cases these diagnostics can be downloaded from their electronic bulletin boards, or it may have to be purchased from the manufacturer. Some of the PC-compatible vendors like Gateway and Dell include a limited version of one of the aftermarket packages that has been customized for their systems. In some cases, however, the diagnostics are installed on a special partition on the hard drive and can be accessed during bootup. This is a convenient way for system manufacturers to make sure you always have diagnostics available.

- *Aftermarket diagnostics software.* There are a number of manufacturers making general purpose diagnostics software for PC-compatible systems. This includes utilities—Symantec's Norton Utilities, Microscope by Micro 2000, Qa-Plus by Diagsoft, PC-Technician by Windsor Technologies, and others—that provide detailed diagnostics of any PC-compatible systems. This chapter also mentions software from numerous other companies.

Many computer operators use the first and last of these software systems to test and troubleshoot most systems—the POST tests and a third-party diagnostic package.

Manufacturer diagnostics can sometimes be expensive, but they are usually complete and work well with the systems they are designed for.

The Power-On Self Test (POST)

When IBM first began shipping the IBM PC in 1981, it included safety features that had never been seen in a personal computer. These features were the POST and parity-checked memory. The parity-checking feature is explained in Chapter 7, "Memory." The following provides much more detail on the POST, a series of program routines buried in the motherboard ROM-BIOS chip that tests all the main system components at power-on time. This program series causes the delay when you turn on an IBM-compatible system; the POST is executed before the computer loads the operating system.

What Is Tested?

Whenever you start up your computer, it automatically performs a series of tests that check the primary components in your system. Items such as the CPU, ROM, motherboard support circuitry, memory, and major peripherals (such as an expansion chassis) are tested. These tests are brief and not very thorough compared with available disk-based diagnostics. The POST process provides error or warning messages whenever a faulty component is encountered.

Although the diagnostics performed by the system POST are not always very thorough, they are the first line of defense, especially in handling severe motherboard problems. If the POST encounters a problem severe enough to keep the system from operating properly, it halts bootup of the system and produces an error message that often leads you directly to the cause of the problem. Such POST-detected problems are sometimes called fatal errors. The POST tests normally provide three types of output messages: audio codes, display-screen messages, and hexadecimal numeric codes to an I/O port address.

POST Audio Error Codes

POST audio error codes usually are audio codes consisting of a number of beeps that identify the faulty component. If your computer is functioning normally, you hear one short beep when the system starts up. If a problem is detected, a different number of beeps sound—sometimes in a combination of short and long beeps. These BIOS-dependent codes can vary among different BIOS manufacturers. Table 21.1 lists the beep codes for IBM systems and the problem indicated by each series of beeps.

Table 21.1 IBM POST Audio Error Codes and Indicated Problem

Audio Code	Sound	Problem (Fault Domain)
1 short beep	.	Normal POST-system OK
2 short beeps	..	POST error-error code
No beep		Power supply, system board
Continuous beep	_____	Power supply, system board
Repeating short beeps	......	Power supply, system board
One long, one short beep	-.	System board
One long, two short beeps	-..	Display adapter (MDA, CGA)
One long, three short beeps	-...	Enhanced Graphics Adapter (EGA)
Three long beeps	- - -	3270 keyboard card

. = *short beep*
- = *long beep*

In Table 21.2, the Audio POST Codes are listed for AMI BIOS. Tables 21.3 and 21.4 list audio codes for Phoenix BIOS. You'll notice that both lists are far superior to the IBM fatal error codes.

Table 21.2 AMI BIOS Audio POST Codes

Beep Code	Fatal Error
1 short	DRAM refresh failure
2 short	Parity circuit failure
3 short	Base 64K RAM failure
4 short	System timer failure
5 short	Processor failure

(continues)

Table 21.2 Continued

Beep Code	Fatal Error
6 short	Keyboard controller Gate A20 error
7 short	Virtual mode exception error
8 short	Display memory Read/Write test failure
9 short	ROM BIOS checksum failure
10 short	CMOS Shutdown Read/Write error
11 short	Cache Memory error

Beep Code	Nonfatal Errors
1 long, 3 short	Conventional/extended memory failure
1 long, 8 short	Display/retrace test failed

Table 21.3 Phoenix BIOS Fatal System Board Errors

Beep Code	Code at Port 80h	Description
None	01h	CPU register test in progress
1-1-3	02h	CMOS write/read failure
1-1-4	03h	ROM BIOS checksum failure
1-2-1	04h	Programmable interval timer failure
1-2-2	05h	DMA initialization failure
1-2-3	06h	DMA page register write/read failure
1-3-1	08h	RAM refresh verification failure
None	09h	First 64K RAM test in progress
1-3-3	0Ah	First 64K RAM chip or data line failure, multibit
1-3-4	0Bh	First 64K RAM odd/even logic failure
1-4-1	0Ch	Address line failure first 64K RAM
1-4-2	0Dh	Parity failure first 64K RAM
2-1-1	10h	Bit 0 first 64K RAM failure
2-1-2	11h	Bit 1 first 64K RAM failure
2-1-3	12h	Bit 2 first 64K RAM failure
2-1-4	13h	Bit 3 first 64K RAM failure
2-2-1	14h	Bit 4 first 64K RAM failure
2-2-2	15h	Bit 5 first 64K RAM failure
2-2-3	16h	Bit 6 first 64K RAM failure
2-2-4	17h	Bit 7 first 64K RAM failure
2-3-1	18h	Bit 8 first 64K RAM failure
2-3-2	19h	Bit 9 first 64K RAM failure
2-3-3	1Ah	Bit 10 first 64K RAM failure
2-3-4	1Bh	Bit 11 first 64K RAM failure

The Power-On Self Test (POST) 841

Beep Code	Code at Port 80h	Description
2-4-1	1Ch	Bit 12 first 64K RAM failure
2-4-2	1Dh	Bit 13 first 64K RAM failure
2-4-3	1Eh	Bit 14 first 64K RAM failure
2-4-4	1Fh	Bit 15 first 64K RAM failure
3-1-1	20h	Slave DMA register failure
3-1-2	21h	Master DMA register failure
3-1-3	22h	Master interrupt mask register failure
3-1-4	23h	Slave interrupt mask register failure
None	25h	Interrupt vector loading in progress
3-2-4	27h	Keyboard controller test failure
None	28h	CMOS power failure/checksum calculation in progress
None	29h	Screen configuration validation in progress
3-3-4	2Bh	Screen initialization failure
3-4-1	2Ch	Screen retrace failure
3-4-2	2Dh	Search for video ROM in progress
None	2Eh	Screen running with video ROM
None	30h	Screen operable
None	31h	Monochrome monitor operable
None	32h	Color monitor (40 column) operable
None	33h	Color monitor (80 column) operable

Table 21.4 Nonfatal System Board Errors

Beep Code	Code at Port 80h	Description
4-2-1	34h	Timer tick interrupt test in progress or failure
4-2-2	35h	Shutdown test in progress or failure
4-2-3	36h	Gate A20 failure
4-2-4	37h	Unexpected interrupt in protected mode
4-3-1	38h	RAM test in progress or address failure > FFFFh
4-3-3	3Ah	Interval timer Channel 2 test or failure
4-3-4	3Bh	Time-of-day clock test or failure
4-4-1	3Ch	Serial port test or failure
4-4-2	3Dh	Parallel port test or failure
4-4-3	3Eh	Math coprocessor test or failure
Low 1-1-2	41h	System board select failure
Low 1-1-3	42h	Extended CMOS RAM failure

POST Visual Error Codes

On the XT, AT, PS/2, and most compatibles, the POST also displays on the system monitor the test of system memory. The last number displayed is the amount of memory that tested properly. For example, a modern system might display the following:

```
32768 KB OK
```

In most cases, the number displayed by the memory test should agree with the total amount of memory installed on your system motherboard, including conventional and extended memory. Some systems display a slightly lower total because they deduct all or part of the 384K of UMA (Upper Memory Area) from the count. The RAM on an expanded memory card is not tested by the POST and does not count in the numbers reported. However, if you are using an expanded memory driver, such as EMM386.EXE or Quarterdeck's QEMM, to configure extended memory installed on the motherboard as expanded, the POST executes before this driver is loaded so that all installed memory is counted. If the POST memory test stops short of the expected total, the number displayed often indicates how far into system memory a memory error lies. This number alone is a valuable troubleshooting aid.

If an error is detected during the POST procedures, an error message is displayed onscreen. These messages usually are in the form of a numeric code several digits long; for example, 1790-Disk 0 Error. The information in the hardware-maintenance service manual identifies the malfunctioning component.

I/O Port POST Codes

A lesser-known feature of the POST is that at the beginning of each POST, the BIOS sends test codes to a special I/O port address. These POST codes can be read only by a special adapter card plugged into one of the system slots. These cards originally were designed to be used by the system manufacturers for burn-in testing of the motherboard during system manufacturing without the need for a video display adapter or display. Several companies now make these cards available to technicians. Micro 2000, JDR Microdevices, Data Depot, Ultra-X, Quarterdeck, and Trinitech are just a few manufacturers of these POST cards.

On the Web

Here are some Web sites to visit for information on some of the POST cards. The first site is the home of Microscope, the second JDR Microdevices, which sells a large variety of specialized electronics, and the final is a link to a PHD16 post card:

http://sacb.co.za/dion/micro2.htm

http://www.jdr.com/

http://www.merriweb.com.au/cblock/phd16.html

When one of these adapter cards is plugged into a slot, during the POST you see two-digit hexadecimal numbers flash on a display on the card. If the system stops unexpectedly or hangs, you can just look at the two-digit display on the card for the code indicating the test in progress during the hang. This step usually identifies the failed part.

Most BIOS on the market in systems with an ISA or EISA bus output the POST codes to I/O port address 80h. Compaq is different: its systems send codes to port 84h. IBM PS/2 models with ISA bus slots, such as the Model 25 and 30, send codes to port 90h. Some EISA systems send codes to port 300h (most EISA systems also send the same codes to 80h). IBM MCA bus systems universally send codes to port 680h.

Several cards read only port address 80h. This port address is certainly the most commonly used and works in most situations, but those cards would not work in Compaq systems, some EISA systems, and IBM PS/2 systems. A POST card designed specifically for the PS/2 MCA bus needs to read only port address 680h because the card cannot be used in ISA or EISA bus systems anyway.

> **Note**
>
> With all these different addresses, make sure that the card you purchase reads the port addresses you need.

The two most common types of POST cards are those that plug into the 8-bit connector that is a part of the ISA or EISA bus, and those that plug into the MCA bus. Some companies offer both types of POST cards—one for MCA bus systems and one for ISA/EISA bus systems. Micro 2000 and Data Depot do not offer a separate MCA bus card; rather, they have slot adapters that enable their existing ISA bus cards to work in MCA bus systems as well as in ISA and EISA systems. Most other companies offer only ISA/EISA POST cards and ignore the MCA bus.

The POST I/O port error codes for various BIOS are listed in the 6th edition of this book, located on the CD.

IBM Diagnostics

IBM systems usually have two levels of diagnostics software. One is a general-purpose diagnostics that is more user-oriented, and the other is a technician-level program that can be somewhat cryptic at times. In many cases, both programs are provided free with the system when it is purchased, and in some cases, the diagnostics and documentation have to be purchased separately. Because the troubleshooting procedures for most systems these days are fairly simple, most people have no problems running the diagnostics software without any official documentation. IBM runs a BBS system that has virtually all of its general and advanced diagnostics available free for downloading. You can find the number for this BBS listed in the vendor list in Appendix B.

IBM Advanced Diagnostics

For technician-level diagnostics, IBM sells hardware-maintenance and service manuals for each system, which include the Advanced Diagnostics disks for that system.
These disks contain the real diagnostics programs and, combined with the hardware-maintenance service manuals, represent the de facto standard diagnostics information and software for IBM and compatible systems. For PS/2 machines, IBM includes the Advanced Diagnostics on the Reference Disk that comes with the system; however, the instructions for using the diagnostics are still found in the service manuals available separately.

If you need a copy of the Advanced Diagnostics for any IBM system, check the IBM National Support Center (NSC) Bulletin Board System (BBS). The IBM BBS has virtually all of the IBM Advanced Diagnostics and Reference Disks available for download at no charge! They are stored on the BBS in a compressed disk image format, and you will need one of two utilities to uncompress the file depending on how it was originally compressed. Follow the instructions presented online for more information on which uncompress program you need. The phone number for the IBM NSC BBS is listed in the Vendor list under the IBM PC Company.

These programs produce error messages in the form of numbers you can use to identify the cause of a wide range of problems. The number codes used are the same as those used in the POST and general-diagnostics software. The meaning of the numbers is consistent across all IBM diagnostic programs. This section explores the advanced diagnostics and lists most of the known error-code meanings. IBM constantly adds to this error-code list as it introduces new equipment.

Using IBM Advanced Diagnostics. If you have a PS/2 system with the MCA (Micro Channel Architecture) bus slots (models produced later than the Models 25 to 40), you may already have IBM's Advanced Diagnostics, even if you don't know it. These diagnostics are usually hidden on the PS/2 Reference Disk. To access these diagnostics, boot the PS/2 Reference Disk. When the main menu is displayed, press Ctrl+A (for Advanced). The program changes to the Advanced Diagnostics menu. In some of the PS/2 systems, the Advanced Diagnostics were large enough to require a separate disk or disks. All the PS/2 Reference and Diagnostics disks are available for downloading on the IBM NSC BBS (see Appendix A).

Examining Error Codes. Most personal computer error codes for the POST, general diagnostics, and advanced diagnostics are represented by the display of the device number followed by two digits other than 00. When the tests display the device number plus the number 00, they indicate that a test was completed without an error being found.

The following list is a compilation from various sources including technical reference manuals, hardware-maintenance service manuals, and hardware-maintenance reference manuals. In each three-digit number, the first number indicates a device. The other two digits indicate the exact problem. For example, 7xx indicates the math coprocessor. A display of 700 means all is well. Any other number (701 to 799) indicates that the math coprocessor is bad or having problems. The last two digits (01 to 99) indicate what is wrong. Table 21.5 lists the basic error codes and their descriptions.

Table 21.5	Personal Computer Error Codes
Code	**Description**
1xx	System Board errors
2xx	Memory (RAM) errors
3xx	Keyboard errors
4xx	Monochrome Display Adapter (MDA) errors
4xx	PS/2 System Board Parallel Port errors

IBM Diagnostics

Code	Description
5xx	Color Graphics Adapter (CGA) errors
6xx	Floppy Drive/Controller errors
7xx	Math Coprocessor errors
9xx	Parallel Printer Adapter errors
10xx	Alternate Parallel Printer Adapter errors
11xx	Primary Async Communications (serial port COM1:) errors
12xx	Alternate Async Communications (serial COM2:, COM3:, and COM4:)
13xx	Game Control Adapter errors
14xx	Matrix Printer errors
15xx	Synchronous Data Link Control (SDLC) Communications Adapter errors
16xx	Display Station Emulation Adapter (DSEA) errors (5520, 525x)
17xx	ST-506/412 Fixed Disk and Controller errors
18xx	I/O Expansion Unit errors
19xx	3270 PC Attachment Card errors
20xx	Binary Synchronous Communications (BSC) Adapter errors
21xx	Alternate Binary Synchronous Communications (BSC) Adapter errors
22xx	Cluster Adapter errors
23xx	Plasma Monitor Adapter errors
24xx	Enhanced Graphics Adapter (EGA) errors
24xx	PS/2 System Board Video Graphics Array (VGA) errors
25xx	Alternate Enhanced Graphics Adapter (EGA) errors
26xx	XT or AT/370 370-M (Memory) and 370-P (Processor) Adapter errors
27xx	XT or AT/370 3277-EM (Emulation) Adapter errors
28xx	3278/79 Emulation Adapter or 3270 Connection Adapter errors
29xx	Color/Graphics Printer errors
30xx	Primary PC Network Adapter errors
31xx	Secondary PC Network Adapter errors
32xx	3270 PC or AT Display and Programmed Symbols Adapter errors
33xx	Compact Printer errors
35xx	Enhanced Display Station Emulation Adapter (EDSEA) errors
36xx	General Purpose Interface Bus (GPIB) Adapter errors
38xx	Data Acquisition Adapter errors
39xx	Professional Graphics Adapter (PGA) errors
44xx	5278 Display Attachment Unit and 5279 Display errors
45xx	IEEE Interface Adapter (IEEE-488) errors
46xx	A Real-Time Interface Coprocessor (ARTIC) Multiport/2 Adapter errors
48xx	Internal Modem errors
49xx	Alternate Internal Modem errors
50xx	PC Convertible LCD errors
51xx	PC Convertible Portable Printer errors

(continues)

Table 21.5 Continued	
Code	**Description**
56xx	Financial Communication System errors
70xx	Phoenix BIOS/Chip Set Unique Error Codes
71xx	Voice Communications Adapter (VCA) errors
73xx	3 1/2-inch External Disk Drive errors
74xx	IBM PS/2 Display Adapter (VGA card) errors
74xx	8514/A Display Adapter errors
76xx	4216 PagePrinter Adapter errors
84xx	PS/2 Speech Adapter errors
85xx	2M XMA Memory Adapter or Expanded Memory Adapter/A errors
86xx	PS/2 Pointing Device (Mouse) errors
89xx	Musical Instrument Digital Interface (MIDI) Adapter errors
91xx	IBM 3363 Write-Once Read Multiple (WORM) Optical Drive/Adapter errors
096xxxx	SCSI Adapter with Cache (32-bit) errors
100xx	Multiprotocol Adapter/A errors
101xx	300/1200bps Internal Modem/A
104xx	ESDI Fixed Disk or Adapter errors
107xx	5 1/4-inch External Disk Drive or Adapter errors
112xxxx	SCSI Adapter (16-bit without Cache) errors
113xxxx	System Board SCSI Adapter (16-bit) errors
129xx	Model 70 Processor Board errors; Type 3 (25MHz) System Board
149xx	P70/P75 Plasma Display and Adapter errors
165xx	6157 Streaming Tape Drive or Tape Attachment Adapter errors
166xx	Primary Token Ring Network Adapter errors
167xx	Alternate Token Ring Network Adapter errors
180xx	PS/2 Wizard Adapter errors
194xx	80286 Memory Expansion Option Memory Module errors
208xxxx	Unknown SCSI Device errors
209xxxx	SCSI Removable Disk errors
210xxxx	SCSI Fixed Disk errors
211xxxx	SCSI Tape Drive errors
212xxxx	SCSI Printer errors
213xxxx	SCSI Processor errors
214xxxx	SCSI Write-Once Read Multiple (WORM) Drive errors
215xxxx	SCSI CD-ROM Drive errors
216xxxx	SCSI Scanner errors
217xxxx	SCSI Optical Memory errors
218xxxx	SCSI Jukebox Changer errors
219xxxx	SCSI Communications errors

Tables 21.6 and 21.7 list error codes that were documented or encountered for several BIOS manufacturers. POST codes for older hardware can be found in the sixth edition, Appendix A, which is included on the CD-ROM that accompanies this book.

Table 21.6 Hewlett Packard 486/U POST Error Codes

Code	Description
00Ax, 00Bx, 00Cx, 00Dx	Adapter ROM (read-only memory) checksum error. Check configuration.
008x	Video ROM (read-only memory) checksum error. Check video ROM or adapter.
009x	Adapter ROM (read-only memory) checksum error in addresses between C8000h and CFFFFh. Check configuration and adapter.
0111x, 0120	CMOS real-time clock is not updating. Check battery and system board.
0130	CMOS real-time clock has invalid time and/or date. Reset date and time.
0240, 0241	CMOS memory information is incorrect. Check the clear configuration switch on the system board; it should be OFF.
0250	CMOS configuration does not match installed devices.
0280, 0282	CMOS configuration information has been corrupted.
02C0	EEPROM memory has not been set or was corrupted.
0301, 0302, 0303, 0305, 0306, 0307, 0311, 0312, 03E0, 03E1, 03E2, 03E3, 03E4, 03E5, 03EE, 03EC	System board keyboard/mouse controller did not respond.
0342, 0343, 0344, 0345, 0346, 0350, 0351	System board keyboard/mouse controller self-test failure. Check keyboard controller.
0352, 0353	Keyboard not responding to POST tests. Check cable and keyboard controller.
0354	Keyboard self-test failure. Check keyboard.
03E6, 03E7, 03E8, 03E9	Mouse interface test failure. Check mouse, cable, or keyboard/mouse controller.
03EA, 03EB	Keyboard/mouse reset failure. Check mouse and cable.
0401	Gate A20 failure. Check keyboard/mouse controller (8042) on system board or the system board itself.
0503, 0505	Serial port error or conflict. Check system board or adapters.
0543, 0545	Parallel port or configuration failure. Check configuration, system board, or adapters.
06xx	Keyboard stuck key failure; xx = Scan code (hex) of the key.
1100, 1101	System timer failure. Check system board.
1300	Floppy controller conflict. Check configuration.
13x1	Adapter communications error; x = slot containing adapter (for example, 1351 = slot 5).
13x2	CMOS indicates a slot is empty, but a board is installed; x = slot.
13x3	CMOS indicates a slot contains a board with no readable identification, but a board with a readable identification is present; x = slot.

(continues)

Table 21.6 Continued

Code	Description
13x4	CMOS configuration information does not match the board in slot x, where x = slot.
13x5	CMOS configuration information is incomplete.
2002	SIMM not detected. Check SIMMs and system board.
2003, 2005, 2007	Incorrect SIMM configuration; for example, when you have 2M and 8M memory modules installed at the same time, the 8M modules must be in the first sockets.
21xx, 22xx	DMA (Direct Memory Access) controller is not functioning correctly. Check system board.
4F0x	SIMM error; x = SIMM socket (For example,. 4F02 = socket 2).
61xx	Memory addressing error. Check installed SIMMs.
62F0	Memory parity error. Check SIMMs or system board.
62F1	Memory controller error. Check system board.
6300	Adapter RAM error. Check installed adapters and memory.
6500	System board ROM BIOS shadowing error. Check system board and setup for conflicts.
6510	Video ROM shadowing error. Check system board or video adapter.
6520	Adapter ROM shadowing error. Check system board adapters and memory.
65C0, 65D0, 65E0	Reserved memory for shadowing failed tests. Segment indicated by third digit (For example, 65D0 = segment D000h).
70xx, 71xx, 7400, 7500	Interrupt controller failure. Check system board and adapters.
8003, 8103	Hard disk configuration (number of sectors) is not correct.
8004, 8104	CMOS hard disk parameters are not correct, where 8004 = drive C, and 8104 = drive D.
8005, 8105	CMOS hard disk parameters not supported, where 8005 = drive C, and 8105 = drive D.
8x06	BIOS shadow RAM on your system board must be functioning if you have either a hard disk drive type 33 or type 34 installed.
8007, 8107	The number of hard disk drive cylinders specified for your type 33 or type 34 hard disk drive is not correct, where 8007 = drive C, and 8107 = drive D.
800D, 8010, 800E, 800F	Hard drive controller not responding. Check controller or cables.
8011	Hard disk test failure.
8012, 8013	Hard disk controller test failure.
8020, 8120	Hard drive not ready, where 8020 = drive C, and 8120 = drive D.
8021, 8121	Unable to communicate with hard disk controller, where 8021 = drive C and 8121 = drive D is at fault.
8028	Hard disk controller is configured for drive splitting, but splitting is not supported or is not functioning. Check configuration.
8030, 8130	Identify drive failure, where 8030 = drive C, and 8130 = drive D is at fault. Check the EISA Configuration Manager Utility.

IBM Diagnostics

Code	Description
8038, 8138, 803A, 813A, 803B, 813B 803C, 813C	Hard disk (Recalibrate) error, where 8039, 803A, or 803C = hard disk or controller for drive C, and 8139, 8013A, or 813C = drive D or its controller is at fault.
8040, 8140, 8041, 8141, 8042, 8142, 8043, 8143, 8044, 8144, 8045, 8145	Hard disk (Read Verify) command failure, where 804x = hard disk drive or controller for C, and 814x = hard drive or controller for D.
8048, 8148, 804A, 814A	Hard disk (Drive Identify) command failure, where 804x = drive C, and 814x = drive D.
8049, 8149, 804B, 814B	Hard disk (Set Multiple Mode) command failure, where 804x = drive C, and 814x = drive D.
8400	No boot sector (or corrupted boot sector) on hard disk.
900A, 910A, 920A	CMOS floppy configuration does not match actual drives installed, where 900A = drive A, 910A = drive B, and 920A = a third floppy drive.
9000, 9100, 9200, 9001, 9101, 9201	Floppy controller communication error, where 90xx = drive A, 91xx = drive B, and 92xx = a third floppy drive.
9002, 9102, 9202	Floppy drive (Seek) error, where 90xx = drive A, 91xx = drive B, and 9202 = a third floppy drive.
9003, 9103, 9203	Floppy drive (Recalibrate) error, where 90xx = drive A, 9103 = drive B, and 9203 = a third floppy drive.
9005, 9105, 9205	Floppy drive (Reset) error, where 9005 = drive A, 9105 = drive as B, and 9205 = a third floppy drive.
9008, 9108, 9208	Floppy drive command error, where 9008 = drive A, 9108 = drive B, and 9208 = a third floppy drive.
9009, 9109, 9209	Floppy drive track zero error, where 9009 = drive A, 9109 = drive B, and 9209 = a third floppy drive.
A001, A002, A003, A004, A005, A006, A007, A008, A009, A00A, A00B, A00C, A00D, A00E	Math coprocessor failure.
B300	CPU Level 2 cache failure.
Exxx	Memory board failure (non-HP).

Table 21.7 IBM POST and Diagnostics Error-Code List

Code	Description
1xx	**System Board Errors**
101	System board interrupt failure (unexpected interrupt).
102	System board timer failure.
102	PS/2; real-time clock (RTC)/64-byte CMOS RAM test failure.
103	System board timer interrupt failure.
103	PS/2; 2K CMOS RAM extension test failure.
104	System board protected mode failure.
105	System board 8042 keyboard controller command failure.
106	System board converting logic test failure.

(continues)

Chapter 21—Software and Hardware Diagnostic Tools

Table 21.7 Continued

Code	Description
1xx	**System Board Errors**
107	System board Non-Maskable Interrupt (NMI) test failure; hot NMI.
108	System board timer bus test failure.
109	System board memory select error; low MB chip select test failed.
110	PS/2 system board parity check error (PARITY CHECK 1).
111	PS/2 I/O channel (bus) parity check error (PARITY CHECK 2).
112	PS/2 Micro Channel Arbitration error; watchdog time-out (NMI error).
113	PS/2 Micro Channel Arbitration error; DMA arbitration time-out (NMI error).
114	PS/2 external ROM checksum error.
115	Cache parity error, ROM checksum error, or DMA error.
116	System board port read/write failure.
118	System board parity or L2-cache error during previous power-on.
119	"E" Step level 82077 (floppy controller) and 2.88M drive installed (not supported).
120	Microprocessor self-test error.
121	256K ROM checksum error (second 128K bank).
121	Unexpected hardware interrupts occurred.
131	PC system board cassette port wrap test failure.
131	Direct memory access (DMA) compatibility registers error.
132	Direct memory access (DMA) extended registers error.
133	Direct memory access (DMA) verify logic error.
134	Direct memory access (DMA) arbitration logic error.
151	Battery or CMOS RAM failure.
152	Real-time clock or CMOS RAM failure.
160	PS/2 system board ID not recognized.
161	CMOS configuration empty (dead battery).
162	CMOS checksum error or adapter ID mismatch.
163	CMOS error; date and time not set (clock not updating).
164	Memory size error; CMOS setting does not match memory.
165	PS/2 Micro Channel adapter ID and CMOS mismatch.
166	PS/2 Micro Channel adapter time-out error (card busy).
167	PS/2 CMOS clock not updating.
168	CMOS configuration error (math coprocessor).
169	System board and processor card configuration mismatch. Run Setup.
170	ASCII setup conflict error.
170	PC Convertible; LCD not in use when suspended.
171	Rolling-bit-test failure on CMOS shutdown address byte.
171	PC Convertible; base 128K checksum failure.
172	Rolling-bit-test failure on NVRAM diagnostic byte.

Code	Description
1xx	**System Board Errors**
172	PC Convertible; disk active when suspended.
173	Bad CMOS/NVRAM checksum.
173	PC Convertible; real-time clock RAM verification error.
174	Bad configuration.
174	PC Convertible; LCD configuration changed.
175	Bad EEPROM CRC #1.
175	PC Convertible; LCD alternate mode failed.
176	Tamper evident.
177	Bad PAP (Privileged-Access Password) CRC.
177	Bad EEPROM.
178	Bad EEPROM.
179	NVRAM error log full.
180x	Sub Address data error, where *x* equals the slot number that caused the error.
181	Unsupported configurations.
182	Privileged-access switch (JMP2) is not in the write-enable position.
183	PAP is needed to boot from the system programs.
183	Privileged-access password required.
184	Bad power-on password checksum—erase it.
184	Bad power-on password.
185	Bad startup sequence.
186	Password-protection hardware error.
187	Serial number error.
188	Bad EEPROM checksum CRC #2.
189	Excessive incorrect password attempts.
191	82385 cache controller test failure.
194	System board memory error.
199	User indicated INSTALLED DEVICES list is not correct.
2xx	**Memory (RAM) Errors**
20x	Memory error.
201	Memory test failure; error location may be displayed.
202	Memory address error; lines 00–15.
203	Memory address error; lines 16–23 (ISA) or 16–31 (MCA).
204	Memory remapped due to error (run diagnostics again).
205	Base 128K memory error; memory remapped.
207	ROM failure.
210	System board memory parity error.
211	PS/2 memory; base 64K on system board failed.
212	Watchdog time-out error (reported by NMI interrupt handler).

(continues)

Chapter 21—Software and Hardware Diagnostic Tools

Table 21.7 Continued

Code	Description
1xx	**System Board Errors**
213	DMA bus arbitration time-out (reported by NMI interrupt handler).
215	PS/2 memory; base 64K on daughter/SIP 2 failed.
216	PS/2 memory; base 64K on daughter/SIP 1 failed.
221	PS/2 memory; ROM to RAM copy failed (ROM shadowing).
225	PS/2 memory; wrong-speed memory on system board, unsupported SIMM.
230	Overlapping adapter and planar memory (Family 1).
231	Non-contiguous adapter memory installed (Family 1).
231	2/4-16M Enhanced 386 memory adapter; memory module 1 failed.
235	Stuck data line on memory module, microprocessor, or system board.
241	2/4-16M Enhanced 386 memory adapter; memory module 2 failed.
251	2/4-16M Enhanced 386 memory adapter; memory module 3 failed.
3xx	**Keyboard Errors**
301	Keyboard reset or stuck key failure (SS 301, SS = scan code in hex).
302	System unit keylock is locked.
303	Keyboard-to-system board interface error; keyboard controller failure.
304	Keyboard or system board error; keyboard clock high.
305	Keyboard +5v dc error; PS/2 keyboard fuse (on system board) error.
306	Unsupported keyboard attached.
341	Keyboard error.
342	Keyboard cable error.
343	Keyboard LED card or cable failure.
365	Keyboard LED card or cable failure.
366	Keyboard interface cable failure.
367	Keyboard LED card or cable failure.
4xx	**Monochrome Display Adapter (MDA) Errors or PS/2 System Board Parallel Port Errors**
401	Monochrome memory, horizontal sync frequency, or video test failure.
401	PS/2 system board parallel port failure.
408	User indicated display attributes failure.
416	User indicated character set failure.
424	User indicated 80525 mode failure.
432	Parallel port test failure; Monochrome Display Adapter.
5xx	**Color Graphics Adapter (CGA) Errors**
*501	CRT error.
501	CGA memory, horizontal sync frequency, or video test failure.
503	CGA adapter controller failed.
508	User indicated display attribute failure.

Code	Description
5xx	**Color Graphics Adapter (CGA) Errors**
516	User indicated character set failure.
524	User indicated 80×25 mode failure.
532	User indicated 40×25 mode failure.
540	User indicated 320×200 graphics mode failure.
548	User indicated 640×200 graphics mode failure.
556	User indicated light-pen test failed.
564	User indicated paging test failure.
6xx	**Floppy Drive/Controller Errors**
601	Floppy drive/controller Power-On Self Test failure; disk drive or controller error.
602	Disk boot sector is not valid.
603	Disk size error.
604	Non-media sense.
605	Disk drive locked.
606	Disk verify test failure.
607	Write protect error.
608	Drive command error.
610	Disk initialization failure; track 0 bad.
611	Drive time-out error.
612	Controller chip (NEC) error.
613	Direct memory access (DMA) error.
614	Direct memory access (DMA) boundary overrun error.
615	Drive index timing error.
616	Drive speed error.
621	Drive seek error.
622	Drive cyclic redundancy check (CRC) error.
623	Sector not found error.
624	Address mark error.
625	Controller chip (NEC) seek error.
626	Disk data compare error.
627	Disk change error.
628	Disk removed.
630	Index stuck high; drive A.
631	Index stuck low; drive A.
632	Track 0 stuck off; drive A.
633	Track 0 stuck on; drive A.
640	Index stuck high; drive B.
641	Index stuck low; drive B.
642	Track 0 stuck off; drive B.

(continues)

Chapter 21—Software and Hardware Diagnostic Tools

Table 21.7 Continued

Code	Description
6xx	**Floppy Drive/Controller Errors**
643	Track 0 stuck on; drive B.
645	No index pulse.
646	Drive track 0 detection failed.
647	No transitions on read data line.
648	Format test failed.
649	Incorrect media type in drive.
650	Drive speed error.
651	Format failure.
652	Verify failure.
653	Read failure.
654	Write failure.
655	Controller error.
656	Drive failure.
657	Write protect stuck protected.
658	Changeline stuck changed.
659	Write protect stuck unprotected.
660	Changeline stuck unchanged.
7xx	**Math Coprocessor Errors**
701	Math coprocessor presence/initialization error.
702	Exception errors test failure.
703	Rounding test failure.
704	Arithmetic test 1 failure.
705	Arithmetic test 2 failure.
706	Arithmetic test 3 (80387 only) failure.
707	Combination test failure.
708	Integer load/store test failure.
709	Equivalent expressions errors.
710	Exception (interrupt) errors.
711	Save state (FSAVE) errors.
712	Protected mode test failure.
713	Special test (voltage/temperature sensitivity) failure.
9xx	**Parallel Printer Adapter Errors**
901	Printer adapter data register latch error.
902	Printer adapter control register latch error.
903	Printer adapter register address decode error.
904	Printer adapter address decode error.
910	Status line(s) wrap connector error.

Code	Description
9xx	**Parallel Printer Adapter Errors**
911	Status line bit 8 wrap error.
912	Status line bit 7 wrap error.
913	Status line bit 6 wrap error.
914	Status line bit 5 wrap error.
915	Status line bit 4 wrap error.
916	Printer adapter interrupt wrap error.
917	Unexpected printer adapter interrupt.
92x	Feature register error.
10xx	**Alternate Parallel Printer Adapter Errors**
1001	Printer adapter data register latch error.
1002	Printer adapter control register latch error.
1003	Printer adapter register address decode error.
1004	Printer adapter address decode error.
1010	Status line(s) wrap connector error.
1011	Status line bit 8 wrap error.
1012	Status line bit 7 wrap error.
1013	Status line bit 6 wrap error.
1014	Status line bit 5 wrap error.
1015	Status line bit 4 wrap error.
1016	Printer adapter interrupt wrap error.
1017	Unexpected printer adapter interrupt.
102x	Feature register error.
11xx	**Primary Async Communications (Serial COM1:) Errors**
1101	16450/16550 chip error; serial port A error.
1102	Card selected feedback error.
1102	PC Convertible internal modem test failed.
1103	Port 102h register test failure.
1103	PC Convertible internal modem dial tone test 1 failed.
1104	PC Convertible internal modem dial tone test 2 failed.
1106	Serial option cannot be put to sleep.
1107	Cable error.
1108	Interrupt request (IRQ) 3 error.
1109	Interrupt request (IRQ) 4 error.
1110	16450/16550 chip register failure.
1111	Internal wrap test of 16450/16550 chip modem control line failure.
1112	External wrap test of 16450/16550 chip modem control line failure.
1113	16450/16550 chip transmit error.
1114	16450/16550 chip receive error.

(continues)

Table 21.7 Continued

Code	Description
11xx	**Primary Async Communications (Serial COM1:) Errors**
1115	16450/16550 chip receive error; data not equal to transmit data.
1116	16450/16550 chip interrupt function error.
1117	16450/16550 chip baud rate test failure.
1118	16450/16550 chip receive external data wrap test failure.
1119	16550 chip first-in first-out (FIFO) buffer failure.
1120	Interrupt enable register error; all bits cannot be set.
1121	Interrupt enable register error; all bits cannot be reset.
1122	Interrupt pending; stuck on.
1123	Interrupt ID register; stuck on.
1124	Modem control register error; all bits cannot be set.
1125	Modem control register error; all bits cannot be reset.
1126	Modem status register error; all bits cannot be set.
1127	Modem status register error; all bits cannot be reset.
1128	Interrupt ID error.
1129	Cannot force overrun error.
1130	No modem status interrupt.
1131	Invalid interrupt pending.
1132	No data ready.
1133	No data available interrupt.
1134	No transmit holding interrupt.
1135	No interrupts.
1136	No received sine status interrupt.
1137	No received data available.
1138	Transmit holding register not empty.
1139	No modem status interrupt.
1140	Transmit holding register not empty.
1141	No interrupts.
1142	No interrupt 4.
1143	No interrupt 3.
1144	No data transferred.
1145	Maximum baud rate error.
1146	Minimum baud rate error.
1148	Time-out error.
1149	Invalid data returned.
1150	Modem status register error.
1151	No data set ready and delta data set ready.
1152	No data set ready.

Code	Description
11xx	**Primary Async Communications (Serial COM1:) Errors**
1153	No delta data set ready.
1154	Modem status register not clear.
1155	No clear to send and delta clear to send.
1156	No clear to send.
1157	No delta clear to send.
12xx	**Alternate Async Communications (Serial COM2:, COM3:, and COM4:) Errors**
1201	16450/16550 chip error.
1202	Card selected feedback error.
1203	Port 102h register test failure.
1206	Serial option cannot be put to sleep.
1207	Cable error.
1208	Interrupt request (IRQ) 3 error.
1209	Interrupt request (IRQ) 4 error.
1210	16450/16550 chip register failure.
1211	Internal wrap test of 16450/16550 chip modem control line failure.
1212	External wrap test of 16450/16550 chip modem control line failure.
1213	16450/16550 chip transmit error.
1214	16450/16550 chip receive error.
1215	16450/16550 chip receive error; data not equal to transmit data.
1216	16450/16550 chip interrupt function error.
1217	16450/16550 chip baud rate test failure.
1218	16450/16550 chip receive external data wrap test failure.
1219	16550 chip first-in first-out (FIFO) buffer failure.
1220	Interrupt enable register error; all bits cannot be set.
1221	Interrupt enable register error; all bits cannot be reset.
1222	Interrupt pending; stuck on.
1223	Interrupt ID register; stuck on.
1224	Modem control register error; all bits cannot be set.
1225	Modem control register error; all bits cannot be reset.
1226	Modem status register error; all bits cannot be set.
1227	Modem Status Register error; all bits cannot be reset.
1228	Interrupt ID error.
1229	Cannot force overrun error.
1230	No modem status interrupt.
1231	Invalid interrupt pending.
1232	No data ready.
1233	No data available interrupt.
1234	No transmit holding interrupt.

(continues)

Table 21.7 Continued	
Code	Description
12xx	**Alternate Async Communications (Serial COM2:, COM3:, and COM4:) Errors**
1235	No interrupts.
1236	No received sine status interrupt.
1237	No receive data available.
1238	Transmit holding register not empty.
1239	No modem status interrupt.
1240	Transmit holding register not empty.
1241	No interrupts.
1242	No interrupt 4.
1243	No interrupt 3.
1244	No data transferred.
1245	Maximum baud rate error.
1246	Minimum baud rate error.
1248	Time-out error.
1249	Invalid data returned.
1250	Modem status register error.
1251	No data set ready and delta data set ready.
1252	No data set ready.
1253	No delta data set ready.
1254	Modem status register not clear.
1255	No clear to send and delta clear to send.
1256	No clear to send.
1257	No delta clear to send.
13xx	**Game Control Adapter Errors**
1301	Game control adapter test failure.
1302	Joystick test failure.
17xx	**ST-506/412 Fixed Disk and Controller Errors**
1701	Fixed disk general POST error.
1702	Drive/controller time-out error.
1703	Drive seek error.
1704	Controller failed.
1705	Drive sector not found error.
1706	Write fault error.
1707	Drive track 0 error.
1708	Head select error.
1709	Error-correction code (ECC) error.
1710	Sector buffer overrun.

Code	Description
17xx	**ST-506/412 Fixed Disk and Controller Errors**
1711	Bad address mark.
1712	Internal controller diagnostics failure.
1713	Data compare error.
1714	Drive not ready.
1715	Track 0 indicator failure.
1716	Diagnostics cylinder errors.
1717	Surface read errors.
1718	Hard drive type error.
1720	Bad diagnostics cylinder.
1726	Data compare error.
1730	Controller error.
1731	Controller error.
1732	Controller error.
1733	BIOS undefined error return.
1735	Bad command error.
1736	Data corrected error.
1737	Bad track error.
1738	Bad sector error.
1739	Bad initialization error.
1740	Bad sense error.
1750	Drive verify failure.
1751	Drive read failure.
1752	Drive write failure.
1753	Drive random read test failure.
1754	Drive seek test failure.
1755	Controller failure.
1756	Controller error-correction code (ECC) test failure.
1757	Controller head-select failure.
1780	Seek failure; drive 0.
1781	Seek failure; drive 1.
1782	Controller test failure.
1790	Diagnostic cylinder read error; drive 0.
1791	Diagnostic cylinder read error; drive 1.
24xx	**Enhanced Graphics Adapter (EGA) or Video Graphics Array (VGA) Errors**
2401	Video adapter test failure.
2402	Video display error.
2408	User indicated display attribute test failed.
2409	Video display error.

(continues)

Table 21.7 Continued

Code	Description
24xx	**Enhanced Graphics Adapter (EGA) or Video Graphics Array (VGA) Errors**
2410	Video adapter error; video port error.
2416	User indicated character set test failed.
2424	User indicated 80×25 mode failure.
2432	User indicated 40×25 mode failure.
2440	User indicated 320×200 graphics mode failure.
2448	User indicated 640×200 graphics mode failure.
2456	User indicated light-pen test failure.
2464	User indicated paging test failure.
25xx	**Alternate Enhanced Graphics Adapter (EGA) Errors**
26xx	**XT or AT/370 370-M (Memory) and 370-P (Processor) Adapter Errors**
27xx	**XT or AT/370 3277-EM (Emulation) Adapter Errors**
28xx	**3278/79 Emulation Adapter or 3270 Connection Adapter Errors**
29xx	**Color/Graphics Printer Errors**
30xx	**Primary PC Network Adapter Errors**
3001	Processor test failure.
3002	ROM checksum test failure.
3003	Unit ID PROM test failure.
3004	RAM test failure.
3005	Host interface controller test failure.
3006	[p/m]12v test failure.
3007	Digital loopback test failure.
3008	Host detected host interface controller failure.
3009	Sync failure and no Go bit.
3010	Host interface controller test OK and no Go bit.
3011	Go bit and no command 41.
3012	Card not present.
3013	Digital failure; fall through.
3015	Analog failure.
3041	Hot carrier; not this card.
3042	Hot carrier; this card.
31xx	**Secondary PC Network Adapter Errors**
3101	Processor test failure.
3102	ROM checksum test failure.

Code	Description
31xx	**Secondary PC Network Adapter Errors**
3103	Unit ID PROM test failure.
3104	RAM test failure.
3105	Host interface controller test failure.
3106	[p/m]12v test failure.
3107	Digital loopback test failure.
3108	Host detected host interface controller failure.
3109	Sync failure and no Go bit.
3110	Host interface controller test OK and no Go bit.
3111	Go bit and no command 41.
3112	Card not present.
3113	Digital failure; fall through.
3115	Analog failure.
3141	Hot carrier; not this card.
3142	Hot carrier; this card.
32xx	**3270 PC or AT Display and Programmed Symbols Adapter Errors**
33xx	**Compact Printer Errors**
35xx	**Enhanced Display Station Emulation Adapter (EDSEA) Errors**
36xx	**General-Purpose Interface Bus (GPIB) Adapter Errors**
37xx	**System Board SCSI Controller Error**
38xx	**Data Acquisition Adapter Errors**
39xx	**Professional Graphics Adapter (PGA) Errors**
44xx	**5278 Display Attachment Unit and 5279 Display Errors**
45xx	**IEEE Interface Adapter (IEEE-488) Errors**
46xx	**A Real-Time Interface Coprocessor (ARTIC) Multiport/2 Adapter Errors**
48xx	**Internal Modem Errors**
49xx	**Alternate Internal Modem Errors**
50xx	**PC Convertible LCD Errors**
51xx	**PC Convertible Portable Printer Errors**
56xx	**Financial Communication System Errors**
70xx	**Phoenix BIOS/Chipset Unique Error Codes**
7000	Chipset CMOS failure.
7001	Chipset shadow RAM failure.
7002	Chipset CMOS configuration error.

(continues)

Table 21.7 Continued	
Code	Description
71xx	Voice Communications Adapter (VCA) Errors
73xx	3 1/2-Inch External Disk Drive Errors
74xx	IBM PS/2 Display Adapter (VGA Card) Errors
74xx	8514/A Display Adapter Errors
76xx	4216 PagePrinter Adapter Errors
84xx	PS/2 Speech Adapter Errors
85xx	2MB XMA Memory Adapter or XMA Adapter/A Errors
86xx	PS/2 Pointing Device (Mouse) Errors
89xx	Musical Instrument Digital Interface (MIDI) Adapter Errors
91xx	IBM 3363 Write-Once Read Multiple (WORM) Optical Drive/Adapter Errors
96xx	SCSI Adapter with Cache (32-Bit) Errors
100xx	Multiprotocol Adapter/A Errors
101xx	300/1200bps Internal Modem/A Errors
104xx	ESDI or MCA IDE Fixed Disk or Adapter Errors
107xx	5 1/4-Inch External Disk Drive or Adapter Errors
112xx	SCSI Adapter (16-bit without Cache) Errors
113xx	System Board SCSI Adapter (16-Bit) Errors
129xx	Processor Complex (CPU Board) Errors
149xx	P70/P75 Plasma Display and Adapter Errors
152xx	XGA Display Adapter/A Errors
164xx	120M Internal Tape Drive Errors
165xx	6157 Streaming Tape Drive or Tape Attachment Adapter Errors
16520	Streaming tape drive failure.
16540	Tape attachment adapter failure.
166xx	Primary Token Ring Network Adapter Errors
167xx	Alternate Token Ring Network Adapter Errors
180xx	PS/2 Wizard Adapter Errors
185xx	DBCS Japanese Display Adapter/A Errors

Code	Description
194xx	80286 Memory-Expansion Option Memory-Module Errors
200xx	Image Adapter/A Errors
208xx	Unknown SCSI Device Errors
209xx	SCSI Removable Disk Errors
210xx	SCSI Fixed Disk Errors
210PLSC	"PLSC" codes indicate errors P = SCSI ID number (Physical Unit Number, or PUN) L = Logical unit number (LUN, usually 0) S = Host Adapter slot number C = SCSI Drive capacity: A = 60M B = 80M C = 120M D = 160M E = 320M F = 400M H = 1,024M (1G) I = 104M J = 212M U = Undetermined or Non-IBM OEM Drive
211xx	SCSI Tape Drive Errors
212xx	SCSI Printer Errors
213xx	SCSI Processor Errors
214xx	SCSI Write-Once Read Multiple (WORM) Drive Errors
215xx	SCSI CD-ROM Drive Errors
216xx	SCSI Scanner Errors
217xx	SCSI Magneto Optical Drive Errors
218xx	SCSI Jukebox Changer Errors
219xx	SCSI Communications Errors
243xxxx	XGA-2 Adapter/A Errors
I998xxxx	Dynamic Configuration Select (DCS) Information Codes
I99900xx	Initial Microcode Load (IML) Error
I99903xx	No Bootable Device, Initial Program Load (IPL) Errors
I99904xx	IML-to-System Mismatch
I99906xx	IML Errors

General-Purpose Diagnostics Programs

A large number of third-party diagnostics programs are available for PC-compatible systems. Specific programs are available also to test memory, floppy drives, hard disks, video boards, and most other areas of the system. Although some of these utility packages should be considered essential in any tool kit, many fall short of the level needed by professional-level troubleshooters. Many products, geared more toward end users, lack the accuracy, features, and capabilities needed by technically proficient people who are serious about troubleshooting. Most of the better diagnostics on the market offer several advantages over the IBM diagnostics. They usually are better at determining where a problem lies within a system, especially in IBM-compatible systems. Serial- and parallel-port loopback connectors, or wrap plugs, are often included in these packages, or are available for a separate charge. The plugs are required to properly diagnose and test serial and parallel ports. (IBM always charges extra for these plugs.)

Many of these programs can be run in a batch mode, which enables a series of tests to be run from the command line without operator intervention. You then can set up automated test suites, which can be especially useful in burning in a system or executing the same tests on many systems.

These programs test all types of memory, including conventional (base) memory, extended memory, and expanded memory. Failures can usually be identified down to the individual chip or SIMM (bank and bit) level.

> **Tip**
> Before trying a commercial diagnostic program to solve your problem, look in your operating system. Most operating systems today provide at least some of the diagnostic functions that diagnostic programs do. You may be able to save some time and money. Operating system-based diagnostics are covered in Chapter 22, "Operating Systems Software and Troubleshooting."

Unfortunately, there is no clear leader in the area of diagnostic software. Each program presented here has unique advantages. As a result, no program is universally better than another. When deciding which diagnostic programs, if any, to include in your arsenal, look for the features that you need.

AMIDiag

AMI (American Megatrends, Inc.) makes the most popular PC ROM BIOS software in use today. The AMI BIOS can be found on the majority of newer IBM compatible systems that are currently being sold. If you have seen the AMI BIOS, you know that most versions have a built-in diagnostic program. Few people know that AMI now markets an enhanced disk-based version of the same diagnostics that are built into the AMI ROM.

AMIDiag, as the program is called, has numerous features and enhancements not found in the simpler ROM version. AMIDiag is a comprehensive, general purpose diagnostic that is designed for any IBM compatible system, not just those with an AMI ROM BIOS.

AMI's Web site has a demo version of AMIDiag available for downloading:

http://www.megatrends.com

On the Web

Checkit Pro

Touchstone Software Corporation's Checkit products offer an excellent suite of testing capabilities, including tests of the system CPU; conventional, extended, and expanded memory; hard and floppy drives; and video card and monitor (including VESA-Standard cards and monitors, mouse, and keyboard). Several versions of the Checkit product are available—Checkit Pro Deluxe is the company's most complete hardware diagnostic program. Checkit Pro Analyst for Windows performs Windows-based diagnostics. Checkit Plus, which is included by some system manufacturers with their systems, is less complete.

Checkit Pro Deluxe provides limited benchmarking capabilities but gives detailed information about your system hardware such as the following: total installed memory, hard drive type and size, current memory allocation (including upper memory usage), IRQ availability and usage, modem/fax modem speed, and a variety of other tests important to someone troubleshooting a PC. Checkit Pro Deluxe includes a text-editing module that opens automatically to CONFIG.SYS and AUTOEXEC.BAT. If you use Windows, Checkit Pro's Windows option makes it easy to edit your Windows SYSTEM.INI and WIN.INI files.

Some of the testing performed by Checkit Pro is uncommon for diagnostic utility packages (for example, its capability to test modem/fax settings). Still, Checkit Pro lacks important features such as an easy-to-use listing of available DMA channels, which is crucial if you are trying to install a sound card and other hardware devices.

For additional information on Checkit, be sure to check their Web site:

http://www.checkit.com/products/index.htm

On the Web

Microscope

Microscope by Micro 2000 is a full-featured, general purpose diagnostic program for IBM compatible systems. It has many features and capabilities that can be very helpful in troubleshooting or diagnosing hardware problems.

The Microscope package is one of only a few diagnostics packages that are truly PS/2 aware. Microscope not only helps you troubleshoot PS/2 systems, but also does some things that even IBM advanced diagnostics cannot do. For example, it can format industry-standard ESDI hard disk drives attached to the IBM PS/2 ESDI controller. When you attach an ESDI drive to the IBM ESDI controller, the BIOS on the controller queries the drive for its capacity and defect map information. IBM apparently chose a proprietary format for this information on its drives; if the controller cannot read the information, you cannot set up the drive nor format it by using the PS/2 Reference Disk.

Although IBM used an ESDI controller in its PS/2 system, you could not get just any ESDI drive to work on that system. Some drive manufacturers produced special PS/2 versions of their drives that had this information on them. Another way around the problem was to use an aftermarket ESDI controller in place of the IBM controller so that you could use the IBM ESDI drive as well as any other industry-standard ESDI drive. With this method, however, you could not use the Reference Disk format program anymore because it works only with IBM's controller. Microscope solves many of these problems because it can format an industry-standard ESDI drive attached to the IBM ESDI controller and save you from having to purchase an aftermarket controller or a special drive when you add drives to these systems.

Microscope also has a hardware interrupt and I/O port address check feature that is more accurate than the same feature in most other software. It enables you to accurately identify the interrupt or I/O port address that a certain adapter or hardware device in your system is using—a valuable capability in solving conflicts between adapters. Some user-level diagnostics programs have this feature, but the information they report can be grossly inaccurate, and they often miss items installed in the system. Microscope goes around DOS and the BIOS. Because the program has its own operating system and its tests bypass the ROM BIOS when necessary, it can eliminate the masking that occurs with these elements in the way. For this reason, the program also is useful for technicians who support PCs that run under non-DOS environments, such as UNIX or on Novell file servers. For convenience, you can install Microscope on a hard disk and run it under regular DOS.

Finally, Micro 2000 offers excellent telephone technical support. Its operators do much more than explain how to operate the software—they help you with real troubleshooting problems. This information is augmented by good documentation and online help built in to the software so that, in many cases, you don't have to refer to the manual.

On the Web

You can find more on Microscope at

http://sacb.co.za/dion/micro2.htm

Norton Utilities Diagnostics

When you consider that Norton Diagnostics (NDIAGS) comes with the Norton Utilities, and that Norton Utilities is already an essential collection of system data safeguarding, troubleshooting, testing, and repairing utilities, NDIAGS probably is one of the best values in diagnostic programs.

If you already have a version of Norton Utilities earlier than 8.0, get an upgrade. They also have a version that is designed for Windows 95. If you don't already have Norton Utilities, you'll want to strongly consider this package, not only for NDIAGS, but also for enhancements to other utilities such as Speedisk, Disk Doctor, and Calibrate. These three hard drive utilities basically represent the state of the art in hard drive diagnostics and software-level repair. SYSINFO still handles benchmarking for the Norton Utilities, and it does as good a job as any other diagnostic package on the market.

NDIAGS adds diagnostic capabilities that previously were not provided by the Norton Utilities, including comprehensive information about the overall hardware configuration of your system—the CPU, system BIOS, math coprocessor, video adapter, keyboard and mouse type, hard and floppy drive types, amount of installed memory (including extended and expanded), bus type (ISA, EISA, or MCA), and the number of serial and parallel ports. Unlike some other programs, loopback plugs do not come in the box for NDIAGS, but a coupon is included that enables you to get loopback plugs free. Note that this program uses wrap plugs that are wired slightly different than what has been commonly used by others. The different wiring allows you to run some additional tests. Fortunately, the documentation includes a diagram for these plugs, allowing you to make your own if you desire.

NDIAGS thoroughly tests the major system components and enables you to check minor details such as the NumLock, CapsLock, and ScrollLock LEDs on your keyboard. NDIAGS also provides an on-screen grid you can use to center the image on your monitor and test for various kinds of distortion that may indicate a faulty monitor. The Norton Utilities 8.0, as mentioned previously, is available for registered users of a previous version and can be purchased for $100 or less.

For information about all the Symantec utilities, see:

http://www.symantec.com/lit/util/doswinut/doswinut.html

PC Technician

PC Technician by Windsor Technologies is one of the longest running PC diagnostics products on the market. As such, it has been highly refined and continuously updated to reflect the changing PC market.

PC Technician is a full-featured comprehensive hardware diagnostic and troubleshooting tool, and tests all major areas of a system. Like several of the other more capable programs, PC Technician has its own operating system that isolates it from problems caused by software conflicts. The program is written in assembly language and has direct access to the hardware in the system for testing. This program also includes all the wrap plugs needed for testing serial and parallel ports.

PC Technician has long been a favorite with field service companies, who equip their technicians with the product for troubleshooting. This program was designed for the professional service technician; however, it is easy for the amateur to use. As a bonus, PC Technician costs much less than many of the other programs in its class.

Windsor Technologies can be found on the Internet:

http://www.windsortech.com/

QAPlus/FE

QAPlus/FE by Diagsoft is one of the most advanced and comprehensive sets of diagnostics you can buy for 386, 486, or Pentium-based computers, including PS/2s. Its testing is extremely thorough, and its menu-based interface makes it downright easy to use, even for someone who is not particularly well-versed in diagnosing problems with personal computers. QAPlus/FE also includes some of the most accurate system benchmarks you can get, which can be used to find out if that new system you are thinking of buying is really all that much faster than the one you already have. More importantly, QAPlus/FE comes on bootable 3 1/2- and 5 1/4-inch disks that (regardless of whether your operating system is DOS, OS/2, Windows NT, or UNIX) can be used to start your system when problems are so severe that your system hardware cannot even find the hard drive. You also can install QAPlus/FE on your hard drive if you are using DOS 3.2 or later.

Many of you may already have a less comprehensive version of this program called QAPlus, which is oriented toward end users. The basic QAPlus version is often included with systems sold by a number of different PC system vendors. Although the simple QAPlus program is okay, the full-blown QAPlus/FE version is much better for serious troubleshooting.

QAPlus/FE can be used to test your motherboard, system RAM (conventional, extended, and expanded), video adapter, hard drive, floppy drives, CD-ROM drive, mouse, keyboard, printer, and parallel and serial ports (the QAPlus/FE package includes loopback plugs for full testing of these ports). It also provides exhaustive information on your system configuration, including the hardware installed on your system, its CPU, and the total amount of RAM installed on your system. It provides full interrupt mapping—crucial when installing new adapter boards and other hardware devices—and gives you a full picture of the device drivers and memory resident programs loaded in CONFIG.SYS and AUTOEXEC.BAT, as well as other information about DOS and system memory use.

QAPlus/FE also includes various other utilities that are more likely to appeal to the serious PC troubleshooter than to the average PC user. These special capabilities include a CMOS editor that can be used to change system date and time, as well as the hard drive type; installed memory size and other CMOS information; a COM port debugger; a hard drive test and low-level formatting utility; a floppy drive test utility; and a configuration file editor that can be used to edit AUTOEXEC.BAT, CONFIG.SYS, a remote system communication host program that enables service people with the full remote package to operate your computer via modem, as well as other text files.

Unlike some diagnostics programs, QAPlus/FE has a system burn-in capability, meaning it can be used to run your system non-stop under a full load of computations and hardware activity for the purpose of determining whether any system component is likely to fail in real life use. Many people use a burn-in utility when they receive a new system, and then again just before the warranty runs out. A true system burn-in usually lasts 48 to 72 hours, or even longer. The amount of time QAPlus/FE can burn-in a system is user-configurable by setting the number of times the selected tests are to be run.

On the Web

Diagsoft can be found on the Internet:

http://www.diagsoft.com/

Disk Diagnostics

All the general-purpose diagnostics programs can test both floppy and hard disk drives. However, because these programs are general-purpose in nature, the drive tests are not always as complete as one would like. For this reason, there are a number of specific programs designed expressly for performing diagnostics and servicing on disk drives. The following section discusses some of the best disk diagnostic and testing programs on the market and what they can do for you.

Drive Probe

Many programs on the market evaluate the condition of floppy disk drives by using a disk created or formatted on the same drive. A program that uses this technique cannot make a proper evaluation of a disk drive's alignment. A specially-created disk produced by a tested and calibrated machine is required. This type of disk can be used as a reference standard by which to judge a drive. Accurite, the primary manufacturer of such reference standard floppy disks, helps specify floppy disk industry standards. Accurite produces the following three main types of reference standard disks used for testing drive function and alignment:

- Digital Diagnostic Disk (DDD)
- Analog Alignment Disk (AAD)
- High-Resolution Diagnostic Disk (HRD)

The HRD disk, introduced in 1989, represents a breakthrough in floppy disk drive testing and alignment. The disk is accurate to within 50µ-inches (millionths of an inch)—accurate enough to use not only for precise testing of floppy drives, but also for aligning drives. With software that uses this HRD disk, you can align a floppy drive without having to use special tools or an oscilloscope. Other than the program and the HRD disk, you need only an IBM-compatible system to which to connect the drive. This product has lowered significantly the cost of aligning a drive and has eliminated much hassling with special test equipment.

The Accurite program Drive Probe is designed to work with the HRD disks (also from Accurite). Drive Probe is the most accurate and capable floppy disk testing program on the market, thanks to the use of HRD disks. Until other programs utilize the HRD disks for testing, Drive Probe is my software of choice for floppy disk testing. Because the Drive Probe software also acts as a disk exerciser, for use with AAD disks and an oscilloscope, you can move the heads to specific tracks for controlled testing.

Disk Manager

Disk Manager by Ontrack stands today as the most comprehensive and capable hard disk test and format utility available. This program works with practically every hard disk and controller on the market, including the newer SCSI and IDE types.

> **Note**
>
> Disk Manager unfortunately got the nickname "disk mangler" in its earlier versions because of bugs and system incompatibilities. While those problems have been long since removed, some technicians refuse to use it. In today's market of IDE and SCSI drives, the need for this software is limited anyway.

The Disk Manager program allows testing of the controller as well as the drive. Read-only testing may be performed as well as read/write tests. One of the best features is the comprehensive low-level formatting capability, which enables a user to set not only interleave but skew factors as well. The low-level format portion is also capable of truly formatting most IDE drives, a feature that few other programs have.

If you do any testing and formatting of hard disks, this program should be in your utility library. For more information about Disk Manager, see "Hard Disk Drives and Controllers" in Chapter 14.

On the Web

Ontrack can be found on the Internet:

http://www.ontrack.com/ontrack/products.html

Data Recovery Utilities

There are several programs designed for data recovery rather than just hardware troubleshooting and repair. These data recovery programs can troubleshoot and repair disk formatting structures (boot sectors, file allocation tables, directories) as well as files and file structures (database files, spreadsheet files, and so on).

The Norton Utilities by Symantec stands as perhaps the premier data recovery package on the market today. This package is very comprehensive and will automatically repair most types of disk problems.

What really makes this package stand out is the fantastic Disk Editor program. Currently, there is no other program as comprehensive or as capable of editing disks at the sector level. The Disk Editor included with the Norton Utilities can give the professional PC troubleshooter or repairperson the ability to work directly with any sector on the disk. Unfortunately, this does require extensive knowledge of sector formats and disk structures. The documentation with the package is excellent and can be very helpful if you are learning data recovery on your own.

> **Note**
>
> Data recovery is a lucrative service that the more advanced technician can provide. People are willing to pay much more to get their data back than to simply replace a hard drive.

For more automatic recovery that anybody can perform, Norton Utilities has several other useful modules. Disk Doctor and Calibrate are two of the modules included with the Norton Utilities version 8.0 and later, including the Windows 95 version. Together, these two utilities provide exhaustive testing of the data structures and sectors of a hard drive. Disk Doctor works with both hard disks and floppies and tests the capability of the drive to work with the system in which it is installed, including the drive's boot sector, file allocation tables (FAT), file structure, and data areas. Calibrate, which is used for the most intensive testing of the data area of a drive, also tests the hard drive controller electronics.

Calibrate also can be used to perform deep-pattern testing of IDE, SCSI, and ST-506/412-interface drives, writing literally millions of bytes of data to every sector of the drive to see whether it can properly retain data; moving data if the sector where it is stored is flawed; and marking the sector as bad in the FAT.

> **Note**
>
> A stand-alone product called SpinRite, now in version 3.1, performs many of the same features as Calibrate, including re-interleaving drive sectors, and it is widely regarded as the best program for re-interleaving drives. However, the need for Calibrate and SpinRite has greatly diminished as controllers have become quicker and drives have had their low-level formats performed at the factory at optimum settings.

Due to the excellent Disk Editor, anybody serious about data recovery needs a copy of Norton Utilities. The many other modules that are included are excellent as well, and the latest versions now include NDIAGS, which is a comprehensive PC hardware diagnostic.

Symantec and its complete list of product offerings can be found on the Internet:

http://www.symantec.com/lit/util/doswinut/doswinut.html

On the Web

Shareware and Public-Domain Diagnostics

Many excellent public-domain diagnostic programs are available, including programs for diagnosing problems with memory, hard disks, floppy disks, monitors and video adapters, as well as virtually any other part of the system. These programs are excellent for users who do not perform frequent troubleshooting or who are on a budget.

Chapter 22

Operating Systems Software and Troubleshooting

This chapter focuses on the problems that occur in PC systems because of faulty or incompatible software. First, it describes the structure of DOS and how DOS works with hardware in a functioning system. Topics of particular interest are as follows:

- FAT file structure
- FAT disk organization
- Programs for data and disk recovery (their capabilities and dangers)

The chapter also examines two other important software-related issues: using memory-resident software (and dealing with the problems it can cause), and distinguishing a software problem from a hardware problem. Finally, the chapter examines the Windows 95 and Windows NT operating systems that have all but taken over the desktop, and how their relationship with the PC hardware differs from that of DOS.

Disk Operating System (DOS)

Information about DOS may seem out of place in a book about hardware upgrade and repair, but if you ignore DOS and other software when you troubleshoot a system, you can miss a number of problems. The best system troubleshooters and diagnosticians know the entire system—hardware and software.

Note that Windows 95, by default, still uses the same structures on the disk as DOS does, such as the Master Boot Record (MBR), DOS Boot Record (DBR), File Allocation Tables (FATs), and directories. There are a few enhancements to the directory structure in order to support long file names, but that's about it. However, the OEM Service Release 2 of Windows 95 includes a 32-bit FAT file system that breaks the current partition size barrier of 2G for DOS and Windows 95 partitions. Note that the OS/2 HPFS (High Performance File System) supports single partitions of up to 8G and NTFS (the Windows NT File System) can support 2T partitions (2T = 2,000G).

This section describes the basics of DOS: where it fits into the PC system architecture, what its components are, and what happens when a system boots (starts up). Understanding the booting process can be helpful when diagnosing startup problems. This section also explains DOS configuration—an area in which many people experience problems—the file formats DOS uses, as well as how DOS manages information on a disk.

Operating System Basics

DOS is just one component in the total system architecture. A PC system has a distinct hierarchy of software that controls the system at all times. Even when you are operating within an application program such as a word processor, several other layers of programs are always executing underneath. Usually the layers can be defined distinctly, but sometimes the boundaries are vague.

Communications generally occur only between adjoining layers in the architecture, but this rule is not absolute. Many programs ignore the services provided by the layer directly beneath them and eliminate the middleman by skipping one or more layers. An example is a program that ignores the DOS and ROM BIOS video routines and communicates directly with the hardware in the interest of the highest possible screen performance. Although the high performance goal is admirable, many operating systems (such as OS/2 and Windows NT) no longer allow direct access to the hardware. Programs that do not play by the rules must be rewritten to run in these new environments.

The hardware is at the lowest level of the system hierarchy. By placing various bytes of information at certain ports or locations within a system's memory structure, you can control virtually anything connected to the CPU. Maintaining control at the hardware level is difficult; doing so requires a complete and accurate knowledge of the system architecture. The level of detail required in writing the software operating at this level is the most intense. Commands to the system at this level are in *machine language* (binary groups of information applied directly to the microprocessor). Machine language instructions are limited in their function: You must use many of them to perform even the smallest amount of useful work. The large number of instructions required is not really a problem because these instructions are executed extremely rapidly, wasting few system resources.

Programmers can write code consisting of machine language instructions, but generally they use a tool—an *assembler*—to ease the process. They write programs using an *editor*, and then use the assembler to convert the editor's output to pure machine language. Assembler commands are still very low level, and using them effectively requires that programmers be extremely knowledgeable. No one (in his or her right mind) writes directly in machine code anymore; assembly language is the lowest level programming environment typically used today. Even assembly language, however, is losing favor among programmers because of the amount of knowledge and work required to complete even simple tasks, and because of its lack of portability between different kinds of systems.

When you start a PC system, a series of machine code programs, the ROM BIOS, assumes control. This set of programs, always present in a system, talks (in machine code) to the hardware. The BIOS accepts or interprets commands supplied by programs above it in the system hierarchy and translates them to machine code commands that then are passed on to the microprocessor. Commands at this level typically are called *interrupts* or *services*. A programmer can use nearly any language to supply these instructions to the BIOS.

DOS itself is made up of several components. It attaches to the BIOS, and part of DOS actually becomes an extension of the BIOS, providing more interrupts and services for other programs to use. DOS provides for communication with the ROM BIOS in PCs and with higher level software (such as applications). Because DOS gives the programmer interrupts and services to use in addition to those provided by the ROM BIOS, a lot of "reinventing the wheel" in programming routines is eliminated. For example, DOS provides a rich set of functions that can open, close, find, delete, create, and rename files, as well as perform other file-handling tasks. When programmers want to include some of these functions in their programs, they can rely on DOS to do most of the work.

This standard set of functions that applications use to read data from and write it to disks makes data recovery operations possible. Imagine how tough writing programs and using computers would be if every application program had to implement its own custom disk interface, with a proprietary directory and file retrieval system. Every application would require its own special disks. Fortunately, DOS provides a standard set of documented file storage and retrieval routines that can be used by all software applications. As a result, you can make some sense out of what you find on a typical disk.

Another primary function of DOS is to load and run other programs. As it performs that function, DOS is the *shell* within which another program can be executed. DOS provides the functions and environment required by other software—including operating environments such as Windows 3.x—to run on PC systems in a standard way. Windows 95 finally marries DOS and the Windows environment into a more seamless operating system. You can still drop to a DOS prompt within Windows 95, however the graphical interface is now the operational standard.

The System ROM BIOS

Think of the system ROM BIOS as a form of compatibility glue that sits between the hardware and an operating system. Why is it that the same DOS operating system can run on the original IBM PC and on the latest Pentium systems—two very different hardware platforms? If DOS were written to communicate directly with the hardware on all systems, it would be a very hardware-specific program. Instead, IBM developed a set of standard services and functions that each system should be capable of performing, and coded them as programs in the ROM BIOS. Each system then gets a completely custom ROM BIOS that talks directly to the hardware in the system and knows exactly how to perform each specific function on that hardware only.

This convention enables operating systems to be written to what is essentially a standard interface that can be applied to many different types of hardware. Any applications written to the operating system standard interface can run on that system. Figure 22.1 shows that two very different hardware platforms can each have a custom ROM BIOS that talks directly to the hardware, and still provides a standard interface to an operating system.

876   Chapter 22—Operating Systems Software and Troubleshooting

The two different hardware platforms described in Figure 22.1 can run not only the exact same version of DOS, but also the same application programs because of the standard interfaces provided by the ROM BIOS and DOS. Keep in mind, however, that the actual ROM BIOS code differs among the specific machines and that it is usually not possible to run a ROM BIOS designed for one system in a different system. ROM BIOS upgrades must come from a source that has an intimate understanding of the specific motherboard on which the chip will be placed, because the ROM must be custom written for that particular hardware.

FIG. 22.1   A representation of the software layers in an IBM-compatible system.

The portion of DOS shown in Figure 22.1 is the system portion, or core, of DOS. This core is physically manifested as the two system files on any bootable DOS disk. These hidden system files are called IO.SYS and MSDOS.SYS in MS-DOS and versions of DOS licensed from Microsoft by original equipment manufacturers (OEMs), or IBMIO.COM and IBMDOS.BOM in IBM's PC-DOS. In Windows 95, the IO.SYS and MSDOS.SYS files still exist, but perform slightly different functions. The IO.SYS file actually contains all of the code previously found in both system files, while MSDOS.SYS is a text file containing configuration settings for the boot process. These two system files are normally the first files listed in the directory on a bootable disk.

Figure 22.1 represents a simplified view of the system; some subtle but important differences exist. Ideally, application programs are insulated from the hardware by the ROM BIOS and by DOS, but in reality many programmers write portions of their programs to talk directly to the hardware, circumventing DOS and the ROM BIOS. A program may therefore work only with specific hardware, even if the proper DOS and ROM BIOS interfaces for the hardware in the machine are present.

Programs designed to communicate directly with the hardware are written that way mainly to increase performance. For example, many programs directly access the video hardware to improve screen update performance. These applications often have install programs that require you to specify exactly what hardware is present in your system so that the program can load the correct hardware-dependent routines into the application.

Additionally, some utility programs absolutely must talk directly to the hardware to perform their function. For example, a low-level format program must talk directly to the hard disk controller hardware to perform the low-level format of the disk. Such programs are very specific to a certain controller or controller type. Another type of system-specific utility, called a *memory manager*, enables extended memory in a DOS system to function as expanded memory. These drivers work by accessing the system processor directly and using specific features of the chip.

Another way that reality might differ from the simple view is that DOS itself communicates directly with the hardware. The DOS system files can contain low-level drivers designed to supplant and supersede ROM BIOS code in the system. When DOS loads, it determines the system type and ID information from the ROM and loads different routines depending on which version of ROM it finds. For example, there are at least four different hard disk code sections in IBM DOS, but only one is loaded for a specific system.

I have taken a single DOS boot disk with only the system files (plus COMMAND.COM and CHKDSK.COM) on it, and booted the disk on both an XT and an AT system, each one with an identical 640K of memory. After loading DOS, CHKDSK reported different amounts of free memory, which showed that DOS had taken up different amounts of memory in the two systems. This is because of the different code routines loaded, based on the ROM ID information. In essence, DOS, the ROM BIOS, and the hardware are much more closely related than most people realize.

DOS Components

DOS consists of two primary components: the input/output (I/O) system and the shell. The I/O system consists of the underlying programs that reside in memory while the system is running; these programs are loaded first when DOS boots. The I/O system is stored in the IO.SYS and MSDOS.SYS (or IBMIO.COM and IBMDOS.COM) files that are hidden on a bootable DOS disk. No matter what the exact names are, the function of these two files is basically the same for all versions of DOS.

The user interface program, or shell, is stored in the COMMAND.COM file, which also is loaded during a normal DOS boot sequence. The shell is the portion of DOS with which the user communicates with the system, providing the DOS prompt and access to internal commands like COPY and DIR.

The following sections examine the DOS I/O system and shell in more detail to help you properly identify and solve problems that are related to DOS rather than to hardware. Also included is a discussion on how DOS allocates disk file space.

The following sections describe the two files that make up the I/O system: IO.SYS (or IBMBIO.COM) and MSDOS.SYS (or IBMDOS.COM), as well as the DOS command processor (COMMAND.COM).

IO.SYS (or IBMBIO.COM)

IO.SYS is one of the hidden files found on any system (bootable) disk. This file contains the low-level programs that interact directly with devices on the system and the ROM BIOS. During boot-up, the DOS volume boot sector loads the file into low memory and gives it control of the system (see the section "DOS Volume Boot Sectors" later in this chapter). The entire file, except the system initializer portion, remains in memory during normal system operation.

For a disk to be bootable, IO.SYS or its equivalent must be listed as the first file in the directory of the disk and must occupy at least the first cluster on the disk (cluster number 2). The remainder of the file might be placed in clusters anywhere across the rest of the disk. The file normally is marked with hidden, system, and read-only attributes, and placed on a disk by the FORMAT command (with the /S switch) or the SYS command.

MSDOS.SYS (or IBMDOS.COM)

MSDOS.SYS, the core of DOS, contains the DOS disk-handling programs. The routines present in this file make up the DOS disk and device-handling programs. MSDOS.SYS is loaded into low memory at system bootup by the DOS volume boot sector and remains resident in memory during normal system operation.

MSDOS.SYS or its equivalent originally had to be listed as the second entry in the root directory of any bootable disk. This file usually is marked with hidden, system, and read-only attributes, and is normally placed on a disk by the FORMAT /S command or the SYS command. There are no special requirements for the physical positioning of this file on a disk.

The Shell or Command Processor (COMMAND.COM)

The DOS command processor COMMAND.COM is the portion of DOS with which users normally interact. The commands can be categorized by function, but IBM DOS divides them into two types according to how they are made available: *resident* or *transient*.

Resident commands are built into COMMAND.COM and are available whenever the DOS prompt is present. They are generally the simpler, frequently used commands such as CLS and DIR. Resident commands execute rapidly because the instructions for them are already loaded into memory. They are *memory-resident*.

When you look up the definition of a command in the DOS manual, you find an indication of whether the command is resident or transient. You then can determine what is required to execute that command. A simple rule is that, at a DOS prompt, all resident commands are instantly available for execution, with no loading of additional files required. Resident commands are also sometimes termed *internal*. Commands run from a program on disk are termed *external*, or *transient*, and also are often called *utilities*.

Transient commands are not resident in the computer's memory, and the instructions to execute the command must be located on a disk. Because the instructions are loaded into memory only for execution and then are overwritten in memory after they are used, they are called *transient commands*. Most DOS commands are transient; otherwise, the memory requirements for DOS would be much larger than they are. Transient commands are used less frequently than resident commands and take longer to execute because they must be found and loaded before they can be run. DOS' transient commands take the form of individual executable files, such as FORMAT.COM and XCOPY.COM, that are located in the DOS home directory (typically C:\DOS).

Most executable files operate like transient DOS commands. The instructions to execute the command must be located on a disk. The instructions are loaded into memory only for execution and are overwritten in memory after the program is no longer being used.

DOS Command File Search Procedure
One of the most commonly seen DOS errors is the `Bad command or filename` message that appears when you attempt to issue a command that DOS cannot process. This can happen for a number of reasons, and your troubleshooting efforts should begin at the highest level, the software itself, before you begin to suspect that a hardware problem may be at fault.

Whenever you issue a transient command or run a software application's executable file, DOS attempts to find the instructions needed to execute that command by looking in several places, in a specific order. The instructions that represent the command or program are located in files on one or more disk drives. Files that contain execution instructions have an extension of either COM (command files), EXE (executable files), or BAT (batch files). COM and EXE files are machine code programs; BAT files contain ASCII text specifying a series of commands and instructions using the DOS batch facilities. DOS attempts to locate these executable files by searching the current directory and the directories specified in the `PATH` command.

In other words, if you type several characters, like **WIN**, at the DOS prompt and press the Enter key, DOS attempts to find and run a program named WIN by performing a two- or three-level search for the program instructions (the file). The first step in looking for command instructions is to see whether the command is a resident in COMMAND.COM and, if so, to run it from the program code already loaded in memory. If the command is not resident, DOS looks in the current directory for a file called WIN with a COM, EXE, and BAT extension (in that order), and loads and executes the first file it finds with the specified name. Therefore, if two files in that directory are called WIN.COM and WIN.BAT, the WIN.COM file will always be executed in response to the `WIN` command.

If the command is not resident and no file by that name is found in the current directory, DOS looks in each of the directories specified in the DOS `PATH` environment variable in turn, searching for the file using the same extension order just indicated. Finally, if DOS fails to locate the required instructions, it displays the error message `Bad command or filename`. As you can see, this error message can be misleading. You may puzzle at the inability of DOS to run a command file that clearly is on the disk, and suspect a hardware problem concerning the disk drive itself, when actually the problem stems from the fact that the command instructions are simply missing from the search areas.

Suppose that, at the DOS prompt, you type the command **XYZ** and press Enter. This command sends DOS on a search for the XYZ program's instructions. If DOS is successful, the program starts running within seconds. If DOS cannot find the proper instructions, an error message is displayed. Here is what happens:

1. DOS checks internally to see whether it can find the XYZ command as one of the resident commands whose instructions are already loaded. It finds no XYZ command as resident.

2. DOS looks next in the current directory on the current drive for a file named XYZ.COM, then for a file named XYZ.EXE, and finally for a file named XYZ.BAT.

3. DOS looks to see whether the PATH environment variable exists. If not, the search ends here. If so, DOS checks every directory listed in that PATH for the first file that it can find named XYZ.COM, XYZ.EXE, or XYZ.BAT (in that order). Your PATH lists several directories, but DOS does not find an appropriate file in any of them.

4. The search ends, and DOS generates the message Bad command or filename.

For this search-and-load procedure to be successful, you must ensure that the desired program or command file exists in the current directory on the current drive. Or, you must set your DOS PATH to point to the drive and directory in which the program does exist.

A common practice is to place all simple command files or utility programs in one directory and set the PATH to point to that directory. Each of those programs (or commands) is then instantly available simply by typing its name from any DOS prompt, just as though it were resident.

This practice works well only for single-load programs such as commands and other utilities. Major applications often consist of many individual files and might have problems if they are called up from a remote directory or drive using the DOS PATH. This is because the PATH variable has no effect when the application looks for its overlay and accessory files.

On a hard disk system, users typically install all transient commands and utilities in subdirectories and ensure that the PATH points to those directories. The path literally is a list of directories and subdirectories specified in the AUTOEXEC.BAT file that tells DOS where to search for files when the command cannot be found in the current directory. A path on such a hard drive may look like this:

```
PATH=C:\DOS;C:\BAT;C:\UTILS;
```

In the previous example, all of the ancillary programs included with the DOS operating system will be immediately locatable because of the inclusion of C:\DOS in the PATH command.

The PATH normally cannot exceed 128 characters in length (including colons, semicolons, and backslashes). As a result of that limitation, you cannot have a PATH that contains all your directories if the directory names exceed 128 characters.

You can also completely short circuit the DOS command search procedure simply by entering the complete path to the file at the command prompt. For example, rather than include C:\DOS in the PATH and enter this command:

C:\>CHKDSK

You can enter the full name of the program:

C:\>C:\DOS\CHKDSK.COM

The latter command immediately locates and loads the CHKDSK program with no search through the current directory or PATH setting. This method of calling up a program speeds the location and execution of the program and works especially well to increase the speed of DOS batch file execution. It also allows you to immediately eliminate path problems as the source of the Bad command message.

DOS Versions

In more than a decade and a half of development, a great many DOS versions have been released. IBM released version 1.0 of the operating system in 1981, but by version 3.x Microsoft too began releasing its own DOS, using the same version numbers as IBM in most cases. Early versions of DOS were frequently designed for the hardware configurations of specific machines. At one time, IBM, Compaq, and other original equipment manufacturers would have their own versions of DOS (created by IBM or Microsoft), designed to support only their hardware. You could not, in many cases, boot an IBM DOS computer using a Compaq DOS boot disk, and gain full functionality.

DOS 5.x. By the time that DOS 5.0 was released by Microsoft, however, this situation was all but eliminated. DOS 5 was the first version of the operating system to be marketed on a retail level, and users turned out in droves to upgrade their systems. Both the IBM and Microsoft versions of DOS 5.0 and later can be used on almost any system.

DOS 5 offered vastly improved memory management, and incorporated many of the features that users had come to rely on third-party utilities for. At this time, there are some people who still swear by DOS 5, and resist upgrading to version 6 which, truth to tell, is more of an enhancement than a major overhaul. However, there is no reason why any DOS version below 5.0 should still be in use on any computer (except for museum pieces that can handle nothing but their native versions).

IBM and MS DOS 6.xx. After DOS 5.0, there were several different versions of DOS 6.xx from both Microsoft and IBM. The original release of MS DOS 6.0 came from Microsoft. One of the features included in 6.0 was the new DoubleSpace disk compression. Unfortunately, DoubleSpace had some problems with certain system configurations and hardware types. In the meantime, IBM took DOS 6.0 from Microsoft, updated it to fix several small problems, removed the disk compression, and sold it as IBM DOS 6.1. Microsoft had many problems with the DoubleSpace disk compression used in 6.0 and released 6.2 as a free bug fix upgrade.

Microsoft then ran into legal problems in a lawsuit brought by Stacker Corporation that accused Microsoft of having infringed on its rights to the compression algorithm used by its Stacker software product. Microsoft was ultimately vindicated of any wrongdoing, but not before it had removed the DoubleSpace compression feature from DOS 6.2, which was released as 6.21. Microsoft then quickly developed a non-infringing disk compression utility called DriveSpace, which was released in version 6.22, along with several minor bug fixes. IBM skipped over the 6.2 version number and released DOS 6.3 (now called PC DOS), which also included a different type of compression program than that used by Microsoft. By avoiding the DoubleSpace software, IBM also avoided the bugs and legal problems that Microsoft had encountered. Also included in the updated IBM releases were enhanced PCMCIA and power management commands.

The Boot Process

The term *boot* comes from the term bootstrap and describes the method by which the PC becomes operational. Just as you pull on a large boot by the small strap attached to the back, a PC can load a large operating system program by first loading a small program that then can pull in the operating system. A chain of events begins with the application of power and finally results in an operating computer system with software loaded and running. Each event is called by the event before it and initiates the event after it.

Tracing the system boot process might help you find the location of a problem if you examine the error messages that the system displays when the problem occurs. If you can see an error message displayed only by a particular program, you can be sure that the program in question was at least loaded and partially running. Combine this information with the knowledge of the boot sequence, and you can at least tell how far along the system's startup procedure has progressed before the problem occurred. You usually want to look at whatever files or disk areas were being accessed during the failure in the boot process. Error messages displayed during the boot process as well as those displayed during normal system operation can be hard to decipher, but the first step in decoding an error message is to know where the message came from—what program actually sent or displayed the message. The following programs are capable of displaying error messages during the boot process:

- Motherboard ROM BIOS
- Adapter card ROM BIOS extensions
- Master partition boot sector
- DOS volume boot sector
- System files (IO.SYS/IBMBIO.COM, and MSDOS.SYS/IBMDOS.COM)
- Device drivers (loaded through CONFIG.SYS or the Windows 95 Registry SYSTEM.DAT)
- Shell program (COMMAND.COM in DOS)
- Programs run by AUTOEXEC.BAT
- Windows (WIN.COM)

This section examines the system startup sequence and provides a detailed account of many of the error messages that might occur during this process.

How DOS Loads and Starts

If you have a problem with your system during startup and you can determine where in this sequence of events your system has stalled, you know what events have occurred and you probably can eliminate each of them as a cause of the problem. The following steps occur in a typical system startup:

1. You switch on electrical power to the system.

2. The power supply performs a self-test. When all voltages and current levels are acceptable, the supply indicates that the power is stable and sends the Power Good signal to the motherboard. The time from switch-on to Power Good is normally between .1 and .5 seconds.

3. The microprocessor timer chip receives the Power Good signal, which causes it to stop generating a reset signal to the microprocessor.

4. The microprocessor begins executing the ROM BIOS code, starting at memory address FFFF:0000. Because this location is only 16 bytes from the very end of the available ROM space, it contains a JMP (jump) instruction to the actual ROM BIOS starting address.

5. The ROM BIOS performs a test of the central hardware to verify basic system functionality. Any errors that occur are indicated by audio codes because the video system has not yet been initialized.

6. The BIOS performs a video ROM scan of memory locations C000:0000 through C780:0000, looking for video adapter ROM BIOS programs contained on a video adapter card plugged into a slot. If a video ROM BIOS is found, it is tested by a checksum procedure. If it passes the checksum test, the ROM is executed; the video ROM code initializes the video adapter; and a cursor appears on-screen. If the checksum test fails, the following message appears:

    ```
    C000 ROM Error
    ```

7. If the BIOS finds no video adapter ROM, it uses the motherboard ROM video drivers to initialize the video display hardware, and a cursor appears on-screen.

8. The motherboard ROM BIOS scans memory locations C800:0000 through DF80:0000 in 2K increments for any other ROMs located on any other adapter cards. If any ROMs are found, they are checksum-tested and executed. These adapter ROMs can alter existing BIOS routines as well as establish new ones.

9. Failure of a checksum test for any of these ROM modules causes this message to appear:

    ```
    XXXX ROM Error
    ```

10. The address xxxx indicates the segment address of the failed ROM module.

11. The ROM BIOS checks the word value at memory location 0000:0472 to see whether this start is a cold start or a warm start. A word value of 1234h in this location is a flag that indicates a warm start, which causes the memory test portion of the POST (Power-On Self Test) to be skipped. Any other word value in this location indicates a cold start and full POST.

12. If this is a cold start, the POST executes. Any errors found during the POST are reported by a combination of audio and displayed error messages. Successful completion of the POST is indicated by a single beep.

13. The ROM BIOS searches for a DOS volume boot sector at cylinder 0, head 0, sector 1 (the very first sector) on the A: drive. This sector is loaded into memory at 0000:7C00 and tested. If a disk is in the drive but the sector cannot be read, or if no disk is present, the BIOS continues with the next step.

14. If the first byte of the DOS volume boot sector loaded from the floppy disk in A: is less than 06h, or if the first byte is greater than or equal to 06h, and the first nine words contain the same data pattern, this error message appears and the system stops:

    ```
    602-Diskette Boot Record Error
    ```

15. If the disk was prepared with FORMAT or SYS using DOS 3.3 or an earlier version and the specified system files are not the first two files in the directory, or if a problem was encountered loading them, the following message appears:

    ```
    Non-System disk or disk error
    Replace and strike any key when ready
    ```

16. If the disk was prepared with FORMAT or SYS using DOS 3.3 or an earlier version and the boot sector is corrupt, you might see this message:

    ```
    Disk Boot failure
    ```

17. If the disk was prepared with FORMAT or SYS using DOS 4.0 and later versions, and the specified system files are not the first two files in the directory, or if a problem was encountered loading them, or the boot sector is corrupt, this message appears:

    ```
    Non-System disk or disk error
    Replace and press any key when ready
    ```

18. If no DOS volume boot sector can be read from drive A:, the BIOS looks for a master partition boot sector at cylinder 0, head 0, sector 1 (the very first sector) of the first fixed disk. If this sector is found, it is loaded into memory address 0000:7C00 and tested for a signature.

19. If the last two (signature) bytes of the master partition boot sector are not equal to 55AAh, software interrupt 18h (Int 18h) is invoked on most systems. On an IBM PS/2 system, a special character graphics message is displayed that depicts inserting a floppy disk in drive A: and pressing the F1 key. For non-PS/2 systems made by IBM, an Int 18h executes the ROM BIOS-based Cassette BASIC Interpreter. When this occurs, the message looks like this:

    ```
    The IBM Personal Computer Basic
    Version C1.10 Copyright IBM Corp 1981
    62940 Bytes free
    Ok
    ```

Because no BIOS versions other than IBM's systems ever had the Cassette BASIC interpreter in ROM, other BIOS manufacturers had to come up with different messages to display for the same situations in which an IBM system would invoke this BASIC. PCs that have an AMI BIOS in fact display a confusing message as follows:

```
NO ROM BASIC - SYSTEM HALTED
```

This message is a BIOS error message that is displayed by the AMI BIOS when the same situations occur that would cause an IBM system to dump into Cassette BASIC, which of course is not present in an AMI BIOS (or any other compatible BIOS for that matter). Other BIOS versions display different messages. For example, under the same circumstances, a Compaq BIOS displays the following:

```
Non-System disk or disk error
replace and strike any key when ready
```

This is somewhat confusing on Compaq's part because this very same (or similar) error message is contained in the DOS Boot Sector, and would normally be displayed if the DOS system files were missing or corrupted.

In the same situations that you would see Cassette BASIC on an IBM system, a system with an Award BIOS would display the following:

```
DISK BOOT FAILURE, INSERT SYSTEM DISK AND PRESS ENTER
```

Phoenix BIOS systems will display either:

```
No boot device available -
strike F1 to retry boot, F2 for setup utility
```

or

```
No boot sector on fixed disk -
strike F1 to retry boot, F2 for setup utility
```

The first or second Phoenix message displays depending on exactly which error actually occurred.

Although the message displayed varies from BIOS to BIOS, the cause for all of them relates to specific bytes in the Master Boot Record, which is the first sector of a hard disk at the physical location Cylinder 0, Head 0, Sector 1.

The problem involves a disk that has either never been partitioned or has had the Master Boot Sector corrupted. During the boot process, the BIOS checks the last two bytes in the Master Boot Record (first sector of the drive) for a "signature" value of 55AAh. If the last two bytes are not 55AAh, an Interrupt 18h is invoked, which calls the subroutine that displays the message you received as well as the others indicated, or on an IBM system invokes Cassette (ROM) BASIC itself.

The Master Boot Sector (including the signature bytes) is written to the hard disk by the DOS FDISK program. Immediately after you low-level format a hard disk, all the sectors are initialized with a pattern of bytes, and the first sector does *not* contain the 55AAh signature. In other words, these ROM error messages are exactly what you see if you attempt to boot from a hard disk that has been low-level formatted, but has not yet been partitioned.

20. The master partition boot sector program searches its partition table for an entry with a system indicator byte indicating an extended partition. If the program finds such an entry, it loads the extended partition boot sector at the location indicated. The extended partition boot sector also has a table that is searched for another extended partition. If another extended partition entry is found, that extended partition boot sector is loaded from the location indicated. The search continues until either no more extended partitions are indicated, or the maximum number of 24 total partitions has been reached.

21. The master partition boot sector searches its partition table for a boot indicator byte marking an active partition.

22. On an IBM system, if none of the partitions are marked active (bootable), ROM BIOS-based Cassette BASIC is invoked. On most IBM-compatible systems, some type of disk error message is displayed.

23. If any boot indicator in the master partition boot record table is invalid, or if more than one indicates an active partition, the following message is displayed, and the system stops:

    ```
    Invalid partition table
    ```

24. If an active partition is found in the master partition boot sector, the volume boot sector from the active partition is loaded and tested.

25. If the DOS volume boot sector cannot be read successfully from the active partition within five retries because of read errors, this message appears and the system stops:

    ```
    Error loading operating system
    ```

26. The hard disk DOS volume boot sector is tested for a signature. If the DOS volume boot sector does not contain a valid signature of 55AAh as the last two bytes in the sector, this message appears and the system stops:

    ```
    Missing operating system
    ```

27. The volume boot sector is executed as a program. This program checks the root directory to ensure that the first two files are IO.SYS (or IBMBIO.COM) and MSDOS.SYS (or IBMDOS.COM). If these files are present, they are loaded.

28. If the disk was prepared with FORMAT or SYS using DOS 3.3 or an earlier version and the specified system files are not the first two files in the directory, or if a problem is encountered loading them, the following message appears:

    ```
    Non-System disk or disk error
    Replace and strike any key when ready
    ```

29. If the disk was prepared with FORMAT or SYS using DOS 3.3 or an earlier version and the boot sector is corrupt, you might see this message:

    ```
    Disk Boot failure
    ```

30. If the disk was prepared with FORMAT or SYS using DOS 4.0 or a later version and the specified system files are not the first two files in the directory, or if a problem

is encountered loading them, or the boot sector is corrupt, the following message appears:

```
Non-System disk or disk error
Replace and press any key when ready
```

31. If no problems occur, the DOS volume boot sector executes IO.SYS/IBMBIO.COM.

32. The initialization code in IO.SYS/IBMBIO.COM copies itself into the highest region of contiguous DOS memory and transfers control to the copy. The initialization code copy then relocates MSDOS.SYS over the portion of IO.SYS in low memory that contains the initialization code, because the initialization code no longer needs to be in that location. Windows 95's IO.SYS combines the functions of DOS' IO.SYS and MSDOS.SYS.

33. The initialization code executes MSDOS.SYS (or IBMDOS.COM), which initializes the base device drivers, determines equipment status, resets the disk system, resets and initializes attached devices, and sets the system default parameters.

34. The full DOS filing system is active, and control is returned to the IO.SYS initialization code.

35. The IO.SYS initialization code reads the CONFIG.SYS file multiple times. In Windows 95, IO.SYS also looks for the SYSTEM.DAT Registry file.

36. When loading CONFIG.SYS, DEVICE statements are first processed in the order in which they appear, and any device driver files named are loaded and executed. Then any INSTALL statements are processed in the order in which they appear, and the programs named are loaded and executed. The SHELL statement is processed and loads the specified command processor with the specified parameters. If the CONFIG.SYS file contains no SHELL statement, the default \COMMAND.COM processor is loaded with default parameters. Loading the command processor overwrites the initialization code in memory (because the job of the initialization code is finished).

    In Windows 95, the COMMAND.COM program is loaded only if an AUTOEXEC.BAT exists, so it can process the commands contained within.

    During the final reads of CONFIG.SYS, all of the remaining statements are read and processed in a predetermined order. Thus, the order of appearance for statements other than DEVICE, INSTALL, and SHELL in CONFIG.SYS is of no significance.

37. If AUTOEXEC.BAT is present, COMMAND.COM loads and runs AUTOEXEC.BAT. After the commands in AUTOEXEC.BAT have been executed, the DOS prompt appears (unless the AUTOEXEC.BAT calls an application program or shell of some kind, in which case the user might operate the system without ever seeing a DOS prompt).

38. If no AUTOEXEC.BAT is present, COMMAND.COM executes the internal DATE and TIME commands, displays a copyright message, and displays the DOS prompt.

    In Windows 95, IO.SYS automatically loads HIMEM.SYS, IFSHLP.SYS, and SETVER.EXE. Finally, it loads WIN.COM and Windows 95 is officially started.

Some minor variations from this scenario are possible, such as those introduced by other ROM programs in the various adapters that might be plugged into a slot. Also, depending on the exact ROM BIOS programs involved, some of the error messages and sequences might vary. Generally, however, a computer follows this chain of events in "coming to life."

You can modify the system startup procedures by altering the CONFIG.SYS and AUTOEXEC.BAT files, or the Windows 95 Registry. These files control the configuration of DOS or Windows 95 and allow special startup programs to be executed every time the system starts.

File Management

DOS uses several elements and structures to store and retrieve information on a disk. These elements and structures enable DOS to communicate properly with the ROM BIOS as well as application programs to process file storage and retrieval requests. Understanding these structures and how they interact help you to troubleshoot and even repair these structures.

DOS File Space Allocation

DOS allocates disk space for a file on demand (space is not preallocated). The space is allocated one *cluster* (or allocation unit) at a time. A cluster is always one or more sectors. (For more information about sectors, refer to Chapter 14, "Hard Disk Drives.")

The clusters are arranged on a disk to minimize head movement for multisided media. DOS allocates all the space on a disk cylinder before moving to the next cylinder. It does this by using the sectors under the first head, and then all the sectors under the next head, and so on until all sectors of all heads of the cylinder are used. The next sector used is sector 1 of head 0 on the next cylinder. (You find more information on floppy disks and drives in Chapter 13, "Floppy Disk Drives" and on hard disks in Chapter 14, "Hard Disk Drives.")

The algorithm used for file allocation in DOS 3.0 and later versions is called the *Next Available Cluster algorithm*. In this algorithm, the search for available clusters in which to write a file starts not at the beginning of the disk, as in previous DOS versions, but rather from where the last write occurred. Therefore, the disk space freed by erasing a file is not necessarily reused immediately. Rather, DOS maintains a *Last Written Cluster pointer* indicating the last written cluster and begins its search from that point. This pointer is maintained in system RAM and is lost when the system is reset or rebooted, or when a disk is changed in a floppy drive.

The Next Available Cluster algorithm in DOS 3.0 and later versions is faster than the First Available Cluster algorithm of earlier versions and helps to minimize fragmentation. Sometimes this type of algorithm is called *elevator seeking* because write operations occur at higher and higher clusters until the end of the disk area is reached. At that time, the pointer is reset, and writes work their way from the beginning of the disk again.

Files still end up becoming fragmented using the new algorithm, because the pointer is reset after a reboot, a disk change operation, or when the end of the disk is reached. Nevertheless, a great benefit of the newer method is that it makes unerasing files more likely to succeed even if the disk has been written to since the erasure, because the file just erased is not likely to be the target of the next write operation. In fact, it might be some time before the clusters occupied by the erased file are reused.

Even when a file is overwritten under DOS 3.0 and later versions, the clusters occupied by the file are not actually reused in the overwrite. For example, if you accidentally save on a disk a file using the same name as an important file that already exists, the existing file clusters are marked as available, and the new file (with the same name) is written to the disk in other clusters. It is possible, therefore, that the original copy of the file can still be retrieved. You can continue this procedure by saving another copy of the file with the same name, and each file copy is saved to higher-numbered clusters. Then, each earlier version overwritten might still be recoverable on the disk. This process can continue until the system is rebooted or reset, or until the end of the available space is reached. Then the pointer is set to the first cluster, and the previous file data is overwritten.

Because DOS always uses the first available directory entry when it saves or creates a file, the overwritten or deleted files whose data is still recoverable on the disk no longer appear in a directory listing. No commercial quick unerase or other unerase utilities, therefore, can find any record of the erased or overwritten file on the disk—true, of course, because these programs look only in the directory for a record of an erased file. Some undelete programs have a memory-resident delete tracking function that, in essence, maintains a separate directory listing from DOS. Unless an unerase program has such a function, and that function has been activated before the deletion, no program can recall the files overwritten in the directory entry.

Because unerase programs do not look at the FAT, or at the data clusters themselves (unless they use delete tracking), they see no record of the files' existence. By scanning the free clusters on the disk one by one using a disk editor tool, you can locate the data from the overwritten or erased file and manually rebuild the FAT and directory entries. This procedure enables you to recover erased files even though files have been written to the disk since the erasure took place.

Interfacing to Disk Drives

DOS uses a combination of disk management components to make files accessible. These components differ slightly between floppies and hard disks and between disks of different sizes. They determine how a disk appears to DOS and to applications software. Each component used to describe the disk system fits as a layer into the complete system. Each layer communicates with the layer above and below it. When all the components work together, an application can access the disk to find and store data. Table 22.1 lists the DOS format specifications for floppy disks.

Table 22.1 Floppy Disk Format Specifications

Disk Size (in.) Disk Capacity (K)	Current Formats	
	3 1/2" 2,880	3 1/2" 1,440
Media Descriptor Byte	F0h	F0h
Sides (Heads)	2	2
Tracks per side	80	80
Sectors per track	36	18
Bytes per sector	512	512
Sectors per cluster	2	1
FAT length (Sectors)	9	9
Number of FATs	2	2
Root Dir. Length (Sectors)	15	14
Maximum Root Entries	240	224
Total sectors per disk	5,760	2,880
Total available sectors	5,726	2,847
Total available clusters	2,863	2,847

The four primary layers of interface between an application program running on a system and any disks attached to the system consist of software routines that can perform various functions, usually to communicate with the adjacent layers. These layers are shown in the following list:

- DOS Interrupt 21h (Int 21h) routines
- DOS Interrupt 25/26h (Int 25/26h) routines
- ROM BIOS disk Interrupt 13h (Int 13h) routines
- Disk controller I/O port commands

Each layer accepts various commands, performs different functions, and generates results. These interfaces are available for both floppy disk drives and hard disks, although the floppy disk and hard disk Int 13h routines differ widely. The floppy disk controllers and hard disk controllers are very different as well, but all the layers perform the same functions for both floppy disks and hard disks.

Interrupt 21h. The DOS Int 21h routines exist at the highest level and provide the most functionality with the least amount of work. For example, if an application program needs to create a subdirectory on a disk, it can call Int 21h, Function 39h. This function performs all operations necessary to create the subdirectory, including updating the appropriate directory and FAT sectors. The only information this function needs is the name of the subdirectory to create. DOS Int 21h would do much more work by using one of the lower-level access methods to create a subdirectory. Most applications access the disk through this level of interface.

Interrupt 25h and 26h. The DOS Int 25h and Int 26h routines provide much lower-level access to the disk than the Int 21h routines. Int 25h reads only specified sectors from a disk, and Int 26h only writes specified sectors to a disk. If you were to write a program that used these functions to create a subdirectory on a disk, the amount of work would be much greater than that required by the Int 21h method. For example, your program would have to perform all of these tasks:

- Calculate exactly which directory and FAT sectors need to be updated.
- Use Int 25h to read these sectors.
- Modify the sectors appropriately to contain the new subdirectory information.
- Use Int 26h to write the sectors back out.

The number of steps would be even greater considering the difficulty in determining exactly what sectors have to be modified. According to Int 25/26h, the entire DOS-addressable area of the disk consists of sectors numbered sequentially from 0. A program designed to access the disk using Int 25h and Int 26h must know the location of everything by this sector number. A program designed this way might have to be modified to handle disks with different numbers of sectors or different directory and FAT sizes and locations. Because of all the overhead required to get the job done, most programmers would not choose to access the disk in this manner, and instead would use the higher-level Int 21h—which does all the work automatically.

Only disk- and sector-editing programs typically access a disk drive at the Int 25h and Int 26h level. Programs that work at this level of access can edit only areas of a disk that have been defined to DOS as a logical volume (drive letter). For example, DEBUG can read sectors from and write sectors to disks with this level of access.

Interrupt 13h. The next lower level of communications with drives, the ROM BIOS Int 13h routines, usually are found in ROM chips on the motherboard or on an adapter card in a slot. However, an Int 13h handler also can be implemented by using a device driver loaded at boot time. Because DOS requires Int 13h access to boot from a drive (and a device driver cannot be loaded until after boot-up), only drives with ROM BIOS-based Int 13h support can become bootable. Int 13h routines need to talk directly to the controller using the I/O ports on the controller. Therefore, the Int 13h code is very controller-specific.

Table 22.2 lists the different functions available at the Interrupt 13h BIOS interface. Some functions are available to floppy drives or hard drives only, whereas others are available to both types of drives.

Table 22.3 shows the error codes that may be returned by the BIOS INT 13h routines. In some cases, you may see these codes referred to when running a low-level format program, disk editor, or other program that can directly access a disk drive through the BIOS.

Table 22.2 Int 13h BIOS Disk Functions

Function	Floppy Disk	Hard Disk	Description
00h	X	X	Reset disk system
01h	X	X	Get status of last operation
02h	X	X	Read sectors
03h	X	X	Write sectors
04h	X	X	Verify sectors
05h	X	X	Format track
06h		X	Format bad track
07h		X	Format drive
08h	X	X	Read drive parameters
09h		X	Initialize drive characteristics
0Ah		X	Read long
0Bh		X	Write long
0Ch		X	Seek
0Dh		X	Alternate hard disk reset
0Eh		X	Read sector buffer
0Fh		X	Write sector buffer
10h		X	Test for drive ready
11h		X	Recalibrate drive
12h		X	Controller RAM diagnostic
13h		X	Controller drive diagnostic
14h		X	Controller internal diagnostic
15h	X	X	Get disk type
16h	X		Get floppy disk change status
17h	X		Set floppy disk type for format
18h	X		Set media type for format
19h		X	Park hard disk heads
1Ah		X	ESDI—Low-level format
1Bh		X	ESDI—Get manufacturing header
1Ch		X	ESDI—Get configuration

Table 22.3 BIOS INT 13h Error Codes

Code	Description	Code	Description
00h	No error	06h	Media change error
01h	Bad command	07h	Initialization failed
02h	Address mark not found	09h	Cross 64K DMA boundary
03h	Write protect	0Ah	Bad sector flag detected
04h	Request sector not found	0Bh	Bad track flag detected
05h	Reset failed	10h	Bad ECC on disk read
11h	ECC corrected data error	BBh	Undefined error
20h	Controller has failed	CCh	Write fault
40h	Seek operation failed	0Eh	Register error
80h	Drive failed to respond	FFh	Sense operation failed
AAh	Drive not ready		

If you design your own custom disk controller device, you need to write an IBM-compatible Int 13h handler package and install it on the card using a ROM BIOS that will be linked into the system at boot time. To use Int 13h routines, a program must use exact cylinder, head, and sector coordinates to specify sectors to read and write. Accordingly, any program designed to work at this level must be intimately familiar with the parameters of the specific disk on the system on which it is designed to run. Int 13h functions exist to read the disk parameters, format tracks, read and write sectors, park heads, and reset the drive.

A low-level format program for ST-506/412 drives needs to work with disks at the Int 13h level or lower. Most ST-506/412 controller format programs work with access at the Int 13h level because virtually any operation a format program needs is available through the Int 13h interface. This is not true, however, for other types of controllers (such as IDE, SCSI, or ESDI), for which defect mapping and other operations differ considerably from the ST-506/412 types. Controllers that must perform special operations during a low-level format, such as defining disk parameters to override the motherboard ROM BIOS drive tables, would not work with any formatter that used only the standard Int 13h interface.

For these reasons, most controllers require a custom formatter designed to bypass the Int 13h interface. Most general-purpose, low-level reformat programs that perform a non-destructive format access the controller through the Int 13h interface (rather than going direct) and therefore cannot be used for an initial low-level format; the initial low-level format must be done by a controller-specific utility.

Few high-powered disk utility programs, other than some basic formatting software, can talk to the disk at the Int 13h level. The DOS FDISK program communicates at the Int 13h level. The Norton DISKEDIT and older NU programs can communicate with a disk at the Int 13h level when these programs are in their absolute sector mode; they are some of the few disk-repair utilities that can do so. These programs are important because they can be used for the worst data recovery situations, in which the partition tables have been corrupted. Because the partition tables, as well as any non-DOS partitions, exist outside the area of a disk that is defined by DOS, only programs that work at the Int 13h level can access them. Most utility programs for data recovery work only at the DOS Int 25/26h level, which makes them useless for accessing areas of a disk outside of DOS' domain.

Disk Controller I/O Port Commands. In the lowest level of interface, programs talk directly to the disk controller in the controller's own specific native language. To do this, a program must send controller commands through the I/O ports to which the controller responds. These commands are specific to the particular controller and sometimes differ even among controllers of the same type, such as different ESDI controllers. The ROM BIOS in the system must be designed specifically for the controller because the ROM BIOS talks to the controller at this I/O port level. Most low-level format programs also need to talk to the controller directly because the higher-level Int 13h interface does not provide enough specific features for many of the custom ST-506/412 or ESDI and SCSI controllers on the market.

Figure 22.2 shows that most application programs work through the Int 21h interface, which passes commands to the ROM BIOS as Int 13h commands; these commands then are converted into direct controller commands by the ROM BIOS. The controller executes the commands and returns the results through the layers until the desired information reaches the application. This process enables developers to write applications without worrying about such low-level system details, instead leaving them up to DOS and the ROM BIOS. This also enables applications to run on widely different types of hardware, as long as the correct ROM BIOS and DOS support is in place.

FIG. 22.2 Relationships between various interface levels.

Any software can bypass any level of interface and communicate with the level below it, but doing so requires much more work. The lowest level of interface available is direct communication with the controller using I/O port commands. As Figure 22.2 shows, each different type of controller has different I/O port locations as well as differences among the commands presented at the various ports, and only the controller can talk directly to the disk drive.

If not for the ROM BIOS Int 13h interface, a unique DOS would have to be written for each available type of hard and floppy disk drive. Instead, DOS communicates with the ROM BIOS using standard Int 13h function calls translated by the Int 13h interface into commands for the specific hardware. Because of the standard ROM BIOS interface, DOS can be written relatively independently of specific disk hardware and can support many different types of drives and controllers.

DOS Structures

To manage files on a disk and enable all application programs to see a consistent disk interface no matter what type of disk is used, DOS uses several structures. The following list shows all the structures and areas that DOS defines and uses to manage a disk, in roughly the same order that they appear:

- Master and extended partition boot sectors
- DOS volume boot sector
- Root directory
- File allocation tables (FAT)
- Clusters (allocation units)
- Data area
- Diagnostic read-and-write cylinder

A hard disk has all of these DOS disk-management structures allocated, and a floppy disk has all but the master and extended partition boot sectors and the diagnostic cylinder. These structures are created by the DOS FDISK program, which cannot be used on a floppy disk because they cannot be partitioned. Figure 22.3 is a simple diagram showing the relative locations of these DOS disk-management structures on the 32M hard disk in an IBM AT Model 339.

Each disk area has a purpose and function. If one of these special areas is damaged, serious consequences can result. Damage to one of these sensitive structures usually causes a domino effect, limiting access to other areas of the disk or causing further problems in using the disk. For example, DOS cannot read and write files if the FAT is damaged or corrupted. Therefore, you should understand these data structures well enough to be able to repair them when necessary. Rebuilding these special tables and areas of the disk is essential to the art of data recovery.

Chapter 22—Operating Systems Software and Troubleshooting

FIG. 22.3 DOS disk management structures on an IBM AT Model 339 32M hard disk.

Master Partition Boot Sectors. To share a hard disk among different operating systems, the disk might be logically divided into one to four master partitions. Each operating system, including DOS (through versions 3.2), might own only one partition. DOS 3.3 and later versions introduced the extended DOS partition, which allows multiple DOS partitions on the same hard disk. With the DOS FDISK program, you can select the size of each partition. The partition information is stored in several partition boot sectors on the disk, with the main table embedded in the master partition boot sector. The master partition boot sector is always located in the first sector of the entire disk (cylinder 0, head 0, sector 1). The extended partition boot sectors are located at the beginning of each extended partition volume.

Each DOS partition contains a DOS volume boot sector as its first sector. With the DOS FDISK utility, you might designate a single partition as active (or bootable). The master partition boot sector causes the active partition's volume boot sector to receive control when the system is started or reset. Additional master disk partitions can be set up for Novell NetWare, and for OS/2's HPFS, NTFS, AIX (UNIX), XENIX, or other operating systems. These foreign operating system partitions cannot be accessed under DOS, nor are DOS partitions normally accessible using other operating systems. (OS/2 and Windows NT can access FAT partitions, the high-performance file system (HPFS) is exclusive to OS/2, and the NTFS is exclusive to Windows NT.)

A hard disk must be partitioned in order to be accessible by an operating system. You must partition a disk even if you want to create only a single partition. Table 22.4 shows the format of the Master Boot Record (MBR) with partition tables.

Table 22.5 shows the standard values and meanings of the System Indicator Byte.

Table 22.4 Master Boot Record (Partition Table)

Partition Table Entry #1

Offset	Length	Description
1BEh 446	1 byte	Boot Indicator Byte (80h = Active, else 00h)
1BFh 447	1 byte	Starting Head (or Side) of Partition
1C0h 448	16 bits	Starting Cylinder (10 bits) and Sector (6 bits)
1C2h 450	1 byte	System Indicator Byte (see Table 22.5)
1C3h 451	1 byte	Ending Head (or Side) of Partition
1C4h 452	16 bits	Ending Cylinder (10 bits) and Sector (6 bits)
1C6h 454	1 dword	Relative Sector Offset of Partition
1CAh 458	1 dword	Total Number of Sectors in Partition

Partition Table Entry #2

Offset	Length	Description
1CEh 462	1 byte	Boot Indicator Byte (80h = Active, else 00h)
1CFh 463	1 byte	Starting Head (or Side) of Partition
1D0h 464	16 bits	Starting Cylinder (10 bits) and Sector (6 bits)
1D2h 466	1 byte	System Indicator Byte (see Table 22.5)
1D3h 467	1 byte	Ending Head (or Side) of Partition
1D4h 468	16 bits	Ending Cylinder (10 bits) and Sector (6 bits)
1D6h 470	1 dword	Relative Sector Offset of Partition
1DAh 474	1 dword	Total Number of Sectors in Partition

Partition Table Entry #3

Offset	Length	Description
1DEh 478	1 byte	Boot Indicator Byte (80h = Active, else 00h)
1DFh 479	1 byte	Starting Head (or Side) of Partition
1E0h 480	16 bits	Starting Cylinder (10 bits) and Sector (6 bits)
1E2h 482	1 byte	System Indicator Byte (see Table 22.5)
1E3h 483	1 byte	Ending Head (or Side) of Partition
1E4h 484	16 bits	Ending Cylinder (10 bits) and Sector (6 bits)
1E6h 486	1 dword	Relative Sector Offset of Partition
1EAh 490	1 dword	Total Number of Sectors in Partition

(continues)

Table 22.4 Continued

Partition Table Entry #4

Offset	Length	Description
1EEh 494	1 byte	Boot Indicator Byte (80h = Active, else 00h)
1EFh 495	1 byte	Starting Head (or Side) of Partition
1F0h 496	16 bits	Starting Cylinder (10 bits) and Sector (6 bits)
1F2h 498	1 byte	System Indicator Byte (see Table 22.5)
1F3h 499	1 byte	Ending Head (or Side) of Partition
1F4h 500	16 bits	Ending Cylinder (10 bits) and Sector (6 bits)
1F6h 502	1 dword	Relative Sector Offset of Partition
1FAh 506	1 dword	Total Number of Sectors in Partition

Signature Bytes

Offset	Length	Description
1FEh 510	2 bytes	Boot Sector Signature (55AAh)

A WORD equals 2 bytes read in reverse order, and a DWORD equals two WORDs read in reverse order.

Table 22.5 Partition Table System Indicator Byte Values

Value	Description
00h	No allocated partition in this entry
01h	Primary DOS, 12-bit FAT (Partition < 16M)
04h	Primary DOS, 16-bit FAT (16M <= Partition <= 32M)
05h	Extended DOS (Points to next Primary Partition)
06h	Primary DOS, 16-bit FAT (Partition > 32M)
07h	OS/2 HPFS Partition
02h	MS-XENIX Root Partition
03h	MS-XENIX usr Partition
08h	AIX File System Partition
09h	AIX boot Partition
50h	Ontrack Disk Manager READ-ONLY Partition
51h	Ontrack Disk Manager READ/WRITE Partition
56h	Golden Bow Vfeature Partition
61h	Storage Dimensions Speedstor Partition
63h	IBM 386/ix or UNIX System V/386 Partition
64h	Novell NetWare Partition
75h	IBM PCIX Partition
DBh	Digital Research Concurrent DOS/CPM-86 Partition
F2h	Some OEM's DOS 3.2+ second partition
FFh	UNIX Bad Block Table Partition

DOS Volume Boot Sectors. The *volume boot sector* is the first sector on any area of a drive addressed as a volume (or logical DOS disk). On a floppy disk, for example, this sector is the first one on the floppy disk because DOS recognizes the floppy disk as a volume without the need for partitioning. On a hard disk, the volume boot sector or sectors are located as the first sector within any disk area allocated as a nonextended partition, or any area recognizable as a DOS volume.

This special sector resembles the master partition boot sector in that it contains a program as well as some special data tables. The first volume boot sector on a disk is loaded by the system ROM BIOS for floppies or by the master partition boot sector on a hard disk. This program is given control; it performs some tests and then attempts to load the first DOS system file (IO.SYS). The volume boot sector is transparent to a running DOS system; it is outside the data area of the disk on which files are stored.

You create a volume boot sector with the DOS FORMAT command (high-level format). Hard disks have a volume boot sector at the beginning of every DOS logical drive area allocated on the disk, in both the primary and extended partitions. Although all the logical drives contain the program area as well as a data table area, only the program code from the volume boot sector in the active partition on a hard disk is executed. The others are simply read by the DOS system files during boot-up to obtain their data tables and determine the volume parameters.

The volume boot sector contains program code and data. The single data table in this sector is called the *media parameter block* or *disk parameter block*. DOS needs the information it contains to verify the capacity of a disk volume as well as the location of important features such as the FAT. The format of this data is very specific.

Errors can cause problems with booting from a disk or with accessing a disk. Some OEM versions of DOS have not adhered to the standards set for the format of this data, which can cause interchange problems with disks formatted by different versions of DOS. The later versions can be more particular, so if you suspect that boot sector differences are causing inability to access a disk, you can use a utility program such as DOS DEBUG or Norton Utilities to copy a boot sector from the newer version of DOS to a disk formatted by the older version. This step should enable the new version of DOS to read the older disk and should not interfere with the less particular older version. This has never been a problem in using different DOS versions from the same OEM, but might occur when mixing different OEM versions. Table 22.6 shows the format and layout of the DOS Boot Record (DBR).

Table 22.6 DOS Boot Record (DBR) Format

Offset			
Hex	**Dec**	**Field Length**	**Description**
00h	0	3 bytes	Jump Instruction to Boot Program Code
03h	3	8 bytes	OEM Name and DOS Version (IBM 5.0)
0Bh	11	1 word	Bytes/Sector (usually 512)
0Dh	13	1 byte	Sectors/Cluster (must be a power of 2)

(continues)

Table 22.6 Continued

Offset Hex	Dec	Field Length	Description
0Eh	14	1 word	Reserved Sectors (Boot Sectors, usually 1)
10h	16	1 byte	FAT Copies (usually 2)
11h	17	1 word	Maximum Root Directory Entries (usually 512)
13h	19	1 word	Total Sectors (If Partition <= 32M, else 0)
15h	21	1 byte	Media Descriptor Byte (F8h for Hard Disks)
16h	22	1 word	Sectors/FAT
18h	24	1 word	Sectors/Track
1Ah	26	1 word	Number of Heads
1Ch	28	1 dword	Hidden Sectors (If Partition <= 32M, 1 word only)

For DOS 4.0 or Higher Only, Else 00h

Hex	Dec	Field Length	Description
20h	32	1 dword	Total Sectors (If Partition > 32M, else 0)
24h	36	1 byte	Physical Drive No. (00h=floppy, 80h=hard disk)
25h	37	1 byte	Reserved (00h)
26h	38	1 byte	Extended Boot Record Signature (29h)
27h	39	1 dword	Volume Serial Number (32-bit random number)
2Bh	43	11 bytes	Volume Label ("NO NAME" stored if no label)
36h	54	8 bytes	File System ID ("FAT12" or "FAT16")

For All Versions of DOS

Hex	Dec	Field Length	Description
3Eh	62	448 bytes	Boot Program Code
1FEh	510	2 bytes	Signature Bytes (55AAh)

A WORD is 2 bytes read in reverse order, and a DWORD is two WORDs read in reverse order.

Root Directory. A *directory* is a simple database containing information about the files stored on a disk. Each record in this database is 32 bytes long, with no delimiters or separating characters between the fields or records. A directory stores almost all of the information that DOS knows about a file: name, attribute, time and date of creation, size, and where the beginning of the file is located on the disk. (The information a directory does not contain about a file is where the file continues on the disk and whether the file is contiguous or fragmented. The FAT contains that information.)

There are two basic types of directories: the *root directory* and *subdirectories*. Any given volume can have only one root directory, and the root directory is always stored on a disk in a fixed location immediately following the two copies of the FAT. Root directories vary in size because of the different types and capacities of disks, but the root directory of a given disk is fixed. After a root directory is created, it has a fixed length and cannot be extended to hold more entries. Normally, a hard disk volume has a root directory with room for 512 total entries. Subdirectories are stored as files in the data area of the disk and therefore have no fixed length limits.

Every directory, whether it is the root directory or a subdirectory, is organized in the same way. A directory is a small database with a fixed record length of 32 bytes. Entries in the database store important information about individual files and how files are named on a disk. The directory information is linked to the FAT by the starting cluster entry. In fact, if no file on a disk were longer than one single cluster, the FAT would be unnecessary. The directory stores all of the information needed by DOS to manage the file, with the exception of the list of clusters that the file occupies other than the first one. The FAT stores the remaining information about the other clusters that the file occupies.

To trace a file on a disk, you start with the directory entry to get the information about the starting cluster of the file and its size. Then you go to the file allocation table, where you can follow the chain of clusters that the file occupies until you reach the end of the file.

DOS directory entries are 32 bytes long and are in the format shown in Table 22.7.

Table 22.7 DOS Directory Format

Offset Hex	Dec	Field Length	Description
00h	0	8 bytes	File name
08h	8	3 bytes	File extension
0Bh	11	1 byte	File attributes
0Ch	12	10 bytes	Reserved (00h)
16h	22	1 word	Time of creation
18h	24	1 word	Date of creation
1Ah	26	1 word	Starting cluster
1Ch	28	1 dword	Size in bytes

File names and extensions are left-justified and padded with spaces (32h). The first byte of the file name indicates the file status as follows:

Hex	File Status
00h	Entry never used; entries past this point not searched
05h	Indicates that the first character of the file name is actually E5h
E5h	σ (lowercase sigma) indicates that the file has been erased
2Eh	. (period) indicates that this entry is a directory. If the second byte is also 2Eh, the cluster field contains the cluster number of the parent directory (0000h, if the parent is the root).

Table 22.8 describes the DOS directory file attribute byte.

Table 22.8 DOS Directory File Attribute Byte

Bit Positions 7 6 5 4 3 2 1 0	Hex Value	Description
0 0 0 0 0 0 0 1	01h	Read-only file
0 0 0 0 0 0 1 0	02h	Hidden file
0 0 0 0 0 1 0 0	04h	System file
0 0 0 0 1 0 0 0	08h	Volume label
0 0 0 1 0 0 0 0	10h	Subdirectory
0 0 1 0 0 0 0 0	20h	Archive (updated since backup)
0 1 0 0 0 0 0 0	40h	Reserved
1 0 0 0 0 0 0 0	80h	Reserved
Examples		
0 0 1 0 0 0 0 1	21h	Read-only, archive
0 0 1 1 0 0 1 0	32h	Hidden, subdirectory, archive
0 0 1 0 0 1 1 1	27h	Read-only, hidden, system, archive

File Allocation Tables. The *file allocation table (FAT)* is a table of number entries describing how each cluster is allocated on the disk. The data area of the disk has a single entry for each cluster. Sectors in the nondata area on the disk are outside the range of the disk controlled by the FAT. The sectors involved in any of the boot sectors, file allocation table, and root directory are outside the range of sectors controlled by the FAT.

The FAT does not manage every data sector specifically, but rather allocates space in groups of sectors called *clusters* or *allocation units*. A cluster is one or more sectors designated by DOS as allocation units of storage. The smallest space a file can use on a disk is one cluster; all files use space on the disk in integer cluster units. If a file is one byte larger than one cluster, two clusters are used. DOS determines the size of a cluster when the disk is high-level formatted by the DOS FORMAT command.

You can think of the FAT as a type of spreadsheet that tracks the allocation of the disk's clusters. Each cell in the spreadsheet corresponds to a single cluster on the disk; the number stored in that cell is a code indicating whether the cluster is used by a file, and if so, where the next cluster of the file is located.

The numbers stored in the FAT are hexadecimal numbers that are either 12 or 16 bits long. The 16-bit FAT numbers are easy to follow because they take an even two bytes of space and can readily be edited. The 12-bit numbers are 1 1/2 bytes long, which presents a problem because most disk sector editors show data in byte units. To edit the FAT, you must do some hex/binary math to convert the displayed byte units to FAT numbers. Fortunately, (unless you are using the DOS DEBUG program), most of the available tools and utility programs have a FAT editing mode that automatically converts the numbers for you. Most of them also show the FAT numbers in decimal form, which most people find easier to handle.

The DOS FDISK program determines whether a 12-bit or 16-bit FAT is placed on a disk, even though the FAT is written during the high-level format (FORMAT). All floppy disks use a 12-bit FAT, but hard disks can use either. On hard disk volumes of more than 16M (32,768 sectors), DOS creates a 16-bit FAT; otherwise, DOS creates a 12-bit FAT.

DOS creates two copies of the FAT. Each one occupies contiguous sectors on the disk, and the second FAT copy immediately follows the first. Unfortunately, DOS uses the second FAT copy only if sectors in the first FAT copy become unreadable. If the first FAT copy is corrupted, which is a much more common problem, DOS does not use the second FAT copy. Even the DOS CHKDSK command does not check or verify the second FAT copy. Moreover, whenever DOS updates the first FAT, large portions of the first FAT automatically are copied to the second FAT.

If the first copy was corrupted and then subsequently updated by DOS, a large portion of the first FAT would be copied over to the second FAT copy, damaging it in the process. After the update, the second copy is usually a mirror image of the first one, complete with any corruption. Two FATs rarely stay out of sync for very long. When they are out of sync and DOS writes to the disk, causing the first FAT to be updated, it also causes the second FAT to be overwritten by the first FAT. This is why disk repair and recovery utilities warn you to stop working as soon as you detect a FAT problem. Programs like Norton Disk Doctor use the second copy of the FAT as a reference to repair the first one, but if DOS has already updated the second FAT, repair may be impossible.

Clusters (Allocation Units). The term *cluster* was changed to *allocation unit* in DOS 4.0. The newer term is appropriate because a single cluster is the smallest unit of the disk that DOS can handle when it writes or reads a file. A cluster is equal to one or more sectors. Although a cluster can be a single sector, it is usually more than one. Having more than one sector per cluster reduces the size and processing overhead of the FAT and enables DOS to run faster because it has fewer individual units to manage. The trade-off is in wasted disk space. Because DOS can manage space only in full-cluster units, every file consumes space on the disk in increments of one cluster.

Table 22.9 shows the default cluster (or allocation unit) sizes used by DOS for the various floppy disk formats.

Table 22.9 Default Floppy Disk Cluster (Allocation Unit) Sizes	
Drive Type	**Cluster (Allocation Unit) Size**
5 1/4-inch 360K	2 sectors (1,024 bytes)
5 1/4-inch 1.2M	1 sector (512 bytes)
3 1/4-inch 720K	2 sectors (1,024 bytes)
3 1/4-inch 1.44M	1 sector (512 bytes)
3 1/4-inch 2.88M	2 sectors (1,024 bytes)

It seems strange that the high-density disks, which have many more individual sectors than low-density disks, sometimes have smaller cluster sizes. The larger the FAT, the more entries DOS must manage, and the slower DOS seems to function. This sluggishness is due to the excessive overhead required to manage all the individual clusters; the more clusters to be managed, the slower things become. The trade-off is in the minimum cluster size.

Smaller clusters generate less slack (space wasted between the actual end of each file and the end of the cluster). With larger clusters, the wasted space grows larger. High-density floppy drives are faster than their low-density counterparts, so perhaps IBM and Microsoft determined that the decrease in cluster size balances the drive's faster operation and offsets the use of a larger FAT.

For hard disks, the cluster size can vary greatly among different versions of DOS and different disk sizes. Table 22.10 shows the cluster sizes that DOS selects for a particular volume size.

Table 22.10 Default Hard Disk Cluster (Allocation Unit) Sizes

Hard Disk Volume Size	Cluster (Allocation Unit) Size	FAT Type
0M to less than 16M	8 sectors or 4,096 bytes	12-bit
16M through 128M	4 sectors or 2,048 bytes	16-bit
More than 128–256M	8 sectors or 4,096 bytes	16-bit
More than 256–512M	16 sectors or 8,192 bytes	16-bit
More than 512–1,024M	32 sectors or 16,384 bytes	16-bit
More than 1,024–2,048M	64 sectors or 32,768 bytes	16-bit

In most cases, these cluster sizes, selected by the DOS FORMAT command, are the minimum possible for a given partition size. Therefore, 8K clusters are the smallest possible for a partition size of greater than 256M. Although most versions of DOS work like this, some versions might use cluster sizes different from what this table indicates.

The effect of these larger cluster sizes on disk use can be substantial. A drive containing about 5,000 files, with average slack of one-half of the last cluster used for each file, wastes about 20M [5000*(.5*8)K] of file space.

Note that Windows NT and OS/2 already have more sophisticated file systems that do away with the FAT structure, and which are not subject to the limitations of FAT partitions. The FAT32 file system included in the Windows 95 SR2 release allows for more than 64K clusters. Because there can be more clusters, the individual clusters can be smaller. This alleviates the large cluster size problem for larger drives, and extends the maximum size for a partition on a hard disk from 2G to 2T. The cluster sizes used on FAT32 drives of various sizes are as follows:

Drive Size	Cluster Size
0M to less than 260M	512 bytes
260M–8G	4,096 bytes
6–16G	8,192 bytes
16–32G	16,384 bytes
32G–2T	32,768 bytes

The Data Area. The *data area* of a disk is the area that follows the boot sector, file allocation tables, and root directory on any volume. This area is managed by the FAT and the root directory. DOS divides it into allocation units sometimes called clusters. These clusters are where normal files are stored on a volume.

Diagnostic Read-and-Write Cylinder. The FDISK partitioning program always reserves the last cylinder of a hard disk for use as a special diagnostic read-and-write test cylinder. That this cylinder is reserved is one reason FDISK always reports fewer total cylinders than the drive manufacturer states are available. DOS (or any other operating system) does not use this cylinder for any normal purpose, because it lies outside the partitioned area of the disk.

On systems with IDE, SCSI, or ESDI disk interfaces, the drive and controller might allocate an additional area past the logical end of the drive for a bad-track table and spare sectors. This situation may account for additional discrepancies between FDISK and the drive manufacturer.

The diagnostics area enables software such as a manufacturer-supplied Advanced Diagnostics disk to perform read-and-write tests on a hard disk without corrupting any user data. Low-level format programs for hard disks often use this cylinder as a scratch-pad area for running interleave tests or preserving data during nondestructive formats. This cylinder is also sometimes used as a head landing or parking cylinder on hard disks that do not have an automatic parking facility.

Potential DOS Upgrade Problems

You already know that the DOS system files have special placement requirements on a hard disk. Sometimes these special requirements cause problems when you are upgrading from one version of DOS to another.

If you have attempted to upgrade a PC system from one version of DOS to another, you know that you use the DOS SYS command to replace old system files with new ones. The SYS command copies the existing system files (stored on a bootable disk with hidden, system, and read-only attributes) to the disk in the correct position and with the correct names and attributes. The COPY command does not copy hidden or system files (nor would it place the system files in the required positions on the destination disk if you modify the file attributes in order to use COPY). In addition to transferring the two hidden system files from one disk to another, SYS also updates the DOS volume boot sector on the destination disk so that it is correct for the new version of DOS.

When you execute the SYS command, you are usually greeted by one of two messages:

    System transferred

or

    No room for system on destination disk

If a disk has data on it before you try to write the system files to it, the SYS command from DOS versions 3.3 and earlier probably will fail because they are not capable of moving other files out of the way. The SYS command in DOS 4.0 and higher versions rarely fail because they can move files out of the way.

Some users think that the cause of the No room message on a system that has an older version of DOS is that the system files in any newer version of DOS are always larger than the previous version, and that the new version files cannot fit into the space allocated for older versions. Such users believe that the command fails because this space cannot be provided at the beginning without moving other data away. This is incorrect. The SYS command fails in these cases because you are trying to install a version of DOS that has file names different from those already on the disk. There is no normal reason for the SYS command to fail when you update the system files on a disk that already has them.

The system files can be placed virtually anywhere on the disk, except that the first clusters of the disk must contain the first cluster of the IO.SYS file (or its equivalent). As long as that requirement is met, the IO.SYS and MSDOS.SYS files can be fragmented and placed just about anywhere on the disk, and the SYS command implements them with no problems whatsoever. The only other requirement is that the names IO.SYS and MSDOS.SYS (or their equivalents) must use the first and second directory entries.

DOS 4.0 and Later Versions. Because the system files must use the first two entries in the root directory of the disk as well as the first cluster (cluster 2) of the disk, the versions of the SYS command in DOS 4.0 and later versions automatically move any files that occupy the first two entries that do not match the new system file names to other available entries in the root directory. The SYS command also moves the portion of any foreign file occupying the first cluster to other clusters on the disk. The SYS command in older versions of DOS would fail and require a user to make adjustments to the disk.

The SYS command in DOS versions 5.0 and 6.0 go one step further: They replace old system files with the new ones. Even if the old system files had other names, DOS 5.0 and later ensure that they are overwritten by the new system files. With the enhanced SYS command in DOS 4.0 and later versions, it is difficult to make a DOS upgrade fail.

Windows 95. When you install Windows 95 on a system running DOS, the Setup program renames the existing system files with a DOS extension and replaces them with the Windows 95 versions of IO.SYS and MSDOS.SYS. Once the operating system is installed, users can invoke a Boot Manager utility that allows them to boot the system to the old DOS version, if needed. To do this, Boot Manager simply renames the Windows 95 system files with the extension W95 and renames the DOS files back to SYS.

Known Bugs in DOS

Few things are more frustrating than finding out that software you depend on every day has bugs. It's even worse when DOS does. Every version of DOS ever produced has had bugs, and users must learn to anticipate them. Some problems are never resolved; you must live with them.

Sometimes the problems are severe enough, however, that Microsoft and IBM issue a patch that corrects the problems.

Both companies maintain extensive libraries of patch files and troubleshooting information on their Web sites, at the following addresses:

On the Web

http://www.microsoft.com/kb/softlib/

http://ps.software.ibm.com/pbin-usa-ps/getobj.pl?/pdocs-usa/alldos.html

As of this writing, the current version of MS-DOS is 6.22, which contains fixes for the previous 6.2x releases. IBM has since released PC-DOS 7.0, as well as a number of patches designed to address specific problems in the operating system. The currently available patch releases are as follows:

- *D70DCOMP.ZIP*. The DISKCOMP A: A: command generates an erroneous message about the disk being defective. DISKCOMP B: B: generates a message about the disk being compressed when it is not.

- *D70DCOPY.ZIP*. If A: drive is automounted, an incorrect message prompting the user to insert a disk in the E: drive is generated.

- *D70E.ZIP*. Addresses a problem with the TEMPFILENAME parameter in the E.INI file.

- *D70EMM.ZIP*. The Ctrl+Alt+Delete key combination fails to function.

- *D70MODE.ZIP*. A Function not supported error is generated when issuing the mode con rate=xx command.

- *D70POWER.ZIP*. The DX register is not saved when POWER is called, causing possible system hangs or data loss.

- *D70SHARE.ZIP*. Loading the SHARE program generates Out of memory errors.

- *D70STAC.ZIP*. Allows the SETUP program to function on systems with processors prior to the 80286.

- *D70TVL.ZIP*. Enables the Windows 95 versions of the XTREE and PCTOOLS utilities to run with PC DOS 7.0.

- *D70XDF.ZIP*. The XDFCOPY command fails to recover free space on a drive that does not have enough room for temp files.

DOS Disk and Data Recovery

The CHKDSK, RECOVER, and SCANDISK commands are the DOS damaged disk recovery team. These commands are crude, and their actions sometimes are drastic, but at times they are all that is available or needed. RECOVER is best known for its function as a data recovery program, and CHKDSK usually is used for inspection of the file structure. Many users are unaware that CHKDSK can implement repairs to a damaged file structure. DEBUG, a crude, manually controlled program, can help in the case of a disk disaster, if you know exactly what you are doing.

ScanDisk is a safer, more automated, more powerful replacement for CHKDSK and RECOVER. It should be used in their place if you have DOS 6 or higher.

The *CHKDSK* Command. The useful and powerful DOS CHKDSK command is frequently misunderstood. To casual users, the primary function of CHKDSK seems to be providing a disk space allocation report for a given volume as well as a memory allocation report. CHKDSK does those things, but its primary value is in discovering, defining, and repairing problems with the DOS directory and FAT system on a disk volume. In handling data recovery problems, CHKDSK is a valuable tool, although it is crude and simplistic compared to some of the aftermarket utilities that perform similar functions.

The output of the CHKDSK command when it runs on a typical (well, maybe not typical, but my own personal) hard disk is as follows:

```
Volume 4GB_SCSI     created 08-31-1994 5:05p
Volume Serial Number is 1882-18CF

2,146,631,680 bytes total disk space
      163,840 bytes in 3 hidden files
   16,220,160 bytes in 495 directories
  861,634,560 bytes in 10,355 user files
1,268,613,120 bytes available on disk

       32,768 bytes in each allocation unit
       65,510 total allocation units on disk
       38,715 available allocation units on disk

      655,360 total bytes memory
      632,736 bytes free
```

A little-known CHKDSK function is its ability to report on a specified file's (or group of files') level of fragmentation. CHKDSK can also produce a list of all files (including hidden and system files) on a particular volume, like a super DIR command. By far, the most important CHKDSK capabilities are its detection and correction of problems in the DOS file system.

The name of the CHKDSK program is misleading: It seems to be a contraction of CHECK DISK. The program does not actually check a disk, or even the files on a disk, for integrity. CHKDSK cannot even truly show how many bad sectors are on a disk, much less locate and mark them. The real function of CHKDSK is to inspect the directories and FATs to see whether they correspond with each other or contain discrepancies. CHKDSK does not detect (and does not report on) damage in a file; it checks only the FAT and directory areas (that is, the table of contents) of a disk.

CHKDSK also can test files for contiguity. Files loaded into contiguous tracks and sectors of a disk or floppy disk naturally are more efficient. Files spread over wide areas of the disk make access operations take longer. DOS always knows the location of all of a file's fragments by using the pointer numbers in the FAT. These pointers are data that direct DOS to the next segment of the file. Sometimes, for various reasons, these pointers might be lost or corrupted and leave DOS incapable of locating some portion of a file. Using CHKDSK can alert you to this condition and even enable you to reclaim the unused file space.

CHKDSK Command Syntax. The syntax of the CHKDSK command is as follows:

```
CHKDSK [d:\path\] [filename] [/F] [/V]
```

The *d:* specifies the disk volume to analyze. The *\path* and *filename* options specify files to check for fragmentation in addition to the volume analysis. Wild cards are allowed in the file name specification, to specify multiple files in a specified directory for fragmentation analysis. One flaw with the fragmentation analysis is that it does not check for fragmentation across directory boundaries, only within a specified directory.

The /F (Fix) switch enables CHKDSK to perform repairs if it finds problems with the directories and FATs. If /F is not specified, the program cannot write to the disk, and no repairs are performed.

The /V (Verbose) switch causes the program to list all of the entries in all of the directories on a disk and give detailed information in cases where errors are encountered.

The drive, path, and file specifiers are optional. If no parameters are given for the command, CHKDSK processes the default volume or drive and does not check files for contiguity. If you specify [*path*] and [*filename*] parameters, CHKDSK checks all specified files to see whether they are stored contiguously on the disk. One of two messages is displayed as a result:

```
All specified file(s) are contiguous
```

or

```
[filename] Contains xxx non-contiguous blocks
```

The second message is displayed for each file on the disk that is found to be fragmented and displays the number of fragments that comprise the file. A *fragmented file* is one that is scattered around the disk in pieces rather than existing in one contiguous area of the disk. Fragmented files are slower to load than contiguous files, which reduces disk performance. Fragmented files are also much more difficult to recover if a problem with the FAT or directory on the disk occurs.

If you have only DOS, there are several ways to accomplish a full defragmentation. To defragment files on a floppy disk, you can format a new floppy disk and use COPY or XCOPY to copy all the files from the fragmented disk to the replacement. For a hard disk, you must completely backup, format, and then restore the disk. This procedure is time-consuming and dangerous, which is why so many defragmenting utilities have been developed.

CHKDSK Limitations. In several instances, CHKDSK operates only partially or not at all. CHKDSK does not process volumes or portions of volumes that have been created in the following ways:

- SUBST command volumes
- ASSIGN command volumes
- JOIN command subdirectories
- Network volumes

***SUBST* Problems.** The SUBST command creates a virtual volume, which is actually a subdirectory on an existing volume that uses a different volume specifier (drive letter) as an alias. To analyze the files in a subdirectory created with SUBST, you must give the TRUENAME or actual path name to the files. TRUENAME is an undocumented command in DOS 4.0 and later versions that shows the actual path name for a volume that has been created by the SUBST command.

You also can use the SUBST command to find out the TRUENAME of a particular volume. Suppose that you use SUBST to create volume E: from the C:\AUTO\SPECS directory, as follows:

```
C:\>SUBST E: C:\AUTO\SPECS
```

When you attempt to execute a CHKDSK of the E: volume and the files there, you see the resulting error message:

```
E:\>CHKDSK *.*
Cannot CHKDSK a SUBSTed or ASSIGNed drive
```

To run CHKDSK on the files on this virtual volume E:, you must find the actual path the volume represents. You can do so by entering the SUBST command (with no parameters):

```
E:\>SUBST
E: => C:\AUTO\SPECS
```

You can also find the actual path with the undocumented TRUENAME command (in DOS 4.0 and later versions only), as follows:

```
E:\>TRUENAME E:
C:\AUTO\SPECS
```

After finding the path to the files, you can issue the appropriate CHKDSK command to check the volume and files:

```
E:\>CHKDSK C:\AUTO\SPECS\*.*
```

The output of the CHKDSK command, listing the properties of the disk, is as follows:

```
Volume 4GB_SCSI     created 08-31-1994 5:05p
Volume Serial Number is 1882-18CF

2,146,631,680 bytes total disk space
      163,840 bytes in 3 hidden files
   16,220,160 bytes in 495 directories
  861,634,560 bytes in 10,355 user files
1,268,613,120 bytes available on disk

       32,768 bytes in each allocation unit
       65,510 total allocation units on disk
       38,715 available allocation units on disk

      655,360 total bytes memory
      632,736 bytes free

All specified file(s) are contiguous
```

ASSIGN Problems. Similarly, CHKDSK does not process a disk drive that has been altered by the ASSIGN command. For example, if you have used the command ASSIGN A=B, you cannot analyze drive A: unless you first unassign the disk drive with the ASSIGN command, that is, ASSIGN A=A.

***JOIN* Problems.** CHKDSK does not process a directory tree section created by the JOIN command (which joins a physical disk volume to another disk volume as a subdirectory), nor does it process the actual joined physical drive, because such a drive is an invalid drive specification, according to DOS. On volumes where you have used the JOIN command, CHKDSK processes the actual portion of the volume and then displays this warning error message:

```
Directory is joined
tree past this point not processed
```

This message indicates that the command cannot process the directory on which you have used JOIN. CHKDSK then continues processing the rest of the volume and outputs the requested volume information.

Network Problems. CHKDSK does not process a networked (shared) disk on either the server or workstation side. In other words, at the file server, you cannot use CHKDSK on any volume that has any portion of itself accessible to remote network stations. At any network station, you can run CHKDSK only on volumes physically attached to that specific station and not on any volume accessed through the network software. If you attempt to run CHKDSK from a server or a workstation on a volume shared on a network, you see this error message:

```
Cannot CHKDSK a network drive
```

If you want to run CHKDSK on the volume, you must go to the specific PC on which the volume physically exists and suspend or disable any sharing of the volume during the CHKDSK.

***CHKDSK* Command Output.** CHKDSK normally displays the following information about a disk volume:

- Volume name and creation date
- Volume serial number
- Number of bytes in total disk space
- Number of files and bytes in hidden files
- Number of files and bytes in directories
- Number of files and bytes in user files
- Number of bytes in bad sectors (unallocated clusters)
- Number of bytes available on disk
- Number of bytes in total memory (RAM)
- Number of bytes in free memory
- Error messages if disk errors are encountered

By using optional parameters, CHKDSK also can show the following:

- Names and number of fragments in noncontiguous files
- Names of all directories and files on disk

If a volume name or volume serial number does not exist on a particular volume, that information is not displayed. If no clusters are marked as bad in the volume's FAT, CHKDSK returns no display of bytes in bad sectors.

For example, suppose that a disk was formatted under DOS 6.2 with the following command:

```
C:\>FORMAT A: /F:720 /U /S /V:floppy_disk
```

The output of the FORMAT command looks like this:

```
Insert new diskette for drive A:
and press ENTER when ready...

Formatting 720K
Format complete.
System transferred

    730,112 bytes total disk space
    135,168 bytes used by system
    594,944 bytes available on disk

      1,024 bytes in each allocation unit.
        581 allocation units available on disk.

Volume Serial Number is 266D-1DDC

Format another (Y/N)?
```

The status report at the end of the FORMAT operation is similar to the output of the CHKDSK command. The output of the CHKDSK command when run on this disk would appear as follows:

```
C:\>CHKDSK A:

Volume FLOPPY_DISK created 01-16-1994 10:18p
Volume Serial Number is 266D-1DDC

    730,112 bytes total disk space
     79,872 bytes in 2 hidden files
     55,296 bytes in 1 user files
    594,944 bytes available on disk

      1,024 bytes in each allocation unit
        713 total allocation units on disk
        581 available allocation units on disk

    655,360 total bytes memory
    632,736 bytes free
```

In this case, CHKDSK shows the volume name and serial number information because the FORMAT command placed a volume label on the disk with the /V: parameter, and FORMAT under DOS 4.0 and later versions automatically places the volume serial number on a disk. Note that three total files are on the disk, two of which have the HIDDEN attribute. DOS versions earlier than 5.0 report the volume label FLOPPY_DISK as a third hidden file. To see the names of the hidden files, you can execute the CHKDSK command with the /V parameter, as follows:

```
C:\>CHKDSK A: /V

Volume FLOPPY_DISK created 01-16-1994 10:18p
Volume Serial Number is 266D-1DDC
Directory A:\
A:\IO.SYS
A:\MSDOS.SYS
A:\COMMAND.COM

    730,112 bytes total disk space
     79,872 bytes in 2 hidden files
     55,296 bytes in 1 user files
    594,944 bytes available on disk

      1,024 bytes in each allocation unit
        713 total allocation units on disk
        581 available allocation units on disk

    655,360 total bytes memory
    632,736 bytes free
```

With the /V parameter, CHKDSK lists the names of all directories and files across the entire disk, which in this example is only three total files. CHKDSK does not identify which of the files are hidden, it simply lists them all. The DOS System files are the first two files on a bootable disk and normally have hidden, system, and read-only attributes.

During the FORMAT of the disk in the example, the FORMAT program did not find any unreadable sectors. Therefore, no clusters were marked in the FAT as bad or unusable, and CHKDSK did not display the message

```
xxxxxxxx Bytes in bad sectors
```

Even if the disk had developed bad sectors since the FORMAT operation, CHKDSK still would not display any bytes in bad sectors because it does not test for and count bad sectors. CHKDSK reads the FAT and reports on whether the FAT says that there are any bad sectors. CHKDSK does not really count sectors; it counts clusters (allocation units) because that is how the FAT system operates.

Although bytes in bad sectors sounds like a problem or error message, it is not. The report is simply stating that a certain number of clusters are marked as bad in the FAT and that DOS, therefore, will never use those clusters. Because nearly all hard disks are manufactured and sold with defective areas, this message is not uncommon. In fact, the higher quality hard disks on the market tend to have more bad sectors than the lower quality drives, based on the manufacturer defect list shipped with the drive (indicating all the known defective spots). Many of the newest controllers allow for sector and track sparing, in which the defects are mapped out of the DOS readable area so that DOS never has to handle them. This procedure is almost standard in drives that have embedded controllers, such as IDE (Integrated Drive Electronics) or SCSI (Small Computer Systems Interface) drives.

Suppose that you use a utility program to mark two clusters (150 and 151, for example) as bad in the FAT of the 720K floppy disk formatted earlier. CHKDSK then reports this information:

```
Volume FLOPPY_DISK created 01-16-1994 10:18p
Volume Serial Number is 266D-1DDC

    730,112 bytes total disk space
     79,872 bytes in 2 hidden files
     55,296 bytes in 1 user files
      2,048 bytes in bad sectors
    592,896 bytes available on disk

      1,024 bytes in each allocation unit
        713 total allocation units on disk
        579 available allocation units on disk

    655,360 total bytes memory
    632,736 bytes free
```

CHKDSK reports 2,048 bytes in bad sectors, which corresponds exactly to the two clusters just marked as bad. These clusters, of course, are perfectly good—you simply marked them as bad in the FAT. Using disk editor utility programs such as that supplied with the Norton Utilities, you can alter the FAT in almost any way you want.

CHKDSK Operation. Although bytes in bad sectors do not constitute an error or problem, CHKDSK reports problems found in a disk volume's FAT or directory system with one of several descriptive messages that vary to fit the specific error. Sometimes the messages are cryptic or misleading. CHKDSK does not specify how an error should be handled; it does not tell you whether CHKDSK can repair the problem, whether you must use some other utility, or what the consequences of the error and the repair will be. Neither does CHKDSK tell you what caused the problem or how to avoid repeating the problem.

The primary function of CHKDSK is to compare the directory and FAT to determine whether they agree with one another—whether all the data in the directory for files (such as the starting cluster and size information) corresponds to what is in the FAT (such as chains of clusters with end-of-chain indicators). CHKDSK also checks subdirectory file entries, as well as the special "dot" (.) and "double dot" (..) entries that tie the subdirectory system together.

The second function of CHKDSK is to implement repairs to the disk structure. CHKDSK patches the disk so that the directory and FAT are in alignment and agreement. From a repair standpoint, understanding CHKDSK is relatively easy. CHKDSK almost always modifies the directories on a disk to correspond to what is found in the FAT. There are only a few special cases in which CHKDSK modifies the FAT. When it does, the FAT modifications are always the same type of simple change.

Think of CHKDSK's repair capability as a directory patcher. Because CHKDSK cannot repair most types of FAT damage effectively, it simply modifies the disk directories to match whatever problems are found in the FAT.

CHKDSK is not a very smart repair program and often can do more damage repairing the disk than if it had left the disk alone. In many cases, the information in the directories is correct and can be used (by some other utility) to help repair the FAT tables. If you have run CHKDSK with the /F parameter, however, the original directory information no longer exists, and a good FAT repair is impossible.

> **Caution**
>
> You should never run CHKDSK with the /F parameter without first running it in read-only mode (without the /F parameter) to determine whether and to what extent damage exists.

Only after carefully examining the disk damage and determining how CHKDSK would fix the problems do you run CHKDSK with the /F parameter. If you do not specify the /F parameter when you run CHKDSK, the program is prevented from making corrections to the disk. Rather, it performs repairs in a mock fashion. This limitation is a safety feature because you do not want CHKDSK to take action until you have examined the problem. After deciding whether CHKDSK will make the correct assumptions about the damage, you might want to run it with the /F parameter.

> **Caution**
>
> Sometimes people place a CHKDSK /F command in their AUTOEXEC.BAT file—this is *a very dangerous practice*. If a system's disk directories and FAT system become damaged, attempting to load a program whose directory and FAT entries are damaged might lock the system. If, after you reboot, CHKDSK is fixing the problem because it is in the AUTOEXEC.BAT, it can irreparably damage the file structure of the disk. In many cases, CHKDSK ends up causing more damage than originally existed, and no easy way exists to undo the CHKDSK repair. Because CHKDSK is a simple utility that makes often faulty assumptions in repairing a disk, you must run it with great care when you specify the /F parameter.

Problems reported by CHKDSK are usually problems with the software and not the hardware. You rarely see a case in which lost clusters, allocation errors, or cross-linked files reported by CHKDSK were caused directly by a hardware fault, although it is certainly possible. The cause is usually a defective program or a program that was stopped before it could close files or purge buffers. A hardware fault certainly can stop a program before it can close files, but many people think that these error messages signify fault with the disk hardware, which is almost never the case.

I recommend running CHKDSK at least once a day on a hard disk system because it is important to find out about file structure errors as soon as possible. Accordingly, placing a CHKDSK command in your AUTOEXEC.BAT file is a good idea, but do not use the /F parameter. Also, run CHKDSK whenever you suspect that directory or FAT damage might have occurred. For example, whenever a program terminates abnormally or a system crashes for some reason, run CHKDSK to see whether any file system damage has occurred.

Common Errors. All CHKDSK can do is compare the directory and FAT structures to see whether they support or comply with one another; as a result, CHKDSK can detect only certain kinds of problems. When CHKDSK discovers discrepancies between the directory and the FAT structures, they almost always fall into one of the following categories (these errors are the most common ones you will see with CHKDSK):

- Lost allocation units
- Allocation errors
- Cross-linked files
- Invalid allocation units

The *RECOVER* Command

The DOS RECOVER command is designed to mark clusters as bad in the FAT when the clusters cannot be read properly. When a file cannot be read because of a problem with a sector on the disk going bad, the RECOVER command can mark the FAT so that those clusters are not used by another file. Used improperly, this program is highly dangerous.

Many users think that RECOVER is used to recover a file or the data within the file in question. What really happens is that only the portion of the file preceding the location of the defect is recovered and remains after the RECOVER command operates on it. RECOVER marks the defective portion as bad in the FAT and returns to available status all of the data located after the defect, thus destroying undamaged parts of the file. Always make a copy of the file to be recovered before using RECOVER because the COPY command can get all of the data, including the portion of the file after the location of the defect.

Suppose that you are using a word processing program. You start the program and tell it to load a file called DOCUMENT.TXT. The hard disk has developed a defect in a sector used by this file, and in the middle of loading it, you see this message appear on-screen:

```
Sector not found error reading drive C
Abort, Retry, Ignore, Fail?
```

You might be able to read the file on a retry, so try several times. If you can load the file by retrying, save the loaded version as a file with a different name, to preserve the data in the file. You still have to repair the structure of the disk to prevent the space from being used again.

After multiple retries, if you still cannot read the file, the data will be more difficult to recover. This operation has two phases, as follows:

- Preserve as much of the data in the file as possible.
- Mark the FAT so that the bad sectors or clusters of the disk are not used again.

Preserving Data. To recover the data from a file, use the DOS COPY command to make a copy of the file with a different name. For example, if the file you are recovering has the name DOCUMENT.TXT and you want the copy to be named DOCUMENT.NEW, enter the following at the DOS prompt:

```
COPY document.txt document.new
```

In the middle of the copy, you see the `Sector not found` error message again. The key to this operation is to answer with the (I)gnore option. Then the bad sectors are ignored, and the copy operation can continue to the end of the file. This procedure produces a copy of the file with all the file intact, up to the error location and after the error location. The bad sectors appear as gibberish or garbage in the new copied file, but the entire copy is readable. Use your word processor to load the new copy and remove or retype the garbled sectors.

If this file were a binary file (such as a part of a program), you would have to consider the file a total loss because you do not have the option of retyping the bytes that make up a program file. Your only hope then is to replace the file from a backup. This step completes phase one, which recovers as much of the data as possible. Now you go to phase two, in which you mark the disk so that these areas will not be used again.

Marking Bad Sectors. You mark bad sectors on a disk by using the `RECOVER` command. After making the attempted recovery of the data, you can use the following `RECOVER` command at the DOS prompt to mark the sectors as bad in the FAT:

```
RECOVER document.txt
```

In this case, the output of the `RECOVER` command looks like this:

```
Press any key to begin recovery of the file(s) on drive C:
XXXXX of YYYYY bytes recovered
```

The DOCUMENT.TXT file still is on the disk after this operation, but it has been truncated at the location of the error. Any sectors the `RECOVER` command cannot read are marked as bad sectors in the FAT and will show up the next time you run CHKDSK. You might want to run CHKDSK before and after running `RECOVER` to see the effect of the additional bad sectors.

After using `RECOVER`, delete the DOCUMENT.TXT file because you have already created a copy of it that contains as much good data as possible.

This step completes phase two—and the entire operation. You now have a new file that contains as much of the original file as possible, and the disk FAT is marked so that the defective location will not be a bother.

> **Caution**
>
> Be very careful when you use `RECOVER`. Used improperly, it can do much damage to your files and the FAT. If you enter the `RECOVER` command without a file name for it to work on, the program assumes that you want every file on the disk recovered, and operates on every file and subdirectory on the disk. It converts all subdirectories to files, places all file names in the root directory, and gives them new names (FILE0000.REC, FILE0001.REC, and so on). This process essentially wipes out the file system on the entire disk. *Do not use `RECOVER` without providing a file name for it to work on.* This program should be considered as dangerous as the `FORMAT` command.

ScanDisk

ScanDisk is included with DOS 6 and higher versions as well as Windows 95. This program is more thorough and comprehensive than CHKDSK or RECOVER, and can perform the functions of both of them. It is more like a scaled-down version of the Norton Disk Doctor program, and it can verify both file structure and disk sector integrity. If ScanDisk finds problems, the directory and FATs can be repaired. If the program finds bad sectors in the middle of a file, it marks the clusters (allocation units) containing the bad sectors as bad in the FAT, and attempts to read the file data by re-routing around the defect. Although ScanDisk is good, I would recommend using one of the commercial packages like the Norton Utilities for any major problems. These utilities go far beyond what is included in DOS or Windows.

Third-Party Programs

When you get a `Sector not found` error reading drive C:, by far the best course of action to take is to use one of the third-party disk repair utilities on the market, rather than DOS' RECOVER or even ScanDisk. Programs like the Norton Disk Doctor can perform much more detailed repairs, with a greater amount of safety. If the error is on a floppy disk, use Norton's DiskTool before you use Disk Doctor. DiskTool is specially designed to help you recover data from floppy disks. Disk Doctor and DiskTool preserve as much of the data in the file as possible, and can mark the FAT so that the bad sectors or clusters of the disk are not used again. These Norton Utilities also save Undo information, making it possible for you to reverse any data recovery operation. The Norton Utilities are now distributed by Symantec.

On the Web

Information is available from the Symantec Web site at:

http://www.symantec.com/lit/util/doswinut/doswinut.html

Memory-Resident Software Conflicts

One area that gives many users trouble is a type of memory-resident software called *Terminate and Stay Resident (TSR)* or *pop-up utilities*. This software loads itself into memory and stays there, waiting for an activation key (usually a keystroke combination).

The problem with pop-up utilities is that they often conflict with each other, as well as with application programs and even DOS. Pop-up utilities can cause many types of problems. Sometimes the problems appear consistently, and at other times they are intermittent. Some computer users do not like to use pop-up utilities unless absolutely necessary because of their potential for problems.

Other memory-resident programs, such as MOUSE.COM, are usually loaded from the AUTOEXEC.BAT file. These memory-resident programs usually do not cause the kind of conflicts that pop-up utilities do, mainly because pop-up utilities are constantly monitoring the keyboard for the hotkey that activates them. (Pop-up utilities are known to barge into memory addresses being used by other programs in order to monitor the keyboard, or to activate.) Memory-resident programs like MOUSE.COM are merely installed in memory, do not poll the keyboard for a hotkey, and generally do not clash with the memory addresses used by other programs.

Device drivers loaded in CONFIG.SYS are another form of memory-resident software and can cause many problems.

If you are experiencing problems that you have traced to any of the three types of memory-resident programs, a common way to correct the problem is to eliminate the conflicting program. Another possibility is to change the order in which device drivers and memory-resident programs are loaded into system memory. Some programs must be loaded first, and others must be loaded last. Sometimes this order preference is indicated in the documentation for the programs, but often it is discovered through trial and error.

Unfortunately, conflicts between memory-resident programs are likely to be around as long as DOS is used. The light at the end of the tunnel is operating systems like Windows 95, Windows NT, and OS/2. The problem with DOS is that it establishes no real rules for how resident programs must interact with each other and the rest of the system. Windows 95, Windows NT, and OS/2 are built on the concept of many programs being resident in memory at one time, and all multitasking. These operating systems should put an end to the problem of resident programs conflicting with each other.

Hardware Problems versus Software Problems

One of the most aggravating situations in computer repair is opening up a system and troubleshooting all the hardware just to find that the cause of the problem is a software program, not the hardware. Many people have spent large sums of money on replacement hardware, all on the premise that the hardware was causing problems, when software was actually the culprit. To eliminate these aggravating, sometimes embarrassing, and often expensive situations, you should be able to distinguish a hardware problem from a software problem.

Fortunately, making this distinction can be relatively simple. Software problems often are caused by device drivers and memory-resident programs loaded in CONFIG.SYS and AUTOEXEC.BAT on many systems. One of the first things to do when you begin having problems with your system is to boot the system from a DOS disk that has no CONFIG.SYS or AUTOEXEC.BAT configuration files on it. Then test for the problem. If it has disappeared, the cause was probably something in one or both of those files.

To find the problem, begin restoring device drivers and memory-resident programs to CONFIG.SYS and AUTOEXEC.BAT one at a time (starting with CONFIG.SYS). For example, add one program back to CONFIG.SYS, reboot your system, and then determine if the problem has reappeared. When you discover the device driver or memory-resident program causing the problem, you might be able to solve the problem by editing CONFIG.SYS and AUTOEXEC.BAT to change the order in which device drivers and memory-resident programs are loaded. Or, you might have to upgrade or even eliminate the problem device driver or memory-resident program.

Windows 95

While many users still rely on the DOS command line as their last resort for perfoJ5ing file-management tasks, DOS is no longer the working environment of choice in the PC world. Windows 3.1 is the most prevalent desktop interface today, with Windows 95 rapidly approaching it in popularity. Ultimately, however, Windows 3.1 cannot be considered to be an operating system (although debate concerning this subject has raged for years). It runs on top of DOS, and is completely reliant on the DOS mechanisms discussed in this chapter for startup, file storage, and file maintenance.

Windows 95 can indeed be called an operating system, but at the system level, it is not the radical innovation that it was purported to be before its release. In fact, Windows 95 is actually a combination of a new version of MS-DOS (DOS 7.00, according to the VER command) and a new Windows interface (called the *Explorer*).

Windows 95 marries DOS and the Windows environment into a more cohesive operating system than the DOS/Windows 3.1 combination. Booting a Windows 95 system automatically loads the GUI, but changing one character of the MSDOS.SYS text file causes the computer to boot to a DOS prompt, after which you must type **WIN** to load the Windows interface. Sound familiar?

Windows 95 and DOS Compared

Much of Windows 95 is based on the same concepts as DOS and Windows 3.1, but developed to the next logical stage. The same two system files, IO.SYS and MSDOS.SYS, still exist in Windows 95, except that all of the system file code is now located in IO.SYS, while the MSDOS.SYS file is now an ASCII text file that contains configuration settings for the system's boot behavior.

During the system startup, IO.SYS automatically loads the equivalents of HIMEM.SYS, IFSHLP.SYS, and SETVER.EXE into memory. CONFIG.SYS and AUTOEXEC.BAT files can still be used to load drivers and memory-resident programs into memory, but the 32-bit device drivers designed for use with Windows 95, as well as most of its configuration settings, are loaded by entries in the Windows 95 Registry. Finally, the WIN.COM file is loaded and Windows 95 is officially started.

The Registry is a database of reference information, configuration settings, and parameters that is continuously available to all Windows 95 modules. It replaces not only the functionality of the CONFIG.SYS and AUTOEXEC.BAT files, but the Windows 3.1 INI files as well. The troubleshooting process described earlier in this chapter, in which memory-resident programs and drivers are systematically eliminated by modifying the configuration files, can be performed in Windows 95 as well, by modifying the Registry.

> **Note**
>
> Be aware that when upgrading a Windows 3.1 computer to Windows 95, many of the program-specific settings located in configuration files like SYSTEM.INI and WIN.INI are copied to the Windows 95 Registry. Once this has occurred, changing those settings in the INI file will have no effect on the system, because the actual operative setting is located in the Registry.

The Registry is manifested on disk as two files called SYSTEM.DAT and USER.DAT. SYSTEM.DAT contains machine-specific settings, while USER.DAT contains the settings specific to the user that logs into the system. By maintaining multiple USER.DAT files, different people can share the same computer, with each user maintaining his or her own system configuration and desktop preferences. Registry files can be imported, exported, modified, backed up, and restored in order to maintain, modify, and protect the settings for a particular user or machine.

As far as disk storage is concerned, Windows 95 by default still uses the same FAT file system that DOS does, maintaining familiar structures such as the Master Boot Record (MBR), DOS Boot Record (DBR), FATs, and directories. The primary enhancement to the file system is the capability to use file and directory names that are up to 255 characters in length, while retaining backwards compatibility with existing FAT file systems and utilities.

Windows 95 does this by maintaining two names for every file and directory—a long name and a truncated name—that fit the standard DOS 8.3 format. This way, a Windows 95 file can be opened by any DOS or Windows 3.1 application, although saving the file can strip away the long file name. If, for example, you ran an older version of a disk repair utility like Norton Disk Doctor on a Windows 95 FAT volume, you could effectively lose the long names of all the files and directories on your system. Upgrade versions of most Windows applications are now available that support Windows 95 long names.

FAT32

The original Windows 95 release contained only the FAT file system, but a subsequent upgrade offers a new alternative called FAT32. The Windows 95 OEM Service Release 2 is currently available only with the purchase of a new computer or hard drive from an authorized Microsoft original equipment manufacturer. Most of the other patches and improvements to the operating system included in this release are freely available from Microsoft's Web site, but FAT32 will not be widely available until the release of Windows 98 (code-named Memphis). The OSR2 version of Windows 95 was released in this way not to thwart and irritate millions of users (which it has), but to prevent a backlash of incompatibilities that may occur when the operating system is installed on older hardware.

The primary advantage of FAT32 is its ability to support larger hard drives. Surely no one involved in the development of the FAT file system could ever have dreamed that a midrange home computer would come with a 2G hard drive, but that is now the standard. It is also the largest drive supported by the FAT file system. The other problem with FAT is that the larger cluster sizes used with high-capacity hard drives are extremely wasteful in terms of the disk space lost to the slack caused by unused bits in allocated clusters.

FAT32 addresses both of these problems, by supporting drives up to 2T (or 2,000G) in size, and with much smaller clusters. A 2G FAT drive uses 32K clusters, while the clusters on the same size FAT32 drive are only 4K. This results in a file system that is more efficient when it comes to storing the maximum possible amount of data on a hard drive, by a factor of 10 to 15 percent. Incidentally, while 2T may seem to be an outrageously large amount of data, consider that a typical PC hard drive has gone from 10M to 2G in less than 15 years, an increase of 20,000 percent. At this rate of growth, your home computer in the year 2010 should be equipped with a 400T hard drive (probably running the FAT256 file system).

FAT32 also overcomes some of the other obvious limitations of the FAT system. For example, FAT32 still has two file allocation tables, but it can now make use of either one, switching to the backup if the first table is corrupted. Also, the root directory of a drive is no longer restricted to a specific size. It is composed of cluster chains like any other directory, and can be located anywhere on the disk.

> **Note**
>
> Although it will not be implemented right away, the design of the FAT32 system will eventually allow partitions to be resized as needed. This ability will be almost as significant an advance as when DOS 4 first allowed partitions greater than 32M in size.

FAT32 volumes are implemented by the FDISK program included with the SR2 Windows 95 release. When you attempt to create a partition larger than 512M, the program asks if you want to enable large disk support. Answering yes causes all partitions larger than 512M to use the FAT32 file system.

FAT32, like Windows 95, is designed to provide the greatest possible backwards compatibility, along with its advanced features. It will continue to support real mode DOS programs as well as today's protected mode applications. This means that you will be able to boot from any DOS disk and still access FAT32 drives. However, applications designed for use on FAT drives that address the hardware directly, such as disk repair programs, will not function on (and may damage) FAT32 volumes.

In the course of providing all of its additional functionality, what FAT32 generally lacks is additional speed. FAT32 drives do not perform any faster than their FAT counterparts and may in fact be slower.

Windows NT

In complete contrast to DOS, Windows 3.1, and Windows 95 is Windows NT, a 32-bit operating system that was designed from the ground up to point towards the future of both network and desktop computing. The primary problem that consistently holds back the advancement of computing technology is backwards compatibility. It is difficult to sell a product that forces users to junk the investment that they have already made in software or hardware.

Windows 95 is much closer to DOS/Windows 3.1 than it is to Windows NT for this very reason. Corporations will not consider converting to a new operating system on a large scale if it forces them to waste millions of dollars spent on 16-bit software and user training. Windows NT is just such a product, and its acceptance in the marketplace since its original release in 1993 has been gradual but steady. Windows NT 4.0 benefits both from the Windows 95 Explorer interface and from the marketing program that has led to a massive 32-bit software development effort. If sales of operating systems like Windows

NT have lagged in the past because of a lack of 32-bit productivity applications, the popularity of Windows 95 has certainly remedied the situation.

Windows NT is a completely different operating system from DOS. Although you can open a DOS session window from within the GUI, it is not a shell in the traditional sense. It is rather a DOS emulation that is designed to provide a familiar command-line interface to users who want it. Many DOS programs will not run in a Windows NT DOS session, nor is it possible to boot the operating system to a character-based state that precedes the loading of the graphical interface, as with Windows 95.

Like Windows 95, Windows NT uses a Registry to store its configuration settings and load drivers. There are no CONFIG.SYS, AUTOEXEC.BAT, or INI files. What's more, there is not even an upgrade path from Windows 95 to Windows NT. You must reinstall and reconfigure all of your applications after setting up the operating system.

Windows NT can use the FAT file system, in which case you can boot the computer from a DOS disk and still access its drives. Some of Windows NT's most advanced features, however, are provided by the NT File System (NTFS). NTFS (like FAT32) allows you to create partitions up to 2T in size, but it also provides the file compression, security, and auditing features that are important to Windows NT computers in network environments.

During the Windows NT installation process, the initial setup is performed on a FAT drive, which is converted to NTFS at the end of the installation process, if you want. You can also convert the drives later, using a CONVERT.EXE utility provided with the operating system. This is one of the few instances in which you can convert an existing volume to another file system without losing data. From the time that a partition is converted to NTFS, however, it is accessible by any other operating system. To switch the machine back to Windows 95, Windows 3.1, or DOS, the NTFS partitions must be removed and FAT partitions created from scratch.

As a result of this, virtually none of the troubleshooting techniques outlined earlier in this chapter can be applied to NTFS drives, nor can the disk utilities intended for use on FAT drives address them. However, although they have been a long time in coming, there are now third-party utilities that can repair and defragment NTFS drives.

Chapter 23
IBM Personal Computer Family Hardware

Although IBM no longer seems in a position to dictate the majority of PC standards (Intel and Microsoft seem to have taken on that role), all of the original PC specifications and standards were determined by IBM and set forth in its original line of personal computers. From these original IBM PC, XT, and AT systems came many of the standards to which even today's systems must still conform. This includes motherboard form factors, case and power supply designs, ISA Bus architecture, system resource usage, memory mapping and architecture, system interfaces, connectors, pinouts, and more. As such, nearly every PC-compatible system on the market today is based in some form on one or more of the original IBM products. The original line of systems are often called *Industry Standard Architecture (ISA) systems*, or *Classic PCs*. IBM calls them *Family/1 systems*.

This chapter serves as a technical reference to IBM's original family of personal computer systems. Much of the information in this chapter serves as a sort of history lesson; it is easy to see how far IBM-compatible computing has come when you look over the specifications of the original systems the PC standard is based on! I find the information valuable to teach others the origins of what we call a PC-compatible system today.

Because the PC compatibles are mostly based on the IBM XT and especially AT systems, you can see where things like the motherboard, case, and power supply shapes came from, the positions of slots, connectors and other components on the boards, and the levels of performance these systems originally offered.

Although these systems have long since been discontinued, I am amazed that I still find many of these systems in use. From individuals to large corporations to the government and military, I still occasionally encounter these old systems in my training and consulting practice. Often the only part that remains of the original system is the case and power supply, because newer

Baby-AT form factor motherboards easily fit in most of the original IBM machines. In fact, I still have several of the original IBM XT and AT cases around which now sport modern Pentium motherboards, large hard drives, and all new components!

System-Unit Features by Model

The following sections discuss the makeup of all the various versions or models of the original IBM systems, and also technical details and specifications of each system. Every system unit has a few standard parts. The primary component is the *motherboard*, which has the CPU (central processing unit, or microprocessor) and other primary computer circuitry. Each unit also includes a case with an internal power supply, a keyboard, certain standard adapters or plug-in cards, and usually some form of disk drive.

There is an explanation of each system's various submodels and details about the differences between and features of each model. Also shown are the changes from model to model and version to version of each system.

Included for your reference is part-number information for some of the systems and options. This information is for comparison and reference purposes only; all these systems have been discontinued and generally are no longer available. However, it is interesting to note that IBM still stocks and sells component parts and assemblies for even these discontinued units. IBM still stocks replacement parts even for the original PC, XT, and AT systems!

The original IBM systems can be identified not only by their name, but by a number assigned to each system. IBM normally put the name of the computer on a small 1×1-inch square brushed metal plate on the front cover, and the system number on a similar metal plate on the rear of the chassis. The system names and numbers correspond as follows:

System Number	**System Name**
4860	PCjr
5140	PC Convertible (laptop)
5150	PC
5155	Portable PC (really a portable XT)
5160	XT
5162	XT-286 (really an AT)
5170	AT

Note that because modern PC components are often designed to be physically compatible with the original IBM systems, you can (and usually should) replace any failed or obsolete components in the older IBM systems with non-IBM replacement parts. Invariably, you will be able to obtain upgraded or improved components compared to the originals, and at a greatly reduced price. An example is one original 286 IBM AT that I have that now sports a Pentium MMX motherboard, 64M of RAM, 9G SCSI drive, 12x CD-ROM, and a host of other options. Of course, the only original IBM parts left in the system are the case and power supply, which are both more than 14 years old!

An Introduction to the PC (5150)

IBM introduced the IBM Personal Computer on August 12, 1981, and officially withdrew the machine from marketing on April 2, 1987. During the nearly six-year life of the PC, IBM made only a few basic changes to the system. The basic motherboard circuit design was changed in April 1983 to accommodate 64K RAM chips. Three different ROM BIOS versions were used during the life of the system; most other specifications, however, remained unchanged. Because IBM no longer markets the PC system, and because of the PC's relatively limited expansion capability and power, the standard PC is obsolete by most standards.

The system unit supports only floppy disk drives unless the power supply is upgraded or an expansion chassis is used to house the hard disk externally. IBM never offered an internal hard disk for the PC, but many third-party companies stepped in to fill this void with upgrades. The system unit included many configurations with single or dual floppy disk drives. Early on, one version even was available with no disk drives, and others used single-sided floppy drives.

The PC motherboard was based on the 16-bit Intel 8088 microprocessor and included the Microsoft Cassette BASIC language built into ROM. For standard memory, the PC offered configurations with as little as 16K of RAM (when the system was first announced) and as much as 256K on the motherboard. Two motherboard designs were used. Systems sold before March 1983 had a motherboard that supported a maximum of only 64K of RAM, and later systems supported a maximum of 256K on the motherboard. In either case, you added more memory (as much as 640K) by installing memory cards in the expansion slots.

The first bank of memory chips in every PC is soldered to the motherboard. Soldered memory is reliable but not conducive to easy servicing because it prevents you from easily exchanging failing memory chips located in the first bank. The chips must be unsoldered and the defective chip replaced with a socket so that a replacement can be plugged in. When IBM services the defective memory, IBM advises you to exchange the entire motherboard. Considering today's value of these systems, replacing the motherboard with one of the many compatible motherboards on the market may be a better idea. Repairing the same defective memory chip in the XT system is much easier because all memory in an XT is socketed.

The only disk drive available from IBM for the PC is a double-sided (320 or 360K) floppy disk drive. You can install a maximum of two drives in the system unit by using IBM-supplied drives, or four using half-height third-party drives and mounting brackets.

The system unit has five slots that support expansion cards for additional devices, features, or memory. All these slots support full-length adapter cards. In most configurations, the PC included at least a floppy disk controller card. You need a second slot for a monitor adapter, which leaves three slots for adapter cards.

All models of the PC have a fan-cooled, 63.5-watt power supply. This low-output power supply doesn't support much in the way of system expansion, especially power-hungry items such as hard disks. Usually, this low-output supply must be replaced by a higher-output unit, such as the one used in the XT. Figure 23.1 shows an interior view of a PC system unit.

An 83-key keyboard with an adjustable typing angle is standard equipment on the PC. The keyboard is attached to the rear of the system unit by a six-foot coiled cable. Figure 23.2 shows the back panel of the PC.

Most model configurations of the PC system unit included these major functional components:

- Intel 8088 microprocessor
- ROM-based diagnostics (POST)
- BASIC language interpreter in ROM
- 256K of dynamic RAM
- Floppy disk controller
- One or two 360K floppy drives
- A 63.5-watt power supply
- Five I/O expansion slots
- Socket for the 8087 math coprocessor

PC Models and Features

Although several configurations of the IBM PC were available before March 1983, only two models were available after that time. The later models differ only in the number of floppy drives: one or two. IBM designated these models as follows:

- *IBM PC 5150 Model 166.* 256K RAM, one 360K drive.
- *IBM PC 5150 Model 176.* 256K RAM, two 360K drives.

The IBM PC was never available with a factory-installed hard disk (XT systems came with hard disks), primarily because the system unit had limited room for expansion and offered few resources with which to work. After IBM started selling XTs with only floppy disk drives (on April 2, 1985), the PC essentially became obsolete. The XT offered much more for virtually the same price, so investing in a PC after the XT introduction was questionable.

An Introduction to the PC (5150)

FIG. 23.1 The IBM PC interior view.

FIG. 23.2 The IBM PC rear view.

IBM finally officially withdrew the PC from the market on April 2, 1987. IBM's plans for the system became obvious when the company didn't announce a new model with the enhanced keyboard, as it did with other IBM systems. In retrospect, it is amazing that the system was sold over a period of nearly six years with few changes!

Table 23.1 shows the part numbers for the IBM PC system units and options.

Table 23.1 IBM PC Models and Part Numbers	
Description	**Number**
PC system unit, 256K, one double-sided drive	5150166
PC system unit, 256K, two double-sided drives	5150176
Options	**Number**
PC expansion-unit Model 001 with 10M hard disk	5161001
Double-sided disk drive	1503810
8087 math coprocessor option	1501002
BIOS update kit (10/27/82 BIOS)	1501005

With some creative purchasing, you could make a usable system of a base PC by adding the requisite components, such as a full 640K of memory as well as hard disk and floppy drives. Only you can decide when your money is better invested in a new system.

Before you think of expanding a PC beyond even a simple configuration, and to allow for compatibility and reliability, you must address the following two major areas:

- ROM BIOS level (version)
- 63.5-watt power supply

In most cases, the low output power supply is the most critical issue because all PCs sold after March 1983 already had the latest ROM BIOS. If you have an earlier PC system, you also must upgrade the ROM because the early versions lack some required capabilities, in particular the ability to scan the memory range C0000-DFFFF in the Upper Memory Area (UMA) for adapter card ROMs.

PC BIOS Versions

There have been three different BIOS versions used in the IBM PC. They can be identified by their date and summarized as follows:

- April 24, 1981: The first PC BIOS version would only support a maximum of 544K of RAM, plus it would not scan the UMA for adapter card ROMs, such as are found on EGA/VGA video adapters, hard disk controllers, and SCSI adapters. This BIOS is very rare, and any such machine is almost a collector's item as it represents one of the first PCs ever made!

- October 19, 1981: The second PC BIOS has the same 544K RAM and UMA scan limitations as the first BIOS, but it does fix a couple of minor display bugs. Even this BIOS is not very common.

- October 27, 1982: The third and final PC BIOS has support for a full 640K of base RAM plus the necessary UMA scan to support adapter cards with ROMs on them.

To be useful at all, a PC must have this BIOS revision. If your PC BIOS is one of the older two versions, note that IBM sells a BIOS update kit under part number 1501005.

Table 23.2 Lists the different IBM Family/1 (PC, XT, and AT) BIOS versions. It also shows the ID, Submodel, and Revision bytes that can be determined by a software function call

```
Int 15h, C0 = Return System Configuration Parameters
```

Some of the systems such as the PC and earlier XT and AT systems only supports the ID byte; the submodel and revision bytes had not been established when those systems were developed. The table also shows the number of drive types supported in the AT and XT-286 systems BIOS.

Table 23.2 IBM Family/1 (PC, XT, AT) System BIOS Dates

System	CPU	Speed	BIOS Date	ID, Submodel, Revision	BIOS Drive Types
PC	8088	4.77MHz	04/24/81	FF - -	-
PC	8088	4.77MHz	10/19/81	FF - -	-
PC	8088	4.77MHz	10/27/82	FF - -	-
PCjr	8088	4.77MHz	06/01/83	FD - -	-
PC-XT, PPC	8088	4.77MHz	11/08/82	FE - -	-
PC-XT	8088	4.77MHz	01/10/86	FB 00 01	-
PC-XT	8088	4.77MHz	05/09/86	FB 00 02	-
PC Convertible	80C8	4.77MHz	09/13/85	F9 00 00	-
PC-AT	286	6MHz	01/10/84	FC - -	15
PC-AT	286	6MHz	06/10/85	FC 00 01	23
PC-AT	286	8MHz	11/15/85	FC 01 00	23
PC-XT 286	286	6MHz	04/21/86	FC 02 00	24

The ID, Submodel, and Revision byte numbers are in hexadecimal.
- = This feature is not supported.

The BIOS date is stored in all PC compatible systems at memory address FFFF5h. To display the date of your BIOS, a simple DEBUG command can be used to view this address. DEBUG is a command program supplied with MS-DOS. At the DOS prompt, execute the following commands to run DEBUG, display the date stored in your BIOS, and then exit back to DOS:

```
C:\>DEBUG
-D FFFF:5 L 8
FFFF:0000            30 31 2F-32 32 2F 39 37                    01/22/97
-Q
```

In this example, the system queried shows a BIOS date of 01/22/97.

Chapter 23—IBM Personal Computer Family Hardware

PC Technical Specifications

Technical information for the Personal Computer system and keyboard is described in this section. Here, you find information about the system architecture, memory configurations and capacities, standard system features, disk storage, expansion slots, keyboard specifications, and physical and environmental specifications. This kind of information may be useful in determining what parts you need when you are upgrading or repairing these systems. Figure 23.3 shows the layout and components on the PC motherboard.

FIG. 23.3 The IBM PC motherboard.

System Architecture	
Microprocessor	8088
Clock speed	4.77MHz
Bus type	ISA (Industry Standard Architecture)
Bus width	8-bit
Interrupt levels	8 (6 usable)
Type	Edge-triggered
Shareable	No
DMA channels	4 (3 usable)
Bus masters supported	No
Upgradable processor complex	No

Memory

Standard on system board	16K, 64K, or 256K
Maximum on system board	256K
Maximum total memory	640K
Memory speed (ns) and type	200ns dynamic RAM chips
System board memory-socket type	16-pin DIP
Number of memory-module sockets	27 (3 banks of 9 chips)
Memory used on system board	27 16K×1-bit or 64K×1-bit DRAM chips in 3 banks of 9, one soldered bank of 9 16K×1-bit or 64K×1-bit chips
Memory cache controller	No
Wait states:	
System board	1
Adapter	1

Standard Features

ROM size	40K
ROM shadowing	No
Optional math coprocessor	8087
Coprocessor speed	4.77MHz
Standard graphics	None standard
RS232C serial ports	None standard
UART chip used	NS8250B
Maximum speed (bits per second)	9,600 bps
Maximum number of ports supported	2
Pointing device (mouse) ports	None standard
Parallel printer ports	None standard
Bi-directional	No
Maximum number of ports supported	3
CMOS real-time clock (RTC)	No
CMOS RAM	None

Disk Storage

Internal disk and tape drive bays	2 full-height
Number of 3 1/2-/5 1/4-inch bays	0/2
Standard floppy drives	1×360K
Optional floppy drives:	
5 1/4-inch 360K	Optional

(continues)

(continued)

Disk Storage

5 1/4-inch 1.2M	No
3 1/2-inch 720K	Optional
3 1/2-inch 1.44M	No
3 1/2-inch 2.88M	No
Hard disk controller included	None

Expansion Slots

Total adapter slots	5
Number of long and short slots	5/0
Number of 8-/16-/32-bit slots	5/0/0
Available slots (with video)	3

Keyboard Specifications

101-key Enhanced keyboard	No, 83-key
Fast keyboard speed setting	No
Keyboard cable length	6 feet

Physical Specifications

Footprint type	Desktop
Dimensions:	
Height	5.5 inches
Width	19.5 inches
Depth	16.0 inches
Weight	25 pounds

Environmental Specifications

Power-supply output	63.5 watts
Worldwide (110/60,220/50)	No
Auto-sensing/switching	No
Maximum current:	
104-127 VAC	2.5 amps
Operating range:	
Temperature	60–90° F
Relative humidity	8–80 percent
Maximum operating altitude	7,000 feet
Heat (BTUs/hour)	505
Noise (Average db, operating, 1m)	43
FCC classification	Class B

An Introduction to the PC (5150)

Tables 23.3 and 23.4 show the Switch Settings for the PC (and XT) motherboard. The PC has two eight-position switch blocks (Switch Block 1 and Switch Block 2), whereas the XT has only a single Switch Block 1. The PC used the additional switch block to control the amount of memory the system would recognize, and the XT automatically counted up the memory amount.

Table 23.3 IBM PC/XT Motherboard Switch Settings

SWITCH BLOCK 1 (PC and XT)

		Switch 1	**IBM PC Function (PC Only):**
		Off	Boot From Floppy Drives
		On	Do Not Boot From Floppy Drives
		Switch 1	**IBM XT Function (XT Only):**
		Off	Normal POST (Power-On Self Test)
		On	Continuous Looping POST
		Switch 2	**Math Coprocessor (PC/XT):**
		Off	Installed
		On	Not Installed
Switch 3		**Switch 4**	**Installed Motherboard Memory (PC/XT):**
On		On	Bank 0 only
Off		On	Banks 0 and 1
On		Off	Banks 0, 1 and 2
Off		Off	All 4 Banks
Switch 5		**Switch 6**	**Video Adapter Type (PC/XT):**
Off		Off	Monochrome (MDA)
Off		On	Color (CGA) - 40×25 mode
On		Off	Color (CGA) - 80×25 mode
On		On	Any Video Card w/onboard BIOS (EGA/VGA)
Switch 7		**Switch 8**	**Number of Floppy Drives (PC/XT):**
On		On	1 floppy drive
Off		On	2 floppy drives
On		Off	3 floppy drives
Off		Off	4 floppy drives

Table 23.4 Switch Blocks 2 (PC Only) Memory Settings

Memory	Switch Number (Switch Block 2, PC Only)							
	1	2	3	4	5	6	7	8
16K	On	On	On	On	On	Off	Off	Off
32K	On	On	On	On	On	Off	Off	Off
48K	On	On	On	On	On	Off	Off	Off
64K	On	On	On	On	On	Off	Off	Off

(continues)

Table 23.4 Continued

Memory	Switch Number (Switch Block 2, PC Only)							
	1	2	3	4	5	6	7	8
96K	Off	On	On	On	On	Off	Off	Off
128K	On	Off	On	On	On	Off	Off	Off
160K	Off	Off	On	On	On	Off	Off	Off
192K	On	On	Off	On	On	Off	Off	Off
224K	Off	On	Off	On	On	Off	Off	Off
256K	On	Off	Off	On	On	Off	Off	Off
288K	Off	Off	Off	On	On	Off	Off	Off
320K	On	On	On	Off	On	Off	Off	Off
352K	Off	On	On	Off	On	Off	Off	Off
384K	On	Off	On	Off	On	Off	Off	Off
416K	Off	Off	On	Off	On	Off	Off	Off
448K	On	On	Off	Off	On	Off	Off	Off
480K	Off	On	Off	Off	On	Off	Off	Off
512K	On	Off	Off	Off	On	Off	Off	Off
544K	Off	Off	Off	Off	On	Off	Off	Off
576K	On	On	On	On	Off	Off	Off	Off
608K	Off	On	On	On	Off	Off	Off	Off
640K	On	Off	On	On	Off	Off	Off	Off

An Introduction to the PC Convertible (5140)

IBM marked its entry into the laptop computer market on April 2, 1986, by introducing the IBM 5140 PC Convertible. The system superseded the 5155 Portable PC (IBM's transportable system), which was discontinued. The IBM 5140 system wasn't a very successful laptop system. Other laptops offered more disk storage, higher processor speeds, more readable screens, lower cost, and more compact cases, which pressured IBM to improve the Convertible. Because the improvements were limited to the display, however, this system never gained respect in the marketplace. It is significant in two respects; the first is that it marked IBM's entry into the laptop and notebook portable system market, a market they have tremendous success in today with the ThinkPad systems. The second is that the Convertible was the first IBM PC system supplied with 3 1/2-inch floppy drives.

The PC Convertible was available in two models. The Model 2 had a CMOS 80C88 4.77MHz microprocessor, 64K of ROM, 256K of Static RAM, an 80-column×25-line detachable liquid crystal display (LCD), two 3 1/2-inch floppy disk drives, a 78-key keyboard, an AC adapter, and a battery pack. Also included were software programs called Application Selector, SystemApps, Tools, Exploring the IBM PC Convertible, and Diagnostics. The Model 22 is the same basic computer as the Model 2 but with the diagnostics software. You can expand either system to 512K of RAM by using 128K RAM memory cards, and you can include an internal 1,200 bps modem in the system unit. With aftermarket memory expansion, the computers can reach 640K.

Although the unit was painfully slow at 4.77MHz, one notable feature is the use of Static memory chips for the system's RAM. Static RAM does not require the refresh signal that normal Dynamic RAM (DRAM) requires, which would normally require about 7 percent of the processor's time in a standard PC or XT system. This means that the Convertible is about 7 percent faster than an IBM PC or XT, even though they all operate at the same clock speed of 4.77MHz. Because of the increased reliability of the Static RAM (compared to DRAM) used in the Convertible, as well as the desire to minimize power consumption, none of the RAM in the Convertible is parity checked.

At the back of each system unit is an extendable bus interface. This 72-pin connector enables you to attach the following options to the base unit: a printer, a serial or parallel adapter, and a CRT display adapter. Each feature is powered from the system unit. The CRT display adapter operates only when the system is powered from a standard AC adapter. A separate CRT display or a television set attached through the CRT display adapter requires a separate AC power source.

Each system unit includes a detachable LCD. When the computer is not mobile, the LCD screen can be replaced by an external monitor. When the LCD is latched in the closed position, it forms the cover for the keyboard and floppy disk drives. Because the LCD is attached with a quick-disconnect connector, you can remove it easily to place the 5140 system unit below an optional IBM 5144 PC Convertible monochrome or IBM 5145 PC Convertible color display. During the life of the Convertible, IBM offered three different LCD displays. The first display was a standard LCD, which suffered from problems with contrast and readability. Due to complaints, IBM then changed the LCD to a Super Twisted type LCD display, which had much greater contrast. Finally, in the third LCD, IBM added a fluorescent backlight to the Super Twisted LCD display, which not only offered greater contrast, but made the unit usable in low light situations.

The PC Convertible system unit has these standard features:

- Complementary Metal-Oxide Semiconductor (CMOS) 80C88 4.77 MHz microprocessor

- Two 32K CMOS ROMs containing these items:

    POST (Power On Self Test) of system components
    BIOS (basic input-output system) support
    BASIC language interpreter

- 256K CMOS Static RAM (expandable to 512K)

- Two 3 1/2-inch 720K (formatted) floppy drives

- An 80-column×25-line detachable LCD panel (graphics modes: 640×200 resolution and 320×200 resolution)

- LCD controller

- 16K RAM display buffer
- 8K LCD font RAM
- Adapter for optional printer (#4010)
- Professional keyboard (78 keys)
- AC adapter
- Battery pack

The system-unit options for the 5140 are shown in this list:

- 128K Static RAM memory card (#4005)
- Printer (#4010)
- Serial/parallel adapter (#4015)
- CRT display adapter (#4020)
- Internal modem (#4025)
- Printer cable (#4055)
- Battery charger (#4060)
- Automobile power adapter (#4065)

The following two optional displays were available for the PC Convertible:

- IBM 5144 PC Convertible Monochrome Display Model 1
- IBM 5145 PC Convertible Color Display Model 1

PC Convertible Specifications and Highlights

This section lists some technical specifications for the IBM 5140 PC Convertible system. The weights of the unit and options are listed because weight is an important consideration when you carry a laptop system. Figure 23.4 shows the PC Convertible motherboard components and layout.

Dimensions	
Depth:	360 mm (14.17 inches)
	374 mm (14.72 inches) including handle
Width:	309.6 mm (12.19 inches)
	312 mm (12.28 inches) including handle
Height:	67 mm (2.64 inches)
	68 mm (2.68 inches) including footpads

Weight	
Models 2 and 22 (including battery)	5.5 kg (12.17 pounds)
128K/256K memory card	40 g (1.41 ounces)

Printer	1.6 kg (3.50 pounds)
Serial/parallel adapter	470 g (1.04 pounds)
CRT display adapter	630 g (1.40 pounds)
Internal modem	170 g (6 ounces)
Printer cable	227 g (8 ounces)
Battery charger	340 g (12 ounces)
Automobile power adapter	113 g (4 ounces)
5144 PC Convertible monochrome display	7.3 kg (16 pounds)
5145 PC Convertible color display	16.9 kg (37.04 pounds)

FIG. 23.4 The PC Convertible motherboard.

To operate the IBM 5140 PC Convertible properly, you must have PC DOS version 3.2 or later. Previous DOS versions aren't supported because they don't support the 720K floppy drive.

PC Convertible Models and Features

This section covers the options and special features available for the PC Convertible. Several kinds of options were available, from additional memory to external display adapters, serial/parallel ports, modems, and even printers.

Memory Cards. A 128K or 256K memory card expands the base memory in the system unit. You can add two of these cards, for a system-unit total of 640K with one 256K card and one 128K card.

Optional Printer. A special printer is available that attaches to the back of the system unit or to an optional printer-attachment cable for adjacent printer operation. The printer's intelligent, microprocessor-based, 40cps, non-impact dot-matrix design makes it capable of low-power operation. The printer draws power from and is controlled by the system unit. Standard ASCII 96-character, upper- and lowercase character sets were printed with a high-resolution, 24-element print head. A mode for graphics capability is provided also. You can achieve near-letter-quality printing by using either a thermal transfer ribbon on smooth paper or no ribbon on heat-sensitive thermal paper.

A special printer cable is available that is 22 inches (0.6 meters) long with a custom 72-pin connector attached to each end. With this cable, you can operate the Convertible printer when it is detached from the system unit and place the unit for ease of use and visibility.

Serial/Parallel Adapter. A serial/parallel adapter attaches to the back of the system unit, a printer, or other feature module attached to the back of the system unit. The adapter provides an RS-232C asynchronous communications interface and a parallel printer interface, both compatible with the IBM personal computer asynchronous communications adapter and the IBM personal computer parallel printer adapter.

CRT Display Adapter. A CRT display adapter attaches to the back of the system unit, printer, or other feature module attached to the back of the system unit. This adapter enables you to connect a separate CRT display to the system, such as the PC Convertible monochrome display or PC Convertible color display. By using optional connectors or cables, you can use the CRT display adapter also to attach a standard Color Graphics Adapter (CGA) monitor. Because composite video output is available, you also can use a standard television set.

Internal Modems. IBM offered two different internal modems for the Convertible. Both run Bell 212A (1,200 bps) or Bell 103A (300 bps) protocols. The modems came as a complete assembly, consisting of two cards connected by a cable. The entire assembly is installed inside the system unit. The original first design modem was made for IBM by Novation, and did not follow the Hayes standard for commands and protocols. This rendered the modem largely incompatible with popular software designed to use the Hayes command set. Later, IBM changed the modem to one that was fully Hayes compatible; this resolved the problems with software. IBM never introduced a modem faster than 1,200 bps for the Convertible. Fortunately, you can operate a standard external modem through the serial port, although you lose the convenience of having it built in.

Battery Charger/Auto Power Adapter. The battery charger is a 110-volt input device that charges the system's internal batteries. It does not provide sufficient power output for the system to operate while the batteries are being charged.

An available automobile power adapter plugs into the cigarette-lighter outlet in a vehicle with a 12-volt, negative-ground electrical system. You can use the system while the adapter also charges the Convertible's battery.

Optional Displays. The 5144 PC Convertible monochrome display is a 9-inch (measured diagonally) composite video display attached to the system unit through the CRT display adapter. It comes with a display stand, an AC power cord, and a signal cable that connects the 5144 to the CRT display adapter. This display does not resemble—and is not compatible with—the IBM monochrome display for larger PC systems. The CRT adapter emits the same signal as the one supplied by the Color Graphics Adapter for a regular PC. This display is functionally equivalent to the display on the IBM Portable PC.

The 5145 PC Convertible color display is a 13-inch color display attached to the system unit through the CRT display adapter. It comes with a display stand, an AC power cord, a signal cable that connects the 5145 to the CRT display adapter, and a speaker for external audio output. The monitor is a low-cost unit compatible with the standard IBM CGA display.

Table 23.5 shows the part numbers of the IBM Convertible system units.

Table 23.5 IBM Convertible Part Numbers

5140 PC Convertible System Units	Number
Two drives, 256K with system applications	5140002
Two drives, 256K without system applications	5140022

An Introduction to the XT (5160)

Introduced March 8, 1983, the PC XT with a built-in 10M hard disk (originally standard, later optional) caused a revolution in personal computer configurations. At the time, having even a 10M hard disk was something very special. *XT* stands for *eXTended*. IBM chose this name because the IBM PC XT system includes many features not available in the standard PC. The XT has eight slots, allowing increased expansion capabilities; greater power-supply capacity; completely socketed memory; motherboards that support memory expansion to 640K without using an expansion slot; and optional hard disk drives. To obtain these advantages, the XT uses a different motherboard circuit design than the PC.

The system unit was available in several models, with a variety of disk drive configurations: one 360K floppy disk drive, two 360K floppy disk drives, one floppy disk and one hard disk drive, or two floppy disk drives and one hard disk drive. The floppy disk drives were full-height drives in the earlier models, and half-height drives in more recent models. With the four available drive bays, IBM had standard configurations with two floppy drives and a single hard disk, with room for a second hard disk, provided all half-height units were used.

IBM offered only 10M and 20M full-height hard disks. In some cases, they also installed half-height hard disks, but they were always installed in a bracket and cradle assembly that took up the equivalent space of a full-height drive. If you wanted half-height hard disks (to install two of them stacked, for example), you had to use non-IBM supplied drives or modify the mounting of the IBM supplied half-height unit so that two could fit. Most aftermarket sources for hard disks had mounting kits that would work.

IBM also used double-sided (320/360K) floppy disk drives in full- or half-height configurations. A 3 1/2-inch 720K floppy disk drive was available in more recent models. The 3 1/2-inch drives were available in a normal internal configuration or as an external device. You could install a maximum of two floppy disk drives and one hard disk drive in the system unit, using IBM-supplied drives. With half-height hard disks, you could install two hard drives in the system unit.

The XT is based on the same 8- and 16-bit Intel 8088 microprocessor (the CPU has 16-bit registers but only an 8-bit data bus) as the PC and runs at the same clock speed. Operationally, the XT systems are identical to the PC systems except for the hard disk. All models have at least one 360K floppy disk drive and a keyboard. For standard memory, the XT offers 256K or 640K on the main board. The hard disk models also include a serial adapter.

The system unit has eight slots that support cards for additional devices, features, or memory. Two of the slots support only short option cards because of physical interference from the disk drives. The XT has at least a disk drive adapter card in the floppy-disk-only models, and a hard disk controller card and serial adapter in the hard disk models. Either five or seven expansion slots (depending on the model) therefore are available. Figure 23.5 shows the interior of an XT.

FIG. 23.5 The IBM PC XT interior.

All XT models include a heavy-duty, fan-cooled, 130-watt power supply to support the greater expansion capabilities and disk drive options. The power supply has more than double the capacity of the PC's supply, and can easily support hard disk drives as well as the full complement of expansion cards.

An 83-key keyboard was standard equipment with the early XT models, but was changed to an enhanced 101-key unit in the more recent models. The keyboard is attached to the system unit by a six-foot coiled cable.

All models of the PC XT system unit contain these major functional components:

- Intel 8088 microprocessor
- ROM-based diagnostics (POST)
- BASIC language interpreter in ROM
- 256K or 640K of dynamic RAM
- Floppy disk controller
- One 360K floppy drive (full- or half-height)
- 10M or 20M hard disk drive with interface (enhanced models)
- Serial interface (enhanced models)
- Heavy-duty, 135-watt power supply
- Eight I/O expansion slots
- Socket for 8087 math coprocessor

XT Models and Features

The XT was available in many different model configurations, but originally only one model was available. This model included a 10M hard disk, marking the first time that a hard disk was standard equipment in a personal computer and was properly supported by the operating system and peripherals. This computer helped change the industry standard for personal computers from normally having one or two floppy disk drives only to now including one or more hard disks.

Today, most people wouldn't consider a PC to be even remotely usable without a hard disk. The original XT was expensive, however, and buyers couldn't unbundle, or delete, the hard disk from the system at purchase time for credit and add it later. This fact distinguished the XT from the PC and misled many people to believe that the only difference between the two computers was the hard disk. People who recognized and wanted the greater capabilities of the XT without the standard IBM hard disk unfortunately had to wait for IBM to sell versions of the XT without the hard disk drive.

The original Model 087 of the XT included a 10M hard disk, 128K of RAM, and a standard serial interface. IBM later increased the standard memory in all PC systems to 256K. The XT reflected the change in Model 086, which was the same as the preceding 087 except for a standard 256K of RAM.

On April 2, 1985, IBM finally introduced new models of the XT without the standard hard disk. Designed for expansion and configuration flexibility, the new models enabled you to buy the system initially at a lower cost and add your own hard disk later. The XT therefore could be considered in configurations that previously only the original PC could fill. The primary difference between the PC and the XT is the XT's expansion capability, provided by the larger power supply, eight slots, and better memory layout. These models cost only $300 more than equivalent PCs, rendering the original PC no longer a viable option.

The extra expense of the XT can be justified with the first power-supply replacement you make with an overworked PC. The IBM PC XT is available in two floppy disk models:

- 5160068 XT with one full-height 360K disk drive
- 5160078 XT with two full-height 360K disk drives

Both these models have 256K of memory and use the IBM PC XT motherboard, power supply, frame, and cover. The serial (asynchronous communications) port adapter isn't included as a standard feature with these models.

IBM introduced several more models of the PC XT on April 2, 1986. These models were significantly different from previous models. The most obvious difference, the 101-key enhanced keyboard, was standard with these newer computers. A 20M (rather than 10M) hard disk and one or two half-height floppy disk drives were included. The new half-height floppy disk drives allow for two drives in the space that previously held only one floppy drive. With two drives, backing up floppy disks became easy. A new 3 1/2-inch floppy disk drive, storing 720K for compatibility with the PC Convertible laptop computer, was released also. These newer XT system units were configured with a slightly different memory layout, allowing for 640K of RAM on the motherboard without an expansion slot. This feature conserves power, improves reliability, and lowers the cost of the system.

One 5 1/4-inch, half-height, 360K floppy disk drive and 256K of system-board memory was standard with the XT Models 267 and 268. Models 277 and 278 have a second 5 1/4-inch floppy disk drive. Models 088 and 089 were expanded PC XTs with all the standard features of the Models 267 and 268, a 20M hard disk, a 20M fixed disk drive adapter, a serial port adapter, and an additional 256K of system-board memory—a total of 512K.

The following list shows the highlights of these new models:

- Enhanced keyboard standard on Models 268, 278, and 089; 101 keys, and no status LEDs (XT interface cannot drive LEDs)
- Standard PC XT keyboard on Models 267, 277, and 088
- More disk capacity (20M)
- Standard 5 1/4-inch, half-height, 360K floppy drive
- Available 3 1/2-inch, half-height, 720K floppy drive

- Capacity for four half-height storage devices within the system unit
- Capacity to expand to 640K bytes memory on system board without using expansion slots

These newest XT models have an extensively changed ROM BIOS. The new BIOS is 64K and is internally similar to the BIOS found in ATs. The ROM includes support for the new keyboard and 3 1/2-inch floppy disk drives. The POST also was enhanced.

The new XTs were originally incompatible in some respects with some software programs. These problems centered on the new 101-key enhanced keyboard and the way the new ROM addressed the keys. These problems weren't major and were solved quickly by the software companies.

Seeing how much IBM changed the computer without changing the basic motherboard design is interesting. The ROM is different, and the board now could hold 640K of memory without a card in a slot. The memory trick is a simple one. IBM designed this feature into the board originally and chose to unleash it with these models of the XT.

During the past several years, I have modified many XTs to have 640K on the motherboard, using a simple technique designed into the system by IBM. A jumper and chip added to the motherboard can alter the memory addressing in the board to enable the system to recognize 640K. The new addressing is set up for 256K chips, installed in two of the four banks. The other two banks of memory contain 64K chips—a total of 640K.

Complete instructions for how to install 640K of memory on the XT motherboard can be found on the CD which accompanies this book.

XT BIOS Versions

There have been three different BIOS versions used in the IBM PC-XT. They can be identified by their date and summarized as follows:

- **November 8, 1982:** The original XT BIOS had all of the features of the latest 10/27/82 PC BIOS, including 640K base memory and UMA scan support. This BIOS version was also used in the XT motherboards found in the IBM Portable PC (PPC).
- **January 10, 1986:** The second revision XT BIOS added support for the 101-key Enhanced keyboard, plus full support for 3 1/2-inch 720K floppy drives.
- **May 9, 1986:** This final revision contained some fixes for minor keyboard bugs related mainly to the enhanced keyboard.

Table 23.1 lists the different IBM Family/1 (PC, XT, and AT) BIOS versions. It also shows the ID, Submodel, and Revision bytes that can be determined by the software function call

```
Int 15h, C0 = Return System Configuration Parameters
```

Some of the systems, such as the PC and earlier XT and AT systems, only supports the ID byte; the submodel and revision bytes had not been established when those systems were developed. The table also shows the number of drive types supported in the AT and XT-286 systems BIOS.

The BIOS date is stored in all PC compatible systems at memory address FFFF5h. To display the date of your BIOS, a simple DEBUG command can be used to view this address. DEBUG is a command program supplied with MS-DOS. At the DOS prompt, execute the following commands to run DEBUG, display the date stored in your BIOS, and then exit to DOS:

```
C:\>DEBUG
-D FFFF:5 L 8
FFFF:0000              30 31 2F-32 32 2F 39 37              01/22/97
-Q
```

In this example, the system queried shows a BIOS date of 01/22/97.

XT Technical Specifications

Technical information for the XT system, described in this section, provides information about the system architecture, memory configurations and capacities, standard system features, disk storage, expansion slots, keyboard specifications, and also physical and environmental specifications. Figure 23.6 shows the layout and components on the XT motherboard.

FIG. 23.6 The XT motherboard.

System Architecture

Microprocessor	8088
Clock speed	4.77MHz
Bus type	ISA (Industry Standard Architecture)
Bus width	8-bit
Interrupt levels	8 (6 usable)
Type	Edge-triggered
Shareable	No
DMA channels	4 (3 usable)
Bus masters supported	No
Upgradable processor complex	No

Memory

Standard on system board	256K or 640K
Maximum on system board	256K or 640K
Maximum total memory	640K
Memory speed (ns) and type	200ns dynamic RAM chips
System board memory-socket type	16-pin DIP
Number of memory-module sockets	36 (4 banks of 9)
Memory used on system board	36 64K×1-bit DRAM chips in 4 banks of 9, or 2 banks of 9 256K×1-bit and 2 banks of 9 64K×1-bit chips
Memory cache controller	No
Wait states:	
System board	1
Adapter	1

Standard Features

ROM size	40K or 64K
ROM shadowing	No
Optional math coprocessor	8087
Coprocessor speed	4.77MHz
Standard graphics	None standard
RS232C serial ports	1 (some models)
UART chip used	NS8250B
Maximum speed (bits per second)	9,600 bps
Maximum number of ports supported	2
Pointing device (mouse) ports	None standard
Parallel printer ports	1 (some models)
Bi-directional	No
Maximum number of ports supported	3
CMOS real-time clock (RTC)	No
CMOS RAM	None

Disk Storage

Internal disk and tape drive bays	2 full-height or 4 half-height
Number of 3 1/2 or 5 1/4-inch bays	0/2 or 0/4
Standard floppy drives	1×360K
Optional floppy drives:	
5 1/4-inch 360K	Optional
5 1/4-inch 1.2M	No
3 1/2-inch 720K	Optional
3 1/2-inch 1.44M	No
3 1/2-inch 2.88M	No
Hard disk controller included:	ST-506/412 (Xebec Model 1210)
ST-506/412 hard disks available	10/20M
Drive form factor	5 1/4-inch
Drive interface	ST-506/412
Drive capacity	10M	20M
Average access rate (ms)	85	65
Encoding scheme	MFM	MFM
BIOS drive type number	1	2
Cylinders	306	615
Disk storage		
Heads	4	4
Sectors per track	17	17
Rotational speed (RPMs)	3600	3600
Interleave factor	6:1	6:1
Data transfer rate (kilobytes/second)	85	85
Automatic head parking	No	No

Expansion Slots

Total adapter slots	8
Number of long/short slots	6/2
Number of 8-/16-/32-bit slots	8/0/0
Available slots (with video) 4	

Keyboard Specifications

101-key Enhanced keyboard	Yes
Fast keyboard speed setting	No
Keyboard cable length	6 feet

Physical Specifications

Footprint type	Desktop
Dimensions:	

Height	5.5 inches	
Width	19.5 inches	
Depth	16.0 inches	
Weight	32 pounds	

Environmental Specifications

Power-supply output	130 watts
Worldwide (110v/60Hz, 220v/50Hz)	No
Auto-sensing/switching	No
Maximum current:	
90-137 VAC	4.2 amps
Operating range:	
Temperature	60–90 degrees F
Relative humidity	8–80 percent
Maximum operating altitude	7,000 feet
Heat (BTUs/hour)	717
Noise (Average db, operating, 1m)	56
FCC classification	Class B

Table 23.6 shows the XT motherboard switch settings. The XT motherboard uses a single eight-position switch block to control various functions, as detailed in the table.

Table 23.6 IBM PC/XT Motherboard Switch Settings

SWITCH BLOCK 1 (PC and XT)

		Switch 1	**IBM PC Function (PC Only):**
		Off	Boot From Floppy Drives
		On	Do Not Boot From Floppy Drives
		Switch 1	**IBM XT Function (XT Only):**
		Off	Normal POST (Power-On Self Test)
		On	Continuous Looping POST
		Switch 2	**Math Coprocessor (PC/XT):**
		Off	Installed
		On	Not Installed
Switch 3	Switch 4		**Installed Motherboard Memory (PC/XT):**
On	On		Bank 0 only
Off	On		Banks 0 and 1
On	Off		Banks 0, 1, and 2
Off	Off		All 4 Banks
Switch 5	Switch 6		**Video Adapter Type (PC/XT):**
Off	Off		Monochrome (MDA)
Off	On		Color (CGA); 40×25 mode

(continues)

Table 23.6 Continued

SWITCH BLOCK 1 (PC and XT)

On	Off	Color (CGA); 80×25 mode
On	On	Any Video Card w/onboard BIOS (EGA/VGA)
Switch 7	**Switch 8**	**Number of Floppy Drives (PC/XT):**
On	On	1 floppy drive
Off	On	2 floppy drives
On	Off	3 floppy drives
Off	Off	4 floppy drives

Table 23.7 shows the part numbers of the XT system units.

Table 23.7 IBM XT Model Part Numbers

Description	Number
XT system unit/83-key keyboard, 256K:	
one full-height 360K drive	5160068
one half-height 360K drive	5160267
two full-height 360K drives	5160078
two half-height 360K drives	5160277
XT system unit/101-key keyboard, 256K:	
one half-height 360K drive	5160268
two half-height 360K drives	5160278
XT system unit/83-key keyboard, 256K, one serial, one full-height 360K drive, 10M hard disk	5160086
XT system unit/83-key keyboard, 640K, one serial, one half-height 360K drive, 20M fixed disk	5160088
XT system unit/101-key keyboard, 640K, one serial, one half-height 360K drive, 20M fixed disk	5160089
Option Numbers	
PC expansion-unit Model 002, 20M fixed disk	5161002
20M fixed disk drive	6450326
20M fixed disk adapter	6450327
10M fixed disk drive	1602500
10M fixed disk adapter	1602501
5 1/4-inch, half-height, 360K drive	6450325
5 1/4-inch, full-height, 360K drive	1503810
3 1/2-inch, half-height, 720K internal drive	6450258
3 1/2-inch, half-height, 720K external drive	2683190
8087 math coprocessor option	1501002
Asynchronous serial adapter	1502074

http://www.quecorp.com

Enhanced Keyboard Accessories	
Clear keycaps (60) with paper inserts	6341707
Blank light keycaps	1351710
Blank dark keycaps	1351728
Paper inserts (300)	6341704
Keycap-removal tools (6)	1351717

An Introduction to the Portable PC

IBM introduced the Portable PC on February 16, 1984. The IBM Portable PC, a "transportable" personal computer, is a small suitcase-sized system that has a built-in 9-inch, amber composite video monitor; one 5 1/4-inch, half-height floppy disk drive (with space for an optional second drive); an 83-key keyboard; two adapter cards; a floppy disk controller; and a CGA. The unit also has a universal-voltage power supply capable of overseas operation on 220-volt power. Figure 23.7 shows the Portable PC exterior.

FIG. 23.7 The IBM Portable PC.

The system board used in the IBM Portable PC is the same board used in the original IBM XTs, with 256K of memory. Because the XT motherboard was used, eight expansion slots are available for the connection of adapter boards, although only two slots can accept a full-length adapter card due to internal space restrictions. The power supply is basically the same as an XT's, with physical changes for portability and a small amount of power drawn to run the built-in monitor. In function and performance, the Portable PC system unit has identical characteristics to an equivalently configured IBM PC XT system unit. Figure 23.8 shows the Portable PC interior view.

IBM withdrew the Portable PC from the market on April 2, 1986, a date that coincides with the introduction of the IBM Convertible laptop PC. The Portable PC is rare because not many were sold, although it compared to, and in many ways was better than, the highly successful Compaq Portable that was available at the time. The system was largely misunderstood by the trade press and user community. Most did not understand that the system was really a portable XT and had more to offer than the standard IBM PC. Maybe if IBM had called the system the Portable XT, it would have sold better!

FIG. 23.8 The IBM Portable PC interior.

The Portable PC system unit has these major functional components:

- Intel 8088 4.77MHz microprocessor
- ROM-based diagnostics (POST)
- BASIC language interpreter in ROM
- 256K of dynamic RAM
- Eight expansion slots (two long slots, one 3/4-length slot, and five short slots)
- Socket for 8087 math coprocessor
- Color/Graphics Monitor Adapter
- 9-inch, amber, composite video monitor
- Floppy disk interface
- One or two half-height 360K floppy drives
- 114-watt universal power supply (115–230V, 50–60Hz)
- Lightweight 83-key keyboard
- Enclosure with carrying handle
- Carrying bag for the system unit

Seen previously, Figure 23.6 showed the XT motherboard, which is also used in the Portable PC. The following is the technical data for the Portable PC system:

System Architecture

Microprocessor	8088
Clock speed	4.77MHz
Bus type	ISA (Industry Standard Architecture)
Bus width	8-bit
Interrupt levels	8 (6 usable)
Type	Edge-triggered
Shareable	No
DMA channels	4 (3 usable)
Bus masters supported	No
Upgradable processor complex	No

Memory

Standard on system board	256K
Maximum on system board	256K
Maximum total memory	640K
Memory speed (ns) and type	200ns dynamic RAM chips
System board memory-socket type	16-pin DIP
Number of memory-module sockets	36 (4 banks of 9)
Memory used on system board	36 64K×1-bit DRAM chips in 4 banks of 9 chips
Memory cache controller	No
Wait states:	
System board	1
Adapter	1

Standard Features

ROM size	40K
ROM shadowing	No
Optional math coprocessor	8087
Coprocessor speed	4.77MHz
Standard graphics	CGA adapter with built-in 9-inch amber CRT
RS232C serial ports	None standard
UART chip used	NS8250B
Maximum speed (bits per second)	9,600 bps
Maximum number of ports supported	2
Pointing device (mouse) ports	None standard
Parallel printer ports	None standard
Bi-directional	No
Maximum number of ports supported	3
CMOS real-time clock (RTC)	No
CMOS RAM	None

Disk Storage

Internal disk and tape drive bays	2 half-height
Number of 3 1/2-/5 1/4-inch bays	0/2
Standard floppy drives	1 or 2×360K
Optional floppy drives:	
5 1/4-inch 360K	Optional
5 1/4-inch 1.2M	No
3 1/2-inch 720K	Optional
3 1/2-inch 1.44M	No
3 1/2-inch 2.88M	No
Hard disk controller included	None

Expansion Slots

Total adapter slots	8
Number of long/short slots	2/6
Number of 8-/16-/32-bit slots	8/0/0
Available slots (with video)	6

Keyboard Specifications

101-key Enhanced keyboard	No
Fast keyboard speed setting	No
Keyboard cable length	6 feet

Physical Specifications

Footprint type	Desktop
Dimensions:	
Height	8.0 inches
Width	20.0 inches
Depth	17.0 inches
Weight	31 pounds

Environmental Specifications

Power-supply output	114 watts
Worldwide (110/60, 220/50)	Yes
Auto-sensing/switching	No
Maximum current:	
90-137 VAC	4.0 amps
Operating range:	
Temperature	60–90° F
Relative humidity	8–80 percent

Maximum operating altitude	7,000 feet
Heat (BTUs/hour)	650
Noise (Average db, operating, 1m)	42
FCC classification	Class B

Table 23.8 shows the part numbers for the Portable PC.

Table 23.8 IBM Portable PC Model Part Numbers

Description	Number
256K, one 360K half-height drive	5155068
256K, two 360K half-height drives	5155076
Half-height 360K floppy disk drive	6450300

The disk drive used in the Portable PC was a half-height drive, the same unit specified for use in the PCjr. When the Portable PC was introduced, PCjr was the only other IBM sold with the same half-height drive.

An Introduction to the AT

IBM introduced the *Personal Computer AT (Advanced Technology)* on August 14, 1984. The IBM AT system included many features previously unavailable in IBM's PC systems such as increased performance, an advanced 16-bit microprocessor, high-density floppy disk and hard disk drives, larger memory space, and an advanced coprocessor. Despite its new design, the IBM AT incredibly retained compatibility with most existing hardware and software products for the earlier systems.

In most cases, IBM AT system performance was from three to five times faster than the IBM XT for single applications running DOS on both computers. The performance increase is due to the combination of a reduced cycle count for most instructions by the 80286 processor, an increased system clock rate, 16-bit memory, and faster hard disk and controller.

The AT system unit has been available in several models: a floppy-disk-equipped base model (068) and several hard-disk-enhanced models. Based on a high-performance, 16-bit, Intel 80286 microprocessor, each computer includes Cassette BASIC language in ROM and a CMOS (Complementary Metal Oxide Semiconductor) clock and calendar with battery backup. All models are equipped with a high-density (1.2M) floppy disk drive, a keyboard, and a lock. For standard memory, the base model offers 256K, and the enhanced models offer 512K. In addition, the enhanced models have a 20M or a 30M hard disk drive and a serial/parallel adapter. Each system can be expanded through customer-installable options. You can add memory (up to 512K) for the base model by adding chips to the system board. You can expand all models to 16M by installing memory cards.

Besides the standard drives included with the system, IBM only offered two different hard disks as upgrades for the AT:

- 30M hard disk drive
- 20M hard disk drive

IBM also offered only three different types of floppy drives for the AT:

- A second, high-density (1.2M) floppy disk drive
- A double-density (320/360K) floppy disk drive
- A new 3 1/2-inch 720K drive

The original 068 and 099 models of the AT did not support the 720K drive in the BIOS; you had to add a special driver (DRIVER.SYS—supplied with DOS) for the drive to work properly. The later model ATs supported the 720K drive directly in the BIOS, and also added support for the 1.44M high-density 3 1/2-inch floppy drive, although IBM never sold or officially supported such a drive in the AT.

You can install as many as two floppy disk drives and one hard disk drive or one floppy disk drive and two hard disk drives in the system unit. To use the high-density 5 1/4-inch floppy disk drives properly, you must have special floppy disks—5 1/4-inch, high-coercivity, double-sided, soft-sectored disks. Due to track width problems between the high-density (1.2M) drives and the double-density (360K) drives, a double-density floppy disk drive (320/360K) was available for compatibility with the standard PC or XT systems. You can exchange disks reliably between the 1.2M and the standard 360K drives if you use the proper method and understand the recording process. For transferring data between a system with a 1.2M drive to a system with a 360K drive, you must start with a blank (never previously formatted) 360K disk, which must be formatted and written only by the 1.2M drive. No special precautions are needed to transfer the data the other way. This information is covered in Chapter 13, "Floppy Disk Drives." For complete interchange reliability and to simplify the process however, IBM recommends you purchase the 360K drive.

The AT motherboard has eight slots that support cards for additional devices, features, or memory. Six slots support the advanced 16-bit or 8-bit cards. Two slots support only 8-bit cards. All system-unit models use one 16-bit slot for the fixed disk and floppy disk drive adapter. The enhanced models use an additional 8-bit slot for the serial/parallel adapter. The result is seven available expansion slots for the base model and six available expansion slots for enhanced models. Figure 23.9 shows the interior of an AT system unit.

All AT models include a 192-watt universal power supply; a temperature-controlled, variable-speed cooling fan; and a security lock with key. The user selects the power supply for a country's voltage range. The cooling fan significantly reduces the noise in most environments; the fan runs slower when the system unit is cool and faster when the system unit is hot. When the system is locked, no one can remove the system-unit cover, boot the system, or enter commands or data from the keyboard, thereby enhancing the system's security.

An Introduction to the AT   **957**

FIG. 23.9 The IBM AT unit interior.

The keyboard is attached to the system unit by a 9-foot coiled cable that enables the AT to adapt to a variety of workspace configurations. The keyboard includes key-location enhancements and mode indicators for improved keyboard usability. Figure 23.10 shows the rear panel of an AT.

FIG. 23.10 The IBM AT rear panel.

Every system unit for the AT models has these major functional components:

- Intel 80286 (6MHz or 8MHz) microprocessor
- Socket for 80287 math coprocessor
- Eight I/O expansion slots (six 16-bit, two 8-bit)
- 256K of dynamic RAM (base model)

- 512K of dynamic RAM (enhanced models)
- ROM-based diagnostics (POST)
- BASIC language interpreter in ROM
- Hard/floppy disk controller
- 1.2M hard disk floppy drive
- 20M or 30M hard disk drive (enhanced models)
- Serial/parallel interface (enhanced models)
- CMOS Clock-calendar and configuration with battery backup
- Keylock
- 84-key keyboard or Enhanced, 101-key keyboard (standard on newer models)
- Switchable worldwide power supply

AT Models and Features

Since the introduction of the AT, several models have become available. First, IBM announced two systems: a *base model (068)* and an *enhanced model (099)*. The primary difference between the two systems is the standard hard disk that came with the enhanced model. IBM has introduced two other AT systems since the first systems, each offering new features.

The first generation of AT systems has a 6MHz system clock that dictates the processor cycle time. The *cycle time*, the system's smallest interval of time, represents the speed at which operations occur. Every operation in a computer takes at least one or (usually) several cycles to complete. Therefore, if two computers are the same in every way except for the clock speed, the system with the faster clock rate executes the same operations in a shorter time proportional to the difference in clock speed. Cycle time and clock speed are two different ways of describing the same thing. Discussions of clock speed are significant when you consider buying the AT because not all models have the same clock speed.

All models of the AT included a combination hard/floppy disk controller that was really two separate controllers on the same circuit board. The board was designed by IBM and Western Digital (WD), and manufactured for IBM by WD. This controller had no on-board ROM BIOS like the Xebec hard disk controller used in the XT. In the AT, IBM built full support for the hard disk controller directly into the motherboard ROM BIOS. To support different types of hard disks, IBM encoded a table into the motherboard ROM that listed the parameters of various drives that could be installed. In the first version of the AT, with a ROM BIOS dated 01/10/84, only the first 14 types in the table were filled in. Type 15 itself was reserved for internal reasons, and was not usable. Other table entries from 16 through 47 were left unused and were actually filled with zeros. Later versions of the AT added new drive types to the tables, starting from Type 16 and up.

The first two AT models were the 068 (base) model, which had 256K on the motherboard and a single 1.2M floppy disk drive; and the model 099 (enhanced), which had a 20M hard disk drive, a serial/parallel adapter, and 512K on the motherboard. IBM designated the motherboard on these computers as Type 1, which is larger than the later Type 2 board and used an unusual memory layout. The memory is configured as four banks of 128K chips—a total of 512K on the board. This configuration sounds reasonable until you realize that a 128K chip does not really exist in the physical form factor that IBM used. IBM actually created this type of memory device by stacking one 64K chip on top of another 64K chip and soldering the two together. My guess is that IBM had many 64K chips to use, and the AT was available to take them.

On October 2, 1985, IBM announced a new model of the AT, the Personal Computer AT Model 239. The system has all the standard features of the AT Model 099, but also has a 30M hard disk rather than a 20M hard disk. A second, optional 30M hard disk drive expands the Model 239's hard disk storage to 60M. This unit's motherboard, a second-generation design IBM calls Type 2, is about 25 percent smaller than the Type 1 but uses the same mounting locations for physical compatibility. All important items, such as the slots and connectors, remain in the same locations. Other major improvements in this board are in the memory. The 128K memory chips were replaced by 256K devices. Now only two banks of chips were needed to get the same 512K on the board.

The AT Model 239 includes these items:

- 512K of RAM (standard)
- 6MHz Type 2 motherboard with 256K memory chips
- Serial/parallel adapter (standard)
- 30M hard disk (standard)
- New ROM BIOS (dated 06/10/85). ROM supports 3 1/2-inch 720K floppy drives without using external driver programs, and 22 usable hard disk types (up to Type 23), including the supplied 30M disk. POST "fixes" clock rate to 6MHz.

The Type 2 motherboard's design is a big improvement on Type 1's; the Type 2 motherboard improved internal-circuit timing and layout. Improvements in the motherboard indicated that the system would be pushed to higher speeds—exactly what happened with the next round of introductions.

In addition to obvious physical differences, the Model 239 includes significantly different ROM software from the previous models. The new ROM supports more types of hard and floppy disks, and its new POST prevents alteration of the clock rate from the standard 6MHz models. Because support for the 30M hard disk is built into the new ROM, IBM sold a 30M hard disk upgrade kit that included the new ROM for the original AT systems. This $1,795 kit represented the only legal way to obtain the newer ROM.

The 30M hard disk drive upgrade kit for the Personal Computer AT Models 068 and 099 included all the features in the 30M hard disk drive announced for the AT Model 239.

The upgrade kit also had a new basic input-output subsystem (BIOS), essential to AT operation. The new ROM BIOS supports 22 drive types (compared to the original 14 in earlier ATs), including the new 30M drive. To support the 30M hard disk drive, a new diagnostics floppy disk and an updated guide-to-operations manual are shipped with this kit.

The 30M update kit includes these items:

- 30M hard disk drive
- Two new ROM BIOS modules
- Channel keeper bar (a bracket for the fixed disk)
- Data cable for the hard disk
- Diagnostics and Setup disk
- An insert to the AT guide-to-operations manual

Some people were upset initially that IBM had "fixed" the microprocessor clock to 6MHz in the new model, thereby disallowing any possible "hot rod" or overclocking modifications. Many people realized that the clock crystal on the AT models was socketed so that the crystal could be replaced easily by a faster one. More importantly, because the AT circuit design is modular, changing the clock crystal does not have repercussions throughout the rest of the system, as is the case in the PC and PC XT. For the price of a new crystal (from $1 to $30) and the time needed to plug it in, someone easily could increase an AT's speed by 30 percent, and sometimes more. Unfortunately, due to the POST in the newer model's BIOS, you no longer can implement a simple speedup alteration without also changing the ROM BIOS as well.

Many people believed that this change was made to prevent the AT from being "too fast" and therefore competing with IBM's minicomputers. In reality, the earlier motherboard was run intentionally at 6MHz because IBM did not believe that the ROM BIOS software and critical system timing was fully operational at a higher speed. Also, IBM used some components that were rated only for 6MHz operation, starting of course with the CPU. Users who increased the speed of their early computers often received DOS error messages from timing problems, and in some cases, total system lockups due to components not functioning properly at the higher speeds.

Many companies selling speedup kits sold software to help smooth over some of these problems, but IBM's official solution was to improve the ROM BIOS software and motherboard circuitry, and to introduce a complete new system running at the faster speed. If you want increased speed no matter what model you have, several companies used to sell clock-crystal replacements that were frequency synthesizers rather than a fixed type of crystal. The units can wait until the POST is finished and change midstream to an increased operating speed. Unfortunately, I don't know of anyone who is still making or selling these upgrades.

If you really want to speed up your AT by installing a faster clock crystal, instructions on how to burn your own set of BIOS without the check can be found on the CD accompanying this book. However, it requires the use of a specialized PROM or EPROM burner, or access to one.

On April 2, 1986, IBM introduced the Personal Computer AT Models 319 and 339. These were the last and best AT models, and were an enhancement of the earlier Model 239. The primary difference from the Model 239 is a faster clock crystal that provides 8MHz operation. The Model 339 has a new keyboard—the Enhanced keyboard—with 101 keys rather than the usual 84. Model 319 is the same as Model 339, but includes the original keyboard.

Highlights of the Models 319 and 339 are shown in this list:

- Faster processor speed (8MHz)
- Type 2 motherboard, with 256K chips
- 512K of RAM (standard)
- Serial/parallel adapter (standard)
- 30M hard disk (standard)
- New ROM BIOS (dated 11/15/85). ROM support for 22 usable types (up to type 23) of hard disks, and 3 1/2-inch drives, at both 720K and 1.44M capacities. POST "fixes" clock rate to 8MHz.
- 101-key Enhanced keyboard (standard on Model 339)

The most significant physical difference in these new systems is the Enhanced keyboard on the Model 339. The keyboard, similar to a 3270 keyboard, has 101 keys. It could be called the IBM "corporate" keyboard because it is standard on all new desktop systems. The 84-key PC keyboard still was available, with a new 8MHz model, as the Model 319.

These new 8MHz systems were available only in an enhanced configuration with a standard 30M hard drive. If you wanted a hard disk larger than IBM's 30M, you could either add a second drive or simply replace the 30M unit with something larger.

ROM support for 3 1/2-inch disk drives at both 720K and 1.44M exists only in Models 339 and 319. In particular, the 1.44M drive, although definitely supported by the ROM BIOS and controller, was never offered as an option by IBM. This means that the IBM Setup program found on the Diagnostics and Setup disk did not offer the 1.44M floppy drive as a choice when configuring the system! Anybody adding such a drive had to use one of the many Setup replacement programs available in the public domain, or "borrow" one from an IBM-compatible system that used a floppy disk-based setup program. Adding the 1.44M drive became one of the most popular upgrades for the AT systems because many newer systems came with that type of drive as standard equipment. Earlier AT systems still can use the 720K and 1.44M drives, but they need to either upgrade the ROM to support it (recommended) or possibly use software drivers to make them work.

AT BIOS Versions

There have been three different BIOS versions used in the IBM AT. They can be identified by their date and summarized as follows:

- January 1, 1984: The first AT BIOS version supported only 1.2M and 360K floppy drives directly. Only 14 hard disk types were supported. It came on the Model 068 and 099 systems with the Type 1 motherboard.

- June 10, 1985: The second AT BIOS added support for 720K 3 1/2-inch drives directly (no drivers required). Also more hard disk drive types were added, for a total of 22 usable types. A new test was added to the POST which causes the POST to fail if the clock speed is altered from 6MHz. This BIOS was used on the Model 239 with a Type 2 motherboard.

- November 15, 1985: The third and final AT BIOS added support for a 1.44M 3 1/2-inch drives (no drivers required). Enhanced 101-key keyboard support was added. The POST test checks for 8MHz operation, and fails if the system is running at any other speed. This BIOS was used on Model 319 and 339 systems, and came on a Type 2 motherboard.

Table 23.1 Lists the different IBM Family/1 (PC, XT, and AT) BIOS versions. It also shows the ID, Submodel, and Revision bytes which can be determined by the software function call

```
Int 15h, C0 = Return System Configuration Parameters
```

Some of the systems such as the PC and earlier XT and AT systems only support the ID byte; the submodel and revision bytes had not been established when those systems were developed. The table also shows the number of drive types supported in the AT and XT-286 systems BIOS.

The BIOS date is stored in all PC-compatible systems at memory address FFFF5h. To display the date of your BIOS, a simple DEBUG command can be used to view this address. DEBUG is a command program supplied with MS-DOS. At the DOS prompt, execute the following commands to run DEBUG, display the date stored in your BIOS, and then exit back to DOS:

```
C:\>DEBUG
-D FFFF:5 L 8
FFFF:0000                   30 31 2F-32 32 2F 39 37              01/22/97
-Q
```

In this example, the system queried shows a BIOS date of 01/22/97.

AT Motherboard BIOS Hard Drive Tables. The AT BIOS contains a special table that is used by the hard disk controller driver to determine the hard drive parameters. When a hard disk is installed into this type of system, the "type" of drive is entered into the CMOS RAM by whoever has installed the drive. Then every time the system boots, it looks up the parameters by consulting the CMOS RAM for the particular type selected.

Older systems were, therefore, limited to what different drives they could support or recognize by the entries burned into their BIOS table. The table used in IBM AT and PS/2 systems is shown here in this section.

The various IBM AT and PS/2 systems that use a BIOS drive table do not necessarily have all of the entries shown here. The number of table entries contained in a particular system BIOS can vary from one version to the next. For example, the original AT BIOS (01/10/84) only had Types 1–14 usable, while the later AT BIOS versions (06/10/85 and 11/15/85) had 1–14 and 16–23 usable. The XT-286 had 1–14 and 16–24 as usable types. Some of the PS/1 and PS/2 systems had the table filled as far as Type 44.

Non-IBM systems quickly adopted special "User Definable" or even "Auto-Detect" types where you could either manually enter the complete table entry (rather than selecting a predetermined "type"), or the system would automatically read the type information directly from the drive.

> **Note**
>
> If you have a non-IBM PC-compatible system, the IBM table may be inaccurate for many of the entries past Type 15. Instead, you should consult your CMOS Setup program; most will show the available types as you scroll through them. Another option is to consult your system, motherboard, or BIOS documentation to see if it shows what the correct table entries are. A final alternative is a program such as the Seagate FINDTYPE program which will scan your BIOS, locate the table, and display or print it for viewing. This program can be downloaded from the Seagate Web site or BBS. Most compatibles follow the IBM table for at least the first 15 entries.

Most PS/2 systems have the drive's defect map written as data on the drive one cylinder beyond the highest reported cylinder. This special data is read by the IBM PS/2 Advanced Diagnostics low-level format program. This process automates the entry of the defect list and eliminates the chance of human error, as long as you use only the IBM PS/2 Advanced Diagnostics for hard disk low-level formatting on those systems.

This type of table does not apply to IBM Enhanced Small Device Interface (ESDI) or SCSI hard disk controllers, host adapters, and drives. Because the ESDI and SCSI controllers or host adapters query the drive directly for the required parameters, no table-entry selection is necessary. Note, however, that the table for the ST-506/412 drives can still be found currently in the ROM BIOS of most of the PS/2 systems, even if the model came standard with an ESDI or SCSI disk subsystem.

Table 23.9 shows the IBM motherboard ROM BIOS hard disk parameters for AT or PS/2 systems using ST-506/412 (standard or IDE) controllers.

Table 23.9 IBM AT and PS/2 BIOS Hard Disk Table

Type	Cylinders	Heads	WPC	Ctrl	LZ	S/T	Meg	M
1	306	4	128	00h	305	17	10.16	10.65
2	615	4	300	00h	615	17	20.42	21.41

(continues)

Table 23.9 Continued

Type	Cylinders	Heads	WPC	Ctrl	LZ	S/T	Meg	M
3	615	6	300	00h	615	17	30.63	32.12
4	940	8	512	00h	940	17	62.42	65.45
5	940	6	512	00h	940	17	46.82	49.09
6	615	4	65535	00h	615	17	20.42	21.41
7	462	8	256	00h	511	17	30.68	32.17
8	733	5	65535	00h	733	17	30.42	31.90
9	900	15	65535	08h	901	17	112.06	117.50
10	820	3	65535	00h	820	17	20.42	21.41
11	855	5	65535	00h	855	17	35.49	37.21
12	855	7	65535	00h	855	17	49.68	52.09
13	306	8	128	00h	319	17	20.32	21.31
14	733	7	65535	00h	733	17	42.59	44.66
15*	0	0	0	00h	0	0	0.00	0.00
16	612	4	0	00h	663	17	20.32	21.31
17	977	5	300	00h	977	17	40.55	42.52
18	977	7	65535	00h	977	17	56.77	59.53
19	1024	7	512	00h	1023	17	59.50	62.39
20	733	5	300	00h	732	17	30.42	31.90
21	733	7	300	00h	732	17	42.59	44.66
22	733	5	300	00h	733	17	30.42	31.90
23	306	4	0	00h	336	17	10.16	10.65
24	612	4	305	00h	663	17	20.32	21.31
25	306	4	65535	00h	340	17	10.16	10.65
26	612	4	65535	00h	670	17	20.32	21.31
27	698	7	300	20h	732	17	40.56	42.53
28	976	5	488	20h	977	17	40.51	42.48
29	306	4	0	00h	340	17	10.16	10.65
30	611	4	306	20h	663	17	20.29	21.27
31	732	7	300	20h	732	17	42.53	44.60
32	1023	5	65535	20h	1023	17	42.46	44.52
33	614	4	65535	20h	663	25	29.98	31.44
34	775	2	65535	20h	900	27	20.43	21.43
35	921	2	65535	20h	1000	33	29.68	31.12
36	402	4	65535	20h	460	26	20.41	21.41
37	580	6	65535	20h	640	26	44.18	46.33
38	845	2	65535	20h	1023	36	29.71	31.15

Type	Cylinders	Heads	WPC	Ctrl	LZ	S/T	Meg	MB
39	769	3	65535	20h	1023	36	40.55	42.52
40	531	4	65535	20h	532	39	40.45	42.41
41	577	2	65535	20h	1023	36	20.29	21.27
42	654	2	65535	20h	674	32	20.44	21.43
43	923	5	65535	20h	1023	36	81.12	85.06
44	531	8	65535	20h	532	39	80.89	84.82
45	0	0	0	00h	0	0	0.00	0.00
46	0	0	0	00h	0	0	0.00	0.00
47	0	0	0	00h	0	0	0.00	0.00

*Table entry 15 is reserved to act as a pointer to indicate that the type is greater than 15.

Type = Table entry number

Cylinders = Total number of cylinders

Heads = Total number of heads

WPC = Write Pre-Compensation starting cylinder

65535 = No Write Pre-Compensation (also shown as -1)

0 = Write Pre-Compensation on all cylinders

Ctrl = Control byte, with values according to the following table:

Bit Number	Hex	Meaning
Bit 0	01h	Not used (XT = drive step rate)
Bit 1	02h	Not used (XT = drive step rate)
Bit 2	04h	Not used (XT = drive step rate)
Bit 3	08h	More than eight heads
Bit 4	10h	Not used (XT = imbedded servo drive)
Bit 5	20h	OEM defect map at (cylinders + 1)
Bit 6	40h	Disable ECC retries
Bit 7	80h	Disable disk access retries

LZ = Landing-Zone cylinder used head parking

S/T = Number of Sectors per Track

Meg = Drive capacity in Megabytes

M = Drive capacity in Millions of bytes

Modifying ROM BIOS Hard Disk Drive Parameter Tables. Because the IBM tables in the AT and XT-286 systems (as well as many of the compatibles of that day) were fixed, technicians often found it necessary to modify the BIOS in those systems to add drive types for new drives I wanted to install. For example, I added two new drive types to one of my old AT systems. Those types—25 and 26—have these parameters:

Type	Cylinders	Heads	WPC	Ctrl	LZ	S/T	Meg	M
25	918	15	65535	08h	918	17	114.30	119.85
26	918	15	65535	08h	918	26	174.81	183.31

WPC = Write Pre-Compensation start cylinder
Ctrl = Control Byte, 08h = More than 8 heads, else 00h
LZ = Landing Zone or head parking cylinder
S/T = Sectors per Track
Meg = Megabytes
M = Millions of bytes

In my old AT system, these table entries originally were unused (zeros), as are the remainder of types from 27–47. By burning a new set of ROMs with these two new completed entries, I was able to use a Maxtor XT-1140 drive to maximum capacity with an MFM 17-sector per track controller (as Type 25) or an RLL 26-sector per track controller (as Type 26). This method precluded the need for a controller with its own separate on-board BIOS to override the motherboard table values and therefore also saved memory in the C000 or D000 UMA segments, where such a hard disk controller ROM normally would reside.

> **Tip**
>
> If you are interested in performing this modification, get the *IBM AT Technical Reference Manual* (sold by IBM or Annabooks), which documents the position and format of the drive tables in the BIOS.

On the CD

Changing the Hard Disk Controller Head Step Rate. Another more complicated modification that you can perform to the AT BIOS is to increase the stepping rate of the hard disk controller. The first edition of this book briefly mentioned this modification, and a reader wrote to me to express interest in it. Details of the modification can be found on the CD; however, the performance is relatively slight.

AT Technical Specifications

Technical information for the AT system is described in this section. You will find information about the system architecture, memory configurations and capacities, standard system features, disk storage, expansion slots, and keyboard specifications, as well as physical and environmental specifications. This type of information can be useful in determining what types of parts are needed when you are upgrading or repairing these systems. Figures 23.11 and 23.12 show the layout and components on the two different AT motherboards.

An Introduction to the AT

FIG. 23.11 The IBM AT Type 1 motherboard.

System Architecture

Microprocessor	80286
Clock speed	6 or 8MHz
Bus type	ISA (Industry Standard Architecture)
Bus width	16-bit
Interrupt levels	16 (11 usable)
Type	Edge-triggered
Shareable	No
DMA channels	8 (7 usable)
Bus masters supported	Yes
Upgradable processor complex	No

Chapter 23—IBM Personal Computer Family Hardware

FIG. 23.12 The IBM AT Type 2 motherboard.

Memory

Standard on system board	512K
Maximum on system board	512K
Maximum total memory	16M
Memory speed (ns) and type	150ns dynamic RAM chips
System board memory-socket type	16-pin DIP
Number of memory-module sockets	18 or 36 (2 or 4 banks of 18)
Memory used on system board 18 256K×1-bit chips in one bank	36 128K×1-bit DRAM chips in 2 banks of 18, or
Memory cache controller	No
Wait states:	
System board	1
Adapter	1

Standard Features

ROM size	64K
ROM shadowing	No
Optional math coprocessor	80287

Coprocessor speed	4 or 5.33MHz
Standard graphics	None standard
RS232C serial ports	1 (some models)
UART chip used	NS16450
Maximum speed (bits per second)	9,600 bps
Maximum number of ports supported	2
Pointing device (mouse) ports	None standard
Parallel printer ports	1 (some models)
Bi-directional	Yes
Maximum number of ports supported	3
CMOS real-time clock (RTC)	Yes
CMOS RAM	64 bytes
Battery life	5 years

Disk Storage

Internal disk and tape drive bays	1 full-height and 2 half-height	
Number of 3 1/2-, 5 1/4-inch bays	0/3	
Standard floppy drives	1×1.2M	
Optional floppy drives:		
5 1/4-inch 360K	Optional	
5 1/4-inch 1.2M	Standard	
3 1/2-inch 720K	Optional	
3 1/2-inch 1.44M	Optional (8MHz models3 1/2-inch 2.88M No	
Hard disk controller included:	ST-506/412 (Western Digital WD1002-WA2 or WD1003-WA2)	
ST-506/412 hard disks available	20/30M	
Drive form factor	5 1/4-inch	
Drive interface	ST-506/412	
Drive capacity:	20M	30M
Average access rate (ms)	40	40
Encoding scheme	MFM	MFM
BIOS drive type number	2	20
Cylinders	615	733
Heads	4	5
Sectors per track	17	17
Rotational speed (RPMs)	3600	3600
Disk storage		
Interleave factor	3:1	3:1
Data transfer rate (K/sec)	170	170
Automatic head parking	Yes	Yes

Expansion Slots	
Total adapter slots	8
Number of long and short slots	8/0
Number of 8-/16-/32-bit slots	2/6/0
Available slots (with video)	5

Keyboard Specifications	
101-key Enhanced keyboard	Yes (8MHz models)
Fast keyboard speed setting	Yes
Keyboard cable length	6 feet

Physical Specifications	
Footprint type	Desktop
Dimensions:	
Height	6.4 inches
Width	21.3 inches
Depth	17.3 inches
Weight	43 pounds

Environmental Specifications	
Power-supply output	192 watts
Worldwide (110/60,220/50)	Yes
Auto-sensing/switching	No
Maximum current:	
90-137 VAC	5.0 amps
Operating range:	
Temperature	60–90° F
Relative humidity	8–80 percent
Maximum operating altitude	7,000 feet
Heat (BTUs/hour)	1229
Noise (Average db, operating, 1m)	42
FCC classification	Class B

Table 23.10 shows the AT system-unit part-number information.

Table 23.10 IBM AT Model Part Numbers

Description	Number
AT 6MHz/84-key keyboard, 256K one 1.2M floppy drive	5170068
AT 6MHz/84-key keyboard, 512K, serial/parallel one 1.2M floppy drive, 20M hard disk	5170099
one 1.2M floppy drive, 30M hard disk	5170239

AT 8MHz/84-key keyboard, 512K, serial/parallel one 1.2M floppy drive, 30M hard disk	5170319
AT 8MHz/101-keyboard, 512K, serial/parallel one 1.2M floppy drive, 30M hard disk	5170339

System Options

20M fixed disk drive	6450205
30M fixed disk drive	6450210
30M fixed disk drive upgrade kit	6450468
360K half-height floppy disk drive (AT)	6450207
1.2M high-density drive	6450206
3 1/2-inch, half-height, 720K external drive (AT)	2683191
Serial/parallel adapter	6450215
80287 math coprocessor option	6450211
Floor-standing enclosure	6450218

Enhanced Keyboard Accessories

Clear keycaps (60) with paper inserts	6341707
Blank light keycaps	1351710
Blank dark keycaps	1351728
Paper keycap inserts (300)	6341704
Keycap-removal tools (6)	1351717

An Introduction to the XT Model 286

On September 9, 1986, IBM introduced a new AT-type system disguised inside the chassis and case of an XT. This XT Model 286 system featured increased memory, an Intel 80286 microprocessor, and as many as three internal drives standard. The computer combined an XT's cost-effectiveness, flexibility, and appearance with the high-speed, high-performance technology of the Intel 80286 microprocessor. This model looked like an XT, but underneath the cover, it was all AT.

The IBM XT Model 286 can operate as much as three times faster than earlier models of the XT in most applications. It has a standard 640K of memory. Various memory-expansion options enable users to increase its memory to 16M.

Standard features in this system include a half-height, 1.2M, 5 1/4-inch, high-density floppy disk drive; a 20M hard disk drive; a serial/parallel adapter card; and the IBM Enhanced keyboard. You can select an optional, internal, second floppy disk drive from the following list:

- Half-height, 3 1/2-inch, 720K floppy drive

- Half-height, 3 1/2-inch, 1.44M floppy drive

- Half-height, 5 1/4-inch, 1.2M floppy drive

- Half-height, 5 1/4-inch, 360K floppy drive

The IBM XT Model 286's performance stems primarily from the AT motherboard design, with 16-bit I/O slots and an Intel 80286 processor running at 6MHz. In addition to the type of processor used, clock speed and memory architecture are the primary factors in determining system performance. Depending on the model, the IBM AT's clock speed is 6 or 8MHz, with one wait state; and the XT Model 286 processes data at 6MHz, with zero wait states. The elimination of a wait state improves performance by increasing processing speed for system memory access. The zero-wait-state design makes the XT Model 286 definitely faster than the original AT models that ran at 6MHz and about equal in speed to the 8MHz AT systems. Based on tests, the XT Model 286 also is about three times faster than an actual XT.

Because the XT Model 286 is an AT-class system, the processor supports both real and protected modes. Operating in real address mode, the 80286 is 8088-compatible; therefore, you can use most software that runs on the standard PC systems. In real address mode, the system can address as much as 1M of RAM. Protected mode provides a number of advanced features to facilitate multitasking operations. Protected mode provides separation and protection of programs and data in multitasking environments. In protected mode, the 80286 can address as much as 16M of real memory and 1G of virtual memory. In this mode, the XT Model 286 can run advanced operating systems such as OS/2 and UNIX. When the XT Model 286 was introduced, it was the least-expensive IBM system capable of running a true multitasking operating system.

The IBM XT Model 286 has a standard 640K of RAM. Memory options enable the system to grow to 15 1/2M, much higher than the 640K limit in other PC XTs. If you add an operating system such as OS/2 or Windows, you can take advantage of the larger memory capacities that the XT Model 286 provides.

A 20M hard disk drive is a standard feature in the XT Model 286, as is a 5 1/4-inch, 1.2M, high-density floppy disk drive. A similar floppy disk drive is standard on all models of the AT. Floppy disks formatted on a 1.2M floppy disk drive therefore can be read by an AT or an XT Model 286. The 1.2M floppy disk drive also can read floppy disks formatted with PC-family members that use a 360K floppy disk drive. Figure 23.13 shows the interior of an XT 286 system unit.

The XT Model 286 features the IBM Enhanced keyboard with indicator lights. Many IBM personal computers use the Enhanced keyboard, but the XT Model 286 was the first PC XT to feature keyboard indicator lights.

Five slots support the advanced 16-bit cards or 8-bit cards; three support only 8-bit cards. Two of the three 8-bit slots support only short cards.

A hard disk and floppy drive adapter card are standard features in the XT Model 286. This multifunction card takes only one 16-bit slot and supports as many as four disk drives (two floppy disk drives and two hard disk drives).

The serial/parallel adapter, another standard feature, is a combination card that requires only one slot (either type) and provides a serial and a parallel port. The parallel portion of the adapter has the capacity to attach devices, such as a parallel printer, that accept 8 bits of parallel data. The fully programmable serial portion supports asynchronous communications from 50 bps to 9,600 bps, although even higher speeds are possible with the right software. The serial portion requires an optional serial-adapter cable or a serial-adapter connector. When one of these options is connected to the adapter, all the signals in a standard EIA RS-232C interface are available. You can use the serial port for interfacing a modem, a remote display terminal, a mouse, or other serial device. The XT Model 286 supports as many as two serial/parallel adapters.

FIG. 23.13 The IBM XT-286 interior.

A standard IBM XT Model 286 offers these features:

- 80286 processor at 6 MHz with 0 wait states
- 640K of motherboard memory
- 1.2M floppy drive
- 20M hard disk
- Five 16-bit and three 8-bit expansion slots
- Fixed disk/floppy disk drive adapter (occupies one 16-bit expansion slot)
- Serial/parallel adapter (occupies one 16-bit expansion slot)
- Enhanced 101-key Keyboard with indicator lights
- CMOS Time-and-date clock with battery backup

XT Model 286 Models and Features

The XT Model 286 processor is as much as three times faster internally than the preceding XT family and as much as 25 percent faster than the AT Model 239, depending on specific applications. A 20M fixed disk and a 1.2M, 5 1/4-inch floppy disk drive were standard on the XT Model 286. One additional floppy disk drive can be installed internally as drive B. Any type of floppy drive can be added as a second half-height floppy drive, including both the double and high-density versions of the 5 1/4- and 3 1/2-inch drives.

If you want to be able to read standard 5 1/4-inch data or program floppy disks created by the XT Model 286 on other PC systems, you might want to add a 5 1/4-inch 360K floppy disk drive, which provides full read/write compatibility with those systems. This is due to the fact that the 1.2M drives write a narrower track than the 360K drives, and are unable to properly overwrite a floppy disk written on first by a 360K drive. If full read/write compatibility with 360K drives is not important, you can add a second 1.2M high-density floppy disk drive.

You can add any 3 1/2-inch drive, including the 720K and 1.44M versions. Because the 1.44M does not have any read/write compatibility problems with the 720K drives, however, and the 1.44M drives always can operate in 720K mode, I suggest adding only the 1.44M 3 1/2-inch drives rather than the 720K versions. The higher-density drive is only a small extra expense compared to the double-density version. Most people do not know that full ROM BIOS support for these 1.44M drives is provided in the XT Model 286. Unfortunately, because IBM never offered the 1.44M drive as an option, the supplied Setup program does not offer the 1.44M drive as a choice in the Setup routine. Instead, you have to use one of the many available public domain AT type setup programs, or "borrow" such a program from an AT-compatible system.

XT Model 286 Technical Specifications

The technical information for the XT 286 system described in this section covers the system architecture, memory configurations and capacities, standard system features, disk storage, expansion slots, keyboard specifications, and also physical and environmental specifications. You can use this information to determine the parts you need when you are upgrading or repairing these systems. Figure 23.14 shows the layout and components on the XT 286 motherboard.

System Architecture	
Microprocessor	80286
Clock speed	6MHz
Bus type	ISA (Industry Standard Architecture)
Bus width	16-bit
Interrupt levels	16 (11 usable)
Type Edge-triggered	
Shareable	No
DMA channels	8 (7 usable)
Bus masters supported	Yes
Upgradable processor complex	No
Memory	
Standard on system board	640K
Maximum on system board	640K
Maximum total memory	16M
Memory speed (ns) and type	150ns dynamic RAM chips/SIMMs

System board memory-socket type	30-pin (9-bit) SIMM
Number of memory-module sockets	2
Memory used on system board	One bank of 4 64K×4-bit and 2 64K×1-bit DRAM parity chips, and one bank of 2 9-bit SIMMs
Memory cache controller	No
Wait states:	
System board	0
Adapter	1

FIG. 23.14 The IBM XT-286 motherboard.

Standard Features

ROM size	64K
ROM shadowing	No
Optional math coprocessor	80287
Coprocessor speed	4.77MHz
Standard graphics	None standard

(continues)

(continued)

Standard Features continued	
RS232C serial ports	1
UART chip used	NS16450
Maximum speed (bits per second)	9,600 bps
Maximum number of ports supported	2
Pointing device (mouse) ports	None standard
Parallel printer ports	1
Bi-directional	Yes
Maximum number of ports supported	3
CMOS real-time clock (RTC)	Yes
CMOS RAM	64 bytes
Battery life	5 years

Disk Storage	
Internal disk and tape drive bays	1 full-height and 2 half-height
Number of 3 1/2-/5 1/4-inch bays	0/3
Standard floppy drives	1×1.2M
Optional floppy drives:	
5 1/4-inch 360K	Optional
5 1/4-inch 1.2M	Standard
3 1/2-inch 720K	Optional
3 1/2-inch 1.44M	Optional
3 1/2-inch 2.88M	No
Hard disk controller included:	ST-506/412 (Western Digital WD1003-WA2)
ST-506/412 hard disks available	20M
Drive form factor	5 1/4-inch
Drive interface	ST-506/412
Drive capacity	20M
Average access rate (ms)	65
Encoding scheme	MFM
BIOS drive type number	2
Cylinders	615
Heads	4
Sectors per track	17
Rotational speed (RPMs)	3600
Interleave factor	3:1
Data transfer rate (K/sec)	170
Automatic head parking	No

Expansion Slots	
Total adapter slots	8
Number of long and short slots	6/2
Number of 8-/16-/32-bit slots	3/5/0
Available slots (with video)	5
Keyboard Specifications	
101-key Enhanced keyboard	Yes
Fast keyboard speed setting	Yes
Keyboard cable length	6 feet
Physical Specifications	
Footprint type	Desktop
Dimensions:	
Height	5.5 inches
Width	19.5 inches
Depth	16.0 inches
Weight	28 pounds
Environmental Specifications	
Power-supply output	157 watts
Worldwide (110v/60Hz, 220v/50Hz)	Yes
Auto-sensing/switching	Yes
Maximum current:	
90-137 VAC	4.5 amps
Operating range:	
Temperature	60–90° F
Relative humidity	8–80 percent
Maximum operating altitude	7,000 feet
Heat (BTUs/hour)	824
Noise (Average db, operating, 1m)	42
FCC classification	Class B

Table 23.11 lists the XT Model 286 system-unit part numbers.

Table 23.11 IBM XT-286 Model Part Numbers

Description	Number
XT Model 286 system unit, 6 MHz 0 wait state, 640K, serial/parallel, 1.2M floppy drive, one 20M hard disk	5162286

Optional Accessories

5 1/4-inch, half-height 360K drive	6450325
3 1/4-inch, half-height 720K internal drive	6450258
3 1/2-inch, half-height 720K external drive	2683190
80287 math coprocessor option	6450211

Enhanced Keyboard Accessories

Clear keycaps (60) with paper inserts	6341707
Blank light keycaps	1351710
Blank dark keycaps	1351728
Paper keycap inserts (300)	6341704
Keycap removal tools (6)	1351717

Chapter 24
A Final Word

The contents of this book cover the components of a PC-compatible system. In this book, you discover how all the components operate and interact, and how these components should be set up and installed. You see the ways that components fail and learn the symptoms of these failures. You review the steps in diagnosing and troubleshooting the major components in a system so that you can locate and replace a failing component. You also learn about upgrades for components, including what upgrades are available, the benefits of an upgrade, and how to obtain and perform the actual upgrade. Because failing components so often are technically obsolete, it is often desirable to combine repair and upgrade procedures to replace a failing part with an upgraded or higher performance part.

The information I present in this book represents many years of practical experience with PC-compatible systems. A great deal of research and investigation has gone into each section. This information has saved companies many thousands of dollars. By reading this book, you also take advantage of this wealth of information, and may save you and your company time, energy, and most importantly, money!

Bringing PC service and support in-house is one of the best ways to save money. Eliminating service contracts for most systems and reducing downtime are just two of the benefits of applying the information presented in this book. As I indicate many times in this book, you can also save a lot of money on component purchases by eliminating the middleman and purchasing the components directly from distributors or manufacturers.

The vendor list in Appendix A provides the best of these sources for you to contact. If you intend to build your own systems, the vendor list will be extremely useful as I list sources for all of the components needed to assemble a complete system—from the screws and brackets all the way to the cases, power supplies, and motherboards. I've found that this list is one of the most frequently used parts of this book. Many people have been unable to make direct purchases because doing so requires a new level of understanding of the components involved. Also, many of the vendors are unable to provide support for beginning users. I hope that this book gives you a deeper level of knowledge and understanding so that you can purchase the components you want directly from the vendors who manufacture and distribute them, saving a great deal of money in the long run.

I used many sources to gather the information in this book, starting with my own real-world experiences. I also taught this information to thousands of people in seminars presented over the last 15 years by my company, Mueller Technical Research. During these seminars, I am often asked where more of this type of information can be obtained and whether I have any "secrets" for acquiring this knowledge. Well, I won't keep any secrets! I can freely share the following four key sources of information that can help you become a verifiable expert in PC upgrading and repairing:

- Manuals
- Modems
- Machines
- Magazines

Manuals

Manuals are the single most important source of computer information. Unfortunately, manuals also are one of the most frequently overlooked sources of information. Much of my knowledge has come from poring over technical-reference manuals and other original equipment manufacturer's (OEM) manuals. I would not even consider purchasing a system that does not have a detailed technical-reference manual available. This statement applies also to system components—whether it's a floppy drive, hard disk, power supply, motherboard, or memory card. I have to have a detailed reference manual to help me understand what future upgrades are possible and to provide valuable insight into the proper installation, use, and support of a product.

Often times these manuals must be obtained from the OEM of the equipment you purchase, meaning the vendor or reseller will not supply them. Wherever possible, you should make an effort to discover who the real OEM of each component in your system is, and try to obtain documentation from them on the product or component.

Large manufacturers such as Intel, IBM, Compaq, Hewlett-Packard, and others both manufacture their own components as well as purchase components from other sources. Many of these manufacturers also make available complete libraries of technical documentation for their systems. I have included a list of some of IBM's technical documents in Appendix A, which are quite detailed and, unfortunately, often fairly expensive. These documents are excellent at detailing the operations of CPU, memory, bus, and other architectures in the system, and are even appropriate when discussing compatible systems because most systems must be compatible with IBM in most elements. In other words, the IBM documentation would be interesting to those who do not even own a single piece of true IBM hardware.

Other companies, such as Compaq and HP, also have extensive documentation libraries. IBM, HP, and Compaq make their technical libraries available in a CD-ROM version, which is very convenient and easy to search. These CD-ROMs contain detailed information about PC systems from these companies. In addition to IBM, both Compaq and HP also have BBS services available for technical support; check the vendor list for phone number information as well as for Web pages and other BBS systems.

A simple analogy explains the importance of manuals, as well as other issues concerning repair and maintenance of a system. Compare your business use of computers to a taxicab company. The company has to purchase automobiles to use as cabs. The owners purchase not one car but an entire fleet of cars. Do you think that they would purchase a fleet of automobiles based solely on reliability, performance, or even gas-mileage statistics? Would they neglect to consider on-going maintenance and service of these automobiles? Would they purchase a fleet of cars that could be serviced only by the original manufacturer and for which parts could not be obtained easily? Do you think that they would buy a car that did not have available a detailed service and repair manual? Would they buy an automobile for which parts were scarce and that was supported by a sparse dealer network with few service and parts outlets, making long waits for parts and service inevitable? The answer (of course) to all these questions is no, no, no!

You can see why most taxicab companies as well as police departments use "standard" automobiles such as the Chevrolet Caprice or Ford Crown Victoria. If ever there were "generic" cars, these models would qualify! Dealers, parts, and documentation for these particular models are everywhere. They share parts with many other automobiles as well, which makes them easy to service and maintain.

Doesn't your business (especially if it is large) use what amounts to a "fleet" of computers? If so, think of this fleet as being similar to the cars of a cab company, which would go out of business quickly if these cars could not be kept running smoothly and inexpensively. Now you know why the Checker Marathon automobile used to be so popular with cab companies: Its design barely changed from the time it was introduced in 1956 until it was discontinued in July 1982. (At last report, there was only one still in service in New York City!)

In many ways, the standard XT- and AT-compatible systems are like the venerable Checker Marathon. You can get technical information by the shelf-full for these systems. You can get parts and upgrade material from so many sources that anything you need is always immediately available and at a discounted price. I'm not saying that you should standardize on using older XT or AT systems. However, there are good reasons for standardizing on systems that follow the "generic" physical design of the XT or AT, but use newer internal components. This results in systems that are completely modern in performance and capabilities, and which are easily supported, repaired, and upgraded.

It's amazing that people purchase computers that have no technical documentation and no spare-parts program, or parts available only through dealers, or that use nonstandard form-factor components, and so on. The upgrade, repair, and maintenance of a company's computer systems always seem to take a back seat to performance and style.

In addition to the system OEM manuals, I like to collect documentation from the different OEMs that make the components used in various systems. For example, I recently worked with Gateway 2000 and Hewlett-Packard systems, both of which use Epson floppy drives. The OEM documentation for these systems did not include detailed information on the Epson floppy drives, so I called Epson and ordered the specification manual for these drives. I also ordered the specification manuals for several other drives used in these systems, including Western Digital and Quantum hard disks. I now have detailed information on these drives, which covers jumper settings, service and repair information, and other technical specifications not provided otherwise.

> **Tip**
>
> I recommend that you inventory each major component of your system by manufacturer and model number. If you don't have the specification or technical reference manuals for these components, call the manufacturers (the vendor list in Appendix A will help), and ask for them. You'll be amazed at the wealth of information you can get.

If you want information about the electronics and chip level components in the system, you can contact the manufacturers of these devices and get their data books. Intel, for example, has volumes of information available on their processors, motherboard chipsets, cache controller chips, and other components they make. Other chipset manufacturers have data books on their chips that tell you about all the esoteric settings you see in your CMOS setup. Most of the BIOS manufacturers also produce documentation specific to their BIOS software. Check the vendor list in Appendix A for the manufacturers of the components in your system and call them to see what documentation they have available.

If you're looking for more general-purpose documentation, especially on operating systems or applications software, try Que Corporation, which specializes in this type of computer book. These books combine basic hardware information with more extensive software and operating system coverage. Microsoft and IBM also publish books of interest to computer enthusiasts and technicians. For example, Microsoft sells both Windows 95 and Windows NT Resource Kits, which should be considered mandatory additions to any technical library, as well as *Platinum Edition Using Windows 95* and *Windows NT Advanced Technical Reference* by Que.

Machines

The term *machines* refers to the systems themselves. Machines are one of my best sources of information. For example, suppose that I need to answer the question, "Will the XYZ SCSI host adapter work with the ABC tape drive?" The answer is as simple as plugging everything in and pressing the switch. (Simple to talk about, that is.)

Seriously, experimenting with and observing running systems are some of the best learning tools at your disposal. I recommend that you try everything; rarely will anything you try harm the equipment. Harming valuable data is definitely possible, if not likely, however, so make regular backups as insurance. You should not use a system you depend on for day-to-day operations as an experimental system; if possible, use a secondary machine. People sometimes are reluctant to experiment with systems that cost a lot of money, but much can be learned through direct tests and studies of the system. I often find that vendor claims about a product are somewhat misleading when I actually install it and run some tests. If you are unsure that something will really work, make sure that the company has a return policy that allows you to return the item for a refund if it does not meet your expectations.

Support people in larger companies have access to quantities of hardware and software I can only dream about. Some larger companies have *toy stores*, where they regularly purchase equipment solely for evaluation and testing. Dealers and manufacturers also have access to an enormous variety of equipment. If you are in this position, take advantage of this access to equipment, and learn from this resource. When new systems are purchased, take notes on their construction and components.

Every time I encounter a system I have not previously worked with, I immediately open it up and start taking notes. I want to know the make and model of all the internal components, such as disk drives, power supplies, and motherboards. As far as motherboards, I like to record the numbers of the primary IC chips on the board, such as the processor (of course), integrated chip sets, floppy controller chips, keyboard controller chips, video chipsets, and any other major chips on the board. By knowing which chipset your system uses, you can often infer other capabilities of the system, such as enhanced setup or configuration capabilities.

I like to know which BIOS version is in the system, and I even make a copy of the BIOS on disk for backup and further study purposes. I want to know the hard drive tables from the BIOS, and any other particulars involved in setting up and installing a system. Write down the type of battery a system uses so that you can obtain spares. Note any unique brackets or construction techniques such as specialized hardware (Torx screws, for example) so that you can be prepared for servicing the system later. Some programs have been designed to help you maintain an inventory of systems and components, but I find that these fall far short of the detail I am talking about here.

This discussion brings up a pet peeve of mine. Nothing burns me up as much as reading a review of computer systems in a major magazine, in which reviewers test systems and produce benchmark and performance results for, let's say, the hard disks or video displays in a system. Then, they do not open up the machines and tell me (and the world) exactly which components the manufacturer of the system is using! I want to know exactly which disk controller, hard drive, BIOS, motherboard, video adapter, and so on are found in each system. Without this information, their review and benchmark tests are useless to me.

Then these reviewers run a test of disk performance between two systems with the same disk controller and drives and say (with a straight face) that the one that came out a few milliseconds ahead of the other wins the test. With the statistical variation that normally occurs in any manufactured components, these results are meaningless. The point is perhaps to be very careful of who you trust in a normal magazine review. If it tells me exactly which components were tested, I can draw my own conclusions and even make comparisons to other systems not included in that review.

Modems

Modems refers to the use of public- and private-information utilities and online services, which are a modem and a phone call away. With a modem, you can tie into everything from local electronic bulletin board systems (BBSes) to major information networks such as CompuServe and, of course, the Internet featuring the World Wide Web. Many hardware and software companies offer technical support and even software upgrades over their own public bulletin boards or the Internet. The public-access information networks such as the Internet, CompuServe, and other BBS systems include computer enthusiasts and technical-support people from various organizations, as well as experts in virtually all areas of computer hardware and software. Bulletin boards are a great way to have questions answered and to collect useful utility and help programs that can make your job much easier. The world of public-domain and user-supported software awaits, as well as more technical information and related experiences than you can imagine.

Appendix A includes not only the name, address, and voice phone number for the company, but also the Internet addresses (Web sites) and BBS numbers where available. If you need more information on a vendor's products, or need technical support, try using the vendor's online connection. Many companies today provide online services to facilitate obtaining updated software or driver files which you can download quickly and easily. When a vendor provides an online connection, I consider that service a major advantage in comparison to other vendors who do not provide such a service. Using vendor-provided online connections either through the Internet or via a private BBS or even CompuServe has saved me money and countless hours of time.

Many companies that provide online services do so through a public access utility, such as CompuServe, or through their own Web site on the Internet, rather than running their own BBS. The *CompuServe Information Service (CIS)* is a public information access utility with an extensive network of dial-in nodes that allows you to log onto its cluster of mainframe systems (based in Ohio) from virtually anywhere in the world through a local telephone call. Among CompuServe's resources are the forums sponsored or attended by most of the major software and hardware companies, as well as enthusiasts of all types. CompuServe also provides access to the Internet, including the World Wide Web. CompuServe or other Internet providers, combined with a local electronic bulletin board or two, can greatly supplement the information you gather from other sources.

In fact, CompuServe electronic mail is probably the most efficient method of reaching me. My CompuServe ID is **73145,1566** (through the Internet, it is **73145.1566@compuserve.com**), and if you have questions or just a comment or useful information you think I might be interested in, please send me a message. Because of the extra steps in processing, my standard mail can get backed up and it can take me quite a while to answer a regular postal letter; electronic mail, however, involves fewer steps for me to send, and always seems to have a higher priority. If you do send a regular letter, be sure to include a SASE (Self-Addressed Stamped Envelope) so that I will be able to reply.

Magazines

The last source of information, magazines, is one of the best sources of up-to-date reviews and technical data. Featured are "bug fixes," problem alerts, and general industry news. Keeping a printed book up-to-date with the latest events in the computer industry is extremely difficult or even impossible. Things move so fast that the magazines themselves barely keep pace. I subscribe to most of the major computer magazines and am hard-pressed to pick one as the best. They all are important to me, and each one provides different information or the same information with a different angle or twist. Although the reviews usually leave me wanting, the magazines still are a valuable way to at least hear about products, most of which I never would have known about without the magazines' reports and advertisements. Most computer magazines are also available on CD-ROM, which can ease the frantic search for a specific piece of information you remember reading about. If CD-ROM versions are too much for your needs, be aware that you can access and search most major magazines on the Internet. This capability is valuable when you want to research everything you can about a specific subject.

One of the best kept secrets in the computer industry is the excellent trade magazines that offer free subscriptions. Although many of these magazines are directed toward the wholesale or technical end of the industry, I like to subscribe to them. Some of my favorites magazines include the following:

- *Computer Design*
- *Computer Hotline*
- *Computer Reseller News*
- *Electronic Design News*
- *Electronic Buyer's News*
- *Electronic Engineering Times*
- *Electronic News*
- *Electronic Products*
- *Processor*
- *Service News*
- *Test and Measurement World*

These magazines offer free subscriptions to anyone who qualifies. Aimed at people in the computer and electronics industries, these magazines offer a much greater depth and breadth of technical and industry information compared to the more "public" magazines that most people are familiar with. You'll find these and other recommended magazines in the vendor list in Appendix A.

The Appendixes

The appendixes provide a collection of technical information, tables, charts, and lists especially useful to people in a computer support, troubleshooting, service, or upgrading role. Whether you're looking for the meaning of a word in the glossary, seeking the address and phone number of a company or vendor in the vendor list, or searching for something as technical as determining the pinout of the ISA bus connector, you'll most likely find the information in the appendixes.

The appendixes started out as a brief collection of essential information, but have grown into a complete reference resource. No other book currently on the market contains such a complete and informative technical reference, which is one reason why so many large companies and educational institutions have standardized on this book for their technicians and students. This book is currently being used as an official textbook for many corporate and college-level computer training courses, as well as my own PC training seminars, for which the book was originally designed.

In Conclusion

I hope that *Upgrading and Repairing PCs,* Eighth Edition, is beneficial to you, and I hope that you have enjoyed reading it as much as I have enjoyed writing it. If you have questions about this book, or if you have ideas for future versions, I can be reached at the following address:

> Scott Mueller
> Mueller Technical Research
> 21718 Mayfield Lane
> Barrington, IL 60010-9733
> Phone: (847)726-0709
> Fax: (847)726-0710
> CompuServe ID: **73145,1566**
> Internet address: **73145.1566@compuserve.com**

Remember that the best way to contact me is through e-mail; often time constraints prevent me from responding to regular mail. If you do need a response through the mail, please include a self-addressed stamped envelope so that I can reply to you. If you are interested in one of my many intensive PC training seminars or videotapes, please call my office.

Thank you again for reading this book, and a special thanks to those people who have been loyal readers since the first edition came out in December 1988.

Sincerely,

Scott Mueller

Part VII

Appendixes

A Vendor List

B Glossary

Appendix A
Vendor List

One of the most frustrating things about supporting PCs is finding a specific adapter board, part, driver program, or whatever you need to make a system work. If you are supporting or installing products, you will often need access to technical support or documentation for products you may not have purchased yourself. Over the years, I have compiled a list of companies whose products are popular or I have found to work exceptionally well. I use these contacts regularly to provide information and components to enable me to support PC systems effectively.

Many of these companies have been mentioned in this book, but others not specifically mentioned have been added here. These companies carry many computer products you often will have contact with or that I simply recommend. I have tried to list as many vendors as possible that are important in day-to-day work with PC systems. These vendors can supply documentation for components you have, provide parts and service, and be used as a source for new equipment and even software. This list is as up-to-date as possible, but companies move or go out of business all the time. If you find any information in this list that no longer is accurate, please call me or leave me a message on CompuServe.

Many of the companies listed also provide support via electronic bulletin board systems (BBSes) and of course now via the World Wide Web (WWW). Ward Christensen (creator of the XMODEM protocol) and Randy Seuss created the first Computerized Bulletin Board System (CBBS) system that went online on February 16, 1978, and is still running today using the original software! You can call Ward and Randy's CBBS at (312)545-8086. Since that first BBS came online, BBS systems have proliferated throughout the world, and have now evolved into the Internet.

While originally exclusively the domain of computer enthusiasts, today many companies use Internet Web sites and BBS systems to provide a high level of technical support. Through a company-run Web site or BBS, you often can receive detailed technical support on that company's products, as well as download product literature and reference materials. I usually find the level of support I can obtain online is superior to traditional phone support, especially because I don't have to wait on hold!

With each company listing, I have included both standard phone numbers as well as 800 numbers where possible, so U.S. and international readers can easily contact these companies. Also included are fax, Internet addresses, and BBS numbers where available. I have not included any communications parameter settings, but virtually all BBS systems support 28.8K (V.34) connections.

Some companies run a *FAXback system*, an automated system through which you can request product and technical information to be sent directly to your own fax machine. FAXback systems are an excellent way to get immediate documentation or technical support to solve tough problems.

Many of these companies also provide online support and services through the *CompuServe Information System (CIS)*. You will find many major hardware and software companies on CIS; however, most of these same companies also run standard BBS systems as well. If you want to access CIS, you can contact them via a voice line and request a startup kit.

Most companies are now providing access through the Internet, including the WWW. I have tried to include Net and WWW addresses for any companies that offer this access. Companies are adding this type of access rapidly these days, so many companies may have added Internet sites after this book has been printed. If you discover any such information which I have not included, please send me e-mail detailing what you have found.

Finally, each listing includes a short description of the products or services the company provides. I use this vendor list constantly myself; I hope you find this list as useful as I do!

3Com Corp.
5400 Bayfront Plaza
P.O. Box 58145
Santa Clara, CA
95052-8145

Phone (408) 764-5000
Sales (800) 638-3266
Fax (408) 764-5001
Web **www.3com.com**

Manufactures network adapters, servers, modems, and other networking equipment.

3M Data Storage Products Division
3M Center Building
#223-5N-01
St. Paul, MN 55144

Phone (612) 733-1110
Support (800) 328-9438
Tech Info Sales
 (800) 854-0033
Web **www.3m.com**

Manufactures magnetic disk and tape media. DC-600 and DC-2000 media are standards for tape backup data cartridges.

Aavid Thermal Technologies, Inc.
One Kool Path
P.O. Box 400
Laconia, NH 03247-0400

Phone (603) 528-3400
Fax (603) 528-1478
Web **www.aavid.com**

Manufactures a line of heat sinks and thermal management materials.

ABIT Computer (USA) Corporation

26 Center Ave.
Sulphur, LA 70663

Phone	(318) 625-9592
Sales	(800) 364-7232
Fax	(318) 625-4830
E-Mail	sales@mssi.com

Manufactures an excellent line of PC motherboards in ATX and Baby-AT form factors. Their motherboards are known for having jumper and switchless software configuration.

ACC Microelectronics Corporation (Renamed Auctor Corporation)

2401-A Walsh Ave.
Santa Clara, CA 95051

Phone	(408) 980-0622
Fax	(408) 980-0624

Manufactures PC motherboard chipsets and other logic.

Accurite Technologies, Inc.

48460 Lakeview Blvd.
Fremont, CA 94538-6532

Phone	(510) 668-4900
Fax	(510) 668-4905
Web	www.accurite.com
E-Mail	sales@accurite.com

Manufactures floppy drive diagnostic products as well as PCMCIA diagnostic products and PCMCIA floppy drive subsystems. Floppy drive diagnostic products include the Accurite Drive Probe floppy disk diagnostics program as well as HRD, DDD, and ADD industry standard test disks. PCMCIA products include the PC Extender Card, the PC ReportCard (a PCMCIA diagnostic card), the HeadstartCard (a PCMCIA developers kit), and the Travel Floppy 144 (a PCMCIA interfaced floppy drive subsystem).

Acer America Corp.

2641 Orchard Pkwy.
San Jose, CA 95134-2073

Phone	(408) 432-6200
Support	(800) 445-6495
Fax	(408) 922-2933
Sales	(800) 223-7763
Parts	(800) 637-7000
BBS	(408) 428-0140
Web	www.acer.com

The second largest worldwide motherboard and PC system component manufacturer. Manufactures everything from components to complete desktop and notebook systems, as well as monitors and printers.

Acer Laboratories Inc. (ALi)

Pacific Technology Group
4701 Patrick Henry Dr.
Ste. 2101
Santa Clara, CA 95054

Phone	(408) 764-0644
Fax	(408) 496-6142
Fax BBS	(408) 492-0107

Manufactures chipsets including PC motherboard, super I/O, disk controller, and others. They make the Aladdin series chips for Pentium systems.

Acme Electric/ Safe Power

9962 Route 446
Cuba, NY 14727

Phone	(716) 968-2400
Sales	(800) 325-5848
Fax	(716) 968-3948

Manufactures uninterruptible power supplies (UPS) systems and power conditioners.

Adaptec

691 S. Milpitas Blvd.
Milpitas, CA 95035

Phone	(408) 945-8600
Support	(408) 945-2550
Tech Support FAXBack	(800) 934-2766
Fax	(408) 262-2533
BBS	(408) 945-7727
Web	www.adaptec.com

A leading supplier of high-performance input/output solutions, including a broad array of SCSI host adapters and software solutions. Their SCSI host adapters have become a defacto standard and have an enormous amount of third-party support.

Acquired Trantor Systems, Ltd., and now manufactures the MiniSCSI Parallel Port SCSI adapters, including hard disk and CD-ROM drivers for a variety of devices. Also acquired Future Domain.

Addison-Wesley Publishing Co, Inc.

One Jacob Way
Reading, MA 01867

Phone	(617) 944-3700
Support	(617) 944-2911
Fax	(617) 944-9338
Web	www.aw.com

Publishes technical publications and books.

Adobe Systems, Inc.

345 Park Ave.
San Jose, CA 95110-2704

Phone	(408) 536-6000
Fax	(408) 537-6000
Support	(800) 833-6687
Web	www.adobe.com

Manufactures (and created) the PostScript language and a variety of graphics software. Publisher of Pagemaker, Pagemill, Illustrator, and PostScript fonts (for DOS and Macintosh systems).

Advanced Digital Information Corporation

10201 Willows Rd.
Redmond, WA 98052

Phone	(206) 881-8004
Sales	(800) 336-1233
Fax	(206) 881-2296
Web	www.adic.com

Manufactures high-capacity tape-backup subsystems.

Advanced Integration Research (AIR)

2188 Del Franco St.
San Jose, CA 95131

Phone	(408) 428-0800
Fax	(408) 428-0950
BBS	(408) 428-1735
Web	www.airwebs.com

Manufactures a line of PC-compatible Pentium class motherboards.

Advanced Logic Research (ALR)

9401 Jeronimo St.
Irvine, CA 92718

Phone	(714) 581-6770
Sales	(800) 444-4257
Fax	(714) 581-9240
Support	(714) 458-0532
BBS	(714) 458-6834
Web	www.alr.com

Manufactures PC compatibles featuring ISA, EISA, and MCA buses.

Advanced Micro Devices (AMD)

One AMD Place
Sunnyvale, CA 94088-3453

Phone	(408) 732-2400
Support	(800) 222-9323
Fax	(408) 749-4753
Web	www.amd.com

Manufactures Intel compatible chips and math coprocessors. They have high-end 486 processors as well as a Pentium class chip called the K5. New K6 technology rivals Pentium II in speed and performance.

Advanced Personal Systems

105 Serra Way Ste. 418
Milpitas, CA 95035

Phone	(408) 298-3703
Fax	(408) 945-0242

Manufactures the excellent SYSCHK diagnostics program, which provides valuable information about devices installed in your system.

Aeronics, Inc.

12741 Research Blvd.
Ste. #500
Austin, TX 78759

Phone	(512) 258-2303
Fax	(512) 258-4392

Manufactures the highest quality active and forced perfect terminators for use in SCSI-bus systems. They are known for solving problems with longer distances or multiple-SCSI devices.

AIWA America, Inc. Computer Systems Division

800 Corporate Dr.
Mahwah, NJ 07430

Phone	(201) 512-3606
Sales	(800) 321-AIWA
Fax	(201) 512-3704
BBS	(407) 241-2929
Web	**www.aiwa.com**

Markets and sells mass storage solutions for network systems and personal workstations, including an impressive line of fault-tolerant RAID subsystems and tape backup devices.

Alaris

47338 Fremont Blvd.
Fremont, CA 94538

Phone	(510) 770-5700
Sales	(800) 317-2348
Fax	(510) 770-5759
BBS	(510) 770-5765
Support	(510) 770-5766
Web	**www.alaris.com**

Alaris designs and manufactures a line of video cards and computer systms, including QuickVideo (which allows you to fit up to 60 seconds of high impact video on a single 1.44 floppy with QuickVideo capture card) and Matinee Pro (a high performance PCI graphics adapter/full motion video).

Alaris no longer markets Matinee Pro; they do distribute QuickVideo Pro which allows the production of videograms. Also a streaming video player for the Internet is available (**http://www.alaris.com/vginfo.htm#stream**).

Alliance Research/ORA Electronics

9410 Owensmouth Ave.
Chatsworth, CA 91311

Phone	(818) 772-2700
Support	(800) 431-8124
Fax	(818) 718-8667
Web	**www.orausa.com**

Manufactures a complete line of computer accessories and peripheral products.

AllMicro, Inc. (Purchased by ForeFront Direct)

18820 U.S. Highway 19 N.
Ste. 215
Clearwater, FL 34624

Phone	(813) 539-7283
Fax	(813) 531-0200
Sales	(800) 653-4933
BBS	(813) 535-9042
Web	**www.allmicro.com**
E-Mail	**allmicro@allmicro.com**

Manufacturer and distributor of the Rescue data recovery software, the Post Plus, Discovery Card, Alert Card, and other various hardware and software diagnostic utilities and troubleshooting tools.

Alloy Computer Products

165 Forest St.
Marlborough, MA 01752

Phone	(508) 486-0001
Sales	(800) 800-2556
Fax	(508) 481-7711
BBS	(508) 486-4044
Support	(900) 680-2556

Manufactures tape-backup subsystems.

ALPS Electric

3553 N. First St.
San Jose, CA 95134

Phone	(408) 432-6000
Sales	(800) 950-ALPS
Support	(800) 449-ALPS
Customer Service	(800) 825-ALPS
Fax	(408) 432-6035
BBS	(408) 432-6424
Web	**www.alpsusa.com**

Manufactures high-quality keyboards and keyboard switches. They have an excellent mechanical keyswitch design with a quality tactile feedback. Also makes printers, floppy drives, mice, and keypads.

Altex Electronics, Inc.

11342 IH 35 North
San Antonio, TX 78233

Phone	(800) 531-5369
Fax	(210) 637-3264
Web	**www.altex.com**
E-Mail	**altex2@dcci.com**

Supplies mail order computer/electronics parts.

Amdek Corporation (A Division of Wyse Technology)

1901 Zanker Rd.
San Jose, CA 95112

Phone	(408) 473-1200
Sales	(800) 722-WYSE
Fax	(408) 473-1972
BBS	(408) 922-4400
Support	(408) 435-2770
Web	www.wyse.com

Manufactures monitors.

America Online

8619 Westwood Center Dr.
Vienna, VA 22182

Phone   (703) 448-8700

Provides a very popular on-line service that allows access to their own network as well as the Internet.

American Megatrends, Inc. (AMI)

6145-F Northbelt Pkwy.
Norcross, GA 30071

Phone	(770) 263-8181
Sales	(800) 828-9264
BBS	(770) 246-8780
Web	www.megatrends.com

Manufactures the most popular IBM-compatible BIOS; excellent ISA, EISA, VL-Bus, and PCI local bus motherboards; and diagnostic software such as AMIDIAG, SCSI DIAG, and Remote.

American National Standards Institute (ANSI)

11 West 42nd St.
13th Floor
New York, NY 10036

Phone	(212) 642-4900
Fax	(212) 398-0023
Web	www.ansi.org

ANSI committees set standards throughout the computer industry. Copies of any ANSI-approved standard can be ordered here.

American Power Conversion (APC)

P.O. Box 278
132 Fairgrounds Rd.
West Kingston, RI 02892

Phone	(401) 789-5735
Service	(800) 800-4APC
Fax	(401) 789-3710
Web	www.apcc.com

Manufactures a line of power protection equipment.

Ameriquest Technology

3 Imperial Promenade
Santa Ana, CA 92707

Phone	(714) 437-0099
Fax	(714) 445-5370
Support	(800) 555-1771
Web	www.cmsemh.com

Division of Ameriquest that distributes a variety of system and peripheral products, and specializes in hard disk drives.

AMP, Inc.

AMP Building
P.O. Box 3608
Harrisburg, PA 17105

Phone	(717) 564-0100
Sales	(800) 522-6752
Fax	(717) 986-7605
Web	www.amp.com

Manufactures a variety of computer connectors, sockets, and cables used by many OEMs. They also offer 5v to 3.3v adapters for DX4 processors.

Andromeda Research

P.O. Box 222
Milford, OH 45150

Phone	(513) 831-9708
Fax	(513) 831-7562

Manufactures an excellent EPROM programmer that runs from a PC parallel port. The device can program up to 4M EPROMS and includes software for menu driven operation on IBM-compatible systems.

Annabooks

11838 Bernardo Plaza Ct.
Ste. 102
San Diego, CA 92128-2417

Phone	(619) 673-0870
Sales	(800) 462-1042
Fax	(619) 673-1432
Web	www.annabooks.com
E-Mail	info@annabooks.com

Publishes and sells an excellent line of technical books and information on PC hardware and software design. Teaches workshops on PCI, Cardbus, and USB design.

Anthem Technology Systems (ATS)

1160 Ridder Park Dr.
San Jose, CA 95131

Phone	(408) 453-1200
Sales	(800) 359-3580
Fax	(800) 359-9877

A large distributor of Hewlett-Packard DAT tape and hard disk drives. They also distribute other hard disk and storage products.

Anvil Cases

15650 Salt Lake Ave.
Industry, CA 91745

Phone	(818) 968-4100
Sales	(800) 359-2684
Fax	(818) 968-1703

Manufactures heavy-duty equipment cases.

Apple Computer, Inc.

1 Infinite Loop
Cupertino, CA 95014

Phone	(408) 996-1010
Sales	(800) 538-9696
Fax	(612) 919-2976
Web	www.apple.com

Manufactures a line of Apple-compatible systems, peripherals, and software.

Apricot Computers, Ltd.

3500 Parkside
Birmingham Business Park
Birmingham, B37 7YS
England

Phone	+44 (021) 717-7171
Fax	+44 (021) 717-7799
Web	www.apricot.co.uk

Manufactures a popular line of PC-compatible systems sold primarily in Europe. Acquired by Mitsubishi Electric in 1990.

Arco Computer Products, Inc.

2750 N. 29th Ave. Ste. 316
Hollywood, FL 33020

Phone	(954) 925-2688
Fax	(954) 925-2889
BBS	(954) 925-2791

Manufactures a complete line of Micro Channel ATA IDE adapters used to upgrade IBM PS/2 systems.

Arrowfield International, Inc.

2822-C Walnut Ave.
Tustin, CA 92780

Sales	(800) 227-9628
Phone	(714) 669-0101
Fax	(714) 669-0526
E-Mail	arowfld@ix.netcom.com

Manufactures an incredible array of disk drive brackets, rails, slides, cable adapters, bezels, cabinets, and complete drive upgrade and repair assemblies for IBM, Compaq, and IBM-compatible systems.

Association of Shareware Professionals (ASP)

545 Grover Rd.
Muskegan, MI 49442

Phone	(616) 788-5131
Fax	(616) 788-2765
Web	www.asp-shareware.org

The ASP sets standards for shareware products and provides an ombudsman for disputes between users and authors as well as marketing information for shareware authors.

AST Research, Inc.

16215 Alton Pkwy.
Irvine, CA 92718-9658

Phone	(714) 727-4141
Sales	(800) 876-4278
Fax	(714) 727-9355
BBS	(817) 230-6850
Web	www.ast.com

Manufactures an extensive line of adapter boards and peripherals for IBM and compatible computers, as well as a line of IBM-compatible systems.

Astec America Inc.

6339 Paseo Del Largo
Carlsbad, CA 92009

Phone   (619) 757-1880
Fax   (619) 930-4739
Web   www.astec.com

Manufactures high-end power supplies for PC systems as well as many other applications. Astec power supplies are used as OEM equipment in many of the top manufacturers' systems, including IBM and others.

Asus Computer International (ASUStek)

721 Charcot Ave.
San Jose, CA 95013

Phone   (408) 474-0567
Fax   (408) 474-0568
Web   www.asus.com.tw

Manufactures a line of 486 and Pentium class PC-compatible motherboards.

AT&T National Parts Sales Center/Lucent Technologies

7424 Scott Hamilton Dr.
Little Rock, AK 72209

Phone   (800) 222-7278
Support   (800) 628-2888
Fax   (800) 527-4360

Supplies parts and components for AT&T computer systems. Call and ask for the free AT&T parts catalog.

ATI Technologies, Inc.

33 Commerce Valley Dr. E.
Thornhill, ONT L3T7N6
Canada

Phone   (905) 882-2600
Support   (905) 882-2626
Fax   (905) 882-2620
BBS   (905) 764-9404
Web   www.atitech.ca

Manufactures a popular line of high-performance PC video adapters and chipsets.

Autodesk, Inc.

111 McInnis Pkwy.
San Rasael, CA 94903

Phone   (415) 507-5000
Sales   (800) 445-5415
Fax   (415) 507-5100
Web   www.autodesk.com

Manufactures AutoCAD software.

Autotime Corporation

6605 S.W. Macadam
Portland, OR 97201

Phone   (503) 452-8577
Fax   (503) 452-8495
Web   www.autotime.com
E-Mail   info@autotime.com

Manufactures the Hypercable which transmits high-speed parallel data up to 200 feet. The new bi-directional cable supports parallel-ported CD-ROM and tape backup peripherals. They also convert DIP chips to SIMMs and sell 30-pin to 72-pin SIMM adapters.

Award Software International, Inc.

777 E. Middlefield Rd.
Mountain View, CA 94043

Phone   (415) 968-4433
Fax   (415) 968-0274
BBS   (415) 968-0249
Web   www.award.com

Manufactures a line of IBM-compatible ROM BIOS software.

AZ-COM, Inc.

3343 Vincent Rd., Ste. D
Pleasant Hills, CA 94523

Phone   (510) 254-5400
Fax   (510) 947-1900
Web   az-com.com

Manufactures a complete line of Bus-Extender cards for ISA, EISA, MCA, VL-Bus, PCI, and others. These extenders allow you to easily insert and remove adapter cards for testing with the power on.

Belden Wire and Cable

P.O. Box 1980
Richmond, IN 47375

Phone   (317) 983-5200
Sales   (800) 235-3362
Fax   (317) 983-5656
Web   www.belden.com

Manufactures cable and wire products.

Berkshire Products

P.O. Box 1015
Suwanee, GA 30174

Phone   (770) 271-0088
Fax   (770) 932-0082
Web   **www.berkprod.com**

Manufactures the Serial Watchdog and PC Watchdog system monitor including an optional temperature alarm. This board can automatically re-start a server or other system that has locked up.

Best Power Technology, Inc.
P.O. Box 280
Necedah, WI 54646

Phone   (608) 565-7200
Sales   (800) 356-5794
Fax   (608) 565-2221
Web   **www.bestpower.com**

Manufactures an excellent line of computer power protection equipment from high-end ferroresonent UPS systems to line conditioners and standby power protection systems.

Bitstream, Inc.
215 First St.
Cambridge, MA 02142

Phone   (617) 497-6222
Sales   (800) 522-3668
Fax   (617) 868-0784
Web   **www.bitstream.com**
E-Mail   **sales@bitstream.com**

Manufactures fonts and font software.

Black Box Corporation
P.O. Box 12800
Pittsburgh, PA 15241

Phone   (412) 746-5530
Fax   (412) 746-0746
Web   **www.blackbox.com**
E-Mail   **info@blackbox.com**

Manufactures and distributes a variety of communications products, including network adapters, cables, and connectors for a variety of applications.

Boca Research, Inc.
1377 Clint Moore
Boca Raton, FL 33487

Phone   (407) 997-6227
Support   (407) 241-8088
Fax   (407) 994-5848
BBS   (407) 241-1601
Web   **www.bocaresearch.com**

Manufactures a low-cost line of adapter card products for IBM compatibles. Recently acquired Hayes, and now carries the Hayes modem line.

Borland International
100 Borland Way
Scotts Valley, CA 95066-3249

Phone   (408) 431-1000
Sales   (800) 331-0877
Support   (800) 523-7070
BBS   (408) 431-5096
Web   **www.borland.com**

Software manufacturer that features Turbo language products, Paradox, as well as dBASE 5. Also the software manufacturer of Delphi.

Bose Corp.
The Mountain
Framingham, MA 01701

Phone   (508) 879-7330
Fax   (508) 879-1157

Manufactures speakers and integrated amplifiers.

Boston Computer Exchange
55 Temple Place
Boston, MA 02111

Phone   (617) 542-4414
Fax   (617) 542-8849

A broker for used IBM and compatible computers.

Brooktree Corporation (Purchased by Rockwell)
9868 Scanton Rd.
San Diego, CA 92121-3707

Phone   (619) 452-7580
Sales   (800) 228-2777
Fax   (619) 452-2104
Web   **www.brooktree.com**

Manufactures a line of digital-to-analog converter (DAC) chips, as well as multimedia chipsets.

Buerg, Vernon D.
850 Petaluma Blvd. North
Petaluma, CA 94952

Phone	(707) 778-1811
Fax	(707) 769-5479
BBS	(707) 778-8944
Web	**www.buerg.com**

Manufactures an excellent line of utility programs, including the popular LIST program. Buerg Software is distributed through BBSes and CompuServe.

Byte Information Exchange (BIX)

1030 Massachusetts Ave.
Cambridge, MA 02138

Phone	(800) 695-4775
Fax	(617) 491-6642
Web	**www.bix.com**
E-Mail	**info@bix.com**

An online computer information and messaging system.

Byte Magazine/McGraw Hill

One Phoenix Mill Ln.
Peterborough, NH 03458

Phone	(603) 924-9281
Service	(603) 924-7507
BBS	(617) 861-9764
E-Mail	**editors@bix.com**

A monthly magazine covering all lines of microcomputers.

Byte Runner Technologies

406 Monitor Ln.
Knoxville, TN 37922

Sales	(800) 274-7897
Phone	(423) 966-0058
Fax	(423) 675-3458
Support	(423) 966-3667
Web	**www.byterunner.com**
E-Mail	**sdudley@byterunner.com**

Carries a line of high-performance I/O cards featuring FIFO (16550 type) serial port UART chips, EPP/ECP parallel ports, and high-speed floppy (1M/sec). They also carry adapters that allow any IRQ setting (including IRQs 9-15) to prevent conflicts with other existing ports.

CTG (Formerly Cables to Go)

1501 Webster St.
Dayton, OH 45404

Phone	(513) 224-8646
Sales	(800) 826-7904
Fax	(800) 331-2841

Manufactures a variety of cable, connector, and switch products.

CAIG Laboratories

16744 W. Bernardo Dr.
San Diego, CA 92127-1904

Phone	(619) 451-1799
Sales	(800) CAIG-123
Fax	(619) 451-2799
Web	**www.caig.com**
E-Mail	**caig123@aol.com**

Manufactures and sells cleaners and lubricants for electronic applications, featuring contact enhancer for gold-plated contacts and connectors.

Cal-Abco

6041 Variel Ave.
Woodland Hills, CA 91367

| Phone | (800) 669-2226 |
| Fax | (818) 704-7733 |

Distributes computer systems and peripherals.

Canon USA, Inc.

One Canon Plaza
Lake Success, NY 11042

Phone	(516) 488-6700
Fax	(516) 354-5805
BBS	(516) 488-6528

Manufactures a line of printer and video equipment as well as floppy drives. Supplies floppy drives to Compaq and IBM.

Casio, Inc.

570 Mt. Pleasant Ave.
Dover, NJ 07801

Phone	(201) 361-5400
Sales	(800) 962-2746
Fax	(201) 361-3819
Web	**www.casio-usa.com**

Manufactures digital cameras, personal data systems, and digital watches.

Centon Electronics, Inc.

20 Morgan
Irvine, CA 92718

Phone	(714) 855-9111
Fax	(714) 855-3132
Web	www.centon.com

Manufactures memory enhancement kits, SIMM and DIMM modules, expansion boards, credit cards, and PCMCIA cards.

Chemtronics, Inc.
8125 Cobb Center Dr.
Kennesaw, GA 30144

Phone	(770) 424-4888
Sales	(800) 645-5244
Fax	(770) 424-4267
Web	www.chemtronics.com

Manufactures and sells a complete line of computer and electronic grade chemicals, materials, and supplies.

Cherry Electrical Products
3600 Sunset Ave.
Waukegan, IL 60087

Phone	(847) 662-9200
Fax	(847) 360-3498
Web	www.industry.net/cherry.electrical

Manufactures a line of high-quality keyboards for IBM-compatible systems. Also produces a line of industrial Gas Plasma displays.

Chicago Case Company
4446 S. Ashland Ave.
Chicago, IL 60609

Phone	(312) 927-1600
Fax	(800) 333-8172

Manufactures equipment-shipping and travel cases.

Chinon America, Inc.
615 Hawaii
Torrance, CA 90503

Phone	(310) 533-0274
Sales	(800) 441-0222
Fax	(310) 533-1727
BBS	(310) 320-4160

Manufactures a line of floppy disk and CD-ROM drives.

Chips and Technologies, Inc.
2950 Zanker Rd.
San Jose, CA 95134

Phone	(408) 434-0600
Fax	(408) 894-2079
BBS	(408) 456-0721

Designs, markets, and supports a broad line of semiconductor products that provide peripheral solutions in the areas of media, graphics, and core logic. The company's cutting-edge product family of HiQVideo flat panel video/graphics controllers for portable computers currently leads the market.

Ci Design Company
1695 W. McCarther Blvd.
Costa Mesa, CA 92626

Phone	(714) 556-0888
Fax	(714) 556-0890

Manufactures custom-made 3 1/2-inch drive mounting kits used by Toshiba, Panasonic, and NEC for their drive products. Also makes drive faceplates, enclosures, and custom cable assemblies.

CIE America
2701 Dow Ave.
Tustin, CA 92680

Phone	(714) 573-2942
Sales	(800) 877-1421
Fax	(714) 757-4488
BBS	(714) 573-2645

Manufactures PC printers and other peripherals.

Cirrus Logic, Inc.
3100 W. Warren Ave.
Fremont, CA 94538

Phone	(510) 623-8300
Fax	(510) 252-6020
FAXBack	(800) 359-6414
BBS	(510) 440-9080
Web	www.cirrus.com

Manufactures PC motherboard chipsets for mobile and desktop systems and a line of chipsets for disk controller, video, and communications circuits.

Citizen America Corporation
2450 Broadway Ste. 600
Santa Monica, CA 90404

Phone	(310) 453-0614
Fax	(310) 453-2814
Web	www.citizen-america.com

Manufactures a line of printers and floppy disk drives.

CMD Technology, Inc.

1 Vanderbilt
Irvine, CA 92618

Phone	(714) 454-0800
Sales	(800) 426-3832
Fax	(714) 455-1656
BBS	(714) 454-0795

Manufactures EISA adapters, PCI and VL-Bus IDE, and SCSI disk adapters.

Colorado Memory Systems, Inc. (A Division of Hewlett-Packard)

800 S. Taft Ave.
Loveland, CO 80537

Phone	(970) 669-8000
Fax	(970) 667-0997
BBS	(970) 635-0650

Manufactures tape-backup subsystems specializing in QIC-80 and QIC-40 systems that attach through an interface card, floppy controller, or parallel port connection.

Columbia Data Products

1070B Rainer Dr.
Altamonte Springs, FL 32714

Phone	(407) 869-6700
Fax	(407) 862-4725
BBS	(407) 862-4724
Web	www.cdp.com

Manufactures image backup software for all PC platforms and tools for quick replication of servers and workstations.

Compaq Computer Corporation

20555 State Highway 249
Houston, TX 77070

Phone	(713) 370-0670
Sales	(800) 231-0900
Support	(800) 652-6672
Fax	(713) 378-8754
BBS	(713) 378-1418
Web	support@compaq.com

Manufactures high-end IBM-compatible computer systems.

CompTIA (Computing Technology Industry Association)

450 E. 22nd St. Ste. 230
Lombard, IL 60148-6158

Phone	(847) 268-1818
Fax	(847) 268-1384

A non-profit trade association who sponsors the A+ Certification program.

Compton's NewMedia, Inc. (A Division of Softkey International, Inc.)

1 Anthanaeum St.
Cambridge, MA 02142

Phone	(617) 494-1200
Fax	(617) 494-1279
Web	www.softkey.com

Produces entertainment, multimedia, and education software for floppy and CD-ROM users. CD-ROM titles include Compton's Interactive Encyclopedia.

CompUSA, Inc.

15167 Business Ave.
Dallas, TX 75244

Phone	(214) 888-5700
Sales	(800) 266-7872
Fax	(800) 329-2212

Computer retail superstore and mail-order outlet.

CompuServe Information Service (CIS)

5000 Arlington Centre
Columbus, OH 43220

Phone	(614) 457-8600
Sales	(800) 848-8990
Fax	(614) 529-1610

Online information and messaging service; offers Internet access and manufacturer- and vendor-sponsored forums for technical support.

Computer Component Source, Inc.

135 Eileen Way
Syosset, NY 11791-9022

Phone	(516) 496-8727
Sales	(800) 356-1227
Fax	(800) 926-2062

Distributes a large number of computer components for repair. Specializes in display parts such as flyback transformers and other components.

Computer Design Magazine

PennWell Publishing Co.
Advanced Technology Group
10 Tara Blvd., 5th Floor
Nashua, NH 03062-2801

Phone (603) 891-0123
Fax (603) 891-0539
Web **atd.pennwell.com**

An excellent industry magazine for electronic engineers and engineering managers, featuring articles on all types of computer components and hardware.

Computer Discount Warehouse (CDW)

1020 E. Lake Cook Rd.
Buffalo Grove, IL 60089

Phone (708) 465-6000
Sales (800) 726-4239
Support (800) 383-4239
Fax (708) 465-6800
BBS (708) 465-6899

Computer retail superstore and mail order catalog outlet.

Computer Graphics World Magazine

PennWell Publishing Co.
Advanced Technology Group
10 Tara Blvd., 5th Floor
Nashua, NH 03062-2801

Phone (603) 891-0123
Fax (603) 891-0539

An industry magazine covering graphics hardware, software, and applications.

Computer Hotline Magazine

15400 Knoll Trail Ste. #500
Dallas, TX 75248

Phone (214) 233-5131
Sales (800) 999-5131
Fax (214) 233-5514

A publication that features advertisers offering excellent sources of replacement and repair parts as well as new and used equipment at wholesale prices.

Computer Library

1 Park Ave.
New York, NY 10016

Phone (212) 503-4400
Sales (800) 419-0313
Fax (212) 503-4414
Web **www.iacnet.com**

Manufactures the Computer Select CD-ROM database including full text and abstracts from more than 120 computer publications. This is a valuable research tool.

Computer Reseller News Magazine

CMP Media, Inc.
1 Jericho Plaza
Jericho, NY 11753

Phone (516) 733-6700
Fax (516) 733-6916

An excellent industry trade weekly news magazine featuring news for computer professionals involved in value-added reselling of computer equipment. Subscriptions are free to those who qualify.

Computer Retail Week Magazine

CMP Publications, Inc.
1 Jericho Plaza
Jericho, NY 11753

Phone (516) 733-6700
Fax (516) 733-8577

An excellent industry trade weekly news magazine featuring news for computer superstores, mass merchants, and retailers. Subscriptions are free to those who qualify.

Computer Shopper Magazine

Ziff-Davis Publishing
One Park Ave.
New York, NY 10016

Phone (212) 503-5926

Monthly magazine for experimenters and bargain hunters; features a large number of advertisements.

Computer Technology Review Magazine

West World Productions, Inc.
924 Westwood Blvd.
Ste. 650
Los Angeles, CA 90024-2910

Phone (310) 208-1335
Fax (310) 208-1054

An excellent monthly technical magazine for systems integrators, value-added resellers, and original equipment manufacturers. Subscriptions are free to those who qualify.

Comtech Publishing Ltd.
P.O. Box 12340
Reno, NV 89510

Phone	(702) 825-9000
Sales	(800) 456-7005
Fax	(702) 825-1818
Web	www.accutek.com/comtech

Manufactures dSalvage Professional, the best and most comprehensive xBASE data-recovery and file repair software available.

Connector Resources Unlimited (CRU)
1005 Ames Ave.
Milpitas, CA 95035

Phone	(408) 957-5757
Sales	(800) 260-9800
Fax	(408) 942-0862
Web	www.cruinc.com

Manufactures a large variety of disk enclosures, mounting kits, cables, and connectors for IBM and Mac systems.

Conner Peripherals, Inc.
Seagate Technology
920 Disc Dr.
Scotts Valley, CA 95066

Phone	(408) 438-6550
Fax	(408) 429-6356
FAXBack	(408) 438-2620
Service	(800) 468-3472
BBS	(408) 438-8771

Manufactures a line of hard disk drives, tape-backup products, and CD-ROM drives. They are an OEM supplier to Compaq and other companies.

Conner Tape Products, Inc. (A Division of Seagate Technology)
Seagate Technology
1650 Sunflower Ave.
Costa Mesa, CA 92626

Phone	(714) 641-1230
Sales	(800) 626-6637
Fax	(714) 641-2590
BBS	(408) 456-4415
Web	www.seagate.com

Manufactures a line of tape-backup products and high-capacity tape drives.

Corel Systems, Inc.
1600 Carling Ave.
Ottawa, ONT K1Z8R7
Canada

Phone	(613) 728-8200
Fax	(613) 728-9790
BBS	(613) 728-4752
Web	www.corel.com

Manufactures the CorelDRAW! graphics program as well as Corel SCSI, a SCSI driver kit featuring drivers for a variety of SCSI host adapters and devices. Also manufactures the WordPerfect Suite.

Creative Labs, Inc.
1901 McCarthy Blvd.
Milpitas, CA 95035

Phone	(408) 428-6600
Sales	(800) 544-6146
Service	(800) 998-1000
Support	(408) 742-6600
Fax	(408) 428-6611
BBS	(405) 742-6660
Web	www.creaf.com

Manufactures the Sound Blaster series of audio cards for multimedia and sound applications.

CS Electronics
1342 Bell Ave.
Tustin, CA 92780

Phone	(714) 259-9100
Fax	(714) 259-0911
Web	www.scsi-cables.com/scsi
E-Mail	cablescs@aol.com

Manufactures a very high-quality line of disk and tape drive cables, specializing in SCSI-1, SCSI-2, and SCSI-3 applications. They offer custom lengths, connectors, and impedances for a proper match with an existing installation, and use the highest quality raw cable available.

CST
2336 Lu Field Rd.
Dallas, TX 75229

Phone	(214) 241-2662
Fax	(214) 241-2661

BBS (214) 241-3782
Web **www.simmtester.com**

Manufacturer of memory/SIMMs testers.

CTX International, Inc.
20470 Walnut Dr.
Walnut, CA 91789

Phone (909) 595-6146
Sales (800) 888-9052
Fax (909) 595-6293

Manufactures a line of high-performance notebook computers.

Curtis Manufacturing Co, Inc.
225 Secaucus
Secaucus, NJ 07094

Phone (201) 422-0240
Fax (201) 422-0254

Manufactures a complete line of computer accessories, including copy holders, glare filters, keyboard drawers, media storage, printer stands, data switches, cleaning and toolkits, notebook cases, travel accessories, and surge protectors.

CyberMedia
3000 Ocean Park Blvd.
Ste. 2001
Santa Monica, CA 90405

Phone (800) 721-7824
Fax (310) 581-4700
Web **www.cybermedia.com**

Manufactures diagnostic software for Windows including First Aid 97.

Cypress Semiconductor Corporation
3901 N. First St.
San Jose, CA 95134

Phone (408) 943-2600

Manufactures PC chipsets and other semiconductor devices.

Cyrix Corporation
2703 N. Central Exwy.
Richardson, TX 75080

Phone (214) 968-8388
Sales (800) 462-9749
Fax (214) 699-9857
FAXBack (800) GO-CYRIX
Web **www.cyrix.com**

Manufactures the 6X86 processor and offers a complete line of computer systems.

D. W. Electrochemicals, Ltd.
97 Newkirk Rd. N., Unit 3
Richmond Hill, ONT
L4C 3G4 Canada

Phone (905) 508-7500
Fax (905) 508-7502

Manufactures and sells Stabilant 22 contact enhancer and treatment. Stabilant 22 is the gel concentrate, and Stabilant 22a is a 4-to-1 isopropanol diluted form.

DakTech
4900 Ritter Rd.
Mechanicsburg, PA 17055

Phone (717) 795-9544
Sales (800) 325-3238
Fax (717) 795-9420
Web **www.daktech.com**
E-Mail **daktech@ix.netcom.com**

Distributor of new and used original equipment IBM and Compaq parts.

Da-Lite Screen Co.
3100 N. Detroit St.
P.O. Box 137
Warsaw, IN 46581-0137

Phone (219) 267-8101
Sales (800) 622-3737
Web **www.da-lite.com**

Manufactures a line of projection screens and computer furniture.

Dallas Semiconductor
4401 S. Beltwood Pkwy.
Dallas, TX 75244-3292

Phone (214) 450-0400
Service (214) 450-0448
Fax (214) 450-3715
Web **www.dalsemi.com**

Manufactures real-time clock and non-volatile RAM modules used by a number of OEMs, including IBM, Compaq, and others.

Damark International, Inc.
7101 Winnetka Ave. North
Minneapolis, MN 55429

Phone   (612) 531-0066
Sales   (800) 729-9000
Fax   (612) 531-0281
Web   www.damark.com

Liquidates and distributes a variety of discontinued products, including PC-compatible systems and peripherals.

Darkhorse Systems
12201 Technology Blvd. Ste. 135
Austin, TX 78727

Phone   (512) 258-5721
Fax   (512) 257-0296

Manufactures the SIGMA.LC memory test system. This is a high-quality memory test device that can accurately test SIMMs, individual chips, and other types of memory modules.

Data Base Advisor Magazine
Advisor Publications
4010 Morena Blvd. Ste. 200
San Diego, CA 92117

Phone   (619) 483-6400
Fax   (619) 483-9851
Subscriptions
(800) 336-6060
Web   www.advisor.com
E-Mail   70007.1614@compuserve.com

An excellent magazine featuring articles on database applications software and programming routines. They also publish *Access Visual Basic Advisor, Internet Advisor, FoxPro Advisor, Lotus Notes Advisor,* and *PowerBuilder Advisor.*

Data Communications Magazine
McGraw-Hill Inc.
1221 Avenue of the Americas
New York, NY 10020

Phone   (212) 512-2000
Subscriptions
           (800) 525-5003
Fax   (212) 512-6833
Web   www.data.com

An excellent industry publication featuring articles on networking and communications.

Data Depot
1710 Drew St.
Clearwater, FL 34615-6213

Phone   (813) 446-3402
Sales   (800) SOS-DIAG
Fax   (813) 443-4377
Web   www.datadepo.com/datadepo.htm
E-Mail   datadepo@ix.net_com.com

Manufactures the Pocket-POST diagnostic card for ISA and EISA systems, as well as several other excellent diagnostics hardware and software products.

Data Exchange Corporation
3600 Via Pescador
Camarillo, CA 93012

Phone   (805) 388-1711
Sales   (800) 237-7911
Fax   (805) 482-4856
Web   www.dex.com
E-Mail   sales@dex.com

Specializes in contract manufacturing, end-of-life support, and depot repair. A complete repair and refurbishment facility, providing depot repair of most major computer components.

Data Retrieval Services, Inc.
1040 Kapp Dr.
Clearwater, FL 34625

Phone   (813) 461-5900
Fax   (813) 461-5668

Specialists in data retrieval from head-crashed disk packs, damaged disk drives, floppies, and tapes.

Data Technology Corporation (DTC)
1515 Centre Pointe Dr.
Milpitas, CA 95035-8010

Phone   (408) 942-4000
support   (408) 262-7700
Fax   (408) 942-4027
FAXBack   (408) 942-4005
BBS   (408) 942-4197
Web   www.datatechnology.com

Manufactures a complete line of PC peripherals and multimedia products.

Datamation Magazine

Cahners Publishing Co.
275 Washington St.
Newton, MA 02158-1630

Phone	(617) 964-3030
Subscriptions	(800) 446-6551
Fax	(617) 558-4506
Web	www.datamation.com

An excellent industry publication, featuring articles on networking and communications.

Datastorm Technologies, Inc.

2401 Lemone Blvd.
Columbia, MO 65205

Phone	(573) 443-3282
Sales	(800) 474-1573
Fax	(573) 875-0595
Support	(573) 875-0530
BBS	(573) 875-0503
Web	www.datastorm.com

Manufactures ProCOMM, ProCOMM Plus, and ProCOMM Plus for Windows Internet, Fax, and data communications software.

Dell Computer Corporation

2214 W. Braker Ln. Ste. D
Austin, TX 78759

Phone	(512) 338-4400
Sales	(800) 426-5150
Support	(800) 624-9896
Fax	(800) 727-8320
BBS	(512) 338-8528
Web	www.dell.com

Manufactures a line of low-cost, high-performance IBM-compatible computer systems.

DigaSoft, Inc.

5615 Scotts Valley Dr.
Ste. 140
Scotts Valley, CA 95066

Phone	(408) 438-8247
Sales	(800) 342-4763
Fax	(408) 438-7113
Web	www.diagsoft.com

Manufactures the QAPlus user-level PC diagnostics software, as well as the high-end QAPlus/FE (Field Engineer) software, an excellent program that includes complete high-resolution floppy drive testing and the Power Meter benchmarking utility.

Diamond Flower, Inc. (DFI)

135 Main Ave.
Sacramento, CA 95838

Phone	(916) 568-1234
Fax	(916) 568-1233
Web	www.dfiusa.com

Manufactures a line of PC-compatible systems, motherboards, adapter cards, and other products.

Diamond Multimedia Systems, Inc.

2880 Junction Ave.
San Jose, CA 95134-1922

Phone	(408) 325-7000
Sales	(800) 468-5846
Fax	(408) 325-7070
Web	www.diamondmm.com

Manufactures a line of high-performance video and multimedia adapters. Also makes and sells the Supra line of modem and telephony products.

Digi-Key Corporation

701 Brooks Ave. South
P.O. Box 677
Thief River Falls, MN 56701-0677

Phone	(218) 681-6674
Sales	(800) 344-4539
Fax	(218) 681-3380
Web	www.digikey.com

Sells an enormous variety of electronic and computer components, tools, and test equipment. Publishes a complete catalog listing all items.

Distributed Processing Tech. (DPT)

140 Candace Dr.
Maitland, FL 32751

Phone	(407) 830-5522
Sales	(800) 322-4378
Fax	(407) 260-5366
BBS	(407) 831-6432
Web	www.dpt.com

Manufactures high-performance caching, SCSI host adapters, and disk array (RAID) controllers.

Diversified Technology
P.O. Box 748
Ridgeland, MS 39158

Phone	(601) 856-4121
Sales	(800) 443-2667
Fax	(601) 856-2888

Manufactures industrial and rack-mount PC-compatible systems as well as a variety of backplane-design CPU boards and multifunction adapters.

Dolch Computer Systems
3178 Laurelview Ct.
Fremont, CA 94538

Phone	(510) 661-2220
Fax	(510) 490-2360
Web	www.dolch.com

Manufactures a series of very powerful portable computers that are also very expandable and rugged. If you need something more powerful than a laptop, they have lunchbox-sized portables with large hard disks and high-end video displays.

DTK Computer, Inc.
770 Epperson Dr.
City of Industry, CA 91748

Phone	(818) 810-0098
Fax	(818) 810-0090
BBS	(818) 854-0797
Web	www.dtk.com

Manufactures PC-compatible systems and BIOS software.

Dukane Corporation
2900 Dukane Dr.
St. Charles, IL 60174

Phone	(630) 584-2300
Sales	(800) 676-2485
Fax	(630) 584-5156
Web	www.industry.net/dukane.av

Manufactures a complete line of high-intensity overhead projectors, LCD panels, and LCD data/video projectors. They specialize in portable high brightness overhead projectors units designed for LCD-panel projection applications.

Duracell, Inc.
Berkshire Industrial Park
Bethel, CT 06801

Phone	(203) 796-4000
Sales	(203) 791-3257
Web	www.duracell.com

Manufactures high-performance consumer application batteries including alkaline, lithium, and standard-sized nickel-metal hydride rechargeable batteries.

Edmund Scientific
101 E. Gloucester Pike
Barrington, NJ 08007-1380

Phone	(609) 573-6280
Fax	(609) 573-6233
Sales	(609) 573-6250
Web	www.edsci.com

They offer a wide range of optical components and scientific equipment for industry and research. Volume discounts offered. Free catalog offered to those who qualify.

Electrocution
P.O. Box 52083
Winnipeg MB
R2M 5P9
Canada

Phone	(204) 257-9721
Web	www.mbnet.mb.ca/electrocution

Publishes *The BIOS Companion*, an invaluable book covering in detail the different BIOS versions on the market including detailed setup, configuration, and diagnostics information.

Electronic Buyers' News Magazine
CMP Publications, Inc.
600 Community Dr.
Manhasset, NY
11030-3875

Phone	(516) 562-5000
Subscriptions	(800) 291-5215
Fax	(516) 562-5123

An excellent industry trade weekly magazine featuring news and information for those involved in electronics purchasing, materials, and management. Subscriptions are free to those who qualify.

Electronic Engineering Times Magazine

CMP Publications, Inc.
600 Community Dr.
Manhasset, NY
11030-3875

Phone   (516) 562-5000
Subscriptions
              (800) 291-5215
Fax   (516) 562-5325

An excellent industry trade weekly news magazine featuring news for engineers and technical management. Subscriptions are free to those who qualify.

Electronic Products Magazine

Hearst Business
Publications, Inc.
645 Stewart Ave.
Garden City, NY 11530

Phone   (516) 227-1300
Fax   (516) 227-1444
Web   **www.electronicproducts.com**

An excellent industry trade magazine featuring engineering type information on electronic and computer components and in-depth technical articles. Subscriptions are free to those who qualify.

Electroservice Laboratories

6085 Sikorsky St.
Ventura, CA 93003

Phone   (805) 644-2944
Fax   (805) 644-5006
BBS   (805) 644-7810
Web   **www.esl.com**

Provides repair parts for most major computer OEMs, including all major PC components.

Elek-Tek, Inc.

7350 North Linder Ave.
Skokie, IL 60077

Phone   (847) 677-7660
Sales   (800) 395-1000
Fax   (847) 677-1081
Web   **www.elektek.com**

Computer retail superstore offering a large selection of brand-name equipment at discount pricing.

Elitegroup Computer Systems, Inc.

45401 Research Ave.
Fremont CA 94539

Phone   (510) 226-7333
Sales   (800) 829-8890
Fax   (510) 226-7350
Web   **www.ecsusa.com**

One of the largest Taiwan-based PC motherboard manufacturers.

Endl Publications

14426 Black Walnut Ct.
Saratoga, CA 95070

Phone   (408) 867-6642
Fax   (408) 867-2115
FAXBack   (408) 741-1600
E-Mail   **2501752@mclmail.com**

Publishes the SSF Reflector, containing specs for local bus disk drive attachments. Also publishes SCSI technical documentation such as *The SCSI Bench Reference* and *The SCSI Encyclopedia*.

Epson America, Inc. OEM Division

20770 Madrona Ave.
Torrance, CA 90509-2842

Phone   (310) 787-6300
Fax   (310) 782-5350
FAXBack   (800) 922-8911
BBS   (408) 782-4531
Web   **www.epson.com**

Manufactures printers, floppy disk drives, and complete PC-compatible systems.

Everex Systems, Inc.

5020 Brandin Ct.
Fremont, CA 94538

Phone   (510) 498-1111
Sales   (800) 821-0806
Support   (510) 498-4411
Fax   (510) 683-2062
BBS   (510) 226-9694
Web   **www.everex.com**

Manufactures PC-compatible systems and peripherals.

Exabyte Corporation

1685 38th St.
Boulder, CO 80301

Phone   (303) 442-4333
Fax   (303) 417-7170
Web   **www.exabyte.com**

Manufactures high-performance 8mm and minicartridge tape-backup systems, and 8mm and 4mm tape libraries. Also produces the Eagle Nest modular storage systems.

Extron Electronics

1230 S. Lewis St.
Anaheim, CA 92805

Phone	(714) 491-1500
Sales	(800) 633-9876
Fax	(714) 491-1517
Web	www.extron.com

Manufactures computer-video interface products used to connect PCs to large-screen video projectors and monitors. The company also manufactures VGA, Mac, and RGB distribution amplifiers and switchers used to connect multimedia classroom and boardroom equipment, and VGA- and Mac-to-NTSC/PAL converters for recording computer information and graphics on videotape.

Fantasy Productions (A Division of Fortner & Associates)

1305 Bert St.
Claremore, OK 74017

Sales	(800) 358-5887
Phone	(918) 341-4577
Support	(918) 445-1586

The source for discontinued IBM reference manuals and technical support.

Fedco Electronics, Inc.

184 W. 2nd St.
Fond du Lac, WI 54936

Phone	(414) 922-6490
Sales	(800) 542-9761
Fax	(414) 922-6750

Manufactures and supplies a large variety of computer batteries.

Fessenden Technologies

116 N. 3rd St.
Ozark, MO 65721

Phone	(417) 485-2501
Fax	(417) 485-3133
Web	www.oznet.com/fessenden/
E-Mail	76660.1035@Compuserve.com

Service company that offers monitor and terminal depot repair. They also repair hard drives for older Seagate and Miniscribe MFM/RLL drives.

First International Computer, Inc (FIC)

980-A Mission Ct.
Fremont, CA 94539

Phone	(510) 252-7777
Sales	(800) FICA-OEM
Fax	(510) 252-8888
Web	www.fica.com

The largest Taiwan-based manufacturer of PC-compatible motherboards.

Fluke, John Manufacturing Company, Inc.

6920 Seaway Blvd.
P.O. Box 9090
Everett, WA 98206-9090

Phone	(206) 347-6100
Sales	(800) 443-5853
Fax	(206) 356-5019
Web	www.fluke.com

Manufactures a line of high-end digital troubleshooting tools, including the Scopemeter hand-held scope.

Folio Corporation

5072 N. 300 W.
Provo, UT 84604

Phone	(801) 229-6700
Fax	(801) 229-6787
Sales	(800) 543-6546
Web	www.folio.com

Manufactures the Folio VIEWS infobase software. Also publishes the annual COMDEX exhibitors' list on disk.

Framatome Connectors USA

51 Richards Ave.
Norwalk, CT 06856

Phone	(203) 838-4444
Fax	(203) 852-8629

Manufactures electronic connector products for portable and desktop PCs and workstations.

Fujitsu America, Inc.

3055 Orchard Dr.
San Jose, CA 95134

Phone	(800) 626-4686
Support	(408) 894-3950
Fax	(408) 432-1318
BBS	(408) 944-9899
Web	**www.fujitsu.com**

Manufactures a line of high-capacity hard disk drives. Also manufactures a line of notebook computers, monitors, and peripherals.

Future Domain Corporation (Purchased by Adaptec)

9701 Jeronimo Rd.
Irvine, CA 92718

Sales	(800) 959-7274
Support	(408) 934-7274
Fax	(408) 957-6776
BBS	(408) 945-7727
Web	**www.adaptec.com**

Manufactures a line of high-performance SCSI host adapters and software. Acquired by Adaptec.

Gateway 2000

P.O. Box 2000
610 Gateway Dr.
North Sioux City, SD 57049

Phone	(605) 232-2000
Sales	(800) 523-2000
Support	(800) 846-2000
Fax	(605) 232-2023
BBS	(605) 232-2224
Web	**www.gw2k.com**

Manufactures a popular line of PC-compatible systems sold by mail order. Their systems primarily use Micronics Motherboards, Phoenix BIOS, and industry standard form factors.

Gazelle/GTM Software

289 E. 950 South
Orem, UT 84058

Phone	(801) 235-7000
Fax	(801) 235-7099
Web	**www.shopsite.com/gtm**

Manufactures the Optune disk defragmenter and disk performance utility program.

Giga-Byte Technology Co., Ltd.

18305 Valley Blvd. Ste. A
LaPuente, CA 91744

Phone	(818) 854-9338
Fax	(818) 854-9339
BBS	(818) 854-9340
Web	**www.giga-byte.com**

One of the top 10 largest Taiwan-based motherboard manufacturers.

GigaTrend, Inc.

2234 Rutherford Rd.
Carlsbad, CA 92008

Phone	(619) 931-9122
Sales	(800) 743-4442
Fax	(619) 931-9959
BBS	(619) 931-9469
Web	**www.gigatrend.com**

Manufactures high-capacity tape drives.

Global Engineering Documents

15 Inverness Way East
Englewood, CO 80112-5704

Phone	(303) 792-2181
Sales	(800) 854-7179
Fax	(303) 792-2192

A source for various ANSI and other industry standard documents, including SCSI-1, 2, and 3, ATA IDE, ESDI, and many others. Unlike ANSI, they sell draft documents of standards that are not yet fully ANSI approved.

Globe Manufacturing, Inc.

1159 Route 22
Mountainside, NJ 07092

Phone	(908) 232-7301
Sales	(800) 227-3258
Fax	(908) 232-4729
Web	**www.akstamping.com**

Manufactures assorted PC adapter card brackets.

Golden Bow Systems

P.O. Box 3039
San Diego, CA 92163-1039

Phone	(619) 298-9349
Sales	(800) 284-3269

Fax   (619) 298-9950
Web   **www.goldenbow.com**

Manufactures VOPT, the best and fastest disk optimizer software available. They also offer Vcache, VQ, and VLock

GoldStar Technology, Inc.
1000 Sylvan Ave.
Englewood Cliff, NJ 07632

Phone   (201) 816-2000
Fax   (201) 816-0636
Web   **www.goldstar.co.kr/english/main.html**

Manufactures a line of color monitors and a full line of computer and electronics products.

GRACE Specialty Polymers/WR GRACE, Emerson & Cuming Inc.
869 Washington St.
Canton, MA 02021

Phone   (617) 828-3300
Sales   (800) 472-2391
Fax   (617) 828-3104
Support   (800) 832-4929
Orders   (800) 225-9936

Manufactures structurally, thermally, and electronically conductive epoxy and silicone adhesives, coatings, and encapsulates. Also room temperature, heat-cured, and UV-cured systems as well as circuit board fabrication materials. These include solder mask, solder resist, and polymer thick films.

GSI, Inc.
17951-H Skypark Circle
Irvine, CA 92614-6343

Phone   (714) 261-7949
Sales   (800) 486-7800
Fax   (714) 757-1778
Web   **www.gsi-inc.com**

Manufactures an extremely flexible and powerful line of IDE adapters and floppy controllers, including units with security locks, and support for 2.88M drives. Also offers complete 2.88M drive upgrade kits. Their IDE controllers have a flexible on-board BIOS that allows them to coexist with other drive interfaces. They also sell a Cable Select type IDE cable.

Harbor Electronics
650 Danbury Rd.
Ridgefield, CT 06877

Phone   (203) 438-9625
Fax   (203) 431-3001

Manufactures a line of high-quality SCSI-1, -2, and -3 interconnect cables.

Hauppauge Computer Works, Inc.
91 Cabot Ct.
Hauppauge, NY 11788

Phone   (516) 434-1600
Sales   (800) 443-6284
Service   (516) 434-3197
Fax   (516) 434-3198
BBS   (516) 434-8454
Web   **www.hauppauge.com/hcw/index.htm**

Manufactures video capture cards.

Hayes Microcomputer Products
5835 Peachtree Corners E.
Norcross, GA 30092-3405

Phone   (770) 840-9200
Sales   (800) 874-3734
Fax   (770) 441-1213
FAXBack (800) 429-3739
BBS   (770) 429-3734
Web   **www.hayes.com**

Manufactures a complete line of modems.

Heathkit Education Systems
Heath Company
455 Riverview Dr.
Benton Harbor, MI 49023

Phone   (616) 925-6000
Sales   (800) 253-0570
Fax   (616) 925-2982

Sells courses and training materials for learning electronics and computer design, including A+ Certification for Computer Technicians.

Helm, Inc.
Publications Division
P.O. Box 07130
Detroit, MI 48207

Phone   (313) 865-5000
Fax   (313) 865-5927

Publishes General Motors service manuals and documentation.

Hermann Marketing

1400 North Price Rd.
St. Louis, MO 63132-2308

Phone	(800) 523-9009
Fax	(314) 432-1818

Distributes a line of "Uniquely Intel" products and accessories. My favorite are the T-shirts, coffee cups, and especially the keychain containing actual Intel 486 and Pentium processors encased in clear plastic.

Hewlett-Packard

16399 W. Bernardo Dr.
San Diego, CA 92127-1899

Sales	(800) 752-0900
Service	(970) 635-1000
FAXBack	(800) 333-1917
Audio Tips	(800) 333-1917
BBS	(408) 720-3416
Web	www.hp.com

Manufactures an extensive line of excellent printers and PC-compatible systems and high-end minicomputers.

Hewlett-Packard, Disk Memory Division

11413 Chinden Blvd.
Boise, ID 83714

Sales	(800) 826-4111
Phone	(208) 396-6000
Fax	(208) 396-2896
Web	www.hp.com

Manufactures high-capacity 3 1/2-inch hard disk drives.

Hitachi America, Ltd.

Semiconductor & IC Div.
2000 Sierra Point Pkwy.
Brisbane, CA 94005

Phone	(415) 589-8300
Fax	(415) 583-4207
Web	www.hitatchi.com

Manufactures a variety of memory and other semiconductor devices. Also manufactures computer peripherals, including Office automation, digital graphics products, and LCD devices.

Hypertech

1910 Thomas Rd.
Memphis, TN 38134

Phone	(901) 382-8888
Fax	(901) 373-5290

Manufactures and sells a wide variety of well-engineered, high-performance automotive computer EPROM replacements for many different types of vehicles. Also makes the Power Programmer for reprogramming vehicle PCMs with EEPROMs (Flash ROMs).

Hyundai Electronics America

3101 N. 1st St.
San Jose, CA 95134

Phone	(408) 473-9200
Web	www.hea.com

Manufactures PC-compatible systems.

Also makes monitors, memory, chips, and other peripherals.

IBM Fullfilment Center

P.O. Box 3558
Shiremans Town, PA 17011

Phone	(800) 426-7282

The source for OS/2 software developer kits, reseller literature, and orders for server guides.

IBM Microelectronics

3605 Hwy. 52
Rochester, MN 55901

Phone	(507) 253-4011
Fax	(507) 253-3256

Manufactures a variety of processors, memory, and other semiconductor devices, including the IBM 486SLC2, Blue Lightning, PowerPC, and other processors. Also makes high-speed Static RAM for cache, and produces processor chips and motherboards for a variety of PC-compatible manufacturers.

IBM National Publications

4800 Falls of The Neause
Raleigh, NC 27609

Phone	(800) 879-2755
Fax	(800) 445-9269

The source for current books, reference manuals, documentation, software toolkits, and language products for IBM systems.

For discontinued publications, contact Fantasy Productions or Annabooks.

IBM OEM Division

44 Broadway Rd.
White Plains, NY 10601

Phone   (914) 288-3000
Fax   (914) 686-4527

Manufactures and distributes IBM products such as high-capacity 3 1/2-inch hard disk drives, networking, and chipset products.

IBM Parts Order Center

P.O. Box 9022
Boulder, CO 80301

Phone   (303) 924-4100

IBM's nationwide service parts ordering center.

IBM PC Company

11400 Burnet Rd.
Austin, TX 78758

Phone   (512) 823-0000
Sales   (800) IBM-3333
FAXBack   (800) 426-4329
BBS   (919) 517-0001
Web   **www.ibm.com**

Manufactures and supports IBM personal computers.

IBM PC Direct

3039 Cornwallis Rd.
Building 203
Research Triangle Park, NC 27709-9766

Sales   (800) IBM-2YOU
Canada Sales
          (800) 465-7999
Fax   (800) 426-4182
Info   (800) 426-3332
Orders   (800) 426-2968
Web   **www.pc.ibm.com**

IBM PC's direct mail order catalog sales division. They sell IBM and approved third-party systems and peripherals at a discount from list price, and publish a catalog listing all items.

IBM Personal Systems Technical Solutions Magazine

NCM
P.O. Box 165447
Irving, TX 75016

Sales   (800) 678-8014
Phone   (214) 550-0433
Fax   (214) 518-2507

Publishes an excellent bi-monthly magazine covering IBM personal computer systems and software.

Illinois Lock

301 West Hintz Rd.
Wheeling, IL 60090-5754

Phone   (847) 537-1800
Fax   (847) 537-1881
E-Mail   **iillock@aol.com**

Manufactures keylocks used in many different IBM and IBM-compatible computer systems.

Information Access Company

One Park Ave.
New York, NY 10016

Phone   (212) 503-4400

Manufactures the Computer Library and Computer Select CD-ROM information databases.

***InfoWorld* Magazine**

375 Cochituate Rd.
Framingham, MA 01701

Phone   (508) 879-0700
Sales   (800) 227-8365
Fax   (508) 879-0446
Web   **www.infoworld.com**

Features excellent product reviews.

Inline, Inc.

22860 Savi Ranch Pkwy.
Yorba Linda, CA 92887

Phone   (714) 921-4100
Sales   (800) 882-7117
Fax   (714) 921-4160

Manufactures a complete line of video-connection accessories, including distribution amplifiers, scan converters, line drivers, projector interfaces, and cables. They also offer interactive training systems for computer-based training facilities.

Innerworks Technology, Inc.

319 Sundance Dr.
Bartlett, IL 60103

Phone (630) 372-0884
Fax (630) 372-0885

Manufactures an excellent PC diagnostic program called the Third Degree.

Integrated Device Technology, Inc.

2975 Stender Way
Santa Clara, CA
95054-3090

Phone (408) 727-6116
Sales (800) 345-7015
Web **www.idt.com**

Manufactures chipsets and other semiconductor devices.

Integrated Micro Solutions, Inc.

2085 Hamilton Ave,
3rd Floor
San Jose, CA 95125

Phone (408) 369-8282
Fax (408) 369-0128
Web **users.aol.com\
imsteksup**

Manufactures graphic accelerator chips and boards, and ATM network products.

Intel Corporation

2200 Mission College Blvd.
Santa Clara, CA
95054-1537

Phone (408) 765-8080
Service (800) 468-3548
 (916) 356-7368
Fax (408) 765-9904
Web **www.intel.com**

Manufactures microprocessors used in IBM and compatible systems. Also makes a line of memory and accelerator boards, as well as one of the most popular lines of PC-compatible Pentium motherboards.

Intel PC Enhancement Operations

5200 N.E. Elam Young Pkwy.
Hillsboro, OR 97124

Phone (503) 629-7354
Service (800) 321-4044
Support (800) 628-8686
Sales (800) 538-3373
Fax (503) 264-7969
BBS (503) 264-7999

Manufactures OverDrive CPU upgrades and networking devices.

International Electronic Research Corp. (IERC)

135 W. Magnolia Blvd.
Burbank, CA 91502

Phone (818) 842-7277
Fax (818) 848-8872
Web **www.iercdya.com**

Manufactures a line of excellent CPU heat sink products, including clip-on, low-profile models especially for 486 and Pentium processors that do not require a special socket.

Iomega Corporation

1821 West Iomega Way
Roy, UT 84067

Phone (801) 778-1000
Sales (800) 777-6654
Fax (801) 778-3461
BBS (801) 778-5888
Web **www.iomega.com**

Manufactures the Jaz, Ditto, and Zip removable-cartridge drives.

J. Bond Computer Systems

93 W. Montague Exwy.
Milpitas, CA 95035

Phone (408) 946-9622
Fax (408) 946-2898
Web **www.jbond.com**

Manufactures PC motherboards.

Jameco Computer Products

1355 Shoreway Rd.
Belmont, CA 94002

Phone (415) 592-8097
Sales (800) 831-4242
Fax (415) 592-2503
BBS (415) 637-9025
Web **www.jameco.com**

Supplies computer components, parts, and peripherals by mail order.

JDR Microdevices

1850 S. 10th
San Jose, CA 95112

Phone (408) 494-1400
Sales (800) 538-5000

BBS (408) 494-1430
Web www.jdr.com

A vendor for chips, disk drives, and various computer and electronic parts and components.

Jensen Tools

7815 S. 46th St.
Phoenix, AZ 85044

Phone (602) 968-6231
Sales (800) 426-1194
Fax (800) 366-9662
Web www.jensentools.com

Supplies and manufactures high-quality tools and test equipment.

JTS Corporation

1289 Anvilwood Ave.
Sunnyvale, CA 94089

Phone (408) 468-1800
Fax (408) 747-1319
Web www.jtscorp.com

Manufactures a line of low-cost 3 1/2-inch hard disk drives.

JVC Information Products

17811 Mitchell Ave.
Irvine, CA 92714

Phone (714) 261-1292
Fax (714) 261-9690

Manufactures CD-Recordable and CD-ROM drives.

Kensington Microware, Ltd.

2855 Campus Dr.
San Mateo, CA 94403

Phone (415) 572-2700
Fax (415) 572-9675
Sales (800) 535-4242
Web www.kensington.com

Manufactures and supplies computer accessories.

Key Tronic Corporation

P.O. Box 14687
Spokane, WA 99214

Phone (509) 928-8000
Sales (800) 262-6006
Fax (509) 927-5248
BBS (509) 927-5288
Web www.keytronic.com

Manufactures a variety of high-quality keyboards and mice for PC-compatible systems. Acquired the Honeywell Keyboard division. The Honeywell mouse uses revolutionary new technology that never needs cleaning and works on any surface, unlike traditional ball and roller mice. Supplies Compaq and Microsoft with keyboards.

Kingston Technology Corporation

17600 Newhope St.
Fountain Valley, CA 92708

Phone (714) 435-2600
Sales (800) 835-6575
Fax (714) 435-2699
Web www.kingston.com

Manufactures an excellent line of direct processor upgrade modules for 286 and 386 IBM and Compaq systems, as well as the slot-based MCMaster bus master processor upgrade card for Micro Channel systems. They also sell numerous SIMM memory modules and disk upgrades for other systems.

Labconco Corporation

8811 Prospect
Kansas City, MO 64132

Phone (816) 333-8811
Sales (800) 821-5525
Fax (816) 363-0130

Manufactures a variety of clean room cabinets and clean benches for use in hard disk drive and other sensitive component repair.

Labtec Enterprises, Inc.

3801 N.E. 109 Ave., Ste. J
Vancouver, WA 98682

Phone (360) 896-2000
Fax (360) 896-2020
Web www.labtec.com

Imports amplified speakers for multimedia applications.

Lantronix

15353 Barranca Pkwy.
Irvine, CA 92718-2216

Phone (714) 453-3990
Sales (800) 422-7055
Fax (714) 453-3995
Web www.lantronix.com

Manufactures a variety of network hardware

including servers, bridges, repeaters, hubs, converters, and transceivers.

Laser Magnetic Storage

4425 Arrowswest Dr.
Colorado Springs, CO 80907

Phone (719) 593-7900
Fax (714) 599-8713
BBS (719) 593-4081

Division of DPMG that manufactures a variety of optical and tape disk products.

LearnKey, Inc.

1845 W. Sunset Blvd.
St George, UT 84770

Sales (800) 937-3279
Phone (801) 674-9733
Fax (801) 674-9734
Web www.learnkey.com

Produces and distributes the highest quality computer training videos.

Lexmark

740 New Circle Rd.
Lexington, KY 40511

Phone (606) 232-2000
Fax (606) 232-3557
BBS (606) 232-5238
Web www.Lexmark.com

Manufactures IBM keyboards and printers for retail distribution. Spun off from IBM in 1991, now sells to other OEMs and distributors.

Liebert

1050 Dearborn Dr.
Columbus, OH 43229

Phone (614) 888-0246
Sales (800) 877-9222
Fax (614) 841-6022
Web www.liebert.com

Manufactures a line of computer power-protection devices.

Liuski International

6585 Crescent Dr.
Norcross, GA 30071

Phone (770) 447-9454
Web www.liuski.com

Hardware distributor that carries a variety of peripherals and systems. They are the exclusive distributor of Magitronic PC systems and motherboards.

Logicraft Information Systems, Inc. (Renamed Microtest Enterprises)

22 Cotton Rd.
Nashua, NH 03063

Phone (603) 880-0300
Sales (800) 880-5644
Fax (603) 880-7229
Web www.logicraft.com

Manufacturer of CD-ROM networking and optical storage solutions for the DOS, Windows, Window 95, Windows NT, and Macintosh environments. The company's products provide fast access to CD-ROM databases over a wide range of networks and technologies in the industry, featuring the FastCD PersonalEdition. FastCD has been renamed Virtual CD, which also allows CD-based programs to be run from any local or network disk.

Longshine Microsystems, Inc.

10400-9 Pioneer Blvd.
Santa Fe Springs, CA 90670

Phone (310) 903-0899
Fax (310) 944-2201

Manufactures PC interface boards including disk controllers, super I/O adapters, network cards, and more.

Lotus Development Corporation (A Division of IBM)

55 Cambridge Pkwy.
Cambridge, MA 02142

Phone (617) 577-8500
Service (800) 343-5414
Fax (617) 693-3899
BBS (617) 693-7000
Web www.lotus.com

Manufactures Lotus 1-2-3, Symphony, and Magellan software. Acquired by IBM.

LSI Logic, Inc.

1551 McCarthy Blvd.
Milpitas, CA 95035

Phone (408) 433-8000
Sales (800) 433-8778
Fax (408) 433-2882
Web www.lsilogic.com

Manufactures motherboard logic and chipsets.

Ma Laboratories, Inc.
1972 Concourse Dr.
San Jose, CA 95131

Phone   (408) 954-8188
Fax   (408) 954-0944
Web   **www.malabs.com**

Manufactures and supplies CPUs and SIMMs, PC boards, hard disk drives, floppy drives, motherboards, and math coprocessors. They also manufacture a dummy parity chip that allows fake parity SIMMs to be constructed, which they also sell.

Macworld Communications Inc.
501 Second St.
San Francisco, CA 94107

Phone   (415) 243-0505
Fax   (415) 442-1891

Produces an excellent publication covering news in the Macintosh universe.

MAG InnoVision
2801 S. Yale St.
Santa Ana, CA 92704

Phone   (714) 751-2008
Sales   (800) 827-3998
Fax   (714) 751-5522
Web   **www.maginnovision.com**

Manufactures Flat Square Technology monitors with advanced performance features.

MAGNI Systems, Inc.
9500 S.W. Gemini Dr.
Beaverton, OR 97008

Phone   (503) 626-8400
Sales   (800) 624-6465
Fax   (503) 626-6225

Manufactures a line of products for converting VGA graphics screens to either NTSC (VHS) or S-video (S-VHS).

MapInfo Corporation
One Global View
Troy, NY 12180

Phone   (518) 285-6000
Fax   (518) 285-6070
Sales   (800) 552-2511
Web   **www.mapinfo.com**

Produces desktop mapping software for Windows, Mac, Sun, HP, and DOS systems.

Mastersoft, Inc. (Acquired by Adobe Systems)
8737 E. Via de Commercio
Scottsdale, AZ 85258

Phone   (602) 948-4888
Sales   (800) 624-6107
Fax   (602) 948-8261
BBS   (602) 596-5871
Web   **www.mastersoft.com**

Manufactures Word for Word, a word processing file-conversion program.

Matrox Graphics Inc.
1025 St. Regis Blvd.
Dorval, PQ
H9P 2T4
Canada

Phone   (514) 969-6300
Fax   (514) 969-6363
Sales   (514) 969-6330

Manufactures a line of high-performance PC graphics chipsets and adapters.

Maxell Corporation of America
22-08 Route 208
Fair Lawn, NJ 07410

Phone   (800) 533-2836
Fax   (201) 796-8790

Manufactures magnetic media products, including disks and tape cartridges.

Maxi Switch, Inc.
2901 East Elvira Rd.
Tuscon, AZ 85706

Phone   (602) 294-5450
Fax   (602) 294-6890
BBS   (602) 741-9230
Web   **www.maxiswitch.com**

Manufactures a line of high-quality PC keyboards, including some designed for harsh or industrial environments, and programmable keyboards. Maxi Switch keyboards are used by many compatible system manufacturers, including Gateway 2000.

Maxoptix
3342 Gateway Blvd.
Fremont, CA 94538

Phone	(800) 848-3092
Fax	(510) 353-1845
BBS	(510) 353-1448
Web	www.maxoptix.com

Manufactures a line of optical WORM and magneto-optical drives. Joint venture with Maxtor and Kubota Corporations.

Maxtor Corporation
211 River Oaks Pkwy.
San Jose, CA 95134

Phone	(408) 432-1700
Sales	(800) 262-9867
Fax	(408) 432-4510
BBS	(303) 678-2222
Web	www.maxtor.com

Manufactures a line of large-capacity, high-quality hard disk drives.

Maynard Electronics, Inc. (Seagate Technologies)
36 Skyline Dr.
Lake Mary, FL 32746

Phone	(407) 263-3500
Sales	(800) 821-8782
FAXBack	(800) 732-4283
Fax	(407) 262-4225
BBS	(407) 263-3662
TDD	(408) 438-5382
Web	www.seagate.com

Manufactures a line of tape-backup products. Acquired by Seagate Technologies.

McAfee Associates
2710 Walsh Ave.
Santa Clara, CA 95051

Phone	(408) 988-3832
Sales	(800) 707-1274
Fax	(408) 970-9727
BBS	(408) 988-4044
Web	www.mcafee.com

Manufactures the famous McAfee antivirus software as well as a diagnostic program called PC Medic 97.

McKenzie Technology
910 Page Ave.
Fremont, CA 94538

Phone	(510) 651-2700
Fax	(510) 651-1020
Web	www.bergelect.com/mckenzie

Manufactures sockets for processors and IC chips.

Megahertz Corporation (A Division of 3Com)
605 N5600W
Salt Lake City, UT 84116

Phone	(801) 320-7000
Sales	(800) 527-8677
FAXBack	(800) 856-1045
Fax	(801) 320-6022
Web	www.megahertz.com

Manufactures laptop modems and external network adapters. Also makes AT-speedup products.

Mentor Electronics, Inc.
7560 Tyler Blvd. #E
Mentor, OH 44060

Phone	(216) 951-1884
Fax	(216) 951-0107

Supplies ICs.

Merisel
200 N. Continental Blvd.
El Segundo, CA 90245

Phone	(310) 615-3080
Sales	(800) 542-9955
Service	(800) 462-5241
Fax	(800) 845-3744
Web	www.merisel.com

World's largest distributor of PC hardware and software products from many manufacturers.

Meritec
1359 West Jackson St.
P.O. Box 8003
Painesville, OH 44077

Phone	(216) 354-3148
Fax	(216) 354-0509
Sales	(800) 627-7752

Manufactures a line of SCSI 8-bit to 16-bit (Wide SCSI) adapters in a variety of configurations. These adapters allow Wide SCSI devices to be installed in a standard 8-bit SCSI bus and vice versa.

Merritt Computer Products, Inc.
5565 Red Bird Center Dr. #150
Dallas, TX 75237

Phone	(214) 339-0753
Fax	(214) 339-1313

Manufactures the SafeSkin keyboard protector.

Methode Electronics, Inc.
DataMate Division
7444 W. Wilson Ave.
Chicago, IL 60656

Phone (708) 867-9600
Fax (708) 867-3149

Manufactures and sells a complete line of SCSI terminators.

Micro 2000, Inc.
1100 E. Broadway
3rd Floor
Glendale, CA 91205

Phone (818) 547-0125
Fax (818) 547-0397
Web www.micro2000.com

Manufactures the MicroScope PC diagnostics program, as well as the POSTProbe ISA, EISA, and MCA POST diagnostics card.

Micro Accessories, Inc.
6036 Stewart Ave.
Fremont, CA 94538

Phone (510) 226-6310
Sales (800) 777-6687
Fax (510) 226-6316

Manufactures a variety of cables and disk drive mounting brackets and accessories, including PS/2 adapter kits.

Micro Channel Developers Association
169 Hartnell Ave. Ste. 200
Redding, Ca 96002

Phone (916) 222-2262
Sales (800) GET-MCDA
Fax (916) 222-2528
Web www.microchannel.inter.net/microchannel

An independent organization established to facilitate the evolution and support of the Micro Channel Architecture (MCA). The association also provides microchannel products direct to ender users. They publish the *International Catalog of Micro Channel Products and Services.*

Micro Computer Cable Company, Inc.
12200 Delta Dr.
Taylor, MI 48180

Phone (313) 946-9700
Fax (313) 946-9645
Web www.microccc.com

Manufactures and sells a complete line of computer cables, connectors, switchboxes, and cabling accessories.

Micro Design International (MDI)
6985 University Blvd.
Winter Park, FL 32792

Phone (407) 677-8333
Sales (800) 228-0891
Fax (407) 677-8365
BBS (407) 677-4854

Manufactures the SCSI Express driver software for integration of SCSI peripherals in a variety of environments. Recently acquired PC-Kwik Corporation.

Micro House International
2477 N. 55th St.
Boulder, CO 80301

Phone (303) 443-3388
Sales (800) 926-8299
Fax (303) 443-3323
BBS (303) 443-9957

Publishes the Micro House Technical Library on CD-ROM. The technical library is a Windows-compatible reference tool designed for PC service technicians that covers adapter cards, network cards, motherboards, and disk drives. Also produces DrivePro, EZ Drive, EZ Copy, and many other hard drive formatting and protection products. EZ Drive is the utility shipped with many of the new large IDE hard drives (allows bypass of the BIOS).

Micro Industries Corporation
8399 Green Meadows Dr. N.
North Westerville, OH
43081-9486

Phone	(614) 548-7878	
Sales	(800) 369-1086	
Fax	(614) 548-6184	

Manufactures PC-compatible motherboards.

Micro Solutions, Inc.

132 W. Lincoln Hwy.
DeKalb, IL 60115

Phone	(815) 756-3411
Sales	(800) 890-7227
BBS	(815) 756-9100
Web	www.microsolutions.com

Manufactures a complete line of floppy controllers and subsystems, including 2.88M versions. Also offers floppy drive and tape-backup systems that run from a standard parallel port using no expansion slots. Also make the backpack line of hard drives, CD-ROMS, disk drives, and tape drives.

Micro Solutions, Inc.

40 Old Ridgebury Rd.
Ste. 106
Danbury, CT 06810

Phone	(203) 748-4633
Fax	(203) 797-9849
Web	www.micsol.com

A Premier Service center for Toshiba America, specializing in sales, service, and upgrades for laptop and portable computers.

Micro Warehouse

535 Conneticut Ave.
Norwalk, CT 06854

Phone	(203) 899-4000
Fax	(203) 853-2267
Sales	(800) 547-5444

Distributes a large variety of computers, computer supplies, floppy disks, cables, and so on.

Microcom, Inc.

500 River Ridge Dr.
Norwood, MA 02062

Phone	(617) 551-1000
Sales	(800) 822-8224
BBS	(617) 255-1125
Web	www.microcom.com

Manufactures error-correcting modems and remote access products; created and develops the MNP communications protocols.

Micrografx, Inc.

1303 E. Arapaho Rd.
Richardson, TX 75081

Phone	(214) 234-1769
Sales	(800) 417-8312
Support	(214) 234-2684
Fax	(214) 994-6476
BBS	(214) 644-4194
Web	www.micrografx.com

Manufactures the Micrografx Designer, Windows Draw, ABC Toolkit, Photomagic, and Charisma software. Specializes in Windows and OS/2 development.

Microid Research, Inc.

1538 Turnpike St.
North Andover, MA 01845

Phone	(508) 686-8209
Fax	(508) 683-1630
Web	www.mrbios.com

Manufactures the MR BIOS, one of the most flexible and configurable BIOS versions available. They have versions available for a variety of different chip sets and motherboards.

Microlink/Micro Firmware, Inc.

330 West Gray St. Ste. 170
Norman, OK 73069-7111

Sales	(800) 767-5465
Fax	(405) 573-5535
BBS	(405) 573-5538
Web	www.firmware.com

The largest distributor of Phoenix ROM BIOS upgrades. Develops custom versions for specific motherboards, and supplies many other BIOS vendors with products.

Micron Technologies (Parent Company of Micron Electronics and Micron Custom Manufacturing)

8000 S. Federal Way
Boise, ID 83707

Phone	(208) 368-3900
Sales	(800) 388-6334
Fax	(208) 368-3809
BBS	(208) 368-4530
Web	www.micron.com

Manufactures various memory boards, memory chips, SIMMs, DRAM, SRAM, and other semiconductors, as well as a line of IBM-compatible systems.

Micronics Computers, Inc.

45365 Northport Loop W.
Fremont, CA 94538

Phone	(510) 651-2300
Fax	(510) 651-6692
Sales	(800) 577-0977
Support	(510) 661-3000
FAXBack	(510) 661-3199
BBS	(510) 651-6837
Web	www.micronics.com

Manufactures PC-compatible motherboards and complete laptop and portable systems. Micronics motherboards feature the Phoenix BIOS. Acquired Orchid Technology.

Micropolis Corporation

21211 Nordhoff St.
Chatsworth, CA 91311

Phone	(818)709-3300
Sales	(800)395-DRIV
Fax	(818)709-3396
BBS	(818)709-3310

Manufactures a line of high-capacity 5 1/4- and 3 1/2-inch hard disk drives.

Microprocessors Unlimited, Inc.

24000 S. Peoria Ave.
Beggs, OK 74421

Phone	(918) 267-4961
Fax	(918) 267-3879

Distributes memory chips, SIMMs, math coprocessors, UART chips, and other integrated circuits.

Microsoft Corporation

One Microsoft Way
Redmond, WA 98052-6399

Phone	(206) 882-8080
Sales	(800) 426-9400
Fax	(206) 936-7329
BBS	(206) 936-6735
Web	www.microsoft.com

Manufactures MS-DOS, Windows, Windows NT, and a variety of applications software.

Micro-Star International

4059 Clipper Ct.
Fremont, CA 94538

Phone	(510) 623-8818
Fax	(510) 623-8585
BBS	(510) 623-7398
Web	www.achme.com

One of the top 10 largest Taiwan-based motherboard manufacturers.

MicroSystems Development Tech., Inc.

4100 Moorpark Ave. #104
San Jose, CA 95117

Phone	(408) 296-4000
Fax	(408) 296-5877
BBS	(408) 296-4200
Web	www.msd.com/diags

Manufactures a line of excellent hardware diagnostics products including Post Code Master, Port Test, and Test Drive.

MicroWay, Inc.

Research Park
Box 79
Kingston, MA 02364

Phone	(508) 746-7341
BBS	(508) 746-7946
Web	www.microway.com

Manufactures a line of accelerator products for IBM and compatible systems. Also specializes in math coprocessor chips, math chip accelerators, alpha-based systems, and language products.

Mini Micro

4900 Patrick Henry Ln.
Santa Clara, CA 95054

Phone	(408) 327-0388
Sales	(800) 275-4642
Fax	(408) 327-0389
BBS	(408) 434-9319

Partly owned by Greenleaf Corporation, a wholesale distributor of Conner Peripherals, Inc.

Mitsubishi Electronics America, Inc.

FaxElectronic Device Group
1050 E. Arques Ave.
Sunnyvale, CA 94086

Phone	(408) 730-5900
Sales	(800) 843-2515

Support   (800) 344-6352
Web   **www.mitsubishi.com**

Manufactures monitors, printers, and consumables. For hard disks and floppy disk storage products, contact the Electronic Device Group.

Mitsumi Electronics Corporation

6210 N. Beltline Rd.
Ste. 170
Irving, TX 75063

Phone   (214) 550-7300
Fax   (214) 550-7424
Web   **www.mitsumi.com**

Manufactures a line of CD-ROM and floppy drives, as well as keyboards.

Molex Inc.

2222 Wellington Ct.
Lisle, IL 60532

Phone   (630) 969-4550
Sales   (800) 78-MOLEX
Fax   (630) 969-2321
Web   **www.molex.com**

Manufactures a variety of connectors used in PC systems.

Mosel Vitelic

3910 N. First St.
San Jose, CA 95134

Phone   (408) 433-6000
Fax   (408) 433-0952

Manufactures memory modules.

Motor Magazine

Hearst Corporation
645 Stewart Ave.
Garden City, NY 11530

Phone   (516) 227-1300
Sales   (800) AUTO-828
Fax   (516) 227-1444

The essential trade magazine for the automotive technician, including troubleshooting tips and service product information. Subscriptions are free to those who qualify.

Motorola, Inc.

Microprocessor and Memory Technology Group
3501 Ed Bluestein Blvd.
Austin, TX 78762

Phone   (512) 891-2000
Sales   (800) 521-6274
Fax   (512) 891-2652

Manufactures PC memory including fast static RAM for cache. Also makes the Macintosh, Power PC, and Motorola processors. Also produces the Starmax line of Macintosh-compatible systems.

Mountain Network Solutions, Inc.

360 El Pueblo Rd.
Scotts Valley, CA 95066

Phone   (800) 458-0300
Fax   (408) 438-7623
BBS   (408) 438-2665

Manufactures tape drives and backup subsystems, including hardware and software.

Mustang Software

P.O. Box 2264
Bakersfield, CA 93303

Phone   (805) 873-2500
Sales   (800) 999-9619
Fax   (805) 873-2599
BBS   (805) 873-2400
Web   **www.mustang.com**

Manufactures Wildcat! BBS software.

Mylex Corporation

34551 Ardenwood Blvd.
Fremont, CA 94555

Phone   (510) 796-6100
Sales   (800) 776-9539
Fax   (510) 745-8016
Web   **www.mylex.com**

Manufactures high-performance motherboards, SCSI RAID, and SCSI host adapters.

Myoda Computer Centers

1070 N. Roselle Rd.
Hoffman Estates, IL 60195

Phone   (847) 885-7600
Fax   (847) 885-7661
FaxWeb   **www.myoda.com**

Assembles PC systems for retail sale.

National Semiconductor Corporation

2900 Semiconductor Dr.
Santa Clara, CA
95052-8090

Phone	(408) 721-5000
Fax	(408) 721-7582
BBS	(408) 245-0671
Web	www.national.com

Manufactures a variety of chips for PC circuit applications. Known especially for its UART and Super I/O chips.

NCL America, Inc.

1221 Innsbruck Dr.
Sunnyvale, CA 94086

Phone	(408) 734-1006
Fax	(408) 774-0709

Manufactures IDE host adapters.

NCR Microelectronics

1635 Aeroplaza
Colorado Springs, CO
80916

Phone	(719) 596-5795
Sales	(800) 334-5454
Fax	(719) 573-3286
BBS	(719) 574-0424
Web	www.ncr.com

Manufactures a variety of integrated circuits for PC systems. They also sponsor the SCSI BBS, an excellent source for standard documents covering SCSI, IDE, and other interfaces.

NEC Electronics, Inc.

475 Ellis St.
Mountain View, CA
94039-7241

Phone	(415) 960-6000

Manufactures memory and other semiconductor devices.

NEC Technologies, Inc.

1414 Massachusetts Ave.
Boxborough, MA 01719

Phone	(508) 264-8000
Sales	(800) 632-4636
Fax	(508) 264-8245
BBS	(708) 860-2602
Web	www.nec.com

Manufactures Multisync monitors, CD-ROM drives, video adapters, printers, and other peripherals, as well as complete PC-compatible systems.

Newark Electronics

4801 N. Ravenswood
Chicago, IL 60640-4496

Phone	(312) 784-5100
Fax	(312) 907-5217
Web	www.newark.com

An electronic component and product supplier with a huge catalog of products. Its 1500+ page catalog is an excellent source of components and information.

NexGen, Inc. (A Division of AMD)

1623 Buckeye Dr.
Milpitas, CA 95035

Phone	(408) 432-2400
Sales	(800) 8NEXGEN
Fax	(408) 435-0262
Web	www.amd.com

Manufactures the Nx586 family of processors which are being marketed as alternatives to the Intel Pentium family.

Northgate Computer Systems, Inc.

6840 Hayvenhurst
VanNuys, CA 91406

Phone	(818) 781-0300
Sales	(800) 947-6211
Fax	(818) 779-3767
BBS	(612) 947-4640
Web	www.northgate.net

Manufactures PC-compatible systems and keyboards sold through mail order.

Novell, Inc.

122 E. 1700 South
Provo, UT 84601

Phone	(801) 379-5588
Sales	(800) 526-7937
Fax	(801) 429-5157
BBS	(801) 429-3030
Web	www.novell.com

Manufactures the NetWare LAN operating system.

Number Nine Visual Technology Corporation

18 Hartwell Ave.
Lexington, MA 02173

Phone (617) 674-0009
Fax (617) 674-2919
BBS (617) 862-7502
Web **www.numbernine.com**

Manufactures a line of high-end PC video graphics accelerator cards.

Oak Technology, Inc.

139 Kifer Ct.
Sunnyvale, CA 94086

Phone (408) 737-0888
Fax (408) 737-3838
BBS (408) 774-5308
Web **www.oaktech.com**

Manufactures graphics chipsets.

Ocean Information Systems

688 Arrow Grand Circle
Covina, CA 91722

Phone (818) 339-8888
Fax (818) 859-7668
Web **www.ocean-usa.com/ocean**

Manufactures high-performance PC motherboards.

OEM Magazine

CMP Publications
600 Community Dr.
Manhasset, NY 11030

Phone (516) 562-5000

An excellent magazine for the systems integrator or systems assembler. Free subscription for those who qualify.

Okidata

532 Fellowship Rd.
Mount Laurel, NJ 08054

Phone (609) 235-2600
Sales (800) OKIDATA
Fax (609) 424-7423
BBS (800) 283-5474
Web **www.okidata.com**

Manufactures printers and modems.

Olivetti

765 U.S. Hwy. 202
Somerville, NJ 08876

Phone (908) 526-8200
Fax (908) 526-8405
Sales (800) 243-2324

Manufactures Olivetti and many AT&T PC systems.

Ontrack Data Internationa, Inc. (Formerly Ontrack Computer Systems)

6321 Bury Dr. Ste. 13–21
Eden Prairie, MN 55346

Phone (612) 937-1107
Fax (612) 937-5815
Sales (800) 752-1333
Support (612) 937-2121
BBS (612) 937-8567
Web **www.ontrack.com**

Manufactures the Disk Manager hard disk utilities for PC, PS/2, and Macintosh. Disk Manager is the most comprehensive and flexible low-level format program available, supporting even IDE drives. Also provides extensive data recovery services.

Opti, Inc.

888 Tasman Dr.
Milpitas, CA 95035

Phone (408) 486-8000
Sales (800) 398-6784
Fax (408) 486-8001
BBS (408) 486-8051
Web **www.opti.com**

Manufactures PC motherboard chipsets including the Viper series for Pentium systems.

Orchid Technology (A Division of Micronics)

232 E. Warren Ave.
Fremont, CA 94539

Phone (510) 683-0300
Service (800) 767-2443
Sales (510) 651-2300
Fax (510) 651-5612
Support (510) 661-3000
FAXBack (510) 661-3199
BBS (510) 651-6837
Web **www.orchid.com**

Manufactures a line of video and memory board products for IBM and compatible systems. Also produces 32-bit sound cards.

Pacific Data Products

9855 Scranton Rd.
San Diego, CA 92121

Phone (619) 552-0880
Fax (619) 552-0889
BBS (619) 452-6329

Manufactures the Pacific Page XL and PacificPage PE PostScript-compatible enhancement products for HP LaserJet printers.

Packard Bell
31717 La Tienda Dr.
Westlake Village, CA 91362

Phone	(818) 865-1555
Sales	(800) 733-4411
Fax	(818) 865-0379
BBS	(818) 313-8601

Manufactures a popular line of low-cost PC-compatible computer systems.

Palo Alto Design Group
360 University Ave.
Palo Alto, CA 94301

Phone	(415) 327-9444

Manufactures enclosures that accept Intel ATX motherboards.

Panasonic Communications & Systems
2 Panasonic Way
Secaucus, NJ 07094

Phone	(201) 392-6502
Sales	(800) 233-8182
Fax	(201) 392-4858
BBS	(201) 863-7845
Web	www.panasonic.com

Manufactures monitors, optical drive products, floppy drives, printers, and PC-compatible laptop systems.

Panasonic Industrial Co.
2 Panasonic Way
Secaucus, NJ 07094

Sales	(800) 848-3979

Manufactures IC memory cards, batteries (nickel metal hydride), cellular components (planar filters and resonators), optical and floppy disk drives, CD-ROM drives, printer mechanisms, power supplies (custom AC adapters), semiconductors (video digital signal processors, CCD card camera), microphones, speakers, high-resolution color monitors, TV tuners, ceramic receivers, and video camera modules.

Parallel Technologies, Inc.
P.O. Box 3009
Redmond, WA 98073

Phone	(206) 813-8728
Sales	(800) 789-4784
Fax	(206) 813-3730
Web	www.lpt.com/lpt

Manufactures the Parallel Port Information Utility, as well as a line of cables and software supporting the Windows 95 Direct Cable Connection (DCC). It sells a special Universal Cable offering the highest possible speed connection using DCC.

PARTS NOW!, Inc.
810 Stewart St.
Madison, WI 53713

Phone	(608) 276-8688
Fax	(608) 276-9134

Sells a large variety of laser printer parts for HP, Canon, Apple, and other laser printers using Canon engines.

PC & MAC Connection
6 Mill St.
Marlow, NH 03456

Phone	(603) 446-7721
Sales	(800) 800-5555
Fax	(603) 446-7791

Distributes many different hardware and software packages by way of mail order.

PC Magazine
Ziff Communications Co.
One Park Ave.
New York, NY 10016

Phone	(212) 503-3500
Fax	(212) 503-5799

Magazine featuring product reviews and comparisons.

PC Portable Manufacturer Inc.
1431 Potrero Ave. Unit E
Monte, CA 91733

Phone	(818) 444-3585
Sales	(800) 966-7237
Fax	(818) 444-1027

Manufactures a line of portable cases that accept standard Baby-AT and ATX motherboards, which are ideal for building your own portable systems.

PC Power & Cooling, Inc.

5995 Avenida Encinas
Carlsbad, CA 92008

Phone	(619) 931-5700
Sales	(800) 722-6555
Fax	(619) 931-6988
Web	www.pcpowercooling.com

Manufactures a line of high-quality, high-output power supplies and cooling fans for IBM and compatible systems. Known for high-power output and quiet fan operation.

PC Week Magazine

10 Presidents Landing
Medford, MA 02155

Phone	(617) 393-3700
Fax	(617) 393-3859

Weekly magazine featuring industry news and information.

PC World Magazine

375 Chochituate Rd.
Framingham, MA 01701

Phone	(508) 879-0700
Sales	(800) 435-7766
Fax	(508) 620-7739

A monthly magazine featuring product reviews and comparisons.

PCI Special Interest Group

2727 NE Stanton St.
Portland, OR 97212

Phone	(503) 693-6232
Sales	(800) 433-5177
Fax	(503) 693-8344
Web	www.teleport.com/~pc2/pcisigindex.html

Formed in June 1992, the PCI SIG (Peripheral Component Interconnect Special Interest Group) is the industry organization that owns and manages the PCI Local Bus Specification. More than 500 industry-leading companies are active PCI SIG members. The organization is chartered to support new requirements, while maintaining backward compatibility for all PCI revisions; maintain the specification as an easy-to-implement, stable technology; and contribute to the technical longevity of PCI and its establishment as an industry-wide standard.

PC-Kwik Corporation (Acquired by Micro Design International)

3800 S.W. Cedar Hills Blvd. Ste. 260
Beaverton, OR 97005

Phone	(503) 644-5644
Fax	(503) 646-8267

Formerly Multisoft, it manufactures the PC-Kwik Power Pak system performance utilities, Super PC-Kwik disk cache, and WinMaster Windows utility programs.

PCMCIA—Personal Computer Memory Card International Association

2635 N. First St., Ste. 209
San Jose, CA 95314

Phone	(408) 433-2273
Fax	(408) 433-9558
BBS	(408) 433-2270
Web	www.pc-card.com

An independent organization that maintains the PCMCIA bus standard for credit card-sized expansion adapters.

Philips Consumer Electronics

One Philips Dr.
Knoxville, TN 37914

Phone	(423) 521-4316
Fax	(423) 521-4586
Web	www.magvavox.com

Manufactures Magnavox PCs, monitors, and CD-ROM drives.

Phoenix Technologies, Ltd.

2770 De La Cruz Blvd.
Santa Clara, CA 95050

Phone	(408) 654-9000
Fax	(408) 452-1985
BBS	(714) 440-8026
Web	www.ptltd.com

Designs IBM-compatible BIOS software for a number of ISA, EISA, and MCA systems.

Pivar Computing Services, Inc.

165 Arlington Heights Rd.
Buffalo Grove, IL 60089

Phone	(847) 459-6010
Sales	(800) 266-8378
Fax	(847) 459-6095
Web	www.pivar.com

Service company that specializes in data and media conversion.

PKWare, Inc.

9025 N. Deerwood Dr.
Brown Deer, WI 53223

Phone	(414) 354-8699
Fax	(414) 354-8559
BBS	(414) 354-8670

Manufactures the PKZIP, PKUNZIP, and PKLite data compression software. Widely used on BBS systems and by manufacturers for software distribution.

Plextor

4255 Burton Dr.
Santa Clara, CA 95054

Phone	(408) 980-1838
Sales	(800) 886-3935
Fax	(408) 986-1010
BBS	(408) 986-1569
Web	www.plextor.com

Manufactures a line of high-performance CD-ROM drives.

PowerQuest Corporation

1083 N. State St.
Orem, UT 84057

Phone	(801) 226-8977
Sales	(800) 379-2566
Fax	(801) 226-8941
Web	www.powerquest.com

Manufactures the invaluable PartitionMagic program that enables dynamic hard disk partition management. It also makes DriveCopy which allows transferring complete partitions from one drive to another with all applications intact.

Practical Enhanced Logic

22695 Old Canal Rd.
Yorba Linda, CA 92887

Phone	(714) 282-6188
Fax	(714) 282-6199
Sales	(800) 345-7274
Web	www.pelogic.com

Manufactures the Systo Tek CPU fan failure alarm, as well as the SCSI-Link parallel-to-SCSI converter and other high-performance SCSI adapters.

Precision Plastics

340 Roebling Rd.
San Francisco, CA 94080

Phone	(415) 588-4450
Fax	(415) 588-5336

Manufactures a line of PCMCIA card jewel cases, which are great for protecting PC Cards when not in use.

Processor Magazine

P.O. Box 85518
Lincoln, NE 68501

Sales	(800) 247-4880
Fax	(402) 479-2120
BBS	(402) 477-2283
Web	www.peed.com

Publication that offers excellent sources of replacement and repair parts as well as new equipment at wholesale prices.

Programmer's Shop

33 Riverside Dr.
Pembroke, MA 02359

Phone	(617) 740-2510
Sales	(800) 421-8006
Fax	(617) 829-5009

Distributes programming tools and utility software.

Public Software Library

P.O. Box 35705
Houston, TX 77235

Phone	(713) 524-6394
Sales	(800) 242-4775
Fax	(713) 524-6398
BBS	(713) 442-6704
Web	www.pslonline.com

Distributor of high-quality public domain and shareware software. Its library is the most well-researched and tested available. Also offers an excellent newsletter that reviews the software.

Qlogic Corporation

3545 Harbor Blvd.
P.O. Box 5001
Costa Mesa, CA
92628-5001

Phone	(714) 438-2200
Support	(714) 668-5037
Fax	(714) 668-5324
Web	**www.qlc.com**

Manufactures a line of high-end PCI SCSI adapters.

Qualitas, Inc.

7101 Wisconsin Ave. #1024
Bethesda, MD 20814

Phone	(301) 907-6700
Fax	(301) 907-0905
BBS	(301) 907-8030
Web	**www.qualitas.com**

Manufactures the Qualitas Max 8 memory-manager utility programs.

Quantum Corporation

500 McCarthy Blvd.
Milpitas, CA 95035

Phone	(408) 894-4000
Sales	(800) 624-5545
Support	(800) 826-8022
FAXBack	(800) 434-7532
BBS	(800) 894-3214
Web	**www.quantum.com**

Manufactures a line of 5.24 to 2.5-inch hard disk drives. Supplies drives to Apple Computer, Compaq, IBM, Dell, and HP. Also produces DLT and SSD (solid state disk).

Quarterdeck Corporation

13160 Mindanao
Marina Del Ray, CA 90292

Phone	(310) 309-3700
Fax	(310) 314-4218
BBS	(310) 3094-3227
Web	**www.qdeck.com**

Manufactures the popular ProCOMM Plus/Rapid Remote, CleanSweep, Iware Connect, QEMM, HiJaak Pro, Winprobe, Zip It, Fix It, Partition It, and Remove It utility and diagnostics software.

Quarter-Inch Cartridge Drive Standards, Inc. (QIC)

311 E. Carrillo St.
Santa Barbara, CA 93101

Phone	(805) 963-3853
Fax	(805) 962-1541
Web	**www.qic.org**

An independent industry group that sets and maintains Quarter-Inch Cartridge (QIC) tape drive standards for backup and archiving purposes.

Que Corporation

201 W. 103rd St.
Indianapolis, IN 46290

Phone	(317) 581-3500
Sales	(800) 428-5331
Fax	(800) 448-3804
Web	**www.quecorp.com**

Publishes the highest-quality computer software and hardware books in the industry.

Qume Corporation (Acquired by Wyse Technologies)

500 Yosemite Dr.
Milpitas, CA 95035

Phone	(408) 473-1500
Sales	(800) 538-3777

Manufactures a variety of peripherals.

Radio Shack (A Division of Tandy Corporation)

1800 One Tandy Center
Fort Worth, TX 76102

Phone	(817) 390-3011
Fax	(817) 390-2774

Manages the Radio Shack electronics stores, which sell numerous electronics devices, parts, and supplies. Also manufactures a line of PC-compatible computers and computer accessories and supplies.

Ramtron International Corporation

1850 Ramtron Dr.
Colorado Springs, CO 80921

Phone	(719) 481-7000

Manufactures special memory components including EDRAM dynamic RAM products that combine high-speed DRAM with an even faster SRAM cache on a single chip.

Rancho Technology, Inc.

10783 Bell Ct.
Rancho Cucamonga, CA 91730

Phone   (909) 987-3966
Fax   (909) 989-2365
BBS   (909) 980-7699
Web   **www.rancho.com**

Manufactures an extensive line of SCSI products, including host adapters for ISA, EISA, and MCA bus systems; interface; and converters from single-ended to differential, and vice versa.

Rip-Tie Company

P.O. Box 77394
San Francisco, CA 94107

Phone   (415) 543-0170
Fax   (415) 777-9868
Web   **www.riptie.com**

Manufactures a line of velcro cable ties.

Rockwell Semiconductor Systems

4311 Jamboree Rd.
Newport Beach, CA 92660-3095

Phone   (714) 221-4600

Manufactures communications chipsets used in many PC-compatible modems and high-speed data, fax, business audio, voice-mail and mobile-communication applications.

Roland Corporation U.S.

7200 Dominion Circle
Los Angeles, CA 90040-3696

Phone   (213) 685-5141
Fax   (213) 722-0911
Web   **www.rolandus.com**

Manufactures a variety of musical equipment and MIDI interfaces for computers.

Rosenthal Engineering

P.O. Box 1650
San Luis Obispo, CA 93406

Phone   (805) 541-0910
Fax   (805) 541-2676

Manufactures a unique line of system and disk utilities including The Disk Drive Cleaner, Conflict Resolver, and System Workout.

Rupp Technology Corporation

3228 E. Indian School Rd.
Phoenix, AZ 85018

Phone   (602) 941-4789
Sales   (800) 852-7877
Support   (800) 941-5602
Fax   (602) 224-0898

Developer of the DOS Interlink software used in MS- and PC-DOS. Also sells a commercial version called Fastlynx Lite for DOS that offers many enhancements over Interlink. WinLynx is a full windows file transfer and management program. Also makes custom-length parallel transfer cables using a high-speed, 18-wire design supported by virtually all parallel transfer programs.

S3 Inc.

P.O. Box 58058
2770 San Tomas Expressway
Santa Clara, CA 95052-8058

Phone   (408) 980-5400
Fax   (408) 980-5444
BBS   (408) 654-5676
Web   **www.s3.com**

Manufactures a line of very popular high-performance video chipsets.

Safeware Insurance Agency, Inc.

P.O. Box 656
5760 N. High St.
Worthington, OH 43085

Phone   (614) 781-1492
Sales   (800) 848-3469
Fax   (614) 781-0559
Web   **www.safeware-ins.com**

Insurance company that specializes in insurance for computer equipment.

SAMS
201 W. 103rd St.
Indianapolis, IN 46290

Phone   (317) 581-3500
Web   **www.mcp.com**

Publishes technical books on computers and electronic equipment.

Samsung Semiconductor, Inc.
3655 N. First St.
San Jose, CA 95134

Phone   (405) 954-7000

Manufactures memory and semiconductor devices.

Seagate Software Storage Management Group (Formerly Sytron)
37 Skyline Dr.
Lake Mary, FL 32746

Phone   (407) 333-7500
Fax   (407) 333-7730
Sales   (800) 327-2232
Web   **www.sssmg.seagate.com**

Manufactures the SyTOS tape-backup software for DOS and OS/2, the most widely-used tape software in the industry.

Seagate Technology
920 Disc Dr.
Scotts Valley, CA 95066

Phone   (408) 438-6550
Fax   (408) 429-6356
Service   (800) 468-3472

FAXBack   (408) 438-2620
BBS   (408) 438-8771

The largest hard disk manufacturer in the world. Offers the most extensive product line of any disk manufacturer, ranging from low-cost units to the highest-performance, -capacity, and -quality drives available. Also a complete line of backup software including Backup Exec for Windows 95.

Sencore
3200 Sencore Dr.
Sioux Falls, SD 57107

Phone   (605) 339-0100
Sales   (800) 736-2673
Fax   (605) 335-6379

Manufactures a line of computer monitor signal generators and repair equipment.

Service News Magazine
United Publications Inc.
38 Lafayette St.
P.O. Box 995
Yarmouth, ME 04096

Phone   (207) 846-0600
Fax   (207) 846-0657
Web   **www.servicenews.com**

An excellent monthly newspaper for computer service and support personnel featuring articles covering PC service and repair products. Subscriptions are free to those who qualify.

SGS-Thomson Microelectronics, Inc.
55 Old Bedford Rd.
Lincoln, MA 01773

Phone   (617) 259-0300
Fax   (617) 259-4421
Web   **www.st.com**

Manufactures a variety of memory and semiconductor devices.

Sharp Electronics Corporation
Sharp Plaza
Mahwah, NJ 07430-2135

Phone   (201) 529-8200
Fax   (201) 529-8413
Sales   (800) BE SHARP
Web   **www.sharp-usa.com**

Manufactures a wide variety of electronic and computer equipment, including the best LCD monochrome and active matrix color displays and panels, as well as scanners, printers, and complete laptop and notebook systems.

Sharp Microelectronics Group
5700 NW Pacific Rim Blvd.
Camas, WA 98607

Phone   (800) 642-0261

Manufactures memory and semiconductor devices.

Sigma Data
17 Newport Rd.
New London, NH 03257-4565

Phone	(603) 526-6909
Sales	(800) 446-4525
Fax	(603) 526-6915
Web	www.sigmadata.com

Manufacturer/distributor of personal computer add-on and peripheral products specializing in easy-to-install hard drives, processors, and memory upgrades. It offers a unique line of "Quick Easy" upgrades including the QED (Quick Easy Disk) and QEP (Quick Easy Processor). Its product line also includes high-speed, high-capacity drives for a variety of popular portable, laptop, and notebook computers.

Silicon Integrated Systems Corp. (SiS)

240 N. Wolfe Rd.
Sunnyvale, CA 94086

Phone	(408) 730-5600
Fax	(408) 730-5639

Manufactures PC motherboard chipsets.

Silicon Valley Research

6360 San Ignacio Ave.
San Jose, CA 95119

Phone	(415) 962-3000
Fax	(415) 962-3001
Web	www.svri.com

Manufactures a complete line of IDE interface adapters, including a unique model that supports 16-bit IDE (ATA) drives on PC and XT systems (8-bit ISA bus) and models, including floppy drive support as well as serial and parallel ports.

Simple Technology

3001 Daimler St.
Santa Ana, CA 92705

Phone	(714) 476-1180
Sales	(800) 854-3900
Fax	(714) 476-1209
Web	www.simpletech.com

Manufactures the SIMMswitch, which replaces the soldered resistors on a SIMM, allowing it to be easily reconfigured. It also sells SIMMs with the switch already installed.

SL Waber

520 Fellowship Rd.
Mt. Laurel, NJ 08054

Phone	(690) 866-888

Manufactures a complete line of power protection equipment for PC computers.

Smart Cable Inc.

13625 NE 126th Place
Ste. 400
Kirkland, WA 98034

Phone	(206) 823-2273
Sales	(800) 752-6526
Fax	(206) 821-3961

Manufactures the SmartCable universal serial RS-232 cable.

Softbank COMDEX, Inc.

300 First Ave.
Needham, MA 02194-2722

Phone	(617) 449-6600
Fax	(617) 449-6953

Producer of the world's leading computer trade shows.

Softkey International, Inc.

1 Anthenaeum St.
Cambridge, MA 02142

Phone	(617) 494-1200
Sales	(800) 227-5609
Fax	(617) 494-5898
BBS	(423) 670-2023
Web	www.softkey.com

Manufactures WordStar 7, and distributes more than 500 other software programs including Compton's Encyclopedia and various educational titles.

SofTouch Systems, Inc.

1300 S. Meridian Ste. 600
Oklahoma City, OK 73108-1751

Phone	(405) 947-8080
Fax	(405) 947-8169
Web	www.softouch.com

Manufactures GammaTech Utilities for OS/2 that can undelete and recover files running under OS/2 even on an OS/2 HPFS partition, and UniMaint, a desktop repair and recovery program.

Software Testing Lab (STL)

P.O. Box 19771
Indianapolis, IN 46219

Phone	(317) 974-0805
Fax	(317) 974-0699
E-Mail	murney@ai2a.net

Sola Heavy Duty Electric

1717 Busse Rd.
Elk Grove, IL 60007

Phone	(708) 439-2800
Sales	(800) 289-7652
Fax	(800) 626-6299

Manufactures a line of computer power-protection devices.

Sonera Technologies

P.O. Box 565
Rumson, NJ 07760

Phone	(908) 747-6886
Sales	(800) 932-6323
Fax	(908) 747-4523
Web	www.displaymate.com

Manufactures the DisplayMate video display utility and diagnostic program. DisplayMate exercises, troubleshoots, and diagnoses video display adapter and monitor problems.

Sony Corporation of America

Sony Drive
Park Ridge, NJ 07656

Phone	(408) 894-0555
Fax	(408) 955-5171
BBS	(408) 955-5107
Web	www.sony.com

Manufactures all types of high-quality electronic and computer equipment, including displays and magnetic- and optical-storage devices.

SOYO Tek Inc.

1209 John Reed Ct.
City of Industry, CA 91745

Phone	(818) 330-1712
Fax	(818) 968-4164
Web	www.soyo.com

One of the top 10 largest Taiwan-based motherboard manufacturers.

Specialized Products Company

3131 Premier Dr.
Irving, TX 75063

Phone	(214) 550-1923
Sales	(800) 866-5353
Fax	(800) 234-8286
Web	www.specializedproducts.com

Distributes a variety of tools and test equipment.

Sprague Magnetics, Inc.

12806 Bradley Ave.
Sylmar CA 91342

Phone	(818) 364-1800
Fax	(818) 364-1810
Sales	(800) 553-8712
Web	www.sprague-magnetics.com

Distributes a unique and interesting magnetic developer fluid that can be used to view sectors and tracks on a magnetic disk or tape. Also repairs computer tape drives.

Stac Incorporated

12636 High Bluff Dr.
San Diego, CA 92130

Phone	(619) 794-4300
Sales	(800) 522-7822
Fax	(619) 794-3715
BBS	(619) 794-3711

Manufactures the Stacker real-time data-compression adapter and software for OS/2 and DOS/Windows. They also have new products which include Reach Out Remote Access/Control software and Replica Server disaster recovery software for NetWare and CD quick share.

Standard Microsystems Corporation

80 Arkay Dr.
Hauppauge, NY 11788

Phone	(516) 273-3100
Sales	(800) SMC-4YOU
Fax	(516) 273-1803
FAXBack	(800) 762-8329
BBS	(516) 434-3162
Web	www.smc.com

Manufactures Ethernet and ARCnet network adapters, as well as a complete line of Super I/O chipsets, hubs, and switches.

Star Micronics America, Inc.

70-D Ethel Rd. West
Piscataway, NJ 08854

Phone	(908) 572-5550
Fax	(908) 572-3129
BBS	(908) 572-5010
Web	www.starmicronics.com

Manufactures a line of low-cost printers, receipt printers, and visual card systems.

STB Systems, Inc.

1651 N. Glenville
Richardson, TX
75085-0957

Phone	(214) 234-8750
Fax	(214) 234-1306
BBS	(214) 437-9615
Web	www.stb.com

Manufactures various adapter boards, and specializes in a line of high-resolution VGA video adapters.

Storage Dimensions, Inc.

1656 McCarthy Blvd.
Milpitas, CA 95035

Phone	(408) 954-0710
Fax	(408) 944-1200
BBS	(408) 944-1221
Web	www.storagedimensions.com

Manufactures high-performance disk and tape storage solutions for open system environments. Distributes Maxtor hard disk and optical drives as complete subsystems.

Sun Moon Star

1941 Ringwood Ave.
San Jose, CA 95131

Phone	(408) 452-7811

Manufactures CD-ROM, multimedia kits, and power supplies for PC compatibles.

Supermicro Computer, Inc.

2051 Junction Ave.
San Jose, CA 95131

Phone	(408) 895-2000
Sales	(800) 943-8818
Fax	(408) 895-2008
BBS	(408) 895-2022
Web	www.supermicro.com

Manufactures a high-quality line of Pentium class motherboards.

Superpower Supply, Inc.

990 Norcross Industrial Ct.
Norcross, GA 30071

Phone	(800) 736-0007
Fax	(310) 906-2621

Manufactures a line of PC-compatible power supplies and cases. They also distribute PC networking components.

Symantec Corporation

175 W. Broadway
Eugene, OR 97401

Phone	(800) 441-7234
Fax	(541) 334-7400
BBS	(541) 484-6669
Web	www.symantec.com

Manufactures a line of utility and applications software featuring the Norton Utilities for IBM and Apple systems and PC Tools. Also distributes Winfax Pro.

SyQuest Technology

47071 Bayside Pkwy.
Fremont, CA 94538

Phone	(510) 226-4000
Sales	(800) 245-2278
Support	(800) 249-2440
Fax	(510) 226-4102
BBS	(510) 656-0473
Web	www.syquest.com

Manufactures removable-cartridge hard disk drives.

Tadiran

2 Seaziew
Port Washington, NY 11050

Phone	(516) 625-8488
Sales	(800) 537-1368
Fax	(516) 621-4517
Web	www.echo-on.net\net\mob\tadiran.htm

Manufactures a variety of batteries for computer applications.

Tandy Corporation

1800 One Tandy Center
Fort Worth, TX 76102

Phone (817) 390-3700
Fax (817) 390-2647

Manufactures a line of IBM-compatible systems, peripherals, and accessories.

Tatung Company of America, Inc.

2850 El Presidio St.
Long Beach, CA 90810

Phone (310) 637-2105
Sales (800) 827-2850
Fax (310) 637-8484

Manufactures monitors and complete compatible systems.

TDK Corporation of America

12 Harbor Park Dr.
Port Washington, NY 11050

Phone (516) 625-0100
Fax (516) 625-0651

Manufactures a line of magnetic and optical media, including disk and tape cartridges. Also produces modems, ICs, semiconductors, and power supply products.

Teac America, Inc.

7733 Telegraph Rd.
Montebello, CA 90640

Phone (213) 726-0303
Fax (213) 727-7656
BBS (213) 727-7660
FAXBack (213) 727-7629

Manufactures a line of floppy and tape drives, including a unit that combines both 3 1/2-inch and 5 1/4-inch drives in one half-height package.

Tech Data Corporation

5350 Tech Data Dr.
Clearwater, FL 34620

Phone (813) 539-7429
Sales (800) 237-8931
Fax (813) 538-7876
BBS (813) 538-7090

Distributes computer equipment and supplies.

Tech Spray Inc.

P.O. Box 949
Amarillo, TX 79105-0949

Phone (806) 372-8523
Fax (806) 372-8750

Manufactures a complete line of computer and electronic cleaning chemicals and products.

Tecmar Technologies, Inc.

1900 Pike Rd.
Longmont, CO 80501

Phone (303) 682-3700
Sales (800) 4-BACKUP
Support (800) 344-4463
Service (800) 992-9916
Fax (303) 776-7706
Web **www.tecmar.com**

Manufactures Wangtech, WangDAT, and Proline tape back up drives.

Tekram Technologies

11500 Metric Blvd. Ste. 190
Austin, TX 78758

Phone (512) 833-6550
Fax (512) 833-7276
Web **www.tekram.com**

Manufactures a complete line of caching and non-caching disk controllers, PCI motherboards, multimedia products, CD-ROM servers, printer servers, and video cards. Specializes in IDE and SCSI adapters that are fast and flexible.

Test and Measurement World Magazine

275 Washington St.
Newton, MA 02158-1611

Phone (617) 558-4671
Fax (617) 558-4470
E-Mail **tmw@cahneis.com**

A magazine for quality control and testing in the electronics industry. Free for those who qualify.

Texas Instruments, Inc.

Box 14149
12501 Research Blvd.
Austin, TX 78714-9149

Phone (512) 250-7111
Sales (800) TI-TEXAS

Manufactures memory and other semiconductor devices.

The Learning Curve
P.O. Box 1797
Dunedin, FL 34697

Sales   (800) 736-2295

Manufactures a disk diagnostic program called Drive Wizard on the Wire.

Thermalloy Inc.
2021 W. Valley View Ln.
P.O. Box 810839
Dallas, TX 75381-0839

Phone   (214) 243-4321
Fax   (214) 241-4656
Web   www.thermalloy.com

Manufactures a line of excellent CPU heat sink products, including versions with built-in fan modules, DC-DC converters, and other thermal management solutions.

THYNX
619 Alexander Rd.
Princeton, NJ 08540

Phone   (609) 514-1600
Fax   (609) 514-1818
Web   www.Thynx.com

Distributes and publishes software on CD-ROM disks.

Toshiba America, Inc.
9740 Irvine Blvd.
Irvine, CA 92718

Phone   (714) 583-3926
Sales   (800) 999-4823
Fax   (800) 950-4373
BBS   (714) 837-2116

Manufactures a complete line of 5 1/4- and 3 1/2-inch floppy and hard disk drives, CD-ROM drives, display products, printers, and a popular line of laptop and notebook IBM-compatible systems.

TouchStone Software Corporation
2124 Main St.
Huntington Beach, CA 92648

Phone   (714) 969-7746
Sales   (800) 531-0450
Fax   (714) 960-1886
Web   www.checkit.com

Manufactures the CheckIt user level and CheckIt Pro Deluxe high-end PC diagnostics and troubleshooting programs. CheckIt Diagnostic Kit also includes CheckIt IV, a self-booting portable diagnostic.

Trace Research and Development Center
University of Wisconsin
S-151 Waisman Center
1500 Highland Ave.
Madison, WI 53705

Phone   (608) 263-2309
TDD   (608) 263-5408
E-Mail   info@trace.wisc.edu

The Trace Center is an interdisciplinary research, development, and resource center on technology and disability.

Traveling Software, Inc.
18702 N. Creek Pkwy.
Bothell, WA 98011

Phone   (206) 483-8088
Sales   (800) 662-2652
Fax   (206) 485-6786
BBS   (206) 485-1736
Web   www.travsoft.com

Manufactures the LapLink file-transfer program for PC and Mac systems as well as several other utility programs.

Trident Microsystems
189 N. Bernado Ave.
Mountain View, CA 94043

Phone   (415) 691-9211
Fax   (415) 691-9260
BBS   (415) 961-1016
Web   www.trid.com

Manufactures a line of high-end video chipsets and multimedia video adapters.

TriniTech, Inc.
1430 Court St., Ste. 3
Clearwater, FL 34616

Phone   (813) 442-8882
Sales   (800) 909-3424
Fax   (813) 442-5897

Manufactures a complete line of PC diagnostics products including the OmniPOST, IRQuest Plus, and PC Power Sentry diagnostics cards, and Expertrace diagnostics software.

Tripp Lite Manufacturing

500 N. Orleans
Chicago, IL 60610

Phone (312) 329-1777
Fax (312) 644-6505
Web www.tripplite.com

Manufactures a complete line of computer power-protection devices.

Tseng Labs, Inc.

6 Terry Dr.
Newtown, PA 18940

Phone (215) 968-0502
Fax (215) 860-7713
BBS (215) 579-7536
Web www.tseng.com

Manufactures video controller chipsets, BIOS, and board design for OEMs.

TTI Technologies

5124 Ralston
Ventura, CA 93003

Sales (800) 541-1943
Fax (805) 650-6515
Web www.ttiteck.com

Distributes AMI, Award, Phoenix MR BIOS upgrades, and microid research.

Twinhead Corporation

1537 Centre Pointe Dr.
Milpitas, CA 95035

Phone (408) 945-0808
Sales (800) 552-8946
Web www.twinhead.com

Manufactures notebook, subnotebook, and desktop computer systems.

Tyan Computer Corporation

1753 S. Main St.
Milpitas, CA 95035

Phone (408) 956-8000
Fax (408) 956-8044
Support (408) 935-7884
BBS (408) 956-8171
Web www.tyan.com

Manufactures an excellent line of PC motherboards in ATX and Baby-AT form factors.

U.S. Robotics, Inc. (Merged with 3Com)

8100 N. McCormick Blvd.
Skokie, IL 60076

Phone (847) 982-5010
Sales (800) 550-7800
Fax (847) 933-5300
FAXBack (800) 762-6163
BBS (847) 982-5092
Web www.usr.com

Manufactures a complete line of modems and ISDN communications products.

Ultra-X, Inc.

1765 Scott Blvd. Ste. 101
Santa Clara, CA 95050

Phone (408) 261-7090
Sales (800) 722-3789
Fax (408) 261-7077
Web www.ultrax.com

Manufactures the excellent QuickPost PC, QuickPost PCIS/2, QuickPost PRO, and Racer II diagnostic cards, as well as the Quicktech PRO and Diagnostic Reference diagnostic software packages. The Racer II is one of the most complete troubleshooting hardware cards on the market today.

Underwriters Laboratories, Inc.

Corporate Headquarters
333 Pfingsten Rd.
Northbrook, IL
60062-2096

Phone (847) 727-8800
Fax (847) 272-8129

The leading third-party product safety certification organization in the United States, and the largest in North America. Established in 1894.

Unicomp, Inc.

2501 W. Fifth St.
Santa Ana, CA 92703

Phone (800) 359-5092
Fax (714) 571-1909

Distributes new and refurbished printer repair parts for all types of printers.

UNISYS

Township Line and Union Meeting Rd.
Blue Bell, PA 19424

Phone (800) 448-1424
Fax (716) 742-6671

Manufactures PC-compatible systems that are part of the government Desktop IV contract. Also offers a complete line of information management software solutions.

V Communications, Inc.

4320 Stevens Creek Blvd. #120
San Jose, CA 95129

Phone   (408) 296-4224
Fax   (408) 296-4441
Web   **www.v-com.com**

Manufactures the Sourcer disassembler and other programming tools.

Varta Batteries, Inc.

300 Executive Blvd.
Elmsford, NY 10523

Phone   (914) 592-2500
Fax   (914) 592-2667

Manufactures a complete line of computer batteries.

Verbatim Corporation

1200 WT Harris Blvd.
Charlotte, NC 28262

Phone   (704) 547-6500

Manufactures a line of storage media, including optical and magnetic disks and tapes.

VESA—Video Electronic Standards Association

2150 N. First St. Ste. 440
San Jose, CA 95131-2029

Phone   (408) 435-0333
Fax   (408) 435-8225
Web   **www.vesa.org**

An organization of manufacturers dedicated to setting and maintaining video display, adapter, and bus standards. It has created the VESA video standards as well as the VESA Video Local Bus (VL-Bus) standard.

VIA Technologies, Inc.

5020 Brandin Ct.
Fremont, CA 94538

Phone   (510) 683-3300
Fax   (510) 683-3301

Manufactures PC motherboard chipsets.

ViewSonic

20480 Business Pkwy.
Walnut, CA 91789

Phone   (909) 869-7976
Fax   (909) 869-7958
BBS   (909) 444-5219

Manufactures a line of high-quality monitors and displays with Plug and Play as well as Energy Star compliance. Also produces network-level power backup systems.

Visiflex Seels

16 E. Lafayette St.
Hackensack, NJ 07601

Phone   (201) 487-8080

Manufactures form-fitting clear keyboard covers and other computer accessories.

VLSI Technology, Inc.

1109 McKay Dr.
San Jose, CA 95131

Phone   (408)434-3000

Manufactures chipsets and circuits for PC-compatible motherboards and adapters.

Volpe, Hank

P.O. Box 43214
Baltimore, MD 21236

Phone   (410) 256-5767
BBS   (410) 256-3631
E-Mail **modem.doctor@ghawk.com**

Manufactures the Modem Doctor Version 6 serial port and modem diagnostics program.

Walling Company

4401 Juniper St.
Tempe, AZ 85282

Phone/Fax
(602) 838-1277

Manufactures the DataRase EPROM eraser, which can erase as many as four EPROM chips simultaneously using ultraviolet light.

Wang Laboratories, Inc.

600 Technology Park Dr.
Billerica, MA 01821-4130

Phone   (508) 656-1550
Sales   (800) 225-0654

Manufactures a variety of PC-compatible systems, including some with MCA bus slots.

Warshawski/Whitney & Co.

1104 S. State St.
Chicago, IL 60605

Phone (312) 431-6100
Fax (312) 431-5625
E-Mail **70007.1524@ compuserve.com**

Distributes an enormous collection of bargain-priced tools and equipment. Its products are primarily for automotive applications, but many of the tools have universal uses.

Washburn & Co.

3800 Monroe Ave.
Pittsford, NY 14534

Phone (716) 385-5200
Sales (800) 836-8026
Fax (716) 381-7549
E-Mail **70305.1211@ compuserve.com**

The largest distributor of AMI BIOS and AMI motherboard products, known for providing very high-end technical information and support.

Watergate Software

2000 Powell St. Ste. 1200
Emeryville, CA 94608

Phone (510) 596-1770
Fax (510) 653-4784
Web **www.ws.com**

Manufactures the excellent PC Doctor diagnostic program for PC troubleshooting and repair.

Wave Tech

9145 Balboa Ave.
San Diego, CA 92123

Phone (619) 279-2200
Sales (800) 854-2708
Fax (619) 627-0132
BBS (619) 278-5034
Web **www.wavetech. com**

Manufactures diagnostics and test equipment.

Weitek Corporation

2801 Orchard Pkwy.
San Jose, CA 95134

Phone (408) 526-0300
Fax (408) 577-1066
BBS (408) 522-7512
Web **www.weitek.com**

Manufactures high-performance math coprocessor chips.

Western Digital Corporation

8105 Irvine Center Dr.
Irvine, CA 92718

Phone (714) 932-5000
Sales (800) 832-4778
Fax (714) 932-4012
FAXBack (714) 932-4300
BBS (714) 753-1068
Web **www.wdc.com**

Manufactures many products, including IDE and SCSI hard drives; SCSI and ESDI adapters for ISA, EISA, and MCA bus systems; and Ethernet, Token Ring, and Paradise video adapters. Supplies IBM with IDE and SCSI drives for PS/2 systems.

Winbond (Formerly Symphony Laboratories)

2730 Orchard Pkwy.
San Jose, CA 95134

Phone (408) 943-6666
Fax (408) 474-1600
Web **www.winbond. com.tw**

Manufactures PC motherboard chipsets.

Windsor Technologies, Inc.

130 Alto St.
San Rafael, CA 94901

Phone (415) 456-2200
Fax (415) 456-2244

Manufactures PC Technician, an excellent high-end technician level PC diagnostics and troubleshooting program.

WordPerfect (A Division of Corel Software)

1555 N. Technology Way
Orem, UT 84057

Phone (801) 225-5000
Sales (800) 453-1267
Fax (801) 229-1566
BBS (801) 225-4414

Manufactures the popular WordPerfect word processing program. Acquired by Novell, then sold to Corel.

Wyse Technology

3471 N. 1st St.
San Jose, CA 95134

Phone	(408) 473-1200
Sales	(800) 438-9973
Fax	(408) 473-1972
BBS	(408) 922-4400
Web	www.wyse.com

Manufactures terminals and monitors.

Xerox Corporation

Xerox Square
Rochester, NY 14644

Phone	(203) 968-3000
Fax	(203) 968-3368

Manufactures the Ventura desktop publishing software, as well as an extensive line of computer equipment, copiers, and printers.

Xircom

2300 Corporate Center Dr.
Thousand Oaks, CA 91320

Phone	(805) 376-9300
Sales	(800) 874-7875
Support	(805) 376-9200
Fax	(805) 376-9311
BBS	(805) 376-9130
Web	www.xircom.com

Manufactures external Token Ring and Ethernet adapters that attach to a parallel port, and PCMCIA cards for laptops.

Y-E Data America, Inc.

5824 Peachtree Corners E.
Ste. A
Norcross, GA 30092

Phone	(404) 446-8655
Fax	(404) 291-4203
E-Mail	yea_hq@usa.pipeline.com

Manufactures a line of floppy disk drives, tape drives, and printers. Supplied 5 1/4-inch floppy drives to IBM for use in XT, AT, and PS/2 systems.

Zenith Data Systems

2150 E. Lake Cook Rd.
Buffalo Grove, IL 60089

Phone	(847) 808-5000
Sales	(800) 553-0331
Fax	(800) 472-7211
Web	www.zds.com

Manufactures a line of IBM-compatible systems.

Zeos International, Ltd. (Purchased by Micron Electronics)

900 E. Karcher Rd.
Napa, ID 83687

Phone	(208) 893-3434
Sales	(800) 438-3343
Fax	(208) 893-3424
BBS	(208) 893-8982
Web	www.mei.micron.com

Manufactures a line of good, low-cost, PC-compatible ISA and EISA bus systems sold by way of mail order.

Appendix B
Glossary

This Glossary contains computer and electronics terms that are applicable to the subject matter in this book. This Glossary is meant to be as comprehensive as possible on the subject of upgrading or repairing PCs. Many terms correspond to the latest technology in disk interfaces, modems, video and display equipment, and many standards that govern the PC industry. Although a glossary is a resource not designed to be read from beginning to end, you should find that scanning through this one is interesting, if not enlightening, with respect to some of the newer PC technology.

The computer industry is filled with acronyms used as shorthand for a number of terms. This Glossary defines many acronyms, as well as the term on which the acronym is based. The definition of an acronym usually is included under the acronym. For example, *Video Graphics Array* is defined under the acronym *VGA* rather than under *Video Graphics Array*. This organization makes it easier to look up a term—IDE, for example—even if you do not know in advance what it stands for (Integrated Drive Electronics).

For additional reference, Que's *Computer User's Dictionary* is a comprehensive, general-purpose computer dictionary of computer terminology.

The Web sites can also help you with terms that are not included in this chapter:

On the Web

http://zeppo.cnet.com/Resources/Info/Glossary/

http://www-edlab.ucdavis.edu/ed180/hardwarepracticum.html

10Base2   IEEE standard for baseband Ethernet at 10Mbps over RG-58 coaxial cable to a maximum distance of 185 meters. Also known as *Thin Ethernet*.

10Base5   IEEE standard for baseband Ethernet at 10Mbps over thick coaxial cable to a maximum distance of 500 meters. Also known as *Thick Ethernet*.

10BaseT   A 10Mbps CSMA/CD Ethernet local area network that works on Category 3 or better twisted-pair wiring that is very similar to standard telephone cabling. The 10BaseT Ethernet local area networks work on a "star" configuration in which the wire from each workstation routes directly to a 10BaseT hub. Hubs may be joined together.

100BaseT   A 100Mbps CSMA/CD Ethernet local area network that works on Category 5 twisted-pair wiring. The 100BaseT Ethernet local area networks work on a "star" configuration in which the wire from each workstation routes directly to a central 100BaseT hub. This is the new standard for 100Mbps Ethernet.

100BaseVG The joint Hewlett Packard-AT&T proposal for Fast Ethernet running at 100 million bits per second. It uses four pairs of Category 5 cable, using the 10BaseT twisted-pair wiring scheme to transmit or receive. The 100BaseVG splits the signal across the four wire pairs at 25MHz each. This standard has not found favor with corporations and has been almost totally replaced by 100BaseT.

80286 An Intel microprocessor with 16-bit registers, a 16-bit data bus, and a 24-bit address bus. Can operate in real and protected virtual modes.

80287 An Intel math coprocessor designed to perform floating-point math with much greater speed and precision than the main CPU. The 80287 can be installed in most 286- and some 386DX-based systems, and it adds more than 50 new instructions to what is available in the primary CPU alone.

80386 See *80386DX*.

80386DX An Intel microprocessor with 32-bit registers, a 32-bit data bus, and a 32-bit address bus. This processor can operate in real, protected virtual, and virtual real modes.

80386SX An Intel microprocessor with 32-bit registers, a 16-bit data bus, and a 24-bit address bus. This processor, designed as a low-cost version of the 386DX, can operate in real, protected virtual, and virtual real modes.

80387 An Intel math coprocessor designed to perform floating-point math with much greater speed and precision than the main CPU. The 80387 can be installed in most 386DX-based systems, and it adds more than 50 new instructions to what is available in the primary CPU alone.

80486 See *80486DX*.

80486DX An Intel microprocessor with 32-bit registers, a 32-bit data bus, and a 32-bit address bus. The 486DX has a built-in cache controller with 8K of cache memory as well as a built-in math coprocessor equivalent to a 387DX. The 486DX can operate in real, protected virtual, and virtual real modes.

80486DX2 A version of the 486DX with an internal clock doubling circuit that causes the chip to run at twice the motherboard clock speed. If the motherboard clock is 33MHz, the DX2 chip will run at 66MHz. The DX2 designation applies to chips sold through the OEM market, while a retail version of the DX2 is sold as an overdrive processor.

80486DX4 A version of the 486DX with an internal clock-tripling circuit that causes the chip to run at three times the motherboard clock speed. If the motherboard clock is 33.33MHz, the DX4 chip will run at 100MHz.

80486SX An Intel microprocessor with 32-bit registers, a 32-bit data bus, and a 32-bit address bus. The 486SX is the same as the 486DX except that it lacks the built-in math coprocessor function and was designed as a low-cost version of the 486DX. The 486SX can operate in real, protected virtual, and virtual real modes. Many 80486SX chips were 80486DX chips whose floating-point processor failed Intel's tests.

8086 An Intel microprocessor with 16-bit registers, a 16-bit data bus, and a 20-bit address bus. This processor can operate only in real mode.

8087 An Intel math coprocessor designed to perform floating-point math with much greater speed and precision than the main CPU. The 8087 can be installed in most 8086- and 8088-based systems and adds more than 50 new instructions to what is available in the primary CPU alone.

8088 An Intel microprocessor with 16-bit registers, an 8-bit data bus, and a 20-bit address bus. This processor can operate only in real mode and was designed as a low-cost version of the 8086.

8514/A An analog video display adapter from IBM for the PS/2 line of personal computers. Compared to previous display adapters such as EGA and VGA, it provides a high resolution of 1,024×768 pixels with as many as 256 colors or 64 shades of gray. It provides a video coprocessor that performs two-dimensional graphics functions internally, thus relieving the CPU of graphics tasks. It uses an interlaced monitor and scans every other line whenever the screen is refreshed.

abend Short for *abnormal end*. Used when the execution of a program or task is terminated unexpectedly because of a bug or crash.

AC Alternating current. The frequency is measured in cycles per seconds (cps) or hertz (Hz). The standard value running through a wall outlet is 120 volts at 60Hz through a fuse or circuit breaker that usually can handle about 20 amps.

accelerator board An add-in board replacing the computer's CPU with circuitry that enables the system to run faster.

access time The time that elapses from the instant information is requested to the point that delivery is completed. Usually described in nanoseconds (ns) for memory chips. The IBM PC requires memory chips with an access time of 200 ns, and the AT requires 150 ns chips. For hard disk drives, access time is described in milliseconds (ms). Most manufacturers rate average access time on a hard disk as the time required for a seek across one-third of the total number of cylinders plus one-half of the time for a single revolution of the disk platters (latency).

accumulator A register (temporary storage) where the result of an operation is formed.

active high Designates a digital signal that has to go to a high value to produce an effect. Synonymous with *positive true*.

active low Designates a digital signal that has to go to a low value to produce an effect. Synonymous with *negative true*.

actuator The device that moves a disk drive's read/write heads across the platter surfaces. Also known as an *access mechanism*.

adapter The device that serves as an interface between the system unit and the devices attached to it. Used by IBM to be synonymous with circuit board, circuit card, or card.

adapter description files (ADF) Refers to the setup, configuration files, and drivers necessary to install an adapter card, such as a network adapter card.

address bus One or more electrical conductors used to carry the binary-coded address from the microprocessor throughout the rest of the system.

address Refers to where a particular piece of data or other information is found in the computer. Also can refer to the location of a set of instructions.

aliasing Undesirable visual effects (sometimes called *artifacts*) in computer-generated images caused by inadequate sampling techniques. The most common effect is jagged edges along diagonal or curved object boundaries. See *dithering*.

alphanumeric characters A character set that contains only letters (A–Z) and digits (0–9). Other characters, such as punctuation marks, also may be allowed.

ampere The basic unit for measuring electrical current. Also called *amp*.

analog loopback A modem self-test in which data from the keyboard is sent to the modem's transmitter, modulated into analog form, looped back to the receiver, demodulated into digital form, and returned to the screen for verification.

analog signals Continuously variable signals in which the slightest change may be significant. Analog circuits are more subject to distortion and noise but are capable of handling complex signals with relatively simple circuitry. An alternative to analog is *digital*, in which signals are in only one of two states.

analog video A video signal represented by an infinite number of smooth gradations between given video levels. By contrast, a digital video signal assigns a finite set of levels. See also *digital video*.

analog The representation of numerical values by physical variables such as voltage, current, and so on; continuously variable quantities whose values correspond to the quantitative magnitude of the variables.

analog-to-digital converter An electronic device that converts analog signals to digital form.

AND gate A logic gate in which the output is 1 only if all inputs are 1.

AND A logic operator having the property that if P is a statement, Q is a statement, R is a statement, ..., then the AND of P, Q, R, ... is true if all statements are true and is false if any statement is false.

animation The process of displaying a sequential series of still images to achieve the effect of continuous motion.

ANSI American National Standards Institute. A non-governmental organization founded in 1918 to propose, modify, approve, and publish data processing standards for voluntary use in the United States. Also, the U.S. representative to the International

Standards Organization (ISO) in Paris and the International Electrotechnical Commission (IEC). For more information, see the vendor list. Contact ANSI, 1430 Broadway, New York, NY 10018.

answer mode A state in which the modem transmits at the predefined high frequency of the communications channel and receives at the low frequency. The transmit/receive frequencies are the reverse of the calling modem, which is in originate mode.

anti-aliasing Software adjustment to make diagonal or curved lines appear smooth and continuous in computer-generated images. See also *aliasing*.

APA All points addressable. A mode in which all points of a displayable image can be controlled by the user or a program.

API Application Program Interface. A system call (routine) that gives programmers access to the services provided by the operating system. In IBM-compatible systems, the ROM BIOS and DOS together present an API that a programmer can use to control the system's hardware.

APM Advanced Power Management. A specification sponsored by Intel and Microsoft originally proposed to extend the life of batteries in battery-powered computers. The APM enables application programs, the system BIOS, and the hardware to work together to reduce power consumption. An APM-compliant BIOS provides built-in power management services to the operating system. The application software communicates power-saving data via predefined APM interfaces.

arbitration A method by which multiple devices attached to a single bus can bid or arbitrate to get control of that bus.

archive bit The bit in a file's attribute byte that sets the archive attribute. Tells whether the file has been changed since it last was backed up.

archive medium A storage medium (floppy disk, tape cartridge, or removable cartridge) to hold files that need not be accessible instantly.

ARCnet Attached Resource Computer Network. A baseband, token-passing local area network technology offering a flexible bus/star topology for connecting personal computers. Operating at 2.5Mbit/sec, it is one of the oldest LAN systems and was popular in low-cost networks. Originally developed by John Murphy of Datapoint Corporation, although ARCnet interface cards are available from a variety of vendors.

areal density A calculation of the bit density (bits per inch, or BPI) multiplied by the track density (tracks per inch, or TPI), which results in a figure indicating how many bits per square inch are present on the disk surface.

ARQ Automatic repeat request. A general term for error-control protocols that feature error detection and automatic retransmission of defective blocks of data.

ASCII character A 1-byte character from the ASCII character set, including alphabetic and numeric characters, punctuation symbols, and various graphics characters.

ASCII American Standard Code for Information Interchange. A standard 7-bit code created in 1965 by Robert W. Bemer to achieve compatibility among various types of data processing equipment. The standard ASCII character set consists of 128 decimal numbers, ranging from 0 through 127, assigned to letters, numbers, punctuation marks, and the most common special characters. In 1981, IBM introduced the extended ASCII character set with the IBM PC, extending the code to 8 bits and adding characters from 128 through 255 to represent additional special mathematical, graphical, and foreign characters.

ASME American Society of Mechanical Engineers (**http://www.asme.org/**). ASME International has nearly 600 codes and standards in print, and its many committees involve more than 3,000 individuals, mostly engineers but not necessarily members of the society. The standards are used in more than 90 countries throughout the world.

aspect ratio The measurement of a film or television viewing area in terms of relative height and width. The aspect ratio of most modern motion pictures varies from 3:5 to as large as 3:7, which creates a problem when a wide-format motion picture is transferred to the more square-shaped television screen, which has an aspect ratio of 3:4.

assemble To translate a program expressed in an assembler language into a computer machine language.

assembler language A computer-oriented language whose instructions are usually in one-to-one correspondence with machine language instructions.

asymmetrical modulation A duplex transmission technique that splits the communications channel into one high-speed channel and one slower channel. During a call under asymmetrical modulation, the modem with the greatest amount of data to transmit is allocated the high-speed channel. The modem with less data is allocated the slow, or back, channel (450 bps). The modems dynamically reverse the channels during a call if the volume of data transfer changes.

asynchronous communication Data transmission in which the length of time between transmitted characters may vary. Timing is dependent on the actual time for the transfer to take place, as opposed to synchronous communication, which is timed rigidly by an external clock signal. Because the receiving modem must be signaled when the data bits of a character begin and end, start and stop bits are added to each character.

ATA The AT Attachment interface. An IDE disk interface standard introduced in March 1989 that defines a compatible register set and a 40-pin connector and its associated signals. See also *IDE*.

ATA-2 The second-generation AT Attachment interface specification. This version defines faster transfer modes and Logical Block Addressing schemes to allow high-performance large-capacity drives. Also called *Fast ATA*, *Fast ATA-2*, and *Enhanced IDE (EIDE)*.

ATAPI The AT Attachment Packet Interface. A specification that defines device-side characteristics for an IDE-connected peripheral, such as CD-ROM or tape drives. ATAPI is essentially an adaptation of the SCSI command set to the IDE interface.

ATM Asynchronous Transfer Mode. A high bandwidth, low-delay, packet-like switching and multiplexing technique. Usable capacity is segmented into fixed-size cells, consisting of header and information fields allocated to services on demand. ATM will be the basis for the future broadband network, in view of its flexibility and suitability for both transmission and switching.

attribute byte A byte of information, held in the directory entry of any file, that describes various attributes of the file, such as whether it is read-only or if it has been backed up since it last was changed. Attributes can be set by the DOS ATTRIB command.

audio frequencies Frequencies that can be heard by the human ear (approximately 20 to 20,000Hz).

audio A signal that can be heard, such as through the speaker of the PC. Many PC diagnostics tests use both visual (on-screen) codes and audio signals.

auto answer A setting in modems enabling them to answer incoming calls over the phone lines automatically.

auto dial A feature in modems enabling them to dial phone numbers without human intervention.

AUTOEXEC.BAT A special batch file that DOS executes at startup. Contains any number of DOS commands that are executed automatically.

automatic head parking Disk drive head parking performed whenever the drive is powered off. Found in all hard disk drives with a voice-coil actuator.

average access time The average time it takes a disk drive to begin reading any data placed anywhere on the drive. This includes the *average seek time*, which is when the heads are moved, as well as the *latency*, which is the average amount of time required for any given data sector to pass underneath the heads. Together these make up the average access time.

average latency The average time required for any byte of data stored on a disk to rotate under the disk drive's read/write head. Equal to one-half the time required for a single rotation of a platter.

average seek time The average amount of time it takes to move the heads from one random cylinder location to another, usually including any head settling time. In many cases, the average seek time is tested across one-third of the total number of cylinders for consistency in measurement.

AVI Audio Video Interleave. A storage technique developed by Microsoft for its Video for Windows product that combines audio and video into a single frame or track, saving valuable disk space and keeping audio synchronized with the corresponding video.

backup disk Contains information copied from another disk. Used to make sure that original information is not destroyed or altered.

backup The process of duplicating a file or library onto a separate piece of media. Good insurance against loss of an original.

bad sector A disk sector that cannot hold data reliably because of a media flaw or damaged format markings.

bad track table A label affixed to the casing of a hard disk drive that tells which tracks are flawed and cannot hold data. The listing is entered into the low-level formatting program.

balanced signal Refers to signals consisting of equal currents moving in opposite directions. When balanced or nearly balanced signals pass through twisted-pair lines, the electromagnetic interference effects such as crosstalk caused by the two opposite currents largely cancel each other out. *Differential signaling* is a method that uses balanced signals.

balun Short for *balanced/unbalanced*. A type of transformer that enables balanced cables to be joined with unbalanced cables. Twisted-pair (balanced) cables, for example, can be joined with coaxial (unbalanced) cables if the proper balun transformer is used.

bandwidth Generally, the measure of the range of frequencies within a radiation band required to transmit a particular signal. Measures in millions of cycles per second the difference between the lowest and highest signal frequencies. The bandwidth of a computer monitor is a measure of the rate that a monitor can handle information from the display adapter. The wider the bandwidth, the more information the monitor can carry and the greater the resolution. This term is also used to describe the data-carrying capacity of a given network circuit. The bandwidth of a network circuit is a measure of the rate at which a network can handle information. The higher the bandwidth, the more information the network can carry.

bank The collection of memory chips that make up a block of memory readable by the processor in a single bus cycle. This block, therefore, must be as large as the data bus of the particular microprocessor. In PC systems, the processor data bus (and therefore the bank size) is usually 8, 16, 32, or 64 bits wide. Optionally, some systems also incorporate an optional parity bit for each 8 data bits, resulting in a total of 9, 18, 36, or 72 bits (respectively) for each bank.

bar code The code used on consumer products and inventory parts for identification purposes. Consists of bars of varying thicknesses that represent characters and numerals that are read with an optical reader. The most common version is called the *Universal Product Code (UPC)*.

baseband The transmission of digital signals over a limited distance. ARCnet and Ethernet local area networks use baseband signaling. Contrasts with *broadband transmission*, which refers to the transmission of analog signals over a greater distance.

BASIC Beginner's All-purpose Symbolic Instruction Code. A popular computer programming language. Originally developed by John Kemeny and Thomas Kurtz in the mid-1960s at Dartmouth College. Normally an interpretive language, meaning that each statement is translated and executed as it is encountered; can be a compiled language, in which all the program statements are compiled before execution.

batch file   A set of commands stored in a disk file for execution by the operating system. A special batch file called *AUTOEXEC.BAT* is executed by IBM DOS each time the system is started. All DOS batch files have a BAT file extension.

baud rate   See *baud*.

baud   A unit of signaling speed denoting the number of discrete signal elements that can be transmitted per second. The word *baud* is derived from the name of J.M.E. Baudot (1845-1903), a French pioneer in the field of printing telegraphy and the inventor of Baudot code. Although technically inaccurate, *baud rate* commonly is used to mean *bit rate*. Because each signal element or baud may translate into many individual bits, *bits per second (bps)* normally differs from baud rate. A rate of 2,400 baud means that 2,400 frequency or signal changes per second are being sent, but each frequency change may signal several bits of information. Most people are surprised to learn that 2,400 and 1,200 bps modems transmit at 600 baud, and that 9,600 and 14,400 bps modems transmit at 2,400 baud.

Baudot code   A 5-bit code used in many types of data communications, including teletype (TTY), radio teletype (RTTY), and telecommunications devices for the deaf (TDD). Baudot code has been revised and extended several times.

bay   An opening in a computer cabinet that holds disk drives.

BBS   Bulletin board system. A computer that operates with a program and a modem to enable other computers with modems to communicate with it, often on a round-the-clock basis. Thousands of PC IBM- and Apple-related BBSes offer a wealth of information and public-domain software that can be downloaded.

Betacam   A half-inch video recording format developed by Sony that offers near 1-inch tape quality on a portable system.

bezel   A cosmetic panel that covers the face of a drive or some other device.

Bezier curve   A mathematical method for describing a curve, often used in illustration and CAD programs to draw complex shapes.

bi-directional   Refers to lines over which data can move in two directions, such as a data bus or a telephone line. Also refers to the capability of a printer to print from right to left and from left to right alternately.

binary   Refers to the computer numbering system that consists of two numerals, 0 and 1. Also called *base-2*.

BIOS   Basic Input/Output System. The part of an operating system that handles the communications between the computer and its peripherals. Often burned into read-only memory (ROM) chips.

bisynchronous   Binary synchronous control. An earlier protocol developed by IBM for software applications and communicating devices operating in synchronous environments. The protocol defines operations at the link level of communications—for example, the format of data frames exchanged between modems over a phone line.

bit density Expressed as bits per inch (BPI). Defines how many bits can be written onto one linear inch of a track. Sometimes also called linear density.

bit depth The number of bits used to describe the color of each pixel on a computer display. For example, a bit depth of two means that the monitor can display only black and white pixels; a bit depth of four means the monitor can display 16 different colors; a bit depth of eight allows for 256 colors, and so on.

bit map A method of storing graphics information in memory in which a bit devoted to each pixel (picture element) on-screen indicates whether that pixel is on or off. A bit map contains a bit for each point or dot on a video display screen and allows fine resolution because any point or pixel on-screen can be addressed. A greater number of bits can be used to describe each pixel's color, intensity, and other display characteristics.

bit Binary digit. Represented logically by 0 or 1 and electrically by 0 volts and (typically) 5 volts. Other methods are used to represent binary digits physically (tones, different voltages, lights, and so on), but the logic is always the same.

blank or blanking interval A period in which no video signal is received by a monitor, while the videodisc or digital video player searches for the next video segment or frame to display.

block diagram The logical structure or layout of a system in graphics form. Does not necessarily match the physical layout and does not specify all the components and their interconnections.

block A string of records, words, or characters formed for technical or logical reasons to be treated as an entity.

BMP Bit MaP. A Windows graphics format that may be device-dependent or independent. Device-independent BMP files (DIB) are coded for translation to a wide variety of displays and printers.

BNC British National Connector. A type of connector plug and jack system. Originally designed in England for television set antennas, the BNC is a type of connector designed for use with coaxial cabling. Male and female BNCs are available. Although the term is redundant, BNCs usually are referred to as *BNC connectors*. Often used in local area network cabling systems that use coaxial cable, such as Ethernet and ARCnet, and also used frequently for video cabling systems.

Boolean operation Any operation in which each of the operands and the result take one of two values.

boot record A one-sector record that tells the computer's built-in operating system (BIOS) the most fundamental facts about a disk and DOS. Instructs the computer how to load the operating system files into memory, thus booting the machine.

boot To load a program into the computer. The term comes from the phrase "pulling a boot on by the bootstrap."

bootstrap A technique or device designed to bring itself into a desired state by means of its own action. The term is used to describe the process by which a device such as a PC goes from its initial power-on condition to a running condition without human intervention.

bps Bits per second. The number of binary digits, or bits, transmitted per second. Sometimes confused with baud.

bridge In local area networks, an interconnection between two similar networks. Also the hardware equipment used to establish such an interconnection.

broadband A term used to describe analog transmission. Requires modems for connecting terminals and computers to the network. Using frequency division multiplexing, many different signals or sets of data can be transmitted simultaneously. The alternative transmission scheme is baseband, or digital, transmission.

broadcast quality In the U.S., a standard of 525 lines of video picture information at a rate of 60Hz. See also *NTSC format*.

bubble memory A special type of nonvolatile read/write memory introduced by Intel where magnetic regions are suspended in crystal film and data is maintained when the power is off. A typical bubble memory chip contains about 512K, or more than 4 million bubbles. Failed to catch on because of slow access times measured in several milliseconds. Has found a niche use as solid-state "disk" emulators in environments in which conventional drives are unacceptable, such as military or factory use.

buffer A block of memory used as a holding tank to store data temporarily. Often positioned between a slower peripheral device and the faster computer. All data moving between the peripheral and the computer passes through the buffer. A buffer enables the data to be read from or written to the peripheral in larger chunks, which improves performance. A buffer that is *x* bytes in size usually holds the last *x* bytes of data that moved between the peripheral and CPU. This method contrasts with that of a *cache*, which adds intelligence to the buffer so that the most often accessed data rather than the last accessed data remains in the buffer (cache). A cache can improve performance greatly over a plain buffer.

bug An error or a defect in a program.

burn-in The operation of a circuit or equipment to establish that components are stable and to screen for failures.

bus master An intelligent device that, when attached to the Micro Channel, EISA, VLB, or PCI bus, can bid for and gain control of the bus to perform its specific task.

bus A linear electrical signal pathway over which power, data, and other signals travel. It is capable of connecting to three or more attachments. A bus is generally considered to be distinct from radial or point-to-point signal connections. The term comes from the Latin *omnibus* meaning "for all." When used to describe a topology, bus always implies a linear structure.

byte A collection of bits that makes up a character or other designation. Generally, a byte is 8 data bits. When referring to system RAM, an additional parity (error-checking) bit also is stored (see *parity*), making the total 9 bits.

C A high-level computer programming language frequently used on mainframes, minis, and PC computer systems.

cache An intelligent buffer. By using an intelligent algorithm, a cache contains the data that is accessed most often between a slower peripheral device and the faster CPU.

CAM Common Access Method. A committee formed in 1988 that consists of a number of computer peripheral suppliers and is dedicated to developing standards for a common software interface between SCSI peripherals and host adapters. The CAM committee also has set a standard for IDE drives called the ATA interface.

capacitor A device consisting of two plates separated by insulating material and designed to store an electrical charge.

card A printed circuit board containing electronic components that form an entire circuit, usually designed to plug into a connector or slot. Sometimes called an *adapter*.

carpal tunnel syndrome A painful hand injury that gets its name from the narrow tunnel in the wrist that connects the ligament and bone. When undue pressure is put on the tendons, they can swell and compress the median nerve, which carries impulses from the brain to the hand, causing numbness, weakness, tingling, and burning in the fingers and hands. Computer users get carpal tunnel syndrome primarily from improper keyboard ergonomics that result in undue strain on the wrist and hand.

carrier detect signal A modem interface signal that indicates to the attached data terminal equipment (DTE) that it is receiving a signal from the distant modem. Defined in the RS-232 specification. Same as the received line-signal detector.

carrier A continuous-frequency signal capable of being either modulated or impressed with another information-carrying signal. The reference signal used for the transmission or reception of data. The most common use of this signal with computers involves modem communications over phone lines. The carrier is used as a signal on which the information is superimposed.

cathode ray tube (CRT) A device that contains electrodes surrounded by a glass sphere or cylinder and displays information by creating a beam of electrons that strikes a phosphor coating inside the display unit. This device is most commonly used in computer monitors and terminals.

CAV Constant Angular Velocity. An optical disk recording format where the data is recorded on the disk in concentric circles. CAV disks are rotated at a constant speed. This is similar to the recording technique used on floppy disk drives. CAV limits the total recorded capacity compared to CLV (Constant Linear Velocity), which is also used in optical recording.

CCITT An acronym for the Comité Consultatif Internationale de Télégraphique et Téléphonique (the International Telegraph and Telephone Consultative Committee). Renamed ITU (International Telecommunications Union). See *ITU*.

CCS Common Command Set. A set of SCSI commands specified in the ANSI SCSI-1 Standard X3.131-1986 Addendum 4.B. All SCSI devices must be capable of using the CCS in order to be fully compatible with the ANSI SCSI-1 standard.

CD Compact Disc or compact audio disc. A 4.75-inch (12cm) optical disc that contains information encoded digitally in the constant linear velocity (CLV) format. This popular format for high-fidelity music offers 90 decibels signal/noise ratio, 74 minutes of digital sound, and no degradation of quality from playback. The standards for this format (developed by NV Philips and Sony Corporation) are known as the *Red Book*. The official (and rarely-used) designation for the audio-only format is CD-DA (compact disc-digital audio). The simple audio format is also known as CD-A (compact disc-audio). A smaller (3-inch) version of the CD is known as CD-3.

CD Video A CD format introduced in 1987 that combined 20 minutes of digital audio and 6 minutes of analog video on a standard 4.75-inch CD. Upon introduction, many firms renamed 8-inch and 12-inch videodiscs as CDV in an attempt to capitalize on the consumer popularity of the audio CD. The term fell out of use in 1990 and was replaced in some part by *laser disc*.

CD+G Compact Disc-Graphics. A CD format that includes extended graphics capabilities as written into the original CD-ROM specifications. Includes limited video graphics encoded into the CD subcode area. Developed and marketed by Warner New Media.

CD+MIDI Compact Disc-Musical Instrument Digital Interface. A CD format that adds digital audio, graphics information, and musical instrument digital interface (MIDI) specifications and capabilities to the CD+G format. Developed and marketed by Warner New Media.

CD-DA Compact Disc Digital Audio. Also known as *Red Book Audio* and is the digital sound format used by audio CDs. CD-DA uses a sampling rate of 44.1KHz and stores 16 bits of information for each sample. CD audio is not played through the computer, but through a special chip in the CD-ROM drive. Fifteen minutes of CD-DA sound can require about 80M. The highest quality sound that can be used by multimedia PCs is the CD-DA format at 44.1KHz sample rate. See also *CD*.

CD-I Compact Disc-Interactive. A compact disk format released in October 1991 that provides audio, digital data, still graphics, and motion video. The standards for this format (developed by NV Philips and Sony Corporation) are known as the *Green Book*.

CD-R Compact Disc Recordable, sometimes called CD-Writable. CD-R disks are compact discs that can be recorded and read as many times as desired. CD-R is part of the Orange Book standard defined by ISO. CD-R technology is used for mass production of multimedia applications. CD-R discs can be compatible with CD-ROM, CD-ROM XA, and CD audio. Orange Book specifies multi-session capabilities, which allows data recording on the disk at different times in several recording sessions. Kodak's Photo CD is an example of CD-R technology, and it fits up to 100 digital photographs on a single CD. Multi-session capability allows several rolls of 35mm film to be added to a single disc on different occasions.

CD-ROM   Compact Disc-Read Only Memory. A 4.75-inch laser-encoded optical memory storage medium with the same constant linear velocity (CLV) spiral format as audio CDs and some videodiscs, CD-ROMs can hold about 650M of data. CD-ROMs require more error-correction information than the standard prerecorded compact audio disc. The standards for this format (developed by NV Philips and Sony Corporation) are known as the *Yellow Book*. See also *CD-ROM XA*.

CD-ROM drive   A device that retrieves data from a CD-ROM disc; differs from a standard audio CD player by the incorporation of additional error-correction circuitry. CD-ROM drives usually can also play music from audio CDs.

CD-ROM XA   Compact Disc Read Only Memory eXtended Architecture. The XA standard was developed jointly by Sony, Philips, and Microsoft in 1988 and is now part of the Yellow Book standard. XA is a built-in feature of newer CD-ROM drives, and it supports simultaneous sound playback with data transfer. Non-XA drives support either sound playback or data transfer, but not both simultaneously. XA also provides for data compression right on the disk, which can also increase data transfer rates.

CD-WO   Compact Disc-Write Once. A variant on CD-ROM that can be written to once and read many times; developed by NV Philips and Sony Corporation. Also known as *CD-WORM* (CD-write once/read many). Standards for this format are known as the *Orange Book*.

CD-WORM   See *CD-WO*.

ceramic substrate   A thin, flat, fired ceramic part used to hold an IC chip (usually made of beryllium oxide or aluminum oxide).

CERN   Conseil Européen pour la Recherche Nucléaire (The European Laboratory for Particle Physics). The site in Geneva where the World Wide Web was created in 1989.

CGA   Color Graphics Adapter. A type of PC video display adapter introduced by IBM on August 12, 1981, that supports text and graphics. Text is supported at a maximum resolution of 80×25 characters in 16 colors with a character box of 8×8 pixels. Graphics is supported at a maximum resolution of 320×200 pixels in 16 colors or 640×200 pixels in two colors. The CGA outputs a TTL (digital) signal with a horizontal scanning frequency of 15.75KHz and supports TTL color or NTSC composite displays.

CGI   Common Gateway Interface. An API (Application Programming Interface) for HTTP that provides the server with the capability to run scripts or compiled applications when requested.

channel   A path along which signals can be sent.

character   A representation, coded in binary digits, of a letter, number, or other symbol.

checksum Short for *summation check*, a technique for determining whether a package of data is valid. The package, a string of binary digits, is added up and compared with the expected number.

chip carrier A ceramic or plastic package that carries an integrated circuit.

chip Another name for an *IC*, or *integrated circuit*. Housed in a plastic or ceramic carrier device with pins for making electrical connections.

CHS Cylinder Head Sector. The term used to describe the non-translating scheme used by the BIOS to access IDE drives that are less than or equal to 528M in capacity. See also *LBA*.

CIF Common Image Format. The standard sample structure that represents the picture information of a single frame in digital HDTV, independent of frame rate and sync/blank structure. The uncompressed bit rate for transmitting CIF at 29.97 frames/sec is 36.45Mbps.

circuit board A collection of circuits gathered on a sheet of plastic, usually with all contacts made through a strip of pins. The circuit board usually is made by chemically etching metal-coated plastic.

circuit A complete electronic path.

CISC Complex instruction-set computer. Refers to traditional computers that operate with large sets of processor instructions. Most modern computers, including the Intel 80*xxx* processors, are in this category. CISC processors have expanded instruction sets that are complex in nature and require several to many execution cycles to complete. This structure contrasts with *RISC (reduced instruction-set computer) processors*, which have far fewer instructions that execute quickly.

clean room A dust-free room where certain electronic components (such as hard disk drives) must be manufactured and serviced to prevent contamination. Rooms are rated by Class numbers. A Class 100 clean room must have fewer than 100 particles larger than 0.5 microns per cubic foot of space.

clock speed A measurement of the rate at which the clock signal for a device oscillates, usually expressed in millions of cycles per second (MHz).

clock The source of a computer's timing signals. Synchronizes every operation of the CPU.

clone An IBM-compatible computer system that physically as well as electrically emulates the design of one of IBM's personal computer systems, usually the AT or XT. For example, an AT clone has parts (motherboard, power supply, and so on) that are physically interchangeable with the same parts in the IBM AT system.

cluster Also called *allocation unit*. A group of sectors on a disk that forms a fundamental unit of storage to the operating system. Cluster or allocation unit size is determined by DOS when the disk is formatted.

CLV Constant Linear Velocity. An optical recording format where the spacing of data is consistent throughout the disk, and the rotational speed of the disk varies, depending on what track is being read. Additionally, more sectors of data are placed on the outer tracks compared to the inner tracks of the disk, which is similar to Zone Recording on hard drives. CLV drives will adjust the rotational speed to maintain a constant track velocity as the diameter of the track changes. CLV drives rotate faster near the center of the disk and slower toward the edge. Rotational adjustment maximizes the amount of data that can be stored on a disk. CD audio and CD-ROM use CLV recording.

CMOS Complementary Metal-Oxide Semiconductor. A type of chip design that requires little power to operate. In an AT-type system, a battery-powered CMOS memory and clock chip is used to store and maintain the clock setting and system configuration information.

coated media Hard disk platters coated with a reddish iron-oxide medium on which data is recorded.

coaxial cable Also called *coax cable*. A data-transmission medium noted for its wide bandwidth, immunity to interference, and high cost compared to other types of cable. Signals are transmitted inside a fully shielded environment, in which an inner conductor is surrounded by a solid insulating material and then an outer conductor or shield. Used in many local area network systems such as Ethernet and ARCnet.

COBOL Common business-oriented language. A high-level computer programming language. The business world's preferred programming language on mainframe computer systems, it has never achieved popularity on smaller computers.

code page switching A DOS feature in versions 3.3 and later that changes the characters displayed on-screen or printed on an output device. Primarily used to support foreign-language characters. Requires an EGA or better video system and an IBM-compatible graphics printer.

CODEC CODer-DECoder. A device that converts voice signals from their analog form to digital signals acceptable to more modern digital PBXs and digital transmission systems. It then converts those digital signals back to analog so that you can hear and understand what the other party is saying.

coercivity A measurement in units of oersteads of the amount of magnetic energy to switch or "coerce" the flux change in the magnetic recording media. High-coercivity disk media require a stronger write current.

Color Graphics Adapter See *CGA*.

COM port A serial port on a PC that conforms to the RS-232 standard. See also *RS-232*.

COMDEX The largest international computer trade show and conference in the world. COMDEX/Fall is held in Las Vegas during October, and COMDEX/Spring usually is held in Chicago or Atlanta during April.

COMMAND.COM An operating system file that is loaded last when the computer is booted. The command interpreter or user interface and program-loader portion of DOS.

command An instruction that tells the computer to start, stop, or continue an operation.

common mode noise Noise or electrical disturbances that can be measured between a current- or signal-carrying line and its associated ground. Common mode noise is frequently introduced to signals between separate computer equipment components through the power distribution circuits. It can be a problem when single-ended signals are used to connect different equipment or components that are powered by different circuits.

common The ground or return path for an electrical signal. If a wire, it usually is colored black.

compiler A program that translates a program written in a high-level language into its equivalent machine language. The output from a compiler is called an *object program*.

complete backup A backup of all information on a hard disk, including the directory tree structure.

composite video Television picture information and sync pulses combined. The IBM Color Graphics Adapter (CGA) outputs a composite video signal.

composite video The complete visual wave form of the color video signal, composed of chrominance and luminance picture information; blanking pedestal; field, line, and color sync pulses; and field equalizing pulses. See also *RGB*.

computer Device capable of accepting data, applying prescribed processes to this data, and displaying the results or information produced.

computer-based training CBT. The use of a computer to deliver instruction or training; also known as Computer-Aided (or Assisted) Instruction (CAI), Computer-Aided Learning (CAL), Computer-Based Instruction (CBI), and Computer-Based Learning (CBL).

CONFIG.SYS A file that can be created to tell DOS how to configure itself when the machine starts up. Can load device drivers, set the number of DOS buffers, and so on.

configuration file A file kept by application software to record various aspects of the software's configuration, such as the printer it uses.

console The unit in your system, such as a terminal or a keyboard, with which you communicate with the computer.

contiguous Touching or joined at the edge or boundary, in one piece.

continuity In electronics, an unbroken pathway. Testing for continuity normally means testing to determine whether a wire or other conductor is complete and unbroken (by measuring 0 ohms). A broken wire shows infinite resistance (or infinite ohms).

control cable The wider of the two cables that connect an ST-506/412 or ESDI hard disk drive to a controller card. A 34-pin cable that carries commands and acknowledgments between the drive and controller.

controller card An adapter holding the control electronics for one or more devices such as hard disks. Ordinarily occupies one of the computer's slots.

controller The electronics that control a device such as a hard disk drive and intermediate the passage of data between the device and the computer.

convergence Describes the capability of a color monitor to focus the three colored electron beams on a single point. Poor convergence causes the characters on-screen to appear fuzzy and can cause the user to have headaches and eyestrain.

coprocessor An additional computer processing unit designed to handle specific tasks in conjunction with the main or central processing unit.

core An "old-fashioned" term for computer memory.

CP/M Control Program/Microcomputer. An operating system created by Gary Kildall, the founder of Digital Research. Created for the old 8-bit microcomputers that used the 8080, 8085, and Z-80 microprocessors. Was the dominant operating system in the late 1970s and early 1980s for small computers used in a business environment.

cps Characters per second. A data transfer rate generally estimated from the bit rate and the character length. At 2,400 bps, for example, 8-bit characters with start and stop bits (for a total of 10 bits per character) are transmitted at a rate of approximately 240 cps. Some protocols, such as V.42 and MNP, employ advanced techniques such as longer transmission frames and data compression to increase cps.

CPU Central Processing Unit. The computer's microprocessor chip; the brains of the outfit. Typically, an IC using VLSI (very-large-scale integration) technology to pack several different functions into a tiny area. The most common electronic device in the CPU is the transistor, of which several thousand to several million or more are found.

crash A malfunction that brings work to a halt. A *system crash* usually is caused by a software malfunction, and ordinarily you can restart the system by rebooting the machine. A *head crash*, however, entails physical damage to a disk and probable data loss.

CRC Cyclic Redundancy Checking. An error-detection technique consisting of a cyclic algorithm performed on each block or frame of data by both sending and receiving modems. The sending modem inserts the results of its computation in each data block in the form of a CRC code. The receiving modem compares its results with the received CRC code and responds with either a positive or negative acknowledgment. In the ARQ protocol implemented in high-speed modems, the receiving modem accepts no more data until a defective block is received correctly.

crosstalk The electromagnetic coupling of a signal on one line with another nearby signal line. Crosstalk is caused by electromagnetic induction, where a signal traveling through a wire creates a magnetic field that induces a current in other nearby wires.

CRT Cathode-Ray Tube. A term used to describe a television or monitor screen tube.

current The flow of electrons, measured in amperes (amp)s.

cursor The small flashing hyphen that appears on-screen to indicate the point at which any input from the keyboard will be placed.

cyclic redundancy checking See *CRC*.

cylinder The set of tracks on a disk that are on each side of all the disk platters in a stack and are the same distance from the center of the disk. The total number of tracks that can be read without moving the heads. A floppy drive with two heads usually has 160 tracks, which are accessible as 80 cylinders. A typical 4G hard disk has 10 platters with 20 heads (19 for data and one servo head) and 4,000 cylinders, in which each cylinder is composed of 19 tracks.

D/A Converter DAC. A device that converts digital signals to analog form.

daisy chain Stringing up components in such a manner that the signals move serially from one to the other. Most microcomputer multiple-disk drive systems are daisy-chained. The SCSI bus system is a daisy-chain arrangement, in which the signals move from computer to disk drives to tape units, and so on.

daisywheel printer An impact printer that prints fully formed characters one at a time by rotating a circular print element composed of a series of individual spokes, each containing two characters that radiate from a center hub. Produces letter-quality output.

DAT Digital Audio Tape. A small cassette tape for storing large amounts of digital information, it is sometimes called *4mm tape*. DAT technology emerged in Europe and Japan in 1986 as a way to produce high-quality, digital audio recordings. One DAT cassette can hold anywhere from 1G to 8G of data.

data cable Generically, a cable that carries data. Specific to HD connections, the narrower (20 pin) of two cables that connect an ST-506/412 or ESDI hard disk drive to a controller card.

data communications A type of communication in which computers and terminals can exchange data over an electronic medium.

data compression A technique where mathematical algorithms are applied to the data in a file to eliminate redundancies and therefore reduce the size of the file. There are two types of compression: lossy and lossless. *Lossy* compression deletes some of the original (uncompressed) data needed to reconstruct a file and is normally used only for graphic image or sound files, where the loss of some resolution or information is acceptable. *Lossless* compression completely maintains the integrity of the original file, allowing it to be reconstructed exactly, and is most commonly used for program or data files.

data separator A device that separates data and clock signals from a single encoded signal pattern. Usually the same device does both data separation and combination and is sometimes called an *endec*, or *encoder/decoder*.

data transfer rate The maximum rate at which data can be transferred from one device to another.

data   Groups of facts processed into information. A graphic or textual representation of facts, concepts, numbers, letters, symbols, or instructions used for communication or processing.

DC   Direct current, such as that provided by a power supply or batteries.

DC-600   Data Cartridge 600, a data-storage medium invented by 3M in 1971 that uses a quarter-inch-wide tape 600 feet in length.

DCE   Data Communications Equipment. The hardware that performs the communication—usually a dial-up modem that establishes and controls the data link through the telephone network. See also *DTE*.

DDE   Dynamic Data Exchange. A form of interprocess communications used by Microsoft Windows to support the exchange of commands and data between two applications running simultaneously. This capability has been enhanced further with Object Linking and Embedding (OLE).

DEBUG   The name of a utility program included with DOS, used for specialized purposes such as altering memory locations, tracing program execution, patching programs and disk sectors, and performing other low-level tasks.

decibel (dB)   A logarithmic measure of the ratio between two powers, voltages, currents, sound intensities, and so on. Signal-to-noise ratios are expressed in decibels.

dedicated line   A user-installed telephone line that connects a specified number of computers or terminals within a limited area, such as a single building. The line is a cable rather than a public-access telephone line. The communications channel also may be referred to as nonswitched because calls do not go through telephone company switching equipment.

dedicated servo surface   In voice-coil-actuated hard disk drives, one side of one platter given over to servo data that is used to guide and position the read/write heads.

default   Any setting assumed at start-up or reset by the computer's software and attached devices and operational until changed by the user. An assumption the computer makes when no other parameters are specified. When you type **DIR** without specifying the drive to search, for example, the computer assumes that you want it to search the default drive. The term is used in software to describe any action the computer or program takes on its own with embedded values.

defragmentation   The process of rearranging disk sectors so that files are stored on consecutive sectors in adjacent tracks.

density   The amount of data that can be packed into a certain area on a specific storage media.

desktop   A personal computer that sits on a desk.

device driver   A memory-resident program loaded by CONFIG.SYS that controls an unusual device, such as an expanded memory board.

Dhrystone A benchmark program used as a standard figure of merit, indicating aspects of a computer system's performance in areas other than floating-point math performance. Because the program does not use any floating-point operations, performs no I/O, and makes no operating system calls, it is most useful for measuring the processor performance of a system. The original Dhrystone program was developed in 1984 and was written in Ada, although the C and Pascal versions became more popular by 1989.

diagnostics Programs used to check the operation of a computer system. These programs enable the operator to check the entire system for any problems and to indicate in what area the problems lie.

differential An electrical signaling method where a pair of lines are used for each signal in "push-pull" fashion. In most cases, differential signals are balanced so that the same current flows on each line in opposite directions. This is unlike single-ended signals, which use only one line per signal referenced to a single ground. Differential signals have a large tolerance for common-mode noise and little crosstalk when used with twisted-pair wires, even in long cables. Differential signaling is expensive because two pins are required for each signal.

digital loopback A test that checks the modem's RS-232 interface and the cable that connects the terminal or computer and the modem. The modem receives data (in the form of digital signals) from the computer or terminal and immediately returns the data to the screen for verification.

digital signals Discrete, uniform signals. In this book, the term refers to the binary digits 0 and 1.

digitize To transform an analog wave to a digital signal that a computer can store. Conversion to digital data and back is performed by a *Digital to Analog Converter (DAC)*, often a single chip device. How closely a digitized sample represents an analog wave depends on the number of times the amplitude of a wave is measured and recorded (the rate of digitization) as well as the number of different levels that can be specified at each instance. The number of possible signal levels is dictated by the resolution in bits.

DIP Dual Inline Package. A family of rectangular, integrated-circuit flat packages that have leads on the two longer sides. Package material is plastic or ceramic.

DIP switch A tiny switch (or group of switches) on a circuit board. Named for the form factor of the carrier device in which the switch is housed.

direct memory access (DMA) A process by which data moves between a disk drive (or other device) and system memory without direct control of the central processing unit, thus freeing up the CPU for other tasks.

directory An area of a disk that stores the titles given to the files saved on the disk and serves as a table of contents for those files. Contains data that identifies the name of a file, the size, the attributes (system, hidden, read-only, and so on), the date and time of creation, and a pointer to the location of the file. Each entry in a directory is 32 bytes long.

disc Flat, circular, rotating medium that can store various types of information, both analog and digital. "Disc" is often used in reference to optical storage media, while "disk" refers to magnetic storage media. Disc is often used as a short form for videodisc or compact audio disc (CD).

disk Alternative spelling for "disc" that generally refers to magnetic storage medium on which information can be accessed at random. Floppy disks and hard disks are examples.

diskette An alternate reference to a floppy disk.

dithering The process of creating more colors and shades from a given color palette. In monochrome displays or printers, dithering will vary the black and white dot patterns to simulate shades of gray. Gray scale dithering is used to produce different shades of gray when the device can produce only limited levels of black or white outputs. Color screens or printers use dithering to create colors by mixing and varying the dot sizing and spacing.

DLL (dynamic link library) An executable driver program module for Microsoft Windows that can be loaded on demand and linked in at runtime and subsequently unloaded when the driver is no longer needed.

DMA See *Direct Memory Access*.

DMI Desktop Management Interface. DMI is an operating system- and protocol-independent standard for managing desktop systems and servers.

docking station Equipment that enables a laptop or notebook computer to use peripherals and accessories normally associated with desktop systems.

DOS Disk Operating System. A collection of programs stored on the DOS disk that contain routines enabling the system and user to manage information and the hardware resources of the computer. DOS must be loaded into the computer before other programs can be started.

dot pitch A measurement of the width of the dots that make up a pixel. The smaller the dot pitch, the sharper the image.

dot-matrix printer An impact printer that prints characters composed of dots. Characters are printed one at a time by pressing the ends of selected wires against an inked ribbon and paper.

double density (DD) An indication of the storage capacity of a floppy drive or disk in which eight or nine sectors per track are recorded using MFM encoding. See *MFM*.

down-time Operating time lost because of a computer malfunction.

DPMI DOS Protected Mode Interface. An industry standard interface that allows DOS applications to execute program code in the protected mode of the 286 or higher Intel processor. The DPMI specification is available from Intel.

DRAM Dynamic Random Access Memory. The most common type of computer memory, DRAM can be made very inexpensively compared to other types of memory. DRAM chips are small and inexpensive because they normally require only one transistor and a capacitor to represent each bit. The capacitors must be energized every 15ms or so (hundreds of times per second) in order to maintain their charges. DRAM is volatile, meaning it will lose data with no power or without regular refresh cycles.

drive A mechanical device that manipulates data storage media.

driver A program designed to interface a particular piece of hardware to an operating system or other standard software.

DSM Digital Storage Media. A digital storage or transmission device or system.

DTE Data Terminal (or Terminating) Equipment. The device, usually a computer or terminal, that generates or is the final destination of data. See also *DCE*.

duplex Indicates a communications channel capable of carrying signals in both directions.

DVI Digital Video Interactive. A standard that was originally developed at RCA Laboratories and sold to Intel in 1988. The DVI integrates digital motion, still video, sound, graphics, and special effects in a compressed format. The DVI is a highly sophisticated hardware compression technique used in interactive multimedia applications.

Dvorak keyboard A keyboard design by August Dvorak that was patented in 1936 and approved by ANSI in 1982. Provides increased speed and comfort and reduces the rate of errors by placing the most frequently used letters in the center for use by the strongest fingers. Finger motions and awkward strokes are reduced by more than 90 percent in comparison with the familiar QWERTY keyboard. The Dvorak keyboard has the five vowel keys, AOEUI, together under the left hand in the center row, and the five most frequently used consonants, DHTNS, under the fingers of the right hand.

EBCDIC Extended Binary Coded Decimal Interchange Code. An IBM-developed 8-bit code for the representation of characters. It allows 256 possible character combinations within a single byte. EBCDIC is the standard code on IBM mini-computers and mainframes, but not on the IBM microcomputers, where ASCII is used instead.

edit The process of rearranging data or information.

EEPROM Electrically Erasable Programmable Read Only Memory. A type of nonvolatile memory chip used to store semi-permanent information in a computer such as the BIOS. An EEPROM can be erased and reprogrammed directly in the host system without special equipment. This is used so manufacturers can upgrade the ROM code in a system by supplying a special program that erases and reprograms the EEPROM chip with the new code. Also called a *Flash ROM*.

EGA Enhanced Graphics Adapter. A type of PC video display adapter first introduced by IBM on September 10, 1984, that supports text and graphics. Text is supported at a maximum resolution of 80×25 characters in 16 colors with a character box of 8×14 pixels. Graphics is supported at a maximum resolution of 640×350 pixels in 16 (from a palette of 64) colors. The EGA outputs a TTL (digital) signal with a horizontal scanning frequency of 15.75, 18.432, or 21.85KHz, and supports TTL color or TTL monochrome displays.

EIA   Electronic Industries Association, which defines electronic standards in the United States.

EIDE   Enhanced Integrated Drive Electronics. A specific Western Digital implementation of the ATA-2 specification. See also *ATA-2*.

EISA   Extended Industry Standard Architecture. An extension of the Industry Standard Architecture (ISA) bus developed by IBM for the AT. The EISA design was led by Compaq Corporation. Later, eight other manufacturers (AST, Epson, Hewlett-Packard, NEC, Olivetti, Tandy, Wyse, and Zenith) joined Compaq in a consortium founded September 13, 1988. This group became known as the "gang of nine." The EISA design was patterned largely after IBM's Micro Channel Architecture (MCA) in the PS/2 systems, but unlike MCA, EISA allows for backward compatibility with older plug-in adapters.

electronic mail   A method of transferring messages from one computer to another.

electrostatic discharge (ESD)   The grounding of static electricity. A sudden flow of electricity between two objects at different electrical potentials. ESD is a primary cause of integrated circuit damage or failure.

embedded servo data   Magnetic markings embedded between or inside tracks on disk drives that use voice-coil actuators. These markings enable the actuator to fine-tune the position of the read/write heads.

EMM   Expanded Memory Manager. A driver that provides a software interface to expanded memory. EMMs were originally created for expanded memory boards, but can also use the memory management capabilities of the 386 or higher processors to emulate an expanded memory board. EMM386.EXE is an example of an EMM that comes with DOS.

EMS   Expanded Memory Specification. Sometimes also called the *LIM spec*, because it was developed by Lotus, Intel, and Microsoft. Provides a way for microcomputers running under DOS to access additional memory. EMS memory management provides access to a maximum of 32M of expanded memory through a small (usually 64K) window in conventional memory. EMS is a cumbersome access scheme designed primarily for pre-286 systems that could not access extended memory.

emulator   A piece of test apparatus that emulates or imitates the function of a particular chip.

encoding   The protocol by which data is carried or stored by a medium.

encryption   The translation of data into unreadable codes to maintain security.

endec (encoder/decoder) A device that takes data and clock signals and combines or encodes them using a particular encoding scheme into a single signal for transmission or storage. The same device also later separates or decodes the data and clock signals during a receive or read operation. Sometimes called a *data separator*.

Energy Star A certification program started by the Environmental Protection Agency. Energy Star certified computers and peripherals are designed to draw less than 30 watts of electrical energy from a standard 110-volt AC outlet during periods of inactivity. Also called *Green PCs*.

Enhanced Graphics Adapter See *EGA*.

Enhanced Small Device Interface See *ESDI*.

EPROM Erasable Programmable Read-Only Memory. A type of read-only memory (ROM) in which the data pattern can be erased to allow a new pattern. Usually is erased by ultraviolet light and recorded by a higher-than-normal voltage programming signal.

equalization A compensation circuit designed into modems to counteract certain distortions introduced by the telephone channel. Two types are used: fixed (compromise) equalizers and those that adapt to channel conditions (adaptive). Good-quality modems use adaptive equalization.

error control Various techniques that check the reliability of characters (parity) or blocks of data. V.42, MNP, and HST error-control protocols use error detection (CRC) and retransmission of error frames (ARQ).

error message A word or combination of words to indicate to the user that an error has occurred somewhere in the program.

ESDI Enhanced Small Device Interface. A hardware standard developed by Maxtor and standardized by a consortium of 22 disk drive manufacturers on January 26, 1983. A group of 27 manufacturers formed the ESDI steering committee on September 15, 1986, to enhance and improve the specification. A high-performance interface used primarily with hard disks, ESDI provides for a maximum data transfer rate to and from a hard disk of between 10 and 24Mbit/sec.

Ethernet A type of network protocol developed in the late 1970s by Bob Metcalf at Xerox Corporation and endorsed by the IEEE. One of the oldest LAN communications protocols in the personal computing industry, Ethernet networks use a collision-detection protocol to manage contention.

expanded memory Otherwise known as *EMS memory*, memory that conforms to the EMS specification. Requires a special device driver and conforms to a standard developed by Lotus, Intel, and Microsoft.

eXtended graphics array See *XGA*.

extended memory Direct processor-addressable memory that is addressed by an Intel (or compatible) 286, 386, or 486 processor in the region beyond the first megabyte. Addressable only in the processor's protected mode of operation.

extended partition A nonbootable DOS partition containing DOS volumes. Starting with DOS v3.3, the DOS FDISK program can create two partitions that serve DOS: an ordinary, bootable partition (called the primary partition) and an extended partition, which may contain as many as 23 volumes from D: through Z:.

extra-high density (ED) An indication of the storage capacity of a floppy drive or disk in which 36 sectors per track are recorded using a vertical recording technique with MFM encoding.

Fast ATA Fast AT Attachment interface. Also called *Fast ATA-2*, these are specific Seagate and Quantum implementations of the ATA-2 interface. See also *ATA-2*.

FAT File Allocation Table. A table held near the outer edge of a disk that tells which sectors are allocated to each file and in what order.

FDISK The name of the disk partitioning program under several operating systems to create the Master Boot Record and allocate partitions for the operating system's use.

FIFO First-in first-out. A method of storing and retrieving items from a list, table, or stack so that the first element stored is the first one retrieved.

file A collection of information kept somewhere other than in random-access memory.

file attribute Information held in the attribute byte of a file's directory entry.

file name The name given to the disk file. For DOS, it must be one to eight characters long and may be followed by a file name extension, which can be one to three characters long. Windows 95 eases these constraints by allowing file names of up to 255 characters.

firmware Software contained in a read-only memory (ROM) device. A cross between hardware and software.

fixed disk Also called a *hard disk*, a disk that cannot be removed from its controlling hardware or housing. Made of rigid material with a magnetic coating and used for the mass storage and retrieval of data.

Flash ROM A type of EEPROM developed by Intel that can be erased and reprogrammed in the host system. See *EEPROM*.

floating-point unit (FPU) Sometimes called the math coprocessor; handles the more complex calculations of the processing cycle.

floppy tape A tape standard that uses drives connecting to an ordinary floppy disk controller.

flow control A mechanism that compensates for differences in the flow of data input to and output from a modem or other device.

FM encoding Frequency modulation encoding. An outdated method of encoding data on the disk surface that uses up half the disk space with timing signals.

folder   In a graphical user interface, a simulated file folder that holds documents (text, data, or graphics), applications, and other folders. A folder is like a DOS subdirectory.

form factor   The physical dimensions of a device. Two devices with the same form factor are physically interchangeable. The IBM PC, XT, and XT Model 286, for example, all use power supplies that are internally different but have exactly the same form factor.

FORMAT   The DOS format program that performs both low- and high-level formatting on floppy disks but only high-level formatting on hard disks.

formatted capacity   The total number of bytes of data that can fit on a formatted disk. The unformatted capacity is higher because space is lost defining the boundaries between sectors.

formatting   Preparing a disk so that the computer can read or write to it. Checks the disk for defects and constructs an organizational system to manage information on the disk.

FORTRAN   Formula translator. A high-level programming language for programs dealing primarily with mathematical formulas and expressions similar to algebra and used primarily in scientific and technical applications. One of the oldest languages still widely used because of its compact notation, the many mathematical subroutines available, and the ease with which arrays, matrices, and loops can be handled. FORTRAN was written in 1954 by John Backus at IBM; the first successful FORTRAN program was executed by Harlan Herrick.

frame buffer   A memory device that stores, pixel by pixel, the contents of an image. Frame buffers are used to refresh a raster image. Sometimes they incorporate local processing ability. The "depth" of the frame buffer is the number of bits per pixel, which determines the number of colors or intensities that can be displayed.

frame rate   The speed at which video frames are scanned or displayed—30 frames per second for NTSC, 25 frames a second for PAL/SECAM.

frame   A data communications term for a block of data with header and trailer information attached. The added information usually includes a frame number, block size data, error-check codes, and start/end indicators.

frame   A single, complete picture in a video or film recording. A video frame consists of two interlaced fields of either 525 lines (NTSC) or 625 lines (PAL/SECAM), running at 30 frames per second (NTSC) or 25 frames per second (PAL/SECAM).

FTP   File Transfer Protocol. A method of transferring files over the Internet. FTP can be used to transfer files between two machines on which the user has accounts. Anonymous FTP can be used by a user to retrieve a file from a server without having an account on that server.

full duplex   Signal flow in both directions at the same time. In microcomputer communications, also may refer to the suppression of the online local echo.

full-height drive A drive unit that is 3.25 inches high, 5.75 inches wide, and 8 inches deep.

full-motion video A video sequence displayed at full television standard resolutions and frame rates. In the U.S., this would equate to NTSC video at 30 frames per second.

function keys Special-purpose keys that can be programmed to perform various operations. Serve many different functions, depending on the program being used.

gas-plasma display Commonly used in portable systems, a type of display that operates by exciting a gas, usually neon or an argon-neon mixture, through the application of a voltage. When sufficient voltage is applied at the intersection of two electrodes, the gas glows an orange-red. Because gas-plasma displays generate light, they require no backlighting.

gateway Officially, an application-to-application conversion program or system. For example, an e-mail gateway would convert between SMTP (Internet) e-mail format to MHS (Novell) e-mail format. The term gateway is also used as a slang term for router. See also *router*.

genlocking The process of aligning the data rate of a video image with that of a digital device to digitize the image and enter it into computer memory. The machine that performs this function is known as a *genlock*.

GIF Graphics Interchange Format. A popular raster graphics file format developed by CompuServe that handles 8-bit color (256 colors) and uses the LZW method to achieve compression ratios of approximately 1.5:1 to 2:1.

giga A multiplier indicating 1 billion (1,000,000,000) of some unit. Abbreviated as g or G. When used to indicate a number of bytes of memory storage, the multiplier definition changes to 1,073,741,824. One gigabit, for example, equals 1,000,000,000 bits, and one gigabyte equals 1,073,741,824 bytes.

gigabyte (G) A unit of information storage equal to 1,073,741,824 bytes.

Green Book The standard for Compact Disc-Interactive (CD-I). Philips developed CD-I technology for the consumer market, to be connected to a television instead of a computer monitor. CD-I is not a computer system but a consumer device. CD-I disks require special code and are not compatible with standard CD-ROMs. A CD-ROM cannot be played on the CD-I machine, but Red Book audio can be played on CD-I devices.

GUI Graphical User Interface. A type of program interface that enables users to choose commands and functions by pointing to a graphical icon using either a keyboard or pointing device such as a mouse. Windows and OS/2 are the most popular GUIs available for PC systems.

half duplex Signal flow in both directions but only one way at a time. In microcomputer communications, may refer to activation of the online local echo, which causes the modem to send a copy of the transmitted data to the screen of the sending computer.

half-height drive   A drive unit that is 1.625 inches high and either 5.75 or 4 inches wide and 4 or 8 inches deep.

half toning   A process that uses dithering to simulate a continuous tone image such as a photograph or shaded drawing using various sizes of dots. Newspapers, magazines, and many books use half toning. The human eye will merge the dots to give the impression of gray shades.

hard disk   A high-capacity disk storage unit characterized by a normally non-removable, rigid substrate media. The platters in a hard disk normally are constructed of aluminum or glass.

hard error   An error in reading or writing data that is caused by damaged hardware.

hardware   Physical components that make up a microcomputer, monitor, printer, and so on.

HDLC   High-Level Data Link Control. A standard protocol developed by the ISO for software applications and communicating devices operating in synchronous environments. Defines operations at the link level of communications—for example, the format of data frames exchanged between modems over a phone line.

head actuator   The device that moves read/write heads across a disk drive's platters. Most drives use a stepper-motor or a voice-coil actuator.

head crash   A (usually) rare occurrence in which a read/write head strikes a platter surface with sufficient force to damage the magnetic medium.

head parking   A procedure in which a disk drive's read/write heads are moved to an unused track so that they will not damage data in the event of a head crash or other failure.

head seek   The movement of a drive's read/write heads to a particular track.

head   A small electromagnetic device inside a drive that reads, records, and erases data on the media.

heat sink   A mass of metal attached to a chip carrier or socket for the purpose of dissipating heat.

helical scan   A type of recording technology that has vastly increased the capacity of tape drives. Invented for use in broadcast systems and now used in VCRs. Conventional longitudinal recording records a track of data straight across the width of a single-track tape. Helical scan recording packs more data on the tape by positioning the tape at an angle to the recording heads. The heads spin to record diagonal stripes of information on the tape.

hexadecimal number   A number encoded in base 16, such that digits include the letters A through F as well as the numerals 0 through 9 (for example, 8BF3, which equals 35,827 in base 10).

Hi8 video The high-quality extension of the Video 8 (or 8mm) format, which features higher luminance resolution.

hidden file A file that is not displayed in DOS directory listings because the file's attribute byte holds a special setting.

high density (HD) An indication of the storage capacity of a floppy drive or disk in which 15 or 18 sectors per track are recorded using MFM encoding.

high sierra format A standard format for placing files and directories on CD-ROMs, proposed by an ad hoc committee of computer vendors, software developers, and CD-ROM system integrators. (Work on the format proposal began at the High Sierra Hotel at Lake Tahoe, Nevada.) A revised version of the format was adopted by the ISO as ISO 9660.

high-definition television (HDTV) Any one of a variety of video formats offering greater visual accuracy (or resolution) than current NTSC, PAL, or SECAM broadcast standards. Current formats generally range in resolution from 655 to 2,125 scanning lines, having an aspect ratio of 5:3 (or 1.67:1) and a video bandwidth of 30 to 50MHz (5+ times greater than NTSC standard). Digital HDTV has a bandwidth of 300MHz. HDTV is subjectively comparable to 35mm film.

high-level formatting Formatting performed by the DOS FORMAT program. Among other things, it creates the root directory and FATs.

history file A file created by utility software to keep track of earlier use of the software. Many backup programs, for example, keep history files describing earlier backup sessions.

HMA High Memory Area. The first 64K of extended memory, which is controlled typically by the HIMEM.SYS device driver. Real-mode programs can be loaded into the HMA to conserve conventional memory. Normally DOS 5.0 and higher use the HMA exclusively to reduce the DOS conventional memory footprint.

home page A top-level Web document that relates to an individual or an organization. Other pages in the document are accessible by links from the home page.

HPT High-pressure tin. A PLCC socket that promotes high forces between socket contacts and PLCC contacts for a good connection.

HST High-speed technology. The USRobotics proprietary high-speed modem-signaling scheme, developed as an interim protocol until the V.32 protocol could be implemented in a cost-effective manner. Incorporates trellis-coded modulation for greater immunity from variable phone-line conditions and asymmetrical modulation for more efficient use of the phone channel at speeds of 4,800 bps and above. The forward channel transmits at either 9,600 bps (older designs) or 14,400 bps, and the reverse channel transmits at 450 bps. This technique eliminated the need for the V.32 echo-cancellation hardware that was more costly at the time HST was developed. HST also incorporates MNP-compatible error-control procedures adapted to the asymmetrical modulation.

HTML HyperText Markup Language. A language used to describe and format plain-text files on the Web. HTML is based on pairs of tags which enable you to mix graphics with text, change the appearance of text, and create hypertext documents with links to other documents.

HTTP HyperText Transfer Protocol. The protocol that describes the rules that a browser and server use to communicate over the World Wide Web. HTTP allows a Web browser to request HTML documents from a Web server.

Huffman coding A technique that minimizes the average number of bytes required to represent the characters in a text. Huffman coding works for a given character distribution by assigning short codes to frequently occurring characters and longer codes to infrequently occurring characters.

hypertext A technology that allows for quick and easy navigation between and within large documents. Hypertext links are pointers to other sections within the same document, other documents, or other resources such as FTP sites, images, or sounds.

Hz An abbreviation for hertz, a frequency measurement unit used internationally to indicate one cycle per second.

I/O Input/output. A circuit path that enables independent communications between the processor and external devices.

IBMBIO.COM One of the DOS system files required to boot the machine. The first file loaded from disk during the boot that contains extensions to the ROM BIOS.

IBMDOS.COM One of the DOS system files required to boot the machine. Contains the primary DOS routines. Loaded by IBMBIO.COM, it in turns loads COMMAND.COM.

IC Integrated circuit. A complete electronic circuit contained on a single chip. May consist of only a few transistors, capacitors, diodes, or resistors, or thousands of them, and generally is classified according to the complexity of the circuitry and the approximate number of circuits on the chip. SSI (small-scale integration) equals 2 to 10 circuits. MSI (medium-scale integration) equals 10 to 100 circuits. LSI (large-scale integration) equals 100 to 1,000 circuits. VLSI (very-large-scale integration) equals 1,000 to 10,000 circuits. ULSI (ultra-large-scale integration) equals more than 10,000 circuits.

IDE Integrated Drive Electronics. Describes a hard disk with the disk controller circuitry integrated within it. The first IDE drives commonly were called hard cards. Also refers to the *ATA interface standard*, the standard for attaching hard disk drives to ISA bus IBM-compatible computers. IDE drives typically operate as though they were standard ST-506/412 drives. See also *ATA*.

incremental backup A backup of all files that have changed since the last backup.

initiator A device attached to the SCSI bus that sends a command to another device (the target) on the SCSI bus. The SCSI host adapter plugged into the system bus is an example of a SCSI initiator.

inkjet printer A type of printer that sprays one or more colors of ink on the paper. Can produce output with quality approaching that of a laser printer at a lower cost.

input Data sent to the computer from the keyboard, telephone, video camera, another computer, paddles, joysticks, and so on.

instruction Program step that tells the computer what to do for a single operation.

integrated circuit See *IC*.

interface A communications device or protocol that enables one device to communicate with another. Matches the output of one device to the input of the other device.

interlacing A method of scanning alternate lines of pixels on a display screen. The odd lines are scanned first from top to bottom and left to right. The electron gun goes back to the top and makes a second pass, scanning the even lines. Interlacing requires two scan passes to construct a single image. Because of this additional scanning, interlaced screens often seem to flicker unless a long persistence phosphor is used in the display.

interleave ratio The number of sectors that pass beneath the read/write heads before the "next" numbered sector arrives. When the interleave ratio is 3:1, for example, a sector is read, two pass by, and then the next is read. A proper interleave ratio, laid down during low-level formatting, enables the disk to transfer information without excessive revolutions due to missed sectors.

internal command In DOS, a command contained in COMMAND.COM so that no other file must be loaded in order to perform the command. `DIR` and `COPY` are two examples of internal commands.

internal drive A disk or tape drive mounted inside one of a computer's disk drive bays (or a hard disk card, which is installed in one of the computer's slots).

Internet A computer network that joins many government, university, and private computers together over phone lines. The Internet traces its origins to a network set up in 1969 by the Department of Defense. You can connect to the Internet through many online services such as CompuServe, BIX, and America Online. Internet computers use the TCP/IP communications protocol. There are several million hosts on the Internet. A *host* is a mainframe, mini, or workstation that directly supports the Internet protocol (the IP in TCP/IP).

interpreter A program for a high-level language that translates and executes the program at the same time. The program statements that are interpreted remain in their original source language, the way the programmer wrote them—that is, the program does not need to be compiled before execution. Interpreted programs run slower than compiled programs and always must be run with the interpreter loaded into memory.

interrupt A suspension of a process, such as the execution of a computer program, caused by an event external to that process and performed in such a way that the process can be resumed. An interrupt can be caused by internal or external conditions, such as a signal indicating that a device or program has completed a transfer of data.

interrupt vector A pointer in a table that gives the location of a set of instructions that the computer should execute when a particular interrupt occurs.

IO.SYS One of the DOS system files required to boot the machine. The first file loaded from disk during the boot. Contains extensions to the ROM BIOS.

IPX Internet Packet eXchange. Novell NetWare's native LAN communications protocol used to move data between server and/or workstation programs running on different network nodes. The IPX packets are encapsulated and carried by the packets used in Ethernet and the similar frames used in Token-Ring networks.

IRQ Interrupt Request. Physical connections between external hardware devices and the interrupt controllers. When a device such as a floppy controller or a printer needs the attention of the CPU, an IRQ line is used to get the attention of the system to perform a task. On PC and XT IBM-compatible systems, eight IRQ lines are included, numbered IRQ0 through IRQ7. On the AT and PS/2 systems, 16 IRQ lines are numbered IRQ0 through IRQ15. IRQ lines must be used only by a single adapter in the ISA bus systems, but Micro-Channel Architecture (MCA) adapters can share interrupts.

ISDN Integrated Services Digital Network. An international telecommunications standard that enables a communications channel to carry digital data simultaneously with voice and video information.

ISO International Standards Organization. The ISO, based in Paris, develops standards for international and national data communications. The U.S. representative to the ISO is the American National Standards Institute (ANSI).

ISO 9660 An international standard that defines file systems for CD-ROM disks, independent of the operating system. ISO (International Standards Organization) 9660 has two levels. Level one provides for DOS file system compatibility, while Level two allows file names of up to 32 characters.

ITU International Telecommunications Union. Formerly called CCITT. An international committee organized by the United Nations to set international communications recommendations, which frequently are adopted as standards, and to develop interface, modem, and data network recommendations. The Bell 212A standard for 1,200 bps communication in North America, for example, is observed internationally as CCITT V.22. For 2,400 bps communication, most U.S. manufacturers observe V.22bis, while V.32, V.32bis, V34, and V34+ are standards for 9,600, 14,400, 28,800, and 33,600 bps, respectively. Work is now under way to define a new standard for 56Kbps.

Java An object-oriented programming language and environment similar to C or C++. Java was developed by Sun Microsystems and is used to create network-based applications.

JEDEC Joint Electron Devices Engineering Council. A group that establishes standards for the electronics industry.

J-lead J-shaped leads on chip carriers that can be surface-mounted on a PC board or plugged into a socket that then is mounted on a PC board, usually on .050-inch centers.

JPEG Joint Photographic Experts Group. The international consortium of hardware, software, and publishing interests that, under the auspices of the ISO, has defined a universal standard for digital compression and decompression of still images for use in computer systems. JPEG compresses at about a 20:1 ratio before visible image degradation occurs. It is lossy data compression standard that was originally designed for still images but can also compress real-time video (30 frames per second) and animation. Lossy compression permanently discards unnecessary data, resulting in some loss of precision.

jumper A small, plastic-covered, metal clip that slips over two pins protruding from a circuit board. Sometimes also called a *shunt*. When in place, the jumper connects the pins electrically and closes the circuit. By doing so, it connects the two terminals of a switch, turning it "on."

Kermit A protocol designed for transferring files between microcomputers and mainframes. Developed by Frank DaCruz and Bill Catchings at Columbia University (and named after the talking frog on *The Muppet Show*), Kermit is widely accepted in the academic world. The complete Kermit protocol manual and the source for various versions is available from Kermit Distribution at the Columbia University Center for Computing Activities.

key disk In software copy protection, a distribution floppy disk that must be present in a floppy disk drive for an application program to run.

keyboard macro A series of keystrokes that automatically input when a single key is pressed.

kilo A multiplier indicating one thousand (1,000) of some unit. Abbreviated as k or K. When used to indicate a number of bytes of memory storage, the multiplier definition changes to 1,024. One kilobit, for example, equals 1,000 bits, and one kilobyte equals 1,024 bytes.

kilobyte (K) A unit of information storage equal to 1,024 bytes.

local area network (LAN) The connection of two or more computers, usually via a network adapter card or NIC.

landing zone An unused track on a disk surface on which the read/write heads can land when power is shut off. The place that a parking program or a drive with an autopark mechanism parks the heads.

LAPM Link-Access Procedure for Modems. An error-control protocol incorporated in CCITT Recommendation V.42. Like the MNP and HST protocols, uses cyclic redundancy checking (CRC) and retransmission of corrupted data (ARQ) to ensure data reliability.

laptop computer A computer system smaller than a briefcase but larger than a notebook that usually has a clamshell design in which the keyboard and display are on separate halves of the system, which are hinged together. These systems normally run on battery power.

laser printer A type of printer that is a combination of an electrostatic copying machine and a computer printer. The output data from the computer is converted by an interface into a raster feed, similar to the impulses that a TV picture tube receives. The impulses cause the laser beam to scan a small drum that carries a positive electrical charge. Where the laser hits, the drum is discharged. A toner that also carries a positive charge is then applied to the drum. This toner, a fine black powder, sticks only to the areas of the drum that have been discharged electrically. As it rotates, the drum deposits the toner on a negatively charged sheet of paper. Another roller then heats and bonds the toner to the page.

latency The amount of time required for a disk drive to rotate half of a revolution. Represents the average amount of time to locate a specific sector after the heads have arrived at a specific track. Latency is part of the average access time for a drive.

LBA Logical Block Addressing. A method used with SCSI and IDE drives to translate the cylinder, head, and sector specifications of the drive to those usable by an enhanced BIOS. LBA is used with drives that are larger than 528M and causes the BIOS to translate the drive's logical parameters to those usable by the system BIOS.

LCC Leadless Chip Carrier. A type of integrated circuit package that has input and output pads rather than leads on its perimeter.

LCD Liquid Crystal Display. A display that uses liquid crystal sealed between two pieces of polarized glass. The polarity of the liquid crystal is changed by an electric current to vary the amount of light that can pass through. Because LCD displays do not generate light, they depend on either the reflection of ambient light or backlighting the screen. The best type of LCD, the active-matrix or thin-film transistor (TFT) LCD, offers fast screen updates and true color capability.

LED Light-Emitting Diode. A semiconductor diode that emits light when a current is passed through it.

LIF Low Insertion Force. A type of socket that requires only a minimum of force to insert a chip carrier.

light pen A hand-held input device with a light-sensitive probe or stylus connected to the computer's graphics adapter board by a cable. Used for writing or sketching on-screen or as a pointing device for making selections. Unlike mice, not widely supported by software applications.

local bus A generic term used to describe a bus that is directly attached to a processor that operates at the processor's speed and data transfer width.

local echo A modem feature that enables the modem to send copies of keyboard commands and transmitted data to the screen. When the modem is in command mode (not online to another system), the local echo normally is invoked through an ATE1 command, which causes the modem to display your typed commands. When the modem is online to another system, the local echo is invoked by an ATF0 command, which causes the modem to display the data it transmits to the remote system.

logical drive A drive as named by a DOS drive specifier, such as C: or D:. Under DOS 3.3 or later, a single physical drive can act as several logical drives, each with its own specifier.

logical unit number See *LUN*.

lossless compression A compression technique that preserves all the original information in an image or other data structures.

lossy compression A compression technique that achieves optimal data reduction by discarding redundant and unnecessary information in an image.

lost clusters Clusters that have been marked accidentally as "unavailable" in the FAT even though they don't belong to any file listed in a directory.

low-level formatting Formatting that divides tracks into sectors on the platter surfaces. Places sector-identifying information before and after each sector and fills each sector with null data (usually hex F6). Specifies the sector interleave and marks defective tracks by placing invalid checksum figures in each sector on a defective track.

LUN Logical Unit Number. A number given to a device (a logical unit) attached to a SCSI physical unit and not directly to the SCSI bus. Although as many as eight logical units can be attached to a single physical unit, normally a single logical unit is a built-in part of a single physical unit. A SCSI hard disk, for example, has a built-in SCSI bus adapter that is assigned a physical unit number or SCSI ID, and the controller and drive portions of the hard disk are assigned a LUN (usually 0). Also see *PUN*.

LZW Lempel Zev Welch. A compression scheme used in the GIF graphic format.

magnetic domain A tiny segment of a track just large enough to hold one of the magnetic flux reversals that encode data on a disk surface.

magneto-optical recording An erasable optical disk recording technique that uses a laser beam to heat pits on the disk surface to the point at which a magnet can make flux changes.

master partition boot sector On hard disks, a one-sector record that gives essential information about the disk and tells the starting locations of the various partitions. Always the first physical sector of the disk.

MCA Micro-Channel Architecture. Developed by IBM for the PS/2 line of computers and introduced on April 2, 1987. Features include a 16- or 32-bit bus width and multiple master control. By allowing several processors to arbitrate for resources on a single bus, the MCA is optimized for multitasking, multiprocessor systems. Offers switchless configuration of adapters, which eliminates one of the biggest headaches of installing older adapters.

MCGA   MultiColor Graphics Array. A type of PC video display circuit introduced by IBM on April 2, 1987, that supports text and graphics. Text is supported at a maximum resolution of 80×25 characters in 16 colors with a character box of 8×16 pixels. Graphics are supported at a maximum resolution of 320×200 pixels in 256 (from a palette of 262,144) colors or 640×480 pixels in two colors. The MCGA outputs an analog signal with a horizontal scanning frequency of 31.5KHz and supports analog color or analog monochrome displays.

MCI   Media Control Interface. A device-independent specification for controlling multimedia devices and files. MCI is a part of the multimedia extensions and offers a standard interface set of device control commands, making it easy to program multimedia applications. MCI commands are used for audio recording and playback and animation playback. Videodisk players and other optional devices are controlled by MCI. Device types include CD audio, digital audio tape players, scanners, MIDI sequencers, videotape players or recorders, and audio devices that play digitized waveform files. MCI classifies compound and simple device drivers. Compound drivers require a device element (usually a file and a path) during operation. Simple devices do not require a device element for playback.

MDA   Monochrome Display Adapter. A type of PC video display adapter introduced by IBM on August 12, 1981, that supports text only. Text is supported at a maximum resolution of 80×25 characters in four colors with a character box of 9×14 pixels. Colors, in this case, indicates black, white, bright white, and underlined. Graphics modes are not supported. The MDA outputs a digital signal with a horizontal scanning frequency of 18.432KHz and supports TTL monochrome displays. The IBM MDA also included a parallel printer port.

mean time between failure   See *MTBF*.

mean time to repair   See *MTTR*.

medium   The magnetic coating or plating that covers a disk or tape.

mega   A multiplier indicating 1 million (1,000,000) of some unit. Abbreviated as m or M. When used to indicate a number of bytes of memory storage, the multiplier definition changes to 1,048,576. One megabit, for example, equals 1,000,000 bits, and one megabyte equals 1,048,576 bytes.

megabyte (M)   A unit of information storage equal to 1,048,576 bytes.

memory caching   A service provided by extremely fast memory chips that keeps copies of the most recent memory accesses. When the CPU makes a subsequent access, the value is supplied by the fast memory rather than by relatively slow system memory.

memory   Any component in a computer system that stores information for future use.

memory-resident program A program that remains in memory after it has been loaded, consuming memory that otherwise might be used by application software.

menu software Utility software that makes a computer easier to use by replacing DOS commands with a series of menu selections.

MFM Modified Frequency Modulation encoding. A method of encoding data on the surface of a disk. The coding of a bit of data varies by the coding of the preceding bit to preserve clocking information.

MHz An abbreviation for megahertz, a unit of measurement indicating the frequency of one million cycles per second. One hertz (Hz) is equal to one cycle per second. Named after Heinrich R. Hertz, a German physicist who first detected electromagnetic waves in 1883.

MI/MIC Mode Indicate/Mode Indicate Common. Also called *forced* or *manual originate*. Provided for installations in which equipment other than the modem does the dialing. In such installations, the modem operates in dumb mode (no auto-dial capability), yet must go off-hook in originate mode to connect with answering modems.

micro (μ) A prefix indicating one millionth (1/1,000,000 or .000001) of some unit.

microprocessor A solid-state central processing unit much like a computer on a chip. An integrated circuit that accepts coded instructions for execution.

microsecond (μs) A unit of time equal to one millionth (1/1,000,000 or .000001) of a second.

MIDI Musical Instrument Digital Interface. An interface and file format standard for connecting a musical instrument to a microcomputer and storing musical instrument data. Multiple musical instruments can be daisy-chained and played simultaneously with the help of the computer and related software. The various operations of the instruments can be captured, saved, edited, and played back. A MIDI file contains note information, timing (how long a note is held), volume, and instrument type for as many as 16 channels. Sequencer programs are used to control MIDI functions such as recording, playback, and editing. MIDI files store only note instructions and not actual sound data.

milli (m) A prefix indicating one thousandth (1/1,000 or .001) of some unit.

millisecond (ms) A unit of time equal to one thousandth (1/1,000 or .001) of a second.

MIPS Million Instructions Per Second. Refers to the average number of machine-language instructions a computer can perform or execute in one second. Because different processors can perform different functions in a single instruction, MIPS should be used only as a general measure of performance among different types of computers.

mnemonic An abbreviated name for something, which is used in a manner similar to an acronym. Computer processor instructions are often abbreviated with a mnemonic such as JMP (Jump), CLR (Clear), STO (Store), INIT (Initialize). A mnemonic name for an instruction or an operation makes it easy to remember and convenient to use.

MNP Microcom Networking Protocol. Asynchronous error-control and data-compression protocols developed by Microcom, Inc. and now in the public domain. Ensure error-free transmission through error detection (CRC) and retransmission of errored frames. MNP Levels 1 through 4 cover error control and have been incorporated into CCITT Recommendation V.42. MNP Level 5 includes data compression but is eclipsed in superiority by V.42bis, an international standard that is more efficient. Most high-speed modems will connect with MNP Level 5 if V.42bis is unavailable.

MO Magneto-Optical. MO drives use both magnetic and optical storage properties. MO technology is erasable and recordable, as opposed to CD-ROM (Read Only) and WORM (Write Once) drives. MO uses laser and magnetic field technology to record and erase data.

modem Modulator-demodulator. A device that converts electrical signals from a computer into an audio form transmittable over telephone lines or vice versa. Modulates or transforms digital signals from a computer into the analog form that can be carried successfully on a phone line; also demodulates signals received from the phone line back to digital signals before passing them to the receiving computer.

module An assembly that contains a complete circuit or subcircuit.

Monochrome Display Adapter See *MDA*.

morphing Slang term for metamorphosis, the transformation of one object into another. Morphing is performed by software that analyzes two images and creates several in-between images so that one image appears to become the other. Originally requiring expensive, high-powered computer hardware, morphing can now be done on PC systems with sophisticated software now available.

MOS Metal-Oxide Semiconductor. Refers to the three layers used in forming the gate structure of a Field-Effect Transistor (FET). MOS circuits offer low power dissipation and enable transistors to be jammed close together before a critical heat problem arises. PMOS, the oldest type of MOS circuit, is a silicon-gate P-channel MOS process that uses currents made up of positive charges. NMOS is a silicon-gate N-channel MOS process that uses currents made up of negative charges and is at least twice as fast as PMOS. CMOS, Complementary MOS, is nearly immune to noise, runs off almost any power supply, and is an extremely low-power circuit technique.

motherboard The main circuit board in the computer. Also called *planar*, *system board*, or *backplane*.

MPC A trademarked abbreviation for Multimedia Personal Computer. The original MPC specification was developed by Tandy Corporation and Microsoft as the minimum platform capable of running multimedia software. In the summer of 1995, the MPC Marketing Council introduced an upgraded MPC 3 standard. The MPC 1 Specification defines the following minimum standard requirements: a 386SX or 486 CPU; 2M RAM; 30M hard disk; VGA video display; 8-bit digital audio subsystem; CD-ROM drive; and systems software compatible with the Applications Programming Interfaces (APIs) of Microsoft Windows version 3.1 or higher. The MPC 2 Specification defines the following minimum standard requirements: a 25MHz 486SX with 4M RAM; 160M hard disk; 16-bit sound card; 65,536 color video display; double-speed CD-ROM drive; and systems software compatible with the APIs of Microsoft Windows version 3.1 or higher. The MPC 3 Specification defines the following minimum standard requirements: a 75MHz Pentium with 8M RAM; 540M hard disk; 16-bit sound card; 65,536 color video display; quad speed CD-ROM drive; OM-1 compliant MPEG-1 video, and systems software compatible with the APIs of Microsoft Windows version 3.1 and DOS 6.0 or higher.

MPEG (Motion Picture Experts Group) A working committee which, under the auspices of the ISO, has defined standards for lossy digital compression and decompression of motion video/audio for use in computer systems. See also *lossy*. These standards consist of MPEG-1 and MPEG-2. The MPEG-1 standard delivers decompression data at 1.2 to 1.5M/sec, allowing CD players to play full-motion color movies at 30 frames per second. MPEG-1 compresses at about a 50:1 ratio before image degradation occurs, but compression ratios as high as 200:1 are attainable. Building on the MPEG-1 standard is MPEG-2, which extends to the higher data rates (2 to 15Mbps) needed for signals delivered from remote sources (such as broadcast, cable, or satellite). MPEG-2 is designed to support a range of picture aspect ratios, including 4:3 and 16:9. MPEG compression produces about a 50 percent volume reduction in file size.

MSDOS.SYS One of the DOS system files required to boot the machine. Contains the primary DOS routines. Loaded by IO.SYS, it in turn loads COMMAND.COM.

MTBF Mean Time Between Failure. A statistically derived measure of the probable time a device will continue to operate before a hardware failure occurs, usually given in hours. Because no standard technique exists for measuring MTBF, a device from one manufacturer can be significantly more or significantly less reliable than a device with the same MTBF rating from another manufacturer.

MTTR Mean Time To Repair. A measure of the probable time it takes a technician to service or repair a specific device, usually given in hours.

MultiColor Graphics Array See *MCGA*.

multimedia The integration of sound, graphic images, animation, motion video, and text in one environment on a computer. It is a set of hardware and software technologies that is rapidly changing and enhancing the computer environment.

multitask To run several programs simultaneously.

multithread To concurrently process more than one message by an application program. OS/2, Windows 95, and Windows NT are examples of multithreaded operating systems. Each program can start two or more threads, which carry out various interrelated tasks with less overhead than two separate programs would require.

multiuser system A system in which several computer terminals share the same central processing unit (CPU).

nano (n) A prefix indicating one billionth (1/1,000,000,000 or .000000001) of some unit.

nanosecond (ns) A unit of time equal to one billionth (1/1,000,000,000 or .000000001) of a second.

network A system in which a number of independent computers are linked in order to share data and peripherals, such as hard disks and printers.

nonvolatile memory (NVRAM) Random-access memory whose data is retained when power is turned off. Sometimes NVRAM is retained without any power whatsoever, as in EEPROM or flash memory devices. In other cases, the memory is maintained by a small battery. NVRAM that is battery maintained is sometimes called *CMOS memory*. *CMOS NVRAM* is used in IBM-compatible systems to store configuration information. *True NVRAM* often is used in intelligent modems to store a user-defined default configuration loaded into normal modem RAM at power-up.

nonvolatile RAM disk A RAM disk powered by a battery supply so that it continues to hold its data during a power outage.

notebook computer A very small personal computer approximately the size of a notebook.

NTSC The National Television Standards Committee, which governs the standard for television and video playback and recording in the United States. The NTSC was originally organized in 1941 when TV broadcasting first began on a wide scale in black and white, and the format was revised in 1953 for color. The original standard it created was called RS-170A, which is now simply referred to as NTSC. The NTSC format has 525 scan lines, a field frequency of 60Hz, a broadcast bandwidth of 4MHz, line frequency of 15.75KHz, frame frequency of 1/30 of a second, and a color subcarrier frequency of 3.58MHz. It is an interlaced signal, which means that it scans every other line each time the screen is refreshed. The signal is generated as a composite of red, green, and blue signals for color and includes an FM frequency for audio and a signal for stereo. Twenty years later, higher standards were adopted in Europe with the PAL and SECAM systems, both incompatible with the NTSC standard of North America. NTSC is also called *composite video*.

null modem A serial cable wired so that two Data Terminal Equipment (DTE) devices, such as personal computers, or two Data Communication Equipment (DCE) devices, such as modems or mice, can be connected. Also sometimes called a *modem-eliminator*. To make a null-modem cable with DB-25 connectors, you wire these pins together: 1-1, 2-3, 3-2, 4-5, 5-4, 6-8-20, 20-8-6, and 7-7.

object hierarchy Occurs in a graphical program when two or more objects are linked and one object's movement is dependent on the other object. This is known as a *parent-child hierarchy*. In an example using a human figure, the fingers are child objects to the hand, which is a child object to the arm, which is a child to the shoulder, and so on. Object hierarchy provides much control for an animator in moving complex figures.

OCR Optical Character Recognition. An information-processing technology that converts human-readable text into computer data. Usually a scanner is used to read the text on a page, and OCR software converts the images to characters.

ODI Open Data-link Interface. A device driver standard from Novell that enables you to run multiple protocols on the same network adapter card. The ODI adds functionality to Novell's NetWare and network computing environments by supporting multiple protocols and drivers.

OEM Original Equipment Manufacturer. Any manufacturer that sells its product to a reseller. Usually refers to the original manufacturer of a particular device or component. Most Compaq hard disks, for example, are made by Conner Peripherals, which is considered the OEM.

OLE Object Linking and Embedding. An enhancement to the original Dynamic Data Exchange (DDE) protocol that allows you to embed or link data created in one application into a document created in another application and subsequently edit that data directly from the final document.

online fallback A feature that enables high-speed error-control modems to monitor line quality and fall back to the next lower speed if line quality degrades. Some modems fall forward as line quality improves.

operating system (OS) A collection of programs for operating the computer. Operating systems perform housekeeping tasks such as input and output between the computer and peripherals as well as accepting and interpreting information from the keyboard. DOS and OS/2 are examples of popular OSes.

optical disk A disk that encodes data as a series of reflective pits that are read (and sometimes written) by a laser beam.

Orange Book The standard for recordable compact discs (such as CD-ROM, but recordable instead of read-only). Recordable compact discs are called *CD-R* and are becoming popular with the widespread use of multimedia. Part of the Orange Book standard defines rewritable Magneto-Optical disks and another section defines optical Write Once Read Many (WORM) disks.

originate mode A state in which the modem transmits at the predefined low frequency of the communications channel and receives at the high frequency. The transmit/receive frequencies are the reverse of the called modem, which is in answer mode.

OS/2 A universal operating system developed through a joint effort by IBM and Microsoft Corporation. The latest operating system from IBM for microcomputers using the Intel 386 or better microprocessors. OS/2 uses the protected mode operation of the processor to expand memory from 1M to 4G and to support fast, efficient multitasking. The OS/2 Workplace Shell, an integral part of the system, is a graphical interface similar to Microsoft Windows and the Apple Macintosh system. The latest version runs DOS, Windows, and OS/2-specific software.

output Information processed by the computer or the act of sending that information to a mass storage device such as a video display, a printer, or a modem.

OverDrive An Intel trademark name for its line of upgrade processors.

overlay   Part of a program that is loaded into memory only when it is required.

overrun   A situation where data moves from one device faster than a second device can accept it.

overscanning   A technique used in consumer display products that extends the deflection of a CRT's electron beam beyond the physical boundaries of the screen to ensure that images will always fill the display area. See also *underscanning*.

overwrite   To write data on top of existing data, thus erasing the existing data.

package   A device that includes a chip mounted on a carrier and sealed.

PAL   Phase Alternating Line system. Invented in 1961, a system of TV broadcasting used in England and other European countries (except France). PAL's image format is 4:3, 625 lines, 50Hz, and 4MHz video bandwidth with a total 8MHz of video channel width. With its 625-line picture delivered at 25 frames per second, PAL provides a better image and an improved color transmission over the NTSC system used in North America. PAL also can stand for *Programmable Array Logic*, a type of chip that has logic gates specified by a device programmer.

palmtop computer   A computer system smaller than a notebook that is designed so that it can be held in one hand while being operated by the other. Many are now called *PDAs* or *Personal Digital Assistants*.

parallel   A method of transferring data characters in which the bits travel down parallel electrical paths simultaneously—for example, eight paths for 8-bit characters. Data is stored in computers in parallel form but may be converted to serial form for certain operations.

parity   A method of error checking in which an extra bit is sent to the receiving device to indicate whether an even or odd number of binary 1 bits were transmitted. The receiving unit compares the received information with this bit and can obtain a reasonable judgment about the validity of the character. The same type of parity (even or odd) must be used by two communicating computers, or both may omit parity. When parity is used, a parity bit is added to each transmitted character. The bit's value is 0 or 1, to make the total number of 1s in the character even or odd, depending on which type of parity is used.

park program   A program that executes a seek to the highest cylinder or just past the highest cylinder of a drive so that the potential of data loss is minimized if the drive is moved.

partition   A section of a hard disk devoted to a particular operating system. Most hard disks have only one partition devoted to DOS. A hard disk can have as many as four partitions, each occupied by a different operating system. DOS v3.3 or higher can occupy two of these four partitions.

Pascal   A high-level programming language named for the French mathematician Blaise Pascal (1623-1662). Developed in the early 1970s by Niklaus Wirth for teaching programming and designed to support the concepts of structured programming.

PC Card (PCMCIA) Personal Computer Memory Card International Association. A credit card-sized expansion adapter for notebook and laptop PCs. PC Card is the official PCMCIA trademark; however, both PC Card and PCMCIA card are used to refer to these standards. PCMCIA cards are removable modules that can hold numerous types of devices including memory, modems, fax/modems, radio transceivers, network adapters, solid state disks, and hard disks.

Pentium An Intel microprocessor with 32-bit registers, a 64-bit data bus, and a 32-bit address bus. The Pentium has a built-in Level 1 cache which is segmented into a separate 8K cache for code and another 8K cache for data. The Pentium includes an FPU (floating-point unit) or math coprocessor. The Pentium is backward-compatible with the 486 and can operate in real, protected virtual, and virtual real modes.

Pentium Pro An Intel microprocessor with 32-bit registers, a 64-bit data bus, and a 36-bit address bus. The Pentium Pro has the same segmented Level 1 cache as the Pentium, but also includes a 256K or 512K Level 2 cache on a separate die in the same module. The Pentium Pro includes a FPU (floating-point unit) or math coprocessor. The Pentium Pro is backward-compatible with the Pentium and can operate in real, protected virtual, and virtual real modes.

Pentium II An Intel Pentium Pro with MMX capabilities, using Single Edge Contact (SEC) cartridge packaging technology.

peripheral Any piece of equipment used in computer systems that is an attachment to the computer. Disk drives, terminals, and printers are all examples of peripherals.

PGA Pin-Grid Array. A chip package that has a large number of pins on the bottom designed for socket mounting. Also can mean Professional Graphics Adapter, a limited-production, high-resolution graphics card for XT and AT systems from IBM.

Photo CD A technology developed by Eastman Kodak and Philips that stores photographic images on a CD-R recordable compact disc. Images stored on the Photo CD may have resolutions as high as 2,048×3,072 pixels. Up to 100 true-color images (24-bit color) can be stored on one disk. Photo CD images are created by scanning film and digitally recording the images on compact discs (CDs). The digitized images are indexed (given a four-digit code), and thumbnails of each image on the disc are shown on the front of the case along with its index number. Multi-session capability enables several rolls of film to be added to a single disk on different occasions.

physical drive A single disk drive. DOS defines logical drives, which are given a specifier, such as C: or D:. A single physical drive may be divided into multiple logical drives. Conversely, special software can span a single logical drive across two physical drives.

physical unit number See *PUN*.

PIF Program Information File. A file that contains information about a non-Windows application specifying optimum settings for running the program under Windows 3.x. These are called *property sheets* in Windows 95.

pixel A mnemonic term meaning picture element. Any of the tiny elements that form a picture on a video display screen. Also called a *pel*.

planar board A term equivalent to *motherboard*, used by IBM in some of its literature.

plated media Hard disk platters plated with a form of thin metal film media on which data is recorded.

platter A disk contained in a hard disk drive. Most drives have two or more platters, each with data recorded on both sides.

PLCC Plastic Leaded-Chip Carrier. A popular chip-carrier package with J-leads around the perimeter of the package.

Plug and Play (PnP) A hardware and software specification developed by Intel that enables a PnP system and PnP adapter cards to automatically configure themselves. PnP cards are free from switches and jumpers and are configured via the PnP BIOS in the host system, or via supplied programs for non-PnP systems.

port Plug or socket that enables an external device such as a printer to be attached to the adapter card in the computer. Also a logical address used by a microprocessor for communications between itself and various devices.

port address One of a system of addresses used by the computer to access devices such as disk drives or printer ports. You may need to specify an unused port address when installing any adapter boards in a system unit.

portable computer A computer system smaller than a transportable system but larger than a laptop system. Most portable systems conform to the lunchbox style popularized by Compaq or the briefcase style popularized by IBM, each with a fold-down (removable) keyboard and built-in display. These systems characteristically run on AC power and not on batteries, include several expansion slots, and can be as powerful as full-blown desktop systems.

POS Programmable Option Select. The Micro-Channel Architecture's POS eliminates switches and jumpers from the system board and adapters by replacing them with programmable registers. Automatic configuration routines store the POS data in a battery-powered CMOS memory for system configuration and operations. The configuration utilities rely on Adapter Description Files (ADF) that contain the setup data for each card.

POST Power-On Self Test. A series of tests run by the computer at power-on. Most computers scan and test many of their circuits, sounding a beep from the internal speaker if this initial test indicates proper system performance.

PostScript A page-description language developed primarily by John Warnock of Adobe Systems for converting and moving data to the laser-printed page. Instead of using the standard method of transmitting graphics or character information to a printer and telling it where to place dots one-by-one on a page, PostScript provides a way for the laser printer to interpret mathematically a full page of shapes and curves.

power supply   An electrical/electronic circuit that supplies all operating voltage and current to the computer system.

PPP   Point-to-Point Protocol. A protocol that enables a computer to use the Internet with a standard telephone line and a high-speed modem. PPP is a new standard which replaces SLIP. PPP is less common than SLIP; however, it is increasing in popularity.

primary partition   An ordinary, single-volume bootable partition. See also *extended partition*.

processor speed   The clock rate at which a microprocessor processes data. A standard IBM PC, for example, operates at 4.77MHz (4.77 million cycles per second).

program   A set of instructions or steps telling the computer how to handle a problem or task.

PROM   Programmable Read-Only Memory. A type of memory chip that can be programmed to store information permanently—information that cannot be erased.

proprietary   Anything invented by a company and not used by any other company. Especially applies to cases in which the inventing company goes to great lengths to hide the specifications of the new invention. The opposite of *standard*.

protected mode   A mode available in all Intel 80286- or 80386-compatible processors. In this mode, memory addressing is extended to 16 or 4,096M, and restricted protection levels can be set to trap software crashes and control the system.

protocol   A system of rules and procedures governing communications between two or more devices. Protocols vary, but communicating devices must follow the same protocol in order to exchange data. The data format, readiness to receive or send, error detection, and error correction are some of the operations that may be defined in protocols.

PUN   Physical Unit Number. A term used to describe a device attached directly to the SCSI bus. Also known as a *SCSI ID*. As many as eight SCSI devices can be attached to a single SCSI bus, and each must have a unique PUN or ID assigned from 7 to 0. Normally the SCSI host adapter is assigned the highest-priority ID, which is 7. A bootable hard disk is assigned an ID of 0, and other nonbootable drives are assigned higher priorities.

QAM   Quadrature Amplitude Modulation. A modulation technique used by high-speed modems that combines both phase and amplitude modulation. This technique enables multiple bits to be encoded in a single time interval. The V.32bis standard-codes 6 data bits plus an additional trellis coding bit for each signal change. An individual signal is evaluated with respect to phase and amplitude compared to the carrier wave. A plot of all possible QAM signal points is referred to as the signal constellation pattern. The V.32bis constellation pattern has 128 discrete signal points.

QIC   Quarter-Inch Committee. An industry association that sets hardware and software standards for tape-backup units that use quarter-inch-wide tapes.

QWERTY keyboard The standard typewriter or computer keyboard, with the characters Q, W, E, R, T, and Y on the top row of alpha keys. Because of the haphazard placement of characters, this keyboard can hinder fast typing.

rails Plastic strips attached to the sides of disk drives mounted in IBM ATs and compatibles so that the drives can slide into place. These rails fit into channels in the side of each disk drive bay position.

RAM Random-Access Memory. All memory accessible at any instant (randomly) by a microprocessor.

RAM disk A "phantom disk drive" in which a section of system memory (RAM) is set aside to hold data, just as though it were a number of disk sectors. To DOS, a RAM disk looks and functions like any other drive.

random-access file A file in which all data elements (or records) are of equal length and written in the file end to end, without delimiting characters between. Any element (or record) in the file can be found directly by calculating the record's offset in the file.

Random-Access Memory See *RAM*.

raster A pattern of horizontal scanning lines normally on a TV screen. An electromagnetic field causes the beam of the TV tube to illuminate the correct dots to produce the required characters.

raster graphics A technique for representing a picture image as a matrix of dots. It is the digital counterpart of the analog method used in TV. There are several raster graphics standards.

RCA jack Also called a *phono connector*. A plug and socket for a two-wire coaxial cable used to connect audio and video components. The plug is a 1/8-inch thick prong that sticks out 5/16-inch from the middle of a cylinder.

read/write head A tiny magnet that reads and writes data on a disk track.

read-only file A file whose attribute setting in the file's directory entry tells DOS not to allow software to write into or over the file.

read-only memory See *ROM*.

real mode A mode available in all Intel 8086-compatible processors that enables compatibility with the original 8086. In this mode, memory addressing is limited to 1M.

real time The actual time in which a program or event takes place. In computing, real time refers to an operating mode under which data is received and processed and the results returned so quickly that the process appears instantaneous to the user. The term is also used to describe the process of simultaneous digitization and compression of audio and video information.

Red Book More commonly known as Compact Disc Digital Audio (CD-DA) and is one of four compact disc standards. Red Book got its name from the color of the manual used to describe the CD Audio specifications. The Red Book audio standard requires that digital audio is sampled at a 44.1KHz sample rate using 16 bits for each sample. This is the standard used by audio CDs and many CD-ROMs.

refresh cycle A cycle in which the computer accesses all memory locations stored by DRAM chips so that the information remains intact. DRAM chips must be accessed several times per second, or else the information fades.

register Storage area in memory having a specified storage capacity, such as a bit, a byte, or a computer word, and intended for a special purpose.

remote digital loopback A test that checks the phone link and a remote modem's transmitter and receiver. Data entered from the keyboard is transmitted from the initiating modem, received by the remote modem's receiver, looped through its transmitter, and returned to the local screen for verification.

remote echo A copy of the data received by the remote system, returned to the sending system, and displayed on-screen. A function of the remote system.

resolution A reference to the size of the pixels used in graphics. In medium-resolution graphics, pixels are large. In high-resolution graphics, pixels are small.

RFI Radio Frequency Interference. A high frequency signal radiated by improperly shielded conductors, particularly when signal path lengths are comparable to or longer than the signal wavelengths. The FCC now regulates RFI in computer equipment sold in the U.S. under FCC Regulations Part 15, Subpart J.

RGB Red-Green-Blue. A type of computer color-display output signal comprised of separately controllable red, green, and blue signals, as opposed to *composite video*, where signals are combined prior to output. RGB monitors typically offer higher resolution than composite monitors.

RISC An acronym for Reduced Instruction Set Computer, as differentiated from CISC, Complex Instruction Set Computer. RISC processors have simple instruction sets requiring only one or a few execution cycles. These simple instructions can be used more effectively than CISC systems with appropriately designed software, resulting in faster operations.

RLL Run-Length Limited. A type of encoding that derives its name from the fact that the techniques used limit the distance (run length) between magnetic flux reversals on the disk platter. Several types of RLL encoding techniques exist, although only two are commonly used. (1,7)RLL encoding increases storage capacity by about 30 percent over MFM encoding and is most popular in the very highest capacity drives due to a better window margin, while (2,7)RLL encoding increases storage capacity by 50 percent over MFM encoding and is used in the majority of RLL implementations. Most IDE, ESDI, and SCSI hard disks use one of these forms of RLL encoding.

RMA number Return-Merchandise Authorization number. A number given to you by a vendor when you arrange to return an item for repairs. Used to track the item and the repair.

ROM Read-Only Memory. A type of memory that has values permanently or semi-permanently burned in. These locations are used to hold important programs or data that must be available to the computer when the power initially is turned on.

ROM BIOS Read Only Memory-Basic Input Output System. A BIOS encoded in a form of read-only memory for protection. Often applied to important start-up programs that must be present in a system for it to operate.

root directory The main directory of any hard or floppy disk. Has a fixed size and location for a particular disk volume and cannot be resized dynamically the way subdirectories can.

router Hardware that routes messages from one local area network to another. It is used to internetwork similar and dissimilar networks and can select the most expedient route based on traffic load, line speeds, costs, and network failures.

routine Set of frequently used instructions. May be considered as a subdivision of a program with two or more instructions that are related functionally.

RS-232 An interface introduced in August 1969 by the Electronic Industries Association. The RS-232 interface standard provides an electrical description for connecting peripheral devices to computers.

scan lines The parallel lines across a video screen, along which the scanning spot travels in painting the video information that makes up a monitor picture. NTSC systems use 525 scan lines to a screen; PAL systems use 625.

scratch disk A disk that contains no useful information and can be used as a test disk. IBM has a routine on the Advanced Diagnostics disks that creates a specially formatted scratch disk to be used for testing floppy drives.

SCSI Small Computer System Interface. A standard originally developed by Shugart Associates (then called SASI for Shugart Associates System Interface) and later approved by ANSI in 1986.

SCSI-2 Approved in 1994 and is the currently approved SCSI standard.

SCSI-3 Currently in the development process. Normally uses a 50-pin connector and permits multiple devices (up to eight including the host) to be connected in daisy-chain fashion.

SDLC Synchronous Data Link Control. A protocol developed by IBM for software applications and communication devices operating in IBM's Systems Network Architecture (SNA). Defines operations at the link level of communications; for example, the format of data frames exchanged between modems over a phone line.

SECAM Séquential Couleur à Mémoire (Sequential Color within Memory). The French color TV system also adopted in Russia. The basis of operation is the sequential recording of primary colors in alternate lines. The image format is 4:3, 625 lines, 50Hz, and 6MHz video bandwidth with a total 8MHz of video channel width.

sector A section of one track defined with identification markings and an identification number. Most sectors hold 512 bytes of data.

security software Utility software that uses a system of passwords and other devices to restrict an individual's access to subdirectories and files.

seek time The amount of time required for a disk drive to move the heads across one-third of the total number of cylinders. Represents the average time it takes to move the heads from one cylinder to another randomly selected cylinder. Seek time is a part of the average access time for a drive.

semiconductor A substance, such as germanium or silicon, whose conductivity is poor at low temperatures but is improved by minute additions of certain substances or by the application of heat, light, or voltage. Depending on the temperature and pressure, a semiconductor can control the flow of electricity. Semiconductors are the basis of modern electronic-circuit technology.

sequencer A software program that controls MIDI file messages and keeps track of music timing. Because MIDI files store note instructions instead of actual sounds, a sequencer is needed to play, record, and edit MIDI sounds. Sequencer programs allow for recording and playback of MIDI files by storing the instrument, the note's pitch (frequency), duration in real time that each note is held, and loudness (amplitude) of each musical or sound effect note.

sequential file A file in which varying-length data elements are recorded end-to-end, with delimiting characters placed between each element. To find a particular element, you must read the whole file up to that element.

serial The transfer of data characters one bit at a time, sequentially, using a single electrical path.

servo data Magnetic markings written on disk platters to guide the read/write heads in drives that use voice-coil actuators.

session (single or multi-session) A term used in CD-ROM recording to describe a recording event. In a single session, data is recorded on a CD-ROM disc and an index is created. If additional space is left on the disc, another session can be used to record additional files along with another index. The original index cannot be updated because recordable CD-ROM drives are normally Write Once Read Many (WORM) type drives. Many CD-ROM drives do not expect additional recording sessions and therefore will be unable to read the additional session data on the disk. The advent of Kodak's Photo CD propelled the desire for multi-session CD-ROM XA (extended architecture) drives. The first generation of XA drives were capable of single-session reads only. Multi-session CD-ROM XA drives will read all the indices created when images are recorded many times on the same CD-ROM XA drive.

settling time The time required for read/write heads to stop vibrating after they have been moved to a new track.

shadow ROM A copy of a system's slower access ROM BIOS placed in faster access RAM, usually during the start-up or boot procedure. This setup enables the system to access BIOS code without the penalty of additional wait states required by the slower ROM chips. Also called *shadow RAM*.

shell The generic name of any user-interface software. COMMAND.COM is the standard shell for DOS. OS/2 comes with three shells: a DOS command shell, an OS/2 command shell, and the OS/2 Presentation Manager, a graphical shell.

shielded twisted pair (STP) Unshielded Twisted Pair (UTP) network cabling with a metal sheath or braid around it, usually used in Token-Ring networks.

shock rating A rating (usually expressed in G force units) of how much shock a disk drive can sustain without damage. Usually two different specifications exist for a drive powered on or off.

signal-to-noise (S/N) ratio The strength of a video or audio signal in relation to interference (noise). The higher the S/N ratio, the better the quality of the signal.

SIMM Single Inline Memory Module. An array of memory chips on a small PC board with a single row of I/O contacts.

single-ended An electrical signaling method where a single line is referenced to a ground path common to other signals. In a single-ended bus intended for moderately long distances, there is commonly one ground line between groups of signal lines to provide some resistance to signal crosstalk. Single-ended signals only require one driver or receiver pin per signal, plus one ground pin per group of signals. Single-ended signals are vulnerable to common mode noise and crosstalk but are much less expensive than differential signaling methods.

SIP Single Inline Package. A DIP-like package with only one row of leads.

skinny dip Twenty-four- and 28-position DIP devices with .300-inch row-to-row centerlines.

SLIP Serial Line Internet Protocol. An Internet protocol that is used to run the Internet Protocol (IP) over serial lines such as telephone circuits. IP enables a packet to traverse multiple networks on the way to its final destination.

SMPTE time code An 80-bit standardized edit time code adopted by SMPTE, the Society of Motion Picture and Television Engineers. The SMPTE time code is a standard used to identify individual video frames in the video editing process. SMPTE time code controls such functions as play, record, rewind, and forward of video tapes. SMPTE time code displays video in terms of hours, minutes, seconds, and frames for accurate video editing.

soft error An error in reading or writing data that occurs sporadically, usually because of a transient problem such as a power fluctuation.

software   A series of instructions loaded in the computer's memory that instructs the computer how to accomplish a problem or task.

SO-J   Small Outline J-lead. A small DIP package with J-shaped leads for surface mounting or socketing.

spindle   The central post on which a disk drive's platters are mounted.

SQL   Structured Query Language. A standard relational database language used especially on midrange and mainframe computers.

SRAM   Static Random Access Memory. A form of high speed memory. SRAM chips do not require a refresh cycle like DRAM chips and can be made to operate at very high access speeds. SRAM chips are very expensive because they normally require six transistors per bit. This also makes the chip larger than conventional DRAM chips. SRAM is volatile, meaning it will lose data with no power.

ST-506/412   A hard disk interface invented by Seagate Technology and introduced in 1980 with the ST-506 5M hard drive.

stair-stepping   Jagged raster representation of diagonals or curves; corrected by anti-aliasing.

standby power supply   A backup power supply that quickly switches into operation during a power outage.

start/stop bits   The signaling bits attached to a character before the character is transmitted during asynchronous transmission.

starting cluster   The number of the first cluster occupied by a file. Listed in the directory entry of every file.

stepper motor actuator   An assembly that moves disk drive read/write heads across platters by a sequence of small partial turns of a stepper motor.

storage   Device or medium on or in which data can be entered or held and retrieved at a later time. Synonymous with *memory*.

streaming   In tape backup, a condition in which data is transferred from the hard disk as quickly as the tape drive can record the data so that the drive does not start and stop or waste tape.

string   A sequence of characters.

subdirectory   A directory listed in another directory. Subdirectories themselves exist as files.

subroutine   A segment of a program that can be executed by a single call. Also called *program module*.

surface mount   Chip carriers and sockets designed to mount to the surface of a PC board.

surge protector A device in the power line that feeds the computer and provides protection against voltage spikes and other transients.

S-VHS or Super VHS A higher-quality extension of the VHS home videotape format, featuring higher luminance and the capability to produce better copies.

S-Video (Y/C) Type of video signal used in the Hi8 and S-VHS videotape formats in which the luminance and chrominance (Y/C) components are kept separate, providing greater control and quality of each image. S-video transmits luminance and color portions separately, thus avoiding the NTSC encoding process and its inevitable loss of picture quality.

synchronous communication A form of communication in which blocks of data are sent at strictly timed intervals. Because the timing is uniform, no start or stop bits are required. Compare with *asynchronous communication*. Some mainframes support only synchronous communications unless a synchronous adapter and appropriate software have been installed.

system crash A situation in which the computer freezes up and refuses to proceed without rebooting. Usually caused by faulty software. Unlike a hard disk crash, no permanent physical damage occurs.

system files The two hidden DOS files IBMBIO.COM and IBMDOS.COM; they represent the interface between the BIOS and DOS (IBMBIO) and the interface between DOS and other applications (IBMDOS).

system integrator A computer consultant or vendor who tests available products and combines them into highly optimized systems.

target A device attached to a SCSI bus that receives and processes commands sent from another device (the initiator) on the SCSI bus. A SCSI hard disk is an example of a target.

TCM Trellis-coded modulation. An error-detection and correction technique employed by high-speed modems to enable higher-speed transmissions that are more resistant to line impairments. In TCM encoding, the first 2 data bits of an encoded group are used to generate a third TCM bit that is added to the group. For example, in V.32bis, the first 2 bits of a 6-bit group are used to generate the TCM bit, which then is placed as the first bit of a new 7-bit group. By reversing the encoding at the other end, the receiving modem can determine whether the received group is valid.

TCP/IP Transmission Control Protocol/Internet Protocol. A set of protocols developed by the U.S. Department of Defense (DoD) to link dissimilar computers across many kinds of networks. This is the primary protocol used by the Internet. It was developed in the 1970s by the DoD's Advanced Research Projects Agency (DARPA) as a military standard protocol. TCP/IP is supported by many manufacturers of minicomputers, personal computers, mainframes, technical workstations, and data communications equipment.

temporary backup A second copy of a work file, usually having the extension BAK. Created by application software so that you easily can return to a previous version of your work.

temporary file A file temporarily (and usually invisibly) created by a program for its own use.

tera A multiplier indicating 1 trillion (1,000,000,000,000) of some unit. Abbreviated as t or T. When used to indicate a number of bytes of memory storage, the multiplier definition changes to 1,099,511,627,776. One terabit, for example, equals 1,000,000,000,000 bits, and one terabyte equals 1,099,511,627,776 bytes.

terabyte (T) A unit of information storage equal to 1,099,511,627,776 bytes.

terminal A device whose keyboard and display are used for sending and receiving data over a communications link. Differs from a microcomputer in that it has no internal processing capabilities. Used to enter data into or retrieve processed data from a system or network.

terminal mode An operational mode required for microcomputers to transmit data. In terminal mode, the computer acts as though it were a standard terminal such as a teletypewriter rather than a data processor. Keyboard entries go directly to the modem, whether the entry is a modem command or data to be transmitted over the phone lines. Received data is transmitted directly to the screen. The more popular communications software products control terminal mode and enable more complex operations, including file transmission and saving received files.

terminator A piece of hardware that must be attached to both ends of an electrical bus. Functions to prevent the reflection or echoing of signals that reach the ends of the bus and to ensure that the correct impedance load is placed in the driver circuits on the bus.

thin-film media Hard disk platters that have a thin film (usually three-millionths of an inch) of medium deposited on the aluminum substrate through a sputtering or plating process.

through-hole Chip carriers and sockets equipped with leads that extend through holes in a PC board.

throughput The amount of user data transmitted per second without the overhead of protocol information such as start and stop bits or frame headers and trailers.

TIFF Tagged Image File Format. A way of storing and exchanging digital image data. Developed by Aldus Corporation, Microsoft Corporation, and major scanner vendors to help link scanned images with the popular desktop publishing applications. Supports three main types of image data: black-and-white data, halftones or dithered data, and grayscale data.

time code A frame-by-frame address code, time reference recorded on the spare track of a videotape or inserted in the vertical blanking interval. The time code is an eight-digit number encoding time in hours, minutes, seconds, and video frames.

Token Ring A type of local area network (LAN) in which the workstations relay a packet of data called a *token* in a logical ring configuration. When a station wants to transmit, it takes possession of the token, attaches its data, and then frees the token after the data has made a complete circuit of the electrical ring. Transmits at speeds of 16 million bps. Because of the token-passing scheme, access to the network is controlled, unlike the slower 10BaseX Ethernet system where collisions of data can occur, which waste time. The Token-Ring network uses shielded, twisted-pair wiring, which is cheaper than the coaxial cable used by 10Base2 and 10Base5 Ethernet and ARCnet.

tower A personal computer that normally sits on the floor, and which is mounted vertically rather than horizontally.

TPI Tracks per inch. Used as a measurement of magnetic track density. Standard 5 1/4-inch 360K floppy disks have a density of 48 TPI, and the 1.2M disks have a 96 TPI density. All 3 1/2-inch disks have a 135.4667 TPI density, and hard disks can have densities greater than 3,000 TPI.

track One of the many concentric circles that holds data on a disk surface. Consists of a single line of magnetic flux changes and is divided into some number of 512-byte sectors.

track density Expressed as tracks per inch (TPI); defines how many tracks are recorded in 1 inch of space measured radially from the center of the disk. Sometimes called *radial density*.

track-to-track seek time The time required for read/write heads to move between adjacent tracks.

transportable computer A computer system larger than a portable system, and similar in size and shape to a portable sewing machine. Most transportables conform to a design similar to the original Compaq portable, with a built-in CRT display. These systems are characteristically very heavy, and run only on AC power. Because of advances primarily in LCD and plasma-display technology, these systems are largely obsolete and have been replaced by portable systems.

troubleshooting The task of determining the cause of a problem.

true-color images True-color images are also called 24-bit color images because each pixel is represented by 24 bits of data, allowing for 16.7 million colors. The number of colors possible is based on the number of bits used to represent the color. If 8 bits are used, there are 256 possible color values (2 to the 8th power). To obtain 16.7 million colors, each of the primary colors (red, green, and blue) is represented by 8 bits per pixel, which allows for 256 possible shades for each of the primary red, green, and blue colors, or 256×256×256 = 16.7 million total colors.

TSR Terminate-and-Stay-Resident. A program that remains in memory after being loaded. Because they remain in memory, TSR programs can be reactivated by a predefined keystroke sequence or other operation while another program is active. Usually called *resident programs*.

TTL Transistor-to-Transistor Logic. Digital signals often are called TTL signals. A TTL display is a monitor that accepts digital input at standardized signal voltage levels.

tweens The name given to a series of animation or video frames between the key frames. When one object is transformed (morphed) into another, the initial object and the final object are set on the computer. Tweens are the frames that transpose the first object into the final image.

twisted pair A type of wire in which two small insulated copper wires are wrapped or twisted around each other to minimize interference from other wires in the cable. Two types of twisted-pair cables are available: unshielded and shielded. Unshielded Twisted-Pair (UTP) wiring commonly is used in telephone cables and provides little protection against interference. Shielded Twisted-Pair (STP) wiring is used in some networks or any application in which immunity from electrical interference is more important. Twisted-pair wire is much easier to work with than coaxial cable and is cheaper as well.

UART Universal Asynchronous Receiver Transmitter. A chip device that controls the RS-232 serial port in a PC-compatible system. Originally developed by National Semiconductor, several UART versions are in PC-compatible systems: The 8250B is used in PC- or XT-class systems, and the 16450 and 16550A are used in AT-class systems.

unformatted capacity The total number of bytes of data that can fit on a disk. The formatted capacity is lower because space is lost defining the boundaries between sectors.

uninterruptible power supply (UPS) A device that supplies power to the computer from batteries so that power will not stop, even momentarily, during a power outage. The batteries are recharged constantly from a wall socket.

Universal Asynchronous Receiver Transmitter See *UART*.

UPC Universal Product Code. A 10-digit computer-readable bar code used in labeling retail products. The code in the form of vertical bars includes a five-digit manufacturer's identification number and a five-digit product code number.

update To modify information already contained in a file or program with current information.

URL An acronym for Uniform Resource Locator. The primary naming scheme used to identify a particular site or file on the World Wide Web. URLs combine information about the protocol being used, the address of the site where the resource is located, the subdirectory location at the site, and the name of the particular file (or page) in question.

utility Programs that carry out routine procedures to make computer use easier.

UTP Unshielded Twisted Pair. A type of wire often used indoors to connect telephones or computer devices. Comes with two or four wires twisted inside a flexible plastic sheath or conduit and uses modular plugs and phone jacks.

V.21 An ITU standard for modem communications at 300 bps. Modems made in the U.S. or Canada follow the Bell 103 standard but can be set to answer V.21 calls from overseas. The actual transmission rate is 300 baud and employs FSK (Frequency Shift Keying) modulation, which encodes a single bit per baud.

V.22 An ITU standard for modem communications at 1,200 bps, with an optional fallback to 600 bps. V.22 is partially compatible with the Bell 212A standard observed in the U.S. and Canada. The actual transmission rate is 600 baud, using DPSK (Differential-Phase Shift Keying) to encode as many as 2 bits per baud.

V.22bis An ITU standard for modem communications at 2,400 bps. Includes an automatic link-negotiation fallback to 1,200 bps and compatibility with Bell 212A/V.22 modems. The actual transmission rate is 600 baud, using QAM (Quadrature Amplitude Modulation) to encode as many as 4 bits per baud.

V.23 An ITU standard for modem communications at 1,200 or 600 bps with a 75-bps back channel. Used in the United Kingdom for some videotext systems.

V.25 An ITU standard for modem communications that specifies an answer tone different from the Bell answer tone used in the U.S. and Canada. Most intelligent modems can be set with an ATB0 command so that they use the V.25 2,100Hz tone when answering overseas calls.

V.32 An ITU standard for modem communications at 9,600 bps and 4,800 bps. V.32 modems fall back to 4,800 bps when line quality is impaired and fall forward again to 9,600 bps when line quality improves. The actual transmission rate is 2,400 baud using QAM (Quadrature Amplitude Modulation) and optional TCM (Trellis-Coded Modulation) to encode as much as 4 data bits per baud.

V.32bis An ITU standard that extends the standard V.32 connection range and supports 4,800; 7,200; 9,600; 12,000; and 14,400 bps transmission rates. The V.32bis modems fall back to the next lower speed when line quality is impaired, fall back further as necessary, and fall forward to the next higher speed when line quality improves. The actual transmission rate is 2,400 baud using QAM (Quadrature Amplitude Modulation) and TCM (Trellis-Coded Modulation) to encode as much as 6 data bits per baud.

V.32terbo A proprietary standard proposed by several modem manufacturers that will be cheaper to implement than the standard V.32 fast protocol, but which will only support transmission speeds of up to 18,800 bps. Because it is not an industry standard, it is not likely to have widespread industry support.

V.34 An ITU standard that extends the standard V.32bis connection range, supporting 28,800 bps transmission rates as well as all the functions and rates of V.32bis. This was called V.32fast or V.fast while under development.

V.34+ An ITU standard that extends the standard V.34 connection range, supporting 33,600 bps transmission rates as well as all the functions and rates of V.34.

V.42 An ITU standard for modem communications that defines a two-stage process of detection and negotiation for LAPM error control. Also supports MNP error-control protocol, Levels 1 through 4.

V.42bis An extension of CCITT V.42 that defines a specific data-compression scheme for use with V.42 and MNP error control.

vaccine A type of program used to locate and eradicate virus code from infected programs or systems.

VCPI Virtual Control Program Interface. A 386 and higher processor memory management standard created by Phar Lap software in conjunction with other software developers. VCPI provides an interface between applications using DOS extenders and 386 memory managers.

Vertical Blanking Interval (VBI) Lines 1–21 of the video top field and lines 263–284 of the bottom field, in which frame numbers, picture stops, chapter stops, white flags, closed captions, and more may be encoded. These lines do not appear on the display screen, but maintain image stability and enhance image access.

VESA Video Electronics Standards Association. Founded in the late 1980s by NEC Home Electronics and eight other leading video board manufacturers with the main goal of standardizing the electrical, timing, and programming issues surrounding 800×600 resolution video displays, commonly known as *Super VGA*. VESA has also developed the Video Local Bus (VL-Bus) standard for connecting high speed adapters directly to the local processor bus.

VGA Video Graphics Array. A type of PC video display circuit (and adapter) first introduced by IBM on April 2, 1987, that supports text and graphics. Text is supported at a maximum resolution of 80×25 characters in 16 colors with a character box of 9×16 pixels. Graphics is supported at a maximum resolution of 320×200 pixels in 256 (from a palette of 262,144) colors or 640×480 pixels in 16 colors. The VGA outputs an analog signal with a horizontal scanning frequency of 31.5KHz, and supports analog color or analog monochrome displays.

VHS Video Home System. A popular consumer videotape format developed by Matsushita and JVC.

Video 8 or 8mm Video Video format based on the 8mm videotapes popularized by camcorders.

video graphics array See *VGA*.

video A system of recording and transmitting primarily visual information by translating moving or still images into electrical signals. The term video properly refers only to the picture, but as a generic term, video usually embraces audio and other signals that are part of a complete program. Video now includes not only broadcast television but many non-broadcast applications such as corporate communications, marketing, home entertainment, games, teletext, security, and even the visual display units of computer-based technology.

video-on-CD or video CD A full-motion digital video format using MPEG video compression and incorporating a variety of VCR-like control capabilities. See also *White Book*.

virtual disk A RAM disk or "phantom disk drive" in which a section of system memory (usually RAM) is set aside to hold data, just as though it were a number of disk sectors. To DOS, a virtual disk looks like and functions like any other "real" drive.

virtual memory A technique by which operating systems (including OS/2) load more programs and data into memory than they can hold. Parts of the programs and data are kept on disk and are constantly swapped back and forth into system memory. The applications' software programs are unaware of this setup and act as though a large amount of memory is available.

virtual real mode A mode available in all Intel 80386-compatible processors. In this mode, memory addressing is limited to 4,096M, restricted protection levels can be set to trap software crashes and control the system, and individual real-mode compatible sessions can be set up and maintained separately from one another.

virus A type of resident program designed to replicate itself. Usually at some later time when the virus is running, it causes an undesirable action to take place.

Visual Basic A high-level, graphically oriented, fourth-generation programming language only used in the Windows operating environment.

VL-Bus (VESA Local Bus) A standard 32-bit expansion slot bus specification used in 486 PCs. Now replaced by PCI bus.

VMM Virtual Memory Manager. A facility in Windows enhanced mode that manages the task of swapping data in and out of 386 and higher-processor virtual real-mode memory space for multiple non-Windows applications running in virtual real mode.

voice-coil actuator A device that moves read/write heads across hard disk platters by magnetic interaction between coils of wire and a magnet. Functions somewhat as an audio speaker, from which the name originated.

voltage regulator A device that smoothes out voltage irregularities in the power that's fed to the computer.

volume A portion of a disk signified by a single drive specifier. Under DOS v3.3 and later, a single hard disk can be partitioned into several volumes, each with its own logical drive specifier (C:,D:,E:, and so on).

volume label An identifier or name of up to 11 characters that names a disk.

VRAM Video Random-Access Memory. VRAM chips are modified DRAMs on video boards that enable simultaneous access by the host system's processor and the processor on the video board. A large amount of information thus can be transferred quickly between the video board and the system processor. Sometimes also called *dual-ported RAM*.

VxD Virtual Device Driver. A special type of Windows driver for 386 Enhanced Mode. VxDs run at the most privileged CPU mode (ring 0) and allows low-level interaction with DOS and Windows programs running under Windows.

wait states Pause cycles during system operation that require the processor to wait one or more clock cycles until memory can respond to the processor's request. Enables the microprocessor to synchronize with lower-cost, slower memory. A system that runs with "zero wait states" requires none of these cycles because of the use of faster memory or a memory cache system.

wide area network (WAN) A LAN that extends beyond the boundaries of a single building.

Web browser An application that locates a document on the Internet using a URL (Uniform Resource Locator), retrieves it, and formats the document for display. Netscape Navigator, Spyglass Mosaic, and Microsoft Internet Explorer are examples of Web browsers.

Web site An individual Web document collection named by a unique URL.

Whetstone A benchmark program developed in 1976 and designed to simulate arithmetic-intensive programs used in scientific computing. Remains completely CPU-bound and performs no I/O or system calls. Originally written in ALGOL, although the C and Pascal versions became more popular by the late 1980s. The speed at which a system performs floating-point operations often is measured in units of Whetstones.

White Book A standard specification developed by Philips and JVC in 1993 for storing MPEG standard video on CDs. An extension of the Red Book standard for digital audio, Yellow Book standard for CD-ROM, Green Book standard for CD-I, and Orange Book standard for CD Write Once.

Whitney technology A term referring to a magnetic disk design that usually has oxide or thin film media, thin film read/write heads, low floating height sliders, and low mass actuator arms that together allow higher bit densities than the older Winchester technology. Whitney technology was first introduced with the IBM 3370 disk drive, circa 1979.

Winchester drive Any ordinary, nonremovable (or fixed) hard disk drive. The name originates from a particular IBM drive in the 1960s that had 30M of fixed and 30M of removable storage. This 30-30 drive matched the caliber figure for a popular series of rifles made by Winchester, so the slang term *Winchester* was applied to any fixed platter hard disk.

Winchester technology The term *Winchester* is loosely applied to mean any disk with a fixed or non-removable recording medium. More precisely, the term applies to a ferrite read/write head and slider design with oxide media that was first employed in the IBM 3340 disk drive, circa 1973. Most drives today actually use Whitney technology.

wire frames   The most common technique used to construct a three-dimensional object for animation. A wire frame is given coordinates of length, height, and width. Wire frames then are filled with textures, colors, and movement. Transforming a wire frame into a textured object is called *rendering*.

word length   The number of bits in a data character without parity, start, or stop bits.

World Wide Web   Also called simply the Web. A graphical information system based on hypertext that enables a user to easily access documents located on the Internet.

WORM   Write Once, Read Many (or Multiple). An optical mass-storage device capable of storing many megabytes of information but that can be written to only once on any given area of the disk. A WORM disk typically holds more than 200M of data. Because a WORM drive cannot write over an old version of a file, new copies of files are made and stored on other parts of the disk whenever a file is revised. WORM disks are used to store information when a history of older versions must be maintained. Recording on a WORM disk is performed by a laser writer that burns pits in a thin metallic film (usually tellurium) embedded in the disk. This burning process is called *ablation*. WORM drives are frequently used for archiving data.

write precompensation   A modification applied to write data by a controller in order to alleviate partially the problem of bit shift, which causes adjacent 1s written on magnetic media to read as though they were farther apart. When adjacent 1s are sensed by the controller, precompensation is used to write them closer together on the disk, thus enabling them to be read in the proper bit-cell window. Drives with built-in controllers normally handle precompensation automatically. Precompensation normally is required for the inner cylinders of oxide media drives.

XGA   eXtended Graphics Array. A type of PC video display circuit (and adapter) first introduced by IBM on October 30, 1990, that supports text and graphics. Text is supported at a maximum resolution of 132×60 characters in 16 colors with a character box of 8×6 pixels. Graphics is supported at a maximum resolution of 1024×768 pixels in 256 (from a palette of 262,144) colors or 640×480 pixels in 65,536 colors. The XGA outputs an analog signal with a horizontal scanning frequency of 31.5 or 35.52KHz, and supports analog color or analog monochrome displays.

XMM   eXtended Memory Manager. A driver that controls access to extended memory on 286 and higher processor systems. HIMEM.SYS is an example of an XMM that comes with DOS.

Xmodem   A file-transfer protocol—with error checking—developed by Ward Christensen in the mid-1970s and placed in the public domain. Designed to transfer files between machines running the CP/M operating system and using 300 or 1,200 bps modems. Until the late 1980s, because of its simplicity and public-domain status, Xmodem remained the most widely used microcomputer file-transfer protocol. In standard Xmodem, the transmitted blocks are 128 bytes. 1K-Xmodem is an extension to Xmodem that increases the block size to 1,024 bytes. Many newer file-transfer protocols that are much faster and more accurate than Xmodem have been developed, such as Ymodem and Zmodem.

XMS eXtended Memory Specification. A Microsoft developed standard that provides a way for real-mode applications to access extended memory in a controlled fashion. The XMS standard is available from Microsoft.

XON/XOFF Standard ASCII control characters used to tell an intelligent device to stop or resume transmitting data. In most systems, pressing Ctrl+S sends the XOFF character. Most devices understand Ctrl+Q as XON; others interpret the pressing of any key after Ctrl+S as XON.

Y-connector A Y-shaped splitter cable that divides a source input into two output signals.

Yellow Book standards See *CD-ROM*.

Yellow Book The standard used by Compact Disc Read Only Memory (CD-ROM). Multimedia applications most commonly use the Yellow Book standard, which specifies how digital information is to be stored on the CD-ROM and is to be read by a computer. EXtended Architecture (XA) is currently an extension of the Yellow Book that allows for the combination of different data types (audio and video, for example) onto one track in a CD-ROM. Without XA, a CD-ROM can only access one data type at a time. Many CD-ROM drives are now XA capable.

Ymodem A file-transfer protocol first released as part of Chuck Forsberg's YAM (Yet Another Modem) program. An extension to Xmodem designed to overcome some of the limitations of the original. Enables information about the transmitted file, such as the file name and length, to be sent along with the file data and increases the size of a block from 128 to 1,024 bytes. Ymodem-batch adds the capability to transmit "batches" or groups of files without operator interruption. YmodemG is a variation that sends the entire file before waiting for an acknowledgment. If the receiving side detects an error in midstream, the transfer is aborted. YmodemG is designed for use with modems that have built-in error-correcting capabilities.

ZIF Zero Insertion Force. Sockets that require no force for the insertion of a chip carrier. Usually accomplished through movable contacts and used primarily in test devices in which chips will be inserted and removed many times.

ZIP Zigzag Inline Package. A DIP package that has all leads on one edge in a zigzag pattern and mounts in a vertical plane.

Zip drive An external drive manufactured by Iomega that supports 100M magnetic media on a 3 1/2-inch removable drive.

Zmodem A file-transfer protocol commissioned by Telnet and placed in the public domain. Like Ymodem, it was designed by Chuck Forsberg and developed as an extension to Xmodem to overcome the inherent latency when using Send/Ack-based protocols such as Xmodem and Ymodem. It is a streaming, sliding-window protocol.

Index

Symbols

1K bit memory chips, 10
1x-4x, 6x, 8x CD-ROM drives
 access times, 731
 data transfer rate, 729
3Com Corp., 990
3-D graphic accelerators, 423-424
3M
 Data Storage, 990
 magnetic media drives, 781
3 1/2-inch floppy disks, see floppy disks
3.3v PCI (Peripheral Component Interconnect) bus pinouts, 132-134
4-bit microprocessors, 10
4-pin inline connectors (floppy drives), 525-527
4-way set associative cache, 174
4B/5B scheme (FDDI), 484
5 1/4-inch floppy disks, see floppy disks
5-pin DIN connectors, 358
-5v current, 291
5v PCI (Peripheral Component Interconnect) bus pinouts, 129-131
6-pin mini-DIN connectors, 358

8-bit
 ISA (Industry Standard Architecture) bus, 111
  DMA channels, 145
  IRQs (Interrupt ReQuests), 142, 691
 microprocessors, 10
 sound, 497-498
 systems, see XT systems
8-inch floppy disk drives, see floppy disks
8mm tape drives, 771
9-pin serial cable adapter connections, 432
10Base2 IEEE standard, 1039
10Base5 IEEE standard, 1039
10BaseT, 1039
-12v current, 291
+12v power, 292
16-bit
 EISA (Enhanced Industry Standard Architecture) bus interrupts, 142-144
 Intel 8088 microprocessor, 942
 ISA (Industry Standard Architecture) bus, 112-115
  DMA channels, 692
  interrupts, 142-144
 MCA (Micro Channel Architecture) bus interrupts, 142-144

 sound, 497-498
 systems, see AT (Advanced Technolocy) PCs
21M floptical drives, 564-565
25-pin
 parallel port connector pinout, 447
 serial cable adapter connections, 432
 serial-port specifications, 431-432
30-pin SIMMs (Single Inline Memory Modules), 265, 274, 802
 capacities, 266
 IBM-style, 267
 pinouts, 269
32-bit
 ISA (Industry Standard Architecture) bus, 115
 systems, see AT (Advanced Technology) PCs
34-pin connectors (floppy drives), 525-527
56K modems, 445-446
72-pin SIMMs (Single Inline Memory Modules), 265-266, 274, 802
 EDO RAM, 272
 pinouts, 270
 presence detect pins, 271, 278

83-key PC/XT keyboards, 336
  cable part numbers, 365-366
  compatibility, 341-342
  interface, 345-346
  key numbers, 349-351
  replacements, 365-366
  scan codes, 349-351
84-key AT keyboards, 336-337
  cable part numbers, 365-366
  compatibility, 341-342
  interface, 345-346
  key numbers, 351-352
  replacements, 365-366
  scan codes, 351-352
100BaseT Ethernet cables, 484, 1039
100BaseVG, 1040
101-key (or 102-Key) keyboards, 337-339
  cable part numbers, 365-366
  compatibility, 341-342
  interface, 345-346
  key numbers, 353-357
  replacements, 365-366
  scan codes, 353-357
104-key keyboards, 339-341
  scan codes, 358
168-pin DIMMs (Dual Inline Memory Modules), 275
286 Intel processors, 167-168
386 Intel processors, 168-169
  386DX, 169-170
  386SL, 170-171
  386SX, 170
  protected mode, 169
  real mode, 169
  virtual real mode, 169
486 (80486) Intel processors, 171-173
  burst-mode memory cycles, 171
  instruction-execution time, 171
  internal (level 1) cache, 171, 174-175
  math coprocessors, 171
  upgrading
    to 487SX, 178
    to DX2/OverDrive, 178-182

486DX Intel processors, 175-213
  internal (level 1) cache, 174-175
  math coprocessors, 176
  OverDrive chips, 182-213
  protected mode, 176
  real mode, 176
  upgrading to OverDrive, 178-182
  virtual real mode, 176
486DX2 Intel processors, 178-213
  bus interface unit, 179
  designations, 190
  internal (level 1) cache, 174-175
  speed-rated versions, 172, 179
  upgrade sockets, 180-182
  see also OverDrive Intel processors
486DX4 Intel processors
  internal (level 1) cache, 174-175
  memory bus, 108
  speed rating, 172
486SL Intel processors, 176-177
486SX Intel processors, 177-178
  internal (level 1) cache, 174-175
  OverDrive chips, 182-213
1167 math coprocessor (Weitek), 210
4167 math coprocessors (Weitek), 210
5140 PC Convertible laptop, 936-941
  automobile power adapters, 940
  battery chargers, 940
  extendable buses, 937
  features, 937-938
  LCD display, 937
  memory cards, 939
  modems, 940
  part numbers, 941
  printers, 939-940
  serial/parallel adapters, 940-941
  specifications, 938
  Static RAM, 937

  system-unit options, 938
  video displays, 938-940
8008 microprocessors, 10
8080 microprocessors, 10
8086 Intel processors, 166-167, 1041
8087 Intel processors, 208-209, 1041
8088 Intel processors, 166-167, 932, 942, 947, 1041
8250 chip (UART), 434
8250A chip (UART), 434
8250B chip (UART), 434
8514 display adapters, 403
8514/A processors, 1041
16450 chip (UART), 434
16550 chip (UART), 434
16550A chip (UART), 434
80186 Intel processors, 167
80188 Intel processors, 167
80286 Intel processors, 1040
80287 Intel math coprocessor, 209
80287 Intel processors, 1040
80386 Intel processors
  markings for 32-bit multiply bugs, 211
  testing, 211-212
80386DX processors, 1040
80386SX processors, 1040
80387 processors, 209-210, 1040
80486 Intel processors, *see* **486 Intel processors**
80486DX processors, 1040
80486DX2 processors, 1040
80486DX4 processors, 1040
80486SX processors, 1040
80487 math coprocessors (Intel), 210
82430FX PCI (Peripheral Component Interconnect) set, 799

A

A-Cable
  Differential Connector, 671
  Standard SCSI, 666
A20 line, 244
AAD (Analog Alignment Diskette), 869

adapters

Aavid Thermal
 Technologies, Inc., 990
ABIT Computer (USA)
 Corporation, 991
Above Boards (expanded
 memory), 245
AC (alternating current),
 1041
 voltage, measuring, 34-35
ACC Microelectronics
 Corporation, 991
accelerator boards, 1041
access
 keys, 112
 time, 1041
  average access time,
   1045
  CD-ROM drives,
   730-731
accumulators, 1041
Accurite Technologies,
 Inc., 991
 reference standard
  disks, 869
Acer America Corp., 991
Acme Electric/Safe
 Power, 991
acoustic couplers, 833
active low (digital signal),
 1041
active matrix displays,
 815-816
active media sensors, 534
active terminators
 (SCSI), 674
active-matrix LCD monitors,
 387-388
actuators, 1041
Adaptec, 991
 AHA-1542CF SCSI
  adapter, 238
 SCSI (Small Computer
  System Interface) host
  adapters, 683
adapter boards
 conflicts, 154-156
 removing, 46-47
 see also boards
adapter description files,
 see ADF
adapters, 1041
 5140 PC Convertible
  laptop, 937
 access keys, 112

cable adapters (9-pin/
 25-pin connections), 432
CD-ROM drives, 745
controller cards, 1056
EGA (Enhanced Graphics
 Adapter), 1061
EISA bus (Enhanced
 Industry Standard
 Architecture), 117
game, 381-383
hard disk controller BIOS,
 234-236
host adapters (SCSI),
 683-684
installing, 153
MCA (Micro Channel
 Architecture) bus, 116
memory
 auto-configure adapter
  boards, 250
 configuration, 250-251
 moving to resolve
  conflicts, 251
 optimizing, 251-252
 scratch pad memory, 232
 UMA (Upper Memory
  Area), 251
 see also memory
network adapters, 236-238
 Adaptec AHA-1542CF
  SCSI, 238
 IPL (Initial Program
  Load) ROM, 236-238
 shared memory (RAM),
  236-238
 Token Ring memory
  map, 237
 see also NICs (Network
  Interface Cards)
PCI (Peripheral Component
 Interconnect) bus, 127
ROM (Read Only Memory),
 233-234
 hard disk controller
  BIOS, 234-236
 video adapter BIOS, 234
SCSI (Small Computer
 System Interface) adapter
 BIOS, 234-236
 conflicts, 155
sound cards
 accessories, 504-507
 audio CDs, 495

buying/selection
 criteria, 499-504
concepts, 495-496
Game Blaster, 489
games, 490-491
installation, 508-509
MIDI (Musical
 Instrument Digital
 Interface), 492-493
multimedia, 491-492
patching into stereo
 systems, 509-510
presentations, 493
proofreading, 495
recording sounds,
 493-494
Sound Blaster, 489
sound mixers, 495
terminology, 495-499
troubleshooting
 problems, 510-515
voice annotation, 494
voice recognition,
 494-495
three-prong, 323
VESA local bus, 123
video adapters, 396-424,
 805-806
 8514 display, 403
 bus mastering, 406
 buying criteria, 417
 CGA (Color Graphics
  Adapter), 398-400
 chipsets, 417-418
 codecs, 422
 DisplayMate, 427
 EGA (Enhanced
  Graphics Adapter),
  400-402
 frame buffer
  technology, 414
 HGC (Hercules Graphics
  Card), 398
 MCGA (MultiColor
  Graphics Array),
  403-404
 MDA (Monochrome
  Display Adapter),
  396-398
 memory, 229, 412-413
 NTSC-to-VGA adapter,
  422
 output devices, 419-420

1103

adapters

PCI (Peripheral Component Interconnect), 416
PGA (Professional Graphics Adapter), 402-403
speed improvements, 414-417
SVGA (Super Video Graphics Array), 408-409
troubleshooting, 425-427
VESA SVGA standards (VESA BIOS Extension), 410-412
VGA (Video Graphics Array), 404-409
VMC (VESA Media Channel), 418-419
XGA/XGA-2 (eXtended Graphics Array), 406-409
Adaptive Differential Pulse Code Modulation (ADPCM), 499, 741
Addison-Wesley Publishing Co, Inc., 992
address bus, 108, 1042
processors, 162-163
addresses, 1042
I/O port, 147-148
addresses, configuring controllers, 693-694
parallel ports, 148
serial ports, 148
logical, 224
memory
linear, 227-228
segment, 226-228
Mueller, Scott (author), 986
vendors, 989-1038
ADF (adapter description files), 1042
AdLib sound cards, 496
Adobe Systems, Inc., 992
ADPCM (Adaptive Differential Pulse Code Modulation), 499, 741
ADS (analog-to-digital converters), 497

Advanced CMOS settings, chipset documentation, 23
Advanced Diagnostics (IBM), 707, 843-863
MCA (Micro Channel Architecture) bus, 844
POST error codes, 844-863
Hewlett-Packard 486/U, 847-849
IBM, 849-863
personal computer, 844-846
Advanced Digital Information Corp., 992
Advanced Integration Research (AIR), 992
Advanced Logic Research (ALR), 992
Advanced Micro Devices (AMD), 992
Advanced Personal Systems, 992
Advanced Power Management (APM), 424-425, 830, 1043
Advanced Run Length Limited (ARLL), 578
Advanced SCSI Programming Interface (ASPI), 680
Advanced Technology PCs, *see* **AT (Advanced Technology) PCs**
Aeronics, Inc., 992
AHA-2940AU (SCSI adapter), 683
AHA-2940UW (SCSI adapter), 683
AIR (Advanced Integration Research), 992
air filters (hard disk drives), 607
airport X-ray machines, effects on disks, 557-559
AIWA America, Inc. Computer Systems Division, 992
Alaris, 993
algorithms (Next Available Cluster), 888-889
ALI Aladdin chipset, 800

aliasing, 1042-1043
aligning
floppy disk drives, 563-564
read/write heads (floppy drives), 522
All Points Addressable (APA), 1043
Alliance Research/ORA Electronics, 993
AllMicro, Inc. (Purchased by ForeFront Direct), 993
allocation units (clusters), 543, 903-904, 1053
floppy disks, 903
hard disks, 585, 904
lost clusters, 1074
space allocation in DOS, 888-889
starting cluster, 1090
Alloy Computer Products, 993
alphanumeric characters, 1042
ALPS Electric, 993
Alps ergonomic keyboards, 360
ALR (Advanced Logic Research), 992
Altair kit (MITS), 10
Altex Electronics, Inc., 993
AMD (Advanced Micro Devices), 992
Intel-compatible processors, 205
Amdek Corporation, 994
America Online, 994
American Megatrends, Inc. (AMI), *see* **AMI**
American National Standards Institute (ANSI), 994, 1042
SCSI (Small Computer System Interface) standards, 655-657
American Power Conversion (APC), 994
American Society of Mechanical Engineers (ASME), 1044
American Standard Code for Information Interchange (ASCII), 1044
characters, 1043

Ameriquest Technology, 994
AMI (American Megatrends, Inc.), 287-288, 994
  AMIDiag, 864-865
  ROM BIOS
    audio POST codes, 839-840
    compatibility, 85-88
    problems, 288
AMP, Inc., 994
amperes, 1042
amplitude, 496
analog, 1042
  Analog Alignment Diskette, 869
  loopback, 1042
  signals, 1042
    VGA adapters (Video Graphics Array), 404
  telecommunications, *see* ISDN
  video, 1042
analog-to-digital converters, 1042
AND gate, 1042
AND logic operator, 1042
Andromeda Research, 994
animation, 1042
Annabooks, 994
annotations (voice recordings), sound cards, 494
ANSI (American National Standards Institute), 994, 1042
  SCSI (Small Computer System Interface) standards, 655-657
answer modes, 1043
Anthem Technology Systems (ATS), 995
anti-aliasing, 1043
anti-flicker circuits, 420
Anvil Cases, 995
APA (All Points Addressable), 1043
APC (American Power Conversion), 994
APIs (Application Program Interfaces), 1043
APM (Advanced Power Management), 424-425, 830, 1043

appendixes, 985-986
Apple Computer, Inc., 995
  Apple I, II
    competition with IBM PC-compatible systems, 13
  Lisa computer, 368
  Macintosh, *see* Macintosh
Application layer (OSI model), 482
Application Program Interfaces (APIs), 1043
applications
  configuration file, 1055
  Dhrystone, 1059
  diagnostics, 1059
  mouse problems, 377
Apricot Computers, Ltd., 995
arbitration, 1043
architecture
  FireWire (IEEE-1394), 138-139
  I/O buses
    EISA (Enhanced Industry Standard Architecture), 117
    local buses, 120-138
    MCA (Micro Channel Architecture), 115-117
    ISA (Industry Standard Architecture) bus, 110-115
    USB (Universal Serial Bus), 139-140
archive
  bits, 1043
  media, 1043
ARCnet (Attached Resource Computer Network), 1043
  adapters (NICs), 467
  LANs (local area networks), 483
Arco Computer Products, Inc., 995
areal density, 1043
ARLL (Advanced RLL), 578
ARQ (Automatic Repeat Request), 1043
Arrowfield International, Inc., 995
artifacts, *see* aliasing

ASCII (American Standard Code for Information Interchange), 1044
  characters, 1043
ASME (American Society of Mechanical Engineers), 1044
ASP (Association of Shareware Professionals), 995
aspect ratio, 1044
ASPI (Advanced SCSI Programming Interface), 680
  CD-ROM drives, 732-733
assembler language, 1044
assemblying
  system, 807
  see also installing
ASSIGN command, 910-911
Association of Shareware Professionals (ASP), 995
AST Research, Inc., 995
Astec, 313, 995
  power supplies, 322
Asus Computer International (ASUStek), 996
asymmetrical modulation, 1044
asynchronous
  communication, 1044
  serial interface, *see* serial ports
Asynchronous Transfer Mode, 486, 1045
AT (Advanced Technology) PCs, 15-16, 955
  automatic drive typing, 695
  components, 957-958
  disk management, 896
  expansion slots, 16, 956
  floppy internal controller connector, 537
  ISA (Industry Standard Architecture) bus, 16
  keyboards, 336-337
    cable part numbers, 365-366
    compatibility, 341-342
    interface, 345-346
    key numbers, 351-352
    replacements, 365-366
    scan codes, 351-352

manual drive typing,
 696-698
models, 955
 068, 958
 099, 958
 239, 959
 319, 961
 339, 961
 keyboard accessories
  (enhanced), 971
 part numbers, 970-971
 system options, 971
processors, 16
 see also processors
serial ports
 9-pin connector
  specifications, 430
 25-pin specifications,
  431
specifications, technical,
 966-971
Type 2 motherboard
 disk storage, 969
 environmental
  specifications, 970
 expansion slots, 970
 keyboard specifications,
  970
 memory, 968
 physical specifications,
  970
 standard features,
  968-969
UART chips, 434
XT systems, compared, 17
AT BIOS motherboard, hard
 drive tables, 962-965
AT bus expansion board
 dimensions, 115
 see also ISA (Industry
  Standard Architecture) bus
AT&T National Parts Sales
 Center/Lucent
 Technologies, 996
AT/Desk power supply style,
 294-295
AT/Tower power supply
 style, 294-295
 connectors, 299-300
 switches, 301-302
ATA (AT Attachment) IDE
 interface, 636-637, 1044
 cables, 639, 647-648
 CAM ATA specification,
  637-641

commands, 639-641
configurations, 647-655
connectors, 638
Conner Peripheral drives,
 648-650
drive jumper settings, 648
dual-drive configuration,
 637-638
EIDE (ATA-2), 643-646
I/O connector, 638
intelligent drives, 642-643
intelligent Zoned
 Recording drives, 643
non-intelligent drives,
 641-642
signals, 639
ATA-2 (Enhanced IDE),
 643-646, 1044
 ATAPI (ATA Packet
  Interface), 646
 data transfer, 645-646
 DMA transfer modes, 646
 Extended CHS, 644
 LBA (Logical Block
  Addressing), 644
 PIO (Programmed
  I/O Modes), 645
 Standard CHS, 644
ATAPI (ATA Packet
 Interface), 646, 1044
 CD-ROM drives
  (IDE/ATAPI), 733
ATI Technologies, Inc., 996
ATM (Asynchronous
 Transfer Mode), 486, 1045
ATS (Anthem Technology
 Systems), 995
Attached Resource
 Computer Network,
 see ARCnet
ATX
 form factors (Pentium Pro
  processors), 203
 motherboards, 796
  form factors, 94-97
  interface connectors,
   98-99
 power supply style,
  297-300
audio, 1045
 CD-DA (Compact
  Disc Digital Audio), 1051
 CDs, sound cards, 495
 connectors (sound
  cards), 503

dBs (decibels), 1058
hardware, see sound cards
MCP standards, 491
POST error codes, 839-841
 AMI BIOS, 839-840
 nonfatal system board
  errors, 841
 Phoenix BIOS, 840-841
Audio Video Interleave
 (AVI), 1045
auto answer, 1045
auto dial, 1045
auto-configure adapter
 boards, 250
Autodesk, Inc., 996
AUTOEXEC.BAT file,
 880, 1045
automated setup, EISA
 (Enhanced Industry
 Standard Architecture)
 bus, 120
automatic head parking,
 1045
Automatic Repeat Request
 (ARQ), 1043
automobile power adapters
 (5140 PC Convertible
 laptop), 940
Autotime Corporation, 996
average access time, 1045
 CD-ROM drives, 730-731
average latency, 1045
average seek time, 1045
 hard disk drive
  interfaces, 628
 hard drive speed, 616
AVI (Audio Video
 Interleave), 1045
Award Software
 International, Inc., 287, 996
 ROM BIOS compatibility, 88
AZ-COM, Inc., 996
azimuth, 600

B

B channels (ISDN), 445
Baby-AT
 motherboards, 796
  form factors, 92-93
  interface connectors, 99
 power supply style, 296
backlash (head
 actuators), 598

backplane systems,
    motherboards, 91-92
backups, 57-58, 759-780, 1046
    complete backups, 1055
    disks, 1045
    floppy drives, 760
    low-level formatting, 699
    power-protection devices,
        326-329
        SPS (Standby Power
            Supplies), 326-327
        UPSs (Uniteruptible
            Power Supplies),
            327-329
    software
        data compression, 778
        tape drives, 778-780
    tape drives, 760
        8mm tape drives, 771
        backup software,
            778-780
        bundled backup
            software, 779
        capacity, 773-774
        compatible QIC-
            standard drives,
            768-769
        cost, 775
        DAT (digital audio)
            tape, 770
        data throughput, 775
        development of
            standards, 761
        DLT (Digital Linear
            Tape), 771
        high-capacity
            QIC-standard drives,
            767-773
        installation issues,
            775-777
        portable, 767
        QIC standards, 761-767
        selecting, 773-775
        standards, 774
        third-party backup
            software, 779-780
        Travan cartridge tapes,
            772-773
    temporary backups, 1092
    see also preventive
        maintenance
bad sectors, 1046
bad track tables, 1046

balanced signals, 1046
balun (balanced/
    unbalanced), 1046
bandwidth, 1046
    buses
        EISA bus (Enhanced
            Standard Industry
            Architecture), 117
        processor, 106
banks (memory chips),
    259-260, 268, 275, 1046
    widths, 259-260
bar codes, 1046
barometric filters
    (breather filter), hard
    disk drives, 607
base memory
    (conventional), 224
baseband transmission, 1046
BASIC (Beginner's
    All-purpose Symbolic
    Instruction Code),
    927, 1046
Basic Input/Output System,
    see BIOS
batch files, 879, 1047
batteries
    chargers (5140 PC
        Convertible laptop), 940
    connectors, 100
    portable systems, 828-830
    recording placement prior
        to disassembly, 45
    RTC/NVRAM (Real Time
        Clock/Non-Volatile
        Random Access Memory),
        329-331
baud rate, 438, 1047
Baudot code, 1047
bays, 1047
BBSs (Bulletin Board
    Systems), 1047
    IBM, 844
    vendors, 989
beam splitters
    (CD-ROMs), 727
Beginner's All-purpose
    Symbolic Instruction
    Code (BASIC), 927, 1046
Belden Wire and Cable, 996
Bell 103 (modulation
    standard), 439

Bell 212A (modulation
    standard), 439
bench testing, power
    supply, 318
Berkshire Products, 996
Bernoulli magnetic media
    drives, 782-783
Best Power Technology,
    Inc., 997
Betacams, 1047
bezels, 525, 1047
Bezier curves, 1047
bi-directional, 1047
    interfaces, keyboards, 337
    parallel ports
        Type 1, 448
        Type 3, 448-449
binaries, 1047
    digital signals, 1059
binary digits, see bits
binary synchronous control,
    see bisynchronous
BIOS (Basic Input/Output
    System), 13, 239, 801, 1047
    AMI, audio POST codes,
        839-840
    dates, displaying, 962
    disk functions, Int 13h
        interface (DOS), 892
    distributors, 287
    error codes, Int 13h
        interface (DOS), 893
    error messages, 239-242
    hard disk controllers,
        234-236
    keyboard-controller, 286
    manufacturers, 286-287
    memory conflicts and
        overlap, 246
    modifications, 288-289
        Flash BIOS, 289
        IML (Initial Microcode
            Load), 289-290
    motherboards, 238-290
        bootstrap loader, 238
        IBM Cassette Basic,
            239-290
        Power-On Self Test, 238
        selection criteria, 81-82
        see also motherboards
    Phoenix, audio POST
        codes, 840-841

BIOS (Basic Input/Output System)

Plug and Play
  component, 157
problems, 287-288
recording settings prior to
  disassembly, 42-45
ROM BIOS, 930
  addresses, 689-690
  capacity limitations, 686
  compatibility, 84-89
  DOS (Disk Operating
    System), 875-877
  replacement, 698
  running setup programs
    (motherboard
    installation), 56-57
  SCSI (Small Computer
    System Interface)
    adapters, 234-236
  upgrading, 283-285
  versions, 930-931
    IBM AT, 962
    IBM PC-XT, 945-946
  video adapters, 234
  Web site, 89
bisynchronous (binary
** synchronous control), 1047**
bits (binary digits), 9, 1048
  archive bits, 1043
  bit density, 1043, 1048
  bit depth, 1048
  bit map, 1048
  cells (transition cells),
    hard disk drives, 573-575
  identification (ID), 726
  parity, 261
  synchronizing (Sync), 726
bits per second (bps), 1049
  modems, 438
Bitstream, Inc., 997
BIX (Byte Information
** Exchange), 998**
Black Box Corporation, 997
blanking interval, 1048
blind systems, 597
block diagrams, 1048
blocks, 1048
BMP (Bit MaP), 1048
BNC (British National
** Connector), 1048**
  connectors, 472
boards
  cleaning, 65
  motherboards, *see*
    motherboards

removing, 46-47, 50-51
  adapter boards, 46-47
  motherboards, 50-51
see also adapter boards;
  cards
Boca Research, Inc., 997
boolean operations, 1048
booting, 1048
  DOS, 882, 899
  drives (comparing AT/XT
    systems), 17
  records, 1048
bootstraps, 1049
  loader, 239
Borland International, 997
Bose Corp., 997
Boston Computer
** Exchange, 997**
bps (bits per second), 1049
  modems, 438
branch predictions
** (Pentiums), 194**
Branch Target Buffer
** (BTB), 194**
breather filter
** (barometric), 607**
bridges, 1049
British National Connector
** (BNC), 1048**
  connectors, 472
broadband transmissions,
** 1049**
broadcast quality, 1049
Brooktree Corporation
** (Purchased by**
** Rockwell), 997**
brushes, dusting
** components, 63**
BTB (Branch Target
** Buffer), 194**
bubble memory, 1049
Buerg, Vernon D., 997
buffers, 1049
  CD-ROM drives, 731
bugs, 1049
  80386 processors, 211-212
  DOS, 906-907
  Pentiums, 212-213,
    215-222
    Floating Point Divide
      (FPU), 212-215
    power management, 215
see also errors

Bulletin Board Systems
** (BBSs), 1047**
  IBM, 844
  vendors, 989
bundled software, 779
  sound cards, 502
burn-ins, 1049
burst-mode memory cycles
** (486 Intel processors), 171**
bus interface units (486DX2
** Intel processors), 179**
bus mouse, 372-373
bus snooping, 174
bus versions (IDE
** interfaces), 635-650**
  ATA (AT Attachment),
    636-637
    commands, 639-641
    dual-drive
      configurations,
      637-638
    I/O cable, 639
    I/O connector, 638
    signals, 639
    specification, 637-641
  ATA-2 (Enhanced IDE),
    643-646
    ATAPI (ATA Packet
      Interface), 646
    data transfer, 645-646
    DMA transfer
      modes, 646
  drive categories, 641-643
    intelligent IDE, 642-643
    intelligent Zone
      Recording, 643
    non-intelligent IDE,
      641-642
  drive configuration,
    647-655
    cable connections,
      647-648
    Conner Peripherals
      drives, 648-650
    drive jumper settings,
      648
buses, 474, 1049
  address bus, 108
  processors, 162-163
  bus mastering, 109, 1049
  MCA (Micro Channel
    Architecture) bus, 116
  calculating power
    consumption per slot, 309

cache **1109**

data bus
  Pentium, 162
  processor sizes, 161
  processors, 159-161
defined, 105
EISA (Enhanced
  Industry Standard
  Architecture), 117
  16-bit DMA channels,
    145-146
  16-bit interrupts,
    142-144
  configuring controllers,
    693
  DMA channels, 146-147
  IRQs (Interrupt
    ReQuests), 690-691
I/O bus, 105, 109-140
  expansion slots,
    108-109
  FireWire (IEEE-1394),
    138-139
  local buses, 120-138
  USB (Universal Serial
    Bus), 139-140
ISA (Industry Standard
  Architecture) bus,
  110-115
  8-bit DMA channels, 145
  8-bit interrupts, 142
  16-bit DMA channels,
    145-146, 692
  16-bit interrupts,
    142-144
  IRQs (Interrupt
    ReQuests), 690-691
mastering, 109, 406
MCA (Micro Channel
  Architecture), 115-117
  16-bit DMA channels,
    145-146
  16-bit interrupts,
    142-144
  Advanced Diagnostics,
    844
  DMA channels, 147
  IRQs (Interrupt
    ReQuests), 690-691
  power supply, 292
memory bus, 107-108
  486DX4 processor, 108
  Pentium, 108
motherboards, *see*
  motherboards

PCI (Peripheral Component
  Interconnect) bus
  systems, configuring
  controllers, 693
processor bus, 105-107
system resources, 140-148
  conflicts, 148-158
  DMA channels (Direct
    Memory Access),
    145-147
  I/O (Input/Output) port
    addresses, 147-148
  IRQ channels (Interrupt
    ReQuest), 140-145
  versions (IDE interfaces),
    see bus versions
video adapters, 416
buying
  monitors, 392-396
  motherboards, 799
  Pentium chipsets, features
    to look for, 800-801
  tape drives, 773-775
  video adapters, 417
**Byte Information Exchange
(BIX), 998**
Byte **Magazine
(McGraw Hill), 998**
**Byte Runner
Technologies, 998**
bytes, 466, 1050
  gigabytes, 1066
  kilobytes, 1072
  megabytes, 1075
  terabytes, 170

C

C programming, 1050
cables, 806-807
  10Base2 IEEE standard,
    1039
  10Base5 IEEE standard,
    1039
  10BaseT, 1039
  100BaseT, 1039
  100BaseVG, 1040
  adapters, 9-pin/25-pin
    serial connections, 432
  cleaning, 66
  coaxial cables, 471-473,
    1054
    figure, 473

    Standard Ethernet, 471
    Thinnet (CheaperNet),
      471
  connecting motherboard
    installation, 54-56
  control cables, 1055
  data cables, 1057
  fiber-optic cables, 471,
    473-474
    connectors, 474
    daisy-chain topology
      (bus), 474
    multimode, 473
    single mode, 473
    star topology, 474-475
  hard disk drive interfaces
    ATA IDE, 639
    IDE connectors,
      647-648
    SCSI (Small Computer
      System Interface),
      665-675
  Interlink (parallel ports),
    452-453
  keyboards, defective,
    361-362
  networks, LANs (local
    area networks), 471
  recording placement prior
    to disassembly, 44-45
  S-Video (S-VHS)
    connector, 423
  twisted pair cables,
    471, 1094
cache, 1050
  486 Intel processors
    (Internal Level 1),
    171, 174-175
  CD-ROM drives, 731
  controller (386SL
    processors), 170
  external cache, 280
  file servers, 463
  hard disk drives, 617-618
  hits, 279
  internal cache, 280
  memory, motherboards,
    81, 802-803
  misses, 279
  Pentium processors, 194
    L2 cache, 202
    write-back cache, 174
  RAM chips, 279-280
  unified, 174

Cache On A STick
  (COAST), 802
CACP (Central Arbitration
  Control Point), 116
caddies (CD-ROM drives), 734
CAIG Laboratories, 998
Cal-Abco, 998
calculating
  bandwidth, 106
  power consumption,
    308-310
    floppy drives, 309
    hard disks, 309
    motherboards, 309
    per bus slot, 309
    SCSI (Small Computer
      System Interface) hard
      drives, 310
Calibrate program
  (formatting), 711, 870
CAM (Common Access
  Method), 680, 1050
  ATA specification, 637-641
Canon USA, Inc., 998
capacitive key switches
  (keyboards), 344-345
capacitors, 1050
capacity
  measurements
    (hard disks), 568
  tape drives, 773-774
card edge connectors,
  CD-ROM drives
  (internal), 748-750
Card Edge Low Profile
  (CELP), 802
cards, 1050
  adapter, *see* adapters
  installing, 153
  PC
    cards services, 824-825
    enablers, 825-826
    pinouts, 822-823
    portable systems,
      821-826
    socket service, 824
    software support,
      823-828
    Type III, 821
    Type IV, 821
  services (PC cards),
    824-825
  sound, 806

video, *see* video cards
  see also boards
Carpal Tunnel Syndrome,
  360, 1050
carrier detect signal, 1050
Carrier Sense, Multiple
  Access/Collision Detection,
  see CSMA/CD
carriers, 1050
  chip carriers, 1053
cases
  assembling systems,
    794-795
  covers, removing, 45-46
Casio, Inc., 998
cassette basic (ROM-BIOS
  memory map), 239-290
cathode-ray tubes *see* CRTs
CAV (Constant Angular
  Velocity), 1050
CBT (computer-based
  training), 1055
CCITT (Comité Consultatif
  Internationale de
  Télégraphique)
  modem standards, 436-437
    Bell 103, 439
    Bell 212A, 439
    BeV.21, 439
    data-compression
      (V.42bis), 441-442
    error-correction
      protocols, 441
    modulation, 439-441
    V.22, 439
    V.22bis, 439
    V.23, 439
    V.29, 440
    V.32, 440
    V.32bis, 440
    V.32fast, 440
    V.34, 440
    V.42 (error-
      correction), 441
    see also proprietary
      standards
CCS (Common Command
  Set), 1051
CD Video, 1051
CD+ (CD format), 738
CD+G (Compact
  Disc-Graphics), 1051

CD+MIDI (Musical
  Instrument Digital
  Intreface), 1051
CD-DA (Compact
  Disc-Digital Audio),
  726, 738, 1051
CD-E, 742
CD-I (Compact
  Disc-Interactive), 1051
CD-R (Compact Disc
  Recordable) drives,
  741-742, 787-789, 1051
  history, 787-788
  mass storage, 788-789
  software, 788
  writing CDs, 787-788
CD-ROM (Compact
  Disc-Read Only Memory)
  drives, 804, 1052
  ADPCM (Adaptive
    Differential Pulse Code
    Modulation), 741
  audio sound cards, 495, 501
  beam splitter, 727
  CD-ROM XA (extended
    Architecture), 1052
  components, 727
  data CDs, 726-728
  development of, 724
  ECC (Error Correcting
    Code), 726
  external, 735-736
  formats, 736
    CD+, 738
    CD-DA (Compact
      Disc-Digital Audio),
      738, 1051
    CD-E, 742
    CD-R (CD-Recordable),
      741-742, 1051
    DVD (Digital Video
      Disk), 742-743
    High Sierra Format,
      737-738
    ISO 9660 (first data
      standard), 737
    PhotoCD, 738-740
    Volume Table of
      Contents, 737
    XA (eXtended
      Architecture), 740-741
  installation, 744
    adapter cards, 745
    card edge connector,
      748-750

chip/chipsets **1111**

CD-ROM software, 752-754
  device driver, 753
  external drives, 746-747
  internal drives, 747-748
  jumpers, 745-746
  Microsoft CD Extensions, 753-754
  ribbon cable, 748-750
  SCSI (Small Computer System Interface) chains, 750-752
  test run, 754-756
interfaces, 731
  IDE/ATAPI (EIDE), 733
  proprietary, 733
  SCSI/ASPI, 732-733
internal, 735-736
interpolated data, 728
lands, 725
laser diode, 727
loading mechanisms, 733-735
maintenance, 725
mass-producing, 725
MCP standards, 491
multimedia (MPC), 743-744
pits, 725
playing
  in Windows 3.x, 755
  in Windows 95, 755-756
power cable splitter, 748
recording, CLV (Constant Linear Velocity), 726
removing, 47-48
single-speed, 729
special features
  drive sealing, 735
  self-cleaning lenses, 735-740
specifications, 728
  access time, 730-731
  buffers/cache, 731
  data transfer rate, 729-730
  speeds, 729
technology, 724-726
troubleshooting, 756-757
types, 728-736
CD-WO (Compact Disc-Write Once), 741-742, 1052

CDs (compact discs), 1051
  CD Video, 1051
  CD+G (Compact Disc-Graphics), 1051
  CD+MIDI (Musical Instrument Digital Interface), 1051
  CD-DA (Compact Disc Digital Audio), 738, 1051
  CD-I (Compact Disc-Interactive), 1051
  CD-R (Compact Disc Recordable), 1051
  CD-ROM (Compact Disc-Read Only Memory), see CD-ROM
  CD-ROM XA (eXtended Architecture), 1052
  CD-WO (Compact Disc-Write Once), 741-742, 1052
CDW (Computer Discount Warehouse), 1001
CELP (Card Edge Low Profile), 802
Centon Electronics, Inc., 998
Central Arbitration Control Point (CACP), 116
central processing units, see CPUs
CERN (Conseil Européen pour la Recherche Nucléaire), 1052
certification, Energy Star, 1063
CGA (Color Graphics Adapter), 398-400, 1052
  adapter BIOS memory, 234
  flicker, 398
  memory map, 230-233
  pinouts, 400
  snow, 398
  specifications, 398-399
CGIs (Common Gateway Interfaces), 1052
channels (ISDN), 1052
  B channels, 445
  D channels, 445
characters, 1052
  alphanumeric characters, 1042
  ASCII (American Standard Code for Information Interchange), 1043

cps (characters per second), 1056
EBCDIC (Extended Binary Coded Decimal Interchange Code), 1061
characters per second, see cps
CheapNet cables (Thinnet), 471
Checkit Pro (Touchstone Software Corp.), 865
  Web site, 865
checksums (hard drives), 581, 1053
chemicals, 27, 37-39
  cleaning, 60-61
    brushes/swabs, 63
    CFCs (chlorofluoro-carbons), 60-61
    contact cleaner/lubricants, 62
    dusters, 62
    HCFCs (hydrochloro-fluorocarbons), 61
    obtaining, 64
    standard solutions, 61-62
    vacuum cleaners, 62-63
  freeze sprays, 38-39, 62
  Freon R12, 38
  lubricants, 62-63
  Stabilant 22, 37-38
Chemtronics, Inc., 999
Cherry Electrical Products, 999
Chicago Case Company, 999
Chinon America, Inc., 999
chip/chipsets, 1053
  carriers, 1053
  creep, defined, 268
  documentation, 18, 21-23
    Advanced CMOS settings, 23
    motherboard manufacturers, identifying, 22
    Pentium Pro 200MHz system, 22
    processors, identifying, 21
    video chipset, 22
  math chips, see math corprocessors

Pentium-specific
   motherboards, 799-800
   features, 800-801
Pentium II
   motherboards, 800
PnP (Plug and Play),
   801-802
ROM (Read Only
   Memory), 801
speed rating reliability,
   89-90
Super I/O chip, 22
VESA BIOS Extension
   (SVGA standards),
   410-412
video adapters, 414,
   417-418
**Chips and Technologies,
Inc., 999**
CHKDSK command, 881
   ASSIGN command
      problems, 910-911
   data recovery, 908
   errors, 915-916
   JOIN command
      problems, 911
   network problems, 911
   operation, 914-915
   output, 908, 911-914
   SUBST command
      problems, 909-910
   syntax, 908-909
CHS (Cylinder Head Sector),
   1053
Ci Design Company, 999
CIE America, 999
CIF (Common Image
   Format), 1053
cigarette smoke hazards, 59
Cinepak (codec
   program), 422
circuits, 1053
   anti-flicker, 420
   boards, 525, 1053
   equalization, 1063
   ICs (integrated circuits), 10
   testing, logic probes/
      pulsers, 35
Cirrus Logic, Inc., 999

CIS (CompuServe
   Information Service),
   984, 1000
CISC (Complex
   Instruction-Set
   Computer), 1053
Citizen America
   Corporation, 999
clean rooms, 1053
cleaning, 58-67
   brushes/swabs, 63
   chemicals, 60-61
      CFCs (chlorofluoro-
         carbons), 60-61
      contact cleaner/
         lubricants, 62
      dusters, 62
      HCFCs (hydrochloro-
         fluorocarbons), 61
      obtaining, 64
      standard solutions,
         61-62
   drives, floppy disk drives,
      562-563
   dusting
      brushes, 63
      compressed air, 38, 62
      preventing dust/
         pollutants, 75-76
      procedures, 65
      vacuum cleaners, 62-63
   keyboards, 364-365
   lubricants, 62-65
   mouse, 373-375
   procedures, 64
      boards, 65
      connectors/contacts,
         63, 66
      keyboards/mouse, 66-67
      tools needed, 60
      vacuum cleaners, 62-63
clock
   signals, 163
      hard disk drives, 575
   speeds, 163, 1053
clones, 1053
closed loop (servo-controlled
   mechanisms), 599
clusters (allocation units),
   543, 903-904, 1053
   floppy disks, 903
   hard disks, 585, 904

   lost clusters, 1074
   space allocation in
      DOS, 888-889
   starting cluster, 1090
CLV (Constant Linear
   Velocity), 726, 1054
CMD Technology, Inc., 1000
CMOS (Complementary
   Metal-Oxide
   Semiconductor), 170,
   329-331, 1054
   memory/clock, AT/XT
      systems, 17
   RAM addresses,
      motherboards, 101-104
   recording settings prior to
      disassembly, 42-45
   running setup programs
      (motherboard
      installation), 56-57
   settings, chip/chipset
      documentation, 23
COAST (Cache On A
   Stick), 802
coated media, 1054
coaxial cables (LANs),
   471-473, 1054
   10Base2 IEEE standard,
      1039
   10Base5 IEEE standard,
      1039
   figure, 473
   Standard Ethernet, 471
   Thinnet BNC connectors,
      471-472
COBOL (Common Business-
   Oriented Language), 1054
code page switching, 1054
CODEC (CODer-DECoder),
   1054
codecs, 1054
   Cinepak (codec
      program), 422
   hardware, 422
   Indeo codec program, 422
   JPEG (Joint Photographic
      Experts Group), 422
   Microsoft Video 1 codec
      program, 422

MPEG (Motion Pictures
  Expert Group), 422
    software, 422
coercivity, 1054
  floppy disks, 555
**coil actuator drives,
  temperature changes, 700**
Color Graphics Adapter,
  see CGA
color monitors, 388-389
  5140 PC Convertible
    laptop, 941
  convergence, 1056
  dot pitch, 391
**Colorado Memory
  Systems, Inc., 1000**
colors, dithering, 1060
**Columbia Data Products,
  1000**
COM files, 879
COM ports, 1054
  adapters, conflicts, 156
  I/O addresses, 148
  IRQ conflicts, 145-147
COMDEX, 1054
**Comité Consultatif
  Internationale de
  Télégraphique,** *see* CCITT
**COMMAND.COM file,
  877-879, 1054**
commands, 1055
  DOS
    ASSIGN, 910-911
    CHKDSK, errors,
      915-916
    CHKDSK, operation,
      914-915
    CHKDSK, output, 908,
      911-914
    FORMAT, 583, 899, 904
    JOIN, 911
    RECOVER, 916-917
    RECOVER, marking bad
      sectors, 917
    RECOVER, preserving
      data, 916-917
    ScanDisk, 918
    search procedure,
      879-881
    SUBST, 909-910
    SYS, 905, 906
    TRUENAME, 910

files, 879
hard disk drive interfaces
  (ATA IDE), 639-641
I/O port, 894-895
modems (Hayes/U.S.
  Robotics brands), 438
queuing, SCSI (Small
  Computer System
  Interface), 664
XDFCOPY, 907
**common (electrical signals),
  1055**
Common Access Method,
  see CAM
**Common Business-Oriented
  Language,** *see* COBOL
**Common Command Set
  (CCS), SCSI (Small
  Computer System
  Interface) commands, 655**
**Common Gateway
  Interfaces,** *see* CGIs
Common Image Format,
  see CIF
common mode noise, 1055
communications
  asynchronous, 1044
  data communications,
    1057
  modem, *see* modems
**Compact Disc Recordable
  (CD-R) drives, 787-789**
  history, 787-788
  mass storage, 788-789
  software, 788
  writing CDs, 787-788
Compact Disc-Digital Audio,
  see CD-DA
companies
  manufacturers, *see*
    manufacturers
  vendors, 989-1038
  see also the individual
    names of companies
**Compaq Computer
  Corporation, 980, 1000**
  diagnostic software, 838
  EISA (Enhanced Industry
    Standard Architecture)
    bus development, 117
compatibility
  keyboards, 341-342
  OverDrive processors,
    191-192

sound cards, 499-500
AT (Advanced
  Technology) PCs
  automatic drive
    typing, 695
  manual drive typing,
    696-698
  see also AT (Advanced
    Technology) PCs
compilers, 1055
**Complementary Metal-
  OxideSemiconductor,**
  see CMOS
complete backups, 1055
**Complex Instruction-Set
  Computer,** *see* CISC
components, 794
  documentation, 18-21
  DOS (Disk Operating
    System), 877
  assembling system, 807
  cables, *see* cables
  cards, *see* cards
  case, 794-795
  CD-ROM drives,
    see CD-ROMs
  cooling fans, 80
  floppy disk drives,
    see floppy disks
  hard disk drives, *see* hard
    disk drives
  heat sinks, 806
  I/O ports, 803-804
  inventory of, 982
  keyboards, *see* keyboards
  motherboards, *see*
    motherboards
  mouse, *see* mouse
  power supply, *see* power
    supply
  sound cards, *see* sound
    cards
  testing with POST, 838-839
    audio error codes,
      839-841
    visual error codes,
      842-843
  vendors, *see* vendors
  video adapters, *see* video
    adapters
composite ferrite heads, 593
composite video, 1055

compressed air, 38
  dusting, 62
compression
  data compression, 1057
    backup software, 778
  Lempel Zev Welch (LZW), 1074
  lossless compression, 1057, 1074
  lossy compression, 1057, 1074
  sound cards (ADPCM), 499
CompTIA (Computing Technology Industry Association), 1000
Compton's NewMedia, Inc., 1000
CompuCom
  proprietary standards (DIS), 442
  Speed Protocol, see CSP
CompUSA, Inc., 1000
CompuServe Information Service (CIS), 984, 1000
Computer Component Source, Inc., 1000
Computer Design Magazine, 1001
Computer Discount Warehouse (CDW), 1001
Computer Graphics World Magazine, 1001
Computer Hotline Magazine, 1001
Computer Library, 1001
Computer Reseller News Magazine, 1001
Computer Retail Week Magazine, 1001
Computer Shopper Magazine, 1001
Computer Technology Review Magazine, 1001
computer-based training, see CBT
computers, 1055
  consoles, 1055
  crashes, 1056
  desktop, 1058
  down-time, 1060
  guest, defined, 458
  host, defined, 458
  laptops, 9

PCs (personal computers)
  Altair kit (MITS), 10
  Apple I (Apple Computer), 11
  history of computing, 9-11
  laptops, 9
  Model 5100 (IBM), 10
  Model 5110 (IBM), 11
  Model 5120 (IBM), 11
  Model 5150 (IBM), 11
  see also PCs
portable systems, see portable systems
computing history, 9-11
Computing Technology Industry Association (CompTIA), 1000
Comtech Publishing Ltd., 1002
conductors, address bus, 1042
CONFIG.SYS file, 1055
configuring
  controllers, 688-694
    DMA channels, 692-693
    I/O port addresses, 693-694
    IRQs (Interrupt Request Channel), 690-691
    ROM addresses, 689-690
  configuration file, 1055
  floppy disk drives
    disk changeline jumper, 530-533
    drive select jumpers, 527-529
    media sensor jumper, 533-538
    terminating resistors, 529-530
  hard disk drives
    AT-class systems, 695-698
    IDE, 637-638, 647-655
    physical installation, 694-695
    SCSI (Small Computer System Interface), 675-681
    system configuration, 695-698

memory (adapter), 250-251
ports
  parallel, 451-453
  serial, 435-436
recording prior to disassembly, 42-45
  accessing setup programs, 43-44
  hard disk type settings, 42-43
  physical configuration, 44-45
connecting
  cables, motherboard installation, 54-56
  cables in LANs, 477
  power supplies, motherboard installation, 54
  to Internet, 487
Connector Resources Unlimited (CRU), 1002
connectors
  BNC (British National Connector), 1048
  cleaning, 63, 66
  EISA (Enhanced Industry Standard Architecture) bus cards, 117
  floppy disk drives, 525-527
  hard disk drives
    ATA IDE, 638
    grounding tab, 613
    interface connectors, 612
    power connectors, 613
    SCSI (Small Computer System Interface), 665-675
  IDE connectors
    primary, 153
    secondary, 153
  motherboards, 98-101
  power supply, 299-303
    AT/Tower style, 299-300
    ATX style, 300
    disk drives, 302-303
    PC/XT style, 299-300
    physical connectors, 303
    switches, 301-302
    voltage ranges, 301
  sound cards, 502-504

Conner Peripherals, Inc., 710, 1002
  IDE drives, 648-650
Conner Tape Products, Inc., 1002
Conseil Européen pour la Recherche Nucléaire, *see* CERN
consoles, 1055
Constant Angular Velocity, *see* CAV
Constant Linear Velocity, *see* CLV
Consultative Committee on International Telephone and Telegraph, *see* CCITT
Contact cleaner/lubricants, 62
contacts, cleaning, 63, 66
contiguous, 1055
continuity, 1055
contracts (service contracts), 23-25
control cables, 1055
Control Program/Microcomputer, *see* CP/M
controllers, 688-694, 1056
  cards, 1056
  configuring, 689-690
    DMA channels, 692-693
    I/O port addresses, 693-694
    IRQs (Interrupt Request Channel), 690-691
  error codes, 719-721
  floppy disk controller, 534-538
controls
  error controls, 1063
  monitors (analog/digital), 395
conventional memory, 224
  barrier, 223, 228
convergence, 1056
converting
  analog-to-digital converter, 1042
  assembling, 1044
  compilers, 1055
  digitize, 1059
cooling
  fans, 806
  problems, 222

coprocessors, 1056
  486 Intel, 171
  486DX Intel, 176
  487SX Intel, 178
  8087 Intel, 208-209
  80287 Intel, 209
  80387 Intel, 209-210
  80487 Intel, 210
  list of, 207-222
  Pentium, FPU (floating-point unit), 197
  specifications, 208
  speed rates, 207
  Weitek, 210
  see also processors
core, 1056
Corel Systems, Inc., 1002
costs
  meters, 34
  SIMM testers, 36
  Stabilant 22a chemical, 38
  tape drives, 57
  tools, 30
covers
  removing, 45-46
  replacing, motherboard installation, 56
CP/M (Control Program for Microprocessors), 10, 1056
cps (characters per second), 1056
CPUs (central processing units), 1056
  address bus, 162-163
  AMD, 205
  cooling
    fans, 314
    problems, 222
  Cyrix, 205-206
  data bus, 159-161
  file servers, 462
  Future Pentium OverDrive Processor, 188
  heating problems, 222
  Intel
    286, 167-168
    386, 168-169
    386DX, 169-170
    386SL, 170-171
    386SX, 170
    486, 171-173
    486DX, 175-176
    486DX2, 178-180
    486DX2 speed-rated versions, 179

    486DX2 upgrade sockets, 180-182
    486SX, 177-178
    487SX, 178
    8086, 166-167
    8088, 166-167
    80186, 167
    80188, 167
    80386, 168-169
    compatible, 204-206
    memory-addressing capabilities, 163
    object-code compatibility, 168
  internal registers, 162
  OverDrive processors, 178, 180-182, 185
    compatibility problems, 191-192
    installation, 190-191
  Pentium, 193-197
    branch predictions (BTB), 194
    first-generation, 197-198
    internal architecture, 195
    math coprocessor (FPU), 197
    motherboard speeds, 198
    second-generation, 198-200
    specifications, 193
    speed, 198
    superscalar technology, 193
    third-generation (P55C), 200
    twin-data pipelines, 193
    u-pipe, 194
    v-pipe, 194
    write-back cache, 174
  Pentium II processors, 203-204
  Pentium OverDrive processors, 182-190
    active heat sink, 185
    designations, 190
    for DX2 and 486SX2 processors, 192-193
    heat sink, 184
    installation, 190-191
    Socket 1, 182
    Socket 2, 184

Socket 3, 186
Socket 4 pinout
   specification, 188
Socket 5, 188
Socket 5 pin
   configuration, 189
Socket 6, 188
Socket 6 pin
   configuration, 190
Socket 7, 188
VRM (Voltage Regulator
   Module), 188
Pentium Pro processors,
   201-203
   ATX form factor, 203
   L2 cache, 202
   MPS (Multi-Processor
      Specification), 202
RAM, see memory; RAM
   (Random Access Memory)
speed ratings, 163-166
   Intel ICOMP index
      ratings, 164
   Pentiums, 165
standards, MCP
   standards, 491
tests, 210-211, 222
   early 80386s, 211-212
   Pentiums, 212-222
   software, 210
see also processors
crashes, 1056
   system crashes, 1091
CRC (Cyclic Redundancy
   Checking), 1056
Creative Labs, Inc., 490, 1002
crosstalk, 1056
CRTs (cathode-ray tubes)
   monitors, 386, 1050, 1056
   displays, 5140 PC
      convertible laptop, 937
   persistence, 386
   raster, 386
   refresh rate, 386
CRU (Connector Resources
   Unlimited), 1002
CS Electronics, 1002
CSEL (Cable SELect), 639, 647
CSMA/CD (Carrier Sense,
   Multiple Access/Collision
   Detection), 468
   Ethernet, 482
CSP (CompuCom Speed
   Protocol), 443
CST, 1002

CTG (Formerly Cables to
   Go), 998
CTX International, Inc., 1003
currents, 1056
cursors, 1057
Curtis Manufacturing
   Co, Inc., 1003
curves, Bezier curves, 1047
Custom mode (MEMMAKER
   program), 255
CyberMedia, 1003
Cyclic Redundancy
   Checking, see CRC
Cylinder Head Sector,
   see CHS
cylinder skew, hard disk
   speed, 620-622
cylinders (floppy drives),
   543-554, 569, 1057
Cypress Semiconductor
   Corporation, 1003
Cyrix Corporation, 1003
   Intel-compatible
      processors, 205-206

D

D channels (ISDN), 445
D. W. Electrochemicals,
   Ltd., 1003
D/A Converter (DAC), 1057
D70DCOMP.ZIP, 907
D70DCOPY.ZIP, 907
D70E.ZIP, 907
D70EMM.ZIP, 907
D70MODE.ZIP, 907
D70POWER.ZIP, 907
D70SHARE.ZIP, 907
D70STAC.ZIP, 907
D70TVL.ZIP, 907
D70XDF.ZIP, 907
Da-Lite Screen Co., 1003
DACs (D/A Converter),
   497, 1057
daisy chains (floppy drives),
   527, 1057
daisy-chain topology
   (cables), 474
daisywheel printers, 1057
DakTech, 1003
Dallas Semiconductor, 1003
Damark International, Inc.,
   1004

Darkhorse Systems, 1004
DAT (Digital Audio Tape),
   770, 1057
data, 1058
   area, 905-906
   backups, see backups
   bus
      Pentium, 162
      processors, 159-161
   cables, 1057
   compression, 1057
      backup software, 778
      sound cards, 501
      standards (modems),
         441-442
   encoding schemes,
      see encoding frames,
         1065
   recovery, see data recovery
   storage
      Compact Disc
         Recordable (CD-R)
         drives, 787-789
      comparing removable
         drives, 785-786
      magnetic media drives,
         781-783
      magneto-optical drives,
         783-785
      QIC-40 tape drive, 766
      QIC-80 tape drive, 766
      removable storage
         drives, 780-789
      WORM drives, 786-789
Data Base Advisor Magazine,
   1004
Data Cartridge 600,
   see DC-600
data communications, 1057
Data Communications
   Magazine, 1004
Data Depot, 1004
   POST code cards, 842
Data Exchange Corporation,
   1004
Data Link layer
   (OSI model), 481
data recovery
   CHDSK command,
      908-909
      ASSIGN command
         problems, 910-911
      JOIN command
         problems, 911

diagnostic software **1117**

network problems, 911
SUBST command
problems, 909-910
DOS (Disk Operating
System), 875
memory-resident
programs, 918-919
pop-up utilities, 918-919
programs, 870-871
RECOVER command,
916-917
ScanDisk command, 918
third-party disk repair
utilities, 918
**Data Retrieval Services, Inc.,
1004**
data separator, 1057
**Data Technology
Corporation (DTC), 1004**
Data Terminal Equipment,
see DTE
**data throughput, tape
drives, 775**
data transfer rates, 1057
CD-ROM drives, 729-730
QIC-40 tape drive, 766
QIC-80 tape drive, 766
DataMaster design, 11-12
Datamation **Magazine, 1005**
**Datastorm Technologies,
Inc., 1005**
DBR (DOS Boot Record), 873
format, 899-900
dBs (decibels), 1058
**DC (Direct Current), 34-35,
1058**
**DC (Diskette Changeline),
530-533**
**DC-600 (Data Cartridge
600), 762, 1058**
**DCE (Data Communications
Equipment), 1058**
DD (double density), 1060
**DDD (Digital Diagnostic
Diskette), 869**
**DDE (Dynamic Data
Exchange), 1058**
DDS-2 drives, 770
DDS-3 drives, 770
de facto standards, 490
DEBUG, 899, 1058
decibels (dBs), 1058

decoding, endec (ENcoder/
DEcoder), 1063
**decompression, sound
cards, 499**
dedicated lines, 1058
dedicated servo
mechanism, 605-606
surface, 1058
defaults, 1058
**defect mapping (hard
disk drives), 702-703**
manufacturer's defect
list, 704
scans, 703-721
surface analysis, 704-705
**DEFRAG (disk
defragmenter), 542**
defragmentation, 1058
floppy disks, 542, 909
hard disks, 67-68
**Dell Computer Corporation,
1005**
density, 1058
DD (double density), 1060
floppy disks, 554-555
hard disk drives, areal
density, 568-569
linear, 554
longitudinal, 554
**depot repair, power
supplies, 319**
design
DataMaster, 11-12
PCs (personal computers),
11-12
portable systems, 811-812
desktop, 1058
DMI (Desktop
Management
Interface), 1060
video (DTV) boards,
421-423
desoldering tools, 30-33
Deutsche Industrie Norm,
see DIN
devices
actuators, 1041
adapters, 1041
arbitration, 1043
bootstraps, 1049
capacitors, 1050
CD-ROM drives, 1052
clocks, 1053

CODEC (COder-DECoder),
1054
controllers, 1056
CRTs (cathode ray tubes),
1050
data separator, 1057
drivers, 1058, 1061
CD-ROM drive
installation, 753
DOS, HIMEM.SYS
(configuring
memory), 253
Microsoft CD
Extensions, 753-754
drives, 1061
ESDI (Enhanced Small
Device Interface), 1063
form factors, 1065
**DFI (Diamond Flower, Inc),
1005**
Dhrystone, 1059
diagnostic equipment,
see test equipment
**diagnostic read-and-write
cylinder, 905**
**diagnostic software,
283-285, 837-838, 1059**
AMIDiag, 864-865
Checkit Pro, 865
data recovery, 870-871
Disk Diagnostics, 868-870
Disk Manager, 869-870
Drive Probe, 869-871
IBM, 843-863
Advanced Diagnostics,
843-863
keyboard error codes, 362
loopback testing, serial
port testing, 454-455
Micro-Scope, 865-866
MSD (Microsoft
Diagnostics), serial
port testing, 453
NDIAGS (Norton
Diagnostics), 866-867
PC Technician (Windsor
Technologies), 867
POST, 837-843
audio error codes,
839-841
system component
tests, 838-839
visual error codes,
842-843

public-domain, 871
QAPlus/FE, 867-868
dial-up networking, 458
Diamond Flower, Inc (DFI), 1005
Diamond Multimedia Systems, Inc., 1005
differential, 1059
differential SCSI (Small Computer System Interface), 662-663
A-Cables, 671
P-Cables, 672
Q-Cables, 673
universal symbols, 662
DigaSoft, Inc., 1005
Web site, 868
Digi-Key Corporation, 1005
digital audio
CD-DA (Compact Disc Digital Audio), 1051
Digital Audio Tape (DAT), *see* DAT
digital circuits, logic probes/pulsers, 35
Digital Diagnostic Diskette, *see* DDD
Digital Linear Tape, *see* DLT
digital loopback, 1059
Digital Multi-Meters, *see* DMMs
digital signals, 1059
active low, 1041
VGA adapters (Video Graphics Array), 404
Digital Storage Media, *see* DSM
digital technology (ISDN), 444-445
Digital Video Interactive, *see* DVI
digital-to-analog converters, *see* DACs
digitized sound (waveform audio), 497, 1059
DIMMs (dual inline memory modules), 264-269
168-pin, 266, 275
installing, 53, 274-280
removing, 52
Synchronous DRAM (SDRAM) memory, 267
see also SIMMs (Single Inline Memory Modules)

DIN (Deutsche Industrie Norm), 359
DIPs (Dual Inline Pins), 274, 1059
chips, 257
installing broken/bent chips, 282
polarity notches, 282
direct cable connections, 458
Direct Current, *see* DC
Direct Memory Access, *see* DMA (Direct Memory Access) channels
directories, 1059
DOS (Disk Operating System)
file attribute bytes, 902
formats, 901
root, 900-902
DIS (Dynamic Impedance Stabilization) proprietary standard, 442
disassembling systems, 40-52
keyboards, 362
preparations, 41-45
ESD (electrostatic discharge) protection, 41-42
recording physical configuration, 44-45
recording setup/configuration, 42-44
removing
adapter boards, 46-47
covers, 45-46
disk drives, 47-48
motherboards, 50-51
power supplies, 48-50
SIMMs/DIMMs, 52
tools, 27-33, 45
hand tools, 28-30
soldering/desoldering, 30-33
Disk Change (floppy drives), 530, 560-561
Disk Diagnostics, 868-870
disk drives
actuators, 1041
automatic head parking, 1045
bad sectors, 1046
bad track tables, 1046

bays, 1047
cleaning, *see* cleaning
hard disk drives, *see* hard disk drives
latency, 1073
power connectors, 302-303
removing, 47-48
Disk Editor (Norton Utilities), 870
Disk Manager program, 642, 707, 869-870
formatting hard drives, 708
Disk Operating System, *see* DOS
disk-sweep (servo mechanisms), 603
DISKEDIT (Norton), 893
diskette changeline jumper (floppy drives), 530-533
diskless workstations, 460
disks, 1060
backup disks, 1045
coated media, 1054
cylinders, 1057
data area, 905-906
data recovery, *see* data recovery
defragmentation, 1058
diagnostic programs
Disk Manager, 869-870
Drive Probe, 869
ED (extra-high density), 1064
embedded servo data, 1062
fixed, defined, 1064
floppy, *see* floppy disks
formatting, 1065
functions, BIOS, Int 13h interface (DOS), 892
hard disks, *see* hard disks drives
interleave ratios, 1070
key disks, 1072
landing zones, 1072
medium, 1075
optical disks, 1080
reference standards, 869
scratch disks, 1087
storage
AT Model 286, 976
AT Type 2 motherboard, 969
IBM PCs, 933-934

DOS (Disk Operating System) **1119**

PC XTs, 948
Portable PC, 954
virtual disks, 1097
see also drives
Display Power-Management Signaling, *see* **DPMS**
DisplayMate, 427
displays
 portable systems, 813-817
  active matrix displays, 815-816
  dual scan displays, 814-815
  external, 830-832
  screen resolution, 816-817
 screen savers, 72
 see also monitors
distance limitations for LAN cables, 478
distortion (speakers), 505
Distributed Processing Tech. (DPT), 1005
distributed termination (floppy drives), 529
distributors, ROM BIOS, 287
dithering, 1060
Diversified Technology, 1006
DLLs (Dynamic Link Libraries), 1060
DLT (Digital Linear Tape), 771
DMA (Direct Memory Access) channels, 145-147, 510, 1059
 8-bit ISA (Industry Standard Architecture) bus channels, 145
 16-bit EISA/ISA/MCA bus channels, 145-146
 AT/XT systems, compared, 17
 configuring controllers, 692-693
 EISA (Enhanced Industry Standard Architecture) bus, 146-147, 693
 ISA (Industry Standard Architecture) bus, 692
 MCA (Micro Channel Architecture) bus, 147
 PCI (Peripheral Component Interconnect) bus , 693

DMI (Desktop Management Interface), 1060
DMMs (Digital Multi-Meters), 316-318
 cost, 34
 features, 316-317
 measuring voltage, 34-35, 317-318
  cautions, 34-35
 selecting, 316-317
docking stations, 832-833, 1060
documentation, 17-18
 chip/chipsets, 18, 21-23
  motherboard manufacturers, identifying, 22
  Pentium Pro 200MHz system, 22
  processors, identifying, 21
  video chipset, 22
 components, 18-21
 hard disk drives, installation, 687
 keyboards, 367-368
 manuals, 980-982
 manufacturers, 23
 motherboard selection criteria, 83-84
 OEMs (Original Equipment Manufacturers) manuals, 18, 981
 Pentium chipsets, 801
 system-level, 18-19
Dolch Computer Systems, 1006
DOS (Disk Operating System), 873-919, 1060
 booting, 882
  errors, 899
 bugs, 906-907
 code page switching, 1054
 COMMAND.COM, 878-879
 commands
  ASSIGN, 910-911
  CHKDSK errors, 915-916
  CHKDSK operation, 914-915
  CHKDSK output, 908, 911-914
  FORMAT, 583, 899, 904

 JOIN, 911
 RECOVER, 916-917
 ScanDisk, 918
 search procedure, 879-881
 SUBST, 909-910
 SYS, 905-906
 TRUENAME, 910
 compared to Windows 95, 920-921
 components, 877
 CONFIG.SYS, 1055
 data recovery, 875
  CHDSK command, 908-909
 DEBUG program, 899, 1058
 device drivers,
  HIMEM.SYS (configuring memory), 253
 directories
  file attribute bytes, 902
  formats, 901
 DPMI (DOS Protected Mode Interface), 1060
 extended partitions, 1064
 FATs (File Allocation Tables), 902-903
 FDISK program, 893, 903
 files
  IO.SYS, 876-878
  management, 888
  MSDOS.SYS, 876-878
  names, 901
  space allocation, 888-889
  status, 901
 floppy disk format specifications, 890
 hardware, 874
 I/O system, 877
 interfaces, 890
  disk drives, 889-895
  I/O port commands, 894-895
  Interrupt 13h, 891-894
  Interrupt 21h, 890-891
  Interrupt 25/26h, 891
 loading, 882-888
 patches, Web sites for finding, 907
 ROM BIOS, 875-877
 root directories, 900-902
 shell, 877-879

DOS (Disk Operating System)

starting, 882-888
structures, 895-905
   allocation units, 903-904
   data area, 905-906
   diagnostic read-and-write cylinder, 905
   FATs (file allocation tables), 902-903
   master partition boot sectors, 896-898
   root directories, 900-902
   volume boot sectors, 899-900
upgrading
   DOS 4.0, 906
   troubleshooting, 905-906
   Windows 95, 906
DOS 4.0, upgrading to, 906
DOS 5.x, 881
DOS 6.xx, 881-882
DOS Boot Record, *see* **DBR**
dot pitch (monitors), 391, 394, 1060
dot-matrix printers, 1060
double density (DD), 1060
   disks (floppy), 545, 554
double stepping, 546
double-sided floppy disks, 554-555
double-sided MIG heads, 593
double-speed CD-ROM drives
   access times, 731
   data transfer rate, 729
down-time, 1060
DPMI (DOS Protected Mode Interface), 1060
DPMS (Display Power Management Signaling) monitors, 391
DPT (Distributed Processing Tech.), 1005
DRAM (Dynamic Random Access Memory), 1061
   installing, 273-274
   see also RAM (Random Access Memory)
Drive Probe, 869
   aligning floppy drives (High-Resolution Diagnostic disk), 563

drive-select jumpers (floppy drives), 527-529
drivers, 1061
   device drivers, 1058
   software, mouse problems, 375-383
   sound cards, 502
drives, 1061
   30M for AT Models 068 and 099, 960
   actuators, 1041
   AT (Advanced Technology), 956
   automatic head parking, 1045
   bad sectors, 1046
   bad track tables, 1046
   CD-ROMs, 498, 804, 1052
      CD+, 738
      CD-DA (Compact Disc-Digital Audio), 738
      CD-E, 742
      CD-R (CD-Recordable), 741-742
      components, 727
      drive sealings, 735
      DVD (Digital Video Disc), 742-744
      external, 735-736
      formats, 736
      High Sierra Format, 737-738
      installation, 744-754
      interfaces, 731-733
      internal, 735-736
      ISO 9660 (first data standard), 737
      loading mechanisms, 733-735
      MCP standards, 491
      performance specifications, 728-731
      PhotoCD, 738-740
      self-cleaning lenses, 735-740
      single-speed, 729
      sound cards, 501
      speeds, 729
      technology, 724-726
      XA (eXtended Architecture), 740-741
   cleaning, *see* cleaning
   Compact Disc Recordable (CD-R) drives, 787-789

history, 787-788
mass storage, 788-789
software, 788
writing CDs, 787-788
disk drives, latency, 1073
embedded servo data, 1062
floppy disk drives, 544, 804
   3 1/2-inch, 541, 546-554
   5 1/4-inch, 540, 545-546
   8-inch, 519
   aligning, 563-564
   AT controller internal connector, 537
   backups, 760
   caring for, 556-557
   circuit boards, 525
   cleaning, 562-563
   clusters (allocation units), 543
   connectors, 525-527
   cylinders, 543-554
   development of, 519-520
   diskette changeline jumper, 530-533
   double stepping, 546
   drive select jumpers, 527-529
   faceplate (bezel), 525
   floppy disk controller, 534-538
   floptical drives, 564-566
   head actuator, 521, 523-524
   installation, 559
   logical DOS-format parameters, 544
   logical operation, 540-543
   magnetic properties, 538-540
   media sensor jumper, 533-538
   mini-floppy disk drive, 519
   PC/XT controller internal connector, 535
   physical specifications/operations, 536-538
   read/write heads, 520-523

drives

repairing, 562-564
root directories, 541
SA-400 interface, 525
sectors, 540
sensors, 550
single-sided, 520
spindle motor, 524-525
ST-412, 520
ST-506, 520
terminating resistors, 529-530
track-width specifications, 538
tracks, 540
troubleshooting, 560-561
full-height drive, 1066
half-height drive, 1067
hard disk drives, 804
air filters, 607-608
areal density, 568-569
bit cells (transition cells), 573, 575
buying recommendations, 624-625
capacity, 623-624
capacity measurements, 568
checksums, 581
clock signals, 575
components, 588
configuring controllers, 688-694
connectors, 612-613
cost, 623
cylinders, 569
data encoding, 575-579
defined, 567
development of, 568
encoding method, 573
encoding scheme comparisons, 579-580
Endec (ENcoder/ DECoder), 575, 630
faceplate (bezel), 613-614
flux, 573
flux reversal, 573, 575
FM (Frequency Modulation) encoding, 576
grounding strap, 610-611
HDAs (Head Disk Assemblies), 570, 588
head actuators, 596-606
head crashes, 570
magnetic data storage, 572-575
media, 589-591
MFM (Modified Frequency Modulation) encoding, 576-577
motherboard, 611-612
MTBF (Mean Time Between Failures), 615
operation, 569-572
physical installation, 694-695
platters (disks), 588-589
prefix portions (headers), 581
racks, 569
read/write heads, 591-595
RLL (Run Length Limited) encoding, 577-579
Seagate ST-12550N Barracuda 2 specifications, 571
sectors, 580-587
shock mounted, 622
sliders, 595-596
speed/performance, 615-622
spindle motors, 609-610
suffix portions (trailers), 581
system configuration, 695-698
temperature acclimation, 608-609
Winchester drive, 1098
Zone Recording, 584
IBM PCs, 927
internal drives, 1070
jumpers, IDE connectors, 648
logical drives, 1074
magnetic media drives, 781-783
magneto-optical drives, 783-785
PC XTs, 941-942
power connectors, 302-303
QIC-standard, 764-767
8mm tape drives, 771
backup software, 778-780
bundled backup software, 779
capacity, 773-774
compatible, 768-769
cost, 775
DAT (digital audio) tape, 770
data throughput, 775
DLT (Digital Linear Tape), 771
high-capacity, 767-773
installation issues, 775-777
portable tape drives, 767
QIC-40, 764-767
QIC-80, 764-767
selecting, 773-775
standards, 774
third-party backup software, 779-780
Travan cartridge tapes, 772-773
removable storage drives, 780-789
Bernoulli, 782-783
Compact Disc Recordable (CD-R) drives, 787-789
comparing removable drives, 785-786
magnetic media drives, 781-783
magneto-optical drives, 783-785
SyQuest, 783
WORM drives, 786-787
removing, 47-48
ST-506/412, 893
tape
8mm tape drives, 771
backups, 760, 778-780
bundled backup software, 779
capacity, 773-774

compatible QIC-standard drives, 768-769
cost, 57, 775
DAT (Digital Audio Tape), 770
data throughput, 775
development of standards, 761
DLT (Digital Linear Tape), 771
high-capacity QIC-standard drives, 767-773
installation issues, 775-777
portable, 767
QIC standards, 761-767
selecting, 773-775
standards, 774
third-party backup software, 779-780
Travan cartridge tapes, 772-773
thermal expansion, 311
WORM drives, 786-789
see also disks
DSM (Digital Storage Media), 1061
DSP (Digital Signal Processors) sound cards, 502
DTC (Data Technology Corporation), 1004
DTE (Data Terminal Equipment), 1061
DTK Computer, Inc., 1006
DTV (Desktop Video) boards, 421-423
Dual Cavity PGA (Pin Grid Array) package, 201
Dual Inline Pins, *see* DIPs
dual scan displays, 814-815
Dukane Corporation, 1006
duplex, 1061
duplex transmission, asymmetrical modulation, 1044
Duracell, Inc., 1006
dusting, 62, 65
brushes, 63
dust-caused problems, 58-60

ESD protection, 65
preventing dust/pollutants, 75-76
procedures, 65
vacuum cleaners, 62-63
see also cleaning
DVD (Digital Video Disc), 742-743
DVI (Digital Video Interactive), 1061
Dvorak keyboard, 1061
Dvorak-Dealy keyboards, 360
DX4 Overdrive processor, 185
Dynamic Data Exchange, *see* DDE
Dynamic Impedance Stabilization, *see* DIS
Dynamic Link Libraries, *see* DLLs
Dynamic Random Access Memory, *see* DRAM

E

e-mail (electronic mail) addresses, vendors, 989-1038
EBCDIC (Extended Binary Coded Decimal Interchange Code), 1061
ECC (Error Correcting Code), 726
ECP (Enhanced Capabilities Port), 449-450
ED (extra-high density), 1064
edge-triggered interrupt sensing, ISA (Industry Standard Architecture) bus, 141
editing, 1061
Edlab Web site, 1039
Edmund Scientific, 1006
EDO (Extended Data Out) memory, 803
Pentiums, 272
EEPROM (Electrically Erasable Programmable Read-Only Memory), 289, 1061
EGA (Enhanced Graphics Adapter), 400-402, 1061

adapter BIOS memory, 234
memory map, 230-233
specifications, 402
EIA (Electronic Industries Association), 1062
EIDE (Enhanced Integrated Drive Electronics), 643-646, 1062
ATAPI (ATA Packet Interface), 646
CD-ROM drives, 733
data transfer, 645-646
DMA transfer modes, 646
Extended CHS, 644
LBA (Logical Block Addressing), 644
PIO (Programmed I/O modes), 645
Standard CHS, 644
eight-speed CD-ROM drives
access times, 731
data transfer rate, 729
EISA bus (Enhanced Industry Standard Architecture), 117, 1062
16-bit DMA channels, 145-146
16-bit interrupts, 142-144
auto-configure adapter boards, 250
automated setup, 120
bandwidth, 117
card specifications, 117
connectors, 117
DMA channels, 146-147, 693
IRQs (Interrupt ReQuests), 690-691
level-sensitive interrupts, 141
Electrically Erasable Programmable Read-Only Memory, *see* EEPROM
electricity
AC, 1041
amperes, 1042
analog-to-digital converter, 1042
cards, 1050
common, 1055
conductors, address bus, 1042
currents, 1056

errors 1123

dBs (decibels), 1058
DC (Direct Current), 1058
differential, 1059
ESD (electrostatic
    discharge)
  outlet testers, 35-36
  shock, system failures,
    310-312
  Stabilant 22 chemical
    semiconducter, 37-38
Electro Motive Force,
  see EMF
electrocution, 1006
electromagnetic radiation
  (monitors), 391-392
electromagnetic theory, 163
electromagnetism (hard disk
  drives), 572
Electronic Buyers' News
  Magazine, 1006
Electronic Engineering Times
  Magazine, 1007
Electronic Industries
  Association, *see* EIA
electronic mail, *see* e-mail
Electronic Products
  Magazine, 1007
Electroservice Laboratories,
  1007
electrostatic discharge,
  see ESD
Elek-Tek, Inc., 1007
ELF magnetic emissions
  (radiation), 391-392
Elitegroup Computer
  Systems, Inc., 1007
embedded servo
  mechanism, 604-605, 1062
EMF (Electro Motive
  Force), 606
EMM (Expanded Memory
  Manager), 1062
EMM386.EXE program
  (memory management),
  253
EMS (Expanded
  Memory Specification),
  244-246, 1062
emulators, 1062
enablers (PC cards), 825-826

encoding, 1062
  hard disk drives, 573,
    575-579
    clock signals, 575
    comparisons, 579-580
    FM (Frequency
      Modulation)
      encoding, 576
    MFM (Modified
      Frequency
      Modulation)
      encoding, 576-577
    RLL (Run Length
      Limited) encoding, 7,
      577-579
    ST-506/412 interface,
      629-631
encryption, 1062
endec (ENcoder/DECoder),
  630, 1063
  hard disk drives, 575
Endl Publications, 1007
Energy Star systems
  (energy-efficient),
  215, 312, 1063
  monitors, 391
energy-saving monitors
  DPMS (Display
    Power Management
    Signaling), 391
  Energy Star, 391
Englebart, Douglas
  (mouse inventor), 368
Enhanced Capabilities Port,
  see ECP, 449-450
Enhanced Graphics Adapter,
  see EGA
Enhanced Integrated Drive
  Electronics, *see* EIDE
Enhanced Parallel Port,
  see EPP
Enhanced Small Device
  Interface, *see* ESDI
Ensoniq chip set, 500
Ensoniq Corp, 492
Entry Systems Division
  (IBM), 11
environmental
  specifications, 934
    AT (Advanced Technology)
      AT Model 286, 977
      Type 2 motherboard,
        970

    PC XTs, 949
    Portable PCs, 954-955
EPP (Enhanced Parallel
  Port), 449
EPROM (Erasable
  Programmable Read-Only
  Memory), 284, 1063
Epson America, Inc. OEM
  Division, 1007
equalization, 1063
ergonomic keyboards, 360
Error Correcting Code
  (ECC), 726
Error Correcting Code,
  see ECC
errors
  audio error codes (POST),
    839-841
      AMI BIOS, 839-840
      nonfatal system board
        errors, 841
      Phoenix BIOS, 840-841
  BIOS
    error codes, Int 13h
      interface (DOS), 893
    error messages, 239-242
  booting DOS, 899
  "Cannot CHKDSK a
    SUBSTed or ASSIGNed
    drive" message, 910
  CHKDSK command,
    915-916
  controls, 1063
  correction protocols
    (modems), 441
  crashes, 1056
  CRC (Cyclic Redundancy
    Checking), 1056
  data recovery, *see* data
    recovery
  diagnostics, 1059
  hard errors, 1067
  hardware error codes,
    719-721
  keyboards, diagnostic and
    POST error codes, 362
  messages, 1063
  "No room for system on
    destination disk"
    message, 905-906
  parity checking, 315
    memory, 261-264

POST, Advanced
  Diagnostics (IBM)
  codes, 844-863
SCSI (Small Computer
  System Interface) drives,
  679-686
"Sector not found error
  reading drive C"
  message, 918
"Sector not found"
  message, 917
"System transferred"
  message, 905
visual error codes (POST),
  842-843
see also bugs;
  troubleshooting
ESD protection (electrostatic
  discharge), 1062
  aluminum foil, 42
  cleaning contacts, 63
  disassembling systems,
    41-42
  dusting boards, 65
  grounding straps, 281
  installing memory, 281
  kits, 30, 41
  vacuum cleaner use, 63
ESDI (Enhanced Small
  Device Interface), 632-633,
  1063
  capacity limitations, 684
  system configuration, 698
ESP (Enhanced Serial Ports),
  434-435
Ethernet, 1063
  10Base2 IEEE standard,
    1039
  10Base5 IEEE standard,
    1039
  10BaseT, 1039
  100BaseT, 484, 1039
  100BaseVG, 1040
  adapters (NICs), 467
Everex Systems, Inc., 1007
Exabyte Corporation, 1007
executable files (EXE), 879
Expanded Memory
  Manager, *see* EMM
Expanded Memory
  Specification, *see* EMS

expansion
  boards, ISA (Industry
    Standard Architecture)
    bus, 115
  bus, *see* I/O bus
  cards, PCs, 928
  slots, 108-109
    ISA (Industry Standard
      Architecture) bus, 112
    Portable PCs, 954
    riser-card slots, 109
expansion chassis, 262
expansion slots
  AT (Advanced
    Technology), 16, 956
    Model 286, 977
    Type 2 motherboard, 970
  IBM PCs, 934
  ISA bus, *see* ISA (Industry
    Standard Architecture) bus
  PC XTs, 942, 948
  widths, AT/XT systems, 17
  XT systems, 17
Express mode (MEMMAKER
  program), 255
Extended Binary Coded
  Decimal Interchange
  Code, *see* EBCDIC
Extended Data Out, *see* EDO
Extended Graphics Array
  (XGA), 1099
Extended Industry Standard
  Architecture, *see* EISA
extended memory, 224, 242,
  1063
  A20 line, 244
  configuring with
    HIMEM.SYS device
    driver, 253
  HMA (High Memory Area),
    243-244
  protected mode, 242
  real mode, 242
  virtual real mode, 242
  XMS (eXtended Memory
    Specification), 242-243
Extended Memory Manager
  (XMM), 1099
Extended Memory
  Specification (XMS), 1100

extended parallel ports, *see*
  bi-directional parallel ports
extended partitions, 1064
extended PCs, *see* XT
  systems
extended-length warranties,
  23-25
Extened Graphics Array,
  see XGA
external cache, 280
external CD-ROM drives,
  735-736
  installation, 746-747
    CD-ROM software,
      752-754
    SCSI (Small Computer
      System Interface)
      chains, 750-752
external displays (portable
  systems), 830-832
  LCD panels, 831
  LCD projectors, 831
  TV-Out feature, 831-832
external hardware interrupts
  (maskable interrupts), 142
external loopback tests,
  serial ports, 454
external terminators, SCSI
  (Small Computer System
  Interface) drives, 677
extra-high density, *see* ED
Extron Electronics, 1008

F

faceplate (bezel), 525
failures
  data recovery, *see* data
    recovery
  system, *see* system failures
fans, 806
Fantasy Productions, 1008
Fast ATA, 1064
Fast Mode parallel port
  (EPP), 449
fast SCSI (Small Computer
  System Interface), 663
Fast-20 (Ultra) SCSI, 663
FAT32, 585, 921-922

FATs (file allocation tables),
  585, 873, 902-903
    clusters (allocation
      units), 585
    defined, 1064
    floppy disk drives, 541
faxes, protocols, 444
FAXModem standards, 444
FDDI (Fiber Distributed Data
  Interface), 484-486
FDISK program (DOS),
  711-712, 893, 903
    defined, 1064
    undocumented functions,
      712-713
FDIV bug, 212-213
    testing for, 213-215
Fedco Electronics, Inc., 1008
feedback loop (closed
  loop), 599
ferrite heads (hard
  disk drives), 593
Fessenden Technologies,
  1008
Fiber Channel SCSI
  (Small Computer System
  Interface), 664
Fiber Distributed Data
  Interface, *see* FDDI
fiber-optic cables, 473-474
    connectors, 474
    daisy-chain topology
      (bus), 474
    star topology, 474-475
    types
      multimode, 473
      single mode, 473
FIC (First International
  Computer, Inc), 1008
FIFO (first-in first-out), 1064
File Allocation Tables,
  see FATs
file attributes, 1064
file servers, 459-461
    hard disks, evaluating, 462
    hardware
      CPU, 462
      evaluations, 461
      keyboard, 464
      monitor, 464
      mouse, 464

NICs (network interface
  cards), 463-464
power supply, 464
RAM, 462-463
files
  FAT (file allocation table),
    see FATs
  ADF (adapter description
    files), 1042
  AUTOEXEC.BAT, 880
  BAT, 879
  batch files, 1047
  COM, 879
  COMMAND.COM,
    877-879
  configuration file, 1055
  defined, 1064
  defragmentation
    floppy disks, 909
    hard disks, 67-68
  DOS
    IO.SYS, 876-877
    IO.SYS file, 878
    management, 888
    MSDOS.SYS, 876-878
    names, 901
    space allocation,
      888-889
    status, 901
  EXE (executable), 879
  FAT clusters (allocation
    units), 585
  folders, 1065
  hidden files, 1068
  history files, 1068
  HPFS (High Performance
    File System), 585
  IBMBIO.COM, 1069
  IBMDOS.COM, 1069
  incremental backups, 1069
  IO.SYS, 876, 1071
  memory swap, 830
  MSDOS.SYS, 876, 1078
  names, 1064
  NTFS (Windows NT File
    System), 585
  random-access files, 1085
  read-only file, 1085
  sequential files, 1088
  sound file formats, 499
  system files, 1091
  temporary files, 1092

filters (hard disk drives)
  barometric (breather)
    filters, 607
  recirculating filters, 607
FireWire (IEEE-1394),
  138-139
firmware, 1064
First International
  Computer, Inc (FIC), 1008
fixed disk drives, *see* hard
  disk drives
Flash BIOS, 289
  see also EPROM; PROM
Flash ROM, 1064
flicker (monitors), 398
floating-point errors
  (Pentium processors), 212
floating-point unit, *see* FPUs
floppy controllers (AT/XT
  systems), 17
floppy disk drives, 544, 804
  3 1/2-inch
    1.44M, 547-548
    2.88M, 548-549
    720K, 546-547
    formats, 541
    recording problems,
      549-554
    sensors, 550
  5 1/4-inch
    1.2M, 545-546
    360K, 545
    formats, 540
  8-inch, 519
  backups, 760
  caring for, 556-557
    airport x-ray machines,
      effects of, 557-559
    metal detectors, effects
      of, 558-559
  cleaning, *see* cleaning
  components
    circuit boards, 525
    clusters (allocation
      units), 543
    connectors, 525-527
    cylinders, 543-554
    diskette changeline
      jumper, 530-533
    drive select jumpers,
      527-529

floppy disk drives

faceplate (bezel), 525
floppy disk controller,
   534-538
head actuator, 521-524
logical operation,
   540-543
magnetic properties,
   538-540
media sensor jumper,
   533-538
physical specifications/
   operations, 536-538
read/write heads,
   520-523
spindle motor, 524-525
terminating resistors,
   529-530
controller internal
   connectors, 534-538
   AT systems, 537
   PC/XT systems, 535
development of, 519-520
double stepping, 546
floptical drives, 564-566
   21M floptical drives,
      564-565
   Iomega Zip drives, 565
   LS-120 (120M) floptical
      drive, 565-566
logical DOS-format
   parameters, 544
mini-floppy disk
   drive, 519
power consumption, 309
removing, 47-48
repairing
   aligning, 563-564
   cleaning, 562-563
root directory, 541
SA-400 interface, 525
sectors, 540
single-sided, 520
ST-412, 520
ST-506, 520
track-width
   specifications, 538
tracks, 540
troubleshooting, 560
   clamping off-center, 561
   phantom directory
      (Disk Change),
      560-561

floppy disks
   3 1/2-inch, construction
      of, 553-554
   5 1/4-inch
      construction of,
         551-552
      media-access hole, 552
      write-enable notch, 552
   allocation units, 903
   caring for, 556-557
      airport x-ray machines,
         effects of, 557-559
      metal detectors, effects
         of, 558-559
   coercivity, 555
   defragmentation of
      files, 909
   defragmenting, 542
   density, 554-555
   double-density, 554
   format specifications, 890
   formatting, 555-556
   high density, 554
   key disks, 1072
   physical specifications/
      operation, 536-538
   standards, MCP
      standards, 491
   thickness, 555
   tracks, 540
floppy tape, 1064
floptical drives, 564-566
   21M floptical drives,
      564-565
   Iomega Zip drives, 565
   LS-120 (120M) floptical
      drive, 565-566
flow control, 1064
Fluke, John Manufacturing
   Company, Inc., 1008
flux reversals (hard disk
   drives), 573, 575
FM (Frequency Modulation)
   encoding
      encoding, 1064
      hard disk drives, 576
         ASCII character
            waveforms, 579
         comparisons to MFM/
            RLL encoding,
            579-580

foam element key switches
   (keyboards), 343
folders, 1065
Folio Corporation, 1008
Forced Perfect Termination,
   see FPT
foreign language
   keyboards, 339
Form 1 (CD-ROM XA), 741
Form 2 (CD-ROM XA), 741
form factors, 1065
   ATX (Pentium Pro
      processors), 203
   portable systems, 809-811
   power supply, 293-299
      AT/Desk style, 294-295
      AT/Tower style, 294-302
      ATX style, 297-300
      Baby-AT style, 296
      PC/XT style, 293-300
      Slimline style, 296-297,
         301-302
FORMAT command, 583,
   899, 904, 1065
formats
   CD-ROM discs/drives, 736
      CD+, 738
      CD-DA (Compact Disc-
         Digital Audio), 738
      CD-E, 742
      CD-R (CD-Recordable),
         741-742
      DVD (Digital Video
         Disk), 742-743
      High Sierra Format,
         737-738
      ISO 9660 (first data
         standard), 737
      PhotoCD, 738-740
      XA (eXtended
         Architecture), 740-741
   DBR (DOS Boot Record),
      899-900
   DOS directories, 901
   floppy disk specifications,
      890
formatted capacity (disks),
   1065
formatting
   disks, 1065
   floppy disks, 555-556

hard disk drives
  data backups, 699
  defect mapping, 702-703
  high-level formatting (HLF), 583-584, 587, 716-718
  low-level formatting (LLF), 583-584, 699-711
  manufacturer's defect list, 704
  operating position of drives, 700-701
  partitioning, 583-587, 711-716
  surface analysis, 704-705
  temperature changes, 699-700
high-level formatting, 1068
low-level formatting, 1074
tape drives
  QIC-40, 766
  QIC-80, 766
FORTRAN (FORmula TRANslator), 1065
FPT (Forced Perfect Termination), SCSI (Small Computer System Interface), 675
FPUs (floating-point unit), 197
  bug in Pentiums, 212-215
  defined, 1064
Framatome Connectors USA, 1008
frame buffers, 1065
frames, 478-479
  buffer technology (video adapters), 414
  data, 1065
  layers, 479-480
  rate, 393, 1065
  video, 1065
freeze sprays, 38-39, 62
Freon, 38
Frequency Modulation (FM) encoding, 1064
frequency response
  defined, 496
  speakers, 505

frequency-shift keying, *see* FSK
FSK (frequency-shift keying), 439
FTP (File Transfer Protocol), 486
  defined, 1065
Fujitsu America, Inc., 1009
full duplex, 1065
full-height drive, 1066
full-motion video, 1066
full-size AT motherboards, 92, 796
function keys, 1066
  101-key (or 102-key) keyboards, 338
fuses, repairing, 320
Future Domain Corporation (Purchased by Adaptec), 1009
Future Pentium OverDrive Processor, 188

G

G (gigabyte), 1066
games
  adapter (joystick) interface, 381-383
  Game Blaster, 489
  ports, sound card accessory, 506
  sound cards, 490-491
gas plasma displays, 816, 1066
gates (AND gate), 1042
Gateway 2000, 1009
gateways, 1066
Gazelle/GTM Software, 1009
genlocking, 1066
German Industrial Norm committee (DIN), 359
GIF (Graphics Interchange Format), 1066
giga, 1066
Giga-Byte Technology Co., Ltd., 1009
gigabytes (G), 1066
GigaTrend, Inc., 1009
glass platters (hard disks), 589
Glidepoint, 381

Global Engineering Documents, 1009
Globe Manufacturing, Inc., 1009
Golden Bow Systems, 542, 1009
GoldStar Technology, Inc., 1010
GRACE Specialty Polymers/ WR GRACE, Emerson & Cuming Inc., 1010
Graphical User Interface (GUI), 1066
graphics
  animation, 1042
  CD+G (Compact Disc-Graphics), 1051
  EGA (Enhanced Graphics Adapter), 1061
graphics cards, *see* video adapters
Graphics Interchange Format (GIF), 1066
gray code (servo mechanisms), 601
Green Book, 1066
Green PCs, 215
grounding straps (hard drives), 281, 610-611
grounding tab (connector), hard disk drives, 613
Group I (FAXModem protocol), 444
Group II (FAXModem protocol), 444
Group III (FAXModem protocol), 444
GSI, Inc., 1010
guest computer (networking), 458
GUI (Graphical User Interface), 1066

H

half duplex, 1066
half toning, 1067
half-height drive, 1067
hand tools, 28-30
Harbor Electronics, 1010
hard disk drive interfaces, 627-628

hard disk drive interfaces

average seek time, 628-635
capacity limitations,
    684-686
controllers, 683
ESDI (Enhanced Small
    Device Interface),
    632-633
host adapters, 683-684
IDE (Integrated Drive
    Electronics), 633-652
  ATA (AT Attachment),
    636-650
  bus versions, 635-650
  CAM ATA specification,
    637-641
  comparisons to SCSI
    (Small Computer
    System Interface),
    681-684
  interposer cards, 635
  MCA IDE, 651-652
  origins, 635
  system configuration,
    698
  XT-Bus, 650-651
SCSI (Small Computer
    System Interface),
    653-681
  ANSI standards,
    655-657
  ASPI (Advanced SCSI
    Programming
    Interface), 680
  cable pinouts, 665-675
  cables, 665-673
  CAM (Common Access
    Method), 680
  Common Command
    Set, 655
  comparisons to IDE,
    681-684
  configurations, 675-681
  connector pinouts,
    665-675
  construction, 657-658,
    661
  data-transfer rates, 656
  development of,
    657-658, 661
  differential, 662-663,
    671-673

Fast SCSI (Small
    Computer System
    Interface), 663
Fast-20 (Ultra) SCSI, 663
host adapters, 683-684
SCSI-1, 663-664
SCSI-2, 663-664
SCSI-3, 664-665
Serial SCSI, 664
single-ended, 662-663
single-ended
    connectors, 666-670
system configuration,
    698
termination, 674-675
Wide SCSI, 664
ST-506/412, 629-631
hard disk drives, 804, 1067
air filters
  barometric (breather)
    filters, 607
  recirculating filters, 607
allocation units, 904
areal density, 568-569
bit cells (transition cells),
    573, 575
buying recommendations,
    624-625
capacity, 568, 623-624
coated media, 1054
coil actuators, temperature
    changes, 700
components, 588
connectors
  grounding tab, 613
  interface connectors, 612
controllers, head step
    rate, 966
cost, 623
cylinders, 569
data encoding schemes,
    575-579
  ASCII character
    waveforms, 579
  clock signals, 575
  comparisons, 579-580
  endec (ENcoder/
    DECoder), 575
  FM (Frequency
    Modulation)
    encoding, 576

MFM (Modified
    Frequency
    Modulation)
    encoding, 576-577
  read circuits, 580
  RLL (Run Length
    Limited) encoding,
    577-579
defined, 567
defragmenting files, 67-68
development of, 568
endec (ENcoder/DECoder),
    630
file servers, evaluating, 462
flux reversals, 573, 575
grounding strap, 610-611
HDAs (Head Disk
    Assemblies), 570, 588
head actuators, 596
  backlash, 598
  blind systems, 597
  parking (automatic
    head parking), 606
  rack-and-pinion gear
    mechanism, 598
  servo mechanisms,
    601-606
  split-metal-band
    mechanism, 597
  stepper motor, 596-598
  temperature fluctuation
    problems, 598-599
  voice coil, 596
  voice coil actuators,
    599-601
head crashes, 570
installation procedures
  AT-class systems,
    695-698
  configuring controllers,
    688-694
  data backups, 699
  defect mapping,
    702-703
  high-level formatting,
    716-718
  low-level formatting
    (LLF), 699-707
  low-level formatting
    software, 707,711
  manufacturer's defect
    list, 704

operating position of drive, 700-701
partitioning, 711-716
physical installation, 694-695
surface analysis, 704-705
system configuration, 695-698
temperature changes, 699-700
interfaces, *see* hard disk drive interfaces
magnetic data storage, encoding method, 573
master partition boot sector, 1074
media, 589
  oxide media, 589
  thin-film media, 590
  thin-film sputtered media, 590
motherboards, 611-612
operation, 569-572
  magnetic data storage, 572-575
partitioning, MBR (Master Boot Record), 897
platters (disks), 588-589
portable systems, 819-820
power consumption, 309
racks, 569
read/write heads, 591-595
  ferrite heads, 593
  HDA (Head Disk Assembly), 592
  Metal-In-Gap (MIG) heads, 593
  MR (Magneto-Resistive) heads, 594-595
  single-gap, 595
  TF (Thin Film) heads, 593-594
  voice coil actuator assembly, 591
recording type settings, 42-43
reliability, MTBF (Mean Time Between Failures), 615
removing, 47-48

SCSI (Small Computer System Interface), power consumption, 310
Seagate ST-12550N Barracuda 2
  capacities, 624
  specifications, 571
sectors, 580-587
  checksums, 581
  clusters (allocation units), 585
  format, 582
  formatting, 583-584
  high-level formatting (logical), 583, 587
  low-level formatting (physical), 583-584
  partitioning, 583, 585-587
  prefix portion (headers), 583
  prefix portions (headers), 581
  suffix portions (trailers), 581
  Zone Recording, 584-585
shock mounted, 622
sliders, 595-596
speed/performance, 615
  average seek time, 616
  cache controllers/ programs, 617-618
  cylinder skew, 620-622
  head skew, 619-622
  interleaving, 616-618
  latency, 616
  sector translation, 616
  transfer rate, 616-617
spindle motors, 609-610
standards, MCP standards, 491
temperature acclimation, 608-609
thermal expansion, 311
tracks, format, 582
troubleshooting problems, 718-721
virus scanning, 68-69
Winchester drives, 1098
hard errors, 1067
hardware, 1067

cards, *see* cards; video cards
codecs, 422
components, 807
conflicts, 510-512
DOS (Disk Operating System), 874
file servers, evaluating, 461
interrupts, 140-145
  external (maskable interrupts), 142
  see also IRQs
layer (OSI model), 481
metric/English, 40
monitors, *see* monitors
motherboards, *see* motherboards
mouse problems, *see* mouse
Plug and Play (PnP), 157
portable systems, 813-830
  batteries, 828-830
  displays, 813-817
  hard disk drives, 819-820
  keyboards, 826
  memory, 819
  PC cards, 821-826
  pointing devices, 827-828
  processors, 817-819
  removable media, 820-821
repairing, 919
screws, 39-40
Hauppauge Computer Works, Inc., 1010
Hayes
  compatible modems commands, 438
  proprietary standards (V-Series), 443
Hayes Microcomputer Products, 1010
hazards
  cigarette smoking, 59
  see also safety
HD (high density), 1068
HDAs (Head Disk Assembly), 570, 588
  hard disk drives, 592
HDLC (High-Level Data Link Control), 1067

HDtest program, 707-709
HDTV (high-definition television), 1068
head actuators, 521, 523-524
  defined, 1067
  hard disk drives, 596
    backlash, 598
    blind systems, 597
    parking (automatic head parking), 606
    rack-and-pinion gear mechanism, 598
    servo mechanisms, 601-606
    split-metal-band mechanism, 597
    stepper motor, 596
    stepper motor actuators, 597-598
    temperature fluctuation problems, 598-599
    voice coil, 596, 599-601
  stepper motors, 523
head crashes
  hard disk drives, 570
  defined, 1067
Head Disk Assembly, *see* HDA
head parking, 1067
  automatic head parking, 1045
headers (prefix portion), hard disk drives, 581, 583
headphone/speaker connectors (sound cards), 503
heads
  hard disk drives
    ferrite heads, 593
    HDA (Head Disk Assembly), 592
    MIG (Metal-In-Gap) heads, 593
    MR (Magneto-Resistive) heads, 594-595
    single-gap, 595
    TF (Thin Film) heads, 593-594
    voice coil actuator assembly, 591

seek, defined, 1067
skew, hard disk speed, 619-622
heat sinks, 806, 1067
  Pentium OverDrive processors, 184-185
Heathkit Education Systems, 1010
heating problems, 222
helical scans, 1067
Helm, Inc., 1010
Hercules Graphics Card, *see* HGC
Hermann Marketing, 1011
hertz (Hz), 163, 1069
Hertz, Heinrich Rudolph, 163
Hewlett-Packard, 313, 980, 1011
  diagnostic software, 838
  Disk Memory Division, 1011
  POST error codes, 847-849
hexadecimal numbers, 1067
HGC (Hercules Graphics Card), 398
Hi8 video, 1068
hidden files, 1068
high density (HD), 554, 1068
High Memory Area, *see* HMA
High Performance File System, *see* HPFS
High Sierra Format (CD-ROM discs/drives), 737-738, 1068
high-definition television (HDTV), 1068
High-Level Data Link Control, *see* HDLC
high-level formatting (HLF), 1068
  hard disk drives, 583-584, 587, 716-718
high-pressure tin (HPT), 1068
High-Resolution Diagnostic Disk, *see* HRD
high-speed networking technologies, 483-486
  100BaseT Ethernet cables, 484

ATM (Asynchronous Transfer Mode), 486
high-speed serial-bus ports, 455
high-speed technology (HST), 1068
HIMEM.SYS (device driver), 243, 253
history files, 1068
Hitachi America, Ltd., 1011
HLF, *see* high-level formatting
HMA (High Memory Area), 243-244, 1068
home pages, 1068
horizontal frequency (monitors), 393
horizontal scan rate, 386
host adapters, SCSI (Small Computer System Interface), 683-684
host computers (networking), 458
hot air rework stations, 32
HP DDS-3 drive (Model C1537A), 770
HPFS (High Performance File System), 585
HPT (high-pressure tin), 1068
HRD (High-Resolution Diagnostic Disk), 563, 869
HST proprietary standard (modems), 442, 1068
HTML (HyperText Markup Language), 1069
HTTP (HyperText Transfer Protocol), 1069
Huffman coding, 1069
Hypertech, 1011
hypertext, 1069
HyperText Markup Language (HTML), 1069
HyperText Transfer Protocol (HTTP), 1069
Hyundai Electronics America, 1011
Hz (hertz), 1069

I

I/O (input/output), 1069
  chips, super I/O chip, 22
  connectors, hard disk drive
    interfaces (ATA IDE), 638
  port addresses, 147-148, 510
    parallel ports, 148
    serial ports, 148
I/O bus, 105, 109-140
  EISA (Extended Industry
    Standard Architecture),
    117
    automated setup, 120
    bandwidth, 117
    card specifications, 117
    connectors, 117
  expansion slots, 108-109
  FireWire (IEEE-1394),
    138-139
  ISA (Industry Standard
    Architecture), 110-115
    8-bit, 111
    16-bit, 112-115, 692
    32-bit, 115
    access keys, 112
    expansion board
      dimensions, 115
    IRQs (Interrupt
      ReQuests), 690-691
  local bus
    development of, 120
    VESA local bus,
      122-127
  MCA (Micro Channel
    Architecture) bus,
    115-117
  USB (Universal Serial Bus),
    139-140
I/O ports
  addresses, configuring
    controllers, 693-694
  commands, 894-895
  motherboards, 803-804
  system (DOS), 877
IBM, 980
  5140 PC Convertible,
    936-941
  AT (Advanced Technology)
    disk management, 896
    BIOS versions, 962

BBS (Bulletin Board
  System), 844
competition with Apple
  Computer, 13
diagnostic software, 838,
  843-863
Entry Systems Division, 11
Fulfillment Center, 1011
Lexmark keyboards, 367
Microelectronics, 1011
Model 5100, 10
Model 5110, 11
Model 5120, 11
Model 5150, 11
motherboard, hard disk
  parameters, 963-965
National Publications,
  1011
NSC (National Support
  Center), 844
OEM Division, 1012
Options, 366
Parts Order Center, 1012
PC Company, 1012
PC Direct, 1012
PCs, *see* PCs (personal
  computers)
PC-XT BIOS versions,
  945-946
*Personal Systems Technical
  Solutions* Magazine, 1012
POST (Power-On Self Test),
  see POST
power-protection
  systems, 324
ROM BIOS, 930
Thinkpad 700, 378
XT Model 286, 971-978
IBMBIO.COM, 1069
IBMDOS.COM, 1069
IC (integrated circuits),
  see chips/chipsets
ICOMP (Intel Comparative
  Microprocessor
  Performance) index, 164
ICs (integrated circuits), 10
ID (identification bits), 726
  pins (monitors), 424
  settings, SCSI (Small
    Computer System
    Interface) drives, 675-678

IDE (Integrated Drive
  Electronics), 633-652, 1069
  ATA (AT Attachment),
    636-637
    cable connections,
      647-648
    cables, 639
    CAM ATA specification,
      637
    commands, 639-641
    configurations, 647-655
    connector, 638
    Conner Peripheral
      drives, 648-650
    drive jumper settings,
      648
    dual-drive
      configurations,
      637-638
    EIDE (ATA-2), 643-646
    I/O connector, 638
    intelligent drives,
      642-643
    intelligent Zoned
      Recording drives, 643
    non-intelligent drives,
      641-642
    signals, 639
  bus versions, 635-650
  capacity limitations, 684
  CD-ROM drives (ATAPI/
    EIDE), 733
  comparisons to SCSI
    interface, 681-684
    controllers, 683
    host adapters, 683-684
  connectors, 153, 683-684
  drives, setup programs,
    42-43
  formatting, LLF
    software, 710
  host adapters, 683-684
  interposer cards, 635
  low-level formatting (LLF),
    705-707
  MCA IDE, 651-652
  origins, 635
  system configuration, 698
  XT-Bus (8-bit), 650-651
**identification, motherboard
  manufacturers, 22**
identification bits (ID), 726

Identify Drive command
  (ATA IDE), 639
IEEE (Institute of
  Electrical and Electronic
  Engineers), 483
    10Base2, 1039
    10Base5, 1039
    1284 standard
      (parallel ports), 450
    1394 high-speed local
      serial bus, 138-139, 457
    standards
      IEEE 802.3 (Ethernet),
        483
      IEEE 802.5 (Token
        Ring), 483
Illinois Lock, 1012
images, true-color images,
  1093
IML (Initial Microcode
  Load), 289-290
incremental backups, 1069
Indeo codec program, 422
index holes (5 1/4-inch
  floppy disks), 551
indexes
  ICOMP (Intel Comparative
    Microprocessor
    Performance), 164
  marks, 603
Industry Standard
  Architecture Bus, *see* ISA
Information Access
  Company, 1012
InfoWorld Magazine, 1012
Initial Microcode Load,
  see IML
inkjet printers, 1070
Inline, Inc., 1012
Innerworks Technology,
  Inc., 1012
Inport mouse (bus mouse),
  372-373
input, 1070
input devices
  game adapter (joystick)
    interface, 381-383
  keyboards, 335-368
    83-key PC/XT keyboard,
      336
    84-key AT keyboard,
      336-337
    101/102-key, 337-339

104-key (Windows
  keyboards), 339-341
automatic enabling
  numeric keypad
  feature, 342
cable part numbers, 365
compatibility, 341-342
interface, 345-346
interface protocol, 337
key numbers, 348-358
key switch design,
  342-345
keyboard/mouse
  interface connectors,
  358-359
membrane, 344
repairing, 361-367
scan codes, 337,
  348-358
special features, 359-360
troubleshooting,
  361-367
typematic functions,
  347-348
mouse
  components, 369
  development of,
    368-370
  hardware problems,
    373-375
  interfaces, 371-373
  software problems,
    375-377
  Trackpoint, 377-381
  Trackpoint II, 378
input/output (I/O), 1069
installing
  adapter cards, 153
    sound cards, 508-509
  CD-ROM drives, 744
    adapter cards, 745
    card edge connector,
      748-750
    CD-ROM software,
      752-754
    device driver, 753
    external drives, 746-747
    internal drives, 748-750
    jumpers, 745-746
    Microsoft CD
      Extensions, 753-754
    ribbon cable, 748-750

SCSI (Small Computer
  System Interface)
  chains, 750-752
  test run, 754-756
floppy disk drives, 559
hard disk drives
  AT-class systems,
    695-698
  configuring controllers,
    688-694
  data backups, 699
  defect mapping,
    702-703
  high-level formatting
    (HLF), 716-718
  IDE, 637-638
  low-level formatting
    (LLF), 699-711
  manufacturer's defect
    list, 704
  operating position,
    700-701
  partitioning, 711-716
  physical installation,
    694-695
  surface analysis,
    704-705
  system configuration,
    695-698
  temperature changes,
    699-700
  troubleshooting
    problems, 718-719
memory
  adapter boards, 280-281
  diagnostics programs,
    283
  DRAM (Dynamic
    Random Access
    Memory), 273-274
  ESD problems, 281
  jumper setting
    adjustments, 282
  leads broken/bent, 282
  RAM chips, 274-280
  switch setting
    adjustments, 282
  total, 248-250
motherboards, 52-57
  connecting cables,
    54-56
  connecting power
    supplies, 54

memory modules, 53
mounting, 53-54
preparing, 52-53
replacing covers, 56
running setup
programs, 56-57
RAM chips, ESD
(electrostatic
discharge), 281
SIMMs/DIMMs, 53
sound cards, 155
tape drives, 775-777
**instruction pipelines
(Pentiums), 194**
instructions, 1070
Int 13h interface (DOS)
BIOS disk functions, 892
BIOS error codes, 893
integrated chipsets, 285
integrated circuits, *see*
chips/chipsets; ICs
**Integrated Device
Technology, Inc., 1013**
**Integrated Drive Electronics
(IDE),** *see* **IDE**
**Integrated Micro Solutions,
Inc., 1013**
**Integrated Services Digital
Network,** *see* **ISDN**
Intel, 980
Comparative
Microprocessor
Performance, *see* ICOMP
CPU memory-addressing
capabilities, 163
ICOMP index ratings, 164
PC Enhancement
Operations, 1013
Pentium Pro
microprocessors, 10
processors
286, 167-168
386, 168-169
386DX, 169-170
386SL, 170-171
386SX, 170
486, 171-175, 178
486DX, 174, 176
486DX OverDrive chips,
182-213

486DX2, 172-175,
179-182, 190
486DX4, 172, 174-175
486SL (80486), 176-177
486SX, 174-178
486SX OverDrive chips,
182-213
487SX (math
coprocessor), 178
4004 microprocessors, 10
8086, 166-167
8087 math
coprocessors, 208-209
8088, 166-167
8088 microprocessor,
942
80186, 167
80188, 167
80287 math
coprocessors, 209
80386, 168-169
80387 math
coprocessors, 209-210
80487 math
coprocessors, 210
compatible, 204-206
math coprocessors,
207-222
object-code-
compatibility, 168
OverDrive, 178-213
Weitek math
coprocessor, 210
Triton chips, 799
**intelligent ATA-IDE drives,
642-643**
**intelligent media
sensors, 534**
**intelligent Zoned Recording
ATA-IDE drives, 643**
**IntelliMouse (Microsoft),
370-371**
interactive CDs (CD-I), 1051
interfaces, 1070
adapters, 1041
CD-ROM drives, 731
IDE/ATAPI (EIDE), 733
proprietary, 733
SCSI/ASPI, 732-733
connectors
hard disk drives, 612
motherboards, 98-101

DOS, 890
I/O port commands,
894-895
Interrupt 13h, 891-894
Interrupt 21h, 890-891
Interrupt 25/26h, 891
game (joystick) adapter,
381-383
hard disk drives, 627-628
average seek time,
628-635
capacity limitations,
684-686
ESDI (Enhanced Small
Device Interface),
632-633
IDE (Integrated Drive
Electronics), 633-652
SCSI (Small Computer
System Interface),
653-681
ST-506/412, 629
keyboards, 345-346,
358-359
mouse, 371-373
bus mouse, 372-373
motherboard mouse
port, 371-372
serial and motherboard
mouse port (KEEP), 372
serial interface, 371
RS-232 interface, 1087
**interlaced monitors/video
adapters, 391**
interlacing, 1070
interleaving
CD-ROM XA (eXtended
Architecture), 740
hard disk speed, 618
hard drive speed, 616
memory (RAM chip
architecture), 279
ratios, 1070
internal cache, 280
**internal CD-ROM drives,
735-736**
installation, 748-750
CD-ROM software,
752-754
SCSI (Small Computer
System Interface)
chains, 750-752

internal commands, 1070
internal drives, 1070
internal modems, 5140 PC Convertible laptop, 940
internal registers, 162
internal stack overflow error (IRQ channels), 141
International Electronic Research Corp. (IERC), 1013
International Standards Organization (ISO), 1071
International Telecommunications Union, *see* ITU
Internet, 1070
    network connections, 486
    Packet Exchange (IPX), 1071
interpolated data CD-ROMs, 728
interposer cards (IDE interface), 635
interpreters, 1070
Interrupt 13h interface, 891-894
Interrupt 21h interface (DOS), 890-891
Interrupt 25/26h interface (DOS), 891
Interrupt Requests, *see* IRQs
interrupts
    AT/XT systems, 17
    conflicts, 374-375
    vectors, 1071
IO.SYS file, 876-878, 1071
Iomega Corporation, 1013
    Zip drives, 565
IPL (Initial Program Load) ROM, 236
IPX (Internet Packet eXchange), 1071
IRQs (Interrupt Requests), 140-145, 1071
    8-bit ISA (Industry Standard Architecture) bus interrupts, 142
    16-bit EISA/ISA/MCA bus interrupts, 142-144
    configuring controllers, 690-691
    conflicts, 144-145, 511
    EISA/ MCA buses, 141
    external interrupts (maskable interrupts), 142
    internal stack overflow error, 141
    ISA (Industry Standard Architecture) bus, 141
ISA bus (Industry Standard Architecture), 15-16, 110-115
    8-bit, 111
        DMA channels, 145
        interrupts, 142
        IRQs (Interrupt ReQuests), 691
    16-bit, 112-115
        DMA channels, 145-146, 692
        interrupts, 142-144
    32-bit, 115
    access keys, 112
    AT systems (Advanced Technology PCs), 16
    expansion boards, 115
    IRQs (Interrupt ReQuests), 141, 690-691
    XT systems, 17
    see also AT bus expansion board dimensions
ISDN (Integrated Services Digital Network), 444-445, 1071
    connections to the Internet, 488
    terminal adaptor, 445
ISO (International Standards Organization), 1071
ISO 9660 (CD-ROM discs/drives), 737, 1071
ISP (integrated system peripheral) chips
    bus mastering, 109
ITU (International Telecommunications Union), 1051, 1071

J

J-lead, 1072
J. Bond Computer Systems, 1013
Jameco Computer Products, 1013
Java, 1071
JDR Microdevices, 1013
    POST code cards, 842
JEDEC (Joint Electron Devices Engineering Council), 1071
Jensen Tools, 1014
JOIN command, 911
Joint Electron Devices Engineering Council (JEDEC), 1071
Joint Photographic Experts Group, *see* JPEG
joysticks, 506-507
    connectors (sound cards), 504
    interface, 381-383
    problems, 514
JPEG (Joint Photographic Experts Group), 422, 1072
JTS Corporation, 1014
jumpers, 1072
    CD-ROM drives, 745-746
    recording settings prior to disassembly, 44
    selection (media sensor jumper), 533-538
    settings
        adjusting, 282
        SCSI (Small Computer System Interface) ID, 676
JVC Information Products, 1014

K

K (kilobyte), 1072
Kensington Microware, Ltd., 1014
Kermit protocol, 1072
key disks, 1072
Key Tronic Corporation, 1014
keyboards, 335-368, 805
    83-key PC/XT, 336
    84-key AT, 336-337
    101-key (or 102-key), 337-339
    104-key (Windows keyboard), 339-341
    accessories (enhanced), AT models, 971

automatic enabling numeric keypad feature, 342
bidirectional interface, 337
cable part numbers, 365
carpal tunnel syndrome, 1050
cleaning, 66-67, 364-365
compatibility, 341-342
controller, 286
documentation, 367-368
Dvorak keyboard, 1061
Dvorak-Dealy, 360
ergonomic keyboards, 360
foreign language, 339
IBM PCs, 928
IBM/Lexmark, 367
interfaces, AT/XT systems, 17
key numbers, 348-358
   83-key PC/XT keyboards, 349
   84-key AT keyboards, 351-352
   101-key (or 102-key), 353-357
key switch designs, 342-345
   capacitive switches, 344-345
   foam element switches, 343
   mechanical, 343
   rubber dome switches, 344
LAN file servers, 464
macros, 1072
membrane, 344
PC XTs, 943
   parts numbers, 951
portable systems, 826
QWERTY keyboard, 1085
repairing, 361-367
replacements, 365-367
scan codes, 337, 348-358
   83-key PC/XT keyboards, 349
   84-key AT keyboards, 351-352
   101-key (or 102-key), 353-357
   104-key Windows, 358

specifications
   AT Model 286, 977
   AT Type 2 motherboard, 970
   IBM PCs, 934
   PC XTs, 948
technology
   interface, 345-346
   keyboard/mouse interface connectors, 358-359
   typematic functions, 347-348
Trackpoint pointing devices, 367
troubleshooting errors, 361
   defective cables, 361-362
   diagnostic and POST error codes, 362
   stuck keys, 361
keypads (numeric)
   101-key (or 102-key) keyboards, 338
   automatic enabling feature, 342
   portable systems, 826
kilo, 1072
kilobyte (K), 1072
Kingston Technology Corporation, 1014

L

L2 cache (Pentium Pro processors), 202
Labconco Corporation, 1014
Labtec Enterprises, Inc., 1014
landing zones, 1072
Landmark POST code cards, 842
lands (CD-ROMs), 725
languages
   assembler, 1044
   BASIC (Beginner's All-purpose Symbolic Instruction Code), 1046
   C programming, 1050

   COBOL (Common Business-Oriented Language), 1054
   Microsoft Cassette BASIC, 927
LANs (local area networks), 457-459, 1072
   10BaseT, 1039
   100BaseT, 1039
   100BaseVG, 1040
   bridges, 1049
   cables, 471
      coaxial, 471-473
      connections, 477
      fiber-optic, 471, 473-474
      selecting, 476
      twisted pair, 471
   components, 458-459
   data-transfer speeds, 466-467
   direct cable connections, 458
   file servers, 459-461
      caching, 463
      CPU, 462
      keyboard, 464
      monitor, 464
      mouse, 464
      NICs (network interface cards), 463-464
      power supply, 464
      RAM, 462-463
   network adapters, functions, 469
   network interface cards (NICs), 464-471
      ARCnet adapters, 467
      Ethernet adapters, 467
      Token Ring adapters, 468
      Token Ring cards, 465
   peer-to-peer networks, 458
   Token Ring early token release, 468
   types, 483
   workstations, 459-460
LANtastic, 483
Lantronix, 1014

LAPM (Link-Access Procedure for Modems), 441, 1072
laptops, 9, 810, 1073
  IBM 5140 PC Convertible, 936-941
larger cluster sizes, 586
laser diode (CD-ROMs), 727
Laser Magnetic Storage, 1015
laser printers, 1073
latency, 1073
  average latency, 1045
  hard drive speed, 616
LBA (Logical Block Address), 1073
  SCSI (Small Computer System Interface) interfaces, 685
LCC (Leadless Chip Carrier), 1073
LCDs (Liquid Crystal Display), 1073
  active-matrix, 387-388
  monochrome, 388
  panels, external displays, 831
  passive-matrix, 387-388
  projectors, external displays, 831
  screen, 5140 PC Convertible laptop, 937
  triple-supertwist, 388
Leadless Chip Carrier (LCC), 1073
leads, broken/bent during memory installation, 282
LearnKey, Inc., 1015
LED (Light-Emitting Diode), 1073
Lempel Zev Welch (LZW), 1074
level-sensitive interrupts (EISA/MCA buses), 141
Lexmark, 1015
  Select-Ease ergonomic keyboards, 360
Li-Ion (Lithium-Ion), 828
Liebert, 1015
LIF (Low-Insertion-Force), 1073
  sockets, 181

light pens, 1073
Light-Emitting Diode (LED), 1073
LIM (Lotus Intel Microsoft), 171
line conditioners, 326
line testers, 833
linear
  actuators (voice coil actuators), 600
  density, floppy disks, 554
linear addresses (memory), 227-228
linearity, defined, 496
Link Access Procedure for Modems, see LAPM
Liquid Crystal Displays, see LCDs
Lisa computer (Apple), 368
Lithium Polymer, 828
Lithium-Ion (Li-Ion), 828
Liuski International, 1015
LLF (Low-Level Formatting)
  hard disk drives, 699-707
  data backups, 699
  defect mapping, 702-703
  Disk Manager program, 708
  HDtest program, 708-709
  IDE software, 710
  manufacturer's defect list, 704
  nondestructive software, 711
  SCSI (Small Computer System Interface) software, 709
  software, 707-711
  surface analysis, 704-705
load resistors, bench testing power supply, 318
loading
  DOS, 882-888
  mechanisms (CD-ROM drives)
    caddy system, 734-735
    tray loading, 734-735

loads (power supply), 304-305
local area networks, see LANs
local buses, 1073
  development of, 120
  PCI (Peripheral Component Interconnect) bus
    3.3v pinouts, 132-134
    5v pinouts, 129-131
    adapter cards, 127
    universal bus pinouts, 135-137
  VESA Local bus (VL-Bus), 122-127
    card limitations, 123
    disadvantages of, 123
    electrical limitations, 123
    pinouts, 124-126
    speed, 123
local echo, 1074
local resistors (power supply testing), 318
logic
  AND gate, 1042
  block diagrams, 1048
  boards, see circuits
  operators, AND, 1042
  probes/pulsers, 35
logical addresses, 224
Logical Block Addressing (LBA), 1073
logical drives, 1074
Logical Unit Number (LUN), 1074
Logicraft Information Systems, Inc., 1015
Logitech mouse, 369
longitudinal density (floppy disks), 554
Longshine Microsystems, Inc., 1015
loopback connectors, see wrap plugs
loopback testing (serial ports), 454-455
loose components, reseating, 64-65
lossless compression, 1057, 1074

lossy compression,
    1057, 1074
lost clusters, 1074
Lotus Development
    Corporation, 1015
Lotus Intel Microsoft
    (LIM), 171
Low Insertion Force
    (LIF), 1073
low-cost service, 24
low-density drives, *see*
    double density (DD)
Low-Insertion Force, *see* LIF
low-level formatting, 1074
    hard disk drives, 583-584
low-profile computers, 109
LPT ports (I/O addresses), 148
LPX motherboards, 796
    form factors, 93-94
LS-120 (120M) floptical
    drives, 565-566
LSI Logic, Inc., 1015
lubricants (cleaning), 62-63
LUN (Logical Unit Number),
    1074
LZW (Lempel Zev Welch),
    1074

M

M (megabyte), 1075
Ma Laboratories, Inc., 1016
machines as sources,
    982-983
Macintosh (Apple), 368
macros, 1072
Macworld Communications,
    Inc., 1016
MAG InnoVision, 1016
magazines, 985
    Computer Design, 1001
    Computer Graphics World,
        1001
    Computer Hotline, 1001
    Computer Reseller News,
        1001
    Computer Retail Week, 1001
    Computer Shopper, 1001
    *Computer Technology
        Review*, 1001
    Data Base Advisor, 1004
    Data Communications, 1004

Datamation, 1005
Electronic Buyers' News,
    1006
Electronic Engineering Times,
    1007
Electronic Products, 1007
*IBM Personal Systems
    Technical Solutions*, 1012
InfoWorld, 1012
Motor, 1021
OEM, 1023
PC, 1024
PC Week, 1025
PC World, 1025
Processor, 1026
Service News, 1029
*Test and Measurement
    World*, 1033
trade, 985
magnetic data storage
    (hard disk drives), 572-575
magnetic media drives
    Bernoulli, 782-783
    SyQuest, 783
Magneto-Optical (MO), 1077
    drives, 783-785
    recording, 1074
Magneto-Resistive heads,
    see MR heads
MAGNI Systems, Inc., 1016
maintenance, 57-58
    CD-ROMs, 725
    cleaning, 58-67
        boards, 65
        brushes/swabs, 63
        chemicals, 60-64
        connectors/contacts,
            63, 66
        keyboards/mouse, 66-67
        procedures, 64-67
        tools needed, 60
        vacuum cleaners, 62-63
    devloping maintenance
        programs, 58-76
    hard disk care, 67-69
        defragmenting files,
            67-68
        virus scanning, 68-69
    lubricants, 62-63
    operating environment,
        69-76
        dust/pollutants, 75-76
        on/off cycles, 70-72

power-line noise, 73-74
            radio-frequency
                interference (RFI),
                74-75
            static electricity, 72-73
            temperature, 69-71
        power supplies, 70-71
        reseating socketed
            components, 64-65
        screen savers, 72
        see also backups
    manuals, 980-982
        hard disk drives,
            installation, 687
        see also documentation
    manufacturers, 980
        keyboards, 367
        motherboards,
            identifying, 22
        mouse, 369
        power supply
            replacements, 322-323
        ROM BIOS, 286-287
        specific documentation, 23
        see also vendors
MapInfo Corporation, 1016
mapping hard disk drives,
    702-703
marketplace, PC-compatible
    systems in, 13-14
maskable interrupts
    (IRQs), 142
mass-producing
    CD-ROMs, 725
Master Boot Record, *see* MBR
Master Boot Sector, *see* MBS
master configuration
    (IDE drives), 648
master partition boot sector,
    1074
Mastersoft, Inc., 1016
Mate-N-Lock (floppy drive
    connector), 525
math coprocessors, 206-208
    Intel
        486 processors, 171
        486DX processors, 176
        487SX processors, 178
        8087 processors,
            208-209
        80287 processors, 209
        80387 processors,
            209-210

80487 processors, 210
  list of, 207-222
  specifications, 208
  speed rates, 207
  Weitek, 210
Pentium, FPU (floating
  point unit), 197
see also processors
Matrox Graphics, Inc., 1016
Maxell Corporation of
  America, 1016
Maxi Switch, Inc., 1016
  keyboards, 360
Maxoptix, 1017
Maxtor Corporation,
  632, 1017
Maynard Electronics, Inc.,
  1017
MBR (Master Boot Record),
  587, 873
  partition tables, 897
MBS (Master Boot
  Sector), 587
MC (minicartridge), 762
MCA (Micro Channel
  Architecture) bus, 115-117,
  1074
  16-bit DMA channels,
    145-146
  16-bit interrupts, 142-144
  adapter cards, 116
  Advanced Diagnostics, 844
  auto-configure adapter
    boards, 250
  bus mastering, 116
  DMA channels, 147
  IRQs (Interrupt ReQuests),
    141-144, 690-691
  level-sensitive
    interrupts, 141
  power supply, 292
  setup programs, 44
MCA IDE (IDE interfaces),
  651-652
McAfee Associates, 1017
MCGA (MultiColor Graphics
  Array), 403-404, 1075
MCI (Media Control
  Interface), 1075
McKenzie Technology, 1017
MDA (Monochrome Display
  Adapter), 396-398, 1075

adapter BIOS memory, 234
  memory map, 229-233
  pinouts, 397-398
MDI (Micro Design
  International), 1018
MDRAM (Multibank
  DRAM), 415
Mean Time Between Failure
  (MTBF), 1078
Mean Time To Repair
  (MTTR), 1078
measuring
  coercivity, 1054
  dot pitch, 1060
mechanical key switches
  (keyboards), 343
  foam element, 343
  rubber dome, 344
media
  archive media, 1043
  hard disk drives, 589
    oxide media, 589
    thin-film sputtered
      media, 590
Media Control Interface
  (MCI), 1075
media sensor jumper (floppy
  drives), 533-538
media-access holes
  (5 1/4-inch floppy
  disks), 552
medium, 1075
mega, 1075
megabytes (M), 1075
megahertz (MHz), 1076
Megahertz Corporation,
  1017
membrane keyboards, 344
MemCor (platters), 589
MEMMAKER program
  (memory management),
  253-255
memory, 1075
  adapter memory
    configuration, 250-251
    moving to resolve
      conflicts, 251
    optimizing, 251-252
    UMA (Upper Memory
      Area), 251

AT (Advanced Technology)
  Model 286, 974-975
  Type 2 motherboard, 968
banks, 259-260, 268,
  275, 1046
bubble memory, 1049
buffers, 1049
bus, 107-108
cache, 279, 1050
  caching (RAM chip
    architecture), 279-280
cards, 5140 PC Convertible
  laptop, 939
chips (1Kbit), 10
configuring
  with HIMEM.SYS
    (device driver), 253
  conventional, 224
    barrier, 223, 228
  core, 1056
DIMMs (Dual Inline
  Memory Modules),
  264-269
  168-pin, 275
  168-pin capacities, 266
  installing, 274-280
  Synchronous DRAM
    (SDRAM) memory, 267
DMA (Direct Memory
  Access), 1059
DRAM (Dynamic Random
  Access Memory), 1061
  installing, 273-274
EDO (Extended Data
  Out), 803
EDO RAM (Pentiums), 272
EMM (Expanded Memory
  Manager), 1062
EMS (Expanded Memory
  Specification), 1062
EPROM (Erasable
  Programmable Read-Only
  Memory), 1061, 1063
expanded memory,
  244-246, 1063
extended memory,
  224, 242
  A20 line, 244
  HMA (High Memory
    Area), 243-244
  protected mode, 242
  real mode, 242

virtual real mode, 242
XMS (Extended Memory Specification), 242-243
frame buffers, 1065
IBM PCs, 933
installing
  adapter boards, 280-281
  diagnostics programs, 283
  ESD problems, 281
  jumper setting adjustments, 282
  leads broken/bent, 282
  switch setting adjustments, 282
  total, 248-250
integrated chipset, 285
management programs (freeing UMA), 252-253
  EMM (Expanded Memory Manager), 1062
  EMM386.EXE (DOS), 253-255
  MEMMAKER (DOS), 253-255
  QEMM (Quarterdeck), 255-290
motherboards, 802-803
  selection criteria, 81
parity checking, 261-264
  errors, 315
  NMI (non-maskable interrupt), 263
  odd parity, 261
  parity bits, 261
  power supply problems, 315
  saving after, 264
PC XTs, 947
physical memory, 256-257
Portable PC, 953
portable systems, 819
RAM chips, 257
  capacity, 275-276
  DIPs (Dual Inline Pin), 257, 274
  installing, 274-280
  interleaved memory architecture, 279
  list of, 257-259

markings, 259, 275
memory caching, 279-280
paged memory architecture, 278
part numbers, 259
  removing, 282
SIPPs (Single Inline Pin Package), 257, 274
speed, 271-272, 276-278
storage capacities, 257-259
VRAM (Video Random Access Memory), 414-416
wait states, 276-277
registers, 1086
reserved memory, 226
resident programs, 918-919, 1076
ROM BIOS
  distributors, 287
  keyboard-controller, 286
  manufacturers, 286-287
  modifications, 288-290
  preventing conflicts and overlap, 246
  problems, 287-288
  upgrading, 283-285
scratch pad memory, 232
SDRAM (Pentiums), 272-273
shadow memory (shadow ROM), 246-248
SIMMs (Single Inline Memory Modules), 257, 264-269, 274, 802
  30-pin, 266-267, 269, 274
  72-pin, 266, 270-271, 274
  chip creep, 268
  installing, 274-280
SRAM (Static Random Access Memory), 279
swap files, 830
switch settings, IBM PC/XT, 935-936
terabytes, defined, 170
testing, 36-37

UMA (Upper Memory Area), 224-226, 842
  adapter ROM, 233-238
  linear addresses, 227-228
  motherboard ROM BIOS, 238-239
  segment addresses, 226-228
  Video RAM, 226, 228-233
usable memory, total, 248-250
video adapters, 412-413
virtual memory, 1097
XT Model 286, 972
see also SIMMs (Single Inline Memory Modules)
Mentor Electronics, Inc., 1017
menu software, 1076
Merisel, 1017
Meritec, 1017
Merritt Computer Products, Inc., 1018
messages (errors), *see* **errors**
metal detectors, effects on disks, 558-559
Metal-In-Gap, *see* **MIG**
Metal-Oxide Semiconductor (MOS), 1077
meters
  cost, 34
  DMMs (Digital Multi-Meters)
    features, 316-317
    measuring voltage, 317-318
    selecting, 316-317
  measuring voltage, 34-35
Methode Electronics, Inc., 1018
metric screws, 40
mezzanine bus, *see* **PCI (Peripheral Component Interconnect) bus**
MFM (Modified Frequency Modulation), 1076
  encoding hard disk drives, 576-577

hard disk drives
    ASCII character waveforms, 579
    comparisons to FM/RLL encoding, 579-580
MHz (megahertz), 1076
MI/MIC (Mode Indicate/Mode Indicate Common), 1076
micro, 1076
Micro 2000, Inc., 1018
    POST code cards, 842
Micro Accessories, Inc., 1018
Micro Channel Architecture, *see* MCA
Micro Channel Developers Association, 1018
Micro Computer Cable Company, Inc., 1018
Micro Design International (MDI), 1018
Micro Firmware, Inc. (ROM BIOS distributor), 287
Micro House International, 1018
Micro Industries Corporation, 1018
Micro Solutions, Inc., 1019
Micro Warehouse, 1019
Micro-Star International, 1020
Microcom, Inc., 1019
Microcom Networking Protocol, *see* MNP
Micrografx, Inc., 1019
Microid Research, Inc., 1019
Microlink/Micro Firmware, Inc., 1019
Micron Technologies, 1019
Micronics Computers, Inc., 1020
microphone in connectors (sound cards), 503
microphones, 506
Micropolis Corporation, 1020
microprocessors, 1076
    286, 167-168
    386, 168-169
    386DX, 169-170
    386SL, 170-171
    386SX, 170
    486 (80486), 171-173
    486DX (80486), 175-176
    486DX2, 178-213
        speed-rated versions, 179
        upgrade sockets, 180-182
    486DX4 memory bus, 108
    486SL (80486), 176-177
    486SX (80486), 177-178
    487SX, 178
    8086, 166-167, 1041
    8087, 1041
    8088, 166-167, 1041
    8514/A, 1041
    80186, 167
    80188, 167
    80286, 1040
    80287, 1040
    80386, 168-169
    80386DX, 1040
    80386SX, 1040
    80387, 1040
    80486DX, 1040
    80486DX2, 1040
    80486DX4, 1040
    80486SX, 1040
    accelerator boards, 1041
    address bus, 162-163
    AMD, 205
    AT systems (Advanced Technology PCs), 16
    AT/XT systems, comparing, 17
    bus, 105-107
        bandwidth, 106
        see also buses
    CISC (Complex Instruction-Set Computer), 1053
    cooling problems, 222
    coprocessors, 1056
    CPUs (central processing units), *see* CPUs
    Cyrix, 205-206
    data bus, 159-161
        sizes, 161
    file servers, 462
    Future Pentium OverDrive Processor, 188
    heating problems, 222
    identifying chip/chipset documentation, 21
    Intel-compatible, 204-206
    internal registers, 162
    math coprocessor list, 207-222
    memory-addressing capabilities, 163
    motherboard selection criteria, 80-81
        chip speed rating reliability, 89-90
    National Semiconductor 87308, 22
    object-code compatibility, 168
    OverDrive, 178-213
        active heat sink, 185
        compatibility problems, 191-192
        designations, 190
        DX2 and 486SX2 processors, 192-193
        DX4 processor, 185
        heat sink, 184
        installation, 190-191
        Socket 1, 182
        Socket 2, 184
        Socket 3, 186
        Socket 4 pinout specification, 188
        Socket 5, 188-189
        Socket 6, 188, 190
        Socket 7, 188
        socket designs, 182-190
        upgrade sockets, 180-182
        VRM (Voltage Regulator Module), 188
    Pentium, 193-197
        branch predictions (BTB), 194
        first-generation, 197-198
        internal architecture, 195
        math coprocessor (FPUs), 197
        motherboard speeds, 198
        second-generation, 198-200
        specifications, 193
        speeds, 198

modems **1141**

superscalar technology, 193
third-generation (P55C), 200
twin-data pipelines, 193
u-pipe, 194
v-pipe, 194
write-back cache, 174
Pentium II, 203-204
Pentium Pro, 201-203
  ATX form factor, 203
  L2 cache, 202
  MPS (Multi-Processor Specification), 202
portable systems, 817-819
  TPC (Tape Carrier Packaging), 817-818
  voltage reduction, 818-819
speed ratings, 163-166
  chip speed rating reliability, 89-90
  Intel ICOMP index ratings, 164
  Pentiums, 165
standards, MCP standards, 491
tests, 210-211, 222
  early 80386s, 211-212
  Pentium models and steppings, 215-222
  Pentiums, 212-215
  software, 210
see also CPUs (central processing units)
Microprocessors Unlimited, Inc., 1020
MicroScope (Micro 2000), 838, 865-866
  Web site, 866
microsecond, 1076
Microsoft, 1020
  BASIC (Beginners All-purpose Symbolic Instruction Code), 10
  Cassette BASIC language, 927
  CD Extensions
    command-line options, 754
    installing, 753-754
  Diagnostics (MSD), 251
  IntelliMouse, 369-371

Natural ergonomic keyboards, 360
PC development, 12
Video 1 codec program, 422
MicroSystems Development Tech., Inc., 1020
Microtest Enterprises, 1015
MicroWay, Inc., 1020
MIDI (Musical Instrument Digital Interface), 1076
  CD+MIDI, 1051
  connectors (sound cards), 504, 507
  sound cards, 492-493, 501
MIG (Metal-In-Gap) heads (hard disk drives), 593
milli, 1076
Million Instructions Per Second (MIPS), 1076
millisecond, 1076
Mini Micro, 1020
mini-floppy disk drive, *see* **floppy disk drives**
minicartridge (MC), 762
MIPS (Million Instructions Per Second), 1076
MITS Altair kit, 10
Mitsubishi Electronics America, Inc., 1020
Mitsumi Electronics Corporation, 1021
mixers (sound), 495
mnemonic, 1076
MNP (Microcom Networking Protocol), 1077
  modem proprietary standards, 442
  proprietary standard, 443
MO (Magneto-Optical), 1077
Mode 1 (CD-ROM XA), 741
Mode 2 (CD-ROM XA), 741
Mode Indicate/Mode Indicate Common (MI/MIC), 1076
Model 068 AT (Advanced Technology), 958
Model 087 XT, 943-944
Model 089 XT, 944
Model 099 AT (Advanced Technology), 958
Model 2 IBM PC Convertible laptop, 936

Model 22 IBM PC Convertible laptop, 936
Model 239 AT (Advanced Technology), 959
Model 268 XT, 944
Model 278 XT, 944
Model 319 Personal Computer AT (Advanced Technology), 961
Model 339 Personal Computer AT (Advanced Technology), 961
Model 5100 (IBM), 10
Model 5110 (IBM), 11
Model 5120 (IBM), 11
Model 5150 (IBM), 11
Model 5160068 XT, 944
Model 5160078 XT, 944
modems, 1077
  56K modems, 445-446
  5140 PC Convertible laptop, 940
  analog loopback, 1042
  answer modes, 1043
  auto answer, 1045
  auto dial, 1045
  baud rate, 438
  bps (bits per second), 438
  carrier detect signal, 1050
  commands (Hayes/U.S. Robotics brands), 438
  DCE (Data Communications Equipment), 1058
  digital loopback, 1059
  flow control, 1064
  ISDN (Integrated Services Digital Network), 444-445
  local echo, 1074
  online fallback, 1080
  originate mode, 1080
  recommendations, 444
  resources, 984
  standards, 436-437
    data-compression (V.42bis), 441-442
    error-correction protocols, 441
    FAXModem, 444
    LAPM (Link Access Procedure for Modems), 441

modulation, 439-441
ping-pong protocol, 443
proprietary, 437
proprietary standards,
  442-443
V.21, 439
V.22, 439
V.22bis, 439
V.23, 439
V.29, 440
V.32, 440
V.32bis, 440
V.32fast, 440
V.34, 440
V.42 (error-
  correction), 441
V.F.C. (Fast Class), 440
**Modified Frequency
Modulation encoding,
see MFM**
**modulation standards
(modems), 439-441**
**modulator-demodulator
(modem), 1077**
modules, 1077
Molex, Inc., 1021
monitors, 385-396
  APM (Advanced Power
    Management), 424-425
  buying, 392-396
  CGA (Color Graphics
    Adapter)
    flicker, 398
    snow, 398
  color, 388-389
  convergence, 1056
  CRTs (cathode-ray tubes),
    386, 1050, 1056
    displays, 5140 PC
      Convertible laptop, 937
    persistence, 386
    raster, 386
    refresh rate, 386
  digital controls
    (analog/digital), 395
  energy-saving
    DPMS (Display Power
      Management
      Signaling), 391-392
    Energy Star, 391
  horizontal frequency, 393
  ID pins, 424
  interlaced, 391

LAN file servers, 464
LCDs (liquid-crystal
  displays), 387-388
monochrome, 388-390, 940
multiple-frequency, 393
noninterlaced, 391
Professional Graphics
  Monitor, 402
resolution, 390-391
  dot pitch, 391, 394
  pixels, 390
safety, radiation (magnetic
  emissions), 391-392
screen savers, 72
sizes, 389-390
testing, 395-396
troubleshooting, 425-427
vertical frequency
  (refresh/frame rate), 393
**mono in connectors
(sound cards), 503**
**Monochrome Display
Adapter, see MDA**
**monochrome LCDs (liquid
crystal displays), 388**
**monochrome monitors,
388-389**
  5140 PC Convertible
    laptop, 940
  resolution, 390
**monophonic sound cards,
500-501**
morphing, 1077
**MOS (Metal-Oxide
Semiconductor), 1077**
Mosel Vitelic, 1021
motherboards, 795-803, 1077
  AT BIOS hard drive tables,
    962-965
  ATX, 796
  Baby-AT, 796
  buses
    address bus, 108
    defined, 105
    I/O bus, 105
    memory bus, 107-108
    processor, 105-107
    see also buses
  buying, 799
  CMOS RAM addresses,
    101-104
  connectors, 98-101
  documentation, 20

expansion slots, 108-109
form factors, 82, 90-98
  ATX, 94-97
  Baby-AT, 92-93
  backplane systems,
    91-92
  full-size AT, 92
  LPX, 93-94
  NLX, 97-98
full-size AT, 796
hard disk drives, see hard
  disk drives
I/O ports, 803-804
IBM PCs, 932
installing, 52-57
  connecting cables,
    54-56
  connecting power
    supplies, 54
  memory modules, 53
  mounting
    motherboards, 53-54
  preparing, 52-53
  replacing covers, 56
  running setup
    programs, 56-57
LPX, 796
manufacturers,
  identifying, 22
memory, see memory
mouse port, 371-372
PC XTs, 947
Pentium, 798
  chipsets, 799-802
  memory, 802-803
  speeds, 165, 198
Pentium II chipsets, 800
Pentium Pro National
  Semiconductor 87308, 22
Pentium Pro Natoma
  chipsets, 800
power supply, 291-292
  consumption of
    power, 309
  Power_Good signal,
    292, 301-304, 317
  PS_ON signal, 293
  processors, 801-802
RAM chips
  capacity, 275-276
  installing, 274-280
  interleaved memory
    architecture, 279

multimedia

memory caching, 279-280
paged memory architecture, 278
speeds, 276-278
removing, 50-51
replacement boards, 79
ROM BIOS (Basic Input/Output), 238-290, 801
    bootstrap loader, 238
    distributors, 287
    IBM Cassette Basic, 239-290
    keyboard-controller, 286
    manufacturers, 286-287
    modifications, 288-290
    problems, 287-288
    upgrading, 283-285
selection criteria, 79-90
    checklist, 80-83
    chip speed rating reliability, 89-90
    documentation, 83-84
    ROM BIOS compatibility, 84-89
Super I/O chip, 108
switch settings, 935, 949-950

Motion Pictures Expert Group, *see* **MPEG**
Motor Magazine, 1021
Motorola, Inc., 1021
Mountain Network Solutions, Inc., 1021
mounting motherboards, 53-54
mouse, 805
    cleaning, 66-67
    components, 369
    development of, 368-370
    Glidepoint, 381
    hardware problems, cleaning mouse, 373-375
    interfaces
        bus mouse, 372-373
        motherboard mouse port, 371-372
        serial, 371-372
    LAN file servers, 464
    Macintosh, 368
    manufacturers, 369
    software problems, 375-377
    standard components, 369
    Trackpoint, 377-381
moving adapter memory, 251
MPC (Multimedia PC), 491, 1077
    CD-ROMs (multimedia), 743-744
    Marketing Council, 491
MPEG (Motion Pictures Expert Group), 422, 499, 1078
MPS (Multi-Processor Specification), 202
MR (Magneto-Resistive) heads (hard disk drives), 594-595
MS jumper, *see* media sensor jumper
MS-DOS 6.x MEMMAKER program (memory management), 253-255
MSD (Microsoft Diagnostics), 251
    POST code cards, 842
    serial port testing, 453
MSDOS.SYS file, 876-878, 1078
MTBF (Mean Time Between Failures), 1078
    hard disk drives, 615
MTTR (Mean Time To Repair), 1078
Mueller, Scott (author)
    address/telephone number, 986
    Mueller Technical Research (author's company), 980
Multi-Processor Specification, *see* **MPS**
Multibank DRAM, 415
MultiColor Graphics Array, *see* **MCGA**
multimedia, 1078
    audio, 1045
    CD-ROMs (MPC CD-ROMs), 743-744
        ADPCM (Adaptive Differential Pulse Code Modulation), 741
        audio sound cards, 495, 501
        beam splitter, 727
        CD-ROM XA (eXtended Architecture), 1052
        components, 727
        data CDs, 726-728
        development of, 724
        ECC (Error Correcting Code), 726
        external, 735-736
        formats, 736-743, 1051
        installation, 744-756
        interfaces, 731-733
        internal, 735-736
        interpolated data, 728
        lands, 725
        laser diode, 727
        loading mechanisms, 733-735
        maintenance, 725
        mass-producing, 725
        MCP standards, 491
        multimedia (MPC), 743-744
        pits, 725
        playing, 755-756
        power cable splitter, 748
        recording, CLV (Constant Linear Velocity), 726
        removing, 47-48
        single-speed, 729
        special features, 735-740
        specifications, 728-731
        technology, 724-726
        troubleshooting, 756-757
        types, 728-736
        see also CD-ROMs
    defined, 491
    sound cards, 491-492
    video adapters
        3-D graphic accelerators, 423-424
        blanking interval, 1048
        desktop video (DTV) boards, 421-423
        NTSC-to-VGA adapter, 422
        output devices, 419-420
        still-image video capture cards, 420
        VFC (Video Feature Connector), 418-419

Multimedia Personal Computer (MPC), 1077
multimeters
  cost, 34
  measuring voltage, 34-35
multimode fiber-optic cables, 473
multiple-frequency monitors, 393
multiport boards, defined, 436
multitasking, 242, 1078
multithread, 1078
multiuser systems, 1078
Musical Instrument Digital Interface, *see* MIDI
Mustang Software, 1021
Mylex Corporation, 1021
Myoda Computer Centers, 1021

N

names
  DOS files, 901
  files, 1064
nano, 1078
nanosecond (ns), 271, 1079
nanosliders, 595
National Semiconductor 87308, 22
National Semiconductor Corporation, 1022
National Support Center (NSC), 844
National Television Standards Committee (NTSC), 1079
Natoma chipsets, 800
NCL America, Inc., 1022
NCR Microelectronics, 1022
NDIAGS (Norton Diagnostics), 866-867
NEC Electronics, Inc., 1022
NEC Technologies, Inc., 1022
negative voltages (power supply)
  -5v, 291
  -12, 291
NetBEUI network (NetBIOS Extended User Interface), 458

network interface cards, *see* NICs
Network layer (OSI model), 482
networks, 1079
  adapters, 236-238
    Adaptec AHA-1542CF SCSI, 238
    functions, 469
    IPL (Initial Program Load) ROM, 236-238
    shared memory (RAM), 236-238
    Token Ring memory map, 237
  Ethernet, *see* Ethernet
  high-speed LAN technologies, 483-486
    100BaseT Ethernet cables, 484
    ATM (Asynchronous Transfer Mode), 486
    Internet connections, 486
  LANs (local area networks), 457-459
    cables, 471-474
    components, 458-459
    data-transfer speeds, 466-467
    Dial-Up Networking, 458
    direct cable connections, 458
    file servers, 459-461
    network interface cards (NICs), 464-471
    peer-to-peer networks, 458
    types, 483
    workstations, 459-460
  NetBEUI network (NetBIOS Extended User Interface), 458
  NICs (network interface cards), 463-471
    ARCnet adapters, 467
    conflicts, 155
    Ethernet adapters, 467
    Token Ring adapters, 465, 468
  peer-to-peer networks
    Dial-Up Networking, 458
    Windows 95 setup, 458

protocols
  frames, 478-480
  collision-sensing (CSMA/CD; KEEP), 482
  FDDI (Fiber Distributed Data Interface), 483-48
  OSI (Open System Interconnection), 480-483
  token-passing (Token Ring), 482
Newark Electronics, 1022
NexGen, Inc., 1022
Next Available Cluster algorithm, 888-889
NiCad (Nickel Cadmium), 828
Nickel Metal-Hydride (NiMH), 828
NICs (network interface cards), 463-471
  ARCnet adapters, 467
  conflicts, 155
  Ethernet adapters, 467
  Token Ring adapters, 465, 468
NiMH (Nickel Metal-Hydride), 828
NLX motherboards
  form factors, 97-98
  NLX Motherboard Specification Web site, 98
NMI (non-maskable interrupt), 263
No room for system on destination disk message (error), 905-906
non-intelligent ATA-IDE drives, 641-642
Non-Maskable Interrupt, *see* NMI
nondestructive format programs, 599
noninterlaced monitors/video adapters, 391
nonvolatile memory (NVRAM), 1079
Northgate Computer Systems, Inc., 1022
Norton
  Diagnostics, 866-867
  Disk Doctor, 918

DISKEDIT, 893
Utilities, 704, 838, 870
**notebook computers,
810-811, 1079**
Novell, Inc., 1022
ns (nanosecond), 271
**NSC (National Support
Center), 844**
**NTFS (Windows NT File
System), 585**
**NTSC (The National
Television Standards
Committee), 1079**
NTSC-to-VGA adapter, 422
null modem cable, 1079
**Number Nine Visual
Technology Corporation,
1022**
numeric keypads
101-key (or 102-key)
keyboards, 338
automatic enabling
feature, 342
portable systems, 826
**NVRAM (nonvolatile
memory), 1079**

O

Oak Technology, Inc., 1023
object hierarchy, 1079
**Object Linking and
Embedding (OLE), 1080**
**Ocean Information
Systems, 1023**
**OCR (Optical Character
Recognition), 1079**
odd parity, 261
**ODI (Open Data-link
Interface), 1080**
**OEMs (Original Equipment
Manufacturers), 18, 1080**
documentation, 981
motherboards, 20-23
OEM Magazine, 1023
ROM BIOS compatibility,
84-85
Okidata, 1023
**OLE (Object Linking and
Embedding), 1080**

Olivetti, 1023
Omninet (LAN), 483
on-site service, 24
online fallback, 1080
**Ontrack Data International,
Inc., 1023**
Web site, 870
**Open Data-link Interface
(ODI), 1080**
**Open System
Interconnection,** *see* OSI
operating systems, *see* OSes
operators, logic AND, 1042
Opti, Inc., 1023
Opti Viper, 799
**Optical Character
Recognition (OCR), 1079**
optical disks, 1080
Orange Book, 1080
Orchid Technology, 1023
**Original Equipment
Manufacturers,** *see* OEMs
originate mode, 1080
OS/2, 1080
OS/2 1.x requirements, 15
**OSI (Open System
Interconnection), 480-483**
**OSes (operating systems),
1080**
OS/2, 1080
OS/2 1.x requirements, 15
DOS (Disk Operating
System)
booting, 882
COMMAND.COM,
878-879
compared to Windows
95, 920-921
components, 877
data recovery, 875
file management, 888
floppy disk format
specifications, 890
hardware, 874
I/O system, 877
interfaces, 890
interfacing to disk
drives, 889-895
Interrupt 13h, 891-894
Interrupt 21h interface,
890-891

Interrupt 25/26h
interface, 891
loading, 882-888
master partition boot
sectors, 896-900
MSDOS.SYS file, 878
ROM BIOS, 875-877
shell, 877, 877-879
starting, 882-888
structures, 895-905
volume boot sectors,
899-900
see also DOS (Disk
Operating System)
DOS 5.x, 881
DOS 6.xx, 881-882
software, 807
Windows 95, 919-922
Windows NT, 922-923
see also systems
outlets, testing, 35-36
output, 1080
CHKDSK command, 908,
911-914
devices, video, 419-420
ratings, power supply,
305-307
**OverDrive Intel processors,
178-213, 1080**
486DX4 processor, 185
compatibility problems,
191-192
Socket 2 pinout
configuration, 184
Socket 3 pinout
specification, 186
socket design types,
182-190
speed-rated versions, 179
upgrade sockets, 180-182
see also 486DX2 Intel
processors; Future
Pentium OverDrive
Processor
**overheating (power supply
problems), 313-314**
overlay, 1081
overrun, 1081
overscanning, 1081
overwriting, 1081
oxide media (hard disks), 589

P

P-Cable
  Differential Connector, 672
  SCSI (Small Computer System Interface), 669
  Single-Ended, 669
P5 microprocessors, *see* **Pentium**
P55C (third-generation Pentium), 200
Pacific Data Products, 1023
packages, 1081
Packard Bell, 1024
paddle boards (IDE interface), 635
paged memory (RAM chip architecture), 278
PAL (Phase Alternating Line system), 1081
palmtop computers, 1081
Palo Alto Design Group, 1024
Panasonic Communications & Systems, 1024
Panasonic Industrial Co., 1024
parallel method, 1081
parallel ports, 446-451
  25-pin connector pinouts, 447
  bi-directional, 448-449
  configurations, 451-453
  defined, 429
  ECP (Enhanced Capabilities Port), 449-450
  EPP (Enhanced Parallel Port), 449
  IEEE 1284 standard, 450
  I/O addresses, 148, 452
  Interlink cables, 452-453
  testing, 455
  unidirectional, 448
  upgrading to EPP/ECP ports, 450-451
  wrap plugs, 33
Parallel Technologies, Inc., 1024
parallel/serial adapters, 5140
  PC Convertible laptop, 940

parity bits, 261
  parity checking, 261-264
    errors, 315
    NMI (non-maskable interrupt), 263
    odd parity, 261
    parity bits, 261
    power supply problems, 315
    saving after, 264
  method, 1081
  SCSI (Small Computer System Interface) drives, 679-686
  SIMMs (Single Inline Memory Modules), 802
park programs, 1081
parking head actuators, 606-617
part numbers, AT models, 970-971
Partial-Response, Maximum-Likelihood technology, *see* **PRML**
partitions, 585, 1081
  DOS (Disk Operating System)
    master boot sectors, 896-900
    volume boot sectors, 899-900
  extended, 1064
  hard disk drives, 583-587, 711-716
    FDISK program, 711-713
    MBS (Master Boot Sector), 587
    software, 713-716
PARTS NOW!, Inc., 1024
passive media sensor (floppy drives), 533
passive terminators, SCSI (Small Computer System Interface), 674
passive-matrix LCD monitors, 387-388
patches (DOS), Web sites for finding, 907
PC & MAC Connection, 1024

PC bus, *see* **I/O bus**
PC cards
  cards services, 824-825
  enablers, 825-826
  pinouts, 822-823
  portable systems, 821-826
  socket service, 824
  software support, 823-828
  Type III, 821
  Type IV, 821
PC Keyboard Design (boot-disk package), 367
PC Magazine, 1024
PC Net (LANs), 483
PC Portable Manufacturer, Inc., 1024
PC Power & Cooling, Inc., 313, 1025
  power supplies, 322
PC Technician (Windsor Technologies), 867
PC Week Magazine, 1025
PC World Magazine, 1025
PC XT systems, 941-951
  disk storage, 948
  drives, 941-942
  expansion slots, 942, 948
  features, 943-945
  floppy internal controller, 535
  IRQs (Interrupt Requests), 691
  keyboards, 336, 943
    cable part numbers, 365-366
    compatibility, 341-342
    interface, 345-346
    key numbers, 349-351
    replacements, 365-366
    scan codes, 349-351
    specifications, 948
  memory switch settings, 935-936
  microprocessors, 942
  Model 087, 943-944
  Model 089, 944
  Model 268, 944
  Model 278, 944
  Model 5160068, 944
  Model 5160078, 944
  models, 943

motherboard switch
settings, 935, 949-950
parts numbers, 950
power supply, 293-294, 943
connectors, 299-300
serial ports,
25-pin connector
specifications, 432
technical specifications,
946-958
UART chips, 434
see also AT (Advanced
Technology) PCs
PC-Kwik Corporation, 1025
PC-Probe (Landmark), 838
**PCI (Peripheral Component
Interconnect) bus**
3.3v pinouts, 132-134
5v pinouts, 129-131
adapter cards, 127
DMA channels, 693
universal bus pinouts,
135-137
video adapters, 416
**PCI Special Interest Group,
1025**
**PCMCIA (Personal
Computer Memory Card
International Association),
1025**
PCs (personal computers), 15
5100, 10
5110, 11
5120, 11
5150, 11, 928-930
Advanced Technology PCs,
see AT (Advanced
Technology) PCs
Altair kit (MITS), 10
Apple I (Apple
Computer), 11
compatibility in
marketplace, 13-14
design, 11-12
disk storage, 933-934
drives, 927
Energy Star systems
(energy-efficient), 312
expansion cards, 928
expansion slots, 934
extended PCs, *see* XT
systems (Extended PCs)

history of
IBM, 927-936
computing, 9-11
keyboards, 928, 934
laptops, 9
memory, 933, 947
physical specifications, 934
Portable PC, 951-955
power supply, 928
XT model, *see* XT systems
(Extended PCs)
peer-to-peer networks, 458
Dial-Up Networking, 458
Windows 95 setup, 458
Pentium, 193-197
BiCMOS (Bipolar
Complementary
Metal Oxide
Semiconductor), 196
branch predictions (BTB),
194
bugs, 212-213
floating point divide,
212-215
power management,
215
buses
memory, 108
processor bus, 106
see also buses
CPU speeds, 165
data bus, 162
first-generation, 197-198
internal architecture, 195
math coprocessor
(FPU), 197
memory
EDO RAM, 272
SDRAM, 272-273
motherboards, 798
chipsets, 799-802
memory, 802-803
speeds, 198
OverDrive processors,
182-190
active heat sink, 185
designations, 190
for DX2 and 486SX2
systems, 192-193
Future Pentium
OverDrive
Processor, 188
heat sink, 184
installation, 190-191

Socket 1, 182
Socket 2, 184
Socket 3, 186
Socket 4 pinout
specification, 188
Socket 5, 188
Socket 5 pin
configuration, 189
Socket 6, 188
Socket 6 pin
configuration, 190
Socket 7, 188
VRM (Voltage Regulator
Module), 188
processors
testing, 215-222
write-back cache, 174
second-generation,
198-200
specifications, 193
speeds, 198
superscalar technology, 193
tape carrier packaging
(TCP), 196
third-generation
(P55C), 200
twin-data pipelines, 193
u-pipe, 194
v-pipe, 194
write-back cache, 174
**Pentium II processors,
203-204**
chipsets, 800
Pentium Pro, 201-203
200MHz system, 22
motherboard, National
Semiconductor 87308, 22
MPS (Multi-Processor
Specification), 202
processors, 201-203
ATX form factor, 203
Dual Cavity PGA
package, 201-212
L2 cache, 202
**performance, CD-ROMs,
728-731**
**Peripheral Component
Interconnect**, *see* PCI
**peripherals for portable
systems, 830-833**
acoustic couplers, 833
docking stations, 832-833
external displays, 830-832
line testers, 833

persistence (CRTs), 386
Personal Computer AT (Advanced Technology), see AT (Advanced Technology) PCs
Personal Computer Memory Card International Association, see PCMCIA
personal computers, see PCs; AT (Advanced Technology) PCs; XT systems (Extended PCs)
PGA (Professional Graphics Adapter), 402-403
phantom directories (floppy drives), 560-561
Phase Alternating Line system (PAL), 1081
phase-shift keying, see PSK
Philips Consumer Electronics, 1025
Phillips-head screws, 39
Phoenix BIOS
  audio POST codes, 840-841
  ROM BIOS compatibility, 88-89
Phoenix Technologies, Ltd., 1025
phones, surge protectors, 325-326
phono connectors, 1085
PhotoCD (CD-ROM discs/drive format), 738
  CD sessions, 739
  photo production, 739
physical
  configuration, recording prior to disassembly, 44-45
  connectors, 303
  installation (hard disk drives), 694-695
  specifications
    AT Type 2 motherboard, 970
    XT Model 286, 977
Physical layer (OSI model), 481
Physical Unit Number (PUN), 1084

PIF (Program Information File), 1082
ping-pong protocol (V.29), 443
pinouts
  motherboard connectors, 98-101
  OverDrive processors, 186, 188
  PC Card interface, 822-823
  PCI (Peripheral Component Interconnect) bus
    3.3v, 132-134
    5v, 129-131
    universal, 135-137
  power supply disk drives, 302-303
  SIMMs (Single Inline Memory Modules)
    30-pin, 269
    72-pin, 270
  VESA Local bus, 124-126
  video adapters
    EGA (Enhanced Graphics Adapter), 400
    MDA (Monochrome Display Adapter), 397-398
PIO (Programmed I/O Modes), 645
pitch, defined, 496
pits, CD-ROMs, 725
Pivar Computing Services, Inc., 1026
pixels, 1083
  monitors, 390
pizza-box computers, 109
PKWare, Inc., 1026
planar boards, 1083
plasma displays, 816
Plastic Leaded-Chip Carrier (PLCC), 1083
plated media (thin-film media), 590, 1083
platters (disks), 1083
  hard disk drives, 588-589
  oxide media, 589
  thin-film sputtered media, 590

playing
  CD-ROMs
    in Windows 3.x, 755
    in Windows 95, 755-756
  sounds (sound cards), 493-494
PLCC (Plastic Leaded-Chip Carrier), 1083
Plextor, 1026
PnP (Plug and Play)
  BIOS component, 157
  hardware component, 157
  motherboard selection criteria, 82
  motherboards, 801
  operating-system component, 158
  Pentium chipsets, 801
  SCSI (Small Computer System Interface), 679
  systems, 156-158
  Universal Serial Bus, 456
Point-to-Point Protocol, see PPP
pointing devices
  portable systems, 827-828
  see also mouse
polarity notches, 282
pop-up utilities, 918
Port Finder program, 436
portable systems, 809, 951, 1083
  design, 811-812
  disk storage, 954
  displays, external, 830-832
  environmental specifications, 954-955
  expansion slots, 954
  form factors, 809-811
    laptops, 810
    notebooks, 810-811
    subnotebooks, 811
  hardware, 813-830
    batteries, 828-830
    displays, 813-817
    hard disk drives, 819-820
    keyboards, 826
    memory, 819, 953
    PC cards, 821-826

power supply **1149**

pointing devices,
  827-828
processors, 817-819
removable media,
  820-821
parts numbers, 955
peripherals, 830-833
  acoustic couplers, 833
  docking stations,
    832-833
  external displays,
    830-832
  line testers, 833
repairing, 812-813
standard features, 953
system architecture, 953
upgrading, 812-813
**portable tape drives,
  767-769**
ports
  COM ports, 1054
    IRQ conflicts, 145-147
  I/O (Input/Output)
    motherboards, 803-804
    port addresses, 147-148
  parallel, 446-451
    25-pin connector
      pinouts, 447
    bidirectional, 448-449
    configurations, 451-453
    defined, 429
    ECP (Enhanced
      Capabilities Port),
      449-450
    EPP (Enhanced Parallel
      Port), 449
    I/O addresses and
      interrupts, 452
    IEEE 1284 standard, 450
    Interlink cables,
      452-453
    testing, 455
    unidirectional, 448
    upgrading to EPP/ECP
      ports, 450-451
  serial, 429-434
    25-pin connector
      specifications, 431-432
    adapter conflicts, 156
    cable adapters,
      9-pin/25-pin
      connections, 432

configurations, 435-436
defined, 429
high-speed (ESP/Super
  High-Speed Serial
  Ports), 434-435
multiport boards, 436
power supply, 292
start bits, 429
testing, 453-455
UART (Universal
  Asynchronous
  Receiver/Transmitter)
  chips, 433-434
wrap-plug part
  numbers, 454
wrap plugs, 33
**POS (Programmable Option
  Select), 1083**
**positive voltages
  (power supply), 292**
**POST (Power-On Self Test),
  837-843, 1083**
  Advanced Diagnostics
    (IBM) error codes,
    844-863
      Hewlett-Packard 486/U,
        847-849
      IBM, 849-863
      personal computer,
        844-846
  audio error codes, 839-841
    AMI BIOS, 839-840
    nonfatal system board
      errors, 841
    Phoenix BIOS, 840-841
  keyboard error codes, 362
  motherboard ROM
    BIOS, 238
  system component tests,
    838-839
  visual error codes, 842-843
PostScript, 1083
**power cable splitter
  (CD-ROM drives), 748**
power supply
  -5v, 291
  +12v, 292
  -12v, 291
  5140 PC Convertible
    laptop
      automobile adapters, 940

assembling systems,
  794-795
calculating power
  consumption, 308-310
  floppy drives, 309
  hard disks, 309
  motherboards, 309
  per bus slot, 309
  SCSI (Small Computer
    System Interface) hard
    drives, 310
connecting, motherboard
  installation, 54
connectors, 299-303
  AT/Tower style, 299-300
  ATX style, 300
  disk drives, 302-303
  PC/XT style, 299-300
  physical connectors, 303
  switches, 301-302
  voltage ranges, 301
form factors, 293-299
  AT/Desk style, 294-295
  AT/Tower style,
    294-295, 299-302
  ATX style, 297-300
  Baby-AT style, 296
  PC/XT style, 293-294,
    299-300
  Slimline style, 296-297,
    301-302
function of, 291-310
IBM PCs, 928, 930, 934
LAN (local area networks)
  file servers, 464
loads, 304-305
manufacturers of
  replacements, 322-323
MCA (Micro Channel
  Architecture), 292
motherboards, 291-292
  consumption of
    power, 309
  Power_Good signal,
    292, 301-304, 317
  PS_ON signal, 293
output ratings, 305-307
PC XTs, 943, 949
portable systems, 829-830
power-line noise,
  reducing, 73-74

1150 power supply

power-protection systems, 323-329
  line conditioners, 326
  phone line surge protectors, 325-326
  Standby Power Supplies (SPS), 326-327
  surge protectors, 325
  Uninterruptible Power Supplies (UPS), 327-329
Power_Good signal, 292, 301, 303-304
preventive maintenance, 70-71
problems, 313-314
PS_ON signal, 293
removing, 48-50
repairing, 319-320
  depot repair, 319
  internal fuse, 320
replacements, selecting new power supply, 321-322
RTC/NVRAM batteries (Real Time Clock/ Non-Volatile Random Access Memory), 329
serial ports, 292
specifications, 307
testing with DMMs (Digital Multi-Meters), 317-318
thermal shock, 310-312
troubleshooting, 314-319
  DMM (Digital Multi-Meters), 316-318
  local resistors (test equipment), 318
  test equipment, 318-319
power surges (power-protection systems), 323-329
  line conditioners, 326
  phone line surge protectors, 325-326
  Standby Power Supplies (SPS), 326-327
  surge protectors, 325
  Uninterruptible Power Supplies (UPS), 327-329

Power-On Self Test, *see* POST
power-protection systems, 323-329
  IBM, 324
  line conditioners, 326
  phone line surge protectors, 325-326
  Standby Power Supplies (SPS), 326-327
  surge protectors, 325
  Uninterruptible Power Supplies (UPS), 327-329
Power_Good signal, 292, 301-304
  measuring power supply, 317-318
PowerQuest Corporation, 1026
PPP (Point-to-Point Protocol), 487
Practical Enhanced Logic, 1026
Precision Plastics, 1026
prefix portions (hard disk sectors), 581, 583
presence detect pins (72-pin SIMMs), 271, 278
Presentation layer (OSI model), 482
presentations, sound cards, 493
preventive maintenance, 57-58
  CD-ROMs, 725
  cleaning, 58-67
    boards, 65
    brushes/swabs, 63
    chemicals, 60-64
    connectors/contacts, 63, 66
    keyboards/mouse, 66-67
    procedures, 64-67
    tools needed, 60
    vacuum cleaners, 62-63
  developing maintenance programs, 58-76
  hard disk care, 67-69
    defragmenting files, 67-68
    virus scanning, 68-69
  lubricants, 62-63

operating environment, 69-76
  dust/pollutants, 75-76
  on/off cycles, 70-72
  power-line noise, 73-74
  radio-frequency interference (RFI), 74-75
  static electricity, 72-73
  temperature, 69-71
power supplies, 70-71
reseating socketed components, 64-65
screen savers, 72
see also backups
primary IDE connectors, 153
primary partition, 1084
printers
  5140 PC Convertible laptop, 937, 939
  cable, 940
  daisywheel, 1057
  dot-matrix printers, 1060
  inkjet printers, 1070
  laser printers, 1073
  optional, 939-940
PRML (Partial-Response, Maximum-Likelihood), 580
problems, *see* errors; troubleshooting; repairing
Processor Magazine, 1026
processors, 801-802
  286, 167-168
  386, 168-169
  386DX, 169-170
  386SL, 170-171
  386SX, 170
  486 (80486), 171-173
  486DX (80486), 175-176
  486DX2, 178-213
    speed-rated versions, 179
    upgrade sockets, 180-182
  486DX4 memory bus, 108
  486SL (80486), 176-177
  486SX (80486), 177-178
  8086, 166-167, 1041
  8087, 1041
  8088, 166-167, 1041
  8514/A, 1041
  80186, 167

programs **1151**

80188, 167
80286, 1040
80287, 1040
80386, 168-169
80386DX, 1040
80386SX, 1040
80387, 1040
80486DX, 1040
80486DX2, 1040
80486DX4, 1040
80486SX, 1040
accelerator boards, 1041
address bus, 162-163
AMD, 205
AT systems (Advanced Technology PCs), 16
AT/XT systems, comparing, 17
bus, 105-107
   bandwidth, 106
   see also buses
CISC (Complex Instruction-Set Computer), 1053
cooling problems, 222
coprocessors, 1056
CPUs (central processing units), *see* CPUs
Cyrix, 205-206
data bus, 159-161
file servers, 462
Future Pentium OverDrive Processor, 188
heating problems, 222
identifying chip/chipset documentation, 21
Intel-compatible, 204-206
internal registers, 162
math coprocessor list, 207-222
memory-addressing capabilities, 163
motherboard selection criteria, 80-81
   chip speed rating reliability, 89-90
National Semiconductor 87308, 22
object-code compatibility, 168
OverDrive, 178-213
  active heat sink, 185
  compatibility problems, 191-192
  designations, 190
  DX2 and 486SX2 processors, 192-193
  DX4 processor, 185
  heat sink, 184
  installation, 190-191
  Socket 1, 182
  Socket 2, 184
  Socket 3, 186
  Socket 4 pinout specification, 188
  Socket 5, 188
  Socket 5 pin configuration, 189
  Socket 6, 188
  Socket 6 pin configuration, 190
  Socket 7, 188
  socket designs, 182-190
  upgrade sockets, 180-182
  VRM (Voltage Regulator Module), 188
Pentium, 193-197
  branch predictions (BTB), 194
  first-generation, 197-198
  internal architecture, 195
  math coprocessor (FPU), 197
  motherboard speeds, 198
  second-generation, 198-200
  specifications, 193
  speeds, 198
  superscalar technology, 193
  third-generation (P55C), 200
  twin-data pipelines, 193
  u-pipe, 194
  v-pipe, 194
  write-back cache, 174
Pentium II, 203-204
Pentium Pro, 201-203
  ATX form factor, 203
  L2 cache, 202
  MPS (Multi-Processor Specification), 202
portable systems, 817-819
  TPC (Tape Carrier Packaging), 817-818
  voltage reduction, 818-819
speed ratings, 163-166
  chip speed rating reliability, 89-90
  Intel ICOMP index ratings, 164
  Pentiums, 165
standards, MCP standards, 491
tests, 210-211, 222
  early 80386s, 211-212
  Pentium models and steppings, 215-222
  Pentiums, 212-215
  software, 210
see also CPUs (central processing units)
Professional Color Adapter, *see* PGA
Professional Graphics Monitor, 402
Program Information File (PIF), 1082
Programmable Option Select (POS), 1083
Programmable Read-Only Memory (PROM), 1084
Programmed I/O Modes, *see* PIO
Programmer's Shop, 1026
programming
  BASIC (Beginner's All-purpose Symbolic Instruction Code), 1046
  C programming, 1050
  COBOL (Common Business-Oriented Language), 1054
programs
  Advanced Diagnostics, 707
  caching programs (hard disk drives), 617-618

programs

Calibrate program (formatting), 711
CHKDSK, see CHKDSK command
data recovery, 870-871
   Calibrate, 870
   Norton Utilities, 870
   SpinRite, 871
DEBUG, 899
diagnostic, 283-285
   AMIDiag (American Megatrends, Inc.), 864-865
   Checkit Pro (Touchstone Software Corp.), 865
   Disk Diagnostics, 868-870
   Disk Manager, 869-870
   Drive Probe, 869-871
   Micro-Scope (Micro 2000), 865-866
   Microsoft Diagnostics (MSD), 251
   PC Technician (Windsor Technologies), 867
   public-domain, 871
   QAPlus/FE (Diagsoft), 867-868
Disk Manager, 642, 707
   formatting hard drives, 708
DISKEDIT (Norton), 893
Drive Probe program, aligning floppy drives, 563
FDISK (DOS), 893, 903
HDtest, 707, formatting hard drives, 708-709
LLF (Low-Level Formatting)
   IDE, 710
   SCSI (Small Computer System Interface), 709
memory management, 252-253
   EMM386.EXE (DOS), 253-255
   MEMMAKER (DOS), 253-255
   QEMM (Quarterdeck), 255-290

   memory-resident, 918-919, 1076
   park programs, 1081
   partitioning, 713-716
      FDISK, 711-713
   SpinRite program (formatting), 711
PROM (Programmable Read-Only Memory), 1084
ProNet (LAN), 483
proofreading sound cards, 495
proprietary interfaces (CD-ROM drives), 733
proprietary standards (modems), 437, 442-443
   DIS (Dynamic Impedance Stabilization), 442
   HST, 442
   MNP (Microcom Networking Protocol), 443
   V-Series, 443
protected mode, 242
   286 Intel processors, 168
   386 Intel processors, 169
   486DX Intel processors, 176
protocols, 1084
   defined, 436
   Kermit, 1072
   modems
      error-correction protocols, 441
      LAPM (Link Access Procedure for Modems), 441
      ping-pong protocol (V.29), 443
   networks
      collision-sensing (CSMA/CD), 482
      FDDI (Fiber Distributed Data Interface), 483-486
      frame layers, 479-480
      frames, 478-479
      OSI (Open System Interconnection), 480-483
      token-passing (Token Ring), 482
   PPP (Point-to-Point Protocol), 487

   SLIP (Serial Line Internet Protocol), 487
   TCP/IP (Transmission Control Protocol/Internet Protocol), 486-488
   see also standards
PS/2 SCSI (Small Computer System Interface) connectors, 668
PS_ON signal, 293
PSK (phase-shift keying), 439
Public Software Library, 1026
public-domain diagnostic programs, 871
PUN (Physical Unit Number), 1084
purchasing, see buying

Q

Q-Cable
   Differential Connector, 673
   SCSI (Small Computer System Interface), 670
   Single-Ended, 669
Qa-Plus (Diagsoft), 838
QAM (Quadrature Amplitude Modulation), 439, 1084
QAPlus/FE (Diagsoft), 867-868
QEMM program (memory management), 255-290
QIC standards (tape backups), 761-763, 1027
   backup software, 778-780
      bundled, 779
      third-party, 779-780
   drive types, 764-767
      8mm tape drives, 771
      compatible, 768-769
      DAT (digital audio) tape, 770
      DLT (Digital Linear Tape), 771
      high-capacity, 767-773
      portable, 767
      QIC-40, 764-767
      QIC-80, 764-767
      Travan cartridge tapes, 772-773

installing, 775-777
  external installation, 777
  internal installation, 776-777
selecting drive types, 773-775
  capacity, 773-774
  cost, 775
  data throughput, 775
  standards, 774
QIC-02, 761
QIC-5B-DC, 762
QIC-40 tape drive, 764-767
  data storage, 766
  data transfer rates, 766
  formatting, 766
QIC-80 tape drive, 764-767
QIC-5010-MC, 762
Qlogic Corporation, 1027
Quad-speed CD-ROM drives
  access times, 731
  data transfer rate, 729
Quadrature Amplitude Modulation, *see* QAM
Qualitas, Inc., 1027
Quantum Corporation, 1027
Quarter-Inch Cartridge Drive Standards, Inc., 761, 1027
Quarterdeck Corporation, 1027
Quarterdeck QEMM program (memory management), 255-290
Que Corporation, 1027
QWERTY keyboard, 1085

R

rack-and-pinion gear mechanism (head actuators), 598
racks (hard disk drives), 569
radiation, monitors (magnetic emissions), 391-392
Radio Frequency Interference (RFI), 74-75, 1086
Radio Shack, 1027

rails, 1085
RAM (Random Access Memory), 257, 1085
  architectures
    interleaved memory, 279
    paged memory, 278
  AT/XT systems, comparing, 17
  cache, 279-280
  capacity, 275-276
  CMOS RAM addresses, motherboards, 101-104
  DIMMs (Dual Inline Memory Modules), 264-269
  DIPs (Dual Inline Pins), 257, 274
  DRAM (Dynamic Random Access Memory), 1061
  file servers, 462-463
  installing, 274-280
  list of, 257-259
  markings on, 258, 275
  memory banks, 259-260, 268, 275
  motherboard selection criteria, 81
  network cards, shared memory, 236
  part numbers, 259
  removing, 282
  SIMMs (Single Inline Memory Modules), 257, 264-269
  SIPPs (Single Inline Pin Packages), 257, 274
  speed, 271-272, 276-278
  standards, MCP standards, 491
  Static, 937
  storage capacities, 257-259
  testing, 36-37
  VRAM (Video Random Access Memory), 414-416
  wait states, 276-277
  Window, 415
  see also DRAM, SRAM; SIMMs
RAM disk, 1085
Ramtron International Corporation, 1027

Rancho Technology, Inc., 1028
Random Access Memory, *see* RAM
random-access files, 1085
raster, 386, 1085
raw physical mode, intelligent ATA-IDE drives, 642
RCA jack, 1085
Read Multiple command (ATA IDE), 640
Read Only Memory, *see* ROM
read-only file, 1085
read/write heads, 1085
  alignment, 522
  floppy disk drives, 520-523
  hard disk drives, 591-595
    ferrite heads, 593
    HDA (Head Disk Assembly), 592
    MIG (Metal-In-Gap) heads, 593
    MR (Magneto-Resistive) heads, 594-595
    single-gap, 595
    TF (Thin Film) heads, 593-594
    voice coil actuator assembly, 591
  head actuator, 521
  tunnel erasure, 521
real mode, 242, 256
  286 Intel processors, 168
  386 Intel processors, 169
  486DX Intel processors, 176
real time, 1085
recirculating filters (hard disk drives), 607
recording
  CD-ROMs, CLV (Constant Linear Velocity), 726
  setup/configuration, 42-45
    accessing setup programs, 43-44
    hard disk type settings, 42-43
    physical configuration, 44-45

sounds (sound cards), 493-494
voice annotations, sound cards, 494
records, *see* **sectors**
RECOVER command
marking bad sectors, 917
preserving data, 916-917
Red Book, 1086
Reduced Instruction Set Computer (RISC), 1086
reference standards (disks), 869
refresh cycle, 1086
refresh rates (monitors), 386, 393
registers, 1086
Registry, 920
remote
digital loopback, 1086
echo, 1086
power switches, 301
removable media, portable systems, 820-821
removable storage drives, 780-789
Compact Disc Recordable (CD-R) drives, 787-789
history, 787-788
mass storage, 788-789
software, 788
writing CDs, 787-788
comparing removable drives, 785-786
magnetic media drives, 781-783
Bernoulli, 782-783
SyQuest, 783
magneto-optical drives, 783-785
WORM drives, 786-789
removing
adapter boards, 46-47
case covers, 45-46
disk drives, 47-48
motherboards, 50-51
power supplies, 48-50
SIMMs/DIMMs, 52
repairing
data recovery, *see* data recovery
hardware, compared to software, 919

keyboards, 361-367
disassembly, 362
monitors, 426
portable systems, 812-813
power supply, 319-320
depot repair, 319
internal fuse, 320
software, compared to hardware, 919
see also troubleshooting
reproducing CD-ROMs, mass-production, 725
requirements
OS/2 1.x, 15
Windows 3.x, 15
Windows NT 4.x, 15
reseating socketed components, 64-65
reserved memory, 226
resolution (screen), 390-391, 1086
dot pitch, 391, 394
pixels, 390
portable systems, 816-817
SVGA, 394
VGA, 394
resource conflicts, 511
adapter boards, 154-156
NICs (network interface cards), 155
Plug and Play systems, 156-158
resolving, 148-149
manually, 149-150
system-configuration templates, 150-154
serial ports, 156
sound cards, 154-155
resources
appendixes, 985-986
machines, 982-983
magazines, 985
manuals, 980-982
modems, 984
Return-Merchandise Authorization number, 1087
RFI (Radio Frequency Interference), 74-75, 1086
RGB (Red-Green-Blue), 1086
ribbon cable, CD-ROM drives (internal), 748-750
Rip-Tie Company, 1028

RISC (Reduced Instruction Set Computer), 1086
riser-card slots (expansion slots), 109
RLL (Run Length Limited) encoding, 1086
hard disk drives, 577-579
ASCII character waveforms, 579
comparisons to FM/MFM encoding, 579-580
RLL 2,7 version, 577-578
RLL 3,9 version (Advanced RLL; ARLL), 578
system configuration, 698
RMA number, 1087
Rockwell Semiconductor Systems, 1028
Roland Corporation U.S., 1028
ROM (Read Only Memory), 233-234, 801, 1087
addresses, configuring controllers, 689-690
Flash, defined, 1064
hard disk controller BIOS, 234-236
IPL (Initial Program Load), 236
motherboard BIOS, 238-290
bootstrap loader, 238
IBM Cassette Basic, 239-290
Power-On Self Test, 238
preventing conflicts and overlap, 246
SCSI (Small Computer System Interface) adapter BIOS, 234-236
shadow memory, 246-248
video adapter BIOS, 234
ROM BIOS, 801, 930, 1087
capacity limitations, 686
compatibility, 84-89
AMI, 85-88
Award, 88
OEMs, 84-85
Phoenix, 88-89
distributors, 287
DOS (Disk Operating System), 875-877

hard disk parameter tables, modifying, 965
keyboard-controller, 286
manufacturers, 286-287
modifications, 288-289
  Flash BIOS, 289
  IML (Initial Microcode Load), 289-290
  problems, 287-288
  ROM replacement, 698
  tables, 697-698
  upgrading, 283-285
root directories, 900-902
  floppy disk drives, 541
Rosenthal Engineering, 1028
rotary actuators (voice coil actuators), 601
routers, 1087
routines, 1087
RS-232 interface, 1087
RTC/NVRAM batteries (Real Time Clock/ Non-Volatile Random Access Memory), 329-331
rubber dome key switches (keyboards), 344
Run Length Limited encoding, *see* RLL
Rupp Technology Corporation, 1028
Rutledge, Joseph (Trackpoint inventor), 377

S

S-Video (S-VHS) connector, 423
S-Video (Y/C), 1091
S/N (signal-to-noise) ratio, 1089
S3, Inc., 1028
SA-400 interface (floppy drives), 525
safety
  monitors, radiation (magnetic emissions), 391-392
  see also hazards
Safeware Insurance Agency, Inc., 1028

sampling
  defined, 497
  sound cards, 500
SAMS, 1029
Samsung Semiconductor, Inc., 1029
SASE (Self-Addressed Stamped Envelope), 984
SASI (Shugart Associates System Interface), 519
saving after parity checking errors, 264
scan codes (keyboards), 337, 348-358
  83-key PC/XT keyboards, 349-351
  84-key AT keyboards, 351-352
  101-key (or 102-key), 353-357
  104-key Windows, 358
scan lines, 1087
ScanDisk (DOS/Windows) command, 704, 918
scratch disks, 1087
scratch pad memory, 232
screens
  resolution, 390-391, 1086
  dot pitch, 391, 394
  pixels, 390
  portable systems, 816-817
  SVGA, 394
  VGA, 394
  savers, 72
screws
  metric/English, 40
  Torx, 320
  types, 39
SCSI (Small Computer System Interface), 519, 653
  adapter cards, conflicts, 155
  ANSI standards, 655-657
  ASPI (Advanced SCSI Programming Interface), 680
  cables, 665
    A-cables, 671
    P-cables, 669, 672

    pinouts, 665-675
    Q-cables, 670, 673
    single-ended, 666-670
  CAM (Common Access Method), 680
  capacity limitations, 685
  CD-ROM drives, 732-733
    chains, 750-752
    installing adapter driver, 752-753
  Common Command Set, 655
  comparisons to IDE interfaces, 681-684
    controllers, 683
    host adapters, 683-684
  configurations, 675-681
    ID jumper settings, 675-679
    parity, 679-686
    Plug and Play SCSI, 679-680
    Start on command (delayed start), 678-679
    synchronous negotiation, 679
    termination, 676-679
    terminator power, 679-686
  connectors, 665
    A-Cable, 671
    P-Cable, 669, 672
    pinouts, 665-675
    Q-Cable, 670, 673
    single-ended, 666-670
  construction, 657-658, 661
  data-transfer rates, 656
  development of, 657-658, 661
  differential, 662-663
    A-Cables, 671
    P-Cables, 672
    Q-Cables, 673
    universal symbols, 662
  fast SCSI, 663
  Fast-20 (Ultra) SCSI, 663
  formatting, LLF
    software, 709
  hard drives, power consumption, 310

host adapters, 683-684
LBA (Logical Block Address), 685
low-level formatting (LLF), 705-707
SCSI-1, 663-664
SCSI-2, 663-664
SCSI-3, 664-666
Serial SCSI, 664
setup programs, 42-43
single-ended, 662-663
   connectors, 666-670
   P-Cables, 669
   Q-Cables, 669
   universal symbols, 662
system configuration, 698
termination, 674-675
Wide SCSI, 664
SDL (Shielded Data Link), 359
SDLC (Synchronous Data Link Control), 1087
SDRAM (Pentiums), 272-273
Seagate Software Storage Management Group, 1029
Seagate ST-12550N Barracuda 2 hard drive
   capacities, 624
   specifications, 571
Seagate Technology, 520, 1029
SECAM (Séquential Couleur à Mémoire), 1088
secondary IDE connectors, 153
Sector not found error message, 917
Sector not found error reading drive C message, 918
sectors, 888-889
   bad sectors, 1046
   defragmentation, 1058
   floppy disks, 540
   hard disk drives, 580-587
      checksums, 581
      clusters (allocation units), 585
      formatting, 582-584
      high-level formatting (logical), 583, 587
      low-level formatting (physical), 583-584

partitioning, 583, 585-587
prefix portions (headers), 581, 583
speed, 616
suffix portions (trailers), 581
Zone Recording, 584-585
security
   Energy Star, 1063
   software, 1088
seek time, 1088
   average seek time, 1045
   hard disk drives, 616, 628
segment addresses (memory), 226-228
selecting
   DMMs (Digital Multi-Meters), 316-317
   tape drives, 773-775
      capacity, 773-774
      cost, 775
      data throughput, 775
      standards, 774
Self-Addressed Stamped Envelope (SASE), 984
self-cleaning lenses (CD-ROM drives), 735-740
Selker, Ted (Trackpoint inventor), 377
semiconductors, 9, 1088
Sencore, 1029
sensors, floppy disk drives, 550
separators (data), 1057
sequencers, 1088
Séquential Couleur à Mémoire (SECAM), 1088
sequential files, 1088
serial and motherboard mouse port (KEEP), 372
Serial Line Internet Protocol, *see* SLIP
serial ports, 429-434
   25-pin connector specifications, 431-432
   adapters, conflicts, 156
   AT-style, 9-pin connector specifications, 430

AT/XT systems, comparing, 17
configurations, 435-436
defined, 429
high-speed, 434-435, 455
I/O addresses, 148
IEEE 1394 high-speed, 457
IRQ conflicts, 145-147
multiport boards, 436
power supply, 292
start bits, 429
testing
   loopback testing, 454-455
   MSD (Microsoft Diagnostics), 453
UART (Universal Asynchronous Receiver/Transmitter) chips, 433-434
USB (Universal Serial Bus), 456-457
wrap plugs, 33, 454
Serial SCSI, 664
serial/parallel adapters (5140 PC Convertible laptop), 940-941
service contracts, 23-25
Service Diagnostics (processor test), 210
Service News Magazine, 1029
servo data, 1062, 1088
servo mechanisms, 599-606
   dedicated servo, 605-606
   disk-sweep, 603
   embedded servo, 604-605
   gray code, 601
   servowriter, 601
   wedge servo, 603-604
servo surface, dedicated, 1058
servo-controlled mechanism, 599
servowriters, 601
Session layer (OSI model), 482
settings
   recording prior to disassembly, 42-45
   accessing setup programs, 43-44

skewing **1157**

hard disk type settings, 42-43
physical configuration, 44-45
time, 1089
setup, automated, EISA bus (Enhanced Industry Standard Architecture), 120
setup programs
accessing, 43-44
recording settings prior to disassembly, 42-45
accessing setup programs, 43-44
hard disk type settings, 42-43
physical configuration, 44-45
running, motherboard installation, 56-57
SGRAM (Synchronous Graphics RAM), 415
SGS-Thomson Microelectronics, Inc., 1029
shadow memory (shadow ROM), 246-248, 1089
Shannon's Law, 446
shared memory (network cards), 236
shareware
ASP (Association of Shareware Professionals), 995
diagnostic, 871
Sharp Electronics Corporation, 1029
Sharp Microelectronics Group, 1029
shells, 877-879, 1089
Shielded Data Link, see **SDL**
shielded twisted pair (STP), 1089
shock mounted (hard disk drives), 622
shock ratings, 1089
Shugart, Alan (floppy drive inventor), 519
Shugart Associates System Interface, see **SASI**
Sigma Data, 1029

signal-to-noise (S/N) ratio, 1089
signals
analog signals, 1042
balanced signals, 1046
carrier detect signal, 1050
carriers, 1050
channels, 1052
common, 1055
common mode noise, 1055
crosstalk, 1056
daisy chains, 1057
differential, 1059
digital signals, 1059
duplex, 1061
hard disk drive interfaces (ATA IDE), 639
Silicon Integrated Systems Corp. (SIS), 1030
Silicon Valley Research, 1030
silicone lubricants, 63-64
SIMMs, 274, 802 (Single Inline Memory Modules), 264-269, 1089
30-pin, 265, 267, 274, 802
capacities, 266
IBM-style, 267
pinouts, 269
72-pin, 265, 267, 274, 802
capacities, 266
EDO RAM, 272
pinouts, 270
presence detect pins, 271, 278
chip creep, 268
installing, 53, 274-280
motherboard selection criteria, 81
parity, 802
polarity notches, 282
removing, 52
testing, 36-37
see also RAM
Simple Technology, 1030
Single Density encoding, see **FM (Frequency Modulation) encoding**
Single Inline Memory Modules, see **SIMMs**
Single Inline Packages (SIPPs), see **SIPPs**

single mode fiber-optic cables, 473
single-drive configuration (IDE drives), 648
single-ended method, 1089
single-ended SCSI, 662-663
connectors, 666-670
P-cables, 669
Q-cables, 669
universal symbols, 662
single-gap heads, see **ferrite heads; MIG heads; TF heads**
single-sided floppy disks, 520
coercivity, 555
density, 554-555
thickness, 555
single-sided MIG heads, 593
single-speed CD-ROM drives, 729
access times, 731
data transfer rate, 729
SIPPs (Single Inline Packages), 274, 1089
installing broken/bent pins, 282
memory chips, 258
SIS (Silicon Integrated Systems Corp.), 1030
sites (Web)
AMIDiag, 865
ASME, 1044
BIOS information, 89
Checkit, 865
Diagsoft, 868
DOS bug patches, 907
Edlab, 1039
Microscope, 866
NLX Motherboard Specification page, 98
Ontrack, 870
POST code cards, 842
Symantec, 867, 871, 918
Windsor Technologies, 867
Zeppo Glossary, 1039
six-speed CD-ROM drives
access times, 731
data transfer rate, 729
size
monitors, 389-390
video display, 389-390
skewing, 618-622

calculating skew factors, 621-622
cylinder skew, 620-621
head skew, 619-620
SL Waber, 1030
slave configuration (IDE drives), 648
sliders (hard disk drives), 595-596
slimline computers, 109
Slimline power supply style, 296-297
    connector switches, 301-302
SLIP (Serial Line Internet Protocol), 487, 1089
slots, AT/XT systems, comparing, 17
Small Outline J-lead (SO-J), 1090
Smart Cable, Inc., 1030
SMI (System Management Interrupt), 170, 176
SMM (System Management Mode), 176
smoking (cigarettes) hazards, 59
SMPTE time code, 1089
SMTP (Simple Mail Transfer Protocol), 486
snow (monitors), 398
SO-J (Small Outline J-lead), 1090
socket services (PC Cards), 824
sockets
    LIF (Low-Insertion Force), 181
    Overdrive
        Socket 1, 182
        Socket 2, 184
        Socket 3, 186
        Socket 4, 188
        Socket 5, 188-189
        Socket 6, 188, 190
        Socket 7, 188
    upgrading 486 processors, 180-182
    ZIF (Zero-Insertion Force), 181
soft errors, 1089
Softbank Comdex, Inc., 1030

Softkey International, Inc., 1030
SofTouch Systems, Inc., 1030
software
    AT/XT systems, comparing, 17
    backup
        bundled, 779
        data compression, 778
        tape drives, 778-780
        third-party, 779-780
    bundles, sound cards, 502
    CD-ROMs, installation, 752-754
    codecs, 422
    diagnostic, 837-838
        AMIDiag, 864-865
        Checkit Pro, 865
        data recovery, 870-871
        Disk Diagnostics, 868-870
        Disk Manager, 869-870
        Drive Probe, 869
        IBM, 843-863
        Micro-Scope, 865-866
        NDIAGS (Norton Diagnostics), 866-867
        PC Technician (Windsor Technologies), 867
        POST, 837-843
        public-domain, 871
        QAPlus/FE, 867-868
    firmware, defined, 1064
    LLF (Low-Level Formatting), 707-711
        Disk Manager program, 708
        HDtest program, 708-709
        IDE, 710
        nondestructive, 711
        SCSI, 709
    menu software, 1076
    mouse problems, 375-377
    OSes (operating systems), 807
    PC Cards, 823-828
    repairing, compared to hardware, 919
    security software, 1088

    standards, MCP, 491
    TSR (Terminate and Stay Resident), 918
Software Testing Lab (STL), 1031
Sola Heavy Duty Electric, 1031
soldering/desoldering, 30-33
Sonera Technologies, 1031
Sony Corporation of America, 1031
Sound Blaster, 489, 496
sound cards, 806
    accessories
        joysticks (game port), 506-507
        microphone, 506
        MIDI connectors, 507
        speakers, 504-506
        synthesizers, 507
    AdLib, 496
    applications, 490
        audio CDs, 495
        games, 490-491
        MIDI (Musical Instrument Digital Interface), 492-493
        multimedia, 491-492
        presentations, 493
        proofreading, 495
        recording sounds, 493-494
        sound mixers, 495
        voice annotation, 494
        voice recognition, 494-495
    buying criteria
        bundled software, 502
        CD-ROM drives, 501
        compatibility, 499-500
        connectors, 502-504
        data compression, 501
        drivers, 502
        DSP (Digital Signal Processors), 502
        MIDI interface, 501
        monophonic, 500-501
        sampling capability, 500
        stereophonic, 500-501
        volume control, 504

standards **1159**

concepts/terminology
8-bit/16-bit sound, 497-498
ADS (analog-to-digital converters), 497
amplitude, 496
CD-ROM drives, 498
compression/ decompression, 499
DACs (digital-to-analog converters), 497
file formats, 499
frequency response, 496
linearity, 496
pitch, 496
sampling, 497
total harmonic distortion, 496
waveform audio, 497
conflicts, 154-155
Game Blaster, 489
installation, 155, 508-509
patching into stereo systems, 509-510
Sound Blaster, 489, 496
troubleshooting problems
computer won't start, 514
hardware conflicts, 510-512
joystick problems, 514
lockups, 514
no sound, 512
one-sided sound, 513
parity errors, 514
scratchy sound, 514
volume is low, 513
see also audio
sound mixers, 495
SOYO Tek, Inc., 1031
space allocation, 888-889
spare-parts inventory, 24
speakers, 504-506
connectors, 100
distortion (total harmonic distortion), 505
frequency response, 505
headphone connectors (sound cards), 503
watts, 505
Specialized Products Company, 1031

specifications
8514 display adapters, 403
AT technical, 966-971
CGA (Color Graphics Adapter), 398-399
EGA (Enhanced Graphics Adapter), 402
EISA adapter cards, 117
floppy disk format specifications, 890
MCGA (MultiColor Graphics Array), 404
PGA (Professional Graphics Adapter), 403
power supply, 307
VGA (Video Graphics Array), 406
XGA/XGA-2 (Extended Graphics Array), 408
speed
AT/XT systems, comparing, 17
CD-ROM drives, 729
CPUs (central processing units)
Pentium, 165
ratings, 163-166
hard disk drives, 615
average seek time, 616
cache controllers/ programs, 617-618
cylinder skew, 620-622
head skew, 619-620
interleaving, 616, 618
latency, 616
sector translation, 616
transfer rate, 616-617
math coprocessors, 207
memory, RAM chips, 271-272, 276-278
Pentium CPUs/ motherboards, 165
processors
486 compared to motherboard clock speed, 172
Intel ICOMP index ratings, 164
VESA Local bus, 123
video adapters, 414-417
buses, 416

video processors, 414
VRAM (Video Random Access Memory), 414-416
spindle motors
floppy disk drives, 524-525
grounding strap, 610-611
hard disk drives, 609-610
SpinRite program (formatting), 711, 871
split-metal-band mechanism (head actuators), 597
Sprague Magnetics, Inc., 1031
SPS (Standby Power Supplies), 326-327
sputtered media (thin-film media), 590
sputtering, 590
SQL (Structured Query Language), 1090
SRAM (Static Random Access Memory), 279, 1090
see also DRAM; RAM
ST-412 floppy disk drive, 520
ST-506 floppy disk drive, 519-520
ST-506/412, 1090
capacity limitations, 684
drives, 893
encoding schemes, 629-632
interface, 629
Stabilant 22, 37-38
Stac Incorporated, 1031
stair-stepping, 1090
stamped multisession, 738
Standard Ethernet cable, 471
Standard Microsystems Corporation, 1031
standards
modems
bps (bits per second), 438
data-compression (V.42bis), 441-442
error-correction protocols, 441
FAXModem, 444

LAPM (Link Access
 Procedure for
 Modems), 441
modulation, 439-441
proprietary, 437
proprietary standards,
 442-443
V.21, 439
V.22, 439
V.22bis, 439
V.23, 439
V.29, 440
V.32, 440
V.32bis, 440
V.32fast, 440
V.34, 440
V.42 (error-correction),
 441
V.F.C. (Fast Class), 440
**Standby Power Supplies
 (SPS), 326-327**
**Star Micronics America, Inc.,
 1032**
**star topology (fiber-optic
 cables), 474-475**
StarLan (LAN), 483
start bits (serial ports), 429
**Start on Command SCSI
 drives, 678-679**
start/stop bits, 1090
starting cluster, 1090
startup
 DOS, 882-888
 problems, 514
**static electricity, preventing,
 72-73**
 see also ESD protection
**Static RAM PC
 Convertible, 937**
**Static Random Access
 Memory,** *see* **SRAM**
status, DOS files, 901
STB Systems, Inc., 1032
**stepper motor actuators,
 523, 1090**
 hard disk drives, 596-597
  mechanical links,
   597-598
  split-metal-band
   mechanism, 597
  temperature fluctuation
   problems, 598-599

**stereo line in connectors
 (sound cards), 503**
**stereo line out connectors
 (sound cards), 503**
**stereo systems, patching
 sound cards, 509-510**
**stereophonic sound cards,
 500-501**
**STL (Software Testing Lab),
 1031**
storage
 accumulators, 1041
 archive media, 1043
 data
  Compact Disc
   Recordable (CD-R)
   drives, 787-789
  comparing removable
   drives, 785-786
  magnetic media drives,
   781-783
  magneto-optical drives,
   783-785
  QIC-40 tape drive, 766
  QIC-80 tape drive, 766
  removable storage
   drives, 780-789
  WORM drives, 786-787
 DC-600 (Data Cartridge
  600), 1058
 DD (double density), 1060
 directories, 1059
 DSM (Digital Storage
  Media), 1061
 DTE (Data Terminal
  Equipment), 1061
 ED (extra-high density),
  1064
**Storage Dimensions, Inc.,
 1032**
**STP (shielded twisted pair),
 1089**
**Structured Query Language
 (SQL), 1090**
structures, DOS, 895-905
 allocation units,
  903-904
 data area, 905-906
 diagnostic read-and-write
  cylinder, 905

 FATs (file allocation
  tables), 902-903
 master partition boot
  sectors, 896-900
 root directories, 900-902
 volume boot sectors,
  899-900
stuck keys, 361
subdirectories, 900-902
subnotebooks, 811
subroutines, 1090
SUBST command, 909-910
**suffix portions (hard
 drives), 581**
summation check,
 see **checksum**
Sun Moon Star, 1032
**Super High-Speed Serial
 Ports, 434-435**
Super I/O chip, 22, 108
**Super Twisted LCD display
 (5140 PC Convertible
 laptop), 937**
**Super VGA (Super Video
 Graphics Array), 408-409**
 adapter BIOS memory, 234
 memory map, 231-233
 recommended, 394
 resolution, 390
**Supermicro Computer, Inc.,
 1032**
**Superpower Supply, Inc.,
 1032**
**superscalar technology
 (Pentiums), 193**
surge protectors, 325
surges (power)
 power-protection systems,
  323-329
  line conditioners, 326
  phone line surge
   protectors, 325-326
  Standby Power Supplies
   (SPS), 326-327
  surge protectors, 325
  Uninterruptible Power
   Supplies (UPS),
   327-329
**SVGA (Super Video Graphics
 Array), 408-409**
 VESA standards (VESA
  BIOS Extension), 410-412

swabs, cleaning connectors/
  contacts, 63, 66
SWEDAC (Swedish monitor-
  emission standard), 392
switches, 9
  adjusting settings, 282
  DIP switches, 1059
  key switch designs
    (keyboards), 342-345
      capacitive switches,
        344-345
      foam element
        switches, 343
      mechanical switch, 343
      rubber dome
        switches, 344
  power supply connectors,
    301-302
  recording settings prior to
    disassembly, 44
  settings (motherboards)
    IBM PC/XT, 935, 949-950
Symantec Corporation, 1032
  Web site, 867, 871, 918
sync (synchronizing
  bits), 726
synchronous
  communication, 1091
Synchronous Data Link
  Control (SDLC), 1087
Synchronous DRAM
  (SDRAM) memory, 267
Synchronous Graphics
  RAM, 415
synchronous negotiation
  (SCSI drives), 679
synthesized sounds, 499
synthesizers, 507
SyQuest Technology, 1032
  magnetic media drives,
    781, 783
SYS command, 905-906
system components, 794
  assemblying system, 807
  cables, *see* cables
  case, 794-795
  CD-ROM drives, 804
  cooling fans, 806
  floppy disk drives, 804

hard disk drives, *see* hard
  disk drives
heat sinks, 806
I/O ports, 803-804
inventory of, 982
keyboards, *see* keyboards
motherboards, *see*
  motherboards
mouse, *see* mouse
power supply, *see* power
  supply
sound cards, *see* sound
  cards
testing with POST, 838-839
  audio error codes,
    839-841
  visual error codes,
    842-843
vendors, *see* vendors
video adapters, *see* video
  adapters
System Management
  Interrupt, *see* SMI
System Management Mode,
  see SMM
system options, AT
  models, 971
system resources, 140-148
  conflicts, 148-158
    adapter boards, 154-156
    Plug and Play systems,
      156-158
    resolving manually,
      149-150
    system-configuration
      templates, 150-154
  DMA channels (Direct
    Memory Access), 145-147
  8-bit ISA (Industry
    Standard Architecture)
    bus channels, 145
  16-bit EISA/ISA/MCA
    bus channels, 145-146
  EISA (Enhanced
    Industry Standard
    Architecture) bus,
    146-147
  MCA (Micro Channel
    Architecture) bus, 147
  I/O port addresses, 147-148

IRQ channels (Interrrupt
  ReQuests), 140-145
  8-bit ISA (Industry
    Standard Architecture)
    bus interrupts, 142
  16-bit EISA/ISA/MCA
    bus interrupts,
    142-144
  conflicts, 145-147
  internal stack overflow
    error, 141
  network interface cards,
    see NICs
  SCSI adapter card
    conflicts, 155
  serial ports, conflicts, 156
  sound cards
    conflicts, 154-155
    installing, 155
**System transferred message
  (error), 905**
systems, 15-17
  architecture
    AT Model 286, 974
    IBM PCs, 932
    PC XTs, 947
    Portable PC, 953
  AT (Advanced Technology)
    PCs, 15-17
    expansion slots, 16
    ISA (Industry Standard
      Architecture) bus, 16
    processors, 16
    XT systems,
      compared, 17
  cleaning, 58-67
    brushes/swabs, 63
    chemicals, 60-64
    connectors/contacts,
      63, 66
    keyboards/mouse, 66-67
    lubricants, 62-63
    procedures, 64-67
    tools needed, 60
    vacuum cleaners, 62-63
  components
    assemblying system, 807
    cables, *see* cables
    case, 794-795
    CD-ROM drives, 804

systems

  cooling fans, 806
  floppy disk drives, 804
  hard disk drives, *see*
    hard disk drives
  heat sinks, 806
  I/O ports, 803-804
  inventory of, 982
  keyboards, *see*
    keyboards
  motherboards, *see*
    motherboards
  mouse, *see* mouse
  power supply, *see* power
    supply
  sound cards, *see* sound
    cards
  testing with POST,
    838-842
  vendors, *see* vendors
  video adapters, *see* video
    adapters
configuration
  hard disk drives,
    695-698
  templates, 150-154
crashes, 1056, 1091
  power supply,
    troubleshooting,
    314-319
  thermal shock, 310-312
disassembling, *see*
  disassembling systems
documentation, 18-19
files, 1091
integrators, 1091
operating systems, *see* OSes
XT systems (Extended
  PCs), 15-17

T

T-1 connections to the
  Internet, 488
T-3 connections to the
  Internet, 488
Tadiran, 1032
Tagged Image File Format
  (TIFF), 1092
Tandy Corporation, 1032
tape carrier packaging
  (TCP), 196
tape drives
  8mm tape drives, 771
  backups, 760
  compatible
    QIC-standard
    drives, 768-769
  development of
    standards, 761
  high-capacity
    QIC-standard
    drives, 767-773
  QIC standards, 761-763
  QIC-standard drives,
    764-767
  software for, 778-780
costs, 57
DAT (Digital Audio
  Tape), 770
DLT (Digital Linear
  Tape), 771
installing, 775-777
portable, 767
QIC-40, 764-767
QIC-80, 764-767
selecting, 773-775
Travan cartridge tapes,
  772-773
targets, 1091
Tatung Company of
  America, Inc., 1033
TCM (Trellis-coded
  modulation), 1091
TCP (tape carrier
  packaging), 196
TCP/IP (Transmission
  Control Protocol/Internet
  Protocol), 486-488
TDK Corporation of
  America, 1033
Teac America, Inc., 1033
teardown, *see* disassembling
  systems
Tech Data Corporation,
  1033
Tech Spray, Inc., 1033
technical specifications
  AT, 966-971
  Model 087 XT, 946-958
Tecmar Technologies, Inc.,
  1033
Tekram Technologies, 1033
telephone numbers
  Mueller, Scott (author), 986
  vendors, 989-1038
telephones, surge protectors,
  325-326
Telnet (Terminal
  Emulation), 486
temperature
  damage, preventing, 69-71
  hard disk drives
    acclimation, 608-609
    installation, 699-700
    head actuators, 598-599
    thermal shock, 310-312
templates, system
  configuration, 150-154
temporary backups, 1092
temporary files, 1092
tera, 1092
terabytes, 170, 1092
terminal adapters
  (ISDN device), 445
terminal mode, 1092
Terminate and Stay Resident
  (TSR), 918, 1094
terminating resistors,
  529-530
termination
  hard disk drive interfaces
    (SCSI), 674-675
  SCSI drives, 664, 676-678
terminators, 1092
  SCSI (Small Computer
    System Interface) drives,
    power, 679-686
*Test and Measurement
  World* Magazine, 1033
test equipment, 33-37
  breakout boxes, 33
  logic probes/pulsers, 35
  meters, 34-35
  outlet testers, 35-36
  SIMM testers, 36-37
  wrap plugs, 33
testing
  monitors, 395-396
  parallel ports, 455
  POST, 837-843
    audio error codes,
      839-841
    system component
      tests, 838-839
    visual error codes,
      842-843

troubleshooting **1163**

power supply, 317-319
processors, 210-211, 222
  heating and cooling
    problems, 222
  known-defective chips,
    211-212, 215-222
  Pentium, 212-215
  software, 210
serial ports, 453-455
video adapters, 427
Texas Instruments, Inc.,
  1033
TF (thin film) heads, hard
  disk drives, 593-594
TFT (thin-film transistor), 388
THD (total harmonic
  distortion), 505
thermal recalibration, 602
thermal shock, 310-312
Thermalloy, Inc., 1034
Thick Ethernet (10Base5
  IEEE standard), 1039
Thin Ethernet (10Base2 IEEE
  standard), 1039
thin-film media, 1092
thin-film sputtered media
  (hard disks), 590
Thinkpad 700, 378
Thinnet cables, 471
  BNC connectors, 472
third-party disk repair
  utilities, 918
third-party software,
  779-780
three-prong adapters, 323
through-holes, 31, 1092
throughput, 1092
  tape drives, 775
THYNX, 1034
TIFF (Tagged Image File
  Format), 1092
time, access time, 1041
time code, 1093
TLB (Translation Lookaside
  Buffer), 195
Token Ring, 482, 1093
  adapters (NICs), 468
  cards (NICs), 465
  LANs, early token
    release, 468
  memory map, 237
  networks, 474
tools, 27-33

chemicals, 37-39
cleaning systems, 60
compressed air, 38
costs, 30
hand tools, 28-30
hardware types, 39
kits, 28-29
metric/English, 40
soldering/desoldering,
  30-33
test equipment, 33-37
  breakout boxes, 33
  logic probes/pulsers, 35
  meters, 34-35
  outlet testers, 35-36
  SIMM testers, 36-37
  wrap plugs, 33
Torx drivers, 29-30
topology, 474-475
Torx
  drivers, 29-30
  screws, 39, 320
Toshiba America, Inc., 1034
total harmonic distortion
  (THD), 505
TouchStone Software
  Corporation, 1034
TPC (tape carrier
  packaging), 817-818
TPI (tracks per inch), 1093
Trace Research and
  Development Center, 1034
track density, 1093
track following system,
  see voice coil actuators
track-to-track seek time,
  1093
Trackball portable
  systems, 827
Trackpad portable
  systems, 827
Trackpoint, 367-368,
  377-381
  portable systems, 827
Trackpoint II, 377-381
Trackpoint III, 377-381
tracks
  floppy disks, 540
  hard disk drives,
    format, 582
tracks per inch (TPI), 1093
trade magazines, 985
trailers (suffix portions), 581

transfer rates, hard drive
  speed, 616-617
transformers (variable
  voltage), testing power
  supply, 318-321
Transistor-to-Transistor
  Logic (TTL), 1094
transistors, 9-10
transition cells, 573-575
transitions (flux transitions),
  hard disk drives, 573
Translation Lookaside
  Buffer, *see* TLB
translation mode, intelligent
  ATA-IDE drives, 642
transmissions
  asymmetrical modulation,
    1044
  asynchronous
    communication, 1044
  baseband, 1046
  broadband, 1049
  data transfer rate, 1057
Transport layer
  (OSI model), 482
transportable computers,
  1093
Travan cartridge tapes,
  772-773
Traveling Software, Inc.,
  1034
tray loading mechanisms
  (CD-ROM drives), 734-735
Trellis-coded modulation
  (TCM), 1091
tri-connector wrap plugs, 33
Trident Microsystems, 1034
TriniTech, Inc., 1034
Triple-speed CD-ROM drives
  access times, 731
  data transfer rate, 729
triple-supertwist LCDs, 388
Tripp Lite Manufacturing,
  1035
Triton chips, 799
Triton II chips, 799
troubleshooting
  CD-ROMs, 756-757
  data recovery, *see* data
    recovery
  DOS
    loading, 882-888
    starting, 882-888
    upgrade problems,
      905-906

floppy disk drive problems, 560-561
hard disk drives, 718-721
keyboard problems, 361
    cleaning, 364-365
    defective cables, 361-362
    diagnostic and POST error codes, 362
    disassembly, 362
    replacements, 365-367
    stuck keys, 361
monitors, 425-427
mouse
    hardware, 373-375
    software, 375-377
power supply problems, 314-319
    DMMs (Digital Multi-Meters), 316-318
    test equipment, 318-319
    ventilation, 313
sound card problems
    computer won't start, 514
    hardware conflicts, 510-512
    joystick problems, 514
    lockups, 514
    no sound, 512
    one-sided sound, 513
    parity errors, 514
    scratchy sound, 514
tools, *see* tools
video adapters, 425-427
see also problems; repairing
true-color images, 1093
TRUENAME command, 910
Tseng Labs, Inc., 1035
TSR (Terminate and Stay Resident), 918, 1094
TTI Technologies, 1035
TTL (Transistor-to-Transistor Logic), 1094
tunnel erasure, 521
TV-Out feature, external displays, 831-832
tweens, 1094
twin-data pipelines (Pentiums), 193
Twinhead Corporation, 1035
twisted pair cables, 471, 1094
    10BaseT, 1039
    100BaseT, 1039
    100BaseVG, 1040
    unshielded twisted pair cables, 471
Tyan Computer Corporation, 1035
Type 1 parallel ports (bidirectional), 448
Type 3 parallel ports (bidirectional), 448
Type III PC Card, 821
Type IV PC Card, 821
typematic functions (keyboards), 347-348

U

u-pipe (Pentiums), 194
U.S. Robotics, Inc., 1035
    modems
        commands, 438
        HST (proprietary standards), 442
UART (Universal Asynchronous Receiver/Transmitter), 1094
    AT or PC/XT systems, 434
    chips, 433-434
Ultra (Fast-20) SCSI, 663
Ultra-X, Inc., 1035
Ultra-X POST code cards, 842
UMA (Upper Memory Area), 224-226, 842
    adapter ROM, 233-234
        hard disk controller BIOS, 234-236
        network adapters, 236-238
        SCSI (Small Computer System Interface) adapter BIOS, 234-236
        video adapter BIOS, 234
    adapters, 251
    configuring with HIMEM.SYS (device driver), 253
    linear addresses, 227-228
    memory configuration programs, MEMMAKER (DOS), 253-255
    memory management programs, 252-253
        EMM386.EXE (DOS), 253-255
        QEMM (Quarterdeck), 255-290
    motherboard ROM BIOS, 238-290
    segment addresses, 226-228
    Video RAM memory, 226-229
        CGA memory map (Color Graphics Adapter), 230
        EGA memory map (Enhanced Graphic Adapter), 230-231
        MDA memory map (Monochrome Display Adapter), 229-230
        VGA memory map (Video Graphics Array), 231-233
UMBs (Upper Memory Blocks), 254
Underwriters Laboratories, Inc., 1035
    surge protectors, 325
unformatted capacity, 1094
Unicomp, Inc., 1035
unidirectional parallel ports, 448
unified cache, 174
Uniform Resource Locator (URL), 1094
Uninterruptible Power Supplies (UPS), 327-329
UNISYS, 1035
Universal Asynchronous Receiver/Transmitter, *see* UART
universal PCI (Peripheral Component Interconnect) bus, *see* PCI
Universal Serial Bus, *see* USB
unlatched mode, 614
unshielded twisted pair (UTP), 471, 1089, 1095

UPC (Universal Product Code), 1094
updating, 1094
upgrading
    DOS, 905-906
    portable systems, 812-813
Upper Memory Area, see UMA
Upper Memory Blocks, see UMBs
UPS (Uninterruptible Power Supplies), 327-329
URL (Uniform Resource Locator), 1094
USB (Universal Serial Bus), 139-140, 456-457
utilities, pop-up, 918
UTP (unshielded twisted pair), 1089, 1095
UVGA resolution, 390

V

V Communications, Inc., 1036
v-pipe (Pentiums), 194
V-Series proprietary standards (modems), 443
V.21 modem standard, 439
V.22 modem standard, 439
V.22bis modem standard, 439
V.23 modem standard, 439
V.29 modem standard, 440, 443
V.32 modem standard, 440
V.32bis modem standard, 440
V.32fast modem standard, 440
V.34 modem standard, 440
V.42 modem standard (error-correction), 441
V.42bis modem standard (data-compression), 441
V.F.C. (Fast Class) modem standard, 440
vaccine programs, 1096
vacuum cleaners, 62-63
VAFC (VESA Advanced Feature Connector), 418-419

variable voltage transformers, testing power supply, 318-321
Varta Batteries, Inc., 1036
VBI (Vertical Blanking Interval), 1096
VBS (Volume Boot Sector), 587
VCPI (Virtual Control Program Interface), 1096
vendors, 989-1038
    system components, 807
    see also manufacturers
ventilation, troubleshooting power supply problems, 313
Verbatim Corporation, 1036
Vertical Blanking Interval (VBI), 1096
vertical frequency (refresh/frame rate), 393
Very Large Scale Integration (VLSI) circuit, 169
VESA Advanced Feature Connector (VAFC), 418-419
VESA BIOS Extension (SVGA standards), 410-412
VESA Local bus (VL-Bus), 122-127, 1036
    card limitations, 123
    disadvantages of, 123
    DPMS monitors (Display Power Management Signaling), 391
    electrical limitations, 123
    pinouts, 124-126
    speed, 123
VESA Media Channel (VMC), 418-419
VFC (Video Feature Connector), 418-419
VGA (Video Graphics Array), 404-406
    adapters
        BIOS memory, 234
        recommended, 394
    analog signals, 404
    digital signals, 404
    memory map, 231-233
    resolution, 390
    specifications, 406
    video standards (MCP), 491
VIA Technologies, Inc., 1036

video
    analog video, 1042
    blanking interval, 1048
    broadcast quality, 1049
    CD Video, 1051
    composite video, 1055
    DVI (Digital Video Interactive), 1061
    EGA (Enhanced Graphics Adapter), 1061
    frames, 1065
    full-motion video, 1066
    Hi8 video, 1068
video adapters, 396-424, 805-806
    8514 display, 403
    bus mastering, 406
    buying criteria, 417
    CGA (Color Graphics Adapter), 398-400
        memory map, 230
        pinouts, 400
        specifications, 398-399
    chipsets, 417-418
    codecs, 422
    EGA (Enhanced Graphics Adapter), 400-402
        memory map, 230-231
        specifications, 402
    HGC (Hercules Graphics Card), 398
    MCGA (MultiColor Graphics Array), 403-404
    MDA (Monochrome Display Adapter), 396-398
        memory map, 229-230
        pinouts, 397-398
    memory, 229, 412-413
    multimedia
        3-D graphic accelerators, 423-424
        desktop video (DTV) boards, 421-423
        NTSC-to-VGA adapter, 422
        output devices, 419-420
        still-image video capture cards, 420
        VFC (Video Feature Connector), 418-419
    PCI (Peripheral Component Interconnect), 416

PGA (Professional Graphics Adapter), 402-403
ROM BIOS, 234
speed improvements, 414-417
  buses, 416
  frame buffer technology, 414
  video processors (chipsets), 414
  VRAM (Video Random Access Memory), 414-416
SVGA (Super Video Graphics Array), 408-409
  recommended, 394
  resolution, 390
  VESA SVGA standards (VESA BIOS Extension), 410-412
troubleshooting, 425-427
UVGA resolution, 390
VGA (Video Graphics Array), 404-406
  analog signals, 404
  digital signals, 404
  memory map, 231-233
  recommended, 394
  resolution, 390
  specifications, 406
VMC (VESA Media Channel), 418-419
XGA/XGA-2 (eXtended Graphics Array), 406-409
  operation modes, 407
  resolution, 390
  specifications, 408
video chipset, 22
video conferencing, *see* ISDN
video displays (monitors), 385-396
  5140 PC Convertible laptop, 938, 940
  APM (Advanced Power Management), 424-425
  buying, 392-396
  CGA (Color Graphics Adapter), 398
  color, 388-389
  controls (analog/digital), 395

CRTs (cathode-ray tubes), 386
dot pitch, 391
energy-saving, 391-392
horizontal frequency, 393
ID pins, 424
interlaced, 391
LAN file servers, 464
LCDs (liquid-crystal displays), 387-388
monochrome, 388-389
multiple-frequency, 393
noninterlaced, 391
resolution, 390-391
  dot pitch, 394
  pixels, 390
safety, radiation (magnetic emissions), 391-392
sizes, 389-390
troubleshooting, 425-427
vertical frequency (refresh/frame rate), 393
Video Electronics Standards Association, *see* **VESA**
Video Feature Connector, *see* **VFC**
Video Graphics Array, *see* **VGA**
Video Random-Access Memory, *see* **VRAM**
ViewSonic, 1036
virtual 86 mode, 386 Intel processors, 169
Virtual Control Program Interface (VCPI), 1096
Virtual Device Driver (VxD), 1098
virtual disks, 1097
virtual memory, 1097
  286 Intel processors, 168
Virtual Memory Manager (VMM), 1097
virtual real mode, 242, 1097
  386 Intel processors, 169
  486DX Intel processors, 176
virus scanning, 68-69
viruses, 149
Visiflex Seels, 1036
VistaLan, 483
visual error codes (POST), 842-843

VL-Bus, *see* VESA Local bus
VLF magnetic emissions (radiation), 391-392
VLSI (Very Large Scale Integration) circuit, 169
VLSI Technology, Inc., 1036
VMC (VESA Media Channel), 418-419
VMM (Virtual Memory Manager), 1097
voice annotation, sound cards, 494
voice coil actuators, hard disk drives, 596, 599-601, 1097
  azimuth, 600
  closed loop (servo-controlled mechanisms), 599
  linear actuators, 600
  rotary actuators, 601
  servo mechanisms, 599-606
voice recognition, sound cards, 494-495
volatile storage, *see* RAM chips
Volpe, Hank, 1036
voltage
  measuring, 34-35, 317-318
  positive (power supply), 292
  power supply ranges, 301
  reduction, portable systems, 818-819
Voltage Regulator Module, *see* VRM
voltage regulators, 1097
Volume Boot Sector, *see* VBS
Volume Table of Contents (CD-ROM drives), 737
Vopt utility (disk defragmenter), 542
VRAM (Video Random Access Memory), 226-229, 414-416, 1097
  adapter ROM, 233-234
  hard disk controller BIOS, 234-236
  network adapters, 236-238

SCSI (Small Computer
 System Interface)
 adapter BIOS, 234-236
 video adapter BIOS, 234
CGA memory map (Color
 Graphics Adapter), 230
EGA memory map
 (Enhanced Graphics
 Adapter), 230-231
MDA memory map
 (Monochrome Display
 Adapter), 229-230
VGA memory map (Video
 Graphics Array), 231-233
Window RAM, 415
VRM (Voltage Regulator
 Module), Pentium
 OverDrive processors, 188
VxD (Virtual Device Driver),
 1098

W

wait states, 163, 1098
 RAM chips, 276-277
Walling Company, 1036
Wang Laboratories, Inc.,
 1036
warranties, 23-25
Warshawski/Whitney & Co.,
 1037
Washburn & Co., 287, 1037
Watergate Software, 1037
watts (speakers), 505
WAV files (waveform audio),
 497, 499
Wave Tech, 1037
WD1002-WA2 controller, 632
Web sites
 AMIDiag, 865
 ASME, 1044
 BIOS information, 89
 CERN, 1052
 Checkit, 865
 Diagsoft, 868
 DOS bug patches, 907
 Edlab, 1039
 Microscope, 866
 NLX Motherboard
  Specification page, 98
 Ontrack, 870
 POST code cards, 842

Symantec, 867, 871, 918
Windsor Technologies, 867
Zeppo Glossary, 1039
wedge servo mechanism,
 603-604
Weitek Corporation, 1037
Weitek math coprocessor
 (Intel), 210
Western Digital
 Corporation, 1037
what-you-see-is-what-you-get
 (WYSIWYG), 390
Whetstone, 1098
White Book, 1098
Whitney technology, 1098
Wide SCSI, 664
Winbond, 1037
Winchester drives, 1098
Winchester technology,
 1098
Window RAM, 415
Windows 3.x,
 requirements, 15
Windows 95, 919-922
 32-bit protected mode
  drivers, 252
 compared to DOS, 920-921
 FAT32, 921-922
 LANs, peer-to-peer network
  setup, 458
 Registry, 920
 upgrading DOS, 906
Windows NT, 922-923
Windows NT 4.x,
 requirements, 15
Windows NT File System,
 see NTFS
Windsor Technologies, Inc.,
 1037
 Web site, 867
wire frames (animation),
 1099
WordPerfect, 1037
workstations, LANs (Local
 Area Networks), 459-460
WORM drives, 786-789
wrap plugs, 33, 454
wrist straps, *see* ESD
 protection, kits
Write Multiple command
 (ATA IDE), 640
write precompensation,
 1099

write-enable notch
 (5 1/4-inch floppy
 disks), 552
Wyse Technology, 1038
WYSIWYG (what-you-see-is-
 what-you-get), 390

X

X-ray machines, effects on
 disks, 557-559
XA (eXtended Architecture)
 CD-ROM discs/drives, 740
XDFCOPY command, 907
Xebec 1210 controller,
 631-632
Xerox Corporation, 1038
XGA (eXtended Graphics
 Array), 406-409, 1099
 operation modes, 407
 resolution, 390
 specifications, 408
XGA-2 (eXtended Graphics
 Array), 406-409
Xircom, 1038
XMM (eXtended Memory
 Manager), 1099
Xmodem, 1099
XMS (eXtended Memory
 Specification), 242-243,
 1100
XON/XOFF, 1100
XT Model 286, 971-973
 adapter cards, 972
 disk drives, 972
 disk storage, 976
 Enhanced keyboard, 972
 environmental
  specifications, 977
 expansion slots, 977
 features, 973-974
 keyboard specifications, 977
 memory, 972-975
 models, 973-974
 motherboard design, 972
 part numbers, 977
 physical specifications, 977
 processor modes,
  supporting, 972
 serial/parallel adapter, 972
 standard features, 971,
  975-976

system architecture, 974
technical specifications, 974-978
XT systems (eXtended PCs), 15-17, 941-951
   disk storage, 948
   drives, 941-942
   expansion slots, 942, 948
   features, 943-945
   floppy internal controller, 535
   IRQs (Interrupt Requests), 691
   keyboards, 336, 943
      cable part numbers, 365-366
      compatibility, 341-342
      interface, 345-346
      key numbers, 349-351
      replacements, 365-366
      scan codes, 349-351
      specifications, 948
   memory switch settings, 935-936
   microprocessors, 942
   Model 087, 943-944
   Model 089, 944
   Model 268, 944
   Model 278, 944
   Model 5160068, 944
   Model 5160078, 944
   models, 943
   motherboard switch settings, 935, 949-950
   parts numbers, 950
   power supply, 293-294, 299-300, 943
   serial ports, 25-pin connector specifications, 432
   technical specifications, 946-958
   UART chips, 434
   see also AT (Advanced Technology) PCs
XT-Bus (IDE interfaces), 650-651

Y

Y-E Data America, Inc., 1038
Yellow Book, 1100
Ymodem, 1100

Z

Zenith Data Systems, 1038
Zeos International, Ltd., 1038
Zeppo Glossary Web site, 1039
ZIF (Zero Insertion Force), 29, 181, 1100
ZIP (Zigzag Inline Package), 1100
Zmodem, 1100
Zone Recording, hard disk drives, 584-585
   intelligent Zoned Recording IDE drives, 643
zones (hard disk drives), 584

Complete and Return this Card for a *FREE* Computer Book Catalog

Thank you for purchasing this book! You have purchased a superior computer book written expressly for your needs. To continue to provide the kind of up-to-date, pertinent coverage you've come to expect from us, we need to hear from you. Please take a minute to complete and return this self-addressed, postage-paid form. In return, we'll send you a free catalog of all our computer books on topics ranging from word processing to programming and the internet.

Mr. ☐ Mrs. ☐ Ms. ☐ Dr. ☐

Name (first) ☐☐☐☐☐☐☐☐☐☐☐☐☐ (M.I.) ☐ (last) ☐☐☐☐☐☐☐☐☐☐☐☐☐☐☐

Address ☐☐☐☐☐☐☐☐☐☐☐☐☐☐☐☐☐☐☐☐☐☐☐☐☐☐☐☐☐

☐☐☐☐☐☐☐☐☐☐☐☐☐☐☐☐☐☐☐☐☐☐☐☐☐☐☐☐☐

City ☐☐☐☐☐☐☐☐☐☐☐☐☐☐ State ☐☐ Zip ☐☐☐☐☐☐☐☐☐☐

Phone ☐☐☐☐☐☐☐☐☐☐ Fax ☐☐☐☐☐☐☐☐☐☐

Company Name ☐☐☐☐☐☐☐☐☐☐☐☐☐☐☐☐☐☐☐☐☐☐☐☐

E-mail address ☐☐☐☐☐☐☐☐☐☐☐☐☐☐☐☐☐☐☐☐☐☐☐☐

1. Please check at least (3) influencing factors for purchasing this book.

- Front or back cover information on book ☐
- Special approach to the content ☐
- Completeness of content ☐
- Author's reputation ☐
- Publisher's reputation ☐
- Book cover design or layout ☐
- Index or table of contents of book ☐
- Price of book ☐
- Special effects, graphics, illustrations ☐
- Other (Please specify): _____ ☐

2. How did you first learn about this book?

- Saw in Macmillan Computer Publishing catalog ☐
- Recommended by store personnel ☐
- Saw the book on bookshelf at store ☐
- Recommended by a friend ☐
- Received advertisement in the mail ☐
- Saw an advertisement in: _____ ☐
- Read book review in: _____ ☐
- Other (Please specify): _____ ☐

3. How many computer books have you purchased in the last six months?

- This book only ☐
- 2 books ☐
- 3 to 5 books ☐
- More than 5 ☐

4. Where did you purchase this book?

- Bookstore ☐
- Computer Store ☐
- Consumer Electronics Store ☐
- Department Store ☐
- Office Club ☐
- Warehouse Club ☐
- Mail Order ☐
- Direct from Publisher ☐
- Internet site ☐
- Other (Please specify): _____ ☐

5. How long have you been using a computer?

☐ Less than 6 months ☐ 6 months to a year
☐ 1 to 3 years ☐ More than 3 years

6. What is your level of experience with personal computers and with the subject of this book?

	With PCs	With subject of book
New	☐	☐
Casual	☐	☐
Accomplished	☐	☐
Expert	☐	☐

Source Code ISBN: 0-7897-1295-4

7. Which of the following best describes your job title?

Administrative Assistant .... ☐
Coordinator .... ☐
Manager/Supervisor .... ☐
Director .... ☐
Vice President .... ☐
President/CEO/COO .... ☐
Lawyer/Doctor/Medical Professional .... ☐
Teacher/Educator/Trainer .... ☐
Engineer/Technician .... ☐
Consultant .... ☐
Not employed/Student/Retired .... ☐
Other (Please specify): _____ ☐

8. Which of the following best describes the area of the company your job title falls under?

Accounting .... ☐
Engineering .... ☐
Manufacturing .... ☐
Operations .... ☐
Marketing .... ☐
Sales .... ☐
Other (Please specify): _____ ☐

9. What is your age?

Under 20 .... ☐
21-29 .... ☐
30-39 .... ☐
40-49 .... ☐
50-59 .... ☐
60-over .... ☐

10. Are you:

Male .... ☐
Female .... ☐

11. Which computer publications do you read regularly? (Please list)

_____
_____
_____
_____
_____
_____
_____
_____
_____

Comments: _____
_____
_____

Fold here and scotch-tape to mail.

NO POSTAGE
NECESSARY
IF MAILED
IN THE
UNITED STATES

BUSINESS REPLY MAIL
FIRST-CLASS MAIL PERMIT NO. 9918 INDIANAPOLIS IN

POSTAGE WILL BE PAID BY THE ADDRESSEE

ATTN MARKETING
MACMILLAN COMPUTER PUBLISHING
MACMILLAN PUBLISHING USA
201 W 103RD ST
INDIANAPOLIS IN 46290-9042

Check out Que® Books on the World Wide Web
http://www.quecorp.com

As the biggest software release in computer history, Windows 95 continues to redefine the computer industry. Click here for the latest info on our Windows 95 books

Make computing quick and easy with these products designed exclusively for new and casual users

Examine the latest releases in word processing, spreadsheets, operating systems, and suites

The Internet, The World Wide Web, CompuServe®, America Online®, Prodigy® —it's a world of ever-changing information. Don't get left behind!

Find out about new additions to our site, new bestsellers and hot topics

In-depth information on high-end topics: find the best reference books for databases, programming, networking, and client/server technologies

A recent addition to Que, Ziff-Davis Press publishes the highly-successful *How It Works* and *How to Use* series of books, as well as *PC Learning Labs Teaches* and *PC Magazine* series of book/disc packages

Stay on the cutting edge of Macintosh® technologies and visual communications

Find out which titles are making headlines

With 6 separate publishing groups, Que develops products for many specific market segments and areas of computer technology. Explore our Web Site and you'll find information on best-selling titles, newly published titles, upcoming products, authors, and much more.

- Stay informed on the latest industry trends and products available
- Visit our online bookstore for the latest information and editions
- Download software from Que's library of the best shareware and freeware

Copyright © 1997, Macmillan Computer Publishing-USA, A Viacom Company

The CD-ROM that accompanies this book will automatically start the install process by using Windows 95's auto-play feature. If you have disabled this feature, or are using Windows 3.x, please see the README files in \ZDBENCH\WB96 (WinBench 96), \ZDBENCH\WS96 (Winstone 96), and ZDBENCH\WS32 (Winstone 32). If you have problems with this disc, please contact Macmillan Technical Support at (317) 581-3833. We can be reached by e-mail at **support@mcp.com**.

License Agreement

This package contains one CD-ROM that includes software described in this book. See applicable chapters for a description of these programs and instructions for their use.

By opening this package you are agreeing to be bound by the following:

This software is copyrighted and all rights are reserved by the publisher and its licensers. You are licensed to use this software on a single computer. You may copy the software for backup or archival purposes only. Making copies of the software for any other purpose is a violation of United States copyright laws. THIS SOFTWARE IS SOLD AS IS, WITHOUT WARRANTY OF ANY KIND, EITHER EXPRESSED OR IMPLIED, INCLUDING BUT NOT LIMITED TO THE IMPLIED WARRANTIES OF MERCHANTABILITY AND FITNESS FOR A PARTICULAR PURPOSE. Neither the publisher nor its licensers, dealers, or distributors assumes any liability for any alleged or actual damages arising from the use of this software. (Some states do not allow exclusion of implied warranties, so the exclusion may not apply to you.)

The entire contents of this disc and the compilation of the software are copyrighted and protected by United States copyright laws. The individual programs on this disc are copyrighted by the authors or owners of each program. Each program has its own use permissions and limitations. To use each program, you must follow the individual requirements and restrictions detailed for each. Do not use a program if you do not agree to follow its licensing agreement.